THE OXFORD HANDBOOK OF

BUDDHIST PRACTICE

THE OXFORD HANDBOOK OF

BUDDHIST PRACTICE

Edited by

PAULA ARAI *and* KEVIN TRAINOR

OXFORD
UNIVERSITY PRESS

OXFORD
UNIVERSITY PRESS

Oxford University Press is a department of the University of Oxford. It furthers the University's objective of excellence in research, scholarship, and education by publishing worldwide. Oxford is a registered trade mark of Oxford University Press in the UK and certain other countries.

Published in the United States of America by Oxford University Press
198 Madison Avenue, New York, NY 10016, United States of America.

Library of Congress Cataloging-in-Publication Data
Names: Trainor, Kevin, editor. | Arai, Paula Kane Robinson, editor.
Title: The Oxford handbook of Buddhist practice / Paula Arai and Kevin Trainor.
Description: New York : Oxford University Press, 2022. |
Series: Oxford handbooks series | Includes index.
Identifiers: LCCN 2021051385 | ISBN 9780190632922 (hardback) |
ISBN 9780190632939 (UPDF) | ISBN 9780190632946 (epub) | ISBN 9780190632953 (Digital-Online)
Subjects: LCSH: Buddhism. | Religious life—Buddhism. |
Buddhism—Doctrines. | Spiritual life—Buddhism.
Classification: LCC BQ4950 .O94 2022 | DDC 294.3/4—dc23/eng/20220223
LC record available at https://lccn.loc.gov/2021051385

DOI: 10.1093/oxfordhb/9780190632922.001.0001

1 3 5 7 9 8 6 4 2

Printed by Sheridan Books, Inc., United States of America

Contents

Contributors ix

1. Introduction: Embodiment and Sense Experience 1
PAULA ARAI AND KEVIN TRAINOR

PART I. REGIONAL PERSPECTIVES

2. Buddhist Practice in South Asia 21
MIRANDA SHAW

3. Buddhist Practice in Southeast Asia 37
NATHAN McGOVERN

4. Buddhist Practice in East Asia 53
PAULA ARAI AND EUN-SU CHO

5. Buddhist Practice in Central Asia/Himalayas 70
TODD LEWIS

6. Buddhist Practice in Europe and North America 93
SCOTT MITCHELL

7. Globalized Forms of Buddhist Practice 112
INKEN PROHL

PART II. MATERIAL MEDIATIONS

8. Relics and Images 131
JOHN S. STRONG

9. The Agency of Images 148
SUSAN L. HUNTINGTON

10. Texts and Rituals 176
NATALIE GUMMER

11. Interactions with Built Environments 191
Abhishek Singh Amar

12. Buddhism and the "Natural" Environment 213
Julia Shaw

PART III. BODIES IN TRANSITION

13. Buddhist Healing Practices 235
Sienna R. Craig

14. Pilgrimage 251
Ian Reader

15. Dance as Vajrayana Practice 266
Miranda Shaw

16. Buddhist Death Practices 284
Margaret Gouin

PART IV. BODY-MIND TRANSFORMATIONS

17. Aural Practices of Chanting and Protection 301
Mahinda Deegalle

18. Pure Land Practice 320
Charles B. Jones

19. Koan Practice 336
Jeff Shore

PART V. HUMAN AND NONHUMAN INTERACTIONS

20. Practices of Veneration and Offering 355
Jeffrey Samuels

21. Ritual Identification and Purification in Esoteric Practice 368
Richard K. Payne

22. Heavenly Rebirth and Buddhist Soteriology 384
Stephen Jenkins

PART VI. DOMESTIC AND MONASTIC PRACTICES

23. Women's Ordination 405
Hiroko Kawanami

24. Monastic Authority in Medieval Japan: The Case of the Convent Hokkeji 421
Lori Meeks

25. Monastic Discipline and Local Practice 435
Vesna A. Wallace

26. Disciplining the Body-Mind 453
Charles Korin Pokorny

27. Home Altars 469
Linda Ho Peché

28. Calendrical, Life-Cycle, and Periodic Rituals 486
Jonathan S. Walters

29. Food Practices 501
Lisa Grumbach

PART VII. MODERNITIES AND EMERGENT FORMS OF PRACTICE

30. Nation-State and Monastic Identity 519
Thomas Borchert

31. Tree Ordinations and Global Sustainability 535
Susan M. Darlington

32. An Embodied Dharma of Race, Gender, and Sexuality 550
Jasmine Syedullah

33. Buddhist Chaplaincy 564
Jitsujo T. Gauthier

34. Buddhist and Non-Buddhist Practitioner Relations 581
Elizabeth J. Harris

35. Internet-Based Practices 597
Louise Connelly

36. Contemplative Science and Buddhist Science 613
John D. Dunne

37. Seeing through Mindfulness Practices 632
Erik Braun

Index 649

Contributors

Abhishek Singh Amar is an Associate Professor in Asian Studies at Hamilton College, New York. He received his PhD from the School of Oriental & African Studies, University of London. He specializes in the archaeological history of Buddhism in premodern India. He has held fellowships in UK, Germany, US, and India. He has published a coauthored book, *Archaeological Gazetteer of Gaya District* (KPJRI, 2017), a co-edited volume, *Cross-Disciplinary Perspectives on a Contested Buddhist Site: Bodhgaya Jataka* (Routledge, 2012), and several articles on Buddhist and Hindu material culture. He also directs a digital Humanities project, *Sacred Centers in India*, which developed a database of temples and sculptures of Hindu Gaya, and is currently developing a database of Indian Buddhist Monasteries.

Paula Arai received her PhD in Buddhist Studies from Harvard University, specializing in Japanese Sōtō Zen. She trained at Aichi Senmon Nisōdō under the tutelage of Aoyama Shundō Rōshi. She is author of *Painting Enlightenment: Healing Visions of the Heart Sutra--The Buddhist Art of Iwasaki Tsuneo* (Shambhala Publications, 2019), *Bringing Zen Home: The Healing Heart of Japanese Buddhist Women's Rituals* (University of Hawai'i Press, 2011), and *Women Living Zen: Japanese Buddhist Nuns* (Oxford University Press, 1999). Her research has received a range of support, including from Fulbright, the American Council of Learned Societies, the American Academy of Religion, the Reischauer Institute, the Mellon Foundation, the Lilly Foundation, and Awards to Louisiana Artists and Scholars. She has curated exhibits of Iwasaki's *Heart Sutra* paintings at the Museum of Art at Louisiana State University, the Crow Collection of Asian Art in Dallas, and the Morikami Museum in Delray Beach Florida. Arai is currently a Professor of Buddhist Studies at Louisiana State University, holding the Urmila Gopal Singhal Professorship in Religions of India.

Thomas Borchert is Professor of Religion at the University of Vermont, and is the author of *Educating Monks: Minority Religion on China's Southwest Border* (University of Hawai'i Press, 2017), and the editor of *Theravada Buddhism in Colonial Contexts* (Routledge, 2018). His research interests focus on the intersection of monasticism, nationalism, and citizenship in Thailand, China, and Singapore.

Erik Braun is an associate professor in the Department of Religious Studies at the University of Virginia. In addition to various articles, he is the author of *The Birth of Insight: Meditation, Modern Buddhism, and the Burmese Monk Ledi Sayadaw* (University of Chicago Press, 2013) and co-edited with David McMahan the volume *Buddhism,*

Meditation, and Science (Oxford University Press, 2017). His research focuses on Burmese Buddhism in the nineteenth and early twentieth centuries, Pali literature, and globalizing forms of meditative practice. He received his PhD in the Study of Religion from Harvard University.

Eun-su Cho is Professor of Buddhist Philosophy in the Department of Philosophy at Seoul National University (SNU). She received her PhD in Buddhist Studies from the University of California. Before she joined SNU in 2004, she was an assistant professor in the Department of Asian Languages and Cultures at the University of Michigan. She has published articles ranging from Indian Abhidharma Buddhism to Korean Buddhist thought and history, including "The Uses and Abuses of Wŏnhyo and the '*T'ong* Pulgyo' Narrative," "Wŏnhyo's Theory of 'One Mind': A Korean Way of Interpreting Mind" and "Repentance as a Bodhisattva Practice—Wŏnhyo on Guilt and Moral Responsibility"; co-translated (with John Jorgensen) *Jikji: The Essential Passages Directly Pointing at the Essence of the Mind*; and edited an anthology on Korean Buddhist nuns, *Korean Buddhist Nuns and Laywomen: Hidden Histories, Enduring Vitality* (SUNY, 2012). A monograph titled *Language and Meaning Buddhist Interpretations of the "Buddha's Word" in Indian and East Asian Perspective* (University of Hawai'i Press, 2020).

Louise Connelly is a Teaching Fellow in Digital Education and Convenor of the Human Ethical Review Committee (HERC) at the University of Edinburgh, and is a Senior Fellow of the Higher Education Academy UK (SFHEA). She received her PhD from the University of Edinburgh in 2012, titled "Aspects of the Self: An Analysis of Self Reflection, Self Presentation, and the Experiential Self within Selected Buddhist Blogs." Her research interests include internet research and ethics; media, religion, and culture; digital Buddhism; digital material religion; and digital education. Her recent publications include "Virtual Buddhism: Online Communities, Sacred Places and Objects," in *The Changing World Religion Map*, ed. S. Brunn (Springer, 2015); and "Towards a Typology and Mapping of the Buddhist Cyberspace," in *The Pixel in the Lotus: Buddhism, the Internet and Digital Media*, ed. G. Grieve and D. Veidlinger (Routledge, 2015).

Sienna R. Craig is Professor of Anthropology at Dartmouth College in Hanover, New Hampshire. She received her PhD from Cornell University in 2006. Craig is the author of *The Ends of Kinship: Connecting Himalayan Lives between Nepal and New York* (University of Washington Press, 2020), *Mustang in Black and White*, with photographer Kevin Bubriski (Vajra Publications, 2018), *Healing Elements: Efficacy and the Social Ecologies of Tibetan Medicine* (University of California Press, 2012), and *Horses like Lightning: A Story of Passage through the Himalayas* (Wisdom Publications, 2008), as well as a co-editor of *Medicine between Science and Religion: Explorations on Tibetan Grounds* (Berghahn Books, 2010), and *Studies of Medical Pluralism in Tibetan History and Society* (IITBS, 2010), among other publications. Craig enjoys writing across genres and has published poetry, creative nonfiction, fiction, and children's literature, in addition to scholarly works in medical and cultural anthropology. Her work has been supported by the National Science Foundation, the John Simon Guggenheim

Foundation, the Social Science Research Council, and the Wenner Gren Foundation for Anthropological Research. From 2012 to 2017 she served as co-editor of *HIMALAYA, Journal of the Association for Nepal and Himalayan Studies*, and she is an Executive Council member of the International Association for the Study of Traditional Asian Medicine (IASTAM).

Susan M. Darlington currently serves as President of Deep Springs College in California. She was Professor of anthropology and Asian studies at Hampshire College in Amherst, Massachusetts, for thirty years before this. Her research focuses on the ways in which monks in Thailand use their interpretation of Buddhism to promote environmental conservation and to help relieve suffering caused by globalization and agricultural intensification. Her book *The Ordination of a Tree: The Thai Buddhist Environmental Movement* (2012) was translated and published in Thailand in 2015. A scholar of socially engaged Buddhism, she has published numerous articles and book chapters on Buddhism and ecology, critically examining how Buddhism is interpreted and used to deal with contemporary social, economic, political, and environmental issues.

Mahinda Deegalle is Professor Emeritus of Religions, Philosophies and Ethics at Bath Spa University, United Kingdom. He held the Numata Professorship at McGill University and the NEH Professorship at Colgate University. He has conducted postdoctoral research at Kyoto University and Aichi Gakuin University under the Japan Society for the Promotion of Science and Bukkyo Dendo Kyokai fellowships. He is a recipient of the British Academy/Leverhulme Trust, British Council, and Fulbright grants. He is the author of *Popularizing Buddhism* (SUNY, 2006) and editor of *Buddhism, Conflict and Violence in Modern Sri Lanka* (Routledge, 2006), *Dharma to the UK* (2008), *Vesak, Peace and Harmony* (2015), *Justice and Statecraft* (2017), and co-editor of *Pali Buddhism* (1996). He regularly appears in the media such as BBC and has conducted fieldwork in Sri Lanka, Japan, Korea, and China. His research concentrates on Buddhism and politics, war, violence, and religious extremism. He is currently researching on pilgrimage to Adam's Peak (Śrī Pāda).

John D. Dunne serves on the faculty of the University of Wisconsin-Madison, where he holds the Distinguished Chair in Contemplative Humanities at the Center for Healthy Minds. He is also Chair of the Department of Asian Languages and Cultures. His work focuses on Buddhist philosophy and contemplative practice, especially in dialogue with cognitive science and psychology. His publications appear in venues ranging across both the humanities and the sciences, including *Foundations of Dharmakīrti's Philosophy* (2004) and *Science and Philosophy in the Indian Buddhist Classics: The Mind* (2020). He is a Fellow of the Mind and Life Institute, where he has previously served on the Board of Directors, and he is an academic advisor to the Ranjung Yeshe Institute in Kathmandu, Nepal.

Jitsujo T. Gauthier is the current Chair and Assistant Professor of the Buddhist Chaplaincy Department at University of the West. She teaches courses such as Buddhist

Homiletics, Spiritual Care and Counseling, Service Practicum, and Engaged Zen for both the Master of Divinity and Doctorate of Buddhist Ministry programs. Her research focuses on the practical application of Buddhism within fields of contemplative education, clinical ministry, and interfaith work. Her dissertation, "An On-the-Job Mindfulness Intervention for Pediatric ICU Nurses," was published in the *Journal of Pediatric Nursing* (2015). She is the author of "Hope in the Midst of Suffering: A Buddhist Perspective" in the *Journal of Pastoral Theology* (2016), "I Am a Woman: Finding Freedom in Seeing Clearly," *American Buddhist Woman Quarterly from Sakyadhita USA* (2016), and "Formation and Supervision in Buddhist Chaplaincy" in *Reflective Practice: Formation and Supervision in Ministry* (2017). She is a Dharma Holder and Priest residing at the Zen Center of Los Angeles.

Margaret Gouin obtained her PhD in Buddhist Studies at the University of Bristol, and until her retirement in 2017 was an Honorary Research Fellow at the School of Theology, Religious Studies, and Islamic Studies at the University of Wales Trinity Saint David. Her primary field of research has been death and dying, with particular reference to the rituals of various schools of Buddhism. She is the author of *Tibetan Rituals of Death: Buddhist Funerary Practices* (Routledge, 2010), and contributed the chapter on "The Buddhist Way of Death" to the second edition of *Death and Bereavement across Cultures* (ed. Parkes, Laungani, and Young; Routledge, 2015).

Lisa Grumbach teaches at Ryukoku University, Kyoto, Japan, and the Institute of Buddhist Studies, Berkeley, California. Her research examines the interactions between Buddhism and local deity (*kami*) religions in medieval Japan, with a focus on the role of food and animal offerings in these interactions. Recent publications include "The Creation of Ritual Meat Avoidance by Japanese State Systems," in *Sacred Matters, Stately Concerns: Faith and Politics in Asia, Past and Present*, ed. John M. Thompson (Peter Lang, 2014) and "When Food Becomes Tresspass: Buddhism and the Kami in Local Economies," in *Methods in Buddhist Studies: Essays in Honor of Richard Payne*, ed. Scott A. Mitchell and Natalie E. F. Quli (Bloomsbury, 2019).

Natalie Gummer is Professor of Religious Studies at Beloit College in Beloit, Wisconsin, where she has taught since 2001. She graduated with a PhD from Harvard University in Buddhist Studies in 2000. Her research examines premodern South Asian Mahayana Buddhist literary theory and practice, especially forms of ritual-poetic poiesis and performative embodiment. She also explores how Mahayana literature might offer us critical purchase on a range of contemporary ethical and philosophical debates. She is editor of *The Language of the Sūtras: Essays in Honor of Luis Gómez*, and the author of several articles on Buddhist ritual and literary culture. She is currently completing a monograph entitled *Performing the Buddha's Body: Mahāyāna Sūtras as Ritual Speech Acts.*

Elizabeth J. Harris is an Honorary Senior Research Fellow at the Edward Cadbury Centre for the Public Understanding of Religion, University of Birmingham (UK), and was an associate professor at Liverpool Hope University. She is former President of the European Network of Buddhist-Christian Studies and is currently President of the UK Association for Buddhist Studies. She specializes in the study of contemporary Theravada Buddhism, with particular reference to Sri Lanka, Buddhist-Christian Studies, and Inter-Religious Studies. Her publications include: *What Buddhists Believe* (Oneworld, 1998); *Theravāda Buddhism and the British Encounter: Religious, Missionary and Colonial Experience in Nineteenth Century Sri Lanka* (Routledge, 2006); ed. *Hope: A Form of Delusion? Buddhist and Christian Perspectives* (EOS, 2013); and *Religion, Space and Conflict in Sri Lanka: Colonial and Postcolonial Perspectives* (Routledge, 2018).

Susan L. Huntington is Distinguished University Professor, Emerita, at The Ohio State University. Her publications include *The "Pāla-Sena" Schools of Sculpture*; *Art of Ancient India*; *Leaves from the Bodhi Tree: The Art of Pāla India (8th–12th Centuries) and Its International Legacy*; *Lay Ritual in the Early Buddhist Art of India*; and various articles, particularly on the issue of aniconism in early Buddhist art. She has received awards from the John Simon Guggenheim Memorial Foundation, the Fulbright Award program, the National Endowment for the Humanities, and the Smithsonian Institution. From Ohio State, she has received the Distinguished Scholar Award, the Distinguished University Professorship, and two awards for outstanding teaching. In 1998, she was the Numata Distinguished Visiting Professor at Bailliol College at Oxford University, in 2005 she was the Mary Jane Crowe Visiting Professor at Northwestern University, and from 2011 to 2012, she was a Member of the Institute for Advanced Study in Princeton.

Stephen Jenkins, Professor Emeritus at Humboldt State University, was trained at Harvard. His recent talks argue for the soteriological importance of *devaloka*s as precedents for pure lands. Recent publications include: "Compassion Blesses the Compassionate: The Basis of Social and Individual Wealth, Health, Happiness, Power and Security in Indian Buddhist Thought," in *Buddhist Visions of the Good Life for All*, ed. Sallie King (Routledge, 2021); "Buddhism: Confronting the Harmful with Compassion," in *Nonviolence in World Religions*, ed. Mark Juergensmeyer (Routledge, 2021); "Once the Buddha Was a Warrior," in *The Nature of Peace and the Morality of Armed Conflict*, ed. Florian Demont-Biaggi (2017); "Debate, Magic, and Massacre: The High Stakes and Ethical Dynamics of Battling Slanderers of the Dharma in Indian Narrative and Ethical Theory," *Journal of Religion and Violence* (2016); and "Waking into Compassion: The Three *Ālambana* of *Karuṇā*," in *Moonpaths*, ed. Jenkins et al. (2015).

Charles B. Jones earned his PhD in History of Religions from the University of Virginia in 1996. Since that time he has been a member of the faculty of the School of Theology and Religious Studies at The Catholic University of America. His early research focused on Buddhism in Taiwan, and later moved into the study of Chinese Pure Land Buddhism, the Jesuit missions in late Ming dynasty China, and inter-religious dialogue.

Hiroko Kawanami is Professor of Buddhism and Society in the Department of Politics, Philosophy and Religion at Lancaster University. She has conducted extensive research on the Buddhist monastic community in Myanmar, examining its social transactions in areas of knowledge transmission, religious donations, international relief work, and more generally the relationship between politics and religion. Her edited publications include *Buddhism, International Relief Work and Civil Society* (2013); "Special Issue on Burmese-Myanmar Religion," *Asian Ethnology* (2009); and *Buddhism and the Political Process* (2016). She is author of *Renunciation and Empowerment of Buddhist Nuns in Myanmar-Burma* (2013) and *The Culture of Giving in Myanmar: Buddhist Offerings, Reciprocity and Interdependence* (2020).

Todd Lewis is the Distinguished Professor of Arts and Humanities and Professor of Religion at the College of the Holy Cross. His primary research since 1979 has been on Newar Buddhism in the Kathmandu Valley and the social history of Buddhism. Since completing his PhD (Columbia, 1984), Lewis has authored many articles on the Buddhist traditions of Nepal and the book *Popular Buddhist Texts from Nepal: Narratives and Rituals of Newar Buddhism* (SUNY Press, 2000). Recent books include the co-edited *Teaching Buddhism: New Insights on Understanding and Presenting the Traditions* (Oxford, 2016); *Buddhists: Understanding Buddhism through the Lives of Practitioners* (Wiley-Blackwell, 2014), and the co-authored textbook *World Religions Today* (Oxford, seventh edition, 2021). His translation, *Sugata Saurabha: A Poem on the Life of the Buddha by Chittadhar Hridaya of Nepal* (Oxford, 2010), received awards from the Khyentse Foundation and the Numata Foundation as the best book on Buddhism in 2011. His most recent publication, with Jinah Kim, is *Dharma and Punya: Buddhist Ritual Art of Nepal* (Brill, 2019).

Nathan McGovern is Associate Professor in the Department of Philosophy and Religious Studies at the University of Wisconsin-Whitewater. His work focuses on interrogating the boundary between Buddhism and Brahmanism/Hinduism in early South Asia and contemporary Thailand. In his book, *The Snake and the Mongoose* (2019), he questions the received narrative that Buddhism arose in opposition to Brahmanism and argues that the divide between "Brahmanical" and "non-Brahmanical" religions in ancient India arose through contestation over the word "Brahman."

Lori Meeks (BA, Columbia; PhD, Princeton) is Associate Professor of Religion and East Asian Languages and Cultures at the University of Southern California, where she has taught since 2004. She has served as President of the Society for the Study of Japanese Religions and as Co-Chair for the Buddhism Section of the American Academy of Religion. Meeks is the author of the award-winning *Hokkeji and the Reemergence of Female Monastic Orders in Premodern Japan* (Kuroda Series in East Asian Buddhism, University of Hawai'i Press, 2010) and has also written many articles and book chapters on nuns and women in East Asian Buddhism, and on Buddhism in pre-modern Japan. Meeks is currently working on a book-length study of Japanese cults to the Blood Bowl Sutra, and on translations of Eison's teachings, with Professor Paul Groner. She typically teaches "Introduction to Buddhism," a large lecture course at USC, every year.

Scott Mitchell is the Dean and holds the Yoshitaka Tamai Professorial Chair at the Institute of Buddhist Studies, Berkeley, California. He teaches and writes about

Buddhism in the West, Buddhist modernism, Pure Land Buddhism, and Buddhism and media. Mitchell is the co-editor with Natalie Quli of *Buddhism beyond Borders* (SUNY, 2015) and *Methods in Buddhist Studies* (Bloomsbury, 2019); and co-editor with Ann Gleig of the forthcoming *Oxford Handbook of American Buddhism.* He is the author of *Buddhism in America: Global Religion, Local Contexts* (Bloomsbury, 2016), and the forthcoming *Mid-Century Modern Buddhism: Japanese Americans, Beat Poets, and the Making of American Buddhism* (Oxford).

Richard K. Payne (PhD, 1985, Graduate Theological Union) is Yehan Numata Professor of Japanese Buddhist Studies at the Institute of Buddhist Studies, Berkeley. In the course of his dissertation research on the *homa*, he completed the training program on Mount Kōya, becoming a Shingon priest. He is Editor-in-Chief of the *Oxford Bibliographies, Buddhism*, and Co-Editor-in-Chief of the *Oxford Encyclopedia of Buddhism* (online, and forthcoming in print). He chairs the Editorial Committee for *Pacific World: Journal of the Institute of Buddhist Studies*, and Editorial Board of the Pure Land Buddhist Studies Series, University of Hawai'i Press. Recent publications include *Language in the Buddhist Tantra of Japan* (Bloomsbury Academic), *Pure Lands in Asian Texts and Contexts: An Anthology* (co-edited with Georgios Halkias, University of Hawai'i Press), *Homa Variations: The Study of Ritual Change across the* Longue Durée (co-edited with Michael Witzel, Oxford University Press), and *Secularizing Buddhism: New Perspectives on a Dynamic Tradition* (edited volume, Shambhala Publications). His continuing area of research is tantric Buddhist ritual.

Linda Ho Peché is an independent scholar and project director for the Vietnamese in the Diaspora Digital Archive—a digital humanities project, and director of oral history archives for the Vietnamese American Heritage Foundation—a non-profit organization. She is co-editor of the forthcoming volume, *Toward a Framework for Vietnamese American Studies: History, Community, and Memory,* to be published by Temple University Press. She earned a doctorate in cultural anthropology from The University of Texas at Austin in 2013 and has taught courses there and at Rice University's Chao Center for Asian Studies.

Charles Korin Pokorny began Sōtō Zen practice in 1991 at the San Francisco Zen Center and trained as a resident at Tassajara and Green Dragon Temple (Green Gulch Farm) from 1994 to 2006. He received a master's degree in religious studies at Stanford University in 1994. He was ordained as a Sōtō Zen priest in 1999 by Tenshin Reb Anderson, and received dharma transmission in 2018. He and his wife, Sarah Dojin Emerson, were head priest at Stone Creek Zen Center in Graton, California from 2014 to 2022 and are now transitioning to teaching at Brooklyn Zen Center. He teaches graduate courses at the Institute of Buddhist Studies in Berkeley, with a current focus on ritual practice in East Asian Buddhist traditions.

Inken Prohl is Professor of Religious Studies at the University of Heidelberg (since 2006). After studying at the Free University of Berlin, Keiō University, and the University of Tōkyō, she received her PhD in Religious Studies in 1999. For several years she has been conducting fieldwork in Japan, the United States, and Germany. Her research interests focus on modern transformations of Buddhism, the recent history of religions in Germany, Japan, and the United States, new approaches of "Material Religion," as well as Sensory Experiences of Modern Spirituality. Together with John Nelson she published *The Handbook of Contemporary Japanese Religions* (Brill, 2012). Her publications also include *Religiöse Innovationen: Die Shinto-Organisation World Mate in Japan* (Reimer, 2005), *Zen für Dummies* (Wiley, 2010), and "Buddhism in Contemporary Europe" in *The Wiley Blackwell Companion to East and Inner Asian Buddhism*, ed. Mario Poceski, 2014).

Ian Reader is Professor Emeritus at the University of Manchester. His main academic interests include the study of pilgrimage across cultures, contemporary religious practices in Japan, and studies of religion and violence. Among recent books are *Pilgrims until We Die: Unending Pilgrimage in Shikoku*, coauthored with John Shultz, about people who live as permanent pilgrims in Shikoku (Oxford University Press, 2021), *Pilgrimage in the Marketplace* (Routledge, 2014), *Pilgrimage: A Very Short Introduction* (Oxford University Press, 2015), *Health-Related Votive Tablets from Japan: Ema for Healing and Well-being*, coauthored with Peter de Smet (Leiden University Press, 2017), and *Dynamism and the Ageing of a Japanese "New" Religion* (Bloomsbury, 2019), with Erica Baffelli.

Jeffrey Samuels is Professor Emeritus in the Department of Philosophy and Religion at Western Kentucky University. His research includes Buddhist monastic culture in Sri Lanka. He has also been working on a social history of Buddhism in Malaysia, with a particular focus on Theravada communities. His publications include *Attracting the Heart: Social Relations and the Aesthetics of Emotion in Sri Lankan Monastic Culture* and *Figures of Buddhist Modernity in Asia* (co-edited with Justin McDaniel and Mark Rowe), along with numerous articles in books and academic journals. His research has been funded by the National Endowment for the Humanites, the American Academy of Religion, the Asian Research Institute (at the National University of Singapore), the Metanexus Institute, and Fulbright.

Julia Shaw is Associate Professor in South Asian Archaeology at University College London, Institute of Archaeology. Current research interests include South Asian environmental and socio-religious history; archaeology as environmental humanities; religious and medico-environmental worldviews and disability studies; interfaces between environmental archaeology, ecological public health, and global climate-change activism. She has been conducting archaeological fieldwork in India since 1998 and directs the Sanchi Survey Project. She is author of *Buddhist Landscapes in Central India* (Routledge, 2007), articles on topics related to the archaeology of Buddhism, Hinduism, socio-ecological history, land and water governmentality, and landscape survey archaeology and remote-sensing; and editor of four special volumes of *World Archaeology* (Archaeologies of Water; Religious Change; Environmental Ethics, and Medicine and Healthcare).

Miranda Shaw (PhD, Harvard University) is Professor Emerita of Religious Studies at the University of Richmond in Virginia. With a regional focus on South Asia and the Himalayas, her research centers on women, cultural constructions of gender, female deities, and sacred dance in Buddhist literary, visual, and ceremonial arts. Shaw's extensive field research in India and Nepal has been funded by the Fulbright Foundation, National Endowment for the Humanities, and American Academy of Religion. Her publications include two books, *Passionate Enlightenment: Women in Tantric Buddhism* (1994), which has been translated into six languages, and *Buddhist Goddesses of India* (2006). She contributed entries for the Buddhism section of the *Encyclopedia of Women in World Religions* (ABC-CLIO, 2019) and is currently preparing book manuscripts on the Vajrayana dance of Nepal and Buddhist goddesses of Tibet and Nepal.

Jeff Shore is Professor Emeritus of Zen Studies at Hanazono University in Kyoto, the sole Rinzai-affiliated university in the world, where he has taught full-time since 1987. Publications include *Great Doubt: Practicing Zen in the World* (Wisdom, 2016), *Zen Classics for the Modern World: Translations of Chinese Zen Poems and Prose with Contemporary Commentary* (Diane, 2011), and *Being without Self: Zen for the Modern World* (Asoka, 2008). Following graduate studies in philosophy and religion at the University of Hawaiʻi and at Temple University in his hometown of Philadelphia, he went to Japan in 1981 to practice Zen Buddhism. According to leading Zen scholar-monk Victor Sōgen Hori, "Jeff Shore is the first Westerner to complete the Rinzai koan training in Japan under a Japanese Zen master."

John S. Strong is Charles A. Dana Professor Emeritus of Religious Studies and Asian Studies at Bates College in Lewiston, Maine, where he taught for forty years. He has also had visiting appointments at the University of Peradeniya (Sri Lanka), at the University of Chicago, and at Stanford, Princeton, and Harvard Universities. His research has focused on Buddhist legendary and biographical traditions mostly in South Asia. His book publications include *The Legend of King Aśoka* (1983), *The Legend and Cult of Upagupta* (1992), *The Buddha: A Beginner's Guide* (2001), *Relics of the Buddha* (2004), *Buddhisms: An Introduction* (2015), and *The Buddha's Tooth* (2021). He now lives, happily retired, in a house on a lake in a woods in Maine.

Jasmine Syedullah is a queer black feminist, theorist of modern freedom and abolition struggles, and coauthor of *Radical Dharma: Talking Race, Love, and Liberation* (North Atlantic Books, 2016). She joined the Program of Africana Studies to teach prison studies at Vassar College in 2019 and holds the first Assistant Professor line there. Previously, Syedullah taught at the University of San Francisco and the University of California Santa Cruz where she completed her PhD in Politics with a designated emphasis in Feminist Studies and History of Consciousness. Dr Sy, as she is affectionately called, is also a certified yoga teacher and mindfulness facilitator. Her talks and workshops bridge contemplative practice and radical politics, bringing embodied practices of collective liberation to spaces of social justice, community organizing, and institutional change across occupied Turtle Island.

Kevin Trainor is Professor of Religion at the University of Vermont. His work has centered on Buddhist relic practices in South Asia, and his publications include *Relics, Ritual and Representation in Buddhism: Rematerializing the Sri Lankan Theravada Tradition* (Cambridge University Press, 1997), *Embodying the Dharma: Buddhist Relic Veneration in Asia*, co-edited with David Germano (SUNY Press, 2004), *Buddhism: The Illustrated Guide*, editor (Oxford University Press, 2004), and *Relics in Comparative Perspective*, editor, a special double issue of *Numen* (2010). His current research centers on Buddhist pilgrimage in Sri Lanka.

Vesna A. Wallace is Professor of Religious Studies, with specialization in South Asian and Mongolian Buddhist traditions, in the Department of Religious Studies at the University of California, Santa Barbara. She has produced over eighty publications, including six books, related to Buddhism in India and Mongolia.

Jonathan S. Walters is Professor of Religion and George Hudson Ball Endowed Chair of Humanities at Whitman College in Walla Walla, Washington. He is the author of *The History of Kelaniya* (Colombo, 1996) and *Finding Buddhists in Global History* (American Historical Association, 1998), coauthor of *Querying the Medieval: Texts and the History of Practices in South Asia* (Oxford, 2000), co-editor of *Constituting Communities: Theravāda Buddhism and the Religious Cultures of South and Southeast Asia* (SUNY, 2003), and translator of the Pali *Apadāna* (published online in 2018 as *Legends of the Buddhist Saints*, www.apadanatranslation.org), in addition to numerous book chapters and journal articles exploring various periods of Buddhist history, past and present. He has conducted fieldwork in rural Anuradhapura on and off since 1982.

CHAPTER 1

INTRODUCTION: EMBODIMENT AND SENSE EXPERIENCE

PAULA ARAI AND KEVIN TRAINOR

Situating Practice in the Field of Buddhist Studies

Why a handbook of Buddhist practice? During the past half century, the academic study of religion in Europe and North America has undergone significant change. Well into the twentieth century, it was rooted in assumptions about human religiosity characteristic of the prevailing impulses in Western civilization, with a focus on textual, philosophical, and historical developments in the major monotheistic traditions. This orientation provided the broad framework within which all religious traditions were studied and understood, and indeed what counted as worthy of study. Toward the latter half of the twentieth century, however, the field expanded as more voices and orientations were included within the scope of scholarly inquiry. Approaches that highlight the methodological implications of human embodiment increasingly found their place alongside textual and philosophical representations associated with religious elites.

While the trajectory of scholarship on Buddhism broadly parallels the contours of the general field of religion, the field of Buddhist studies has expanded more tentatively beyond philological, philosophical, and "Protestant" modes of analysis.[1] The field's criteria for authoritative scholarship have continued to reflect the scholarly priorities of nineteenth-century Buddhologists, whose academic inquiries gave relatively little attention to the implications of human embodiment and lived experience. Instead they looked to authoritative collections of texts, especially sources judged to provide insight into the historical origins of Buddhism, as they sought to construct a coherent representation of Buddhism that could be compared with the belief systems of the other major world religions. Mid-nineteenth-century efforts to differentiate Buddhism from

Hinduism also reinforced the tendency to represent Buddhism as rational, philosophical, and anti-ritualistic.

The expansion of Buddhist studies from practices that privilege the editing, reading, and analysis of Buddhist texts to those centered on the observation and analysis of contemporary Buddhists engaged in embodied actions of varying degrees of formality have been accompanied by concerns about authenticity and authority. In fact, the relationship between text and practice in the pursuit of authentic knowledge has been central to the work of both Western academics and Buddhist practitioners.[2] For example, debates about the relationship between *pariyatti*, a Pali term that refers to the study of Buddhist texts, and *paṭipatti*, which denotes the practice of the Buddha's teachings, have concerned members of the Theravada Buddhist sangha at least since the compilation of the highly influential Pali commentaries in the fifth century CE. As George Bond has noted, debates about the proper relationship between text and practice emerged in the nineteenth century as a key feature of Buddhist modernism, as different communities of Sri Lankan Buddhists debated the place of *bhavanā*, mental cultivation or meditation, in the lives of lay and monastic Buddhists.[3]

When examined from the standpoint of embodied practice, this contrast between textual study and meditation becomes more complicated than it might first appear. Because the earliest Indian Buddhist texts existed exclusively in oral forms and textual knowledge resided within the bodies of Buddhist monastics, early Buddhist textual practice was embodied and linked with living face-to-face forms of transmission quite different from later reading practices, which depended upon externalized written texts and their continued reinscription. Likewise, what counts as a form of practice has been complicated by nineteenth-century Euro-American scholars' tendency to sharply differentiate meditation, associated with individualized forms of rationality, from other kinds of embodied behavior linked with collective display and affective expression, such as forms of offering and veneration directed toward relics. Thus a focus on practice opens up a broader consideration of what constitutes a Buddhist text and the diversity of practices centered upon it, and turns our attention to how particular forms of knowledge and their attendant practices are given authority by both scholars and practitioners, and scholar-practitioners.

The emergence of Buddhist practice as a category of scholarly inquiry has also brought into sharper focus the role of practice in defining and maintaining analytical boundaries. Attention to embodied practices within diverse communities of Buddhists works against efforts to clearly define and represent Buddhism as a singular coherent religion. The project of defining Buddhism was linked to the emergence of religion in the West as a key analytical category, a form of conceptualization largely absent from traditional Asian forms of knowledge construction. While nineteenth-century scholars recognized to varying degrees the diversity of Buddhist histories, their studies were often organized around a master narrative that began with an original philosophical purity, associated with the Buddha and his early monastic followers and constructed through a selective reading of Pali canonical sources, that over time became corrupted (i.e., ritualized) under the influence of later generations of Buddhists whose affective needs transformed the Buddha into a god-like object of devotion. This narrative of pristine origins and decline was consonant with efforts to clearly differentiate the religions of Buddhism and Hinduism from one another, and resonated with accounts of the history of Christianity influenced by Protestant critiques of Catholic ritualism. As scholars turned to texts outside the Pali canon, which was for some time erroneously believed to represent the earliest forms of Buddhist tradition, a narrative of three distinct streams of Buddhist tradition came to dominate scholarly representations of Buddhism. Early Indian Buddhism was identified with the Hinayana/Theravada, followed by the emergence of the Mahayana and Vajrayana traditions, each defined by their distinctive collections of Buddhist texts in different languages that formed the basis for scholars' efforts to delineate their distinctive systems of belief and practice.

In contrast, the increasing prominence of field-based studies of diverse communities of Buddhists over the past several decades has illuminated the porous and contested nature of the boundaries that define different groups of Buddhists. These studies have also highlighted the role of embodied performance in constituting and defending a range of modern social identities that intersect in complex ways with other markers of belonging, such as gender, race, ethnicity, and citizenship in modern nation-states. Such representations of Buddhism tend toward more localized and particularized frames of analysis, and they commonly foreground the ways in which Buddhist beliefs and practices are embedded in local sociocultural dynamics.

While the field of religious studies has historically tended to foreground the "Eastern" or "non-Western" character of Buddhism, both in terms of its origins and historical lineages, during the past several decades increasing attention has been drawn to the establishment of Buddhist traditions in Europe and North America, and to the emergence of globalized forms of Buddhism deeply shaped by modern forms of transnational capitalism and new communication technologies. Once again, debates about the authenticity and authority of specific practices continue to shape the analysis and representation of these traditions, just as they continue to inform the internal dynamics of new communities of Buddhist practitioners. Among the issues that have emerged are the following: the centrality of meditation as the foundation for the authentic practice of Buddhism, in contrast to forms of devotional ritual; discourses centered on "mindfulness" as a generic form of mental discipline grounded in secular scientific discourses and practices; debates about the importance of foundational Buddhist cosmological principles such as karma and rebirth for authentic practice in the West; and discussions about the proper place of renunciant traditions in the sangha and the role that social hierarchies should play in its internal organization. Such negotiations increasingly take place within globalized frameworks of discourse and practice, marked by flows of Buddhist teachers, practitioners, and scholars across geographical and cultural boundaries that, until the late nineteenth century, supported the characterization of Buddhism as an "Asian" religion.

From Rite to Practice: Embodied Action and Formalization

What do we mean by practice, and how does it differ from ritual? There is a long history of scholarship on religious ritual, and as Catherine Bell has noted, Western scholars of religion have frequently employed a binary contrast between belief and ritual in their analyses. Paralleling this conceptual dichotomy are a number of other conceptual contrasts with which the belief/ritual dyad is implicitly or explicitly linked, including paired contrasts between mind and body, and reason and emotion. Bell also observes that these analytical binaries have often served discursively to evoke and reinforce social hierarchies, in particular, a contrast between the detached outside observer (the scholar), implicitly associated with mind and rational analysis, and religious practitioners, whose embodied participation in the powerful sensory engagements of ritual action are assumed to preclude the possibility of their understanding the ritual's true meaning within its sociocultural context.[4] This contrast between belief and ritual is central to Durkheim's influential definition of religion, and it finds a classic expression in Geertz's analysis of religion as a cultural system, where he observes that outside observers can only aesthetically appreciate or scientifically dissect religious performances, in contrast to participants, for whom they are "enactments, materializations, realizations" of a particular religious perspective.[5]

This dichotomous characterization of the relationship between belief and ritual on the one hand, and of the divergent perspectives of outside analysts and inside participants on the other, parallels a binary opposition that has structured an influential narrative of Buddhism's historical origins in ancient India. This account highlights the Buddha's rejection of brahmanic sacrifice, which construed karma as ritual action, in favor of an individualized and ethicized conception of karma, reconceived as an individual's intentional actions. The Buddhist reconfiguration of karma's significance, according to this narrative, is tied to the centrality of Buddhist meditation, which is understood to facilitate the individual's process of gaining analytical distance from the body and its sensory attachments.[6] Once again, this tendency to privilege mind over body and detached rationality over somatically grounded sensation and emotion, linked with a powerful discourse of normative monastic renunciation and social disengagement, has contributed to problematic characterizations of Buddhism as anti-ritualistic, and has deflected attention from the centrality of embodied practices in Buddhist communities. It has, for example, tended to obscure the ways in which Buddhist meditation can be understood as a kind of embodied practice, and neglected forms of engagement with Buddhist texts that aren't focused on their semantic content.

We have chosen to organize this handbook around the category of Buddhist practice, rather than Buddhist ritual, because "practice" foregrounds the centrality of embodied action without necessarily implying that the action in question is highly formalized and repetitious. It points instead to the fluid and open-ended character of ritualization, which we regard as a wide-ranging behavioral dynamic marked by varying degrees of formalization and improvisation, a dynamic that is most fruitfully engaged when the observable actions of embodied individuals are explored in connection with the particular material and social environments that frame those actions. We thus seek to keep in continuous play the interactions of three analytically distinct registers: individuals' bodies, marked by complex internal systems of psycho-physical interaction; distinct material environments that afford those individuals a range of concrete possibilities for sensory engagement; and particular forms of social organization linked to power and authority that shape human interactions. In this sense, practice can be understood as fundamentally about kinds of strategic behavior, as the sometimes convergent and sometimes divergent aims of particular individuals and social groups play out through their embodied interactions. What marks a particular practice as "Buddhist" is itself a matter of strategic engagement, and this includes a given person's self-identification along the scholar-practitioner continuum, an identification that may change according to context.

Continuum of Contexts

Our attention to embodied thought and action invites attention to the implications of positionality and context. Analytically highlighting the relationships among the three foci of individual person, material surround, and social interactions foregrounds the interactive and emergent properties of human practice, and points to the diversity of analytical standpoints that potentially come into play in the work of Buddhist scholars and practitioners. Consider, for example, the interactions of these three registers within the confines of a library, which is both an independent physical structure and a socially constituted site that shapes the interactions between the people who use it and the objects that it preserves and controls for particular purposes. Those granted access to it commonly embody a set of authoritative skills cultivated over many years (e.g., language mastery, paleography), skills finely calibrated to the effective use of the texts that it contains (e.g., reading, transcription, memorization, oral recitation), and that form the basis for other practices that extend beyond the library's walls (e.g., writing, teaching, publication, chanting, invocation). Thus while the library as physical structure and social institution represents a key location for understanding some formative "Buddhist" practices for both scholars and practitioners, the broader significance of those practices emerges only when they are viewed in relationship to additional practices that unfold outside its walls, practices around which various forms of authority and authenticity are constellated and performed. Moreover, how one understands a given library practice varies depending upon one's standpoint, whether framed by the experience of particular library users and their individual motivations, by the material characteristics of the library itself as it impinges upon those who enter and use it (or are excluded from its use), or viewed in relation to broader social dynamics that set the terms for how the texts preserved in the library can and should be used and how possible interpretations of their meaning are secured.

The human body is constituted of complex biologically conditioned features, including sexual organs, skin color, and a complex sensory apparatus, as well as socially constructed markers of identity and status such as gender, sexual orientation, race, and ethnicity. Human orientations toward and engagements with surrounding materiality emerge interactively in accordance with the constraints and possibilities imposed by particular physical bodies, the impact of specific material features of their surrounding environments, and in relation to the particular behavioral and linguistic codes into which people have been socialized. Among the culturally inflected variables that influence these human orientations are foundational constructions of the relationship between the mind and body, between the self and others, and of the proper ordering of community, for example, by assumptions about inalienable individual rights and the justness of hierarchical power differentials.

Our focus on religious practice highlights the role of ritualized behavior in mediating the complex and ongoing sensory interactions of human bodies with their material surroundings. One particular sense may be foregrounded in a given practice, such as touch when holding prayer beads, mind when visualizing Avalokiteśvara, or taste when sipping ceremonial tea. How these interactions affect the body and what the encounter might mean to a practitioner or scholarly observer is simultaneously constrained and open-ended. One person may be transported through an olfactory encounter with incense that intensifies attention to the present moment, while another may experience an allergic reaction and choose in the future to only practice in spaces that mandate unscented offerings. Participants in religious practice function simultaneously in all three registers, embedded in rich milieux with individual, material, and social dimensions. For example, an encounter with monastics in silk brocade robes chanting before a golden Buddha creates a sensorium of auditory, visual, and mental activity that may strengthen the monks' religious authority for one practitioner, provoke an anti-clerical response in another, while inclining a scholarly observer to theorize about Buddhist cosmologies, social hierarchies, or the aesthetics of Buddhist practice. And the criteria for judging who has the privileged perspective on the significance of this encounter are likewise deeply linked to diverse forms of practice that extend well beyond the confines of the temple in which the encounters take place.

Varying ontological and cosmological worldviews augment the range of sensory encounters with materiality. Some Buddhists, for example, hold that a rock can manifest Buddha-nature, while others, Buddhist and non-Buddhist, regard a rock as mere materiality lacking potential sentience. Buddhist practitioners who cohabit a world with living bodhisattvas may feel exaltation upon seeing His Holiness the Dalai Lama, an incarnation of the bodhisattva of compassion, or may feel protected by wearing a red cord he has blessed. Some would never let a text they consider sacred touch the floor, while others remain aloof as dust accumulates on a book that they devoted years of their lives to writing. Practices like pilgrimage follow the contours of a textually narrated Buddhist geography, marked out by stupas and images, even as the moving bodies of pilgrims bring those pathways to life. Predisposed as social beings to coordinate with others and sharing deep somatic capacities for synchronization through shared sensory stimulation, religious practices often engender powerful integrative experiences, even as they potentially sharpen the divide between insiders and outsiders and heighten conflict over territorial control.

Each person has a distinct experiential perspective influenced by physical differences and personal memories, yet each individual is also deeply socialized in ways that can be analyzed from a variety of theoretical perspectives. Attention to forms of embodied social interaction illuminates the ebbs and flows of inclusion and estrangement, the orchestration of unequal access to prestige, authority, and material resources, and broad dynamics of conflict and cooperation orchestrated by markers of difference and solidarity, such as gender, ethnicity, sexual orientation, and racialization. For example, in the history of conflict over women's ordination, one can observe how different sangha institutions, in some cases aligned with state-directed forms of political power, have acted in particular circumstances to support or suppress the struggles of Buddhist women to pursue their highest religious aspirations. And ordination itself is a powerful form of practice that significantly alters the lives of those who undertake it through transformations of their bodies (removing hair and donning robes), changes in their material surroundings (ranging from solitary forest dwellings to large urban monastic complexes), and, in many cases, significant status elevation closely keyed to restrictive behavioral codes and expectations of ritual proficiency.

Viewing Buddhist Practice through Lenses of Emotion, Embodiment, and Agency

As an exercise in conceptual cartography, this *Handbook* seeks to nurture the emergence of innovative and self-reflective Buddhist studies scholarship by providing some analytical landmarks for orienting readers to the rich diversity of practices that animate Buddhist lives and cultures. Facing this potentially overwhelming panoply of actions undertaken by countless Buddhists across a vast geographical, historical, and cultural expanse, it is reasonable to ask: What, if anything, do they have in common? One possible answer: these forms of practice share an orientation toward reducing suffering (*duḥkha*). In keeping with this core concern, this volume explores a number of strategic practices that diverse communities of Buddhists have undertaken as they navigate the perils of samsara and pursue diverse liberatory ideals.

We have organized our mapping of the terrain of Buddhist practice through the heuristic lenses of three key dimensions of religious practice. Whatever else they might entail, Buddhist practices evoke and direct a wide range of emotions, are grounded in human embodiment, and support the agency of those who undertake them to realize particular goals. While it is a commonplace of modern scholarship to presume a clear division between the aims and methods of scholars of Buddhism on the one hand, and of "religious" or "spiritual" practitioners on the other, this volume seeks to explore what these distinctive forms of practice have in common, as well as what distinguishes them, whether the goals articulated for undertaking them be the gaining of insight or tenure. The approaches and methods that scholars and practitioners undertake—whether discursively framed as first-person, second-person, or third-person—reflect the dynamics entailed by human emotion, embodiment, and agency. Issues of authenticity and authority likewise inform the actions that scholars and practitioners perform, even if the criteria for identifying and resolving those issues may vary greatly depending upon their respective contexts.

Emotion

Emotion and religion have a long and tangled history in Western analytical traditions.[7] Emotion or "feeling" has, at times, been identified as the essence of religion and, when linked with private forms of subjective experience, functioned as a bulwark against the deconstructive power of scientific rationality. There is also a long history of debate over the primary location of emotions: Are they best understood as sense-based mental disturbances, as somatically grounded instinctual responses linked to human evolution, or as fundamentally social phenomena with complex histories and a wide range of distinctive cultural forms? Where one locates emotions, whether as fundamentally biological and universal across the human species or as socially and culturally differentiated, has powerful analytical and epistemological consequences. Are emotions susceptible to rational inquiry? What is their relationship to cognitive processes? And what role do they or should they play in authoritative knowledge construction?[8]

It is important to note at the outset that traditional Buddhist discourses lack any direct lexical equivalent to the term "emotion." A wide range of particular emotions have been clearly differentiated in various Buddhist analytical projects, often broadly evaluated as either "skillful" or "unskillful" (*kuśala/akuśala*) with respect to their role in one's advance or retreat along the path to ultimate liberation from suffering.[9] Generalized discussions about the role of emotion in Buddhism are thus potentially misleading, since using the broad category of emotion tends to aggregate things that diverse Buddhist discourses have typically differentiated. And there is also the enduring legacy of nineteenth-century representations of Buddhism as a religion of systematic emotional detachment, programmatically devoid of sentiments of devotion, at least in its earliest and ostensibly more authentic forms. Thus one might be surprised, for example, that the practice of cultivating *upekṣā*, "equanimity" (one of the four *brahmavihāra*s, or "divine abidings"), aims at developing a positive emotion, not extirpating emotion altogether.[10]

As recent Buddhist studies scholarship has highlighted, Buddhist communities have, through their religious practices, cultivated and orchestrated a wide range of somatically grounded emotional responses. Examples include the powerful effects of drawing near the glorious bodies of buddhas and bodhisattvas (present in the flesh or materially mediated through relics, texts, and images), of setting forth on extended pilgrimages to access the powerful effects of localized forms of religious presence, and of accessing virtual worlds through the mediation of Buddhist websites and smartphone apps.

The increasing prevalence of ethnographically based scholarship has contributed greatly to an appreciation of the disparate emotional valences of lived religion within a diversity of contemporary Buddhist communities, and ethnographic methodology has recognized the intersubjective and affective dimensions of ethnographic fieldwork. Text-based scriptural analyses, whether pursued in secular academic contexts or within communities of Dharma practice, have generally been less attuned to the positive role of emotion in Buddhist traditions, though creative engagements with different genres of Buddhist texts have also played a key role in foregrounding the capacity of narrative to evoke powerful feelings.[11] Consider, for example, this seemingly disembodied aphorism in the *Dhammapada* "No sons there are for protection, / Neither father nor even relations, / For one seized by the End-Maker; Among relations there is no protection. / Knowing this fact, The wise one, restrained by virtue, / Would make clear, right quickly, / The path leading to Nibbāna." Theravada commentarial tradition links this verse to a story about Paṭācārā, who loses her husband, children, and parents on a single day, descends into a grief so profound that she walks about the city naked, and returns to sanity through an encounter with the Buddha's profound compassion.[12] This narrative grants the verses an embodied emotional urgency, and opens up a social world marked by class and gender difference.

Attention to the emotional power of visual images and their behavioral force reveals an additional dimension of Buddhist practice. Consider these two visual representations of the Paṭācārā story in Sri Lanka, the first a version of the narrative painted in the 1990s at Bellanvila Temple near Colombo (Figure 1.1), the second a nineteenth-century depiction from Kataluva Temple in the south (Figure 1.2). The Bellanvila scene shown here depicts Paṭācārā using her body to shelter her children from a torrential downpour, powerfully evoking the embodied force of her fierce love and self-sacrificing desire to protect them. The tragic limits of this maternal care and its cost in suffering soon become apparent when both of her children are swept to their deaths as they attempt to cross a stream engorged by the rains.

The depth of Paṭācārā's suffering, brought to a climax when she learns that her mother, father, and brother have all perished from the collapse of their house during the storm, appears in the nineteenth-century painting from Kataluva; here Paṭācārā is shown wandering about, deranged by her grief and oblivious to the loss of her clothing until she encounters the Buddha, whose compassion returns her to her senses, and she requests permission to go forth as a member of the women's monastic community. Subsequent scenes depict her life as a *bhikkhuṇī*, later known as "foremost in the mastery of the Vinaya" (a striking contrast to her earlier naked disorientation) and spiritual preceptor

FIGURE 1.1. Detail from temple mural depicting Paṭācārā sheltering her children from the storm with her body. Painted in the 1990s by Somabandu Vidyapati, Bellanvila Rajamaha Viharaya.

Photo: Kevin Trainor.

to a large community of Buddhist nuns. These depictions propel their viewers through a complex web of interdependent and emergent emotional forces linked to the visually mediated story of Paṭācārā, as well as to the viewers' own diverse emotional histories. As a relatively distanced observer, I can easily catalog the distinct series of emotions evoked in Paṭācārā's story, from her socially disruptive love for the lower-class servant who became her husband, her continued longing to return to the family she disgraced, her maternal care to protect and nurture her children, her overpowering grief and disorientation elicited by the loss of all her loved ones, her return to equanimity through the Buddha's compassionate presence, and finally her own compassionate nurturing of the religious lives of the women in her community. What I cannot confidently assess is how these emotional potentials, embodied quite differently in these two distinct temple paintings,[13] gain force and consequence in the emotional lives of the individuals who encounter them in real time, each shaped by unique individual stories as well as a diversity of social identities and roles.[14] Even if one must acknowledge the relative analytical indeterminacy of these affective forces, their connection to Buddhist practice remains clear, particularly when we situate these paintings in the temple settings that frame them, which provide the immediate opportunity for merit-making offerings and acts of veneration.

FIGURE 1.2. Detail from temple mural depicting the naked, mentally deranged Paṭācārā as she approaches the Buddha. Unknown 19th-century artist, Kataluva Purvarama Maha Viharaya.

Photo: Kevin Trainor.

Embodiment

Bodies are primary sites of Buddhist practice. Buddhist discourses commonly investigate the body as a privileged location for observing and analyzing the dynamic, interactive forces that shape human perception, intentionality, and action. Embodiment as a heuristic lens highlights the interdependence of internal and external factors that shape individual experiences, which can be seen both as a manifestation of those factors, as well as the basis upon which subsequent perceptions and actions predictably unfold in time and space. Exploring Buddhist practice through the lens of embodiment illuminates a plethora of stark and subtle distinctions between people and reveals patterns rippling through a cross section of socio-historical milieux.

When viewing Buddhist practice through the lens of embodiment, two broad dynamics come into focus: body as problem and body as solution. These different notions of the body elucidate a range of practice strategies that are based upon varying understandings of the relationship of practice to awakening. Practices that observe the body as problem home in on impermanent, impure, and sensory distortions associated with the body. Practices to address these problems are diverse, ranging from meditating on a decomposing corpse to simply avoiding activities perceived as stimulating sensory desires and attachments. One could argue that the Buddhist monastic discipline codified in the Vinaya aims at addressing the body as problem.

In contrast, two major currents run through the body-as-solution orientation. One current delineates body as process and highlights transformation; here body is a primary medium for development and improvement. Practices that characterize this current include such practices as chanting, seated meditation, making offerings at an altar, and pilgrimage. The other current sees the body as the site of realization. Viewed from this perspective, the body is not a means to an end, but rather the locus of awakening. Practice is approached as a matter of acting in accord with the inherently enlightened nature of the body, fully present in the most mundane of activities, from eating to defecating. Looking through the lens of embodiment thus reveals how diverse Buddhist body-centered discourses construct a continuum of valorizations, from body as font of impurity and fountainhead of suffering to body as carriage of bliss and manifestation of buddha-nature.

The lens of embodiment also throws into relief how current communities and institutions of Buddhist practice and scholarship wrestle with a multiplicity of embodied identities. All bodies are subject to taxonomies of identity formation, including race/ethnicity, sexual orientation, gender identity, and variations of bodily shape and ability. These differences, variably identified with individual bodies, are often indexed to hierarchies of social authority and authenticity. Such value-based differentiations define and police the boundaries of social groups by marking particular bodies as included or excluded. Examining the possibilities and limitations that forms of embodiment foster sheds light on how power, agency, and value are culturally and socially encoded and distributed. How one perceives a body and which social constructs are attended to has a wide range of potential effects for practitioners, whether they locate themselves within academic or Dharma-based communities.

Social constructions of embodiment can impose positive or negative valences on bodily features, according to context. Those recognized as belonging to the hegemonic norm display embodied markers that are assessed positively and are accorded authority and power. Those whose embodiment does not match dominant norms are prone to being devalued and marginalized. Under some circumstances, however, markers of marginality are positively assessed by the majority, such as when dominant members of the group pursue ideals of inclusion and diversity. In either case, imposed negative and positive identities have an impact on individuals and groups. While not all group members internalize the assumptions of the dominant value system, the conditions within which they must seek their own well-being create very different possibilities for flourishing, depending on their relative congruence with the ideological and institutional constraints imposed by the dominant group.

Discourses on non-self in Dharma community contexts illustrate the complexity of issues that come into play when attention is directed toward dynamics of embodiment. Recourse to the principle of non-self may direct attention away from the effects of embodied social differences, allowing members of the dominant community to ignore incidents of micro-aggression and conditions of structural injustice. Moreover, an emphasis on individual responsibility for one's life circumstances, reinforced by constructions of karmic agency and the primacy of individual perceptions, may blunt an awareness of the need for collective action to dismantle systematic oppression. Thus invoking non-self discourses may privilege the dominant group and reinforce marginalization. At the same time, practitioners outside the dominant group may find that cultivating an awareness of non-self heightens their insight into the conditioned and transient nature of the self and supports the deconstruction of harmful perceptions and attitudes, providing resources for resistance.

In academic contexts, scholarship that ignores the implications of embodiment, especially of marginalized bodies, deflects attention away from power differentials tied to embodied differences and reinforces a normativity that unconsciously supports the privileged majority. Problematic perceptions of scholars' bodies linked to assumptions about differentials of intelligence and authority may influence search committees, letters of recommendation, course evaluations, and performance reviews. Attention to embodied differences, for example, gender and race/ethnicity, opens up a critical understanding of how particular religious texts, commonly assumed to represent the shared perspectives of the members of a religious community, may in fact represent the views of a dominant minority whose authority those texts support. Analyses that are inattentive to the social force of embodied differences obscure the forms of practice, self-understanding, and agency of members of the community outside the dominant group. A focus on embodiment is thus vital to critical scholarship, for it highlights how unconscious assumptions about embodied differences potentially influence scholarly interpretations, and it directs attention to the lives of community members whose perspectives and practices may not be visible or accurately represented in the authorized representations of particular religious communities.

Recognizing the bodily conditions of scholarly practice can in turn illuminate how our own bodily particularities and those of the people with whom we engage might affect our selection of topics and authoritative sources, and predispose us to dismiss or favor certain methodological and theoretical approaches. Being conscious of our embodied particularity and its implications leads us to acknowledge the limitations and incompleteness of any analytical project, and encourages us to open our scholarship to a broader community of conversation partners.

Academic analysis informed by an understanding of the ways that scholarly practice is itself shaped by the scholar's own embodiment and particular forms of practice supports the production of qualitative knowledge that is richly contextualized, thus foregrounding the diversity of Buddhist communities and highlighting the dangers of static and essentialized generalizations about "Buddhist" ideas and ideals. In highlighting the particularities of embodied life, the dynamics of the tradition as practiced—whether in the present day or in historically distant communities—come more clearly into view, making palpable the local, somatic, and kinesthetic dimensions of lived religion. In this way, the emergent properties of practice are brought to the fore and, depending upon the scholar's analytical focus, a clearer understanding of their cognitive, social, psychological, aesthetic, political, or spiritual dimensions becomes available.

Agency

In focusing on agency as a key dimension of practice, we take as a starting point the observation that practice has a strong strategic orientation. In other words, it is purposive behavior that is typically formalized in ways that set it apart from more random, spontaneous activities, and those who undertake it do so to pursue particular aims, shaped by individual and communal interests. In this respect, both Buddhist and academic practitioners engage in forms of practice that they perceive to be efficacious and empowering. But by what criteria are particular acts determined to be efficacious, and toward what ends? Whose authority and what material constraints set the conditions within which efficacy is experienced and assessed?

Central to notions of agency are basic assumptions about how individual agents are constituted. For example, do the kinds of relatively formalized behaviors that we identify as strategic presume a self-conscious agent performing actions directed toward realizing intentional ends that can be explicitly articulated? Given the powerful role of sensory interactions in human behavior and their links to somatically grounded affects, is it perhaps apposite to consider the agency of human bodies that seek their own ends apart from and possibly contrary to conscious choice? In addition, how do particular foundational assumptions, for example Buddhist teachings of *anātman* (the absence of a stable and enduring self) or scientific models of material causation, enable or thwart particular forms of human agency?

Our focus on the dynamics of Buddhist practice, in keeping with the continuum of contexts identified previously (internal psycho-physical dynamics, sensory engagements with material environments, social dynamics), highlights the interactive and emergent character of human agency, and recognizes that agency takes on different appearances depending upon the viewer's location and the analytical frameworks they employ. Broadly speaking, scholars of Buddhist traditions located in Euro-American traditions of scholarship work within institutions that value objectivity and support practices aimed at intersubjective validation as a means of securing authoritative knowledge. Consequently, claims to knowledge grounded in private forms of experience and personal subjectivity are commonly met with professional skepticism, particularly in the natural and social sciences. Ideals and disciplines of scientific rigor and objective analysis are socially and materially supported through funding agencies, research laboratories, libraries, academic presses, and elaborate peer-review practices aimed at minimizing the distorting effects of personal bias. At the same time, ideals of individual creativity and ownership of the scholar's unique intellectual products are affirmed through formal citation practices and copyright laws devised to protect private property.

An alternative practice of intersubjective validation informs the increasing prominence of field-based research within contemporary Buddhist communities. Grounded in epistemologies that affirm the value of emotion and embodied experience for interpersonal understanding, these forms of scholarship commonly foreground the impact of a scholar's subject-position within a field of unequal power relationships and potentially heighten awareness of the ethical implications of scholarly representations in ways that text-based analyses of historically distant Buddhist communities have not.

A perceived disjunction between those who work in academic institutions and those who participate in Dharma communities is heightened in the United States by constitutionally based prohibitions against public funding for religious groups. Many scholars of Buddhism working in state-supported religious studies departments take pains to sharply differentiate their "study" of religion from its "practice" by Buddhists. Emerging debates over "mindfulness" practices illuminate the fraught nature of this distinction. Whether mindfulness counts as "Buddhist" and "religious" depends upon the contexts in which it is practiced, as well as on the contested meanings of those categories and the forms of agency that they enable. Secularized forms of mindfulness are widely practiced in hospitals and in state-supported educational institutions, reflecting what Jeff Wilson has termed a process of "mystification" that obscures the practice's historical and cultural roots.[15] Critics of the incorporation of these practices in public schools characterize them as forms of "stealth Buddhism," deeply embedded in a system of ethical values that they regard as religious.[16] Collaborative research undertaken by scientists and practitioners of "contemplative wisdom"[17] over the past three decades under the aegis of the Mind and Life Institute likewise points to an extensive framework of shared inquiry and practice that strategically blurs the boundaries between the domains of science and spirituality as these have been formulated within the context of Western modernity.

A focus on agency in the context of Buddhist practice directs scholarly attention away from static generalizations about what Buddhists believe and toward the enormous diversity of cultural and historical contexts within which Buddhists have taken up particular forms of action aimed at the alleviation of suffering. However multiform these practices, they have generally been framed within a worldview in which the effects of "skillful" and "unskillful" actions play out over multiple lifetimes, and in which access to the Dharma and the sangha, linked to the compassionate activities of buddhas and bodhisattvas, provides essential guidance along the path to awakening.

While some authoritative Buddhist discourses frame action and its consequences primarily in terms of conscious intentionality and foreground individual agency as determinative for progressing along the path to awakening, others emphasize modes of interdependence. These include accounts of supportive relationships forged within Buddhist communities, both lay and monastic, and stories of the liberative force of embodied encounters with extraordinary human and nonhuman agents (buddhas, arhats, bodhisattvas, deities). Such accounts are often tied to privileged locations set apart through various formal ritual strategies (temples, domestic shrines, stupas, mountains) and are frequently linked to aesthetically powerful objects (relics and reliquaries, images, mandalas) that materially mediate the presence of those powerful agents of liberation.

These latter settings, which foreground interactive relationships between the bodies of individual agents and the material and social settings within which they are situated, figure prominently in the essays collected in this volume. While the idea of a handbook implies a certain comprehensiveness and hands-on practicality, we have organized this collection with a keen awareness that the dynamics of practice, embedded in individual bodies and particular locations, push against efforts to generalize and systematize. In place of comprehensiveness, we have sought to include a diversity of examples from various Buddhist traditions, cultural locations, and historical periods, organized around several interpretive settings useful for observing the dynamics of Buddhist practice. These include broad regional perspectives, formative examples of material mediation, physical bodies as sites of transformation and body-mind interaction, powerful sites of human and nonhuman interaction, relationships within and between lay and monastic communities, and several emergent forms of Buddhist practice shaped by conditions of modernity and the influence of globalization. By including essays written by scholars whose work is informed by a variety of critical methodologies (textual analysis, historical research, archaeology, field-based ethnography) and relationships to Dharma practice (hospital chaplain, Dharma teachers, ordained, lay, and non-practitioners), we have sought to showcase a wide range of potential approaches, and we are hopeful this volume will support an expanding dialogue as our readers make use of it, creating new conversations as they selectively engage the perspectives of individual contributors while pursuing their own areas of research.

Notes

1. Gregory Schopen, "Archaeology and Protestant Presuppositions in the Study of Indian Buddhism," *History of Religions* 31 (1991): 1–23.
2. Charles Hallisey, "Roads Taken and Not Taken in the Study of Theravāda Buddhism," in *Curators of the Buddha: The Study of Buddhism under Colonialism*, ed. Donald S. Lopez, Jr. (Chicago: University of Chicago Press, 1995), 31–61.
3. George D. Bond, *The Buddhist Revival in Sri Lanka: Religious Tradition, Reinterpretation and Response* (Columbia, SC: South Carolina Press, 1988), 147–48.
4. Catherine Bell, *Ritual Theory, Ritual Practice* (New York: Oxford University Press, 1992).
5. Clifford Geertz, *The Interpretation of Cultures* (New York: Basic Books, 1973), 113–14; Geertz critiques functionalist analyses that simply reduce religious representations to underlying social dynamics.
6. See, for example, Gombrich's account of this: ". . . for brahminism morality remained mainly extrinsic, like ritual: realized in action which derives its value from the social context. It was the Buddha who first completely ethicized the concept: in Hinduism ritual and moral obligations remain lumped together"; Richard F. Gombrich, *Theravāda Buddhism: A Social History from Ancient Benares to Modern Colombo* (London: Routledge & Kegan Paul, 1988), 46.
7. John Corrigan, "Introduction: How Do We Study Religion and Emotion?," in *Feeling Religion*, ed. John Corrigan (Durham, NC: Duke University Press, 2017), 1–21; see also

Corrigan, "Introduction: The Study of Religion and Emotion," in *The Oxford Handbook of Religion and Emotion*, ed. John Corrigan (New York: Oxford University Press, 2008), 3–13.

8. The role of emotion or "affect" in the study of religion is explored in Donovan Schaefer, *Religious Affect: Animality, Evolution, and Power* (Durham, NC: Duke University Press, 2015). Donovan demonstrates the power of affect studies to reorient the study of religion from approaches that privilege linguistically based analysis to those grounded in somatically based affects and the priority of human intersubjectivity.
9. Maria Heim, "Buddhism," in *The Oxford Handbook of Religion and Emotion*, ed. John Corrigan (New York: Oxford University Press, 2008), 17–34.
10. Heim, "Buddhism," 25.
11. Stephen C. Berkwitz, "Emotions and Ethics in Buddhist History: The Sinhala *Thupavamsa* and the Work of Virtue." *Religion* 31, no. 2 (April 2001): 155–73.
12. Translation of *Dhammapada* vss. 288–89 quoted from John Ross Carter and Mahinda Palihawadana, trans., *The Dhammapada* (New York: Oxford University Press, 1987), 318; the fifth-century Pali commentary on these verses narrates Paṭācārā's story and an embellished Sinhala version, dating to the thirteenth century, is included in the *Saddharmaratnāvaliya*. See H. C. Norman, ed., *The Commentary on the Dhammapada* (London: Pali Text Society, 1970), 2:260–70.; E. W. Burlingame, trans., *Buddhist Legends* (London: Pali Text Society, 1990), 2:250–56; Rajini Obeyesekere, trans., *Portraits of Buddhist Women: Stories from the* Saddharmaratnāvaliya (Albany: State University of New York Press, 2001), 126–33.
13. It is noteworthy that the twentieth-century depiction at Bellanvila Temple does not depict the nude body of Paṭācārā, even though other paintings in that temple, by the same painter, depict female nudity.
14. David Freedburg's *The Power of Images* (Chicago: University of Chicago Press, 1989) explores the power of religious images to evoke powerful and even violent emotional responses; for a Sri Lankan example situated in postcolonial political dynamics, see H. L. Seneviratne, "Revolt in the Temple: Politics of a Temple Paintings Project in Sri Lanka," in *The Anthropologist and the Native: Essays for Gananath Obeyesekere*, ed. H. L. Seneviratne (London: Anthem Press, 2011), 179–202. doi:10.7135/UPO9780857289919.011.
15. Jeff Wilson, *Mindful America* (New York: Oxford University Press, 2014).
16. Candy Gunther Brown, *Debating Yoga and Mindfulness in Public Schools: Reforming Secular Education or Reestablishing Religion?* (Chapel Hill: University of North Carolina Press, 2019).
17. See https://www.mindandlife.org/mission/.

Further Reading

Bell, Catherine. *Ritual Theory, Ritual Practice*. New York: Oxford University Press, 1992.

Corrigan, John, ed. *The Oxford Handbook of Religion and Emotion*. New York: Oxford University Press, 2008.

David Morgan. *The Thing about Religion: An Introduction to the Material Study of Religions*. Chapel Hill: University of North Carolina Press, 2021.

Samuels, Jeffrey. *Attracting the Heart: Social Relations and the Aesthetics of Emotion in Sri Lankan Monastic Culture*. Honolulu: University of Hawaiʻi Press, 2010.

Schaefer, Donovan. *Religious Affect: Animality, Evolution, and Power*. Durham, NC: Duke University Press, 2015.

Tsomo, Karma Lekshe, *Eminent Buddhist Women and Buddhist Women across Cultures: Realizations*. Albany: State University of New York Press, 2020.

Tsomo, Karma, Lekshe, ed. *Buddhist Feminisms and Femininities*. Albany: State University of New York Press, 2019.

Williams, Angel Kyodo, Rod Owens, and Jasmine Syedullah. *Radical Dharma: Talking Race Love & Liberation*. Berkeley, CA: North Atlantic Press, 2016.

Wilson, Jeff. *Mindful America: The Mutual Transformation of Buddhist Meditation and American Culture*. New York: Oxford University Press, 2014.

PART I

REGIONAL PERSPECTIVES

THE first five chapters in Part I provide an orientation to broader dynamics of Buddhist practice, framed within one of five commonly differentiated geographical regions; a sixth chapter explores globalized dynamics of twenty-first-century forms of practice. Each of the five regions is, to varying degrees, characterized by shared historical, cultural, or linguistic influences that have shaped the transmission and adaptation of distinctive forms of Buddhist tradition and practice. These essays are intended to provide a more comprehensive orientation, in contrast to the essays organized in the subsequent six parts, which are grouped together by distinctive dimensions of Buddhist practice that the authors explore in greater particularity, reflecting the embeddedness of their research into Buddhist practices in local contexts. Foregrounding these regional perspectives, rather than the commonly differentiated traditions of Theravada, Mahayana, and Vajrayana, underscores the embodied nature of Buddhist practice and highlights its great multiplicity and diversity.

Inevitably, a focus on regional dynamics draws attention away from the complex flows of people, ideas, and practices across regional boundaries that have characterized Buddhist traditions over more than two millennia. Consider, for example, the case of Sri Lankan Buddhist traditions, which are historically grounded in South Asian linguistic and cultural dynamics, but which here are primarily explored in the context of Southeast Asian cultural and political formations. This points to the value of reading the regional overviews in relation to each other, attuned to broader movements of people and practices across regional boundaries, enabled in part by modern technologies and forms of categorization, not least of which is the idea of "Buddhism" itself.

CHAPTER 2

BUDDHIST PRACTICE IN SOUTH ASIA

MIRANDA SHAW

THE South Asian subcontinent spans areas presently designated as India, Pakistan, Bangladesh, and the Nepal Terai. As a geographic region, the landmass of South Asia is bordered by the Hindu Kush and Himalayan mountain ranges, the Arabian Sea, and the Indian Ocean.[1] The topography of the region afforded overland routes, waterways, and seaports for the royal emissaries and trade networks that carried Buddhism from its heartland in the fertile Indo-Gangetic Plain throughout the subcontinent and across Asia, where it took root and gained diverse cultural and local inflections. The kingdom in which Shakyamuni was born and grew to adulthood is within the current border of Nepal, while his religious quest and post-enlightenment activities were concentrated in northeastern India. There are scant archaeological records of Buddhist practice during the lifetime of the Buddha in perhaps the fifth or early fourth century BCE. However, scholars seeking to reconstruct and understand the practices of South Asian Buddhists of millennia past encounter an abundance of architectural, artistic, and inscriptional evidence from the third century BCE onward, eventually joined by scriptural literature, that remains rich and challengingly complex through the close of the Pāla period in the twelfth century CE.

In what follows, my discussion adheres to a broadly chronological treatment of South Asian Buddhism as it evolved through the early formative period (third century BCE through second century CE), Mahayana movement (first century CE onward), and Vajrayana tradition (seventh through twelfth centuries CE). This is not a literal periodization and does not imply supersession of a given practice or movement by another but is, rather, a way to identify trends whose emergence builds on and extends previous developments that persisted alongside them.

My thematic focus is the recognition and veneration of female generative power that is rooted in the cultural substrate of the South Asian subcontinent and wends through Buddhist thought, iconography, and practice. Gender roles have been scripted and negotiated throughout Buddhist history in ways to which scholars are attending with increasing nuance. Nonetheless, an enduring feature of South Asian Buddhism is a recognition of female bodies—from maternal earth and feminine facets of nature to lofty goddesses—as sources of life, birth, vital energies, and transformative power, which in turn are conditions of spiritual practice and attainment. Moreover, Buddhism has never posited a separation of mind and matter that might demand a rejection of bodily existence and the material world (matter, matrix, mother) as a condition of spiritual progress. Buddhism has located the primary sources of suffering and illusion within the purview of consciousness, which is inextricable from embodiment.

Early Buddhism

Among the earliest and most enduring records of Buddhist practice are sites centering on stupas, monuments that at once commemorate Shakyamuni and make him tangibly present in the form of relics. South Asian stupa sites are the focus of voluminous scholarship and ongoing archaeological discovery, continuously augmenting evidence of Buddhist practices in South Asia. My discussion begins with the earliest extant examples, the base from which the stupa began its long course of evolution. The early stupa of the first century BCE through second century CE was a solid hemispheric dome topped by a modest pinnacle and surrounded by circumambulatory paths and a railing (*vedikā*) whose gates, pillars, and crossbars were elaborately carved with sacred imagery, worship scenes, and supernatural and divine beings.[2]

The primary purpose of a stupa is to serve as a womb for the relics of Shakyamuni Buddha (and, over time, other Buddhist venerables). This purpose is inherent in the origin, design, and designations of the stupa mound. The earliest roots of the stupa mound are arguably traceable to a global Paleolithic and Neolithic practice spanning millennia of burial in a womb-shaped space—be it a cave, pottery vessel, or built structure—to signal not the end of life, but return to the birth source for transition to the next phase of the life cycle. In South Asia, the stupa mound has historical precedent in the tumulus, a low, earthen burial mound in which remains were deposited at the core, just at or below ground level.[3] The outward appearance of the mound resembles the swelling of a pregnant stomach, perhaps indicating a place where the maternal earth swells with pregnancy, casting the tomb not as a final resting place but as a repository for regeneration and rebirth.

That the stupa is a womb is reflected in the Buddhist terminology. The mound is termed "womb" (*garbha*), while the central receptacle encasing the relics is the "egg" (*aṇḍa*). A womb provides the conditions for gestation, while an egg contains an embryo and a concentration of nutrients. Another term for the stupa dome is *kumbha*, referring to a rotund vessel with a narrowed neck that has served as a womb in ritual practice and visual symbolism from the Vedic period to the present and across traditions. The many uses of the *kumbha* as a burial urn, reliquary, ritual vessel, and iconographic motif stem from the primary understanding of the vessel as a womb, a vessel of generation and transformation that implicitly contains life-giving water, the nectar of immortality, or the vital elixir of life.

The function of the stupa-as-womb helps us understand why the mound is solid (rather than hollow) and remains relatively plain. A womb is by nature a dark, safely sheltered space whose purpose is enclosure rather than display. The vitality of life forces within the chthonic womb is conveyed by the exuberant imagery carved on the surrounding railing and gates. The iconographic program abounds with burgeoning vegetation, fruit-laden trees, treasure-bearing vines (*kalpa-latā*), brimming vessels, pearl garlands, and female figures whose ample breasts and hips proclaim their fertility. Aquatic motifs include conch shells, water birds, turtles, crocodilian creatures (*makara*), fish-tailed mammals, elephants spraying water, and, foremost among them, the water-borne lotus. The unfurling tendrils and branching stalks of lotus rhizomes wend through the stupa reliefs, while open-faced blossoms in astonishing array and inventiveness of design animate the stupa-railing pillars and crossbars. The lotuses may sprout from a *kumbha* whose amniotic elixir sustains luxuriant growth. The prominence of water imagery celebrates the life-sustaining rains that renew the growth cycle in an arid climate punctuated by monsoons and reflects what Ananda Coomaraswamy terms a "water cosmology," which recognizes water (rather than earth or space) as the primordial source of life.[4]

A unifying theme of this imagery is primary generative power: water as the source of existence, the lotus that self-generates from its own rhizome, the female body, and rainfall as a condition of agrarian life. The life-giving fluids and forces flow as well through fruit-bearing trees, undulating vines, vases of plenty, and blossoming nature. All the aforementioned motifs have a feminine resonance. Those steeped in that iconographic realm would recognize this integrated body of imagery as the visual vocabulary of a theology of female generative power.

Female figures, too, found prominent placement at several of the earliest stupa sites, where their large-scale effigies variously appear on railing pillars, the towering gates, and at one site completely encircling the stupa on outward-facing pillars. Most of the figures are identifiable by inscription or iconography as *yakṣiṇīs*, members of a populous class of divinities revered in India for a broad range of benefactions. Although rendered in different stylistic idioms, their manner of portrayal consistently emphasizes their femaleness through curvaceous bodily contours, deeply carved pudenda, diaphanous clothing, and detailed embellishments of feminine beauty: layers of bracelets and necklaces, elaborately coifed hair, and gracefully cascading scarves. The most articulated feature is a hip belt (*mekhalā*) fashioned of multiple strands of beads of varying shapes and materials (seeds, valuable stones, gems, precious metals, coins) and a clasp of ornate design.

The understanding of the stupa as womb is confirmed by the visual parallel between the shape of the stupa mound and the abdominal contours of the *yakṣiṇī*. The abdomen and hips, as they expand from a tapered waist, form a half-circle that replicates the hemispheric stupa dome. The intricately carved stupa railings resemble the hip belt that adorns *yakṣiṇīs*' hips and serve a comparable role. The stupa-womb itself requires no embellishment but is glorified by adornment, just as the hips of women and goddesses have been adorned by bands and elaborate hip girdles in South Asian figural arts from the earliest extant strata to the present.

The imagery in the stupa sculptural programs conveys symbolic meanings but does not simply portray ideals or promised realities. In the South Asian cultural sphere, sacred images are not simply illustrations of what they depict. They have an active potency imbued by the materials from which they are made (in this case, living stone), ritual processes during their creation, and properties inherent in the designs. The forces, energies, and beings they represent are made present by their portrayal. On this principle, the imagery surrounding a stupa serves as a repository of life-enhancing energies. The inexhaustible fertility of the rhizome, ever-flowing vessel, and female bodies form a matrix of vitalizing forces that nurture and enliven the relics within, perpetually fertilizing the field of merit.

Stupa sites accommodated a range of religious practices: individual and communal, lay and clergy-led, meditative and celebratory. The open-air complex that constellated around a main stupa included processional paths for circumambulation, paved walkways and areas for assembly, water tanks, wells, gardens, and other sacra, such as additional stupas, subsidiary shrines, pillars, and Dharma wheels. Worship scenes among the stupa carvings show devotees standing before the sacra with hands pressed together at the heart in a gesture of reverence, gazing upward in adoration or with head bowed. Some kneel; some touch their forehead to the ground or render full body prostration. Votaries come bearing platters and flasks of offerings and flower garlands. There are gatherings of worshippers making musical offerings with flutes, drums, and stringed instruments and bodies swaying in celebratory dance. Such practices were drawn from a common South Asian vocabulary of devotion and remain central to the Buddhist reverential and merit-making repertoire.[5] Among the worshippers are individuals, couples, adults accompanied by children in what appear to be family groups, and people of different geographic origins and social standing, including royalty, a diversity reflected in donative inscriptions as well.

The main stupa was the visual and spiritual focal point of a given site, but other sacra also received worship. These included footprints, Dharma wheels atop pillars, sacred trees, and votive stupas of other esteemed persons. Many divinities and supernatural beings appear in stupa reliefs among the celebrants of Shakyamuni, but some were singled out for independent portrayal and reverence. Figures chosen for this emphasis include the guardian kings of the four directions, *yakṣa*s, and, most numerous among them, the *yakṣiṇī*s discussed earlier. Their effigies are featured on gateway pillars and the outward face of railing pillars, where they could be venerated during a preliminary round of circumambulation on the outermost walkway before entrance through the eastern gate to circumambulate the stupa itself.

These images, as living repositories of the beings or genre of beings they portray, would receive votive offerings (such as food, incense, lamplight, and flowers) and be supplicated for their customary blessings of abundance, offspring, flourishing health and fortunes, bountiful crops, safe travels, and protection from natural dangers and mischievous and malevolent spirits. Buddhist narratives are replete with tales of divine and supernatural beings who joined the congregation of Shakyamuni, pledged to support and protect his followers, and imparted the means of their invocation. Votaries may have chanted liturgies to the divine benefactors during circumambulation. Suitable formulae are found in varied texts, such as the *Āṭānāṭiya-sutta*, which relates spells that summon the divine benefactors—the guardian kings and their retinues of *yakṣa*s, *yakṣiṇī*s, and spirit beings—from the four quarters of the universe, beginning in the east and proceeding clockwise to the south, west, and north, a pattern that corresponds to the starting point and direction of stupa circumambulation.

Stupa reliefs, combined with literary sources and the ethnographic present, help us envision the sensorium and performance modalities of the early South Asian Buddhist world. The sculptural reliefs reflect full somatic engagement as votaries render gestures and postures of devotion. Instrumental music, singing, and the hum of chanting reverberated through the soundscape. The fragrance of incense, sandalwood paste, and tropical blossoms sweetened the air. Twinkling lamps, colorful floral offerings, and gleaming silken banners lent visual vibrancy. Add to this scenario the bustle of vendors catering to pilgrims from afar and the occasional fanfare of a royal cavalcade.[6] Activities reached a crescendo during the celebration of holy days. Buddhists have long observed (lunar) monthly days auspicious for merit-making and a day marking Shakyamuni's birth, enlightenment, and *parinirvāṇa* that bring monastics and laity together for elaborate communal outpourings of veneration and lavish donative activity.

Festivals were celebrated across the early South Asian Buddhist world at stupas, monasteries, sites of events commemorated, and public thoroughfares. The consecration of a stupa and ritual displays of relics enjoyed royal patronage.[7] Most of the events, however, were under monastic supervision. Annual festivals were dedicated to votive stupas of Śāriputra and other Arhats on monastery grounds. The end of the annual rain retreat drew laity to the monastery for an all-night ceremony of sutta-recitation, lamp-lighting, and offerings. Monastics held ritual services for sacra in their keeping, such as an annual rite of bathing Buddha images that required multiple scented liquids for lustration, pure silk, and heaps of flowers. The most elaborate ceremonial display was the chariot procession. A Bodhisattva image or other sacra, adorned with silks, precious ornaments, and layers of flower garlands, was installed on a festooned palanquin or many-storied chariot serving as a portable shrine that was drawn through the streets with banners waving high, accompanied by music and drumming.[8] Gregory Schopen's Vinaya research has revealed the ongoing involvement of monastics in the planning and staging of festivals, sometimes in remote places remarkable only for a marvelous event in the life of Shakyamuni. Considerable organization was required to prepare the site, publicize the event, and arrange for the arrival, feeding, and protocols of hundreds and perhaps thousands of monks and nuns converging for the festival. Administrative offices were even created for the purpose.[9]

Dramatic performances were part of the performative landscape and festival life. Aśvaghoṣa (late first to early second century CE) composed several plays on Buddhist themes, crafting the narratives for dramatic enactment with sumptuous portrayal of the beauties and pleasures to be renounced, scenes requiring music and dance, and Buddhist principles rendered in poetic verse. We know little of the venues in which his plays were performed, but large gatherings of people at festivals were a customary setting for plays in the early centuries of the Common Era. Traveling troupes and solo performers composed plays for specific audiences and festivals. Gregory Schopen found evidence that one such actor, determined to develop a play for a Buddhist festival in Rajagriha, sought and received instruction for his narrative from an erudite nun gifted in eloquence. A Buddhist festival might incorporate plays as an obligatory feature. Schopen also reports of an annual festival commemorating a gift to Shakyamuni by *nāgās* at which two plays were staged, one of them a play written by nuns and performed by monks.[10]

It is increasingly apparent that monastics, performing artists, artisans, and laity devoted their resources and talents to conveying Buddhist ideas and ideals in material and embodied media. Jatakas lent themselves to narration and dramatization. A seventh-century Chinese pilgrim to India reported that stories of Shakyamuni's previous life, including the *Vessantara Jataka*, were set to verse and music and enacted as dramas incorporating recitation, acting, singing, and dancing.[11] More than a millennium later, at the dawn of the twenty-first century, ethnomusicologist Martina Claus-Bachmann encountered a similarly vibrant performative landscape during her fieldwork in Sri Lanka, namely, "continuous performances of *Jataka* narratives" by actors, singers, storytellers, and puppeteers in explicitly religious settings (temples, festivals, funerals, pandals) and quasi-secular venues (theaters, television, pop music videos, and recordings).[12] We may surmise that Buddhists across times and locales have employed a full range of expressive media to transmit Dharma with emotionally engaging sensory immediacy.

Mainstays of monastic life may have been memorizing texts, meditative pursuits, and Vinaya adherence, but monks and nuns had a range of clerical responsibilities, in addition to the regular involvement in the festival round discussed earlier. An important ritual role was to act as mediators with the supernatural realm. They were equipped with many means to ward off dangers to themselves, the laity, and the broader locale or region. Foremost among the methods was recitation of spells (*paritta*) commended by Shakyamuni to secure safety, peace of mind, and well-being by affording protection from all manner of natural and supernatural dangers, such as venomous snakes, wild animals, poisonous insects and plants, disease, and demonic interference.

Monks and nuns maintained cults of *yakṣas*, *yakṣiṇīs*, and *nāgas* on monastic premises. The supernatural being in question might be an original inhabitant of the monastic site, a being of local import, or a pan-Buddhist figure, such as the great *yakṣiṇī* Hāritī. Monasteries incorporated painted and sculpted images and shrines, made regular offerings (generally of food) to their nonhuman residents, and supplicated them to guard the monastery and, in the case of *nāgas*, to ensure timely rainfall.[13]

Monastics served as intercessors on behalf of those who had died, offering rites for transferring merit to deceased relatives to improve their afterlife destiny and for pacifying restless spirits and ghosts that haunt the living. Some monastic sites had extensive mortuary stupa grounds adjacent to the *vihāra*.[14] Monks and nuns were also obligated to lend their presence at important domestic events (e.g., celebration of a birth or marriage), the dedication of a construction project (e.g., a dwelling, stable, park, or lotus pond), and a major donation to a stupa (e.g., a pillar, parasol, or banner), on which occasions the monastics performed the ceremonial dedication of merit.[15]

Teachings, practices, and institutional patterns stemming from the earliest documented layers of Buddhism persisted through the Pāla period and had taken root in Sri Lanka and Southeast Asia beginning in the third century BCE, where they underwent varied localized trajectories under shifting geopolitical conditions but retained many elements traceable to the early period of Buddhism, including the Pāli language textual tradition.

Mahayana Buddhism

Innovations that came to mark the Mahayana movement had begun to percolate by the first century BCE and were efflorescing by the first century CE. An outpouring of scriptural creativity generated streams of thought and practice that eventually coalesced in what we now call Mahayana. Proponents of Mahayana bequeathed their ideas to us in abundant array, albeit through complex textual histories.[16] Their teachings voice a soaring imagination that opened visionary realms of wonder and vistas of infinite time and space. Their oratory took flight in devotional poesy and elaborate narrative. They introduced a firmament of divinities who served as exemplars of progress on a spiritual path spanning eons and culminating in buddhahood. Under Mahayana purview, the Buddhist imaginaire expanded to encompass innumerable worlds inhabited by countless buddhas and bodhisattvas, equal in number to the grains of sand in the Ganges river and to the atoms in the universe.

The proliferation of enlightened beings and beings well advanced toward enlightenment ushered in new sources of revelation. Shakyamuni remained the authoritative source of *buddha-vacana*, but other speakers of truth came to the fore. Countless *bodhisattva-mahāsattvas* were endowed with the ability to turn the wheel of Dharma. Laypersons, too, could reveal Dharma through "inspired eloquence" (*pratibhāna*). Innovative though the new revelations may be, they proclaimed access to the living stream of wisdom at the heart of the tradition.

New developments in the sphere of thought reverberated through the terrain of practice. Mahayana scriptures themselves acquired great sanctity, joining buddhas and stupas as worthy of supreme reverence. By virtue of being suffused with liberating wisdom, a text or portion of a text could serve as a relic, on grounds that the Dharma pulses with the living presence of a buddha just as surely as bodily remains. Hyperbole reigns in discourse on the merit accruing from honoring a given Mahayana scripture, which is greater (as the argument goes) than the merit of making offerings in the presence of a buddha for thousands of years or filling the earth with stupas of gold and jewels.

Ways of honoring a text include the homage and offerings rendered to a buddha or stupa, such as flowers, incense, lamplight, and banners. Powerfully meritorious and transformative effects attend the text as an oral and aural medium. Hearing, memorizing, retaining, reciting, contemplating, copying, and dispensing the text are heralded as fully liberating practices in their own right.[17] The skilled orator (*dharma-bhāṇaka*) who could recite and illuminate scripture in a compelling manner was a revered figure, worthy of honor as a living repository and voice of the Dharma. A *dharma-bhāṇaka* was to be enthroned, served, and showered with offerings in the same manner as a buddha.[18]

Whereas the earlier tradition placed Shakyamuni within a sequence of buddhas of ages past and Maitreya, the future Buddha, Mahayana envisioned innumerable Buddhas throughout the cosmos, each inhabiting and presiding over a world, or buddha-field (*buddha-kṣetra*). Earth is the buddha-field of Shakyamuni. Ascending to another buddha-field and continuing one's spiritual journey in the presence of a buddha became a new focus of practice and aspiration. Abhirati, the realm of Akṣobhya, and Sukhāvatī, the realm of Amitābha, came to the fore by the second century CE as paradisal destinations where the fortunate could enjoy heavenly comforts in a land of jeweled splendor and dwell in the radiant presence of the enlightened one. There, they would receive teachings and advance toward buddhahood in surrounds of beauty and plenty, their every need instantly met.

Practices devoted to these buddhas centered on strong aspiration to be reborn in one of those realms and envisioning the realm and its wonders. Intricate scriptural descriptions of the marvels that await—the kaleidoscopically dazzling ever-shifting palette of the trees of precious gems, musical clouds, palatial pavilions, and fragrant breezes—may be intended not simply to describe the buddha-fields but to guide their visualization.[19] The goal was to be reborn there and continue one's spiritual journey at the feet of the buddha, without descending again into the six realms of rebirth.

Abhirati was the more difficult of access of the two, requiring a vast accumulation of merit. A practitioner sufficiently advanced in meditative disciplines and moral purity to be reborn there would take birth through a brief pregnancy and easeful birth process for the mother. Abhirati served as a launching pad for travel to other worlds to gather wisdom from many buddhas. The goal of Abhirati was eclipsed by that of Sukhāvatī, entrance to which was more readily accessible.[20] The buddha-fields offer nourishment (whatever food and drink one desires), clothing and adornments growing on trees, and the necessary spiritual sustenance to advance to awakening. Thus, a buddha-field serves as a womb, providing all that is needed for the gestation of a buddha. In addition to meaning "field," *kṣetra* denotes a "place of origin" and "fertile womb."

A practitioner need not wait until the next life, however, to come into the presence of a buddha. A meditative discipline termed *buddha-anusmṛti* offered a means to encounter a buddha face-to-face. The practice is to hold a vivid mental image of a given buddha in singular focus, envisioning him enthroned in his buddha-field amid an illustrious assembly and steadily contemplating his virtues, perfections, beauties, and, above all, radiance. The *locus classicus* of this technique, dating from the second century CE, prescribes uninterrupted concentration for seven days and nights. No other ritual is required, although use of an image to aid visualization is permitted. The goal is to induce a profound meditative state (*samādhi*) in which one is experientially transported to the buddha-field to receive Dharma teachings directly from the buddha while basking in his resplendent presence.[21]

The practice of *dhāraṇī* recitation also gained currency. The Mahayana *dhāraṇī* expanded on the protective role and beneficial properties of the Pāli *paritta* to encompass fulfillment of soteriological aims.[22] The *Kāraṇḍavyūha*, a circa fifth-century CE scripture featuring Avalokiteśvara, extols his *dhāraṇī* (*oṃ maṇi padme hūṃ*) as his supreme essence, the essence of Dharma, the highest meditation, and the entrance to liberation. Its recitation confers mental brilliance, the six perfections, highest wisdom, pure compassion, and mastery of liberative skills. Reciters are endowed with such potent liberating power that simply inhaling their breath or brushing by them will set one on the stage of an irreversible bodhisattva. Setting eyes on them frees women, men, children, oxen, deer, and birds from suffering and establishes them as virtuoso yoga practitioners and bodhisattvas in their last samsaric rebirth.[23]

The maternal matrix of enlightenment received new iterations in Mahayana movements. Female generativity is epitomized by the feminine gender of liberating wisdom as *prajñā*, the source and "mother" of all enlightened ones (*sarva-buddha-mātā*) and her personification as a goddess, Prajñāpāramitā, the overarching cosmic reality and eternal wisdom that gives birth to buddhas.[24] The *dhāraṇī*, too, is a female generative source. The efficacy attributed to *dhāraṇī* is based on a long-standing principle of South Asian metaphysics that sound is a primary creative force that operates at the subtlest levels of reality in the form of vibrational waves that give rise to denser, tangible phenomena. The term *dhāraṇī* is a feminine noun derived from a verbal root (*dhṛ*) whose meanings have a range of female connotations in reference to the roles of bearing, giving birth, and sustaining life. Thus, the feminine gender of the word accords with the generative power of recitation, which yields every spiritual goal, including supreme awakening. A synonym for *dhāraṇī* is *vidyā*, another feminine noun. The six-syllable spell of Avalokiteśvara in the *Kāraṇḍavyūha* is often hailed as the "queen of great *vidyās*" and is personified in the work as a white goddess holding a rosary of jewels for recitation practice.[25]

The stupa-as-womb is the forerunner and arguably the prototype of *tathāgata-garbha* ("buddha-womb"), a teaching that found authoritative expression in a circa third-century CE scripture revealed by Queen Śrīmālā Devī to her female retinue and attendants, after which she led all the women of her city onto the Mahayana path, followed by the king and male citizenry. The queen taught that every being is a "womb" (*garbha*) in which resides the pure essence of a buddha (*tathāgata*). Until the buddhahood is realized, it remains an "embryo" (also *garbha*). The queen universalizes the womb, proclaiming the *tathāgata-garbha* to be "the womb of the Dharma realm, the womb of the Dharma body, the womb of the supramundane, the womb of intrinsic purity."[26] She asserts that the *tathāgata*-womb has no beginning or end, casting it as the source of all: phenomenal arising, living beings, enlightened beings. In Mahayana more broadly, reality (*dharma-dhātu*) has the qualities of a womb. Emptiness is akin to a womb as the matrix of infinite potentiality, giving rise to the stream of insubstantial, interdependent, impermanent (i.e., empty)—and ultimately pure—phenomena. The arising of phenomena is nuanced with the insight that, in an ultimate sense, there is no arising and hence phenomena are "unborn," meaning that phenomena unfold within and yet never leave the womb, making all of reality, the vast realm of Dharma (*dharma-dhātu*), the womb.

In the *Gaṇḍavyūha*, Sudhana's quest for enlightenment unfolds in a womblike environment suffused with feminine wisdom and compassion, populated by female divinities, and replete with female guides.[27] The female divinities express their compassion through trees, flowers, ponds, rivers, caves, and clouds; they voice their wisdom through water, wind, ocean wave, and birdsong. The aspect of nature most akin to the womb is the night sky, which is dark and vitally alive. The nocturnal firmament is radiant with goddesses (*devatā*) who manifest as celestial bodies to protect travelers and impart wisdom gleaned from lifetimes of spiritual purification and the vast panorama of their vision. Sudhana's illuminating encounters with night goddesses occupy a quarter of the narrative with exultations of their beauty, lofty realizations, and illustrious discourse.[28] The same work glorifies the womb of Mayadevī as a magnificent jeweled pavilion of cosmic expanse in which countless bodhisattvas complete their journey to awakening within the harmonious, luminous weave of phenomenal reality.

Late Mahayana, or what is increasingly recognized as the proto-Tantric phase, saw the emergence of a new genre of practice in texts dating from the mid-fifth through seventh centuries CE.[29] *Dhāraṇī* practice remained central. The new development was an elaborate ritual technology to invoke a deity into the ritual space. Avalokiteśvara, Mañjuśrī, and Vajrapāṇi recur in the revelation scenarios, while the deities to be invoked were mainly figures of non-Buddhist genesis, such as Lakṣmī, Sarasvatī, and an array of *yakṣiṇīs* endowed with distinctive identities in this context. Ritual details vary, but the general pattern is to prepare a seat for the arrival of the deity in a specified place (e.g., on the ground, in a cave, by a river) and assemble the offerings to be rendered, such as ghee lamps, incense, food, and flowers. The practitioner draws, paints, sculpts, or commissions an image of the deity. Visualization (creating a mental image) and ceremonial hand gestures (*mudrā*) do not have a role. The focus is on *dhāraṇī* recitation in requisite number (e.g., 1,008, 8,000, or 100,000) for a specified duration (e.g., nightly from full moon to full moon). If the rite has been performed correctly, the deity will appear and confer promised benefactions, fulfill requests, or grant extraordinary powers.[30]

VAJRAYANA

Vajrayana has as its doctrinal edifice the teachings of preceding centuries. Tantric scriptures regularly refer to non-self, the four *brahmavihāra*, emptiness, compassion, nondual wisdom, and attainment of buddhahood as the goal. Buddhahood, however, was no longer a distant goal to be attained after eons of practice, but rather a transformation attainable in the present lifetime and body. The practice landscape shifted accordingly. As an accelerated path, Vajrayana offers methods designed for intensive karmic purification, toward the aim of fully embodying buddhahood. Vajrayana raised esteem for the body as a locus of immense resources and divine qualities, glorifying the human body as a microcosm in which all the energies and powers throughout the universe are present. Different Tantric systems mapped the internal cosmos and geography differently, but they share the vision of the body as a universe within. The varied Tantric deities and methods (mantra, visualization, subtle body yoga) offer multiple templates and routes for full transformation, a transformation expressed in Tantric terms as attaining the body, speech, and mind of a buddha.

From an ultimate perspective, the Vajrayana path is one of revealing innate divinity. From an experiential perspective, however, a dramatic apotheosis will occur: a new being, an enlightened being, will be born. The womb for the gestation of the divine body is the mandala, an evolution of the stupa. A mandala is envisioned and ritually constructed in three-dimensional form, but when represented in two-dimensional form (as a diagram, painting, or sand mandala), the resemblance to the stupa becomes clear. The center, the location of the relics in the stupa, becomes the seat of the deity in the mandala. Both have a circular surround and four gates in the cardinal directions, with the point of entry in the east. The clockwise circumambulation of the stupa becomes the clockwise meditative path through the mandala. Whereas the stupa enshrines relics, the mandala provides an environment through which the practitioner journeys, eventually to reach the center. The sectors, retinue figures, and imagery represent psycho-physiological dynamics that will be purified of egoic toxicity and transformed into divine qualities and powers.

The womblike nature of the mandala is conveyed by the lotus on which a mandala rests. The lotus has a feminine association that extends deep into the substrate of Vedic and Upanishadic thought as the womb from which the world is born and the support on which the world then rests. A lotus and the primordial waters in which it is rooted are the primary conditions of life. The lotus, as the womb of the world, is likened to the human womb and serves as its emblem (*yoni-rūpatvam*) in visual imagery.[31] The female association of the lotus was amplified in Vajrayana, wherein elements that are unified through Tantric practice, such as wisdom and skillful means, or bliss and emptiness, are expressed as male-female pairings in which the female element is represented by a lotus and the male by a vajra. In Tantric scripture as well, the vulva is referred to as "lotus" (*padma*). In mandala symbolism, the lotus is the foundation of the new world into which the practitioner will take birth as the presiding deity. The meaning of purity that accrued to the lotus is also present as the purifying nature of the mandala journey, which culminates in the purity of vision that reveals the world as it truly is, as the sacred realm of perfection, beauty, and harmony represented by the mandala.

Primary generative source as female finds many expressions in Vajrayana metaphysics, symbolism, and ritual. Mantra recitation is an essential Vajrayana practice, directing the creative power of sound to specific ritual aims and to the attainment of buddhahood. The root source of mantras (and all language) is the Sanskrit letter "a" (pronounced "ah"), the release of breath required to vocalize, whether to speak or to recite. "A" is the first letter of the Sanskrit alphabet, recognizing its primacy. In the Vajrayana pantheon, "a" is personified by the female Buddha Nairātmyā. Her body is blue, the color of infinite space. She is universal and all-pervading, the unbounded consciousness that encompasses all. She is the *dharma-dhātu*, the spacious expanse in which illusory phenomena momentarily shimmer. She is the space of breath ("ah"), the primary sound and source of all others and the realities they shape. Whereas ordinary language and the dualism it entails generate samsaric realities, mantras purify awareness and reveal the sacred realities represented by the mandalas and deities.[32]

A range of other liberating powers are cast in explicitly female terms and personified by female deities in the Tantric pantheon. Wisdom as female force and maternal source received new emphasis. The ascent of Vajrayana brought a resurgence of interest in *Prajñāpāramitā* texts in the ninth century CE. A high proportion of illuminated palm leaf manuscripts produced between the tenth and twelfth centuries are *Aṣṭa-sahasrikā-prajñāpāramitā* texts.[33] The costly, time-consuming production of an illuminated manuscript required the largesse of a wealthy or royal purse to sponsor the labor for its planning, manufacture, and copying and the materials, time, and artistic effort to illustrate its folia with diminutive, meticulously rendered paintings. The selection of this early *Prajñāpāramitā* text for illumination and ritual veneration endorses the generative nature of the work as the primary expression of liberating wisdom and honors the wisdom goddess whom it extols. As Jinah Kim has demonstrated, the portrayal of the goddess in a given manuscript casts her as the emanating source of the scenes and figures of awakening that animate its leaves. Events of Shakyamuni's life, pilgrimage sites, celestial bodhisattvas, and esoteric deities bear no relation to the content of the text. Their inclusion illustrates the role of Prajñāpāramitā as the source of the enlightenment that flows from her illuminating presence.[34]

Wisdom was in turn homologized with another primary force of transformation envisioned as female, the inner heat, or fire, of yogic purification (*caṇḍālī*) that is kindled in the navel chakra in esoteric yoga practice and spread through the subtle body, incinerating karmic dross just as transcendent wisdom (*prajñā*) dissolves dualistic conceptuality. The inner flame, too, is personified as a goddess that shares its name, Caṇḍālī.

Vajrayoginī, the supreme female Buddha in many Tantric lineages, encompasses all creative, liberating, transforming powers. She is the focus of several Tantric scriptures and mandalas, numerous rituals, and dozens of *sādhanas*, not counting those in which she is paired with a consort or those introduced beyond the South Asian purview.[35] She wears a garland of fifty-one heads, the number of letters in the Sanskrit alphabet, representing her mastery of the creative power of sound, language, and mantra. She blazes bright with flames of wisdom that consume delusion and burns hot with the transforming heat of yogic purification. Vajrayoginī is a cosmogonic figure, the one from whom the universe is born and into whom it dissolves. Her womb, as the universal source, is represented in geometric form as a red, downward-pointing triangle. The triangular shape is an abstract rendering of the pudendum, the threshold of creation, while red is the prototypically female color in Tantric symbolism. Termed *dharmodayā*, "source of all things," her womb is a common feature of ritual construction of a mandala, regardless of the deity on whom the mandala centers. The *dharmodayā* (sometimes doubled, sometimes containing a lotus design) is typically drawn with red powder on a cleared and cleansed surface to serve as the base on which the mandala will be formed, visually expressing and ritually invoking the source of the world to be created, the mandala in which the practitioner will be transformed and reborn as a deity. Thus, her womb is the source for the rebirth of the practitioner in a divine mode of bodily being on earth. Vajrayoginī also presides over a favored paradisal afterlife destination for Vajrayana practitioners, a blissful realm inhabited by *ḍākiṇīs* in rainbow array, ever celebrating the victory of awakening with supernal dance and song. A practitioner who has sufficiently purified his or her subtle body may ascend directly to her realm at death, dissolving into rainbow light and leaving no bodily remains.

Alongside its meditative and metaphysical pursuits, Buddhism has been a prodigious producer of material culture, shaping landscapes with pilgrimage routes and monuments, constructing worship and practice spaces, crafting votive and ritual objects, and generating hand-copied and printed texts. New evidence of Buddhist practice is continuously brought to light by archaeological discoveries, newly unearthed caches of manuscripts, and analysis of objects and sites with scientific techniques (e.g., carbon dating, radiography, GPS mapping, forensic palynology). Digital archives of sites, images, texts, and textual translations put masses of data at scholars' fingertips and accelerate the pace of research, collaboration, and dissemination. The burgeoning record provides a wealth of evidence so staggering in its abundance and complexity that its interpretation will engage scholars for time to come, ever expanding and refining our understanding of Buddhist practices, past and present.

Notes

1. South Asia is variously defined in different classificatory systems (geographical, cultural, economic, political, historical, and contemporary) and may encompass adjacent countries and islands such as Afghanistan, Bhutan, and Sri Lanka.
2. Extant portions of Bhārhut (Madhya Pradesh), Bhūteśvara (Uttar Pradesh), Sanghol (Punjab), and Sanchi Stupa I (Madhya Pradesh) form the composite from which my interpretations derive. Contemporaneous sites further afield, in Gandhāra, Andhra Pradesh (Amarāvatī), and Karnataka (Kanaganahalli), warrant site-specific consideration and comparison.
3. The tumulus burial is not limited to South Asia, but is documented globally, particularly during the Neolithic and Megalithic periods and continuing in some areas into the Bronze and Iron Ages and beyond.
4. Ananda Coomaraswamy, *Yakṣas: Essays in the Water Cosmology*, 1931, revised ed. (Delhi: Indira Gandhi National Centre for the Arts, 1993), chaps. 10–11.
5. For documentation of the full range of practices, see Susan L. Huntington, *Lay Ritual in Early Buddhist Art: More Evidence against the Aniconic Theory* (Amsterdam: Royal Netherlands Academy of Arts and Sciences, 2012).

6. On musical instruments, dancing, processions, and festival scenes in early Buddhist reliefs, see Garima Kaushik, *Symphony in Stone: Festivities in Early Buddhism* (Jaipur: Literary Circle, 2007).
7. Ulrich Pagel, "Stūpa Festivals in Buddhist Narrative Literature," in *Indica et Tibetica: Festscrift für Michael Hahn*, ed. Konrad Klaus and Jens-Uwe Hartmann (Vienna: Arbeitskreis für Tibetische und Buddhistische Studien Universitat Wien, 2007), 368–94.
8. Chinese pilgrims to India in the fifth and seventh centuries remarked on elaborate chariot processions. See, e.g., H. A. Giles, trans., *The Travels of Fa-hsien (399–414 A.D.), or Record of the Buddhist Kingdoms* (1923; reprint, Westport, CT: Greenwood Press, 1981), 5–6. For the earliest known and well-detailed account of such a procession, see Gregory Schopen, "Taking the Bodhisattva into Town: More Texts on the Image of 'the Bodhisattva' and Image Processions in the *Mūlasarvāstivāda-vinaya*," *East and West* 55 (2005): 299–311.
9. Gregory Schopen, *Buddhist Nuns, Monks, and Other Worldly Matters: Recent Papers on Monastic Buddhism in India* (Honolulu: University of Hawai'i Press, 2014), 363–66, 369–72.
10. Schopen, *Buddhist Nuns, Monks, and Other Worldly Matters*, 265, 419–21.
11. J. Takakusu, trans., *A Record of the Buddhist Religion as Practised in India and the Malay Archipelago (A.D. 671–695), by I-Tsing* (1896; reprint, Delhi: Munshiram Manoharlal, 1998), 163–64; for his description of an image procession, see 87.
12. Martina Claus-Bachmann, "*Jataka* Narrations as Multimedial Reconstructive Embodiments of the Mental System Buddha Shakyamuni," *The World of Music* 44, no. 2 (2002): 115–34, quote on 117.
13. Robert DeCaroli, *Haunting the Buddha: Indian Popular Religions and the Formation of Buddhism* (New York: Oxford University Press, 2004), 58–62, 76–85, 91.
14. DeCaroli, *Haunting the Buddha*, 94–102.
15. Gregory Schopen, "Ritual Obligations and Donor Roles of Monks in the Pāli Vinaya," *Journal of the Pali Text Society* 16 (1992): 87–107.
16. For helpful summation of the textual genealogies that challenge a search for an "original" text, see Daniel Boucher, "What Do We Mean by 'Early' in the Study of Early Mahāyāna--and Should We Care?" *Bulletin of the Asia Institute*, n.s., 23 (2009): 33–41.
17. For the technical vocabulary for engaging with a text in oral and written forms, see David Drewes, "Oral Texts in Indian Mahāyāna," *Indo-Iranian Journal* 58, no. 2 (2015): 117–41.
18. David Drewes, "*Dharmabhāṇakas* in Early Mahāyāna," *Indo-Iranian Journal* 54, no. 2 (2011): 331–72.
19. Paul Harrison, "Mediums and Messages: Reflections on the Production of Mahāyāna Sūtras," *The Eastern Buddhist*, n.s., 35, no. 1–2 (2003), 121–22.
20. On Abhirati and its differentiation from Sukhāvatī, see Jan Nattier, "The Realm of Akṣobhya: A Missing Piece in the History of Pure Land Buddhism," *Journal of the International Association of Buddhist Studies* 23, no. 1 (2000): 71–102.
21. Paul M. Harrison, "Buddhānusmṛti in the Pratyutpanna-buddha-saṃmukhāvasthita-samādhi-sūtra," *Journal of Indian Philosophy* 6, no. 1 (Sept. 1978): 35–57.
22. Peter Skilling, "The Rakṣā Literature of the Śrāvakayāna," *Journal of the Pali Text Society* 16 (1992): 109–82.
23. Peter Alan Roberts and Tulku Yeshi, trans., *The Basket's Display:* Kāraṇḍavyūha (n.p.: 84000, 2013), 53–54, 61–62, and passim.
24. Miranda Shaw, *Buddhist Goddesses of India* (Princeton, NJ: Princeton University Press, 2016), chap. 8.

25. Roberts and Yeshi, trans., *Basket's Display*, viii, 57–59.
26. Translation by John S. Strong in *The Experience of Buddhism: Sources and Interpretations*, 2nd ed. (Belmont, CA: Wadsworth/Thompson Learning, 2002), 159.
27. Shaw, *Buddhist Goddesses of India*, chap. 7. A third of the text is devoted to goddesses as primary guides, additional goddesses appear throughout, and Mayadevī is exalted to cosmic status.
28. Slightly more than a quarter of the pilgrimage account is devoted to meetings with night goddesses. For discussion of them and implications of their spatial arrangement in a mandala formation, see Douglas Osto, *Power, Wealth and Women in Indian Mahāyāna Buddhism: The Gaṇḍavyuha-sutra* (New York: Routledge, 2008), 23, 88, 97–100, 122–23.
29. On the dating of this phase, see Jacob P. Dalton, "How *Dhāraṇīs* WERE Proto-Tantric," in *Tantric Traditions in Transmission and Translation*, ed. David B. Gray and Ryan Richard Overbey (New York: Oxford University Press, 2016), 214–16, 219.
30. For specific rites, see Richard S. Cohen, *The Splendid Vision: Reading a Buddhist Sutra* (New York: Columbia University Press, 2012), 32–39; Shaw, *Buddhist Goddesses of India*, 105–6, 136–40, 237–38.
31. Ananda Coomaraswamy, *Elements of Buddhist Iconography*, 3rd. ed. (New Delhi: Munshiram Manoharlal, 1979), 17–21.
32. Shaw, *Buddhist Goddesses of India*, chap. 17.
33. Jinah Kim, *Receptacle of the Sacred: Illustrated Manuscripts and the Buddhist Book Cult in South Asia* (Berkeley: University of California Press, 2013), 9–10, 31, 36–37, 249.
34. Kim, *Receptacle of the Sacred*, chaps. 2–5.
35. For detailed treatment of Vajrayoginī manifestations, mandalas, rituals, and meditation practices in a twelfth-century Sanskrit compendium, see Elizabeth English, *Vajrayoginī: Her Visualizations, Rituals, and Forms* (Boston: Wisdom Publications, 2002).

Further Reading

DeCaroli, Robert. *Haunting the Buddha: Indian Popular Religions and the Formation of Buddhism*. Oxford and New York: Oxford University Press, 2004.

Fogelin, Lars. *An Archaeological History of Indian Buddhism*. Oxford and New York: Oxford University Press, 2015.

Garling, Wendy. *Stars at Dawn: Forgotten Stories of Women in the Buddha's Life*. Boulder. CO: Shambhala, 2016.

Huntington, Susan L. *The Art of Ancient India: Buddhist, Hindu, Jain*. New York and Tokyo: Weatherhill, 1985.

Kaushik, Garima. *Symphony in Stone: Festivities in Early Buddhism*. Jaipur: Literary Circle, 2007.

Kim, Jinah. *Receptacle of the Sacred: Illustrated Manuscripts and the Buddhist Book Cult in South Asia*. Berkeley: University of California Press, 2013.

Linrothe, Robert N. *Ruthless Compassion: Wrathful Deities in Early Indo-Tibetan Esoteric Buddhism*. Boston: Shambhala, 1999.

Nattier, Jan. *A Few Good Men: The Bodhisattva Path according to* The Inquiry of Ugra (Ugraparipṛcchā). Honolulu: University of Hawai'i Press, 2003.

Osto, Douglas. *Power, Wealth and Women in Indian Mahāyāna Buddhism: The Gaṇḍavyuha-sutra*. New York: Routledge, 2008.

Schopen, Gregory. *Buddhist Nuns, Monks, and Other Worldly Matters: Recent Papers on Monastic Buddhism in India*. Honolulu: University of Hawai'i Press, 2014.

Shaw, Miranda. *Buddhist Goddesses of India*. Princeton, NJ: Princeton University Press, 2016.

Shaw, Miranda. "Magical Lovers, Sisters, and Mothers: *Yakṣiṇī Sādhana* in Tantric Buddhism." In *Breaking Boundaries with the Goddess: New Directions in the Study of Śāktism, Essays in Honor of Narendra Nath Bhattacharyya*, ed. Cynthia Hume and Rachel Fell McDermott. New Delhi: Manohar, 2008, 265–96.

Skilling, Peter. "Nuns, Laywomen, Donors, Goddesses: Female Roles in Early Indian Buddhism." *Journal of the International Association of Buddhist Studies* 24, no. 2 (2001): 241–74.

Snellgrove, David L. *Indo-Tibetan Buddhism: Indian Buddhists and Their Tibetan Successors*. London: Serindia, 1987.

Wedemeyer, Christian K. *Making Sense of Tantric Buddhism: History, Semiology, and Transgression in the Indian Traditions*. New York: Columbia University Press, 2013.

CHAPTER 3

BUDDHIST PRACTICE IN SOUTHEAST ASIA

NATHAN MCGOVERN

IN recent decades, scholars of Buddhism have come to the increasing realization that "Buddhist Studies" as a discipline of Western knowledge creation was established on a set of premises with roots in Protestant theology that, especially when combined with orientalism, have greatly distorted the perception of Buddhism in the West. In particular, the Protestant emphasis on scripture as the locus of "true religion," the rejection of tradition, and the devaluation of ritual and thus "practice" in general led early Buddhologists to focus on the earliest texts in their construction of knowledge about Buddhism, largely ignoring or subordinating actual Buddhist practice in the present and even in the past, in proportion to its distance from the time of the Buddha. When their construction of "Buddhism" clashed with actual Buddhist practice, their orientalist prejudices against Asian Buddhist actors made it easy for them to dismiss the latter as a degeneration of "true Buddhism," the product of the fanciful and infantile "oriental mind."

Perhaps no form of traditional Buddhism has been more affected by this Protestantizing and orientalist legacy than that which has come to be called "Theravada Buddhism," the predominant form of Buddhism found in Southeast Asia today. The reason for this lies in the fact that Theravada Buddhists look to the *Tipiṭaka* ("Triple Basket") in Pali as their authoritative set of scriptures, rather than the later Mahayana sutras written in Sanskrit. Once European scholars in the mid-nineteenth century identified the Pali texts of the *Tipiṭaka* as the oldest Buddhist textual sources, they became the locus of Western efforts to (re)construct "true Buddhism." Concomitantly, Theravada Buddhism came to be seen as the "earliest" and "purest" form of Buddhism. But this "Theravada Buddhism" was of course not primarily the Buddhism practiced in Sri Lanka and mainland Southeast Asia; it was an abstraction equated with early (Indian) Buddhism, bearing a mostly unexamined relationship with actual contemporary practice in Southeast Asia. This uncritical and fallacious equation of "Theravada Buddhism" with "early Buddhism" is still sometimes found within Buddhology today, especially among more philologically inclined scholars who do not specialize in Southeast Asia. The theoretical basis for the study of Southeast Asian Buddhism is the rejection of this equation, allowing space for the study of Theravada Buddhism on its own terms as a contemporary and recent historical phenomenon of the second millennium CE, with reference to the actual practices of Buddhists in Southeast Asia and Sri Lanka, independent of what the Pali texts supposedly say Theravada Buddhists do and believe.

In part as a reflection of the need to overcome the persistent conflation of "Theravada" with "early Buddhism," but also for the sake of space, I will present in this chapter an account of Southeast Asian Buddhist practice that is mostly synchronic, rooted in the present and recent past. In addition, the scope of my essay will not map exactly onto "Southeast Asia" as defined in solely physical geographical terms. Rather, my focus will be on the forms of Buddhism that have come in the modern period to be known as "Theravada." The physical and demographic center of gravity of Theravada Buddhism is firmly within Southeast Asia, as four of the five major Theravada countries (Myanmar, Thailand, Laos, and Cambodia) are in mainland Southeast Asia. The fifth, Sri Lanka, is an island just off the coast of India in South Asia, but given the extensive ties between the sangha in Sri Lanka and those in mainland Southeast Asia going back nearly 1,000 years, as well as the prestige that Lanka has held in the Southeast Asian Buddhist imaginary for as much time, it is impossible to discuss Southeast Asian Buddhism without reference to Sri Lanka. Vietnam, on the other hand, will not be discussed in this chapter, in spite of being part of mainland Southeast Asia. With the exception of ethnic Khmers near the border with Cambodia who practice Theravada Buddhism, most Vietnamese practice Mahayana forms of Buddhism that are heavily Sinicized due to historic links with China. Readers interested in Vietnam are therefore referred to Chapter 4 on East Asian Buddhism.

I will begin with an overview of Southeast Asian practice, including a bit of historical background and a synchronic account of Theravada Buddhist practice today. This will then be followed by several short discussions of important trends and themes in scholarship on Southeast Asian Buddhist practice.

Overview

The Religio-Historical Geography of Southeast Asia

Pali Buddhism historically has been but one player in a very complex history of religion in Southeast Asia that led to the religious geography we find there today. Trade with South Asia in the first millennium CE led to the adoption across Southeast Asia, both mainland and insular, of a variety of cultural traits and systems from South Asia, many of which in modern eyes could be termed "religious." An earlier generation of scholars referred to this process as "Indianization";[1] today, scholars prefer to use the term "localization" to emphasize the agency of Southeast Asians in this process. In any case, the adoption of South Asian "religious" practices, beliefs, and motifs was quite eclectic and not limited to any one form of Buddhism or even Buddhism itself. Thus, in the first millennium CE, and continuing into the first few centuries of the second millennium, we find depictions of and references to not only the Buddha, but also Viṣṇu, Śiva, other "Hindu" gods, Mahayana bodhisattvas, and even deities of Buddhist Tantra.

During the first millennium CE, Pali Buddhism was confined to the Pyu people of the Irrawaddy Valley in what is now Myanmar, followed by the Burmese who established Bagan in that area in the ninth century, and the (probably Mon) people of what is conventionally known as "Dvāravatī," in the Chaophraya Valley of what is now Thailand. A variety of circumstances in the first few centuries after the turn of the second millennium conspired to make Pali Buddhism dominant in mainland Southeast Asia and thus create the "Theravada world" as it exists today. First, Tai-speaking peoples began migrating south and west from their homeland in the border region between what is now northern Vietnam and Guangxi Province in China, adopting Pali-medium Buddhism in the process. This led to the establishment of four major Tai polities in central mainland Southeast Asia, all of which patronized Pali Buddhism: Lan Xang in what is now Lao, Lanna in what is now northern Thailand, Sukhothai in what is now central Thailand, and Siam around the Gulf of Thailand. The early history of the last of these polities, Siam, is poorly understood, but it appears that its rise represented a shift in power in the old Khmer sphere of influence, away from the old inland capital of Angkor toward maritime polities closer to the coast (Siam and Phnom Penh). Siam retained much of its older Khmer culture, but became increasingly "Tai-ified," especially in the fifteenth century as it merged with Sukhothai. Pali Buddhism became dominant not only in Siam, but also (perhaps under the influence of increasingly powerful Siam) in the more central Khmer realms to the east.

In the late twelfth century, King Parākramabāhu I (r. 1153–1186) of the Polonnaruwa kingdom in Lanka undertook a "reform" of the sangha on the island in which he recognized only one monastic *nikāya*, that of the Mahāvihāra, as legitimate, and forced all other monks to re-ordain in that lineage or disrobe. Other *nikāya*s, most importantly the Abhayagiri, had participated in Sanskrit-medium developments in Buddhism on the mainland, most importantly the Mahayana. The Mahāvihāra, on the other hand, had throughout the first millennium been more conservative and anti-cosmopolitan in outlook, sticking to its older texts in Pali.[2] Parākramabāhu's reform, however, thrust the Mahāvihāra into a cosmopolitan role, as monks who practiced Pali-oriented forms of Buddhism in Southeast Asia (Burmese, Mon, Tai, and Khmer) came to Lanka to re-ordain in the newly purified lineage and then return home to re-ordain other monks and establish "Lankan" lineages there. This new cosmopolitan relationship between Lanka and Southeast Asian polities that looked to Lanka as a center of monastic purity led to a renaissance in Pali culture, with the sudden efflorescence of Pali literature after a hiatus of hundreds of years, especially grammatical literature that often was written in imitation of earlier Sanskrit grammatical literature.[3] Moreover, the prestige of Lanka in this newly emergent "Pali cosmopolis" was rooted in what, ironically, was originally the *least* cosmopolitan of the Lankan *nikāya*s, which had therefore eschewed developments in first-millennium Buddhism, namely the Mahayana and Vajrayana. It therefore bequeathed to modern "Theravada Buddhism," at least on the normative level, a "primitive" and non-Mahayana identity, which unfortunately played into the conflation of "Theravada Buddhism" with "early Buddhism" in early Western scholarship.

The geography of Theravada Buddhism today maps roughly, but not exactly, onto national boundaries. Its practice is widely spread among Sinhala, Burmese, Mon, Tai, and Khmer ethnic groups. It is therefore the majority religion in Sri Lanka (majority Sinhala), Myanmar (majority Burmese and minority Mon), Laos (majority Tai), Thailand (majority Tai and minority Mon), and Cambodia (majority Khmer). Contiguous with this five-country core, it is also a minority religion practiced by Tai groups in Bangladesh, southern China, and northern Malaysia, as well as ethnic Khmers in southern Vietnam.[4]

Theravada Buddhist Practice

Theravada Buddhism today can be defined as that form of Buddhism that uses Pali as its sacred language, looks to the *Tipiṭaka* and other texts preserved in Pali as authoritative, and at least normatively is the only surviving form of Buddhism that does not self-identify as Mahayana. These qualities should be understood not as innate, but as emerging historically from the Pali cosmopolis of the second millennium CE. Nevertheless, they do describe the rough contours of Buddhist practice in the "Theravada world." Certain shared features can be found throughout the Theravada Buddhist world due to the Pali cosmopolis. The lack of any central authority, however, has ensured that there is considerable regional and local variation in Theravada Buddhist practice. The only centralizing forces in Theravada Buddhism have been the appointment of *saṅgharāja*s and monastic reforms performed by kings at the regional level. Sri Lanka has a unique regional Theravada culture due to its physical isolation from the rest of the Theravada world. In mainland Southeast Asia, one can see a regional split between the Burmese cultural sphere to the west and the Tai/Lao and Khmer cultural sphere to the east. The latter, while broad and involving several countries and ethnic groups, bears a certain amount of unity due to the historical significance of Siam, which itself arose out of a fusion of Tai and Khmer cultures and came to have hegemony over other Tai and Khmer polities at a crucial point in the nineteenth century. Even within a single modern nation-state, however, one finds particular regional variation to this day.

The focal point of practice for most Theravada Buddhists is the local temple. The word "temple" here refers to religious compounds referred to as *wat* or *vat* in the Tai-Lao-Khmer cultural sphere, *kyaung* in the Burmese cultural sphere, and *vihāraya* in Sri Lanka. Usually, these religious compounds can be considered simultaneously "temples" and "monasteries." They are "temples" insofar as they provide an opportunity for public

FIGURE 3.1. Stupa at Kelaniya Raja Maha Vihara near Colombo.

Photo: Nathan McGovern.

Buddhist worship, almost always in the form of a Buddha image or images, and often with stupas (more commonly referred to as *cetiya*s in mainland Southeast Asia) as well (Figure 3.1). They are "monasteries" insofar as they house monks. There are some Theravada "temples" that are not "monasteries" (i.e., they do not house monks), and there are some Theravada "monasteries" that are not "temples" (i.e., they house monks but provide no opportunity for public worship), but for the sake of simplicity I will use the term "temple" here to refer to the vast majority that perform both functions.

Theravada temple architecture displays great architectural variation, especially among the three zones I defined earlier, but also within each of the three zones. Generally speaking, they will include residential spaces for monks and at least one prominent Buddha image for public worship, often with many other images and stupas as well. In addition, Theravada temples that have the requisite number of monks in residence will include a special area defined by a *sīmā*-boundary, as described in the Pali Vinaya. This area is used for special acts of the sangha, most importantly the recitation of the *pāṭimokkha* (the 227 rules followed by Theravada monks) on *uposatha* days and the ordination of new monks. In mainland Southeast Asia, the *sīmā* area is usually a formal structure that serves as the primary "sanctuary" of the temple. In Sri Lanka, however, the *sīmā* area may be open-air.

The primary "clergy" of Theravada Buddhism are the monks (*bhikkhu* in Pali) that reside in each temple. As with monks in most Buddhist traditions, Theravada Buddhist monks completely shave the hair off their heads. Also like other Buddhist monks, they wear distinctive robes. In Theravada traditions, monks wear a "triple robe" that is intended to conform to canonical prescriptions, to a greater degree than is found in Mahayana traditions. Still, the degree of adherence to, and interpretation of, canonical descriptions of the robes and how to wear them is hotly contested within Theravada monastic lineages and has frequently been a marker of *nikāya* differences. The most obvious variation found in Theravada robes is color. Monks in the Tai-Lao-Khmer cultural sphere tend to wear robes that are an orange or yellowish color. Monks in the Burmese cultural sphere, on the other hand, tend to wear robes that a reddish color, and monks in Sri Lanka tend to wear robes of a color corresponding to whether they belong to the Siyam Nikāya or one of the Burmese-derived *nikāya*s.

All Theravada monks theoretically belong to a single "Theravada" *nikāya* insofar as they all follow the same Vinaya preserved in Pali. This Vinaya and its associated *nikāya* is one of only three with surviving lineages today, the other two being the Mūlasarvāstivāda (Tibet/Mongolia) and the Dharmaguptaka (East Asia). As in other traditions, there are two levels of ordination for Theravada monks. The first, *pabbajjā*, allows one to become a "novice" (*sāmaṇera*), who follows ten precepts. The higher ordination, *upasampadā*, allows one to become a fully ordained monk, or *bhikkhu*, who follows the entire *pāṭimokkha*, which in the Pali Vinaya contains 227 rules. One must be twenty years old to receive the higher ordination, but the age for lower ordination is defined vaguely by the Vinaya as "old enough to scare crows away," which is interpreted in various ways. Often very young boys will live in robes in Theravada temples, either because they are orphans or to receive an education.

Conformity to the rules of *pāṭimokkha* is perhaps a greater concern among Theravada monks than those of Mahayana traditions, but there is still room for interpretation, as well as some notable exceptions. Theravada monks generally speaking do not eat after noon, in accordance with the Vinaya prescription, although there is wide latitude for consuming "liquids" and "medicine." Unlike many East Asian monks, Theravada monks usually do eat meat, which, contrary to popular belief in the West, was allowed by the Buddha as long as the animal was not killed specifically for the sake of the monk being fed. With the exception of a very small number of "forest monks" who undertake the *dhutaṅga* practice of wandering in the forest nine months out of the year, Theravada monks generally reside in a temple year-round. Still, the three-month *vassa* or "rains retreat" is ceremonially observed in Theravada countries, and monks' movement is generally restricted during that time. In spite of the fact that the handling of gold and silver by monks is prohibited in the Vinaya, most Theravada monks do use money, although there may be arrangements in place to ritually avoid their direct handling of currency.

Although all Theravada monks theoretically belong to a single *nikāya* insofar as they all follow the same Vinaya, in practice they are divided into separate ordination lineages that are themselves referred to as *nikāya*s. Most of these *nikāya*s have their origins in the eighteenth or nineteenth century. In Thailand and Cambodia, there are two major *nikāya*s: the Thammayut and the Mahānikāi. The Thammayut was founded in the nineteenth century in Siam by the man who was to become King Mongkut (Rāma IV), and the majority of monks who did not join this reformist lineage became known as the Mahānikāi. Since Siam asserted hegemony over Laos and Cambodia at that time, the Thammayut-Mahānikāi division spread to those countries as well and remained after Siam ceded them to the French. This division in the sangha still exists today in Cambodia, but after the communist Pathet Lao took control of Laos in the 1970s, it abolished *nikāya* distinctions and nationalized the sangha as an organ of the state. In Myanmar, there are several *nikāya*s, but only two major ones: the Thudhamma Nikāya, established by King Bodawpaya (r. 1782–1819), and the Shwegyin Nikāya, founded by the Shwegyin Sayadaw during the reign of King Mindon (1853–1878). Higher ordination lineages in Sri Lanka died out by the eighteenth century; all three existing *nikāya*s in Sri Lanka derive from the reimportation of lineages of higher ordination from mainland Southeast Asia. The oldest, the Siyam Nikāya, was founded in 1753 from a Siamese lineage; the other two are Burmese: the Amarapura Nikāya, founded in 1803, and the Rāmañña Nikāya, founded in 1864.[5]

The Pali Vinaya, like all Vinayas, recounts the Buddha's establishment of an order of fully ordained nuns, called *bhikkhunī*s, and contains a *pāṭimokkha* of 311 rules, plus the eight *garudhammā* imposed on the Buddha's aunt Mahāpajāpatī at the foundation of the order. All *bhikkhunī* lineages following the Pali Vinaya, however, died out many centuries ago. It appears that there were *bhikkhunī* lineages until the eleventh century in Lanka and until the thirteenth century in Burma. To the east of the Burmese cultural area, there is only scant evidence that an order of fully ordained nuns might have once existed in Cambodia.[6] In the absence of a *bhikkhunī* order, some women live a monastic lifestyle in Theravada countries under a lower form of ordination, taking either eight or ten precepts. These "precept nuns" are called *dasasilmātā* in Sri Lanka and wear robes similar to those of monks; in Burma, they are called *thilashin* and wear pink, brown, or yellow robes; and in the Tai-Lao-Khmer cultural area, they wear white and are called either *mae chi* (Tai) or *don chi* (Khmer). There are far fewer precept nuns than monks, and their life is often difficult because they receive less respect and thus less material support from laypeople. Since the late 1980s, attempts have been made to reinstate the *bhikkhunī* order, but they have been controversial. While ordinations of monks require a quorum only of already ordained monks, ordinations of nuns require a quorum of both monks *and* nuns, posing a quandary when the order of nuns has died out. Recent ordinations of *bhikkhunī*s have fulfilled the quorum using nuns from the only surviving *bhikṣuṇī* lineage, the Dharmaguptaka of East Asia. This approach has been most successful in Sri Lanka. Ten Sri Lanka women, led by Kusuma Devendra, were ordained in Sarnath in 1996, and now over 1,000 nuns have been ordained in their lineage, receiving varying degrees of popular support. In defiance of the fact that the conservative state-supported sanghas of Myanmar and Thailand have rejected their validity, women from other Theravada countries have also ordained in the newly rekindled Sri Lankan lineage.[7]

Theravada monastics, the vast majority of them male, have an important ritual role to play as a "field of merit," but in terms of motivation and practice, they should be seen as in continuity with ordinary laypeople. This is particularly true given that most Theravada monks do not remain ordained for life. In mainland Southeast Asia, in fact, it is completely culturally acceptable, and in fact encouraged of young men before they marry, to ordain temporarily, even for as short a time as a few months or days. In Sri Lanka, the cultural expectation is that monks will ordain for life, but the reality is that Sri Lankan monks disrobe at about the same rate as those in mainland Southeast Asia. The old textbook generalizations that Buddhist monks are completely detached from society, or that "monks meditate, laypeople donate," bear little resemblance to the reality on the ground. Meditation is not the primary pursuit of most monks, and few enter the order with the expectation that they will attain *nibbāna* in this life. The most common motivation for ordination is to make merit, both for oneself and for one's relatives. Given the restricted options for women's ordination, it is common for a son to ordain at the death of his mother, leading to the saying in Thailand that "a woman goes to heaven clinging to the monastic robes of her son." Monks may have other mundane motivations for ordaining, including getting an education or simply having a place to live if they are poor.

Most practitioners of Theravada Buddhism are of course neither monks nor nuns, but laypeople. The practice of ordinary laypeople revolves around the making of merit (*puñña*), both to improve one's circumstances in this life and to ensure a favorable rebirth. Although theoretically any good deed counts as merit, merit-making tends to focus specifically on *saṅghadāna*, or donations to the sangha. The most everyday form of *saṅghadāna* is giving food to monks (Figure 3.2).

FIGURE 3.2. Monks going on an alms round in Salaya, Thailand.

Photo: Nathan McGovern.

This can be done from one's own home when the monks go on their early-morning alms-round; alternatively, one can arrange to feed all the monks of a temple lunch (usually served around 11:00 a.m.) at the temple itself. Given traditional gender roles, women play an outsized role in this type of merit-making. Aside from the giving of food, which is the most ritualized form of merit-making, one can also make merit as one wishes by donating robes, household goods, buildings, Buddha images, or simply cash to the sangha or (as appropriate) a particular monastic.

Laypeople tend to go to the temple to worship the Buddha and make merit on annual cultural and religious holidays, their own birthday, and whenever they have the fancy. At the bare minimum, laypeople visiting a temple will prostrate themselves three times before the main Buddha image and usually make some sort of offering to the image (candles, joss sticks, flowers). There are usually collection boxes for simple monetary donations, but often laypeople prefer to make donations, even of cash, more formally to monastics.

The "liturgies" employed by monastics when laypeople come to make merit vary widely by both occasion and location. The biggest common denominator is that prayers are recited in Pali, although they may in some cases also be recited in the local vernacular. Sermons are given when there are large numbers of laypeople in attendance and are of course given in the vernacular. Most ceremonies involving laypeople will begin with the prayer *namo tassa bhavagato arahato sammāsambuddhassa* ("Homage to the Blessed One, the Worthy One, the Rightly Self-Awakened One"), recited three times, followed by the triple refuge (to the Buddha, *Dhamma*, and Sangha), recited three times, followed in turn by the taking of the five precepts (to abstain from killing, stealing, wrong speech, sexual misconduct, and intoxicants). The "term of validity" of these precepts may be understood as being quite short, especially for the last of the five, since the consumption of alcohol is quite common in Theravada countries. Another common prayer recited by Theravada laypeople is the *iti pi so* formula that lists the qualities of the Buddha. If the visiting laypeople have formally made *saṅghadāna*, there will likely be a ceremony for the transfer of merit to one's dead relatives. This ceremony involves pouring water from a cup or small cruet into a bowl or the ground while the monastics chant in Pali. The whole transfer of merit in these ceremonies is conceived of in quite physical terms. Monastics are understood to generate sacred power, especially through the chanting of Pali verses. This power can be transmitted through direct contact, or through a string that is held by the monks while they chant and then tied directly to the laypeople or submersed in water, which is in turn sprinkled on the laypeople by a monk, much like Catholic holy water.

The largest crowds of laypeople are drawn to the temple on annual festivals and holidays. These vary by country and even by region within each country. In addition, the holidays that draw laypeople may not be specifically "Buddhist." For example, now that the Western calendar has been adopted, many laypeople go to the temple on December 31 or January 1 because they want to start the year by making merit. All five

Theravada countries also have a traditional New Year that falls in the middle of April and is a common time to visit the temple. This traditional New Year is shared with certain parts of India (including Tamil Nadu) and appears to reflect the very old cultural world shared between South and Southeast Asia. Likewise, one finds various festivals of lights celebrated late in the year in Theravada countries, similar to Dīwālī festivals in India. Particularly important is the Loi Krathong festival celebrated in Thailand and by other Tai peoples in November. Within a strictly Buddhist calendar of the year, the first day of the rains retreat and the last day of the rains retreat, followed by the *kaṭhina* ceremony for donating monastic robes, have a particular significance. There are also certain holidays corresponding to events in the Buddha's life. The most important of these is Vesākha Pūjā, observed according to the lunar calendar in April or May. It commemorates the Buddha's birth, enlightenment, and death, which are supposed to have occurred on the exact same date of the lunar calendar. This holiday is celebrated extravagantly in Sri Lanka, but it is of far lesser importance in mainland Southeast Asia.

Finally, it should be noted that Theravada *Buddhist* practice is fully integrated with a variety of practices that, according to the very limited modern paradigm of "world religions," may appear *religious* but not *Buddhist*. Buddhism is, like Christianity, a universalist religion that does not simply involve local traditions for negotiating with supernatural agents, but rather makes general claims over *all* supernatural agents. Unlike Christianity, however, Buddhism did not go through a phase in which the very existence of most supernatural agents came to be denied—with the exception of Buddhist Modernism, more influential in Sri Lanka than in mainland Southeast Asia, which developed directly under the influence of Protestant Christianity and post-Protestant Enlightenment rationalism. Generally speaking, Buddhism does not deny the existence of gods and spirits; rather, it subordinates all such supernatural beings to the Buddha by regarding them, like animals and human beings, as trapped in samsara, subject to the law of karma and eventually to death and rebirth. Supernatural beings may still live a long time and have superhuman powers, making them, aside from their technical lack of immortality, indistinguishable from such beings in polytheistic traditions. Although there is some controversy over doing so, even in traditional (non-modernist) contexts, Theravada Buddhists may worship and otherwise negotiate with supernatural beings, sometimes using technologies provided by the Buddhist sangha and sometimes others provided by lay specialists. The supernatural beings in question include local spirits (*phī* in the Tai cultures, *neak ta* in Cambodia, and the *nat*s in Burma), as well as Hindu gods (especially Brahmā and Indra, who are mentioned in the Pali *Tipiṭaka*, but also Śiva, Viṣṇu, and forms of the Goddess). In addition, all Buddhist monarchs in the Theravada Buddhist world once made use of royal court Brahmans to perform rituals on their behalf, and the two Theravada monarchies that still exist, those of Thailand and Cambodia, continue to do so to this day.

Themes in Scholarship on Southeast Asian Buddhist Practice

What, if Anything, Is Theravada Buddhism?

The study of Buddhism in Southeast Asia has struggled to liberate itself from the persistent conflation of "Theravada Buddhism" with "early Buddhism." Given that this conflation occludes practice, the very study of Theravada Buddhism or Southeast Asian Buddhism itself must inherently be a project focused on Buddhist practice. Luckily, an increased focus on Buddhist practice in general in recent decades has allowed for the growth of a true field of *Theravada* Buddhist studies, apart from early Buddhist studies. Unfortunately, until very recently, it was difficult to find a comprehensive study of Theravada or Southeast Asian Buddhism in English. Richard Gombrich's *Theravada Buddhism* partially reinforced the old conflation by addressing only early Buddhism and modern Sri Lanka.[8] Donald Swearer's *The Buddhist World of Southeast Asia* eschewed the conflation of early and Theravada Buddhism, but lacked comprehensiveness insofar as it focused mostly on Buddhist practice in Thailand.[9] It is only in the second decade of the twenty-first century that we have gotten a truly comprehensive account of Theravada Buddhism *as such* with Kate Crosby's *Theravada Buddhism*.

Ironically, no sooner has the study of Theravada Buddhism come into its own than has its very basis been questioned. Several scholars, beginning with Peter Skilling, have pointed out that "Theravada" as a term of sectarian identity is rarely used by Buddhists in Sri Lanka and Southeast Asia.[10] Todd Pereira has shown that the use of the term "Theravada" to refer to the type of non-Mahayana Buddhism practiced in Sri Lanka and Southeast Asia can only be traced back to Ananda Metteyya, a Westerner ordained as a Burmese monk, in the early twentieth century.[11] Although "Theravada" has become the standard sectarian label within the modern discourse of world religions, most Buddhist practitioners in Sri Lanka, Myanmar, Laos, Thailand, and Cambodia would simply describe what they do as "Buddhism." "Theravada Buddhism" is not only not the same thing as early Buddhism; it is, in a sense, a modern invention.

Buddhism in the Religious Landscape of Southeast Asia

As the study of Theravada Buddhism as a contemporary form of practice emerged in the twentieth century, early scholars grappled with what they saw as non-Buddhist components in the religion of Sri Lankan and Southeast Asian Buddhists—in the form of the worship of and negotiation with gods and spirits. Michael Ames, studying Sri Lanka, referred to a non-Buddhist component that he called "magical-animism," and Melford Spiro, studying Burma, referred to a non-Buddhist component that he called "supernaturalism" or "animism."[12] Stanley Tambiah's *Buddhism and the Spirit Cults in North-East Thailand* marked a turning point insofar as it saw the different aspects of Thai religion not as separate "components," but as interrelated parts of a single religious "field."[13] Other studies of Thai religion by Kirsch and Terwiel published around the same time analyzed this "field" into two (Buddhism and animism) or three (Buddhism, Brahmanism, and animism) parts, with different origins, that contribute to the religious lives of Thai people.[14]

Such studies relied on a model of "syncretism," the theory that practical religion is the product of the "mixing" of different religious components. Syncretism has fallen into disfavor among scholars of religion in recent years, and in particular scholars of Buddhism, because it posits pure religious types prior to "mixing" that often have no referent in the real world. Scholars of Buddhism now understand that there was no "pure Buddhism," even in its earliest centuries in India, free from the "contamination" of gods and spirits. The idea that Buddhism does not or should not involve gods and other supernatural beings is the modern product of an extremely selective reading of the Pali *sutta*s through the lens of Protestant and Enlightenment rationalism. Recent studies, such as those by Hayashi, McDaniel, Holt, and Davis,[15] have sought to resituate what were once considered non-Buddhist components in Theravada practice as instead normal and expected facets, often central to its practice.

Vipassanā and a "Tantric" Theravada?

As part of the conflation of Theravada Buddhism with early Buddhism and its fetishization as the most "primitive" and therefore "pure" form of Buddhism, there has been great interest in the modern West in the Theravada form of meditation known as *vipassanā* or "insight" meditation. The study of Theravada Buddhism on its own terms has led to the realization that meditation in general is far less central to its practice than the modernist image would have us believe, but it has also revealed a more complex set of traditions among those Theravada practitioners who do meditate. In the 1970s, on the verge of the takeover by the Khmer Rouge, François Bizot discovered an esoteric meditation tradition in Cambodia and salvaged some of their texts, which he then published over the following decades. Bizot noted certain similarities in this tradition with the Tantric traditions of Mahayana Buddhism and Hinduism, including secret initiation, visualization techniques, and the use of sacred diagrams (*yantra*s) and esoterically encoded *mantra*s. The work of Bizot and a small group of followers thus led to what was at first referred to as the study of "Tantric Theravada" or "esoteric Southern Buddhism."[16] This terminology has fallen into disfavor, however, especially under the criticism of Justin McDaniel, who has argued that such practices are firmly rooted in the Pali tradition, with no relationship to the Mahayana or Hinduism, and actually form the *mainstream* of traditional Theravada practice.[17]

While much of what had been dubbed "Tantric" in Theravada, such as the use of *yantras* and *mantras*, is indeed mainstream, Bizot's discovery of an esoteric *meditative* tradition that is different from modern *vipassanā* and the para-canonical model provided by Buddhaghosa still stands. This tradition, which is now practiced only in a few places in Thailand and Cambodia, has been studied extensively by Kate Crosby. Crosby, preferring now to use the Thai term *borān kammatthān* ("old meditation") to describe this tradition, rather than "Tantric," estimates that it was once practiced widely in Sri Lanka and the Tai-Lao-Khmer region, prior to the modern period.[18] It has now been replaced by various meditation methods that have their origins in the colonial period and typically place emphasis on their ties to canonical models, while appealing to a broad, including lay, audience. The most important and widespread of these is *vipassanā*, which originated in nineteenth-century Burma, in particular through the teachings of Ledi Sayadaw, and has since spread under various auspices across the traditional Theravada world and the world at large.[19]

Other Trends in the Study of Theravada Buddhist Practice

Unfortunately, space limitations prevent me from going into much detail about other trends in the study of Theravada Buddhist practice. Southeast Asian and Sri Lankan Buddhisms have rich material cultures. Kevin Trainor's work on the material culture of Sri Lankan Buddhism played an important role in the growth of interest in material culture in Buddhism.[20] Unfortunately, much work remains to be done, although encouraging work has emerged recently on the culture of Buddha images[21] and manuscripts.[22] Theravada Buddhist studies has participated in the growth of interest in women in Buddhism and feminist studies of Buddhism. Within the context of Theravada Buddhism, this has often focused on recent efforts to restart the *bhikkhunī-saṅgha*.[23] Finally, Theravada Buddhist studies has been on the forefront of efforts to recognize the role that violence plays in Buddhist traditions. While the essentialist understanding of Buddhism promoted the perception that Buddhism is a uniquely "peaceful" religion, cases of state-sponsored violence against religious minorities in Theravada Buddhist countries, particularly Muslims and Hindus, have led to studies of the ways in which Buddhism in Sri Lanka and Southeast Asia has been marshalled to the cause of violence.[24]

Theravada Buddhist Practice and Modernity

The earlier conflation of Theravada Buddhism with a supposedly "pristine" early Buddhism was not simply academic; it actually gave rise to new forms of Buddhism that attempted to conform to the rationalist expectations that arose out of the Western academic construction of "original" Buddhism. This was particularly true in Sri Lanka under British colonial rule, where reformers sought to expunge Buddhism of any "non-rational" elements (mythology, belief in gods and spirits, etc.) and present it as a philosophy more "scientific" than any other religion, in particular Christianity, and therefore uniquely suited to the modern world. Gombrich and Obeyesekere dubbed this phenomenon "Protestant Buddhism," where "Protestant" here has a double meaning. On the one hand, these reformers were "protesting" against the incursions of Christian missionaries in Sri Lanka. On the other hand, the reformed Buddhism they promoted in many ways imitated the structures and values of Protestant Christianity.[25] More recent research has situated this particular movement in Sri Lanka within the context of a broader global growth of "rational" Buddhisms that suppress traditional supernatural aspects of the tradition, referred to as "Buddhist Modernism."[26]

Within the context of Theravada Buddhist practice, however, several scholars have questioned the degree to which modern Theravada Buddhist practice should be understood as a reaction to Western modernity. These authors, including Anne Blackburn, Michael Charney, Anne Hansen, Justin McDaniel, and Alicia Turner,[27] have typically focused on particular Buddhist actors in Sri Lanka or Southeast Asia during the colonial period and the way in which they navigated the particular world that they inhabited. These scholars emphasize *continuity* with earlier Buddhist technologies, customs, thought-patterns, and mores that were employed by these actors within the context of colonialism, thus making them active participants in the construction of local modernities, rather than passive reactors to a hegemonic Western modernity.

Notes

1. The classic work by the creator of the theory of "Indianization" is George Coedès, *The Indianized States of Southeast Asia*, ed. Walter F. Vella, trans. Susan Brown Cowing (Honolulu: East-West Center Press, 1968).
2. Jonathan S. Walters, "Buddhist History: The Sri Lankan Pāli Vaṃsas and Their Community," in *Querying the Medieval: Texts and the History of Practices in South Asia*, ed. Ronald Inden et al. (New York: Oxford University Press, 2000), 99–164.
3. Alastair M. Gornall, "Buddhism and Grammar: The Scholarly Cultivation of Pāli in Medieval Laṅkā" (PhD diss., Cambridge University, 2013).
4. There are also modern international converts to Theravada Buddhism, such as among the Newars of Nepal and Western Buddhists, but these are beyond the scope of this chapter.
5. Kate Crosby, *Theravada Buddhism: Continuity, Diversity, and Identity* (West Sussex, UK: Wiley Blackwell, 2014), 213–14.

6. Crosby, *Theravada Buddhism*, 225.
7. Crosby, *Theravada Buddhism*, 226–27.
8. Richard F. Gombrich, *Theravāda Buddhism: A Social History from Benares to Colombo*, 2nd ed. (London: Routledge, 2006).
9. Donald K. Swearer, *The Buddhist World of Southeast Asia* (Albany: State University of New York Press, 1995).
10. Peter Skilling, "Theravāda in History," *Pacific World* 3, no. 11 (Fall 2009): 61–94; Peter Skilling et al., eds., *How Theravāda Is Theravāda? Exploring Buddhist Identities* (Chiang Mai: Silkworm Books, 2012).
11. Todd LeRoy Perreira, "Whence Theravāda? The Modern Genealogy of an Ancient Term," in Skilling et al., *How Theravāda Is Theravāda?*
12. Michael M. Ames, "Magical-Animism and Buddhism: A Structural Analysis of the Sinhalese Religious System," *Journal of Asian Studies* 23 (1964): 21–52; and Melford Spiro, *Burmese Supernaturalism* (Englewood Cliffs, NJ: Prentice Hall, 1967).
13. Stanley Tambiah, *Buddhism and the Spirit Cults of North-East Thailand*, Cambridge Studies in Social Anthropology, ed. J. R. Goody, no. 2 (Cambridge: Cambridge University Press, 1970).
14. A. Thomas Kirsch, "Complexity in the Thai Religious System: An Interpretation," *Journal of Asian Studies* 36, no. 2 (1977): 241–66, and B. J. Terwiel, *Monks and Magic: An Analysis of Religious Ceremonies in Central Thailand*, Scandinavian Institute of Asian Studies Monograph Series, no. 24 (Lund, Sweden: Studentlitteratur, 1975), esp. p. 5.
15. Hayashi Yukio, *Practical Buddhism among the Thai-Lao: Religion in the Making of a Region* (Kyoto: Kyoto University Press, 2003); Justin McDaniel, *The Lovelorn Ghost and the Magical Monk: Practicing Buddhism in Modern Thailand* (New York: Columbia University Press, 2011); John Clifford Holt, *The Buddhist Viṣṇu: Religious Transformation, Politics, and Culture* (New York: Columbia University Press, 2005); John Clifford Holt, *Spirits of the Place: Buddhism and Lao Religious Culture* (Honolulu: University of Hawai'i Press, 2009); Erik Davis, *Deathpower: Buddhism's Ritual Imagination in Cambodia* (New York: Columbia University Press, 2016).
16. The best overview of this early work is Kate Crosby, "Tantric Theravāda: A Bibliographic Essay on the Writings of François Bizot and Others on the Yogāvacara Tradition," *Contemporary Buddhism* 1, no. 2 (2000): 141–98.
17. McDaniel, *The Lovelorn Ghost*, 100–109.
18. Crosby, *Theravada Buddhism*, 157–59; Kate Crosby, *Traditional Theravada Meditation and Its Modern-Era Suppression* (Hong Kong: Buddha Dharma Centre of Hong Kong, 2013).
19. Erik Braun, *The Birth of Insight: Meditation, Modern Buddhism, and the Burmese Monk Ledi Sayadaw* (Chicago: University of Chicago Press, 2013).
20. Kevin Trainor, *Relics, Ritual, and Representation in Buddhism: Rematerializing the Sri Lankan Theravāda Tradition* (Cambridge: Cambridge University Press, 1997).
21. Angela S. Chiu, *The Buddha in Lanna: Art, Lineage, Power, and Place in Northern Thailand* (Honolulu: University of Hawai'i Press, 2017).
22. Daniel M. Veidlinger, *Spreading the Dhamma: Writing, Orality, and Textual Transmission in Buddhist Northern Thailand* (Honolulu: University of Hawai'i Press, 2006).
23. For a useful bibliography, see Crosby, *Theravada Buddhism*, 235–37.
24. Michael K. Jerryson, *Buddhist Fury: Religion and Violence in Southern Thailand* (New York: Oxford University Press, 2011); John Clifford Holt, ed., *Buddhist Extremists and Muslim Minorities: Religious Conflict in Contemporary Sri Lanka* (New York: Oxford University Press, 2016).
25. Richard Gombrich and Gananath Obeyesekere, *Buddhism Transformed: Religious Change in Sri Lanka* (Princeton, NJ: Princeton University Press, 1988), 202–40.

26. David L. McMahan, *The Making of Buddhist Modernism* (New York: Oxford University Press, 2008).
27. Anne M. Blackburn, *Buddhist Learning and Textual Practices in Eighteenth-Century Lankan Monastic Culture* (Princeton, NJ: Princeton University Press, 2001); Anne M. Blackburn, *Locations of Buddhism: Colonialism and Modernity in Sri Lanka* (Chicago: University of Chicago Press, 2010); Michael W. Charney, *Powerful Learning: Buddhist Literati and the Throne in Burma's Last Dyansty, 1752–1885* (Ann Arbor: University of Michigan Centers for South and Southeast Asian Studies, 2006); Anne Ruth Hansen, *How to Behave: Buddhism and Modernity in Colonial Cambodia, 1860–1930* (Honolulu: University of Hawai'i Press, 2007); Justin Thomas McDaniel, *Gathering Leaves and Lifting Words: Histories of Buddhist Monastic Education in Laos and Thailand* (Seattle: University of Washington Press, 2008); McDaniel, *The Lovelorn Ghost*; Alicia Turner, *Saving Buddhism: The Impermanence of Religion in Colonial Burma* (Honolulu: University of Hawai'i Press, 2014).

Further Reading

Blackburn, Anne M. *Locations of Buddhism: Colonialism and Modernity in Sri Lanka*. Chicago: University of Chicago Press, 2010.

Braun, Erik. *The Birth of Insight: Meditation, Modern Buddhism, and the Burmese Monk Ledi Sayadaw*. Chicago: University of Chicago Press, 2013.

Charney, Michael W. *Powerful Learning: Buddhist Literati and the Throne in Burma's Last Dyansty, 1752–1885*. Ann Arbor: University of Michigan Centers for South and Southeast Asian Studies, 2006.

Chiu, Angela S. *The Buddha in Lanna: Art, Lineage, Power, and Place in Northern Thailand*. Honolulu: University of Hawai'i Press, 2017.

Crosby, Kate. *Theravada Buddhism: Continuity, Diversity, and Identity*. West Sussex, UK: Wiley Blackwell, 2014.

Davis, Erik. *Deathpower: Buddhism's Ritual Imagination in Cambodia*. New York: Columbia University Press, 2016.

Gombrich, Richard, and Gananath Obeyesekere. *Buddhism Transformed: Religious Change in Sri Lanka*. Princeton, NJ: Princeton University Press, 1988.

Hansen, Anne Ruth. *How to Behave: Buddhism and Modernity in Colonial Cambodia, 1860–1930*. Honolulu: University of Hawai'i Press, 2007.

Hayashi Yukio, *Practical Buddhism among the Thai-Lao: Religion in the Making of a Region*. Kyoto: Kyoto University Press, 2003.

Holt, John Clifford. *The Buddhist Viṣṇu: Religious Transformation, Politics, and Culture*. New York: Columbia University Press, 2005.

Jerryson, Michael K. *Buddhist Fury: Religion and Violence in Southern Thailand*. New York: Oxford University Press, 2011.

McDaniel, Justin Thomas. *The Lovelorn Ghost and the Magical Monk: Practicing Buddhism in Modern Thailand*. New York: Columbia University Press, 2011.

Skilling, Peter, et al., eds. *How Theravāda Is Theravāda? Exploring Buddhist Identities*. Chiang Mai: Silkworm Books, 2012.

Trainor, Kevin. *Relics, Ritual, and Representation in Buddhism: Rematerializing the Sri Lankan Theravāda Tradition*. Cambridge: Cambridge University Press, 1997.

Turner, Alicia. *Saving Buddhism: The Impermanence of Religion in Colonial Burma*. Honolulu: University of Hawai'i Press, 2014.

CHAPTER 4

BUDDHIST PRACTICE IN EAST ASIA

PAULA ARAI AND EUN-SU CHO

Introduction

Buddhist practices transformed the East Asian cultural landscape even as the culture transformed the Indic-inspired practices. Tailoring the aesthetics, values, and social dynamics to fit the people in a manner that moved their heart-minds was an integral and critical feature of transmission. The early trickles that made their way into the Middle Kingdom during the first century CE swelled into burgeoning rivers that continuously shaped and reshaped the Chinese, Korean, and Japanese environments through which they flowed. Intermingling with indigenous colors and cares, the currents are notably materially embodied in orientation. In contrast to South Asian forms of Buddhist practice that highlighted the dangers of sensory attachments and material impurity, East Asian teachings and practice generally affirmed the potentiality of nature and materiality to manifest Buddhist awakening.

Deeply entrenched Confucian values gave rise to a this-worldly, socially focused mode of practice. Taoist expressions are seen in notions of nature as both a conducive environment for practice as well as a guide. Shamanic influence pulses through Buddhist practice in the Korean peninsula. Shinto ideals of purity and a seamless harmony with nature gave rise to not only clean temples but to a shift in the understanding of the senses, suffering, and who/what is a buddha. From translating key Buddhist terms to how and what to eat, where to go for guidance, and what to do with death, all aspects of daily life found a place in East Asian Buddhist modes of practice. The themes that come into focus when viewing the East Asian landscape include concerns for methods and skills that have practical value for daily life.

Practice in China

When Buddhists first brought their teachings into China in the first century CE, they entered a civilization that assumed a continuity of being where all things are animated by a unifying principle and through which the vital energy of *qi* flows.[1] The decline of the Han dynasty (206 BCE–220 CE) opened avenues for a creative harmonization of Buddhist, Daoist, and Confucian impulses. Although the relationship between these traditions is complicated and negotiations are ongoing, the sinification of the Buddhist teachings is evident in the earliest translations of Sanskrit texts into Chinese. The indigenous Chinese organizing concept of *dao* (path, way) to communicate *bodhi* (awakening) places focus on the type and quality of activity ones does in the present moment in the midst of social interactions and engagements with nature.[2] Translating nirvana with the Daoist term *wuwei* ("non-doing" or "non-interference") casts the Buddhist concern as non-interference with the path. Path intimates moving in harmony with *qi* as it flows through people, plants, rocks, and rivers. Activities from chopping wood to viewing the moon can be opportunities to experience the interconnectedness of phenomena, making such actions integral to the Buddhist path. This approach reached its fullest expression in Chan practice, whereas other schools developed different inflections and emphases.

Daoist and Confucian Influences

The earliest echelon of translations set the trajectory for the Buddhist path to wend its way through the terrain of Chinese civilization. Prominent loci include emphasis on this-worldly, mundane, and concrete concerns. Time is commonly apportioned in units of a life span, generations, or political eras. These contrast with the abstract cosmic expanses of space and time that informed Indian civilization.

The Buddhist landscape was literally shaped by Daoist teachings that center on nature as a locus of positive meaning and engagement. Chinese Buddhists established monasteries in mountainous settings to fulfill both the Buddhist monastic ideal of retreat from the world and the Daoist sense that mountains are the most suitable place for self-cultivation. Buddhists integrating Daoist teachings was not only an indication of the sinification of the Buddhist tradition, it also indicates contestation regarding who has power over sacred geography. Among the prominent mountain monasteries is the Monastery of the Eastern Grove on Mount Lu. In 380 CE, Huiyuan (334–416), the posthumously recognized founder of the Pure Land School, located his monastery on this mountain because it was one of the numinous mountains of the Daoist tradition associated with an immortal and various miraculous events and visions. Along with fellow monastics and laity, Huiyuan considered the landscape "to be an integral part of their spirituality."[3] The physical beauty of the monastic site, situated near a ravine and waterfall, might have influenced its choice as well. One of Huiyuan's biographers describes how the natural surroundings enhanced the monastery: "The *vihāra* which Huiyuan had founded fully profited by the beauty of the mountain. . . . Inside the monastery he . . . made a special grove for meditation, where among the trees . . . the stony paths were covered with moss. Every spot . . . was full of spiritual purity and majesty of atmosphere."[4] The monastery was the most prominent center of Buddhism in southern China during his lifetime and for several centuries thereafter. Lush and dramatic mountain sites across the vast geographical expanse of the Middle Kingdom are the natural settings of privileged Chinese Buddhist monastic practice.

To be palatable to an intensely family-centered society, the practice of becoming an ordained member of the sangha required reframing the meaning and significance of "leaving home." Structuring monastic relationships with familial terms ameliorates the monastic experience for the ordinand. Upon leaving their birth family, they join a Dharma family, complete with brothers, sisters, parents, uncles, aunts, and grandparents. The day you are ordained is your new birthday and your teacher is your new parent. Those who were ordained earlier by your teacher are your older brothers and sisters. The practice of painting a realistic portrait of a respected teacher derives from the Chinese practice associated with ancestor commemoration. It was originally a mortuary practice that later became also a signifier of Dharma transmission.[5]

Knowing your progeny has joined a new family is of little comfort for a culture driven by filial piety. Even the practice of tonsuring was considered an unfilial act, for it defaced the body given by the parents. Eventually arguments and scriptures were enlisted to make a case that ordained Buddhists could be even more filial than the level aspired to in Confucian practices, for they could practice great filial piety by considering "all sentient beings equal to their own parents."[6] Since the Song Period (960–1276) the Buddhist notion of karmic causation merged with indigenous notions of causation (reward and retribution). It gave rise to an understanding that karma runs through family lines. This approach to karma worked well with filial piety for it heightened a sense of gratitude to ancestors. It also intensified moral responsibility, for one generates the conditions for their progeny. Engaging in Buddhist mortuary rituals, most notably the Ghost Festival, is part of one's moral responsibility and contributed to the robust Chinese practice of venerating ancestors.

Main Schools and Practices

The Huayan school's influential meditation manual, *Discernments of the Dharmadhatu of Avatamsaka* (*Huayan Fajie Guanmen*), offers thirty avenues for meditating on *dharmadhātu*.[7] Instructing that insight into true emptiness is "not something to be discussed, nor is it to be understood; it is the realm of practice,"[8] invokes two Chinese terms: *li* (principle) and *shi* (phenomena), respectively referencing *śūnyatā* (emptiness) and *rūpa* (form). Woven into Chinese Buddhist philosophy in the fourth century, these Daoist terms facilitate expressing a distinctly Chinese interpretation of the dynamics of emptiness, interdependence, and phenomena, stressing the all-pervading and all-embracing nature of the myriad things. The *Awakening Mahāyāna Faith* text, widely recognized as originating in China, develops the teaching of *tathāgathagarbha* in terms of the interpenetration of *li* and *shi.* Seeing *tathāgathagarbha* as the ontological basis of reality makes the conditions and activities of everyday life potentially efficacious in achieving enlightenment. Philosophical justification for a this-worldly focus supported the positive valorization of farming and artistic refinement as Buddhist practices and affirmed the sociopolitical realm as a locus of practice.

Tiantai school founder, Zhiyi (531–597), exhibited the Chinese impulse to harmonize in his hermeneutical scheme that sought order out of the multiplicity, even contradictory, Buddhist teachings that entered China from different times and regions. His teachings were eventually systematized into the "Five Periods and Eight Teachings" that correspond to a hierarchical ordering of Shakyamuni's discourses. Zhiyi acknowledges Huayan as most sublime, but its inaccessibility inspired him to rank the pedagogically more practical teachings next. The scheme asserts that the *Lotus Sutra* expresses the highest level, culminating in the teaching: "Three Thousand Realms in a Single Thought." Zhiyi's meditation manual, *Mohe Zhiguan*, articulates a curriculum of practices ranging from stillness to motion in daily life. In his view, balancing these two modes are critical for effective practice. Zhiyi's teachings and practice methods continue to undergird the Chinese Buddhist tradition.

Chan school practices are fundamentally influenced by the work ethic and ritualized behaviors characteristically cultivated in the Confucian tradition. In part due to the laity valuing hard work as an indicator of moral and social responsibility, alms gathering was not a viable practice to sufficiently sustain a Chinese monastic community. Farming and other types of manual labor became authorized forms of Buddhist monastic practice. Baizhang Huaihai (720–814), the putative creator of the *Pure Rules of Baizhang*, integrated a rigorous work ethic that prescribes behavior into his new vision of a Chan monastery. He is famous for not eating until his disciples returned the elder teacher's tools to him, exemplifying his dictum: "A day without work--a day without eating." Traces of the Vinaya regulation to not eat after the noon hour linger in that an evening meal available to hard-toiling monastics is known as a "Medicine Meal," since medicine is permitted after noon. The Confucian concern for embodied expressions of moral principles is evident in the intricate prescriptive instructions delineated in Chan monastic regulations. The Confucian term *li*, ritualized activity, refers to precise gestures that are encoded with moral import to be enacted in appropriate contexts. Ordained Chan monastic practitioners are trained to embody proper behavior by precisely adhering to detailed regulations that specifically describe how a plethora of activity is to be performed, from eating to face-washing and sleeping to table-wiping. For example, respectfully offering an item requires bowing at the angle appropriate for the relationship you have with the recipient. Such ritualized behaviors are associated with sincerity of movement, integrity of action, and mindful intent. In this way, training the body-mind moves in concert with Dharma values by stressing the action of the body. Koan (Ch. *kong'an*) practice is also part of the training, focusing on the action of the mind. In the Tang dynasty (618–907), Yanshou (904–975) is attributed with converging the practices of Chan and Pure Land by asserting that *nianfo* was a Chan koan: "Who is the one calling the name of the Buddha?"[9] This exemplifies the non-sectarian impulse that runs through Chinese Buddhist practice.

The ubiquitous practice of reciting Amituofo's name heralds the most important buddha in the Chinese context. The practice is associated with Pure Land Buddhist teachings. It is practiced in distinctive ways in formal and informal contexts. A fascinating example is a ritual practiced in the rural southeastern region of Ninghua. Lay women practice a purification ritual to recognize menopausal women as *nianfo mama*, or Amituofo recitation mother.[10] Prayer beads are gifted to the women, along with numerous other prescribed gifts, from the mother of a menopausal woman and her own married daughter. In this way, the ritual weaves together three generations that the male social order tried to separate and facilitates elderly women forming a supportive community. They take on a new identity with a Dharma name, and thereafter can be addressed by that name, rather than wife of X or some other family-relation term like "auntie" or "granny." This practice flourishes precisely because it is non-institutionalized, and it demonstrates how women can exercise agency to generate practices that help them meet their emotional needs and embody their values.

Known in China as Guanyin, the bodhisattva of compassion is the most important bodhisattva. Guanyin transformed into female form through knitting together Buddhist culture with folk tales of women respected for powerful acts of compassion—the most beloved being the Princess Miaoshan. Pilgrimages to Guanyin are a popular practice, most notably to the island of Mount Putuo.[11] Many local traditions have constellated around Guanyin. Several demonstrate how women exercise their agency to creatively develop extra-canonical practices that demonstrate dedicated embodiment of their Buddhist values. A notable one that is recorded in Tang (618–917) and Song (960–1276) writings on Buddhist embroidery underscores three critical features of a practice that involves lay Buddhist women embroidering Buddhist images with their hair.[12] Each stitch symbolizes a buddha, repetition multiplies buddhas and merit, and demonstrates how women wove their bodies into a devotional practice. Guanyin is the most common icon to stitch, but Buddha and Bodhidharma are also sewn. Examples of this practice are extant from Ming (1368–1644) and Qing (1644–1911) China. They are associated with stories of filial piety, including how after a daughter embroidered Guanyin, her father was miraculously healed. Women who engaged in this domestic practice exercised agency by cultivating virtue with their own hands. Sacrificing their own hair intensified the meaning and affective force of the practice.

Chinese Buddhist practices had a formative influence on developments in Korea and Japan, though each forged their own trajectories shaped by indigenous traditions and sociopolitical contexts.

Practice in Korea

Historical Overview

Buddhism came to Korea around the fourth century, introducing the Three Kingdoms of Korea (fourth century–676 CE) to a systematic spiritual worldview that challenged the existing shamanistic understandings of the world. The Kingdom of Silla, in particular, actively promulgated Buddhism to the masses not only to cultivate an ethic based on the ideas of karma and rebirth, but also to develop the social consciousness that drove their unification of the Korean peninsula. During this period, numerous Buddhist sutras were brought into Korea by monks, which formed the basis for a diversity of schools, including Madhyāmaka (Samnon), Vinaya (Kyeyul), Huayan (Hwaŏm), and Yogacāra (Pŏpsang).

Wŏnhyo (617–686) is widely respected as Korea's premier Buddhist thinker. By his time, numerous Buddhist sutras and treatises had made their way into Korea from China. He offered an interpretation of teachings that revealed a unifying foundation undergirding an otherwise confusing diversity of texts. A scholar-monk, his practice of the teachings centered on embodying the bodhisattva ideal. He furthered the Pure Land practice of *yŏmbul*, reciting the name of Amitābha, and he sought to engage the world non-dualistically, eventually marrying and connecting with village people through song, dance, and drink. In this way, Buddhist teachings and practices made inroads into Korean society.

Buddhism was revered as a national religion through the Unified Silla (676–935 CE). The Koryŏ Dynasty (918–1392 CE) saw a flourishing of Buddhist arts, including architecture, painting, literature, and sculpture. During the Koryŏ, Buddhist institutions enjoyed court support as a state religion. State protection was sought through building monasteries according to geomantic principles. In the tenth century, a monastic examination system facilitated the Buddhist sangha's integration into the state bureaucracy. Chinul (1158–1210) established the investigation of the "critical phrase" *hwadu* (Ch. *huatou*; J. *koan*) method for Sŏn (Ch. Chan; J. Zen) meditation practice. He linked the speculative metaphysics of Hwaŏm, the predominant doctrinal tradition, with the experiential emphasis of Sŏn (known as "cultivating both *samādhi* and *prajñā*"), emphasizing that the understanding of the sutras is just as important as meditative practice. During the thirteenth century, over 80,000 woodblocks were carved into the *Tripiṭaka Koreana*, underscoring the importance placed upon Buddhist texts; these are still preserved in the Haein Monastery.

The Chosŏn dynasty (1392–1910) was a Confucian regime that largely promoted an anti-Buddhist policy. Not only was state support of Buddhism withdrawn, but monastics were prohibited from entering large cities. However, the effects of this policy were highly dependent on particular kings and a shifting social milieu. The long-held notion of Chosŏn Buddhism as a period of suppression throughout is being challenged by scholars with evidence that it was practiced even at the highest levels of society, including the royal palace. Though Buddhist faith was banned in the public sphere, it never lost its foothold in the private realms, remaining a part of everyday emotional and spiritual life.

During the decades of Japanese colonialism (1910–1945), Buddhists sought to recover from long-held disdain and suppression, sometimes seeking help from the Japanese Buddhists. Later, the Buddhist community was divided as anti-Japanese and pro-nationalist Korean Buddhist groups emerged. However, during the colonial period, the Buddhist society began to change its religious and social outlook and developed a new agenda. Their aim was to modernize and elevate Korean Buddhism and re-establish the identity of a national religion.[13] When colonization ended in 1945, there had been widespread effort to shed the influence of colonial Japanese Buddhist influence. In particular, tension over the married cleric system that had been introduced during the Japanese colonial period and had permeated the culture of Korean Buddhist temples gave rise to a "purification movement" during the 1950s and 1960s.[14]

Characterizing Korean Buddhism: Harmonious and Unifying

During the colonial period, two key concepts emerged, and they persist in shaping the character of Korean Buddhism. The first, *T'ong Pulgyo* (holistic Buddhism), was invented by a historian Ch'oe Namsŏn as part of a nationalist agenda for promoting Korean thought. For Ch'oe, Wŏnhyo provided the perfect representative for his progressive developmental theory of Korean Buddhism, which culminates in Wŏnhyo's formulation of Buddhism as "integration." The second, *Hoguk Pulgyo* (nation-protecting Buddhism), appeared during the same time by colonial scholars, with a reference to Buddhism in the Three Kingdoms and Koryŏ periods, as part of modern theorization of the religion. In the 1980s, exploration into the "uniqueness" of the Korean Buddhist tradition was heightened, which highlighted Wŏnhyo's teaching of *hwajaeng* (harmonization) in support of social ideals promoting the spirit of harmony, unity, and cooperation.[15] Due to its inclusiveness and openness to a range of teachings, such ecumenical tendencies still hold significant currency in Buddhist society, especially through the belief that Buddhism supports harmony and reconciliation of social conflict.

Religious Landscape

For a long time, Buddhism had been the dominant religion in Korea; however, according to the 2015 national census, the number of those who identify as Buddhist during this period has declined, while the number of those who identify as Protestant and Christian has markedly risen. The Buddhist population comprised 15.53% of the nearly 50 million people in South Korea, while Protestants represented 19.73% and Catholics 7.93%. This demographic shift may reflect the common view that the Buddhist tradition is a staid religion that has not kept up with the times.

The *Chogye-jong* (The Chogye Order of Korean Buddhism) is currently the largest order of Buddhism. It is recognized as a representative of the Korean Buddhist community, reinforced by its historically continuous identity that stretches back to the twelfth century. Other orders, mostly married orders, were established and registered with the government in recent decades. As of 2018, there were 482 orders registered in the Ministry of Culture under the Buddhism category. Recent data provided by Chogye Order says that the number of the monastics are about 13,000. Currently 80% of Buddhist temples are affiliated with the Chogye Order. The T'aego and Ch'ŏnt'ae Orders both include married clergy, each comprising 10% of current Buddhist temples. The Chogye Order maintains that celibacy and vegetarianism are the monastic norms for Korean Buddhism, holding that *taech'ŏ'* (having a wife) and *yuksik* (eating meat) are impure practices. Although statistics are not available, it is rather widely known that a large percentage of monastics do not keep the practice of vegetarianism.

Women are observably prominent. A half of the current sangha is composed of celibate nuns, and lay women make up 80% of Buddhist laity.[16] South Korea is currently one of the few countries where the Buddhist nuns' sangha includes full ordination. Nuns receive the same education and training in scriptures and meditation as their male counterparts, and consequently the laity hold nuns with the same high regard as monks.

Contemporary Organizations and Practices

Numerous innovative organizations and practices emerged in response to the changing concerns, socioeconomic conditions, and needs of Buddhist monastics and laity, especially notable since the 1970s.

Korean temples—traditional large monasteries and small hermitages—have served as the basis for the monastics' livelihood, and also places for studying, practicing, and guiding lay people. In the contemporary Buddhist scene, urban temples and Dharma centers have emerged to serve as more regular and accessible bases for laypeople.

Contemporary monastic curriculum in Korea exhibits traces of Chinul's legacy to develop doctrinal understanding before engaging in meditation practice. Typically it begins with four years of seminary for doctrinal study of the scriptures and is followed by Sŏn meditation training. Sŏn meditation practice is known as the representative form of practice, intimating that Sŏn is the quintessential form of Korean Buddhism. *Ch'amsŏn*, sitting meditation, and *kanhua* i.e., *hwadu* observation method, are the central practices of the three-month long monastic retreats held in summer and winter. The Sŏn patriarch Sŏngch'ŏl (1912–1993) is credited with reviving the spirit of meditation practice and Sŏn superiority in 1970s.

A superior assessment of *hwadu* mediation as a direct path to enlightenment has continued straight through since the medieval period. Despite this, devotional practices such as praying, chanting, and prostrations are the most prevalent types of practice for monastic and lay alike. These daily-life devotional practices, called *Kibok Pulgyo* (Prayer for Good Fortune Buddhism), resonate with forms of Buddhist practice aimed at health, prosperity, protection, and safety, concerns that stretch into the earliest strata of Buddhist practice. Temples are crowded with mothers praying for their children's success on entrance exams, their family members' recovery from illness, or the overcoming of some other adversity. Temples also perform memorial rituals, called *Sasipguje*, to mark the forty-ninth day after a death and *Ch'ŏndoje* rituals for pacifying the souls of the dead. These rituals provide a major source of income for temples. Another popular practice is the recitation of the names of deities, called *kido* and translated as "prayers." The practice includes extended sessions of reciting the names of the various buddhas and bodhisattvas, the most popular being Avalokiteśvara (*Kwanseŭmbosal*), Amitabha (*Amitabul*), or Shakyamuni Buddha (*Sŏkkamonibul*). Prostrations (*chŏl*) are another popular form of devotional practice. Prostrations are recognized for having a positive effect on health and longevity, especially in light of the heightened stress of modern South Korean society.

Temples offer Sunday Dharma services and occasional meditation courses and Buddhist education classes. Sunday services usually begin with the Three Refuges and conclude with the Four Vows, accompanied by piano music. Choral music is one of the most popular group activities for temple members. Adopting western music for Dharma services originated during the colonial period as an effort toward modernization. Temple choirs perform in front of the congregation on special occasions. More serious choirs perform in contests with other groups and produce music CDs.

Major Buddhist temples run Buddhist Education Colleges as a requirement for new lay disciples. The curriculum commences with the Buddha's biography and moves to the doctrines of Early Buddhism, Abhidharma Buddhism, and Mahayana Buddhist philosophical treatises such as Madhyāmaka and Yogacāra Buddhist traditions. Focus on doctrinal and textual study in lay introductory courses reflects the scholastic orientation of Korean Buddhism.

Publishing books aimed at a lay readership is another avenue through which monastics have reached out and have connected with the general public. Beopjeong (Pŏpjŏng, 1932–2011), an intellectual monk and writer, published nearly twenty books, gaining him the trust and respect of the late twentieth-century South Korean populace. Some of his books remain on the bestseller list a decade after his passing, such as *Musoyu* (*No Possession*). It sold over a million copies, and provides the masses with a thoroughly contemporary and authentically Korean Buddhist alternative to rampant materialism.

Monastics also developed novel organizations focused on leading the laity in various modalities that served monastic concerns to engage the Dharma. Starting in the 1970s, Buddhists responded to the dictatorial government's push for economic growth with what they called *Minjung Pulgyo* (People's Buddhism). They argued that the Buddhist message centered on establishing an equal society by overcoming injustice. Two contemporary movements among these engaged Buddhist groups stand out: the Jungto (Pure Land) Society, founded by Pŏmnyun (b. 1953) in 1988, and Indra's Net

Community, founded by Tobŏp (b. 1949) in 1999. Founded as grassroots communities based on Buddhist principles, Buddhist monks and nuns initiated these organizational attempts to develop values and ways of living that served as alternatives to the contemporary world's emphasis on mass consumption, commercialism, and the exploitation of natural resources.

Urban mega temples also began to emerge amidst the vibrancy of the 1970s. Two temples that met with immediate and unprecedented success in attracting new members are Hanmaŭm Sŏn Center, founded by the late female Sŏn master Daehaeng (Taehaeng, 1927–2012), and Nŭng'in Sŏn Center, founded by the monk Jigwang (Chigwang, b. 1951). A majority of members are politically conservative, with affluent backgrounds and traditional Buddhist orientations.

Reflecting technological developments, the internet (notably YouTube) and social media are avenues that followers of Pŏmnyun (b. 1953) of the Jungto Society have employed to help him build a huge following. He has become a leading celebrity among Korean Buddhists through his engaging televised talk show, "Direct Questions and Direct Discussions with Pŏmnyun." He also tours constantly around the country, holding mass lectures in city halls, universities, and other public spaces. His dialogues display the curative power of authentic Sŏn as applied to daily problems, using the method of providing provocative responses grounded in the non-dualistic logic of emptiness.[17] These conversations encourage audiences to talk openly about their family- or work-related problems, while he responds to them in a way that reveals how the roots of their questions lie within their own attachments, wrong views, greed, or other internal problems. Among the other figures regarded as celebrities are a nun, Chŏngmok, who owns an internet radio station featuring soft music and commentary on various topics and an intellectual monk with a Ph.D., Hyemin, who became a media sensation upon returning to Korea after teaching in the United States. Hugely popular among the young people, his books feature collections of aphorisms on love, relationships, and various contemporary concerns.

In addition to these innovations, many temples led by young and popular monastics also hold cultural events at their temples. The events are frequently musical, such as "concerts under the moonlight," and they aim to draw people who would not otherwise come to the temple without the lure of experiencing a serene temple atmosphere surrounded by mountains. There is also a growing new trend of non-Buddhist interest in meditation as self-care and an interest in temple food.

Temple Stay programs are another mode of inventive monastic activity that helps the Buddhist sangha reach a greater body of people. Originally conceived to support foreign tourists during the World Cup in 2002, attracting Koreans as well as well as international travelers, now Korean Buddhist temples are increasingly recognized as tourist destinations for unique cultural experiences and healing. An increasing number of temples, spreading even to urban city temples, now offer a mix of spiritual, cultural, and tourist activities that provide participants with a "transformative experience" and the "occasion to connect with Korean tradition, nature, and one's peace of mind."[18]

Western, Theravada, and Tibetan Buddhism have drawn a new generation of youth and intellectuals to meditation, theory, and non-traditional perspectives. These developments are emblematic of the last half century of Buddhist activities in South Korea that facilitate a more globalistic and modern mode of Buddhist practice.

Practice in Japan

Surveying the landscape of Japanese Buddhist practice reveals traces of Vedic, Daoist, and Confucian impulses and a deep well of Chinese and Korean Buddhist ways, intermingled with indigenous Shinto colors and sensibilities. The current of influences began to flow in 538 CE when Korean King Seong of Paekche sent Emperor Kimmei (r. 539–571 CE) a statue of a buddha and scriptures. It gained momentum in 590 CE when three nuns—Zenshin-ni, Ezen-ni, and Zenzō-ni—launched the monastic practice of Buddhism upon returning to Japan after *bhikṣuṇī* ordination in Paekche.[19] Since this watershed moment, practices have continued to transmute to suit the aesthetics, values, social dynamics, and institutional structures as they shape the ongoing transformation of people in a primarily world-affirming mode.

To help Buddhists navigate the land of "eight million *kami*," the *honji-suijaku* (origin-manifestation) interpretive scheme associated a Buddhist figure with a Shinto figure. This practice lubricated the wheels of power as it helped Buddhist practices take root in Japan. Centered on a range of Buddhist figures and sutras, sects—including the Nara schools, Heian schools of Shingon and Tendai, and the Kamakura schools of Jōdo, Jōdo Shin, Rinzai and Sōtō Zen, and Nichiren—began to establish distinctive practices that animate the Buddhist terrain. The majority of people, however, did not formally affiliate with a particular sect until the Tokugawa period (1603–1868), when the feudal government girded its power by requiring people to register at a Buddhist temple in an effort to eliminate threats from the Christian West. As before this systematized organization, people continued to engage in Buddhist practices outside the domain of such institutional structures, with the most widespread ritual practices focusing on protection and healing, Amida Buddha, the bodhisattvas Kannon and Jizō, and the *Lotus* and *Heart Sutras*.

Practices in Relationship to Concepts of Enlightenment

Two concepts that have influenced the shape of many Japanese Buddhist practices are *mappō* (degenerate age of the Dharma) and *hongaku*, original enlightenment. The concept of *mappō* stretches back to the Nara period (710–794), but a series of natural disasters, conflagrations, and the upheaval of the governmental structure intensified salience of the concept in the shift from the Heian period (794–1185) to the Kamakura period (1185–1333). In a spectrum of direct and subtle ways, the notion of *mappō* has affected the contours and sense of effectiveness of practice as it focuses attention on conditions for the current world. A range of interpretations of *hongaku*[20] gave rise to a host of practices that generated numerous applications that focused on activity in and for this world.

Within this milieu, concepts of enlightenment affected the types of practices advanced. After training in China, Kūkai (774–835) returned to Japan and made *sokushin jōbutsu*, "become Buddha in this body," a central feature of Shingon esoteric teaching. A complex web of practices is available to facilitate this, including Diamond Realm and Womb Realm Mandala meditations, chanting, mudras, mantras, the Ajikan *siddham* syllable visualization on the letter "A," and the *goma* ritual. Other teachings in Japan had resonant views on the nature of enlightenment, though the specific articulation and attending practices varied. Tendai's rich assortment of teachings and practices spawned a burst of inspiration often dubbed "Kamakura Buddhism." Though they differ in significant ways, the Pure Land practices of Hōnen (1133–1212) and Shinran (1173–1263) institutionalized *nembutsu* practice, chanting "Praise to Amida Buddha," in the Jōdo and Jōdo Shin sects, respectively. The goal of enlightenment had to be routed through rebirth in the Pure Land, where rebirth had more to do with Amida's compassionate vow to help beings than it had to do with disciplined practice. Nonetheless, *nembutsu* practice is associated with humble and grateful behavior in social relationships. In Sōtō Zen, Dōgen (1200–1253) suggested *shikan taza*, "just sitting," as an effective method to actualize his insight into the relationship of practice and enlightenment: *shushō-ittō*, "Practice *is* enlightenment." "Sitting" is the prototypical activity that can be transposed to any manner of actions, including eating, cleaning, and walking. Rinzai Zen also stresses zazen augmented by koan practice. Nichiren (1222–1282), whose sect takes his name, focused on chanting the title of the *Lotus Sutra*, known as the *daimoku*, to reach enlightenment, for the *daimoku* embodies "the reality of the Buddha's enlightenment."[21] The aim of the practice is to manifest this reality here and now. Distilling practice to one method is a feature that continues to undergird much of sect-based Japanese Buddhist practice, though most people engage in an array of practices that extend beyond the direct purview of institutional boundaries.

Practices Engaged with Nature and Art

Nature is a useful hermeneutical lens for illuminating significant dimensions of Japanese Buddhist practice, though the meaning of nature and relationships with nature have involved a range of ontological and soteriological understandings.[22] There is no singular assessment as to whether and how much Japanese indigenous ideas and practices regarding nature have shaped or influenced the Buddhist transformation. It is clear that Japan adopted the Daoist-inspired Chinese practice of establishing temples and monastic complexes on mountains, though on plains the association with a mountain only took eponymous form. Engaging with natural phenomena from a Japanese Buddhist perspective not only reveals aesthetic preferences; it also illuminates how Buddhist concepts were transformed in the Japanese context. Though predating the Japanese encounter with *sōmoku jōbutsu*, "plants become buddhas," deliberations about this concept animated ninth-century Japanese discourse, knitting notions of nature, however conceived, into the fabric of Japanese Buddhist practice.[23] Kūkai not only taught that the heretofore formless concept of *dharmakāya* took the form of natural phenomena, but that this Dharma body itself taught the Dharma: *hosshin seppō*. To understand the teachings, then, is a practice of appreciating the activity of the present moment and refining attunement to change. Doing so facilitates cultivating awareness about the nature of all things, including the seasons of human life and death.

Artistic paths of practice emerged from the impulse to experience the beauty of impermanence in natural phenomena. These practices require refining the senses to perceive nature imbued with Buddhist concepts of impermanence, interrelatedness, and emptiness. Sense perceptions are often implicated in fueling delusion, but contemplative art practices, such as Way of Tea (*sadō*), opened a path of transformative experience that engaged the senses. The Heian-period literary concept of *mono no aware* (awareness of the fleeting nature of things) enriched the Buddhist teachings on impermanence, amplifying appreciation of the present precisely because it is evanescent. The Way of Flowers (*kadō*), Way of Fragrance (*kōdō*), and Way of Poetry (*kadō*), which highlight natural imagery to express subtle emotions, also engage the senses to attune to the beauty of ephemerality. Other practices that cultivate attunement to a Buddhist-based interpretation of natural phenomena include Zen ink painting and garden design. Rinzai Zen, especially during the Muromachi period (1336–1573 CE), is the epicenter of art as practice. More informally, yet more commonly, the practice of viewing the annual blossoming of cherry trees interprets these flowers as the quintessence of ephemeral beauty. Seen as having no fear to burst forth their full potential for beauty in the face of imminent demise, they are heralded as exemplars of the Buddhist virtue of non-attachment. These arts shift the valence of impermanence from a source of suffering to a source of beauty. By refining the senses, these contemplative art practices teach one how to stop suffering by attuning to and embodying the beauty of impermanence.

Monastic and Domestic Practices

Monastic practice in Japan includes a range of meditation techniques, chanting, and ritual ceremonies. Monastics have also refined vegetarian cooking into an artful practice called *shōjin ryōri*. Monastic regulations and understandings about the nature of precepts vary according to time period and sect. Tōdai-ji leaders controlled the ordination platform during the Nara period (710–794) where monastics received the *Caturvarga Vinaya* of the Dharmagupta School. Saichō (767–822), founder of the Tendai Buddhist sect in Japan, was successful in augmenting the criteria for acknowledging full monastic status. He adopted the bodhisattva precepts delineated in the *Bramajāla Sūtra*. Eventually most Buddhist sects adopted them over the Vinaya-based ordination, with monks and nuns taking the same precepts.[24] In the thirteenth century, Jōdo Shinshū openly permitted clerics to marry, following Shinran's example of "not monastic, not lay." In 1872 the government encouraged monks to marry and decriminalized clerical marriage, eating meat, and not keeping the head tonsured, blurring the distinction between monastic and domestic practice.

Rituals at home altars (*butsudan*) are a prominent feature of domestic practice.[25] In addition to a Buddhist figure or consecrated piece of calligraphy, mortuary tablets (*ihai*) of deceased family members are commonly honored in the altar. *Ihai* have the posthumous Buddhist name of the deceased, who is often recognized as a buddha upon passing. After making offerings of light (candles), incense, flowers, and food at the altar, it is common for people to hold prayer beads (*juzu*) while interacting with their deceased loved ones as "personal buddhas." These "personal buddhas" listen without judgment and offer support, affirmation, and care as needed, making home altars sites of healing.[26] Such practices that recognize the significance of continuing relationships between ancestors and their living descendants suggest an embodied awareness that karmic connections continue to flow through familial lines.

A host of *kuyō* memorial rites weave together interaction between monastics and laity. Monastics come into the home to chant sutras for ancestor memorial rites, and laity go to temples to engage in a range of public rituals. The most prominent one is *obon*, where special offerings welcome ancestors home for a few days. Laity also go to gravesites, usually on temple grounds, to make offerings. Typically, a temple organizes an *obon* dance on a summer evening during this period. Although grief can be poignant during the first *obon* following the death of a loved one, *obon* is not primarily a solemn practice. It reinforces family connections as it subtly affirms that no one is alone, even after death. *Mizuko kuyō* rituals are memorials for unborn fetuses, whether miscarried, stillborn, or aborted. This practice recognizes the loss and grief as it ushers the *mizuko* to be reborn in more auspicious conditions. *Kuyō* rituals are also offered for objects, including needles, dolls, and brushes,[27] suggesting the porous character of the boundaries between inanimate and animate forms.

Engaging in practices to experience enlightenment is not the primary focus of most Buddhist practices in Japan. Rather, numerous practices focus on "this-worldly benefits" (*genze riyaku*), including protection from natural disasters, fire, illness, and harm. Buddhist practice flourished with state projects to protect the nation through meritorious activities, including building temples, ordaining monastics, and copying sutras. Sutra copying (*shakyō*) and chanting are non-hermeneutical text practices that weave through Buddhist practice from early on.[28] As with the contemplative art practices, the practice of sutra copying and chanting involves body-mind activity to enact the teachings of non-duality and are thereby healing. Other healing practices include drinking water from a source known for healing, carrying an amulet (*omamori*), or placing a paper or wooden talisman (*ofuda*) in the home to aid its inhabitants. Healing is a predominant motivation for embarking on a pilgrimage. A number of pilgrimage routes lace through mountains and across plains, including the longest one making a circuit of 88 temples around Shikoku Island, founded by Kūkai, and the 100 Kannon Pilgrimage, which connects the Saigoku, Bandō, and Chichi-bu routes. Bowing, especially out of respect and gratitude, is the most ubiquitous practice. People bow at their home altars; when arriving at a temple or departing a temple on a pilgrimage route; doing a *kuyō* for ancestors or needles; performing a ritual for lifetime monastic vows; commencing a meditation session; making a bowl of tea; or ending a chant. Bows can involve forehead to the floor, lowering body with palms together, or just a distinct lowering of the head while in an upright posture.

In addition to recent developments in *Shin Shūkyō* (New Religions) and *Shinshin Shūkyō* (New New Religions)—largely syncretic Buddhist traditions that aim to address modern needs heightened by urbanization—several innovative practices have emerged in response to the 2011 Fukushima tragedy. Buddhist chaplaincy, which takes cues from Christian models and does not necessitate ordination, is emerging as a way to offer spiritual counseling. *Kaze no denwa* (wind phone) is a telephone booth in an open field to talk with deceased loved ones.[29] "Café de Monk" is a mobile café that offers a casual place for people to gather with a monk for informal counseling. The name invokes a triple entendre of "monk": (1) it means "monastic"; (2) the Japanese pronunciation, "monku," is a homonym for "complain"; (3) it is a reference to Thelonious Monk, whose tunes are played in the background.[30]

Japanese Buddhist practice continues to transform with the changing needs of the times, though the current of concern for this-worldly needs of people remains constant as ritualized practices embed meaning into daily activities.

Notes

1. Tu Wei-ming, "The Continuity of Being: Chinese Visions of Nature," in *On Nature*, ed. Leroy S. Rouner (Notre Dame, IN: Notre Dame University Press, 1984), 113–32.
2. Saitō Akira, "Buddhist Translations Past, Present, and Future: With a Focus on Chinese and Tibetan Renderings," *Journal of Cultural Interaction in East Asia* 8 (2017): 17–26.
3. Miranda Shaw, "Buddhist and Taoist Influences on Chinese Landscape Painting," *Journal of the History of Ideas* 49, no. 2 (April–June 1988): 190.
4. Erik Zürcher, *The Buddhist Conquest of China: The Spread and Adaptation of Buddhism in Early Medieval China* (Leiden: E. J. Brill, 1959), 241.
5. Foulk T. Griffith and Robert H. Sharf, "On the Ritual Use of Ch'an Portraiture in Medieval China," *Cahiers d'Extrême-Asie* 7 (1993): 149–219.
6. Fa-lin, *Pien-cheng lun* (*Taishō* 52.529b). Cited in Kenneth Chen, "Filial Piety in Chinese Buddhism," *Harvard Journal of Asiatic Studies* 28 (1968): 97.
7. Its authorship is uncertain, though it is attributed to Dushun (557–640), the posthumous first head of the Huayan lineage.
8. *Fa-tsang, Hua-yen Fa-p'u-ti-hsin-chang* (Taishō 45. 652c20 f).
9. Chung-fan Yu, *Chinese Buddhism: A Thematic History* (Honolulu: University of Hawai'i Press, 2020), 212.
10. Neky Tak-Ching Cheung, "Receiving Prayer Beads: A Lay-Buddhist Ritual Performed by Menopausal Women in Ninghua, Western Fujian," in *Recovering Buddhism in Modern China*, ed. Jan Kiely and J. Brooks Jessup (New York: Columbia University Press, 2016), 545–623..

11. Chun-fang Yu, *Kuan Yin: The Chinese Transformation of Avalokiteshvara* (New York: Columbia University Press, 2001).
12. Yuhang Li, "Embroidering Guanyin: Constructions of the Divine through Hair," *East Asian Science, Technology, and Medicine* 36 (2012): 131–66.
13. Hwansoo Ilmee Kim, *Empire of the Dharma: Korean and Japanese Buddhism, 1877–1912* (Cambridge, MA: Harvard University Asia Center, 2012), and *The Korean Buddhist Empire: A Transnational History 1910–1945* (Cambridge, MA: Harvard University Asia Center, 2018).
14. Pori Park, *Trial and Error in Modernist Reforms: Korean Buddhism under Colonial Rule* (Berkeley, CA: Institute of East Asian Studies, UC Berkeley, Center for Korean Studies, 2009).
15. Eun-su Cho, "The Uses and Abuses of Wŏnhyo and the 'T'ong Pulgyo' Narrative," *The Journal of Korean Studies* 9, no. 1 (Fall 2004): 36.
16. The government report published in 2018 based on the 2015 Census indicates about 56 percent of those who identified as Buddhist are women. However, regarding temple activities, scholars usually estimate 80 percent of the temple goers are women.
17. See Hyekyung (Lucy) Jee, "Application of Zen Rhetoric to Daily Issues: The Case of 'Conversation with Pŏmnyun,'" *Contemporary Buddhism* 17, no. 2 (2016): 236–51.
18. Florence Galmiche, "A Space of Mountains within a Forest of Buildings? Urban Buddhist Monasteries in Contemporary Korea," in *Sociology and Monasticism: Between Innovation and Tradition*, ed. Isabelle Jonveaux, Enzo Pace, and Stefania Palmisano (Leiden: Brill, 2014), 235–36.
19. *Nihongi*, trans. by W. G. Aston (Rutland, VT: Charles E. Tuttle, 1972), vol. 2, p. 101. *Gangōji Garan Engi* in *Jisha Engi*, compiled by Ienaga Saburō, Fujieda Akira, Hayashima Kyōshō, and Tsukushima Hiroshi (Tokyo: Iwanami Shoten, 1975), 11.
20. Jacqueline Stone has examined original enlightenment in terms of Tendai and Nichiren orientations, in *Original Enlightenment and the Transformation of Medieval Japanese Buddhism* (Honolulu: University of Hawai'i Press, 1999).
21. Jacqueline Stone, "Medieval Tendai *hongaku* Thought and the New Kamakura Buddhism: A Reconsideration," *Japanese Journal of Religious Studies* 22, no. 1–2 (1995): 22.
22. See Fabio Rambelli, *Buddhist Materiality: A Cultural History of Objects in Japanese Buddhism* (Stanford, CA: Stanford University Press, 2007); and Bonaventura Ruperti, Silvia Vesco, and Carolina Negri, eds., *Rethinking Nature in Contemporary Japan: From Tradition to Modernity* (Venice: Edizioni Ca' Foscari, 2017).
23. For a well-researched discussion, see chapter 1 of Rambelli's *Buddhist Materiality*.
24. Sōtō Zen adopted a 16-vow version.
25. Paula Arai, "Domestic Dharma in Japan," in *Oxford Encyclopedia of Buddhism*, ed. Richard Payne (New York: Oxford University Press, 2020) https://doi.org/10.1093/acrefore/9780199340378.013.965.
26. Paula Arai, *Bringing Zen Home: The Healing Heart of Japanese Women's Rituals* (Honolulu: University of Hawai'i Press, 2011): 65–107.
27. Rambelli, *Buddhist Materiality*, chapter 6.
28. Rambelli, *Buddhist Materiality*, chapter 3.
29. https://www.citylab.com/life/2017/01/otsuchi-wind-phone-japanese-mourners/512681/.
30. https://www.pri.org/stories/2015-10-23/cafe-de-monk-tsunami-survivors-can-get-coffee-cake-and-someone-listen-their-woes.

Further Reading

China

Gregory, Peter. *Tsung-mi and the Sinification of Buddhism*. Princeton, NJ: Princeton University Press, 1991.

McRae, John, *Seeing through Zen: Encounter, Transformation, and Genealogy in Chinese Chan Buddhism*. Berkeley: University of California Press, 2004.

Swanson, Paul. *Clear Serenity, Quiet Insight: T'ien-t'ai Chih-i's Mo-ho-chih-kuan*, 3-volume set. Honolulu: University of Hawai'i Press, 2017.

Yü, Chün-fang. *Chinese Buddhism: A Thematic History*. Honolulu: University of Hawai'i Press, 2020.

Yü, Chün-fang. *Kuan Yin: The Chinese Transformation of Avalokiteshvara*. New York: Columbia University Press, 2001.

Korea

Buswell, Robert E., Jr. *Currents and Countercurrents: Korean Influences on the East Asian Buddhist Traditions*. Honolulu: University of Hawai'i Press, 2005.

Buswell, Robert E., Jr. *The Zen Monastic Experience: Buddhist Practice in Contemporary Korea*. Princeton, NJ: Princeton University Press, 1992.

Cho, Eun-su, ed. *Korean Buddhist Nuns and Laywomen: Hidden Histories, Enduring Vitality*. Albany: State University of New York Press, 2011.

Kim, Hwansoo Ilmee. *The Korean Buddhist Empire: A Transnational History 1910-1945*. Cambridge, MA: Harvard University Asia Center, 2018.

Park, Jin Y., ed. *Makers of Modern Korean Buddhism*. Albany: State University of New York Press, 2010.

Japan

Arai, Paula. *Bringing Zen Home: The Healing Heart of Japanese Women's Rituals*. Honolulu: University of Hawai'i Press, 2011.

Rambelli, Fabio. *Buddhist Materiality: A Cultural History of Objects in Japanese Buddhism*. Stanford, CA: Stanford University Press, 2007.

Reader, Ian, and George J. Tanabe, Jr. *Practically Religious: Worldly Benefits and the Common Religion of Japan*. Honolulu: University of Hawai'i Press, 1998.

Swanson, Paul, and Clark Chilson, eds. *Nanzan Guide to Japanese Religions*. Honolulu: University of Hawai'i Press, 2005.

Tanabe, George, Jr., ed. *Religions of Japan in Practice*. Princeton, NJ: Princeton University Pres, 1999.

CHAPTER 5

BUDDHIST PRACTICE IN CENTRAL ASIA/HIMALAYAS

TODD LEWIS

ARRAYED on the Himalayan periphery of both North India and Tibet, Buddhist traditions across this 1,600-mile long montane arc have been shaped by monastic networks, pilgrimage routes, itinerant saints, and modern states. Peoples sharing a common language, kinship ties, and institutional connections have come to occupy ethnographic niches across this extraordinary mountainous region, with their usually small-scale settlements subsisting through unique combinations of fixed crop agriculture, animal husbandry, and trade. Nowhere in the Buddhist world is it more evident that celibate monastic Buddhism is a luxury for societies: in the Himalayan frontier zone, many communities adopted Buddhism, but in a more minimalist form, with small monastery-temples (Figure 5.1), often with householders as monk-ritualists.

Himalayan Buddhists speak dialects of Central Tibetan or "Tibeto-Burman" languages, the latter a linguistic designation of limited utility; it indicates their being speakers of non-Indo-European languages whose native tongue is also largely unintelligible to central Tibetan speakers.

The known Buddhist groups to be discussed here—in Kashmir, Himachal Pradesh, Sikkim, and Arunachal Pradesh, as well as those in modern Nepal and Bhutan—share many common traits, as well as exceptional differences. As is the case for the environment across the Himalayan range, where the landforms include a rich variety of ecological niches, so too have the various Himalayan peoples adopted Buddhism according to the logic of their own geographic sociocultural and political circumstances. Much remains unknown, both regarding group origins and contemporary practices; scholarship has been scant, and most of the first studies completed in the past fifty years have become, by 2021, outdated, as many changes have altered the lives of individuals and entire communities across the Himalaya regions.

One variable of profound significance is how each Buddhist community in the region was tied to the region's political states. Today, being part of India, China, Pakistan, or Nepal compels each group to comply with different laws regarding land tenure and

FIGURE 5.1. A Tibet-styled *chorten* (stupa) in the Himalayan frontier.

Photo: Todd Lewis.

taxation, and to integrate themselves into very different national cultures. Only one Himalayan state, Bhutan, has Buddhism as its state religion; in all the others, Himalayan Buddhists exist as minorities in their respective greater polities.

Ancient History

Although the Himalayas could have been seen on a clear day from some places in ancient Kapilavastu, the Buddha's hometown, there is no evidence in the early canonical records of Shakyamuni Buddha visiting, or an early sangha being established, in the Himalayan middle hills or beyond during his lifetime or in the first centuries that followed. What is found in the popular stories of the early canons is an awareness of Mount Kailash and Lake Manosarowar as holy places, and of "snow mountains" or "Himavat" as unpopulated forested regions for ascetic retreat, as well as venues where gods and other spirits dwell. Since the broad alluvial Gangetic plain was still only dotted by early cities and villages, and most ancient agricultural lands then were surrounded by vast tracts of jungle, humans could find new lands to clear nearby, and so had no compelling reason to settle in the mountains where the easily arable land was rare, soils less fertile, and subsistence much harder.

Earliest to affect the region were diaspora traders, spiritual seekers, and pioneer settlers. Settlement occurred first, in all likelihood, in relation to pilgrimage routes to sacred locations close to the Himalayan peaks, holy lakes, or river confluences (*tīrthas*). These incursions drew areas of the region under the influence of itinerant ascetics, both brahmanas and heterodox holy men; by this time, individual Buddhists followed these expanding economic and religious networks that began to link the plains to the mountains. Among the inscriptions set up by the great King Ashoka (r. 273–232 BCE), there are several among the dozens of places mentioned where he sent "emissaries of Dharma" that were in the northwest Himalayas.

As the first large empires formed in South Asia, the Himalayan region was identified as a border, or frontier zone (*pratyanta*). It is likely that the Buddhist sangha had by the turn of the common era been established in this region. One archaeological discovery that suggests this was found at the important stupa complex at Sanchi, where a relic container of a monk named Majjhima had the following words inscribed: "relics of the great teacher of Himalayan people."[1] What exactly was meant by "Himavat" in this record, however, cannot be determined.

It is certain that early Buddhist monks and monasteries, following the missionary ethos of the Buddha, spread out initially across the trade routes. The great northern route, the *Uttarapatha*, linked the northern Gangetic plain westward to the Indus watershed; it joined trade routes going toward Central Asia and the Silk routes, facilitating the spread of the faith to highland Gandhara and Kashmir, a process that with Emperor Kaniṣka (ca. 100 CE) grew in significance.

The introduction of Buddhism elsewhere across the Himalayas likely followed the same pattern as in the Gangetic plain and Kashmir. Merchants and rulers built the first modest monasteries in emerging settlements and along trade routes, seeking legitimation, ritual protections, and merit for themselves; as these towns grew, so did their Buddhist institutions. In several cultural centers that left records, a great deal is specifically known.

Kashmir Valley

The great expanse of the fertile Kashmir Valley, and its location as a prosperous entrepôt on a southern branch from the great trans-Eurasian Silk routes, enabled this region to eventually become a second key center of early Indic Buddhism. It was so important that, according to a succession of accounts from visiting Chinese pilgrims from the fifth to seventh centuries, it was a land dotted with over a hundred impressive monasteries and home to great monk-scholars and sages. Ideas and Buddhist institutions seem to have evolved creatively in this region that was connected with adjacent Gandhara; Buddhism and Hinduism existed in harmony, with kings supporting both. On the former, we have the remarkable history of Kashmir written by Kalhana in 1148 CE, the

Rājatarangaṇī, which reports that in its later stages, the Buddhist sangha included both "celibate" and "married" members, a comment of intriguing historical importance.[2]

What is certain is that it was Gandhara and Kashmir Buddhists who were important to spreading Buddhist culture up into Central Asia, China, and the Tibetan plateau. Indeed, the Kashmir-Gandhara region is recalled by later Tibetan Buddhist historians as the place of origin for Mahayana and later Vajrayana traditions.

Although Buddhism endured in the Vale of Kashmir until at least 1400 CE, it declined in competition with Muslim missionaries and the campaigns of destruction by a succession of increasingly intolerant rulers. Little of the tradition's material culture survives to testify to this Valley's former magnificence or importance in the history of Indic Buddhism.

Kathmandu Valley

By contrast, the far smaller but also richly fertile Kathmandu Valley endures as an oasis of an indigenous Buddhist tradition until the present day. Its connections to the very proximate Gangetic plain dating back almost two thousand years are clear from the earliest extant epigraphic records there, written in Sanskrit in Gupta script beginning in the fifth century. There are also stray image finds suggesting that Buddhist presence likely began there at least several centuries earlier, doubtless the result of its proximity to Magadha and the earliest Buddhist holy places such as Lumbini, which is 120 miles distant, and Bodhgaya, 200 miles.

After 464 CE, the Sanskrit inscriptions indicate donations by householders and kings of a ruling dynasty that referred to themselves by the name Licchavi. Reflecting the same pattern of diversity found up until today, records of Hindu temples and Buddhist monasteries are found "side by side" there, a harmonious relationship that is confirmed by Chinese pilgrim Xuanzang's journal covering the period 629–645 CE.

The Licchavi inscriptions and the earliest known art reveal connections between the Nepal Valley and the traditions of monastic art that originated on the Gangetic plains from the early Buddhist centuries, as well as patronage by kings and merchants, and the existence of a *bhikṣunī* sangha. Devotees of Shiva, Vishnu, and other Hindu gods are also well represented, especially in royal circles. Multi-roof wooden religious sanctuaries, as seen in Figure 5.2, illustrate an example of peoples in the Valley importing cultural forms originating from the Indic cultural centers to the south.

The indigenous people of the Kathmandu Valley, the Tibeto-Burman language-speaking Newars, supported the work of resident Buddhist scholars, ritualists, and leaders in the sangha who since then have received, preserved, and adapted Indic traditions. From this time, resident scribes copied Sanskrit manuscripts, some perhaps traveling to monastic centers in the Gangetic plains by the Pala era. Newar Buddhist artisans were also important. So renowned were they that in subsequent centuries they

FIGURE 5.2. Skyline of the Newar town of Bhaktapur, with the Himalayan peaks to the north.
Photo: Todd Lewis.

were called upon to build most of the major temples, monasteries, and stupas across Tibet and as far away as China. After the destruction of most great Gangetic monasteries (by 1300 CE), Tibetan Buddhist saints and scholars also traveled south to this valley to build monasteries, erect and restore its great stupas, give and take initiations, and collect Sanskrit texts. These fruitful exchanges (still little studied) shaped the development of both Newar and Tibetan Buddhist traditions up to the present day.

Himachal Pradesh

The existence of Buddhism now located primarily in the Indian state of Himachal Pradesh (H.P.) dates back over two thousand years, as numismatic evidence has established the presence of Buddhism in the lower hills of the upper Beas River watershed. In the H.P. highlands, Buddhist monasticism is attested back at least one thousand years, when monasteries associated with the southern Tibetan kingdom of Guge were built. Legends recount the presence of Padmasambhava (active 750 CE?) and other tantric *siddhas* in this region, founding retreats and temples. No records exist regarding the premodern establishment of Buddhism outside of the two important valleys and besides the few attested sites in the region between them. Undoubtedly, in some rural regions after 900 CE, Nyingma, the "ancient" school, spread among the hill peoples, and this tradition is still widespread in small communities across the Himalayan region until today.

Himalayan Buddhism after 1200

After the Second Introduction of Buddhism into Tibet (1000 CE onward), Indic saints and teachers definitively established and strengthened Buddhist traditions across the region. Sources have the translator-missionary Rinchen Zangpo (958–1055 CE) coming to Himachal, where legends state that he built 108 monasteries in the Lahul, Kinnaur, and Spiti valleys. A few survive, including the large complexes at Tabo and Lalung. The continuous movement of figures from the plains, such as Naropa (956–1041), Atiṣa (982–1057), Marpa (1012–1096), and Dharmasvamin (d. 1234), is documented by their biographers; these accounts depict their travel in small entourages across trails and passes, to visit the many settlements. One gets the impression of many other such travelers—originating from both the Indic plains and the Tibetan highlands—who endured many hardships establishing the Dharma across the Himalayan frontier. These hagiographic stories typically recount the recurring need to subdue local deities and convert local chieftains to the Buddhist path.

As Tibetan polities after 1150 CE were politically and religiously controlled by the new trans-regional monastic schools founded in central Tibet, and with the eventual triumph by 1650 of the Gelugpas led by the Dalai Lamas, the dominant school extended regional monastic centers across their own southern Himalayan frontier, in what is today highland India and Nepal. Notable was this process in the eastern Himalayas, where Bhutan was settled by members of the Drukpa school who sought refuge from Gelugpa persecution in central Tibet.

Long before the borders of modern nations were drawn, an extensive "web of Tibetan monasticism" existed that drew aspiring young monks from all the remote Himalayan regions to larger institutions, some as far as to central Tibet, for education and religious training. In fact, the greatest monasteries in Lhasa and Shigatse were divided into sub-institutions according to the linguistic areas of the monks' origins. Movement across this expanding Tibetan Buddhist network went both ways: the isolated locations far from the great centers of population at times drew saints seeking spiritual retreat amidst the fierce isolation of the beautiful mountainous terrain; and the missionary ethos of Buddhism, along with the lure of travel (that always existed among some monastics from the beginning of Buddhism), also gave many of these remote outposts, at times, rich infusions of doctrinal teaching and spiritual inspiration.

One early example of this important phenomenon from the late fifteenth century was gTsan-smyon Heruka (1452–1507), a famous mendicant tantric yogin of the Kargyupa order born in central Tibet. After gaining renown as a young meditation master, he became restless with settled monasticism, and periodically undertook long and arduous pilgrimages along the southern Himalayan periphery, visiting the Kathmandu Valley and then other more highland Tibetan Buddhist communities. A spiritual virtuoso renowned for his "holy madness," the saint's life was marked by long periods of solitary meditation, scholarly projects (his biography of the *siddha* Milarepa is one of the classics of popular Tibetan literature), and long expeditions spent on pilgrimages to give teachings to those he met. gTsan-smyon is credited with founding many monasteries in remote places, presumably by more conventional methods, as was the case with other missionary lamas crossing the region like him.

The premodern era was also a time of groups migrating over the high passes into the valleys of the Himalayan periphery. Whether it was to seek better lands, follow kin, or the result of groups fleeing times of tumult from Mongol or other incursions across the Tibetan plateau, people speaking similar languages came to populate the highland regions. Some nomadic groups on the Tibetan plateau crossed the high passes to reach less harsh conditions on ridges and valleys located at lower altitudes south of the great peaks. Scholars of the Sherpas from the Mount Everest region, for example, have surmised that this group migrated less than four hundred years ago from the eastern Tibetan plateau.[3]

Early Modern Himalayan Buddhism(s)

By 1600, the Himalayas can be described as a dual religious frontier, the intersection of Tibetan Buddhist civilization from the north interspersed with Indic civilization from the south, with the Kathmandu Valley the last outpost of ancient and medieval Indic Buddhism. In many regions, peoples migrating from the Tibetan plateau settled into preferred or available ecological niches, and there adapted their life centered on Buddhism to their own newfound circumstances. But the region was also by then being populated from the Gangetic plains as well, according to another pattern: Indic migrants, usually bearers of brahmanical or "Hindu" traditions, who settled in the alluvial river valleys and introduced intensive rice cultivation and cow-centered subsistence. The intersection of migrants can still be seen in watershed peaks and valleys across the region today: where lower down there are rice cultivators speaking Nepali, an Indo-European language, in the highlands above and to their north are migrants speaking Tibeto-Burman languages, who rely on yaks (and yak-cow hybrids) along with high-altitude grains (barley, buckwheat), grown on irrigated fields according to a totally different subsistence pattern. Trade has been long-standing linking these groups: highland peoples carried rock salt quarried on the Tibetan plateau and mounted caravans to bring it to the lowlands, where they traded it for rice and goods.

Each region has its own history, including in some cases violent conversion to Tibetan Buddhism. The Lepcha of Sikkim offer a case study of "spiritual conquest": in their myths, this group (who refer to themselves as Rong-pa) retains a memory of missionary lamas destroying all evidence of their indigenous culture upon their subjugation and conversion:

> Later the sons of *zo khe bu* and their [Central Tibetan noble] families came down to Sikkim with their followers, invaded and conquered the country. At that time . . . [the lamas] collected all the Lepcha manuscripts and books containing historical records, myths, legends, laws, literature and burned them. They took the ashes to the high hills and blew them into the air and built monasteries on the hills from which they scattered the ashes . . . and forced Lepcha scribes to translate their scriptures and venerate them. . . .[4]

Tibeto-Burman peoples were thus affected by both brahmanical and Tibetan migrants, as distant institutional leaders from both directions sought to incorporate them into their larger polities. In most Himalayan regions, the rice-growing Indic populations typically came to dominate mid-montane political systems, so that the press to "Sanskritize" and adopt brahmanical traditions was faced by the many Buddhist ethnic groups in the regional and early modern states. After 1600 CE, two material influences arrived to affect the entire Himalayan region: corn and the potato from the "new world." The former staple, indigenous to North America, could be cultivated on dry, non-irrigated mountain terraces in the mid-hills; the potato, indigenous to highland South America and so adapted to thrive in high altitudes, could be grown up to 12,000 feet. Both increased the food that could be grown, and so enabled populations there to add nourishing additions to their diets. As monasticism depends on a community's surplus wealth, these developments doubtless abetted the vitality of Himalayan Buddhism over the past 400 years.

Until the last decades, most Tibeto-Burman groups had contacts with Tibetan Buddhism to their north, both within the corridors of trade, and with monastic centers. It was these ties that were instrumental in establishing and sustaining Buddhist culture and Himalayan Buddhist ethnic group identity, and it was these ties that had been unraveled, or reoriented, in the later twentieth century. After 1959, a new wave of Tibetan Buddhist influence came in the form of refugee spiritual leaders resettling and building new monastic centers outside Chinese-controlled territory.

Modern Borders and Anomalous Cultural Survivals

The continuity of independent Tibetan Buddhist culture in some Himalayan localities is due to the "accidents" of colonial rule: Ladakh and highland Buddhist areas of the modern states of Himachal Pradesh (Kulu, Manali, Kinnaur) ended up within modern India due to the British ceding this territory to rulers of "princely states"; the British

Raj successfully defended their princely states until Indian independence (1947). Sikkim and Bhutan were likewise allowed to remain independent kingdoms by the British only insofar as their foreign policies were consistent with colonial interests, a position continued by independent India after 1947 to the present day. (Sikkim, however, was annexed back into India within the state of West Bengal in 1975.) In the same way, highland Tibetanized communities in Arunachal Pradesh that were claimed by British India (Tawang and vicinity) also remain as Indian territory today, though these regions, like some of those cited previously, are still claimed by China.

Buddhism in the Hindu State of Nepal

The modern country of Nepal was created in 1769 when a hill king from Gorkha united many other rulers to conquer hill regions from Sikkim to Himachal Pradesh. Centered in the Kathmandu Valley, this Shah dynasty sought to rule with brahmans administering *dharmaśastra*-based laws, and its kings claiming to be incarnations of Vishnu, ruling a Hindu country protected by Shiva in the form of Pashupati ("Lord of Creatures"). The Shiva temple in Kathmandu became the object of lavish patronage. (The modern borders were reduced to their current sites after skirmishes with the British in the early nineteenth century.)

For the Tibetans, Tibeto-Burman peoples, and Newars, this new political order was problematic and oppressive. So difficult did life under Shah rule become in many hill communities that tens of thousands migrated to the less-populated "frontier" Himalayan regions to the east: to British-held Sikkim, to Darjeeling and Arunachal Pradesh, to independent Bhutan, and even as far east as Burma. Many of these migrants retained kin ties in Nepal, and some brought their Buddhist traditions with them. The influence of these displaced Buddhist groups, whose experiences outside Nepal were considerably more "modern" (exposed to British-mediated Protestant Christianity, science, government, law, etc.), was an important factor that influenced their Nepal Buddhist communities in subsequent decades.

When the Ranas usurped power from the Shah kings in 1846, they sought to unify the dozens of ethnic groups autocratically, using stronger versions of Hinduism and Hindu law. State practices fostered conversion to Hinduism and laws punished groups that refused to give up or radically curb their non-Hindu religious practices. (Eating yak meat, for example, was viewed as an act of "cow killing.") Tamangs, the largest Tibeto-Burman group in Nepal, whose mid-montane settlements are closest to the Kathmandu Valley, suffered the most from Rana despotism in the form of losing land ownership and being enslaved.

The history of a much smaller and more remote ethnic group, the Thakalis, living on the upper Kali Gandaki River, provides another case study of Tibeto-Burman Buddhist response. Since the north-south trade route through their territory garnered so much wealth and depended on relationships with high-caste state officials, the

Thakali strategically adapted to the Hindu state by almost completely suppressing their Buddhist identity: they had their literati compose new historical accounts asserting ancient Hindu origins, celebrated Hindu festivals, adopted brahmanical life cycle rituals, and dropped Buddhist ritualism. Other Tibeto-Burman groups did not go this far, but most tried to limit conflict with the Hindu state of Nepal. Even after 1950, when the Ranas were deposed and the Shah kings reassumed power, coercive Hindu identity practices still continued. Government schools taught in Nepali only and included Hinduism, and every government center in every district of Nepal established a small temple to Pashupati, and each also built a temple for Durgā worship where government officials performed sacrifices during the fall Dashara festival.

These practices fostered resentments that eventually led to the revolution of 1991, an uprising that led to multiparty democracy. This ushered in a new era of ethnic politics in which mostly Buddhist Tibeto-Burman groups across the nation rallied to oppose Hindu and brahmanic cultural hegemony. Eventually this movement added to the political forces spearheaded by a Maoist uprising (1996–2006) that eventually removed the Shah dynasty and made Nepal a secular state in 2008.

Modern Tibetan Monasticism across Nepal's Highlands

Until 1959, the region's Tibetan or Tibeto-Burman connections to the Tibetan plateau Buddhist institutions were still vital, from Ladakh and Himachal Pradesh, to Humla in far-western Nepal, as well as (from west to east) in Dolpo, Lo-Mustang, Nyeshang, Nupri, Manang, Langtang, Helambu, Solu-Khumbu, and Walung. Local boys interested in training to become senior monks would do what their ancestors had done for centuries: travel to central Tibet and return to maintain local institutions that typically sheltered, at most, a few resident monks whose main occupation was local ritual service. This web of monasticism changed with the exodus of the Dalai Lama to India, and since 1960, the network has been partially realigned to refugee institutions in Dharamsala, Sikkim, and Kathmandu.

Also affected was the "second tier" of connection between central Tibet and the Tibeto-Burman peoples (whose main settlements are typically lower than 10,000 feet): Magars, Gurungs, Thakalis, Manangis, Tamangs, Sherpas, and Lepchas. Most of the Buddhist ritualists among them follow the Nyingmapa school, and the people rely on householder lamas to perform their rituals. To train for this service, young Tibeto-Burman men typically live for several years as apprentices with elder householder lamas or in the regional highland monasteries. (Before 1959, some of these might have trained in Tibet.) A few great saints who became famous across Tibet were born in places like Dolpo or Yolmo[5] in the Nepal Himalayas. Most return to their villages to marry and maintain shrines long-established as their family's own property. Thus, most "Buddhist monasteries" among Tibeto-Burman peoples today are family shrine-residences, and sons usually continue to follow their fathers as the local Buddhist ritualists.

The growing presence of Tibetan Buddhist monasteries and teachers in the Kathmandu Valley also altered the religious landscape of the Tibeto-Burman groups. Back to the later Malla era (post-1600), Tibetan monks became an integral if small part of the landscape, with most centered around monasteries built around the great stupas of Bauddha and Svayambhu. Throughout the twentieth century, each of the main Tibetan sects also established branch monasteries with major resident scholars and spiritual teachers in Nepal. Up to the present, resident Tibetan householders have been drawn to worship at major Newar shines (*bāhā*).

The Maoist uprising abetted this Tibetan monastic expansion in the Valley after 1990. Growing rural violence and intimidation drove many of the affluent Tibeto-Burman Buddhists from across the mid-hills to resettle in Kathmandu. This influx has fueled a spate of new residential building, as well as the construction of dozens of new monasteries. Driven by this migration and remittances from overseas, by 2021 many immense Tibetan monasteries have been built across the breadth of the Valley proximate to traditional sacred centers. These now attract refugee monks and nuns from the Tibetan plateau, the refugee diaspora, as well as a growing number of those from the Tibeto-Burman communities seeking ordination. To be ordained and study with great Tibetan lamas today, one need not walk overland to Central Tibet, but only take a short bus trip to monasteries dotted around the nation's capital.

The Kathmandu Valley is now one of the most important centers of Tibetan Buddhism in the world for several reasons. First, in addition to the Tibeto-Burman influx, one of the largest concentrations of Tibetan refugees in the world has settled there. Given the wealth generated by carpet-weaving enterprises, the tourist industry, and foreign remittances, some of this surplus has been dedicated to providing patronage to dozens of new monasteries. Second, as Tibetan Buddhism has become increasingly attractive to Westerners, a number of prominent Tibetan lamas oriented to them—and funded by their donations—have established "Dharma centers" at Bauddha and other places that in most ways resemble traditional monasteries. Here one can find textual study and meditation being pursued by both ethnic Tibetans and Westerners clad in red robes.

Examples of Highland Buddhism(s) in Nepal and India

Among Himalayan peoples, the most familiar term used for a Buddhist ritualist is *lama*, a Tibetan word usually meaning "tantric guru," but one that has also become a family

FIGURE 5.3. Tibetan monks playing long horns, inviting the local deities to the yearly masked dance festival.

Photo: Charles Ramble.

surname of individuals with a history of serving as Buddhist ritualists. The term can designate a celibate monk as well as a married priest.

Tibetan Buddhists characteristically mark the Himalayan landscape with meritorious devotional items, sacred objects imparting protection, and the sound of rituals (as seen in Figure 5.3). Stupas are found in and around the villages; settlements are decorated with prayer-walls at village entranceways (most inscribed with the Avalokiteśvara mantra, "*Om mani padme hum*") and fluttering prayer flags with protective mantras fly above the houses and shrines.

Most villages have one or two temple-shrines. Usually small, these typically contain images or paintings of Guru Rimpoche (Padmasambhava), the founding saint of the prevalent Nyingma school; the Buddha Shakyamuni; and Chenrizi, the celestial bodhisattva known in Sanskrit as Avalokiteśvara. Many temples house block-printed texts, ritual paraphernalia, and a variety of icons or paintings. A yearly festival that commemorates the monastery's founding is typically one of the major events of the village ritual year.

The Buddhist sangha in these communities is almost never a celibate elite, but is composed of householders, as this vocation is inherited. The Tamang of the central Himalayas are representative in the composition of a Tibeto-Burman sangha: "Tamang lamas are married householders who farm like their kinsfolk, although they avoid

FIGURE 5.4. Tamang Nyingma-pa Lama (second from the left) performing a death ritual, 1982.
Photo: Todd Lewis.

plowing. During rituals, they don red robes, chant texts, display scroll paintings, and employ ritual implements. At these times villagers address them by the honorific *sangkye*, the word for "Buddha."[6]

The most common Tibeto-Burman Buddhist rituals (*ghyawa*) are those concerned with merit-making and death, in which the lamas chant and meritorious gifts are made to ensure a positive future birth. The essential Buddhist death rite among the Tamang is called *ghyewa* or *gral* (lit. "rescue"), which includes the last rites and a memorial death feast afterward. When someone dies, lamas are invited to come sit with the body to chant texts with drum and cymbal accompaniment, to pacify the *bla* ("soul"). They also supervise the last rites, usually cremation, to send off the dead successfully to a favorable rebirth (Figure 5.4).

A traditional spiritual practice for householders that has grown in popularity across Himalayan Buddhist societies is that of *nyungne*, a two-day fasting and Mahayana meditation rite dedicated to the celestial bodhisattva Chenrizi. On the first day, each participant takes vows to observe the rules, and abide by the eight moral precepts; each can eat only one vegetarian meal, with water the only drink. The second day entails a complete fast with no meals or liquids, as each participant must remain silent until the end. The purpose of the rite is to heighten awareness of suffering, and to deepen the individual's connection to this bodhisattva, the most popular in all Himalayan traditions.

Being Buddhist: Shamanism and the Himalayan "Religious Field"

Since most Himalayan Buddhists follow other traditions, it is important to think of a larger "religious field" that includes ceremonies performed by other ritual specialists that are directed to local and clan deities. These often mesh with local Buddhist traditions, but at times they can clash. On the village level, every ethnic group across the region regularly venerates its lineage ancestors as living gods, whose wrath or protection can affect the living.

The Himalayan landscape contains a welter of spirits inhabiting local mountains, springs, rocks, caves, trees, and rivers. Some deities when pleased bring local blessings like the seasonal rains and the land's fertility; others in the local pantheon can cause misfortunes, including illnesses. In both cases—for venerating their ancestors and worshipping local deities—villagers mostly call upon spirit mediums. Across the region, these shamans perform dramatic all-night séances to contact the gods. By drumming and singing, they enter trance; in this state, they converse with and hear the divinities express their wishes, and then work to satisfy their demands with songs, sacrifices, offerings, and mantras.

Himalayan shamanic traditions vary across the region, and may even differ within the same group; crossing over from watershed to watershed moving west to east, the religious life of the people shifts as regularly as changes in dialect. The Tamang of central Nepal are typical in their reliance on several different independent religious specialists: they have a tradition of a *lambu* who limit their service to exorcising evil spirits, as shown in Figure 5.5; and their *bombo* contact the gods for protection, healing, or to secure more general blessings.

In most times and places, this coexistence of lamas and spirit mediums represents an amiable division of labor; but at other times and some places, this is not the case. Stan Mumford's study (1989) of Buddhists in Manang, in west-central Nepal, explored a conflict that divided Buddhists in one village when newly settled refugee Tibetan Buddhist lamas opposed deer sacrifice. For centuries, this ritual had been done to appease a local mountain deity, and most devotees argued that without this deity's blessing, their tenuous farming life would be endangered. But the lamas insisted that blood sacrifice inevitably generated bad karma for individuals and the entire locality; it was this act of taking life that actually endangered the community. The lamas instead performed a "sacrifice" of a dough deer effigy; but the shaman loyalists found this dangerously inadequate. Life has gone on with both traditions contending and continuing.

The populations in the Lo-Mantang region proximate to the Dhaulagiri Himalaya have also fostered this coexistence of blood sacrifice traditions with Buddhism. In his study of the village of Te, Charles Ramble (2007) has shown that while the people are

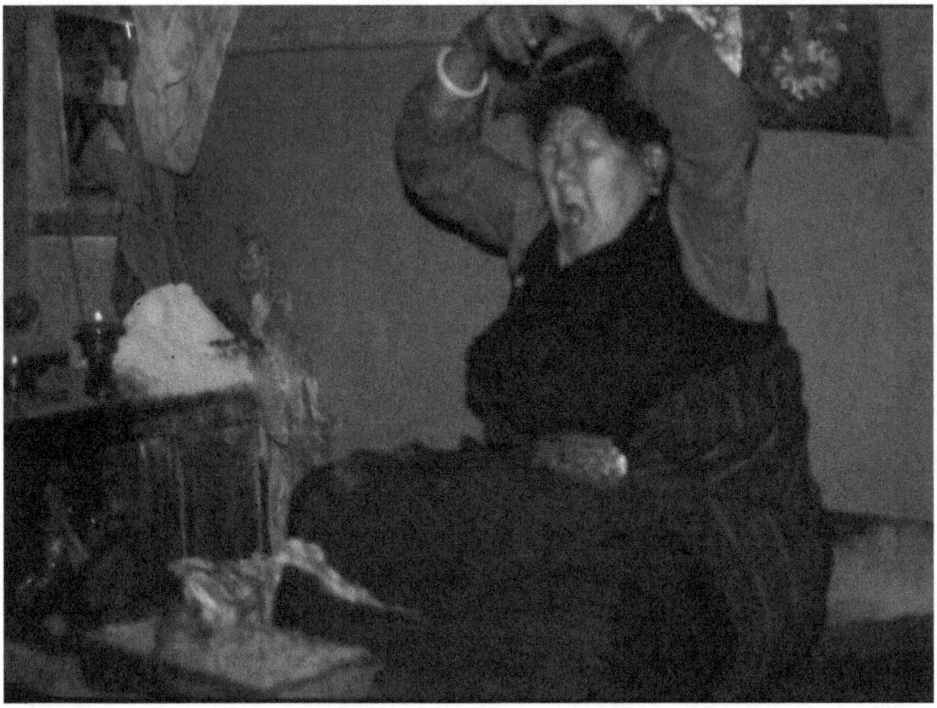

FIGURE 5.5. Spirit medium in Darjeeling, possessed in healing ritual.

Photo: Todd Lewis.

nominally Buddhist and support Buddhist tantric priests to perform a variety of rituals, they are also devotees of a local religion that involves blood sacrifices of animals to wild, unassimilated local gods and goddesses. Again, Himalayan peoples shape religion to the pragmatic demands of community survival.

Among many Tibeto-Burman groups, this multi-specialist religious life is seen in the death rituals that involve multiple practitioners, not just Buddhist lamas. Among the Gurungs of Nepal (and similar to the Tamangs, discussed earlier) there are exorcists (*pucu*) who conduct rituals to drive off demons, shamans (*khilbri*) who pacify the disembodied soul, and lamas who do rituals to garner merit and guide the being to a favorable next rebirth. It is the same among the Lepchas of Sikkim, where householders called *bóngthíng* preside at recurring religious ceremonies and may be called upon to heal acute illness; but it is a shaman called the *mun* who heals by exorcising demons.

Overall, amidst all the pragmatic traditions, it is Buddhist doctrine and worldview that are nonetheless acknowledged as the dominant ideology across the Himalayan frontier.[7] Just as the buddhas and bodhisattvas reign supreme over lesser gods and local spirits in the cosmos, karma provides the central moral principle that guides individual moral life as a natural law. Still, living in the high Himalayas requires vigilance and community action, as well as flexibility.

"Upgrading Buddhism": Recent Changes among Sherpas and Gurungs

The most studied highland Buddhist group in the Himalayas is the Sherpas, who early in the modern era achieved unparalleled prosperity by the eighteenth century due to their involvement in Indo-Tibetan trade, so much so that wealthy families there began to invest in Buddhist traditional learning and practices in their communities. In 1850, they funded several Sherpa villagers to travel to Tibet. This group came to study with the well-known lama scholar Choki Wangchuk, who instructed them in ritual and meditation cycles, some of which are still popular throughout the villages of Solu-Khumbu, the Sherpa homeland in proximity to Mount Everest. As Matthew Kapstein has noted, "The liturgies for these rites are often profound and beautiful, as their titles suggest, e.g., 'The Union of All that is Precious,' 'The Spontaneous Freedom of an Enlightened Intention,' 'The Celestial Doctrine of the Land of Bliss.'"[8]

Sherpas later were the first to enter the trekking industry in Nepal, and this plus support from foreign donors counteracted the loss of their trading enterprises north into Tibet after the border was closed in 1959. In the 1970s and 1980s, however, those prospering from trekking and mountaineering were not as interested in Buddhist patronage and instead oriented themselves toward Western culture. Many settled in the Kathmandu Valley, and the Buddhist material culture of the highland Sherpa settlements was neglected. Since 1990, however, Sherpa patrons have resumed their interest in maintaining their homeland Buddhist institutions, and they now support celibate monastics both there and in new monasteries in the Kathmandu Valley.

There are now two types of Sherpa *gompa*. Private monasteries, the property of a senior member of a clan, are located in homes and are under the control of lineage priests, *gyudpi*; all relatives gather in these precincts when rituals need to be performed. The public *gompa*s, notably in Chiwong and Tengboche, which were built beginning in 1930, are for everyone in the community. They preserve a large collection of texts copied in Tibet, and own woodblocks for printing many manuscripts, these the result of Sherpa artisans who learned to carve woodblocks for printing that are said to rival those produced elsewhere in Tibet. Supported by wealthy Sherpa patrons, some Sherpa lamas today have entered the world of global Tibetan Buddhist monasticism and have attained an international following.

The Gurungs of central Nepal (pop. 534,000), though less well-known than Sherpas (pop. 150,000), have also benefited from new opportunities. Their employment in British and Indian "Gorkha" military regiments, their prosperity from the development of tourism in their home region, and remittances from Gurungs who have emigrated abroad to work have all brought new wealth and innovations in their group's practice of Buddhism. Southern Gurungs have hired their own elders to compose from oral legends a written historical text called the *Tamu Pye*. Drawing on sections extracted from recent Nepali histories, this work documents the uniqueness of their group's history and asserts the great antiquity of the Gurungs' devout Buddhist practice. The Tamu Pye states that Gurung adherence to Buddhism dates back to the age of buddhas coming before Shakyamuni, and that devotees then in fact are their ancestors.[9] As with other Tibeto-Burman groups, their new compositions claim that their group once possessed its own calendar as well as Gurung works of literature in their own language, written in their own script; and there are stories in the *Tamu Pye* that maintain that these landmarks of high culture had been destroyed by Newar king Jaya Sthiti Malla (r. 1382–1395) "at the instigation of the Hindu sage Shankara."[10] While accounts of this sort contain little that can be historically authenticated, they indicate how greatly their leaders and community wish to assert the validity of their own traditions, and their pride in Buddhist identity.

Modern Newar Buddhism

By 1500 CE, the Newar sangha was led by an elite calling themselves *vajrācāryas* whose ancestors had developed a highly ritualized Buddhist culture. Although the exact when and why of this development remain unknown, there was a literal domestication of the sangha as former celibate Newar monks became married "householders-monks" and membership was based on patrilineal descent. Most Newars followed exoteric Indic Mahayana Buddhism; it was Vajrayana Buddhism and tantric initiation that assumed the highest position in local understanding, though only a few actually practiced the esoteric traditions. Newar monastic architecture still reflects this development: in the large courtyards that define the monastic space, the shrines facing the entrance have on the ground floor an image of Shakyamuni or Avalokiteśvara (Figure 5.6); but on the first floor above is the *āgama*, a shrine with a Vajrayana deity, with access limited to those with a tantric initiation.

As Hindu shrines and law were in the ascendancy from the late Malla period right through the late twentieth century, Newar Buddhism adapted. A system of main and branch monasteries developed in Patan and Kathmandu to organize this sangha community. Newar "householder monks" with ties to their own monastery (New. *bāhā*) called themselves either *Bare* (from the Sanskrit term *Vande* or *vandanā*, an ancient Indic term of respect for monks), *śākyabhikṣu*, or *vajrācārya*, and began to function as endogamous castes. This meant that one had to be born into this sangha and, with a few exceptions, everyone else was denied ordination. (This left only the Tibetan sanghas in the Kathmandu Valley where ordination into a celibate monastic Mahayana life was possible for Newars men or women wishing to become monastics.)

The masters in the Newar sangha definitely adapted their local ritual traditions to conform to the state's caste laws and thereby preserve the social and legal standing of the Buddhist community, including its once-extensive monastic landholdings. Many Newar monasteries today, especially in Patan, still bear the name of their founding patrons, and date back to the Early Malla period (1300–1428). Local Buddhist monks, like Hindu

FIGURE 5.6. Image of Avalokiteśvara in Kathmandu, from late Licchavi period (c. 800 CE).
Photo: Todd Lewis.

panditas, were especially active in manuscript copying; Buddhist monastic libraries in the Kathmandu Valley in the modern era became known worldwide as the greatest repository of Sanskrit texts; they include ancient copies spanning a great breadth of subject matter, from popular narratives and canonical texts to astrology and daily ritual practices. Thousands of medieval Sanskrit texts recorded on paper or palm leaf folios like that seen in Figure 5.7 are still found in private homes, archives, and monasteries.

Unlike the monastic institutions of Tibet that fostered in-depth philosophical inquiry and vast commentarial writings, Newar Buddhists have produced few original

FIGURE 5.7. Buddhist text cover with painted folio page showing Shakyamuni Buddha, late Malla era (1700 CE).

Photo: Todd Lewis.

contributions to Buddhist philosophical scholarship. The Newar sangha's special focus has been the performance of rituals drawing upon deities and powers of the Mahayana-Vajrayana Buddhist tradition. Like married Tibetan monks of the Nyingmapa order, the householder Newar *vajrācārya* priests serve the community's ritual needs, with some specializing in textual study, medicine, astrology, and meditation. Their ritual services are vast, including Buddhist versions of Hindu life-cycle rites (*samskāras*), fire rites (*homa*), daily temple rituals (*nitya pūjās*), mantra chanting protection rites, merit-producing donation rites, stupa rituals, image consecrations, "chariot festivals" (*ratha jātras*), tantric singing and dance,[11] and vajrayana initiations (*abhisekhas*). Many very ancient practices originating in later Indic Buddhism continue to exist today. To cite one example: in Kathmandu's Itum Bāhā, one can still see the ritual of marking time by a monk rapping on a wooden gong, a monastic custom begun over 2,000 years ago in ancient India. To cite another, "the cult of the Mahayana book" also endures at yearly rites in Patan and Kathmandu when devotees make offerings to special *Prajñāpāramitā* texts.[12] And processions of Buddha images—like those mentioned by the Chinese pilgrims in the fifth–seventh centuries—are still found on the streets of the major cities during festivals.

The Newar Buddhist traditions that developed in these unusual ways have faced a host of challenges since its kings fell in 1769. Shah discrimination against Buddhists and changes in land tenure laws undermined the land tenancy system, and many of the endowments that had been created to underwrite the Newar Buddhist tradition since the Malla era (1428–1769) were lost. Today, of the 300 monasteries still extant, roughly 10 percent of these have all but disappeared, and more than 60 percent are in perilous structural condition. Only a few dozen Newar monasteries across the Valley maintain the daily morning and evening cycle of ritual practices that draw modest numbers of householders to participate daily. Despite the decline of the monasteries as buildings and institutions, much is still preserved in the elaborate monastic architecture, thousands of archived texts, and the wealth of cultural observances. A small circle of Newar tantric practitioners still exists as well.

Newar Buddhism also had a regional diaspora. One of the most important changes that Shah rule brought to the middle hill regions of the country was the expansion of trade, and this was largely in the hands of Newars who migrated to the new trade towns. The thousands who left the Valley to seek these new opportunities also took their culture, prominently Buddhism, with them. Thus, in towns such as (from east to west) Daran, Dhankuta, Chainpur, Bhojpur, Dolakha, Trisuli, Bandipur, Pokhara, Tansen, Ridi, and Baglung, Newar Buddhists built small monasteries as branch institutions of those in their home cities; in most places, these continue to be active today.

Despite the control of the Newar sangha by caste and age-seniority systems, and in the face of state discrimination, revitalization efforts have been mounted in recent years. Across the Kathmandu Valley, Buddhist householders have established *Jñānamalla Bhajans* to sing newly written and composed Buddhist songs performed in the style of Hindu *bhakti* groups, with the leader playing the harmonium, accompanied by a tabla, cymbals, and chorus. These groups have also undertaken service projects for their local tradition, including Buddhist festival participation.

In the last decades, Kathmandu teachers Badri Bajracharya (1946–2018) and Naresh Bajracharya have offered new teachings, initiations, and festival practices. Programs and new texts have been organized to train *Bare* in Sanskrit, literature, philosophy, and ritual practice. In Patan, the Lotus Research Center, led by Min Bahadur Shakya (1951–2012), has brought together Newar and Tibetan traditions, as well as publishing in modern Newari the great works of Sanskrit Mahayana Buddhism. The construction of a Newar Vajrayana *vihāra* in Lumbini (2012–2021) has been a source of community revitalization due to these leaders, as well as the support of patrons enriched by the vast expansion of the Kathmandu markets due to the Valley's more than tripling in population since 1980.

Modern Theravada Buddhism in the Himalayas

Since the 1920s, Newars disenchanted with their ritually rich, but explanation-poor Mahayana tradition have supported the establishment of Theravada Buddhist reform institutions in the Kathmandu Valley. Inspired by teachers from Sri Lanka, Burma,

Thailand, and India, Newars "entered the robes" and some founded institutions in the large cities that are dedicated to the revival of Buddhism based upon Theravada doctrine, popular preaching, new Buddhist schools, and lay meditation.

Beginning with the Anandakuti monastery at Svayambhū for monks, the Dharmakirti monastery for "nuns" in central Kathmandu, and several dozen smaller institutions, Newars have been ordained and have renounced the householder life to live as monastics. (Technically, the ancient order of nuns, the *bhikkhunī* sangha, died out in the Theravada countries; the term *anagarika* is used locally, although several young women have recently traveled to China to take the *bhikkhunī* ordination.)[13]

The Theravadin institutions have been instrumental to promoting the modernist "Protestant Buddhism" originating in colonial Sri Lanka: they have subtly critiqued Newar and Tibetan Mahayana beliefs and practices, while seeking to revive the faith by promoting textual study and translations of Pali texts into Newari. In the last twenty years, prominent monks have acquired foreign Theravada patrons who have funded new monasteries being built in the Valley in the Burmese or Thai styles. The Theravadins have also been very influential in spreading the practice of *vipassanā* meditation, including centers affiliated with Goenka (1924–2013), a lay teacher from India. Since the early 1980s, these have gained considerable popularity, but primarily among middle-class Newars.

Recent Trends in Himalayan Buddhism(s)

Most villages today across the Buddhist mid-hills and highlands are populated for most of the year only by new mothers, elders, and their grandchildren. Many young people now engage in a form of circular migration, staying away most of the year to pursue cash-income jobs in Kathmandu, India, the Gulf states, or in the West. This is changing the nature of rural life across the region, but has also opened new possibilities for Himalayan peoples. Indeed, a formidable new influence in the region's Buddhism are the remittances being sent home from Himalayan Buddhists working abroad; some of this wealth is being used to fund rituals and for the patronage of temples back in the home regions.

Since 1960, responding to strings attached to the considerable developmental aid from the Chinese government, Nepal has refused to admit the exiled Dalai Lama. In recent years, the state's northern border guards turn back refugees, and officials now restrict granting asylum to refugees making it to the capital. The entire region's status as haven for Tibetan refugees, and their further diaspora, may soon be nearly ended.

Today, Buddhists from the Tibetan and Tibeto-Burman groups originating across the Himalayan region now coexist among Newar and Theravada adherents amidst the Kathmandu Valley's remarkable religious pluralism. In addition to a rich variety of Hindu temples and traditions, ancient and new, there are Sikh temples and Muslim mosques built by their resident trader communities; one can also find centers for a half-dozen Japanese "new religions." Nepal's capital today is one of the most diverse religious locations in the world.

Himalayan Buddhists have absorbed a diversity of outside influences from their earliest history; in the future, its adherents will doubtless continue to shape their own lives with reference to both the venerable Buddhist traditions of their ancestors and the new ideas and possibilities that will make their way into their mountain vistas.

Notes

1. Huu Phuoc Le, *Buddhist Architecture* (London: Grafikol, 2010), 148.
2. M. A. Stein (trans.), *Kalhana's Rajatarangani* (New Delhi: Motilal Banarsidass, 1979 [1935]), 9, 74.
3. James Fisher, *Sherpas: Reflections on Change in Himalayan Nepal* (Berkeley: University of California Press, 1990), 61.
4. Halfdan Siiger, *The Lepchas: Culture and Religion of a Himalayan People* (Copenhagen: National Museum of Denmark, 1967), 28.
5. One such famous example is the seventeenth century tantric adept, teacher, author, and painter Yolmowa Tenzin Norbu, whose life has been thoroughly documented in Benjamin Bogin, *The Illuminated Life of the Great Yolmowa* (Chicago: Serindia, 2013).
6. David H. Holmberg, *Order in Paradox: Myth, Ritual, and Exchange among Nepal's Tamang* (Ithaca, NY: Cornell University Press, 1989), 697.
7. Graham E. Clarke, "The Ideas of Merit (*Bsod nams*), Virtue (*Dge ba*), Blessing *Byin rlabs*) and Material Prosperity (*Rten 'brel*) in Highland Nepal," *Journal of the Anthropological Society of Oxford* 21, no. 2 (1990): 165–84, and "The Great and Little Traditions in the Study of Yolmo, Nepal," *Wiener Studien zur Tibetologie Buddhismuskunde* 10 (1983): 21–37.
8. Matthew Kapstein, "Sherpas: Religion and the Printed Word," *Cultural Survival Quarterly* (September 1983): 12.
9. Heinz Bechert, "The Original Buddha and the Recent Buddha: A Preliminary Report on Buddhism in a Gurung Community," *Ancient Nepal* 119 (2003): 10.
10. Bechert, "The Original Buddha," 11.
11. See Miranda Shaw's Chapter 15 in this volume on dance practices of the Newar *vajrācāryas*.
12. See Natalie Gummer's Chapter 10 in this volume on texts and rituals.
13. See Hiroko Kawanami's Chapter 23 in this volume on Buddhist nuns.

Further Reading

Bogin, Benjamin. *The Illuminated Life of the Great Yolmowa*. Chicago: Serindia, 2013.

Clarke, Graham E. "The Ideas of Merit (*Bsod-nams*), Virtue (*Dge-ba*), Blessing (*Byin-rlabs*) and Material Prosperity (*Rten-'brel*) in Highland Nepal." *Journal of the Anthropological Society of Oxford* 21, no. 2 (1990): 165–84.

Fisher, James F. *Trans-Himalayan Traders: Economy, Society, and Culture in Northwest Nepal* [Dolpo]. Berkeley: University of California Press, 1986.

Gellner, David N. *Monk, Householder and Tantric Priest: Newar Buddhism and Its Hierarchy of Ritual.* Cambridge: Cambridge University Press, 1992.

Gorer, Geoffrey. *Himalayan Village: An Account of the Lepchas of Sikkim.* 2nd ed. New York: Basic Books, 1967.

Holmberg, David H. *Order in Paradox: Myth, Ritual, and Exchange among Nepal's Tamang.* Ithaca, NY: Cornell University Press, 1989.

Levine, Sarah, and David Gellner. *Rebuilding Buddhism: The Theravada Movement in Twentieth-Century Nepal.* Cambridge, MA: Harvard University Press, 2007.

Lewis, Todd T. *Popular Buddhist Texts from Nepal: Narratives and Rituals of Newar Buddhism.* Albany: State University of New York Press, 2000.

Lewis, Todd T. "Newars and Tibetans in the Kathmandu Valley: Ethnic Boundaries and Religious History." *Journal of Asian and African Studies* 38 (1989): 31–57.

Lewis, Todd T., and Naresh Bajracharya. "Vajrayāna Traditions in Nepal." In *Tantric Traditions in Transmission and Translation*, ed. David B. Gray and Ryan Richard Overbey. New York: Oxford University Press, 2016, 87–198.

Locke, John K. *Karunamaya.* Kathmandu: Sahiyogi, 1980.

Messerschmidt, Donald A. *The Gurungs of Nepal: Conflict and Change in a Village Society.* New Delhi: Oxford University Press, 1976.

Mumford, Stan Royal. *Himalayan Dialogue: Tibetan Lamas and Gurung Shamans in Nepal.* Madison: University of Wisconsin Press, 1989.

Ortner, Sherry B. *Sherpas through Their Rituals.* Cambridge: Cambridge University Press, 1978.

Ramble, Charles. *The Navel of the Demoness: Tibetan Buddhism and Civil Religion in Highland Nepal.* New York: Oxford University Press, 2007.

CHAPTER 6

BUDDHIST PRACTICE IN EUROPE AND NORTH AMERICA

SCOTT MITCHELL

Introduction

This chapter examines Buddhism as it is practiced in North America and Europe, locations where Buddhists have been balancing the twin necessities of preserving tradition and adapting to new cultural locales for over a century and a half. As an object of intellectual fascination, Buddhism first entered North American and European consciousness in the mid-nineteenth century. Not long after, Buddhist immigrants from Asia began arriving and establishing practice communities. Both of these trajectories are important for understanding the historical foundations of the tradition; this chapter will focus most of its attention on current developments as well as scholarly debates and research vistas.

Beginning with a brief overview of the history of Buddhism in North America and Europe, we will pay particular attention to the distinctive histories of Buddhist engagements in Hawaiʻi, mainland North America, and Europe. From there, the chapter will survey various lenses through which to examine the issue of practice, including adaptation in response to translation and legal or political systems, identity, race, and gender. To explore these topics in more specific depth, a series of case studies is offered, demonstrating the various ways practice is embodied and performed in North American and European contexts.

At the outset, two items should be stressed. As no single chapter could possibly cover everything, attempts have been made to limit the scope of study to specific geopolitical locales, privileging, for better or worse, the United States, Canada, and Western Europe. The reader should note, however, that more sustained research on burgeoning Buddhist communities in Mexico and the reinvigoration of Buddhism in Russia and former

Soviet bloc countries is sorely needed. Moreover, contemporary Buddhism is fluid, dynamic, and inherently connected to transnational and global cultural flows. These connections make it difficult, if not impossible, to fully understand local Buddhist forms without attending to international networks and the grand sweep of history. A temple located in a residential neighborhood in Lincoln, Nebraska, for example, can only exist because of the United States' involvement in Vietnam half a century earlier, involvement that was the end result of centuries of European colonial activities in the area that gave shape to the specific forms of Buddhism brought to Nebraska during the refugee crisis after the fall of Saigon. The following chapter, then, should be read as a mere pointer to much larger research projects.

Buddhist Histories

Buddhism's trajectory into North America and Europe is complex and diverse. Attention will be paid, here, to Hawai'i, the mainland United States and Canada, and Europe.

Hawai'ian Buddhism

Following James Cook's eighteenth-century visits to the islands, European and American corporations began the process of settling what was, then, the Kingdom of Hawai'i, largely for agriculture, and began trading with both the United States and Asian nations and colonies. Protestant missionaries followed, and, combined with the introduction of European diseases, the native Hawai'ian population was decimated and traditional culture displaced. At the same time, these trading ventures brought migrant workers to the islands from China, Korea, and Japan through the latter half of the nineteenth century, workers who began establishing cultural and religious communities. Whereas Chinese and Korean immigrants would have undoubtedly brought Buddhist practices with them, Japanese immigrants were the first to establish Buddhist communities in the Kingdom of Hawai'i before it was annexed as a US territory in 1898.[1]

The first Jōdo Shinshū priest, Soryu Kugai, arrived in Hawai'i in 1889, and he established a temple several years later. Over the next few decades, both Zen and Shingon communities were established. These nascent Buddhist temples served multiple roles as community centers for the Japanese immigrant community, including both explicitly Buddhist or religious centers, as well as language and cultural schools.[2] Due to the six-day-a-week working conditions on plantations, services began to be held on Sundays, mirroring Protestant Christian norms. By the 1920s, modernist priests such as Enyō Imamura began attempts to reach out to non-Japanese, some of whom, such as Ernest and Dorothy Hunt, further Anglicized the community by composing Buddhist hymns and services, many of which are still in use today and have been exported to the US mainland.[3]

Because many of these communities were established when Hawai'i was still nominally independent from the United States, their Japanese headquarters treated them as separate missions from later established mainland communities. Moreover, because of the unique culture of Hawai'i, with a highly diverse population and the largest per-capita population of both Buddhists and Asians of any US state, Buddhism's development on the islands is somewhat unique as compared to the mainland. At present, Buddhism in Hawai'i is simultaneously facing a decline and increased international attention. Japanese Buddhist communities continue to decline as the population ages, younger generations are less interested in Buddhism or religion generally, and evangelical Christian groups increase across the islands.[4] On the other hand, other Buddhist groups fare quite well and have made significant inroads to the culture at large, as is the case with the new Japanese Buddhist religious movement, Shinnyoen. Rising in popularity in the postwar years, Shinnyoen has a growing presence in Hawai'i. Since 1998 the group has hosted an annual lantern floating ceremony in Honolulu which attracts thousands of participants who set lighted candles into the harbor for peace.[5]

Mainland United States and Canada

Before Chinese and Japanese immigrants brought Buddhism to the mainland, there was a sizable interest in Buddhism, especially on the East Coast, in American intellectual circles going back to the early nineteenth century. Transcendentalists were nominally interested in Buddhism largely through translations and other scholarly studies of Buddhist texts produced in Europe. The Transcendentalists' newsletter, *The Dial*, is credited as publishing the first translation in America of the *Lotus Sutra* by Elizabeth Palmer Peabody.[6] By the early nineteenth century, casual interest in Buddhism was so prevalent in New England that Protestant writers of the day worried that all of Boston would convert to the Asian religion.[7]

This intellectual interest in Buddhism is exemplified by the World's Parliament of Religions held in conjunction with the Chicago World's Fair in 1893. Representatives of the world's religions, including notable Buddhists such as Anagarika Dhamapala, Shaku Soen, and a young D. T. Suzuki (who was there to assist Soen), presented their views on religion to an American audience. The Parliament's organizers convened the meeting in a spirit of "universal brotherhood"; however, they also clearly hoped to showcase the superiority of both Protestant Christianity and the United States.[8] Regardless of how the organizers framed the event, and regardless of the success or failure for any representative to accurately promote their tradition, sustained interest in Buddhism seems to have waned over the first few decades of the twentieth century as the nation moved through the Great Depression and two world wars.

At the same time, immigrants from China and Japan were arriving on the West Coast and were establishing Buddhist communities. Chinese laborers forced off, first,

California's gold mines and, second, the transcontinental railroad, and segregated into Chinatowns in Los Angeles and San Francisco, established the first Buddhist temples in the United States. However, the overt racism of the time led to the Chinese Exclusion Act of 1882 and pressure to convert to Christianity, which prohibited many communities from thriving into the twentieth century. Japanese Buddhists were more successful, having established Pure Land (1889), Shingon (1913), and Zen (1922) temples along the West Coast, including Canada. Umbrella organizations oversaw many of these communities in the United States and Canada, such as the Buddhist Mission of North America (now the Buddhist Churches of America), which by 1940 oversaw forty-four temples with an estimated membership of 45,000.[9]

Intellectual interest in Buddhism rekindled in the 1950s and 1960s. At the same time, anti-Asian immigration laws were repealed in the United States. Until the passage of the Hart-Cellar Act in 1965, persons from virtually the whole of Asia were barred from immigrating to the United States; this and restrictive citizenship and discriminatory laws hampered the development of Asian American and Buddhist communities. Following 1965, and combined with the Southeast Asian refugee crises, a large influx of Asian immigrants began arriving and establishing Buddhist communities across the United States and Canada from the late 1960s and into the 1980s. Simultaneously, a renewed popular interest in Buddhism was fueled, in part, by intellectual and academic study of Buddhism and Asia, countercultural interests in non-Western spiritual traditions, and Buddhist propagation programs on the part of Asian Buddhists in the postwar era. This new North American religious landscape led increasing numbers of non-Asian Americans to convert to the Buddhist tradition and, in some cases, to establish new communities in tandem with or separate from pre-established Buddhist communities. For example, Shunryu Suzuki, who was dispatched to the Sokoji Zen temple (established in the 1930s) in San Francisco's Japantown, attracted the attention of young white converts who wanted to learn meditation. Eventually, Suzuki and his followers established the San Francisco Zen Center and would go on to train a new generation of Zen Buddhists in the United States.

Thus, by the century's end, the North American Buddhist landscape was extraordinarily diverse, with virtually all major strands of the tradition having some representation, and Buddhist groups were present in all fifty states. Buddhism is now practiced by fifth-generation Asian Americans, recent converts and their children, and meditation practices are taken up by the curious who may not identify as Buddhist at all.

Canadian Buddhism follows a trajectory similar to the United States. As mentioned previously, many early twentieth-century communities were established at the same time on both sides of the border. Canada enacted similarly restrictive immigration laws as the United States. They interned Japanese Canadians or relocated them from the West Coast during World War II and similarly repealed race-based immigration quotas in the 1960s. However, unlike the United States, the Canadian government has been generally more active in promoting multiculturalism and policies to help immigrants and refugees settle in Canada. Moreover, different immigrant groups have migrated to Canada than to the United States, which has a direct impact on the number and types of

Buddhists in both countries. Thus, attention should be paid to significant demographic and historical differences between the two countries.[10]

Europe

Buddhism's first entrée to the continent came, in a general sense, as a result of colonial expansion across Asia.[11] As empires expanded and Jesuit missionaries were dispatched to spread Christianity, Europeans became increasingly aware of "the obscure cult of the 'False God' called 'Bod.' "[12] By the mid-1800s, this awareness began to flourish as the nascent scholarly field of modern Buddhists studies developed due to texts dispatched to Europe from the colonies and translated by European scholars. Scholarly work was supported by projects such as the Pali Text Society (made possible by the establishment of European colonies in India), which were dedicated to studying and translating Buddhist texts. This work overlapped with a nascent interest in the practice of Buddhism on the part of Europeans; however, until the latter half of the twentieth century, this interest was minimal at best.

Two exceptions should be made, however. First, as evidenced by a large body of recent scholarship, there was considerable interest in Theravada Buddhism across the British Isles in the late nineteenth century. This included the conversion and ordination of several British and Irish figures to Buddhism, perhaps most notably U Dhammaloka (neé Laurence Carroll), who ordained as a Theravada monk in Burma sometime in the late 1890s. His travels through the United States and Southeast Asia are a notable example of the transnational nature of Buddhism's spread in the modern period, as well as the fact that Buddhism was more than merely an elite intellectual curiosity.[13] Second, there has been a Buddhist presence in eastern Europe for centuries owing to the spread of Mongolian culture as far west as the Kalymik region of Russia. Beyond Batchelor's notes on the existence of Tibetan-derived forms of Buddhism across Russia, little additional scholarship has taken up this potentially rich historical field.[14]

Unlike the United States, which had a sizable influx of Buddhist immigrants from the 1800s and again post-1965, there has been no comparable migration of Buddhists to Europe. Nevertheless, since the immediate postwar years, Europeans began searching for alternative religions and spiritualities at the same time that Asian Buddhist missionary activities began in earnest, especially in western Europe. By the 1960s and 1970s, this interest began to manifest in the so-called "Zen boom" (which swept North America at roughly the same time); and the popularization of Zen Buddhism was quickly followed by the popularization of Tibetan Buddhism as lamas emigrated to the West following the Chinese invasion of Tibet. All of this activity led to the remarkable increase and diversification of European Buddhism; the number of Buddhist centers in Britain, for example, increased from seventy-four to four hundred between 1980 and 2000.[15]

Since the beginning of the twenty-first century, mindfulness meditation's popularity has spread on both sides of the Atlantic. Recent and forthcoming scholarship, largely from a sociological perspective, promises to increase our understanding of the dynamics of spiritual practice and secularization in Europe. Moreover, recent scholarship on European Buddhism has begun to unpack intergenerational dynamics as younger generations of European Buddhists come of age:[16] the continued popularization and commodification of Zen and Buddhism more generally;[17] and the development and spread of Buddhist communities via studies of architecture and place.[18] By all indications, the study of contemporary Buddhism in Europe is growing in volume and sophistication.

ADAPTATION

Arguably, Buddhist practice began the process of adaptation to Western cultural norms before it left Asia. For example, Braun's exhaustive study of Mahasi Sayadaw demonstrates how the Burmese monk adapted meditation practices to suit, first, a rising middle class of Burmese Buddhists.[19] This practice was then disseminated across Southeast Asia, where white Westerners were exposed to the practice during the 1960s and 1970s. Once trained, these teachers (many of whom ordained as monastics) returned to the United States or Europe to further spread this now adapted practice in new cultural contexts. Even a practice such as the Hunts' Anglicized hymns mentioned earlier have Japanese antecedents; Japanese Buddhists had begun composing Buddhist songs set to Western music not long after the Meiji Restoration in 1868. Once Buddhist practice took root in Europe and North America, further adaptation was accelerated and shaped by several factors, two of which will be considered in the following: language and sociopolitical structures.

Language

Buddhists need to translate both specific words and whole concepts into a new vernacular as the tradition moves across borders. These translations have an obvious impact on how the tradition is received in its new context. For example, translations of *duhkha* as "suffering" or *anatman* as "self-annihilation" were used as evidence of Buddhism's pessimism by nineteenth-century European thinkers.

Such translations are more than merely linguistic or philosophical; there is a *relationship* between translation and practice. For example, the largest Jōdo Shinshū Buddhist organization in North America is the Buddhist *Churches* of America (BCA). At BCA-affiliated temples, one can attend a weekly religious service officiated by a *minister*. The decision by the community, more than a century ago, to begin calling temples "churches" and priests "ministers" was neither arbitrary nor accidental. Sustained discussions were held to determine the appropriate English titles for ordained clergy. The decision to call a building a "church" has an effect on practice; a church is a specific kind of religious community, a place where one attends services and enters into communion with others. This is a departure from Japanese Buddhist norms where, generally speaking, rituals and services are conducted at a temple by priests regardless of whether there are lay members of the community in attendance, and priests more often visit the homes of temple members to perform services at the family home altar. Thus, there is a different relationship between a specific type of religious building or community reflected in the nomenclature.

A further example can be seen in the meeting of Buddhist philosophies of mind and Western psychology, which has led to the emergence of a specific "Buddhist psychology." It is clear that many forms of Buddhist practice are designed to allow one to critically investigate how one's mind functions; it is also clear that different Buddhist philosophical schools spent much time mapping the mind, as it were. These practices and systems, however, are not "psychology" in the Western sense of the word, and certainly were not intended to be therapeutic but, rather, had the soteriological aim of releasing one from samsara. Nevertheless, the translation of such practices and systems of thought into Western vernacular has contributed to the possibility of Buddhist practices being put into service of therapeutic ends (for example, mindfulness meditation). Or, as Payne argues, this meeting of Buddhism and Western psychology has led to three overlapping discourses, that "Buddhism is a precursor to psychotherapy, that Buddhism can be exploited for psychotherapeutic resources, and that Buddhism can be interpreted as a form of psychotherapy."[20] Thus there is a relationship between the casual acceptance of the fact of Buddhist psychology and the notion that Buddhist practices are in and of themselves therapeutic.

Sociopolitical Structures

It would be naive to believe that translation has a causative relationship to practice; it would also be naive to believe that translation decisions happen in a vacuum. Indeed, the decision to name a specific building a "church" instead of "temple" was made within a specific socio-historical context, namely, the early half of the twentieth century in the United States, a time of extreme anti-Japanese and anti-Buddhist sentiment.[21] On the one hand, this cultural atmosphere created the conditions whereby Japanese American Buddhists felt a strong urge to "blend in," to adapt their practices and communities to American norms. On the other hand, there were specific legal structures in place that required a certain nomenclature: to be recognized as a religious community in the eyes of the state, one needed to organize as a church. Thus, to enjoy the benefits, especially in the United States, of religious freedom, there is a certain pragmatism to translation choices.

Even in the absence of anti-Japanese or anti-Buddhist sentiment, however, conforming Buddhist communities to North American religious norms further affects practice at the institutional level. To be a recognized religious nonprofit, such a community needs to be organized in a specific way; namely, it needs a board of directors, bylaws, and so forth. This structure changes the relationship of members to their community and, potentially, between lay and monastic members of the community. A board of directors, for example, is ordinarily composed of lay members of the community who have the authority to hire and fire religious professionals—monks, priests, ministers, etc. Both Quli and Numrich have noted how this legal structure, which is a marked departure from the symbiotic relationship of monastic and lay sangha in pre-modern Theravada, has led to disputes within communities.[22]

Such political structures can also affect issues of doctrine. Baumann notes how pan-Buddhist organizations are encouraged in parts of Western Europe.[23] Such organizations make navigating political systems easier for Buddhist communities; however, they also require that all members adhere to similar doctrines. Whereas most Buddhist communities may be able to agree on some basic points (e.g., the Four Noble Truths), not all Buddhist traditions agree on the finer points (e.g., the efficacy of the *Lotus Sutra* above all other practices). Thus, to join a pan-Buddhist organization is to deny or alter one's doctrinal beliefs; to not join means willingly disenfranchising oneself from the benefits of government recognition.

Thus, adaptations to Buddhist practice must be viewed within their larger socio-historical contexts. Whereas Buddhists may adapt their practices to suit the needs of new members, to make Buddhism relevant to new audiences, often these changes are nuanced and are directed by larger legal, political, or social contexts that can be both extremely influential and subtle in their effect on Buddhist practice.

Identity

Adaptation and change intersect with the embodied practice of Buddhism which, in turn, intersects with larger cultural discourses around embodied identities. In North American and European contexts, these identities are often expressed through discourses of ethnicity and race, gender, and sexual identity. To say that these identities are discourses is to gesture toward the social contexts that shape and define embodied identities. Leaving aside essentialist questions of the nature of the self (from a Buddhist perspective or otherwise), social and legal structures that implicitly define and explicitly legislate embodied persons exist. Whether through social customs or discrimination that disenfranchise non-white persons, legal barriers to same-sex marriage, or the subtle everyday reinscription of normative gender roles and overt forms of sexual harassment, persons' lived realities are expressed and experienced through embodied identities that are shaped by forces beyond their control. Buddhists in North America and Europe, in addition to being Buddhists, are also persons of color, women, and sexual minorities. And these experiences invariably shape how Buddhism is practiced.[24]

In the case of racial or ethnic identity, the experience of Japanese American Buddhists serves as a useful starting point. When the first Japanese Buddhists emigrated to the United States, the only persons eligible for citizenship were white persons and freed African American slaves. When Japanese immigrants sued the government for citizenship, cases were generally dismissed on the grounds that Japanese belonged to the "Mongolian race," were not white, and therefore were ineligible for citizenship and the rights it conferred. This process of legislating racial categories is how racial identities are constructed and maintained. Once classified as a racial "other," Japanese immigrants, and eventually their children, were further denied equal opportunity in housing, unions, and workplaces; and politicians and labor leaders routinely laid the blame for economic distress on Japanese immigrants. These racist discourses led to the widespread anti-Japanese sentiment in the decades before World War II.[25]

Prior to the Empire of Japan's attack on Pearl Harbor in 1941, the US Federal Bureau of Investigation was already tracking Japanese leaders in the Buddhist community on the spurious assumption that those who had not converted to Christianity were more likely to be loyal to Japan; such persons, and whole communities, were routinely derided as "emperor worshipers."[26] Following the attack on Pearl Harbor and the United States' declaration of war on Japan, the US government then targeted Buddhists first for relocation and incarceration in American internment camps. Rather than capitulating to the pressure to convert, Japanese American Buddhism persisted in the camps and was re-established in its pre-war homes following incarceration. Thus we see the intersection of racial and religious identities in the experience and practice of Buddhism.

Buddhism and gender have garnered a significant amount of research since the 1990s. Initially, much attention was paid to the supposed "democratization" of Buddhist practice—that is, an increase in the number of laypersons engaged in meditation practice which has, historically, been the purview of a monastic elite—and the positive effects this has had on gender equality.[27] However, two problems are left unanswered by this argument. First, a casual acceptance that both lay women and lay men are meditating does not address the question of how gender informs the types of practices in which Buddhists engage. Suh, for example, has shown that such gender parity is hardly universal across the North American Buddhist landscape, and that gender plays a significant role, discursively, in how both women and men approach Buddhist practice, community, and notions of authority.[28] Second, even if both women and men have access to meditation, this does not mean that both women and men have access to leadership roles (power) within Buddhist communities. Cadge notes that Buddhists often fall back on normative gender roles outside of the meditation hall, with men disproportionately represented in leadership positions and women disproportionately represented in supportive roles.[29]

In part as a response to these concerns, some Buddhist communities have created spaces specifically for traditionally marginalized groups to practice from their embodied experiences. Gleig has perhaps done the most work on these communities, specifically the Oakland, California, East Bay Meditation Center (EBMC).[30] The Center has both explicit programs and sitting groups for persons of color, for LGBTQI identified persons, and modifies its practices to be inclusive to differently abled persons. Its leadership structure encourages collaboration and equality, and the center is run on a fully donation basis to ensure that even economically marginalized persons have access to Buddhist practice. In this way, the EBMC's model not only reflects an awareness of the embodied nature of practice, but also serves as an example of how Buddhists are adapting the tradition in new cultural contexts.

Two (or More) Buddhisms

A note should be added here in regard to the so-called two Buddhisms typology that preoccupied the study of North American Buddhism for several decades at the turn of the twenty-first century. In short, beginning with Layman's and Prebish's foundational texts in the 1970s, scholars have sought to understand the diversity of Buddhist traditions in the West that, especially at that time, often tracked along racial lines.[31] The dichotomy was made explicitly about race following the publication of a 1992 editorial in *Tricycle* magazine wherein Helen Tworkov wrote that Asian Americans had not participated in the development of an authentically "American Buddhism." Subsequent scholarly and popular essays by Prebish, Nattier, Numrich, Hickey, and others sought to clarify, complicate, support, or reject the dichotomy.[32]

Hickey's work on the subject is perhaps the most straightforward in explicitly connecting the racial implications of the dichotomy and the scholar's role in perpetuating those same divisions. Academic "taxonomies that include an 'ethnic Buddhism' category apply the term 'ethnic' *only* to people who are not white. To presume that whiteness is the norm against which 'ethnic' is measured is another example of unconscious white privilege. . . . More important, European American converts are *also* 'ethnic Buddhists.'"[33] Quli links these typologies to Buddhist studies' foundation in a "salvage studies" academic milieu where the only acceptable subjects for study were in Asia and in the ancient past.[34] This attitude renders all of North American Buddhism an inappropriate site for normative Buddhist studies; and it is particularly deleterious to Asian American communities who are rendered unsuitable objects of study "because not only do they reside in 'unnatural' places [the West], they have appropriated some Western ideas, rendering their Buddhisms (and themselves) inauthentic 'distortions.'"[35] Such strict binaries between "Asian/ethnic" and "white/convert" Buddhists are undermined by ethnographic and demographic studies; Spencer's work on the BCA—dismissed as an "ethnic fortress" of Japanese American Buddhism by some—demonstrates the internal diversity of the community, while arguing for a more nuanced approach to our scholarly typologies.[36]

Indeed, Hickey argues for developmental models of North American Buddhism that allow for change over time. In this way, her work anticipates that of Han's study of young adult Asian American Buddhists. Han argues "that considering the experiences and perspectives of young adult Asian American Buddhists (YAAABs) as a pan-ethnic, pan-Buddhist group further reveals the limitations of the 'two Buddhisms' typology. . . [and that] the diverse practices and nuanced beliefs of [YAAABs] challenge reductionist representations of Asian American Buddhists as not meditating, engaging exclusively in 'ritual' or 'devotional' practices" and belonging exclusively to their parents' Buddhist traditions.[37] Thus, with more sustained and nuanced ethnographic work on North

American and European Buddhism, scholarship will develop increasingly nuanced and sophisticated ways to describe diverse and necessarily complex religious traditions.

Case Studies

To further explore how Buddhists practice in North America and Europe, in the following we will examine several specific case studies.

Zen Ritual and Practice

There has long been a presumption that one of Zen Buddhism's allures for young white converts in the mid- to late twentieth century was its iconoclasm and lack of rituals. In essence, so the theory goes, young people disaffected by normative Christianity embraced Zen Buddhism as it was presented to them by Alan Watts or D. T. Suzuki who (over)emphasized the value of pure experience. In rejecting rituals, these converts embraced the practice of Zen meditation in the hopes of having a direct experience of awakening, or *satori*. Thus, when one surveys the North American Zen Centers that proliferated from the 1980s on, one finds a preponderance of meditation and a lack of ritual practice.

This caricature, however, is just that, a caricature, and belies the actual preponderance of ritual in North American Zen Buddhism. The full range of both large and small rites one would normally experience in a Zen community is alive and well within the tradition—from prostrations and offerings at altars, to bodily gestures such as the *shashu*,[38] to the highly ritualized question-and-answer session with a teacher (*dokusan*) and receiving dharma transition to become an authorized teacher. (And, it might go without saying, the practice of meditation is a ritual in itself.)

Further, ethnographic fieldwork reveals not only a plethora of ritual behavior[39] but a desire for ritual, especially around life transitions. Wilson's work on the *mizuko kuyo* ceremony is a prime example.[40] In Japan, the *mizuko kuyo* ceremony is a ritual generally conducted by priests on behalf of women who have lost a child through abortion, miscarriage, or stillbirth. Like other Japanese Buddhist rituals around death, the ceremony bestows a Buddhist name on the deceased child or fetus and is intended to help it navigate the afterlife. The ceremony itself was not widely popular in pre-war Japan when Zen was first established in the United States; hence, it was not well known in the United States when convert communities were first being established. However, in the past few decades, an increased awareness of the full range of Japanese Zen rituals, combined with a need among the community for rituals to mark life transitions, has prompted the importation and development of new ritual forms.

In convert Zen communities, the ritual has been adapted for its American context. There are overlaps, to be sure, such as the sewing of a bib or hat for statues of the

Bodhisattva Jizo (who watches over children) and a service conducted by a priest. However, in the North American context, priests also serve a pastoral role, and the ritual includes time for group discussion where the family can express grief and can be comforted by the community. In both Japanese and American contexts, the ritual serves an important function in the healing process for someone in a state of grief and psychological distress; the method by which this healing happens, however, is expressed in unique ways owing to differing cultural contexts and expectations.

Meditation (Secular and Otherwise)

The Zen emphasis on meditation speaks to the widespread popular assumption that meditation is the normative Buddhist practice; as Bieldfeldt notes, the question "do you practice" has become synonymous with "do you practice *meditation*?"[41] Of course, this assumption is problematic due to the wide diversity of practices across Buddhist traditions, times, and locations (including the West). Nevertheless, the prevalence of meditation at present is deserving of sustained research. Preston and Coleman have done some of the initial work in this regard, focusing ethnographic studies on predominantly white or convert communities in the United States.[42] Cambell's study of meditation-based communities in Toronto explicitly links the processes of embodied learning and Buddhist practice;[43] her work is supported by other sociological studies of Canadian Buddhism that puts white or convert communities into conversation with Asian-immigrant groups. Gleig's work, *American Dharma*, on US-based convert groups points to inter-generational dynamics and the complexity of these communities and their relationship to meditative practices both within Buddhist communities and their overlap to secular spaces.[44]

In this regard, the secularization of mindfulness and other meditation practices has, over the last decade, received a substantial amount of scholarly attention. Due in no small part to Jon Kabat-Zinn's popularization of a therapeutic, Buddhist-informed meditation program that has been deployed in a host of secular spaces from hospitals to prisons to public schools to the military, mindfulness meditation has emerged as both a significant cultural force and the signifier for Buddhism's general acceptance by the culture at large. Moreover, this phenomenon seems to be spreading on both sides of the Atlantic, with mindfulness programs and scholarship on mindfulness proliferating in both North America and Europe. A key point of debate is the question of how "Buddhist" this practice is, a point of contention for scholars, practitioners, advocates, and detractors alike. If rendered "Buddhist," mindfulness is both a proper subject of scholarly investigation as well as a potential violator of the principle of separation of church and state. If not considered "Buddhist," mindfulness is merely another fad in a long line of self-help and quasi-spiritual techniques that promise health and happiness, as well as a religious practice appropriated from its original context in service to the demands of the capitalist marketplace.[45]

Of course, these positions are not mutually exclusive. The popularization and/or secularization of mindfulness represents an explicit attempt on the part of Buddhists to make and remake practices in new cultural contexts. It is also a symptom of larger (neo-)orientalist processes that appropriate Asian religious practices into Western and consumerist spaces for decidedly non-religious purposes.[46]

Pagodas and Stupas (for Peace and Otherwise)

Nippozan-Myōhōji, a small sect of Nichiren Buddhism, has built dozens of peace pagodas throughout the world since the 1980s. In many ways, the denomination is normatively Nichiren-shu in orientation; practitioners recite the Japanese title of the *Lotus Sutra* (*namyō-hō-renge-kyō*) for the benefit of sentient beings' awakening. At the same time, the group's focus on peace work and advocacy for nonviolence make them distinct among Japan's various Nichren-derived groups. In addition to constructing more than eighty peace pagodas around the world, the group also participates in nonviolent protests, often marching, chanting, and beating small hand drums in opposition to nuclear arms, environmental destruction, and police brutality.[47]

The purpose of the pagodas is to promote nonviolence and peace, specifically anti-nuclear arms and warfare. Pagodas are erected in highly visible and public spaces but are presided over by members of the Nippozan-Myōhōji sect. The practice of constructing pagodas is thus a mixture of modern and traditional Buddhist concerns.[48] On the one hand, pagodas—like stupas—serve as visual and symbolic reminders of the Buddha and Buddhist ideas of enlightenment and compassion; on the other hand, being constructed specifically for the purpose of nuclear disarmament, they are decidedly modern in nature.

In addition to the half-dozen Nippozan-Myōhōji constructed peace pagodas, Europe is also home to more than 200 stupas constructed by Kagyu-derived Tibetan Buddhist organizations. The meaning and purpose of these stupas dovetail with their Nichiren counterparts—many were erected specifically with peace work and activism in mind. Many are also fully functioning Buddhist practice centers, large enough to host regular meditation and ritual services. In this way, the stupas represent a "combination of religious and secular performances," both a place for Buddhists to meditate or receive Tibetan Buddhist empowerments as well as a location for tourism, socializing, and commerce.[49] One stupa, built in the mid-1990s in the Spanish city of Benalmádena, was the direct result of a former mayor's desire to compete with the stupa of a neighboring city. The Benalmádena stupa, overseen by a local Karma Kagyu association, was designed by a German-based Polish architect who consulted traditional Tibetan builders to ensure that the Spanish stupa was built appropriately. The large structure is open to the public as a tourist attraction, but also hosts regular Buddhist lectures and meditation courses. Thus, it represents a blending of competing religious/secular/economic/activist needs that point to the messy ways in which Buddhist practice manifests in Western cultural contexts.

Social Engagement

Perhaps one of the most visible adaptations Buddhists have made in North American and European contexts has been the articulation of a specifically Buddhist social ethic. The rise of "engaged Buddhism" has certainly been met with both warmth and strong critique. Some have called into question the notion that there is a necessarily happy congruence between Buddhist ethics and socially progressive ethics,[50] while others have pointed to Buddhism's mixed historical (and current) record on matters of social justice, human rights, and pacifism.[51] As valid as these criticisms may be, they will be left aside, as we are here concerned with the fact of a particular practice, not its validity.

To say that engaged Buddhism is a practice is to move our attention away from ethical or philosophical debates about Buddhism and instead to Buddhist/activist discourses that explicitly claim engagement as a form of practice. Some engaged Buddhists claim that "one's engagement with the problems of society is part and parcel of one's spiritual practice, an application and testing of that practice in demanding situations."[52] Such discourses have lead Queen to claim that engaged Buddhism represents a potential new "*yana*" or vehicle of Buddhism, one distinct from Mahayana, etc., by virtue of its focus on engaged action.[53] (Not all Buddhists would agree with this point of view, however, and instead might claim that the bodhisattva path, say, necessitates compassionate action and is therefore normatively Mahayana, not something separate from it.)

There are, of course, various forms of engaged Buddhist practice. Nippozan-Myōhōji's construction of peace pagodas mentioned previously is arguably a type of political or social engagement. Members of the community have also been more explicitly engaged in social protests.[54] Whereas engaged practices such as these are spurred by local events, the worldwide spread of peace pagodas speaks to the transnational nature of contemporary engaged Buddhist practice. The Taiwan-based Fo Guang Shan, for instance, has a global spread and an explicit socially engaged ethos in the form of "humanistic Buddhism," regularly framed as establishing a pure land on earth through charitable work, education, and social outreach. The work of Bernie Glassman, founder of the Zen Peacemaker Order, while being initially locally constrained to the United States, similarly has a global appeal. Some of his organization's early efforts at social outreach included socially conscious businesses in New York, as well as "bearing witness" meditation programs for homeless outreach. The Order also conducts regular pilgrimages to Holocaust sites to bear witness to the horrors of war and to be reminded of humanity's propensity for violence and intolerance.[55]

Further Research Vistas

By way of conclusion, two final matters are raised here as potential research vistas. First, this volume is concerned with the idea of Buddhist practice, and the editors and contributors have made it clear that scholarship is itself a form of practice. Scholarship *about* Buddhism is not often thought of as "Buddhist practice" per se owing to the commitment scholars have, not to the Buddhist sangha or the dharma, but to their (usually) secular or public research institutions and communities. However, this easy bifurcation between Buddhist scholarship and Buddhist practice is disrupted first by the overlap of Buddhist communities and Buddhist scholarship and, second, the growing preponderance of individuals who are *both* scholars of Buddhism and Buddhist practitioners.

Of the former, scholarly output does not exist in a vacuum. It is often both funded by Buddhist communities or philanthropic organizations and consumed by practicing Buddhists. Buddhist scholars (even and especially those who do not identify as Buddhists) contribute to Buddhist publications in North America such as *Tricycle* or *Lion's Roar* magazines; and translations of sutras or historical accounts of Buddhism produced by scholars are read by Buddhist practitioners. Thus, there is an overlap between Buddhist scholarship-as-practice and Buddhist practice itself. Our scholarly work has implications for the tradition, implications that cannot be easily separated by relying on a naive appeal to "objective" scholarship.

Perhaps more importantly, it is also naive to assume that scholars are never practitioners or that practitioners cannot also be scholars. Prebish first noted the existence of what he called "scholar-practitioners" some twenty years ago, and argued that they often felt as though they needed to keep their Buddhist identities hidden within academic circles that were invested in maintaining the scholar/practitioner divide.[56] Anecdotally, the number of self-identified scholar-practitioners is undoubtedly higher than it was when Prebish first advanced this thesis, evidenced by, if nothing else, the success of such organizations as the Buddhist Critical-Constructive Reflection Unit at the American Academy of Religion and the publication of work such as *Buddhist Theology*.[57] Regrettably, the number of self-professed scholar-practitioners, Buddhist theologians, or whatever we may call the category is just that—anecdotal. Despite Prebish calling our attention to the phenomenon, no one else seems to have taken up the charge to do any sustained research on this population. Such research would both answer the question of how widespread the phenomenon is and, perhaps more importantly, reveal how this relationship changes the nature of Buddhist practice in North America and Europe.

The second potential research vista similarly challenges our conceptual categories, and relates to the nature of "the West" as much as the limitation of this chapter. Of necessity, this chapter has focused on the Anglo-American cultural sphere and related developments in, primarily, western Europe. Much therefore has been left out, most notably: Buddhism in Russia and former Soviet states; Buddhism in Mexico, Central America, and South America; Buddhism in other parts of the Anglicized world, including Australia and New Zealand; and Buddhism across the "Global South," including South Africa. While some of these areas have received substantial scholarly attention, much remains uncovered.

The existence of Buddhism in these other non-Asian, Anglicized, Westernized, and/or postcolonial locations both complicates our definition of "Western Buddhism" and calls our attention to the necessity of studies that are focused on the local. Whereas

Buddhism's history in, say, Australia mirrors in some ways its history in North America, there are significant differences as well. These locations are bound up in globalized cultural flows and they necessarily have an effect on one another. This was the case in 2009 when Theravada monk Ajahn Brahm ordained four nuns in Australia. The event prompted Brahm's Thai Theravada lineage to expel him, speaking engagements in Vietnam were canceled, and the news spread across the global Buddhist world. Regardless of the politics of ordination internal to, in this case, the Thai Theravada tradition, such events serve to highlight the tension between the local and the global, a tension which compels scholars to rethink our conceptual frameworks and the heuristics we employ in our study of contemporary Buddhisms, Buddhists, practices, and communities.

Notes

1. Hawai'i became a US state in 1959.
2. Noriko Asato, "The Japanese Language School Controversy in Hawaii," in *Issei Buddhism in the Americas*, ed. Duncan Ryūken Williams and Tomoe Moriya (Urbana: University of Illinois Press, 2010), 45–64.
3. George J. Tanabe, "Glorious Gathas: Americanization and Japanization in Honganji Hymns," in *Engaged Pure Land Buddhism: Challenges Facing Jōdo Shinshū in the Contemporary World: Studies in Honor of Professor Alfred Bloom*, ed. Kenneth Tanaka and Eisho Nasu (Berkeley, CA: Wisdom Ocean, 1998), 221–40; Keiko Wells, "The Role of Buddhist Song Culture in International Acculturation," in *Issei Buddhism in the Americas*, ed. Duncan Ryūken Williams and Tomoe Moriya (Urbana: University of Illinois Press, 2010), 164–81.
4. For more on the declaim of Buddhism in Hawai'i, see the film *Aloha Buddha*, http://alohabuddhafilm.com.
5. Victoria Rose Montrose, "Floating Prayer: Localization, Globalization, and Tradition in the Shinnyo-en Hawaii Lantern Floating," *Journal of Religion in Japan* 3 (2014): 177–97.
6. Scott A. Mitchell, *Buddhism in America: Global Religion, Local Contexts* (London: Bloomsbury Academic, 2016), 37.
7. Thomas A. Tweed, *The American Encounter with Buddhism, 1844–1912: Victorian Culture and the Limits of Dissent* (Bloomington: Indiana University Press, 1992), 26–8.
8. James Edward Ketelaar, "Strategic Occidentalism: Meiji Buddhists at the World's Parliament of Religions," *Buddhist-Christian Studies* 11 (1991): 37–56; Judith Snodgrass, *Presenting Japanese Buddhism to the West: Orientalism, Occidentalism, and the Columbian Exposition* (Chapel Hill: University of North Carolina Press, 2003).
9. Tetsuden Kashima, *Buddhism in America: The Social Organization of an Ethnic Religious Organization*. (Westport, CT: Greenwood Press, 1977), 142.
10. Jeff Wilson, "What Is Canadian about Canadian Buddhism?" *Religion Compass* 5 (2011): 536–48.
11. Baumann has arguably done some of the most extensive work, in English, on Buddhism in Western Europe. See, for example, Martin Baumann, "Creating a European Path to Nirvāna: Historical and Contemporary Developments of Buddhism in Europe," *Journal of Contemporary Religion* 10 (1995): 55–70; "The Dharma Has Come West: A Survey of

Recent Studies and Sources," *Journal of Buddhist Ethics* 4 (1997): 194-211; "Buddhism in Europe: An Annotated Bibliography," *Journal of Global Buddhism* (2001), http://www.globalbuddhism.org/bib-bud.html (accessed May 3, 2018).

12. Baumann, "Creating a European Path to Nirvana," 55.
13. *The Journal of Contemporary Buddhism* 11, no. 2 (2010), for example, was a special issue dedicated solely to scholarship on U Dhammaloka.
14. Stephen Batchelor, *The Awakening of the West: The Encounter of Buddhism and Western Culture.* (Berkeley, CA: Parallax Press, 1994).
15. Martin Baumann, "Protective Amulets and Awareness Techniques, or How to Make Sense of Buddhism in the West," in *Westward Dharma: Buddhism beyond Asia*, ed. Charles S. Prebish and Martin Baumann (Berkeley: University of California Press, 2002), 51–65.
16. Thanissaro Phra Nicholas, "Almost a Proper Buddhist: The Post-Secular Complexity of Heritage Buddhist Teen Identity in Britain," *Journal of Global Buddhism* 15 (2014): 1–14; Helen Waterhouse, "Sōka Gakkai Families in the UK: Observations from a Fieldwork Study," *Journal of Global Buddhism* 16 (2015): 180–94.
17. Jørn Borup, "Branding Buddha: Mediatized and Commodified Buddhism as Cultural Narrative," *Journal of Global Buddhism* 17 (2016): 41–55.
18. Caroline Starkey and Emma Tomalin, "Building Buddhism in England: The Flourishing of a Minority Faith Heritage," *Contemporary Buddhism* 17 (2016): 326–56.
19. Erik Braun, *The Birth of Insight: Meditation, Modern Buddhism, and the Burmese Monk Ledi Sayadaw* (Chicago: University of Chicago Press, 2013).
20. Richard K. Payne, "Buddhism and the Powers of the Mind," in *Buddhism in the Modern World*, ed. David L. McMahan (New York: Routledge, 2012), 234; see also Ann Gleig, "Wedding the Personal and Impersonal in West Coast Vipassana: A Dialogical Encounter between Buddhism and Psychotherapy," *Journal of Global Buddhism* 13 (2012): 129–46.
21. Duncan Ryūken Williams, "Camp Dharma: Japanese-American Buddhist Identity and the Internment Experience of World War II," in *Westward Dharma: Buddhism beyond Asia*, ed. Charles S. Prebish and Martin Baumann (Berkeley: University of California Press, 2002), 191–200.
22. Paul David Numrich, *Old Wisdom in the New World: Americanization in Two Immigrant Theravada Buddhist Temples* (Knoxville: University of Tennessee Press, 1996); Natalie Quli, *Laicization in Four Sri Lankan Buddhist Temples in Northern California*, dissertation, Graduate Theological Union, 2010.
23. Martin Baumann, "The Transplantation of Buddhism to Germany: Processive Modes and Strategies of Adaptation," *Method and Theory in the Study of Religion* 6 (1994): 43–44.
24. See, for example, Joseph Cheah, *Race and Religion in American Buddhism: White Supremacy and Immigrant Adaptation* (New York: Oxford University Press, 2011).
25. Kashima, *Buddhism in America*, 35–39.
26. Kashima, *Buddhism in America*, 35–39.
27. Richard Hughes Seager, *Buddhism in America* (New York: Columbia University Press, 1999), 185–200; Kenneth K. Tanaka, "Epilogue: The Colors and Contours of American Buddhism," in *The Faces of Buddhism in America*, ed. Charles S. Prebish and Kenneth Tanaka (Berkeley: University of California Press, 1998), 289–90.
28. Sharon A. Suh, *Being Buddhist in a Christian World: Gender and Community in a Korean American Temple* (Seattle: University of Washington Press, 2004).
29. Wendy Cadge, "Gendered Religious Organizations," *Gender and Society* 18 (2004): 777–93.

30. Ann Gleig, "Queering Buddhism or Buddhist De-Queering?" *Theology & Sexuality* 18 (2012): 198–214.
31. Emma McCloy Layman, *Buddhism in America* (Chicago: Nelson-Hall, 1976); Charles S. Prebish, *American Buddhism* (North Scituate, MA: Duxbury Press, 1979).
32. Charles S. Prebish, "Two Buddhisms Reconsidered," *Buddhist Studies Review* 10 (1993): 187–206; Jan Nattier, "Visible and Invisible: On the Politics of Representation in America," *Tricycle: The Buddhist Review* (1995): 42–49; Paul David Numrich, "Two Buddhisms Further Considered," *Contemporary Buddhism* 4 (2003): 55–78; Wakoh Shannon Hickey, "Two Buddhisms, Three Buddhisms, and Racism," *Journal of Global Buddhism* 11 (2010): 1–25.
33. Hickey, "Two Buddhisms, Three Buddhisms, and Racism," 14.
34. Natalie E. Quli, "Western Self, Asian Other: Modernity, Authenticity, and Nostalgia for 'Tradition' in Buddhist Studies," *Journal of Buddhist Ethics* 16 (2009): 1–38.
35. Quli, "Western Self," 24.
36. Anne C. Spencer, "Diversification in the Buddhist Churches of America: Demographic Trends and Their Implications for the Future Study of US Buddhist Groups," *Journal of Global Buddhism* 15 (2014): 35–61.
37. Chenxing Han, "Diverse Practices and Flexible Beliefs among Young Adult Asian American Buddhists," *Journal of Global Buddhism* 18 (2017): 3.
38. *Shashu* is a hand posture where the fisted left hand is wrapped by the right and held at the solar plexus, a posture often held by Zen Buddhists within the community and/or during formal walking meditation.
39. David L. Preston, *The Social Organization of Zen Practice: Constructing Transcultural Reality* (Cambridge: Cambridge University Press, 1988).
40. Jeff Wilson, *Mourning the Unborn Dead: A Buddhist Ritual Comes to America* (New York: Oxford University Press, 2009).
41. Carl Bielefeldt, "Practice," in *Critical Terms for the Study of Buddhism*, ed. Donald S. Lopez (Chicago: University of Chicago Press, 2005), 230.
42. Preston, *The Social Organization of Zen Practice*; James William Coleman, *The New Buddhism: The Western Transformation of an Ancient Tradition* (New York: Oxford University Press, 2001).
43. Patricia Q. Campbell, *Knowing Body, Moving Mind: Ritualizing and Learning at Two Buddhist Centers* (Oxford and New York: Oxford University Press, 2011).
44. Ann Gleig, *American Dharma: Buddhism Beyond Modernity* (New Haven, CT: Yale University Press, 2019).
45. See Jeff Wilson, *Mindful America: The Mutual Transformation of Buddhist Meditation and American Culture* (New York: Oxford University Press, 2014).
46. Tessa Bartholomeusz, "Spiritual Wealth and Neo-Orientalism," *Journal of Ecumenical Studies* 35 (1998): 19–33; Jane Iwamura, *Virtual Orientalism: Asian Religions and American Popular Culture* (New York: Oxford University Press, 2010).
47. Mitchell, *Buddhism in America*, 223.
48. Marilyn Ivy, "Modernity," in *Critical Terms for the Study of Buddhism*, ed. Donald S. Lopez (Chicago: University of Chicago Press, 2005), 312.
49. Eva Seegers, "The Innovative Stūpa Project in Andalusia, Spain: A Discussion on Visual Representations of Tibetan Buddhist Art in Europe," *The Journal of the British Association for the Study of Religions* 17 (2015): 35.

50. Damien Keown, "Buddhist Ethics: A Critique," in *Buddhism in the Modern World*, ed. David L. McMahan (New York: Routledge, 2012), 215–31.
51. Brian Daizen Victoria, "Engaged Buddhism: A Skeleton in the Closet?" *Journal of Global Buddhism* 2 (2001): 72–91.
52. Sallie B. King, "Socially Engaged Buddhism," in *Buddhism in the Modern World*, ed. David L. McMahan (New York: Routledge, 2012), 207.
53. Christopher S. Queen, "Introduction: A New Buddhism," in *Engaged Buddhism in the West*, ed. Christopher S. Queen (Boston: Wisdom Publications, 2000), 1–31
54. Mitchell, *Buddhism in America*, 223.
55. See //web.archive.org/web/20190411122821/http://zenpeacemakers.org/programs/auschwitz-birkenau-bearing-witness-retreat/.
56. Charles S. Prebish, *Luminous Passage: The Practice and Study of Buddhism in America* (Berkeley: University of California Press, 1999).
57. Roger Jackson and John Makransky, eds., *Buddhist Theology: Critical Reflections by Contemporary Buddhist Scholars*. Routledge Critical Studies in Buddhism. (London and New York: Routledge, 2013).

Further Reading

Gleig, Ann. *American Dharma: Buddhism beyond Modernity*. New Haven, CT: Yale University Press, 2019.

Harding, John S, Victor Sogen Hori, and Alexander Soucy. *Flowers on the Rock: Global and Local Buddhisms in Canada*. Montréal, Québec: McGill-Queen's University Press, 2014.

McMahan, David L., ed. *Buddhism in the Modern World*. New York: Routledge, 2012.

Mitchell, Scott A. *Buddhism in America: Global Religion, Local Contexts*. London: Bloomsbury Academic, 2016.

Mitchell, Scott A, and Natalie E. F. Quli, eds. *Buddhism beyond Borders: New Perspectives on Buddhism in the United States*. Albany: State University of New York Press, 2015.

Prebish, Charles S., and Martin Baumann, eds. *Westward Dharma: Buddhism beyond Asia*. Berkeley: University of California Press, 2002.

Williams, Duncan Ryūken, and Tomoe Moriya, eds. *Issei Buddhism in the Americas*. Urbana: University of Illinois Press, 2010.

Wilson, Jeff. *Mindful America: The Mutual Transformation of Buddhist Meditation and American Culture*. New York: Oxford University Press, 2014.

CHAPTER 7

GLOBALIZED FORMS OF BUDDHIST PRACTICE

INKEN PROHL

INTRODUCTION

BUDDHIST institutions in many Asian countries promise their visitors the realization of desires for wealth, happiness, and prosperity through invocation of the power of the buddhas in rituals, amulets, and other forms of offerings. Framed within Buddhist narratives and aesthetics, a seemingly endless stream of books, blogs, articles, and apps, available in many countries around the globe, praise the benefits of practicing meditation for becoming a happier, healthier, and more relaxed person. Pictures of buddhas are being used in marketing campaigns for furniture, food, toys, and many other kinds of goods promising a bettering of one's life, and advertisements rely on the magic of the words "Zen," "mindful," or "nirvana" to promote sales on a global scale. In short, Buddhist semantics, aesthetics, and designs are an integral part of articulating promises of contentment, happiness, success, health, and luck as well as personal advancement in the twenty-first century.

Why are practices and narratives of Buddhism so popular when it comes to the optimization and healing of the modern self? What are the reasons Buddhist signifiers are connected so closely to the practice of consumption and the desire for wealth and success? At first glance, the manifold entanglements between Buddhism and capitalism seem to be at odds with the widespread association of Buddhism with anti-materialism. This association belongs to the orientalist discourse closely related to the "New Buddhism" that emerged out of a confluence of cultures from the West and Asia during the nineteenth and twentieth centuries.[1] As a long-standing orientalist trope, the religious tradition of Buddhism is held to contain both teachings and practices aimed at enlightenment, a target beyond the mundane. Why then are Buddhist narratives and practices so popular in our globalized present, which is deeply affected by the new spirit of capitalism and a resulting ethos of consumerism?[2] Central tenets within this new spirit of capitalism are the responsibility of every person to continually work to constitute and improve the self and one's emotional skills, and the imperative to create a happy life through consumerism.[3] Through the dynamics of hyper-mediatization, all aspects of life are dependent on and shaped by mass media. It is through these channels that the new spirit of capitalism spreads globally, the process being most advanced with the younger generations and in urban centers of highly industrialized societies in East and West alike. This chapter discusses the reciprocal interaction between Buddhist practice and this fundamental transformation of global modernity.[4]

The idea of no-self and the removal of wishes and desires as paths to end suffering are seen as central to Buddhism. Nevertheless, fragments of this very same Buddhism seem to resonate well with the personalized imperatives of the globalized present to manufacture happiness through consumption, as well as manufacturing the self through self-work. Here I intend to show that Buddhist-oriented ideas and practices resonate with the new spirit of capitalism. The chapter will illustrate this resonance by way of the examples of "prosperity Buddhism," the transformation of practices of introversion—commonly called meditation—as well as the spread of Buddhist semantics, practices, and materialities in the field of marketing, branding, and consumption.

The Practice of Bricolage: Mediatization of Religions in Global Societies

The markers of globalized forms of Buddhist practice are strongly influenced by mediatization processes, which means that religious institutions and other individual actors spread their messages via print, radio, television, or the internet. Yet this description covers only a small part of what mediatization means, as the underlying processes are far more deeply embedded in present-day culture. As scholars of religion point out, the way that religion is reproduced, represented, and understood in our contemporary world is fundamentally a function of the media age.[5] An emerging consensus suggests that, thanks to media technologies, religion is everywhere now.[6]

We can describe what we witnessed over the last century as a democratization and a pluralization of objects commonly held to be traditional religious semantics, images, and designs. Due to the ubiquity of media, such as newspapers, books, television, and the internet, dissemination is not limited to cognitive content. On the contrary, in hyper-mediatized society, images, films, music, and all kinds of materialities make practices, aesthetics, and designs commonly held to be religious accessible to everyone. Additionally, how images and designs are ascribed meaning is becoming more important. Because of this global discourse on the subject of religion, the teachings, keywords, architectures, and materialities of the so-called world religions are considered to be traditional religious semantics, images, and designs in the present. In the case of Buddhism, common discourse holds that sutras and commentaries, temples and stupas, monks and nuns, as well as the keywords "Zen," "nirvana," "karma," "reincarnation," and "mindfulness," all belong to Buddhism.[7] The concept of "Buddhism" itself as a separate translocal and transcultural entity was born in Europe.[8] With the aid of the previously mentioned dynamics of mediatization, this modern concept of Buddhism has spread globally and is continually being reified. As a reminder of the fact that this Buddhism is a social construction, I will try to avoid using the term as a singular subject or object. I will instead use such terms as "Buddhist field" or "Buddhist semantics, practices, and designs."

Modern media technologies enable individuals, social groups, and institutions to interpret, mix, and rearrange religious semantics and materialities in order to redistribute these creative arrangements through the media. This phenomenon, which is what is meant when we talk about "mediatized religion," has significant consequences in the field of Buddhism.[9] The easy accessibility of information for actors within the Buddhist field, as well as access to practices and materialities associated with the field, allows these actors to supplement or optimize ideas, practices, or goods toward believers or consumers and to respond to changes in demand. Mediatization has made the production of goods targeted at Buddhist actors easier and quicker. A good example of this trend are the teachings and practices of so-called prosperity Buddhism, which are discussed in the next section. Furthermore, the elements of this pluralistic emergence of what is supposed to be the traditional field of religion do not remain confined to it—people carry innovations across fields. In the case of Buddhist semantics, materialities, and aesthetics, these include psychology, psychotherapy, and self-help. In these fields we find countless examples of the incorporation of Buddhist semantics, images, and designs, with the practices of meditation and mindfulness being the most popular in contemporary societies. The manifold results of bricolage are presented in the second part of this chapter. Further examples are drawn from the realms of medicine, popular culture and entertainment, and marketing and branding.

Prosperity Buddhism

In many Asian Buddhist countries, scholars of religion have observed a growing popularity of Buddhist practices promising this-worldly benefits through the use of religious power.[10] The significant aspects of this change can be made visible by analyzing the New Religions of Japan.[11] Agonshū, one of these New Religions, teaches that problems like illness, relationship troubles, obstacles in education, and even poverty can be traced back to the influence of maleficent spirits of the dead. This is a concern that can be found in many premodern forms of Buddhism in Japan, as well as other Buddhist cultures in East and Southeast Asia. This topic of the evil dead is equally central in many other New Religions of Japan. Kiriyama Seiyū (1921–2016), the founder of Agonshū, claimed to have found the way to salvation for these sad or vengeful wandering spirits in the *Āgama-sūtras* (*Sutta-piṭaka* of the Pali canon). Agonshū offers their members a great number of rituals to harness the power of the *Āgama-sūtras* in order to lead the ancestors to salvation—and solve the life problems claimed to be caused by them. These rituals, the great events of Agonshū, as well as the writings of Kiriyama, are advertised using elaborate marketing campaigns. Listings of prices and registration forms for the rituals are omnipresent within the organization.

Several times each year, Agonshū stages a *goma* ("fire") ritual.[12] During the ritual, as observed during fieldwork between 1992 and 2005, thousands of wooden sticks inscribed with the wishes and concerns of followers of the New Religion are burned.[13] Approximately 2,000 people are in attendance at every event. They are greeted at the entrance of the central *dōjō* (meeting place) at the heart of Tokyo with the words "*okaeri nasai*" ("welcome home"). Deep resonant drumbeats announce Kiriyama's appearance, who enters the altar space adorned with the regalia of a priest of esoteric Buddhism. While he is kneeling, participants keep with the beat of the drums as they recite the *Heart Sutra* and passages from the *Āgama-sūtras*. Each participant places before them wooden sticks (*tōba*) inscribed with the name of the ancestor who is the object of the ritual. The space is filled with the sound of prayer beads, the deep tone of the drums, and the communal recitations. Meanwhile Kiriyama, assisted by almost twenty other priests, proceeds with the *goma* ritual. The first of many thousands of small wooden sticks with the participants' wishes are burned. Others are just held over the flame to be burned later. The beat of the drums speeds up, as do the perfectly choreographed movements of the priests in front of the altar. They offer the participants a dramatic show of nearly synchronous movement. The ceremony invokes the impression of being directed by an invisible hand. The ritual ends with a drumroll, and Kiriyama leaves. After the almost trancelike mood of the ritual, a calm and relaxed atmosphere fills the *dōjō*.

A short time later, Kiriyama reappears. Now he is dressed in a bright yellow kimono in the newly illuminated *dōjō*. He gives a short speech on the necessity of honoring the ancestors to better one's karma. During his speech, he insists on every person's ability to take charge of their destiny and to change it for the better through their actions. Whoever wants to be happy, Kiriyama proclaims, should work hard and should have clear moral stances. A firm belief in oneself and one's own success are also of central importance. Following Kiriyama's speech, the participants stay and talk about their experiences. They are unanimous in voicing the opinion that the *goma* ritual has given them new energy and that they have won a more optimistic outlook on facing the challenges in their lives. In both his books and speeches, Kiriyama invokes semantics associated with traditional Buddhist thought and combines them with New Age ideas, scientific results from evolutionary biology, as well as narratives about well-known places and people to promote his teachings about karma and how to improve it. As with other teachings and practices of New Religions in Japan, Buddhist notions and rituals are innovatively mixed with discourses from other fields in order to increase their attractiveness and the plausibility of Agonshū's teachings.

The strong emphasis on individual responsibility for salvation within is a reflection of the strong synergy of religion and market moralities of the present day.[14] The greeting "welcome home," the high degree of staged performance, including music, light, and priestly actions, and the significant use of media for marketing of the religious promises are visible parallels to the prosperity gospel of the Pentecostal and evangelical organizations currently rising in popularity around the globe. Traditional and familiar elements of Buddhist practice as communal recitation, the penetrating beat of the drums, and the elaborate performance in front of the altar are intensified with the help of elaborate technologies, facilitating an intense experience beyond those of the everyday. However, Agonshū offers more than the sale of carefully produced rituals to solve problems. The concluding remarks by Kiriyama are steeped in the rhetoric of positive thinking. He appeals to the members of Agonshū to meet the challenges in the ordinary course of their lives not only by trusting in the power of the buddhas or the bodhisattvas. Instead, they are to face them with the powers of initiative, self-assurance, and hard work.

Such hybrid forms, combining traditional rituals to access the religious power of the Buddha dharma and rhetoric of empowerment, are typical aspects of the Buddhist-oriented New Religions of Japan, including Sōka Gakkai, Kōfuku no Kagaku, and Shinnyo-en. They too offer rituals and rhetoric aimed at validating and explaining problems and challenges experienced by their adherents in the context of late modern life. The discourses offered by the groups tend to focus on the responsibility and the power of the individual self to solve the problem in question. Emphasizing individual responsibility as the source of contentment and happiness for oneself is something that resonates with the ethos of many contemporary societies, including Asian societies like Japan or Korea. Institutional, familial, or gendered structures, which may be responsible for suffering or conflicts, become invisible in this frame of reference. Instead, they are presented as challenges that the individual has to master on their own. In doing so, these teachings and practices respond to the demands imposed by the new spirit of capitalism. They show an ongoing or even increasing reliance on transcendent[15] powers in order to balance uncertainty and the growing demands imposed on the individual.[16] At the same time, these Buddhist teachings and practices serve to anchor the subjectivities and dispositions that resonate with free market rhetoric, such as an emphasis on the responsibility of the individual as entrepreneur in the market of their own success and happiness, or the therapeutic practice of positive thinking rehearsed in the *dōjō*. This twofold reconfiguration is the reason "prosperity Buddhism" is a proper appellation for these Buddhist-oriented New Religions.

Examples of such prosperity Buddhism can also be found in other Asian countries, such as the Taiwanese Fo Guang Shan and the Chinese Longquan temple. Based on a modern reinterpretation of Buddhist concepts, Buddhist organizations in Thailand offer their adherents empowerment rhetoric and ritual services promising prosperity, success, and luck. A good example is the Dhammakaya temple in Bangkok.[17] Its meditation center is adorned with plaques reading, "sit here and get rich."[18] This motto is reminiscent of the claim made by the Japanese movement Sōka Gakkai that chanting the central mantra *namu myōhō renge kyō* in the right manner will lead to the fulfillment of all wishes. Traditionally, adherents' wishes used to center on harmonious relationships or health issues. Nowadays the chanting is more and more understood as a magical tool for gaining access to material goods.[19]

The ritual services and rhetoric of empowerment made and actualized by Buddhist institutions in Asia promising the realization of success, prosperity, and happiness through a mix of religious intervention and individual work have been harshly criticized. In Thailand the catchphrase *puttha phanit* ("Buddhist business") is used to publicly shame these kinds of goods.[20] The rise of these offers of Buddhist commodities and services in Asia—which can, as we will see, also be observed around the globe—and the attendant elaborate marketing are called "commercialization" or "entertainmentization" by scholars of Buddhism and religion.[21]

However, as scholars of religion also tell us, religious goods have always been for sale, entertainment has always been important in and for religion, and leaders of religious traditions have always had to be good at business in order to finance their institutions. Thus, the marketing of religion and the reliance on messages and aesthetics in order to promote religions are the historical norm. This general norm also holds true for Buddhism, as numerous scholars have shown in the past decades.[22] What is new is the power and effectiveness of the technologies used to spread elements from the field known as religion into society more broadly. Also novel and much more important to note is—as the example of prosperity Buddhism shows—that Buddhist institutions are successfully creating religiously convincing answers that blend traditional practices and beliefs in the power of buddhas and bodhisattvas with rhetoric that resonates with the new spirit of capitalism.

Buddhist Semantics, Practices, Designs, and Self-Optimization

Images and statues of practitioners and buddhas who sit quietly with crossed legs on a cushion can be found in many fields of contemporary mediatized society of the first decades of the twenty-first century. According to common understanding, these images and statues show the central practice of Buddhism: sitting meditation. This sitting practice is said to have led to Shakyamuni Buddha's enlightenment. After philological and hermeneutic studies of Buddhist texts undertaken in the last two centuries have interpreted this practice as an individual method of introversion and concentration, it has become close to impossible to *not* cast this practice as meditation.

Recent scholarship provides alternative interpretations to this view. Images and statues of the silently sitting Buddha can be read as powerful signs for the claim that Buddhism has realized "the truth." Narratives of the Buddha's supernatural abilities, such as levitation, the ability to walk on water and through walls, to multiply his body, to travel at the speed of thought to other places or different universes, and telepathic or clairvoyant abilities can be used as proof of the Buddha's religious knowledge—and his successors' knowledge.[23] Embodied in the contemplating Buddha, enlightenment gains a physical as well as a spiritual dimension.

A good example of the embodied materialization of Buddhist soteriology is the ritualized character of the practice of *zazen* ("seated meditation") in Japanese Sōtō Zen Buddhism.[24] Seated meditation can be interpreted not as a form of introspection, but rather as "a ritual 're-presentation' of the original awakening of the Buddha."[25] *Zazen* acts as a powerful performance for mediating between worldly actors and transcendent agents, powers, or figures—in this case, the transcendental entity of the Buddhist dharma. Again, the terms "transcendent" and "transcendental" are used as comparative analytical tools to describe the dynamics of the practices of Zen Buddhism from the metatheoretical approach of religious studies. These terms denote assumptions concerning something beyond the immanent world, for instance, the miraculous powers of the buddhas and the dharma, the invisible band of lineage, the notion of enlightenment, or the supernatural abilities of religious specialists in Buddhism. Monastics in medieval Japan transformed their practices to cater to the religious needs and demands of the rural population. Through mass ordinations, funeral rites, and pleas for worldly benefits, laypeople could participate in the blessings associated with the Buddha's enlightenment.[26] For centuries, priestly activities have symbolized and evoked impressions of order, symmetry, control, and power. Zen monastic training, as Robert Sharf notes, emphasizes "physical discipline and ritual competence."[27] Speaking of his apprenticeship in Eihei-ji, a priest of a Sōtō temple in rural Nagano explains that the novices' daily lives revolves around the practice of *zazen* and the mindful control of one's body and movements. As he puts it, "During my time in the monastery, the main goal was to incorporate the monastic rules (*sahō*). We learned to express the Buddhist doctrine with our body and its movements when practicing *zazen* and following the temple rules."[28] As a powerful performance, *zazen* offers cognitive as well as sensuous access to the transcendent sphere of Zen Buddhism.[29] The different ceremonies surrounding *zazen* are designed to convince the laity of the clergy's religious competence and their abilities to fulfill their visitors' most common concerns: providing access to worldly benefits and caring for the dead and the ancestors.

The example of the role of *zazen* in the context of Japanese Buddhism shows that this practice need not necessarily be understood in the context of meditation. There are many open research questions regarding the role of meditation in the history of Buddhism, not least how important and frequent the practice actually was.[30] Yet, the confluence of transcultural flows from East and West has led to the predominant understanding of this practice as meditation reinterpreted not as a ritual or a performance, but as a means of individual and psychological introspection. In fact, meditation and the detailed instructions of these meditative practices as tools for religious experiences are often seen as the major reason for the popularity of "modern Buddhism" in a global context.[31]

The practice of this reimagined version of meditation is central in the expansive field of most of the Buddhist organizations, networks, and groups spreading globally in the twentieth and twenty-first centuries, and the opening of centers in large urban areas. In addition to people adopting the Buddhist label, there has been a proliferation of novel meditation practices. Conditions imposed by the mediatization of religious semantics, practices, and designs facilitate the transfer and mixture of narratives and materialities from different contexts. Examples include meditation-yoga, Christian meditation, or mindfulness-based stress reduction therapy. Even though they are not always made explicit, references to Buddhist topoi are fundamental when talking about meditation.[32] One reason for this seems the particular suitability of the icon of the meditating buddha for this field. The figure shows a person allegedly working on his mind and body trying to find insight, transformation, and salvation from ills through experiencing the wisdom of the body. This ascription resonates with the paradigm of self-cultivation in contemporary global societies.

The practice of mindfulness is cast as a non-religious technique in a supposedly secular, therapeutic setting.[33] Its effectiveness is argued to be scientifically measurable, and its use is made independent of creed or worldview, for instance, when mindfulness pioneer Jon Kabat-Zinn talks about mindfulness as "the wisdom and the heart of Buddhist meditation without the Buddhism."[34] The common presentation of mindfulness as involving Buddhist designs and aesthetics, however, leads to the supposition that this practice gains its attractiveness precisely through its references to Buddhist topoi. The analysis of contemporary discourses on mindfulness shows that its ontological foundation rests on transcendental claims. It is supposed to be a universal state of being, independent of its actual discursive and historic forms, self-revealing and capable of bringing about a state of health and well-being.[35]

In contrast to practices of mindfulness globally, the centers of Zen Buddhism that have developed outside of Japan in the last 100 years explicitly understand their activities as Buddhist.[36] The missionary activities of Deshimaru Taisen (1914–1982) resulted in the formation of many Zen Buddhist groups in France and Germany in the tradition of the Sōtō School. The meditation practice of groups in the lineage of Deshimaru commonly takes place in well-kept, austere rooms built around a Buddhist altar.[37] The meditation practice usually consists of two 40-minute *zazen* periods, with a period of walking meditation (*kinhin*) in between. Before the *zazen* session begins, participants enter the room following a prescribed sequence of motions. They move slowly to the front of the altar and then counterclockwise around the room. This sequence, along with other movements, like fluffing up the meditation cushions and folding the *koromo* or *kesa* (special Buddhist cloaks), follows specific instructions. "It's important to do all exercises with your complete concentration—as if your life was at risk," one participant told me. After the bell is rung, the practice of sitting still begins and silence falls over the room. Occasionally, one can hear the rustle of some piece of clothing. "The atmosphere is so tense, I was even afraid to yawn," said a female participant. Another practitioner told me that the powerful atmosphere of the room helped him to forget about the pain in his knees or the itchiness he felt all over his body. He could "leave everything behind and just breathe."

These *zazen* sessions can be described as strictly regimented processes that need to be kept free from any form of spontaneity or improvisation. The strict rules demand total dedication from every practitioner and free them from individual decisions and feelings. From the participants' perspective, the rules concerning motions and behavior soon turn from repressive dogma into helpful guidance that makes many of them feel special about their status as adepts of Zen Buddhism. The leaders of these sessions have a salient role in clothing the events in Buddhist garments by displaying a certain *habitus*, offering narratives from Zen Buddhist literature, and guiding the participants' attention toward the possibility of enlightenment. These narrations blend with the expectations of many practitioners, which are framed by the modern, psychologized ideas of meditation as a search within oneself involving extraordinary experiences.[38] The obligatory concentration on one's own body and its functions can lead to sensations that had been heretofore unknown to many practitioners. The quiet practice, together with the aesthetics of the *dōjō* and the guidance of the supervisors of *zazen*, can lead to strong impressions which take hold of the practitioners and even give them a feeling of getting in touch with something they experience as transcending the mundane world. These sensory aspects help practitioners to actually *feel* what they consider to be a Buddhist experience. Practitioners often emphasize feelings of liberation and refreshment, and elaborate on how they were able to leave behind worrying thoughts and everyday experiences, or even their sense of self.

The dynamics characteristic of the practice of *zazen* in contemporary urban settings described in the preceding paragraphs are to a greater or lesser degree at play in the practice of modern meditation. Due to the dynamics of mediatization, we can find a wide variety of ascriptions toward the practice in books, films, and on the internet. Still, the notion of a special experience that resonates with a truth beyond the mundane occupies the dominant tone in a wide array of specific contextual constructions. These ascriptions, group dynamics, the materialities of the setting, and the confrontation with the body sentenced to stillness, affect interpretation and transformations on the part of the practitioners. An anthropology of meditation therefore has to investigate these transformations from an interdisciplinary perspective. Based on studies undertaken so far, it is safe to argue that the exercise of meditation displays the typical characteristics of self-cultivation practices.[39] Its centerpiece is the assumption of the existence of an inner self that is perceived in need of overcoming, forgetting, discovering, improving, or optimizing itself. The precise goals of practice vary from group to group. It can, however, be observed that groups that stress the orthodox Buddhist understanding of "no self" have lost popularity in the twenty-first century. Guidance and rhetoric, meanwhile, which affirm the ability of the self to get better are increasingly gaining popularity. We can presently witness this process in the field of mindfulness and related practices. The goals and effects assured by the practice of meditation include a means of stress reduction, gaining balance, achieving inner peace and serenity, and recharging energy. Depending on their framing into explicit Buddhist, implicit Buddhist, or other hybrid frames, these practices promise unusual or extraordinary experiences that are supposed to induce therapeutic, healing, or religious effects.

What we witness in the transformed version of the practice of *zazen* and related practices of meditation can be understood as an economization of the self, because the transformed practice centers on the self's production and optimization. As the economy and its associated rhetoric are reified and sacralized, so are the self, its drive for happiness and experience, and the manufacture of individual identity. This is done with the help of religious semantics, be these the narratives and designs of Zen Buddhism, or more or less hidden or hybridized Buddhist semantics. Religious entities—such as the buddhas and bodhisattvas in traditional Buddhism—are no longer relevant in the transformed versions of *zazen* and comparable practices of meditation. The only significant entity left is the self itself. As the individual self constitutes the foundation of consumerism, *zazen* and comparable forms of meditation can be seen as strengthening the ongoing economization of the individual in contemporary urban societies. Witnessing the re-entry of *zazen* to Japan in its reinterpreted, modern guise as a means of self-optimization and seeing the practice of comparable forms of meditation in places like Singapore, Taiwan, Korea, and other highly industrialized areas of Asia, suggests that contemporary religious practices are not primarily influenced by cultural factors. Instead, they are mainly shaped by social contexts and discourses—such as capitalism and the regimes of the self in the case of *zazen* and comparable practices of meditation.

Buddhist Signifiers in the Field of Branding

The branding strategies for a variety of products in a range of settings rely on the magic of the words "Zen," "karma," or "mindful," including products like *Evoke Morning Zen Muesli*,[40] *Karma Milk*, and *Mindful Mayo*.[41] Pictures of buddhas are used in marketing campaigns, brand names, and the packaging of products like furniture, food, toys, and many other kinds of goods. Consumers with no direct relationship to Buddhism are targeted with Buddhist-inspired designs such as those of temples, rock gardens, and silently meditating monks. Ideas and images with a Buddhist "touch" appear to have a powerful influence over consumers. A cursory investigation of the publicly available databases of large advertising agencies in the year 2016 suggests that Buddhist narratives, materialities, and designs are often used in the field of advertisement.[42] In short: Buddhism sells.

What could be the reasons for the proliferation of Buddhist semantics and designs in the world of branding, marketing, and consumption? Contemporary marketing strategies cater to the belief that each individual is *in possession* of a unique personal identity and this identity needs to be *expressed in their possessions* and their ways of consumption. Brands are vehicles for the self-construction of the modern subject.[43] Products and their surrounding narratives need to be materialized in such a fashion as to elicit positive impressions in the body and the senses. Therefore, successful branding has to appeal to and stimulate emotions which customers associate with what they spend their money on.[44] In addition to eliciting positive sensations, the product needs to make the customer feel good about themselves.

One can readily conclude that advertisers would be negligent not to rely on semantics, materialities, and practices of Buddhism, for they are effective. The Buddhist field provides tools for advertisers that are eminently suitable for accomplishing their goals. The semantics and images of the Buddhist field have a distinct positive image in contemporary discourse and are elements of a generally accepted narrative tradition.[45] According to Jørn Borup, Buddhism has become mainstream, and the field of Buddhism can be described as "cool" and "chic."[46] Buddhist semantics are thus highly useful for generating brands that sell.

A brief look at some examples of marketing campaigns imbued with Buddhist semantics, practices, and designs illustrate the dynamics at work. The ice-cream company Häagen-Dazs tried using the attractiveness of Buddhism in an ad shown in Japan in 2004. Their ad for green tea ice cream shows three circles flowing into each other. The graphical design of each circle in different green hues connotes the sand from "Zen Gardens," tea fields, and a scoop of ice cream. The attendant text reads "a cup of Zen."[47] One way to read this is that the green tea ice cream melds the spirit of Zen with the spirit of Japan—as represented by tea fields—into something new that consumers can buy and savor. Through the mixture of Zen with green tea, Häagen-Dazs even offers a taste of nostalgia through a scoop of their ice cream. The authority and authenticity of these claims are reinforced through the respective allusions to the Buddhist field.

An ad from India shows a laughing Buddha holding a tablet with a cornucopia of food and drink. The ad promotes a drug against heartburn from the company Esoz and ran in magazines and newspapers in India in the summer of 2012.[48] Medications and other medicinal products against stress and exhaustion are often advertised in connection with sitting Buddhas. The statues smile calmly—or so the reference of the branding strategy—in the face of adversity. A positive reaction is "triggered" within the consumer and a positive relationship with the product established. For consumers in adverse situations, a salvific promise lies in the product. The world of fashion has discovered the power of the Buddha to drive sales. The logo of the fashion brand True Religion features a very happy looking laughing Buddha, guitar in one hand, the other giving the viewer a thumbs-up.[49]

The icon of the meditating Buddha proves to be particularly suitable for contemporary branding because the figure and materialities of Buddhism evoke an idea of striving for something beyond. Modern forms of marketing and consumption bank on this striving. As Kathryn Lofton puts it: "The product is a material way to access something ineffable."[50] The sitting Buddha has some mystical touch in the eyes of many. Therefore, the figure communicates the promise of extraordinary experiences and the possibility of transcending everyday life, or even this world altogether. It features an individual who is seen as able to bring about their own truth, well-being, and happiness. Buddhist iconographies and narration are appealing to the senses and stimulate positive emotions. These individual emotions are constantly interacting with the globally mediatized ascriptions toward Buddhism as something basically positive. Based on this interaction, the field of Buddhism fuels consumption. Buddhist images affirm the importance of working on the body, individual experience, and the constant drive for optimization. The aesthetics of the Buddhist field pull on the senses, thereby reassuring consumers that they constantly have to buy commodities to better and transform themselves. Succinctly put, Buddhist narration and imagery are capable of sacralizing consumption.

Conclusion: Buddhist Transformations in the Age of Late Capitalism

Based on romantic ideas about the anti-materialistic stance of Buddhism, apologists for a "Buddhist economy" express great hope and expectation for Buddhism as a possible alternative to global materialism and consumption.[51] However, if we move from the level of normative discourse to the level of global practices, Buddhism shows a strong affinity toward the workings of capitalism and consumption. Enabled by the thorough mediatization of religious semantics, we observe a new form of explicitly Buddhist teachings and practices in the emergence of prosperity Buddhism which help their practitioners to internalize the imperatives of capitalism, including self-responsibility and optimization of their soft skills, such as flexibility or resilience in the face of labor or family stress. Especially in the case of women, mindfulness rhetoric may include promises of dealing with the challenges that are imposed on them by the "triple burden" of late capitalist societies.[52] We witness the use of Buddhist narratives and materialities in the immensely popular field of meditation. Whether explicit or implicit, these allusions to the field of Buddhism serve to legitimate and increase the value of these practices as something inherently good that might even enable practitioners to reach the realms beyond the mundane, secularist world. This also holds true for the wide field of mindfulness whose post-secular dynamic is fueled by reinterpreted Buddhist topoi and imagery. While the practice of meditation in its various forms effects manifold transformations perceived as positive by the practitioners, its underlying paradigm strengthens the ceaseless imperative for the individual to strive for improvement. Lastly, we have seen that Buddhist semantics are able to fuel consumption.

Critics of the current entanglements of the field of Buddhism in the practices of self-optimization and consumption suggest that religions, especially Buddhism, have transformed to fit the ideological foundation of capitalism. These analyses convey the message that Buddhism is misunderstood or in some way deformed in the process. The findings on the field of prosperity Buddhism, meditation, and Buddhist-imbued marketing suggest otherwise. These developments are not to be taken as signs of the degeneration of Buddhism from something imagined as a pristine, holy, or somehow "real" religion. Rather, they may be seen as an ordinary way that humans, in interaction with society, use Buddhist narratives, practices, and materialities in the contemporary world. Second, the findings about Buddhist practices on a global scale do not confirm the assumption that Buddhism is deformed or weakened. Our results suggest the opposite. Buddhism is seen as offering means to gain supernatural support. The spiritual aura of Buddhism is either explicitly or implicitly at play in the wide field of meditation and in marketing and branding. This transcendental competency constitutes the global popularity of Buddhism in a wide array of different fields.

Notes

1. David McMahan, *The Making of Buddhist Modernism* (Oxford, New York: Oxford University Press, 2008), 5.
2. See Luc Boltanski and Ève Chiapello, *The New Spirit of Capitalism* (London and New York: Verso, 2018); Francois Gauthier, Linda Woodhead, and Tuomas Martikainen, "Introduction: Consumerism as the Ethos of Consumer Society," in *Religion in Consumer Society: Brands, Consumers and Markets*, ed. Francois Gauthier, Linda Woodhead, and Tuomas Martikainen (Farnham, UK, and Burlington, VT: Ashgate, 2013).
3. Eva Illouz, *Saving the Modern Soul: Therapy, Emotions, and the Culture of Self-Help* (Berkeley: University of California Press, 2008).
4. For a broader theoretical approach on Buddhism and globalization, see Christina Rocha, "Buddhism and Globalization," in *Buddhism in the Modern World*, ed. David McMahan (Abingdon and New York: Routledge, 2012), 289–303.
5. Stewart Hoover, *Religion in the Media Age* (London: Routledge, 2006).
6. Jeremy Stolow, "Religion and/as Media," *Theory, Culture & Society* 22, no. 4 (2005): 119–45.
7. An overview of Buddhism and popular culture in the United States is given by James Mark Shields, "The Conversion of Captain America: Buddhism and Postwar US Popular Culture," in *The Routledge Companion to Religion and Popular Culture*, ed. John C. Lyden and Eric Michael Mazur (London: Routledge, 2015), 401–18.
8. David McMahan and Erik Braun, "Introduction. From Colonialism to Brainscans: Modern Transformations of Buddhist Meditation," in *Meditation, Buddhism, and Science*, ed. David McMahan and Erik Braun (New York: Oxford University Press, 2017), 7.
9. For a general overview on Buddhism and media, see Scott A. Mitchell, "Buddhism and Media," in *Oxford Research Encyclopedia of Religion*, ed. John Barton (Oxford University Press, 2019), https://doi.org/10.1093/acrefore/9780199340378.013.624.
10. See, for instance, Rachelle M. Scott, *Nirvana for Sale? Buddhism, Wealth, and the Dhammakāya Temple in Contemporary Thailand* (Albany: State University of New York Press, 2009); and Inken Prohl, "New Religions in Japan: Adaptations and Transformations in Contemporary Society," in *Handbook of Contemporary Japanese Religions*, ed. Inken Prohl and John K. Nelson (Leiden: Brill, 2012), 241–67.
11. On the New Religions in Japan, see Peter B. Clarke, ed., *Japanese New Religions in Global Perspective* (Richmond, UK: RoutledgeCurzon, 2000).
12. The *goma* fire ritual is derivative of the *homa* ritual practiced in Vedic India for thousands of years. The description of the *goma* ritual is based on fieldwork undertaken in 1992, 1995, and 2005. For more information, see Ian Reader, *Religion in Contemporary Japan* (Basingstoke, UK: Macmillan, 1991), 208–33; Inken Prohl, "Solving Everyday Problems

with the Help of the Ancestors: Representations of Ghosts in the New Religions Agonshū and World Mate," in *Practising the Afterlife: Perspectives from Japan*, ed. Susanne Formanek and William LaFleur (Wien: Verlag der Österreichischen Akademie der Wissenschaften, 2004), 461–83.

13. On more recent developments after Kiriyama's death, see Baffeli, Erica and Ian Reader, *Dynamism and the Ageing of a Japanese 'New' Religion: Transformations and the Founder* (Manchester: Bloomsbury, 2018).
14. Daromir Rudnyckyj and Filippo Osella, *Religion and the Morality of the Market* (Cambridge: Cambridge University Press, 2017).
15. In line with theories of religious studies, the term "transcendent" is used to designate powers, entities, and realms that are thought to exist beyond the immanent; see, for instance, Birgit Meyer, "Religious Sensations: Why Media, Aesthetics, and Power Matter in the Study of Contemporary Religion," in *Religion: Beyond a Concept*, ed. Hent de Vries (New York: Fordham University Press, 2007), 704–23. As an analytical term it is also applicable to Buddhism and corresponds among others with the term "supernatural" that is more often used in the context of Buddhism, for instance by McMahan, *The Making of Buddhist Modernism*.
16. In the case of Thailand, McMahan sees evidence for an increase of the reliance on the supernatural as a reaction to the forces of globalized capitalism; see McMahan, *The Making of Buddhist Modernism*, 38–39.
17. For an ethnographic study of this temple, see Scott, *Nirvana for Sale?*
18. Seth Mydans, "Where Buddhism's Eight-Fold Path Can Be Followed with a Six-Figure Salary," *New York Times* (blog), December 20, 2016, https://www.nytimes.com/2016/12/20/world/asia/thailand-buddhist-temple-praying-wealth.html.
19. This is based on observations and communications at Sōka Gakkai's meeting places in Japan and Germany during the last decade.
20. Pattana Kitiarsa, "Buddha Phanit: Thailand's Prosperity Religion and Its Commodifying Tactics," in *Religious Commodifications in Asia: Marketing Gods*, ed. Pattana Kitiarsa (London and New York: Routledge, 2008), 120–44.
21. For example: Lionel Obadia, "Is Buddhism like a Hamburger? Buddhism and the Market Economy in a Globalized World," in *The Economics of Religion: Anthropological Approaches*, ed. Lionel Obadia and C. Donald Wood (Bingley, UK: Emerald Group, 2011), 99–120; Jørn Borup, "Branding Buddha: Mediatized and Commodified Buddhism as Cultural Narrative," *Journal of Global Buddhism* 17 (2016): 41–55; Mitchell, *Buddhism and Media*; note, however, that Mitchell questions the line between the religious and the commercial (176).
22. For an overview, see Trine Brox and Williams-Oerberg, "Buddhism, Business and Economics," in *The Oxford Handbook of Contemporary Buddhism*, ed. Michael Jerryson (New York: Oxford University Press, 2017), 504–17.
23. Sven Bretfeld, "Verkörperung von Weisheit, Kraft und Schönheit," in *Von Thangka bis Manga: Bild-Erzählungen aus Asien*, ed. Iris Poßegger and Sven Bretfeld (Leipzig: Seemann, 2012), 20–25.
24. The Sōtō School is one of the three Zen schools in Japan.
25. Bernard Faure, *Visions of Power: Imagining Medieval Japanese Buddhism* (Princeton, NJ: Princeton University Press, 1996), 217.
26. William M. Bodiford, *Sōtō Zen in Medieval Japan* (Honolulu: University of Hawai'i Press, 1993), 213–16.

27. Robert H. Sharf, "Buddhist Modernism and the Rhetoric of Meditative Experience," *Numen* 42, no. 3 (1996): 249.
28. Personal communication, Nagano, June 2006.
29. Inken Prohl, "Same Forms, Same Sensations? The Practice of Sitting Still in Traditional Japanese and Contemporary Urban Settings," in *Eastspirit: Transnational Spirituality and Religious Circulation in East and West*, ed. Jørn Borup and Marianne Qvortrup Fibinger (Leiden: Brill, 2017), 100–19.
30. McMahan and Braun, *Meditation, Buddhism, and Science*, 7.
31. McMahan, *The Making of Buddhist Modernism*, 183–214.
32. Jeff Wilson, *Mindful America: The Mutual Transformation of Buddhist Meditation and American Culture* (New York: Oxford University Press, 2014).
33. McMahan and Braun, *Meditation, Buddhism, and Science*, 3–4.
34. Danny Fisher, "Mindfulness and the Cessation of Suffering: An Exclusive Interview with Mindfulness Pioneer Jon Kabat-Zinn," *Lion's Roar*, October 20, 2010, https://www.lionsroar.com/mindfulness-and-the-cessation-of-suffering-an-exclusive-new-interview-with-mindfulness-pioneer-jon-kabat-zinn/.
35. Alp Arat, "'What It Means to Be Truly Human': The Postsecular Hack of Mindfulness," *Social Compass* 64, no. 2 (2017): 167–79.
36. Inken Prohl, *Zen für Dummies: Das Unaussprechliche des Zen* (Weinheim: Wiley-VCH, 2010).
37. The account is based on observations made in France and Germany on numerous occasions, 1985–2016.
38. On the manifold ascriptions toward meditation, see Scott A. Mitchell, "The Tranquil Meditator: Representing Buddhism and Buddhists in US Popular Media," *Social Compass* 8, no. 3 (2014): 81–89.
39. For an overview, see McMahan and Braun, *Meditation, Buddhism, and Science.*
40. Last accessed: September 10, 2017: https://www.amazon.com/Evoke-Morning-Gluten-Muesli-Ounce/dp/B006GKBFN4?th=1.
41. Two of many examples to be found at Whole Foods Market, 2016–2017. On the appeal of "Zen" in advertisement, see: Joshua A. Irizarry, "Putting a Price on Zen: The Business of Redefining Religion for Global Consumption," *Journal of Global Buddhism* 16 (2015): 51–69.
42. Databases searched are: adeevee, Coloribus, and Ads of the World, each in spring 2016, and AdsSpot in November 2021.
43. Adam Arvidsson, *Brands: Meaning and Value in Media Culture* (London and New York: Routledge, 2006).
44. Daryl Travis, *How Does IT Make YOU FEEL?: Why Emotion Wins the Battle of Brands* (Chicago: Brandtrust, 2013).
45. Scott Mitchell, "Buddhism, Media, and Popular Culture," in *Buddhism in the Modern World*, ed. David McMahan (London and New York: Routledge, 2012), 305–23.
46. Jørn Borup, "Branding Buddha: Mediatized and Commodified Buddhism as Cultural Narrative," *Journal of Global Buddhism* 17 (2016): 41.
47. Last accessed 24 November, 2021: https://adsspot.me/media/outdoor/haagen-dazs-green-tea-cup-of-zen-30362cb8bbfa.
48. Last accessed 24 November, 2021: https://adsspot.me/media/prints/esoz-laughing-buddha-9eb6c43c60ff.
49. Last accessed 24 November 2021: https://www.truereligion.com/mens-designer-clothing.

50. Kathryn Lofton, *Consuming Religion* (Chicago and London: University of Chicago Press, 2017), 9.
51. Examples are: Peter Harvey, *An Introduction to Buddhist Ethics: Foundations, Values, and Issues* (London and Cambridge: Cambridge University Press, 2000); Claire Brown, *Buddhist Economics: An Enlightened Approach to the Dismal Science* (New York: Bloomsbury Press, 2017).
52. That is to say the burdens of earning a wage, carrying the bulk of domestic and childcare duties, and bearing the costs of the rising divorce rate. See Linda Woodhead, "Gender Differences in Religious Practice and Significance," in *The Sage Handbook of the Sociology of Religion*, ed. A. James Beckford and J. N. Demerath III (London: SAGE Publications, 2007), 577. See also Illouz, *Saving the Modern Soul.*

Further Reading

Borup, Jørn. "Branding Buddha: Mediatized and Commodified Buddhism as Cultural Narrative." *Journal of Global Buddhism* 17 (2016): 41–55.

Brox, Trine, and Elizabeth Williams-Oerberg. "Buddhism, Business, and Economics." In *The Oxford Handbook of Contemporary Buddhism*, ed. Michael Jerryson. New York: Oxford University Press, 2017, 504–17.

McMahan, David. *The Making of Buddhist Modernism*. Oxford and New York: Oxford University Press, 2008.

McMahan, David L., and Erik Braun, eds. *Meditation, Buddhism, and Science*. New York: Oxford University Press, 2017.

Mitchell, Scott. "Buddhism, Media, and Popular Culture." In *Buddhism in the Modern World*, ed. David McMahan. London and New York: Routledge, 2012, 305–23.

Rocha, Christina. "Buddhism and Globalization." In *Buddhism in the Modern World*, ed. David L. McMahan. London and New York: Routledge, 2012, 289–303.

Rudnyckyj, Daromir, and Filippo Osella. *Religion and the Morality of the Market*. Cambridge: Cambridge University Press, 2017.

Scott, Rachelle M. *Nirvana for Sale? Buddhism, Wealth, and the Dhammakāya Temple in Contemporary Thailand*. Albany: State University of New York Press, 2009.

Shields, James Mark. "The Conversion of Captain America: Buddhism and Postwar US Popular Culture." In *The Routledge Companion to Religion and Popular Culture*, ed. John C. Lyden and Eric Michael Mazur. London: Routledge, 2015, 401–18.

PART II

MATERIAL MEDIATIONS

THE study of Buddhist practice highlights forms of sensory engagement with the social and material environments in which scholars and practitioners are located. Of particular importance are three classes of material objects around which authoritative sets of formalized behaviors have been concentrated over more than two millennia: texts, relics, and images. And preeminent among these objects have been Buddhist texts, which have served as the primary focus of inquiry for European and American scholars of Buddhism since the emergence of the field of Buddhist studies in the nineteenth century. The Western "textualization" of Buddhist studies, which entailed the acquisition and disciplined study of Buddhist manuscripts, including "scientific" editing and philological analysis as well as the publication of critical editions and translations, provided the foundation for the modern discipline of Buddhist studies. This Western scholarly privileging of textual sources has depended upon and in some respects has paralleled the centrality of diverse forms of textual transmission and interpretation within sangha communities. At the same time, Euro-American values and cultural assumptions contributed to a "dematerialization" of Buddhist traditions of practice by constructing and valorizing systems of Buddhist thought, abstracted from textual sources preserved in Western libraries, which were represented as more authentic than devotional practices such as relic and image veneration.

Part II begins with John Strong's inquiry (Chapter 8) into the centrality of relics and images as material objects that mediate the expanded biography of the Buddha. Attention to these objects and the diversity of formalized behaviors that they support opens up a wider framework for understanding the Buddha's embodied presence and its effects on the world, while also pointing to differences in how relics and images have materially mediated that presence. Susan Huntington's Chapter 9 on Buddha images expands upon this by exploring some of the distinctive ways in which images have been imbued with potency and agency through rituals of consecration and veneration. Natalie Gummer in Chapter 10 then turns to an exploration of ritualized engagements with texts in South Asian Buddhist communities, highlighting variegated forms of material agency that differ significantly from dominant Western textual representations.

The final two chapters in this section, both informed by the discipline of archaeology, shift to an examination of the wider social and material environments of two important Indian Buddhist communities: Bodhgaya and Sanchi. While Abhishek Amar focuses in Chapter 11 on the "built environment" and its connection to Buddhist ritual practices centered on the site of the Buddha's enlightenment, Julia Shaw in Chapter 12 explores the potential of archaeological research for illuminating how Buddhist monastic communities at Sanchi engaged with the "natural environment," and its implications for shaping modern environmentalist discourses.

CHAPTER 8

RELICS AND IMAGES

JOHN S. STRONG

Image[s] and relics—that is all that the Buddhists adore.

—Eugène Burnouf, 1844.[1]

DESPITE the fact that "Protestant" presuppositions led many late nineteenth- and twentieth-century Buddhologists to dismiss the worship of relics and images as "un-Buddhist," or as "a sop to the plebeian needs of the unlettered masses,"[2] the centrality of these objects of veneration to any understanding of Buddhist practice is now commonly recognized.[3] Images and relics are pan-Buddhist phenomena in that they are universal features of the tradition, for monastics and laypersons alike. Although, to be sure, there are famous relics (such as the Buddha's tooth in Sri Lanka) and famous images (such as the Udāyana sandalwood image in East Asia), which may draw pilgrims from far and wide, we should not be blind to the myriads of "ordinary" generic relics and images that, simply put, are "everywhere." In Sri Lanka, for instance, there are Buddha relics to be found and Buddha images to be seen in virtually every monastery.[4] In China, Buddhism itself came to be known as the "religion of images" (*xiang jiao*),[5] and, by the Tang dynasty, the proliferation of relics there was so great that one scholar has spoken of it as a "hemorrhage of the sacred."[6] Similarly, profusions of images may be found in Southeast Asia, Tibet, Korea, and Japan, and, throughout the world, in non-Buddhist milieux such as museums or private collections.

This chapter will primarily be concerned with relics and sculpted representations of the Buddha Gautama (Shakyamuni), although it should be recognized that Buddhists also venerate relics of other enlightened beings such as disciples of the Buddha or great masters of the tradition, as well as images of other buddhas and bodhisattvas besides Shakyamuni.[7]

There are some significant differences between Buddha relics and Buddha images, yet from an ideological and devotional perspective, the two may profitably be considered together. Both images and relics are thought to make the sacred power of the Buddha present, even after his complete absence in *parinirvāṇa*.[8] As such, they are facilitators of the spread and persistence of the tradition and serve to localize the Buddha in particular places. Indeed, the arrival of relics and/or images of the Buddha in a given place often marks the introduction (or re-establishment) of the religion there, and can be the subject of legendary chronicles or oral traditions that enhance their pedigrees and prestige.[9] Both relics and images are sometimes said to be "alive"—like the Buddha, they can move about, emit rays of light, and perform other miracles.[10] Both have acted as palladia for Buddhist kingdoms, ensuring the prosperity, well-being, and protection of the realm. As such, both have been, and in some places remain, politically important, serving to legitimate the sovereignty of rulers who possess and honor them.[11] In some places, relic-shrines and images may be conjoined together (Figure 8.1); elsewhere, they may be recognized as variant sorts of "memorials" (*cetiya*) for venerating the Buddha.[12] In Sri Lanka, for instance, devotees, when they visit a monastery, will commonly make separate devotional stops at both the stupa (supposedly containing bodily relics of the Buddha) *and* the Buddha image (as well as at the Bodhi tree, which is another type of relic).[13] Generally, on such occasions, they will make simple offerings of flowers, and utter or think a formulaic verse: "With this heap of flowers, which has color and scent, . . . I make offering at the feet of the Buddha. By this merit may there be release (*mokṣa*) [for me]. Just as this flower fades, so my body goes towards destruction."[14] As is inferred in these words, despite its apparent simplicity, this ordinary act of piety can be expressive of many things: it recognizes the greatness of the Buddha (in his relics or his image), and the importance of making merit and attaining enlightenment, while at the same time prompting a realization of one's own impermanence.

In addition to these various similarities between images and relics, there are also differences to be accounted for. Anthropomorphic images of the Buddha were relatively late in making an appearance (around the first century CE),[15] whereas relics were objects of veneration possibly from the very time of the Buddha's death (fourth century BCE). Relics, because of their original connection with the physical body of the Buddha, tend to emphasize his humanity and historicity,[16] while images may perhaps incline more toward his "divinity." As one authority put it, "From the beginning of its appearance, the anthropomorphic Buddha image was not that of a human being but clearly that of a god."[17] Images, by their very material shape, may in and of themselves be recognized as being of the Buddha, while relics, without identifying markers such as reliquaries, inscriptions, or legendary traditions, remain essentially anonymous.[18] Finally, images only "come alive" as a result of their consecration,[19] while relics *qua* relics generally require no such ritual sanctification,[20] although it can be argued that their enshrinement in stupas or other types of reliquaries is ritually marked and may be seen as a kind of consecration for the devotional site of which they are then a part.

The last decade of the twentieth and first decade of the twenty-first centuries saw a mushrooming of scholarship on images and relics. Much of this revolved around the

FIGURE 8.1. Buddha image in the Grande Pagode de Vincennes, Paris. A set of bodily relics is enshrined in the base of the image.

Photo: John Strong.

question of the Buddha's presence and/or absence in these objects of veneration. Most scholars affirmed that the Buddha is present in some way in both relics and images, though they differed as to how that "presence" is to be understood. Is the Buddha thought to be *literally* present in the relic or image, or only symbolically, affectively, ritually, or functionally present?[21] Within these parameters, a whole gamut of suggestions reflecting different theoretical frameworks have been made for understanding the nature of relics and/or images.[22]

As useful and insightful as the discussions of these issues have been, in what follows, I will seek to move beyond these debates, in part because I suspect most views of presence and absence are ultimately grounded in Western theistic notions of immanence and transcendence. Instead, I will consider relics and images as alternative bodies of the Buddha,[23] and organize my discussion around two sets of polarities: (1) wholeness and fragmentation, or "the one and the many post-mortem bodies of the Buddha"; and (2) aversions and advocacies.

Wholeness and Fragmentation: Oneness and Multiplicity of Postmortem Bodies

We generally think of the Buddha Shakyamuni as having been one person with one body. If, however, we consider (as is now common) accounts of his previous lives (jatakas) as part of his overall biography, then it is clear that he also had many "prenatal bodies" (human, divine, animal, etc.). Similarly, if we view stories of the Buddha's relics and images as extending the continuum of his biography after his *parinirvāṇa*, it is possible to see these relics and images as "postmortem bodies." Somatically speaking, then, in the context of his full biography, the Buddha's birth marks his transition from his having been multiply present *diachronically*, through a succession of individual bodies in his past lives, to his being singularly present as Gautama; and his *parinirvāṇa* marks his transition from having been singularly present as Gautama to being multiply present *synchronically* in his relics and images.

This second transition (which interests us here) is reflected in legendary traditions that oscillate between highlighting wholeness and stressing fragmentation.[24] And here we must consider relics and images separately, if only because the two of them generally emphasize different processes. Relics tend to make the Buddha's body multiple by a process of division, while images do so by a process of replication.

Two Types of Relics: Scattered and Not Scattered

Most scholarly discussions of Buddhist relics begin with the account of the Buddha's death and funeral contained in the *Mahāparinirvāṇa-sūtra*. There we are told that after his passing in Kuśinagarī in northern India, the people of the local tribe, the Mallas, worshipped, then cremated his body, and then collected his relics from the ashes of his pyre. The relics, however, did not remain together long. There quickly arose a dispute over their possession, with eight North Indian kingdoms claiming them for themselves. The dispute, which almost erupted in violence, ended with an arbitration effected by a brahmin named Droṇa, who divided the relics into eight shares and gave one to each of the contending parties. They promptly took them off to their own kingdoms, where they enshrined them in stupas. This was the beginning of the scattering of the Buddha's post-mortem bodies.[25] As Buddhaghosa points out in his commentary on the text, what had been one body (*sarīra*) became many bodies (*sarīrāni*), i.e., relics.[26]

Interestingly, this narrative scenario featuring the dispersal of the relics into the Droṇa-stupas violates the Buddha's directive, given earlier in the sutra, about how his funeral should be conducted. According to his instructions to his disciple Ānanda, the remains of his body were to be buried under a *single* stupa to be erected at a crossroads. Indeed, in the earliest Chinese translation of the text, that is the action that is carried out.[27] In part because of this, a number of scholars have suggested that, alongside the story of the *division* of the relics and their distribution into eight stupas, there was a *single*-sepulture tradition, which saw the Buddha as originally having been buried in one place, and perhaps not even cremated at all.[28]

This proposed dual tradition is echoed in Pali legends about buddhas of the past, where one of the factors that differentiates various *tathāgatha*s is whether their relics stay together and are consequently preserved in a single stupa, or whether their relics are scattered (*vippakiṇṇa*), or made widespread (*vitthārika*), and enshrined in many. The past Buddha Vipassī, for example, has all his relics kept together and placed in a single stupa that is seven leagues high. The past Buddha Konāgamana, however, has his relics spread far and wide into multiple stupas.[29] The same distinction may be found in Sanskrit, Tibetan, and Chinese sources.[30] In the *Bhadrakalpika-sūtra*, each of the thousand buddhas of the Fortunate Aeon (*bhadrakalpa*) is specified as either having his relics remain in "a single mass" (*ekaghana*) or spread extensively (*vaistārika*) into multiple stupas, whose extraordinary numbers are sometimes given.[31] Similarly, in the *Lotus Sutra*, the past Buddha Prabhūtaratna (with whom Shakyamuni famously shares a seat) appears in his "relic form" (*dhātuvigraha*), which is said to be "in a single mass" (*ekaghana*); and in the *Mūlasarvāstivāda Vinaya*, the relics of the past Buddha Kāśyapa's body (which Shakyamuni also exhumes) are said to be his undivided whole skeleton.[32] (Buddhas, it might be noted, are proclaimed to have a unique skeletal structure: unlike humans, whose bones are "placed tip to tip," and *pratyekabuddha*s, whose bones are hooked together, the bones of buddhas are all linked together "like a chain" [Pali, *saṅkhalikā*].)[33]

The scattered/not scattered motif is reiterated in a more diachronic way in subsequent legends about Shakyamuni's relics. According to a number of texts, about twenty years after the Buddha's *parinirvāṇa*, his chief disciple, Mahākāśyapa, goes and collects the relics from the original Droṇa-stupas and buries them in a single new underground chamber built for him by King Ajātaśatru. From having one body divided into eight relic bodies, the Buddha thus goes back to having one relic-body. Two centuries later, however, King Ashoka uncovers that chamber, takes all the relics out of it, and redistributes them into 84,000 stupas that he has newly built all over his realm. In other texts, there is no mention of Mahākāśyapa's chamber and it is Ashoka who gathers together the relics from the original Droṇa-stupas, only to disperse them again into the 84,000 stupas.[34] Either way, the legendary traditions as a whole take us from unity (the Buddha's body or the one stupa tradition) to dispersal (the eight Droṇa stupas) to unity (Mahākaśyapa's underground chamber) to further dispersal (Ashoka's 84,000 stupas).

The 84,000 stupas, however, represent only the start of the dispersal of the post-mortem bodies of the Buddha. In time, both in legend and in history, the relics are spread, in a more disorganized fashion perhaps, throughout the Buddhist world. Even so, the theme of unity is not forgotten, for this further fragmentation is eventually countered by another legend—about the "*parinirvāṇa* of the relics." In this, just prior to the advent of the future Buddha Maitreya, all of Shakyamuni's relics from all over the world fly through the air and reassemble in Bodhgaya, where they come together in a "single mass" of gold, and take on once again the form of the Buddha, before undergoing their own final cremation and disappearing entirely.[35]

What are we to make of all this? Kevin Trainor has observed that Euro-Americans often "prefer wholes to parts."[36] Consequently, there has been a tendency, perhaps especially in analyses of Christian relics, to apply to fragments of bodies the principle of *pars pro toto*, according to which a bodily part may stand in for a whole person. It is not clear, however, that *pars pro toto* always applies to Buddhist relics. Sometimes, it seems to, but at other times, a bodily part of the Buddha, i.e., a relic, may simply stand for the fact of his partition, a kind of *pars pro partitione*. Buddhist relics are thus not only bodies of the Buddha, but also symbols of his body's passing out of integrity, of its impermanence (*anitya*), and selflessness (*anātman*).

As such, relics can be a reminder of the Buddha's sacrificial compassion for others. This is stated explicitly, for example, by the second-century CE poet Mātṛceṭa, who praises the Buddha for "powdering his bones into tiny particles" so that his body will be shared with as many people as possible after his *parinirvāna*.[37] Similarly, in a number of Mahayana texts, the Buddha is described as "pulverizing" or "smashing" his own body into relics for the sake of sentient beings everywhere.[38] Such declarations are often paired with examples from jataka tales in which the Buddha, in a slightly different way, sacrifices his body (or has it variously cut up) for others.[39]

Images: Aniconic and Anthropomorphic

Issues of oneness and multiplicity are prominent in the case of relics, but they may also be found in traditions about images, though in a slightly different way. Art historians, at the beginning of the twentieth century, much debated the question of the origin of the anthropomorphic Buddha image—probably around the first century CE. Was it indigenously Indian (from the land of Mathurā), or a product of "Greek" culture in the northwest region of Gandhāra?[40] At the same time, they noted that many of the early (second–first centuries BCE) bas-reliefs at Bhārhut and Sāñcī do not feature anthropomorphic images of the Buddha, but aniconic signs such as trees, wheels, footprints, thrones, stupas, etc. The significance of this early Buddhist "aniconism" (as it came to be called) has been much discussed. Questions abound, such as: Was there a reluctance or an interdiction with regard to representing the Buddha in human form, given the notion of his *parinirvāṇa* as extinction? What are the relations of these various aniconic signs to pre-Buddhist traditions, such as folk religion or Vedic beliefs? Do these aniconic symbols actually represent the Buddha? Do they depict episodes from his life story, or are they portraits of places of pilgrimage where he was worshipped? Were the aniconic signs intended as supports for meditative visualizations, and, if so, of whom or what?[41]

In recent times, discussions of aniconism have focused on a debate between Susan Huntington and Vidya Dehejia on whether or not these symbols represent the Buddha or pilgrimage sites.[42] What is of interest to me here, however, is that, whatever they signify, these aniconic symbols are *fragmentary* depictions; they show either an episode of the Buddha's biography, or a place where he once did something and is now venerated, but never the whole of him.

In this light, these aniconic symbols in their fragmentariness are akin to scattered relics. In fact, many of them may well be representations of relics and their worship—trees, wheels, seats, or footprints being, in fact, relics of contact or use, and stupas being monuments containing relics.[43] As Huntington has put it, "Devotion to . . . relics comprises the principal artistic theme of these carvings."[44] Rather than view the aniconic friezes at Bhārhut and Sanchi as narrating the presence (or indicating the absence) of Shakyamuni per se, therefore, we may do well to see them as representations of his scattered relics and their worship.

But if the aniconic images at Sanchi and Bhārhut do not seem to be aiming at a total recapture of Shakyamuni, later fully anthropomorphic depictions of him do (though, even here, various hand gestures [mudras] on Buddha images may suggest he is being depicted at a particular time in his life). Thus, generally speaking, the shift from aniconic to iconic art in Buddhism may be said to represent a transition from fragments to wholes. In this, Buddha images are akin to those non-scattered relics that are preserved or gathered in a single mass, sometimes taking on the physical appearance of the Buddha with all his marks as they do so.[45]

Multiplication of Anthropomorphic Images

Yet the question of multiplicity will not go away, since, although images may represent wholes, there are many such wholes. Art historians are not the only ones to have speculated about the origins of the Buddha image. The tradition itself has done that in several legendary sagas.[46] Perhaps the most famous of these is the story of the so-called sandalwood image of King Udāyana, of which there are many versions. In one of them, King Udāyana longs impatiently to see the Buddha when the latter is away spending the three months of the rains-retreat in heaven, preaching to his mother who has been reborn there. To remedy the situation, the king asks the Buddha's disciple Mahāmaudgalyāyana for help, and the latter obliges by sending thirty-two artists up to heaven to sculpt a sandalwood statue of the Buddha from life. Each artist is responsible for one of the thirty-two marks on the Buddha's body, so here again we may have an echo of the theme of an image being a unification of parts. Once the image is made, the artists bring it back down to earth and King Udāyana has it installed in the Buddha's residence in the Jetavana monastery and venerates it there. Here, then, is a clear example of how an image can serve as a replacement for the Buddha when he is absent. When, at the end of the rains-retreat, the Buddha returns to earth—when he becomes present again—a curious thing happens: the sandalwood image is enlivened; it gets up from its/his seat and goes out to welcome him. The Buddha tells it/him to sit back down but predicts it/he will have a great role to play in the propagation of Buddhism, once he himself becomes absent again, i.e., after his own *parinirvāṇa*.[47]

There is much that can be said about this legend, but let me restrict myself to the following points. In this and other stories like it, the image of the Buddha initially comes alive only in the presence of the living Buddha. In this, we seem to have a reflection (or foreshadowing) of the ritual of image consecration in which new images are "empowered" or "enlivened" by being placed in contact with an older, already consecrated image, which in turn was "empowered" by a still older image, and so on and so forth, right back to the Buddha.[48] Alternatively or additionally, in consecration rituals, the biography of the Buddha may be recited to the new image to "instruct" it in the ways of the enlightened one, or the eyes of the image may be "opened" (i.e., painted or sculpted in) to signify its enlightenment.[49] Implicit in all this is the notion of a genealogy or lineage of succession that connects images to the living Shakyamuni. What we glimpse in the legend of the Udāyana image is the beginning of that succession. The Buddha declares that it/he, as his own postmortem body, will succeed him after his passing and will carry out his mission of spreading the dharma. In the meantime, the living Udāyana image coexists with the still living Shakyamuni. There are thus now two buddhas, or at least two buddha bodies, in one place and at one time.

The Buddhist legendary tradition did not stop this multiplication of buddha bodies/images at two. For instance, in his "great miracle" at Śrāvastī, the Buddha initially goes from projecting one image of himself, to gradually filling the whole sky with multiple magically created images, an array reproduced sometimes in the "thousand-buddha" wall paintings of later iconography. In the legends, it is clear that these are not static images; they walk, they talk, they take on different postures; they are, in this sense, alive.[50] This legendary multiplication of buddhas is, of course, paralleled by the artistic production of countless buddha statues, all coexisting throughout the world, or within single temples or monasteries.

Both the legends and the iconography raise important Buddhological questions. For instance, in early Buddhism, it was thought that no two buddhas could coexist simultaneously in the same time and place, although there could be multiple buddhas appearing separately from one another over the eons. The proliferation of buddha images, all felt to be in some sense alive and so to each *be* the Buddha, represented a significant challenge to that one-buddha doctrine, one that both reflected and effected new, ultimately Mahayana, assertions that many buddhas could exist at one time.

This overlap of buddhas can be seen in devotional practices in a variety of ways. In Chinese Mahayana contexts, for example, it is expressed in the veneration of images, all on the same altar, of the so-called "buddhas of the three times" (*sanshi fo*)—past, present, and future. Alternatively, in images inspired by the *Lotus Sutra*, Shakyamuni is shown sharing his seat with the ancient buddha of the past, Prabhūtaratna, and the pair are worshipped together, though the focus is on Shakyamuni as "our" Buddha.[51] In South and Southeast Asian contexts, a different instance of this may be seen in the worship of relics at sites such as the Shwe Dagon pagoda in Yangon or the Mahāthūpa in Anurādhapura, which contain layered within them not only the relics of Shakyamuni, but also relics of his immediate predecessors, the three previous buddhas of this eon.[52]

Aversions and Advocacies: Relics and Images in Cultural Contexts

We have seen so far that, with regard to Buddhist relics and images, there exists what Kevin Trainor calls an "oscillation between division and unity."[53] Sometimes this oscillation takes the form of movement from one pole to the other; sometimes it takes the form of the simultaneous paradoxical affirmation of the two poles at once: the Buddha is both singular and plural, whole and fragmented, in his images and relics.

In the remainder of this chapter, in order to better understand the place of relics and images in Buddhist practice, I want to look at a second set of polarities. First, primarily with regard to relics but touching also on the role of images, I will consider the question of cultural notions of purity and impurity. Then, more briefly, and exclusively with regard to images, I will look at the question of iconophobia (i.e., suspicion of and anxiety toward images) and what I neologistically am calling "iconophilia" (i.e., enthusiasm for images).

Relics: Purity and Impurity

Neither relics nor images were part of the Vedic and Brahmanical religious tradition that stood as an important backdrop to the formation of Buddhism. Although Hindu anthropomorphic images of deities began appearing around the same time as images of the Buddha, and perhaps in the same place (Mathurā), relics never really became a part of Hinduism.[54] One of the reasons for this was Brahmanical feelings about the impurity of dead bodies and things associated with them. Corpses were thought to be highly polluting, and parts of corpses (relics) no fit object for worship. In this context, some scholars have viewed the development of relic worship in Buddhism to be culturally anomalous.[55]

The same observation could be made for other cultural contexts. In China, for instance, the Confucian tradition much valued the integrity of the body and held in horror the kind of fragmentation implied by the relics tradition. Indeed, cremation there does not appear to have become commonplace even for Buddhists until the Song Dynasty (960–1279 CE).[56] The fear of dismemberment of the body even seems to have led to a creation of another kind of "whole relic": the mummification and lacquering of the integral bodies of deceased masters, which bring relics closer to images.[57]

Paradoxically, however, side by side with worries about the possible impurity of bodily remains went affirmations that the relics of the Buddha were also powerful and pure. For one thing, they came from the Buddha's body which, unlike the bodies of ordinary beings, was affirmed to be pure, even in death.[58] Second, although from one perspective relics may be associated with death, from another they are seen to be alive—capable of multiplying themselves, moving about, and glowing with light. As one eleventh-century Chinese author reports: as he was examining a Buddha's tooth relic, it suddenly started producing small relic pellets. "They wafted away in countless numbers, some flying up into the air and others falling to the ground. . . . They sparkled brightly, filling the eyes with light."[59] In India, stories of relics manifesting their power by emitting colored lights from the top of stupas date back at least to the time of the Chinese pilgrims.[60]

Bones, Beads, and Gems

This double affirmation of both purity and impurity, life and death, may be related to the fact that the Buddhist tradition came to recognize two kinds of relics. On the one hand, there are bones or ashes; on the other hand, there are shiny pearls or gemlike beads of various colors.[61] Archaeologists have found these two types of objects side by side in countless reliquaries in unearthed stupas in India and elsewhere (Figure 8.2).

The bones are sometimes thought by Western scholars to represent "true relics," while the beads are sometimes said to be "votive offerings" left there by devotees, but it is clear that the beads and gems are often treated by Buddhists as though they were relics in and of themselves, and today most relics that are viewed by devotees outside of their reliquaries are of second type.[62]

The roots of this tradition, perhaps, may already be found in Buddhaghosa's commentary on the *Mahāparinirvāṇa Sūtra*, which states that, along with various bones and teeth of the Buddha, there were also found in the ashes of his funeral pyre quantities of relics the size of mustard seeds, broken grains of rice or split peas, which resembled "jasmine buds, washed pearls, and [nuggets] of gold."[63] I would like to suggest that in the side-by-side presence of these two kinds of relics—"bones" and "beads"—we have a reflection of the coexistence of the impurity and impermanence of bodily relics, on the one hand, and of their purity and permanence, on the other.

FIGURE 8.2. Stone and pearl (?) beads mixed with earth, bone fragments (?) and probably ashes found with a coin of first century BCE inside a reliquary from a stupa in Swat, Pakistan, now at the Peshawar University Museum.

Photo: Wannaporn Rienjang.

Attitudinal Shifts

At the same time, it is possible to discern a shift from the first of these poles to the second. In Southeast Asia, for instance, it is thought that bits of bone from the funeral pyres of deceased saints may transmogrify into crystalline beads over time.[64] Similarly, in East Asia, bodily relics of the Buddha sometimes become precious wish-fulfilling jewels (*cintāmaṇi*),[65] as though the relics themselves were evolving from impurity to purity.

Recently, Johannes Bronkhorst has revisited the whole question of relics as bones of contention between Buddhist and Brahmanical cultures. He argues that the veneration of relics was part of the culture of what he calls "Greater Magadha," anciently centered in northeastern India—the tradition from which Buddhism emerged. This was distinct from and in competition with Brahmanical culture, located more to the west.[66] As the two cultural streams began to encounter and influence one another, Brahmanical concerns about impurity led to various modifications in Buddhist funerary practices, as well as to "a tendency to reinterpret or modify the worship of bodily relics."[67] Simply put, the perceived impurity of bones and ashes was mitigated by "hiding" them in stupas, or reliquaries, where they remained invisible to devotees. (The Buddha's famous tooth relic in Kandy, for example, is rarely actually seen, enshrined as it is in no less than seven nested reliquaries, which are themselves golden and bejeweled.)[68]

Bronkhorst goes on to argue that not only was there a shift from relic worship to stupa worship,[69] but that this further led to the very development of the cult of anthropomorphic images in Buddhism, as an alternative to relic veneration. Images, he says, "made it possible to venerate the memory of the last Buddha without being *soiled* by the cult of relics."[70] In other words, the worship of Buddha images was seen as a "purer" alternative than the veneration of relics, since they are connected to the living (not the dead) body of the Buddha. For this reason, he states, there was "a gradual decline in the presence of Buddhist relics in India."[71]

Images: Iconophobia and Iconophilia

Some support for Bronkhorst's view may perhaps be found in the archaeological record of Greater Gandhāra which shows, at Buddhist sites, a transition from relic shrines (some for the open-display of relics, some containing stupas) to image shrines.[72] Such a purificatory move, perhaps, is also reflected in another attitudinal shift: some early Buddhists chose to emphasize the Buddha's teaching (his body of doctrine—*dharmakāya*), over the remains of his physical body. Indeed, the notion of "dharma-relics" soon arose, and was, in some circles, privileged over that of bodily relics.[73]

Generally speaking, however, theorizing about the perceived impurity of relics and the mitigating purificatory appeal of images fails to take into account the fact that images themselves were not always seen in a positive light. As Robert DeCaroli has argued, there was considerable ambiguity in early Buddhist attitudes not only toward relics but toward images. At one end of the spectrum, there was a feeling of anxiety, or what he calls "image aversion," i.e., iconophobia. (This may be related to, but is also distinct from, the Buddhist aniconism touched on previously.) At the other end, there was wholehearted acceptance and affirmation of Buddha images, i.e., iconophilia.[74]

As DeCaroli points out, in the cultural context of ancient India, images of *human beings* were often associated with black magic and were thought of as "dangerous,"[75] while those of nonhumans were generally linked with local "regional" deities such as *yakṣas* and *nāgas*. Either way, their veneration generally aimed not at spiritual but at worldly (*laukika*) attainments.[76] This, at least initially, was not what Buddhists were all about. In this light, "depictions of a transcendent religious figure [such as the Buddha] might have been cause for both confusion and alarm."[77] There was thus a tendency for some Buddhists, at least, to eschew images.

According to DeCaroli, it took some time for the tradition to overcome this contextual heritage, but eventually, what he calls "image appeal" won out, as new forms of meditative and devotional worship (e.g., Buddha *bhakti*) arose, and as public attitudes toward embodiment and the use of images for proselytizing purposes changed, not only in Buddhism, but in other Indian religions.[78] There was, in other words, a shift in attitudes toward images from anxiety to affirmation, from iconophobia to iconophilia, paralleling perhaps the shift in views of relics discussed earlier. Even so, iconophobic (and anti-relic) inclinations continued to crop up at various times in the history of the Buddhist tradition, for example, in certain Chan/Zen contexts.[79]

Conclusion

We have seen in this chapter that, when we consider the Buddhist tradition as a whole throughout history (as opposed to the sentiments of individual devotees in particular times and places), we find mixed and ambiguous attitudes with regard to relics and images. We first addressed a basic question: Do both of these objects of devotion, as postmortem bodies of the Buddha, serve to make him singularly or multiply present? The evidence put forward suggests that they may do both. Similarly, in the second half of this chapter, we turned to another set of polarities, and we found that, in the light of certain cultural considerations, relics could be seen as pure and/or impure and images as causing anxiety and/or assurance. At the same time, and not disputing the acceptance that these paradoxical assertions persist at some levels in the tradition, we found a general shift in attitudes which sought out ways of foregrounding the purity of relics and the venerability of images.

Notes

1. Eugène Burnouf, *Introduction to the History of Indian Buddhism*, trans. Katia Buffetrille and Donald Lopez (Chicago: University of Chicago Press, 2010), 330.
2. Robert Sharf, "On the Allure of Buddhist Relics," *Representations* 66 (1999): 78.
3. I would like to thank Kay Rienjang and Kevin Trainor for preliminary comments on this essay.
4. Richard Gombrich, *Precept and Practice: Traditional Buddhism in the Rural Highlands of Ceylon* (Oxford: Clarendon Press, 1971), 106.
5. Cynthea J. Bogel, *With a Single Glance: Buddhist Icon and Early Mikkyō Vision* (Seattle: University of Washington Press, 2009), 40.
6. Bernard Faure, *Visions of Power: Imagining Medieval Japanese Buddhism*, trans. Phyllis Brooks (Princeton, NJ: Princeton University Press, 1996), 153.
7. See Louis Frédéric, *Buddhism*. Flammarion Iconographic Guides (Paris: Flammarion, 1995), 109-200.
8. See, e.g., Steven Collins, *Nirvana and Other Buddhist Felicities* (Cambridge: Cambridge University Press, 1998), 246–47; and Jacob Kinnard, *Imaging Wisdom: Seeing and Knowing in the Art of Indian Buddhism* (Delhi: Motilal Banarsidass, 1999), 25.
9. For a brief survey of Pali relic chronicles, see Stephen Berkwitz, *The History of the Buddha's Relic Shrine* (New York: Oxford University Press, 2007), 3–8; on the inauguratory role of images in various countries, see Robert Sharf and Elizabeth Sharf, *Living Images: Japanese Buddhist Icons in Context* (Stanford, CA: Stanford University Press, 2001), 2.

10. See, e.g., Gregory Schopen, *Bones, Stones, and Buddhist Monks* (Honolulu: University of Hawai'i Press, 1997), 154; John Kieschnick, *The Impact of Buddhism on Chinese Material Culture* (Princeton, NJ: Princeton University Press, 2003), 29–80; Sharf and Sharf, *Living Images*.
11. See, e.g., H. L. Seneviratne, *Rituals of the Kandyan State* (London: Cambridge University Press, 1978); Chen Jinhua, "*Sarīra* and Scepter: Empress Wu's Political Use of Buddhist Relics," *Journal of the International Association of Buddhist Studies* 25 (2002): 33–140; Brian Ruppert, *Jewel in the Ashes: Buddha Relics and Power in Early Medieval Japan* (Cambridge, MA: Harvard University Press, 2000); and, for a modern example: Patrice Ladwig, "Worshipping Relics and Animating Statues: Transformations of Buddhist Statecraft in Contemporary Laos," *Modern Asian Studies* 49, no. 6 (2015): 1875–902.
12. On *cetiya* (Sanskrit, *caitya*), see Peter Skilling, "Relics: The Heart of Buddhist Veneration," in *Relics and Relic Worship in Early Buddhism*, ed. Janice Stargardt (London: British Museum Press, 2018), 2; and the discussion in John S. Strong, *Relics of the Buddha* (Princeton, NJ: Princeton University Press, 2004),19.
13. Gombrich, *Precept and Practice*, 86; Kevin Trainor, *Relics, Ritual, and Representation in Buddhism: Rematerializing the Sri Lankan Theravāda Tradition* (Cambridge: Cambridge University Press, 1997), 89.
14. Gombrich, *Precept and Practice*, 115–16, slightly altered.
15. The origin of the Buddha image is still being debated. The earliest datable and labeled image in Gandhāra appears on a coin in the latter part of Kaniṣka's reign (127–150 CE). See Wannaporn Kay Rienjang, "Chronology of Stupa Relic Practices in Afghanistan and Dharmarajika, Pakistan, and Its Implications for the Rise of Popularity of the Image Cult," in *Gandhāra Connections 1: Problems of Chronology in Gandhāran Art*, ed. P. Stewart and W. Rienjang (Oxford: Archaeopress, 2018). More generally, see Robert DeCaroli, *Image Problems: The Origin and Development of the Buddha's Image in Early South Asia* (Seattle: University of Washington Press, 2015), 12–28.
16. Johannes Bronkhorst, *Buddhism in the Shadow of Brahmanism* (Leiden: E. J. Brill, 2011), 208.
17. Robert Brown, "God on Earth: The Walking Buddha in the Art of South and Southeast Asia." *Artibus Asiae* 50 (1990): 98.
18. Sharf, "Allure," 81.
19. Donald Swearer, *Becoming the Buddha: The Ritual of Image Consecration in Thailand* (Princeton, NJ: Princeton University Press, 2004), 77–172.
20. David Freedberg, *The Power of Images: Studies in the History and Theory of Response* (Chicago: University of Chicago Press, 1989), 97.
21. For the views of various scholars on this, see Swearer, *Becoming the Buddha*, 108–15.
22. For a listing of some of these, see Strong, *Relics*, 4–5.
23. I am inspired here by Michael Radich, "The Somatics of Liberation: Ideas about Embodiment in Buddhism from its Origins to the Fifth Century C.E.," PhD diss., Harvard University, 2007, 588–92. See also Michael Radich, *The* Mahāparinirvāṇa-mahāsūtra *and the Emergence of* Tathāgatagarbha *Doctrine* (Hamburg: Hamburg University Press, 2015), 114–15.
24. Kevin Trainor, "Introduction: *Pars pro toto*: On Comparing Relic Practices," *Numen* 57 (2010): 272.
25. Maurice Walshe, *Thus Have I Heard* (London: Wisdom Publications, 1987), 273–76.

26. An Yang-Gyu, *The Buddha's Last Days: Buddhaghosa's Commentary on the* Mahāparinibbāna Sutta (Oxford: Oxford University Press, 2003), 205. On singular and plural uses of the word "sarīra," see Schopen, *Bones*, 101, and Jonathan Silk, *Body Language: Indic śarīra and Chinese shèlì in the* Mahāparinirvāṇa-sūtra *and* Saddharmapuṇḍarīka (Tokyo: The International Institute for Buddhist Studies, 2006).
27. André Bareau, *Recherches sur la biographie du Buddha dans les sūtrapiṭaka et les vinayapiṭaka anciens: II. Les derniers mois, le parinirvāṇa et les funérailles* (Paris: Ecole Française d'Extrême-Orient, 1970–1971), 2:319–20.
28. Bronkhorst, *Buddhism in the Shadow*, 217. See also Jean Przyluski, "Le partage des reliques du Buddha," *Mélanges chinois et bouddhiques* 4 (1935–1936): 353; and John Strong, "Two Buddha Relic Traditions," *Religion Compass* 1, no. 3 (2007): 342.
29. Strong, *Relics*, 29, 44–48.
30. See Peter Skilling, "Cutting across Categories: The Ideology of Relics in Buddhism," *Annual Report of the International Institute for Advanced Buddhology at Soka University* 8 (2005): 298–99; and Justin Ritzinger and Marcus Bingenheimer, "Whole Body Relics and Chinese Buddhism: Previous Research and Historical Overview," *The Indian International Journal of Buddhist Studies / Bauddha adhyayana ki Bharatiya antarrastriya patrika* 7 (2006): 37–94.
31. Skilling, "Cutting across Categories," 299.
32. Silk, *Body Language*, 60–75; Strong, "Two Traditions," 344–45.
33. An, *Buddha's Last Days*, 113.
34. Strong, *Relics*, 125–36. It should be pointed out that in many sources, Ashoka does not get all of the relics from all of the Droṇa stupas, those at Rāmagrāma remaining uncollected, for a variety of reasons.
35. Strong, *Relics*, 221–28.
36. Trainor, "*Pars pro toto*," 270.
37. Skilling, "Relics," 3.
38. Silk, *Body Language*, 58; Ruppert, *Jewel*, 291 n1; Skilling, "Relics," 3.
39. See Ruppert, *Jewel*, 71, and Strong, *Relics*, 47–48.
40. A. K. Coomaraswamy, "The Origin of the Buddha Image," *Art Bulletin* 9 (1926–1927), 287–329; Alfred Foucher, *The Beginnings of Buddhist Art* (Paris: Paul Geuthner, 1917), 111–38.
41. For the views of various scholars on these and other questions, see Klemens Karlsson, *Face to Face with the Absent Buddha: The Formation of Buddhist Aniconic Art* (Uppsala: Uppsala University Library, 1999), 36–53; and DeCaroli, *Image Problems*, 24–43.
42. On this debate, see Rob Linrothe, "Inquiries into the Origin of the Buddha Image: A Review," *East and West* 43 (1993): 253.
43. Strong, *Relics*,152–57, 85–94.
44. Susan Huntington, *Lay Ritual in the Early Buddhist Art of India: More Evidence against the Aniconic Theory* (Amsterdam: Royal Netherlands Academy of Arts and Sciences, 2012), 24.
45. Trainor, "*Pars pro toto*," 166.
46. See Swearer, *Becoming the Buddha*, 14–24, for a survey of these.
47. Martha Carter, *The Mystery of the Udayana Buddha* (Naples: Istituto Universitario Orientale, 1990), 7; Alexander Soper, *Literary Evidence for Early Buddhist Art in China* (Ascona: Artibus Asiae, 1959), 261.
48. See Alexander Griswold, *Towards a History of Sukhodaya Art* (Bangkok: The National Museum 1967), 47.
49. Swearer, *Becoming the Buddha* 122–51, 94–107.

50. Foucher, *Beginnings*, 147–84.
51. Marsha Weidner, *Latter Days of the Law: Images of Chinese Buddhism 850–1850* (Lawrence: Spencer Museum of Art), 237, and plates 4 and 20.
52. Strong, *Relics*, 78; Trainor, *Relics*, 100.
53. Trainor, "*Pars pro toto*," 272.
54. Robert Brown, "Buddha Images," in *Encyclopedia of Buddhism*, ed. Robert Buswell (New York: Macmillan Reference, 2004), 1: 79–82.
55. See, e.g., Przyluski, "Partage," 353–54.
56. Silk, *Body Language*, 78.
57. Bernard Faure, *The Rhetoric of Immediacy: A Cultural Critique of Chan/Zen Buddhism* (Princeton, NJ: Princeton University Press, 1991), 148–78. See also Ritzinger and Bingenheimer, "Whole Body Relics."
58. Strong, *Relics*, 18.
59. Kieschnick, *Impact*, 51; see also Strong, *Relics*, xiv.
60. Strong, *Relics*, 176. For a nineteenth-century example of "Buddha rays" in Sri Lanka, see John Davy, *An Account of the Interior of Ceylon, and of Its Inhabitants* (London: Longman, 1821), 71.
61. Strong, *Relics*, 10–12; Faure, *Rhetoric*, 137–43; David Germano, "Living Relics of the Buddha(s) in Tibet," in *Embodying the Dharma: Buddhist Relic Veneration in Asia*, ed. David Germano and Kevin Trainor (Albany: State University of New York Press, 2004), 63; Wannaporn Rienjang, "Relic Cult Practice in Eastern Afghanistan with Comparison to Dharmarajika Pakistan," PhD diss., University of Cambridge, 2017, 130–45, 186–94, 232–41, 275–84.
62. Skilling, "Relics," 3
63. An, *Buddha's Last Days*, 206.
64. J. L. Taylor, *Forest Monks and the Nation State* (Singapore: Institute of Southeast Asian Studies, 1993), 175–77. See also Strong, *Relics*, 11.
65. Ruppert, *Jewel*, 130–35.
66. Bronkhorst, *Buddhism in the Shadow*, 194.
67. Bronkhorst, *Buddhism in the Shadow*, 200.
68. A. M. Hocart, *The Temple of the Tooth in Kandy* (London: Luzac, 1931), 1
69. Bronkhorst, *Buddhism in the Shadow*, 197. See also Rienjang, "Chronology."
70. Bronkhorst, *Buddhism in the Shadow*, 200, italics added.
71. Johannnes Bronkhorst, "Les reliques dans les religions de l'Inde," in *Indische Kultur im Kontext*, ed. Lars Göhler (Wiesbaden: Harrassowitz Velag, 2005), 72.
72. Kurt A. Behrendt, *The Buddhist Architecture of Gandhāra* (Leiden: E. J. Brill, 2004), 239–53.
73. Gregory Schopen, *Figments and Fragments of Mahāyāna Buddhism in India* (Honolulu: University of Hawai'i Press, 2005), 25–62. See also Strong, *Relics*, 8–10.
74. DeCaroli, *Image Problems*, 29
75. DeCaroli, *Image Problems*, 53.
76. DeCaroli, *Image Problems*, 53.
77. DeCaroli, *Image Problems*, 59.
78. DeCaroli, *Image Problems*, 116–45.
79. Faure, *Rhetoric*, 143–47; Kieschnick, *Impact*, 69–80; Fabio Rambelli, *Buddhist Materiality: A Cultural History of Objects in Japanese Buddhism* (Stanford, CA: Stanford University Press, 2007), 66–70.

Further Reading

Bronkhorst, Johannes. *Buddhism in the Shadow of Brahmanism*. Leiden: E. J. Brill, 2011.

DeCaroli, Robert. *Image Problems: The Origin and Development of the Buddha's Image in Early South Asia*. Seattle: University of Washington Press, 2015.

Germano, David, and Kevin Trainor, eds. *Embodying the Dharma: Buddhist Relic Veneration in Asia*. Albany: State University of New York Press, 2004.

Huntington, Susan. *Lay Ritual in the Early Buddhist Art of India: More Evidence against the Aniconic Theory*. Amsterdam: Royal Netherlands Academy of Arts and Sciences, 2012.

Kinnard, Jacob. *Imaging Wisdom: Seeing and Knowing in the Art of Indian Buddhism*. Delhi: Motilal Banarsidass, 1999.

Rotman, Andy. *Thus Have I Seen: Visualizing Faith in Early Indian Buddhism*. Oxford: Oxford University Press, 2008.

Ruppert, Brian. *Jewel in the Ashes: Buddha Relics and Power in Early Medieval Japan*. Cambridge, MA: Harvard University Press, 2000.

Schopen, Gregory. *Bones, Stones, and Buddhist Monks*. Honolulu: University of Hawai'i Press, 1997.

Sharf, Robert, and Elizabeth Sharf. *Living Images: Japanese Buddhist Icons in Context*. Stanford, CA: Stanford University Press, 2002.

Silk, Jonathan. *Body Language: Indic śarīra and Chinese shèlì in the Mahāparinirvāṇa-sūtra and Saddharmapuṇḍarīka*. Tokyo: The International Institute for Buddhist Studies, 2006.

Skilling, Peter. "Cutting across Categories: The Ideology of Relics in Buddhism," *Annual Report of the International Institute for Advanced Buddhology at Soka University* 8 (2005): 269–322.

Strong, John. "Two Buddha Relic Traditions." *Religion Compass* 1–3 (2007): 341–52.

Strong, John S. *Relics of the Buddha*. Princeton, NJ: Princeton University Press, 2004.

Swearer, Donald. *Becoming the Buddha: The Ritual of Image Consecration in Thailand*. Princeton, NJ: Princeton University Press, 2004.

Trainor, Kevin. *Relics, Ritual, and Representation in Buddhism: Rematerializing the Sri Lankan Theravāda Tradition*. Cambridge: Cambridge University Press, 1997.

CHAPTER 9

THE AGENCY OF IMAGES

SUSAN L. HUNTINGTON

Introduction

THE words in Buddhism's written texts and oral transmissions record and communicate the extensive body of Buddhist teachings. But simply knowing these words is insufficient for Buddhist attainment. The words must be put into action, as it is through the practices of the devotee that Buddhist aspirations are pursued and ultimately realized.

Underpinning many of the Buddhist practices through which the Buddhist teachings are activated are the material objects designed expressly for that purpose. At the pinnacle is the figural imagery that abounds in Buddhism. In particular, three-dimensional depictions of an array of beings fashioned of stone, metal, wood, lacquer, or other materials are given places of honor on altars, in shrines, and in outdoor settings and processions. Today, regardless of school and geography, images of Shakyamuni, the Buddha of this era, are a focus of devotion in Buddhist monasteries, usually residing in a hall specifically created for his veneration. In addition, depending on lineage and tradition, depictions of other buddhas, bodhisattvas, arhats, teachers, protectors, and other beings are so prevalent in Buddhist settings that such figurative representations are a hallmark of Buddhism.

Where Buddhism has traveled, so have images. Textual accounts concerning the introduction of Buddhism into China focus on images and, indeed, a Chinese term for Buddhism is *xiangjiao*, or religion of images. The official transfer of Buddhism from Korea to Japan in the sixth century is marked by King Song of Baekche's presentation of the famed Amida triad to Emperor Kinmei of Japan. The most sacred image in Tibet, the Jowo Shakyamuni at the Jokhang in Lhasa, is linked with the very foundation of Tibetan Buddhism. In Burma, the Mahāmuni Shakyamuni image (Figure 9.1) is reputed to have been created when Shakymuni visited the region to introduce his teachings and was

FIGURE 9.1. Mahāmuni Buddha with human devotees. Metal with an estimated twelve tons of gold leaf offerings on its surface. Mandalay, Myanmar (Burma).

Photo: Donald M. Stadtner.

enlivened by him personally. Like texts, images have been a core element in the transmission and practice of the Dharma.

The images under consideration are not intended as decoration, nor are they mere illustrations of texts or didactic tools.[1] They are reified as exalted beings whom the monastic and lay communities honor through their devotional and ritual practices. As the focus of many art-historical investigations, these works have been well studied for their style, date, and place in artistic evolution. But, until recently, their vital role in Buddhist praxis had largely been overlooked and even misunderstood. A spate of publications over the past few decades has changed this. Some studies focus on the magical or other powers attributed to individual images. Others document how images are transformed from works of art created by human hands into living beings through the process of consecration. The way has thus been paved to explore additional questions about images and their human devotees.

In this chapter, I describe some of the actions taken by Buddhists in their veneration of images.[2] Further, because image veneration is considered reciprocal, I explore the agency attributed to images, as well as the ways in which they are invested with the powers needed to make them participants in this interactive process. Finally, I attempt to reconstruct the early history of image veneration, asking whether or not this practice can be considered a core feature of Buddhism from its earliest days, or if it was added later to the spectrum of reverent activities.

Image Veneration Practices

In contrast to their presentation in their original contexts, Buddhist images are traditionally displayed in modern museums naked, stripped of their garments, jewelry, flowers, and other adornments presented by their devotees (Figure 9.2). To preserve them in the museum environment, images are often cleaned of the coats of smoke accrued from years of burning incense or oil lamps in their presence. Layers of paint offered as gifts over the centuries are also commonly removed to reveal the work as it appeared at the time it was created. Consecratory materials that had been inserted are extracted for study and preservation. Thus, the evidence of the image's life story and its use in context are frequently eradicated in favor of its conservation and display as a work of art, rather than as a living being. Matters of style, artistic quality, and iconography are more easily studied from these naked, cleaned figures, but these concerns are largely irrelevant to the devotee, to whom the image is a living being and must be treated as such. The value and meaning of the image in the Buddhist context rest less on whether the object is an artistic masterpiece and more on its efficacy in bestowing blessings.

Like many other Buddhist activities, image veneration is a means by which devotees can increase their accumulation of merit (*puṇya*). By showing honor and generosity to the being embodied in the image, the devotee performs a meritorious act. Devotees may ask for assistance on the Buddhist path and make requests for life-enhancing benefits, such as safe childbirth, good health, longevity, and material wealth. In other words, image veneration is intended to bring about results, whether implicit or explicit, supramundane or mundane. More precisely, veneration establishes a reciprocal relationship between the devotee and the image, which is understood to have its own agency to transform the devotee's life.

Even the everyday life of an image reveals something of this rich complexity. For example, images undergo rituals to assure their readiness to greet their devotees, just

FIGURE 9.2. Upper: Image of Shakyamuni Buddha in context at Samye Monastery, Tibet.

Photo: Eric Huntington.

Lower: Image of Vajravarahī/Vajrayoginī displayed in the *Circle of Bliss* exhibition at the Los Angeles County Museum of Art, 2002–2003. Metal. Central Tibet, ca. fifteenth century. Collection of the Los Angeles County Museum of Art.

Photo: John C. Huntington.

as humans might prepare for a special event by bathing, grooming, and dressing. In Burma, at around 4:30 each morning, the chief monk and his lay assistants prepare the renowned golden Mahāmuni image of Shakyamuni (Figure 9.1) for its day of visitors. The ceremony attracts large audiences, particularly on the full moon or other auspicious dates. Those who witness this morning ritual vow to share the merit gained with all sentient beings. During the hour-long ceremony, the face of the Buddha is cleaned with ointment and a paste of ground sandalwood, and an enormous toothbrush polishes its teeth, all while the *Mettā Sutta* is recited. The image is scented with sprays of perfume and is offered food, candles, flowers, and water.[3]

In some Buddhist traditions, images are considered a type of relic known as *uddeśika*. Not surprisingly, many image rituals are identical to the ways in which Buddhists venerate relics.[4] Some image practices show the type of hospitality one might proffer on an honored guest. Others, such as full body prostrations, demand substantial effort. The following are descriptions of some of the most common ways in which devotees venerate images. These particular practices originated in the Indic world, the homeland of Buddhism, and traveled to other regions with the spread of the Dharma.

Beholding (Skt. *darśan*)

Kūkai, the Japanese Buddhist luminary and founder of the esoteric Shingon school, claimed that "[w]ith a single glance [at the images] one becomes a Buddha."[5] While not all Buddhists might agree, the simple act of viewing an image is understood to confer merit, and even accidental glances are credited with bestowing benefit to a casual passerby. As one of the most fundamental Buddhist practices and a key element in image veneration, beholding is almost always the first act taken when a devotee encounters an image.

The term for this action is *darśan*, often translated simply as "seeing." More than just seeing, however, *darśan* is an interactive exchange in which the devotee "takes *darśan*" (*darśan lena*) and the image "gives *darśan*" (*darśan dena*). Although *darśan* may occur with objects other than images, particularly relics such as the Bodhi tree at Bodhgaya under which Shakyamuni attained enlightenment, image *darśan* offers the opportunity for a powerful visual dialogue when the eyes of the devotee and those of the image meet. The practice of painting, incising, or inlaying the image's eyes is typically part of the consecration practice through which the image is awakened, but it also gives prominence to the eyes and thus facilitates *darśan* (Figure 9.3).

The special role that *darśan* plays in Buddhism has led to practices that are specifically intended to foster these visual encounters, such as visiting a particular shrine or undertaking a pilgrimage to see a specific image or object. Some practices bring the sacred image to the devotee, such as festivals and ceremonies in which portable images are brought out into public spaces so that they can be viewed by throngs of devotees (Figure 9.4).

FIGURE 9.3. Upper portion of the main image of Shakyamuni Buddha, showing painted eyes, in the Mahābodhi shrine, Bodhgaya, India. The tenth-century stone figure has been repainted in recent times, including the eyes.

Photo: John C. Huntington.

Salutation and Paying Homage (Skt. *praṇām*)

While interacting with the image, devotees may bow, kneel, prostrate, and perform other gestures of respect and greeting. These reverential salutations are known as *praṇām*. The most common hand gesture is *añjali mudrā*, in which the palms are pressed together in front of the chest and the head is bowed in reverence (Figure 9.4). *Praṇām* can also be offered to respected persons, such as the Dalai Lama, a guru, or a senior member of one's family. As a gesture of respect, *praṇām* is one of the basic actions performed by Buddhists and is often combined with *darśan*. Likely predating its appearance in the surviving archaeological record, *añjali mudrā* is depicted in Buddhist art from the second century BCE onward, and endures as a widespread gesture of greeting among Buddhists today.

FIGURE 9.4. *Praṇām* to an image of Dīpaṅkara Buddha during the Samyak Mahādāna festival in 2003. Kathmandu, Nepal.

Photo: Dina Bangdel.

Offerings and Gift-Giving (Skt. *dāna*)

Making offerings to the image is a core feature of Buddhist devotion. The act demonstrates generosity. Items needed by the image as a living being, such as food and water, are provided every day. Other common contributions include flowers (Figure 9.5), incense, oil lamps, and perfumed water. Luxury items, such as elaborate clothing, jewelry, and gold leaf, are also proffered, particularly on special occasions.

Lustration (Skt. *abhiṣeka*)

Bathing an image with perfumed water, milk, or another liquid is a standard practice in Buddhist image veneration (Figure 9.6). At least two scriptures document this practice in China.[6] Another Chinese source, the Tang-era monk Yijing, devotes an entire chapter of his account of his travels across the Buddhist world to ritual bathing of the Buddha.

FIGURE 9.5. Image of Shakyamuni Buddha adorned with flowers. On platform of Shwesandaw Pagoda. Prome, Myanmar (Burma). Painted marble.

Photo: Donald M. Stadtner.

Yijing comments that the teachings of the Buddha are so profound that they are "beyond the understanding of an uncultivated mind, while the lavation of the holy image [of the Buddha] can be performed with benefit by all people."[7] He further claims that bathing an image of the Buddha regularly can "clear away the evil influence of our deeds caused by idleness"[8] and that to "bathe and venerate a holy image is an action that makes one meet a Buddha in all lives."[9]

Hospitality (Skt. *pūjā*)

Pūjā is a hospitality ritual in which the image is treated as an honored guest. Incorporating multiple elements, such as *darśan*, *praṇām*, offerings, and lustration, into a complex ceremony, a typical *pūjā* involves prayers and invocations, music, burning of incense, lighting of lamps, lustration, and offerings of flowers and foods. A full *pūjā* incorporates the senses of touch, sight, sound, smell, and taste. *Pūjā*s remain an important component of practice throughout the Buddhist world today and are performed regularly at home shrines and in monasteries. More elaborate *pūjā*s are conducted for important occasions and purposes.

FIGURE 9.6. Monk lustrating an image of Shakyamuni Buddha. On platform of Shwesandaw Pagoda. Prome, Myanmar (Burma). Painted marble.

Photo: Donald M. Stadtner.

Clockwise Circumambulation (Skt. *pradakṣiṇa*)

One of Buddhism's most characteristic rituals is *pradakṣiṇa*, that is, clockwise circumambulation around an esteemed relic, image, person, or object. *Pradakṣiṇa* is depicted in the earliest known Buddhist relief carvings from India, which date from the second century BCE, and continues as a major practice to the present day. An entire scripture in Chinese is devoted to circumambulation.[10] Architecture is often designed to allow *pradakṣiṇa*. For example, an image may be set forward from a wall so that devotees have space to walk around it. Even in cave monuments, where the artistic challenge to provide an ambulatory passage entails the laborious extraction of stone matrix from behind the image, passageways were created to enable devotees to perform circumambulation. The mid-sixth century Cave 7 at Aurangabad, India, for example, includes a circumambulatory passage encompassing the entire central shrine and the seated Buddha figure contained within (Figure 9.7).

FIGURE 9.7. Upper: Plan of Cave 7 at Aurangabad, India, showing ambulatory passage around a shrine containing a Buddha image. Lower: Buddha image in Cave 7 shrine at Aurangabad, India, ca. mid-sixth century.

Drawing and photo by John C. Huntington.

The Agency of Images

Throughout the Buddhist world, images are credited with the agency to listen, speak, walk, and act. They can shed tears, sweat, emit light, levitate, perform miracles, and provide blessings. If provoked, they can exact retribution. Their powers are recounted in the many narratives that have endured over Buddhism's lengthy history, and there are doubtless myriad additional examples that are not preserved or known.

The ability to listen is an important power attributed to images of Shakyamuni. Thus, a variety of regular services and activities take place in the main image hall at monasteries, where the enlivened image of Shakyamuni presides. The image may hear individual requests and listen to the recitation of texts and chanting by assemblies of devotees. Taking an oath in front of an image of Shakyamuni is considered by Burmese Theravadins to be "a sacred act that attests to the truth of this affirmation."[11] Actions that include spoken words, such as taking refuge vows[12] or the bodhisattva vow,[13] are undertaken in the presence of the Buddha image.

The abilities attributed to images of Shakyamuni are extensions of the miraculous powers he himself possessed. The very first replicas of Shakyamuni, reputedly created during his lifetime, are credited with agency. Most famous are the images attributed to the patronage of kings Prasenajit and Udāyana, both contemporaries and followers of the Buddha. Not mere statues, these figures were full surrogates for Shakyamuni, intended to serve in his stead during his short-term absences while he was still alive and in perpetuity after his death. Both had agency from the moment of their creation and did not require consecration; both were validated by Shakyamuni himself as worthy stand-ins during his life and successors who would serve as his proxies after his nirvana. The renowned Burmese Mahāmuni image (Figure 9.1) is also reputed to have been created during Shakyamuni's lifetime and enlivened by him personally.[14] The image is described as a younger brother and even a twin whom the Buddha endowed with his own supernatural powers. Shakyamuni himself declared that the image would exist for five thousand years after he entered nirvana.[15] Burmese narratives ascribe nine different miracles to the Mahāmuni Buddha and record that at one time it was able to speak, act as an advisor to kings, and preach sermons.[16]

The powers attributed to images have led to their use as palladia by Buddhist kings. The Emerald Buddha in Bangkok is just one well-known example. Buddhist history records many instances of kings coveting the talismanic powers of images belonging to another monarch and, by capturing the rival's palladia, weakening their competitor and increasing their own power. Images also serve throughout the Buddhist world as guardians and overseers of local communities. In Thailand, for example, every town has a Buddha image that protects the people and place and participates in the social world of its devotees.[17]

While many images are readily accessible to devotees for devotional interactions in the course of their daily lives, some have restricted availability. In Japan, at least fifty images have been identified as secret. These images are available only occasionally, such as once or twice a month, once or twice a year, or even on a cycle of many years.[18] Some are available only on special occasions, and others are never accessible to ordinary devotees. The viewing of such works after long intervals between showings makes them occasions of great rarity and benefit to those who have the good fortune to see them.

Although the Japanese term for secret Buddha (*hibutsu*) did not appear until the thirteenth century, restricted access to images likely occurred earlier, not only in Japan but elsewhere, particularly among esoteric schools. Throughout the Himalayan region and Mongolia, images of wrathful protectors are customarily covered by a cloth to keep them fully or partially hidden. In Nepal, although the Shakyamuni Buddha in the main shrine is accessible to all, each monastery also has a secret shrine that houses an image of Cakrasaṃvara or another tantric "chosen" deity (*iṣṭadevatā*) affiliated with the founding and lineage of the monastery. Access to this shrine and its image is restricted to members of the sangha who have taken the highest initiations and who perform the mandatory rituals out of the public eye.

Creating Agency: From Sculpture to Living Being

The creation of images is in itself a meritorious practice. The Chinese monk Yijing noted that if "a man makes an image even as small as a grain of barley . . . he will obtain special good causes as limitless as the seven seas, and his good rewards will last as long as four rebirths."[19] Image-making merit is also described in Chinese Buddhist texts, such as the *Scripture on the Production of Buddha Images* and the later *Mahāyāna Scripture on the Merit Gained through the Production of Images.*[20] Thai texts on Buddha image creation include the *Manual for Buddha Image Making* and the *Meritorious Blessing for Making Buddha Images.*[21] The latter relates the benefit gained by creating images of Shakyamuni Buddha according to the material out of which the work is fashioned, with the greatest merit, that of blessings for seventy eons, accruing from images made of sandalwood or the wood of the Bodhi tree.[22] In Burma, the most honored title, *hpaya*, is proffered only on those donors who sponsor the creation of an image.[23]

Images with inherent agency, such as those attributed to kings Prasenajit and Udāyana, or those considered self-arisen (*svayambhū*), require no special actions to enliven them. However, a Buddhist image created by human hands must undergo a hallowing process. At some time after the artists create the figure that will serve as the container, the living entity is invited to enter. One Tibetan source likens this process to the manner in which buddhas enter the womb of Māyādevī.[24] The ritual generally spans several days, and, in Tibet, ends with the request for the entity to remain in the image.[25] To maximize the efficacy, consecratory rituals occur on specifically chosen auspicious dates that may be many months after the finishing touches have been completed by the artists. Some moments in the consecration process are even timed to specific times of day. Further, the consecration must be performed perfectly by a ritual master of high attainment. Images are regularly reconsecrated to reinforce their powers and, if an image is going to be moved to a new location or needs restoration, it must be deconsecrated by asking the residing entity to move to a temporary receptacle.

Image consecration occurs in every geographic region where Buddhism has spread and across the broad categories of Buddhist schools. The methods vary. A pervasive consecratory practice in the Himalayas, Mongolia, and East Asia involves inserting objects into the base (Figure 9.8) or a cavity in the head or body of the figure (Figure 9.9). Helmut Brinker calls these "cache images."[26] Because the objects inserted into such images are considered relics, cache images are by nature a form of reliquary. That the practice of inserting objects was known in India as early as the seventh century is suggested by a single known example with a sealed base.[27] Most commonly, cache images contain texts, but they may also hold bodily relics, such as a tooth, a hair, a kidney stone, or fragment of bone, as well as other precious objects, such as coins, gemstones, Bodhi tree leaves, and even smaller images. The most well-studied cache image is the renowned wooden Shakyamuni dated in a Japanese era equivalent to 985 in the Seiryōji in Kyoto, Japan (Figure 9.10), which contained an extensive array of texts and other objects, as well as a heart, stomach, lung, liver, and intestines made of silk.[28] After the objects have been inserted into cache images, the openings are sealed with a base plate or panel.

A dramatic example of what might be considered a cache image recently came to light through CT imaging technology that revealed the mummified body of a Chinese monk encased in a human-created sculpture (Figure 9.11).[29] The inner organs had been removed and replaced with texts written on paper. The monk, possibly an individual named Liuquan who died around 1100 CE, practiced self-mummification by following a special body-preserving diet, allowing his body to become desiccated and finally undergo oxygen deprivation until death, all while engaged in deep meditation. Practitioners of self-mummification are often considered to be buddhas, but it is unknown whether encasement of their remains in a sculpted receptacle was commonplace. That becoming a statue was considered a goal in some Buddhist traditions, however, is suggested in Japan by an elaborate ritual known as a Welcoming Ceremony whereby mask-wearing humans temporarily take the form of statues.[30]

Enlivening rituals commonly incorporate the "*dharma* verse relic," that is, the verse on dependent origination (*ye dharmā hetu . . .*). The verse was routinely incised or stamped onto images made during the Pāla-period in eastern India and Bangladesh (Figure 9.12). In Tibet, a mirror on which the verse is written in saffron is placed atop

FIGURE 9.8. Image of Shakyamuni Buddha showing base both closed and open with inserted texts. Tibet, ca. eighteenth century. Gilded bronze. Private collection.

Photo: John C. Huntington.

grains or flowers. The grains or flowers absorb the reflection of the verse and are then scattered on the object being consecrated.[31]

Perhaps the most universal consecration practice is the ceremony in which the eyes of the image, particularly the pupils, are painted, incised, inlaid, or otherwise "opened" to awaken the image (Figure 9.3). In 752, the eyes of the great Daibutsu image at the Tōdaiji in Nara, Japan were opened in an elaborate event organized by Empress Kōken and attended by the entire Japanese court, along with dignitaries from China and India. In Sri Lanka, the newly opened eyes are considered so powerful that the artist must paint the eyes while looking into a mirror, rather than directly at the image.[32] The eye-opening is commonly the final element of the consecration process, at which time the image of Shakyamuni is considered awakened in the very manner that Shakyamuni was awakened under the Bodhi tree. Thus, like Shakyamuni himself, the image has attained perfect knowledge and the resultant powers.

It is impossible to determine in every case whether an image has been consecrated simply by examining it. Sometimes, the evidence of consecration has been lost over time, as is often the case with painted details. Some consecration methods leave no visible

FIGURE 9.9. Left: Sculpture of Shakyamuni Buddha. Right: X-ray of side view of image showing wooden spine and clay image inside. The base of the image contains rolled up paper texts. Painted and gilded clay. Private collection. Tibet, ca. eighteenth century.

Photo: John C. Huntington.

mark on the image. In Sri Lanka, consecration includes depositing a compartmented stone reliquary called a *yantragala* under an image before it is installed.[33] If the figure is removed from its original context, it bears no evidence of the consecration. A Tibetan consecration practice uses a web of strings to unite the image with other sanctified objects and even the ritual master. After the ceremony, the strings are removed, leaving no trace of the ritual on the image. In Burma and Thailand, the Shakyamuni image is invested with the full knowledge of his past and final lives and the totality of his teachings through extensive recitations by monks during the consecration.[34] Although leaving no mark, through this ceremony, the *dhammakāya*, that is, the sum of the Buddha's teachings, enters into the image, and the image embodies the omniscience and powers of the Buddha.[35]

A consecrated image is differentiated from one that has not undergone the process. In Japan, the term "shadow image" designates an unconsecrated image.[36] But within

FIGURE 9.10. Front and back views of Udāyana-type Shakyamuni Buddha image. Seiryōji, Kyoto, Japan. Wood. Dated equivalent to 985 CE.

Photos after Gregory Henderson and Leon Hurvitz, "The Buddha of Seiryōji: New Finds and New Theory," *Artibus Asiae* 19, no. 1 (1956): pls. 1 and 3. Reproduced with permission of Amy E. McNair.

Buddhist discourse, views differ on whether a consecrated image, or an image at all, can be considered truly alive and, if so, in what ways. At one end of the spectrum is the famed Chan story of the monk from Danxia who burns a wooden image of the Buddha as firewood, explaining that it was in reality only a piece of wood. At the other end,

FIGURE 9.11. Left: Mummified monk, possibly Liuquan, made into a sculpture. Right: CT scan of the image. China, ca. 1100.

Photos: M. Elsevier Stokmans.

one Japanese source holds that the Buddha is already present in the piece of wood, and creating the image is only a matter of freeing the form from the matrix.[37] Even more extreme, the fourteenth-century Japanese thinker Gōhō proposes that only images have actual existence and that the human Buddhas are just appearances.[38] A more nuanced view is offered in an inscription from India that states that the human monks dwell in the monastery, whereas the Buddha image was "established," that is, consecrated.[39] Some Buddhist thinkers contend that consecration might not even be necessary to enliven an image, although it provides merit to the patron and assists those newly embarking on the Buddhist path. One Tibetan writer notes that the entire universe is pervaded by the wisdom-essence of the body, speech, and mind of all buddhas and therefore there is nothing to invite from the outside into the image.[40]

The relationship between the image and the being it represents is an ongoing topic among Buddhist teachers and modern scholars alike. Later Buddhist traditions talk about the relationship between the image and the Buddha himself in terms of the Buddha body (*kāya*) systems. Multiple sources regard the image as an emanation body (*nirmāṇakāya*), the form that the Buddha takes in order to offer his teachings to his followers. Emanation bodies are authoritative duplicates of the Buddha, comparable to the replicas Shakyamuni made of himself during his performance of the Miracle at

FIGURE 9.12. Buddha image with back view showing seal impressed with verse on dependent origination. Pāla period. Kurkihar, India, ca. late ninth or early tenth century. Metal. Patna Museum.

Photo: John C. Huntington.

Śrāvasti. In Tantra, consecrated images are considered an emanation body because the consecration process parallels that by which a Buddha may be emanated into the world of samsara.[41] Within this framework, an image of the Buddha is not simply a representation but, rather, is made of the very thing it represents. The image is the Buddha. It is the signified and not the signifier.

In contrast, the Pāli commentarial literature explains that images were made to fill the void left by the absent Buddha.[42] Yijing observes that, although he is no longer in the world, Shakyamuni's image still exists and should be treated as if he were still in the world.[43] One modern writer proposes that on "the most basic level, the Buddha's disciples wish to be in the Master's presence in order to hear the dharma directly from him."[44] Thus, although Shakyamuni is gone, to devotees living after his nirvana, his image serves in his stead.

Regardless of whether the image is the same as the Buddha or even whether it contains a life force, various writers state that venerating the image is the same as venerating the

Buddha. At the least, consecrated receptacles provide a locus for human interaction, thereby assisting devotees on the Buddhist path.

Originals and Replicas

In modern Western culture, a work of art that is a copy of another is considered creatively flawed. If virtually indistinguishable from the original, it might be condemned as a forgery. In contrast, many of the most important Buddhist images are prized as faithful replicas of a revered original.

The most famous portrait lineage derives from the image of Shakyamuni attributed to King Udāyana, the most renowned example of which is the sculpture at the Seiryōji in Japan (Figure 9.10). There are several accounts of this image. The core narrative is that King Udāyana had the original image created while the Buddha was in Trāyastriṁśa Heaven preaching Abhidharma to his deceased mother. The king, distraught at being unable to see the Buddha, commissioned thirty-two craftsmen to create an exact likeness. With a piece of prized sandalwood, the artisans were transported to the heaven where they could see the Buddha and thereby create a perfect rendering. Brought back to earth and already bestowed with agency, the image greeted the Buddha on his return from Trāyastriṁśa, whereby the Buddha predicted the role of the image in spreading his teachings after his death.

According to some accounts, the original remained in India and only copies made their way to other regions. The image that is now at the Seiryōji in Japan was brought from China by the pilgrim Chōnen in 986; however, there is debate regarding whether that image is a duplicate of the one in China or even the original sculpture made in Trāyastriṁśa that had made its way from India to China. Regardless, the Seiryōji image has become the center of a cult and has spawned some one hundred replicas that have also become the focus of veneration in their own settings.

Even prior to the likely creation of the Seiryōji image in the tenth century, the Udāyana-type, with its distinctive anatomy and drapery, is well known in Buddhist art. Based on style, the likely prototype represents the artistic Indian idiom of Mathura around the fifth century, which, in turn, derives from the artistic styles of Gandhara during the second and third centuries.

Although scholars commonly interpret such similar-looking Buddhist images as types representing a particular style or school of art, the striking sameness indicates faithfulness to a particular model. However, after consecration, each is an individual who will have a unique life story. Numerous examples in painting and sculpture that might be interpreted as generic images are in fact representations of specific individuals. An eleventh-century Nepali manuscript, for example, bears depictions of numerous renowned images, along with labels identifying them as particular individuals (Figure 9.13).

FIGURE 9.13. Painting of Gandhara Lokanātha image being venerated by devotees. Palm-leaf manuscript. Nepal. Dated equivalent to 1015 CE. Cambridge University Library, MS Add.1643, fol. 89.

Photo: John C. Huntington.

Origins of Image Veneration

Figural images are a defining feature of Buddhism. Images of Shakyamuni are ubiquitous in Buddhism today, and representations of other important beings are pervasive depending on the specific teaching lineage. But did Buddhists use figurative images from the start? If not, when, where, and why did this now universal phenomenon begin? Were images enlivened at the outset? If not, when, where, and why might this development have occurred?

Ideally, we might have a "first" image and documents, such as inscriptions or texts, that provide incontrovertible answers to these important questions. Rather than presenting a single "first" image or even a cluster of early images, however, the archaeological record documents a burst of image-making activity in the Indic region around the first and second centuries CE—some five hundred years after the Buddha lived—with thousands of Buddha images simultaneously produced in locations spanning South Asia from southeastern India to Pakistan. Traditional scholarship has vigorously debated which of these disparate centers invented the Buddha image. However, I suggest that the simultaneity of the appearances in the archaeological record is the more noteworthy phenomenon. Instead of documenting the invention of the Buddha image, the sudden appearance of Buddha imagery in multiple places likely reflects the translation of forms from ephemeral media, such as wood, into the enduring stone medium. Indeed, when significant archaeological evidence emerges around the turn of the Common Era, it is not only images of Shakyamuni that appear, but a host of other Buddhist beings, including other buddhas and bodhisattvas, as well as Jain and Hindu images.[45] The invention of all of these fully developed portrayals simultaneously seems unlikely; they must have evolved over time prior to their visibility in the stone record. Further, the mature regional styles and striking iconographic standardization exhibited all at once by Buddhist images from the disparate schools of Gandhara, the Mathura region, and Andhra Pradesh suggest a considerable period of development prior to the translation of forms into stone. The standardized vocabulary of postures, hand gestures, and bodily marks of Buddhist figures implies an extensive period of evolution and perhaps even a common source in ephemeral materials. A parallel translation from wood to stone is clear in the case of architecture since the earliest stone monuments are literal copies of their wooden prototypes.[46] The vast majority of examples likely perished over time, although some might still await discovery. Therefore, the lack of earlier figurative representations is likely due to archaeological lacunae rather than a deliberate choice made by Buddhist adherents.

The lack of early example has led scholars to hypothesize that early Buddhists deliberately avoided creating images of Shakyamuni. Exhaustive searches of Buddhist literature, however, have failed to discover a prohibition or even constraints on creating images of him. Rather than looking for reasons why Buddhists might *not* have used imagery, I propose that it is more productive to understand why they did. The evidence presented in this chapter for the pervasive use of images as a core feature of Buddhism casts doubt on whether there was ever a deliberate anti-image stance. If such a position existed—and indeed one that lasted half a millennium—it seems unimaginable that the views about image use could have been so completely and irrevocably overturned without debate or schisms. Therefore, perhaps more critical than the "when" and "where" questions that have dominated scholarship on the origin of the Buddha image since the nineteenth century, asking "why" and "how" Buddhists use images reveals answers that are more consistent with Buddhist practice.

Because evidence of veneration and vivification practices appear at the very same time that Buddha images emerge in the archaeological record, the prevailing assumption that the Buddha image was a simple artistic invention can be dismissed. That images were venerated is documented in the art itself. A second-century carving from Amaravati,

India, shows a standing Buddha image in an architectural niche accompanied by devotees who perform the *añjali mudrā* gesture of respect that is still ubiquitous in Buddhist practice today (Figure 9.14). And in the Gandhara region, the receptacles atop the heads of Buddha images likely held consecratory insertions.[47] Further, because some methods of consecration leave no visible mark, image enlivenment may have been

FIGURE 9.14. Detail of a relief sculpture showing a statue of a Buddha being venerated by devotees. Amaravati, India, ca. second century. Stone. British Museum.

Photo: John C. Huntington.

more widespread than suggested by any visible method. The simultaneous emergence of Buddha images, proof of their veneration, and evidence implying their consecration, although not in a single example, suggest that the extensive image practices evident in later Buddhism were established during the period prior to their appearance in the known stone record.

Additional evidence supporting an early date for Buddha images comes from the architectural record. Although any separately installed sculptures have long ago vanished, a number of stone halls at early Indian Buddhist monastic sites appear to have locations for images.[48] For example, Cave 8 at Ajanta in western India dating from the second century BCE includes a shrine at the center rear with a platform upon which a Buddha image may have been installed (Figure 9.15). The conception is identical to later fifth-century caves at the site that house permanent Buddha images carved of the stone matrix.

The terminology used for Buddha image halls further suggests an early date for the use of images and, moreover, requires a reformulation of how the image hall and therefore the Buddha image have been viewed in modern scholarship. Buddhist texts use the name *gandhakuṭī*, or "fragrant hall," to describe any residence of the Buddha, particularly his home at the Jetavana monastery, where he spent nineteen rainy seasons and

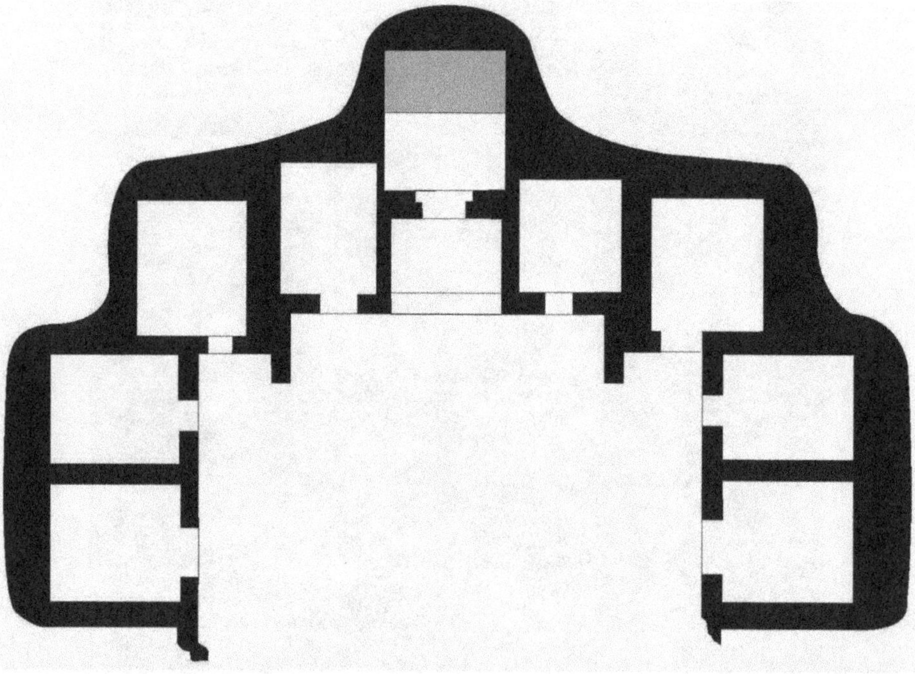

FIGURE 9.15. Ground plan of Cave 8 at Ajanta, India, showing shrine at the rear with a platform upon which a Buddha image could be placed. Ca. second-century BCE.

Drawing: John C. Huntington.

the later years of his life. As early as the second century BCE, the term is used to label a building as the Buddha's residence in a depiction of the Jetavana from Bharhut, India.[49]

More importantly, the term *gandhakuṭī*, or its local equivalent, traveled with Buddha imagery and is used to designate the main Shakyamuni Buddha hall at monasteries throughout Asia.[50] The ubiquitous Buddha image hall is thus clearly conceived not as a temple, as is so commonly thought, but rather as the Buddha's abode. Therefore, just as Shakyamuni resided in the *gandhakuṭī* during his lifetime, his enlivened image, serving as his proxy, dwells in the Shakyamuni image hall at monasteries throughout the world. The Pāli *Samantapāsadikā* commentaries explain this relationship, noting that when he was alive the Buddha was head of the sangha, but now it is an image or reliquary that serves in his stead.[51] Inscriptions from India indicate that these proxies were considered to be alive and residing in the perfumed chamber.[52] Although these sources date from many centuries after the Buddha's lifetime, they do not record a reformulation of the Buddha image or the hall as a *gandhakuṭī* at that time. Instead, they describe this information in a matter-of-fact way, suggesting an ongoing tradition. Indeed, if such a major reconceptualization had occurred, it would surely have been mentioned or have been visible in the artistic and architectural record. In other words, Buddhist monasteries throughout the Buddhist world and over the centuries have been graced with the Buddha's living presence, in his residence, in perpetuity.

The date at which Buddha images were first animated is unknown. However, a date soon after his lifetime can be surmised. Although we do not know where image animation originated or how it spread, it is well documented among the Egyptians and Mesopotamians and, more importantly, contemporary with the Buddha among the Greeks.[53] In the Indic world, representations of various beings in the period prior to the known emergence of Buddhist imagery were also considered to have agency. However, evidence of image animation in the Indic world has been used by modern scholars to conjecture that the early Buddhists feared such powers and therefore avoided creating images of Shakyamuni entirely.[54] In contrast, I propose that the desire to maintain the Buddha's living presence and, indeed, harness these very powers led to actions that may have endowed even his early images with agency. In this way, installed in his residence, the Buddha continued to preside over the monastic community and to be available as an active, living being to his devotees even after his nirvana.

Concluding Comments

That images are considered to have agency in Buddhism is undisputed. Not simply works of art, vivified images are animated beings with whom Buddhist devotees interact on a daily basis. As head of the monastic community even after his nirvana, Shakyamuni lives on in his images, perpetuating his teachings, overseeing the activities of the sangha, and offering assistance to his followers. Veneration of other Buddhist beings in the form of their images is also central to the teachings of a variety of traditions. Such images can be reifications of concepts so abstract that the forms they take in the world of samsara provide a first step toward grasping their significance. Acts of devotion, such as taking *darśan* and providing the image with offerings, are concrete ways that devotees gain merit and cultivate the virtues and mindset necessary for attainment. As with all Buddhist practices, however, these acts must transcend the outer choreography and arise from the correct inner intention. Only then can these practices be expected to yield the desired response from the image.

Notes

1. This essay does not consider figurative imagery in narrative scenes.
2. Images used for other purposes, such as meditation and visualization, are not discussed here as they are not veneration practices per se.
3. Juliane Schober, "In the Presence of the Buddha: Ritual Veneration of the Burmese Mahāmuni Image," in *Sacred Biography in the Buddhist Traditions of South and Southeast Asia*, ed. Juliane Schober (Honolulu: University of Hawaiʻi Press, 1997), 259–88; 264.
4. See Susan L. Huntington, *Lay Ritual in the Early Buddhist Art of India: More Evidence against the Aniconic Theory* (Amsterdam: Royal Netherlands Academy of Arts and Sciences, 2012).
5. Cynthea J. Bogel, *With a Single Glance: Buddhist Icon and Early Mikkyō Vision* (Seattle and London: University of Washington Press, 2009), 3.
6. Robert H. Sharf, "The Scripture on the Production of Buddha Images," in *Religions of China in Practice*, ed. Donald S. Lopez, Jr. (Princeton, NJ: Princeton University Press, 1996), 261–67; 262.
7. Śramaṇa Yijing, *A Record of the Inner Law Sent Home from the South Seas*, trans. Li Rongxi (Berkeley: Numata Center for Buddhist Translation and Research, 2000), 135.
8. Yijing, *Record*, 135.
9. Yijing, *Record*, 138.
10. Sharf, "Scripture," 262.
11. Schober, "Presence," 275.
12. Schober, "Presence," 264.
13. Eric Huntington, "Ritual Structure and Material Culture in the *Guide to Bodhisattva Practice*," in *Readings of Śāntideva's Guide to Bodhisattva Practice* (*Bodhicaryāvatāra*), ed. Jonathan C. Gold and Douglas S. Duckworth, (New York: Columbia University Press, 2019), 132–45; 138.
14. For more on this image, see Schober, "Presence," 259–88; Angela S. Chiu, *The Buddha in Lanna: Art, Lineage, Power, and Place in Northern Thailand* (Honolulu: University of Hawaiʻi Press, 2017), 91–96; and Donald M. Stadtner, *Sacred Sites of Burma. Myth and Folklore in an Evolving Spiritual Realm* (Bangkok: River Books, 2011), 260–75.
15. Schober, "Presence," 268.
16. Schober, "Presence," 269.
17. Chiu, *Buddha*, 1.
18. Summarized from Sarah J. Horton, *Living Buddhist Statues in Early Medieval and Modern Japan* (New York: Palgrave Macmillan, 2007), chapter 6, especially 156.
19. Yijing, *Record*, 138.

20. Sharf, "Scripture," 262.
21. Chiu, *Buddha*, 172–73.
22. Donald S. Lopez, Jr., *From Stone to Flesh: A Short History of the Buddha* (Chicago and London: University of Chicago Press, 2013), 43.
23. Schober, "Presence," 276–77.
24. Yael Bentor, *Consecration of Images and Stūpas in Indo-Tibetan Tantric Buddhism* (Leiden: E. J. Brill, 1996), xx, 19.
25. Bentor, *Consecration*, 5.
26. Helmut Brinker, *Secrets of the Sacred: Empowering Buddhist Images in Clear, in Code, and in Cache* (Lawrence and Seattle: University of Kansas, Spencer Museum of Art, in association with University of Washington Press, 2011), 7.
27. R. D. Banerji, *Eastern Indian School of Mediaeval Sculpture* (Delhi: Manager of Publications, 1933), 131 and pl. LXVIc.
28. For the first description of the contents, see Gregory Henderson and Leon Hurvitz, "The Buddha of Seiryōji: New Finds and New Theory," *Artibus Asiae* 19, no. 1 (1956): 4–55.
29. The 2015 discovery was widely publicized in news releases, such as https://www.history.com/news/ct-scan-reveals-mummified-monk-inside-ancient-buddha-statue.
30. Horton, *Living Buddhist Statues*, 50.
31. Bentor, *Consecration*, 115.
32. Richard Gombrich, "The Consecration of a Buddhist Image," *Journal of Asian Studies* 26, no. 1 (November 1966): 24–26.
33. Senake Bandaranayake, *Sinhalese Monastic Architecture* (Leiden: E. J. Brill, 1974), 100.
34. For examples, see Schober, "Presence," 275–76; Donald K. Swearer, *Becoming the Buddha: The Ritual of Image Consecration in Thailand* (Princeton, NJ: Princeton University Press, 2004), 96–97.
35. Schober, "Presence," 275.
36. Brinker, *Secrets*, 13–14.
37. Fabio Rambelli, *Buddhist Materiality: A Cultural History of Objects in Japanese Buddhism* (Stanford, CA: Stanford University Press, 2007), 85.
38. Rambelli, *Buddhist Materiality*, 81.
39. Gregory Schopen, "The Buddha as an Owner of Property and Permanent Resident in Medieval Indian Monasteries," *Journal of Indian Philosophy* 18, no. 3 (1990): 187. Schopen translates *pratiṣṭ[h]āpita* as "established," but the term denotes consecration.
40. Bentor, *Consecration*, 13–14.
41. Bentor, *Consecration*, 5.
42. Jacob N. Kinnard, "The Field of the Buddha's Presence," in *Embodying the Dharma: Buddhist Relic Veneration in Asia*, ed. David Germano and Kevin Trainor (Albany: State University of New York Press, 2004), 125.
43. Yijing, *Record*, 135.
44. Kinnard, "Field," 122.
45. A few large-scale stone sculptures from India, mainly representing nature deities, are known from the period prior to the explosion of stone carving.
46. For example, see Susan L. Huntington, with contributions by John C. Huntington, *Art of Ancient India* (New York and Tokyo: Weatherhill, 1985), figs. 5.21 and 5.22.
47. Juhyung Rhi, "Relics, and Jewels: The Assimilation of Images in the Buddhist Relic Cult of Gandhāra: Or Vice Versa," *Artibus Asiae* 65, no. 2 (2005): 169–211.

48. Susan L. Huntington, "The Buddha and the Perfumed Hall: Architectural Evidence for the Early Origin of the Buddha Image," in *Buddhist Buildings Past and Present* [working title], ed. Susan L. Huntington (forthcoming, University of Bonn).
49. Huntington, *Art of Ancient India*, fig. 5.16.
50. Huntington, "Buddha and the Perfumed Hall."
51. Kinnard, "Field," 131.
52. Schopen, "Buddha as an Owner," 196.
53. See Deborah Tarn Steiner, *Images in Mind: Statues in Archaic and Classical Greek Literature and Thought* (Princeton, NJ: Princeton University Press, 2001); Sarah Iles Johnston, "Animating Statues: A Case Study in Ritual," *Arethusa* 41, no. 3 (Fall 2008): 445–77.
54. Robert DeCaroli, *Image Problems: The Origin and Development of the Buddha's Image in Early South Asia* (Seattle and London: University of Washington Press, 2015), 28.

Further Reading

Davis, Richard H. *Images, Miracles, and Authority in Asian Religious Traditions*. Boulder, CO: Westview Press, 1998.

Faure, Bernard. "The Buddhist Icon and the Modern Gaze." *Critical Inquiry* 24, no. 3 (Spring 1998): 768–813.

Faure, Bernard. "Buddhism's Black Holes: From Ontology to Hauntology." *International Journal of Buddhist Thought & Culture* 27, no. 2 (December 2017): 89–121.

Gonda, Jan. "Pratiṣthâ." *Saṃjñâvyâkaraṇam*. Studia Indologica Internationalia. Poona and Paris: Center for International Indological Research, 1954, 1:1–37. Reprinted in *Selected Studies of Jan Gonda* (Leiden: E. J. Brill, 1975), 2:338–74.

Granoff, Phyllis, and Koichi Shinohara, eds. *Images in Asian Religions*. Vancouver and Toronto: UBC Press, 2004.

Greene, Eric M. "The 'Religion of Images'? Buddhist Image Worship in the Early Medieval Chinese Imagination." *Journal of the American Oriental Society* 138, no. 3 (July–September 2018): 455–84.

Gyatso, Janet M. "In the Sacred Realm." In *From the Sacred Realm: Treasures of Tibetan Art from the Newark Museum*, ed. Valrae Reynolds. Munich, London, and New York: Prestel, 1999, 171–249.

Kensuke, Nedachi. "The Transfer of Divine Power: Replicas of Miraculous Buddhist Statues." In *Kamakura. Realism and Spirituality in the Sculpture of Japan*, ed. Ive Covaci. New York: Asia Society, 2016, 37–46.

Reedy, Chandra L. "The Opening of Consecrated Tibetan Bronzes with Interior Contents: Scholarly, Conservation, and Ethical Considerations." *Journal of the American Institute for Conservation* 30, no. 1 (April 1991): 13–34.

Sharf, Robert H. "On the Allure of Buddhist Relics." *Representations* 66 (Spring 1999): 75–99; republished in *Embodying the Dharma: Buddhist Relic Veneration in Asia*, ed. David Germano and Kevin Trainor. Albany: State University of New York Press, 2004, 163–91.

Sharf, Robert H., and Elizabeth Horton Sharf, eds. *Living Images: Japanese Buddhist Icons in Context*. Stanford, CA: Stanford University Press, 2001.

Swearer, Donald K. "Hypostasizing the Buddha: Buddha Image Consecration in Northern Thailand." *History of Religions* 34, no. 3 (February 1995): 263–80.

Trainor, Kevin. "Introduction: Beyond Superstition." In *Embodying the Dharma: Buddhist Relic Veneration in Asia*, ed. David Germano and Kevin Trainor. Albany: State University of New York Press, 2004, 1–20.

Wang, Michelle C. "Early Chinese Buddhist Sculptures as Animate Bodies and Living Presences." *Ars Orientalis* 46 (2016): 13–38.

Winfield, Pamela D. *Icons and Iconoclasm in Japanese Buddhism: Kūkai and Dōgen on the Art of Enlightenment*. Oxford: Oxford University Press, 2013.

CHAPTER 10

TEXTS AND RITUALS

NATALIE GUMMER

THE BUDDHA'S SPEECH IN THE SOUTH ASIAN RITUAL COSMOS

THE Buddha speaks a language of fire and light. When he teaches, he "illuminates" the Dharma. And as a result of hearing this radiant speech, his followers are "instructed, excited, fired up, and gladdened": through a process that some texts refer to as "cooking," they attain a higher state.[1] The quality that the Buddha's speech both possesses in abundance and imparts to others is *tejas*, "radiant energy," a term that unites the brilliance of fire and sun with the vital, seminal fluid that infuses healthy beings and prolongs their lives. This full range of meanings resonates when the Buddha speaks, and situates his luminous words—both in their cause and in their effects—squarely in the South Asian sacrificial cosmos.

The Buddha's speech can cook those who hear it because he cooked himself through incalculable eons of self-perfection on the bodhisattva path. In sharp critique of the Vedic sacrificial complex, in which the sacrificer—paradigmatically, the king—obtains an immortal, sunlike body in heaven by substituting a sacrificial victim for himself, the bodhisattva repeatedly sacrifices himself for others. But the results of his self-sacrificial acts are very much at one with the Vedic ritual complex: after receiving ritual consecration (that is, a prediction to buddhahood) as a crown prince (that is, a bodhisattva) from each buddha he encounters, he becomes, like each of them in their own eons, the supreme sovereign. But he exercises his royal command (*śāsana*) not by force (*daṇḍa*), but through the Dharma that he utters. Buddhist texts raise this crucial term in South Asian discourse to prominence by claiming and amplifying the term's nascent associations with sovereignty: the Dharma is "the ruling power of the ruling power," the "very essence of kingship" and "the transcendent power that lies behind the visible power and authority of the king."[2] Whatever else Dharma might mean in Buddhist texts, it also invokes this supreme reality and sovereign essence that governs everything in the world, a reality and essence only fully revealed in the teachings of the Buddha. And by uttering the Dharma, the Buddha consecrates others with this essence. His teachings convey the nature of reality, but (or rather, therefore) they always also convey tremendous ritual power.

These conceptions of the ritual potency of the Buddha's speech participate in broader recalibrations of South Asian ritual efficacy at around the period of their composition, during which ritual speech was in the process of supplanting the sacrificial fire. The degree to which Buddhists instigated or simply participated in this process is impossible to determine with precision, but Buddhist critiques of sacrificial violence and declarations of the Dharma's sovereign power likely played some role.[3] Whatever the case, eloquent speech and rituals of recitation became both means and end, both the fire and food of sacrifice and the radiant, immortal, kingly body thus produced.[4] According to the Dharma, sovereign power is ritually conferred not through fiery sacrifice, but through the ethical import, aesthetic beauty, and fiery radiance of the Dharma itself.

The Buddha's eloquent speech, attained through arduous self-sacrifice, is thus a ritual means of transformation, possessing both the radiant energy of the sacrificial fire and the potent essence of the seminal, sovereign power substances through which transformation is effected in the sacrificial cosmos. Indeed, part of what makes the Buddha a buddha is precisely his ability to teach—to cook others with his speech, that is, others who are incapable of cooking themselves. And, in quite different ways in different Buddhist contexts, his speech is not only means, but also end: like the verses of the Veda in Brahmanical ritual, it is the perfect poetic body in which he continues to remain present after he enters *parinirvāṇa*. His teachings, given voice and long life in the Dharma that he utters, continue to exercise sovereign power in the world long after his physical death (although even the Dharma's worldly manifestations, it is said, eventually decline and die out[5]). As the Buddha insists in his oft-quoted admonishment of Vakkali, the monk who pines so desperately to be in his physical presence, "One who sees the *dhamma* sees me; one who sees me, sees the *dhamma*."[6] This passage might seem to diminish the significance of the Buddha's physical presence, such that his teachings can so easily substitute for him, but it also offers precedent for viewing his teachings as a full-fledged form of embodiment[7]—albeit one that requires ritual resuscitation.

In short, *buddhavacana* is itself both ritual product and ritual process—both the perfected body obtained through self-sacrifice and a means of cooking others through the radiant, potent substance of eloquent speech. It is not too much of a generalization to characterize a wide swath of Buddhist practice as focused on the goal of activating the vital potency of the Buddha's speech, and thereby making him present in some fashion. Yet the mechanisms for achieving this end and the conceptions of embodiment and substance that underlie those mechanisms are multifarious indeed.

The Buddha's Textual Body

Speech is an act of the body—indeed, an act of bodily emission. This basic fact, faintly salacious to contemporary ears, is quite overt in texts attributed to the Buddha, in which his speech produces "sons of his own mouth."[8] Once it has left the body, speech can only be preserved through further bodily processes, whether by internalizing it (through memorization, for instance) or by materializing its external existence (through practices such as inscription). These techniques of preservation—recording technologies, we might say—enable "playback" of the Buddha's speech and allow it to act in the world after his final nirvana: they provide him with new bodies through which to speak. And they act, in no small part, by entering and transforming other bodies through rituals.

Tradition has it that the earliest written record of the Buddha's teachings was the inscription of the Pali canon in the first century BCE in Sri Lanka, precisely to ensure that his words would endure.[9] Notions of the verbal and textual embodiment of the Buddha, however, seem to have emerged most explicitly in those sutras that designate themselves "Mahayana," often in relation to ideas and practices involving the Buddha's bodily relics.[10] John Strong has argued that relics—present manifestations of the Buddha's death and absence—do not so much make the Buddha himself present as extend his biography: they prolong his ability to act in the world, but in new ways, and in different material forms, that generate new stories ("bioramas").[11] By contrast, many Mahayana sutras claim to make the Buddha—indeed, *all* buddhas—present, and to be a true—indeed, *the* true—embodiment of the Buddha, his eternal body of Dharma (*dharmakāya*). But they also claim to be relics,[12] and like relics, these sutras vastly extend the buddha biography, and not only into a seemingly endless future, but also into an infinite past. Or perhaps it is more accurate to say that these sutras make buddha biographies part of their own autobiographies—the stories they tell of their innumerable past and future performances, their ritual powers to produce infinitely plural buddhas reigning over infinitely plural worlds. If the sutras constitute the *dharmakāya* (body of Dharma) of all buddhas, their sovereign essence and transformative powers, as some sutras claim,[13] then buddhas live and teach as long as the sutras circulate. And while they often foretell the decline of the Dharma in this world, these stories of impending decay serve in part to signal the rarity of an encounter with the Dharma, and to spur the preservation of the sutras' potent ritual substance. Yet the same sutras often also imply that their eternal essence remains pure and untouched by the ravages of time, becoming manifest again whenever and wherever buddhas—or buddha-surrogates—utter their words.

Much of the scholarship relevant to the ritual uses of these sutras has circled around the relationship between the mode of their composition and their claims to power. Two contributions in particular have had a substantial impact on subsequent trajectories of inquiry. Gregory Schopen has posited a "cult of the book" focused on the enshrinement of and devotion to various sutras, in tension with devotion to the "relic cult"[14]; and Richard Gombrich has taken the extravagance with which the sutras go about "celebrating their own survival" as evidence of their composition in writing.[15] These two influential (and controversial) studies have directed much subsequent scholarly attention both to the material text as the focus of ritual praxis, and to the function of such sutras as written "manuals" that guide audiences in performing a wide range of mental, verbal, and kinesthetic forms of praxis.[16] But whether the sutras were initially composed orally or in writing—still a matter of debate[17]—scholars have come to recognize that far from being diametrically opposed forms of knowledge production, written texts and oral performance are profoundly intertwined, most especially in manuscript cultures.[18] Perhaps more importantly, across the Buddhist world, both written and oral modes of text production have been understood and performed as ritual acts in their own right—acts that make a buddha's power to transform audiences present and potent in his speech, whether that speech is conceived of as his eternal bodily essence or his living relic, and whether its sound resonates in the world anew or asserts its own "textualized" material presence in the face of the absence of buddhas.[19]

The story of the Buddha Prabhūtaratna in the *Saddharmapuṇḍarīka* (*Lotus Sutra*) vividly encapsulates this conflation of written text, oral performance, living bodily presence, and reliquary monument to absence, as well as the sutra's autobiographical subsumption of the buddhas, past, present, and future, who are its auditors and orators. Because of a vow he made in a past life, the sutra tells us, the colossal stupa of Prabhūtaratna emerges from the ground whenever the sutra is taught. Although he long ago passed into final nirvana, his body, interred in the stupa, seems very much alive, praising the Buddha Shakyamuni for teaching the sutra. And indeed, every time the sutra is performed, every time a performer voices Prabhūtaratna's past vows and their fulfillment in the present moment of utterance, his elaborately described stupa *does* emerge in the minds of auditors; his voice *is* heard again in the present. The stupa—present symbol of pastness—in which his remains are ensconced is a perfect metaphor for the *Lotus Sutra* itself, which enables past buddhas (including Shakyamuni, who joins his predecessor in the stupa/sutra) to become present and active once again, to transform listeners with their potent speech, preserved in the (written and/or memorized) sutra and actualized through oral performance. Read through this story, every time the sutra is performed, the verbal body of the buddha is reincarnated, given new agency and life through the body and voice of its performer.[20] That, too, is a ritual process.

Rituals of Incorporation

Oral or written, then, sutras have vital substance. Rituals enable that substance to enter other bodies and transform them in ways that assume the mechanisms and metaphors of ritual efficacy that pervade the sacrificial cosmos. Buddha-speech is at once food, semen, life essence, and consecratory liquid (all these being productively conflated in sacrificial ritual). And this substance is not distinguishable from its narrative power. In northern

Thailand, for instance, Buddha images are consecrated with his power and presence both through the ritual and recitational re-enactment of key portions of the Buddha biography, and through the chanting of *suttas* designated as *paritta* (protective verses) for their verbal distillation of the Buddha's sovereign protective power.[21] And although life stories and *paritta* are different varieties of speech, their difference cannot be neatly reduced to "meaning" as opposed to "efficacy." The electric potency of *paritta*, which galvanizes a number of Theravadin rituals,[22] is conveyed to the images to be consecrated in part through a recreation of the night of the Buddha's awakening: a thread held by the chanting monks is woven into a canopy above the images, representing the seat of awakening (*bodhimaṇḍa*). Stories of the Buddha's life story, including the self-sacrificial process of perfection he undertook in past lives, not only instruct the image, but also instill it with the verbal essence of the Dharma that the Buddha attained thereby. The words uttered and chanted in the consecration ritual imbue the image with both life essence and life experience.

The coincidence in these rituals of speech as story and speech as sonorous power substance might shed anachronistic yet revealing light on the normative centrality of ritual utterance in Mahayana sutras and elsewhere. "As a gifted actor becomes the person he or she plays by identifying with the character portrayed in the drama, so the Buddha image becomes the Buddha's double after being instructed in the *tathāgata*'s life history," notes Swearer.[23] Yes, and the reverse is true as well: just as the image becomes a buddha-double by hearing the biography, so does the ideal performer of the Dharma (*dharmabhāṇaka*) endowed with inspired eloquence (*pratibhāna*)—a "gifted actor" if ever there was one—become a buddha-surrogate, and eventually a buddha, by uttering the words of buddhas. And by enabling others to hear those words, to be consecrated, like the image, with the narrative and potent substance of speech, he sets them on the same path. Like the buddha image, they must receive the powerful substance and story of the sutras aurally in order to become themselves sources of that substance. Unlike most Buddha images, however, they emit that potent substance orally. Part of what makes the Mahayana the Mahayana is the sutras' ritual power to turn listeners (*śrāvaka*s) into speakers, into buddha-surrogates and buddhas, and thereby to perpetuate a transmission lineage to some extent independent of the earthly existence of any particular buddha. Importantly, however, the sutras represent themselves not as an alternative to a speaking buddha, but as his true and eternal body, his *dharmakāya*, which is alive and active whenever the sutras are uttered.

Moreover, to an extent not adequately appreciated, Mahayana sutras *are* life stories—first and foremost, autobiographies that testify to their own transformative power (past, present, and future). But they also narrate the biographies of the buddhas (past, present, and future) who speak them and the listeners (past, present, and future) who hear them. And like the images in the Thai consecration rituals, the ritual enunciation of such stories, self-referentially indexed to the moment of oral utterance and aural reception, changes the story of those who listen and speak. Suddenly, they are on the path to buddhahood: the sutra reveals the forgotten pasts and undreamed-of futures of its audiences, and thereby infuses them with the life essence and life experience of a bodhisattva, a buddha-to-be. By the sutras' own account, this infusion, at once consecratory and inseminatory, catalyzes a thoroughly ritualized process of mental and bodily transformation that resonates strongly, in its means and ends, with sacrificial ritual.[24]

As the sutras repeatedly insist, in a time without buddhas (aside from the sutras themselves, that is), this ritual infusion is made possible by the *dharmabhāṇaka*, a figure whose prominence in recent scholarship finally begins to approximate his (or, theoretically, her[25]) prominence in the many of the sutras themselves.[26] The reasons for this are clear: if he speaks with sufficient eloquence, the *dharmabhāṇaka*'s performance can resemble that of a buddha, and thus offer listeners a transformative experience that substitutes for and is functionally equivalent to an encounter with a teaching buddha. The obsession of many Mahayana sutras with their own performers suggests that while the material text may preserve and crystallize the Buddha's essence through textualization, that essence only comes fully to life when it is uttered. The eloquent oral performance of these sutras enables the Buddha's transformative *tejas* to continue cooking listeners. But the *dharmabhāṇaka* himself is not only the means of cookery, but also its (interim) result: he has himself been partially cooked by his own encounter with the sutra, by listening, studying, memorizing, and reciting the text.

Sutras thus offer a powerful challenge to common contemporary assumptions about the kinds of practices deemed to be "ritual." Seen through the lens of the sutras, seemingly mundane or rote textual practices—reading, study, memorization, recitation, inscription, exegesis—become potent ritual processes through which the Buddha's verbal essence is progressively incorporated. The metaphors that the sutras use to express their own transformative powers—very much tied to sacrificial ritual and processes of embodiment—make this abundantly clear: the Buddha's verbal essence is food that enters listeners and transforms them into itself; it is vital, seminal essence that gestates within its audiences and bears the future fruit of buddhahood; it is the liquid of unction that consecrates listeners as crown princes. In the words of the *Suvarṇa(pra)-bhāsottamasutra* (*Sūtra of Utmost Golden Radiance*), it is *dharmāmṛtarasa*, the liquid essence of the immortalizing nectar of the Dharma.[27] Ostensibly scholastic practices involving this essence may not be so neatly separable from those that fit our contemporary notions of ritual.

Rituals of (Re)production and Dissemination

Whether the (oral and written) texts that preserve the Buddha's speech are adjudged to be his relics or his eternal body, they open up a rich range of practices focused on the preservation and proliferation of his presence, or the potent presence of his absence, in new material forms and bodily incarnations. Such practices—and the "bioramas" that generate and are generated by them—often conflate the notion of buddha-speech as power substance and vital essence with the notion of buddha-speech as agentive embodiment: the Buddha's ritually activated speech combines both luminous, electric, vital power and material, agentive form. Rituals not only facilitate access to and incorporation of that power and form, but also expand the transmission and circulation of the texts that embody his presence—or, like relics, "substitute for him in his absence."[28] And expanded modes of transmission in turn generate new technologies for releasing and disseminating the power encapsulated in these materializations—technologies that challenge any easy boundary between writing and oration as modes of dissemination.

A paucity of extra-textual documentation limits scholars' ability to determine the extent to which actual ritual practices involving sutras in ancient South Asia were consistent with normative injunctions in the sutras themselves (especially, but not exclusively, Mahayana sutras), although normative claims may also shed light on historical practices.[29] But whatever the case in the context of their initial production and use, other times and places bear eloquent witness to the development of a rich array of ritual technologies for channeling, incubating, and disseminating the potent substance of the Buddha's speech. While many sutras stress the primacy of oratorical practices to their ritual efficacy, in most times and places, if not in the place of their initial composition, those practices have been dependent upon the circulation of the sutras in written form. The ongoing production of the material text makes possible the continued production of the potent oral substance of the sutra, which (so the sutras tell us) enters and transforms its listeners with such immediacy. Yet copying scriptures is not only a means to an end, but also an end in itself: most sutras include inscription among the meritorious practices they encourage.

In scriptoria across the Buddhist world, practices of inscription have been both highly ritualized, involving rigorous practices of purification, preparation, and production, and highly specialized, usually undertaken by a skilled cadre of scribes. Patronage very often came from rulers who demonstrated and generated their devotion to the Dharma, and with it, their capacity to ensure the well-being of the realm, through massive projects of canon production.[30] These concerns of state, coupled with efforts to ward off the prognosticated decline of the Dharma, led to some of the most monumental practices of inscription in Buddhist history: the carving of the canon in stone. Perhaps the earliest such effort was initiated not by those in power, but by a Sui dynasty Chinese monk, Jingwan. Yet the carving of the canon that he began at Fangshan was continued for centuries by the rulers of subsequent dynasties, its stone tablets testifying to their role as protectors of the Dharma.[31] Perhaps the most recent such effort was undertaken by the nineteenth-century Burmese King Mindon. Grappling with the tremendous pressures exerted upon his kingdom by British colonialism, he held a council to purify and establish the Pali canon, which he then had engraved on 729 marble tablets, each interred in its own stupa.[32]

Individuals and associations have also participated actively in the production of manuscripts, both sponsoring scribal efforts and copying sutras in their own hand. Some such rituals of inscription forge a more direct bodily connection between devotee and sutra and imbue the process with sutra-sanctioned self-sacrificial efficacy by mixing the blood of the donor-scribe into the ink, or even using human bones as writing implements.[33] The manuscripts thus produced, relics both of the Buddha and of the devotee, make manifest in material form the karmic and somatic connection forged between sutra and sponsor through transcription practices. The skin itself becomes the material text in the practice of tattooing protective *yantras* (Buddhist mantras and verses arranged in diagrams) in Southeast Asia, infusing the body of the practitioner with the potent textual body of the Buddha.[34]

The function of textualized buddha-speech as relic and reliquary is also evident both in the ritual treatment of texts and in the artistic forms of manuscripts. In communities across the Buddhist world, whole texts or particular parts thereof have been interred in stupas or other vessels.[35] While the motives for such practices are not always clear, in most instances the potent remains of the Buddha's speech seem to be understood as a material (and like his physical remains, in some sense vital) manifestation of perhaps the most important activity of his career: his transmission of the Dharma through utterance. Certain verses and formulae have served as particularly powerful and ubiquitous embodiments of the essence of his teachings. Stupas across Central, South, East, and Southeast Asia enclose clay tablets and miniature stupas stamped with the pithy encapsulation of the Buddha's teachings known as "the verse on interdependent origination" (*pratītyasamutpādagāthā*).[36] The strings of Sanskrit syllables known as mantra and *dhāraṇī*, which likewise condense the Dharma into compact, potent formulations, have served similar functions.[37] Some rulers employed such textual relics to emulate the Buddhist king Ashoka, who reportedly distributed 84,000 relics in 84,000 stupas. Indeed, the benefits attending the rapid and meritorious reproduction of the Buddha's textual body spurred the use of block-print technology, perhaps first by Chinese Tang dynasty Empress Wu Zetian, who interred the relics thus produced throughout her kingdom.[38]

But the Buddha's textualized speech is not only interred in stupas as bodily remains; it also constitutes in itself a reliquary structure that encloses and preserves the Buddha's body, passed on in final nirvana, yet eternally speaking.[39] Some works produced in East Asia take their visual form from this repository function, such as the stupa-shaped image of the Heart Sutra found at Dunhuang,[40] or the many manuscripts in Japan that enclose individual characters or phrases within stupa-like structures, or identify each character with an image of a buddha.[41] The much more elaborate "jeweled pagoda mandalas" (*kinji hoto mandara*) produced in Japan defy distinction among text, art, and potent ritual object: characters of sutras (especially the *Lotus Sutra* and the *Sutra of Utmost Golden Radiance*) in gold and silver on indigo paper are arranged pointillistically in the shape of elaborate, multistoried "architextual" stupas that contain and make visible the teaching bodies of buddhas.[42] Like the content of the sutras themselves, these mandalas make of that quintessential marker of the Buddha's absence, the stupa, a structure within which one can encounter buddhas, witness their (textualized) speech, and be transformed. Other visual renderings of sutras, such as the "transformative sutra paintings" (*jingbian*) in the Mogao cave complex at Dunhuang, while they do not employ the characters of the sutra as a creative medium, serve similar purposes, bringing the viewer face to face with the teaching buddha who gazes out from the center of such paintings.[43] Just as performing a sutra enables the listener to experience the Buddha's auditory presence, so artistic translations of sutras enable the viewer to enter his visible presence.

The ritual production and use of sutras—oral, written, and pictorial—not only make manifest and disseminate the Buddha's teaching body through sound and inscription, but also generate tremendous merit—merit that (at least according to some sutras) exceeds by far that produced through the interment and veneration of relics. This merit has inspired the development of further technologies—including, but by no means limited to, print—for harnessing and proliferating the transformative power of buddha-speech. Take, for instance, the "revolving repository" (*lunzang*), likely invented in China between the sixth and ninth centuries CE. Turning this octagonal cabinet containing the canon was thought to have the same effect as chanting it; repeating the rotations multiplied these effects.[44] The repository exhibits an oscillation between the relative permanence of material texts (and their mobile housing) and the evanescence of specific ritual acts—chanting, turning the repository—that resonates with other ritual technologies. The prayer wheel, like its canon-sized Chinese predecessor, actualizes with each revolution the efficacy of reciting as many written mantras as are contained within. A number of other Tibetan Buddhist practices—processing with sutras through farmer's fields, impressing woodblocks upon flowing water, hanging prayer flags to flutter in the wind—similarly activate the textualized potency of the pervasive and eternal truth of the Dharma through physical contact with the local and fleeting environment.[45] By giving the Buddha's words a material body, the transformative substance of his speech is released into the world with each ephemeral flap of a flag or flick of a wrist—or the whirr of a disk in a computer.[46]

These technologies and practices for activating the power of texts are analogous to (and may well be modeled on) oratorical practices, which similarly make manifest the evanescent presence of the Buddha in speech. Granted, oration conveys not only the sonorous power and presence of the Buddha, but also the content of his speech (at least to those capable of understanding the language in which it is uttered). Yet like other practices that actualize written teachings, oral performance brings life and efficacy to the textualized relic of the Buddha's speech in the body and voice of the performer. Practices of oration are many and varied, from individual chanting (sometimes accompanied by a full-body prostration to each character uttered) to elaborate ceremonies for state protection spanning several days,[47] from high-speed collaborative recitation of the canon to the single-minded repetition of especially powerful mantras, vows, buddha names, or sutra titles. Utterance relocates buddha-speech in new bodies and circumstances, making it present and relevant in new ways, and (according to some Mahayana sutras) eventually transforming those who embody it in their own speech into buddhas.

The complex relationship of written and oral sutras is frequently exemplified in the testimonial tales about their powers collected in East Asia. In one tale, for instance, a devotee's inability to memorize and recite two particular characters of the *Lotus Sutra* is attributed to a past-life encounter with a moth-eaten manuscript.[48] One provocative tale from Japan tells of a man who is led astray by a demon on the way to work. When after many hours of wandering the man comes face to face with the demon (disguised as a beautiful woman), he flees, the demon in ferocious pursuit. He is on the verge of capture when he falls into a deep hole. A voice in the hole commands the demon to desist; suddenly meek, it departs. Filled with gratitude, the man inquires as to the identity of his liberator. The voice responds that it is the first character of the *Lotus Sutra*, the final remains of a manuscript that had been interred in that spot many years previously. Since then, the character tells the man, it has rescued more than seventy thousand people.[49] In this story and others like it, the material text—even in its most fragmentary form—is an embodiment of the Buddha's speech, able to communicate with and act on behalf of beings in need. Like relics, then, these remains of the Buddha's speech have their own biographies—and sometimes voices, as well.

Similar themes emerge in new form in the Tibetan treasure (*gter*) tradition, in which charismatic figures, identified as reincarnations of key personages from Tibet's mythic past, discover new teachings recognized (by some, at least) as buddha-speech. And unlike sutras and tantras, transmitted from teacher to student over centuries and subject to the ravages of time, treasure teachings are considered to be received directly from a buddha. But the two broad categories of treasure—earth treasure and mental treasure—testify to the continued salience of both externalization and internalization in this mode of transmitting the Dharma: like manuscripts and other relics, earth treasures crystallize the Dharma in material forms that can be hidden and discovered in the physical world, while the revelation of mental treasures in the mind-stream of the discoverer suggests that human body-minds make excellent repositories.[50]

Conclusion

Through an investigation of these technologies, including the many stories that attest and give rise to their efficacy, a vision of text and language emerges that contrasts sharply with most contemporary conceptions. Contemporary views, especially in the modern secular academy, usually assume the separation of language from the body, such that language is seen (ideally, at least) as a neutral, formless vehicle for the conveyance of meaning. But the texts that preserve the word of the Buddha gain their power and efficacy—and, indeed, their meaning—precisely through their profound connection to the body, both the Buddha body that uttered them and the bodies that hear and speak and incorporate them anew. Because of this essential connection to the body, I have suggested in this chapter that we interpret those texts that are designated *buddhavacana*, buddha-speech, *as* rituals, at once substance, manual, and agent of transformation. Despite its apparent evanescence, speech is the part of the Buddha's body that survives, that continues to live and act after he enters final nirvana, through ritual processes of textualization, memorization, performance, and dissemination. Needless to say, this is not in any straightforward sense a historical claim. But given how little we know about the so-called historical Buddha, if such a personage even existed, there is an important sense in which the texts in which he speaks—even now, even to us—are, as some Mahayana sutras boldly proclaim, his only true body. In this sense, the practices that extend its agency and life include not only those undertaken by Buddhists, ancient or modern, but also the textual practices of contemporary scholars.

Notes

1. For more on the use of these terms in Buddhist texts, see Natalie Gummer, "Sacrificial Sūtras: Mahāyāna Literature and the South Asian Ritual Cosmos," *Journal of the American Academy of Religion* 82, no. 4 (2014): 1091–126; Susanne Mrozik, *Virtuous Bodies: The Physical Dimensions of Morality in Buddhist Ethics* (New York: Oxford University Press, 2007), 37–59.
2. Patrick Olivelle, *Language, Texts, and Society: Explorations in Ancient Indian Culture and Religion* (Firenze, Italy: Firenze University Press, 2005), 125–26. See also Alf Hiltebeitel, *Dharma: Its Early History in Law, Religion, and Narrative* (New York: Oxford University Press, 2011). For more on Mahayana sutras as rituals for conferring sovereignty, see Natalie Gummer, "Speech Acts of the Buddha: Sovereign Ritual and the Poetics of Power in Mahāyāna Sūtras," *History of Religions* 61, no. 2 (2021), 173–211.
3. Daud Ali, *Courtly Culture and Political Life in Early Medieval India* (New York: Cambridge University Press, 2004), 96–99; Daud Ali, "Kingship," in *Brill's Encyclopedia of Hinduism*, Vol. 3, ed. Knut Jacobsen et al. (Leiden: E. J. Brill, 2009-2014), 92–94.
4. For a survey of trends toward the verbalization of sacrifice in Buddhist literature and in South Asian traditions more broadly, see Gummer, "Sacrificial Sūtras."
5. The now-classic treatment of this complex theme is Jan Nattier, *Once Upon a Future Time: Studies in a Buddhist Prophecy of Decline* (Berkeley, CA: Asian Humanities Press, 1991). On the relationship between the decline of the Dharma and the final nirvana of the relics, see John Strong, *Relics of the Buddha* (Princeton, NJ: Princeton University Press, 2007), 221–26.
6. M. Léon Feer, ed. *Saṃyutta Nikāya* (London: Pali Text Society, 1975–1999 [1884–1898]), 3:120.
7. Mrozik, *Virtuous Bodies*, 84–86.
8. Natalie Gummer, "The Scandal of the Speaking Buddha: Performative Utterance and the Erotics of the Dharma," in *Buddhist Literature as Philosophy, Buddhist Philosophy as Literature*, ed. Rafal Stepien (Albany: State University of New York Press, 2020), 197–229; Alan Cole, *Text as Father: Paternal Seductions in Early Mahayana Buddhist Literature* (Berkeley: University of California Press, 2005), 85–86.
9. Jens-Uwe Hartmann, "From Words to Books: Indian Buddhist Manuscripts in the First Millennium CE," in *Buddhist Manuscript Cultures: Knowledge, Ritual, and Art*, ed. Stephen Berkwitz, Juliane Schober, and Claudia Brown (New York: Routledge, 2009), 96–97.
10. Michael Radich, "The Somatics of Liberation: Ideas about Embodiment in Buddhism from Its Origins to the Fifth Century C.E.," PhD diss., Harvard University, 2007, especially 332–73, 798–824; John Strong, "Buddhist Relics in Comparative Perspective: Beyond the Parallels," in *Embodying the Dharma: Buddhist Relic Veneration in Asia*, ed. David Germano and Kevin Trainor (Albany: State University of New York Press, 2004), 8–10.
11. Strong, *Relics*.

12. Gummer, "Sacrificial Sūtras," 1102–4; Radich, "Somatics of Liberation," 435–684; Strong, "Buddhist Relics in Comparative Perspective," 36–38.
13. On the *dharmakāya*, see Paul Harrison, "Is the *Dharma-kāya* the Real 'Phantom Body' of the Buddha?," *Journal of the International Association of Buddhist Studies* 15 (1992): 44–94, as well as Radich's critique thereof in "Somatics of Liberation," 813–24. On the South Asian ritual context of the term as employed in Mahāyāna sūtras, see Gummer, "Sacrificial Sūtras."
14. Gregory Schopen, "The Phrase *sa pṛthivīpradeśaś caityabhūto bhavet* in the *Vajracchedikā*: Notes on the Cult of the Book in Mahāyāna," *Indo-Iranian Journal* 17 (1975): 147–81. David Drewes offers an influential critique of Schopen's views in "Revisiting the Phrase '*sa pṛthivīpradeśaś caityabhūto bhavet*' and the Mahāyāna Cult of the Book," *Indo-Iranian Journal* 50, no. 2 (2007): 101–43.
15. Richard Gombrich, "How the Mahāyāna Began," in *The Buddhist Forum*, Vol. I, ed. T. Skorupski (New Delhi: Heritage, 1990), 29.
16. For an especially influential study along these lines, see Paul Harrison, "Mediums and Messages: Reflections on the Production of Mahāyāna Sūtras," *Eastern Buddhist* 35, nos. 1&2 (2003): 115–51.
17. See David Drewes, "Oral Texts in Indian Mahāyāna," *Indo-Iranian Journal* 58 (2015): 117–41.
18. A number of publications have made this point in varying ways, including James Apple, "The Phrase *dharmaparyāyo hastagato* in Mahāyāna Buddhist Literature: Rethinking the Cult of the Book in Middle Period Indian Mahāyāna Buddhism," *Journal of American Oriental Society* 134, no. 1 (2014): 25–50; Drewes, "Oral Texts in Indian Mahāyāna"; Natalie Gummer, "Review of *Empty Vision: Metaphor and Visionary Imagery in Mahāyāna Buddhism*, by David McMahan," *Journal of Global Buddhism* 6 (2005): 36–40; Paul Harrison and Jens-Uwe Hartmann, "Introduction," in *From Birch Bark to Digital Data: Recent Advances in Buddhist Manuscript Research* (Vienna: Austrian Academy of Sciences Press, 2014), vii–xxii; Donald S. Lopez, Jr., "Authority and Orality in the Mahāyāna," *Numen* 42, no. 1 (1995): 21–47.
19. Strong, "Buddhist Relics in Comparative Perspective," 38.
20. I examine this story in Natalie Gummer, "Sūtra Time," in *The Language of the Sūtras*: Essays in Honor of Luis Gómez, ed. Natalie Gummer (Berkeley, CA: Mangalam Press, 2021), 293–337.
21. Donald Swearer, *Becoming the Buddha: The Ritual of Image Consecration in Thailand* (Princeton, NJ: Princeton University Press, 2004).
22. On *paritta*, see, e.g., Anne Blackburn, "Magic in the Monastery: Textual Practice and Monastic Identity in Sri Lanka," *History of Religions* 38, no. 4 (1999): 354–72; Paul Greene, "The Dhamma as Sonic Praxis: Paritta Chant in Burmese Theravāda Buddhism," *Asian Music* 35, no. 2 (2004): 43–78; Peter Skilling, "The Rakṣā Literature of the Śrāvakayāna," *Journal of the Pali Text Society* 16 (1992): 109–82; Swearer, *Becoming the Buddha*, especially 88–94.
23. Swearer, *Becoming the Buddha*, 122.
24. Gummer, "The Scandal of the Speaking Buddha."
25. Despite the inclusion of women among their imagined audiences, the sutras themselves usually assume that their performers are men, in part because birth in female form is often (but not invariably) portrayed as an impediment that such revered figures have overcome. Chinese stories that recount the transformative effects of recitation do include women, however; see, for instance, Daniel Stevenson, "Tales of the Lotus Sūtra," in *Buddhism in Practice*, ed. Donald S. Lopez, Jr. (Princeton, NJ: Princeton University Press, 1995), 427–51.

26. On the role of the orator in Mahāyāna sutras and elsewhere, see Mahinda Deegalle, *Popularizing Buddhism: Preaching as Performance in Sri Lanka* (Albany: State University of New York Press, 2006); David Drewes, "Dharmabhāṇakas in Early Mahāyāna," *Indo-Iranian Journal* 54, no. 4 (2011): 331–72; Natalie Gummer, "Listening to the *Dharmabhāṇaka*: The Buddhist Preacher in and of the Sūtra of Utmost Golden Radiance," *Journal of the American Academy of Religion* 80, no. 1 (2012): 137–60; Richard Nance, "Indian Buddhist Preachers Inside and Outside the Sūtras," *Religion Compass* 2, no. 2 (2008): 134–59; Richard Nance, *Speaking for Buddhas: Scriptural Commentary in Indian Buddhism* (New York: Columbia University Press, 2011); Ryan Overbey, "Memory, Rhetoric, and Education in the *Great Lamp of the Dharma Dhāranī Scripture,*" PhD diss., Harvard University, 2010.
27. See Gummer, "Sacrificial Sūtras"; Gummer, "Listening."
28. Strong, *Relics*, 4.
29. Nance, *Speaking for Buddhas: Scriptural Commentary in Indian Buddhism*, 7–12.
30. See, e.g., Bryan Lowe, *Ritualized Writing: Buddhist Practice and Scriptural Cultures in Ancient Japan* (Honolulu: University of Hawaiʻi Press, 2017), 106–45; Kurtis Schaeffer, *The Culture of the Book in Tibet* (New York: Columbia University Press, 2009), 103–19; Sam van Schaik, "Manuscripts and Printing: Tibet," in *Brill's Encyclopedia of Buddhism*, Vol. 1: *Literature and Languages* (Leiden: Brill, 2015), 959–967; Daniel Veidlinger, *Spreading the Dhamma: Writing, Orality, and Textual Transmission in Buddhist Northern Thailand* (Honolulu: University of Hawaiʻi Press, 2006), 145–50; Jiang Wu and Lucille Chia, eds. *Spreading Buddha's Word in East Asia: The Formation and Transformation of the Chinese Buddhist Canon* (New York: Columbia University Press, 2015).
31. Sonya Lee, "The Buddha's Words at Cave Temples," *Ars Orientalis* 36 (2009): 36–76; Sonya Lee, "Transmitting Buddhism to a Future Age: The Leiyin Cave at Fangshan and Cave-Temples with Stone Scriptures in Sixth-Century China," *Archives of Asian Art* 60, no. 1 (2010): 43–78; Wu and Chia, *Buddha's Word*, 20–21.
32. Charles Keyes, *The Golden Peninsula: Culture and Adaptation in Mainland Southeast Asia* (University of Hawaiʻi Press, 1977), 267.
33. Patricia Fister, "Creating Devotional Art with Body Fragments: The Buddhist Nun Bunchi and Her Father, Emperor Gomizuno-o," *Japanese Journal of Religious Studies* 27, no. 3–4 (2000): 213–38; John Kieschnick, "Blood Writing in Chinese Buddhism," *Journal of the International Association of Buddhist Studies* 23, no. 2 (2001): 177–94.
34. Nicola Tannenbaum, "Tattoos: Invulnerability and Power in Shan Cosmology," *American Ethnologist* 14, no. 4 (1987): 693–711. Yantras are also inscribed on parts of the body of a buddha image during consecration; see Swearer, *Becoming the Buddha*, 63–68.
35. T. H. Barrett, *The Woman Who Discovered Printing* (New Haven, CT: Yale University Press, 2008), 64–67; Shih-shan Susan Huang, "Early Buddhist Illustrated Prints in Hangzhou," in *Knowledge and Text Production in an Age of Print: China, 900–1400*, ed. Lucille Chia and Hilde De Weerdt (Leiden: Brill, 2011): 135–66; Jinah Kim, *Receptacle of the Sacred: Illustrated Manuscripts and the Buddhist Book Cult in South Asia* (Berkeley: University of California Press, 2013); D. Max Moerman, "The Death of the Dharma: Buddhist Sutra Burials in Early Medieval Japan," in *The Death of Sacred Texts: Ritual Disposal and Renovation of Texts in World Religions*, ed. Kristina Myrvold (Burlington, VT: Ashgate, 2010), 71–89; Richard Salomon, "Why Did the Gandhāran Buddhists Bury Their Manuscripts?" in *Buddhist Manuscript Cultures: Knowledge, Ritual, and Art*, ed. Stephen Berkwitz, Juliane Schober, and Claudia Brown

(New York: Routledge, 2009), 19–34; Yael Bentor, "On the Indian Origins of the Tibetan Practice of Depositing Relics and Dhāraṇīs in Stūpas and Images," *Journal of the American Oriental Society* 115, no. 2 (1995): 248–61.

36. Daniel Boucher, "The *pratītyasamutpādagātha* and Its Role in the Medieval Cult of the Relics," *Journal of the International Association of Buddhist Studies* 14, no. 1 (1991): 1–27. The verse also appears on numerous images.
37. See, e.g., Bentor, "Indian Origins"; Paul Copp, *The Body Incantatory: Spells and the Ritual Imagination in Medieval Chinese Buddhism* (New York: Columbia University Press, 2014); Huang, "Illustrated Prints."
38. Barrett, *Woman*; see also Huang, "Illustrated Prints."
39. For the text as stupa in South Asian manuscript production practices, see Kim, *Receptacle of the Sacred.*
40. Pratapaditya Pal and Julia Meech-Pekarik, *Buddhist Book Illuminations* (New York: Ravi Kumar, 1988), 228–29.
41. Halle O'Neal, "Performing the Jeweled Pagoda Mandalas: Relics, Reliquaries, and a Realm of Text," *The Art Bulletin* 97, no. 3 (2015), 286–87.
42. O'Neal, "Jeweled Pagoda Mandalas."
43. Eugene Yuejin Wang, *Shaping the Lotus Sutra: Buddhist Visual Culture in Medieval China* (Seattle: University of Washington Press, 2005); Wu Hung, "What Is Bianxiang? On the Relationship between Dunhuang Art and Dunhuang Literature," *Harvard Journal of Asiatic Studies* 52, no. 1 (1992): 111–92.
44. Charlotte Eubanks, "Circumambulatory Reading: Revolving Sutra Libraries and Buddhist Scrolls," *Book History* 13, no. 1 (2010): 1–24; Wu and Chia, *Buddha's Word*, 53–58.
45. See, e.g., Schaeffer, *Culture of the Book*, 5–6.
46. Eubanks, "Circumambulatory Reading," 18–19.
47. See, for instance, Asuka Sango, *The Halo of Golden Light: Imperial Authority and Buddhist Ritual in Heian Japan* (Honolulu: University of Hawai'i Press, 2015).
48. Stevenson, "Tales of the Lotus Sūtra," 437–38.
49. Yoshiko Kurata Dykstra, trans., *Miraculous Tales of the Lotus Sutra from Ancient Japan: The* Dainihonkoku Hokekyōkenki *of Pries Chingen* (Hirakata City, Osaka-fu: Intercultural Research Institute, Kansai University of Foreign Studies, 1983), 128–29.
50. Janet Gyatso, *Apparitions of the Self: The Secret Autobiographies of a Tibetan Visionary* (Princeton, NJ: Princeton University Press, 2001), 147–50.

Further Reading

Barrett, T. H. *The Woman Who Discovered Printing*. New Haven, CT: Yale University Press, 2008.

Berkwitz, Stephen C., Juliane Schober, and Claudia Brown, eds. *Buddhist Manuscript Cultures: Knowledge, Ritual, and Art*. New York: Routledge, 2009.

Copp, Paul. *The Body Incantatory: Spells and the Ritual Imagination in Medieval Chinese Buddhism*. New York: Columbia University Press, 2014.

Gummer, Natalie D. "Sacrificial Sūtras: Mahāyāna Literature and the South Asian Ritual Cosmos." *Journal of the American Academy of Religion* 82, no. 4 (2014): 1091–126.

Kim, Jinah. *Receptacle of the Sacred: Illustrated Manuscripts and the Buddhist Book Cult in South Asia*. Berkeley: University of California Press, 2013.

Lowe, Bryan D. *Ritualized Writing: Buddhist Practice and Scriptural Cultures in Ancient Japan*. Honolulu: University of Hawai'i Press, 2017.
Nance, Richard F. *Speaking for Buddhas: Scriptural Commentary in Indian Buddhism*. New York: Columbia University Press, 2011.
O'Neal, Halle. *Word Embodied: The Jeweled Pagoda Mandalas in Japanese Buddhist Art*. Cambridge, MA: Harvard University Asia Center, 2018.
Sango, Asuka. *The Halo of Golden Light: Imperial Authority and Buddhist Ritual in Heian Japan*. Honolulu: University of Hawai'i Press, 2015.
Veidlinger, Daniel M. *Spreading the Dhamma: Writing, Orality, and Textual Transmission in Buddhist Northern Thailand*. Honolulu: University of Hawai'i Press, 2006.
Wu, Jiang, and Lucille Chia, eds. *Spreading Buddha's Word in East Asia: The Formation and Transformation of the Chinese Buddhist Canon*. New York: Columbia University Press, 2015.

CHAPTER 11

INTERACTIONS WITH BUILT ENVIRONMENTS

ABHISHEK SINGH AMAR

Introduction

THE story of Buddhist tradition has been propagated through places and sites that were touched by the lives of the Buddha, Buddhist monks and nuns, and lay practitioners. Whether one visits an early Buddhist pilgrimage site of eastern India associated with the life of the Buddha or later Buddhist monastic cave sites in western India, one is awestruck by the materially embedded nature of these sites. Many of them have been explored, excavated, and documented in the last two hundred years, first through colonial endeavors and later through the work of the Archaeological Survey of India (ASI) and other institutions. Reports of many excavations have been published, which indicate impressive "built environments" at these sites. The built environment includes structures (temples, shrines, houses), buildings, their spatial subdivisions, and their specific elements within a defined and bounded space.[1] Considering the specific social and institutional contexts, this chapter examines material remains to understand the built environment of Bodhgaya that has resulted from the interactions between the laity and Buddhist institutions in premodern India. In doing so, it also raises questions about the production, meaning, and multiple uses of material remains at different historical moments. A contextual study therefore becomes necessary to map not only the changes and new additions to the built environment, but also the shifts in the meaning of older constituents.[2]

In the last two decades, several scholars have written about Buddhist sacred sites, monastic complexes, and their associated rituals. Moving away from an exclusive focus on sites and monuments, these works, drawing largely from the disciplines of art history and archaeology, have provided a detailed understanding of the emergence, architectural development, and ritual usages of Buddhist sites such as Thotlakonda, Sanchi, Bodhgaya, and Amaravati. While discussing the spatial arrangement of the

Thotlakonda monastic complex, Fogelin explains how the placement of the stupa within the public worship area facilitates its worship.[3] Similarly, Shimada and Becker, through an analysis of the stupa, railing-pillars, inscriptions, and relief sculptures, have argued for the centrality of the stupa and its function as "a faith inducing object" within monastic complexes.[4] These works have challenged the previously held assumptions about the limited importance of rituals and their role in facilitating interactions between the monastic community and laity. J. Z. Smith, while explaining the importance of rituals,

FIGURE 11.1. Mahābodhi temple complex.

Photo: Abhishek Singh Amar.

argues that "ritual is a mode of paying attention. It is a process of marking interest. This characteristic explains the role of place as a fundamental component of ritual: Place directs attention."[5] Being the site of the Buddha's enlightenment, Bodhgaya emerged as a place to venerate the Buddha from the third century BCE onward. All the material remains at Bodhgaya reflect a relationship between this place and specific rituals and devotional practices at different moments. This chapter examines each of those material remains, their forms, and their functions within and around the Mahābodhi temple complex (Figure 11.1) to evaluate the role of laity in the layered development of this site.

Site Historiography

When Bodhgaya was rediscovered as a Buddhist site in the early nineteenth century by Francis Hamilton Buchanan in 1811–1812, the Mahābodhi temple was a place of Hindu worship under the control of Śaiva Giri abbots (*Mahaṇth*).[6] Buchanan described it as the place where the Buddha was born and lived in the sixth century BCE and mentioned the construction of the Mahābodhi temple by King Ashoka, and also that Buddhism was a flourishing religion in ancient India.[7] The most important phase for the study of Bodhgaya began in 1861, when Alexander Cunningham, as the head of the ASI, realized its importance and potential for the study of early Indian Buddhism, and visited it several times (1861, 1871, 1875–1878 and 1880–1881) in the next two decades. Cunningham focused on early Buddhism, which, according to him, dominated the early history of India despite being hardly known in the nineteenth century. His knowledge of Buddhism and subsequent research was further aided by the translations of the travel accounts of the Chinese Buddhist pilgrims Faxian (1836) and Xuanzang (1858), upon which he extensively relied to explore and examine Buddhist sites in India.[8]

Several minor excavations and repairs were conducted at the site in 1860s and 1870s, including a Burmese one. The Burmese repair and its critical review by R. L. Mitra prompted Cunningham to re-examine recently exposed remains in 1879. He noted his disappointment that "[t]heir clearances had not been carried deep enough to expose the more ancient monuments which still existed on or near the original level of the ground on which the Temple was built. The clearances also had not been made with any discrimination. Everything was removed after digging."[9] Cunningham's critical evaluation led to the appointment of J. D. Beglar (one of Cunningham's assistants) to undertake an excavation, repair, and restoration of the temple complex between 1880 and 1885. The subsequent restoration of the temple complex brought a renewed focus on its Buddhist past, leading to a major contestation over the control of this site between the Buddhist group, the Mahabodhi Society of India, and the local Hindu Śaiva Giri abbot.[10] This conflict was intrinsically linked to the nineteenth-century understanding of Hinduism and Buddhism as clearly bounded entities that overlooked the overlaps between these two traditions and their practitioners historically. In fact, the excavated remains, specifically sculptures, were classified as either "Hindu" or "Buddhist" on the basis of colonial categories, without a careful consideration of their complex interactions in the past. Many of these sculptures, aided by inscriptions, suggest the active worship of this site by Hindu and Buddhist followers, a practice that continues in the present as well.

Methodological Constraints

A modern visitor to the Mahābodhi temple complex visualizes it as per the nineteenth-century restoration of Cunningham and Beglar, which also illustrates the impact of methodological approaches employed by these scholars for the study of Buddhism and Buddhist sites at that time. The restoration of the temple complex emphasizes the historical Buddha's stay at the site, which was based predominantly on the account of Xuanzang and supplemented by translated texts such as the *Mahāvaṁsa* and *Lalitavistāra*. Cunningham reported numerous structures, sculptures, and shrines, including a Bodhi tree, railing pillars, and jeweled walk within the courtyard of the complex (see Figure 11.2), and related each of these as markers of a particular act of the Buddha during his stay at Bodhgaya. This literal interpretation could be attributed to the archaeological method of the time, which aimed at validating textual accounts. Several scholars, including Gregory Schopen and Kevin Trainor, have questioned this overtly textual focus.[11] In fact, the nineteenth-century reconstruction of Bodhgaya raises several questions. First, it was based on the seventh-century description of the temple complex, whereas Bodhgaya emerged in the third century BCE. Cunningham did trace the history of the site from the time of King Ashoka Maurya through textual and travel accounts, but these accounts cannot be taken at face value to either develop a historical chronology of the material remains of the temple complex or comprehend their ritual usage. Max Deeg has pointed to the futility of uncritical reliance on Xuanzang's account to undertake archaeology by explaining how this account was written exclusively for the Chinese court.[12] An excellent example of this phenomenon is Cunningham's dating of Bodhgaya's earliest shrine to the time of the Mauryan King Ashoka, which was based anachronistically on Xuanzang's descriptions and on the Bharhut railing depictions, dated now to the second-first centuries BCE.[13] Therefore, Cunningham's dating and reconstruction of the temple complex and undue emphasis on the royal patronage for the overall development needs to be discarded.

Second, the clearance and restoration also resulted in the destruction of the archaeological context and stratigraphic layers of the temple complex, and led to their permanent loss. As a consequence, scholars over the past 150 years have had to study the development of the site primarily on the basis of the extant architectural and, to a lesser extent, inscriptional and sculptural remains, rendering scholarly attempts to reconstruct the relationship between the architectural features and sculptural remains largely inconclusive and open to new interpretations.

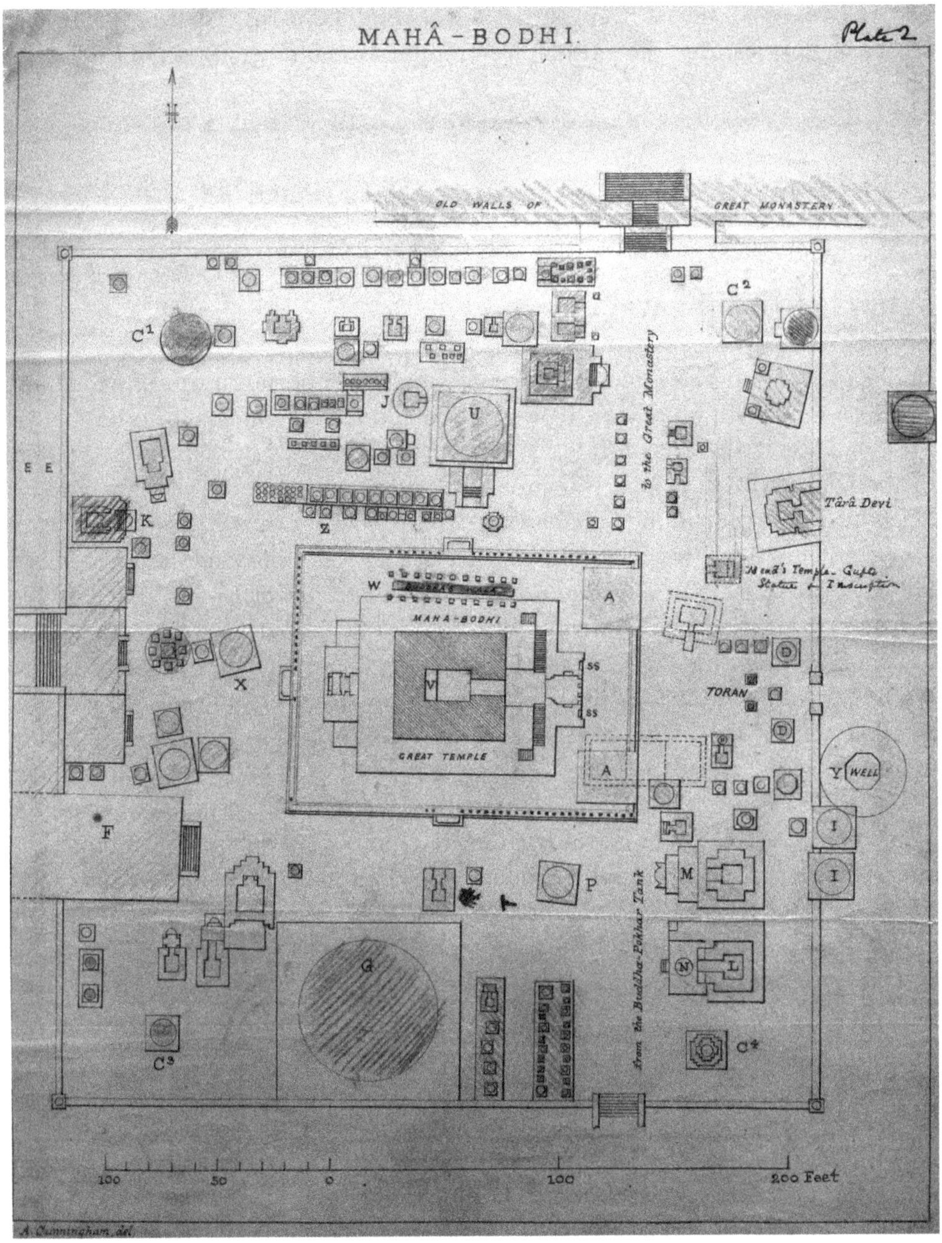

FIGURE 11.2. Courtyard plan of the Mahābodhi temple complex.

Source: A. Cunningham, *Mahābodhi or The Great Buddhist Temple under the Bodhi Tree at Buddha-Gaya* (London: W. H. Allen, 1892).

Cunningham's legacy in the study of Bodhgaya is also visible in the continued focus on the site of temple complex and complete disregard of the surrounding context by later scholarship.[14] Cunningham himself reported other archaeological features in and around Bodhgaya, such as the Bakraur stupa, which is located on the eastern bank of Nirānjana river just across from Bodhgaya. Instead of excluding such archaeological features, they need to be examined as an integral part of Bodhgaya's sacred complex.

BODHGAYA'S DEVELOPMENT

Why Go to Bodhgaya?

Bodhgaya is often presented as drawing its sacred importance from its link with the most important biographical event, the Buddha's enlightenment. The site was prescribed by the Buddha himself as a place to visit in the *Mahāparinibbānasutta* of the *Dīgha Nikāya*, which was probably composed in the third century BCE.[15] Several scholars, including Schopen and Trainor, have analyzed a particular passage from this text, which details an instruction from the Buddha to monastic and lay practitioners to visit four life-event sites and perform rituals. In this particular passage, the monk Ananda asks the Buddha about his replacement after *Mahāparinirvāṇa*, and the Buddha's answer is somewhat ambiguous.[16] It seems that the Buddha's answer does emphasize the importance of visit and veneration to four major life-event sites. His answer is also directed initially at the monks (mentally cultivated and ideal figures), who traveled to these sites in the past to interact with the Buddha. However, the Buddha's answer also seems to suggest that if a layperson wants to interact with the mentally cultivated monks, they should visit these four sites. Since he is interacting with a monk, Ananda in this case, it also indicates that he is simultaneously instructing the monks to base themselves at these four sites, where they can be visited by the practitioners.[17] Perhaps this passage is intended to instruct monks to not only base themselves at such sites, but also act as caretakers to cultivate them.

Schopen, based on a comparison of this passage from the Sanskrit and Pali versions of the *Mahāparinirvāṇa-sūtra*, provides a different interpretation.[18] He correlates the language of this passage with that of two Ashokan inscriptions, on the basis of which he emphasizes the importance of the concept of *darśan* within Buddhism. This concept meant a direct contact with the living presence of the Buddha, who was considered to be present at the life-event sites, such as Bodhgaya.[19] The performance of these acts in Bodhgaya transformed the place itself into a *paribhogika* relic (relic of use), which makes it a place worthy of veneration.[20] Second, Schopen also analyzes the second part of this passage and hints at the practice of "burial *ad sanctos*" that highlights the importance of dying in the surroundings of the life-event sites.[21] The material remains from Bodhgaya indicate both of these practices, which will be investigated in the following.

Early Historic Period: Third Century BCE to Fifth Century CE

The Bodhi-seat and tree shrine (*Bodhighara/Bodhimaṇḍa*), a jeweled walk (*Ratnacaṇkama*), and railing pillars constituted the first shrine at Bodhgaya. Much has been written about their origin, chronological development, and historicity, which I will briefly review here.[22] An important point to consider and question here is Cunningham's assumption that the famous Bharhut relief of the Bodhi tree shrine depicted a historically accurate picture of this early shrine of Bodhgaya. This assumption was founded on the inscription that was written beneath the relief: *bhagvato sakyamunino bodho*.[23] In the last hundred years, this assumption has been questioned by several scholars. Recently, Michael Willis has argued that such depictions of the *Bodhighara* have been found at multiple stupa sites, including Sanchi, Amaravati, and Kanaganahalli, and they do not necessarily match each other; therefore, these depictions should be construed more as an ideal rather than accurate representation.[24] In fact, there are eight depictions of the Bodhi-seat and tree shrine on the railing pillars at Bodhgaya. One of these railings depicts the Bodhi-seat and tree within railings, with two *chatras* (royal canopies) and two garlands on both sides. Another one, commonly accepted as a shrine, is broken on top and depicts the god Sūrya on the bottom panel. All the other depictions show a seat, a tree, and kneeling worshippers, which seem almost generic representations. Was any one of these depictions an actual replica of the Bodhi-seat and tree shrine? The nineteenth-century reconstructions and loss of the original context makes it almost impossible to make a conclusive argument. Instead, what we can be certain of is that these depictions, whether exact or ideal, were aimed at guiding the behaviors of visitors.

The monumentalization of the site began with the construction of the Bodhi-seat, most likely in the Mauryan period. The Mauryan date can be assigned to the Bodhi-seat because of its decoration with geese and palmettes design.[25] A *ratnacaṇkama* (jeweled walk) was erected around the Bodhi-seat shrine in the next two centuries. The sandstone polish and letters inscribed on these pillar-bases indicate that this walk was constructed in the first century BCE to memorialize the Buddha's post-enlightenment walking meditation. Several railing pillars were erected around the Bodhi-seat and tree shrine. Scholars have dated these pillars to the first century BCE by comparative stylistic analysis of pillars from other sites such as Sanchi and Bharhut, and have linked the style to the inscribed pillars from this site.[26] Therefore, it is likely that the Bodhi-seat and tree shrine, along with *ratnacaṇkama* and railing pillars, were in place by the beginning of the Common Era.

In addition to this shrine, a stupa was also constructed on the other side of the river Nirānjana in the village of Bakraur in the second century BCE. A monastery-like structure was excavated right next to this stupa, which contained Dark Grey polished ware and a punch-marked coin. This hints at a monastic presence in the second century BCE at Bakraur.[27] The stupa was named *Sujātā-Kuṭī*, and was probably built to commemorate Sujātā's act of offering milk-rice pudding to the Buddha. Both the *Bodhighara* and stupa were repaired and reconstrued several times over the next few centuries.

Early Medieval Period: Sixth Century to Fourteenth Century CE

Scholars have largely focused on the early historic remains within the temple complex because of the colonial obsession to uncover the early, pure phases of Indian Buddhism. Janice Lesohko, while discussing the trajectory of scholarship, has questioned this phenomenon and has highlighted the copious sculptural production between the eighth and twelfth centuries CE.[28] A majority of these sculptural and architectural materials illustrate the prolific devotional and ritual activities at Bodhgaya in this phase.

The shift of focus from the Bodhi-seat and tree shrine to the Mahābodhi temple with an image of the Buddha was reflective of the transformation that the Buddhist tradition underwent with the introduction of Buddha images in the early centuries CE.[29] Scholars have debated the date of the construction of the first temple at Bodhgaya since the nineteenth-century excavations.[30] Recently, Michael Willis, through an analysis of Cunningham's report and the photographs of the excavations and restorations, has suggested that the first temple was constructed in the late fourth century. This argument is based on the earliest image of a seated Buddha with an inscription dating to the time of King Trikamāla (64th year of the Gupta calendar) (Figure 11.3) that was found at the site.[31] He correlates this with the foundations along the jeweled walk that Cunningham interpreted as railing pillars. In contrast, Willis suggests that these were probably the foundations of the earliest fourth-century temple. This is further substantiated by the "votive deposits" that were found under the altar or pedestal inside the temple. The deposits included a gold amulet case that was made by using a coin of the Kuṣāṇa king Huvishka as a mold. This amulet case was certainly added after the time of this king in the mid-second century CE.[32] This newly plastered altar was constructed over the existing Bodhi-seat, on which a new image was placed to worship the Buddha. In the late sixth century (c. 588/589 CE), the existing temple was replaced by a new, larger structure, the Mahābodhi temple, which is attested by the Mahānāman inscription from the site.[33] The Buddha image within a newly constructed temple was certainly placed on an altar, which may have been used for offerings and devotional purposes. The location of the temple right next to the Bodhi-seat and tree meant that the construction of the temple did not really replace the rituals surrounding the tree or seat. It instead provided an additional avenue to worship the Buddha.

FIGURE 11.3. Buddha image with Trikamāla inscription, Indian Museum Kolkata.
Photo: Abhishek Singh Amar, Courtesy Indian Museum Kolkata.

Images and Sculptures

Several scholars, including Fredrick Asher, Susan Huntington, Janice Leoshko, and Claudine Bautze-Picron, have extensively studied the images and sculptures that were found at Bodhgaya and its surrounding region. Their insightful works have provided a chronological frame for the images, their ritual usage over time, and how that may reflect on the nature of Bodhgaya as a major Buddhist pilgrimage site. Huntington and Asher have pointed to the conservative nature of Bodhgaya because of the high number of Buddha images, specifically in the *bhumisparśa mudra*, when compared to the greater number of bodhisattva and other associated images at other monastic sites in the region, e.g., Nalanda.[34] Asher attributes this to the presence of Sri Lankan Theravada monks, which is known through Xuanzang's account and inscriptional records at the site. Leoshko counters this argument convincingly by listing a variety of images of bodhisattvas found at Bodhgaya, such as Avalokiteśvara, Maṇjuṣṛī, Tāra, and esoteric deities such as Trailōkyavijaya, Cuṇḍa, Nairātmya, and others.[35] Leoshko acknowledges the importance of *bhumisparśa mudra* images of the Buddha from the seventh century CE onward, but attributes their popularity to the depiction of *Māra-vijaya* (victory over Māra) narrative, which was linked to the site and the event of enlightenment.[36] There are at least three images of this type from the seventh and early eighth centuries CE.[37] One such example was found in a single-cell temple east of the Mahābodhi temple in the 1863 excavation of Major Mead at the site.[38] The inscription on the pedestal of this particular headless Buddha image, currently housed in the Indian Museum Kolkata, records the construction of a temple (*bhavana*) by a monk Bodhisena from Dattagalla in honor of the historical Buddha's destruction of worldly desires and his victory over Marā.[39] This inscribed image and its specific context, therefore, highlight how the visiting pilgrims may have been inspired by the event of enlightenment, which made the donation of this image type popular.

New iconographical details were added to this image type in the following centuries. Leoshko has identified three different configurations of such images: the Buddha in the *bhumisparśa mudra* alone, in the *bhumisparśa* mudra attended by two bodhisattvas Avalokiteśvara and Maitrya, and in the *bhumisparśa* mudra surrounded by the eight life events. These configurations began to include features such as the depiction of two earth goddesses, Māra, a tree/leaf motif at the top, a halo, *vajra*/thunderbolt, and devotees at the bottom. Later, crowned Buddha images began to be constructed in the eleventh–twelfth centuries, which indicated his divine and kingly nature and extraordinary status.[40] Leoshko has emphasized that this image type indicates some sort of ritual connection between the historical Buddha and celestial buddhas, who consecrated him during the pre- and post-enlightenment phases of his life. This ritual consecration could also be repeated for a Mahayana or Vajrayana devotee who chose to pursue the ultimate goal of Buddhahood. Similarly, the addition of new features, such as a *vajra* underneath the seat of the Buddha, denotes how Bodhgaya was perceived as the indestructible place of enlightenment for past and future buddhas besides the historical Buddha. These different depictions, therefore, demonstrate numerous ways in which the historical Buddha came to be conceived and ritually invoked.

The biographical links between the place and sculptures are further evident in a particular sculpture type from this site. There are two stone Buddha sculptures from the sixth–seventh century, which are seated under the canopy of *nāga* Mucalinda.[41] These images commemorate the protection of the Buddha from storms and rains after his enlightenment at Bodhgaya. In both images, the Buddha sits in deep meditation (*dhyāna*

FIGURE 11.4 Mucalinda *nāga* with Buddha image and stupa carved on the back.
Photo: Abhishek Singh Amar, Courtesy Indian Museum Kolkata.

mudra) within the coils of the *nāga* Mucalinda. Interestingly, a stupa has been carved on the back of one of these sculptures, which also contains an illegible inscription (Figures 11.4.a and 11.4.b). The depiction of a stupa behind a Buddha sculpture is somewhat unique to Bodhgaya, where another Buddha sculpture with a stupa on its back from the seventh century has also been found.[42] This inscribed sculpture records the donation of this image by a certain general named Manuka. Even though smaller stupa carvings have been found on the stele of sculptures, these two sculptures are unique and appear to convey the equivalency of the Buddha images with the stupas, perhaps also suggesting an equivalency of merit accruing from the construction and donation of stupas and Buddha images. While the motivation behind this sculpture might have been

FIGURE 11.4 Continued

elucidated by its now illegible inscription, the large number of miniature stupas found at Bodhgaya provide important clues about the intent and motivations of donors, which I will address in the following.

Miniature Stupas

Another way in which the monastic and lay community interacted with the site is evident in the number of miniature stupas (Figure 11.5).[43] Cunningham reported a countless number of these structures of various shapes and sizes, made from bricks and stones, dating from different periods.[44] Two different types were found and were documented in the early excavations at the site. Several large ones, made of bricks and stones, were restored at the site, whereas thousands of monolithic or clay stupas, ranging from several centimeters to more than one and half meters in height, were

FIGURE 11.5. Miniature stone stupas in the Mahābodhi temple complex.
Photo: Abhishek Singh Amar.

either plastered haphazardly as a collage at the site or were taken away for rituals and museum collections.[45] Several other stupas disappeared from the site in the nineteenth and twentieth centuries, later reappearing in Asian and European museums or personal collections.

A majority of these smaller stupas are unpublished and hence remain inaccessible for scholarly analyses. However, the Museum für Indische Kunst in Berlin contains sixty-three stone stupas, including a few pedestals, *chatravalis*, and other fragments from Bodhgaya, which were carefully catalogued and published by Claudine Bautze-Picron.[46] Many of these have inscriptions from the tenth through twelfth centuries CE, which record the details of the gift and the donors' intentions. One particular stupa fragment with images of the Buddha, dating from the eleventh century, has a fragmentary inscription, which specifically mentions that it was donated "in order to cross over the ocean of world existence . . . this very beautiful *Caitya*. . . ."[47] Even though it is fragmentary, it does confirm two points: one, that the term used for a miniature stupa was *caitya* in the eleventh century, and two, that they were donated by laity and probably functioned as what Schopen termed "burial *ad sanctos*."[48] He points to the burial function of these *caityas*, also called *kulas*, as many of these contained anonymous bones and ashes in their top sockets.[49] This may have been guided by the understanding among Buddhists that a death burial at a life-event site brought rebirth in heaven. Many such stupas also contained sealings with *dhāraṇī* texts or a portion of those texts. A majority of these *dhāriṇī* texts were associated with issues of death and supposedly had the ability to ensure a better afterlife, including the possibility of a release from a hell for the deceased.[50] With this goal of heavenly rebirth in mind, Buddhist followers combined the earlier practice of erecting stupas with the later *dhāriṇī* texts.[51] For this purpose, what site could be better than Bodhgaya, which was a constant reminder of the historical Buddha?

Devotional and Ritual Activities

Inscribed pillars, sculptures, and carvings depict a range of devotional and ritual activities from different periods at Bodhgaya. Drawing on Kinnard's idea of stupa drum slab depictions as "ritual snapshots" that represented both ideal and actual practice, Becker has argued in her recent book that these depictions were intended to be reflective of ongoing practice as well as a guide for future visitors. They should therefore be examined to understand a range of devotional practices, intentions, and expectations of pilgrims/donors and the role of depictions in shaping those expectations.[52] This approach suggests that the pillars, sculptures, and carvings of Bodhgaya, installed at different moments, may represent either the actual contemporary practices of the visiting pilgrims, or prescriptive ideals for their behavior. Their analysis provides an understanding of how pilgrims interacted with the built environment and in the process contributed to the layered growth of the Mahābodhi temple complex.

The railing pillars from Bodhgaya depict the worship of Buddhist shrines by human, animal, and celestial figures. There are repetitive portrayals of shrines containing stupas, wheels, and Bodhi-seat and tree. In fact, there are eight different depictions of the Bodhi-seat and tree shrine on the pillar railings. One of these depicts the Bodhi-seat and tree within railings, with two *chatras* (royal canopies) and two garlands on both sides. Another one, commonly accepted as a shrine, is broken on top and depicts Sūrya on the bottom panel. Two railing pillars depict the seat and tree being worshipped by celestial deities, and elephants. All the other depictions show a seat, a tree, and kneeling worshippers. The depiction of human and nonhuman worshippers offering garlands, kneeling, and venerating the Bodhi-seat and tree clearly demonstrates the way visitors were expected to interact with the existing shrine, whereas depictions without any worshippers may reflect ideal representations of the shrine, accorded due respect by the addition of royal symbols (*chatra*) and garlands.

Xuanzang, in his mid-seventh century account, also refers to the worship of Bodhi-seat and tree:

> Each year on the day of the Tathāgata's Nirvāṇa, the leaves (of the Bodhi Tree) fade and fall; but they grow out again very soon. On that day the monarchs of various countries and monks and laymen of different places, thousands and myriads in number, gather here by their own will to irrigate and bathe the Bodhi-tree with scented water and milk to the accompaniment of music; with arrays of fragrant flowers and lamps burning uninterruptedly the devotees vie with each other in making the offerings to the tree.[53]

Xuanzang's list of devotional practices matches with the depictions on material remains. The depiction of devotees, either individually or in couples or groups, in the sculptures of Bodhgaya became a popular practice from the eighth century onward. A *bhumisparśa* mudra Buddha image from the early eighth century, currently placed in the *candraśālā* at the entrance of the Mahābodhi temple, is probably the first image that depicts the donor family, who kneel on the square base below the lotus seat of the Buddha.[54] These devotees, along with their donations and devotional activities, are portrayed on a variety of sculptures, including sculptures of the Buddha, Avalokiteśvara, Cuṇḍa, Tāra, and other images. These devotees are often depicted at the bottom pedestal of the sculptures, where they are placed right next to their offerings and any inscriptions. An excellent example is the ninth-century image of Avalokiteśvara from Bodhgaya, which has an elaborate iconographic program.[55] Avalokiteśvara is accompanied by Tārā, the *preta* Sucīmukha, Bhṛkuṭī, and Hayagrīva on its left and right sides. At the top of the stela, the *bhumsparśa* mudra Buddha is accompanied by Vajrasattva on his left and Mañjuśrī on his right. A devotee couple—the man holding a lamp and the smaller female character, probably his wife, holding her hands in the *añjali* mudra—kneels at the feet of the image. It records the name of the central figure as Avalokiteśvara Vajradharma, mantras for each deity above their nimbi, and damaged donor information. The choice of image, along with its specific mantras, clearly delineates a Vajrayana affiliation for the patron. This inscribed image is an excellent example of how a Buddhist practitioner with an exclusive sectarian affiliation engaged with the site.

In fact, Bodhgaya has several donative inscriptions from Mahayana followers. These inscriptions are engraved on donated objects including images, pedestals of images, votive *caitya* fragments, and votive tablets, where donors have clearly identified themselves as a follower of Mahayana.[56] In at least four inscriptions, the donors have used the title of *Śākyabhikṣu*, *Pravara-mahāyānānuyayin*, *Śākyopāsaka*, and *Paramopāsaka*, along with the typical Mahayana formula. *Śākyabhikṣu* refers to a monk from the Mahayana community, whereas *Pravara-mahāyānānuyayin* clearly means a devout follower of Mahayana. *Paramopāsaka* and *Śākyopāsaka* were also used as titles for devout lay Mahayana worshippers. The formula used in these inscriptions is *yad atra puṇyaṃ tad bhavatu*, which means "what here is the merit, may that be," and is often found along the previously mentioned titles. Schopen has argued that this formula refers to the Mahayana idea of "transfer of merit," which was used by Mahayana followers and became a standard across different regions from the sixth century CE.[57] An examination of the objects and their specific features on which these inscriptions were engraved provides information about the ritual usage and intent of donors.

Several sculptural fragments from smaller stone stupas represent the devotees and their offerings besides recording their motives in the inscriptions. Two fragments, probably a part of two different circular *caitya*s, depict several scenes on their different sides, including a row of tiny meditating Buddha images, a kneeling devotee in front of the incense brazier and lamp stand, and a few devotees with jewel stones, respectively. The offerings include a variety of things, including *saptaratna* (seven jewels of the *cakravartin*). All these scenes clearly demonstrate worship and offerings by the donors, who may have sponsored the construction of these stupas. Both these fragments also contain eleventh- and twelfth-century inscriptions that record the name of the donor. The first one is fragmentary, whereas the second one is legible and mentions, "this (is the meritorious gift) of Eḍakā-devī, mother of Sākha (for the welfare) of all sentient beings."[58] This inscription clearly articulates the Mahayana identity of the donor and her intent to acquire and share merit with all beings.

Multiple stupa fragments and votive tablets from the eleventh and twelfth centuries demonstrate the ways in which devotees demonstrated their presence and offerings at Bodhgaya. A pedestal, probably of an image, has an offering of seven jewels, where a kneeling devotee is depicted in *añjali* mudra on its lower left corner. This devotee is venerating the offerings and the accompanying inscription lists him as a Mahayana follower.[59] An inscribed votive tablet demonstrates a similar offering of seven jewels, which has a kneeling devotee in *añjali* mudra on its left side and a devotee couple with a similar sign on the right.[60] Another votive tablet depicts a male and female couple and their offerings. She holds a large offering, whereas he offers both his hands in *añjali* mudra and they have an incense brazier, a lamp stand, two elongated cones on small cups and two smaller cups, and a manuscript.[61] In each of these depictions, the devotees are kneeling and praying with folded hands, which is a way of demonstrating respect and devotion. This is accompanied by the offerings of jewels, light/lamp, incense, garlands, fruits, and flowers, and at times a manuscript.

There are at least ten votive tablets that depict the ritual worship of a manuscript.[62] This clearly hints at "the cult of books," which were not only read but also worshipped on such occasions. Three of these tablets also depict the manuscript along with a ritual expert, who seems to be wearing a conical cap. The manuscript itself rests on a stand and is encircled by a garland, which seems to be an offering. The book cult was an intrinsic part of the Mahayana and specifically Vajrayana tantric visualization practices, which were prevalent in medieval Buddhism.

The previously discussed examples illustrate a range of rituals and devotional acts of monastic and lay communities at Bodhgaya, which were aimed at experiencing the presence of the Buddha, and sought inspiration from his enlightenment. A mere gaze at the

Bodhi tree/seat or an image had the potential to evoke *prasāda*, which Becker defines as a "beneficial mental state experienced by the Buddhist practitioners that produced an overwhelming desire to give."[63] By performing acts of generosity, Buddhist practitioners experienced *prasāda*, which had the power to facilitate mental and spiritual advancement, as well as alter one's postmortem state and future rebirths.

Conclusion

The preceding discussion highlights how the built environment of Bodhgaya was transformed from being the Bodhi-seat and tree shrine in the third century BCE to a massive temple complex in the medieval period. This transformation was a result of ritual and devotional practices of Buddhist followers, who added layers to the built environment of Bodhgaya through their generosity. In doing so, they left material traces that clearly depict festivals, paraphernalia of devotional rituals, and scenes of worship by lay and monastic communities. A careful study of these traces in this chapter exemplifies the role of Buddhist followers in the dynamic growth of Bodhgaya, calling into question the nineteenth-century interpretation of Buddhist practices that relied exclusively on textual accounts to reconstruct Bodhgaya.

Bodhgaya's transformation and its long career raise two questions: What was the effect of new sectarian movements such as Mahayana and Vajrayana on Bodhgaya? And did they in any way diminish the importance of Bodhgaya among its preexisting supporters? In response to the first question, it should be noted that Bodhgaya, despite beginning as a Theravada site, attracted patronage from followers of Mahayana as well as Vajrayana followers. Probably the earliest Mahayana donative inscriptions are from a Sri Lankan monk at Bodhgaya in the sixth century. Several examples of the donation of Mahayana and Vajrayana images, *caitya* stupas, and votive tablets in this chapter demonstrate that they were accepted, installed, and worshipped at the site. Several of these objects were inscribed, which underlined their exclusive Mahayana and Vajrayana affiliations. Despite the acceptance and worship of these new additions, Bodhgaya also continued to emphasize its connections with the historical Buddha, which is reflected in the significant number of *bhumisparśa* mudra images. These images accentuate the narrative of *Mara-vijaya*, "victory over Mara," which established the identity of Bodhgaya as the preeminent Buddhist site. The concurrent coexistence of these multiple streams of thought, ideas, and practices added new layers to the built environment of Bodhgaya and enriched the experience of Buddhist practitioners. This process may have involved complex negotiations among the Theravada and other sectarian groups.

To answer the second question, one needs to highlight the prolific ritual and devotional activities at the site. This is augmented by the presence of Sri Lankan, Chinese, Tibetan, and Burmese inscriptions. Despite belonging to different sectarian groups, practitioners from these countries continued to visit Bodhgaya in the medieval period.

Bodhgaya's popularity is also reflected in the erection of miniature (*kula*) stupas by Mahayana followers, who believed in the preexisting idea of Bodhgaya as the site that had the potential to transform one's postmortem life. In fact, the appeal of Bodhgaya extended beyond Buddhist practitioners, which is noticeable in the recovery of sculptures of several "Hindu" deities from the temple complex. These sculptures demonstrate their subordinated inclusion within the Buddhist tradition and hint at a much more complex story of inter-religious interactions. These examples underscore the dynamic appeal of Bodhgaya, which was in sync with the ever-evolving boundary of premodern Buddhism.

Notes

1. Denis L. Lawrence and Setha M. Low, "The Built Environment and Spatial Form," *Annual Review of Anthropology* 19 (1990): 454.
2. Oskar Verkaiik, *Religious Architecture Anthropological Perspectives* (Amsterdam: Amsterdam University Press, 2013), 11.
3. Lars Fogelin, *Archaeology of Early Buddhism* (Lanham, MD: Altamira Press, 2006), 168–69.
4. Catherine Becker, *Shifting Stones, Shaping the Past: Sculptures from the Buddhist Stupas of Andhra Pradesh* (New York: Oxford University Press, 2015), chs. 2–3. See also Akira Shimada, *Early Buddhist Architecture in Context: The Great Stupa at Amaravati ca. 300 BCE–300 CE* (Leiden and Boston: Brill, 2013), chs. 4–5.
5. J. Z. Smith, *To Take Place: Toward Theory in Ritual* (Chicago: University of Chicago Press, 1987), 103.
6. Francis H. Buchanan, *An Account of the Districts of Bihar and Patna in 1811–12*, ed. John F. W. James (Patna: Bihar Research Society, 1934). Buchanan also reports the visit of two Burmese pilgrims, which suggests that the site was visited, from time to time at least, by Burmese pilgrims.
7. Buchanan, *An Account of the Districts*, 149.
8. A. Cunningham, *Mahābodhi: The Great Buddhist Temple under the Bodhi Tree at Buddha-Gayā* (London: W. H. Allen, 1892), 1–2.
9. Cunningham, *The Great Buddhist Temple*, v.
10. Alan Trevithick, *The Revival of Buddhist Pilgrimage at Bodh Gayā (1811–1949): Anagarika Dharmapala and the Mahābodhi Temple* (New Delhi: Motilal Banarsidass, 2006); also see Tara N. Doyle, "Bodh Gayā: Journeys to the Diamond Throne and the Feet of Gayāsur," PhD diss., Harvard University, 1997.
11. Gregory Schopen, "Archaeology and Protestant Presuppositions in the Study of Indian Buddhism," in *Bones, Stones and Buddhist Monks* (Honolulu: University of Hawai'i Press, 1997), 2. See also Kevin Trainor, "Introduction: Beyond Superstition," in *Embodying the Dharma: Buddhist Relic Veneration in Asia*, ed. David Germano and Kevin Trainor (Albany: State University of New York Press, 2004), 10-11..
12. Max Deeg, "Writing for the Emperor: Xuanzang Between Piety, Religious Propaganda, Intelligence, and Modern Imagination," in *Pāsādikadānam: Festschrift für Bhikkhu Pāsādika*, ed. Martin Straube, J. Soni, M. Hahn, and M. Demoto (Marburg: Indica et Tibetica Verlag, 2009), 32. Deeg also points to the problems of previously published translations of Xuanzang's account.

13. Cunningham, *The Great Buddhist Temple*, 2. See also Vidya Dehejia, *Discourses in Early Buddhist Art: Visual Narratives of India* (New Delhi: Munishiram Manoharlal, 1997), 83. Dehejia dates these pillars to the second–first centuries BCE.
14. Janice Leoshko, "On the Construction of a Buddhist Pilgrimage Site," *Art History* 19, no. 4 (1996): 575.
15. O. v. Hinüber, "Hoary Past and Hazy Memory: On the History of Early Buddhist Texts," *Journal of the International Association of Buddhist Studies* 29, no. 2 (2006): 14. Hinüber argues for the composition of this text or parts of *Mahāparinibbānasutta* around 350 to 320 BCE.
16. Gregory Schopen, "Burial *Ad Sanctos* and the Physical Presence of the Buddha in Early Indian Buddhism," in *Bones, Stones and Buddhist Monks* (Honolulu: University of Hawai'i Press, 1997): 115–16. Schopen provides his own translation of this particular passage from the text.
17. Trainor makes this argument based on a study of the *Mahāparinibbānasutta* and Buddhaghosa's fifth-century CE commentary. See Kevin Trainor, *Relics, Rituals and Representations in Buddhism* (Cambridge: Cambridge University Press, 1997), 50–51.
18. Schopen, "Burial *Ad Sanctos*," 116–17. Schopen chose to rely on the Sanskrit version of *Mahāparinirvāṇa-sūtra*, which was found among the Turfan materials and dates centuries earlier than the Pali redactions of this text. For a detailed discussion of dating of his passage and text, see 136 n.6.
19. Trainor, *Relics, Rituals and Representations*, 178. Trainor also discusses the concept of "Buddha-*dassana*" and devotional practices within Buddhism.
20. Trainor, *Relics, Rituals and Representations*, 89. See also John S. Strong, *Relics of the Buddha* (Delhi: MLBD Publishers, 2007), 8.
21. Schopen, "Burial *Ad Sanctos*," 117.
22. Some recent and important publications include Janice Leoshko, ed., *Bodhgaya: The Site of Enlightenment* (Bombay: Marg Publications, 1988); Doyle, "Journeys to the Diamond Throne"; Fredrick M. Asher, *Bodhgaya: Monumental Legacy* (New Delhi: Oxford University Press, 2008); A. S. Amar, "Sacred Bodh Gaya: The Buddhakṣetra of Gotama Buddha," in *Cross-Disciplinary Perspectives on a Contested Buddhist Site: Bodh Gaya Jataka*, ed. D. Geary, M. R. Sayers, and A. S. Amar (London: Routledge, 2012), 29-42; and Michael D. Willis, "Bodhgayā: From Tree to Temple," in *Modes of Representing Sacred Sites in East Asian Buddhist Art*, ed. Inamoto Yasuo (Kyoto: Kyoto University, 2016), 41–67 (English version).
23. Cunningham, *The Great Buddhist Temple*, 3.
24. Willis, "From Tree to Temple," 46.
25. Asher, *Monumental Legacy*, 3. Asher points to the geese and palmette design on the Bodhi seat that closely resembles those seen on the abacus of several Ashokan pillars, especially the Rampurva and Sankissa pillars.
26. K. K. Chakravarty, *Early Buddhist Art of Bodh-Gayā* (New Delhi: Munshiram Manoharlal, 1997), 47; and Asher, *Monumental Legacy*, 34.
27. K. M. Srivastava, "Excavations at Bakraur *Stūpa*," *Indian Archaeology: A Review* (1973–1974): 10.
28. Leoshko, "Origin of Buddhist Pilgrimage Site," 580.
29. A lot has been written about this controversial issue. For historiographical and other relevant issues, see R. DeCaroli, *Image Problems: The Origin and Development of the Buddha's Image in Early South Asia* (Seattle: University of Washington Press, 2015), chs. 2–3.

30. Fredrick M. Asher, *The Art of Eastern India, 300–800* (Minneapolis: University of Minnesota Press, 1980), 28; Susan Huntington, *The "Pāla-Sena" Schools of Sculpture* (Leiden: E. J. Brill, 1984), 95.
31. The image is currently housed in the Indian Museum, Kolkata (Accession no. A25023). See also Huntington, *The "Pāla-Sena" Schools*, 13.
32. Willis, "From Tree to Temple," 52–53.
33. J. F. Fleet, "Bodhgaya Inscription of Mahanaman," *Corpus Inscriptionum Indicarum* 3 (1888): 277–78. Also see Richard Solomon, *Indian Epigraphy* (New Delhi: M. M. Publishers, 1998), 39.
34. Asher, *The Art of Eastern India*, 76–77; and Huntington, *The "Pāla-Sena" Schools*, 96.
35. Janice Leoshko, "Buddhist Sculptures from Bodhgaya," in *Bodhgaya: The Site of Enlightenment*, ed. Janice Leoshko (Bombay: Marg Publications, 1988), 54.
36. Janice Leoshko, "The Vajrasana Buddha," in *Bodhgaya: The Site of Enlightenment*, ed. Janice Leoshko (Bombay: Marg Publications, 1988), 32, 34. See also Janice Leoshko, "Pilgrimage and the Evidence of Bodhgaya's Images," in *Function and Meaning in Buddhist Art*, ed. K. R. van Kooij and H. van der Veere (Groningen: Egbert Forsten, 1995), 52.
37. Leoshko discusses two of these images that are housed in the Naradah Museum and Indian Museum. For details, see Leoshko, "The Vajrasana Buddha," 32–34. Asher also discusses three such images, including the one in the Naradha Museum, one placed within a *candrasala* of the Mahābodhi Temple, and the third in the Victoria & Albert Museum, UK. For details, see Asher, *The Art of Eastern India*, 75–76.
38. A. Cunningham, *Report for the Year 1871–73*, Vol. III (New Delhi: ASI Publication, 2000, rpt.), 87.
39. H. Lüders, "A List of Brahmi Inscriptions: From the Earliest Times to about 400 AD with the Exception of Those of Asoka ." Appendix to *Epigraphia Indica and Record of the Archaeological Survey of India* 10 (1912): 97.
40. Leoshko, "The Vajrasana Buddha," 40.
41. Asher, *The Art of Eastern India*, 43–44. Asher provides a detailed iconographic and stylistic analysis, on the basis of which he also dates them to the mid-sixth and late seventh centuries, respectively.
42. Asher, *The Art of Eastern India*, 44.
43. Schopen, "Burial *Ad Sanctos*," 119. Even though scholars continue to call them "votive" stupas, Schopen cautions against using the term "votive." Instead, we need to consider the function of these smaller stupas to understand their meaning, discussed later in this chapter.
44. Cunningham, *The Great Buddhist Temple*, 46–49.
45. S. Lawson, "Votive Objects from Bodhgaya," in *Bodhgaya: The Site of Enlightenment*, ed. J. Leoshko (Bombay: Marg Publications, 1988), 63. Lawson cites R. L. Mitra, who reported that at least 2,000 of these were found in the Bodhgaya excavations and at least 500 smaller ones were taken away to Burma.
46. C. Bautze-Picron, *The Art of Eastern India in the Collection of the Museum für Indische Kunst, Berlin* (Berlin: Dietrich Reimer Verlag, 1998).
47. Bautze-Picron, *Collection of the Museum*, 58. (object no. 122).
48. Schopen, "Burial *Ad Sanctos*," 120.
49. Schopen, "Burial *Ad Sanctos*," 117.

50. Schopen, "Burial *Ad Sanctos*," 120–21; see also Lawson, "Votive Objects," 67. Schopen lists eight such texts, whereas Lawson quotes from the *Dhāriṇī* texts, including *Sarvakarmavaraṇaviśodhani Dhāriṇī* and *Vimalośniśa Dhāriṇī*, to illustrate this point.
51. See Stephen Jenkins, Chapter 22 in this volume.
52. Catherine Becker, *Shifting Stones*, 47–48.
53. Xuanzang, *The Great Tang Dynasty Record of the Western Regions*, trans. Ronxi Li (Berkeley: Numata Center for Buddhist Translation and Research, 1996), 245.
54. Asher, *The Art of Eastern India*, 75 (plate 136).
55. Bautze-Picron, *Collection of the Museum*, 34–35 (object no. 50). She has provided a detailed description of the iconographic design of this sculpture, which I use in describing the sculpture.
56. Bautze-Picron, *Collection of the Museum*, 32, 66–67, 73, 75–77 (object nos. 45, 158–59, 183, 193–94, 200–1, 206–8).
57. G. Schopen, "Mahāyāna in Indian Inscriptions," in *Figments and Fragments of Mahāyāna Buddhism in India* (Honolulu: University of Hawai'i Press, 2005), 227–29.
58. Bautze-Picron, *Collection of the Museum*, 76 (object nos. 200–1).
59. Bautze-Picron, *Collection of the Museum*, 67 (object no. 160).
60. Bautze-Picron, *Collection of the Museum*, 75 (object no. 195).
61. Bautze-Picron, *Collection of the Museum*, 74 (object no. 186).
62. C. Bautze-Picron, "Between Men and Gods: Small Motifs in the Buddhist Art of Eastern India, An Interpretation," in *Function and Meaning in Buddhist Art*, ed. K.R. van Kooij and H. van der Veere (Groningen: Egbert Forsten, 1995), 64–69.
63. Becker, *Shifting Stones*, 66–67.

Further Reading

Asher, Fredrick M. *The Art of Eastern India, 300–800*. Minneapolis: University of Minnesota Press, 1980.

Asher, Fredrick M. *Bodhgaya: Monumental Legacy*. New Delhi: Oxford University Press, 2008.

Bautze-Picron, Claudine. *The Art of Eastern India in the Collection of the Museum für Indische Kunst, Berlin*. Berlin: Dietrich Reimer Verlag, 1998.

Becker, Catherine. *Shifting Stones, Shaping the Past: Sculptures from the Buddhist Stupas of Andhra Pradesh*. New York: Oxford University Press, 2015.

Cunningham, Alexander. *Mahābodhi: The Great Buddhist Temple under the Bodhi Tree at Buddha-Gayā*. London: W. H. Allen, 1892.

Geary, D., Matthew R. Sayers, and Abhishek S. Amar. *Cross Disciplinary Perspectives on a Contested Buddhist Site Bodhgaya Jataka*. London: Routledge, 2012.

Huntington, Susan. *The "Pāla-Sena" Schools of Sculpture*. Leiden: E. J. Brill, 1984.

Leoshko, Janice, ed. *Bodhgaya: The Site of Enlightenment*. Bombay: Marg Publications, 1988.

Leoshko, Janice. "On the Construction of a Buddhist Pilgrimage Site." *Art History* 19, no. 4 (1996): 573–97.

Lüders, H. "A List of Brahmi Inscriptions: From the Earliest Times to about 400 AD with the Exception of Those of Asoka." Appendix to *Epigraphia Indica and Record of the Archaeological Survey of India* 10 (1912), 95–97.

Schopen, Gregory. *Bones, Stones and Buddhist Monks: Collected Papers on the Archaeology, Epigraphy and Texts of Monastic Buddhism in India*. Honolulu: Hawai'i University Press, 1997.

Schopen, Gregory. "Mahāyāna in Indian Inscriptions." In *Figments and Fragments of Mahāyāna Buddhism in India*, edited by Gregory Schopen. Honolulu: University of Hawai'i Press, 2005, 223–246.

Trainor, Kevin. *Relics, Ritual, and Representation in Buddhism*. Cambridge: Cambridge University Press, 1997.

Willis, Michael D. "Bodhgayā: From Tree to Temple." In *Modes of Representing Sacred Sites in East Asian Buddhist Art*, edited by Inamoto Yasuo. Kyoto: Kyoto University, 2016, 41–67. (English version).

CHAPTER 12

BUDDHISM AND THE "NATURAL" ENVIRONMENT

JULIA SHAW

INTRODUCTION

THIS chapter explores archaeology's contribution to scholarly understandings of early Indian Buddhist attitudes toward the "natural" environment and the relevance of such material for global discourse on the contemporary climate-change and biodiversity crises. There are two main foci of inquiry: (1) monastic engagement with food production, land and water use in lowland agricultural zones, and (2) attitudes toward, and engagement with, upland forests, including the monastic occupation of prehistoric rock-shelters clustered around hilltops that were developed into structural monastery complexes during the late centuries BCE. Discourse on the related transition from peripatetic mendicancy to sedentary monasticism has tended to focus more on economic linkages with urban-based and agricultural society than with upland forests that are often cast as dangerous places, removed from mainstream economic agency. I argue that both zones need to be viewed together if we are to understand the socio-ecological variables of the transmission of Buddhist monasticism, and the Buddhist literary and artistic motifs of "nature" in "monastic gardens" which are commonly presented as arenas for transcending and viewing "nature." from a distance. I also explore discourse on the often-paradoxical position that forests and mountainous caves occupy in the Buddhist worldview—at once places of refuge and quiet meditation, sources of mystery and hidden treasures including jewels and medico-culinary plants, but also locales of danger and fear. Archaeological correlates of such views include scholarship on timber and non-timber forest products (NTFP) in South Asian and trans-national trading networks, and diachronic landscape archaeology data that illuminate the long-term entanglements between monastics and both upland and lowland environments that supported the development of institutionalized monasticism.

The main case study here is the Sanchi Survey Project (SSP) in central India, which involved the documentation of diachronic landscape data including hilltop monastery complexes, "natural" caves (*guha*) and adapted rock-shelters (*lena*), habitational settlements, sculptures, temples, water resource structures, and land-use patterns. Together with comparative case studies from other parts of South Asia,[1] the evidence for the sangha's engagement with different types of socio-ecological environments in the Sanchi area provides an empirical basis for reassessing scholarly views on the "ecological" credentials of early Buddhism,[2] and their relevance for global discourse on the potential for past human-environmental interactions and "worldviews" to shape current and future sustainability policy.[3]

Archaeology, Religion-and-Ecology, and the Environmental Humanities

Discourse on Buddhist attitudes toward "nature" is characterized by a general lack of integration between Buddhist studies and archaeology, which has been slow to engage with religion-and-ecology discourse[4] and the environmental humanities more broadly speaking.[5] Despite archaeology's long-standing interest in human-environment interactions, it has tended to focus on technological rather than cultural drivers of and responses to environmental change.[6] Hence, idealized assumptions regarding the "eco" credentials of early Indian religions have until recently seen little challenge from archaeology.[7]

Nevertheless, archaeology holds much potential for redressing such views, particularly the notion of pre-colonial India's untouched, and universally revered, upland forests representing the natural "other" of their "cultural" agro-urban lowland counterparts.[8] In Southeast Asia, for example, upland zones previously designated as "virgin" forests are now known to have undergone extensive urban development in antiquity, and in India woodland managing practices were central to Neolithic investment agriculture.[9] However, such recognition of the economic value of forests should not undermine the ritually charged associations of such places.[10]

Similar dislocations characterize archaeology's engagement with Anthropocene and climate change studies, which have been more aligned with the environmental sciences than with the humanities. Studies on the posited links between the weakening of the summer monsoon in 4.1 Ky BP/2100 BCE, the transformation of Harappan urbanism in ca. 1900 BCE, and later changes in land use and food production[11] generally overlook possible intersections with cultural, religio-philosophical, or medical correlates of such processes. Similarly, explanations for the "second" urbanization of the mid-first-millennium-BCE Gangetic valley have emphasized metallurgical innovation as a driver of agricultural expansion into previously inaccessible, forested areas. The archaeological testing of less technologically deterministic models, especially as urban-based polities and religious traditions spread westward from the third century BCE, has been further hampered by the mono-site-type focus of most pre-1990s settlement surveys, and archaeobotany's traditional focus on the earlier, Neolithic origins of crop agriculture.[12]

Buddhist "Landscapes" and Monastic Gardens

Unsurprisingly, therefore, archaeology has had little impact on discourse regarding Buddhist attitudes toward "nature," which may be divided into two main camps: (1) the "eco-apologists," who emphasize the "eco-dharmic" content of early Buddhist teachings,[13] and (2) the "eco-critics," who argue that such claims have been distorted and misappropriated by Western environmentalism.[14] The former emphasize Buddhist preoccupations with nonviolence (*ahiṃsā*) and the alleviation of suffering (*dukkha*) of animals, an expectation of care toward the "natural" world, together with ideals of universal compassion as embodied in later, Mahayana traditions of Avalokiteshvara. Further, Arne Næss's "Deep Ecology" reputedly drew explicitly upon the largely Chinese interpretations of the doctrine of *pratītyasamutpāda*.[15] However, these posited direct linkages between Buddhist teachings and modern environmentalist movements are generally dismissed by the eco-critics as anachronistic and historically inaccurate.[16] Schmithausen, for example, argues that early monastics were impressed less by the "beauty" of "nature" than by its negative and "dangerous" aspects; and that they followed a form of "passive environmentalism" that sought not to transform or "subjugate nature but to transcend it spiritually through detachment."[17]

Schmithausen's emphasis on detachment from and transcendence of "nature" is echoed by art-historical discourse on monastery gardens as ascetic inversions of courtly urban ideals,[18] whereby plant imagery depicted in late-centuries-BCE stupa-railing art represents not "real" plants, but rather idealized utopias, or "dharma spaces," that signal monks' transcendence of, rather than engagement with, "nature."[19] Accordingly, *yakṣī* sculptures are recast as courtesans acting only mnemonically as symbols of monastics' transcendence of worldly pleasures,[20] while Schopen views gardens as places that allowed monastics to enjoy the "views" of the surrounding bucolic countryside from a "safe distance."[21]

A very different view, however, is painted by the SSP multi-type-site landscape data—including 35 hilltop monastery sites and 145 habitational settlements over an area of 750 square kilometers (Figure 12.1)—the suggestion being that by the second century BCE, most hilltops had already been built over by extensive monastic complexes. They overlooked highly cultivated, hydraulically engineered, agrarian landscapes, interspersed by fairly densely distributed, habitational sites.[22] A key feature of such landscapes was a network of reservoirs built in the third to second century BCE, arguably to provide both upstream and downstream irrigation in response to growing monastic

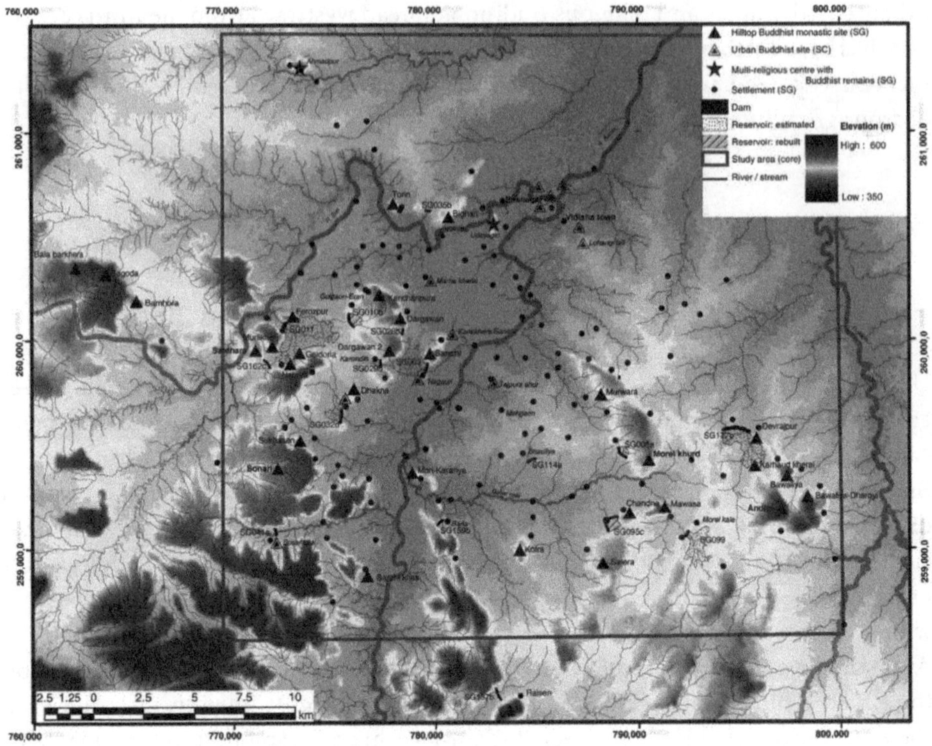

FIGURE 12.1. Map of landscape and archaeological data from the Sanchi Survey Project.
Photo: Julia Shaw.

populations and the need for more sustainable exchange networks than were possible through traditional mendicancy.[23]

This evidence attests to monastic communities that, far from being removed from "nature," excelled in the control and harnessing of its resources. Moreover, the aforementioned monastic gardens and related plant and animal representations symbolized the sangha's direct and skilful *engagement with*, rather than *transcendence of* economically productive "natural" environments.

That the monastery had vested interests in lowland agrarian environments is supported by textual and epigraphical evidence in Sri Lanka, where monastic landlordism was a key instrument of lay patronage from the second century BCE.[24] Recent survey and excavation work presents the idea of "theocratic" hydraulic landscapes in Anuradhapura's hinterland, with comparative studies in eastern India, Bihar, and the Northwest.[25] Similarities between the relative configuration of monasteries, villages, and reservoirs in Sri Lanka and central India justify the assumption of a comparable three-way exchange system between landowners, monasteries, and the agricultural laity in both regions. Water control also plays a key role *within* monastic gardens themselves, as illustrated by ostentatiously displayed water-harvesting and storage facilities at rock-cut monasteries in Gujarat and the western Deccan that evidently doubled as outward displays of the sangha's ability to tame and harness natural resources in regions of climatic uncertainty.[26] While local populations previously depended on rainmaking cults for controlling the onset of the monsoon rains, they were now assured timely water supplies via new *technologies*. Water shortage is a primary cause of *dukkha*, especially in regions where ninety percent of annual rainfall occurs in two to three months, and the sangha's ability to alleviate such suffering was made explicit through ornamental water features that dominate the landscaped monastic "gardens" of places such as Kanheri and Junagadh.

In my view, the eco-dharma debate, with its predominant focus on the non-injury of *animals*, has been hampered by its lack of engagement with the evidence for an environmentally engaged sangha that reflects deeply rooted concerns with *human* suffering (*dukkha*), its causes, and means of alleviation. Further, intersections between Buddhist environmental worldviews, and medical, ritual, and bio-ecological constructions of human and environmental "care," health, and well-being[27] are relevant for scholarly and activist-oriented enquiries into Buddhist "environmentalism," especially given recognition within ecological public health discourse of the behavioral and religo-cultural correlates of planetary and human health.[28]

Monasteries, Reservoirs, Lowland Rice Agriculture, and Rainmaking Cults: "Local" and "Translocal" Landscapes and Representations

The Buddhist monuments at Sanchi overlook a hydraulic landscape that fits with the socially engaged model of "Buddhist economics" that sustained "non-producing" monks and provided a practical means for alleviating human *dukkha*.[29] A key argument is that the irrigation reservoirs here supported rice rather than wheat cultivation, the latter being cultivatable efficiently in the local clay-rich soils without irrigation.[30] By contrast, the agrarian base of the Gangetic valley which supported the "second urbanization" and the earliest Buddhist communities of the mid-first millennium BCE had been rooted in rice cultivation from at least 2000 BCE,[31] with paddy fields figuring prominently in texts as backdrops to Buddhist narratives or as metaphors for monastic discipline. The as-yet untested hypothesis is that the westward spread of rice from this area accompanied the transmission of both Buddhism and urban polities; extant archaeobotanical samples from South India and the Deccan paint a confusing picture, with dates ranging from the late centuries BCE to the mid-first millennium CE. However, it is important to stress that sampling locations seem to have been chosen without due regard to discourse on monastic governmentality and the socio-ecological realities depicted therein. Moreover, despite recent cautions against inferring irrigation facilities from evidence for rice,[32] the obverse situation prevails at Sanchi, where there is irrigation but only a hypothetical presence of rice. However, the high levels of manpower, financial investment, and stored water provisions indicated by the archaeo-hydrological evidence at Sanchi make it difficult to envisage any associated crop *other* than rice.[33]

Further, pollen sequences from the reservoir deposits attest to a predominance of marshland plant species associated with water-logged, upstream rice-cropping environments. The fact that aquatic species—lotus plants, fish, turtles, and snakes—also dominate Sanchi's railing art reinforces my earlier suggestion that such "garden" imagery symbolizes not the sangha's transcendence of "nature," as suggested by others, but rather its direct engagement with the care and management of the kinds of hydraulic environments attested by the SSP landscape data. Such imagery may also reflect "transportable" landscape ideals from the paddy-dominated environments of the Gangetic valley Buddhist "heartland," in similar ways as "translocal" deities from that region, as discussed later, accompanied the spread of Buddhism to new areas. Sanchi's stupas and their "watery" setting also conform with deeper Indic cosmogonic models such as Mount Meru rising from primordial waters, a common motif at sacred sites across South and Southeast Asia. Brancaccio argues that a similar superimposition of "transportable" Buddhist geographies characterized the transmission of Buddhism to the western Deccan, where the natural mountainous terrain of places such as Ajanta, Ellora, and Elephants was re-landscaped according to textual ideals of "palatial abodes in mythical paradises"; the resulting natural-cultural canvas is arguably as crucial to the "reading" of such sites as the rock-cut temples and monasteries themselves.[34]

Of key relevance here are *yakṣa*s and *yakṣī*s, which belong to a class of deity often described as "local" and susceptible to assimilation by "Pan Indian"—Buddhist or Sanskritic—worldviews, and described in early Pali texts as "dangerous" spirits of specific places that can distract forest monks from their meditational duties; like *nāga*s, they require human propitiation to afford protection from the dangerous natural forces—rainfall, pestilence, and disease—that they control.[35] However, most such stories are set in the Gangetic valley, and distinguishing between their "translocal" and *actual* "local" status in other areas is rarely straightforward. Cohen makes a distinction here between Ajanta's Cave-16-*nāga* shrine that he argues helped to "localize" the sangha by honoring "local" rainmaking cults, and *Hārītī*, the child-eating "demoness" from Rajgir in the Gangetic valley, who acts rather as a "portable local deity," symbolizing only in a generalized and "etic" sense the "local" convert.[36] However, although the spatial correlation between *nāga* shrines and water-bodies in the Sanchi area accords with *nāga*s' reputed control over the monsoon rains, because they postdate the establishment of Buddhism here by several hundred years, I argue that many such *nāga*s should, like *Hārītī*, be seen as components of a "transportable" Buddhist landscape, rather than as indicators of preexisting "local" ritual-ecological realities.[37]

How do we get at the latter then, particularly those connected with upland, forest zones, or with devolved, dissenting, or "non-governed" entities with which the latter are often linked.[38] While state-level expansion into forested areas, including the assimilation of regional cults, the settlement of Brahmins, and the establishment of temples, is central to "processural" models of "early-medieval" state development in the Deccan and South India, earlier upland-lowland interactions of this kind remain poorly tested archaeologically,[39] while discourse on the international "spice-trade" has neglected NTFP-urban-rural trading networks within India itself.[40] Other obstacles include Wittfogelian constructions of the highly centralized state-level control of land and water resources.[41] However, although inscriptions attest to the state-funded construction of many "Big Dams,"[42] their day-to-day governance was often overseen by village councils and religious institutions, including, from the mid-first millennium CE, Hindu temples and landowning deities.[43]

Further, although discourse on early Buddhist patronage stresses the role of urban traders and merchants, the relationship between Buddhism and productive society is in fact ambiguous. The sangha's "middle-way" approach to asceticism and agro-urban culture is often contrasted with the more extreme "anti-civilizational" stance of some Hindu ascetic groups, including the rejection of *hiṃsic* cereal-based agriculture in favor of small-scale horticulture.[44] However, Benavides regards Buddhist monasticism as neither a rejection nor affirmation of urban society, but rather a "commentary" on new attitudes toward labor, consumption, wealth and purity, and pollution: while monks are prohibited from engaging in labor, the lay donations (*dāna*) on which they depend comes from others' polluting work. Through a reworking of Hindu purification rites, the donor is cleansed of such pollution through gift-giving rituals that also disguise the sangha's direct involvement in economic exchange, and thus make institutionalized monasticism possible.

This system is reflected in late-centuries-BCE donative inscriptions recording forms of collective patronage that fueled the "second propagation" of Buddhism in central India.[45] However, those epigraphs recording single-identity grants of land, villages, and labor don't appear until the early to mid-first millennium CE[46] and, according to Schopen, these set the bar for dating the transition to fully sedentary monasticism.[47] However, I have argued that Schopen's scheme overlooks crucial evidence for late-centuries-BCE rock-cut monastery architecture in the Deccan, and contemporary structural "platformed" monasteries, as well as associated forms of monastic-governmentality in central India.[48] The latter evidence based on the SSP landscape data, attesting as it does for the sangha's engagement with agriculture, is of crucial relevance also for discourse on "Buddhist environmentalism," and yet has remained absent from text-based discussions to date, with the exception of Elverskog, who cites the SSP landscape data as case studies for *contesting* the eco-dharma thesis.[49] Although Elverskog cites related "anti-environmentalist" activities, including the destruction of forests to make way for monasteries, the implication that agriculture, by itself, is inherently incompatible with an "environmentally friendly" sangha is problematic. Crucially, it ignores broader discourse on "sustainable" agricultural practices, and community-based responses to socio-ecological challenges of which, I have argued, early forms of monastic governmentality are key examples; Elverskog's position also reinforces problematic canonical models of forest monasticism as the "original" ascetic path, set above "later" and "degenerate" forms of socially engaged monasticism.[50]

Forests, Rock-Shelters, and Hilltop Monasteries: Human, Nonhuman, and "More-than-Human" Entanglements

Although lowland agricultural zones were central to the development of monastic-lay exchange in the Sanchi area, the earliest monasteries were established only after periods of pre-monumental engagement with forested upland environments. My argument is that these regions and the medico-culinary resources that they support are crucial for understanding the environmental correlates of socially engaged monasticism, especially given the prominence of the forest motif in Buddhist art and literature, and theories regarding the influence of Buddhism on the spread of Ayurvedic materia medica.[51]

Particularly instructive here is Falk's study of royal forest rituals at *yakṣa* "thrones" in sacred groves (*ārāma*) demarcated from larger expanses of wild "forest" (*jāṅgala*),[52] and Trautmann's argument that elephants, as symbols of both the "wilderness" and imperial power, illustrated the synchronicity of urban and forest economies. Moreover, since elephants were captured in the wild before being trained, rulers were compelled to engage themselves in forest conservation.[53] Against such arguments it is fitting that the elephant, as a symbol in equal measure of the "wild" as well as urban sensibilities, figures so prominently in early stupa railing art, given the sangha's similarly dialectic relationship to both urban and forest lifeways.

The majority of monasteries in the Sanchi area occur on hilltops which, with the exception of the five Archaeological Survey of India protected "Bhilsa Topes" sites, are now covered with fairly dense forest vegetation, a striking indicator of major socio-ecological transformations following the decline of Buddhist monasticism in around the twelfth century CE. Habitational settlement density in the intervening valleys and lower hillsides is also much lower today than attested to by historical patterns.[54] The central Indian hills support valuable plant, animal, and mineral resources, including building materials, semi-precious stones, and iron ores,[55] while the distribution of prehistoric rock-shelters throughout central India, with paintings and tool assemblages dating back in places such as Bhimbetka to the Mesolithic, attest to the deep-historical linkages between hills and hunter-gatherer lifeways.

Hills are also closely associated with place-bound deities such as *yakṣas* that we discussed earlier. For example, the *Āṭānāṭiya-sutta* (Sutta 30) of the *Dīghanikāya* (III.194–206), the great "protective text" that was popular for keeping problematic spirits away as Buddhism spread along the Silk Roads, describes *yakṣas* providing a protective chant to the Buddha dwelling on Vultures Peak in Rajgir.[56] This text is really all about *yakṣas*. Some are described as "good" and as keeping the precepts, but many are not and, since they favor remote places like forests and mountains, can obstruct meditators. Similarly, named *yakṣa* shrines (*cetiya*) connected with groves and trees[57] feature prominently in hilltop festivals (*gir-agga-samajjan*), some of which are mentioned in Aśoka's edicts 1 and 9 as being prohibited for monks and nuns.[58]

The notion that the topography of Buddhist sites followed older cultic conventions has long since informed archaeological assumptions regarding the prevalence of pre-Buddhist ritual practices at early monastic sites,[59] while the term *cetiya*, used in later Pali literature to refer to stupas, has been described as a "deliberate" Buddhist "conversion of terminology."[60] Whether the sangha actively sought out such places due to their prior sacred status, however, is difficult to determine, especially since *yakṣa* or *nāga* worship rarely took on durable forms in these early periods; it is also possible that as a "non-producing" entity, the sangha was restricted to settling non-agricultural spaces that were, according to later texts such as the *Arthaśāstra* (verse 2.2.5), designated for use by peripatetic, "property-renouncing" ascetical and scholarly communities.[61]

Interesting insights into such questions, however, *are* provided by the SSP settlement patterns: although there are increased settlement numbers in "interior" zones during the main phase of Buddhist construction (second–first centuries BCE), older sedentary villages from around 1000 BCE occur throughout the study area.[62] Similarly, the occurrence of rock-shelters, many containing prehistoric paintings and microlithic tools, at fourteen of the hilltop monastic sites—including examples on the eastern edge of the northern saddle of Sanchi hill, and Nagauri hill to the south[63]—attests to much older occupation of such places from at least the Chalcolithic period (2000 BCE). Similar correlations between prehistoric rock-shelters and Buddhist sites are noted in other parts of the Indian subcontinent.[64]

Such shelters may have been used by monastics as temporary residences before the construction of permanent monasteries, or as retreats at the edges of subsequently monumentalized complexes, in keeping with textual accounts of the special ritual or healing properties of "natural" caves (*guha*), to which we will return later.[65] Many such caves, however, show direct evidence for adaptation into monastic dwellings. Although lacking the characteristic "drip ledges" of the third-century-BCE-inscribed *lena*s of Sri Lanka—rock-cut channels cut into their overhangs for diverting rainfall from the interior living spaces, and occurring also in many of the Deccan rock-cut caves[66]—many include simple additions such as external terraced platforms, interior "beds," painted inscriptions and Buddhist imagery, or have small stupas built around their entrances or summits. Such places are thus closer to accepted definitions of modified cave dwellings (*lena*) than to more "isolated," unadapted caves (*guha*), although, as discussed later, the term *lena* comes to be more closely associated with more extreme forms of adaptation, as typified by the Deccan rock-cut caves. At Sanchi itself, three "monastic rock-shelter" clusters were documented on the lower western and southern slope of the hill below the main stupa complex; others have small stupas at their entrances or on their overhanging element, all features that mark them as "significant" locales.[67] At Nagauri to the south, one of many painted shelters clustered around the hill contains prehistoric paintings superimposed by a later painted frieze of an enthroned "royal" couple seated before a procession of horses and elephants with riders, and two *yakṣa*-type, spear-holding figures. The narrative style recalls the first-century-CE carved gateway panels at Sanchi, but Falk's aforementioned work on royal forest rituals may also be relevant here.[68]

The richest collection of "monastic rock-shelters" in the study area occurs at Morel Khurd to the east, a large stupa and monastery complex that forms one of five sites connected to the Hemavata relics.[69] Two such shelters stand immediately below a group of small stupas on the southern part of the hill. Although lacking external platforms, one contains a painted *śankhalipi* inscription; the other contains a painted frieze of a cow, a horse, and a camel with riders, which, as at Nagauri, echo the narrative style of the Sanchi gateway panels.[70] On the northeastern edge of the same hill is a larger group of ten shelters, seven of which have two-meter-high stone platforms and dividing walls at their entrances, and some have raised sleeping areas inside. A large number of one- to two-meter-diameter stupas are arranged over their summits and adjoining plateau, which features a line of sulfurous hot-air holes and outlines of stone structures within which the holes would have been enclosed. These may correspond with the "hot baths" (*jantaghara*) that comprise one of the ten structural components of a *saṅgharama* (*Mahāvagga* I, 30, 4; *Cullavagga* VI, 1, 2).[71] There are large openings inside the shelters that appear to be linked via fault-lines with the hot-air holes, and that may correspond with early Buddhist textual accounts, discussed later, of mountain caves being converted into sweat (*swedana*) chambers, possibly influenced by Ayurvedic therapies described in the *Caraka Saṃhitā* (*Sūtrasthāna* 1, chapter 14). (Figure 12.2).

An example of a more solitary "monastic rock-shelter" occurs on the western edge of Satdhara hill, another of the Hemavata relic-stupa sites, to the west of Sanchi. It contains several painted details, including a Buddha image, two stupas, and a sixth–seventh-century-CE inscription of the Buddhist creed. Given the cave's precarious cliff-side location, there

FIGURE 12.2. Monastic rock-shelter at Morel Khurd.

Photo: Julia Shaw.

is no room for an outer terrace, but its scenic position, set apart from the main stupas and monasteries, and overlooking the river Bes, is suggestive of a quiet meditational retreat.[72]

To the north of Vidisha, at Ahmadpur, and forming part of a complex of fifty-eight prehistoric painted shelters is another single shelter containing a five-line painted Brahmi inscription datable to between the first century BCE and first century CE, in a highly localized, and only partially decipherable, Prakrit.[73] Other paintings include a "tree-in-railing" motif, and a *yakṣa*-type figure holding a spear, similar to the aforementioned example from Nagauri, and numerous *śankhalipi* inscriptions that may be contemporary with a Gupta-period stupa and temple complex on other parts of hill. One of the few decipherable parts of the inscription mentions "*vanehi soḍas-ehi 10 6 ca*" ("with sixteen [forests?]") which, together with the absence of contemporary Buddhist architectural remains, is suggestive of a solitary forest retreat (*āvasā*).

Similar evidence occurs at other central Indian sites, such as Kharwai, Ghatla, and Bhimbetka in Raisen District,[74] the latter containing a single-line Brāhmī inscription that describes it as "*Simhakasa lena*" ("the cave-dwelling of Simhakasa"), and forming part of a complex of painted shelters dating back to the Mesolithic period. By contrast, a large group of "monastic rock-shelters" with external platforms and internal "beds" at the Aśokan edict site of Pangurariya (Hoshangabad District) forms, as at Morel-khurd, part of what is otherwise an extensive monastic complex.[75]

It is possible that some of these "monastic shelters" provided transitional accommodation for monastics before the permanent hilltop monasteries had been completed, although this suggestion requires testing through excavation and palynological investigations. As in Sri Lankan and Southeast Asian two-tiered models of forest/urban monasticism, some such shelters were undoubtedly used also in later periods following the construction of structural monasteries. Moreover, they may have continued to hold special ritual significance in keeping with the meditational, healing, and magical reputation accorded to such places in Buddhist texts. The evidence for this is strongest at Satdhara, while an eleventh-century-CE Mahayana cave retreat near Raisen, to the south of Sanchi, illustrates the continued importance of such places, even after the decline of sedentary monasticism.[76]

Of relevance here is Granoff's study of textual references to remote mountain caves as places for medical therapeutic practice, either by virtue of their perceived inherent healing powers, or through their proximity to "alchemical jewels" and medicinal plants,[77] and of Buddhaghosa's recommendations of certain caves in Sri Lanka as places for meditational retreat.[78] In Mahayana texts of the second-to-third centuries CE, such caves feature as portals into magical "bejeweled" worlds[79] and, in post-Gupta Tantric texts, as locales for esoteric spells and rituals.[80] Granoff makes a clear-cut distinction between the isolated, "wild" *guha* and the sophisticated rock-cut *lena* of the western Deccan sites. However, such a setup overlooks more simply adapted caves such as the Sri Lankan *lena*, and the aforementioned central Indian "monastic rock-shelters," both of which may fit somewhere between these two extremes. Moreover, Granoff's emphasis on the purely "magical" and ritual attributes of such places perpetuates socially constructed notions of the economically disconnected forest, despite oblique reference to the "medicinal plants" to which such locations afforded access. The latter of course fit well with archaeological accounts of the importance of upland forests as sources of medico-culinary "spices,"[81] while textual references to the "Jewel Mountains" in which caves are set may reflect geological as much as "magical" or "ritual" realities; for example, the hill-ranges around Ajanta and other Deccan rock-cut sites are still important source areas for India's precious and semi-precious stones industry.

Further, the ambiguity surrounding the "wild" versus "cultivated" status of *guhas*/*lenas* in Buddhist art and literature may reflect changing social mores and anxieties about "nature" as much as morphological reality. The oft-cited case study here is the Indasālagūha at Rajgir, which, according to the *Sakka pañha sutta*, is where the Buddha, surrounded by wild animals, provided teachings to Indra (Sakka). Artistic representations of this scene from Gandhara, or late first-century-BCE Bharhut, show the cave in its "natural" forest setting, but the later, first-century-CE depictions on Sanchi's northern gateway frieze present it as a rock-cut *caitya*, of the type with which we are familiar from the Deccan sites.[82] Rajgir's mountainous terrain *is* shown, but in a "tamed and mannered" form that arguably mirrors structural shifts from temporary monsoon retreats to permanent monasteries or, as in the Deccan, the direct transformation of natural caves into artificially excavated cave-*like* structures.[83] By the fifth century CE, Buddhaghosa describes the Indasālagūha as having already been transformed from a *guha* into a rock-cut edifice (*lena*) during the Buddha's lifetime, which Brancaccio argues may reflect contemporary anxieties about an unadapted cave being used as the Buddha's residence, or as a place of worship.[84] Obviously if the "artificial" status of the Indasālagūha can be thus exaggerated to fit with changing social mores, the "wild" or "dangerous" element of such places was no doubt equally susceptible to exaggeration. For example, Granoff discusses a *Mahāvastu* verse that recounts the adaptation of a remote Himalayan cave (*guha*) into a therapeutic sweat-chamber inspired by Ayurvedic practices.[85] However, the previously discussed "hot-air hole" at Morel Khurd that was evidently an integral part of the surrounding "monastic rock-shelter" complex there demonstrates that such practices were not always restricted to "remote" mountainous contexts divorced from socially engaged forms of monasticism.

Another important point here is that most of the central Indian "monastic shelters" contain Chalcolithic paintings of everyday forest scenes, unusual "deities," and wild animals depicted in hunting, post-butchery, or hide-preparation scenes, often with their internal organs and skeletal structure visible.[86] This rich repertoire holds much scope for broadening scholarly understanding of interactions between Pan-Indian/Sanskritic and regional cults and related iconographies, as well as the possible impact of prehistoric hunting practices and related conventions of representation—and later Buddhist engagement with such material—on the development of anatomical medical knowledge, which has hitherto focused solely on the Classical Sanskrit tradition; this is of particular relevance given the attested influence of Buddhist monastics on the spread of Ayurveda.[87] It is also interesting to query whether later perceptions, including those of resident monastics, toward the content and meanings of these prehistoric paintings influenced Buddhist textual and artistic portrayals of the "magical" or "dangerous" properties of such places, even if some of the aspects of forest life that the paintings depicted were no longer realities. We may assume, however, that cave-dwelling monastics would have been as familiar with those enduring elements of forest-based culture, such as for example, tree coppicing and swidden agricultural practices that go back to at least 2500 BCE. as they were with lowland agriculture. Indeed, as today, there would have been considerable overlap between the two; forests continue to provide crucial grazing, foraging, and hunting opportunities for villagers, with products such as honey and medico-culinary plants and animals featuring prominently in urban-rural trading networks.

Future excavation is needed to test the degree to which non-ascetical occupation of such rock-shelters persisted during early-historic periods, but extant settlement data suggest that hilltops were *not* favored as places for village occupation during any period. Most settlements are represented by denuded mudbrick mounds on the plains, with around 27 percent of total settlements surviving as poorly dated stone structural remains on the lower slopes of hillsides.[88]

What is clear, however, is that through the construction of hilltop monastic complexes in the late centuries BCE, monastics would have come to represent the principal occupants of such zones. A notable feature here is that key monuments are sited on naturally fortified cliffs, vulnerable points are reinforced with imposing boundary walls, and monasteries follow towering, vertically oriented plans, raised on high platforms and approached by internally set entrances.[89] Such provisions would have ensured protection against floods and potential threats from hostile humans, as well as wildlife, from tigers to insects.[90]

By contrast, the relatively exposed "monastic rock-shelters," as well as the older monsoon rain retreats out of which sedentary monasticism grew, would have ensured that monastics were fully familiar with such threats, and this too may have influenced later architectural traditions. Instructive in this regard is the "*Bhaya-bherava Sutta*" ("Discourse on Fear and Dread") of the *Sutta Piṭaka*, which describes the Buddha teaching forest-dwelling ascetics meditation techniques for overcoming the fear of wild animals.[91] Further, in the Commentary to the *Dhammapada* (verse 40), we have the story of the "Five Hundred *Bhikkhus*" fleeing from their forest encampment after being spooked by forest spirits (*devatas*) there.[92] The latter hide in the trees but soon tire of their guests, conjuring up ghostly apparitions and illnesses to scare them off. The monks seek refuge with the Buddha, who advises them to return to the forest while chanting the *Mettā-Sutta*. This brings about peace with the *devatas*, who descend from the trees, offering their service and devotion to the monks. While this humorous "psychodrama [. . .] captures the spirit of Buddhist meditation,"[93] it also distills Buddhist attitudes toward the "wild" as at once beautiful, frightening, and unpredictable, while illustrating the inevitable disturbance to and control of "nature" that the movement of increasingly large monastic communities into forested environments would have entailed.

The ambiguity surrounding the "human" versus "supranatural" status of the tree-dwellers in this story is also significant, and recalls previously discussed debates surrounding the courtesan/*yakṣī* identity of sculptures in early Buddhist art, whose precise relationship to the plants from which they emerge is not always obvious. Sculptured *śālabañjikās* (the "one that plucks *śāla* flowers") on Sanchi's first-century-CE Stupa 1 gateways, and from sites in the Deccan,[94] belong to a genre of "women standing beneath trees," or plucking flowers as in the Shravasti festival of the *Āvadana Jātaka*.[95] There are also older references in the *Mahābhārata* (Vanaparva III, 265, i-3a), to the *puṣpa shākha dhāra* ("flowering branch holder"), or the "force" that "bends down the branch of the kadama tree," with names varying from *devatā*, *yakṣī*, *dānavī*, *apsara*, "a fair *Daitya* girl," *nāginī*, to *rakṣasī* ("night wanderer in the wood"). Although some such "forces" are bound to specific trees, others have the power to move independently, as though it is the *spirit* of the tree rather than the tree itself that "wills and acts,"[96] while canonical prohibitions against destroying a sacred tree (*cetiyarukkha*) to make way for a monastery has been taken to suggest a belief in the "soul" of the tree. Given the ambiguity surrounding the human, nonhuman, or "more-than-human" status of such beings, it is possible that the *śālabañjikā* embodied all three: the courtesan, the forest-dwelling human, and the "natural" or "supranatural" force of the tree. Moreover, the *śālabañjikā*'s anthropomorphized form implies a "natural" world that has already come under the influence of *human* control and transformation, a process that is epitomized by the prominence of the garden motif, in general, and the śāla tree, more specifically, in Buddhist art, the latter playing such a central role in woodland management practices such as coppicing and swidden from at least the Neolithic period.[97]

Also instructive here is the tale of Aṅgulimāla, who features prominently in early Buddhist art and literature as the forest-dwelling bandit who is converted by the Buddha, but who comes to represent more generally the wilderness as a place of danger that must be "domesticated" by the sangha.[98] Finally, the socio-ecological implications of the *Vessantara Jātaka* and two of the other *Jātakas* that feature on Sanchi's first-century-CE gateways, warrant further analysis in light of the broader landscape context provided by the SSP data, given that they are all set in forests and involve various kinds of exploitation of natural/"wild" resources.

Conclusion

This chapter has explored the potential of archaeologically attested interactions between monastic groups, and the environments, communities, and products of both upland forested and lowland agricultural zones in central India, for interrogating textual and art-historical positions on Buddhist attitudes toward "nature," and for illuminating potential ecological motifs in early stories and narratives. An obvious irony is that the forests that provided refuge for ascetic groups seeking to distance themselves from productive society were valuable sources of timber and medico-culinary products, but also of perceived social "danger" and contagion. Further, the financial viability of physically but not socially removed monasticism depended on its economic interactions with surrounding villagers and townspeople, and in particular its direct involvement with lowland crop-based agriculture. Whether the latter, following Elverskog's arguments, presents "proof" of the sangha's "anti-environmentalist" stance depends on definitions of both "environmentalism" and "sustainability." However, monastic governmentality may be instructive for modern environmental activism, if only by offering examples of community, ideology-based, models of land and water "care," while the rejuvenation of the pre-modern hydraulic structures upon which such systems relied continues to inform localized solutions to the negative fallout of unsustainable agricultural practices introduced following the ironically named "green revolution" of the 1970s.[99]

Hopefully three further points have also been demonstrated: (1) that a socially engaged sangha that managed and cared for land and water resources both as an instrument of patronage and as a means of tackling human suffering helps to diffuse the polarized debate between the "eco-apologists" and their critics, with its narrow focus on whether or not monks were concerned with the suffering of animals or the "beauty" of "nature"; (2) that landscape data from "beyond the monastery walls" help to challenge both Schmithausen's notion of a "passive" Buddhist environmentalism that sought to "transcend" nature through detachment, and related arguments that stress the purely "symbolic" function of early Buddhist garden imagery. My position is that such motifs are less symbols of the sangha's *transcendence* of nature than of its *engagement* with, on the one hand, lowland hydraulic landscapes that reflected a mixture of local ecological-ritual realities and "translocal" ideals from the Gangetic valley and, on the other, its increasing incursion into upland forested zones; and finally (3) that the distribution of hilltop monasteries, habitational settlements, and simply adapted "monastic rock-shelters" challenges clear-cut polarizations between isolated, magical *guha*s, and fully transformed, rock-cut *lena*s and related social constructions of the marginal and dangerous forest. What is clear from the SSP data is that the sangha's ability to straddle both of these socio-ecological environments was crucial for the establishment and development of institutionalized monasticism in the area.

Notes

1. Julia Shaw, "Religion, 'Nature' and Environmental Ethics in Ancient India," *World Archaeology* 48 (2016): 517–43; Krista Gilliland, I. A. Simpson, et al., "The Dry Tank," *Journal of Archaeological Sciences* 40 (2013): 1012–28.
2. Julia Shaw, *Buddhist Landscapes in Central India* (London: Routledge, 2007).
3. Julia Shaw, "Environmentalism as Religio-Medical 'Worldview,'" *Current Swedish Archaeology* 26 (2019): 61–78.
4. M. E Tucker et al., eds., *Routledge Handbook of Religion and Ecology* (London: Routledge, 2016); Mike Hulme, "Varieties of Religious Engagement with Climate Change," in *Routledge Handbook*, 239–48; Julia Shaw, "Archaeology, Climate Change and Environmental Ethics," *World Archaeology* 48 (2016): 453.
5. Felix Riede, "Deep Pasts—Deep Futures," *Current Swedish Archaeology* 26 (2019): 11–28.
6. Felix Riede, "Deep Pasts"; Shaw, "Religion," 520–521.
7. Shaw, "Religion," 521–22.
8. M. D. Morrison and M. T. Lycett, "Constructing Nature," in *The Social Lives of Forests*, ed. Susanna Hecht et al. (Chicago: University of Chicago Press, 2014), 148–60.

9. Damian Evans, "Airborne Laser Scanning as a Method for Exploring Long-Term Socio-Ecological Dynamics in Cambodia," *Journal of Archaeological Science* 74 (2016): 164–75. Eleanor Kingwell-Banham and Dorian Fuller, "Shifting Cultivators in South Asia: Expansion, Marginalisation and Specialisation over the Long Term," Quaternary International 249 (2012): 84–95.
10. Shaw, "Archaeology," 450.
11. Yama Dixit et al., "Abrupt Weakening of the Summer Monsoon in Northwest India 4100 Yr Ago," *Geology* 42 (2014): 339–42.
12. Eleanor Kingwell-Banham et al., "Early Agriculture in South Asia," in *The Cambridge World History*, ed. G. Barker and C. Goucher (Cambridge: Cambridge University Press, 2015), 261–88.
13. C. R. Strain, "Engaged Buddhist Practice and Ecological Ethics," *Worldviews* 20 (2016), 189–210; Shaw, "Religion," 525–26.
14. Lambert Schmithausen, "The Early Buddhist Tradition and Ecological Ethics," *Journal of Buddhist Ethics* 4 (1997): 1–74.
15. Strain, "Engaged," 197.
16. Schmithausen, "The Early," 12–14.
17. Schmithausen, "The Early," 2.
18. Daud Ali, "Gardens in Early Indian Court Life," *Studies in History* 19 (2003): 221–52; Gregory Schopen, "The Buddhist 'Monastery' and the Indian Garden," *Journal of the American Oriental Society* 126 (2006): 487–505.
19. R. L. Brown, "Nature as Utopian Space on the Early Stūpas of India," in *Buddhist Stūpas In South Asia*, ed. J. Hawkes and A. Shimada, 63–80 (New Delhi: Oxford University Press, 2009).
20. Akira Shimada, "The Use of Garden Imagery in Early Indian Buddhism," in *Garden and Landscape Practices in Pre-Colonial India*, ed. D. Ali and E. Flatt (London: Routledge, 2012), 18–38.
21. Schopen, "The Buddhist 'Monastery,'" 498–505.
22. Shaw, *Buddhist*, 228–32
23. Shaw, *Buddhist*, 233–53; Julia Shaw, "Early Indian Buddhism, Water and Rice," in *Water Technologies and Societies in the Past and Present*, ed. Y. Zhuang and M. Altaweel, 223–55 (London: UCL Press, 2018).
24. R. A. L. H. Gunawardana, "Irrigation and Hydraulic Society in Early Medieval Ceylon," *Past and Present* 53 (1971): 3–27.
25. R. A. E. Coningham and P. Gunawardhana, *Anuradhapura*, Vol. 3: *The Hinterland* (Oxford: BAR International Series, 2013); Shaw, "Early Indian," 238.
26. Julia Shaw and J. V. Sutcliffe, "Water Management, Patronage Networks, and Religious Change," *South Asian Studies* 19 (2003): 94–95; Robert DeCaroli, "Snakes and Gutters," *Archives of Asian Art* 69 (2019): 1–19.
27. Vitus Angermeier, "Untangling Multiple Topographical Systems," *eJournal of Indian Medicine* 9 (2017): 39-62; Francis Zimmermann, "May Godly Clouds Rain for You!" in *Du corps humain: Au carrefour de plusieurs savoirs en Inde*, ed. E. Ciurtin (Paris: De Boccard. Studia Asiatica, 2004), 371–84; Giuliano Giustarini, "Healthcare in Pali Buddhism," *Journal of Religion and Health* 57 (2018): 1224–36; Julia Shaw and Naomi Sykes, "New Directions in the Archaeology of Medicine," *World Archaeology* 50 (2019): 367–68; Shaw, "Environmentalism," 70–71.
28. Shaw, "Environmentalism," 67–71.

29. Shaw, "Religion," 519,
30. Shaw, "Early Indian," 242.
31. Kingwell-Banham et al., "Early Agriculture."
32. Kingwell-Banham, "Dry, Rainfed, or Irrigated?" *Archaeological and Anthropological Sciences* 11 (2019): 6489.
33. Shaw, "Early Indian," 242–47.
34. Pia Brancaccio, "Monumentality, Nature and World Heritage Monuments," in *Decolonising Heritage in South Asia*, ed. H. P. Ray (New Delhi: Routledge, 2018), 112–13.
35. Robert DeCaroli, *Haunting the Buddha* (Oxford: Oxford University Press, 2004); Julia Shaw, "Nāga Sculptures in Sanchi's Archaeological Landscape," *Artibus Asiae* 64 (2004): 5–59.
36. R. S. Cohen, "Naga, Yaksini, Buddha: Local Deities and Local Buddhism at Ajanta," *History of Religions* 37 (1988): 340–60.
37. Shaw, "Nāga," 18–19; cf. Jacob Dalton, "The Early Development of the Padmasambhava Legend in Tibet," *Journal of the American Oriental Society* 124, no. 4: 759–72.
38. J. C. Scott, *The Art of Not Being Governed* (New Haven, CT: Yale University Press, 2009); Peter Grave, "Beyond the Mandala," *World Archaeology* 27 (1995): 243–65.
39. Derek Kennet et al, eds., *Excavations at Paithan, Maharashra* (Berlin: De Gruyter, 2020), 4.
40. Morrison and Lycett, "Constructing," 158–60; Shaw and Sykes, "New," 370; Eleanor Kingwell-Banham et al., "Spice and Rice," *Antiquity* 92 (2018): 1552–70.
41. Janice Stargardt, "Water for the State or Water for the People?" in *Water Societies and Technologies from the Past and Present*, ed. Y. Zhuang and A. Altaweel (London: UCL Press, 2018), 256–68.
42. K. D. Morrison, "Dharmic Projects, Imperial Reservoirs, and New Temples of India," *Conservation and Society* 8 (2010): 182–95.
43. G. D. Sontheimer, "Religious Endowments in India," *Zeitschrift für Vergleichende Rechtswissenschaft* 69 (1964): 45–100; M. D. Willis, *The Archaeology of Hindu Ritual* (New York: Cambridge University Press, 2009).
44. Gregory Bailey and I. Mabbett, *The Sociology of Early Buddhism* (Cambridge: Cambridge University Press, 2003), 13; Patrick Olivelle, "The Beast and the Ascetic," in *Ascetics and Brahmins*, ed. P. Olivelle (Florence: University of Florence Press, 2006), 94–96; Francis Zimmermann, "May Godly," 274.
45. G. Benavides, "Economy," in *Critical Terms for the Study of Buddhism*, ed. D.S. Lopez Jr. (Chicago and London: University of Chicago Press, 2005), 77–102.
46. J. D. Hawkes and R. Abbas, "Copper Plates in Context," *Pratnatattva* 22 (2016): 41–71.
47. Gregory Schopen, "Doing Business for the Lord," *Journal of the American Oriental Society* 114 (1994): 527–54.
48. Julia Shaw, "Monasteries, Monasticism, and Patronage in Ancient India," *South Asian Studies* 27, no. 2 (2011): 111–30.
49. Johan Elverskog, "(Asian Studies + Anthropocene),^{4}" *The Journal of Asian Studies* 73 (2014): 963–74.
50. Shaw, "Religion," 529.
51. Kenneth Zysk, *Asceticism and Healing in Ancient India* (New Delhi: Motilal Banarsidass, 1998).
52. N. E. Falk, "Wilderness and Kingship in Ancient South Asia," *History of Religions* 13 (1973): 1–15.
53. T. R. Trautmann, *Elephants and Kings: An Environmental History* (Chicago: University of Chicago Press, 2015), 57. Cf. R. L. Brown, "Telling the Story in Art of the Monkey's Gift

of Honey to the Buddha," *Bulletin of the Asia Institute* 23 (2009): 43–52; Shaw, *Buddhist*, 133–34; Jātaka Stories, https://jatakastories.div.ed.ac.uk/stories-in-art/search/?descriptors=elephant.

54. Shaw, *Buddhist*, 228–32, 250.
55. Shaw, *Buddhist*, 42–43.
56. Sam Van Schaik, *Buddhist Magic* (Boulder, CO: Shambhala, 2020), 43–44; Peter Skilling, "The *Rakṣā* Literature of the *Srāvakayana*," *Journal of the Pali Text Society* 16 (1992): 159, 168. Grateful thanks to Sarah Shaw for helpful discussion.
57. Lance Cousins, "Cetiya and Thupa: The Textual Sources," in *Relic and Relic Worship in Early Buddhism*, ed. J. Stargardt and M. Willis (London: British Museum Press, 2018), 22; A. K. Coomaraswamy, *Yakṣas* (Washington, DC: Smithsonian Institution, 1931), II, 17.
58. Edmund Hardy, "Ueber den upsprung des samajja," in *Album Kern*, ed. H. Kern (Leiden: E. J. Brill, 1903), 61–66.
59. D. D. Kosambi, "At the Crossroads: Mother Goddess Cult Sites in Ancient India, Part I," *The Journal of the Royal Asiatic Society of Great Britain and Ireland* 1, no. 2 (1960): 17–31.
60. Cousins, "Cetiya," 22–23.
61. Shaw, *Buddhist*, 142.
62. Shaw, *Buddhist*, 228–32, figure 13.6.
63. Shaw, Buddhist, 85–86, 136, figure 11.1.
64. L. M. Olivieri et al., "Archaeology and Settlement History in a Test Area of the Swat Valley," *East and West* 56 (2006): 73–150.
65. Shaw, *Buddhist*, 129–130, 135–136, figure 11.23.
66. Di Caroli, "Snakes," 1–19.
67. Shaw, *Buddhist*, 86–87; plate 49.
68. Shaw, *Buddhist*, 110–11; cf Willis, *The Archaeology*, 197.
69. Shaw, *Buddhist*, 115–18; M. D. Willis et al., *Buddhist Reliquaries from Ancient India* (London: British Museum Press, 2000).
70. Shaw, *Buddhist*, 117.
71. Shaw, *Buddhist*, 117.
72. Shaw, *Buddhist*, 113; R. C. Agrawal, "Stupas and Monasteries: A Recent Discovery from Satdhara," in *South Asian Archaeology 1995*, ed. R. Allchin and B. Allchin (Oxford: IBH, 1997), 410–11, figures 9–10.
73. Shaw, *Buddhist*, 129–30.
74. Shaw, *Buddhist*, 36–37.
75. Shaw, *Buddhist*, 37, 117, pl. 52; Harry Falk, "The Preamble at Pāṅgurāriyā," in *Baudd havidyāsudhākaraḥ: Studies in Honour of Heinz Bechert*, ed. H. Bechert et al. (Swisttal-Odendorf: Indica et Tibetica, 1997), 107–21.
76. M. D. Willis, "Avalokiteśvara of the Six Syllables," *Bulletin of the Asia Institute* 23 (2013): 221–29.
77. Phyllis Granoff, "What's in a Name? Rethinking 'Caves,'" in *Living Rock*, ed. P. Brancaccio (Mumbai: Marg Publications), 23–24.
78. Granoff, "What's," 23.
79. Granoff, "What's," 27.
80. Granoff, "What's," 23.
81. Morrison and Lycett, "Constructing"; Kingwell-Banham et al., "Spice"; Shaw and Sykes, "New," 370.
82. Brancaccio, "Monumentality," 113.

83. Pia Brancaccio, "Representations of Indasalaguha," in *South Asian Archaeology and Art 2012*, ed. V. Lefèvre et al. (Tunhout: Brepols, 2016), 427–42.
84. Granoff, "What's," 20.
85. Granoff, "What's," 23–24.
86. Erwin Neumayer, *Prehistoric Rock Art of India* (New Delhi: Oxford University Press, 2011).
87. K. G. Zysk, "The Evolution of Anatomical Knowledge in Ancient India," *Journal of the American Oriental Society* 106 (1986): 687–705.
88. Shaw, *Buddhist*, 215, figure 13.1.
89. Shaw, *Buddhist*, 110–45.
90. Ann Heirman, "How to Deal with Dangerous and Annoying Animals: A Vinaya Perspective," *Religions* 10 (2019).
91. Bhikkhu Nāṇamoli and B. Bodhi, *The Middle Length Discourses of the Buddha* (Somerville, MA: Wisdom Publications, 1995), 102–7.
92. Sarah Shaw, *The Spirit of Buddhist Meditation* (New Haven, CT: Yale University Press, 2014), 370–82.
93. Shaw, *The Spirit*, 369.
94. Pia Brancaccio, *The Buddhist Caves at Aurangabad* (Leiden: Brill, 2011), 11.
95. Coomaraswamy, *Yakṣas*, II, 1–12.
96. Coomaraswamy, *Yakṣas*, II, 1–12, citing *Milindapañha* IV: 3, 20.
97. Cousins, "Cetiya," 22; Lambert Schmithausen, "The Problem of the Sentience of Plants in Earliest Buddhism," *Studia Philologica Buddhica Monograph Series* 6 (Tokyo: International Institute for Buddhist Studies 1991), 26ff; Kingwell-Banham and Fuller, "Shifting," 89–90.
98. Pia Brancaccio, "Aṅgulimāla or the Taming of The Forest," *East and West* 49 (1999): 109, 117.
99. A. Agarwal and S. Narain, *Dying Wisdom* (New Delhi: Centre of Science and Environment, 1997).

Further Reading

Ali, Daud. "Gardens in Early Indian Court Life." *Studies in History* 19, no. 2 (2003): 221–52. https://doi.org/10.1177/025764300301900204

Ali, Daud, and E. Flatt, eds. *Garden and Landscape Practices in Pre-Colonial India: Histories from the Deccan*. London: Routledge, 2012.

Brancaccio, Pia. "Aṅgulimāla or the Taming of the Forest." *East and West* 49, no. 1/4 (1999): 105–118. http://www.jstor.org/stable/29757423

Brancaccio, Pia. "Representations of Indasalaguha: Rock-Cut Monasteries and the Shifting Attitudes Towards Buddhist Asceticism." In *South Asian Archaeology and Art 2012: South Asian Religions and Visual Forms in their Archaeological Context*, edited by V. Lefèvre, A. Didier, and B. Mutin, 427–42. Tunhout: Brepols, 2016.

DeCaroli, Robert. "Snakes and Gutters: *Nāga* Imagery, Water Management, and Buddhist Rainmaking Rituals in Early South Asia." *Archives of Asian Art* 69, no. 1 (2019): 1–19. https://doi.org/10.1215/00666637-7329873

Elverskog, Johan. *The Buddha's Footprint: An Environmental History of Asia*. Philadelphia: University of Pennsylvania Press, 2020.

Granoff, Phyllis. "What's in a Name? Rethinking 'Caves.'" In *Living Rock: Buddhist, Hindu and Jain Cave Temples in Western* Deccan, edited by P. Brancaccio, 18–29. Mumbai: Marg Publication, 2013.

Heirman, Ann. "How to Deal with Dangerous and Annoying Animals: A *Vinaya* Perspective." *Religions* 10, no. 2 (2019): 113. https://doi.org/10.3390/rel10020113

Hidas, Gergely. *A Buddhist Ritual Manual on Agriculture: Vajratuṇḍasamayakalparāja – Critical Edition and Translation*. Berlin/Boston: Walter de Gruyter GmbH, 2019. https://doi.org/10.1515/9783110621051-001

Morrison, Kathleen, D., S.B. Hecht, and C. Padoch, eds. *The Social Lives of Forests: Past, Present, and Future of Woodland Expansion*. Chicago: University of Chicago Press, 2014.

Schmithausen, Lambert. "The Early Buddhist Tradition and Ecological Ethics." *Journal of Buddhist Ethics* 4, no. 1 (1997): 1–74.

Shaw, Julia. *Buddhist Landscapes in Central India: Sanchi Hill and Archaeologies of Religious and Social Change, c. 3rd Century BC to 5th Century AD*. London: Routledge, 2007.

Shaw, Julia. "Religion, 'Nature' and Environmental Ethics in Ancient India: Archaeologies of Human:Non-Human Suffering and Well-being in early Buddhist and Hindu Contexts." *World Archaeology* 48, no. 4 (2016): 517–543. https://doi.org/10.1080/00438243.2016.1250671

Shaw, Julia. The Garden, the Field and the Forest: A Deep-Time Study of Nature and Society in South Asia, In Preparation.

Trautmann, Thomas, R. *Elephants and Kings: An Environmental History*. Chicago: University of Chicago Press, 2015.

Tucker, Mary, E., and D.R. Williams, eds. *Buddhism and Ecology: The Interconnection of Dharma and Deeds*, Cambridge, MA: Harvard University, 1997.

PART III

BODIES IN TRANSITION

EMBODIMENT is fundamental to Buddhist practice. And while it is common to think of the human body as relatively stable when measured against the momentariness of ordinary mental states, Buddhist teachings and practices foreground the body's inherent vulnerability and transience. The foundational teaching of samsara locates the material particularity of each human body at the intersection of an endless sequence of past and future forms of embodiment, each of which defines a distinct set of behavioral possibilities and limitations, ranging from hell beings to celestial deities. Viewed in the context of diverse academic disciplines, the bodies of scholars are likewise accorded a wide range of potential roles in knowledge construction, depending in part on the particular methodologies undertaken, whether sheltered by the relative stillness of a research library or swept up in the swirling kinesthetic force of sacred movement. This diversity of scholarly locations is reflected in the four chapters here, which draw on textual sources, including published ethnographies, as well as the authors' own field-based participant observation.

Each chapter in this section explores human bodies in transition. In the case of Sienna Craig's work (Chapter 13), set amidst the devastation of the 2015 earthquakes in Nepal, bodies are investigated as sites of suffering as well as healing as they are strategically engaged by Tibetan healers who draw on a wide range of material and spiritual methodologies. Ian Reader's exploration of pilgrimage practices in Chapter 14 turns attention to physical movement, with a focus on the personal and social effects of placing those bodies in proximity to special locations that materially mediate the transformative presence of powerful religious agents, including sites in India, Sri

Lanka, Burma, Tibet, and Japan. Miranda Shaw's exploration of Vajrayana dance in Nepal (Chapter 15) highlights bodies as they move through physical space and, through the agency afforded by that movement, come to manifest the presence of powerful deities. And finally, Margaret Gouin's Chapter 16, which returns to Tibetan Buddhism, explores the highly elaborated set of practices that support human bodies as they undergo their most significant and precarious transition, crossing over from life to death to rebirth in a new embodied form, a process imbued with great anxiety and spiritual potential for the deceased as well as for the human community they leave behind. Taken together, the chapters provide a series of portraits that illustrate the efficacy of Buddhist practices for strategically marking and collapsing the boundaries between individuals and social groups, and between human and superhuman agents.

CHAPTER 13

BUDDHIST HEALING PRACTICES

SIENNA R. CRAIG

Introduction

A monk sits in a field of rubble, surrounded by boulders and scree. Beyond him, the landscape is blighted, lunar. A poplar trunk has been turned into a mast on which white prayer flags—symbolizing loss, reckoning lives—have been hoisted. The monk's maroon robes are tucked in around his knees and thighs. He wears a matching claret-colored fleece. A faded orange hat covers his shaved head and the edge of a saffron undershirt peaks out from beneath a zipper. Mountain air surrounds him. The monk's jaw is set in concentration. His eyes flutter toward closed. His right palm rests open on folded legs, and he grips a walking stick in his left hand. To imagine navigating this expanse of rock, soil, and splintered wood without some help to balance seems treacherous, even if it weren't possible that the ground beneath his feet might move again, as it did on April 25, 2015—nearly twelve months earlier.

Tenjing Bista, the monk in this scene, is both a monastic in the Sakya (T. *sa skya*) Tibetan Buddhist tradition and an *amchi* (T. *a mchi*)[1] or practitioner of Sowa Rigpa, the "science of healing" that one might also call Tibetan medicine.[2] Although he is sitting on land enfolded within the Langtang valley in Nepal's Rasuwa district, this is not his home territory. He is from the ancient walled city of Lo Monthang, west of here in Mustang district, bordering Tibet. Tenjing is a visitor in Langtang, and, if not a foreigner, then someone whose language, culture, and religious tradition at once resonate with these local highland communities and remain distinct from them. And yet he is here—one year after a 7.8 magnitude earthquake triggered a massive landslide that buried Langtang village and, along with it, about 300 people in 50 seconds, with half the force of an atomic bomb.[3]

In another image (Figure 13.1), Amchi Tenjing sits at the head of a row of ritual practitioners. They are seated outside on the ground, with only a thin camping pad

FIGURE 13.1. Amchi Tenjing Bista, along with local residents and ritual specialists, conducting a Buddhist ritual in Langtang, Nepal, around the one-year anniversary of the 2015 earthquakes. Photo: Austin Lord, 2016.

between their bodies and the cool spring earth. Behind them, a tangle of metal rebar juts into a hazy sky. One year on, the trauma of that disastrous moment lingers: in piles of debris, in neat stacks of salvaged timber, in torn photos still being pulled from the wreckage. Tenjing holds a ritual bell (T. *dril bu*) in one hand; a thunderbolt scepter (T. *rdo rje*, Skt. *vajra*) and unbound Tibetan text (T. *dpe cha*) rest on flat pieces of granite that serve as a makeshift table in front of Tenjing and the other officiants. To the left of Tenjing, a local lama from Langtang sprinkles grains in offering. A novice *amchi* and monk, also from Mustang, chants beside the lama. After having been defiled by so many violent, untimely deaths, this land is being purified and re-consecrated. Prayers are being offered to local deities of place (T. *yul lha*) and spirits that dwell in water sources, in earth and rock (T. *klu, sa bdag, btsan*), as well as for the well-being of those who survived and the remembrance of the dead.

We might ask: Why is this monk and medical practitioner from a distant region of Nepal here in Langtang on the anniversary of this natural disaster? What is he accomplishing with his meditative practice at the site of an ancient Nyingma (T. *rnying ma*) monastery, in a region that is at once a region associated with Guru Rinpoche (Skt. Padmasambhava), the eight-century saint who brought Buddhism from India to Tibet, and also known as a famous trekking destination, a place of yak herders and hoteliers, along the Tamang Heritage Trail?[4] Aside from these moments of meditation and ritual practice, what other activities has Amchi Tenjing been engaged in? Why do they matter to him and to the people of Langtang? How is this experience an illustration of Buddhist healing? This chapter is an attempt to answer these questions. The framework of Sowa Rigpa responses to the 2015 Nepal earthquakes facilitates a discussion of Buddhist approaches to healing, health, and illness within Himalayan and Tibetan communities.

Not all Sowa Rigpa practice is Buddhist practice. Not all Tibetan physicians frame their clinical work around Buddhism. And yet, as Barbara Gerke points out, "Buddhism and medicine have been interconnected since the earliest descriptions of the life of the Buddha."[5] For many practitioners and patients alike, the relationship between body, mind, and spirit, as well as community, actions and their consequences (T. *las,* Skt. *karma*), and environment—understood through epistemological frames that are at once Himalayan/Tibetan *and* Buddhist—remains crucial to grasping the causes and conditions of illness and the pathways toward health. In addition, an orientation toward the world that not only embraces impermanence (T. *mi rtag pa,* Skt. *anitya*) and dependent-origination (T. *rten 'brel,* Skt. *pratītya-samutpāda*), but that also presumes suffering in the realm of sentient existence (T. *'khor ba,* Skt. *samsāra*)—particularly in this "degenerative age" (Skt. *kali yuga*)—can prove very useful in the face of tragedy. *Amchi* not only are accustomed to addressing ailments of the body and mind, but also, given the socioeconomic uncertainties and political instability of life in contemporary Nepal, are accustomed to what might be called the disaster of everyday life.

Like many of his fellow Sowa Rigpa practitioners in Nepal, Amchi Tenjing felt that it was his duty, his Dharma, to respond to this natural disaster by visiting communities that had been hard hit.[6] In a series of *amchi* medical camps, they brought medicines, food, and emergency relief supplies, but also carried with them their capacity as Buddhist practitioners to address mental and spiritual anguish, to reckon disturbed sacred geographies, and to help settle the *la* (T. *bla*), or souls,[7] of those who were killed. While many of these camps occurred soon after the major April 25 and May 12 seismic events, this series of camps across the Langtang valley were happening around the time of the one-year anniversary, at the request of the Langtangpa,[8] and in coordination with several other relief and response efforts. For the previous twelve months, the people of Langtang not only had struggled with the destruction of lives and livelihoods, but also had been engaged in the excruciating work of sifting through what remained and making cautious plans to rebuild. None of this was easy work: it tore on body (T. *lus*) and heart-mind (T. *sems*).[9]

Nepal's *amchi* reacted with wisdom (T. *shes rab* Skt. *prajñā*), compassion (T. *snying rje,* Skt. *karuṇā*), and skillful means (T. *thabs,* Skt. *upāya*) to these events. They understood that all medicine—be they biomedical drugs, Tibetan medicines, acupuncture, massage, or ritual healing—would be more effective if people had access to food and shelter, and that many post-earthquake illnesses would stem from material precarity. They understood—without the need for awkward hyphens such as "bio-psycho-social care" that are prominent in conventional humanitarianism—that a response to physical injury also demanded attunement to emotional states and psychological responses to collective trauma. Crucially, they recognized that ritually acknowledging death needed to be a part of what it meant to help the living respond to and recover from crisis.

In what follows, Sowa Rigpa is described from a Buddhist and a historical perspective, and core theories of health and disease are summarized. A discussion of Sowa Rigpa's systems of education is followed by an introduction to methods of diagnosis and treatment. With this background, the post-earthquake *amchi* camps are presented in a bit more detail in order to make the larger point that medical practice can be understood as compassion in action, even as it remains embedded within larger political-economies of disaster response. This chapter also asks questions about the nature of causality—of earthquakes, of sickness and death—as a way of understanding the responses that *amchi*, and the Nepali villagers they served, had to these events. Here, Buddhist philosophy meets scientific understanding as well as Himalayan and Tibetan concepts of sacred geography, risk, and what it means to steward a landscape that one calls home. In conclusion, this chapter argues that a Buddhist healing framework speaks to something beyond "resilience"—an orientation to the world that expects suffering but that has meaningful, efficacious responses to it, within the lives of individuals and communities.

The Science of Healing in Theory and Practice

The Tibetan term *sowa rigpa* (T. *gso ba rig pa*) can be translated literally as the science or art (T. *rig*, Skt. *vidya*) of healing (T. *gso ba*). It is an empirical and systematic approach to medical diagnosis and therapeutic practice developed over centuries, with its knowledge transmitted both textually and through oral transmission, in response to human disease; it is also a philosophy of health and illness that is connected to Tibetan Buddhist conceptions of what it means to be human.[10] The transmission of Buddhism from India to Tibet included the spread of medical as well as spiritual practices.[11] One example of this is that Sowa Rigpa is understood as one of the "great five" fields of human knowledge in classical Buddhist education, the others being the study of language and grammar, the creative arts, logic, and "inner science" or philosophy. The fact that medicine was incorporated into monastic education in Tibetan societies is one way of describing the deep links between medicine and Buddhism in these cultural contexts.

At another level, we need look no further than the figure of the Medicine Buddha (T. Sangs rgyas Sman bla, Skt. Bhaiṣajyaguru) to understand this connection. The Medicine Buddha occupies a position of prominence in the form and structure of Sowa Rigpa's core texts, the *Four Tantras* (T. *rGyud bzhi*). This work draws on classical texts from Ayurveda (specifically the *Aṣṭāṅgahṛdayasaṃhitā* of Vāgbhata, translated into Tibetan in the eleventh century), as well as indigenous Tibetan treatises and influences from the Greco-Arab world, and was likely codified in the twelfth century by the figure Yuthog Yontan Gompo (g.Yu thog Yon tan mgon po, 1126–1202).[12] Yet the text presents itself, in verse that resembles tantric scripture, as a teaching by the Medicine Buddha.[13] Each chapter of the *Four Tantras* begins with a dialogue between two sages[14]—both emanations of the Medicine Buddha. This transmission of medical knowledge takes place in Tanadug, a "visionary 'City of Medicine,' surrounded by meadows and mountains rich in medicinal plants and substances."[15] This vision is depicted in the first of seventy-nine seventeenth-century scroll paintings (T. *thang ka*) commissioned by the famous monk-physician Desi Sangye Gyatso (T. sDe srid Sangs rgyas rgya mtsho, 1653–1705) to illustrate the *Four Tantras* and aid in medical education (Figure 13.2).[16] The

FIGURE 13.2. Palace of Buddha Bhaisjyaguru (Sangye Menla), Master of Remedies, in Tanadug, the Land of Medicine. Painted by Master Locho, 2013.
Used with permission of Stephan Kloos. Photo: Stephan Kloos, 2014.

Medicine Buddha remains the ethical exemplar for physicians across the regions where Sowa Rigpa is practiced.

Another way of illustrating this connection between medicine and Buddhism is to note that the three fundamental *nyépa or* "dynamics" (T. *nyes pa*)[17] in Sowa Rigpa theory, wind (T. *rlung*), bile (T. *mkhris pa*), and phlegm (T. *bad kan*), are also mapped onto the three mental poisons (T. *dug gsum*, Skt. *klesha*) of desire, hatred, and delusion. In this sense, the root of human disease as it manifests in the body-mind is linked to what causes us to remain in samsara, to suffer. "In this way, the *rGyud bzhi* makes disease into something that is directly linked to the unenlightened nature of everyday reality and to the central Buddhist project of transcending this everyday world of suffering and rebirth."[18] And yet, the configuration of the *nyépa* and their connections to the five elements (T. *byung ba lnga*)—earth, air, fire, water, and space/consciousness—are ways of tracing the historical connections between Sowa Rigpa and other currents of medical tradition. The three *nyépa* have their equivalencies with the Ayurveda *tridoṣa* system—*vāta*, *pitta*, *kapha*—just as Tibetan and Ayurvedic approaches to the detoxification of substances (such as gems and heavy metals) for use in medicinal formulas are similar. The configuration of the five elements in relation to *nyépa*, as well as aspects of Sowa Rigpa's vast *materia medica* and types of external therapies (cupping, acupuncture, moxibustion, etc.), resonate with many aspects of Chinese, South Asian, and Greco-Arab medical and astrological practices.

This leads to another important point: although Sowa Rigpa is linked to Buddhism in fundamental ways, it is also an articulation of Tibetan conceptions of culture, science, technology, and social relations that extend beyond Buddhist doctrine, that have been influenced by other forms of medical knowledge (including biomedicine), and that include rich regional variation.[19] This variation not only occurs in the plants, minerals, and animal products that are used to make medical formulas, but also in regional therapeutic specializations, pharmacological adaptations to distinct patient populations, and the incorporation or coexistence of Sowa Rigpa practices with many forms of ritual healing linked to localized or "folk" religious and cosmological orientations.[20] In theory and practice, Sowa Rigpa is at once indigenous and local, and an adaptive, flexible, and dynamic tradition. Its shared textual history, in the form of the *Four Tantras* and core commentaries and pharmacopeia, allows for, if not "standardization" in a biomedical sense, then consistent and replicable approaches to education, diagnosis, and treatment over vast territories—from areas of the Russian Federation and Mongolia, across the Tibetan Plateau and Himalaya, and, since the 1960s, to diasporic Tibet and many global locales.[21] Even so, Sowa Rigpa maintains—in theory, if not always in practice—a universalist Buddhist goal of maintaining health and addressing the suffering in all sentient beings.

When it comes to the education of practitioners and the treatment of patients, Sowa Rigpa is a deeply embodied practice. It demands self-cultivation. The physician's own body is the primary diagnostic instrument, and the memorization and recitation of texts, as with Buddhist scripture, remains a foundational component of learning and practice.[22] Here, too, we find resonance and points of intersection with Buddhism.

Historically, *amchi* learned to practice medicine by being connected, via family or religious lineages, to their teachers. Schools and colleges of Sowa Rigpa ranged in scope and size, from major institutions such as Chagpori (T. *lcags po ri*), a monastic medical college founded in Lhasa by Desi Sangye Gyatso in 1696,[23] and Mentsikhang (T. *sman rtsi khang*) founded in Lhasa in 1916, where it still exists, and also re-established in exile in 1961,[24] to smaller lay and monastic schools across the greater Himalayan and Tibetan region as well as newer state institutions in places such as Mongolia and Bhutan. Over the years, in different national contexts, and in response to distinct political-economic pressures, Sowa Rigpa education has changed. For example, anything that could be conceived of as "religious" or "superstitious" was purged from curricula in China and Mongolia during communist eras; today the incorporation of aspects of biomedicine and Western scientific disciplines such as biology and chemistry have become commonplace across Sowa Rigpa institutions in Asia. In the case of Amchi Tenjing, like many other practitioners in Nepal, he studied under his father and his great uncle, alongside his brother. His education as an *amchi* was by turns linked to, and distinct from, his training as a Buddhist monk.

When we say that an *amchi*'s primary diagnostic tool is his or her body, what does that mean? Basically, it refers to the complex methods of pulse analysis, urine analysis, and attuned psychosocial understandings that emerge through questioning a patient and examining her constitution. Pulse analysis can be considered at once the ground truth and the apex of Sowa Rigpa expertise. It is a precise science of the body-as-technology and a sensorial art, honed over many years of practice. Taking a pulse (Figure 13.3), along with testing urine according to its taste, color, viscosity, etc., and looking at a patient and asking some questions, guides a practitioner to sense and determine what particular forms of imbalance in the *nyépa*—in relation to the elements, bodily constituents, the dynamics of heat and cold, and many other factors—are leading to illness.

Sowa Rigpa theory articulates a complex classification of diseases, as well as the causes, conditions, and natures of these afflictions. Some diseases are understood to have direct biophysical roots: poisoning, inflammation, fractured bones, sinus disorders, kidney infections, disruptions to digestion, etc. Although they are not usually described in terms that a biomedical doctor would use, they can be treated with medicines and, in some cases, will heal by themselves with proper attention to diet and behavior. Other diseases, however, can be caused by nefarious spirits or by karma accrued from past lifetimes; aspects of Buddhism as well as cultural understandings from Tibetan and Himalayan worlds intersect with medicine and, at least to some, complicate boundaries between "religion" and "science."[25] Here, too, possibilities for ritual healing emerge. Ritual practice is sometimes used in combination with medicines or external therapies, as well as behavioral practices such as the "prescription" of particular meditation methods, the recitation of mantras, pilgrimage, etc.

Speaking of medicines and other therapies, the production of Sowa Rigpa formulas requires a vast range of expertise that one might bundle into Western disciplines of botany, zoology, pharmacology, chemistry, and toxicology. Historically, the production of formulas (including harvesting and preparing medicinal ingredients) and the

FIGURE 13.3. Amchi Tenjing Bista takes the pulse of Pemba Lama, the senior-most surviving religious practitioner from Langtang.

Photo: Austin Lord, 2016.

practice of prescribing were done by the same individual, or people closely connected within that household or a religious institution. Today, many practicing *amchi* rely on ready-made medicines produced in urban pharmacies under varying degrees of standardization and state oversight.[26] Ingestible medicines, as well as formulas used for herbal baths, decoctions, or poultices, are not single ingredients but rather complex formulas that have as few as five and as many as sixty or more ingredients in them. The most complex of all formulas are called *rinchen rilbu* (T. *rin chen ril bu*). They contain various blessed substances (T. *byin labs*) and precious or semi-precious minerals, gems, or detoxified metals such as mercury-sulfide ash (T. *bso thal*). As is the case with other medicines as well, under certain conditions of production, *rinchen rilbu* are also subject to ritual consecrations (T. *sman grub*). Many patients are aware of this. In a distinct but related way to the sense of care provided by the human touch and concentration involved in the act of taking a pulse, one might argue that part of the efficacy of these very biochemically potent formulas also comes from their connection to forms of Buddhist ritual practice.

With respect to *amchi* responses to the earthquakes, these connections between medical and ritual practice were seen not only in the act of showing up and providing medicines or in how practitioners spoke with patients about their trauma, but also in the ritual protection cords and blessed substances they distributed, along with other more common medicines and external therapies. As was the case with Tenjing in Langtang, these connections also manifested in the Buddhist rituals that *amchi* performed, often alongside local religious practitioners, to help appease local deities of place and spirits who could cause illness or misfortune in the living, to purify a ground defiled by physical damage as well as spiritual pollution (T. *sgrib*), and to honor the dead. And, crucially, as both medical and Buddhist practitioners, *amchi* understood that they would be accruing merit (T. *bsod nams,* Skt. *puṇya*) by participating in acts of compassion in action.

Compassion in Action

It is often said that traditional medicine, including Tibetan medicine, succeeds in the treatment of chronic conditions, but that conventional biomedicine is a better option for the provision of acute or invasive care. These examples represent commonly held ideas about what traditional medicine and biomedicine are "good for." It is important to note that such a dichotomized point of view is not only espoused by biomedical practitioners but also stated by *amchi* as well as by patients of all sorts. Indeed, many of the ways that Sowa Rigpa "brands" itself globally—in line with other so-called "complementary and alternative" healing modalities—follows this logic. While these understandings may be empirically true, they are also incomplete. In discussing their responses to the earthquakes, *amchi* spoke not only of treating individual patients suffering from trauma, poor nutrition, and sleeping on the ground, but also the need to appease deities of place, alleviate mental suffering of the living, and guide the dead toward favorable rebirth.

Unlike its neighbors in India, China, and Bhutan, the Nepali government neither officially recognizes nor grants state public health support to Sowa Rigpa practitioners or institutions. This meant that any "medical charity" (T. *sman sbyin pa*) on the part of Nepal's *amchi* needed to be facilitated by private networks in order to execute the post-earthquake camps. Specifically, Tibetan medicines to be used in these camps were donated or purchased at cost from urban clinic-pharmacies in Nepal, or were donated by pharmacies abroad, specifically from New Delhi and Lhasa. (The socioeconomics of small-scale medicine production in Nepal is such that those *amchi* who still produce their own medicines would have depleted annual supplies to serve their own communities had they used these for the camps.) Foreign and local donors helped to fund these camps, but *amchi* donated their time and made contributions to the cost of transportation, which was significant. Although not all of Nepal's *amchi* get along with each other, this state of emergency fostered trust, collaboration, and shared social knowledge about where to go, when, and why.

Between June 2015 and October 2016, *amchi* conducted medical camps in a range of earthquake-affected areas, from Mustang district, west of the April 25 epicenter, to Kavre, Rasuwa, Dolakha, Dhading, Timure, and Sindhupalchok districts further east, near the epicenter of the May 12 earthquake, as well as in Kathmandu, where many internally displaced people had settled. The eleven camps for which I have data[27] served nearly 2,500 patients. In addition to Tibetan medicines, *amchi* provided biomedical first aid, food, tin sheets, soap, water buckets, and toothbrushes. They used acupuncture, moxibustion, and other external therapies, as well as ritual practice. While some might define "medical pluralism" as distinct medical systems existing side by side, I argue that this concept is an enacted fluidity within and between medical systems, in the provision of care, sometimes in dialogue with patient desire. This idea is mirrored in the ways that *amchi* described their use of multiple healing modalities. As Tenjing Bista commented, "From a Buddhist perspective, *amchi* medicine and *allopathic* medicine go hand in hand, like the relationship between skillful means and wisdom (T. *thabs dang shes rab*). With one hand, it is difficult to accomplish things. With two hands, it is easier to do good work."

While seeing patients, they provided forms of culturally resonant counseling, a process of reckoning impermanence and reminding patients of the "happiness-suffering," the *kyi-dug* or the *sukha-duḥkha*, inherent in sentient existence. Whether spoken in Tibetan or Nepali, this idea that sweetness and pain are linked, that they are more one word than two, resonated with those they served. As Amchi Tsewang Gyurme described, "We have given advice of how to control their emotions and provided them with Medicine Buddha amulets to overcome their sorrow and *semné* [T. *sems gnad*, illness of the heart-mind]. Sometimes special mantras (T. *ngags*) were done on them too." He explained that they also gave medicines, such as *agar* (eaglewood, *Aquilaria malaccensis*) formulas, for wind (T. *rlung*) disorders associated with what might be glossed as a combination of "anxiety" and "depression" in biomedicine, and described what he did as being "like psychiatry."

For all camps, one or two senior *amchi* were accompanied by at least twice as many support staff. In some instances, these included biomedically trained nurses or medical assistants. In others, novice *amchi*, students of Tibetan medicine, or young monastics assisted. In all cases, at least one local liaison was recruited to help manage logistics, including finding space in which the camps could occur and locating housing or tent space for *amchi* teams. *Amchi* brought their own food but relied at times on local fuel. Camps averaged two to three days in each location, with some requiring significant travel (by truck/jeep, pack animal, porters, and walking) and presenting various travel obstacles (landslides, mud and impassable roads, broken-down vehicles, etc.).

Most camps followed a similar structure. The team would arrive the afternoon before a camp would begin, speak with local liaisons about camp logistics, including a plan for patient queuing and the creation of some sort of "waiting area." In Buddhist communities, that first evening would often end with a ritual, in which *amchi* joined in practice with local religious representatives, such as described in the opening vignette of this chapter. A morning prayer session would usually start the day, before patients were seen for approximately 12–14 hours straight. The distribution of other forms of material aid often came at the end of the first day. All consultations included pulse analysis and a brief physical examination; the level of patient questioning, time taken for diagnosis, and privacy varied, but was limited in all instances. Ritual practices for the living (e.g., *tsedrub*, *kag go*, *thün*) and dead toward rebirth (e.g., *ngowa*, *monlam*, *bardo*, *namshé*, *chö shé*) were performed at the end of camps in Buddhist communities. In primarily Hindu communities, public ritual practices in situ were not performed; instead *amchi* made offerings for the dead in these communities at sacred sites such as the Boudhanath and Swayambhunath stupas when they returned to Kathmandu. They did this with the knowledge and appreciation of community members.

The ages of patients varied significantly, from infants to people in their ninth decade of life. The majority of patients were over fifty, with female patients outnumbering men, sometimes by as much as two to one. This demographic detail likely reflects patterns of wage labor outmigration from Nepal's rural areas. The types of illnesses that *amchi* diagnosed and treated varied, but wind (T. *rlung*) disorders predominated. Phlegm (T. *bad kan*) disorders, a range of gastric problems, and arthritis/joint pain as well as upper respiratory problems were also common. *Amchi* attributed the cause of many physical illnesses to the work of deconstruction as well as sleeping under tin sheets and tarpaulins, exposed to the elements, for weeks or months. In some areas, *amchi* noted alcohol use/abuse. Although they counseled villagers against this behavior, they acknowledged that getting drunk was a way of responding to pain and uncertainty. As Amchi Ngawang Namgyal commented, "Some hang in between life and death because of their *semné*."

The care *amchi* provided was often cross-cultural, in that they were treating fellow Nepali citizens with whom they shared very few points of reference: neither the same mother tongue nor, in some cases, the same religion. All *amchi* commented on the ways that the physical and geographic circumstances of rural life, as well as poverty and a lack of government presence, contributed to post-earthquake health problems and exacerbated "old" illnesses. In some cases, practitioners were providing Tibetan medicines to communities who had never heard the word "*amchi*" before, or, in other cases, were aware of Tibetan medicine as a system but had never taken such medicines themselves. *Amchi* found themselves involved in different forms of medical and cultural translation: about the bitter tastes of pills; about how Sowa Rigpa was "like" Ayurveda and dependent on *jadibuti*, medicinal plants; about the premise that these medicines could be slow to take effect but would help get at the root of disease. As Amchi Ngawang Namgyal put it, "Fifty percent of the people haven't heard of Sowa Rigpa. When we give them *rilbu* [Tibetan medicinal pills], they react in awkward manners . . . but many of them also are aware of the side effects of Western medicine. They really liked our medicines and asked where they could get more in Kathmandu for future treatment."

While some practitioners said that they were impressed that roads reached many communities—and saw this as a positive "reach" of the state—others noted the difficulties of life off the road as an example of the failed promises of "development." Participating in these camps impacted *amchi* and their helpers in various ways: intellectual, physical, emotional, and spiritual. They experienced their own country anew ways, and accounted for these differences by speaking not only of material conditions but also affective sensibilities. Many recognized their relative position of socioeconomic privilege, despite the ways that being culturally Tibetan in Nepal carries distinct political liabilities and limitations. As Amchi Gyatso Bista said, "Mustang and Dolakha are sky-and-earth different." When comparing his experience of the earthquake at home in Mustang to those he treated in Rasuwa, Amchi Tenjing Bista said, "People there have become like an abandoned house where the inside is not fit for living, even if it still looks ok on the outside. This is when the *la* is lost." This is a potent simile in a landscape where so many actual houses were damaged or destroyed.

In post-camp interviews, many *amchi* used language akin to how they might describe a religious pilgrimage to characterize these camps. They spoke of encountering obstacles, relying on the generosity of strangers, and moving with humility through precarious living landscapes. They framed these experiences not in abject, grave, or desperate terms directed at the recipients of "aid," as often surface in the description of humanitarian missions, but rather in terms of gratitude. These camps were an opportunity to serve fellow sentient beings, to generate merit, to practice *bodhicitta* (T. *byang chub kyi sems*), to recognize their relative good fortune. It can be argued that this response is distinct from the language of "resilience" so often used in conventional trauma response and mental health work, even as "resilience" might capture aspects of what this practice and orientation to the world allows. The age and physical well-being of *amchi* who participated in these camps varied, from practitioners in their early thirties to those in their late sixties. Some have chronic health problems themselves, including diabetes and hypertension. They worked long hours and exerted themselves, and admitted to feeling physically exhausted at the end of camps, but emotionally energized during the experiences. Their descriptions stood in stark contrast to the language of "burnout" that is so common among conventional humanitarian aid workers and physicians.

Although engaging in "politics" was never an overt aim of these camps, one can say that political aspirations were at work. Some *amchi* evoked a "politics of compassion"[28] when describing their response as compared to the limits of purely biomedical and/or foreign interventions. Many *amchi* felt that such activities would help their case for state recognition in Nepal. Some hoped that their successful response to rural medical need would provide further evidence of their effectiveness as healthcare providers in the eyes of the government. Others held out little hope that the Nepali state would pay attention to their actions, but thought that positive local responses to Sowa Rigpa, as well as the increased "name recognition" that came from these camps among new sectors of Nepali society, could "promote *amchi* medicine" from the grassroots. As Amchi Ngawang Namgyal said, "I don't think these earthquake-related camps have made any difference in the government's position, but it has definitely made impressions among the public. From this, they can argue for [Sowa Rigpa] to be included [in public health services]. This is part of democracy."

Conclusion

In responding to the 2015 earthquakes in Nepal, *amchi* recognized the importance of individual patient's bodies; however, biological "bare life" was not the principal framework through which they provided care. Rather, they responded as medical and religious practitioners through actions that illustrate core aspects of Buddhist healing. *Amchi* recognized that while much of the suffering they were addressing derived from the immediacy of the earthquake, others were rooted in a chronic lack of access to healthcare, poor nutrition, the physical demands of subsistence agriculture, and the emotional weight of economic and environmental precariousness in Nepal. Added to this were their varied understandings of the disaster's cause, from the geologic to the cosmological. They spoke about their grasp of scientific concepts that describe the causes of earthquakes—tectonic plates, etc.—and connected this to understandings of the five elements that make up our planet, even as they noted, as did many of their patients, that earthquakes occur when sacred geography is disturbed, when the mythical animal on whose back the earth sits becomes agitated and shakes, when deities of place are defiled by human actions, when greed and sin (T. *sdig pa*) wax and religious devotion wanes. These are not mutually exclusive conceptions.

In discussing their motivations for executing these camps, *amchi* articulated the idea that we all possess the need to help others. Indeed, when we lose sight of that sensibility, social worlds crack open. We begin to fail each other. As Amchi Gyatso Bista put it, "If we don't do this, or if patients don't come, then being an *amchi* has no purpose. As the saying goes, we must have 'purpose thick as rhino skin.'" Although *amchi* are not perfect or necessarily enlightened human beings, their incentives for action were rooted, at least in part, in an orientation toward the Bodhisattva Vow, which rests on the relationship between one's own liberation and deep attentiveness to others, and toward the value of accruing merit. *Amchi* spoke openly about how this chance to serve others was also an opportunity *for themselves*, and how their relative social positions—including access to wealth and connections to patrons (T. *sbyin bdags*)—placed them in a position of power and authority, if also benevolence and responsibility, in relation to the patients they saw and the communities they visited.

Rather than a framework for humanitarianism that teeters between the poles of "professional aid worker" and "humanitarian volunteer," *amchi* described how it was their duty, their Dharma, to respond to suffering by offering medicine and spiritual counsel. As such, their responses to the Nepal earthquakes not only help to ground what is meant by "Buddhist healing," but may also help us think differently about the relationship between those who provide resources, those who carry out humanitarian missions, and those who receive aid. Instead of heroic efforts that can spiral into "burnout" and forms of self-harm, we see an approach that emerges from an epistemology that expects suffering as part of the human condition and has strategies for addressing it. Instead of a model that presumes sacrifice but that often elides power dynamics, we see a cultural recognition of inequality—in the sense that individual and collective experiences are governed by the dynamics of karma as well as the structural positions in which we find ourselves in this human lifetime—and the possibility of benefit for self and other through compassionate action. Instead of the presumption of biomedical superiority, we see the practical embrace of multiple healing modalities. Instead of privileging the living, we see a balanced attention to the living, the dead, and the forces that animate and govern our world.[29]

Notes

1. The term *amchi* is actually a Mongolian word that has been adopted into the Tibetan lexicon.
2. For a discussion of the issue of naming this practice—Tibetan medicine or Sowa Rigpa—see Sienna R. Craig and Barbara Gerke, "Naming and Forgetting: Sowa Rigpa and the Territory of Asian Medical Systems," *Medicine Anthropology Theory* 3 (2016): 87–122.
3. https://www.nytimes.com/2015/12/19/world/asia/nepal-avalanche-langtang.html.
4. For a description of the earthquake as well as an oral history of the village, see https://wikitravel.org/en/Tamang_Heritage_Trail. For a reflexive analysis of response to this disaster, see Austin Lord and Galen Murton, "Becoming Rasuwa Relief: Practices of Multiple Engagement in Post-Earthquake Nepal," *HIMALAYA* 37, no. 2 (2017): 87–102.
5. Barbara Gerke, "Buddhist Healing and Taming in Tibet," in *Oxford Handbook of Contemporary Buddhism*, ed. Michael Jerryson (New York and Oxford: Oxford University Press, 2016), chap. 32, 576.
6. See this article I wrote for the blog *Savage Minds* for a description of these events as they were taking form: https://savageminds.org/2015/06/23/slow-medicine-in-fast-times/.
7. I use this term "soul" with caution and recognition that the Tibetan *bla* is not the same thing as a Judeo-Christian understanding of the term. *Bla* can also translate, along with *srog*, as "life force," and it also relates to "consciousness," or *gnam bshad.* See Barbara Gerke, *Long Lives and Untimely Deaths: Life-Span Concepts and Longevity Practices among Tibetans in the Darjeeling Hills, India* (Leiden and Boston: Brill, 2012).
8. The suffix "pa" indicates people of an area, in this case, people from Langtang.
9. See https://www.youtube.com/watch?v=8wppxzZbccE for a short film that documents the *amchi* camps that occurred in Langtang, Kyangjin, Gatlang, and Syabru villages, Rasuwa district, and in which Amchi Tenjing Bista is featured.
10. Janet Gyatso, *Being Human in a Buddhist World: An Intellectual History of Medicine in Early Modern Tibet* (New York: Columbia University Press, 2015).
11. Barbara Gerke, "Buddhist Healing and Taming in Tibet," in *Oxford Handbook of Contemporary Buddhism*, ed. Michael Jerryson (New York and Oxford: Oxford University Press, 2016), chap. 32; Geoffrey Samuel, "Healing in Tibetan Buddhism," in *The Wiley Blackwell Companion to East and Inner Asian Buddhism*, ed. Mario Poceski (Oxford: Wiley Blackwell, 2014), 278–96.
12. Yang Ga, "The Sources for the Writing of the "Rgyud bzhi," Tibetan Medical Classic," PhD diss., Harvard University, 2010.
13. Samuel, "Healing in Tibetan Buddhism," 281.
14. The two sages are Rigpa Yeshe (literally, "transcendental wisdom of awareness") who is the teacher, and Yilekye (literally, "born from mind"), who is his principal disciple. See Barbara Gerke and Florian Ploberger, "The Final Doubt and the Entrustment of Tibetan Medical Knowledge," in *Buddhism and Medicine: An Anthology of Premodern Sources*, ed. C. Pierce Salguero (New York: Columbia University Press, 2017), chap. 61.
15. Samuel, "Healing in Tibetan Buddhism," 281.
16. Gyatso, *Being Human in a Buddhist World*; Fernand Meyer, "Introduction," in *Tibetan Medical Paintings: Illustrations to the Blue Beryl Treatise of Sangye Gyamtso (1653–1705)*, ed. Yuri Parfionovitch, Fernand Meyer, and Gyurmed Dorje (London: Serindia Publications, 1992), 2–12; Tawni Tidwell, "Imbibing the Text, Transforming the Body, Perceiving the

Patient: Cultivating Embodied Knowledge for Tibetan Medical Diagnosis," PhD diss., Emory University, 2017.

17. *Nyépa* are also described as "deficiencies" or "faults" and often mistranslated as "humors."
18. Samuel, "Healing in Tibetan Buddhism," 281.
19. Vincanne Adams, Mona Schrempf, and Sienna R. Craig, eds., *Medicine between Science and Religion: Explorations on Tibetan Grounds* (London: Berghahn, 2010); Gyatso, *Being Human in a Buddhist World.*
20. Charles Ramble and Ulrike Roesler, eds., *Tibetan and Himalayan Healing: An Anthology for Anthony Aris* (Kathmandu, Nepal: Vajra Publications, 2015); Samuel, "Healing in Tibetan Buddhism," 288.
21. Laurent Pordié, ed., *Tibetan Medicine in the Contemporary World: Global Politics of Medical Knowledge and Practice* (London: Routledge, 2008); Sienna Craig, *Healing Elements: Efficacy and the Social Ecologies of Tibetan Medicine* (Berkeley: University of California Press, 2012); Theresia Hofer, ed., *Bodies in Balance: The Art of Tibetan Medicine* (New York and Seattle: The Rubin Museum of Art in association with University of Washington Press, 2014).
22. Tidwell, *Imbibing the Text.*
23. The original Chagpori was destroyed by the Red Guards in 1959. It was re-established in Darjeeling, India, by Trogawa Rinpoche in the 1980s.
24. The Lhasa Mentsikhang was founded by Chagpori graduate and brilliant monk-physician Khyenrab Norbu at the behest of the 13th Dalai Lama, and it was the first institution of its kind to allow women and non-monastics to train, formally, in Tibetan medicine. It was considered such an important cultural institution that it was one of the first to be re-established in exile. See Stephan Kloos, "The Politics of Preservation and Loss: Tibetan Medical Knowledge in Exile," *East Asian Science, Technology, and Society: An International Journal (EASTS)* 3 (2017): 135–59.
25. Adams, Schrempf, and Craig, *Medicine between Science and Religion*, 3–9.
26. Stephan Kloos, "The Pharmaceutical Assemblage: Rethinking Sowa Rigpa and the Herbal Pharmaceutical Industry in Asia," *Current Anthropology* 58, no. 5 (2017): 693–717; Martin Saxer, *Manufacturing Tibetan Medicine: The Creation of an Industry and the Moral Economy of Tibeteanness* (Oxford and New York: Berghahn, 2013); Craig, *Healing Elements*, 146–82.
27. Data on *amchi* camps come from three sources: (1) informal conversations with all *amchi* involved in the planning and execution of camps, both before and after they occurred; (2) formal interviews with *amchi* and support staff, conducted either by myself or by a Nepali research assistant, Phurwa Dhondrup, after the camps occurred; (3) reports prepared by *amchi* or their English-language-speaking assistants, provided to me due to my dual positionality as both a researcher and a donor who helped to financially support these camps through DROKPA, a nonprofit organization I helped to found, which has been working with Nepali *amchi* since 2000.
28. Bin Xu, *The Politics of Compassion: The Sichuan Earthquake and Civic Engagement in China* (Stanford, CA: Stanford University Press, 2017).
29. The author would like to acknowledge the support of the Himalayan Amchi Association, the Sowa Rigpa International College, and the Himalayan Guge Organization, and all of their member *amchi,* for their participation in the *amchi* camps. Partial funding for the camps was provided by DROKPA, a non-profit organization co-founded by the author. Additional support for this work was provided by a grant from the Claire Garber

Goodman Fund, Department of Anthropology, Dartmouth College. IRB approvals for this work was granted by Dartmouth's Committee for the Protection of Human Subjects. The author would like to thank Austin Lord as well as Amanda and Nat Needham for their participation in camp documentation, including the creation of the short film "Slow Medicine in Fast Times" <https://www.youtube.com/watch?v=8wppxzZbccE> which further illustrates experiences described in this chapter.

Further Reading

Adams, Vincanne, Mona Schrempf, and Sienna R. Craig, eds. *Medicine between Science and Religion: Explorations on Tibetan Grounds*. London: Berghahn, 2010.

Craig, Sienna. *Healing Elements: Efficacy and the Social Ecologies of Tibetan Medicine*. Berkeley: University of California Press, 2012.

Gerke, Barbara. "Buddhist Healing and Taming in Tibet." In *Oxford Handbook of Contemporary Buddhism*, ed. Michael Jerryson. New York and Oxford: Oxford University Press, 2016, 576–90.

Gerke, Barbara, and Florian Ploberger. "The Final Doubt and the Entrustment of Tibetan Medical Knowledge." In *Buddhism and Medicine: An Anthology of Premodern Sources* ed. C. Pierce Salguero. New York: Columbia University Press, 2017, 593–601.

Gyatso, Janet. *Being Human in a Buddhist World: An Intellectual History of Medicine in Early Modern Tibet*. New York: Columbia University Press, 2015.

Hofer, Theresia, ed. *Bodies in Balance: The Art of Tibetan Medicine*. New York and Seattle: The Rubin Museum of Art in association with University of Washington Press, 2014.

Kloos, Stephan. "The Pharmaceutical Assemblage: Rethinking Sowa Rigpa and the Herbal Pharmaceutical Industry in Asia." *Current Anthropology* 58, no. 5 (2017): 693–717.

Meyer, Fernand. "Introduction." In *Tibetan Medical Paintings: Illustrations to the Blue Beryl Treatise of Sangye Gyamtso (1653–1705)*, ed. Yuri Parfionovitch, Fernand Meyer, and Gyurmed Dorje. London: Serindia Publications, 1992, 2–12.

Pordié, Laurent, ed. *Tibetan Medicine in the Contemporary World: Global Politics of Medical Knowledge and Practice*. London: Routledge, 2008.

Samuel, Geoffrey. "Healing in Tibetan Buddhism." In *The Wiley Blackwell Companion to East and Inner Asian Buddhism*, ed. Mario Poceski. Oxford: Wiley Blackwell, 2014, 278–96.

Samuel, Geoffrey. "Medicine and Healing in Tibetan Societies." *East Asian Science, Technology, and Society: An International Journal* 7 (2013): 1–17.

Saxer, Martin. *Manufacturing Tibetan Medicine: The Creation of an Industry and the Moral Economy of Tibetanness*. Oxford and New York: Berghahn, 2013.

CHAPTER 14

PILGRIMAGE

IAN READER

Introduction

The term "pilgrimage" covers a multiplicity of meanings, practices, and connotations. Its origins are in Latin, and it entered the English language via French and in Christian contexts, to refer to acts of travel and journeys to and from places that are viewed as "sacred" and/or as having some association with religious traditions, for example, because they relate to founding narratives or the purported presence of significant figures in that tradition. The Anglophone term "pilgrimage" has been used as a generalized translation of numerous terms in other languages related to the practice of travel to religious sites. Both Japanese and Chinese, for example, have a variety of terms that are most conveniently rendered in English as "pilgrimage" but that convey different nuances of meaning in the languages concerned.[1] Since the term has also transcended its Christian origins to refer to practices across religious traditions, including Buddhism, for the sake of convenience I will use the Anglophone term when referring to the practices, places, and routes I discuss herein.

Initially, "pilgrimage" focused on travel and movement to/from special sites deemed to be sacred. It implicitly contained ascetic dimensions, and also the idea that the places visited were imbued with sacred powers that could be accessed by supplicants, especially those who made significant efforts to get there. The idea that visitors (i.e., pilgrims) could acquire rewards in terms of spiritual or other benefits for making their journeys also indicates that faith plays a part in the practice. These themes are recurrent in Buddhist pilgrimage, and in this chapter I will focus on such aspects—the practice of going to and participating in acts of veneration at places that have a special significance in the Buddhist tradition—along with some of the symbolic meanings associated with them. At the same time, it should be recognized that these are only some of the broader themes associated with pilgrimage. Pilgrimage also provides ways for people to get away from their everyday lives, and this has been a significant element in encouraging the practice, notably in pre-modern times. Especially in modern times, as developments such as good transport systems and a monetary economy have made travel easier and have opened up the possibility of pilgrimage to people who in earlier times were less able to travel, pilgrimage has encompassed themes beyond the immediate realm of religious action and faith. Issues of cultural identity, heritage, and tourism, for example, now feature significantly in understandings of the dynamics of pilgrimage, and they are important issues in Buddhist pilgrimage in the modern day.[2]

Buddhist pilgrimages express practices and meanings that are rarely specific to Buddhism. Scholars have commonly considered pilgrimage to be a universal phenomenon, evident across and beyond religious traditions and cultures, and the extensive literature on this topic has shown how the practice in one tradition has parallels elsewhere and that common theoretical frameworks can be applied across traditions.[3] Thus Buddhist pilgrimages may be examples of Buddhist practice, but they are rarely specifically or uniquely "Buddhist" in nature, so much as examples of pilgrimage found in Buddhist cultural contexts. In this context, too, one might note that relatively little scholarship on Buddhist pilgrimages has had an impact on broader theoretical studies of pilgrimage until very recently. This has been in part for linguistic reasons; for example, important contributions to the economic history of pilgrimage that have been written in Japanese have not been accessible to the wider academic field.[4]

Ascetic Origins and Phenomenological Meanings

The origins of Buddhist pilgrimage are grounded in the foundations of the tradition and the life of the historical Buddha, which serves as a model for all subsequent Buddhists, who can be viewed as pilgrims walking the same path and following in his footsteps. Such themes are not unique to Buddhism but are recurrent across traditions, as the origins of pilgrimage in Christianity (associated initially with journeys to the Christian Holy Land to visit the places associated with Jesus's life and death) and Islam (where pilgrimage has its roots in Muhammad's farewell pilgrimage to Mecca and Medina) indicate.

The Buddha's life story is a pilgrimage narrative, from his leaving home to be a transient ascetic in search of truth, to his meditation and enlightenment at Bodhgaya, to going to Sarnath to give his first teaching, and then spending many years journeying around northern India preaching and establishing the sangha, before he died. After his death, visits to sites associated with these four key points in his life were encouraged in the Buddhist canon and community. In the *Mahāparinibbāna-sutta* (*Dīgha Nikāya*

Part 5, verses 16–21), the Buddha, on his deathbed, is cited as saying that the pious should visit these four places associated with his birth, enlightenment, turning the Wheel of Law (i.e., his first teaching), and death/entry into final enlightenment. These sites—present-day Lumbini, Bodhgaya, Sarnath, and Kushinagar—thus formed a coherent pilgrimage structure, while the sutra gave the Buddha's canonical sanction to the practice. Pilgrimages to the four sites thus became an element in early Buddhist practice as disciples followed the physical path of the Buddha; thus pilgrimage became embedded from early on as a significant practice in the tradition.

Symbolic Meanings: Pilgrimage as Teaching

The idea of pilgrimage as a metaphor for the journey of life is found across pilgrimage traditions. In Buddhism it serves as a physical iteration of the journey to enlightenment and cessation—a four-stage process in the Buddha's life, reflected elsewhere in Buddhist pilgrimage contexts. In Japan, for example, the Shikoku *henro*,[5] the 88-temple pilgrimage around the island of Shikoku, passes through four Japanese administrative regions,[6] and this fourfold division represents a four-stage symbolic structure associated with the prefectures through which the pilgrimage passes. The first stage (in which the pilgrim visits the first 23 temples located in Awa province, present-day Tokushima prefecture) are the temples of (in Japanese) *hosshin* (awakening to the Buddhist path); the next 16 in Tosa (present-day Kōchi) represent *shugyō* (practice, the performance of austerities); the next 26 temples in Iyo (present-day Ehime prefecture) stand for *bodai* (awakening of the Buddha mind), and the final 23 in Sanuki (Kagawa prefecture) stand for *nehan* (ultimate enlightenment and liberation).[7]

Pilgrimage in such terms is a spiritual journey enacted on the physical level—or "exteriorized mysticism," as Victor and Edith Turner, talking about Christian pilgrimage but using a term that could readily be applied to Buddhist pilgrimage, have called it.[8] It also is a metaphor for journeying in search of the essence of Buddhism, a theme that permeates the accounts of travels by Buddhists across the centuries. Famous examples include the travels of Chinese Buddhist monks such as Faxian to India to the places associated with the Buddha and his early disciples. Faxian walked across much of Asia in the early fifth century CE, to visit Buddhist sites in India and Sri Lanka, and his account provides an example of monastic pilgrimage in search of the origins of the tradition.[9] Japanese Buddhists from early on traveled for similar reasons to China (the main source of Buddhism for the Japanese). The first use of *junrei*—the most normative Japanese term for Buddhist pilgrimages—was by Ennin, a Tendai Buddhist monk who spent nine years in China and whose account of his travels, *Nittō guhō junrei koki*, translates as "Record of a pilgrimage to seek the law in China."[10]

No Fixed Abode

The Buddha's life pilgrimage manifests the religious ideal of having no fixed abode and being detached from worldly bonds. These are core metaphors for the life of Buddhist monastics, although by no means specific to Buddhism. Such travels and the lack of a fixed abode express the notion of transience; as such, pilgrimage is a physical expression of core Buddhist doctrines, and the pilgrim is bodily enacting Buddhist teachings.

The concept of transience is also evident in the symbolism of death and in notions of spiritual renewal evident in many Buddhist pilgrimage contexts. The idea that on pilgrimage one is temporarily outside normative social orders and hence symbolically dead to the mundane world, and that completion or return from pilgrimage thus symbolizes renewal and rebirth, occurs across pilgrimage cultures and is widely found in Buddhist contexts. In Shikoku, for example, the pilgrim wears clothes and carries items that are associated with death and that symbolically make him/her "dead to the world," while completion is seen as a form of rebirth.[11]

Pilgrimage, in expressing themes of detachment from the mundane world, transience, and the search for enlightenment, also serves to provide a mechanism whereby ordinary people can, temporarily, enter the monastic and ascetic path. The Shikoku pilgrim's clothing is modeled on the monastic mendicant figure Kōbō Daishi, who is the main focus of veneration in the pilgrimage, and as such links the pilgrim and the focus of the pilgrimage together. The pilgrim, dressed as a wandering ascetic, also is supposed to follow various prohibitions normally kept by Buddhist monks and nuns. The pilgrim, as such, is temporarily following the path of monastics—who in turn are walking in the footsteps of the founder of the tradition. They are not, however, walking alone. In Shikoku, pilgrims commonly wear white pilgrimage shrouds inscribed with the insignia *dōgyō ninin* (two people, one practice). The "two people" are the pilgrim and Kōbō Daishi who, according to pilgrimage lore, not only created the pilgrimage through his ascetic travels in Shikoku but symbolically travels with and protects every pilgrim. The pilgrim may be making an individual pilgrimage, but is doing so simultaneously in the footsteps and company of the holy figure at its core.

Places and Pilgrimage

It was not just places associated with the life of the Buddha that became places of pilgrimage early on. As Gregory Schopen has shown, from early in Buddhist history, places associated with the lives, relics, and burial sites of Buddhist sages were seen as containing traces of their power and as such drew worshipful visits from people seeking to receive their graces and benefits.[12] As Schopen noted, such ideas are not a preserve of Buddhist pilgrimage but reflect a wider pattern in pilgrimage.[13] They articulate ideas found across multiple religious traditions about the potential of accessing spiritual power in places associated with places where sages were buried or their relics enshrined, or where figures of worship had manifested, or geographically striking locales deemed to be abodes of such figures or representations of celestial realms.

As Buddhism spread across Asia, it promoted the idea that supplicants could go out and encounter, unmediated, the sacred at sites imbued with power, and that making the effort to access such places indicated a worthiness that could bring spiritual rewards. Creating and promoting pilgrimage sites and routes became an element in Buddhist expansion and a means through which Buddhist preachers encouraged both the spread of the faith and the economic support structures of Buddhist temples.[14]

Buddhism thus developed a multiple array of pilgrimage sites, aided by the belief that figures of worship in the tradition could manifest any- and everywhere—a notion that underlies the development of multiple pilgrimage sites to Avalokiteśvara (Guanyin in China and Kannon in Japan), the bodhisattva of compassion, across the Tibetan, Chinese, Korean and Japanese regions. Buddhist temples housing relics said to be of the Buddha or some other significant figure, or containing icons considered to be especially powerful, or that are focused on figures of worship and legends of miraculous intercession, commonly attract pilgrims seeking to share in the power that they believe (or are led by temple proselytizers to believe) can be accessed there. The thirty-three temple Saikoku Kannon pilgrimage route in western Japan, for example, connects a group of temples, each housing images of Kannon associated with stories of Kannon's miraculous intercessions to save people from dire situations.[15] Such associations with miracle tales feature frequently across the Buddhist world and offer would-be pilgrims the hope that, in journeying to such places, their wishes could be fulfilled.

Geographic phenomena regarded as having symbolic and physical significance have also been identified as sacred and, as such, locales for pilgrimage. For example, islands that are seen as microcosmic representations of the universe,[16] or mountains viewed as transcendental places where celestial and physical realms intersect, have frequently been proclaimed as Buddhist pilgrimage sites. The Tibetan mountain Tsari, known in English as Pure Crystal Mountain, is viewed by Tibetan Buddhists in this way.[17] Mountains may be viewed as symbolic representations of the cosmos and circumambulated, a practice especially prominent in the Tibetan Buddhist tradition, to indicate a symbolic embracing of the entire universe. Buddhist pilgrimages to Mount Kailash in the Tibetan region, for example, involve such circumambulation—a practice also done by Tibetan pilgrims to important Buddhist sites such as the Mahabodhi Temple at Bodhgaya, and around the hill where the Dalai Lama's residence in Dharamsala in India is situated.

Mountains may also be viewed as physical representations of Buddhist cosmology and its ten realms of existence. In Japan, numerous mountains are viewed in this light, with pilgrimages on them symbolizing an ascent through the Buddhist realms to enlightenment. The physical ascent of the mountain is thus mirrored by the symbolic meanings of spiritual elevation; the mountain thus is both a physical setting for practice and a spiritual map of the Buddhist path. At times, too, such physical realms are seen as representations on earth of a Buddhist Pure Land. The Yoshino-Kumano mountain region of Japan was visualized as a representation of Fudaraku, the Pure Land of Kannon, and this served as a key theme in the development of pilgrimages there from the eleventh century onward.[18] The Chinese island of Mount Putuo was also viewed as a physical manifestation of Guanyin's Pure Land and developed as a pilgrimage center for such reasons. In Indonesia, the ninth-century Buddhist temple complex at Borobudur served as a graphic representation in stone of Buddhist cosmology; by ascending through the temple's various levels, the pilgrim symbolically traveled through different Buddhist realms, represented in architectural features and iconography, to the highest Buddha realms.

Sites ranged from transnational ones attracting pilgrims from across the Buddhist world, to pilgrimage sites that have particular resonance for specific national, regional, ethnic, or local groups. Bodhgaya is an example of transnationalism, drawing pilgrims from throughout the Buddhist world and across international borders. Others might be more important within specific national or regional contexts than in transnational terms. While prominent Burmese pilgrimage sites such as the Shwe Dagon Pagoda in Yangon—said to house a relic of the Buddha and to be the holiest Buddhist site in Burma—may be immensely significant within their own cultural settings, they nonetheless may get comparatively few Buddhist pilgrims from abroad. At local and regional levels, one can find numerous Buddhist sites that are important for local populations but that may not receive pilgrims from beyond their own localities. As in other traditions, potential pilgrims are offered a multiplicity of sites and routes from the very local to the international, along with choices of how they wish to perform their pilgrimages.

Asceticism and Pilgrimage

The idea that one should return thinner and poorer from pilgrimage and that hardship and taxing bodily practices strengthen and purify the spirit and make one more able to achieve spiritual development are recurrent themes across religious traditions. Buddhist pilgrimages are a good example of this, and the performance of ascetic acts can be seen at numerous Buddhist sites. A common ascetic act performed by Tibetan Buddhist pilgrims, for example, involves not just the prostrations mentioned earlier at sites such as Bodhgaya, but also doing entire pilgrimages through an extended series of prostrations practices.[19] Kataragama in Sri Lanka—a pilgrimage site sacred to the island's Hindus and Buddhists—is known for the severe ascetic and bodily mortification practices of some pilgrims and ascetics. While such activities (notably the mortifications) are more commonly associated with Hindu ascetics, Buddhists have also participated in them. Practices such as fire-walking at Kataragama are done by pilgrims of both traditions, while ascetics who combine Hindu and Buddhist elements in their practices are also prominent at the site.[20]

The Shikoku pilgrimage in Japan has its roots in the travels of ascetics to sites on the island where Kūkai, the Buddhist monk who later became venerated in his posthumous guise of Kōbō Daishi, is said to have performed austerities. This created a tradition of asceticism in the pilgrimage that endures to the present day. In earlier times such asceticism was, in part, simply a practical necessity; pilgrims had to walk (for lack of any alternative choice) and many were poor and subsisted on begging, and as such they lived like Buddhist monastics dependent on the practice of *takuhatsu* (begging for alms). Sleeping rough was commonplace. Some performed the pilgrimage many times—the most famous case being Nakatsukasa Mōhei, who between 1866 and 1922 circled the island over 280 times on foot, existing on alms and living as a permanent wandering ascetic. While modern developments have made asceticism a choice rather than a necessity (see later discussion), a small minority of pilgrims still treat the pilgrimage as an ascetic exercise, walking, begging for alms, and following the practice of *nojuku* (sleeping out).[21]

Merit, Transference, Benefits, and Faith

While images of austerity, transience, enlightenment, and following in the footsteps of Buddhist sages may be embedded in the frameworks of Buddhist pilgrimage, this does not preclude it also having more worldly dimensions. Indeed, for probably the vast majority of pilgrims, the symbolic imagery of pilgrimage as a journey to enlightenment and as an ascetic exercise in the realms of death and rebirth remains an ideal rather than a practical reality and intention. Far more important are pragmatic day-to-day issues, needs, and aspirations. For many pilgrims the primary purpose of a pilgrimage might well be more related to demonstrating one's faith, venerating the figures of worship associated with pilgrimage temples, and seeking boons, rewards, and worldly benefits as a result of that faith. It may also be an act designed to create merit for a departed family member or for oneself in preparation for what follows this life. Studies in Japan, for example, indicate that prominent motivations among Shikoku pilgrims include performing memorial services for deceased kin (there being a popular belief that performing the pilgrimage for oneself or for a deceased kin can enable them to pass to the Buddhist Pure Land at death) and doing it to seek worldly benefits (*riyaku*).[22] Underlying all of this is a basic belief that performing practices that involve a degree of effort and sacrifice—as pilgrimage does, in terms of travel, expenditure, and acts of devotion, even when not done as an austerity—creates merit that in turn can benefit the practitioner and/or his/her kin, both living and deceased.

Access and Convenience

Pilgrimage has developed in Buddhism as a mass popular practice that enables anyone who so wishes to have access to the realms of the sacred. On one level, this mass development expresses the view that no one should be barred from sharing in the merits and benefits bestowed by Buddhist figures of worship and that the more people who participate in acts of veneration and engagement with Buddhist sites, the better for the tradition. Another critical factor has been the influence of modernity and the mechanisms it has produced to enable more people to travel. One of the most salient elements in pilgrimage across cultures—and evident in Buddhist contexts—is that it has constantly adapted to contemporary circumstances, with pilgrims making use of whatever transport and other facilities are available. In the pre-modern era, pilgrims walked to the sites they visited, not necessarily because they wanted to perform ascetic acts but because they had no choice; hardship was as much a product of the wider environment as it was a moral injunction of pilgrimage. Rarely does one find in pilgrimage contexts—and this is not specific to Buddhism—texts or injunctions that set out how (in terms of transport and so on) pilgrims should do their pilgrimages. The Shikoku pilgrimage, for example, may have a tradition of asceticism, but there are no written injunctions historically that say pilgrims must walk or perform austerities. One of the most striking elements in Buddhist pilgrimage culture is that besides offering the (would-be) pilgrim plentiful choice in terms of the sites that could be visited, it tends to make few rules and restrictions on how they should perform their pilgrimages, with this openness of access and choice serving as one of the major attractions of the practice.[23]

Toni Huber has shown how modern developments spurred pilgrimage growth to the Buddhist sites of India that, after Buddhism was virtually eradicated from the region, had fallen into disuse. Under British colonial rule, Buddhist activists from outside India came into conflict with local Hindu authorities as they sought to regain control of Indian Buddhist sites such as Bodhgaya and to revitalize them as Buddhist sites. They were aided in their endeavors by the development of a countrywide transport system and agencies keen to gain custom across all sectors of society. Indian Railways, for example, was keen to encourage the use of its services and worked in conjunction with Buddhist organizations such as the Mahabodhi Society to promote Indian Buddhist sites, to produce what Huber describes as a reimagined Buddhist holy land there.[24] Mass transportation encouraged Tibetans—who previously had had to walk long distances in often harsh conditions to visit Bodhgaya and other Indian Buddhist sites—to become pilgrims. They quickly embraced the new mode of transport, viewing long-distance journeys by train (which were often crowded and uncomfortable) as a form of ascetic hardship. While this meant that pilgrims could pay lip service to the idea that their pilgrimages remained ascetic, it also indicated their general recognition, something that was shared by Buddhist authorities, that convenience of access and mechanisms to make pilgrimage sites more accessible to greater numbers of people were as important—if not more so.

As this example indicates, as new means became available it was common for pilgrims to make use of them. This again is a feature of pilgrimage cultures around the world. Pilgrimages in general are fluid in their modes of development and commonly reflect and incorporate sociocultural, economic, and transport changes in the wider society, which in turn facilitate pilgrimage and make it increasingly accessible to a wider clientele. In the modern era, motorized transport, liberalized travel regimes, the widespread availability of good healthcare, and monetary economics that enable people to travel more extensively have created the circumstances and means through which increasing numbers of people have been able to travel in a variety of guises, notably in terms of tourism but also pilgrimage. Such modern developments have made pilgrimages not just safer but more readily done and have vastly increased the numbers of people who take part in pilgrimages worldwide. They have given a voice and presence to sectors of the population that were once absent from the pilgrim community. Japan again provides a ready example. In pre-modern times, the large majority of pilgrims in Japan (as in most religious contexts) were men, with a preponderance being young and physically able to engage in long-distance walks and endure the rigors of a transient life. This was especially so in Shikoku, where pilgrims were often at the mercy of the elements and diseases; the numerous examples of pilgrims who died on the route indicates that it was a pilgrimage fraught with danger and, as such, rarely done by the elderly or by women. In Shikoku nowadays, because of modern means of transport and facilities, women—once a small and often harassed minority—now outnumber men on the pilgrimage, while people over sixty (an age group rarely found among Shikoku pilgrims before the twentieth century) are the most numerous. Indeed, it is fair to say that modern developments have led to a democratization of pilgrimage, opening it up to greater numbers of people and enabling many who in earlier ages would not have been able—whether through age, gender, or other reasons—to make pilgrimages, especially to distant places.[25]

Buddhist Pilgrimage and Cultural Identity

Making pilgrimages to Buddhist sites need not be specifically seen as a Buddhist activity, but one also suffused with particular issues of cultural identity politics. The Shwe Dagon temple in Yangon, mentioned earlier, is highly significant in Burmese Buddhism, and pilgrimages there clearly express Buddhist devotionalism. Yet the temple is also an important symbol of national and cultural identity that, in the eyes of Burmese Buddhists, indicates the fusion of nation, ethnicity, and Buddhism. Making a pilgrimage to the temple thus may be also an expression of Burmese identity and cultural belonging. It thus serves not simply as a Buddhist site, but as a place of local Burmese meaning, particularly significant in the fraught political context where attacks by Buddhists on a Muslim minority in the country are rife. Such associations between Buddhism, nationalism, and the state have been recurrent themes across Asia, and they have been particularly striking in political terms. In Sri Lanka, for example, militant Sinhalese Buddhists have argued that the island is sacred to Buddhism; in associating Sinhalese national identity with Buddhism, they have sought to emphasize the position of Buddhism as the dominant religious tradition of the island while justifying the war against, and the subjugation of, the Tamil minority.[26] Buddhist pilgrimage sites such as the Temple of the Tooth in Kandy, supposedly housing a tooth relic of the Buddha, have become rallying symbols in this identification of Buddhism, nationalism, and conflict, with pilgrimage serving as a means of mobilizing forces for political and militant purposes.

A somewhat different dynamic on the island is seen at Kataragama, which manifests Hindu and Buddhist elements and as such illustrates some of the syncretic dimensions of Buddhism. The deity Kataragama is one of the four protectors of the island of Sri Lanka in the eyes of its Buddhist Sinhalese population. To Tamil Hindus this deity is known as Skanda (also as Murugan), a powerful Hindu figure, son of Shiva and Parvati and sibling of Ganesh. As is common in the realms of popular practice, many pilgrims at Kataragama are primarily concerned about the benefits and boons Kataragama/Skanda can bestow on them, rather than about differentiating between Kataragama the Buddhist and Skanda the Hindu figure. Indeed, the powerful aura of (Hindu) Skanda/Murugan helps make the pilgrimage site attractive to Buddhist pilgrims, who nowadays constitute the majority of pilgrims to the site. Increased Buddhist participation and interest in Hindu ritual practices at the site also suggest to some an attempt to impart a more overt Buddhist orientation to it.[27] The main temple complex at Kataragama incorporates Hindu and Buddhist themes and iconography, while there are shrines within the main complex to Ganesh and the Buddha, indicating yet another layer in the complex interaction between the traditions. Kataragama thus is both a Sinhalese Buddhist site and a multi-faith site that expresses ideals of island unity (ideals that have been ravaged by the communal conflicts mentioned earlier). Like other Sri Lankan sites, its orientations relate as much to issues of cultural identity and politics on the island as they do specifically to matters of Buddhist faith.

Japanese Buddhist pilgrimages offer another example of the centrality of cultural themes and of how they, for many pilgrims, are as important as issues of Buddhist faith. In his study of the Saikoku pilgrimage, James Foard showed how the pilgrimage in Tokugawa times (1600–1868) came to be seen as a signifier of national culture and history, and was promoted by the regime as a cultural journey that emphasized the enduring depth of Japanese history and helped develop a consciousness about an inherited national culture.[28] In modern times, the Saikoku pilgrimage has become increasingly viewed by participants as a tour of Japan's cultural heritage, and as a means of encountering and expressing a sense of Japanese identity and pride, while its significance as a specifically Buddhist pilgrimage has become rather marginalized.[29]

The Shikoku pilgrimage, widely now viewed as the most important Buddhist pilgrimage in Japan,[30] also exhibits the ways in which an ostensibly Buddhist practice is imbued with questions of cultural identity. In earlier times, not all the sites were Buddhist; seven were, until the 1870s, Shinto shrines, while the cult of Kōbō Daishi, the Buddhist figure at the center of the pilgrimage, is suffused with folk religious themes. As such, the pilgrimage has long been perceived not so much as a Buddhist pilgrimage but as one expressing multiple themes of the wider Japanese folk and religious traditions. In modern times, it has been portrayed in popular culture and literature—including materials produced by the temples themselves and by interested parties such as island tourist offices—as a manifestation of "traditional Japan," where people can get in touch with aspects of culture that have disappeared from urbanized modern Japan. Such images have helped shape the idea of the pilgrimage as a manifestation of Japanese heritage—an image now reaffirmed by attempts to have the pilgrimage inscribed on the UNESCO World Heritage list.[31] While Shikoku does nowadays receive a very small number of pilgrims from overseas (mainly Westerners fascinated by Japanese culture), it is predominantly a Japanese pilgrimage performed by Japanese people, many of whom, when they discuss their pilgrimages in Shikoku, talk about them in terms of cultural identity.

Shikoku is a further example of the point that pilgrimages involving Buddhist sites should not necessarily be regarded as simply Buddhist, but as examples of cultural performance in which local needs and themes, especially about cultural identity, may be as, or more, significant as Buddhist ones. Indeed, studies of pilgrimage in East Asia have commonly incorporated Buddhist pilgrimage studies into a wider rubric that emphasizes cultural over specific religious themes. Naquin and Yü's seminal study of pilgrimage in China, for example, while it includes discussions of Buddhist sites, deals with them as manifestations of Chinese pilgrimage culture alongside and no different from other pilgrimages within that cultural context.[32] Studies of pilgrimage in Japan, too, tend to focus on them as manifestations of Japanese culture that happen to be Buddhist, rather than analyzing them as examples of Buddhist pilgrimages that happen to be found in Japan.[33]

Back to the Origins

To conclude this discussion of Buddhist pilgrimage practice, and to illustrate the modernizing themes that are evident in the practice, I will return to the origins of the tradition, and to Bodhgaya, Buddhism's one truly transnational and universal site. Alongside the Mahabodhi temple, where Buddhists from different countries of the world converge, there are temples from the various places—such as Japan, Thailand, Burma, Tibet, Taiwan, and China—where Buddhism has developed. These temples, while they contribute to the sense of Bodhgaya as a universal center, also express Buddhism's multiple localizations and are markers of its different ethnic and national dimensions. Visitors from these Buddhist countries are able to be pilgrims to the universal nature of Buddhism while at the same time reaffirming their own localized identities at the temples of their countries—and perhaps (as I have heard, for example, Japanese pilgrims comment there) enhancing their views about the preeminence of their localized forms of Buddhism.

Bodhgaya receives pilgrims from across the Buddhist world, as well as Western backpackers interested in Buddhism, and, increasingly, people who visit it as tourists interested in cultural heritage and history. Mass pilgrimage events such as rituals and sermons by the Dalai Lama have at times brought huge crowds of Tibetan pilgrims there—and have produced tensions between them and the local populace, which is overwhelmingly Hindu. Visitor numbers have been increased further by the designation of the main temple area as a UNESCO World Heritage site in 2002. This has spurred a massive growth in tourist and pilgrim visits and concomitant building of facilities such as hotels to cater to them. Areas of settlement around the main temple have been cleared, often forcing local people out of their homes. Resentments at the ways the local Hindu populace has been marginalized for the sake of tourism and the expansion of facilities for Buddhist pilgrims have been balanced by the opportunities for economic advancement and commercial growth that an increased focus on tourism and heritage brings. However, this emphasis on tourism, embraced by local authorities in order to improve the area's economy, causes concern among many Buddhists, who worry that their sacred center is being turned into a tourist and cultural heritage site in which its Buddhist identity is being eroded.[34]

Bodhgaya thus encapsulates multiple themes evident in studies and analyses of pilgrimage in general theoretical terms. It speaks symbolically to the notion of pilgrimage as a universal dynamic related to a return to origins, while Buddhists congregating there can feel part of a shared global phenomenon. Scholars of pilgrimage can here discern manifestations of one of the field's most significant theoretical contributions, Turner's notion of *communitas*, of pilgrimage sites as places that bring people together in spontaneous feelings of common belonging.[35] Yet there are clearly fractures and fissures at Bodhgaya with temples of different orders, indicating that the tradition is not one universal framework but a multiplicity of competing interpretations, and tensions between displaced locals and visiting Buddhists.[36] It thus manifests another predominant theoretical strand in the study of pilgrimage, namely that pilgrimage, rather than being about *communitas*, is primarily an arena of contesting interests.[37] The site thus contains also the themes of heritage and the interweaving of tourist and pilgrimage themes that have been central to theories of modern pilgrimage, and in which the concept of the "sacred" as a singular or self-standing entity, standing in contrast to a supposed notion of the profane or secular realm, has come under challenge.[38] It can also be seen as illustrating another theoretical analysis of pilgrimage as an encompassing phenomenon capable of incorporating multiple seemingly contradictory themes within its wider dynamic.[39] In such terms, Bodhgaya, the Shikoku pilgrimage, and other Buddhist pilgrimages mentioned in this chapter not only illustrate the multiplicity of themes within Buddhist pilgrimage, but they also reflect multiple themes found in pilgrimage contexts across the religious spectrum. Buddhist pilgrimage sites, then, are more than simply manifestations of Buddhist practice.

NOTES

1. See Ian Reader and Paul Swanson, "Introduction: Pilgrimage in Japan," *Japanese Journal of Religious Studies* 24, no. 3–4 (1997): 225–70, and Marcus Bingenheimer "Pilgrimage in China," in *New Pathways in Pilgrimage Studies: Global Perspectives*, ed. Dionigi Albera and John Eade (New York and Abingdon: Routledge, 2017), 18–35, for discussions of this issue.
2. See Ian Reader, *Pilgrimage in the Marketplace* (New York and Abingdon, UK: Routledge, 2014)for a fuller discussion of these issues.
3. See, for example, Simon Coleman and John Elsner, *Pilgrimage Past and Present in the World's Religions* (Cambridge, MA: Harvard University Press, 1995); Simon Coleman and John Eade, eds., *Reframing Pilgrimage: Cultures in Motion* (London: Routledge, 2004); and Ellen Badone and Sharon R. Roseman, eds., *Intersecting Journeys: The Anthropology of Pilgrimage and Tourism* (Urbana and Chicago: University of Illinois Press, 2004).
4. See Ian Reader, "Japanese Studies," in *International Perspectives on Pilgrimage Studies: Itineraries, Gaps and Obstacles*, ed. Dionigi Albera and John Eade (New York and Abingdon: Routledge 2015), 23–46, for a discussion of Japanese academic and theoretical contributions to the study of pilgrimage, notably in the context of economics and social history.
5. *Henro* is the Japanese term used specifically for pilgrimage in Shikoku; it is one of the many Japanese-language terms that are commonly translated as "pilgrimage" (Reader and Swanson, "Introduction," 233).
6. In pre-modern times these were feudal domains; in modern Japanese terms they are now prefectures.
7. Ian Reader, *Making Pilgrimages: Meaning and Practice in Shikoku* (Honolulu: University of Hawai'i Press, 2005), 52–53.
8. Victor and Edith Turner, *Image and Pilgrimage in Christian Culture* (Oxford: Blackwell, 1978), 33.
9. James Legge, *A Record of Buddhistic Kingdoms: Being an Account by the Chinese Monk Fa-Hsien of His Travels in India and Ceylon* (Oxford: Clarendon Press, 1886).
10. Edwin O. Reischauer, *Ennin's Diary, the Record of a Pilgrimage to China in Search of the Law*. Translated from the Chinese by Edwin O. Reischauer (New York: Ronald Press, 1955).
11. Reader, *Making Pilgrimages*, 63–64.
12. Gregory Schopen, "Burial *ad Sanctos* and the Physical Presence of the Buddha in Early Indian Buddhism: A Study in the Archaeology of Religions," *Religion* 17 (1987): 193–225.
13. See Peter Brown, *The Cult of the Saints: Its Rise and Function in Latin Christianity* (Chicago: University of Chicago Press, 1982), a study of how saints' relics and tombs became the focus of the growing Christian pilgrimage tradition.
14. Janet R. Goodwin, *Alms and Vagabonds: Buddhist Temples and Popular Patronage in Medieval Japan* (Honolulu: University of Hawai'i Press, 1994), is a good example of how ascetics associated with prominent temples in Japan encouraged the practice. See also Gorai Shigeru, *Kōya hijiri* (Tokyo: Kadokawa Sensho, 1975), for a general discussion in Japanese, and Ian Reader, *Pilgrimage in the Marketplace*, for a wider discussion of the use of pilgrimage as a way of spreading religious traditions and building their economic support structures.
15. See Hayami Tasuku, *Kannon shinkō* (Tokyo: Hanawa Shobō, 1983), for a full discussion of Kannon pilgrimages and miracle stories associated with them.

16. This is an underlying theme of island pilgrimages in the Japanese Inland Sea, and also Shikoku.
17. Toni Huber, *The Cult of Pure Crystal Mountain* (New York: Oxford University Press, 1999).
18. D. Max Moerman, *Localizing Paradise: Kumano Pilgrimage and the Religious Landscape of Premodern Japan* (Cambridge, MA: Harvard University Asia Center, 2005),provides a discussion of this issue.
19. See http://www.bbc.co.uk/news/av/world-asia-23592764/buddhists-crawl-from-china-to-tibet-temple-for-pilgrimage for a short video of Tibetan pilgrimage prostration practices.
20. Gananath Obeyesekere, *Medusa's Hair: An Essay on Personal Symbols and Religious Experience* (Chicago: University of Chicago Press, 1984), examines such Hindu-Buddhist ascetic fusions at Kataragama.
21. This paragraph draws on my fieldwork in Shikoku and on Reader, *Making Pilgrimages*, including a brief account of Nakatsukasa's travels (86–87) and the tradition of asceticism in Shikoku historically and in the modern era.
22. While this has been a common observation in studies of pilgrimage, I base it especially on my interviews with pilgrims across multiple traditions over the past three decades. See also Ian Reader and George J. Tanabe, *Practically Religious: Worldly Benefits and the Common Religion of Japan* (Honolulu: University of Hawai'i Press, 1998), 199–201.
23. In Reader, *Making Pilgrimages*, for example, attention is drawn to the many ways (and combinations of ways) in which pilgrims in Shikoku can do the pilgrimage—and to the point that there is no set, ordained, or official way that should be followed.
24. Toni Huber, *The Holy Land Reborn: Pilgrimage and the Reinvention of Buddhist India* (Chicago: University of Chicago Press, 2008), 253–304.
25. I discuss these themes in wider pilgrimage contexts in Reader, *Pilgrimage in the Marketplace*, 93–104; see also Robert R. Bianchi, *Guests of God: Pilgrimage and Politics in the Islamic World* (New York: Oxford University Press, 2004); James G. Lochtefeld, *God's Gateway: Identity and Meaning in a Hindu Pilgrimage* (Oxford and New York: Oxford University Press, 2010); and Suzanne K. Kaufman, *Consuming Visions: Mass Culture and the Lourdes Shrine* (Ithaca, NY: Cornell University Press, 2004),for discussions of such themes in Islamic, Hindu and Catholic contexts.
26. Stanley J. Tambiah, *Buddhism Betrayed? Religion, Politics, and Violence in Sri Lanka* (Chicago: University of Chicago Press, 1992) and Tessa Bartholomeusz, "In Defence of Dharma: Just War Ideology in Buddhist Sri Lanka," *Journal of Buddhist Ethics* 6 (1999): 1–16.
27. See, for example, Richard Gombrich and Gananath Obeyesekere, *Buddhism Transformed: Religious Change in Sri Lanka* (Princeton, NJ: Princeton University Press, 1988), 163–99, for a discussion of these issues.
28. James Foard, "The Boundaries of Compassion: Buddhism and National Tradition in Japanese Pilgrimage," *Journal of Asian Studies* 16, no. 2 (1982): 231–51.
29. Reader, *Pilgrimage in the Marketplace*, 137–38.
30. Reader, *Pilgrimage in the Marketplace*, 36–39.
31. Reader, *Pilgrimage in the Marketplace*, 173–82, discusses the 2008 campaign to gain the inscription; a new attempt was launched in 2016 that uses similar themes of heritage and tradition.
32. Susan Naquin and Chün Fang Yü, eds., *Pilgrims and Sacred Sites in China* (Berkeley, Los Angeles, and Oxford: University of California Press, 1982).

33. This is especially so for Japanese academic studies of pilgrimage; see, for example, the three-volume series of collected essays on pilgrimage edited by Shinno Toshikazu, *Nihon no Junrei* (Tokyo: Tōkyōdō, 1996); Hoshino Eiki, *Junrei: Sei to zoku no genshōgaku* (Tokyo: Kōdansha, 1981).
34. For an excellent discussion, see David Geary, *The Rebirth of Bodh Gaya: Buddhism and the Making of a World Heritage Site* (Seattle and London: University of Washington Press, 2017).
35. This concept was developed by Victor Turner in a series of essays and brought to its fullest expression in Turner and Turner, *Image and Pilgrimage.*
36. Geary, *The Rebirth of Bodh Gaya*, discusses the tensions that have arisen around the site, notably since its UNESCO World Heritage designation, which has contributed to displacements of local people.
37. The focus on contest (which critiqued Turner's idea of communitas) was initially developed by Michael Sallnow and then developed in John Eade and Michael Sallnow, eds., *Contesting the Sacred: The Anthropology of Christian Pilgrimage* (London: Routledge, 1991).
38. See, for example, Badone and Roseman, eds., *Intersecting Journeys*, and Reader, *Pilgrimage in the Marketplace*, for explications of these theoretical positions.
39. For a study of how pilgrimages can encompass multiple, sometimes seemingly contradictory, themes, see Reader, *Making Pilgrimages.* See Ellen Badone, "Conventional and Unconventional Pilgrimages: Conceptualizing Sacred Travel in the Twenty-first Century," in *Redefining Pilgrimage: New Perspectives on Historical and Contemporary Pilgrimages*, ed. Anton Pazos (Farnham, UK, and Burlington, VT: Ashgate, 2014), 7–31, for a fuller discussion of theoretical concepts in pilgrimage, which focuses especially on those outlined here.

Further Reading

Geary, David. *The Rebirth of Bodh Gaya: Buddhism and the Making of a World Heritage Site.* Seattle and London: University of Washington Press, 2017.

Huber, Toni. *The Cult of Pure Crystal Mountain.* New York: Oxford University Press, 1999.

Huber, Toni. *The Holy Land Reborn: Pilgrimage and the Reinvention of Buddhist India.* Chicago: University of Chicago Press, 2008.

Legge, James. *A Record of Buddhistic Kingdoms: Being an Account by the Chinese Monk Fa-hsien of His Travels in India and Ceylon.* Oxford: Clarendon Press, 1886.

Moerman, D. Max. *Localizing Paradise: Kumano Pilgrimage and the Religious Landscape of Premodern Japan.* Cambridge, MA: Harvard University Asia Center, 2005.

Naquin, Susan and Chün Fang Yü, eds. *Pilgrims and Sacred Sites in China.* Berkeley, Los Angeles, and Oxford: University of California Press, 1982.

Reader, Ian. *Making Pilgrimages: Meaning and Practice in Shikoku.* Honolulu: University of Hawai'i Press, 2005.

Reader, Ian. *Pilgrimage in the Marketplace.* New York and Abingdon UK: Routledge, 2014.

CHAPTER 15

DANCE AS VAJRAYANA PRACTICE

MIRANDA SHAW

A global cast of Buddhist luminaries gathered in Boston in 1997 for the first Buddhism in America conference. Asian Zen masters, Tibetan lamas, and Theravada elders were joined by American teachers, scholar-practitioners, and authors. When this distinguished company assembled in a hotel auditorium for an evening event, the atmosphere was astir with conversation and bodies and minds not yet settled after the day's activities. Murmurs of impatience about convening at the end of a long day wafted through. I ascended two steps to the low stage and crossed a row of flower blossoms set in place to establish the stage as sacred space. My introduction to the Vajrayana dance to follow barely interrupted the rustling in the room.

A hush finally settled over the audience when sonorous Sanskrit chanting filled the air and a figure emerged from the shadowy depths of the stage. He was moving at an exquisitely slow pace, gliding sideways, taking short steps on the balls of his feet, brushing the ground so softly that he appeared to float along the curving path of flowers. He paused in the illumined area of the stage, facing the audience. Before them stood a figure clothed in white and bathed in light, his silken dhoti and long scarf aglow. His gaze was soft and his facial expression tender with empathy. He wore the royal adornments of a bodhisattva: crown, earrings, armbands, bracelets, anklets, and layers of pearl necklaces. Part of his long black hair was drawn into a topknot, and the rest streamed to his waist, swaying softly as he resumed his graceful dance. The mood of the room settled to alert stillness, the silent immobility of bodies fully at attention and senses riveted, not wanting to stir or blink lest they miss a moment of the sight unfolding before them.

The dancer was Prajwal Ratna Vajracharya, born to the Vajrayana priesthood of Nepal, renowned in his country for his performative eloquence. The audience was spellbound as his dance proceeded with meditative calm and a measured pace, evincing profound patience and impeccable mindfulness. The spell of serenity remained unbroken as the dance unfolded in softly flowing movements and rounded shapes: circular paths, gently curved limbs, and hands undulating into delicate mudras (Figure 15.1). The organically fluid movements conveyed a state of harmonious flow with reality. With never a pause or hesitation, his steady progress bespoke the firm resolve of a being dedicated to the mission of liberating all beings from suffering. The smooth motions communicated the inner quiescence of one who understands the nature of reality and is deeply at peace, knowing that for every form of suffering, there is a form of release.

FIGURE 15.1. Prajwal Ratna Vajracharya during a moment of stillness in the Avalokiteśvara dance.

Photo: Courtesy of the author.

A frisson of recognition had rippled through the room as those present recognized the deity being danced as a figure beloved across the Buddhist world. The bodhisattva of universal compassion was introduced as Avalokiteśvara in Sanskrit texts and is now most commonly known as Lokeśvara in Nepal, Chenrezig in Tibetan Buddhism, Guanyin in China, and Kannon in Japan, among other regional and local names. The bodhisattva is a pervasive presence in Buddhist cultural spaces, appearing in myriad forms and on many scales, from tiny talismans through paintings, statuary, home altars, roadside shrines, temples, far-flung sacred sites, and lengthy pilgrimage routes. The audience consisted of seasoned Buddhist practitioners and scholars. Everyone present had encountered the bodhisattva. Many had intoned his Sanskrit mantra (*oṃ maṇi padme hūṃ*) or had chanted his East Asian liturgy, the *Heart Sutra*. Some had read scriptures about him, prayed and made devotional offerings to him, practiced in a setting where his image was enshrined, worn an amulet invoking his blessings, or made pilgrimage to legendary icons and sanctuaries.

What was it about this performance that stirred them so deeply, riveting their attention, stunning them to silent awe? Familiarity with the bodhisattva of compassion notwithstanding, this was something few, if any, of those present had experienced before: the lord of compassion in embodied form, dancing before them.

Vajrayana Dance of Nepal

The dancer, Prajwal Ratna Vajracharya, was presenting Charya dance (*caryā-nṛtya*), an esoteric art of the Vajrayana lineage into which he was born.[1] The practitioners of Charya dance are the Vajrayana priests—both male and female—of the Kathmandu Valley, who share as their surname the caste name Vajracharya, which designates them as "Vajrayana masters." Because Vajracharyas are descendants of the indigenous Newar inhabitants of the valley, their religion and culture are properly designated as Newar (pronounced *NAY wahr*) rather than Nepalese. Charya dance was held in secrecy over the centuries, transmitted only to Vajracharyas and performed in rituals attended only by Vajracharyas and select patrons. In the latter decades of the twentieth century, several priests made the controversial decision to share their sacred dance practice more broadly, allowing a small selection of dances to be taught and viewed beyond the bounds of Vajracharya circles.[2] The twenty-first century has seen new developments. Charya dance now has a temple base in Portland, Oregon, and a global reach.[3]

The first decade of my research on Charya dance, in the 1990s, took place in Kathmandu.[4] My inquiries ranged afar, from the corpus of dances, movement vocabulary, and transmission process to the textual sources, ritual settings, and musical accompaniment. Ritual master and scholar-priest Ratna Kaji Vajracharya tutored me in the history, doctrinal aspects, and written versions of songs that accompany the dances.[5] His youngest of six sons, Prajwal Ratna Vajracharya, was my dance teacher and guide to the natural and built environments where the dance unfolds. Their family was my entrée into the human, material, and metaphysical worlds—the daily life, ritual arts, social bonds, and communal values—that form the living matrix of the dance tradition.

Charya dance is a meditative, yogic, and ritual practice. The explicit goal of Vajrayana is to attain supreme awakening (*samyak-saṃbodhi*) in one's present lifetime and body and thus to embody enlightenment. A key practice for accomplishing this goal is deity yoga (*deva-yoga*), a discipline in which the practitioner envisions himself or herself as a deity in order to develop the illumined awareness and liberating powers of the deity. The main role of Charya dance is to serve as a form of deity yoga. Deity yoga is commonly undertaken as a seated meditation practice, but in the Vajrayana tradition of the Kathmandu Valley, deity yoga has the added dimension of somatic and kinesthetic dynamism. The meditator forges "union" (the literal meaning of "yoga") with a given deity by donning similar clothing and adornments; by assuming the same postures, hand gestures, and facial expressions; and by aspiring to embody the wisdom, qualities, and presence of the divinity through the movements and energetic tenor of the dance.

The spectrum of dances reflects the breadth of the Newar pantheon.[6] The movement qualities span the gentle flowing of a peaceful bodhisattva, the powerful lunges and ecstatic leaps of dynamic Vajrayana deities, and the pounding stomps of wrathful Dharma-protectors. Vajracharyas distinguish between "outer" (*bāhya*) dances that may be performed in public settings and "secret" (*guhya*) dances that should be hidden within temple walls, esoteric ritual spaces, and circles of initiates. The "outer" dances feature divinities of benevolent persona, such as Avalokiteśvara (whose dance was described earlier), Mañjuśrī, green Tārā (known in Nepal as Ārya Tārā), white Tārā (Saptalocana Tārā), and the Pañca Jina mandala. Guardian deities of fearsome guise, too, can be included in this category. The Dharma-protectors Vajrapāṇi, Mahākāla, and a multi-armed red Gaṇeśa are mainstays. Highly esoteric, or Anuttara Yoga, deities prominent in the Newar pantheon and subject of many dances include Vajrayoginī, the couple Vajravārāhī and Cakrasaṃvara, and the couple Hevajra and Nairātmyā.

Charya dance also has a role in the ritual life of the Vajracharyas. Dance is an integral feature of Anuttara Yoga Tantra rituals, such as initiations, mandala enactments, esoteric fire offerings, and the sacramental feasting and celebration that culminate all major esoteric ceremonies.[7] The main ritual purpose of the dance is to make the deities bodily present in ritual settings. The ritual dance may be that of a single deity, a deity couple, or an entire mandala retinue. Traditionally, men danced as male deities and women danced as female deities in a ritual context.[8] Large-scale mandalas require that dozens of Vajracharyas be prepared to embody and dance as the mandala deities. The dances are sequential, beginning at the perimeter and circling toward the center, creating a living vignette of the mandala. By invoking the presence, blessings, and divine potencies of the deities, the dancing assures the efficacy of the rites.

Roles and occasions of dance are set forth in foundational Vajrayana texts that Vajracharyas consult for guidance. Their main sources of reference and authority on dance include the *Hevajra-tantra*, *Saṃvarodaya-tantra*, *Abhidhānottara-tantra*, and *Mahākāla-tantra*. These works number among the earliest known Vajrayana writings, dating from the eighth through tenth centuries. The oldest extant Sanskrit manuscripts have been preserved in Newar archives, treasured in Nepal as the revelatory font of the living tradition.[9] The brief passages on dance spread throughout these works are often couched in esoteric terminology. They are unambiguous, however, in heralding dance as an essential Vajrayana practice, pronouncing, "a Tantric vow-holder must sing songs, play instruments, and dance."[10] The *Hevajra-tantra* elaborates:

> If songs are sung from bliss,
> They are supreme *vajra*-songs
> When bliss arises, dance for the sake of liberation,
> Dancing the adamantine postures with full awareness.
> . . .
> The songs are mantra and the dance is meditation;
> Therefore, a practitioner of yoga
> Must ever and always sing and dance.[11]

The "adamantine postures" are those of the deity being danced. The songs that accompany the dances are equally valued as sacred speech, or sound—in essence, mantra. The singing and dancing are refined versions of these pastimes, undertaken in a state of deep meditative immersion. The *Hevajra-tantra* directs the yogi or yogini who dances as a deity to do so "with mindfulness, undistracted, meditating with impassioned mind, in a state of unwavering awareness."[12] The passage addresses advanced practitioners for whom concentrating in the midst of dancing is deemed possible.

The authoritative sources under discussion speak to an audience of religious elites who have taken vows, received initiation, attained meditative stability, and cultivated nondual wisdom. In the Vajrayana world, to ascend to this level and receive access to these teachings assumes serious motivation and effort. The texts impart another body of knowledge prerequisite for the dance practice, namely, instructions for ritual preparations of the site, materials, and dance accoutrements. Dance as an esoteric discipline, then, is intended for those with the potential—that is, the background and range of qualifications—to embody deity and thereby to experience the exalted qualities, sublime realizations, transcendent blissfulness, and clarity of consciousness of the deity. The *Abhidhānottara-tantra* tells us that the fruits of dancing as a deity include "reveling with the body, speech, and mind of an enlightened one."[13] Bodily transformation is full transformation, a fullness that in Vajrayana parlance encompasses body, speech, and mind. We have here the threefold scheme of a practice that transforms the body (through dance), speech (through song), and mind (through meditation) into those of a deity.

Explanatory Models

My central concern in this chapter is the role of dance in the Vajrayana quest for bodily transformation. To describe how and in what sense the dance practitioner comes to embody deity is complicated, even at the level of simplest formulation.[14] Has the dancer cultivated spiritual virtues (such as compassion, patience, and serenity) that then emerge in the dance? Has the dancer discovered divine qualities within himself or herself that then shine forth in the dance? Is there an infusion by an external force or an outflow of something internal? Where, in this process, might Newar Vajrayana locate agency and causality?

I long explored the relationship between Charya dance and the goal of embodying deity in my fieldwork. I discovered that the tradition offers several perspectives, or frames for understanding, each of which entails a different role for dance. I raised the issue in multiple settings and lines of questioning over many years, revisiting the matter in order to confirm, clarify, and reconcile the varying answers proffered. The perspectives intertwined and intermingled in the sources from which I drew them, namely, erudite priestly commentary and interviews of advanced practitioners and teachers of Charya dance. There were no didactic sources to consult. The textual sources that pertain to the dance are liturgical (the accompanying songs) and non-discursive (the Vajrayana texts discussed earlier).

The explanations concur that a union ("yoga") between the divine and human states takes place and that the union has a bodily locus: the deity becomes embodied and the human body is transformed. Beyond this core conviction, I sought an overarching principle that would unify the varying accounts but concluded that the differences among them amount to more than alternate formulations of the same ideas. I recognized that the explanations constellated into several internally coherent but mutually exclusive ways of understanding how the dance brings about bodily transformation, which I present in what follows under the headings of cultivating, revealing, and channeling. The first envisions the dance practice as a process of cultivation in which the dancer develops the qualities and awareness of the deity through contemplative and kinesthetic engagement. The practitioner gradually transforms into deity. The second perspective views the dance practice as a means of revealing divine qualities that are already present, awaiting discovery. The practitioner brings forth the deity within. The third approach holds that the deity enters the practitioner in the midst of the dance, and the presence of the deity within gives rise to the movements. The dancer serves as a vessel of the deity.

The three explanatory models share the premise that a genuine bodily transformation takes place but posit a different role for dance, as I elaborate in the following three sections. I take as my main example the aforementioned dance of Avalokiteśvara, bodhisattva of compassion, although the models can apply to any spiritual virtue or quality sought through the practice of Charya dance.

Cultivating Divinity

According to the cultivating mode of explanation, the practitioner fosters qualities such as empathy, patience, and selfless flow through the dance of Avalokiteśvara, gradually developing the pure, universal compassion of the bodhisattva.

Buddhism has perennially recognized the ultimate inseparability of bodily, emotional, and cognitive processes. On this premise, it follows that bodily movements—such as those of dance—will have cognitive and psychological effects. Dancing inherently cultivates mindfulness, requiring full attention to every part of the body and the energetic tenor of every movement. Attunement to the body is attunement to the world, insofar as the body is our field of perception. Therefore, to attend closely to the body is to hone one's instrument of perception and become a more receptive medium of experience. The refined awareness expands into subtler attunement to the environment and more sensitive resonance with other beings, that is, increasing capacity for empathy with others.

In Charya dance, there is an integral connection between the movements and the qualities sought. For instance, moving slowly requires and hence cultivates patience. Patience (*kṣānti*) is one of the six perfections, or root virtues, of a bodhisattva. The concept of patience may be held as a cherished ideal, but the obstacles to patience are lodged in the body as well as the mind. Moving slowly as a somatic discipline deepens familiarity with the feeling tone of patience, which becomes part of the kinesthetic memory and response repertoire the practitioner can summon in daily life. When there is impulse to react with impatience, such as a rush to judgment or urge to restlessness, irritation, or rash action, the slowness retained in muscle memory and the soothing calm that it exudes offer an alternative to the biochemical agitation of impatience. A new pattern of response is generated and reinforced over time.[15]

According to a widespread Buddhist formulation, habitual reaction patterns are rooted in three primary sources of suffering known as *kleśa*. The *kleśa* are *rāga*, *dveṣa*, and *moha*, that is, desire, aversion, and indifference, the three forms of resistance to the flow of reality in the form of grasping, rejecting, and ignoring. Resistance to experience in turn limits skillfulness of response. The softly flowing movement of the dance is a constant state of ease (Figure 15.2).

To move so fluidly and gracefully, without hesitation or changing pace, is remarkably demanding, requiring at once absence of tension and sufficient muscular exertion to maintain steadiness. Dancing softly and smoothly instills a pattern of harmonious, selfless flow with the currents of life as they arise, the ability to move through environments and situations with open awareness—without resistance, without a self-centered agenda—free to participate altruistically, in ways that relieve suffering and enhance well-being. The practitioner becomes subtly aware of his or her reactions as they arise and better able to moderate them and to modulate energy and effort, that is, to become more deliberate and skillful in action. Moreover, expanding the repertoire of bodily movement disrupts the physiologically engrained routes of habitual reaction patterns, creating new cognitive, ethical, and behavioral possibilities. A broader range of responses and more ways to serve and liberate become possible.[16]

The enlightening possibilities set forth in the dances of the deities set the practitioner on a course of greater wisdom, compassion, and other liberating realizations and divine

FIGURE 15.2. Prajwal Ratna Vajracharya dancing as Avalokiteśvara.

Photo: Courtesy of the author.

FIGURE 15.3. Prajwal Ratna Vajracharya dancing as Vajrapāṇi.

Photo: Courtesy of the author.

qualities. Later in the aforementioned program, the audience witnessed a very different dance, when Prajwal manifested the ferocity of the Dharma protector Vajrapāṇi, moving with electrifying intensity, with wide open eyes and menacing grimace, every muscle quivering (Figure 15.3).

He rushed and careened, leapt and bounded with thunderous stomps, and whirled with taut arms whipping the air. No less an agent of wisdom and compassion than Avalokiteśvara, Vajrapāṇi galvanizes volcanic energy for liberating interventions that require dramatic change, acting swiftly to reconfigure energy. In contrast, the dance of the female Buddha Vajrayoginī displays her fiery wisdom and passionate character. She surges with vitality that lends sizzling dynamism to her bold, sweeping movements and powerful stances. The dance of Vajrayoginī exhibits yogic prowess with sudden shifts between rapid motion and stillness, alternating jubilant leaps and balanced repose on a single leg or one knee bent to the ground, demonstrating self-mastery and the spectrum of energetic modalities at her command (Figure 15.4).

The varied dances, like the deities they embody, cultivate different nuances and expressions of wisdom and compassion, culminating, in the Newar Buddhist vocabulary, in realization of emptiness (*nirātma*, *śūnyatā-bhāva*) and enlightenment, variously termed *dharmadhātu-jñāna* (knowledge of all reality), *mahāmudrā-siddhi* (ultimate realization), and *samyak-saṃbodhi* (supreme awakening).

FIGURE 15.4. Helen Fox Appell II dancing as Vajrayoginī.

Photo: Courtesy of the author.

Revealing Divinity

According to this explanatory model, dance is a process of revealing divine qualities that emerge when the obscuring elements are removed. From a metaphysically nuanced perspective, enlightened awareness and divine qualities such as compassion cannot be produced. With the dance of Avalokiteśvara described earlier, the practitioner is not developing compassion but rather activating sensitivities and abilities that converge in compassion, such as empathy, altruism, and patience. Within this frame of understanding, the dance movements provide routes of exploration of innate but untapped potential. The practitioner does not produce patience as a newly acquired virtue; the manner of dancing leads to a wellspring of patience within his or her own bodily being. Learning to move as exquisitely softly and slowly as required for the dance of Avalokiteśvara is a matter of finding an inborn capacity for composure, constancy, moderation of stimulation, and sufficient steadiness of mind to withstand distractions. Patience is not the only appropriate response to every situation, but patience is an essential component of a compassionate response repertoire. With the dances of the deities as templates of exploration, the practitioner gains access to increasing dimensions and depths of his or her potential by engaging in different movement modalities.

The revelation model recognizes dance as a process of purification. The dancer purifies himself or herself of unenlightened mind-states and motivations, allowing intrinsic divine qualities to shine forth. The practitioner is eliminating negative qualities (afflictive mental states and emotional tendencies and complexes) to reveal a divine quality that is already present, awaiting discovery. The premise of this line of explanation is that experiences of many lifetimes are stored within the body as largely unconscious forces that distort perception and motivate behavior. The "body" in the Vajrayana view is not simply the tangible material form, but a psychophysical continuum of corporeal, emotional, mental, and subtle energetic layers. The debris of the past is present as karmic sediment deposited in the energy pathways of the subtle yogic anatomy, creating blocks, fissures, and knots that disrupt the free flow of vital life energies.[17] The subtle body is the matrix of the multilayered bodily system; therefore, karmic formations in the subtle body can manifest as illness and issues in any area of life.

As a somatic phenomenon, karma can manifest as barriers to specific movement modalities. At its esoteric core, Charya dance is a yogic practice for clearing the subtle body of karmic sediment. In the process of dancing, the practitioner seeks to direct energy in specific ways. Each movement is a full-body energy event whose parameters include the origination, pacing, exertion level, degree of variation (e.g., continuous, slowly shifting, swiftly changing), and overall pattern (e.g., smooth, undulating, jagged, pulsating, bursting) of the movement. Although a given movement sequence involves the entire body, the arm motion within a brief segment of the Avalokiteśvara dance can serve as an example. When the arms are opened softly and fluidly in a gesture of welcome and embrace, the impulse generating the movement must emanate from the center of the body and flow outward through the arms and hands in order to express a full-hearted flow of kindness and generosity. Any impediment within the heart or along the energetic pathways can hinder the fluidity of the movement. The impediments can be any permutation of attachment, constriction, contraction, armoring, or dualistic thought that creates barriers to the full offering of self to others. The effort to generate and sustain the arm movement and hence the energy flow from the center of the body through the limbs will reveal and, through repetition, gradually clear residue from the energy pathways. The clearing process can occur without the immediate conscious awareness of the practitioner or bring associated memories and reaction formations to acute awareness as the karmic sludge is dislodged and dissolved.

Purification is possible by virtue of revealing an underlying state of purity that remains undefiled by mental and karmic obscurations.[18] Newars use the term *vajra-deha*, "adamantine body," for the subtle body, drawing attention to its ultimately untainted purity. The fluidic quality of the dance of Avalokiteśvara embodies the culmination of the revelation process, a pristine subtle body in which the energies freely flow.

Channeling Deity

Another way a dance practitioner may embody deity is to serve as a channel, or vessel, for the deity. The deity has the agency and manifests his or her presence in the dancer and the dance. The practitioner experiences the dance occurring without conscious volition. The dancer does not lose consciousness, as happens in some forms of Himalayan trance possession, but rather undergoes a shift in awareness and a sense of infusion by the presence of the deity.[19] The movements arise from the presence of the deity within. As Ratna Kaji described this occurrence, "It is the deity dancing, not us!"[20]

On this line of explanation, the dance practice lays the ground for the arrival and presence of the deity. The practitioner has positioned himself or herself to be a vessel of the deity by previous efforts to form a bond with the deity through the dance practice and other meditative and ritual disciplines. Foremost among these is the chanting of the deity's mantra, the most direct way of fusing awareness and identity with a deity. Sound resonates through the entire spectrum of matter, from the subtlest to the densest. Therefore, intoning the mantra generates a vibratory pattern that attunes the entire organism—mind, emotions, and bodily tissues—to the sonic essence of the deity.

The practitioner's spiritual preparedness deepens the content and expressiveness of a given dance. In the midst of dancing, an emptying of self—made possible by facility with the movements, freedom from self-consciousness, and absorption in the chant-like cadence of the accompanying song—can open space for the deity to fill.[21] The dancer anticipates and welcomes such an occurrence, but the deity as a sovereign agent cannot be compelled. There is an element of grace, of something given that has not been earned or merited. The deity enters a practitioner who has not attained complete karmic purification and full realization. This form of embodiment is temporary. The deity inhabits the dancer for a limited duration and on a specific occasion, which might be a solitary or small group practice or a ritual or performance setting. The practitioner has rendered a service to the deity that Ratna Kaji Vajracharya called "higher devotion," that is, offering oneself to embody the deity so the deity may be tangibly present to dispense divine blessings, benefactions, and inspiration. Channeling the deity is an elating experience for the dancer and a gift for those who behold the deity in dynamic, bodily form, dancing before them.

Explanatory Power and Purpose

Each of the three modes of explanation has explanatory power by virtue of foregrounding a range of elements within the broader scope of Newar Vajrayana. The explanations constellate varying combinations of descriptive, motivational, metaphysical, and cultural content.

Casting Charya dance as a process of cultivating divinity accounts for experiences of incremental progress over the course of practicing a given dance. In the case of the Avalokiteśvara dance, signs of progress would include a diminution of negative qualities and an increasing ability to respond with patience, harmonious intention, and compassion in one's daily life. The concept of cultivation explains the observable connection between the spiritual technique and evidence of advancing along the path of awakening. Progress would not have taken place without the practice and hence is demonstrably the result of practice. This line of explanation also has motivational impetus, affirming the value of effort. Positing a causal relationship between practice and results helps to instill confidence in the effectiveness of the practice. Confidence in turn energizes discipline and bolsters fortitude to persevere through periods of struggle and stasis.

Viewing Charya dance as a process of revealing innate qualities and inherent divinity has ontological authority. Vajrayana shares a Mahayana metaphysical stance that enlightenment and the divine qualities at its core—such as universal compassion and transcendent wisdom—are beyond the reach of ordinary causality. The ultimate attainments are not products of causes and conditions that arise and dissolve in the stream of phenomenal flux. One's enlightened essence is ever present, hidden behind mists of human failings and delusions, just as the sun may be obscured but not dimmed by clouds, or a precious jewel may be coated in mud but remain unsullied.[22] The essence of enlightenment is unchanging, like the radiance of the sun and brilliance of a diamond, while the accumulated karmic residues to be dissolved, however seemingly dense, are impermanent and no more substantial than clouds in the sky or mud on a jewel.

The revelation model provides a basis of confidence that the goal is not forever out of reach or the barriers insurmountable. One may lack opportunity, motivation, or diligence but cannot lack the foundation for attainment, the divine essence within. This assurance can lend courage to surrender cherished illusions and the seeming security of self-centered reactions and impart trust that something deeper and truer will emerge in their wake. Whereas the concept of cultivation emphasizes the necessity and efficacy of the practice, the concept of revelation underscores the enduring reality of a goal that is ever present, underlying and sustaining one's efforts.

Serving as a vessel, or channel, for the deity describes experiences in the midst of Charya dancing that the deity has arrived and taken over the dance. The presence of the deity is palpable for the dance practitioner and observable by onlookers as well. This manner of embodying deity has cultural credence. Channeling and trance phenomena more broadly are mainstays of Newar Buddhist religious life. Charya dance is situated among a spectrum of traditions in which deities use human beings as mediums of their presence and benefactions. Throughout villages and urban areas of the Kathmandu Valley, it is a regular occurrence for the goddess Hāritī to possess, speak, and heal through female trance mediums (*dyaḥ-mā*). The supreme goddess of the Vajrayana pantheon, Vajrayoginī (also known as Vajradevī and Vajravārāhī), continuously indwells prepubescent girls selected to fill the roles of several local Kumārīs and a national Kumārī who gives daily audience and features in a major annual chariot procession. Vajracharyas consecrate themselves to embody Vajrasattva Buddha when they perform their sacerdotal functions. Across the panoply of Newar Buddhist rituals, officiants and participants channel the presence of deities during specified segments of the ceremonial proceedings.

Trance phenomena are also common in the broader religious landscape of the Kathmandu Valley. A tradition with predominantly Hindu content is the public festival dance tradition known as Dyaḥ Pyākhaṃ, translatable as "dance of deities," in which divinities inhabit the bodies of masked dancers, enact mythic narratives, and dispense their blessings to crowds who gather in city squares and byways to witness the sacred spectacle. Within the gamut of these and other modes of embodying deity in the purview and environs of Newar Vajrayana, Charya dance occupies a special place by virtue of serving primarily as an esoteric discipline and path of spiritual transformation for the practitioner.

The three explanatory models dovetail three operative understandings of deities in Newar Vajrayana, namely, as models of aspiration, as the innate divinity of the practitioner revealed by the process of karmic purification, and as active agents in the fabric of reality whose means of intervention to liberate the unenlightened include the use of human beings as mediums of their presence. Avalokiteśvara, the deity whose dance opened this chapter, can serve as an example. In the cultivation model, he is an exemplar of the infinitely compassionate mode of being that the practitioner aspires to attain and into which the practitioner will evolve and transform. In the revelation model, he is the essence of compassion that blossoms in a heart purified of all karmic traces and vestiges of selfish clinging. In the case of channeling, Avalokiteśvara is the lord of compassion who adopts myriad forms and traverses countless realms to serve living beings and fulfill his mission to alleviate suffering and foster universal well-being and awakening.

Belief in the reality of deities such as Avalokiteśvara accords with the goal of Vajrayana practice to become divine and embody enlightenment. In a cosmic purview spanning millennia, many have trod the path and reached its summit. The universe is populated by divinities, and the culmination of the Vajrayana path is to join their ranks.

Tantric Resolutions

The three Newar Vajrayana explanations of the embodiment of deity in Charya dance are conceptually distinct. Their resolution does not lie in the conceptual realm. Intellectual understanding supports Vajrayana practice, but intellect alone cannot carry one across the threshold of non-dual awareness, the unitary state of being in which the merging of the human and the divine takes place as experienced, embodied reality. The unity inherent in "embodying deity" places it beyond conceptual formulation. Vajrayana tells us that the distinction between "human" and "divine" dissolves in the vaunted state of union.

Vajrayana teachings are geared toward experiential realization rather than systematic formulation. The language of Vajrayana writings is purposely enigmatic, employing metaphor, symbol, allusion, paradox, coded vocabulary, and poetic evocation. Entering the esoteric domain requires initiation and the guidance of a guru. A guru has broad latitude in tailoring the teachings and methods for a given disciple, community, or cultural setting. The guru can draw on a vast repertoire of inherited teachings, modify a traditional approach, or invent one anew. The goal of non-dual wisdom (*prajñā*) is singular, but the methods to transmit it skillfully (*upāya*) are infinite and subject to ongoing inspiration and revelation.

For many reasons, then, multiple perspectives and explanations endure within the tradition. Vajrayana practitioners regularly encounter verbal ambiguity and alternate explanations. Robert Thurman contrasts the non-discursive nature of esoteric language with the exactitude of philosophical discourse. The latter aims for clarity and precision in order to present "pathways of thought to the conceptual mind that enable it to see more clearly. . . . But *esoteric* teaching is by definition secret, occult, mysterious. . . . It has no rhetorical or persuasive function" but rather seeks to move the mind "to feeling, to action, to creation, growth, compassion, or bliss" and even "to generate *obscurity*."[23] Thurman likens uses of language in Anuttara Yoga Tantra to poetry, observing that "the poet seeks not to clarify or persuade, but to intrigue and to evoke. . . . Engagement, evocation, embodiment are the life of the poetic."[24]

The esoteric ethos allows for multiple ways to understand "embodying deity," recognizing that there are many ways to attain it and explain what occurs. Words are conventional constructs. The goal is not to determine the "right" set of words, for there is ever a gap between the form of expression and the reality or experience to which it points. Nor is the goal to dispense with all language in order to push the mind beyond its usual fare into the non-dual state of direct knowing. The Vajrayana way is to engage the body, senses, intellect, and imagination in the quest for an enlightened, enlightening bodily presence, a divine mode of being in which one can fulfill the ultimate purpose of embodying deity, namely, to devote body, speech, and mind—that is, every thought, word, and deed—to universal well-being and awakening. Toward this end, Vajrayana is an aesthetically rich tradition, employing many arts of bodily transformation: mantra, poesy, visual imagery, yoga, ritual, song, and dance.

Notes

1. Charya dance (Skt. *caryā-nṛtya*) is not so called with reference to the Caryā category in the fourfold Tibetan classification system of Kriyā, Caryā, Yoga, and Anuttara Yoga Tantra texts and practices. Charya dance is an Anuttara Yoga Tantra practice. Christian Wedemeyer

has established that the term *caryā* has a technical meaning in this genre of texts, referring to a realm of practice that includes dance, singing, sacramental meat and alcohol, cremation ground practices, bone ornaments, skull cups, consort union, inter-caste mingling, and other transgressions of social and religious norms; Christian Wedemeyer, *Making Sense of Tantric Buddhism: History, Semiology, and Transgression in the Indian Traditions* (New York: Columbia University Press, 2013), 134, 138–43.

2. Three Vajracharyas taught at the Royal Academy of the Arts beginning in the 1950s and transmitted several dances that became the mainstay of the performing arts community, college dance curricula, and cultural programs staged for tourists. On the motives, routes, and content of this public line of transmission, see Miranda Shaw, "Tantric Buddhist Dance of Nepal: From the Temple to the Stage and Back," in *Nepal: Nostalgia and Modernity*, ed. Deepak Shimkhada (Bombay: The Marg Foundation, 2011), 101–10.
3. For the website of the temple, see https://www.dancemandal.com.
4. The substance of this essay draws on fieldwork in Kathmandu for two- and three-month stints in 1991, 1992, 1993, 1995, 1997, and 2007. My ongoing research on Charya dance has touched on issues raised in this essay but is focused on other aspects of the tradition.
5. Ratna Kaji Vajracharya authored many books on Newar Buddhism in the Newar language. For his autobiographical reflections and Vajrayana outlook in an English publication, see Prem Saran, *Yoga, Bhoga and Ardhanariswara: Individuality, Wellbeing and Gender in Tantra* (New Delhi: Routledge, 2008), 102–7, 183–89, 194.
6. The majority of dances that center on deities are the focus of my essay. Other dances (less than 5 percent of the oeuvre, in my estimation) are devoted to esoteric yogic practice, metaphysical themes (such as emptiness), and religious sacra other than deities.
7. This ritual list was compiled from interviews with Ratna Kaji spanning 1991 and 1997. Examples of specific rituals within these categories would lead far afield of the present discussion.
8. David N. Gellner reports the same gendered pattern in a Cakrasaṃvara initiation in Patan; *Monk, Householder, Tantric Priest: Newar Buddhism and Its Hierarchy of Ritual* (Cambridge: Cambridge University Press, 1992), 274–75, 277–78. Ratna Kaji Vajracharya imparted this as the customary pattern in Kathmandu over his lifetime and thus one he followed in the 51-deity Cakrasaṃvara mandala enactment he oversaw in 1982. In a relatively recent departure from this pattern, Badri Ratna Vajracharya danced all the parts of a 73-deity Cakrasaṃvara mandala enactment over which he presided in Kathmandu in 2009. I have sought but not garnered explanation for this innovation, which may well have been due to limited preparation time or an insufficient number of Vajracharya participants.
9. The *Kriyāsaṃgraha*, a circa eleventh-century ritual compendium of Newar authorship, cites occasions for dance that overlap but don't dovetail those I ascertained in the current tradition. Mudras and bodily postures identified in the text rarely match or resemble any I documented. Vajracharyas I interviewed did not cite this text as a source on Charya dance, although the compendium warrants further research for its dance content.
10. *Cittaviśuddhiprakaraṇa* vv. 110–11. My translation, from Prabhubhai Patel, ed., *Cittaviśuddhiprakaraṇa of Āryadeva: Sanskrit and Tibetan Texts* (Santiniketan: Viśva-Bharati, 1949), 8.
11. *Hevajra-tantra* I.vi.10, I.vi.13. Translation follows that of G. W. Farrow and I. Menon in *Concealed Essence of the Hevajra Tantra, With the Commentary of Yogaratnamālā* (Delhi: Motilal Banarsidass, 1992), 64, 65, slightly amended.

12. *Hevajra-tantra* I1.iv.9. David Snellgrove, trans., *The Hevajra Tantra: A Critical Study* (London: Oxford University Press, 1959), 1:102, slightly amended.
13. Skt. *bhagavataḥ kāya-vāk-cittena viharanti*; Martin M. Kalff, "Selected Chapters from the *Abhidhānottara-tantra*: The Union of Female and Male Deities," PhD diss., Columbia University, 1979, 327, v. 89b2.
14. Hereafter, at times I use the term "dancer" to refer to one who is dancing and not someone who has dance as a profession.
15. I describe this process of kinesthetic and emotional re-patterning in more detail in "Dancing Compassion: Cultivating a Body of Love in the Tantric Buddhist Dance of Nepal," *Journal of Dance, Movement and Spiritualities* 4, no. 2 (2017): 173–78.
16. Philosopher and scholar of religion and dance Kimerer LaMothe articulates, in neurological and physiological terms, how movements, sensations, and responses perpetually interrelate in a mutually transformative process of "bodily becoming"; *Why We Dance: A Philosophy of Bodily Becoming* (New York: Columbia University Press, 2015), chap. 4, encapsulated on pp. 96–104. Her discussion is applicable to and illuminates Charya dance as a transformative discipline.
17. Newar Vajrayana does not precisely map the subtle body. The operative terms and concepts are those for the subtle body (*vajra-deha*), network of subtle veins (*nāḍī*), central vertical axis (*avadhūtī*) and parallel channels to the left (*lalanā*) and right (*rasanā*), subtle energies that carry breath and thought (*prāṇa*), *cakra*s along the central channel (albeit not systematized into a fixed number), and inner heat (*caṇḍālī*). This vocabulary and level of iteration reflect those found in the songs (*dohā* and *caryā-gīti*) integral to the dance tradition and in the classical Vajrayana sources cited in this chapter, which offer a similar core schema that is adapted for varying iconographic and visualization systems.
18. Francesco Sferra surveys the vocabulary and meanings of purity and purification (*viśuddhi*) in Vajrayana literature and reveals the ongoing tension and distinction, or dichotomy, between purification as a process and purity as an inherent condition in "The Concept of Purification in Some Texts of Late Indian Buddhism," *Journal of Indian Philosophy* 27 (1999): 83–103, especially 85–86.
19. The texts in currency in Newar Vajrayana, cited previously, do not use the main Sanskrit term for possession, *aveśa*, to describe possession by deities. The Newar term *dyaḥ wayegu* is used both for trance possession and for channeling deity.
20. Ratna Kaji Vajracharya, personal communication, first stated to me in July 1991, and subsequently repeated and confirmed by him and several others who reported the experience.
21. Harshita Kamath draws a similar distinction between ritual trance possession and fusion with the mythic or divine character being danced in the classical dance styles of Kuchipudi and Kathakali. For what I term "channeling," she coins the phrase "classical possession" in her essay "Bodied, Embodied, and Reflective Selves: Theorizing Performative Selfhood in South Indian Performance," in *Refiguring the Body: Embodiment in South Asian Religions*, ed. Barbara Holdredge and Karen Pechilis (Albany: State University of New York Press, 2016), 109–29.
22. Vajracharyas promulgate the principle of innate enlightenment but do not, insofar as I could ascertain, use the term *tathāgata-garbha* for the indwelling essence of enlightenment.
23. Robert A. F. Thurman, "Vajra Hermeneutics," in *Buddhist Hermeneutics*, ed. Donald S. Lopez, Jr. (Honolulu: University of Hawai'i Press 1988), 125.
24. Thurman, "Vajra Hermeneutics," 125.

Further Reading

Appell, Helen Fox. "Charya Nritya: Nepalese Ritual Dance of Deity Yoga." In *Dancing with Dharma: Essays on Movement and Dance in Western Buddhism*, ed. Harrison Blum. Jefferson, NC: McFarland Press, 2016, 155–63.

Atlan, Corinne. *Danses de Diamant*. Paris and Pondicherry: Kailash Editions, 2001.

George, David E. R. *Buddhism as/in Performance: Analysis of Meditation and Theatrical Practice*. New Delhi: D. K. Printworld, 1999.

Shaw, Miranda. "Dancing Compassion: Cultivating a Body of Love in the Tantric Buddhist Dance of Nepal." *Journal of Dance, Movement and Spiritualities* 4, no. 2 (2017): 173–78.

Shaw, Miranda. "Tantric Buddhist Dance of Nepal: From the Temple to the Stage and Back." In *Nepal: Nostalgia and Modernity*, ed. Deepak Shimkhada. Bombay: Marg Foundation, 2011, 101–110.

Widdess, Richard. "Caryā: The Revival of a Tradition?" *European Bulletin of Himalayan Research* 12–13 (1997): 12–20.

CHAPTER 16

BUDDHIST DEATH PRACTICES

MARGARET GOUIN

Death is an important event for a Buddhist. It is not just the conclusion of one life, but also the prelude to birth in the next life cycle. At this point, the karmic balance accrued during one's life—and past lives—comes into play; and one's past actions will now influence one's future birth for good or ill. Someone who has not lived a virtuous life may still be able to improve their prospects of a fortunate rebirth (into one of the three higher realms of samsara—human, titan, or god—where it is possible to make further progress toward the ultimate goal of enlightenment) by dying in a calm and composed state with their mind settled on the Buddha and the Dharma (a "good" death). Indeed, for someone who achieves the necessary focus, it is possible to attain enlightenment at the very moment of death. Conversely, a person can negate the accumulated good karma of a life lived in accordance with the Buddha's teachings by dying in a state of confusion or anger. A "bad" death, where one dies suddenly without the opportunity to prepare oneself, is one of the most feared possibilities; bad deaths are usually those that occur by accident or disease, by violence, or in childbirth. The undesirable consequence of a bad death is rebirth in one of the lower realms—as an animal, a hungry ghost, or a hell being—and the consequent loss of opportunity to progress toward enlightenment.

The critical importance of death is recognized in all traditions of Buddhism, and a basic structure underlies practices otherwise differentiated by doctrinal or cultural considerations. These death practices (also referred to herein as funeral or funerary rites/rituals/practices) relate not solely to the disposal of the body, but to a more extensive sequence of activities which commence before death and continue after the body is no longer present. Broadly speaking, these include preparing for death, taking proper care of the body after death, some form of religious ritual, and dedicating the merit of the ritual to the benefit of the deceased.

It must be acknowledged that historically the field of Buddhist studies has for the most part failed to pay adequate attention to the richness and complexity of Buddhist death practices. Much emphasis has been placed on the study of texts, with little or no recognition of differences arising from regional, social, and cultural factors, as well as from variations between traditions.[1]

The focus of this chapter will be on traditional Tibetan Buddhist death practices.[2] In an effort to give a useful overview, these will be described as if there is a standard form of funeral which flows as one coherent whole. In fact, this is far from the truth: existing data indicate a very wide variety of practices throughout Tibetan cultural areas. This account is an amalgam based on written accounts drawn from both ethnographic studies and travelers' descriptions, as well as selected Tibetan Buddhist texts describing mortuary rituals; and the extent of variations will be pointed out where relevant. Similarities with and differences from other traditions will also be noted, but space does not permit much detail in this respect.[3]

Death is the single most important life event for a Tibetan Buddhist: there are few if any other life events attended by such a degree of attention and ritualization. The death rituals start before the person is even dead, but only once it has been determined that death is inevitable. At this point, healing and life-extending practices will be abandoned and the dying person must turn their thoughts to achieving a "good" death. They might be advised to arrange for the distribution of their possessions, to resolve any outstanding disputes, and to reconcile with any estranged family members or neighbors. The concern is to free them from any kind of attachment to the life they are about to leave. To this end also, noisy displays of grief are discouraged, and indeed loved ones may be excluded entirely from the death chamber in case their presence causes thoughts of human love, and therefore worldly attachment, to cloud the sufferer's mind. Religious pictures or other objects may be placed where the dying person can see them, and there may be continuous recitation of prayers and mantras. Friends may visit and recall religious empowerments they received together, or recount memories of religious teachers they have known. They may also recall particularly meritorious actions performed by the dying person, in order to keep their mind on the positive aspects of their life and thereby increase the likelihood of a good rebirth. The sufferer may be encouraged to repeat their refuge vows and to recite mantras, if they are able. Some accounts indicate the dying person may be given a consecrated substance, in particular a bit of sacred relic, to eat.[4]

The emphasis on creating a serene atmosphere allowing a focus on the spiritual importance of dying is found throughout all Buddhist traditions.[5] While the elements vary, deathbed practices usually include religious chanting and the presence of religious objects, both of which help keep the mind properly attuned to the karmic significance of the moment.[6]

The Tibetan concept of when death occurs is complex, but a basic understanding is necessary in order to grasp the significance of the after-death rituals. Three different words are used to describe the elements that together constitute "being alive." The *srog* is the principle that sustains physical life in the body. It ceases to exist when death occurs. The *rnam shes* is consciousness, or the "consciousness principle"; it alone will experience the transition through the bardo (the intermediate state between death and rebirth) to a new birth. The third element, the *bla*, is often translated as "soul" or "spirit" in

Western language; it appears to be a pre-Buddhist term that coexists uneasily with the very Buddhist concept of *rnam shes*. The *bla* is believed to survive death by up to nine years, but is tied to the place death occurred. It must be kept happy, otherwise it can manifest as a harmful influence on the family of the deceased.

For a Tibetan Buddhist, death does not occur at the cessation of physical (visible, "outer") breathing. Even after heart and lungs have ceased to function, "inner" breathing may continue, and as long as it does, the person is not really dead. However, for most people, the cessation of outer breathing and the dissipation of the life force will be almost simultaneous. In order to be certain that the person really is dead, an attempt may be made (by "calling the soul"[7]) to see whether their soul has simply temporarily absented itself, giving the appearance of death. If the soul does not return when called, death is confirmed; and at this point often a white cloth is placed over the face of the corpse.

Ritual activity after death focuses on two important aims, which run in parallel. One sequence of activities is designed to promote the spiritual well-being of the deceased person by assisting them to achieve the best possible rebirth. An equally important sequence operates to protect the deceased person and those around them from the nefarious effects of evil spirits. The two goals often overlap, and frequently one ritual or ritual series will work to accomplish both ends.

One of the first and most important activities undertaken immediately after death is casting the death horoscope. Horoscopes play a central role in Tibetan Buddhist life; the death horoscope will be drawn up according to the time and place of the death, in conjunction with the deceased's birth horoscope data.[8] It is important for determining the cause of death (i.e., what malevolent spiritual entity the survivors need to be protected against), and even more vitally, where the deceased will be reborn. If the foreseen rebirth will be "unfortunate" (in one of the three lower realms of rebirth), the horoscope might also indicate what steps may be taken by the survivors to counteract this and achieve a more fortunate rebirth. In many cases, it appears the horoscope is also used to determine how, where, and when the body should be disposed.

A ritual that may be performed before or after death is *'pho ba*. As with so many elements of the Tibetan Buddhist funeral rites, it appears to be usually but not invariably performed, and in some cultural settings it will not be performed at all until after the corpse has been disposed of. By means of prayers coupled with a series of special vocalized sounds, the consciousness (*rnams shes*) of the dying or deceased person is expelled through the crown aperture in their skull and sent directly to a pure land, usually that of Amitābha.[9] If this occurs sometime after death but before disposal, the consciousness of the deceased may first be recalled into the body to ensure it is properly directed to the pure land by the *'pho ba*. If the body is no longer present, an effigy may be used (see later discussion). Even if a religious professional[10] declares that the *'pho ba* has been successful, the funeral rites proceed as if it were not. Although there are numerous examples in other Buddhist traditions of practices designed to assist the deceased in reaching the desired pure land,[11] the mechanism of *'pho ba* appears to be unique to Tibetan Buddhism.

The element of Tibetan death practices with which Western Buddhists are most familiar is the guidance of the deceased's consciousness (*rnam shes*) through the intermediate state between death and rebirth (the bardo). Indeed, it sometimes appears as if this is thought to be the *only* death practice. This confusion perhaps arose with the publication in 1927 of a translation of a group of texts touted by its editor, W. Y. Evans-Wentz, as "a mystic manual for guidance through the Otherworld of any illusions and realms, whose frontiers are birth and death."[12] Apparently seeking to capitalize on the contemporary popularity of E. Wallis Budge's translation of Egyptian funerary documents, Evans-Wentz rather unfortunately, and certainly inaccurately, entitled it "The Tibetan Book of the Dead." In fact it is *a* "Tibetan Book of the Dead"; there are many different such "guidebooks," with different portrayals of the bardo stages.

Nevertheless, the practice of giving guidance—of some kind—to the deceased's consciousness is consistently found in Tibetan death practices, although there are many variations in the text read, when it is read, how it is read, and the length of time for which it is read. One of the first and most important elements of guidance is simply telling the deceased that they are dead, and assuaging any fear they may experience when they find they are unable to communicate with those around them. This is essentially a continuation of the pre-death efforts to ensure that the person stays calm and aware of what is happening, and now, newly dead, focuses on the important and challenging task of navigating the bardo to a fortunate rebirth, rather than continuing to be preoccupied by matters pertaining to their former life.

In order to assist the deceased in reaching a good rebirth, the harmful effects of their negative karma and mental obscurations (wrong ideas about the nature of reality) must be counteracted. This is usually done by recalling the deceased's consciousness (*rnam shes*) into the body and then performing various *'byang chog* (purification rituals) to eliminate the possibility of rebirth in the lower realms.[13] Guidance may be given as part of the purification ritual or following it,[14] and either the guidance or the purification ritual (or both) may be followed by *'pho ba*. No incongruity seems to be experienced in multiplying the types of ritual—even though they envisage different goals—or in repeating them, sometimes many times over. "More" numerically always appears to be equated with "more effective."

Making and dedicating merit is the largest and arguably the most important element in the ritual sequence(s). "Making merit" is the primary religious activity of most Tibetan Buddhist laypersons, and the accumulation of merit during one's life has a direct effect on one's prospects for obtaining a fortunate rebirth. However, merit made on behalf of the deceased by survivors, and dedicated to their benefit, may also operate to improve their rebirth prospects.

The simplest form of making merit, and the most accessible to laypersons, is any form of generosity; the distribution of food and alms is mentioned frequently in the data. However, any activity that promotes the Dharma is especially meritorious, so in the context of death practices, merit-making activities will include inviting religious professionals to chant texts, and commissioning the creation of religious articles such as texts, paintings, or statues.

Feeding the deceased, and any other spirits that might be in the vicinity, is also a meritorious act; rituals of feeding the dead are found throughout Tibetan Buddhist funerary activities and occur both before and after the disposal of the body. These rituals are not unique to Tibetan Buddhism: for example, Langer provides details of similar activities in the context of Sri Lankan Buddhism, although these appear to take place only after the disposal of the body.[15] There are a variety of ways the feeding may occur. In some cases the food is burned; this appears to be a form of offering known as *tsha gsur* (or *bsur*).[16] In other settings it may be placed on an altar, to be subsequently removed and either thrown away or eaten by the survivors. The essence of the food is believed to nourish the newly deceased,[17] and to strengthen them for the arduous passage through the bardo(s).[18] Offerings may also be made to the buddhas, bodhisattvas, and hungry ghosts, in a ritual called *tshe*. The Tibetan practice appears to be related to an early Chinese Buddhist ritual (which may itself have its foundations in early Indian Buddhism), said to have been introduced into Tibet by a Chinese princess in the eighth century CE.[19]

A constellation of ritual activities is aimed at protecting the survivors from harm by the malevolent entity which caused the death. Death is rarely assumed to be natural and is frequently attributed to the malign activity of some negative spiritual entity, who must be kept away from the survivors.[20] Another potential source of danger to survivors is the spirit (*bla*) of the newly dead person, which may not recognize they are dead and may try to return to the body. Such spirits are always malevolent; the spirits of children and young people who have died without living a full life span are considered particularly dangerous.

The most feared eventuality is that the corpse may actually be reanimated either by a demon or by the spirit (*bla*) of the newly deceased. This is the dreaded *ro langs*, a zombie-like creature that seeks to turn other, living, people into *ro langs*, and that is very difficult to kill.[21] One purpose of the prayers and purification rites is to prevent harmful spirits from invading the fresh corpse, and someone may be delegated to sit by the body at night chanting prayers and mantras to keep such demons at bay. Very commonly the body will be tightly bound in a fetal position, often breaking the back in the process, in order to prevent it from moving if by mischance it is reoccupied. The bodies of those who have died suddenly are considered particularly likely to become *ro langs*, because they were not able to prepare themselves for death.

There is no consistent formula for preparing the body for disposal. In some cultural settings the procedures may be very elaborate as to the setting, the dressing, and the positioning of the corpse.[22] In other contexts there is minimal reference simply to washing and tidying the body. At all times, however, it is clear that the body is treated with dignity and respect. In part this is due to the belief that disturbing the body unnecessarily may distract and upset the newly dead person (who can still hear and see what is going on around their remains) when they should be concentrating on leaving their familiar environment and entering the bardo. There is also the belief that the consciousness (*rnams shes*) may exit through whatever part of the body is touched prematurely before the proper rituals have been undertaken. If the body is touched below the waist, this will lead to an unfortunate rebirth in the lower realms.

The form of disposal, and where and when it will occur, is usually determined by the death horoscope, which may also indicate who may and may not participate in the procession and/or the disposal itself. It appears that all forms of disposal occur away from inhabited areas, so some form of transportation is required to move the body to the disposal area.[23] This must take into account the fact that if the body is put down on the ground at any point in transit, the spirit (*bla*) will stay there, effectively converting the spot into a cemetery. To avoid this possibility, any time the body must be put down, a temporary bier is constructed, even if it is only a few bits of stone to hold the body above the ground. If the journey to the disposal site is long, resting places may be built ahead of time at one or more locations along the route.[24]

In some cultural settings, the procession itself may be an elaborate affair, punctuated by rituals, dancing, and even special meals.[25] An element frequently referred to is the use of a white cloth, which may be a *kha btags* (prayer scarf) or a much longer piece of fabric, tied at one end to the corpse with the other end usually being carried by the officiating religious professional. This cloth is explained in many ways in such ethnographic data as exist, but reference is often made to needing to show the spirit (*bla*) the way to the disposal area,[26] thus reinforcing the emphasis on ensuring that the *bla* makes it safely to a final resting place, first suggested by the need to avoid placing the body on the ground in transit. Other accounts suggest that the cloth is meant to show the deceased (*rnam shes* or *bla*? the literature is unclear) the way to Amitābha's pure land.[27]

The disposal of the body is perhaps more elaborated in Tibetan Buddhism than in other Buddhist traditions. Available ethnographic data indicate that there are four principal methods of disposal: exposure (in the open air), immersion (in water), cremation (burning), and burial (in the earth). The bodies of persons of great spiritual attainment (and also sometimes, it would appear, persons of high social standing) might be preserved by a form of mummification. There are also indications that special considerations apply for the disposal of the bodies of the very young and the very old. There is a major failure of Western scholarship in this area, far too often shown by the uncritical (and unreferenced) repetition of an arbitrary list of disposal methods which has little foundation in fact: "sky burial" (by which is meant exposure)[28] is best, cremation is second-best, earth burial is bad, and water disposal is only for death by disease. This list is simply not supported by the available evidence.[29]

In fact, there are many forms of exposure. In some cases—usually when feeding the corpse to "vultures" (most likely Himalayan griffons and/or bearded lammergeiers)—the body is dismembered and the corpse-cutter(s) may even go so far as to pulverize the bones and mix the resulting powder with the brains, *rtsam pa* (roasted barley flour), and/or butter to make them appetizing to the birds. But the corpse may just be taken to a remote spot and left, untouched or only scored a few times. Accounts list eagles, hawks, crows, ravens, wolves, jackals, foxes, dogs, and pigs as possible scavengers, although not all are acceptable in all areas.

Cremation may be on a large pile of up to nine tiers of logs or—in areas where wood is scarce—in a specially built small cremation oven, where the necessary heat can be achieved by utilizing the updraft created by the chimney. Earth burial may be accomplished by laying the body on the ground and piling stones over it, as well as by interment in caves, or in chambers burrowed into the sides of hills, if the soil cover is not sufficient for an excavated grave. In some areas, earth burial is the first of a two-stage process: once the soft tissues have decayed, the body is dug up again and the remains are burned. The body may also be buried as a temporary measure to await a more appropriate or auspicious time to use a preferred method.

Disposal by immersion in water appears to be primarily a poor person's method. In some areas it is reserved for any form of dishonorable, sudden, or violent death, including death by disease. In other locations, on the contrary, the body may be transported a considerable distance in order to place it in a body of water considered particularly auspicious.

As already mentioned, special rules may apply for the disposal of bodies of religious leaders and nobility, and the usual methods are mummification or cremation. Particularly with regard to "holy persons," a major concern is making possible the production of relics during the disposal process. Much less information is available with regard to the treatment of children's bodies,[30] and almost none about the very old.[31] What little data there are suggest an interesting parallel: children may be (but are not invariably) buried *in the family's house* in order to "preserve the prosperity" of the household, and the only records I have found of burying very old people—just four cases—describe all of them as also being buried in the house.[32] In the case of the old people, no reason is given; but given the similarity of treatment of these widely disparate age groups, further investigation seems merited.

The only possible conclusion from the considerable variety in how the corpse is disposed of is that there is no fixed degree of desirability for one method over any other, and that methods vary widely according to geographic location and cultural grouping. There is a serious deficiency in Western ethnographic data in this area. However, much useful information may be gleaned from personal accounts, memoirs, and travel diaries published by soldiers, merchants, missionaries, and travelers. Although their interpretations may be suspect, they were in general accurate and at times obsessively detailed in writing down what they saw.

Even after the body has been disposed of, rituals of benefit and protection continue. In some cases, the deceased's consciousness (*rnam shes*) will be recalled into an effigy for more purifications and continuing guidance.[33] The effigy may be a simple structure, or an elaborate device dressed with special items of clothing. The most important (sometimes the only) element is the *byang bu* (name card), usually some form of representation of the deceased with their name written on it. The deceased's consciousness (*rnam shes*) is called specifically into the name card and will stay there until dismissed. At the conclusion of the full sequence of death rituals, the name card (and effigy, if there is one) will be burned, thus liberating the consciousness to go on its way through the intermediate state(s) to rebirth.

Often the consciousness is guided by showing the *byang bu* a series of picture cards (*tsa ka li*); the path shown may be through the bardo, or alternatively through the six realms of rebirth, each of which is ritually closed behind the deceased until they arrive at a pure land or the state of enlightenment. The reading of bardo texts may also be undertaken at this point, or may continue if it was started before disposal; and *'pho ba* may be performed even if it had already been done before or shortly after death. The *byang bu* also makes the deceased present for purification rituals (*'byang chog*). Purification rituals for those who died "bad" deaths are particularly urgent, although it appears that there are no special procedures, only the more frequent repetition of the usual purification practices.[34]

An important event is the exorcising of the "death-demon," the malevolent spiritual entity responsible for the death. As already noted, the location and identity of this spirit is usually identified in the death horoscope, as well as the rituals that must be performed to get rid of it.[35] In addition, steps may be taken to ensure that the deceased's spirit (*bla*, which here appears to take on the connotations of "ghost") does not stay attached to its previous dwelling. The spirits of children are particularly feared, and considerable effort may be made to ensure that a child's spirit remains well disposed toward the survivors.[36]

Merit-making activities also continue, including chanting, distributing food and alms, and erecting prayer flags. An activity believed to generate a very high degree of merit is making some of the remains of the deceased into *tsha tsha*. Remains are usually bones, bone fragments, and/or ashes left over from disposal by exposure or cremation, and also the ashes from burning the *byang bu* at the conclusion of the death rites. They may be ground up and mixed with water, clay, and other substances such as spices, to make small clay shapes. These are often consecrated and then placed in locations of particular spiritual significance. The process is believed to purify the deceased's karma and liberate them from the possibility of rebirth in the lower realms.[37]

The *dge ba*[38] is a ritual or series of rituals which contains many of the elements already described. Although it is not performed in every cultural area, where it does exist it may be a very elaborate process extending over several days.[39] An important component is the distribution of food within the village of the deceased. This may be a very elaborate affair if the deceased's family is wealthy, or a simple sharing of home-brewed beer or salt if the family is poor; but the equal distribution of whatever is available to all the villagers without discrimination as to age or social status is of paramount importance,[40] and the portions may be weighed to ensure exact parity. At the end of the *dge ba* and indeed generally at the conclusion of the funerary rites, a formal feast will be held, including a final food offering to the deceased, with the reminder forcibly given to them that they are dead now and should be on their way.[41] There appears to be provision in some cultural areas for a special ritual meal for a dead child which is the equivalent, although much simpler, of an adult's *dge ba*.[42]

There is little evidence of formal memorialization within the first year or two after death and even less after that. The making and placing of physical markers (such as gravestones) is not generally commented on; however, ritual activities may be taken to generate merit for the deceased on the death anniversary.[43] This does not prevent the continuing display of photographs and memorabilia of the deceased on the household altar. The death rituals do not replace the normal processes of grief and mourning, but provide a routine for moving the survivors through the process of loss from its first sharp immediacy to acceptance and letting go. However, continuing emotional displays of grief are frowned upon as demonstrating an unseemly degree of attachment to the deceased, and are discouraged on the grounds that they will hinder the dead person's passage on to their next life.

Many aspects of Tibetan Buddhist funeral rites are almost completely ignored in modern accounts, notably elements of performance, material culture, socioeconomic factors, gender, and "folk" beliefs as opposed to Buddhist philosophy. The absence of these elements in some accounts and their presence in others (most frequently in the older records) leaves the conscientious scholar in a quandary. Are these elements missing because they didn't occur? Or because although they occurred, the person recording the events didn't see them? Or because although they saw them, they didn't think they were important, or were told by their informant(s) that they weren't important? There is no way of knowing.

The role of the laity in the various ritual procedures is largely left unexplored, particularly the part played by women. It would appear, for example, that women do a great deal of the background work for the death practices, such as the preparation of food and looking after the needs and requirements of the religious professionals conducting the rituals, but they are not usually present at the actual disposal of the body or at many of the formal rituals. This may have led ethnographers to conclude that the activities of women in the context of funerary rituals were not worth recording.

Elements of material culture, particularly clothing and food, are almost completely ignored, with one or two important exceptions which only serve to highlight the lack of information elsewhere.[44] There appear to be special rules relating to which materials and/or colors are (or aren't) permitted to be worn by either the corpse or the survivors, and some indication that importance is attached to removing buttons and substituting fastenings, or to wearing clothes inside out or back-to-front. Thupten Sangay mentions a purification ritual that involves a particular usage of the deceased's clothing,[45] but why the clothes should be treated this way is obscure. Very little information is given on costumes worn in the course of death rituals, by either the religious professionals or the corpse.[46] Performative elements such as singing and dancing have been largely ignored.[47]

Is there ritual pollution, and if so, how does it arise, in whom or what, and how is it dissipated? What are the rules for mourning? Who has to observe them, and for how long?[48] There appears to be considerable variation in this area, as in the role of family members, some of whom may have special roles to play and others who may be specifically barred from participation. Sometimes it is mentioned that low-status actors, such as blacksmiths, tailors, and musicians, take part in the ceremonies, but the reason for their presence is rarely examined.

Another element overlooked in almost all accounts is the economic component of death practices. For one thing, they provide an important source of monastic income, both from creating religious artifacts as a part of the merit-making activities and from the performance of the necessary rites.[49] If monks are invited to perform rituals, for example, they must be offered the best food and accommodation available for the duration of their presence in the house. All the materials for necessary ritual objects (e.g., offerings such as *gtor ma* made of butter, sugar, and roast barley flour) must be provided, again of the best quality the household can afford. This can represent a significant expense and may explain why very often monks do not appear to be called in to perform rituals until after death. It would also explain why, in the existing accounts, there is rarely any mention of death rites continuing for the full forty-nine days mandated by the guidance texts as the maximum time the dead may spend in the bardo state before achieving rebirth. Such lengthy rituals are usually found only in the case of wealthy laypersons or major religious figures.

Religious professionals are sometimes paid for their services by giving them clothing or other possessions of the deceased. This may also be considered a merit-making activity, akin to the practice in Theravada and Chinese Buddhism of generating merit by offering food and clothing to the monastic community. Against this interpretation must be placed the fact that apparently religious professionals will not perform the death rituals *unless* they receive some kind of payment. Mumford comments on the unfortunate fate of a blacksmith's young daughter, whose death horoscope indicated she was destined for rebirth as a wandering demon. Because the family had no financial resources for a Buddhist funeral, it was impossible for her to escape this fate; and because she would harm people as a wandering demon, on her next rebirth she would descend even further down the samsaric scale. There was never the slightest suggestion that the local lama should perform the rituals for free to save the child from such an unhappy destiny. On the other hand, a wealthy man's family was able to overturn a horoscope predicting rebirth in the animal realm by paying for a lavish funeral.[50]

The cost of the funeral itself is a barometer of merit—families may bankrupt themselves to provide a "meritorious" (i.e., expensive) funeral, both as a sign of respect and also to generate the maximum amount of benefit for the deceased.[51] The funeral is also an opportunity for the family to settle debts owed by and owing to the deceased, before the estate is passed on to the beneficiaries.

A related aspect that remains largely unexplored is the social importance of economic reciprocity between the family of the deceased and their neighbors. Through the neighbors' participation in ritual events surrounding the death, and in particular by their bringing gifts (usually small amounts of money) and assisting in the preparation of food for the bereaved family, a network of obligations is created that will be called upon when the next death occurs in the community: what I do for you now, you will do for me when the time comes.[52] Persons who assist with preparing the body and carrying it to the disposal site may receive either cash payment or food or some item(s) belonging to the deceased; they may also be feasted by the family at the conclusion of the post-disposal rituals.

Some accounts mention (in passing) popular beliefs associated with death and dying.[53] What other such beliefs are there, from the various different ethnic groups that make up cultural Tibet? What effort is being made to discover and preserve them? Tibetan culture is under siege where ethnically Tibetan areas have been occupied by the People's Republic of China; and in the diaspora, habits and traditions evolve, change, and disappear under the influence of a new environment and new social imperatives. As the older Tibetans die, the beliefs and traditions once central to their culture and their self-identity as Buddhists are lost for lack of any effort to record them. The woefully inadequate state of modern ethnographic data on Tibetan death practices highlights the possibility that many fascinating aspects of a rich and complex culture may be left unexplored due to the inattention of scholars.

Notes

1. The study of texts is of course of major importance, but should not be divorced from the study of practice—the text-in-action. To study practice without ascertaining the text used is equally unhelpful.
2. The designation "Tibetan" includes not only the inhabitants of the area known as the independent country of Tibet prior to 1959, but also any ethnic group having a spoken language within the Tibetan language family, some use of written Tibetan, and shared or related myths and historical narratives. Geographically this covers the former independent Tibet, some areas of China, and parts of North India, Nepal, Bhutan, and Sikkim, as well as the Tibetan diaspora.
3. An additional difficulty that arises with making such comparisons is that Buddhist death practices, generally, are poorly documented in Western academic literature. There are some excellent historical and textual studies, but a lack of ethnographic data. Some valuable additions have been made in recent years.
4. Thupten Sangay, "Tibetan Rituals of the Dead," translated by Gavin Kilty, *Tibetan Medicine* 7 (1984): 30. The most usual form of "relic" in this context is *ring bsrel* (see, for example, Marian H. Duncan, *Customs and Superstitions of Tibetans* [Delhi: Book Faith India, 1998], 118). These are small conglomerations of tiny crystals sometimes found in the ashes of very holy persons following cremation, but which may also be produced from the bodies of saintly living persons: see David Germano, "Living Relics of the Buddha(s) in Tibet," in *Embodying the Dharma: Buddhist Relic Veneration in Asia*, ed. David Germano and Kevin Trainor (Albany: State University of New York, 2004), 51–91. For Theravāda deathbed practices, see Rita Langer, *Buddhist Rituals of Death and Rebirth: Contemporary Sri Lankan Practice and Its Origins* (Abingdon, UK: Routledge, 2007), 10–12. Pure Land practices are particularly elaborated in this regard: see, for example, James C. Dobbins, "Genshin's Deathbed Nembutsu Ritual in Pure Land Buddhism," in *Religions of Japan in Practice*, ed. George J. Tanabe Jr. (Princeton, NJ: Princeton University, 1999), 116–75.
5. It may have been imported into early Buddhism from then-existing Indian practices. Langer, *Buddhist Rituals*, 26–35, gives a detailed examination of the belief that a person's last thoughts could influence their next rebirth, as found in the *Brāhmaṇa*s and *Upaniṣads*.
6. Langer, *Buddhist Rituals*, 11–12. The elaborate deathbed practices of medieval Japan are studied in Jacqueline I. Stone, *Right Thoughts at the Last Moment: Buddhism and Deathbed Practices in Early Medieval Japan* (Honolulu: University of Hawai'i Press, 2016).

7. Michael Vinding, "The Thakālīs as Buddhists: A Closer Look at Their Death Ceremonies," *Kailash* 9 (1982): 296.
8. Tibetan astrology is complex, and appears to be based on the same or similar elements as Chinese astrology. Mumford gives a summary of the basic components of a death horoscope, with a diagram showing the interrelations of the various parts: Stan Royal Mumford, *Himalayan Dialogue: Tibetan Lamas and Gurung Shamans in Nepal* (Madison: University of Wisconsin, 1981), 105–10.
9. Pure Land practices are more extensive in Tibetan Buddhism than is usually reported: see Matthew T. Kapstein, "Pure Land Buddhism in Tibet? From Sukhāvatī to the Field of Great Bliss," in *Approaching the Land of Bliss: Religious Praxis in the Cult of Amitābha*, ed. Richard K. Payne and Kenneth K. Tanaka (Honolulu: University of Hawai'i Press, 2004), 16–51; and Georgios T. Halkias, *Luminous Bliss: A Religious History of Pure Land Literature in Tibet. With an Annotated Translation and Critical Analysis of the Orgyen-ling Golden Short Sukhāvatīvyūha-sūtra* (Honolulu: University of Hawai'i Press, 2013). Halkias treats *'pho ba* specifically in his chapter 5; see also Matthew T. Kapstein, "A Pilgrimage of Rebirth Reborn: The 1992 Celebration of the Drigung Powa Chenmo," in *Buddhism in Contemporary Tibet: Religious Revival and Cultural Identity*, ed. Melvyn C. Goldstein and Matthew T. Kapstein (Berkeley: University of California Press, 1998), 95–119.
10. Death rituals are usually performed by monks, lamas, or tantric yogins. There is no account indicating that the rites may be, or ever are, performed by nuns, although there is mention of nuns participating in a funeral procession (Vinding, "Thakālīs," 301), and having a role in the chanting of a particular ritual; Geoffrey Gorer, *Himalayan Village: The Lepchas of Sikkim*, 2nd ed. (New York: Basic Books, 1967), 355. The only activity that may upon occasion be performed by a layman seems to be the casting of the death horoscope. Various elements of the rituals, however, may be performed by laypersons (usually male) under the direction of the professional(s).
11. For example, see generally Stone, *Right Thoughts*, and Dobbins, "Genshin's Deathbed Nembutsu Ritual".
12. W. Y. Evans-Wentz, ed., *The Tibetan Book of the Dead, or the After-Death Experiences on the Bardo Plane, According to Lama Dawa-Samdup's English Rendering*, 4th ed. (Oxford: Oxford University Press), 2 (from the Introduction to the first edition).
13. See for example Lama Maha-sukha, "A Ritual for Caring for the Dead," in *Death and Dying: The Tibetan Tradition*, edited by Glenn C. Mullin (London: Arkana, 1987), 196–216.
14. Maha-sukha, "Ritual," 207.
15. Langer, *Buddhist Rituals*, 148–49. She suggests these offerings derive from the Hindu practice of *śrāddha*, which is still an important element in contemporary Hindu funerals.
16. Jampa L. Panglung, "On the Origin of the Tsha gsur Ceremony," in *Soundings in Tibetan Civilization*, ed. Barbara Aziz and Matthew T. Kapstein (New Delhi: Manohar Publications, 1985), 269.
17. Evans-Wentz, *Book of the Dead*, 19.
18. Alexandra David-Neel, *Immortality and Reincarnation: Wisdom from the Forbidden Journey*, trans. Jon Graham (Rochester: Inner Traditions, 1997), 37.
19. Pasang Wangdu and Hildegard Diemberger, *dBa'-bzhed: The Royal Narrative Concerning the Bringing of the Buddha's Doctrine to Tibet* (Vienna: Verlag der östrerreichischen Akademie der Wissenschaften, 2000), 35 and n.58.
20. Evans-Wentz, *Book of the Dead*, 27.
21. Turrell V. Wylie, "Ro-langs: The Tibetan Zombie," *History of Religions* 4 (1964): 69–80.

22. See, for example, Brigitte Steinmann, "Le rituel funéraire chez les Tamang de l'est," *Bulletin de l'École française de l'extrême-Orient* 76 (1987): 224–25.
23. This is usually some form of stretcher or bier, ranging from a basic construction (Halfdan Siiger, *The Lepchas: Culture and Religion of a Himalayan People* [Copenhagen: National Museum of Denmark, 1967], vol. 1, 182) to a very elaborate edifice (e.g., Steinmann, "Le rituel funéraire," 227); occasionally the body will be carried by one person, if it has been bound into a small bundle.
24. Thupten Sangay, "Rituals," 36.
25. Vinding is particular useful in describing these elements: "Thakālīs," 300–1.
26. Charles Ramble, "Status and Death: Mortuary Rites and Attitudes to the Body in a Tibetan Village," *Kailash* 9 (1982): 337; L. Austine Waddell, *Tibetan Buddhism: With Its Mystic Cults, Symbolism and Mythology, and in Its Relation to Indian Buddhism* (Delhi: Low Price, 1999), 494.
27. See, for example, Martin Brauen, "Death Customs in Ladakh," *Kailash* 9 (1982): 324.
28. "Sky burial" does not appear to be a Tibetan term at all and may be of Chinese origin: Dan Martin, "On the Cultural Ecology of Sky Burial on the Himalayan Plateau," *East and West* 45, no. 4–5 (1996): 354–55. Leaving a corpse to be consumed by scavengers was a popular medieval Chinese Buddhist practice; Chinese records attesting to this form of disposal predate the earliest mention of the practice in Tibet by several centuries: Liu Shufen, "Death and the Regeneration of Life: Exposure of the Corpse in Medieval Chinese Buddhism," *Journal of Chinese Religions* 28 (2000): 1–30.
29. For a full discussion of the many and varied forms of disposal used, see Margaret Gouin, *Tibetan Rituals of Death: Buddhist Funerary Practices* (Abingdon, UK: Routledge, 2010), 46–95, from which the following summary remarks are drawn and to which reference should be made for citations of sources.
30. The definition of what constitutes a "child" is not settled and varies quite widely throughout the Tibetan cultural region. Particularly useful references with regard to the death rites of children are Anne-Marie Blondeau, "Que notre enfant revienne! Un rituel méconnu pour les enfants morts en bas-âge," in *Les habitants du toit du monde: Études recueillies en hommage à Alexander W. Macdonald*, ed. Samten G. Karmay and Philippe Sagant (Nanterre: Société d'ethnologie, 1997), 193–220, and Ramble, "Status and Death." See also Steinmann, "Le rituel funéraire," 230–32.
31. That is, anyone over eighty years of age: Rinchen Losel, "Burial Customs in Garze," in *Theses on Tibetology in China*, ed. Hu Tan (Beijing: China Tibetology, 1991), 168.
32. Rinchen Losel, "Burial Customs," 174–75.
33. David Snellgrove, *Buddhist Himalaya: Travels and Studies in Quest of the Origins and Nature of Tibetan Religion* (Oxford: Bruno Cassirer, 1957), 264–74.
34. An exemplary recent study of how a Buddhist ethnic minority copes with bad deaths is Alexandra de Mersan, "Funeral Rituals, Bad Death and the Protection of Social Space among the Arakanese (Burma)," in *Buddhist Funeral Cultures of Southeast Asia and China*, ed. Paul Williams and Patrice Ladwig (Cambridge: Cambridge University, 2012), 142–65.
35. Waddell, *Lamaism*, 494–95, n.4, reports at some length on such a procedure.
36. Walter Asboe, "Disposal of the Dead in Tibet," *Man* 36 (1932): 66.
37. Snellgrove, *Buddhist Himalaya*, 274.
38. *dge ba* means "virtue"—anything that is good, auspicious, propitious.
39. An excellent description of a *dge ba* is found in Steinmann, "Le rituel funéraire," 238–53.

40. Christoph von Fürer-Haimendorf, *The Sherpas of Nepal: Buddhist Highlanders* (New Delhi: Sterling, 1979), 242–45.
41. Mumford, *Himalayan Dialogue*, 210.
42. Steinmann, "Le rituel funéraire," 232; a different type of feast is described in Ramble. "Status and Death," 344.
43. Langer records a *matakadāna* (offering in the name of the dead) ten years after the death: Langer, *Buddhist Rituals*, 142–44. Patrice Ladwig describes annual festivals in which Lao Buddhists continue to care for their dead: "Feeding the Dead: Ghosts, Materiality and Merit in a Lao Buddhist Festival for the Deceased," in Williams and Ladwig, *Buddhist Funeral Cultures*, 119–41.
44. Steinmann's "Le rituel funéraire" is by far the most detailed with regard to elements of material culture, and the role of women.
45. Thupten Sangay, "Rituals," 32.
46. See Vinding, "Thakālīs," 300 and Plate 1, for a striking example of special attire worn for a dance performed as part of the funeral procession.
47. Steinmann comments that what matters to the survivors in the performance of the death rites is that the *dge ba* took place, that the texts were read, *and that the lamas danced*: "Le rituel funéraire," 258. See also Vinding, "Thakālīs," 301.
48. Steinmann gives some information on the mourning for a male householder: "Le rituel funéraire," 234–38. See also Brauen, "Death Customs," 328–29.
49. Kapstein, "Pure Land," 26.
50. Mumford, *Himalayan Dialogue*, 203.
51. Duncan, *Customs*, 112–13; see also 118.
52. Brauen, "Death Customs," 330–31.
53. For example: if a hen crows, especially in the evening, someone in the family will die: Duncan, *Customs*, 243.

Further Reading

Blondeau, Anne-Marie. "Que notre enfant revienne! Un rituel méconnu pour les enfants morts en bas-âge." In *Les habitants du toit du monde: Études recueillies en hommage à Alexander W. Macdonald*, ed. Samten G. Karmay and Philippe Sagant. Nanterre: Société d'ethnologie, 1997, 193–220.

Bodiford, William M. "Zen in the Art of Funerals: Ritual Salvation in Japanese Buddhism." *History of Religions* 32, no. 2 (1992): 146–64.

Brauen, Martin. "Death Customs in Ladakh." *Kailash* 9 (1982): 319–32.

Cole, Alan. "Upside Down/Rightside Up: A Revisionist History of Buddhist Funerals in China." *History of Religions* 35, no. 4 (1996): 307–38.

Cuevas, Bryan J., and Jacqueline I. Stone, ed. *The Buddhist Dead: Practices, Discourses, Representations*. Honolulu: University of Hawai'i Press, 2007.

Dobbins, James C. "Genshin's Deathbed Nembutsu Ritual in Pure Land Buddhism." In *Religions of Japan in Practice*, ed. George J. Tanabe, Jr. Princeton, NJ: Princeton University Press, 1999, 166–75.

Gombrich, Richard F. *Buddhist Precept and Practice: Traditional Buddhism in the Rural Highlands of Ceylon*. Delhi: Motilal Banarsidass, 1991.

Gouin, Margaret. *Tibetan Rituals of Death: Buddhist Funerary Practices*. Abingdon, UK: Routledge, 2010.

Halkias, Georgios T. *Luminous Bliss: A Religious History of Pure Land Literature in Tibet. With an Annotated Translation and Critical Analysis of the Orgyen-ling Golden Short Sukhāvatīvyūha-sūtra*. Honolulu: University of Hawai'i Press, 2013.

Langer, Rita. *Buddhist Rituals of Death and Rebirth: Contemporary Sri Lankan Practice and Its Origins*. Abingdon, UK: Routledge, 2007.

Steinmann, Brigitte. "Le rituel funéraire chez les Tamang de l'est." *Bulletin de l'École française de l'extrême-Orient* 76 (1987): 217–80.

Stone, Jacqueline I. *Right Thoughts at the Last Moment: Buddhism and Deathbed Practices in Early Medieval Japan*. Honolulu: University of Hawai'i Press, 2016.

Vinding, Michael. "The Thakālīs as Buddhists: A Closer Look at Their Death Ceremonies." *Kailash* 9 (1982): 291–318.

Watson, James J., and Evelyn S. Rawski, ed. *Death Ritual in Late Imperial and Modern China*. Berkeley: University of California Press, 1988.

Williams, Paul, and Patrice Ladwig, ed. *Buddhist Funeral Cultures of Southeast Asia and China*. Cambridge: Cambridge University Press, 2012.

PART IV

BODY-MIND TRANSFORMATIONS

THE dominance of text-based analysis in Euro-American scholarship on Buddhist traditions has contributed to an unconscious privileging of mind over body, particularly evident in modernist constructions of Buddhism that sharply differentiate meditational practices from embodied rituals, especially practices oriented toward this-worldly benefits. The title of Part IV and the three chapters that it groups together point to the instability of the body-mind divide and problematize the implicit hierarchy of value that it enables. Viewing Buddhist tradition within the framework of body-mind transformations illuminates the great diversity of body-mind practices that Buddhists have undertaken and redirects attention to their role in facilitating a variety of relationships mediated by embodied sense experience.

Consider the different forms of relationship exemplified in the three chapters: interdependent relationships between members of the sangha and lay Buddhists, as well as with powerful superhuman agents, mediated through *paritta* chanting rituals; the multiple forms of practice through which Pure Land practitioners interact with Amitābha Buddha and with one another; and the intense relational dynamics of master and disciple mediated through koan practice. We also find diverse sensory engagements with human language in the three chapters in Part IV: as sensory embodiments of the Buddha's liberative presence in the sounds of *paritta* chanting; of Amitābha's compassion in Pure Land practice; and words as manifestations of buddha-nature in koan practice.

The three chapters also represent a multiplicity of subject positions through which knowledge of Buddhist practice is enabled. Two of the authors are ordained; one is a

Sri Lankan Theravada monk who is a university professor in the United Kingdom, the other is ordained in the Soto Zen tradition as it has taken root in the United States. The third contributor is a historian of Chinese religion teaching in an American university.

Steeped in textual scholarship, primary sources, and deep cultural engagement, Mahinda Deegalle presents in Chapter 17 a rich landscape of Sri Lankan aural practices, ranging from poetic expressions of aural virtuosity to the traditional chants of Buddhist pilgrims, all imbued with the potency of *buddhavacana*, the word of the Buddha, brought to bear on a variety of human concerns and afflictions. In Chapter 18, Charles Jones explores numerous historical and textual sources to flesh out the wide range of practices employed in transforming the body-mind with the goal of rebirth in Amitābha's Pure Land. From forms of recitation to expressions of filial piety, all practices that dedicate merit to rebirth in the Pure Land are brought together under this expansive umbrella. Weaving together scholarly insights with first-person experience to explicate the dynamics of koan practice as a vehicle for Buddhist awakening, Jeff Shore's discussion in Chapter 19 explores how the body-mind is transformed through use of specialized, multivalent, and playful word interchanges between master and disciple where the practice of *zazen* itself is an embodied koan. Taken together, they exemplify the central role of body-mind transformation in a diversity of Buddhist traditions.

CHAPTER 17

AURAL PRACTICES OF CHANTING AND PROTECTION

MAHINDA DEEGALLE

> *"Apē Budun: Api Wan̆dinḍa"* . . . All day long the pilgrims' haunting hymn, with its loudly vociferated chorus of *"Sadhu! Sadhu!"* throbs in the air. . . . Ahead of his flock marches the *"gurun[n]ānse"* . . . book in hand, chanting texts.
>
> —R. H. Bassett, *Romantic Ceylon*[1]

This chapter surveys a range of chanting practices from the Theravada Buddhist traditions of South and Southeast Asia, with a focus on Sri Lanka. Chanting practices in Sri Lankan Theravada Buddhism are varied and diverse, including a wide range of recitation practices. Foremost among these is the rhythmic chanting of selected Buddhist "discourses" (*suttas*) as *paritta* (recitation for protection), found in several specific ritual contexts (Figure 17.1).

Chanting practices also include recitation of Pali texts in prose, as well as chanting of specific verse texts (*gāthā*) such as the *Dhammapada*, which is very popular and frequently heard in sermon contexts. In addition, recitation sessions occur when four-line Sinhala poems (*kavi*) are used in ritual settings, such as making offerings (*pūjā*) to the Bodhi tree.[2] Furthermore, there is a long-established tradition of recitation practices associated with rhythmic reading of Sinhala classical prose texts such as the *Jātaka Pota*, *Saddharmaratnāvaliya* and *Pūjāvaliya*.[3] While some ancient practices such as *paritta* are broadly applicable to all Theravada Buddhist traditions, certain practices, such as reciting *gāthās*, may be unique to Sri Lankan Theravada practice. All of these forms are nevertheless broadly representative of the rich multiplicity of chanting practices employed in diverse Buddhist communities.

In its emphasis on chanting as a meditative or contemplative practice, Sri Lankan Buddhist traditions embrace many forms. Chanting ranges from the simple recitation of

FIGURE 17.1. The *paritta maṇḍapa* (pavilion for protection recitation) constructed with coconut leaves and decorated with medicinal herbs and plants at the annual celebration of Śrī Saddhātissa International Buddhist Centre, London, on February 16, 2019.

Photo: © Mahinda Deegalle.

individual Pali words to very elaborate and extended rhythmic recitations of *sutta*s such as the *Metta Sutta*,[4] and may include poems composed in the Sinhala vernacular such as melodious *kavi*. Together, these practices are recognized as enhancing protection and well-being by ensuring individual and communal happiness.

Pre-Buddhist Chanting Practices Embraced in Theravada Buddhism

The power of words was widely accepted in ancient India. Traditions that derived from the Vedic heritage with an emphasis on the *Ṛg Veda* continued to assert the magical potency of words, mystical expressions, and magical formulas. Words inspired by divine sources were privileged by the Brahmanic tradition. Mīmāṃsā philosophers such as Bhaṭṭa Kumārila asserted *śabda* (word) as an expression of the actual ultimate reality.[5] This ancient Indian heritage extended to embrace even non-Vedic traditions, and appears to have influenced the development of Buddhist traditions. The result was religiously inspired poems, formulaic stanzas, metrically rich *gāthās*, power-laden mantras, and protective *parittas*. Their effective use in guaranteeing this-worldly and other-worldly benefits was seen as potent.

The magical potency of *paritta*[6] highlights the significance of *paritta* as a ritual for dispelling negative forces and securing protection. In Mahāyāna Buddhist traditions, religiously inspired *Siddham* (J. *bonji*) letters originating in northern India appeared to communicate the potency of words and their efficacy in recitations. Letters were seen as having magical potency for various purposes. From India, they spread quite widely to East Asian Buddhist societies such as China and Japan.[7] All Theravada Buddhist traditions of South and Southeast Asia emphasize the importance of chanting as a meditative practice. The act of chanting is acknowledged as a potent means of protecting reciters as well as those around the reciters, as evidenced in daily monastic and lay practice, as well as those described in literary accounts.

History of the Study of *Paritta* Ritual in Asian Studies

During the British colonial period, Oriental Studies scholarship was very much attracted to *paritta* recitation rituals. Many *paritta* manuscripts were acquired for European palm-leaf collections.[8] Scholars of varied academic disciplines such as Indology, textual studies, anthropology, history, and religion drew attention to the *paritta* ritual (Figure 17.2).

Though not comprehensive by any means, the earliest publication on *paritta* appeared in two brief treatments by Robert Spence Hardy (1803–1868). Hardy consulted Sinhala texts and his *A Manual of Buddhism* as well as *Eastern Monachism* included a treatment on *paritta*.[9] More detailed treatments followed in the works of O. Pertold (1923),[10] E. Waldschmidt (1934), and W.A. de Silva (1940). Two detailed treatments with wide-ranging perspectives on *paritta* are the works of Peter Schalk (1972)[11] and Lily de Silva (1981)[12] with textual, historical, anthropological, sociological, and religious data. Using Sinhala, Pali, and Sanskrit sources, de Silva's work (1981) traced contemporary as well as historical aspects of *paritta* ritual. She placed *paritta* ritual in a broader framework, highlighting chanting practices and their symbolic meaning in the history of Buddhism.

FIGURE 17.2. The *Indrakīla* (ceremonial post) constructed within the *paritta maṅḍapa* indicating the location of the central seat at the whole-night *paritta* recitation at Śrī Saddhātissa International Buddhist Centre, London, on February 22, 2020. In the foreground, reels of the *pirit nūl* (protection threads) are visible, which will be distributed to pious listeners as blessings at the conclusion of the ceremony in the early morning.

Photo: © Mahinda Deegalle.

ACCOUNTS OF *PARITTA* IN THE SRI LANKAN PALI CHRONICLES

The post-canonical Sri Lankan Pali chronicle, the *Cūḷavaṃsa* (46: 5–6), refers to actual *paritta* recitations sponsored by King Aggabodhi IV (r. 667–683) by honoring *bhikkhus*. It (51: 78–83) gives more details of *paritta* recitations sponsored by King Sena II by holding a "great festival" in which the *Ratana Sutta* was "written down upon a golden plate." When an image of Venerable Ananda was brought into the town, the king made *bhikkhus* recite the *paritta*. He also arranged "sprinkling" of *paritta* water to protect "against illness" and "danger of plague" and approved the annual performance of *paritta* ritual.[13] The *Cūḷavaṃsa* (52: 80–81; 62: 31–32; 87: 1–13; 99: 25–27) mentions *paritta* recitations during the period of kings Kassapa V, Vikramabāhu I, Parākramabāhu II, and Kīrtī Śrī Rājasiṅha. The recitation practices during the time of King Kīrtī Śrī Rājasiṅha (r. 1747–1782 CE) were particularly varied and rich (99: 15–35). The *Cūḷavaṃsa* account mentioned not only the recitation of *paritta*, but also other activities such as copying manuscripts of canonical texts and recitation practices.

Paritta as Ritual of Prosperity and Protection

Forms of *paritta* remain a ritual for generating prosperity, well-being, and protection. Today *paritta* has become a ritual that celebrates auspicious occasions. To ensure peace and harmony, a *paritta* ceremony is often performed in Buddhist homes and businesses in Sri Lanka. In actual *paritta* recitations, this-worldly benefits (i.e., prosperity) of chanting are highlighted. *Paritta* is recited to enhance prosperity in South and Southeast Asia.[14]

As a ritual of recitation, *paritta* has specific linguistic features. *Paritta* remains a ritual of recitation of canonical and post-canonical Pali texts alone. *Sutta*s are recited by groups of monks in highly ritualized contexts. A potent magical atmosphere is created in which symbolically the Triple Gem is present at the recitation pavilion (Figure 17.1) through relics of the Buddha, palm-leaf manuscripts containing the *dhamma*, and nominally the sangha by the participation of assembled reciters. The construction of a special *pirit* pavilion in which clean water collected in a large pot, cotton threads prepared, an *Indrakīla* (ceremonial post) (Figure 17.2) constructed, and colorful decorations made with medicinal herbs and plants in the pavilion add increasingly rich magical presence to the ritual locus. Vernacular texts, whether they be in Sinhala or in any other language, are not recited in the ceremony and are not considered by practitioners as *paritta*, though some *paritta* texts have already been translated into poetical verse. The proper recitation of *paritta* with appropriate ritualistic apparatus is considered to have potency to generate prosperity by guarding listeners from dangers, disease, and calamities. The recitation of Pali canonical *sutta*s (comprising primarily twenty-nine texts of various lengths) and post-canonical *gāthā*s (such as *Jayamaṅgala Gāthā*)[15] accompanying the ritual performances form the actual *paritta* ceremony.

In Sri Lanka, the collection of *paritta* (Sin. *pirit*) texts is called the *Piruvānā Pot Vahansē* or *Maha Pirit Pota* (Great Book of Protection).[16] The collection consists of *sutta*s drawn from the Pali canon and includes post-canonical Pali compositions that can be considered minor-*paritta* texts.

Some texts recited in the *paritta* ceremony have long-established associations with strong magical potency from the early Buddhist tradition. For example, the recitation of the canonical discourse, the *Ratana Sutta*, has been regarded as an actual *sutta* delivered to Venerable Ananda by the Buddha himself in seeking protection from suffering, fear, and disease caused by famine in Vaiśāli.[17] According to the commentarial tradition,[18] Venerable Ananda protected Vaiśāli by chanting the *Ratana Sutta* and blessed the afflicted community. It is recorded that the recitation that invoked blessings of the Triple Gems (Buddha, Dhamma, and sangha) ensured safety there by generating well-being and prosperity.

The purposes for holding grand *paritta* recitations vary significantly.[19] Some rituals intend to dispel negative powers, such as malevolent spirits who are believed to cause various illnesses and misfortune. The magical potency of the ritual, generated through the rehearsal of *paritta* texts and sounds produced in the process, is believed to have power to pacify malevolent spirits and their influence. Merit generated through *paritta* recitation and attentive listening to it is believed to provide much needed protection in return. Intention to confer blessings on auspicious occasions is overwhelmingly predominant. Occupying a new house, opening a new business, entering into marriage, embarking on a journey, starting a new job, just before childbirth, annual celebrations and commemorations, and assuming political office are just a few examples of occasions when Buddhists would invite Buddhist monks to recite *paritta* to seek blessings. As a ritual, *paritta* can be recited on many occasions, depending on individual preferences. The number of *sutta*s recited at the *paritta* ritual and the length of the ceremony—once a day, several times a day, one night, a week, a fortnight, a month, or a year—are determined by many other factors, such as funding, resources, and the wishes of organizers. In Sri Lanka, it is customary to hold a one-night chanting of *paritta* for prosperity and protection quite frequently in temples as well as in homes.

As a ritual performance of embedded symbolic meaning, *paritta* is conceived to bear great magical potency. This magical potency is perhaps more visible in Southeast Asian countries, for example, in Thailand, where *paritta* water and *paritta* thread are used in a more visible and magically potent manner, in addition to the use of magically animated amulets. In Southeast Asia, amulets and magical formulas written in the form of tattoos are quite widespread. The magical potency of *paritta* recitation is also visible in the way sacred sounds are used in the ritual context of the image consecration ceremony as witnessed in Thailand as well as Sri Lanka.[20]

Theravada Buddhist traditions in Sri Lanka, for example, accepted and adopted the immense efficacy of *paritta* as a potent ritual of recitation. In the case of Theravada Buddhists of the past and present, *paritta* has been the most potent and efficacious method of recitation that secures mundane welfare here and now and ensures benefits for holistic living with mundane and supramundane benefits. On the whole, the ritual enactment of the spoken "word" of the Buddha creates *paritta*'s potency as a Buddhist chanting ritual. A broad participation of monks and laity makes it a public manifestation of the Buddhist religion in a communal setting.

Baṇa as Buddhist Instruction in Ritualized Recitation

Providing Buddhist instruction, an anticipated role of the sangha, was a prominent feature of the development of Theravada Buddhism in Sri Lanka. *Baṇa,* translated here as "preaching," was a significant means for providing religious instruction. The two-pulpit preaching (*āsana dekē baṇa*) ritual that gradually developed from older peaching practices in the early part of the eighteenth century combined religious instruction with chanting and recitations,[21] thus displaying how Buddhist piety was incorporated into the preaching ritual. Combining the vernacular language, Sinhala, with Pali, the Theravada scriptural language, two-pulpit preaching created a rich context for enhancing knowledge of Buddhism in wider circles, including rural communities. To increase pious wisdom and convey the lessons of Buddhism, two-pulpit preaching incorporated popular elements, such as singing, chanting, and dramatic performance, as well as the cultivation of aesthetic pleasure. Two-pulpit preaching became a source of cultural as well as religious instruction among Sri Lankan Buddhists, which continued well into the latter part of twentieth century;[22] other forms of preaching have replaced it today.

The eloquent style resulting from the incorporation of the *cūrṇikāva* (half-metrical and half-prose compositions) became a major attraction in two-pulpit preaching. The eloquent style was enriched by the incorporation into the ritual performance of aesthetic elements, such as verses that are sung and prose sections with alliteration. Though the meaning of what is recited in the ritual in Pali is later explained in Sinhala, it was perhaps difficult for Buddhist laity to comprehend because a vast majority of Buddhists, especially women, were illiterate until the proliferation of Buddhist schools as a result of Buddhist revival in the late nineteenth century. In addition, the alliteration made the language too ornamental, elegant, literary, and elite. Despite challenges to comprehension that the alliterative prose of *vṛttagandhi* (rhythmic prose) posed, it remained a rich repository of aesthetic pleasure for those who listened to it attentively.

Buddhist *dharmadēśanā* (instruction in *dhamma*) such as two-pulpit style had two key aspects: the intoning of a scriptural text as a form of recitation, and the presentation of the meaning of the scripture through detailed explanations in which narratives, metaphors, similes, and anecdotes were used. The two preachers in two-pulpit preaching who perform these two religious roles are known as the *sarabhañña* (the reciter) and the *padabhañña* (the expounder). The *sarabhañña* first chants scriptural passages (*dhammapāṭha*) beautifully in a musical tone according to a recognized meter, and the *padabhañña* then provides a word-for-word explanation of the chant's meaning. The *sarabhañña* is responsible for making the ritual rich in form (*savyañjana*), while excellence in content is achieved through the expounding ability of the *padabhañña*. At times, one person may perform both activities; on other occasions, however, two persons seem to have together performed the two roles of the *desanā* (delivering sermons).

The existence of these two *desanā* roles, *sarabhañña* and *padabhañña*, modeled from the accounts of Buddhist councils (*saṅgāyanā*)[23] and adopted in two-pulpit preaching, provided preachers with the basic performative roles. In two-pulpit preaching, performing alternately, the *sarabhañña* reads out the *dhammapāṭha* from the original Pali manuscript, while the *padabhañña* provides detailed explanations with innovative interpretations of his own as a Sinhala commentary on the sermon.[24] Thus the ritual performance of two-pulpit preaching in Sri Lanka produced "something of the dramatic."[25]

Chanting Practices during Pilgrimage

Various chantings are practiced in Buddhist pilgrimages. During pilgrimage, Buddhist chanting includes recitations of major *paritta suttas* by both monks and laity for their protection during the journey. They also recite specific Pali *gāthās* to make offerings at each sacred site and en route. Important sacred sites linked to the Buddha's three visits to Sri Lanka are enumerated in Sri Lankan Buddhist literature. They are grouped together to eight (Sin. *aṭamasthāna*)[26] or sixteen (Sin. *soḷosmasthāna*) sites as narrated in a Pali *gāthā* (verse).[27] The group of eight sites centers on the ancient capital Anurādhapura, while the sixteen sites are island-wide.

The list of sixteen pilgrimage places (Sin. *soḷosmasthāna*) are as follows: (1) Mahiyaṅgaṇa (the Buddha's first visit, *Mahāvaṃsa* 1: 19–32; *Cūḷavaṃsa* 1: 45–81); (2) Nāgadīpa (second visit, *Mahāvaṃsa* 1: 45–72; *Cūḷavaṃsa* 1: 2–51); (3) Kälaṇiya (third visit, *Mahāvaṃsa* 1: 74–76; *Cūḷavaṃsa* 1: 52–59); (4) Śrī Pāda (*Mahāvaṃsa* 1: 77–78); (5) Divāguhāva (*Mahāvaṃsa* 1: 78); (6) Dīghavāpi (*Mahāvaṃsa* 1: 78–80; *Cūḷavaṃsa* 2: 60); (7) Śrī Mahā Bodhi (*Mahāvaṃsa* 1: 80–81; *Cūḷavaṃsa* 2: 61–63); (8) Ruvanvälisǟya (*Mahāvaṃsa* 1: 81–82); (9) Thūpārāmaya (*Mahāvaṃsa* 1: 82); (10) Silā Cetiya (*Mahāvaṃsa* 1: 82–83); (11) Mutiyaṅgaṇa; (12) Tissa Mahā Vihāraya; (13) Mirisaväṭiya; (14) Abhayagiriya; (15) Jētavanārāmaya; and (16) Kataragama Kiri Vehera.[28]

The tradition of the Buddha's three visits to the island, as recorded in the chronicles (*Mahāvaṃsa* 1: 1–84), is the foundation for the development of the list of sixteen pilgrimage sites. Though the citation of the list of sixteen pilgrimage sites can be varied in some sources,[29] a partial list can be found in the palm-leaf manuscript *Soḷosmasthāna Sāntiya* (Or.6615(27)) in the Hugh Nevill Collection. Some important sites (1 to 10) in the list of sixteen places, referred to in Sri Lanka's two prominent Pali chronicles, became sacred locations because of their explicit connections to the Buddha's three visits. The two chronicles do not mention the remaining six sites (11 to 16), located now in three provinces—Uva (2), Southern (1) and North-central (3)—which may have been added to the list much later, making the complete list of sixteen sites. These latter six sites appear not closely linked to the Buddha's three visits since they are not mentioned explicitly or implicitly in the chronicles. They are recognized as Buddhist holy sites, sometimes as *puññabhūmi* (sacred land);[30] being identified as sites of relic enshrinements makes them pure and highly efficacious for merit-making. They are popular places where many devotees meet today for pilgrimage.

The sixteen pilgrimage sites have given birth to a rich Buddhist religious literature consisting of a large corpus of poetry. Most sites can have their own uniqueness in relation to the Buddha and Buddhism on the island. In liturgical terms, the Pali *gāthā* used for venerating the sixteen sites articulates a strong preoccupation with (bodily) relic enshrinements in those sacred locations, suggesting a kind of presence of the Buddha there even after his death.

In the list of sixteen pilgrimage sites, the fourth is the most famous, adventurous, and challenging pilgrimage center: Śrī Pāda, the location of the Buddha's footprint left on the top of Mount Samanala (h. 7,360 ft). *The Mahāvaṃsa* (1: 77–78) recorded the Buddha's visit to Śrī Pāda on his third visit. Śrī Pāda has been in the Buddhist and non-Buddhist imagination for a long time.[31] It was known to Persians, Arabs, and Europeans as Adam's Peak for centuries.[32] It is the most important and internationally known Sri Lankan Buddhist pilgrimage site.

Śrī Pāda has been the subject of temple mural paintings and literary compositions. As an important religious object, Śrī Pāda became aesthetically attractive for many to compose poetry. A variety of poetic compositions commenced from poets who came from many walks of life. Poets such as Tām̆bugala in the Kandyan period invested a significant amount of time to composing poetry. There are over thirty-seven poetry texts on the theme of Śrī Pāda pilgrimage alone; if *san̆dēśa*s (message poetry) are included, the number may exceed over fifty works. Among them, the most popular Sinhala poetry texts are the *Himagata Varṇanāva* (n.d.) and *Tun Saraṇaya* (1904) of Tām̆bugala. The latter in particular carved out a specific religiosity through a distinctive ritual recitation practice perpetuated through annual pilgrimage to Śrī Pāda. Parts of those two texts are still chanted and recited in the pilgrimage to Śrī Pāda; parts of their poems became sample poetry genres included in the British documentary film *The Song of Ceylon* (1934), filmed before Sri Lankan independence.

This large corpus of poetry, both in printed forms and palm-leaves, is in the Sinhala language, demonstrating the popularity of devotional chantings. The poems composed frequently in *sivupada* (quatrain) poetical genre by numerous, known and anonymous, authors over centuries in the vernacular language are found today in affordable and inexpensive publications, widely available at pilgrimage sites.

In addition to many Sinhala poems used as recitations in the pilgrimage to Śrī Pāda, there are two Pali *gāthās* (stanzas) often used to pay respect the Buddha's footprint. Their content tells a bit of the footprint's history. The first *gāthā* used for expressing devotion to the footprint tells specifically about the footprint of the Buddha in Sri Lanka:

> From Kälaṇiya, by air, the Buddha went to that place [Śrī Pāda] and displayed the footprint bearing beautiful features of the [Dhamma] wheel. I pay respect that footprint located at the summit of Sumana rock, which is like a precious crown for the young lady Lanka.[33]

The second Pali *vandanā gāthā* (veneration stanza), the period of its composition unknown, makes a historical claim: it mentions four footprints of the Buddha. The footprints are enumerated with specific geographic locations, perhaps extending the imagination as far as the Middle East, though the exact location of Yōnaka may remain disputed.

> Bowing down my head, I pay respect to that footprint located on the sand banks of Narmadā River, on Rock Saccabaddha, on Sumana (Saman) Rock, and in the city of Yōnaka.[34]

In addition to these standard Pali verses that are used for paying respect to the footprint and Pali poems such as *Samantakūṭa Vaṇṇanā*, there are also collections of Sinhala poems related to the Śrī Pāda pilgrimage. Some of the poetry used today in the pilgrimage is taken from Sinhala folk poetry such as *Tun Saraṇe*, *Samanala Hālla* (1877), and *Himagata Varṇanāva*. Some poems are passed down from generation to generation by word of mouth. Others are later compositions inspired by piety and devotion. Those who climb the mountain, mostly in the night nowadays, as well as those who descend the mountain after sunrise, recite poems with much enthusiasm. This tradition of recitation varies significantly today depending on pilgrims' piety, their social location, the regions of the country that they come from, whether pilgrims are led by an experienced liturgical leader, as well as factors such as specific days and months of the pilgrimage. Whether the chanting practices are rapidly disappearing or in sharp decline remains to be ascertained through in-depth historical research.[35]

Poems help pilgrims to manage physical tiredness and coordinate the speed of ascent and descent. One could imagine that collective singing by large groups alerted animals and chased them away from the jungle path that leads to the summit of the mountain. Collective recitation generates a rhythmic melody linked to the rhythm of lifting the foot and placing it down on the steps. The rhythm that accompanies the poem enhances the journey's progress, moving the pilgrims step by step to the top of the mountain while reciting the poems in chorus, supporting a collective effort to be one in mind and body in the difficult journey to the summit.

The following poetic composition illustrates the rhythmic aspect of recitation and resulting movement of pilgrim's body.

apē budun—api vaňdinṭa	We go to pay respect [to] our Buddha.
peraḷi peraḷi—api vaňdinṭa	We pay respect [to] him by rolling around from one side to another.[36]

When the first two words—*apē budun*—are sung, the pilgrim lifts their foot toward the next step. When the pilgrim recites *api vaňdinṭa*, the pilgrim places their foot down on the step. This is repeated with the last two verses of the poem. When everyone in the *naḍē* (pilgrims' group) recites the poem together, they raise and lower their feet in unison.

During the pilgrimage up and down the mountain, informal dialogue often takes place among pilgrims who have not previously met; in addition, a group climbing up the mountain responds to a group climbing down by reciting poems such as the following:

> May the deity Sumana Saman bless this group of pilgrims who are coming down after paying respect.[37]

Such verses used in the spontaneous dialogues among ascending and descending pilgrims have similar patterns and rhythms. Their words, tones of recitation, and bodily expressions facilitate the pilgrims' dialogue during the journey. When pilgrims see novice pilgrims (referred to as *kiri kōḍu* or "milk drinking" novices) climbing Śrī Pāda for the first time on the way to the summit (often identified by a white piece of cloth tied to the right arm with a coin, called *pan̆ḍura*), they comment something like the following:

> This novice pilgrim is on the way to pay respect. May the deity Saman have compassion on the novice![38]

Today Śrī Pāda is not only a place of pilgrimage. It has also become a place for relaxation and entertainment. Poetry used on the journey enhances the aesthetic and entertainment aspects of pilgrimage. Poetic recitation is one of the most important means by which most traditional Buddhist pilgrims communicated with their fellow pilgrims in a cordial and friendly manner. These dialogues produce a powerful sense of an extensive community as pilgrims complete the lengthy and arduous journey.

Chanting Practices in Monastic Training

Sri Lankan Theravada tradition represents the Buddhist monastic as the custodian of the *dhamma*. Chanting practices are central primarily to the life and training of Buddhist monks, and to a lesser extent in the newly emerged female novice and higher ordination traditions. How is a Buddhist monk trained to excel in chanting? Monastic training in chanting can vary depending on the specific monastic establishment. In the Kandyan region, in particular, specific attention is paid to the chanting of *paritta*.

On the whole, Buddhist monastic training greatly emphasizes aspects of memorization and chanting. The first lesson for any novice is to excel in chanting.[39] This emphasis can be seen even in *katikāvatas*—conventions agreed upon by the Buddhist monastic community with royal mediation on operational laws of the sangha—which were promulgated in Sri Lanka from the twelfth to eighteenth centuries.[40] The twelfth-century *Mahā Parākramabāhu Katikāvata* states that heads of the sangha "should diligently employ" their pupils to commit "to memory at least" the *Khuddasikkhā* and the *Pātimokkha* and the *Dasadhamma Sutta* and the *Anumāna Sutta*. Those who are unable to excel in the practice of memorization of books are "made to commit to memory" the *Mūlasikkhā* and *Sekhiyā* and "to rehearse" the *Sikhavaḷaňda Vinisa*. They are expected to be "capable of repeating correctly any portion of the text from beginning to the end on being questioned every six months."[41] Memorization and training in chanting are highly valued requirements for novice ordination and the growth of Buddhist monastics. Requirements for higher ordination include a mastery of a collection of chanted texts[42] as well as skills in developing a repertoire for delivering sermons. The development of skills in chanting was highlighted in monastic practices such as the two-pulpit preaching.

In 1921, a leading Buddhist monk in Kandy, Venerable Maḍugallē Siddhārtha, principal of Saṅgharāja Pirivena, prepared a training manual for Buddhist monastics under the heading of *Abhinava Katikāvata saha Baṇadaham Pota* (The New Monastic Convention and The Book of Training in Dhamma).[43] It was a collection of practical guidance and training for Buddhist monastics approved by the Sangha Council of the Malvatu Vihāra of Siyam Nikāya. Both novices and higher ordination candidates were expected to memorize the entire content of the *Baṇadaham Pota* (often called *Sāmaṇera Baṇadaham Pota* with an emphasis on novice trainees) in preparing for the oral examination for higher ordination. Since its compilation, this has become the manual frequently used for training young novices in the Theravada traditions of Sri Lanka even beyond the Siyam Nikāya. The required training in memorization and recitation included a variety of *paritta*s recited in private and communal *paritta* recitations: many *paritta* texts included in the training manual were taken from the *Mahapirit Pota*, a total of twenty-six shared texts.

In addition to the *paritta* texts, the entire *Dhammapada* was included among the texts to be memorized by those seeking novice and higher ordination. The *Dhammapada* continued to be an immensely useful tool in selecting themes for monastic preaching,[44] a fact visible in printed sermon texts. It has provided basic guidance in learning of Buddhist preaching and teaching that is relevant for a Buddhist trainee planning to pursue religious goals of becoming a disciplined monastic with an excellent preaching repertoire.

Daily Chanting at Buddhist Monasteries

Daily worship rituals in Buddhist temples are an important part of Buddhist monastic life. Morning, lunchtime, and evening rituals are prominent features. Special rituals also include those on full moon *pōya* (observance) days[45] recognized as important occasions for celebration in the liturgical calendar. Among them, Vesak[46]—the month of May full moon as the occasion of Siddhārtha Gautama's birth, awakening, and passing away—and Poson—the full moon of the month of June as the day of arrival of Buddhism in Sri Lanka in the third century BCE—stand out as significant communal and public displays of Buddhist religiosity. The period of rain retreat (July–September) ending with an offering of a special and highly treasured robe called *kaṭhina* to the community of monks is also an important opportunity for recitation and chanting.

Chanting is integrated into novice learning and daily practices of Buddhist monasteries. Texts for chanting are drawn from the *Baṇadaham Pota*. Novices have many opportunities to practice what they learn through memorization. They master further refined skills in chanting through participation in daily temple services. Regular chantings in temples, often in mornings, particularly in evenings, include recitations of the three main *paritta suttas*—*Maṅgala*, *Ratana* and *Karaṇīya*—in addition to frequently chanted *parittas* such as the *Jinapañjaraya*, *Aṭavisi Pirita*, *Mahā Jaya Maṅgala Gāthā*, and *Äṇavum Pirita*. On special occasions such as childbirth, in addition to those mentioned previously, texts such as the *Aṅgulimāla Paritta* are recited at the devotee's home. Novices are integrated into the Buddhist system of learning through further listening and memorizing frequently recited texts on ordinary and special rituals.

Domestic Religiosity: Chanting in Making Home a Temple

Today daily chanting is an important religious aspect in most Buddhist homes in Sri Lanka. In the mornings and evenings, family members gather to offer flowers and incense as well as recitations, sitting in front of the Buddha image or a photo of the Buddha hung on the wall. Some of their recitations are memorized Pali verses for making specific offerings to the Buddha; they also recite *parittas* from printed booklets. The intention of these domestic rituals is to seek blessings for their own success and to transfer merit to departed relatives and protective deities.

This practice of domestic rituals finds no divide between the rich and poor. Some affluent households, however, even have small shrine rooms solely dedicated to domestic religiosity. The content and form of this religiosity can vary significantly from one house to another, depending on each individual circumstance and demands of the day. This is a small-scale display of private religiosity, as opposed to the public expression of collective religiosity seen in the participation of all-night *paritta* rituals held at home, in which Buddhist monks often chant *parittas*. Most Buddhists understand the significance of chantings and recitations, as well as forms of meditation, as a way of conferring blessings on themselves and others.

It is not certain when domestic religiosity as it exists today emerged in the Sri Lankan context. Is this domestic religiosity primarily a response in reaction to the persecution of Buddhism during the British colonial period? The renewal movements in the late nineteenth and early twentieth centuries had a significant role in the emergence and popularization of forms of domestic religiosity. This could have happened perhaps in the early decades of the twentieth century around the time of independence from British colonial rule. Domestic religiosity appears to be complex in terms of its historical origins.

The seventeenth-century account of Robert Knox (1640–1720) is a case in point, which informs us that the practice of domestic religiosity is very much a local development in Ceylon in areas around Kandy, where he lived as a captive for nearly twenty years. In terms of historicity of domestic Buddhist religiosity, it is worth considering Knox's detailed observations. Knox noted that many "build in their yards private Chappels," "little houses" similar to "Closets, sometimes so small, that they are not" bigger than two feet in size. They were constructed on "a Pillar three or four foot from the ground" and images of Buddha were placed within them. The devotion was expressed by keeping it "near" and offering services there. Customs observed there were "lighting up candles and lamps" and offering "flowers every morning." Knox noted also offerings of "victuals" and beliefs that motivated such practices: "the more they perform such ceremonious service to him here, the more shall be their reward hereafter before him."[47] Knox captured the richness that he witnessed in domestic Buddhist religiosity, when Buddhist lifestyle was less complex, less modernized, and less open to outside influences. Knox outlined a devotional religious scene that is now more or less a familiar facet of Buddhist life in the twentieth and twenty-first centuries, with small shrine rooms in front of or inside Buddhist homes. Knox's account suggests a home-grown devotional domestic religiosity.

Technological Advances and Commercialization of Buddhist Chanting Practices

In the modern period, at least from the time of adoption of open-economic policy in 1978, Sri Lanka has become increasingly open to commercialized activities. Commercialization of all aspects of life has also influenced religious practices. Chanting and its associated practices had to struggle in the midst of increasing commercialization.

In the past two decades, I have heard stories from informants of commercialization of religious practices and an invasion of the religious realm. Some members of the urban professional elite in Colombo, who lead busy lives and seek shortcuts to everything, pay some entrepreneurial Buddhist monks and laymen regularly for performing certain services for them, such as performing *paritta* rituals in their business premises and dwellings. Such activities are organized almost like any other hiring service such as catering. Paying monks to perform *paritta* chanting,[48] though it may appear controversial at times, is not surprising given the complex circumstances of modern urban life. Such activities also testify to the perceived efficacy of chanting rituals, even in a secularized and complex modern world.

Commercialization is not limited to *paritta* recitation. In the past five decades, an increasing commercialization has taken place in preaching rituals as well. It is another aspect of Buddhist life in Sri Lanka that has been transformed by economics and social forces. Buddhist services such as the administration of the five precepts, chanting *paritta*, delivering sermons, officiating in funerals, etc., were activities that were traditionally available free of charge. Charging fees for any services rendered by Buddhist monks was not advocated in the tradition. In the past decade, a few monks began to charge for providing services related to delivering sermons. The service includes transport, hiring a public announcing system, etc. This has now extended further to include radio and TV. Several Buddhist radio and TV stations now commonly charge a fee from sponsors to record and broadcast sermons. The recording is done in the studio with a live audience present, and offerings are made to the preacher.

Significant improvements in technology, including readily available twenty-four-hour radio stations and Buddhist TV channels, have enlarged the possibilities of listening to a variety of Buddhist chantings of famous and popular reciters. Such technological innovations have made available immense opportunities for seekers and practitioners of *dhamma* to enjoy chanting. The *dhamma*, including rich recitations, are now at one's fingertips everywhere; the Sri Lankan situation is not an exception.

Technological advances have increased accessibility to Buddhist services. Some may not need to visit a Buddhist temple to listen to sermons or to see devotional rituals performed. Though the quality of service may be an issue, in theory, at least, it is possible to have access to religious services through one's computer or smartphone. Modern Buddhist media networks have reached far and wide in providing access to Buddhist sermons, chanting, and devotional rituals. Restrictions posed by Covid-19 have increased the reliance on media outlets for religious services. Covid-19 fatalities required more access to remote, technological facilities to perform essential funeral rituals. In Buddhist contexts, delivering sermons and *paritta* recitations remotely to heal the sorrow stricken communities became essential. The shift to technological provisions is not merely because of increasing commercialization, but it is also a case of using more advanced technology to propagate the teachings of the Buddha far and wide. Contemporary chanting through technology, though associated with increasing commercialization, is valuable. This phenomenon of readily available advanced technological resources on Buddhism and Buddhist practices such as chanting have enhanced the depth and breadth of domestic religiosity.

Conclusion

This chapter has examined the power of words in Theravada ritual practices. It has illustrated the potency of *Buddhavacana*—the "word" of the Buddha in contemporary

Buddhist contexts. It has surveyed varied chanting practices in the Sri Lankan Theravada Buddhist tradition. Recitation practices focus on the rhythmic chanting of Buddhist "discourses" (*suttas*) as *paritta* (recitation for protection), as well as the recitation of Pali prose texts, verses, and popular Sinhala poems (*kavi*). Chanting in the vernacular in the context of pilgrimage to Śrī Pāda has shown some adaptations to local situations and the needs of pilgrims. The ongoing significance of *Buddhavacana*, the role of the sangha in preserving and making it available, and diverse forms of lay practice are still strongly visible in Buddhist chanting practices, and the rich textual, historical, and sociological aspects of Buddhist chanting merit further contextualized investigation.

Notes

1. R. H. Bassett, *Romantic Ceylon* (London: Cecil Palmer, 1929), 152.
2. H. L. Seneviratne and Swarna Wickremeratne, "Bodhi-puja," *American Ethnologist* 7 (4) 1980: 734–43; Richard Gombrich, "A New Theravadin Liturgy," *Journal of the Pali Text Society* 9 (1981): 47–73; Richard Gombrich and Gananath Obeyesekere, *Buddhism Transformed* (Princeton, NJ: Princeton University Press, 1988), 384–410.
3. Mahinda Deegalle, *Popularizing Buddhism* (Albany: State University of New York Press, 2006), 8, 17.
4. Bhikkhu Bodhi (trans.), *The Suttanipāta* (Melksham and Somverville: Pali Text Society and Wisdom, 2017), 179–80.
5. Sheldon Pollock, *The Language of the Gods in the World of Men* (Berkeley: University of California Press, 2006), 51–59; Richard Gombrich, *Buddhism and Pali* (Oxford: Mud Pie Slices, 2018), 69–72.
6. For magical effects of *paritta*, see Mahinda Palihawadana, "Pali Sajjhāya and Sanskrit Svādhyāya," in *Recent Researches in Buddhist Studies*, ed. Kuala Lumpur Dhammajoti et al. (Colombo and Hong Kong: Y. Karunadasa Felicitation Committee and Chi Ying Foundation, 1997), 493–515.
7. *Japanese-English Buddhist Dictionary* (Tokyo: Daito Shuppansha, 1991), 21.
8. During his travels to Sri Lanka in 1821–22, copies acquired by Rasmus Rask (1787–1832) are now in Denmark (C. E. Godakumbura, *Catalogue of Ceylonese Manuscripts* (Copenhagen: The Royal Library, 1980), 25-26). During the long service in Sri Lanka (1865–97), Hugh Nevill (1848–97) collected over 2,227 palm-leaf manuscripts, which are now at the British Library (K. D. Somadasa, *Catalogue of the Hugh Nevill Collection of Sinhalese Manuscripts in the British Library*, 7 vols. (Oxford and London: Pali Text Society and The British Library, 1987–95), 7:81–82).
9. Robert Spence Hardy, *A Manual of Buddhism* (London, 1860), 2, 46, 235–237, 278; Robert Spence Hardy, *Eastern Monachism* (London, 1860), 240–42.
10. O. Pertold, "A Protective Ritual of the Southern Buddhists," *Anthropological Society of Bombay* XII (6) 1923: 744–89.
11. Peter Schalk, *Der Paritta-Dienst in Ceylon* (Lund: Bröderna Ekstrands Tryckeri AB, 1972).
12. Lily De Silva, *Paritta: A Historical and Religious Study of the Buddhist Ceremony for Peace and Prosperity in Sri Lanka* (Colombo: The National Museums of Sri Lanka, 1981).
13. Wilhelm Geiger and C. Mabel Rickmers (trans.), *Culavamsa* (New Delhi: Asian Education Services, 1998), 155.

14. Donald K. Swearer, *Becoming the Buddha* (Princeton, NJ: Princeton University Press 2004), 88–118.
15. Mahinda Deegalle, "Textuality of the *Jayamaṅgala Gāthā* and Its Liturgical Role in Modern Buddhist Marriage Ceremony," in *Buddhist Studies*, ed. P. D. Premasiri et al (Peradeniya: University of Peradeniya, 2002), 188–91.
16. Lional Lokuliyana, *Catubhanavarapali* (Singapore: Singapore Buddhist Meditation Centre, n.d.).
17. Bhikkhu Bodhi (trans.), *The Suttanipāta*, 193–95.
18. H. Smith (ed.), *Khuddakapāṭha, Together with Its Commentary Paramatthajotikā I* (London: Pali Text Society, 1915), 164.
19. Walpola Rahula, *History of Buddhism in Ceylon* (Colombo: M. D. Gunasena, 1956), 278.
20. Donald K. Swearer, *Becoming the Buddha*, 88–118; Richard Gombrich, "The Consecration of a Buddha Image," *Journal of Asian Studies* 26 (1) 1966: 23–36.
21. Deegalle, *Popularizing Buddhism.*
22. Ittǟpāna Dhammālaṅkāra Thera, *Pävidi Paṇ̌ḍi Miṇi Pahan* 6 (Dehivala: Śrīdēvi Printers, 2014), 148–61.
23. The teachings of the Buddha were rehearsed at the three Buddhist councils (*saṅgāyanā*).
24. Deegalle, *Popularizing Buddhism.*
25. E. R. Sarachchandra, *The Folk Drama of Ceylon* (Colombo: Department of Cultural Affairs, 1952), 23.
26. The list of eight (Sin. *aṭamasthāna*) pilgrimage sites in Anurādhapura has variations. According to the administrative body of the *aṭamasthāna* (Sorata Thera, 1963–70: 25), since 1908 they are: (i) Śrī Mahā Bodhi, (ii) Ruvanvälisǟya, (iii) Thūpārāmaya, (iv) Lovāmahāpāya, (v) Mirisaväṭiya, (vi) Abhayagiriya, (vii) Jētavanārāmaya, and (viii) Laṅkārāmaya. The same list with some order variation (i, iv, ii, iii, v, vi, viii, and vii) is found in Candrā Vikramagamagē's *Aṭamasthāna* (Maharagama: Taraṅji Prints, 2001). This list had excluded both Mihintalē and Isurumuniya. The fourteenth-century *Pūjāvaliya* (Sraddhatisya, 1930: 708) added (a) Dakuṇu Mahāsǟya, (b) Piritlä Geya, (c) Dantādara Pokuṇa, and (d) Mihintalē Mahasala Sǟya, replacing all except (i) to (iv). The *Saddharmālaṅkāraya*'s list added (a) Mālaka Sīmā, (b) Jantāghara Pokuṇa, (c) Lahabatgeya, (d) Catuśśālāva, and (e) Mahābhojana śālāva, replacing all except (i), (ii), and (iv). The list in the *Nam Pota* is similar except that (viii) Laṅkārāmaya is replaced with Mihintalē; Rotum̆ba Pēmaratana Thera, *Pärāṇi Pansal Pot* (Piṭakoṭuva: Multi Pot Hala, 2008), 25.
27. The list of sixteen places of pilgrimage is also inconsistent. Except the first ten, the remaining sites are not found in the *Mahāvaṃsa*. According to the Pali *gāthā* that venerates the sixteen sites, the order is: (1) Mahiyaṅgaṇa, (2) Nāgadīpa, (3) Käḷaṇiya, (4) Footprint (Śrī Pāda), (5) Divāguhāva, (6) Dīghavāpi, (7) Mutiyaṅgaṇa Cetiya, (8) Tissa Mahā Vihāraya, (9) Bodhiya (Śrī Mahā Bodhi), (10) Mirisaväṭiya, (11) the Great Cetiya Ruvanvälisǟya, (12) Thūpārāmaya, (13) Bhayāgiriya (Abhayagiriya), (14) Jētavanaya, (15) Sela Cetiya, and (16) Kataragama (Kiri Vehera); D. A. Āryadāsa, *Bauddha Vandanā Gāthā* (Kolam̆ba: Vidyārthaprakāśa Yantrālaya, 1930), 12; H. W. Perērā, *Śrī Laṅkāvē Soḷosmasthāna* (Kandy: Buddhist Publication Society, 1997), 3. Hugh Nevill added a new one—Lōvāmahāpāya (Or.6615(27))—to the two lists (K. D. Somadasa, *Catalogue of the Hugh Nevill Collection of Sinhalese Manuscripts in the British Library*, VI, 30; VII, 203). Kevin Trainor's useful historical and literary study can be found in "A Textualized Landscape," in *Muditā*, ed. Iňdurāgārē Dhammaratana Thera et al. (Kolam̆ba: Goḍagē Pot Mäňdura, 2012), 648–54.

28. Āryadāsa, *Bauddha Vandanā Gāthā*, 12.
29. Välivițiyē Sorata Thera, *Śrī Sumaṅgala Śabdakoṣaya* (Mt. Lavinia: P. Abhayawickrama, 1963–70), 1130; K. D. Somadasa, *Catalogue of the Hugh Nevill Collection of Sinhalese Manuscripts in the British Library*, VII, 203; Kevin Trainor, *Relics, Ritual, and Representation in Buddhism* (Cambridge: Cambridge University Press, 1997), 145–46.
30. *Puññabhūmi* literally means the "land of merit" but is better rendered as "sacred land," perhaps of mid-twentieth-century origin.
31. Mahinda Deegalle, "Sri Pada Sacred to Many," in *Multiculturalism in Asia*, ed. Imtiyaz Yusuf (Bangkok: Mahidol University and Konrad Adenauer Stiftung, 2018), 44–66.
32. Deegalle, "Sri Pada Sacred to Many."
33. My English translation. The Pali verse "*kalyāṇito gaganato* . . ." is taken from E. P. Amarasiṅha's *Purāṇa Himagata Varuṇa Hevat Samanala Śrīpāda Varṇanāva* ([Kolam̆ba]: Ānanda Pustaka Pracārakayō, [n.d.]). This verse is rare compared to frequently found *gāthā* "*yam Nammadāya*. . . ."
34. My English translation. The source of Pali *gāthā* "*yaṃ Nammadāya nadiyā* . . ." is W. D. Andris Appuhāmi's, *Vandanākārayinṭa yōgya gāthā saha Tun Saraṇaya* (Kolam̆ba: Granthālōka Yantrālaya, 1904).
35. Historical and literary research on Śrī Pāda pilgrimage is gradually emerging. See Alexander McKinley, "Mountain at a Center of the World," PhD diss., Duke University, 2018; and Mahinda Deegalle, "Sri Pada Sacred to Many: Sufi Mystics on Pilgrimage to Adam's Peak," in *Multiculturalism in Asia: Peace and Harmony*, ed. Imtiyaz Yusuf (Bangkok: Mahidol University and Konrad Adenauer Stiftung, 2018), 40–69.
36. My English translation. J. B. Disānāyaka, *Siripā Vandanāva* (Kolam̆ba: Goḍagē Pot Män̆dura, 2001), 72; and Markus Aksland, *The Sacred Footprint* (Bangkok: Orchid Press, 2001), 83–84.
37. My English translation. Disānāyaka, *Siripā Vandanāva*, 72.
38. My English translation. Disānāyaka, *Siripā Vandanāva*, 72.
39. Anne Blackburn, *Buddhist Learning and Textual Practice in Eighteenth-Century Lankan Monastic Culture* (Princeton, NJ: Princeton University Press, 2001).
40. Nandasena Ratnapala, *The Katikāvatas* (Munich: Kitzinger 1971), 129–30.
41. Ratnapala, *The Katikāvatas*, 129–30.
42. Jeffrey Samuels, *Attracting the Heart* (Honolulu: University of Hawai'i Press, 2010).
43. Maḍugallē Siddhārtha Thera, *Abhinava Katikāvata saha Baṇadaham Pota* (Kolam̆ba: M. D. Gunasēna, 1976).
44. Deegalle, *Popularizing Buddhism*, 155, 162, 179.
45. In the lunar calendar, there are four days of religious observance (Sin. *satara pōya*). Full moon is the most appropriate day for Buddhist laity to engage in special observances.
46. Mahinda Deegalle, *Vesak, Peace and Harmony* (Bollegala: Nāgānanda International Buddhist University, 2015).
47. Robert Knox, *An Historical Relation of the Island Ceylon*, ed. J. H. O. Paulusz (Dehiwala: Tisara Prakāśakayō, [1681] 2003), 73.
48. Though Buddhist priests in Japan, for example, traditionally receive financial donations from parishioners for performing chanting sessions during the Obon festival, etc., there is no such method of making direct payments for recitation services of Buddhist monks in any of the Theravada countries in South and Southeast Asia.

Further Reading

Amarasiṅha, F. P. *Purāṇa Himagata Varuṇa Hevat Samanala Śrīpāda Varṇanāva*. [Kolaṁba]: Ānanda Pustaka Pracārakayō, n.d.

Anderson, Carol. "'For Those Who Are Ignorant': A Study of the *Bauddha Adahilla*." In *Constituting Communities: Theravada Buddhism and the Religious Cultures of South and Southeast Asia*, ed. John C. Holt et al. Albany: State University of New York Press, 2003, 171–88.

Appuhami, W. D. Andris. *Vandanākārayinṭa yōgya gāthā saha Tun Saraṇaya*. Kolaṁba: Granthālōka Yantrālaya, 1904.

De Silva, Lily. *Paritta: A Historical and Religious Study of the Buddhist Ceremony for Peace and Prosperity in Sri Lanka. Spolia Zeylanica*, vol. 36. Colombo: The National Museums of Sri Lanka, 1981.

Deegalle, Mahinda. *Popularizing Buddhism: Preaching as Performance in Sri Lanka*. Albany: State University of New York Press, 2006.

Deegalle, Mahinda. "Śrī Pāda Sacred to Many: Sufi Mystics on Pilgrimage to Adam's Peak." In *Multiculturalism in Asia: Peace and Harmony*, ed. Imtiyaz Yusuf. Bangkok: Mahidol University and Konrad Adenauer Stiftung, 2018, 40–69.

Deegalle, Mahinda. "Textuality of the *Jayamaṅgala Gāthā* and Its Liturgical Role in Modern Buddhist Marriage Ceremony." In *Buddhist Studies: Essays in Honour of Professor Lily de Silva*, ed. P. D. Premasiri et al. Peradeniya: The Department of Pali and Buddhist Studies, University of Peradeniya, 2002, 183–97.

Gombrich, Richard. "A New Theravadin Liturgy." *Journal of the Pali Text Society* 9 (1981): 47–73.

Hardy, Robert Spence. *A Manual of Buddhism*. London: Williams and Norgate, 1860.

Knox, Robert. *An Historical Relation of the Island Ceylon*. Edited by J. H. O. Paulusz. 2nd edition. Dehiwala: Tisara Prakāśakayō, [1681] 1989.

Lokuliyana, Lional. *Catubhanavara Pali: The Great Book of Protection*. Singapore: Singapore Buddhist Meditation Centre, n.d.

Pertold, O. "A Protective Ritual of the Southern Buddhists." *Anthropological Society of Bombay* 12, no. 6 (1923): 744–89.

Schalk, Peter. *Der Paritta-Dienst in Ceylon*. Lund: Lunds Universitet, 1972.

Seneviratne, H. L., and Swarna Wickremeratne. "Bodhi-puja: Collective Representations of Sri Lanka Youth." *American Ethnologist* 7, no. 4 (1980): 734–43.

Trainor, Kevin. 2012. "A Textualized Landscape: Divā-guhāva and the Sri Lankan Tradition of the Sixteen Great Pilgrimage Sites (*Soḷosmasthāna*)." In *Muditā*, ed. Iṅdurāgārē Dhammaratana Thera et al. Kolaṁba: Goḍagē Pot Mäṅdura, 2012, 648–54.

CHAPTER 18

PURE LAND PRACTICE

CHARLES B. JONES

Introduction

To scholars of East Asian Buddhism, the phrase "Pure Land practice" immediately evokes one term: *nianfo* (Ch.; K. *yŏmbul*; J. *nembutsu*), understood as the practice of orally repeating the name of the Buddha Amitābha. In response, this Buddha will come to the devotee's deathbed and conduct him or her to his buddha-land called Sukhāvatī ("Utmost Bliss") far to the west of this present world. This land is free from distractions, miraculously provides everything one needs, and one has Amitābha as one's teacher, so one will advance to buddhahood with no possibility of backsliding. The practice does not require mastery of difficult concepts, skill in ritual, strict morality, or rigorous austerities, and thus is open to ordinary Buddhist believers as a "path of easy practice."

This picture is not wrong, but it is oversimplified. In this chapter, we will see that *nianfo* is not the only practice that leads to rebirth, and that the term represents a constellation of practices from simple vocalization of the Buddha's name to complex visualizations to deathbed rituals to large-scale group practices. We will also see a number of theoretical understandings of its workings. "Pure Land practice," it turns out, is multifaceted and multiform.

The discussion that follows will define Pure Land as a "tradition of practice" rather than a school or sect. This means: (1) as a tradition, it is something that is transmitted through a variety of avenues (e.g., literature, face-to-face teaching, lay societies); (2) it includes a set of practices bound together by common goals (rebirth in Sukhāvatī and the stage of non-retrogression), an audience that includes non-virtuoso practitioners, and a set of exemplary figures called patriarchs (Ch. *zu*); (3) it engages in an ongoing articulation of the ideas that underwrite its practices and produces apologetic literature defending those ideas and practices. Using "tradition of practice" as our guiding paradigm, we can see Pure Land as an option available to all Buddhists, but a discrete option distinct from others.

Indian Background

In an influential 1977 article, Gregory Schopen demonstrated that between the second and sixth centuries CE, rebirth in Sukhāvatī became a goal for almost any Mahayana religious practice, whether it centered on Amitābha or not.[1] However, this did not mean that there existed a distinctive set of Pure Land practices, since outside of the *Sukhāvatī-vyūha* family of sutras the literature did not specify a practice whose primary purpose was rebirth in Sukhāvatī. Rather, one dedicated the merit of whatever practice one engaged to that goal.

We find a good example of this in the *Ārya-samantabhadra-caryā-praṇidhāna-rāja-sūtra*. In this text, the bodhisattva Samantabhadra vows to engage in numerous practices for the sake of all sentient beings, none of which is identifiably "Pure Land" in orientation. Nevertheless, near the end he declares:

> And when I am dying,
> May I remove all obstacles,
> See Amitābha face to face
> And proceed to the land of Sukhāvatī.
> [...]
> By whatever most excellent, infinite merit
> Obtained through my developing the Good Course,
> May beings submerged in the flood of passions
> Go to the very best city of Amitābha.[2]

The early transmission of Buddhism to China brought in its train literature such as this that put forth Amitābha's land of Sukhāvatī as a goal for everyone.

Inception in China: Huiyuan of Mount Lu

Many lists of Pure Land "patriarchs" (Ch. *zu*) have been proposed as a way to recognize shapers and carriers of the tradition, and all of them place Huiyuan of Mount Lu (334–416) at the head.[3] However, we should examine the extent to which Huiyuan was a "Pure Land Buddhist," and the practices he and his followers pursued.

Around 406 CE, Huiyuan corresponded with the Central Asian monk-translator Kumārajīva with questions about several topics. One set of questions dealt with the practice of the *nianfo samādhi* as described in the *Patyutpanna-samādhi-sūtra* (Ch.: *Banzhou sanmei jing*, T.418). In this practice, one selects a buddha and visualizes him while facing his assigned direction. This should lead to a waking vision or a vivid dream of that buddha. Huiyuan, presuming that the vision was only a product of the practitioner's mind, asked Kumārajīva how a visualized buddha could impart teachings not already known to the practitioner. His letter expressed no particular devotion to the Buddha Amitābha, nor any aspiration for rebirth in Sukhāvatī after death.[4] On his deathbed, Huiyuan expressed concern about his observance of the monastic rules, not rebirth.[5]

Nevertheless, elements of his practices and writings presage later Pure Land themes. Most famously, in the year 402 he convened the "White Lotus Society," a group of 123 lay and monastic followers who gathered before an image of Amitābha to fast, meditate, and support one another in gaining rebirth in "the west" after death.[6] Later figures who listed Huiyuan as the first patriarch cited his encouragement of lay societies and group practice as one justification (e.g., Fazhao, ca. 740–838).[7] In addition, Huiyuan facilitated rituals focused on attaining rebirth in the Pure Land *in extremis*, as when his disciple Sengji fell critically ill and wanted to prepare for death.[8] Here we see an early Pure Land deathbed ritual, later one of the more powerful vehicles for popularizing the tradition. Finally, in his preface to a collection of poems praising the *nianfo samādhi*, Huiyuan stated that this practice is easier to implement and produces results more efficiently than any other method of meditation.[9] This statement became a standard trope in later Pure Land apologetic literature. Thus, although Huiyuan and his community did not adopt the practices and rationales of the developed tradition, they did provide some seeds that later came to fruition.[10]

Shandao's Breakthrough

After Huiyuan, Pure Land practice continued to evolve through the fifth to eighth centuries. Tanluan (476–542) and Daochuo (562–645) contributed to the development of Pure Land practice by introducing the terms "self-power" (*zili*) and "other-power" (*tali*), placing emphasis on the power of Amitābha's vows (*fo yuan li*), and recommending *nianfo* as the most appropriate practice for people of the Age of the Dharma's End (*mofa*). However, most scholars consider Shandao (613–681) to be the founder of the Pure Land tradition.[11] Shandao earned recognition as the second patriarch by contributing four essential ingredients to the Chinese understanding of Pure Land practice:

First, he asserted that even unenlightened worldlings perceived the Pure Land as a "reward-land" (*baotu*). Prior authors had maintained that the Pure Land's inhabitants perceived its purity in accordance with their own attainment of purification. Advanced bodhisattvas could see it as a reward-land; but worldlings with tainted minds saw it only as a "transformation-land" (*huatu*) that accommodated their lower accomplishments.

Shandao declared that, since the Pure Land manifested in accordance with Amitābha's vows, all who dwelt there saw it as a reward-land.[12]

Second, Shandao defined the ambiguous term "ten *nian*" (*shi nian*) as "ten oral invocations" (lit., "ten sounds," *shi sheng*).[13] He said:

> The . . . [sutra text] makes clear that the guilty person, oppressed by the approach of death, has no way to contemplate the Buddha's name. [It next] elucidates how the good friend, knowing that through suffering [the dying person] has lost the contemplation, switches his teaching to oral repetition (*koucheng*) of the Buddha's name.[14]

Shandao applied this interpretation to other sutra passages in which the term *nian* did not clearly indicate oral repetition.[15] Thus, he established that *nianfo* indicated a very easy recitative practice.

Third, Shandao taught that ordinary beings (*fanfu*) attain rebirth in the Pure Land, not superior beings or advanced practitioners. Previous authors had maintained that all who go to rebirth had some level of prior attainment, even if they were only beginning Mahayanists. In his *Commentary on the Contemplation Sutra*, Shandao responded, "The 'people of the three lowest births' refers to evil worldlings (*e fanfu*) on account of their evil deeds. At the end of their lives, they lean upon the good [friend] and ride on the power of the Buddha's vows to go to rebirth. [. . .] How can one say they are beginners in the Mahayana?"[16]

Finally, and most consequentially, Shandao ascribed rebirth in the Pure Land entirely to the power of Amitābha. All previous authors had attributed rebirth to factors operating on the practitioner's side. Either the practice of *nianfo* had some inchoate power that made it unexpectedly effective (e.g., one's mind is most concentrated when facing death), or the practitioner had stored some merit from previous lives. Amitābha's primal vows merely established the Pure Land as a postmortem destination and himself as a suitable object of contemplation.

Shandao contended that one attained rebirth in the Pure Land because Amitābha brought one there: "As the *Larger Sutra* says, all ordinary beings [. . .] who attain rebirth [in the Pure Land] without exception avail themselves of the karmic power of Amitābha's great vows as a predominating condition."[17] Later in the same text, he says, "At first, without the encounter with the 'good friend,' the fires of hell come to welcome them. After meeting the 'good friend,' transformation buddhas come in welcome. This is entirely due to the power of Amitābha's vows."[18]

These four innovations made it possible to conceive of rebirth in the Pure Land as an unearned achievement that the Buddha conferred. In this way, Shandao created space for even the most evil and least accomplished person to gain rebirth. His affirmation of unearned achievement became the hallmark of Pure Land thereafter, leading scholars to consider him the tradition's founder.[19]

Varieties of *Nianfo* Practice

While Shandao opened a path for undeserving people to gain rebirth via a very simple practice, the tradition continued to hold that practitioners could also use higher-level methods to advance, and *nianfo* came to indicate a broad array of practices. In addition, the East Asian tradition maintained the idea that one could dedicate *any* practice to gaining rebirth in the Pure Land. In his *Jingtu huowen* (T.1972), Tianru (d. 1354) pointed out that practices other than visualization (*guanxiang*) and recollection (*yinian*) could bring about rebirth. Even non-Buddhist practices such as filial piety would serve.[20] Tianru did not mean that one should do other practices instead of *nianfo*. Rather, he showed that *nianfo* did not exclude other practices; all could lead to rebirth given the right intention.

Other authors said that *nianfo* could serve as one's sole practice, but it could take many forms and constitute a complete program of practice. This presentation took two forms that I have elsewhere called the "medicine cabinet" approach, and the "graded path" approach.[21] The first describes various modes of *nianfo* from which the master chooses the one most suited to the disciple at hand, much as a physician dispenses medicine according to the patient's symptoms. The second arranges methods of *nianfo* into a path along which the disciple progresses from the simple to the complex.

Kuiji (632–682) provides an early example of the first approach in his *Amituo jing tongzan shu* (T.1758), in which he described three modes of *nianfo*: mental practice (*xinnian*), quiet vocal *nianfo* (*qingsheng nian*), and loud vocal *nianfo* (*gaosheng nian*). He did not arrange these into a three-step path; one chooses the method that serves the moment. For instance, he says that loud vocal *nianfo* can counteract drowsiness and focus the mind as necessary. Any of these methods will do as long as the mind remains engaged.[22] More recently, Yinguang (1861–1940) adopted a pastoral approach and prescribed methods of *nianfo* according to the individual's needs. For example, in an essay entitled "The Great Master Taught Me a Method of *Nianfo*" (*Dashi jiao wo nianfo fangfa*), a disciple describes how Yinguang instructed him to recite the name of Amitābha ten times mentally, but without counting or using a rosary. This served to bring about rebirth in Sukhāvatī and to increase concentration.[23]

The "graded path" approach arranges different methods of *nianfo* into a curriculum from elementary to advanced levels. Zongmi (780–841) set forth a fourfold scheme that became highly influential:

1. "Contemplation of the name" (*chengming nian*), which for Zongmi meant contemplating any buddha's name to gain a vision of all the buddhas.[24] Since the Pure Land tradition took the term *chengming* to mean oral invocation rather than interior contemplation, it assimilated Zongmi's term in that sense.

2. "Contemplating an image" (*guanxiang nian*) meant to contemplate a physical image of a buddha (e.g., a painting or statue).[25]
3. "Contemplating a visualization" (*guanxiang nian*) meant to contemplate the features of a buddha's body mentally without using a physical image.[26] (*Xiang* represents two different Chinese words in these two steps.)
4. Finally, "contemplating the true mark" (*shixiang nian*), a method for advanced practitioners, involves reflecting that buddhas are free of all distinguishing characteristics. One thus contemplates their true reality.[27]

Zongmi was not a Pure Land figure; he called these methods *nian* (contemplation) rather than *nianfo*, and he did not present them as methods for attaining rebirth. Nevertheless, later Pure Land authors modified his fourfold scheme to frame their conceptions of practice. For example, Zhuhong (1535–1615) adapted it in his *Amituo jing shu chao* (CBETA X.424). He excluded the middle two methods as too complex for his contemporaries, and placed the "contemplation of the true mark" below the practice of "holding [Amitābha's] name" (*chiming*, a synonym for *chengming*). The latter method worked in spite of one's ignorance, while the former risked overreaching and hubris.[28] The contemporary Taiwan master Zhiyu (1924–2000) also used Zongmi's schema to frame a set of progressive techniques in an essay entitled "Four Types of Nianfo" (*Si zhong nianfo*).[29]

Pure Land Societies

Human beings naturally gravitate to each other for collective religious practices. They may gather on an ad hoc basis, or they may establish formal associations with charters and membership rolls. In China, Pure Land associations are rare prior to the Song dynasty (960–1270),[30] but during the tenth century, several arose in urban centers under monastic oversight. Still later, lay Buddhists set up their own independent societies.

Pure Land societies formed in two distinct patterns. In the first, a limited number of literati covenanted to support one another's practice. These small associations consciously emulated Huiyuan's White Lotus Society, and they fostered meditative practices alongside oral *nianfo*. The second kind were larger and more inclusive. One reported by Daniel Getz aspired to enroll over ten thousand members to meet annually. Membership in these societies crossed many social lines: lay and monastic, gentry and commoner, and male and female. These never coalesced into durable social structures like Christian denominations, however, and most lasted only a few years. Both kinds of association emphasized the accumulation of merit by obliging members to recite the Buddha's name a certain number of times daily and to contribute funds. They also took advantage of new print technology to have tally-sheets made and distributed, and members handed in their completed sheets when the group met.[31]

Deathbed Rituals

A great deal of Pure Land practice in China also took place in private settings. Since the time of death was critical for the achievement of rebirth in the Pure Land, a set of deathbed rituals developed to help the dying person maintain concentration, and those in attendance watched for signs of successful rebirth. The death of Huiyuan's monastic disciple Sengji on Mount Lu provided an early template for these rituals:

> [Sengji] [. . .] suddenly felt critically ill. Therefore, he wanted sincerely [to seek] the Western Country and visualized an image of the Buddha Amitāyus [i.e., Amitābha]. Huiyuan presented Sengji a candle and said, "By setting your mind on [Sukhāvatī], you may strive against the defilements for a while." Grasping the candle as a support, Sengji stilled his thoughts and was unperturbed, and asked the monks to assemble during the night in order to rotate [in reciting] the *Larger Sukhāvatīvyūha-sūtra*. [. . .] He lay down for a while. In a dream, he saw himself holding a candle and riding in space to see the Buddha Amitāyus. [. . .] Suddenly, he woke up and told the attendant at his sickbed about it. [. . .] His eyes looked out into space as if he saw something. The next moment he lay down again with a look of delight and said to his companions, "I am going!" He turned on his right side, and his breath left him.[32]

Elements of this story became standard in deathbed scenes: the need for concentration, the assembling of others to perform *nianfo* or chant sutras, patient and attendants looking for auspices of rebirth (here, a dream), and signs of success (here, Sengji's self-report and peaceful departure). In a study of Pure Land death rituals, Daniel Stevenson listed other features of the developed ritual: the appearance of Amitābha and his retinue, unearthly fragrances, nimbi appearing on those present, and so on.[33]

There was another side to this conception of the "good death," however. Shandao warned that persons by the bed who had ritually polluted themselves by eating meat, drinking wine, or consuming the five pungent herbs could attract demons and obstruct successful rebirth.[34] Yuan Hongdao (1568–1610) reported a near-failure in the case of a young nephew. The ritual was proceeding well, and the signs were positive: his nephew could see the Buddha coming. Suddenly the vision faded, and an investigation revealed that a menstruating maidservant had entered the room. After she was removed, the ritual resumed and all signs pointed to successful rebirth.[35] Alternatively, a distraction might break the dying person's concentration at the critical moment. In 1992, Zhiyu wrote that a prominent layman had practiced *nianfo* faithfully for twenty years, but had not laid down the mind of greed. Around his deathbed, the ritual was proceeding perfectly and showed every sign of success. Abruptly, one of his wives burst into the room and berated him for leaving her and their child without support. He quickly dictated changes to his will, but he was unable to regain concentration. With his dying breath, he reported seeing the darkness of hell rising before him.[36] Finally, one could not even be sure that the ritual would take place at all. One might die suddenly away from home, or not have the resources to engage the necessary specialists.

These stories notwithstanding, the existence of hundreds of "rebirth biographies" (*wangsheng zhuan*) indicate that nearly all devotees, both male and female, attained rebirth without incident. Nevertheless, these stories point to an important issue for Pure Land Buddhism: If rebirth in Sukhāvatī depends to any degree on the devotee's efforts or circumstances, then one cannot be completely certain that one will make it. The fact that the second story came from a twentieth-century source indicates that Chinese Pure Land is still grappling with this anxiety. These fears migrated to Japan, as vividly reported by Jacqueline Stone.[37] Now we will see how Japanese Pure Land thinkers overcame it.

Japan: Hōnen, Shinran, and Ippen

The Kamakura period in Japan (1185–1333) corresponds to a time in China when Pure Land societies thrived and Pure Land thought achieved greater definition. Hōnen (1133–1212), the founder of the Jōdoshū (Pure Land School), Shinran (1173–1262), who founded the Jōdo Shinshū (True Pure Land School), and Ippen (1239–1289), who established the Jishū (Time Assembly), felt disturbed by the tradition's inability to guarantee rebirth and developed new conceptions of the ways in which Pure Land practice worked. According to Soho Machida, Hōnen's concerns were social, while Shinran's issues were personal.[38] A chance encounter inspired Ippen's innovations.

Hōnen was troubled by violence and political instability, by clergy who robbed people of hope by insisting that rebirth in the Pure Land required their expensive ritual skills, and by anxiety about the possibility of losing the goal at the last moment. He therefore advised people to rely solely on the eighteenth of Amitābha's vows, which promises rebirth to all beings who recite his name as few as ten times as the only reliable path to rebirth.[39] He also declared that rebirth depended exclusively upon the Buddha's other-power, evoked through the chant of *namu Amida butsu*, thus removing human effort from the equation. Finally, he stressed that rebirth in the Pure Land would follow death under all circumstances with no fear of failure,[40] thus eliminating the need for clerical ritual assistance,[41] and assuring believers that rebirth would happen even if they died suddenly or *non compos mentis*. He continued to live as an observant monk himself, engaged in contemplative practices, and enjoyed some accomplishments in *samādhi*.[42]

Shinran took a different tack. Less successful than Hōnen in contemplative practice, he underwent a personal crisis that made him doubt the efficacy of any self-effort. Hōnen's teaching gave him new hope. He came to believe that rebirth did not depend in any degree upon one's own efforts and that rebirth came about through the other-power of Amitābha's vows. Thus, for Shinran, the crucial event occurred when *shinjin* or "true entrusting" arose. So thorough was his conviction of the uselessness of self-power that he decided even the arising of *shinjin* was a gift of Amitābha and not the practitioner's accomplishment.[43] To ascribe rebirth to any religious discipline was to deny the universality of salvation, since this excluded anyone unable to engage in that discipline.[44] When one relied on other-power rather than self-power, practice became effortless and salvation spontaneous (*jinen*). Strictly speaking, then, in Shinran, we reach a point where there *is* no "Pure Land practice" anymore. The Buddha grants the gift of faith which seizes the individual and evokes the cry of "*namu Amida butsu*" free of human contrivance.

This led to another problem, however: If everything is accomplished in the one moment when Amitābha grants the gift of true entrusting, then why do any further practice? This question arose among Hōnen's followers, but Hōnen rejected the reasoning outright and insisted on a lifetime of sustained *nembutsu* practice.[45] Members of the Jōdo Shinshū followed the logic of this question to the position of "once-calling" (*ichi nengi*), meaning that one need say the *nembutsu* with faith only once. Others found this unsatisfactory, and promoted the position of "many-calling" (*ta nengi*), interpreting subsequent recitations as expressions of gratitude.[46]

Shinran's teaching created another puzzle. Amitābha's salvation was universal,[47] but *shinjin* became a kind of conversion experience outside of the individual's control, and it was plain that not everyone underwent it. This forced Shinran and his followers to admit that it was very difficult to attain and only the rare individual experienced it.[48] Thus, Shinran could only counsel those hoping to receive Amitābha's grace to say the *nembutsu* while constantly examining themselves for any trace of self-power and cast themselves entirely on the power of the Buddha's vow. When *shinjin* did arise, then the individual could rest assured that they had achieved the status of the "definitely settled" and would unfailingly be reborn in the Pure Land.[49]

Ippen's solution to the problem of self-power took a different direction and involved fewer paradoxes. He had taken to wandering Japan's highways and handing paper amulets to everyone with the words *namu Amida butsu* inscribed upon them. He assured the recipients that reciting this formula with faith would guarantee their rebirth in the Pure Land. One day, he tried to hand one to a fellow monk, but the monk refused, saying that since he had no faith, reciting the formula would mean nothing. This response distressed Ippen, who wondered if a person's mere lack of faith was enough to thwart Amitābha's vows. Ippen resolved his perplexity by realizing that faith played no role whatsoever in salvation; one attained rebirth automatically when one recited the *nembutsu*. One's state of mind while doing so made no difference. Furthermore, Ippen declared that the moment of reciting the *nembutsu* was the moment of rebirth. He reasoned that the Buddha's name equaled the Buddha's actual presence, and wherever Amitābha was, his immediate environment had to be the Pure Land by definition. No other Pure Land figure had gone this far; all had held that rebirth happened after death when the Buddha came to conduct one to Sukhāvatī.[50]

Self-Power and Other-Power

The terms "self-power" and "other-power" underlie any understanding of rebirth in the Pure Land, and Chinese and Japanese thinkers held very different conceptions of the value and interrelation of these two powers. Put simply, the Chinese believed that the Buddha and the practitioner combined their powers to bring about the result, while some Japanese thinkers held that Amitābha's power alone carried one to rebirth.

In China, Pure Land thinkers had many ways of conceptualizing the relationship between self-power and other-power. Some denied any strict distinction between the two. As Yuan Hongdao argued in his *Xifang helun*, as long as Amitābha and the believer worked together, the contributions of self and other interwove in non-duality.[51] Others made use of the Chinese philosophical concept of *ganying*, or "sympathetic resonance." When one plucks a string on a musical instrument, strings tuned to the same pitch vibrate spontaneously; when the mind focuses on *nianfo*, the mind of Amitābha responds and forms a connection. Zhuhong took this line in his *Da jingtu sishiba wen* (*Answers to 48 Questions about Pure Land*, CBETA X.1158).[52] The modern Chinese Pure Land masters Zhiyu (1924–2000) and Daan (b. 1959) sum up this approach with the apt phrase "the two powers of self and other" (*zi ta er li*).[53]

Chinese authors also provided reasons for Pure Land practitioners to put forth sustained efforts based on the teachings of the *Contemplation Sutra*. In this sutra, not all rebirths in the Pure Land are alike; one is reborn at one of nine levels, ranging from the "highest of the high" to the "lowest of the low." Those who practiced assiduously and maintained morality would be reborn at a high level, meet the Buddha, receive his teaching, and become buddhas themselves in as little as one day. At the other extreme, the worst malefactor imaginable attains rebirth at the periphery of the Pure Land, receives instruction from lesser bodhisattvas, and may take many eons to achieve buddhahood. While both gain rebirth and the guarantee of liberation, the former achieve the ultimate goal much more rapidly than the latter. This mattered, because in Mahayana Buddhism, practitioners ought to seek buddhahood in order to save others, and the faster one attains this goal, the faster one may begin this compassionate work.[54] Self-power and other-power work together, as when one walks up an escalator and gets to the top faster by combining one's efforts with the movement of the machine.

The three major schools of Japanese Pure Land Buddhism rejected this model. Hōnen taught that Amitābha's power was sufficient to bring one to the Pure Land in response to one's sustained practice, and Shinran taught that Amitābha's gift of *shinjin* vouchsafed one's rebirth and practitioners contributed nothing to the process. Ippen dispensed with faith altogether and held that rebirth followed the *nembutsu* automatically. All three formulas resolved the anxieties inherent in the Chinese approach. Hōnen freed practitioners from dependence upon the state-sponsored monastic and ritual system and from fear of interference at the critical moment of death. Shinran and Ippen alleviated the ordinary believer's anxiety that their power was insufficient for liberation by asking them to leave it all to Amitābha. If human effort could not bring about rebirth, then lack of effort could not hinder it either. It was like riding an elevator: it does all the lifting, and one has only to ride it.

Both positions served particular purposes. The Chinese approach reassured devotees that if they truly lacked the power or opportunity to practice, the other-power of Amitābha would carry them to the Pure Land. At the same time, they could still exhort those who *did* have ability and opportunity to do as much practice with as much diligence as they could muster. However, their reliance on the idea of sympathetic resonance to explain the mechanism of rebirth and the metaphors used to imagine deliverance created unease. Chinese thinkers affirmed that sympathetic resonance operated only while the practitioner was engaged in *nianfo*. As soon as one stopped, the connection with the Buddha ceased. Thus, if one lost focus at the critical moment, rebirth might miscarry, as we saw in the story of the layman and his aggrieved wife.

The Japanese approach removed such fears, but at a price. When Hōnen assured his followers that they would be reborn even if death came upon them suddenly and Shinran told his congregations that even their own worst evil could not hinder Amitābha's grace, abuses took place. Some even espoused antinomianism, claiming that followers *should* commit evil deeds as a way to elicit more of Amitābha's grace,[55] and the founders had to find ways to convince their disciples to behave morally. Hōnen had his followers sign a pledge that they would continue to observe ethical rules, and Shinran told his followers that one should not take poison just because there is an antidote,[56] but these were weak compared to the reasoned exhortations to morality that the Chinese tradition formulated.

Shinran hit upon a better approach when he tied his followers' attitudes toward morality to the arising of *shinjin*. Since *shinjin* involved a complete entrusting of one's fate to Amitābha, any idea that one could elicit Amitābha's grace by deliberate wrongdoing demonstrated that one had not yet reached the point of true entrusting. A person of true *shinjin* recognized his or her inability to assist the process of rebirth, and exhibited an attitude of humility and gratitude, not defiance. This provided a stable theoretical paradigm for combating the temptation to abuse Amitābha's grace by flouting morality.[57] Ippen, whose itinerant group depended upon soliciting donations while on the road, enforced a strict code of behavior without theorizing its relation to the process of rebirth.

Thus, we see a tension built into the distinction of self-power and other-power: if success depends to any degree upon one's own effort, then one must accept the corollary that the practice may fail. Conversely, if one removes self-power from the equation, one may assuage this fear but create the potential for antinomianism. The Chinese and Japanese traditions remedied the first and second pitfalls, respectively, and found ways of countering them that have endured.

The "Pure Land in the Human Realm"

By the early twentieth century, Buddhism faced the advent of modernity. Those committed to improving life and reforming politics and society saw Pure Land as too "other-worldly" to be of assistance since it denigrated the present world and directed people's hopes to a realm beyond. The monk-reformer Taixu (1890–1947) receives credit for formulating a new kind of Buddhism capable of addressing the problems of human life here and now under the name "Humanistic Buddhism" (*renjian fojiao*). One outgrowth of Humanistic Buddhism was a novel way of approaching Pure Land called the "Pure Land in the Human Realm" (*renjian jingtu*). He set forth this idea in a 1926 essay entitled "On the Establishment of the Pure Land in the Human Realm" (*Jianshe renjian jingtu lun*).[58]

Taixu did not intend to supplant traditional Pure Land practice. While counseling a concern with human life everywhere, his use of the term "Pure Land in the Human Realm" applied mostly to the proposed creation of a Buddhist utopian community.[59] He also understood that even in the modern world, people worried about their postmortem fates, and so he encouraged continued practices leading to rebirth in Sukhāvatī or other buddha-realms. Nevertheless, the piece contains unambiguous calls for reform and social justice work in order to improve people's lives, especially in a 1930 address appended to this essay called "Creating the Pure Land in the Human Realm" (*Chuangzao renjian jingtu*).[60] His approach is synthetic, putting the traditional and the modern together to meet all human needs both here and in the hereafter.

Modern Buddhists such as Sheng Yen (Shengyan, 1930–2009) have taken up the banner of the "Pure Land in the Human Realm." His Dharma Drum Mountain organization has adopted environmentally friendly practices and espoused social reforms under this slogan. Like Taixu, Sheng Yen did not seek thereby to supersede traditional practices since he agreed that the implementation of Humanistic Buddhism does not conflict with the aspiration for rebirth in Amitābha's land; in fact, he held that the first prepares one for the second. He states that all Mahayana Buddhists ought to generate the desire to save all other beings. When one has this attitude, then one accords with Amitābha's compassionate vows. Normatively, one should vow *both* to bring about the Pure Land in the Human Realm by assisting beings in the present world *and* seek rebirth in Sukhāvatī after death. In this way, one gains a higher rebirth in the Pure Land, becomes a buddha sooner, and can go about aiding other beings.[61] This idea has begun to take hold in Japan as well.

Conclusion: The Varieties of Pure Land Practice

In the preceding remarks, I hope to have shown that "Pure Land practice" goes well beyond the simple action of reciting Amitābha's name. We have seen that *any* means of Buddhist cultivation can become Pure Land practice if one directs the merit toward rebirth. In addition, we have seen that even the single term *nianfo* covers a multitude of practices from buddha-visualization to simple oral repetition of the name. Moreover, the explanations by which people understand how *nianfo* works are as varied as the practices. Self-power and other-power can mix in a variety of ways by invoking the Mahayana philosophical concept of non-duality to show that the two are not ultimately separate, or by positing the mechanism of sympathetic resonance to show how one's efforts evoke the Buddha's response. Finally, one can exclude self-power altogether and rely on Amitābha to provide a moment of true conversion and entrusting that is beyond one's ability to bring about. We have also seen variations between individual practices done alone and ritualized practices such as meetings of large societies and deathbed ceremonies. All of these constitute the highly diffuse field of "Pure Land practice."

Notes

1. Gregory Schopen, "Sukhāvatī as a Generalized Religious Goal in Sanskrit Mahāyāna *Sūtra* Literature," in *Figments and Fragments of Mahāyāna Buddhism in India* (Honolulu: University of Hawai'i Press, 2005), 154–89..
2. Douglas Osto, "A New Translation of the Sanskrit Bhadracarī with Introduction and Notes," *New Zealand Journal of Asian Studies* 12, no. 1 (December 2010): 18–19.
3. Chen Chienhuang, "Lianzong shisan wei zushi de queli guocheng ji qi shiyi," in *Wushang fangbian yu xianxing fale: Mituo jingtu yu renjian jingtu de zhoubian guanxi* (Taipei: Xianghai wenhua, 2010), 22–33.
4. For a translation of the correspondence, see Charles B. Jones, *Chinese Pure Land Buddhism: Understanding a Tradition of Practice* (Honolulu: University of Hawai'i Press, 2019), 150–53.
5. *Gaoseng zhuan*, T.2059, 50:361b1–b13; Erik Zürcher, *The Buddhist Conquest of China: The Spread and Adaptation of Buddhism in Early Medieval China*. Sinica Leidensia 11 (Leiden: Brill, 1959), 253.
6. *Gaoseng zhuan*, T.2059, 50:358c29–a1; Zürcher, *Buddhist Conquest*, 244.
7. Fazhao, *Jingtu wuhui nianfo songjing guanxing yi*, T.2827, 85:1255b11–b13.
8. *Gaoseng zhuan*, T.2059, 50:362b12–b27.
9. *Guang hongming ji*, T.2103, 52:351b20–b24.
10. For more, see Jones, *Chinese Pure Land Buddhism*, chapter 8.
11. For more on Tanluan and Daochuo, see Jones, *Chinese Pure Land Buddhism*, 17–20.
12. Shandao, *Guan wuliangshoufo jing shu*, T.1753, 37:251a6–a9.
13. Chen Chienhuang, *Xingjiao jingtu famen: Tanluan, Daochuo yu Shandao kaizhan Mituo jingtu jiaomen zhi guizhe* (Taipei: Shangzhou, 2009), 146, 167; T.1753, 37:249c28–c29.
14. T.1753, 37:277b14–b17.
15. e.g., Shandao, *Wangsheng lizan jie*, T.1980, 47:447c27–448a9.
16. T.1753, 37:249a24–249b5.
17. T.1753, 37:246b10–b11.
18. T.1753, 37:249a22–a24.
19. Julian Pas, *Visions of Sukhāvatī: Shandao's Commentary on the Kuan Wu-Liang-Shou-Fo Ching* (Albany: State University of New York Press, 1995), 318–19; Chen Yangjiong, *Zhongguo jingtuzong tongshi* (Nanjing: Phoenix, 2000), 270; Jones, *Chinese Pure Land Buddhism*, 20–25.
20. see T.1972, 47:295a24–a27.

21. Charles B. Jones, "Toward a Typology of Nien-fo: A Study in Methods of Buddha-Invocation in Chinese Pure Land Buddhism," *Pacific World: Journal of the Institute of Buddhist Studies*, 3rd series, no. 3 (2001): 219–39. See also Jones, *Chinese Pure Land Buddhism*, chapter 7.
22. T.1758, p. 37:341c11–c18.
23. Yinguang, *Yinguang dashi quanji*, compiled and edited Shi Guangding (Taipei: Fojiao Chubanshe, 1991), 7:471–72.
24. Zongmi, *Huayan jing Puxian xingyuan pin shu chao*. CBETA X.229, 5:280c9–c16.
25. Zongmi, *Huayan jing*, 5:280c16–c20.
26. Zongmi, *Huayan jing*, 5:280c20–a7.
27. Zongmi, *Huayan jing*, 5:281a7–a15.
28. Yunqi Zhuhong, *Amituo jing shu chao*. CBETA X.424, 22:612a15–a18, 612b20–b21.
29. Zhiyu, "Si zhong nianfo," in *Chipan lian chao* (Sanxia: Xilian jingyuan, 1986), 21–24.
30. Daniel A. Getz, "T'ien-t'ai Pure Land Societies and the Creation of the Pure Land Patriarchate," in *Buddhism in the Sung*, ed. Peter Gregory and Daniel Getz (Honolulu: University of Hawai'i Press, 1999), 514 n.30.
31. Getz, "T'ien-t'ai Pure Land," 499.
32. T.2059, 50:362b16–b27.
33. Daniel B. Stevenson, "Death-Bed Testimonials of the Pure Land Faithful," in *Buddhism in Practice*, ed. Donald S. Lopez, Jr. (Princeton, NJ: Princeton University Press, 1995), 594.
34. Shandao, *Guannian Amituofo xianghai sanmei gongde famen*, T.1959, 47:24b29–c2.
35. Yuan Hongdao, *Yuan Hongdao ji jianjiao*. ed. and annotated Qian Bocheng (Shanghai: Shanghai guji chubanshe 1981), 1:476–77. English translation in Jonathan Chaves, *Pilgrim of the Clouds* (New York: Weatherhill, 1978), 82–83.
36. Zhiyu, *Shifu de hua* (Taipei: Xilian jingyuan, 1992), 58.
37. Jacqueline Stone, "By the Power of One's Last Nembutsu: Deathbed Practices in Early Medieval Japan," in *Approaching the Land of Bliss: Religious Praxis in the Cult of Amitābha*, ed. Richard K. Payne and Kenneth K. Tanaka (Honolulu: University of Hawai'i Press 2004), 88–94.
38. Soho Machida, *Renegade Monk: Hōnen and Japanese Pure Land Buddhism* (Berkeley: University of California Press, 1999), 3.
39. Machida, *Renegade*, 77.
40. Machida, *Renegade*, 97–98.
41. Machida, *Renegade*, 79–80, 85, 95.
42. Machida, *Renegade*, 72–73, 106–10.
43. Shinran, *The Collected Works of Shinran*, trans. and annotated by Dennis Hirota et al. (Kyoto: Jōdo Shinshū Hongwanji-ha, 1997), 1:464.
44. Shinran, *Collected Works*, 1:687.
45. James Dobbins, *Jōdo Shinshū: Shin Buddhism in Medieval Japan* (Bloomington: Indiana University Press, 1989), 50–53.
46. Shinran, *Collected Works*, 1:696–97.
47. Shinran, *Collected Works*, 1:457.
48. Shinran, *Collected Works*, 1:464.
49. Shinran, *Collected Works*, 1:455.
50. For more information in Ippen, see Charles B. Jones, *Pure Land: History, Tradition, and Practice* (Boston: Shambhala, 2021), chapter 12.
51. Yuan Hongdao, *Xifang helun*. T.1976, 47:393b28–c9.

52. CBETA X 61n1158_p0510a03.
53. Daan, *Jingtu zong jiaocheng* (Beijing: Zongjiao wenhua chubanshe, 2006), 125; Zhiyu, *Shifu*, 58.
54. See Charles B. Jones, "Foundations of Ethics and Practice in Chinese Pure Land Buddhism," in *Destroying Mara Forever: Buddhist Ethics Essays in Honor of Damien Keown*, ed. John Powers and Charles Prebish (Ithaca, NY: Snow Lion, 2009), 237–59.
55. Dobbins, *Jōdo Shinshū*, 53.
56. Yuien, *Tannishō: A Shin Buddhist Classic*, trans. Taitetsu Unno (Honolulu: Buddhist Study Center Press, 1984), 24.
57. Dobbins, *Jōdo Shinshū*, 55.
58. One may find a full translation of this essay in Charles B. Jones, *Taixu's "On the Establishment of the Pure Land in the Human Realm": A Translation and Study* (New York: Bloomsbury Academic, 2021).
59. Taixu, "Jianshe renjian jingtu lun," in *Taixu dashi quanshu* (Taipei: Shandao Temple Sutra Distribution Center 1956), 24:399–403.
60. Taixu, "Jianshe," 24:425–30.
61. Sheng Yen, *Shengyan fashi jiao jingtu famen*, comp. and ed. Guoxian. Shengyan shuyuan, 5. (Taipei: Fagu wenhua, 2010), 90–93.

Further Reading

Chaves, Jonathan. *Pilgrim of the Clouds*. New York: Weatherhill, 1978.

Dobbins, James. *Jōdo Shinshū: Shin Buddhism in Medieval Japan*. Bloomington: Indiana University Press, 1989.

Getz, Daniel A. "T'ien-t'ai Pure Land Societies and the Creation of the Pure Land Patriarchate." In *Buddhism in the Sung*, ed. Peter N. Gregory and Daniel A. Getz, Jr. Honolulu: University of Hawai'i Press, 1999, 477–523.

Jones, Charles B. *Chinese Pure Land Buddhism: Understanding a Tradition of Practice*. Honolulu: University of Hawai'i Press, 2019.

Jones, Charles B. "Foundations of Ethics and Practice in Chinese Pure Land Buddhism." In *Destroying Mara Forever: Buddhist Ethics Essays in Honor of Damien Keown*, ed. John Powers and Charles Prebish. Ithaca, NY: Snow Lion, 2009, 237–59.

Jones, Charles B. *Pure Land: History, Tradition, and Practice*. Boston: Shambhala, 2021.

Jones, Charles B. *Taixu's "On the Establishment of the Pure Land in the Human Realm": A Translation and Study*. New York: Bloomsbury Academic, 2021.

Jones, Charles B. "Toward a Typology of Nien-fo: A Study in Methods of Buddha-Invocation in Chinese Pure Land Buddhism." *Pacific World: Journal of the Institute of Buddhist Studies*, 3rd series, no. 3 (2001): 219–39.

Machida, Soho. *Renegade Monk: Hōnen and Japanese Pure Land Buddhism*. Berkeley: University of California Press, 1999.

Nattier, Jan. "The Realm of Akṣobhya: A Missing Piece in the History of Pure Land Buddhism." *Journal of the International Association of Buddhist Studies* 23, no. 1 (2000): 71–102.

Pas, Julian. *Visions of Sukhāvatī: Shandao's Commentary on the Kuan Wu-Liang-Shou-Fo Ching*. Albany: State University of New York Press, 1995.

Schopen, Gregory. "Sukhāvatī as a Generalized Religious Goal in Sanskrit Mahāyāna *Sūtra* Literature." In *Figments and Fragments of Mahāyāna Buddhism in India*. Honolulu: University of Hawai'i Press, 2005, 154–89.

Sharf, Robert H. "On Pure Land Buddhism and Chan/Pure Land Syncretism in Medieval China." *T'oung Pao* 88, fasc. 4–5 (2002): 282–331.

Stevenson, Daniel B. "Death-Bed Testimonials of the Pure Land Faithful." In *Buddhism in Practice*, ed. Donald S. Lopez, Jr. Princeton, NJ: Princeton University Press, 1995, 592–602.

Stone, Jacqueline I. *Right Thoughts at the Last Moment: Buddhism and Deathbed Practices in Early Medieval Japan*. Kuroda Studies in East Asian Buddhism, 26. Honolulu: University of Hawai'i Press, 2016.

CHAPTER 19

KOAN PRACTICE

JEFF SHORE

It is always a matter, my darling,
Of life or death . . . .

—Richard Wilbur, "The Writer"

THE koan tradition can be traced to spontaneous encounters attributed to teachers and disciples in Tang Dynasty (618–907) China. This tradition gradually developed into organized curricula used today in monastic training and in lay groups worldwide. While admirers tend to consider koan practice a unique and peerless spiritual treasure, some critics see the developed curricula as little more than a hollow shell. There are good reasons for both views. By inviting the reader to open up to the great doubt directly underfoot, this chapter provides a sense of what koan practice is from the inside.

Recent scholarship has examined koan practice as "instrumentalist," that is, as an irrational problem-challenge to provoke awakening, and as "realizational," that is, as a probe-expression of awakening with a logic all its own. Generally, the instrumentalist argument describes the preliminary koan practice of Rinzai Zen, while the realizational model applies more to the use of koans in Sōtō Zen practice. These are the two major schools of Zen Buddhism. Recent scholarship has even argued that koan practice is little more than ritual re-enactment, or "scriptural exegesis"—a form of textual commentary.[1] The value and limit of such descriptions will become clear as we progress.

For over a thousand years, countless people have devoted their lives and lifeblood to koan practices in the Zen Buddhist tradition. If the story of Gautama Buddha's life stirs something in us—if we have ever been compelled to deeply question who and what we really are—then great doubt is not far away and we can discern the point of koan practice. Gautama Buddha's life, however, has been embellished with myth. So has the Zen tradition. Recent scholarship has shown how classic koans are actually legends or have fictional-legendary elements. They are not historical events, but have been amplified or even created for various purposes, spiritual and otherwise. Critical scholarship can elucidate naïve, romanticized notions. In the context of spiritual practice, however, the point is to resolve the great doubt, that is, the fundamental spiritual dilemma at the core of one's own being.

Beginnings: Muzhou and his Genjō-kōan

The word "koan" (Ch. *gong'an*) did not begin as a Buddhist or religious term, but as a Chinese legal term referring to a public case put before the local magistrate. Usage attributed to early Chan (Chinese Zen) Buddhism retained this juridical sense, often with a scathing, accusatory tone—and penalty attached. During the Tang dynasty, when Muzhou Daoming (780–877) saw a fellow monk approaching, he would often declare: "It's an open-and-shut case, but you're released from thirty blows!" Muzhou used the now popular term, pronounced in Japanese *genjō-kōan*, meaning manifest koan, or case at hand. His usage is closer to the legal phrase *res ipsa loquitur*—the thing speaks for itself—so it has been rendered as "an open-and-shut case." One time he said: "Ever since this old monk [Muzhou] came to preside here, I've not seen one person truly free. Why don't you come forward?" A monk approached. Muzhou: "The supervising monk is not here, so go out of the gate and give yourself twenty blows." Monk: "What have I done wrong?" Muzhou: "You've just added chains to your cangue [a pillory worn by criminals]!"[2]

Taken lightly, such exchanges may seem amusing farce and not particularly significant; taken seriously, great doubt may arise. For it presents the monk, and us, with a problem-challenge that stops us in our tracks: What is wrong with the way I am? Put less bluntly, what did Muzhou discern in the seeking monk? What did Gautama discern that made him leave home and seek the Way? There is, as yet, no method to the seeming madness. Encounters spontaneously occur and take up whatever is at hand. Then they are over. No mention is made of meditating on them or commenting on them. Eventually these "encounter dialogues" were retold, written down, discussed, and became the focus of meditation as koan cases.

In practice, when a koan works, it directly galvanizes one's own great doubt.[3] Cutting through the complex strata of traditional Buddhist thought—and one's own discursive thought—koans tend to use common words, familiar concerns, and immediate situations. Let's consider six classic koans.

Classic Koans

(1) Without thinking this is good or that is bad, right now, what is your original face?

As mentioned, early exchanges were sometimes altered, some were invented, and sectarian and sociopolitical concerns came into play. This koan, and its larger legendary context, is a prime example of these issues. Attributed to Huineng (638–713), also known as the sixth patriarch of Chan, it is found in standard editions of his *Platform Sutra*. "Original face" is a simple and direct way of pointing out buddha-nature, that is, one's selfless, true nature. Does one put on a face for others? For oneself? "Without thinking this is good or that is bad" uses paired opposites (good-bad) to suggest "prior to all opposing positions that arise from discursive mind." This is made clear in the fuller statement of the koan ending, ". . . before the birth of your parents" or ". . . before your parents gave birth to you." The paired opposites mother-father represent the causes and conditions from which self, and self-deception, arise.

In the *Platform Sutra*, Huineng is an impoverished and illiterate barbarian from the south who ekes out a living as a woodcutter. Another classic koan derives from an encounter with an arriving monk. Huineng asks where he came from and the monk answers that he came from Mount Song. Huineng then challenges: "Who is this that's come?" Along with these koans, his renowned "there's never been a single thing," in response to the head monk's poem stressing the need to practice constant vigilance, enshrine Huineng and his *Platform Sutra* as quintessential Chan.

Except for one thing: none of the typical koan statements from the *Platform Sutra*, including "original face," "who's come," and "never been a single thing" are found in earlier manuscript versions uncovered in Dunhuang in 1900. Recent scholarship has been teasing out the complex issues involved, including sectarian rivalry, secular power, and whether awakening is immediate or whether it is gradual and requires constant application. In actual practice, however, these koans are effective because they are palpable and direct. They work as koans despite, or as Zen scholar John McCrae insists, precisely because, they lack historicity.[4] They can strike to the core of our own great doubt.

(2) Who is the one transcending all phenomena?

This was the Chinese layman Pang Yun's (d. 808) koan. With family and home responsibilities, Pang must have struggled long and hard with it in his daily life. Who is this one free from all entanglements inner and outer, that literally "does not go along with the ten thousand phenomena?" Rather than being summarily sentenced by Muzhou, or asked by Huineng what is his original face or who's come, Pang already had zeroed in on his own natural koan when he visited the two most outstanding teachers of his time. Their responses helped bring Pang back to his real senses.

The first teacher, Shitou Xiqian (700–791), responded by placing his hand over Pang's mouth. The layman had an insight. Later Pang visited Mazu Daoyi (709–788). When the layman put this same question to him, Mazu responded: "I'll tell you when you've gulped down all the water in the West River!" The layman awakened. After meeting with Shitou, Pang famously expressed his newfound miraculous powers in a poem ending: "Carrying water, fetching firewood." But where is the one seeking to transcend all phenomena now? Here is the "miracle."[5] Chan koans and Chan literature in general are filled with unpretentious, succinct, and direct expressions of no-self awakening that contrast with more traditional Buddhist ways and mores. These have been replaced with the extraordinarily ordinary mind of carrying wood, returning home to sit by the fire, the daily acts of eating, sleeping, even answering the call of nature.

(3) "What is buddha?" Mazu: "Mind is buddha."

Earlier Buddhist sutras and teachers have made similar claims.[6] But Mazu's succinct and direct expressions, such as "mind is buddha" and "ordinary mind is the Way," along with his legendary strikes, kicks, and shouts, place him at the heart of the nascent koan tradition. In case thirty of the koan collection known as *Gateless Barrier* (*Wumen guan*), compiler Wumen Huikai (1183–1260) illumines the koan with this poem:

> A fine day under clear skies.
> No use foolishly searching here and there.
> You still ask what is buddha?
> Pleading innocence with contraband in hand![7]

As Chan developed on Chinese soil and was shaped by the vernacular, it aimed at awakening in a manner that was untamed and unrestrained by discursive mind or logic. Although the term "Chan" refers to "meditation," an unfettered dynamism also emerges, typified in figures such as Mazu, layman Pang, and Linji Yixuan (d. 866). Ordinary mind produces extraordinary situations and actions, including striking, yelling, overturning tables, and equally extraordinary statements, not just about mind being buddha but about buddha being a privy hole. Anything—even nothing—to help the other awaken to the truth of no-self directly underfoot.

(4) Like a person up a tree, hanging by his teeth for dear life on a high branch, hands cannot grab the bough, feet cannot touch the trunk. Another person comes along and asks the point of Bodhidharma coming from the west. If he does not answer, he fails to meet the questioner's need. If he does answer, he will surely lose his life. Right now, how do you answer?

Xiangyan Zhixian (d. 898) was a brilliant Chan monk. One day his teacher Guishan Lingyou (771–853) told him that he did not want the results of his great learning, but just a word as to who he is before his birth. Whatever Xiangyan offered his teacher rejected. Finally, he begged his teacher to teach it to him, but his teacher refused. Driven into great doubt, Xiangyan left the monastery and lived as a nameless gravekeeper. Then one day while sweeping, he happened to hear the "tock" of stone hitting bamboo and awakened. Back covered in sweat and tears of joy in his eyes, Xiangyan now knows the great compassion his teacher displayed in giving him nothing to help him awaken.

The bizarre koan of a man literally up a tree and out on a limb is case five of *Gateless Barrier*. It is Xiangyan's.[8] Out of great compassion, he condensed his life struggle into this koan. Koan practice involves answering through one's own life and limb. This is the source of Chan's compassionate dynamism.

(5) What is the sound of the single hand?

In Edo period Japan, a thousand years after Huineng, Hakuin Ekaku (1686–1769) created this koan: You know the sound of two hands brought together; what is the sound of one hand? With nothing up his sleeve, Hakuin challenges one to directly embody and manifest what is indivisible, prior to opposition. Like Huineng's original face koan, there is no explicit reference to any Buddhist teaching or doctrine. Hakuin used this koan in training his disciples. He found it more effective in rousing great doubt than Zhaozhou Congshen's (778–897) by then overused and over-interpreted *Wu* koan:

(6) A monk asked: "Does this dog have buddha-nature or not?"
Zhaozhou replied: "*Wu.*" [J. *Mu:* "Nope!" or "Not!"]

All beings have buddha-nature, that is, are without self. Yet here Zhaozhou replied "*Wu.*" *Gateless Barrier* compiler Wumen comments on this first case: "Rouse a massive doubt with your whole being and inquire into *Wu*." Along with the original face and the sound of the single hand, this is the most well-known and oft-used koan.

In sum, self constantly divides itself into me-you, birth-death, like-dislike, good-bad. It could even be said that self **is** this split, this divisiveness. A living koan opens up the great doubt at the root of this existential dilemma so that it can be resolved, once and for all. As seen earlier, Muzhou simply and directly gave his verdict without explanation. An explicit formulation attributed to Shitou essentially challenges: "As you are won't do; not as you are won't do either. Neither will do—now what do you do?"[9] Genuine koan practice serves as a formidable barrier that self cannot enter or get into. Koans are, in this sense, "instrumentalist." No-self awakening is the dissolution of the great doubt that forms this barrier. Now one cannot get out of it: what had been an unsolvable problem-challenge for the self has become wondrous probe-expression through body, mouth, and mind. Thus koans are also "realizational" and genuine zazen meditation can itself be the embodied koan.

Yunmen and the Koan Tradition

Raising spontaneous expressions of the past for purposes of instruction as well as creating his own, Yunmen Wenyan (864–949) could be considered the father of the koan tradition.[10] In a Dharma talk, Yunmen said: "Don't you know that the moment Deshan [Xuanjian (780–865)] saw a monk enter the monastery gate he drove him away with his stick, and when Muzhou saw a monk enter the gate he would say: 'It's an open-and-shut case, but you're released from thirty blows!'" Note that Yunmen is reminding listeners of previous *genjō-kōan*.

In the same Dharma talk, Yunmen explains: "Our predecessors offered entangling vines to aid us." The term "entangling vines" is one of many synonyms for koans. It refers both to hindrances that can snare us as well as to aids that can awaken us. Yunmen then cites three more koans of his predecessors, this time ecstatically redolent and animated ones:

> The whole world is nothing but you!
>
> Get hold of this old monk on the tips of the hundred grasses,
> find the son of heaven in the busy marketplace!
>
> A particle of dust arises and the whole world is contained therein.
> On the tip of a single lion's hair the whole body is manifest!

Yunmen then brings it home: "Get a good grip and inquire thoroughly; after some time an entrance will naturally open. No one can do it for you; it is each person's own task."[11] Yunmen has well summed up koan practice, but he has done so by explicitly quoting entangling vine–koans of his predecessors. According to the Zen tradition, this is due to the great compassion of the teachers as they sought to guide more and more students not primed and ready with their own great doubt in the form of a natural koan.

Over the next two centuries, koan practice transformed into a unique Buddhist method that championed constant, single-minded inquiry on the *huatou*, the essential phrase or point of a koan, in order to rouse one's own great doubt. As shown in the following, Dahui Zonggao (1089–1163) in Song Dynasty (960–1279) China is the crucial figure for developing this practice. But first, how does koan practice work?

How Koan Practice Works: Through Great Doubt to the Heart of the Matter

Whether monastic or lay, one needs to live a wholesome life and learn proper meditative discipline. Otherwise koan practice is bound to be counterproductive, like trying to swim the English Channel by attaching weights instead of a lifejacket. Even if some modicum of insight were attained, such breakthroughs tend to degenerate into breakdowns. Genuine koan practice, despite role-playing imitation and shamelessly spurious teachers, is solidly based in the Buddhist tradition and commitment to moral conduct.

Living a wholesome life provides a solid basis to develop uninterrupted concentration. Preliminary concentration practices, such as focusing on the breath, help stabilize body and mind. Gradually all one's energy gathers in the belly, not merely as endless discursive thought in the head. To prevent the common mistake of thinking about the koan rather than actually being inseparable from it and embodying it, one may be required to gather and sustain all one's energies before one is given a koan. However, a koan may also be given to help bring about this sustained concentration.

Either way, the point is to rouse one's own great doubt. Without doing so, koan practice fails.[12] In Chan, a common formulation which points to this doubt is that one does not know where one comes from at birth or where one goes at death. The real point, however, is that we do not know where we are right now—where **this** really is. Here great doubt opens underfoot. Whether the koan arises naturally or is given by a teacher, if one gives oneself to it, eventually the koan coalesces. One can no longer grasp it as something, anything, even nothing. Rather, now one is grasped by it. The koan may have seemed utterly ungraspable and out of reach; now it is inescapable, a bowling ball in the pit of the stomach, solid and unmovable. Rising from zazen meditation, it rises. No longer limited to time on the sitting cushion, it comes to be what is, whatever and wherever one is. Rather than try to analyze or explain away the felt tension, now the koan throws one directly into the sensation of great doubt as the sensation of great doubt throws one into the koan: *What is it?! Who is this?!* Through great doubt, self comes to a standstill and solidifies as the *huatou* or living core of the koan.

The koan has now taken root; but it has not been resolved. Gradually one's existential doubts coalesce around the koan. Self and doubt become inseparable, one massive doubt or doubt block, as it's called. Hakuin: "It's all a matter of raising or failing to raise this doubt block. It must be understood that this doubt block is like a pair of wings that advances you along the way."[13] Gaofeng Yuanmiao (1238–1295) states in his *Essentials of Chan*: "In India and China, in the past and the present, of all the worthies who spread this light, none did anything more than simply resolve this one doubt. The thousand doubts, the ten thousand doubts, are just this one doubt. Resolve this doubt and no doubt remains."[14]

As Yunmen said: "No one can do it for you; it is each person's own task." If available, however, the genuine guidance of a living exemplar is most helpful, serving as a mirror when one comes in all sincerity, as a formidable wall when not. (Recall Muzhou.) One continues boring into it, without escaping, without wandering into discursive thought about how, when, or why. This state is described as "tasteless" since the usual seeking and evading through sense experience and discursive thought has dried up. Self and all its contortions, including intellect, emotion, and will, have come to a halt. It has nowhere to go. All that I think I know, all that I think I am, becomes as if frozen, good and stuck in a sublime way. Hakuin described it like being "encased in a great sheet of ice," "seated inside a bottle of purest crystal" such that "all the workings of mind—thought, consciousness, emotions—hung suspended. . . ."[15]

In his *Essentials of Chan*, Gaofeng Yuanmiao describes his experience with the koan "All returns to one; to where does the one return?" (*Blue Cliff Record*, case forty-five):

> Unexpectedly in my sleep, there was the doubt: "All returns to one; to where does the one return?" The doubt suddenly arose of itself. I stopped sleeping and forgot to eat, could not distinguish east from west, day from night. Spreading out my sitting mat or putting out my eating bowls, defecating or urinating, active or still, speaking or silent, everything was "to where does the one return?" Without any discursive thought—even if I had wanted to think of something else, it was impossible. Just like being nailed or glued to it, however hard you try to shake loose, it won't budge.[16]

Great care is needed here as well, since sublime insights and ecstatic glimpses may explode on the scene and be mistaken for awakening. From an account of Xueyan Qin (d. 1287):

> All the actions of daily life between heaven and earth, all the things of the world, things seen with the eye and heard with the ear, things I had up until now disliked and discarded, as well as ignorance and the defilements—I saw that from the outset they are my own wonderful brightness and flow from my true nature. For half a month no other characteristics of movement, not even tiny thoughts, arose. Unfortunately, I did not encounter the worthy eye of an expert. I ought not to have just sat in that state. An ancient called this "not dropping off understanding, blocking knowing things as they really are."[17]

No matter how profound the insight or experience, it will not do as long as the old patterns remain, as long as the old mind-wheel still churns. Yet as long as one thread of self-attachment remains, fear may hold one back. Thus self remains in this half-frozen state; thus the seemingly ice-cold words and actions of a compassionate teacher, and the extreme rigor of Zen monastic life.

"Die the one great death, then return to life!" is a common expression for the breaking up of this great doubt, as is "the mind of samsara [birth-death] shattered" and "the iron mountain crumbles." More prosaic expressions abound, such as "the pail of lacquer smashed," and "a bean buried in cold ash explodes." Being without self, the inviolable dignity of each and every thing is now manifest. Chan teacher Ziyong Chengru (ca. 1645–?) sums it up in a Dharma talk she gave during retreat:

> The wise men of old spontaneously pointed at things around them then uttered a phrase. These exclamations were *huatou* that drove practicers into pitch darkness. Suddenly the doubt block shatters—then for the first time you realize people now are no different than the wise men of old and the wise men of old are no different than people now. Thirteen years ago, this mountain monastic [Ziyong Chengru] embraced her *huatou*. Forgetting sleep and food, simple and steady like a fool, I was as if dead. Now thirteen years later: soft spring sun in clear blue sky illumines everywhere without exception![18]

This is what koan practice is for, at least initially: this is one's original face, the mind that is buddha.

From Koan to Huatou: Dahui and Honing the Heart of the Koan

Edo period Japanese Zen scholar-monk Mujaku Dōchū (1653–1744) described Dahui's approach this way. "Dahui considers the shattering of the mind of samsara to be the most important thing. This is not necessarily bound up with zazen meditation."[19] By the time of Dahui in the twelfth century, koans had already been formulated into detailed koan cases. This led to literary feats by learned monks that probed and sublimely expressed awakening. Dahui, on the other hand, fixed the focus of koan practice on the *huatou*, the heart of the koan. Compiler-author of the *Chan Whip Anthology*, Yunqi Zhuhong (1535–1615), described *huatou* as the koan's "compelling single word or phrase." Zen scholar Jeffrey Broughton adds "*that presses in upon one—so urgent, of such great moment that one must do something right now*."[20] *Huatou* is the slippery abyss of the koan where one falls into it. No longer "a koan" or "the koan," now it is one's own quandary that must be resolved.

As seen earlier with Gaofeng Yuanmiao, the *huatou* of the koan "All returns to one; to where does the one return?" is "to where does the one return?" With layman Pang's koan, "Who is the one transcending all phenomena?" the *huatou* is "Who is the one?" This is what is locked onto, rather than "transcending all phenomena," which can lead to endless discursive thought about various phenomena. Dahui even suggested that the *huatou* of this koan inspired him to use *huatou* as a basic teaching tool.[21] The Korean tradition has faithfully followed Dahui's *huatou* practice; the most basic *hwadu* (*huatou*) in Korean Zen is virtually the same: "What is this?" It derives from the previously mentioned sixth patriarch's response to the monk who came from Mount Song: "Who is this that's come?"[22] On the other hand, in Japan the distinction between koan and *huatou* is largely ignored, with the word "koan" covering the basic meaning of both terms.[23]

Unlike koan practice, *huatou* practice developed in Song Dynasty (960–1279) China specifically for laypeople. Monastics stayed for extended periods of sustained practice under a teacher; laypeople usually could not. *Huatou* took the more complex, literary practice developing around koan cases in the monasteries and streamlined it so the basic work could be done directly in the world on one's own. Dahui and others such as Gaofeng Yuanmiao described the lay world as the ideal place for *huatou* practice.[24] Indeed, the Chan term most commonly used for this sustained focus on the *huatou* was not a technical Buddhist term, of which there were many. Rather, the individual was to concentrate (*gongfu*; J. *kufū*) on it as artisans carefully focus on their work. The term suggests paying constant attention to and carefully working on what is at hand.[25]

Dahui's *huatou* focus is considered a crucial innovation in koan practice. It served as a corrective to serious dangers he saw, such as attachment to "silent illumination"[26] (a term he used disparagingly to mean a meditation practice that neither rouses great doubt nor expresses awakening) and "lettered Chan."[27] Genuine concentration (*gongfu*) pares the koan down to its essential point or *huatou*, which is none other than one's original face, that is, mind as buddha. As innovative as Dahui's *huatou* practice seems, it is also the natural and inevitable culmination of koan practice in the world.[28] It could also be considered a return to the roots in an effort to free koan practice of its top-heavy literary leanings.

The Koan of Literary Zen: Living Words, Not Dead Words

Dahui focused on the *huatou* for good reason. There was a strong tendency in his time toward "lettered Chan," where intellectual understanding and clever repartee took precedence over experience. Dahui often criticized Confucian literati and scholar-officials, many practicing under his guidance, for their ability to give brilliant answers to everything under the sun—while failing to illumine the one great doubt underfoot. He recommended a healthy dose of dullness.[29]

Dahui's teacher Yuanwu Keqin (1063–1135) stressed live words or phrases instead of dead ones.[30] Not a matter of avoiding certain "dead" words and using others that are "live," but rather of breathing life into the words used. Certainly some words are more abstract and tend to remove the reader/listener from, rather than usher them into, the subject at hand. More than the words themselves, however, it is a matter of how they are handled. Words can be used to transcend words, to illumine **this**.

Gateless Barrier is a fairly straightforward, straight-shooting koan textbook. *Blue Cliff Record*, on the other hand, is a masterpiece of Chan literature. Compiled and coauthored by Dahui's teacher Yuanwu and based on an earlier work by Xuedou Chongxian (980–1052), simple koan cases are turned into elaborate texts with several layers of interlinear poetry and prose. According to Zen scholar Robert Buswell: "A more complex genre of literature can hardly be imagined, rivaling any of the exegetical commentaries of the doctrinal schools."[31] In Japan, it has become de rigueur for teachers to go even further and add their own commentaries.

The account of Yuanwu's awakening gives a glimpse of the subtlety and sublimity with which he would imbue *Blue Cliff Record*. One day when Yuanwu's teacher Wuzu Fayan (1024?–1104) was visited by an official, the teacher recited the following verse to him, but it was Yuanwu in attendance who got it:

> Repeatedly she calls [her servant] Little Jade, though she needs nothing;
> She just wants her beloved to hear her voice.[32]

At the risk of explaining it away, suffice it to say that through this verse, teeming with worldly sentiment, Wuzu Fayan adroitly expressed effortless, freeflowing sense experience—freed of the very self-attachment and yearning normally associated with such verse. Thus his attending disciple Yuanwu awakened upon hearing his teacher reciting it. However, after finding students in one-on-one encounters blindly repeating statements they memorized from *Blue Cliff Record*, Dahui is said to have destroyed his teacher's work. And it does seem to have gone out of circulation for well over a century after that. An afterword in a Yuan Dynasty (1279–1368) reprint states that Dahui burned the *Blue Cliff Record* to save students from making such mistakes, then adds: "The intention which originally compiled this book and that which burned it were one. How could they be different?"[33] It seems that treating koans as little more than "scriptural exegesis" and "ritual re-enactment" can be traced back at least to Dahui's time.

Koan Practice as *Kōjō*: Continuing On, Ever Further

From the outside, awakening may seem like the end of koan practice. It is also the beginning of "after-awakening practice"—literally "after-satori practice." Terms such as satori and *kenshō* (literally "seeing the nature") were basically synonyms for awakening. They have been avoided here since in much modern literature and practice they have been trivialized into mental states, insights, and glimpses.What is after-awakening practice? In a word, awakening directed toward a specific purpose, such as to clearly express being without self so as to help others realize it, to bring it to life in various circumstances so as to be of service to others, and to remove any stink of awakening. For example:

> Qingliang Taiqin (d. 974) said to the assembly: "At first I intended to pass my time secluded deep in the mountains. But troubled by the unfinished koan of my teacher, I emerged and am now completing it for you." A monk came forward and asked: "What is this unfinished koan?" Qingliang struck the monk and said: "What the ancestors leave unfinished, their descendants must deal with!"[34]

A more general term in Japanese for after-awakening practice is *kōjō*, which refers to continuing on, ever further. Hakuin often mentions, "The further you go the deeper it gets." This sums it up. In its broader sense, *kōjō* can refer to the entire practice after awakening. Inspired by Hakuin, several koan curricula have developed in Japan containing hundreds and hundreds of cases, often with several koans each, not to mention capping phrases. This has made koan practice more approachable as a kind of common currency; it has also subjected it even further to role-playing imitation and ritual re-enactment. The general outline of these koan curricula has already been introduced in English.[35]

Zen scholar-monk Victor Sōgen Hori has detailed how koan practice is both quintessentially Buddhist and Chinese, even how antecedents can be found in Chinese literary games.[36] This in no way dilutes the basic point of koan practice: awakening—truly being without self—is not an end in itself. How could it be? By its very nature, it does not remain stuck to itself, or to anything, but freely and compassionately expresses being without self in thought, word, and deed, without leaving a trace. Why would it? This is body and mind, sense experience in its entirety, resurrected—freely flowing directly from the source, rather than through the lens of self.

The Koan of Koan Practice: Awakening as the Standard

Muzhou's younger brother in the Dharma, Linji (J. Rinzai)—the purported father of koan Zen—clearly struggled with his own great doubt: "In the past, when I had as yet no realization, all was utter darkness."[37] And several statements attributed to Linji have become classic koan cases. However, Linji did not use the term "koan." And when he used similar terms, he was condemning their abuse: "worthless contrivances of the men of old," "seize upon words from the mouths of those old masters and take them to be the true Way," "inscribe the words of some dead old guy in a great big notebook, wrap it up in four or five squares of cloth, and won't let anyone look at it. . . . Blind idiots! What kind of juice are you looking for in such dried-up bones!"[38] Koans were clearly not Linji's standard criterion for awakening.

Guishan Lingyou (see koan four, discussed earlier) lived at the same time as Muzhou and Linji and was known for the statement, "Take awakening as your standard." Centuries later, Dahui often used it in his letters to laypeople.[39] It puts the "eccentricities" of figures like Muzhou and Linji, not to mention Guishan's refusal to "teach" his disciple Xiangyan, in a suggestive light. It serves as a departure point for genuine koan practice and a fine koan in its own right.

The Koan of Authority or the Authority of the Koan

By contrast, several centuries later, Zhongfeng Mingben (1263–1323) stated: "If there is something about a Zen student's realization that the student cannot settle on their own, they will ask the teacher and **the teacher, on the basis of the koans, will settle it for them.**"[40] With Zhongfeng, previous koan cases, rather than the living source from which they come, have taken on a life of their own and have become the standard criterion. Perhaps this view of koans as arbiter had something to do with how koan practice developed in Japan from around this time.

Zen scholar T. Griffith Foulk insightfully argues: "It is a convention of the dialogue genre in Chan/Zen literature that the voice of the master . . . always represents the standpoint of awakening, speaks with the greatest authority. . . . The mark of the master, or rather the formal position of master, is to have the last word and pronounce the ultimate judgment."[41] While the literature can be interpreted this way, and Zhongfeng might even seem to agree, it has little to do with living koan practice. The formal one-on-one interview, commonly called *dokusan* or *sanzen* in Japanese, does begin with the student bowing to the teacher. Once this is done, however, the two face each other without a hair's breadth between. In fact, for a genuine one-on-one encounter, both teacher and student **must** drop all premise, pretense, and posturing. Mere ritual re-enactment or scriptural exegesis will not do here. "Realization equaling the teacher's diminishes its worth by half; only realization surpassing the teacher is worthy of continuing the lineage."[42] Opposite of blind authority or imitation, this statement of Baizhang Huaihai (720–814), a leading Dharma heir of Mazu, is celebrated in the Zen tradition for expressing what is required of a worthy student—and teacher.

Conclusion

What, finally, is a koan? T. Griffith Foulk asserts, "The idea that 'anything can serve as a koan' . . . is a modern development; there is scarcely any precedent for it in the classical literature. . . ."[43] While his point is well taken, classical Japanese Zen teacher Nanpo Jōmyō (aka Daiō Kokushi; 1235–1309) stated: "Although the number of koans is said to be only one thousand seven hundred, actually the mountains and rivers, the great earth, the grasses and trees, the forests—whatever is seen by the eyes, whatever is heard by the ears—all of these are koans."[44] Almost anything can serve as a koan—provided it is taken to the root.

Properly used, koan practice serves as a direct and immediate method that homes in on the root of the problem. Many koans originated naturally as an individual's great doubt that had to be asked and resolved at that time and place. They did not begin as handy cases plucked from published collections with standard answers appended. Over time, koans were passed down or developed specifically to help rouse great doubt by focusing on the problem-challenge inherent in the *huatou*, which is none other than the problem-challenge inherent in and as oneself.

In conclusion, koan practice is a catalyst to awaken as Gautama Buddha did. While this is true, it needs to be tempered with a humble awareness that koan practice often fails. This is a troubling facet of koan practice that requires great care and acumen. Koans are constantly in danger of becoming literary playthings. Koan practice, too, is constantly in danger of becoming imitation and re-enactment, or greed seeking after some insight or experience. Seeking to have all one's problems magically solved through a koan can itself be a huge problem that blinds one to the real issue underfoot. Self can corrupt anything it comes into contact with, including zazen meditation and koans.

Tragically, even these may degenerate into escapes from the fundamental problem they were meant to reveal and heal. After all, depending on what one does with them, koans are priceless treasures or hollow shells.

A living koan is not found in a book or transmitted from someone on high. It is found a bit closer to home. The signboard at the entrance to Zen temples throughout Japan welcomes visitors with "Look underfoot."[45]

Notes

1. See Victor Sōgen Hori, "Kōan and Kenshō in the Rinzai Zen Curriculum," in *The Koan: Texts and Contexts in Zen Buddhism*, ed. S. Heine and D. S. Wright (New York: Oxford University Press, 2000), 280–315; and Victor Sōgen Hori, *Zen Sand: The Book of Capping Phrases for Kōan Practice* (Honolulu: University of Hawai'i Press, 2003), 5–15. For koan as problem, challenge, probe, and expression, see Jeff Shore, "Koan Zen from the Inside" (Kyoto: Hanazono University, 1995): https://beingwithoutself.files.wordpress.com/2011/10/koan-zen-from-the-inside.pdf.
2. *Jingde Transmission of the Lamp*: T2076 .51.0291a28–b03. In English, see Chang Chung-yuan, *Original Teachings of Ch'an Buddhism* (New York: Vintage Books, 1971), 107–15.
3. On the meaning and significance of great doubt, see Boshan and J. Shore, *Great Doubt: Practicing Zen in the World* (Somerville, MA: Wisdom Publications, 2016).
4. John R. McCrae, *Seeing through Zen* (Berkeley: University of California Press, 2003), xix, 5–6. Also see John R. McCrae, *The Platform Sutra of the Sixth Patriarch* (Berkeley: Numata Center for Buddhist Translation and Research, 2006), xiv. Dunhuang version in Philip Yampolsky, *The Platform Sutra of the Sixth Patriarch* (New York: Columbia University Press, 1967). The original face koan can be found in case 23 of Zenkei Shibayama, *Zen Comments on the Mumonkan [Gateless Barrier]* (New York: Harper & Row, 1974). T2005 .48.0295c22.
5. See Yoshitaka Iriya, *Hō-koji Goroku* (Tokyo: Chikuma Shobō, 1973). In English, see James Green, *The Sayings of Layman P'ang: A Zen Classic of China* (Boston: Shambhala, 2009).
6. See Mario Poceski, *Ordinary Mind as the Way: The Hongchou School and the Growth of Chan Buddhism* (New York: Oxford University Press, 2007), 168–70.
7. See case 30, Shibayama, *Zen Comments*. T2005 .48.0296c27.
8. See case 5, Shibayama, *Zen Comments*. T2005 .48.0293c01.
9. See Yoshitaka Iriya, *Baso no Goroku* (Kyoto: Zen Bunka Kenkyūsho, 1984), 107–10.
10. "In all major koan collections, koans featuring Master Yunmen are more numerous than those of any other master." Urs App, *Master Yunmen* (New York: Kodansha International, 1994), 242.
11. *The Record of Yunmen*: T1988 .47.0547a10-26. See App, *Yunmen*, 107–8.
12. See Boshan and Shore, *Great Doubt*.
13. Philip Yampolsky, *The Zen Master Hakuin: Selected Writings* (New York: Columbia University Press, 1971), 146, slightly amended. See Katsuhiro Yoshizawa, *Oradegama* (Kyoto: Zen Bunka Kenkyūsho, 2001), 157, 493–94.
14. Robert E. Buswell, "The Transformation of Doubt," (2012): https://terebess.hu/zen/mesterek/Gaofeng-Buswell.pdf, 1, slightly amended. Also see Robert E. Buswell, "The 'Short-Cut' Approach of *K'an-hua* Meditation: The Evolution of a Practical Subitism in Chinese

Ch'an Buddhism," in *Sudden and Gradual: Approaches to Enlightenment in Chinese Thought*, ed. Peter N. Gregory (Honolulu: University of Hawaii Press, 1988), 373 n.126.

15. Katsuhiro Yoshizawa, *The Religious Art of Zen Master Hakuin* (Berkeley: Counterpoint, 2009), 250. Also see Norman Waddell, *Hakuin's Precious Mirror Cave* (Berkeley: Counterpoint, 2010), 25–26.
16. Buswell, "Transformation," 7–8, slightly amended.
17. Jeffrey L. Broughton, *The Chan Whip Anthology: A Companion to Zen Practice* (New York: Oxford University Press, 2015), 90, slightly amended.
18. *Ziyong Ru chanshi yulu*, in *Zhonghua dazang jing di er ji* (Taipei: Xinwenfeng chubanshe, 1987), Vol. 39, 820b. See Beata Grant, *Eminent Nuns: Woman Chan Masters of Seventeenth Century China* (Honolulu: University of Hawai'i Press, 2009), 168.
19. Broughton, *Chan Whip*, 3, slightly amended. Also see Jeffrey L. Broughton, *The Letters of Chan Master Dahui Pujue* (New York: Oxford University Press, 2017), 26, 34. Also see Broughton, *Chan Whip*, 95 n.153.
20. Broughton, *Chan Whip*, 30.
21. See Broughton, *Letters*, 11.
22. See Robert E. Buswell, *The Zen Monastic Experience* (Princeton, NJ: Princeton University Press, 1992), 155.
23. "In Japanese Rinzai Zen the word *watō* [*huatou*] is a synonym for koan." I. Miura and R. F. Sasaki, *Zen Dust: The History of the Koan and Koan Study in Rinzai (Lin-chi) Zen* (New York: Harcourt, Brace, & World, 1966), 248.
24. See Broughton, *Letters*, 9–15. Also see Miriam Levering, "Ch'an Enlightenment for Laymen: Ta-Hui and the New Religious Culture of the Sung," PhD diss., Harvard University, 1978, 210–13, 310–11. For Gaofeng, see Buswell, "Transformation," 9.
25. See Broughton, *Chan Whip*, 4–5, 64, 80. Also see Broughton, *Letters*, 23–26. Popularly called *kung fu*, though its connection with martial arts is dubious. See Broughton, *Chan Whip*, 4. 工夫 is also written 功夫. See Miura and Sasaki, *Zen Dust*, 257 n.45.
26. See Broughton, *Chan Whip*, 76–78. Also see Broughton, *Letters*, 16–20, and Levering, "Ch'an Enlightenment," 260–82.
27. See Buswell, "Short-Cut," 345.
28. See Buswell, "Transformation," 5.
29. See Broughton, *Letters*, 15–16, 191–94; Levering, "Ch'an Enlightenment," 255–60.
30. Similar terms can already be found among Yunmen's disciples. See Ding-Hwa Evelyn Hsieh, "Yuan-wu K'o-Chin's (1063–1135) Teaching of Ch'an *Kung-an* Practice," *Journal of the International Association of Buddhist Studies* 17 (Summer 1994): 81 n.45.
31. Buswell, "Short-Cut," 345. For another interpretation, see Hsieh, "Yuan-wu."
32. See Hori, *Zen Sand*, 528, slightly amended. Also see Hsieh, "Yuan-wu," 82.
33. Quoted in Levering, "Ch'an Enlightenment," 32–33.
34. Case 75, Thomas Yūhō Kirchner, *Entangling Vines: Zen Koans of the Shūmon Kattōshū* (Kyoto: Tenryu-ji Institute for Religion and Philosophy, 2004), 39, slightly amended.
35. See the pioneering works of Hori such as *Zen Sand*. Also see Miura and Sasaki, *Zen Dust*, and Shore, "Koan Zen from the Inside."
36. See Hori, *Zen Sand*, 5–7, 41–61.
37. Ruth Fuller Sasaki, *The Record of Linji* (Honolulu: University of Hawai'i Press, 2009), 283, slightly amended.
38. Sasaki, *Record of Linji*, 166, 216, 237, 260, 278.

39. "Inquiring exhaustively into the Dharma Principle, take awakening as your standard." See Broughton, *Chan Whip*, 166, and Broughton, *Letters*, 179, 210, 288, 310, 311.
40. My emphasis. Quoted in Miura, *Zen Dust*, 6, slightly amended. See Z. Noguchi and S. Matsubara, *Chūhō Myōhon Sanbō-yawa* (Tokyo: Kyuko-Shoin, 2015), 84, 86.
41. T. Griffith Foulk, "The Form and Function of Koan Literature: A Historical Overview," in Heine and Wright, *The Koan*, 33–34.
42. See Sasaki, *Record of Linji*, 328–29.
43. Foulk, "Form and Function," 26.
44. Quoted in William M. Bodiford, *Soto Zen in Medieval Japan* (Honolulu: University of Hawai'i Press, 1993), 146–47, slightly amended. Hakuin writes: "What is true meditation? It is to make everything: coughing, swallowing, waving the arms, motion, stillness, words, action, the evil and the good, prosperity and shame, gain and loss, right and wrong, into one single koan." Yampolsky, *Hakuin*, 58. See Yoshizawa, *Oradegama*, 38, 265.
45. See case 85, Kirchner, *Entangling Vines*, 44; similar expressions include: "Illumine underfoot" and "Watch your step!"

Further Reading

Boshan and J. Shore. *Great Doubt: Practicing Zen in the World.* Somerville, MA: Wisdom Publications, 2016.

Broughton, Jeffrey L. *The Chan Whip Anthology: A Companion to Zen Practice.* New York: Oxford University Press, 2015.

Broughton, Jeffrey L. *The Letters of Chan Master Dahui Pujue.* New York: Oxford University Press, 2017.

Buswell, Robert E. "The 'Short-Cut' Approach of K'an-hua Meditation: The Evolution of a Practical Subitism in Chinese Ch'an Buddhism." In *Sudden and Gradual: Approaches to Enlightenment in Chinese Thought*, ed. Peter N. Gregory. Honolulu: University of Hawai'i Press, 1988, 321–77.

Buswell, Robert E. *The Zen Monastic Experience.* Princeton, NJ: Princeton University Press, 1992.

Hori, Victor Sōgen. "Kōan and Kenshō in the Rinzai Zen Curriculum." In *The Koan: Texts and Contexts in Zen Buddhism*, ed. S. Heine and D. S. Wright. New York: Oxford University Press, 2000, 280–315.

Hori, Victor Sōgen. *Zen Sand: The Book of Capping Phrases for Kōan Practice.* Honolulu: University of Hawai'i Press, 2003.

Miura, Isshū, R. F. Sasaki. *Zen Dust: The History of the Koan and Koan Study in Rinzai (Lin-chi) Zen.* New York: Harcourt, Brace, & World, 1966.

Mohr, Michel. "Emerging from Nonduality: Kōan Practice in the Rinzai Tradition Since Hakuin." In *The Koan: Texts and Contexts in Zen Buddhism*, ed. S. Heine and D. S. Wright. New York: Oxford University Press, 2000, 244–79.

Sasaki, Ruth Fuller. *The Record of Linji.* Honolulu: University of Hawai'i Press, 2009.

Shibayama, Zenkei. *Zen Comments on the Mumonkan.* New York: Harper & Row, 1974.

Shore, Jeff. "Koan Zen from the Inside." Kyoto: Hanazono University, 1995. https://beingwithoutself.files.wordpress.com/2011/10/koan-zen-from-the-inside.pdf

PART V

HUMAN AND NONHUMAN INTERACTIONS

The dominance of monotheistic religious traditions in Euro-American academic studies of religion has contributed to the widespread characterization of Buddhist traditions as atheistic, at least according to what were taken to be their earliest and most authentic forms, and this perspective has also deeply influenced Buddhist modernist discourses. Because this analysis implicitly drew upon Christian and Jewish cosmologies organized around an all-powerful creator god, the absence of a universal creator deity in Buddhist cosmologies contributed to the characterization of Buddhism as atheistic, despite the prominence of numerous gods and other superhuman agents in Buddhist narratives, including traditional accounts of the Buddha's divine rebirths in his past lives. This orientation likewise resonated with nineteenth-century accounts that represented early Buddhist tradition as a form of rationalistic philosophy sharply contrasted with Hindu theistic cosmologies and forms of devotional practice. Beginning in the mid-twentieth century, field-based ethnographic studies of a diversity of cultural communities shaped by Buddhist traditions have explored in greater depth the dynamics of human interaction with nonhuman agents, though often within an analytical framework informed by a great tradition–little tradition hierarchy in which elite text-based doctrinal systems were contrasted with popular forms of practice focused on pragmatic, this-worldly concerns.

The three chapters in this section highlight the centrality of human and nonhuman interactions in a variety of Buddhist communities. In Chapter 20, Jeffrey Samuels explores a wide range of practices of veneration and offering directed by Buddhists toward the material manifestations of the Triple Gem or Refuge, including buddhas, texts, and members of the sangha. He points, in addition, to the deep integration of such devotional practices with Buddhist ideals of mental discipline. Richard Payne's Chapter 21 focuses on Buddhist *homa* offerings, exploring how these tantric practices facilitate the practitioners' identification of body, speech, and mind with the deities evoked in the rituals. His analysis highlights how tantric practice moves beyond the common Buddhist distinction between sudden and gradual modes of awakening by enabling a praxis of transmutation. In Chapter 22, Stephen Jenkins demonstrates the centrality of heavenly rebirths and pure lands in early Indian Buddhist traditions and illuminates the historical development of a multitude of Buddhist practices directed toward their realization. Taken together, the three essays testify to the central importance accorded forms of practice that mediate human and nonhuman interactions in a wide range of Buddhist traditions and historical periods.

CHAPTER 20

PRACTICES OF VENERATION AND OFFERING

JEFFREY SAMUELS

CENTRAL to the lives of most Buddhists across the globe are practices of veneration and offerings. While archaeological evidence suggests that such practices go back to the very beginnings of Buddhist history,[1] the centrality of veneration and offerings has not always been recognized in earlier Buddhist scholarship.

Practices of veneration and offerings not only punctuate the daily lives of monastic and lay Buddhists (e.g., daily offerings of food or flowers), but also more occasional times when calendrical rituals and ceremonies (such as celebrating the Buddha's birthday and marking the end of the rains retreat) are often focused occasions for such practices.

In most Buddhist countries, many acts of veneration and offerings are preceded by Buddhists paying homage to the Buddha and going for refuge to what is known as the three jewels or gems (*triratana/tiratana*), which are regarded to be at the heart or center of the religion: the Buddha, the teachings (Dharma/*dhamma*), and the community of monastics or Buddhist adepts (sangha). In tantric Buddhism, a fourth refuge is added to the three: one's tantric master or guru.

Given the centrality of these three in the lives of Buddhists, I will, in this chapter, organize the range of practices of veneration and offerings around them. After exploring the practices of veneration and offerings in relation to the three jewels, I will then explore the psychological and sociological dimensions of such practices.

PRACTICES OF VENERATION AND OFFERING TO THE BUDDHA

The key figure in the Buddhist tradition is the Buddha himself, known by his given name as Siddhartha, or in relationship to his family and clan names as Gautama/Gotama or

Shakyamuni/Sakkamuni. As a historical figure who more than probably lived during the fifth century BCE, he is, in many ways, at the center of the religion, as it is from him that we have received the second jewel—the teachings—and from him that the third jewel—the monastic community—emerged.

The Buddha is made present through images and statues found at Buddhist temples, at wayside shrines, in home temples, and so on. The presence of the Buddha is additionally experienced through relics, which are most often housed in reliquary mounds (stupas or *chaityas* or pagodas) which are commonly hemispherical monuments. Like statues, reliquary mounds are often key sites for veneration and offerings, where supplicants may meditate, cicumambulate the structure, and make offerings.[2] These images and sites of relics, regardless of where they are located, are treated with utmost respect and, symbolizing the Buddha's virtue and wisdom, are a focus for offerings and practices of veneration.

While any offering, given with the purity of the supplicant's heart and mind, is acceptable, the most common offerings include light (e.g., lighting a candle or oil lamp), flowers, incense, food, and liquid (most commonly water). What is important in all forms of giving is that the objects donated are considered pure. In Sri Lanka, for instance, some people offering cooked food will not taste the food prior to giving it, as doing so is believed to contaminate it, thus making it impure.

Prior to giving these objects, verses recounting the virtues of the Buddha may be recited, which are then followed by individual verses for each object given. In the Theravada tradition, such verses are recited in the language associated with the Buddha's speech (Pali), rather than in vernacular languages (e.g., Sinhala, Thai, Cambodian, and so on). At temples, one would also find donation boxes near the images of the Buddha and devotees often leave money to support the temple and the community of monks. In making such offerings, supplicants will often kneel in front of the statue and after reciting certain verses in their mind or even audibly, they will bow down in front of the statue, thus physically signifying the Buddha's superior status.

Alongside the Buddha, offerings are also made and verses of veneration are also expressed toward other buddhas. In Theravada Buddhism in South and Southeast Asia, for example, the twenty-eight buddhas (which include Shakyamuni and the twenty-seven buddhas who are believed to have preceded him, along with the future Buddha, Metteyya or Maitreya) are venerated.

BUDDHAS IN EAST ASIA

Just as other buddhas are recognized in the Theravada tradition and are recipients of offerings and veneration by Buddhists living in South and Southeast Asia, so too are other buddhas acknowledged in East Asia. One key difference, though, is that while Shakyamuni is regarded as the central figure in the Theravada world, his popularity—in East Asia—may be eclipsed by other more accessible buddhas.

Out of the plethora of buddhas that are recognized in East Asia, the most popular buddha in China, Korea, and Japan is Amitābha/Amitāyus (Āmítuófó [Chinese] or Amida [Japanese]). Amitābha (i.e., the Buddha of Infinite Light)—also known as Amitāyus (the Buddha of Infinite Life)—is the central buddha of Pure Land Buddhism, one of the most popular forms of Buddhism practiced in East Asia. According to that tradition, Amitābha is said to be currently residing in the Western Pure Land of *sukhāvatī*. As a buddha who has not yet entered final or complete enlightenment, as Shakyamuni did in his eightieth year, Amitābha is regarded to be more accessible to devotees.

Practices of veneration and offerings toward Amitābha are centered around paying homage to him through repeating phrases of recollection, such as "homage to Amitābha" (Sanskrit: *namo Amitābha*; Chinese: *namo Āmítuófó*; Japanese: *namo Amida Butsu*) and by making offerings to images of Amitābha. In doing so, devotees not only are able to direct their minds and hearts toward Amitābha, but also are able to achieve benefits in this world (such as health and well-being) and in the next. Indeed, such practices as recollecting Amitābha's name are believed to result in the accumulation of faith in him; this faith, in turn, will result in the supplicant being reborn in Amitābha's Western Pure Land at the moment of death. Another important practice is visualizing Amitābha and his Pure Land (which includes his attendant bodhisattvas). Finally, as with Shakyamuni, practices of veneration are also accompanied by acts of offerings toward Amitābha. Such offerings include food, water, incense, light, and money.

Buddhas in the Himalayas

Amitābha is not only popular in East Asia; he is also well-recognized in the Himalayan region where Tantric or Vajrayana Buddhism is widely practiced. In that tradition, there are five great buddhas—Amitābha, Amoghasiddhi, Ratnasambhava, Akṣobhya, and Vairocana—to whom practices of veneration (in the form of repeating mantras, practicing meditation, visualizing the Buddha and his mandala) and offerings are made.

In addition to these five, there are a plethora of other buddhas, deities, and bodhisattvas recognized in the Vajrayana tradition and to whom practices of veneration and offerings are made. Some of the more popular deities and buddhas include Maitreya, Mahākāla, Vajrapāṇi, Samantabhadra, Kālacakra, Hevajra, and Vajradhara; popular bodhisattvas include Avalokiteśvara, Mañjuśrī, and Kṣitigarbha. Unlike other Buddhist traditions, there are also female bodhisattvas and deities recognized and to whom offerings are made. They include Tārā, Vajrayoginī, Marīcī, Viśvamātā, Vajravidāraṇa, and many more.

The main forms of veneration to buddhas, bodhisattvas, and other deities involve making eight types of offerings which are, more often than not, done daily: offering water for drinking, water for bathing, flowers, incense, light, perfume scent, celestial food, and sound (such as music, mantras, and prayers). A more simplified version of these offerings is done in the form of eight water bowls, with each of them symbolizing one of the traditional offerings. As in other Buddhist traditions, such offerings are accompanied by verses expressing one's veneration for the buddha.

Pilgrimage as Forms of Veneration and Offerings

Yet another form of veneration to the buddha(s) is pilgrimage. Most commonly, the sites for pilgrimage are those associated with the Buddha and are, largely, in and around the Indian Gangetic plain: Sarnath (outside Varanasi), where the Buddha preached his first sermon; Bodhgaya (in the state of Bihar), where the Buddha attained enlightenment; Kushinara (in Uttar Pradesh), where the Buddha passed away into final enlightenment; Lumbini (southern Nepal), where the Buddha was born; as well as a host of other sites where the Buddha performed a miracle, preached a famous sermon, or had a worthwhile encounter.[3]

Alongside these popular pilgrimage sites, many countries in the Buddhist world have their own specific sites for pilgrimage. For instance, in Sri Lanka, there are sixteen sites for pilgrimage (*solosmasthāna*) which are believed to be places visited by the Buddha. Along with these, there are other sites there and in other Buddhist countries that are said to contain either a relic of the Buddha (such as Shwedagon Pagoda in Myanmar, Tongdosa Temple in Korea, and Giác Lâm Pagoda in Vietnam, to name only a few) or famous Buddha images (such as Wat Pho and Wat Phra Kaeo in Thailand, Todaiji Temple (which houses an image of Vairocana Buddha) in Japan, and Jokhang Temple in Tibet, to name a few). Such places, as Ian Reader has illustrated through his study focused on Japan, have often become major national and international tourist destinations and are regarded as important dimensions of cultural heritage and history.[4]

It is important to bear in mind as one considers Buddhist pilgrimage that such activities are more than acts of veneration. Indeed, as John Holt points out, "[t]he Buddha's relics were popularly believed to be latent manifestation of miraculous power," and that by making a pilgrimage, that power is believed to affect the pilgrims themselves.[5]

Practices of Veneration and Offering to the Dharma

The second jewel that is often a recipient of offerings and practices of veneration is the Dharma which, in the Buddhist context, refers to the teachings. In the Vakkali Sutta in the Pali canon (found in the *Samyutta Nikāya*), the Buddha is purported to have visited the sick monk Vakkali. After a brief exchange about Vakkali's health, Vakkali admits to the Buddha that he is troubled by the fact that while he wanted to visit the Buddha in person, his illness prevented him from doing so. In reply to Vakkali's sense of trouble and remorse, the Buddha first asks, "What is there to see in this vile body?" He then goes on to say that "[h]e who sees Dhamma, Vakkali, sees me; he who sees me sees Dhamma. Truly seeing Dhamma, one sees me; seeing me one sees Dhamma." In saying this, the Buddha established an important relationship between himself, as the founder of the Dharma, and the teaching itself. Implicit in this relationship is that like the Buddha himself, the teachings or Dharma are worthy of veneration and offerings. In fact, just as Buddhists express their veneration by going for refuge to the Buddha and the community of monastics (sangha), so too do they go for refuge to the Dharma and express their veneration toward it through prostrating themselves.

The veneration and reverence expressed toward the Dharma are not only limited to going for refuge. In Buddhism, outward treatment of texts also indicates their important status. In Tibet, as in many other Buddhist regions, Buddhist texts are never placed on the floor, and prior to opening and reading a text, the book or manuscript is lifted up and touched to one's forehead. In certain ritual events in Sri Lanka, Buddhist texts may also be paraded. As a sign of respect and veneration, the texts are often placed on top of one's head, which—regarded as purest part of the body—reflects a form of ritualized obeisance. Some texts, such as the book of protection (*piritpota*) and the collection of tales of the Buddha's past lives (*jātaka*) are outwardly shown honor and veneration by referring to the texts themselves through the use of honorifics, such as *vahanse* or "Venerable One" in Sinhala.

Moreover, just as the Buddha's relics were enshrined in reliquary mounds (stupas or pagodas), so too are Buddhist texts, which—as we have seen—are sometimes equated with the Buddha himself, placed in such mounds. These stupas, which are seen as representing the Buddha through his word (*vacana*), are also honored and the recipient of offerings.

In addition to these practices, the Dharma is venerated by reciting it, copying it, and distributing it. Indeed, a number of Mahayana texts implore people to copy and distribute the texts themselves. For instance, in the *Tathāgatagarbha-sūtra*, we read that when someone finds enjoyment in the text and "accepts it, recites it, copies it, or even reveres but a single one of its metaphors,"[6] they will receive an innumerable amount of merit.

In chapter 10 of the *Lotus Sutra*, a very important and popular Mahayana text, we read that "[t]hose who shall take, read, make known, recite, copy, and after copying always keep in memory, . . . who by that book shall feel veneration for the Buddhas, . . . who shall worship that book with flowers, incense, perfumed garlands, ointment, powder, clothes, umbrellas, flags, banners, music, etc., and with acts of reverence such as bowing and joining hands, . . . I predict their being destined to supreme and perfect enlightenment."

Practices of Veneration and Offering to the Sangha

The third jewel, for which practices of veneration and offerings are often made, is the sangha. While the term *sangha* literally means multitude or assembly, it narrowly refers to the community of monks and nuns.

With the death of the Buddha, the communities of monks and nuns are regarded as playing a key role in keeping the religion and teachings alive. Indeed, as Rupert Gethin points out, the sangha has been responsible for learning the Dharma, teaching the Dharma, and (ideally) living according to the Dharma.[7] Thus, they are regarded not only as a place of refuge, but also as an incomparable field of merit in this world—an ideal recipient of offerings and veneration.

Despite the whole sangha being called an incomparable field of merit in this world, laypeople tend to be a bit more discerning as to who, in fact, is a worthy recipient. As Michael Carrithers's work illustrates, laypeople in Sri Lanka tend to view monastics who are more seriously engaged in meditation as being more worthy of offerings and that for some meditation temples, laypeople have to wait a year in advance to donate the day's meals.[8]

Discussing with laypeople in Sri Lanka how merit is earned, I too have been told that giving to a monastic that one deems more worthy results in more merit accrued. In my research on monastic culture in contemporary Sri Lanka, for instance, it became very evident that merit really only results when the heart-mind (Sinhalese *hita*; Pāli *citta*) feels pleased and happy, a notion that is also expressed in the Pali literature.[9] As aesthetics may play a key role in influencing one's emotions, it can be easily argued that aesthetics are central to practices of veneration and offerings.[10]

There are numerous ways in which laypeople make offerings to the sangha. Key forms of giving include clothing (most commonly in the form of robes), shelter, and medicine. Other forms of giving include the eight monastic requisites (i.e., three robes, alms bowl, razor, belt, water strainer, and sewing needle), or something needed for the monastery (e.g., books) or for the monks themselves (e.g., an umbrella or bed sheets or towels), and so on.

The most common form of giving to the sangha, however, is food. In some countries, such as Thailand and Laos, Buddhist monastics go on alms rounds daily, and the laity can be seen lining the street or the path they take to offer food and drink to them. In other cases, the laity sign up to offer a meal to a monastery or to a group of monastics. Depending on the size of the monastery and the number of lay patrons, several families may coordinate offerings on the same day; depending on the size of the village or city, the same family or families may offer food once a month or once every year or two. While during some acts of offering, such as the daily alms rounds, words are not often exchanged between donors and monastics, in other more formal settings, the monks recite verses that extoll giving as a meritorious act and the donors may also transfer the merit from giving to deceased relatives.

While living members of the monastic community are the most common recipients of offerings and veneration, offerings are also made to past Buddhist arhats and famous figures. As Justin McDaniel documents in his book on Thai Buddhist practices, famous monks who are no longer living are frequent recipients of offerings and practices of veneration.[11] One such monk, documented by McDaniel, is Venerable Somdet Toh, a monk who lived between 1788 and 1872. As someone who is believed to have "cured" the ghost Mae Nak and stopped her from haunting and harming those around her, as well as magically cured soldiers' gunshot wounds and accomplished other supernatural feats, Somdet Toh is regarded to be extremely powerful and is still the recipient of veneration and offerings despite being dead for almost 150 years. In fact, as McDaniel points out, the popularity of Luang Phor Toh, as he is affectionately known and whose images are found in both temples and personal altars, eclipses the Buddha in some temple environments. Other famous monks, such as the meditation master Phra Achan Man and Luang Pho Thuat, are also believed to be very powerful and, as such, are still revered today. Their images may decorate home altars as well as those in temples associated with them, and laity still pay respect to them and make offerings to the images today.

Due to their popularity, deceased Buddhist monks and saints are revered and are still the recipient of offerings in other Buddhist countries as well. In Japan, for instance, the monk Kūkai is extremely popular, and devout Buddhists may go on a long pilgrimage (approximately 1,200 kilometers) to visit the eighty-eight sites associated with him. Known as the Shikoku Pilgrimage, pilgrims frequent temples and other famous sites associated with Kūkai and express their devotion through practices of veneration and offerings at the sites.[12]

In Tibet, there are a plethora of famous monastics of the past who continue to receive veneration and offerings. Padmasambhava, also known as Guru Rinpoche, was a tantric yogi from the eighth century who traveled from India to Tibet to help construct the first Buddhist temple there and is later known for introducing Tantric Buddhism to Tibet and as the founder of the Nyingma lineage. As expressions of veneration, mantras and prayers are recited to Padmasambhava, and offerings are made to him as well. Believed to still be accessible to practitioners through a multitude of forms and emanations, there are immediate and long-term benefits that ensue from such practices of devotion, including health, long life, spiritual powers, peace, happiness, and even enlightenment.

Mental Cultivation Component to Practices of Veneration and Offerings

As I noted in the previous section, acts of veneration and offering to the Buddha, the Dharma, and the sangha are regarded to be highly meritorious actions and, as such, affect our present and future lives. According to Buddhist doctrine, our present lives and experiences are determined by our previous thoughts, words, and actions, which are not only limited to our present lives, but extend over previous lives as well. By doing good deeds, speaking in a proper manner, and thinking good thoughts, we are able to affect not only how we experience the world around us, but also our future lives as we move through the cycle of death and rebirth.

In general, good deeds that ensure our well-being are considered to be wholesome, and the way to accumulate merit falls into three groups of actions (*puññakiriyāvathu*): giving, morality, and mental cultivation. Giving, at the top of the list, is considered to be the easiest way to accumulate merit, as it not only helps others, but also, in the process, helps us reduce our own thoughts of greed and attachments.[13]

In another Buddhist list—the list of ten wholesome actions (*dasakusalakamma*)—giving is once again found at the top of the list. Also included in the list is *apacāyana*, which is often translated as honoring, worshipping, and paying reverence, and includes such people as one's parents, relatives, and teachers (both secular and spiritual). Thus, in this list, practices of offerings and veneration are regarded to be very wholesome activities that increase one's merit in this life and aid one on the path to a better rebirth and enlightenment.

What is worthwhile to keep in mind when we consider practices of veneration and offering, however, is the state of mind of the donor. Indeed, as it has been suggested to me and as I have argued elsewhere, despite the plethora of ways in which one can make offerings and engage in practices of veneration, what ultimately seems to determine whether such actions are efficacious in bringing benefit is the mental state of the donor. For an action to be considered meritorious and beneficial, it must be carried out with the right intention and with such mental qualities as non-greed, non-hatred, and non-confusion. To give an example: If I were to give to a monastic toward whom I felt anger, then I would probably not feel non-hatred and non-greed when I set out to complete the action, when I do the action, or when I reflect on the action. Instead, as I venerate them or make an offering to them, more than likely, my offering and my act of veneration would be accompanied by such thoughts as "Why am I giving to this monastic?" "There are more worthy monks or nuns to whom to make offerings," and so on. This, as both monks and laypeople in Sri Lanka conveyed to me, would affect or even taint any benefit that may come from such activities. What that means, then, is that since practices of veneration and offerings are viewed positively in Buddhism because they are seen as resulting in positive states of mind, the actions themselves must be undertaken with the correct intention and mental states.[14]

Practices of Veneration and Offerings in a Globalized World

In this last section, I would like to explore how practices of veneration and offerings may be used as a process of identity formation in the modern nation-state, drawing specifically on Malaysia as a case study. Implied in many of the examples given earlier is the fact that practices of veneration and offerings are undertaken not necessarily as a solitary affair but, instead, in groups. Whether it is a group of donors bringing food to monastics living in temples, groups of villagers or city dwellers lining the road to offer food to monks, people celebrating the life of the Buddha or deceased monks with fellow pilgrims, practices of giving and veneration also function as a way of bringing groups of people together for a shared purpose. This shared purpose may, in more multiethnic and multi-religious globalized societies, function to unite disparate groups of people under a common cause. The resultant greater sense of cohesion, as the following example suggests, may provide strength to groups for speaking in a single, unified voice and accomplishing things that would not otherwise be possible.

During May 2010, I was fortunate enough to be in Malaysia during Vesak, the full-moon day commemorating the birth, enlightenment, and death of the Buddha. While there, I attended two Vesak celebrations: the first one at the Sri Lankan Temple in Sentul, Kuala Lumpur, and the other at Buddhist Maha Vihara in Brickfields, Kuala Lumpur.

The larger of the two celebrations took place at Buddhist Maha Vihara. I arrived at the temple in the early afternoon where throngs of people—milling about—made donations to the temple, venerated the Buddha, paid their respect to the monks there, received blessings from the temple's resident monks, lit lamps, and stood in a long line to pay their respect to the temple's head monk. As the temple wasn't large enough for the burgeoning crowd, many of the visitors chose to walk around the adjacent streets where Vesak floats stood ready to make the twelve-kilometer procession through the city.

Although Buddhist Maha Vihara is ethnically Sri Lankan, the Sri Lankans who congregated at the temple were far outnumbered by other ethnic groups: Indian Tamils, Tibetans, a few Malays and Taiwanese and—by far the most numerous—Malaysian Chinese. The Vesak floats that were parked on the street mirrored the demographically diverse crowd at the temple: although the Brickfields temple and the other Sri Lankan temple in Sentul, Kuala Lumpur, had their own floats, they were lost in a sea of other floats such as those representing different groups of Theravada (including Burmese and Thai) and Mahayana Buddhists, as well as Vajrayana Buddhists, with some of their followers charged with carrying a hundred-foot-long *tangka* through the streets of Kuala Lumpur.

What is interesting to point out with regard to Vesak in Malaysia as a key and very visible form of veneration and offerings is how it functions socially in drawing together disparate global Buddhist and ethnic communities. Given Malaysia's ethnocracy,[15] the shared participation in large-scale religious celebratory rites such as Vesak provides a sense of unified Buddhist cohesion to otherwise disparate ethnic Buddhist communities (Sinhalese, Chinese, Burmese, and so on) who otherwise feel marginalized vis-à-vis the larger Malay-Muslim majority. In order to understand how this is possible, some background is necessary.

According to records,[16] Ven. K. Gunaratana, who came to Malaysia in 1926 and became the head monk of the Mahindarama Temple in 1933 (and subsequently the chief monk of Malaya and Singapore) played an instrumental role in "getting Vesak day to be gazetted a public holiday in 1949" at a time when Malaya was under British colonial rule.[17] Historical accounts recount that in March 1949, a meeting that was attended by over five hundred people representing thirty-one Buddhist temples, and "all races and nationalities in the Settlement of Penang," was held in Penang. During that meeting, a three-part resolution was put forth and agreed upon: (1) to adopt Wesak Full Moon Day as the Buddha's Birthday, (2) to request the Government to grant a Public Holiday on that occasion, and (3) to form "The Wesak Holiday Committee, Penang" to carry out item 2. That same year, the British High Commissioner, Sir Henry Gurney, gave his support to the idea and requested that the committee "take the matter up with each State or Settlement separately as public holidays were legally under the control of each State and Settlement."[18] In 1949, the states and settlements of Penang, Malacca, Kedah, and Perak approved Vesak as a public holiday, and the other states of Malaysia soon followed suit. Finally, on January 3, 1962—five years after independence—it was announced that "the Federation Government had declared Wesak Full Moon Day a Federation-wide holiday with effect from 1962."[19]

A closer look at the events that led up to declaring Vesak as a national holiday, however, also reveals certain tensions and fissures that existed within the Buddhist community. According to Lim Teong Aik, the decision to make Vesak a public holiday originated with Ven. K. Gunaratana, a Sinhalese monk who preached frequently in Hokkien to the Chinese community that gathered at the Penang Buddhist Association and his own Mahindarama temple. Despite Ven. Gunaratana's social capital among the Chinese and Sinhalese Buddhists in Penang, a division arose along ethnic lines concerning when Vesak should be celebrated. Lim explains that when the "opinions of leading Buddhists including monks were sought . . . [the] Chinese Buddhists wanted to celebrate the occasion on the 8th Day of the Chinese 4th Moon, but the Southern Buddhists (Singhalese, Siamese and Burmese) insisted on the orthodox day[,] i.e. the Wesak Full Moon Day."[20] Realizing that the governor-general at the time, Malcolm McDonald, would only agree to making Vesak a public holiday after the different communities had settled their dispute, a deal was brokered through Khoo Soo Jin and Khoo Soo Ghee, and the Chinese community agreed on the Vesak full moon for the public holiday. It was only at that time that a non-sectarian committee that represented the different Buddhist communities was established.

Although there were previous instances of different ethnic communities coming together, the story of Vesak points to the first concerted effort, of which I am aware, of multiple ethnic Buddhist communities working together to fulfill a common Buddhist aim in Malaysia. Indeed, a look at the fifteen-person Wesak Holiday committee illustrates that while the majority of members were Chinese (including the chairman, secretary, and correspondent), the committee also included Thai (Nai Deng Sararaks and Nai Wan Charasvirochana), Sinhalese (W. A. Ariyadasa and M. B. Jinadasa), and Burmese (Maung Swee Nee and Maung Swee Dong) representatives, as well as an Indian (Mr. M. Saravanamuttu) as the adviser.

When I spoke with a number of the participants in the Vesak celebrations in 2010, many of them were quick to share with me how impressive the Buddhist communities are in Malaysia. They were quick to note how all the different communities of Buddhists are here together as one and how that show of unity for a common purpose is important in Malaysia, where smaller communities are often marginalized by the government and the Malay majority. While it is true that some underlying tensions still exist beneath the surface, the overall sense of social cohesion was definitely palpable, a fact of which most attendees were quite proud.[21]

Despite the fact that the Vesak celebrations in which I participated reflected a diversity of Buddhist traditions and ethnic communities, the shared participation in the ritual allowed smaller, disparate ethnic communities to feel that they are part of something larger vis-à-vis the Malay-Muslim majority. By participating in the ritual, they were no longer confined to their specific ethnic identity. Instead, they were able to adopt a much more encompassing Buddhist identity through which they were able to view themselves as part of a larger gobal society of Buddhists that extended well beyond the Malaysian nation-state.

Notes

1. See, for instance, Gregory Schopen, *Bones, Stones, and Buddhist Monks: Collected Papers on Aracheology, Epigraphy, and Texts of Monastic Buddhism in India* (Honololu: Univerity of Hawai'i Press, 1997).
2. For a more complete discussion of relics, see Kevin Trainor, *Relics, Ritual and Representation in Buddhism: Rematerializing the Sri Lankan Theravada Tradition* (Cambridge: Cambridge University Press, 2007), as well as David Germano and Kevin Trainor, eds., *Embodying the Dharma: Buddhist Relic Veneration in Asia* (Albany: State University of New York Press, 2004). For a discussion of stupas and their religious and historical significance, see Anna Liberta Dallapicccola and Stephanie Zingel-Avé Lallemant, eds. *The Stūpa: Its Religious, Historical, and Architectural Significance* (Wiesbaden, Germany: Steiner, 1980).
3. For a general discussion of pilgrimage, see Ian Reader, *Pilgrimage: A Very Short Introduction* (Oxford: Oxford University Press, 2015). For an exploration of how pilgrimage may function as a way for Tibetans to develop their own relgion and society, see Toni Huber, *The Holy Land Reborn: Pilgrimage and the Tibetan Reinvention of Buddhist India* (Chicago: University of Chicago Press, 2008).
4. Ian Reader, *Making Pilgrimages: Meaning and Practice in Shikoku* (Honolulu: University of Hawai'i Press, 2004).
5. John C. Holt, "Pilgrimage and the Structure of Sinhalese Buddhism," *The Journal of the International Association of Buddhist Studies* 5, no. 2 (1982): 83.
6. William H. Grosnick, "The Tathāgatagarbha Sūtra," in *Buddhism in Practice*, ed. Donald S. Lopez Jr. (Princeton, NJ: Princeton University Press, 1995), 103.
7. Rupert Gethin, *The Foundations of Buddhism* (Oxford: Oxford Paperbacks, 1998).
8. Michael Carrithers, *The Forest Monks of Sri Lanka: An Anthropological and Historical Study* (Oxford: Oxford Univesrity Press, 1983).
9. See Maria Heim, *Theories of the Gift in South Asia: Hindu, Buddhist, and Jain Reflections on Dana* (New York: Routledge Press, 2004).
10. This has been more fully explored in Jeffrey Samuels, *Attracting the Heart: Social Relations and the Aesthetics of Emotions in Sri Lankan Monastic Culture* (Honolulu: University of Hawai'i Press, 2010).

11. Justin T. McDaniel, *The Lovelorn Ghost and the Magical Monk: Practicing Buddhism in Modern Thailand* (New York: Columbia University Press, 2014).
12. This is explored at length in Ian Reader, *Making Pilgrimages: Meaning and Practice in Shikoku* (Honolulu: University of Hawai'i Press, 2004).
13. For a full treatment of giving in Sri Lankan Buddhism, see Toshiici Endo, *Dāna: The Development of Its Concept and Pracitice* (Colombo, Sri Lanka: Gunasena, 1987).
14. Jeffrey Samuels, "Is Merit in the Milk-Powder? Pursuing Puñña in Contempoary Sri Lanka," *Contemporary Buddhism* 9, no. 1 (2008): 123–47..
15. The concept of ethnocracy as it relates to Malaysia is developed in Geoff Wade, "The Origins and Evolution of Ethnocracy in Malaysia," Paper 112 of *The Working Paper Series* (Singapore: Asia Research Institute, 2009).
16. Ven Witanachchi Indaratana, C. Elgiriye, and Lilianne Lim, *Mahindarama Buddhist Temple: 85 Years of History (1918–2003)* (Penang, Malaysia: Mahindarama Dhamma Publications, 2004).
17. Indaratana et al., *Mahindarama*, xxx.
18. Lim, Teong Aik, *Malaysian Buddhist Association Silver Jubilee Anniversary Special Publication (1959–1984)*, n.d., 35–38.
19. Lim, *Malaysian Buddhist Association*, 37.
20. Lim, *Malaysian Buddhist Association*, 36.
21. Some of this is explored in Jeffrey Samuels, "'Forget Not Your Old Country': Absence, Identity, and Marginalization in the Practice and Development of Sri Lankan Buddhism in Malaysia," *South Asian Diaspora* 3, no. 1 (March 2011): 117–32.

Further Reading

Dallapicccola, Anna L., and Stephanie Zingel-Avé Lallemant, eds. *The Stūpa: Its Religious, Historical, and Architectural Significance*. Wiesbaden, Germany: Steiner, 1980.

Endo, Toshiici, *Dāna: The Development of Its Concept and Pracitice*. Colombo, Sri Lanka: Gunasena, 1987.

Carrither, Michael. *The Forest Monks of Sri Lanka: An Anthropological and Historical Study*. Oxford: Oxford Univesrity Press, 1983.

Germano, David, and Kevin Trainor, eds. *Embodying the Dharma: Buddhist Relic Veneration in Asia*. Albany: State University of New York Press, 2004.

Heim, Maria. *Theories of the Gift in South Asia: Hindu, Buddhist, and Jain Reflections on Dana*. New York: Routledge Press, 2004.

Huber, Toni. *The Holy Land Reborn: Pilgrimage and the Tibetan Reinvention of Buddhist India*. Chicago: University of Chicago Press, 2008.

McDaniel, Justin T. *The Lovelorn Ghost and the Magical Monk: Practicing Buddhism in Modern Thailand*. New York: Columbia University Press, 2014.

Reader, Ian. *Pilgrimage: A Very Short Introduction*. Oxford: Oxford University Press, 2015.

Samuels, Jeffrey. *Attracting the Heart: Social Relations and the Aesthetics of Emotions in Sri Lankan Monastic Culture*. Honolulu: University of Hawai'i Press, 2010.

Samuels, Jeffrey. "Is Merit in the Milk-Powder? Pursuing Puñña in Contempoary Sri Lanka." *Contemporary Buddhism* 9, no. 1 (2008): 123–47.

Schopen, Gregory. *Bones, Stones, and Buddhist Monks: Collected Papers on Aracheology, Epigraphy, and Texts of Monastic Buddhism in India*. Honololu: Univerity of Hawai'i Press, 1997.
Siezmore, Russell F., and Donald K. Swearer, eds. *Ethics, Wealth, Wealth and Salvation: A Study in Buddhist Social Ethics*. Columbia: University of South Carolina Press, 1990.
Trainor, Kevin. *Relics, Ritual and Representation in Buddhism: Rematerializing the Sri Lankan Theravada Tradition*. Cambridge: Cambridge University Press, 2007.

CHAPTER 21

RITUAL IDENTIFICATION AND PURIFICATION IN ESOTERIC PRACTICE

RICHARD K. PAYNE

Prefatory Anecdote

THE first time I ever saw a tantric fire ritual (Skt. *homa*, Jpn. *goma*) was long before sunrise on New Year's Day, 1981, at the Shingon temple in Sacramento.[1] The temple was dark inside, with about 200 people in attendance. Sitting there, we watched as the priest, Rev. Taisen Miyata, entered the *naijin*, the inner ritual area at the front of the temple, sat at the altar, and started a fire in a hearth built into the altar itself. As the flames began to glow, a *taiko* drum started a steady beat, and the sangha began chanting the *Heart Sutra* in unison, over and over again.

As the drum and chanting continued, the flames leapt up and died down repeatedly—five times, once each for protectors, bodhisattvas, Chief Deity, and the Celestial and Worldly Deities. Sitting in the dark with the flames rising and falling, the drum beating, and the sangha chanting was a powerful experience—moving, not in a sentimental sense, but rather in the intensity of combined visual and auditory sensations.

Introduction

As indicated by this volume itself, after having long been overshadowed by the study of Buddhist doctrine, the study of practice has become recognized as central to the field of Buddhist studies. Most important to this development is the recognition that meditation is neither the sole, nor normative form of Buddhist practice. Instead, the Buddhist tradition is constituted by a wide range of ritual and yogic practices, including but extending well beyond meditation. This change in perception of Buddhist practice correlates with a change in attitude toward tantric Buddhism. In this chapter we examine a particular tantric ritual, the *homa*, which is paradigmatic for tantric practice more generally. The first section introduces the *homa*, emphasizing its characteristic as a votive rite, its place in the contemporary tantric Buddhist world, its historical background, and the structure of the *homa* found in Shingon—one of the tantric Buddhisms of modern Japan. Next, while modern scholarship has employed the semiotic pairing of sudden and gradual to articulate the process of awakening, if instead we consider different conceptions of purification, we find that there are three identifiably distinct metaphors. The final section looks at what the *homa* with its symbolically central act of ritual identification can tell us about the embodied character of Buddhist ritual more generally.

What Is the *Homa*?: Tantric Votive Rite

Performed in many temples and shrines in contemporary Japan, a *homa* involves a fire built on the altar, with offerings made into it.[2] In terms of the conceptual categories employed in the field of religious studies, the *homa* is better understood as a votive offering than as a sacrifice. Although to an observer a sacrifice and a votive offering may appear indistinguishable, the two categories are marked by distinct attitudes.[3] To sacrifice is to give up something by making it sacred, out of reach of human use, and often this means to destroy what is being made sacred.[4] Such destructive acts are sometimes propitiatory (appeasing a deity, making a deity happy), or expiatory (repentance or contrition: making up for having done something wrong). Though it also places offerings out of human use, a votive offering is a different religious modality—it is more explicitly an act of exchange, and in some cases occurs when a vow has been fulfilled. This includes not only objects given in exchange, but also actions. One might, for example, pledge to go on a pilgrimage if one's son is healed. Performing that pilgrimage is then a votive offering as well.[5]

Homa in the Contemporary Tantric Buddhist Cosmopolis

Throughout the tantric Buddhist cosmopolis today, one can find *homa* (Jpn. *goma*) rituals being performed in a variety of settings. In Japan the *homa* is most commonly associated with Shingon and the tantric dimension of Tendai. However, *homa* rituals are also found in Shugendō and several of the new religious movements of Japan such as Shinnyo-en and Agonshū.

The *homa* has several different ritual functions. Contemporary Japanese thought identifies a set of five: protection, prosperity, subjugation, emotional affinity, and summoning.[6] In addition to these different functions, a variety of different buddhas, bodhisattvas, and protectors can be evoked as the ritual's main figure; "Chief Deity" is the general term used for this central figure, whoever it may be. Changes of function modify such ritual details as the shape of the hearth, time of day best performed, color of the practitioner's garb, and the form of some of the key mantras employed in the course of the ritual.[7] Different Chief Deities receive different mantras, or mantras modified to correspond to them, and are visualized in distinct ways. In the present forms of the *homa* as employed in Shingon, all of these variations are made within a common ritual structure.[8]

Beyond Japan, the *homa* continues today as part of the ritual repertoire throughout the tantric cosmopolis. For example, Tibetan and Nepali traditions have *homa*s that are usually performed outdoors on temporary altars as part of a larger ceremonial complex, making them more similar to Shugendō practices than to Shingon versions, which are most frequently held inside temples and as stand-alone rituals. *Homa* rituals are also quite commonly practiced in Hindu forms of tantra, and the practice of *homa* has been exported internationally.[9] In some of these cases, the contemporary traditions tend toward a sanitization of their own origins, expunging tantric associations because of its modern disrepute. When deploying the *homa*, these traditions may characterize it more in terms of a yogic culture of practice, rather than as an explicitly tantric practice.

Historical Background to the Tantric *Homa*

Contemporary *homa* practice demonstrates a continuity of ritual culture extending back to Vedic and Iranian sources. In much of contemporary scholarship, Vedic rituals of fire offerings are considered to be the predominant source for tantric forms of *homa*, though the details of this continuity remain unclear. The primary action of making offerings into a fire and the appropriated metaphor of feasting an honored guest that organizes the ritual actions are key indicators suggesting continuity. More problematic, however, is the relation between the ritual organization of Vedic and tantric rites—one detailed study, for example, shows that a paradigmatic Vedic rite, the *agnihotra*, and *homa* do not share a common organizational structure.[10]

Vedic ritual forms date back perhaps as much as 4,000 years or more, and along with Iranian rites are themselves rooted in older practices of Indo-European religious culture.[11] One of the threads linking the Buddhist tantric *homa* to Vedic practices as such is the figure of Agni, who will be discussed more fully later in relation to the major sedimentary layers of contemporary tantric Buddhist ritual—two of which are Vedic and tantric ritual cultures.

Ritual Sediment Underlying the *Homa*

Agni is fire, that is, fire as such, not a god who inhabits fire or who is symbolized by fire. Having a critical role in Vedic ritual from its very earliest period, he is one of the oldest of the Vedic deities. Agni is all kinds of fire, from wildfires and lightning to the cremation fire, the fire of digestion, and the fire of sexuality. His function in Vedic ritual is to transform the offerings by burning, converting them to their scent so that they can ascend into the celestial realm of the gods and ancestors. The offerings are part of a feast being given to honored guests, and the transformation of burning makes the feast offerings available to the guests. As Lopez notes, "The burning of the offering in the sacrificial fire transforms or, rather, transubstantiates the nature and character of what is being offered. Every offering is transubstantiated into *medha* 'juice, essence, aroma,' which is then available to the gods for eating, and *asu* 'life force.' "[12] While this constitutes a transformation, it is not a purification in the sense of purifying something material (and therefore impure) into something spiritual (and therefore pure.) The gods cannot consume ordinary food, and need the offerings transformed into the kinds of substances they can eat, which are odors.[13] While this burning does not involve a symbolic purification of an impure (material) substance, the leftovers from the ritual offerings are considered polluted—in the sense of being potent and dangerous, and therefore needing to be disposed of properly. As the god of fire who converts the offerings into a form accessible to the guests, Agni appears as the first deity to receive offerings in the contemporary Shingon *homa*.

Symbols, such as Agni, do not have a singular, universal meaning. What a symbol means depends upon its place in a network of symbolic uses, that is, on its context. Thus, what Agni means in the context of tantric Buddhist ritual practice is not the same as what Agni means in the Vedic context. The symbolism of purifying the offerings by etherealizing them into scent continues as a kind of ritual sediment upon which the tantric Buddhist *homa* is built. While adaptation of the ritual from Vedic antecedents to tantric Buddhist form retained Agni as a key figure, the doctrinal reframing of the ritual changed from that of making purified offerings to the gods and ancestors to awakening through ritual identification, which is both symbolically and structurally central to Buddhist forms of the *homa* ritual.

Structure of the *Homa*

In contemporary Shingon *homa* rituals, the fire offerings as such take place within a larger frame ritual devoted to Fudō Myōō (Acalanātha Vidyārāja, the Immovable Lord, King of Wisdom), who is the paradigmatic Chief Deity for the frame ritual, no matter who the Chief Deity in the sequence of five fire offerings may be. In Shingon rituals, such as those priests learn during their training, the norm is for there to be two sets of offerings, primary and secondary,[14] offered to Fudō Myōō as the Chief Deity of the frame ritual. Following the first four of the seven secondary offerings, the practitioner begins the sequence of *homa* offerings. Upon finishing the *homa* offerings, the balance of the secondary offerings is completed.

While historically different numbers of sets of *homa* offerings are known, in contemporary Shingon *homa*, as mentioned previously, there are usually five sets of offerings. Each set of offerings is directed toward a different deity or set of deities. These are Agni

(Jpn. Katen), the Lord of the Assembly, the Chief Deity (Jpn. *honzon*), the Thirty-Seven Deities (buddhas, bodhisattvas and protectors of the Vajradhātu mandala[15]), and the Worldly Deities (Vedic and astral deities).

Structurally then, although each of the five sets of offerings is made to different deities, they are made in the midst of the larger frame ritual's offerings to Fudō Myōō (Acalanātha Vidyārāja), the Chief Deity of the frame ritual. Significantly, the five sets of offerings fall between the time that the practitioner ritually identifies with Fudō Myōō and dissociates from that identification. Ritual identification does not take place in any of the five sets of offerings. Instead, those sets of offerings are being made by the identity of practitioner and Chief Deity.[16]

Ritual Identification of Practitioner and Deity in the Ritual Program of the *Homa*

Given the lengthy history of the *homa* and its transmission to several different religious cultures, there are a vast number of ritual manuals prescribing different forms of the ritual. In the Shingon tradition, these share a characteristic that is found throughout Buddhist tantric praxis: ritual identification of the practitioner with the deity. This idea itself has different expressions and different doctrinal formulations, as for example in Dzongkhapa's focus on it as the defining characteristic of tantric Buddhism.[17] Ritual identification of the practitioner and the deity evoked into the fire takes place as three ritual acts, known as the "three mysteries" (*sanmitsu*), one each for the identity of the practitioner's body, speech, and mind with those of the deity. These are bodily merging of oneself and deity (*nyūga ga nyū*), spoken invocations (*shōnenju*), and contemplation of the wheel of syllables (*jirinkan*).[18] Actual performances of these are by posture (*āsana*), recitation of mantra, and contemplating the significance of key *bīja* mantra by means of reciting a formulaic text.[19]

The symbolism of ritual identification is that there is another kind of three-way identification, in this case between the deity, the practitioner, and the fire. Thus, the mouth of the hearth is also the deity's mouth and the practitioner's. The fire in the hearth is also digestive fire and at the same time the transformative fire of the deity's wisdom.[20] The material offerings made into the fire are also symbolic offerings made to the deity, and at the same time the practitioner's obscurations (*āvaraṇa*), that is, their own mistaken conceptions and misplaced affections (*jñeyāvaraṇa*, and *kleṣāvaraṇa*, respectively), which are transformed from their negative forms to positive ones. In addition to the five explicit functions identified earlier, tantric rituals were interpreted as conducive to awakening. Ronald Davidson has described this, saying, "Like the transformation of wood into ash, this interpretation emphasized the simultaneous transmutation of the personality afflictions into forms of awakened being, by means of their purification in the fire of gnosis."[21] In the same way that the contextual difference between Vedic ritual and tantric Buddhist ritual affects the significance of Agni, so also does the interpretive context of the nature of the obscurations change the significance of the ritual identification from one of purifying ("etherealizing") to transforming. Looking more specifically at metaphors for the process of awakening allows us to understand ritual identification as an alchemical transmutation, revealing one's always and already awakened state.

Metaphors of the Process of Awakening

Scholarship on the idea of awakening has largely been dominated by a twofold model. In the South Asian context, that has been the dichotomy of "leap" and "path."[22] On the East Asian side, although the conceptual dichotomy is fundamentally the same, the terminology has been "sudden" and "gradual."[23] These metaphors are based on consideration of the nature of the path from ground to goal. Does it require slow, steady progress, such as the accumulation of merit over countless eons, or does it involve a leaping across that can only be done in a moment? Thinking instead from the perspective of "purification," however, we can see a different set of metaphors by which the process of awakening has been described. We suggest that a threefold schema provides a richer, more nuanced basis for understanding conceptions of the path. These three are cleansing, cultivating, and transmuting.

Cleansing: Purity as the Absence of Pollution

Cleansing presupposes that a pure state already exists under the obstacles and debris of negative mental and emotional states, and that one needs to clean those away—purity in this case being conceived in negative terms as the absence of pollution. This negative conception is not only found in the Buddhist tradition, but is grounded in the broader Indic culture, continuing into the present. In his study of the religious culture of modern Chhattisgarh village in the state of Madhya Pradesh, Lawrence A. Babb notes that "pollution is an existent; purity is its absence. To become pure is to rid oneself of pollution; it is not to 'add purity.' "[24] This "negative" understanding is also found in Buddhaghosa's treatment of the ten bad deeds. These are grouped into the three dimensions of human existence, body, speech, and mind: three bodily actions (killing, stealing, and sexual misconduct), four verbal actions (lying, malicious speech, harsh speech, and frivolous speech), and three mental actions (covetousness, malice, and wrong view).[25] The ten good deeds are "described as merely 'abstaining' (*virati*) from the 10 bad deeds."[26] Maria Heim explains that this logic is extended to the idea that "the highest kind of abstinence is not resisting temptation or following precepts, but being so advanced that the thought to commit a bad action never even enters one's head."[27] Here we see a rationale that at least resonates with one version of tantric antinomianism—not that of intentionally breaking the rules of monastic life, but of acting without negative motivation even when performing actions otherwise prohibited. This is consistent with some Theravadin interpretations of karma as consequent upon intentional acts—actions done without conscious intent (*cetanā*) do not create karmic consequences.[28]

One of the best-known instances of a metaphor for this negative conception of purification as cleansing is that of the mirror. This is found, for example, in the origin myth of Sōtō Zen. According to the Platform Sutra of the Sixth Patriarch, in order to select a Dharma heir, the Fifth Patriarch, Hongren, instructed his students to submit a verse demonstrating their attainment. All of the students deferred, thinking that Shenxiu, the senior-most student who was already their instructor, would naturally be chosen. Fearing that his own awakening was inadequate, Shenxiu himself hesitated to show the verse he wrote to his master, eventually writing it anonymously on the wall of a hallway at night. That verse read:

> The body is the *bodhi* tree;
> The mind is like a bright mirror's stand.
> Be always diligent in rubbing it—
> Do not let it attract any dust.[29]

Prior to the invention of modern mercury-coated glass mirrors, mirrors were made of polished metal, such as brass. Such mirrors easily lose their reflective sheen, and require regular polishing in order to maintain their utility. Hence the necessity of polishing the mirror becomes a metaphor for meditation as the means of maintaining a pure mind.

Huineng's response to Shenxiu also refers to this metaphor, but challenges its accuracy as representing the process of awakening:

> *Bodhi* is fundamentally without any tree;
> The bright mirror is also not a stand.
> Fundamentally there is not a single thing—
> Where could any dust be attracted?[30]

Cleansing metaphors also include aquatic imagery in which water is naturally pure. Images such as letting turbid water settle or disturbed water calm operate on the basis of this negative conception of purity as the absence of pollution. Cleansing metaphors reveal a view of the process of awakening in which purity is negatively conceived as the absence of pollution.

Cultivating: Agricultural Metaphors

Metaphors of cultivating point to an understanding of the process of awakening as one of clearing away the obstacles and debris of negative mental and emotional states in order to be able to propagate positive ones. And it also introduces images of merit as something that can be cultivated. A variety of agricultural metaphors found in the literature can be encompassed under cultivation as a general category.

We have already encountered the idea of "good roots" (*kuśala mūla*) in relation to the negative conceptions of cleaning metaphors. But the idea of good roots is itself an agricultural metaphor pointing to wet rice culture. When rice seedlings are transplanted into paddy fields, they need to have good roots—to not be dead, rotted, or withered. Similarly, there is the concept of a "field of merit" (*puṇyakṣetra*). Acts such as making donations to either the sangha as an institution or to individual monks or nuns constitutes planting seeds of merit in a field of merit.

A different use of "field" is the idea of a buddha field (*buddhakṣetra*). The descriptions of buddha fields convey the medieval Indian sense of what characteristics were desired. Maitreya's palace and pleasure grove in Tuṣita is considered by Gelukpa followers of Tsongkhapa to be a "purified field." Along with other characteristics, it is described as having the desirable characteristic of being far from a city, and "all the ground is made from a variety of precious stones that are smooth like the palm of one's hand, soft when pressed down upon and comfortable to walk on. It has lakes, water fountains, waterfalls, grassy meadows, and so forth which produce pleasure to touch."[31] The idea that a pure land is smooth, easy to walk on, and with plentiful water are consistent across many such descriptions, and indicate what is not desired—a dry land, with hills and rough surfaces.

While pure lands are described in such highly positive terms, the English term "pure land" derives from the Chinese *ching tu*, which is interpreted as "land that purifies." The best known of pure lands is Sukhāvatī, the pure land of Amitābha, and what is most critical about Sukhāvatī is that—unlike this realm—it is a place where there are no obstacles to one hearing the Dharma accurately, cultivating practice effectively, and attaining awakening.

Transmuting: An Alchemical Process

A third metaphor is that of alchemical transmutation in which the negative mental and emotional states are converted into positive ones. If not suggested by ideas about the nature of the unbeneficial roots (*akuśala mūla*), this kind of conception is at least compatible with it.[32] In the *Path of Purification* (P. *Visuddhimagga*), Buddaghosa (fl. fifth century CE) gives a typology of six personality types (*cariyā*), three of which are negative (being the three roots of affliction) and three positive—the positive and negative forms being inversions of each other. The greedy temperament correlates with a faithful temperament: "Greed seeks out sense desires as object, while faith seeks out the special qualities of virtue and so on. And greed does not give up what is harmful, while faith does not give up what is beneficial."[33] Similarly, a hating temperament corresponds with an intelligent one: "Hate seeks out only unreal faults, while understanding seeks out only real faults. And hate occurs in the mode of condemning living beings, while understanding occurs in the mode of condemning formations."[34] Lastly, the inverse of a deluded temperament is a speculative one: "For just as delusion is restless owing to perplexity, so are applied thoughts that are due to thinking over various aspects. And just as delusion vacillates owing to superficiality, so do applied thoughts that are due to facile conjecturing."[35] In contrast to Buddhaghosa's description of the ten good deeds as simply the absence of the ten bad deeds, discussed earlier, here the relation between the positive and negative temperaments suggests an alchemical conception that negative (or impure or ordinary, foolish person) can be converted to positive (or pure, or a buddha). This can be taken to imply that there is something like an underlying purity or undifferentiated unity which is expressible either in positive or negative form. In Indian systems of alchemy this is ash, which "is the supreme manifestation of primal matter."[36] Recall the previous quote from Davidson regarding the reduction of obscurations to ash in the *homa* fire.

This same logic is found in the *Laṅkāvatāra-sūtra*, which is an important source for the idea of the comprehensive ground of consciousness, *ālayavijñāna*. *Ālayavijñāna* is the karma-bearing unconscious which is pure in the sense of being neither positive nor negative, but which carries latencies depending on thoughts, decisions, and actions. The *Laṅkāvatāra-sūtra* says:

> Mind [*ālayavijñāna*] is always neutral.
> Mentation [karma producing thought] moves in two ways.
> The arising of consciousness [conscious awareness of objects]
> Is virtuous and nonvirtuous.

and then goes on:

> Mind is naturally clear.
> Mentation is what makes it turbid.
> Mentation together with consciousness
> Always plants latent tendencies.[37]

The idea of an underlying purity which is pure in the sense of being neither positive nor negative enables a logic in which negative or positive expressions can be converted one to another in a kind of mental alchemy.

Later than both the *Lotus Sutra* and Buddhaghosa's *Visuddhimagga*, the metaphor of alchemical transmutation is explicit in Śāntideva's *Bodhicaryāvatāra* (ca. 700 CE), where he adjures his practitioners to "[g]rasp tightly the quicksilver elixir, known as the Awakening Mind, which must be thoroughly worked."[38] Here Śāntideva is likening the conversion of an ordinary person into a bodhisattva to the kind of transformation effected by the alchemists' mercury. Stephen E. Harris has argued that this reference to alchemy is more than simply a literary flourish for Śāntideva. Instead, it is a second logic of awakening found in the text, the most frequent one being that of cleansing. The metaphor of cleansing includes equating the power of *bodhicitta* to eradicate "great vices in an instant" to the destructive power of the rain of fire that destroys the cosmos at the end of time.[39] Harris, however, finds the alchemical conception of transmutation itself to be a consistent enough theme throughout the work to constitute an alternative model of the working of *bodhicitta*. He calls attention to meditations that "invoke all three of the root *kleśas* of anger (*krodha*) craving (*tṛṣṇā*) and delusion (*moha*) and by far the most frequent strategy employed is to waken and redeploy their energy into liberative purposes."[40] Focusing on alchemical imagery, Harris suggests that "the energy of the *kleśas*, though defiled, when combined with *bodhicitta* will naturally fuel its own destruction and replacement by the force of the *kuśala dharmas* themselves."[41]

At the center of the *homa* is ritual identification in which the ritual practitioner and the buddha or bodhisattva evoked into the ritual enclosure become identical. This is a transmutative moment, such that the thought of awakening (*bodhicitta*) is actualized. Embodying the buddha, the practitioner's speech is the speech of the buddha, and his/her view of the world is the buddha's pure vision of the world as empty.

Theorizing Buddhist Ritual

Despite repeated efforts by many scholars, no widely accepted definition of ritual has emerged, suggesting that the task is misdirected by a now outmoded metaphysics. There is nothing about which a correct definition can be constituted. Instead, "ritual" is a socially constructed concept, which means it is constructed by use, rather than being an object about which a definition can be devised. Socially constructed, that concept is employed in both popular religious culture and in academic discourse. Regarding the latter usages, Kevin Trainor has said that "[t]he category of ritual itself has been produced and employed within a community of scholars with its own ritualized strategies for operating in the world."[42] In lieu then of a definition, we can draw on the two usefully general characteristics of ritual that Trainor has identified. Ritual is first "undeniably something that one does, i.e., it entails the use of one's body. . . . [And, second] ritual tends toward formality and away from spontaneity."[43] The first characteristic is relevant in relation to one theory of Buddhist ritual as primarily a matter of "seeing," while the second is evidenced by the historical continuity of ritual structures and metaphors discussed earlier in the chapter.

Four Stages of Ritual Identification

One suggestion about how to understand Buddhist ritual has been to consider it a Buddhist analogue of Hindu *darśan*, "wherein the supplicant ritually invokes the presence of a deity, and both supplicant and deity behold one another."[44] For much of tantric Buddhist thought, however, "deity yoga"—as it is known in Tibetan traditions—is a path of practice that only begins with seeing a buddha. The four interactions between the practitioner and the Buddha in deity yoga frequently begin with seeing, then proceed to laughing, embracing (or holding hands), and culminate in uniting.[45] As conceptualized in the four stages of deity yoga, uniting correlates with ritual identification in the performance of tantric ritual. The critical difference between a Mahayana philosophy of practice and a tantric one is ritual identification, "the act of generating oneself as the deity" (Tib. *bdag bskyed*), or in Shingon terminology, the "three mysteries" (Jpn. *sanmitsu*), which are the unity of the body, speech, and mind of the practitioner with the body, speech, and mind of the deity. José Ignacio Cabezón notes that, along with offerings and expiatory rites at the end of a ritual, ritual identification is "ubiquitous to tantric ritual generally."[46]

Embodied Awakening: Body, Speech, and Mind

Present-day representations of Buddhist practice frequently emphasize its mental aspect. On the one hand, this follows from the highly psychologized nature of contemporary American popular religious culture. On the other, many Buddhist understandings give the mind a central, determinative role in consciousness. Thus, because of the apparent congruence of these two, the representation of practice as a mental exercise is overdetermined. However, the underlying dualism of Western thought, which dichotomizes material and bodily from spiritual and mental, distorts the understanding of awakening by making the goal into a purely mental transformation.

Buddhist thought discusses the totality of human existence as a process having three aspects—body, speech, and mind—as in the three mysteries discussed previously. Highlighting this holistic conception of human existence, awakening involves the integral transformation of body, speech, and mind together. The import of embodiment is made evident in a text centered on Amitābha and Avalokiteśvara, the *Wuliangshou rulai guanxing gongyang yigui*. The practices prescribed by this text "are said to induce a *samādhi* wherein the practitioner's body becomes indistinguishable from the body of the deity. The power of this *samādhi*, claims the text, will bring about the eradication of defilement, allowing the practitioner to attain the highest level of rebirth in the Pure Land at death."[47]

A second characteristic of modern presentations of Mahayana interpret *bodhicitta* as the *intention* to become awakened, structuring this teleologically as a present unawakened state and a future awakened one. The tantric logic, however, asserts that one is always and already awakened, even if one doesn't act like it. Thus, *bodhicitta* is not about intention toward a future state, but rather thinking (*citta*) as awakened (*bodhi*), that is, actualizing the always already awakened state. Ritual actions of actualizing *bodhicitta* are not therefore merely assertions of pious intent, but are linked directly to the central ritual act of ritual identification. Ritual identification by means of the three mysteries of body, speech, and mind "do not bring about this union so much as they give form to it. In other words, the practitioner has always been one with the deity; the rites of the three mysteries merely enact, express, or realize this primordial state of affairs."[48] The performative complexity of the *homa* ritual reflects the complex symbolic and interpretive history of the ritual.[49] As a process of sedimentation, Vedic, Buddhist, Mahayana, and tantric layers have each been laid on top of one another, in some cases accentuating features in the lower layers, and in others blurring them.

Conclusion

Ritual identification as performed in the contemporary Shingon *homa* involves the full range of human existence as categorized by Buddhist thought: body, speech, and mind. It exemplifies the third metaphor of the process of awakening, alchemical transmutation of negative expressions of an underlying undifferentiated state into positive ones. In this case it is the primordial unity of practitioner and buddha that is made manifest in the ritual context. This conception of the process of awakening differs from the other two metaphors, cleansing and cultivating. These three metaphors together provide a fuller and more nuanced analysis of different conceptions than the long-standing semiotic pairing of sudden/leap and gradual/path.

The perspective on Buddhist ritual practice provided by an examination of tantric conceptions of ritual identification as a union proceeding in four steps also provides much greater depth than simply identifying Buddhist ritual as a corollary to Hindu *darśan*. In addition, ritual identification emerges as a tantric doctrinal component that is unique to the tradition. Tantra is more than simply a collection of free-floating yogic and ritual technologies that was "transmitted independent of any theoretical or doctrinal overlay."[50] It is instead a lived tradition in which practice and doctrine are integral to one another.

The *homa* is found throughout the tantric cosmopolis, Hindu, Buddhist, and Jain, and across the full range of Buddhist cultures from Nepal, through all of Inner Asia, to East Asia, and now internationally. It is a dramatic ritual performance, in which a fire is built by the practitioner, and offerings are made into that fire. The offerings are representative of the practitioner's own mental and emotional obscurations, while the fire is the wisdom of emptiness that purifies the practitioner's obscurations, converting them into pure offerings for the buddha. It is ritual identification of the practitioner's body, speech, and mind with the same three existential aspects of the deity that is central to the practice, and that at the same time makes the practice effective.

Notes

1. My thanks to Maria Heim, Dan Lusthaus, Charles Muller, and Gil Fronsdal for the kind assistance they provided.

   A preliminary version of these opening sections was presented as a public lecture at the University of Southern California's Shinso Ito Center for Japanese Culture and Religion. My thanks to Duncan Williams, the Shinso Ito Center, the University of Southern California, and Shannon Takushi for organizing the event.

2. In Japan, *homa* are most commonly encountered either as stand-alone rituals, or as the central event of a more extended ceremony. In other Buddhist cultures, however, *homa* also constitute a smaller part of a larger ceremonial, such as "to expiate faults of omission and commission in the enactment of the rite, and so as to 'satisfy the deity' "; José Ignacio Cabezón, "Introduction," in *Tibetan Ritual*, ed. José Ignacio Cabezón (New York: Oxford University Press, 2010), 16. Such a contextual change also modifies the significance of the ritual.
3. These terms—*sacrifice* and *votive offering*—are sublated from their contexts of origin in Greek, Latin, and early Christian religious practice, and are used here heuristically, rather than as absolutely distinct categories.
4. Douglas Hedley, "Sacrifice," in *The Oxford Handbook of Theology and Modern European Thought*, ed. Nicholas Adams, George Pattison, and Graham Ward (Oxford and New York: Oxford University Press, 2013), 346.
5. David E. Aune, "Prayer," in *The Oxford Handbook of Early Christian Ritual*, ed. Ristro Uro, Juliette J. Day, Rikard Roitto, and Richard E. DeMaris (Oxford and New York: Oxford University Press, 2019), 250–51.
6. Richard K. Payne, "Homa: Tantric Fire Ritual," in *Oxford Research Encyclopedia of Religion*, ed. John Barton (Oxford and New York: Oxford University Press, 2016), n.p..
7. On this latter point, see Richard K. Payne, "Mantra and Grammar: A Linguistic Dimension of Extraordinary Language," in *Investigating Principles: International Aspects of Buddhist Culture, Essays in Honour of Charles Willemen*, ed. Lalji "Shravak" and Supriya Rai (Hong Kong: Buddha-Dharma Centre of Hong Kong, 2019), 277–88.
8. While outside the specific ritual corpus of modern Shingon, ritual programs may vary in different religious traditions. However, other scholars have noted the consistent nature of ritual structures within specific traditions. Stephanie W. Jamison uses the metaphor of "ritual boxes" that are opened and closed in the course of a ritual performance; Stephanie W. Jamison, *Sacrificed Wife/Sacrificer's Wife: Women, Ritual, and Hospitality in Ancient India* (Oxford and New York: Oxford University Press, 1996), 52. Charles Orzech has referred to "boilerplate"; Charles D. Orzech, *Politics and Transcendent Wisdom: The Scripture for Humane Kings in the Creation of Chinese Buddhism* (University Park: Pennsylvania State University Press, 1998), 155; and Yael Bentor to "frames"; Yael Bentor, *Consecrations of Images and Stūpas in Indo-Tibetan Tantric Buddhism* (Leiden: E. J. Brill, 1996), 7–8. José Cabezón refers to this as a "narrative" ("Introduction," 17), which is, however, a second-order analysis of a relation that is dialectically both "model of" and "model for."
9. Richard K. Payne and Michael Witzel, eds., Homa *Variations: The Study of Ritual Change across the* Longue Durée (Oxford and New York: Oxford University Press, 2016).
10. Richard K. Payne, "Ritual Syntax and Cognitive Theory," *Pacific World: Journal of the Institute of Buddhist Studies*, 3rd series, no. 6 (2004): 195–227.
11. There are noteworthy similarities with not only Iranian, but also Greek and Roman ritual practices as well. In recent work, Holly Gether argues that the Iranian practices were not simply part of the Indo-European background to tantra, but had a direct influence in the medieval origins of the tantric *homa*. This is an interesting proposal, and deserves further study, though it remains in a preliminary stage of development. Holly Grether, "Tantric Homa Rites in the Indo-Iranian Ritual Paradigm," *Ritual Studies* 21, no. 1 (2007): 16–32; see also, "The Ritual Interplay of Fire and Water in Hindu and Buddhist Tantras," in Richard K. Payne and Michael Witzel, eds., Homa *Variations: The Study of Ritual Change across the* Longue Durée (Oxford and New York: Oxford University Press, 2016), 47–66.

12. Carlos Lopez, "Food and Immortality in the Veda: A Gastronomic Theology?" *Electronic Journal of Vedic Studies* 3, no. 3 (1997): 11–19 (slightly revised version available at https://www.academia.edu/3647011/Food_and_Immortality_in_the_Veda_A_Gastronomic_Theology; accessed January 11, 2019).
13. Lopez, "Food and Immortality in the Veda," 15.
14. The Japanese terms can be rendered as "regular" and "scattered."
15. The Vajradhātu is one of the two mandalas employed in the Shingon tradition, the other being the Garbhadhātu mandala. These provide an esoteric cosmology that is dialectically the ground for and reflected in the symbolism and organization of ritual practices.
16. Robert Sharf comes to the same conclusion, saying: "The fire ritual is thus framed by the recitations of the dispersed invocations [secondary offerings], and the practitioner is to remain in a state of unity with the principal deity throughout the fire offerings." Sharf, "Thinking through Shingon Ritual," *Journal of the International Association of Buddhist Studies* 26, no. 1 (2003): 81.
17. Jeffrey Hopkins, "Preface," in *The Great Exposition of Secret Mantra*, Vol. I: *Tantra in Tibet*, trans. Jeffrey Hopkins (1977. Reprint, Boulder, CO: Snow Lion, 2016) , vii–xii; viii.
18. Sharf, "Thinking through Shingon Ritual," 69–70.
19. On this last, see Richard K. Payne, *Language in the Buddhist Tantra of Japan: Indic Roots of Mantra* (London and New York: Bloomsbury, 2018), 82–85.
20. Yixing, T.1796: 39.662b7–13; cited in Sharf, "Thinking through Shingon Ritual," 71.
21. Ronald M. Davidson, *Indian Esoteric Buddhism: A Social History of the Tantric Movement* (New York: Columbia University Press, 2002), 141.
22. This dichotomy is the basis of Karl H. Potter's classic study, *Presuppositions of India's Philosophies* (1963. Reprint, Delhi: Motilal Banarsidass, 2002).
23. This was given expression in the collection Peter N. Gregory, ed., *Sudden and Gradual: Approaches to Enlightenment in Chinese Thought* (1987. Reprint, Delhi: Motilal Banarsidass, 1991).
24. Lawrence A. Babb, *The Divine Hierarchy: Popular Hinduism in Central India* (New York: Columbia University Press, 1975), 49.
25. Maria Heim, *The Forerunner of All Things: Buddhaghosa on Mind, Intention, and Agency* (New York: Oxford University Press, 2014), 67–68.
26. Heim, *The Forerunner of All Things*, 74.
27. Heim, *The Forerunner of All Things*, 75.
28. Heim, *The Forerunner of All Things*, 91–92.
29. John R. McRae, trans., *The Platform Sutra of the Sixth Patriarch* (Moraga, CA: BDK America, 2000), 20 (T. 348b).
30. McRae, trans., *The Platform Sutra of the Sixth Patriarch*, 22 (T. 349a).
31. James B. Apple, "Maitreya's Tuṣita Heaven as a Pure Land in Gelukpa Forms of Tibetan Buddhism," in *Pure Lands in Asian Texts and Contexts: An Anthology*, ed. Georgios T. Halkias and Richard K. Payne (Honolulu: University of Hawai'i Press, 2019), 188–222; 196.
32. The term *kusala*, and by implication its negative *akusala*, have been subject to some contestation. While often given ethical connotation (good or meritorious) in the commentarial literature, Lance Cousins argues that earlier usages indicate "produced by wisdom" or "skillful." Lance Cousins, "Good or Skillful? *Kusala* in Canon and Commentary," *Journal of Buddhist Ethics* 3 (1996): 136–64. Heim argues against the notion that the ethical significance is later, however. Instead, she suggests that the two meanings overlap: "there are

ways that moral sensitivity and awareness can be conceived as skillful, and ethically good action as well crafted." Maria Heim, *The Forerunner of All Things*, 57.

33. Buddhaghosa, *The Path of Purification* (Visuddhimagga), trans. Bhikkhu Ñāṇamoli (1975. Reprint, Seattle: BPS Pariyatti Editions, 1999), 97 (Ch. III, § 75).
34. Buddhaghosa, *The Path of Purification* (Visuddhimagga), 97 (Ch. III, § 76).
35. Buddhaghosa, *The Path of Purification* (Visuddhimagga), 97 (Ch. III, § 77).
36. David Gordon White, *The Alchemical Body: Siddha Traditions in Medieval India* (Chicago and London: University of Chicago Press, 1996), 283.
37. Karl Brunnhölzl, "Translator's Introduction," in *A Compendium of the Mahāyāna: Asaṅga's* Mahāyānasaṃgraha *and Its Indian and Tibetan Commentaries*, 3 vols. (Boulder, CO: Snow Lion, 2018), I:3–147; I:65.
38. Ch. 1, verse 10. Śāntideva, *The Bodhicaryāvatāra*, trans. Kate Crosby and Andrew Skilton (Oxford: Oxford University Press, 1995), 6.
39. Stephen E. Harris, "The Skillful Handling of Poison: *Bodhicitta* and the *Kleśas* in Śāntideva's *Bodhicaryāvatāra*," *Journal of Indian Philosophy* 45 (2017): 331–48; 332.
40. Harris, "The Skillful Handling of Poison," 335.
41. Harris, "The Skillful Handling of Poison," 340.
42. Kevin Trainor, *Relics, Ritual, and Representation in Buddhism: Rematerializing the Sri Lankan Theravāda Tradition* (Cambridge: Cambridge University Press, 1997), 137. Trainor is summarizing Catherine Bell, *Ritual Theory, Ritual Practice* (New York: Oxford University Press, 1992), 205f., 219.
43. Trainor, *Relics, Ritual, and Representation in Buddhism*, 137.
44. Robert H. Sharf, "Ritual," in *Critical Terms for the Study of Buddhism*, ed. Donald S. Lopez, Jr. (Chicago and London: University of Chicago Press, 2005), 257. It is important to note that Sharf is here talking not about all Buddhist rituals, but only about Buddhist invocation rituals, giving his claims the character of a tautology.
45. See Jeffrey Hopkins's translation of the introduction to Tsongkhapa's *Sngags rim chen mo*, published as *Tantra in Tibet* (London: George Allen & Unwin, 1977), 156–62. My thanks to Roger Jackson for assistance with this. Jackson further points out that the order is not the same in all instances. He also suggests that the earliest sources seem to be the *Hevajra* and *Saṃpuṭa* tantras (personal communication, email dated December 19, 2018).
46. José Ignacio Cabezón, "Introduction," in *Tibetan Ritual*, ed. José Ignacio Cabezón (Oxford and New York: Oxford University Press, 2010), 1–34; 18.
47. Sharf, "Thinking through Shingon Ritual," 72.
48. Sharf, "Thinking through Shingon Ritual," 70.
49. This history is more complex than the two-strata chronological analysis suggested by Sharf, who in turn draws on work by Phyllis Granoff. Sharf, "Thinking through Shingon Ritual," 83–84.
50. Sharf, "Thinking through Shingon Ritual," 57.

Further Reading

Abé, Ryūichi. *The Weaving of Mantra: Kūkai and the Construction of Esoteric Discourse*. New York: Columbia University Press, 1999.

Aune, David E. "Prayer." In *The Oxford Handbook of Early Christian Ritual*, ed. Risto Uro, Juliette J. Day, Rikard Roitto, and Richard E. DeMaris. Oxford and New York: Oxford University Press, 2018, 245–64.

Babb, Lawrence A. *The Divine Hierarchy*. New York: Columbia University Press, 1975.
Harris, Stephen E. "The Skillful Handling of Poison: *Bodhicitta* and the *Kleśas* in Śāntideva's *Bodhicaryāvatāra*." *Journal of Indian Philosophy* 45 (2017): 331–48.
Hedley, Douglas. "Sacrifice." In *The Oxford Handbook of Theology and Modern European Thought*, ed. Nicholas Adams, George Pattison, and Graham Ward. Oxford and New York: Oxford University Press, 2013, 345–60.
Padmakara Translation Group, trans. *A Feast of the Nectar of the Supreme Vehicle*. Boulder, CO: Shambhala Publications, 2018.
Payne, Richard K. "Homa: Tantric Fire Ritual." In *Oxford Research Encyclopedias, Religion*, ed. John Barton. Oxford and New York: Oxford University Press, 2016, n.p.
Payne, Richard K. "Ritual Syntax and Cognitive Theory." *Pacific World: Journal of the Institute of Buddhist Studies* 3rd series, no. 6 (2004): 195–227.
Payne, Richard K., and Michael Witzel, eds. Homa *Variations: The Study of Ritual Change across the* Longue Durée. Oxford and New York: Oxford University Press, 2016.
Sharf, Robert H. "Ritual." In *Critical Terms for the Study of Buddhism*, ed. Donald S. Lopez, Jr. Chicago and London: University of Chicago Press, 2005, 245–70.
Sharf, Robert H. "Thinking through Shingon Ritual." *Journal of the International Association of Buddhist Studies* 26, no. 1 (2003): 51–96.
Williams, Paul. "Some Mahāyāna Perspectives on the Body." In *Religion and the Body*, ed. Sarah Coakley. Cambridge: Cambridge University Press, 1997, 205–30.

CHAPTER 22

HEAVENLY REBIRTH AND BUDDHIST SOTERIOLOGY

STEPHEN JENKINS

INTRODUCTION

PRACTICES for attaining heavens constitute a theistic side of Buddhism crucial for understanding texts, soteriology, current relationships with deities, and the evolution of Buddhology and cosmology.[1] Such practices have been regarded, and often dismissed, as popular religion, concessions to lay spirituality, Hindu influences, or as distinctively Mahayanist or East Asian.[2] The apparent contradiction with "no-self" casts pursuit of heaven in a heretical light. How could there be identity with the rebirth? Heavens were diversions from the path, and *devatā*[3] must fall when their merit runs out. All these are misconceptions. This chapter focuses on non-Mahayana traditions, but shows that practices and beliefs typical of East Asian Pure Land have antecedents in early Indian tradition. Indic pure lands evolved naturally and explicitly from earlier traditions regarding heavens. Steven Collins wrote:

> It is easy to overlook the Buddhist heavens. Textbook depictions of Buddhism often reduce them to an incidental diversion, something like a pleasant vacation separate from the hard work of the path to *nirvana*. From a certain kind of abstract doctrinal view this is understandable, and it is certainly characteristic of Buddhist modernism; but it seriously distorts the place of the heavens in the pre-modern Pali *imaginaire*.[4]

The Buddhist "*imaginaire*" teems with *devatā*. Representations abound in sacred sites and narratives. Their cult vividly continues in Southeast Asia. Except among modernists, Theravadins still aspire to heavenly rebirth. Even in "abstract doctrinal views," heavens are ideal for attaining nirvana, not diversions, and meditation theory is systematically correlated with heaven-realm cosmology. Most Buddhist *devatā* have no Vedic antecedent, which shows they are not merely rhetorical deployments of "Hindu" deities.[5] The Vedic deities most honored among Buddhists, Brahma (a former monk and non-returner)[6] and Indra (a disciple and stream-winner)[7], are humiliated in the *purāṇas* and largely ignored in Hinduism. Indian traditions made competing claims for effective access to sustained heavenly birth. *Tīrthikas* so resented Maudgalyāyana for gathering converts with reports of celestial travels, where he met Buddhists in heaven and *tīrthikas* in hell, that they had him murdered.[8]

The standard "graduated talk," guiding listeners to "stream entry," has *sagga-kathā*, talk of heaven, as a stock element.[9] It is shown in the following that it is incorrect that *devatā* no longer make spiritual progress and necessarily fall when their merit runs out.[10] Although heavens are impermanent, and some *devatā* are poised to plunge into the hells, this is not so for Buddhists. They either ascend to higher heavens to attain nirvana or do so during their current heavenly lifetime.[11] The *Aṅguttara Nikāya* explains as follows:

> The worldling remains there all his life, and when he has completed the entire life span of those *devatā*, he goes to hell, to the animal realm, or to the sphere of afflicted spirits. But the Blessed One's disciple remains there all his life, and when he has completed the entire life span of those *devatā*, he attains final *nibbāna* in that very same state of existence. This is the distinction, the disparity, the difference between the instructed noble disciple and the uninstructed worldling.[12]

This reasoning is applied to every *devaloka* from that of the Four Great Kings to even, remarkably, the "*devatā* of the base of nothingness," who live sixty thousand eons and appear to be among the so-called long-lived *devatā*.[13]

There are reasons to regard heavenly birth as mistaken, including warnings not to confuse them with salvation or to be seduced by bliss. "Long-lived devata" are listed among "the eight inopportune times" that impede liberation. However, *dīrgha-ayuṣka-devatā* refers to a particular class of extreme longevity in disembodied states so sublime they cannot hear the Dharma.[14] After enumerating these unfortunate "times," the *nikāyas*, *Nāgārjuna* and *Śikṣāsamuccaya* (citing the *Avalokana-sūtra* found in *Mahāvastu*), describe other heavens as fortunate. "He avoids the eight inopportune times . . . he goes to heaven. He even becomes Śakra, king of the *devatā*, a lord on the peak of Meru. He becomes Suyāma, lord of *devatā*. . . . He even becomes Brahma in the Brahma world."[15] Brahmanical aspirations to heaven for its own sake were considered inferior [*hīna*],[16] but Buddhist *devatā* aspire for nirvana.[17] In one case, Sariputta guided a dying Brahmin to heaven, since "[t]hese Brahmins are devoted to the *Brahmaloka*," but was criticized for not teaching nirvana.[18] Jérôme Ducor argued that Sukhāvatī is different from the heavens in not being an end in itself,[19] but this is a common feature. Heavens as an end goal are mistaken, but they can also function as lands of enlightenment. There is a general tension between the glorification of these realms and the need to maintain nirvana as the distant pole star of all spiritual practice. The *Āyuḥparyanta-sūtra*, a Mainstream[20] text, dedicates itself to explaining the life spans of all the realms of birth, but in the end, it disparages the super-longevity of the heavens. "Why is that? Because the manifestation of conditioned existence is suffering. As for instance something that is impure: when already a little of it stinks, how much more so does a lot of it!"[21]

A tale of Vasubandhu illustrates cautionary concerns for getting lost in heavenly bliss. He and Buddhasiṃha agreed to return to his brother Asaṅga after rebirth in Tuṣita. Vasubandhu, reborn pure-land-style in a lotus, met Maitreya and returned. Buddhasiṃha, however, was lost in bliss and ultimately fell into lower births.[22] *Dīgha Nikāya* contains a similar tale of three monks reborn as hedonistic *gandharvas*. Seeing their fate, the laywoman Gopaka, now a *devatā*, reprimanded them, and the two then attained the *brahmaloka*s through meditation. But the third did not make it. Gopaka then declares, "let no disciple doubt that truth may yet be realized by those who dwell in these abodes."[23] The translator suggests this indicates it is "almost impossible for gods to gain enlightenment, but not quite."[24] This is belied by the continuing narrative. Sakka, seeing these *gandharva*s reborn in a higher heaven than his own, is motivated to engage the Buddha, and both he and eighty thousand other *devatā* attain the dharma-eye.[25] Buddhaghosa tells us that eighty million *devatā* attained the dharma eye when the Buddha taught the *Abhidharma* in heaven.[26] Celebrating the realizations of attending *devatā* at the end of a sermon is a stock feature of Mainstream and Mahayana texts.

The key to remaining in heaven is hearing Dharma, so this is a central concern.[27] A *devatā* enjoying the Nandana pleasure grove lamented that, having never heard the Buddha, she would fall after sixty thousand years. The disciple Moggallāna, famous for his visits to the heavens, comforted her: "Do not fear, Uposathā, you are declared by Buddha. He specified you a *sotāpanna* [stream-winner], the miserable destinies are abandoned for you."[28] The *nikāyas* trouble to reassure us that *devatā* receive Dharma from multiple sources,[29] including visits by the Buddha, Moggallāna, and monks with meditative powers. The Buddha is "teacher of gods and humans" and *devatā* are included in stock expressions of his compassion. In *Dīgha Nikāya*, the Buddha visits "pure abodes," and *devatā* attribute their attainment to the previous Buddha Vipassī. Then thousands of *devatā* proclaim they did so under Shakyamuni. He visits every pure abode and in each they declare the same.[30] The Buddha descended to our world from heaven and his famous return to teach his mother was unexceptional.[31] Of the Buddha's ascent to heaven, John Strong writes:

> . . . it is important to note in what sense Trāyastriṃśa is here viewed as a heaven . . . the Buddha's presence there transforms it into a sort of supernatural monastery—a "dharmalogical heaven." Indeed what is emphasized here is the preaching of the Dharma—more specifically the Abhidharma—which the Buddha expounds nonstop to his mother (and the assembled deities).[32]

Many such visits support this dharmalogical transformation. Moggallāna ascended and was greeted by thousands of *devatā*.[33] Monks visit *devaloka*s for afternoon naps,[34] bring sculptors to carve images of Maitreya,[35] or bring disciples to hear his teaching.[36] *Devatā*, born in heaven through advanced practice, also teach. The famous lay teacher Hathaka had a large human following, but now teaches as a Mahābrahma.[37] Tāvatiṃsa heaven has Sudhamma Hall, where various *devatā* teach Dharma.[38] Heavens even have relic shrines for the hair and clothing discarded on the Buddha's renunciation.[39] According to Buddhaghosa's Burmese hagiography, he fulfilled his aspiration at the end of the *Visuddhimagga* and resides in heaven with Maitreya.[40] As seen in many examples that follow, the heavens are filled with great teachers, practitioners, and even celestial bodhisattvas. Their role as ideal places to receive teachings is shared with pure lands.

Devatā also descend to teaching assemblies.[41] In Pali scriptures, the Buddha and his disciples are visited hundreds of times by *devatā*, and many *sutta*s were taught at their request.[42] Celebrated for their spiritual attainments in the thousands after hearing teachings in both Mainstream and Mahayana texts, they are not just cheerleaders, but represent afterlife hopes for oneself and one's ancestors. As seen in the following, *devatā* are the blessed dead whom one hopes to rejoin.[43]

Devatā continued to identify with previous lives, as with Anāthapiṇḍika, Hathaka the lay disciple, Moggallāna's attendant Kakudha, and the mothers of the Buddha and Sariputta.[44] Anāthapiṇḍika reunited with his daughter in Tuṣita and returned to revere Sariputta, who tended his deathbed, facilitating his heavenly birth.[45] Heaven-born ancestors intervene when they see relatives in danger or to relieve their grief.[46] One greets the Buddha as his old friend, Ghatikāra.[47] Vasubandhu returned to Asaṅga. The Buddha's mother descended to his funeral, as he ascended to teach her.[48] The feeling of Japanese Buddhists of continuing connection with their ancestors and hopes to meet them again after death are consistent with Indic traditions. A poor woman, who attained heaven by offering Mahākāśyapa parched rice, returned as the beautiful *devatā* Lājā, determined to serve him.[49] But it is unseemly for monks to have goddesses for servants, so the Buddha intervened and sent her back to heaven. The courtesan Sirimā became a stream-winner after witnessing the power of *mettacitta* to protect a woman she jealously tried to burn with boiling ghee. She died young and was reborn as Chief Queen of the Lord of the Yāma *devatā*. To cure a young monk enamored of her body, the Buddha prevented her cremation, letting her body rot in public and asking who will pay for it now. Sirimā returned with 500 other *devatā* to view her decomposing body. Witnessing this, she became a non-returner.[50] Narrative reminds us that *anātman* includes strong karmic continuities from moment to moment and life to life and illustrates José Cabezón's claim that "doctrine itself cannot be understood independent of culture."[51]

Devatā play important salvific roles. Pure abode *devatā* actively support the sangha's mission. These *deva-anāgāmins* and *deva-arhats*, and others from lower heavens, play salient roles by descending like bodhisattvas and supporting the Buddha's work. They are prominent in the *nikāya*s and *Abhidharma*, act as narrative agents in a widespread literature, including the *Mahāvastu*, *Lalitavistara*, *Buddhacarita*, etc., and appear abundantly in Buddhist art. They had a place in the imaginations of Buddhists of all kinds. In some contexts, the *Śuddhāvāsika*s announce the birth and enlightenment of the Buddha. They appear as the four sights, become Brahmins to prepare royal priests to recognize the Buddha at birth, and even give the Buddha his name.[52] *Devatā* correct, reprimand, test, and cajole monks on matters of Dharma and right conduct.[53] They implore the Buddha to teach. Vajrapāṇi, identified with Indra/Sakka, is the Buddha's bodyguard.[54] Before the rain retreats, the *devatā* collectively assemble and organize the protection of monastics.[55] The *devatā* record humans' merit and demerit on tablets and report to the Four Great Kings and to Yama, the Buddhist Hades, who judges the karma of the dead and assigns them to heaven or hell.[56]

Devatā engage in continuous merit-making. Pure abode *devatā* are broadly depicted in art lifting the Buddha's topknot, enshrining it in heaven. The feet of the dying Buddha are stained with their tears.[57] They build stupas for King Ashoka.[58] When Mahākassapa avoids offerings from Sakka's retinue, preferring alms from the poor, Sakka disguises himself as a weaver. When discovered, Sakka declares: "We too are in need of merit!" and Mahākassapa reassures him.[59] In Thailand today, charismatic monks offer *devatā* merit in exchange for lottery ticket numbers and, in Sri Lanka, offering merit to the gods in exchange for their blessings is routine practice.

In jataka tales and hagiographies, *devatā* take human birth to support the sangha. In *Temiya* Jataka, the bodhisattva, abiding in Tāvatiṃsa, wanted to go to higher heavens, but Sakka convinced him to be born as Temiya, along with 500 other *devatā*.[60] Rupert Gethin points out that Buddhaghosa aspired for Tuṣita to meet Maitreya, and attain nirvana there.[61] In his fifteenth-century Burmese hagiography, he fulfilled this aspiration through deathbed devotion. Knowing his time of death, Buddhaghosa practiced *buddha-anusmṛti* and attained a golden mansion with myriad celestial nymphs. However, Buddhaghosa was actually returning to heaven. Previously, a great elder ascended with Indra to Tāvatiṃsa seeking a translator and appealed to the *devatā* Ghosa. Ghosa replied: "Oh King of the *Devatā*, I wish to go to higher *deva*-worlds. I do not go to the human world, because dwelling in the human world has so much suffering."[62] Ultimately, Ghosa condescended to birth as Buddhaghosa, returning to heaven upon death. Remarkably, venerating Buddhaghosa also assures divine birth.[63] Indeed, Burmese nuns could imagine this monastic exemplar reluctantly descending from heaven, re-ascending by *buddha-anusmṛti*, and as someone they might meet there by means of venerating him. Nāgasena of the Milindapañha has a similar story.[64]

Pure Land Antecedents

Heavenly qualities and nomenclature became conventions for pure lands.[65] These include radiance (*śubha*), longevity (*ayus*), bliss (*sukha*), purity (*śuddha*), and typical powers of bodhisattvas, especially to pervade and travel to worlds.[66] Pure abode residents are called pure beings and dwellers in purity (*Śuddhāvāsika*s, *Śuddhāvāsadevatā, or Śuddhasattva*s) The name Sukhāvatī conforms to heaven being called "blissful rebirth," *Sukha-upapatti*, and those born there are called *sukhin*, blissful.[67] Heavens have increasing levels of bliss, longevity, and radiance. "Deva," cognate with "divinity," derives from a root meaning "to shine." *Svarga*, "heaven," can be etymologically read as "gone to celestial light."[68] Narratives exploring heavenly attainment often ask how *devatā* become as radiant as stars. The name "Amitābha," "Limitless Light," resonates with this attribute, as "Amitāyus" resonates with super-longevity. *Rūpa-dhātu* heavens are called

Parīttābha, *Apramāṇābha*, Measureless Light, and *Bhāsvara*; and *Śubhakṛtsna*, or *Parīttaśubha*, *Apramāṇaśubha*, and *Śubhakṛtsna* limited, measureless, and complete in *śubha*.[69] Some *devatā* are even called *ābhā*, light.[70]

Devatā pervade worlds, shining like gold or beryl.[71] The Pali commentary describes pervasion as knowing others' thoughts, seeing with the divine eye, pervading with radiance, and extending bodily auras to thousands of worlds.[72] Like rays emerging from the Buddha's body and extending limitlessly, divine radiance is not just an expression of purity or beauty, but vision. Expanding bodily auras to pervade worlds suggests the universal pervasion of buddha-bodies. Amitābha's radiance, like other buddhas, expresses omniscience. Buddhist *devatā* have more *ābha*, *ayus*, and *sukha* than non-Buddhists.[73] Similarly, residents of Sukhāvatī outshine *devatā*. In his land of bliss, the Buddha of Limitless Life and Light iconically embodies the super abundance of normative Buddhist hopes for bliss, longevity, and radiance. Julian Pas notes that Amitābha's qualities of limitless life, limitless light, purity, and a boundless form-body are basic to proto-Mahayanistic Buddhology.[74] We can also identify these as characteristic qualities of *devatā*, suggesting a progression from the model of the heaven-born to Mahayana Buddhology. This progression is also suggested by the bodhisattva path. Maitreya is now a *devatā*, as was the Buddha before his last birth, and many of the *bhūmis* of the Mahayana path are associated with heavenly birth at various levels.[75]

Easy accessibility is another feature that heavens share with pure lands. As discussed later, even modest offerings may lead to heaven. Merely "taking refuge" or confirmed confidence in the Buddha, Dharma, and Sangha may guarantee such rebirth.[76] When Bhāviveka grimly resolved to meditate in a cave for vast periods until Maitreya's advent as a buddha, Avalokiteśvara advised him not to go to such trouble: "You should [just] cultivate superior good deeds in order to be reborn in the Tuṣita heaven, where you can speedily see and pay homage [to Maitreya]."[77]

Pure lands, like Sukhāvatī and Abhirati, are explicitly modeled on heaven realms,[78] even their seven-jeweled airborne palaces, foods, and clothes. The *Perfection of Wisdom* asserts that *buddhakṣetras* offer everything that heavens do.[79] Pure lands competed with the "dharmalogical" Mainstream heavens. Since few Buddhists were *yogins* or philosophers, access to heaven may be the primary area of competition between Indic traditions. Mahayanists, mimicking earlier appropriations of *Brahmalokas*, applied a "pure land" overlay to abhidharmic schemes of correlation between aspirants and their respective rebirths. The *Prajñāpāramitā* simply adds on subsequent rebirth in buddha-fields, followed by attainment of enlightenment. For instance, those who practice the "immeasurables" attain *Brahmalokas*, but then pass on to buddha-fields.[80] Similarly, those who attain pure abodes subsequently attain enlightenment in buddha-fields, and so on.[81] Just as Buddhists in pure abodes were described as superior to non-Buddhist *devatā*, now Mahayanists born in pure lands are described as superior to those born in heavens. Mainstream *devatā*, who often ascended through compassion and generosity, actively struggle to enlighten the world. Ideas of rebirth in buddha-fields elaborate old patterns of thought and expectation. It seems natural that pure land sutras are among the earliest Mahayana texts. Through pure lands, heavens became fully dharmalogical and left behind their tension with the goal of nirvana.

How Do You Get There?

As Sukhāvatī became a generalized goal for Mahayanists, so were the heavens for Mainstream Buddhists. All practices generating merit were linked to heavenly rebirth.[82] Simple heartfelt offerings could secure heaven. The *Vimānavatthu*, [Heavenly] Mansion Stories, are a vast lore of heavenly attainment based on ethical practice, devotion, and donations.[83] Offerings such as sandals, flowers, or gruel lead to heavenly rebirth as a stream-winner and so ultimately to nirvana.[84] Gethin argues that the path was always conceived from a multiple-life perspective and graded cosmology.[85] Rebirth was also probably always connected to merit, and merit was based on devotional offerings. After death, the Buddha functioned as a merit-field through his abiding power, *adhiṣṭhāna*, in relics, images, stupas, pilgrimage sites, and texts. For Mainstream Buddhists, the Buddha is the supreme merit-field empowering heavenly birth. In this sense, he is a source of "other power." In contemporary Thailand, buddha-field (*buddhakhetta*) indicates the Buddha as merit-field (*puññakhetta*) to whom offerings still have effect.[86] Through stupa worship and veneration of relics,[87] pilgrimage with reverent hearts, *buddhānusmṛti*, ethical conduct,[88] deathbed aspirations, and "a single mind of faith to the marrow of one's bones,"[89] Mainstream Buddhists strive for heavens that are ideal places to receive Dharma and attain arhatship. According to *Abhidharmakośa*:

> All intelligent persons who reflect on the threefold perfection of the Tathāgatas necessarily produce a profound affection, a profound respect with regard to them. The Buddhas . . . are like mines of jewels. Nevertheless, fools . . . understand in vain the extolling of the merits of the Buddha and they do not conceive affection for the Buddha or his Dharma. The wise on the contrary, understand the explanation of the qualities of the Buddha, conceiving, with respect to the Buddha and his Dharma, a mind of *faith which penetrates to the marrow of their bones*. These persons through this *single mind of faith*--overcome infinite bad karma, get excellent rebirths, and attain *nirvana*.[90]

Here we see the power of faith and seeming transcendence of karma. Surely Hōnen and Shinran would be pleased.

The *Brahmavihāras*: Practices of Compassion Pervasion

There was a belief shared with Brahmanical traditions that the development of compassion leads to birth in *Brahmaloka*s. Disciples of non-Buddhist teachers are credited with attaining such birth.[91] The Buddha describes previous lives as a teacher of the *brahmavihāras* who reached heaven and also as a king who ascended by practicing them on his deathbed.[92] In both stories, the attainments are real, but not the ultimate goal. As Sunetta, a non-Buddhist, he taught the "immeasurables" to disciples. Many practiced incorrectly and reached lesser heavens, but Sunetta himself was reborn among the radiant gods. He states: "The practice of the path by me and my disciples was not in vain, we obtained great reward. But this was not the ultimate completion of holy life—now as a *tathāgata* I teach the ultimate path."[93] Although *Brahmalokas* are a common goal, brahmins are incompetent in attaining them, and the Buddha alone knows the correct path.[94]

Deathbed Practice

Any merit-making practice could be employed to exploit the special potency of the moment of death, but practices were also specifically designed for the dying. We have already seen preaching, compassion practice, and *buddhānusmṛti* as deathbed practices. Peter Masefield notes, "many instances can be found of the Buddha visiting sick and dying individuals and teaching them *Dhamma* whereupon they were, after death, said to become *anāgāmins*. . . . talk to the dying could have the effect of establishing them even in the lofty Brahmaloka in spite of their previous deeds," even for those meriting hell.[95] Just as the *Abhidharmakośa* said a "single mind of faith" overcomes infinite bad karma, the *Milindapañha* says: "though someone should have lived a hundred years an evil life, yet if, at the moment of death thoughts of the Buddha should enter their mind, they will be reborn among the gods."[96] The *Petavatthu* describes an unworthy person attaining heaven by accidentally seeing the Buddha on his deathbed.[97] In another case a lowly frog attains heaven when accidentally killed during the Buddha's sermon.[98] The *Dīgha Nikāya* commentary portrays passengers on a sinking ship attaining heaven by taking refuge just as they drown.[99]

Death at pilgrimage sites also leads to heaven.[100] Gregory Schopen showed that monks and laity believed devout death near relics assured heavenly rebirth without regression. To achieve this, they placed small stupas, enclosed with *dhāraṇī*, in dense clusters and deep layers around major stupas. He notes similar practices for rebirth in Sukhāvatī at Mount Kōya.[101]

A recent study by Jaqueline Stone confirms something I have highlighted in talks since 2015;[102] deathbed practices in Pali texts share striking similarities with East Asian Pure Land practices. Referring to a practice recommended by Buddhaghosa, where families show the dying offerings made on their behalf and assure them of karmic merit, she writes:

> We do not know whether or not some early version of such a ritual may have served as a prototype for the deathbed practices . . . that emerged in China by the same period. But the logic behind them was the same. Not only do the living generate

> merit for the dying by their offerings, but the sight, sound, and fragrance of such offerings engages the senses of the dying and acts to call to mind the Buddha and his Dharma, ensuring that the individual's "proximate karma"—the last thought—will be meritorious.[103]

Another shared feature is attention to signs of rebirth, which may include flames for those bound for hell or heavenly mansions for others. As discussed in the following, in *Abhidharma*, signs of meditative attainments also include seeing, smelling, or hearing heavenly phenomena. In one case from the *Dhammapada Commentary*, a lay disciple, lying on his deathbed while monks chant the *Satipaṭṭhāna Sutta*, is given a choice of *devaloka*s when chariots arrive from six different realms offering to take him away.[104] In contemporary Thailand and Burma, funerary practices, especially for venerated figures, include elaborate constructions designed like heavenly *vimāna* intended as conveyances to the heavens.[105]

Pure Land tradition's concern with the moment of death, *maraṇacitta*, in determining rebirth has deep Indian roots.[106] In teachings expressly for monastics, the *Majjhima Nikāya*'s exposition on "rebirth according to aspiration" elaborates auspicious births from wealthy humans to *devatā*.[107] Practices for attaining heavens are systematically structured paths, requiring faith, ethical discipline, wisdom, and focused aspiration, *praṇidhāna*, for the world concerned.[108]

> A person on his deathbed "fixes his mind on that, establishes it, develops it. These aspirations and this abiding of his, thus developed and cultivated, lead to his reappearance there [in that realm]. This *Bhikkhus* is the path, the way. . . ."[109]

The *nikāyas*' instructions on deathbed counseling include leading laity through successive aspirations for ever higher heavens, with the highest to attain nirvana. The dying should abandon anxiety about their family. Then they are taken step by step through various levels of heaven and told to successively abandon the last and resolve on higher worlds. The Heaven of Four Great Kings up to *Brahmaloka*s are each described as ever more sublime, as if the dying person was progressing upward. Finally, the dying are reminded that even *Brahmaloka*s are impermanent and are directed toward nirvana.[110] Assuming most were not on the brink of nirvana, this practice guides the dying to the highest heaven possible. However, the last advice about nirvana is still crucial, since, without this orientation, *devatā* may even descend to hell when their merit dissipates.[111]

Meditation

From early times, there was a link between meditation and location. The entire Buddhist "path" is conceptualized spatially. Buddhists course, enter, ascend, stand, abide, are fixed or unfixed on *mārga*, *bhūmi*, *āvāsa*, *āsana*, *vihāra*, *kṣetra*, *mukha*, *gocara*, *viṣaya*, *loka*, *maṇḍala*, and *dhātu*. Heavens and pure lands are exquisite refinements of spatial models of spiritual progress. Even nirvana is described as a place.[112] In meditation theory, sources vary on correlations between attainments and resulting heavens,[113] but *nikāyas*, narrative, and *Abhidharmas* tend to agree that those who attain *jhāna* and non-returners are reborn in pure abodes.[114] Levels of pure abodes are correlated with stages of meditative attainment.[115] *Abhidharmakośa* presents types of non-returners, called jumpers and leapers, who skip heavens or ascend ever higher heavens before nirvana.[116] Meditation results in seeing, smelling, or hearing heavenly things.[117] In East Asia, these were anxiously sought-after signs of immanent rebirth in pure lands for those on their deathbeds. This informs the common appearance of pure lands when buddhas or bodhisattvas enter *samādhi*. Attainment of heavens is not a lay matter divorced from the serious business of ascetic meditation, but is integral to meditative pursuits.

Centuries after Buddhaghosa, elite Mahayanist meditation masters continued to engage in practices for attaining heavenly rebirth. According to tradition, Xuanzang, a great figure in Mahayana Yogācāra traditions, shared Buddhaghosa's deathbed aspiration to be born in Tuṣita with Maitreya. Just after visiting the Indian monastery where Asaṅga famously ascended to Tuṣita to receive the Yogācāra teachings from Maitreya, Xuanzang faced death at the hands of river-bandits, who wished to sacrifice him to Durgā. With their permission, he prepared to die. In meditation, he gradually progressed up to Mount Meru and then on through the lower heavens until reaching Tuṣita. This parallels the progression from lower to higher realms in Mainstream deathbed practice, suggesting actual travel up through cosmic realms. Miracles erupted that overawed the bandits and Xuanzang survived, but on his deathbed back in China, he again aspired for birth in Tuṣita. His last words confirmed the certainty of his rebirth and he dedicated his merit toward all those present at his deathbed being reborn there with him. Alan Sponberg, whose work I draw on here, concludes that this practice was probably common among Xuanzang's colleagues.[118] Remarkably, even the iconic Tibetan scholastic Tsong Khapa, who also wrote aspirational prayers to be reborn in Sukhāvatī, aspired to birth in Tuṣita with Maitreya. His tradition regards him as abiding there now.[119] So we have the possibility that Xuanzang, Buddhaghosa, Vasubandhu, Nāgasena, Tsong Khapa, Queen Māyā, Hathaka, and Anāthapiṇḍika are all present together in Tuṣita at the feet of Maitreya, who continuously teaches *Abhidharma* there.

Laity versus Monastic

Deathbed practices for "rebirth according to aspiration" were explicitly addressed to monastics, exemplified by figures like Buddhaghosa and Nāgasena. Meditation theory and stages of the path were directly linked to heavenly cosmology. The *Abhidharma*, normally associated with monastics, was initially taught in heaven to hosts of *devatā*, headed by the Buddha's wise mother.[120] The *Abhidharma* in turn richly elaborated the heavens, their levels, life spans, jeweled ponds, etc., to a degree of complexity not found in Hindu or Abrahamic traditions. Elite meditative and philosophical traditions are framed by and saturated with these cosmological concerns.

Schopen shows that monastics sought heaven through practices exploiting the power of relics. Like Nāgārjuna, Buddhaghosa recommended that monastics practice *deva-anusmṛti*, mindfulness of deities, to attain heaven and the love of the *devatā*. They are to enter private retreat and focus on the range of *devatā* and the qualities they share with them.[121] In Buddhaghosa's scriptural reference, *deva-anusmṛti* is recommended, along with remembrance of the Three Jewels, for noble disciples to attain freedom from the *kleśa*s.

> There are *devatā* [ruled by] the four great kings, Tāvatiṃsa *devatā*, Yāma *devatā*, Tusita *devatā*, *devatā* who delight in creation, *devatā* who control what is created by others, *devatā* of Brahmā's company, and *devatā* still higher than these. There exists in me too such faith as those deities possessed . . . such virtuous behavior . . . learning . . . generosity . . . [and] wisdom as those deities possessed because of which, when they passed away here, they were reborn there. When a noble disciple recollects the faith, [etc.] . . . in oneself and in those deities, on that occasion their mind is not obsessed by lust, hatred, or delusion . . . their mind is simply straight, based on the deities. A noble disciple whose mind is straight gains inspiration in the meaning, . . . in the Dhamma, gains joy connected with the Dhamma. When one is joyful, rapture arises. For one with a rapturous mind, the body becomes tranquil. One tranquil in body feels pleasure. For one feeling pleasure, the mind becomes concentrated. This is called a noble disciple who dwells in balance amid an unbalanced population, who dwells unafflicted amid an afflicted population. As one who has entered the stream of the Dhamma, one develops recollection of the deities. Mahānāma, a noble disciple who has arrived at the fruit and understood the teaching, often dwells in just this way.[122]

The *Aṅguttara Nikāya* even lists *devānusmṛti* among the key practices of which just a finger snap makes one a monastic worthy of alms.[123]

Conclusion

From early tradition to modern times, lay and monastic Buddhists strove for divine longevity, radiance, bliss, and vision in order to pursue Dharma in perfect environments filled with spiritual teachers. The Buddha knows best the path to heaven, and those attaining them with Buddhist aspirations are superior to other *devatā*. Aspiration for nirvana, continued merit-making, and, above all, access to the Dharma assure that one will not fall, but will either be reborn ever higher or attain liberation in the current *devaloka*. Buddhism presented itself as superior in guidance, efficacy, and the quality and sustainability of heavenly attainments.

Devotion and faith, described in *Abhidharmakośa* as "single minded faith to the core of one's bones," are strongly connected to divine rebirth, even overcoming extreme negative karma. The Buddha is still a merit-field after his passing, and devotional offerings generate salvific power; as such, he functions as a source of salvific "other power," even in Mainstream traditions. Taking refuge or stupa worship assured status as a stream-winner, and even the destitute may ascend through modest acts of devotion. The *nikāya*s offer systematically constructed practices for heaven, including deathbed rituals and *devānusmṛti*. Archaeological records reveal that monastics and laity strove for heavens without regression by interning their ashes with *dhāraṇī* in proximity to relics. Since, like Buddhaghosa, most did not anticipate nirvana, it seems reasonable to speculate the central soteriological concern was for rebirth in heavens or the pure lands into which they evolved.

The pure lands were explicitly modeled on heavens like the pure abodes. The *Prajñāpāramitā* appropriates abhidharmic *devaloka* aspirations and simply adds an overlay of rebirth in pure lands. Early appropriations of Brahmanical heavens (or perhaps just unique claims on Gangetic cosmology) were reappropriated in Mahayana sutras. Buddha fields assumed the soteriological functions of heavens. Pure Land Buddhism is a distillation of a common stock of normative Indic ideas into a particular cultic form that has strong parallels and roots in Mainstream Buddhism.

Devatā are relatives that we may meet again. They continue to interact with families and the sangha. They make merit by playing salvific roles in supporting the Buddha's mission and involvement with relics and stupas. Not only do *devatā* descend, but meditators ascend. Systematic thought, meditative practice, and heavenly aspiration are not separate areas of concern. *Devatā* teem around the Buddha as he teaches, instigate hundreds of Pali *sutta*s, and first received the *Abhidharma*. They represent practitioners' future aspirations—aspirations far more in reach than nirvana—which provide a robust and inclusive soteriology capable of motivating not just renunciants, but an entire civilization.

Notes

1. I am deeply indebted to Mattia Salvini and Giuliano Giustarini for devoting a seminar to this research at Mahidol University. Thanks to Allison Aitken for valuable criticism.
2. John Holt discusses misinterpretation of deities and impacts on Theravada cultures: *The Buddhist Viṣṇu: Religious Transformation, Politics, and Culture* (New York: Columbia University Press, 2004), 23–31. Jacqueline Stone does the same, showing impacts on Japanese culture: *Right Thoughts at the Last Moment: Buddhism and Deathbed Practices in Early Medieval Japan* (Honolulu: University of Hawai'i Press, 2016).
3. Females, males, and ungendered beings exist in the heavens. Where possible, I use *devatā*, which can refer to any gender.
4. Steven Collins, *Nirvana and Other Buddhist Felicities* (Cambridge: Cambridge University Press, 1998), 297.

5. "Except for a few, the majority of these gods are not even heard of, either in the brahmanic or any of the other contemporary Gaṅgetic religious traditions . . . majority of the active gods in Buddhism are not . . . brahmanic gods." M. Mārasinghe, *Gods in Early Buddhism: A Study in Their Social and Mythological Milieu as Depicted in the Nikāyas of the Pāli Canon* (Vidyalankara: Uni. Sri Lanka, 1974), 68–69.
6. *Saṃyutta-nikāya*, ed. M. Leon Feer (1884–1904; repr., London: Pali Text Society, 1970–1980), 5.232 (hereafter *SN*). *The Connected Discourses of the Buddha: A New Translation of the Saṃyutta Nikāya*, trans. Bhikkhu Bodhi (Boston: Wisdom Publications, 2000), 1699.
7. *Dīgha-nikāya*, ed. T.W. Rhys Davids and J. Estlin Carpenter (1889–1910; repr., London: Oxford University Press, 1975–1982), 2.285 (hereafter *DN*). *The Long Discourses of the Buddha*, trans. Maurice Walshe (London: Wisdom Publications, 1987), 331.
8. Nyanaponika Thera and Helmut Hecker, *Great Disciples of the Buddha* (Boston: Wisdom Publications, 1997), 102.
9. *Aṅguttara-nikāya*, ed. Richard Morris (1885–1910; repr., London: Pali Text Society, 1961–1976), 4.186 (hereafter *AN*); ethics, giving, and renunciation are elements.
10. *Princeton Dictionary of Buddhism*, ed. Robert Buswell Jr. and Donald Lopez Jr. (Princeton, NJ: Princeton University Press, 2014): s.v. "*Svarga*," states: "Since *devatā* merely enjoy rewards of good deeds rather than performing new wholesome actions, they are considered spiritually stagnant. . . . They are inevitably reborn in lower realms." Cf. s.v. "*deva*."
11. *AN* 1.267; *The Book of Gradual Sayings*, trans. F. L. Woodward (New York: Oxford University Press, 1933), 1.245–6. Cf. MN 1.82; examples follow.
12. *The Numerical Discourses of the Buddha: A Translation of the Aṅguttara Nikāya*, trans. Bhikkhu Bodhi (Boston: Wisdom Publications, 2012), 508. *Muṇḍaka Upaniṣad* says those attaining *svarga* through Vedic rituals eventually fall in distress, but renunciants do not. *Muṇḍaka Upaniṣad*, I.2.7–11.
13. *Numerical Discourses*, 997, 347–48, and 505–8.
14. *Numerical Discourses*, 1157; see note 1689. Sometimes *devatā* intoxicated with bliss are included. See Daniel Stuart, *A Less Traveled Path: Saddharmasmṛtyupasthānasūtra: Chapter 2 Critically Edited with a Study in Its Structure and Significance for the Development of Buddhist Meditation* (Beijing: Austrian Academy of Sciences and China Tibetology Research Center, 2015), 5.1.4.3 and n.69.
15. Śāntideva, *The Training Anthology of Śāntideva*, trans. Charles Goodman, (New York: Oxford University, 2016), 279–80. *The Mahāvastu*, Vol. 2, trans. J. J. Jones (London: Luzac, 1952), 330–31; cf. 325. Nāgārjuna, in a text memorized at Nālandā and followed later by many commentators, deploys this list, warning of the impermanence and seduction of heavens, but also recommending *deva-anusmṛti*, Brahmalokas, Sukhāvatī, and other heavens. *Nāgārjuna's Letter to King Gautamīputra* [*Suhṛllekha*], trans. Lozang Jamspal, Ngawang Samten Chophel, Peter Santina (Delhi: Motilal Banarsidass, 1978), 23, 24, 38.
16. *MN* 2.194–95.
17. SN 4.275; *Connected Discourses of the Buddha*, 1311. Buddhists have greater life span, happiness, beauty, fame, sovereignty, etc.
18. MN 2.194–5. *Middle Length Discourses*, 796. Cf. *Madhyama Āgama*, 187.
19. Jérôme Ducor, "Les Sources de la Sukhāvatī, autour d'une étude récente de Gérard Fussman," *Journal of the International Association of Buddhist Studies* 27, no. 2 (2004): 381.
20. "Mainstream" designates Buddhists often indicated by the insulting "*hīnayāna*."

21. *The Sūtra of the Length of Life, Āyuḥparyantasūtra, tshe'i mtha'i mdo*, trans. Bruno Galasek-Hul and Lama Kunga Thartse Rinpoche (84,000 Project, forthcoming); see the closing statement.
22. Xuanzang, *The Great Tang Dynasty Record of the Western Regions*, trans. Li Rongxi (Berkeley: Numata Center, 1996), 153–4. Cf. DN 2.272; *Long Discourses of the Buddha*, 368.
23. *Long Discourses of the Buddha*, 327.
24. *Long Discourses of the Buddha*, note 600, 586.
25. *Long Discourses of the Buddha*, 334. Sakka says he will take human birth, but then be reborn again in Akaniṣṭha to attain nirvana as a *devatā*.
26. Buddhaghosa, *The Path of Purification: Visuddhimagga*, trans. Bhikkhu Nyanamoli (Berkeley: Shambhala, 1976), 385.
27. The theme of Peter Masefield's *Divine Revelation in Pali Buddhism* (Boston: George Allen & Unwin, 1986).
28. *Vimāna Stories, Elucidation of the Intrinsic Meaning So Named the Commentary on the Vimāna Stories: Paramattha-dīpanī nāma Vimānavatthu-aṭṭhakathā*, trans. Peter Masefield and N. A. Jayawickrama (Lancaster: Pali Text Society, 2007), 171–72. Stream-winners have seven lives until liberation without unfortunate rebirths.
29. *AN* 2.185. *Devatā* receive teachings from four sources: "happy ones," *sukhin*, *devatā*, monks with special powers, and those apparitionally reborn in *devalokas*.
30. *DN* 2.50.
31. *Vimāna Stories*, 166, the Buddha again teaches *devatā Abhidhamma* for months. Cf. 76 Mahāmogallāna taught in heaven and *devatā* attain *sotāpatti;* cf. 426, the Buddha again ascends.
32. John Strong, *The Legend and Cult of Upagupta: Sanskrit Buddhism in North India and Southeast Asia* (Princeton, NJ: Princeton University Press, 1992), 151.
33. *SN* 4.270; *Connected Discourses*, 1309–13.
34. *DN* 2.357.
35. Madhyāntika brought craftsman to Tuṣita three times to observe Maitreya. Xuanzang, *Great Tang Dynasty Record*, 92–93.
36. Devasena brought Guṇaprabha three times to Maitreya. Xuanzang, *Great Tang Dynasty Record*, 129.
37. *AN* 1.279. Cf. *Madhyama Āgama*, ed. Marcus Bingenheimer, Bhikkhu Anālayo, and Roderick Bucknell (Berkeley: Bukkyo Dendo Kyokai America, 2013), 307–15.
38. *Madhyama Āgama*, 369. Frank Reynolds and Mai B. Reynolds, *Three Worlds According to King Ruang: A Thai Buddhist Cosmology* (Berkeley: Asian Humanities Press, 1982), 235–36. Punnadhammo Mahāthero, *The Buddhist Cosmos: A Comprehensive Survey of the Buddhist Worldview According to Theravāda and Sarvāstivāda Sources* (Thunder Bay, Canada: Arrow River Forest Hermitage, 2018), 283.
39. In Southeast Asia, the *Cūḷāmaṇi Cetiya* housing the Buddha's topknot is memorialized in the current cult linking birth years and stupas. Regarding classical texts, see John S. Strong, *Relics of the Buddha* (Princeton, NJ: Princeton University Press, 2004), 158.
40. Discussed later in the chapter.
41. *The Madhyama Āgama*, 476. At *AN* 4.308, diverse *devatā* constitute set types of audience. *Vimāna Stories*, 69: *Devatā* ask why they are divine, receive *Dhamma*, and attain *sotāpatti.*
42. *Gods in Early Buddhism*, 172.
43. Holt notes *devatā* represent progress toward nirvana. *Buddhist Viṣṇu*, 27–28.

44. For Śāriputra see *Petavatthu*, 2.2. *Peta Stories*, U Ba Kyaw and Peter Masefield (Lancaster: Pali Text Society, 2007) 84–89.
45. *AN* 3.122; *AN* 3.331; *Connected Discourses*, 131; Nyanaponika, *Great Disciples*, 362; *DN* 2.206: Bimbisārarāja returns. Examples abound in *Petavatthu* and generally.
46. *Mahāvastu*, Vol. 1, 209. *Peta Stories*, 100.
47. "In the past I was the potter, Ghatikāra . . . your friend. . . ." *Connected Discourses*, 126. Cf. *Connected Discourses*, 299, for Anuruddha's former consort.
48. Xuanzang, *The Great Tang Dynasty Record*, 189.
49. Nyanaponika, *Great Disciples*, 123.
50. Punnadhammo, *The Buddhist Cosmos*, 334–35.
51. Space constrains here, but Stone elaborates. *Right Thoughts*, 12. José Cabezón, "Buddhist Studies as a Discipline and the Role of Theory," *JIABS* 18, no. 2 (1995): 263.
52. *Mahāvastu*, trans. Jones, Vol. 1, 119–120; 156; 182; and Vol. II, 146. Aśvaghoṣa, *Buddhacarita*, I.20; Patrick Olivelle, *Life of the Buddha* (New York: University New York Press, 2009), 11, 434, note I.20; *Buddhacarita*, III.26; Olivelle, *Life of Buddha*, 71.
53. *SN* 1.197–205, *AN* 3.309, *SN* 1.61, *Connected Discourses*, 156–57, 294, 299.
54. Stephen Jenkins, "On the Auspiciousness of Compassionate Violence," *Journal of the International Association of Buddhist Studies* 33, no. 1–2 (2010–11): 299–331.
55. Punnadhammo, *The Buddhist Cosmos*, 282.
56. MN.iii.178–87. *Middle Length Discourses*, 1029–36. Reynolds, *Three Worlds According to King Ruang*, 70.
57. Xuanzang, *Great Tang Dynasty Record*, 191.
58. Xuanzang, *Great Tang Dynasty Record*, 225, 236.
59. *Great Disciples of the Buddha*, 124.
60. Sarah Shaw, *The Jātakas: Birth Stories of the Buddha* (New York: Penguin, 2006), 189.
61. Rupert Gethin, s.v. "Heaven," in *Encyclopedia of Buddhism*, ed. Robert E. Buswell, Jr., Vol. 2 (New York: Macmillan Reference, 2003), 315. Buddhaghosa, *Path of Purification*, trans. Nyanamoli, 838: "May I be reborn in Tāvatiṃsa, hear the teaching of Metteya, and attain the highest fruit."
62. *Buddhaghosuppatti*, ed. and trans. James Gray (London: Luzac, 1892), 38. So "*Devarāja ahaṃ uparidevalokaṃ gamituṃ icchāmi; kasmā manussaloke nivāso nāma bahudukkho bahupāyāso; tena manussalokaṃ na gacchāmi.*"
63. *Buddhaghosuppatti*, 35–36.
64. Dharmasena Thera, *Jewels of the Doctrine: Stories of the Saddharma Ratnāvaliya*, trans. Ranjini Obeyesekere (Albany: State University of New York Press, 1991), 61–62.
65. "Amitābha enjoys—admittedly to a superlative degree—the same qualities of purity, splendor, and dazzling light attributed in India to other inhabitants of celestial spheres, such as the Indian gods, (deva)." Luis Gómez, *The Land of Bliss: The Paradise of the Buddha of Measureless Light: Sanskrit and Chinese Versions of the Sukhāvatīvyūha Sutras* (Honolulu: University of Hawai'i Press, 1996), 35–36; see also 52, 58.
66. *Vimāna Stories*, 424.
67. *DN* 3.219. (*sukhupapatti*). Akira Sadakata, *Buddhist Cosmology* (Tokyo: Kosei, 1997), 65: The first three *dhyāna* realms are *sukha-upapatti*; the fourth is beyond *sukha*. For "*sukhin*," see *AN* 2.185.
68. Thanks to Frederick Smith.
69. Yiu-wing Chan, "An English translation of the Dharmatrāta-Dhyāna Sūtra," PhD diss., Hong Kong University, 2013, 234, n.385. Sadakata, *Buddhist Cosmology*, 65.

70. Franklin Edgerton, *Buddhist Hybrid Sanskrit Grammar and Dictionary*, Vol. 2 (Delhi: Motilal Banarsidass, 1985) s.v. "*deva*," 270.
71. *Vimāna Stories*, 149–51; a rice-scum donor attains great brightness.
72. *The Middle Length Discourses of the Buddha*, trans. Bhikkhu Ñāṇamoli and Bhikkhu Bodhi (Boston: Wisdom Publications, 1995), 1327, n.1134.
73. *SN* 4.275; *Connected Discourses*, 1311.
74. *Visions of Sukhāvatī*, 14–16.
75. See Thomas Cleary, trans., *The Flower Ornament Scripture* (Shambhala: Boston, 1993), 726, 733, 772, 787.
76. *SN* 4.270; *Connected Discourses*, 1309.
77. Xuanzang, *Great Tang Dynasty Record*, 317.
78. Tai-wo Kwan, "A Study of the Teaching Regarding the Pure Land of Akṣobhya Buddha in Early Mahayana," PhD diss., University of California at Los Angeles, 1987, 78–82. Hisao Inagaki. *The Three Pure Land Sutras*, 2nd ed. (Berkeley: Numata Center, 2003), 57–58 [278a]. Gómez, *Land of Bliss*, 86, 88, 90, etc.
79. *The Large Sutra on Perfect Wisdom*, trans. Edward Conze (Berkeley: University of California Press, 1975), 417. "Just like the possessions enjoyed by the various classes of gods, from the gods belonging to the Four Great Kings, to the Highest Gods, so will be the possessions enjoyed by the beings in that Buddha-field."
80. Conze, *Large Sūtra*, 70. Space does not allow full exposition.
81. Conze, *Large Sūtra*, 72.
82. Rita Langer, *Buddhist Rituals of Death and Rebirth: Contemporary Sri Lankan Practice and Its Origins* (London: Routledge, 2007), 37–38 and throughout.
83. Robert DeCaroli notes that Dhammapāla's commentary demonstrates *Vimānavatthu*'s importance. *Haunting the Buddha* (New York: Oxford University Press, 2004), 97.
84. *Vimāna Stories*, see throughout and 205 for thirty-six *devatā* and reasons for rebirth.
85. Rupert Gethin, "Cosmology and Meditation: From the Aggañña-Sutta to the Mahayana," *History of Religions* 36, no. 3 (1997): 188.
86. Donald K. Swearer, *Becoming the Buddha: The Ritual of Image Consecration in Thailand* (Princeton, NJ: Princeton University Press, 2004), 20.
87. *SN* 2.142–43. Offerings at stupas garner heaven; cf. *Mahāvastu* Vol. II, 331.
88. *DN* 3.111–12, Right views and actions result in "happy and unhappy destinations"; cf. A.i.29, *Gradual Sayings*, Vol. 1, 26.
89. See *Abhidharmakośa* later in the chapter.
90. Vasubandhu, *Abhidharmakośabhāṣyam*, trans. Louis de la Vallée Poussin, English trans. Leo Pruden (Berkeley: Asian Humanities Press, 1988–90) v. 4, 1146–47.
91. *AN* 4.103; *AN* 4.135; *AN* 3.371.
92. *Madhyama Āgama*, 475–76. *AN* 4.104.
93. *Madhyama Āgama*, 45–46; cf. *AN* 4.100.
94. *MN* 1.73. It is a stock statement that the Buddha knows the path to *devalokas*. *MN* 2.206–8; *Middle Length Discourses*, 816–17. Cf. *Tevijja Sutta*, *DN* 1.235–52; *Long Discourses of the Buddha*, 187–95. Gombrich argues the Buddha merely jokes when saying "a disciplined monk, after death, . . . should attain union with Brahmā." The Buddha derides Vedic practices for Brahmalokas, but only speculation about intentions and dismissal of contradictory *suttas* would allow us to think he did not actually mean he is the true guide. Even if they "missed the boat," Gombrich acknowledges early tradition, compilers, and commentators took the Buddha literally. Richard Gombrich, *What the Buddha Thought* (London: Equinox, 2009), 80–88.

95. Masefield, *Divine Revelation*, 107–8.
96. *The Questions of King Milinda*, Part One, trans. T. W. Rhys Davids (New York: Dover, 1963), 123–24. [Translation slightly adapted for gender inclusion consistent with the text.]
97. *Peta Stories*, 2.5.
98. *Visuddhimagga*, trans. Ñānamoli, 203.
99. *Connected Discourses*, 363, n.59.
100. *DN* 2.40.
101. Gregory Schopen, *Bones, Stones, and Buddhist Monks* (Honolulu: University of Hawai'i Press, 1997), 108–9; 117–18; 121–22.
102. Stephen Jenkins, "Questioning the Eastern-ness of the Western Pure Land: Revisionist Reflections on Pure Land's Indian Identity," IASBS Conference, Berkeley, 2015. "Buddhist Stairways to Heaven," UC Berkeley and Harvard, 2016.
103. Stone, *Right Thoughts at the Last Moment*, 16. Stone relies on Langer's *Buddhist Rituals of Death and Rebirth*.
104. Punnadhammo, *Buddhist Cosmos*, 341.
105. Rebecca S. Hall, "Onward Toward Heaven: Burning the Nok Hatsadiling." *Ars Orientalis* 44 (2014): 180–99.
106. Langer, *Buddhist Rituals of Death*, traces *maraṇacitta* in India.
107. MN 3.103 *Middle Length Discourses*, 959–62. The commentary says "The 'way' is the five qualities beginning with faith, [i.e., faith, virtue, learning, generosity, and wisdom] together with aspiration." Cf. n.1133, p. 1327.
108. Langer, *Buddhist Rituals of Death*, 38.
109. MN 3.103; *Middle Length Discourses*, 962.
110. *SN* 5.407–410; *Connected Discourses*, Vol. 2, 1833–36. Cf. *SN* 4.271–79; *Connected Discourses*, Vol. 2, 1308–12.
111. Cf. *Vimāna Stories*, 236, on dying with a heart of faith.
112. *SN* 3.109, *nibbāna* as delightful expanse of level ground.
113. *Princeton Dictionary of Buddhism*, s.v. "*deva*," 231. The number of *Rūpadhātu* heavens varies from sixteen to eighteen. AN 2.126–29, *Gradual Sayings*, Vol. II, 129–33. The first *dhyāna* results in *brahmaloka*s or pure abodes. Other *dhyāna*s cause birth either in pure abodes or with "radiant *devatā*." *Brahmalokas* reward *mettā* practice, but other *brahmavihāras* result in birth as Radiant [*Ābhassara*] *Devatā*, Ever Radiant [*Subbhakiṇṇa*] *Devatā*, and *Vehapphala Devatā*. Alternatively, *Brahmavihāras* result in pure abodes; see *Buddhist Cosmology*, 59–67.
114. MN 3.103; *Middle Length Discourses*, 959–62; *Aṅguttara* i.245; *Gradual Sayings*, v.1, 224; DN 3.237; DN 2.253; Buddhaghosa, *Visuddhimagga*, ed. Henry Clarke Warren, rev. Dharmananda Kosambi (Cambridge, MA: Harvard University Press, 1950), 23.57; *Path of Purification*, 834; *SN* 1.26, *Long Discourses of the Buddha*, 552, note 185; P. V. Bapat, *Vimuttimagga and Visuddhimagga* (Poona: Fergusson College, 1937), 308; *Abhidharmakośabhāṣyam*, trans. la Vallée Poussin, English trans. Pruden, iii.6b, 377–78; *Abhidharmakośa-Bhāṣya of Vasubandhu*, trans. Louis de la Vallée Poussin; annotated English translation by Gelong Lodrö Sangpo (Delhi: Motilal Banarsidass, 2012), vi.42–43 <223>, 1959–1960, discusses five types of rebirth in pure abodes, based on levels of meditative purity, referencing *Abhidharmahṛdaya of Dharmaśrī* and *Saṃyuktābhidharma-hṛdaya*. For cross referencing see vii.43, <103>, 2245; vi.37–38 <213–14>, 1950–51; *Abhidharmadīpa with Vibhāshāprabhā[v]ṛitti* [*sic*], Tibetan Sanskrit Works Series, Vol. IV, ed. Padmanabh S. Jaini (Patna: Jayaswal Research

Institute, 1959), 116, 339, also cross-references *Abhidharmakośa* and *Abhidhammāthasaṅgaho*; Asaṅga, *Abhidharmasamuccaya*, trans. Walpola Rahula, English trans. Sara Boin-Webb (Fremont, CA: Asian Humanities Press, 2001), 214. *Dharmatrāta-Dhyāna Sūtra*, 234, n.385; see also 136 and 418.

115. The *Majjihma-nikāya* commentary says non-returners are reborn in pure abodes. Attainment of *jhānas* leads to Brahmalokas. Formless attainments lead to formless worlds. *Middle Length Discourses*, n.1136, 1327.
116. *Abhidharmakośa*, vi.37–38, Sangpo, 1950–51.
117. M. M. J. Mārasinghe, *Gods in Early Buddhism*, 93–4; 280.
118. Alan Sponberg, "Meditation in Fa-Hsiang Buddhism," in *Traditions of Buddhist Meditation in Chinese Buddhism*, ed. Peter Gregory (Honolulu: University of Hawai'i Press, 1986), 22–29.
119. James B. Apple, "Maitreya's Tuṣita Heaven as a Pure Land in Gelukpa Forms of Tibetan Buddhism," in *Pure lands in Asian Texts and Contexts*, ed. George Halkias and Richard Payne (Honolulu: University of Hawai'i Press, 2019), 188–222. Tsong Khapa, *The Splendor of an Autumn Moon*, trans. Gavin Kilty (Boston: Wisdom, 2001), 269–80. Although Tsong Khapa makes no special qualifications about Tuṣita, his tradition regards it as a pure land and emphasizes the separateness of Maitreya's place in Tuṣita. This well illustrates the fluid relationship between conceptions of pure lands and heavens.
120. Caroline Rhys Davids, *A Buddhist Manual of Psychological Ethics: Dhammasaṅgaṇi, Compendium of States or Phenomena*. 3rd edition (Oxford: Pali Text Society, 2004), xxxiii.
121. *Visuddhimagga* 7.115–128; *Path of Purification*, 243–46. Buddhaghosa cites *AN.iii*.287; cf. *Nāgārjuna's Letter*, verse 4.
122. *Numerical Discourses*, 864–65. [Translation slightly adapted for gender inclusion consistent with the text.] Cf. AN.i..210–11: *Devānusmṛti* cleanses defilements. CF. *AN*.iii.452, *Numerical Discourses*, 990: *Devānusmṛti* achieves direct knowledge of lust.
123. *AN*.i.42, *Numerical Discourses*, 128.

Further Reading

Collins, Steven. *Nirvana and Other Buddhist Felicities*. Cambridge: Cambridge University Press, 1998.

DeCaroli, Robert. *Haunting the Buddha*. New York: Oxford University Press, 2004.

Gethin, Rupert. "Cosmology and Meditation: From the Aggañña-Sutta to the Mahayana." *History of Religions* 36, no. 3 (1997): 183–217.

Hall, Rebecca S., "Onward Toward Heaven: Burning the Nok Hatsadiling." *Ars Orientalis* 44 (2014): 180–99.

Holt, John. *The Buddhist Viṣṇu: Religious Transformation, Politics, and Culture*. New York: Columbia University Press, 2004.

Langer, Rita. *Buddhist Rituals of Death and Rebirth: Contemporary Sri Lankan Practice and Its Origins*. London: Routledge, 2007.

Mārasinghe, M. *Gods in Early Buddhism: A Study in Their Social and Mythological Milieu as Depicted in the Nikāyas of the Pāli Canon*. Vidyalankara: University of Sri Lanka, 1974.

Masefield, Peter. *Divine Revelation in Pali Buddhism*. Boston: George Allen & Unwin, 1986.

Masefield, Peter, and N. A. Jayawickrama, trans. *Vimāna Stories, Elucidation of the Intrinsic Meaning So Named the Commentary on the Vimāna Stories: Paramattha-dīpanī nāma Vimānavatthu-aṭṭhakathā*. Lancaster: Pali Text Society, 2007.

Punnadhammo Mahāthero. *The Buddhist Cosmos: A Comprehensive Survey of the Buddhist Worldview According to Theravāda and Sarvāstivāda Sources*. Thunder Bay, Canada: Arrow River Forest Hermitage, 2018.

Reynolds, Frank, and Reynolds, Mai B. *Three Worlds According to King Ruang: A Thai Buddhist Cosmology*. Berkeley: Asian Humanities Press, 1982.

Sadakata, Akira. *Buddhist Cosmology*. Tokyo: Kosei, 1997.

Schopen, Gregory. *Bones, Stones, and Buddhist Monks*. Honolulu: University of Hawai'i Press, 1997.

Stone, Jacqueline. *Right Thoughts at the Last Moment: Buddhism and Deathbed Practices in Early Medieval Japan*. Honolulu: University of Hawai'i Press, 2016.

Strong, John. *The Legend and Cult of Upagupta: Sanskrit Buddhism in North India and Southeast Asia*. Princeton, NJ: Princeton University Press, 1992.

PART VI

DOMESTIC AND MONASTIC PRACTICES

THE roots of domestic and monastic practices for women and men began during the Buddha's lifetime. Scholarship on male monastic practices, however, is currently far more substantially developed. As more women scholars have entered the academy, Buddhist Studies scholarship has increasingly revealed women's agency throughout Buddhist history, especially in regard to ordination. Though domestic practices also emerged in the earliest echelon of the Buddhist tradition, the relative paucity of scholarship reflects a long interpretive orientation that has valorized monastic renunciation as more authentic than lay practice. Although this has partly to do with gender disparities, the practical challenges of studying domestic practices have also been a factor. Unlike monastic practices recorded in historical materials that detail monastic organizational structure, regulations, and forms of patronage, domestic practices are not as clearly codified and institutionalized. Research strategies require investing significant time to cultivating trusting relationships with people and being allowed into their homes. Part VI seeks to introduce more balance to the field by foregrounding the practices of female monastics and encouraging the exploration of the rich diversity of domestic practices.

When focus is placed on domestic and monastic practices, the dynamics that come into view include the agency of women in contradistinction to men; delineating monastic versus lay practice; navigating tensions between hegemonic culture and minority concerns; and defining time, space, and bodies as "Buddhist" or not. Each of these dynamics involves determining who has authority to deem a given practice authentic. Such negotiations are central to the strategic forms of practice undertaken by Buddhists in varying sociocultural contexts.

Two chapters in this section reveal the dynamics that have surrounded women's ordination practices. Hiroko Kawanami's Chapter 23 provides a historically and culturally contextualized overview of challenges and achievements creatively negotiated by women in a diversity of monastic traditions. Lori Meek's Chapter 24 on female monastic practice in thirteenth-century Japan highlights the strategies nuns employed to reinvigorate their practice, including distinctive forms of ritual mastery. Her essay also underscores how differences in socioeconomic status and educational level impacted nuns' agency. Together these chapters further our understanding of how women in a diversity of Buddhist communities have worked to define and undertake authentic ordination practices.

New perspectives on the negotiation of authenticity and authority emerge when viewed in the context of cross-cultural engagements. In Chapter 25, Vesna Wallace highlights how Vinaya practice in Mongolia was adapted to accommodate the ingestion of an indigenous fermented drink so that it did not violate the vow to refrain from intoxicants. In Chapter 26, Charles Korin Pokorny explores socioeconomic and social dynamics that shaped cultural adaptations of monastic practice at the Tassajara Zen Mountain Center in California. Linda Ho Peché's Chapter 27 analyzes how Vietnamese Buddhist home altars in Texas are also sites for cultural expression and creative adaptation for a minority community seeking recognition as authentic members of the local civic community.

Issues of authenticity are also closely aligned with identity construction. The last two chapters in Part VI explicate practices that organize Buddhist identities in both domestic and monastic contexts. In Chapter 28, Jonathan Walters shows how Sri Lankan calendrical, life-cycle, and periodic rituals serve to delineate the boundaries of Buddhist time and space, while Lisa Grumbach in Chapter 29 provides a historically informed analysis of the wide range of food practices by means of which practitioners have sought to embody the Dharma by what they do and do not eat.

CHAPTER 23

WOMEN'S ORDINATION

HIROKO KAWANAMI

INTRODUCTION

THE term "ordination" refers to a ceremonial procedure for accepting a new member into a monastic order or other clearly defined religious community, marking the beginning of his or her new life within it. The original purpose of ordaining Buddhist candidates in ancient India was to allow them to "go forth," implying renunciation: the substitution of one's socially designated role as a lay householder with that of a monastic renunciant. However, no procedure for it was formalized during the time of the Buddha; to accept anyone into his alms-gathering community, he merely uttered the words "*Ehi bhikkhu*": shorthand for "Come, monks, practice the life of purity to bring a complete end to suffering (dukkha)."[1] This exceedingly simple formula for bestowing ordination on a new member was first called into question when Rahula, the Buddha's son, decided to become a monk, and Sariputta, a senior disciple, was appointed to ordain him so that the Buddha would not appear partial to a blood relative. It was only after this point that the act of collectively giving endorsement to a new member was formalized as a ceremony and became known as ordination.[2]

The story in the *Cullavagga* in the Pali canon tells us how the first female renunciant, Mahapajapati Gotami, the Buddha's foster mother, was accepted into his evolving community of renunciants. A few years after the male sangha was established, she arrived with 500 women from the Sakya clan who wanted to renounce their secular lives and join it. The story purports that the Buddha initially hesitated, refusing Mahapajapati's plea three times; but when Ananda, his close disciple, questioned him about the intellectual capacity of women to pursue higher spiritual paths, the Buddha finally relented and accepted her as having equivalent qualities to a male disciple. Nonetheless, it is known that Mahapajapati was accepted only on the condition that she observe the *gurudharma*:[3] eight special rules that oblige even the most senior nun to prostrate herself before a junior *bhikkhu* and accept the authority of the male sangha. On this occasion, the Buddha is said to have compared the admission of women to the mildewing of rice in the fields, implying that his Dharma would not last as long as he had originally intended. The account of the *gurudharma* is critiqued by Buddhist scholars and feminists who perceive these rules as an instrument of discrimination, aimed at subordinating female members of the monastic hierarchy. Some also see these rules to have emerged later in the tradition and even question if they were put in place by the Buddha himself. Regardless of the provenance and motivation of these rules, however, others see them as a practical means of maintaining a calculated distance between the male and female members of the community, and of insulating the latter from the hostility of a wider patriarchal society that perceived renunciation as a male prerogative. Interestingly, even the status of these rules *as* rules (as opposed to matters of etiquette) can be questioned, since infringements of them by female monastics carry no punishments.[4]

In recent years, discussion of women's ordination has focused primarily on its legal procedures, drawing on descriptions in the Vinaya to assess the validity of the restored *bhikkhunī* order in Theravada Buddhist countries, as well as the possibility of it being instated in the Tibetan tradition. Technically speaking, it is possible to ordain a female candidate in the Dharmaguptaka tradition preserved in Mahayana Buddhist countries in East Asia, but the issue of whether she should undergo a "single" or a "dual" ordination continues to divide the opinions of practitioners and scholarly observers, as will be discussed in more detail in the following section. In practice, however, single ordination (i.e., ordination by monks alone or even nuns alone, rather than by a combination of both monks and nuns) has been conducted in many traditions, and female candidates who have undergone it have generally been accepted as legitimate members of the monastic community, without the legality of their position being questioned in the local context.

Today, having evolved over two millennia of Buddhist history, the procedural details surrounding ordination vary widely, and many alternative types of ordination are therefore utilized to accept prospective female members into the Buddhist communal fold. Women's ordination is conducted in China, South Korea, Japan, Taiwan, and Vietnam—all countries in which the influence of *Dharmaguptaka-vinaya* is strong, as it is viewed as "uninterrupted" from the time of the Buddha in transmitting the female monastic lineage. In Theravada Buddhist countries such as Myanmar and Sri Lanka where the *bhikkhunī* lineage has gone extinct, and in Thailand and the Himalayan regions where the lineage was never established in the first place, the male-dominated sangha and governments generally take a conservative view that it is not possible to grant Buddhist women a religious status equivalent to that of monks, whether by ordination or otherwise. Nevertheless, Myanmar, Thailand, and Sri Lanka are home to large numbers of precept nuns who may not be fully ordained according to the recognized canonical procedure, but who adhere to hundreds of normative rules in their monastic communities.[5] Many of these nuns have made the Pali Vinaya their central frame of reference and adhere to as many monastic rules as possible in an attempt to legitimate themselves in the eyes of their supporters and skeptics alike.

In the recent ordination debate of Buddhist nuns, perhaps the plight of Tibetan nuns dispersed over several countries in the Himalayan regions drew the most attention, culminating in the Hamburg conference in July 2007, supported by a consortium of international Buddhist scholars.[6] Despite efforts to foster their monastic education by the 14th Dalai Lama and others, the fact that they did not have access to full ordination meant that Tibetan nuns could not study the *Mulasarvastivada-vinaya*, an integral part of the *geshe* curriculum. Some nuns proceeded to take the novice ordination and observe ten precepts, but others continued to seek ways to become fully ordained as *bhikṣhunī*. In 2012, the Dalai Lama suggested that the nuns of the Gelugpa tradition take the *geshe* examination and created the female title of *geshema* specifically for this purpose, and on December 22, 2016, the first batch of twenty Tibetan nuns from nunneries in India and Nepal was awarded a *geshema* degree in the Gelugpa school; equivalent to a doctorate in Buddhist philosophy.[7] The ordination debate of Tibetan nuns has gained ground ever since. In 2017, the 17th Karmapa advocated his plan to introduce full ordination by inviting *bhikṣhunī* from Taiwan to give novice vows to nuns from six Kagyu nunneries. After a year of probation, a two-year traineeship is expected to follow, and it is hoped that *bhikṣhunī* vows will eventually be conferred to successful female candidates in the Tibetan tradition by a dual ordination of Mulasarvativada monks and Dharmagupta nuns.

Issues and Procedures of a Vinaya-Based Ordination

As noted earlier, the issue of whether a single as opposed to dual ordination is permissible for a female candidate has been hotly debated in recent discussions around the restoration of the *bhikkhunī* lineage.[8] The ordination of Mahapajapati, the first *bhikkhunī*, was administered by the Buddha himself, but her female followers were ordained by his male monastic disciples. In other words, the scripture describes how the Buddha authorized the practice of single ordination, which is self-evidently relevant in parallel situations where there are no ordained females available.[9] A dual ordination, on the other hand, requires a minimum of five ordained nuns to question the female candidate in the first part of the ceremony, and at least five ordained monks in the second part to complete the procedure. Nonetheless, basing his arguments on the Vinaya, Venerable Analayo, a German monk ordained in Sri Lanka, has concluded that a single ordination is as valid as dual ordination, provided that it is necessitated by circumstances.[10] Specifically, these circumstances are (1) a *bhikkhunī* order is not in existence, in which case a female candidate can be ordained by the *bhikkhu* community alone; and (2) a *bhikkhunī* order exists, but the female candidate cannot safely approach the monks, so she is ordained by the *bhikkhunī* community in person, and later by the *bhikkhu* community through a messenger. As Analayo's analysis implies, the Vinaya rules—which were compiled in ancient times and steeped in patriarchal values—did not anticipate the commonplace modern situation in which female monastics independently decide to ordain a female candidate without deferring to their male colleagues.

On the other hand, in Theravada territories with no surviving *bhikkhunī* order capable of ordaining female candidates, a prospective nun may ask the male sangha to confer her higher ordination. In such cases, a quorum of Theravada *bhikkhu* has to act in accordance with the advice of *bhikkhunī* who were ordained in the Dharmaguptaka lineage, and who are therefore normally from Mahayana Buddhist countries. As briefly noted previously, the sangha and state in Buddhist countries in Southeast Asia and Sri Lanka are generally conservative in their interpretation of the central law book, the Pali Vinaya, and insist on the impossibility of reviving the *bhikkhunī* lineages that have died out.[11] Moreover, some Theravada monks perceive the international revival movement as a Mahayana plot to convert Sinhalese or Myanmar nuns to a foreign brand of Buddhism.[12] The priority of others is the retention of decision-making powers by the male sangha, especially where issues of lineage adherence and the transmission of authority are involved. The majority of precept nuns in Theravada Buddhist countries are dependent on their monk teachers for protection as well as tutelage, and they consider it more important to be acknowledged as monastic members in their own tradition—whether fully ordained or not—than to be ordained in another lineage that most perceive as alien or non-authentic.[13]

The initiative for an ordination ultimately has to come from the candidate herself in every Buddhist tradition, who makes a public request for ordination and professes her willingness to renounce her secular identity and all existing ties.[14] In most cases, this is a lifelong commitment and the consequences of her decision are profound, especially for a young woman who opts to lead a celibate life regulated by many abstinence rules. At the start of the ceremony, the female candidate announces the name of her "preceptor," who has to be a senior nun with at least ten years' experience.[15] Sometimes the preceptor is allocated by the host institution, and sometimes is chosen by the candidate herself. The preceptor begins by showing the new member a set of monastic robes, and then instructs her about *pārājika*: the grave offences that could lead to excommunication. There are four *pārājika* offenses for male members and eight for females.[16] The transmission of these and other rules from the preceptor to candidate amounts to instructing on the essential aspects of moral conduct both external and internal, and especially on dispelling lustful thoughts, which are regarded as incompatible with the celibate life that follows. Due to the heavy responsibility of training a new member, a female preceptor is not allowed to take on more than one candidate per year[17]—reminding us that an ordination is not only a life-changing event for the candidate herself, but also a major undertaking on the part of the host institution, which takes full responsibility for the training of a new member before as well as after it occurs.

The ritual site for the higher ordination is called the *sīmā*: a marked space that is cleansed both literally and symbolically before the ordination ceremony, with monks reciting sacred words held to have magical power to dispel malevolent spirits that could disturb the ritual procedure. Women are normally not allowed to enter the *sīmā* or to use it in their own ordinations, and thus it has been another area of contention in discussions of women's ordination, especially in the Theravada tradition. In Sri Lanka, for example, supporters of the newly restored *bhikkhunī* order were accused of violating the consecrated spaces of temples, as its ordination rites were conducted within these, and conservative monks saw women entering them as an act of challenge to the purity of their Theravada legacy.[18]

Qualifications of the Candidate

A female candidate, during the *upasampadā* (a ritual that confers higher ordination), is asked a set of questions aimed at evaluating her suitability and establishing whether she has any "hindrances" that make her ineligible for ordination. Twenty-nine "hindrances" are listed in the *Dharmaguptaka-vinaya*; thirteen major and sixteen minor, which apply to both male and female candidates.[19] The thirteen major hindrances include serious violations that can be classified as *pārājika* offenses, which include having sexually abused a monk or a nun, or having previously joined the sangha and later converted to another religion. Eunuchs, hermaphrodites, "nonhumans," and animals are disqualified, as well as a person whose intention is to ordain only for one's personal benefit.[20] The sixteen minor hindrances point to a person who cannot qualify as long as that hindrance exists, such as a slave, a criminal, a debtor, a royal servant, or a person whose parents do not grant consent. An ideal candidate is expected to be healthy both physically and mentally, and someone without any contagious, incurable, or chronic illnesses.[21]

In the case of a female candidate, she is asked whether she has complete organs and menstruates regularly. She cannot be incontinent or suffering from uterine prolapse. She cannot be pregnant, married, or the mother of an un-weaned child. She also cannot be a female *paṇḍaka*, an androgyne or a hermaphrodite, in other words, a woman with ambiguous sex.[22] Ideally, these questions are asked by a group of senior female monastics on behalf of their male counterparts, to avoid inflicting embarrassment on the female candidate; and it is described in the *Cullavagga* that the need to make such inquiries was a major underlying reason for the emergence of dual ordination.[23] Before her formal acceptance as a prospective nun, a woman's parents or a guardian must grant her permission to renounce the world. If married, she has to obtain a divorce from her husband as part of leaving the family and all domestic responsibilities.[24] Parents in traditional Asian societies are normally reluctant to let an unmarried daughter join the monastic community, not only because of the hardship she may encounter in her life as a nun, but because female renunciation itself is—as discussed earlier—widely held to be subversive of the mores of such societies. During my fieldwork in Myanmar, for example, I was told how a young woman ran away from home under cover of darkness because her family objected to her decision, while another—a newlywed—begged her husband to grant her permission to renounce the world.[25] As well as societal expectations, however, such stories highlight the inner resolution of female candidates who decide to become nuns despite fierce opposition from their immediate family. This contrasts sharply with the social milieu of a male candidate, whose renunciation is widely celebrated and endorsed as a meritorious act for both the candidate and his parents.

However, while renunciation represents a withdrawal from worldly fetters and a cutting of family ties, it does not imply a reclusive lifestyle dedicated merely to one's own spiritual benefit. Once ordained, she is expected to take on wider religious duties as stipulated by the monastic community, and to work toward the common goal of disseminating the Dharma. Thus, a nun is required to dispel selfish tendencies and to immerse herself totally in the moral ethos of the Buddhist community, specifically by adhering to a full set of monastic rules. So that senior nuns can be certain of her general aptitude, a female candidate has to undergo probationary training as a *sikkhamānā*, during which time she observes six rules out of the ten prescribed for a *sāmaṇerī*.[26] Conservative Vinaya experts sometimes argue that a woman who has not done two years of training as a *sikkhamānā* is not a qualified candidate,[27] but in practice, not many female candidates seem to have completed the prescribed period. Besides, the senior nuns' main concern at this point is that the candidate is able to adhere to monastic discipline and live in harmony with other nuns in the community. She is also expected to maintain an amicable relationship with the monks and solicit the support of lay followers. In reality, she continues to be on probation not merely after her ordination, but for many years beyond the induction period, before she is fully transformed into a vocational monastic.

Most Buddhist nunneries are reluctant to accept mature candidates or those who have been married before, since these women are presumed to be unable to adjust to a communal way of living and strict adherence to monastic rules. Although the official minimum age for receiving ordination is twenty, female candidates in traditional Asian countries seem mostly to be in their mid-teens, which is regarded as an age at which a child can decide if she wants to leave home and pursue a life as a nun.[28] A young member starts her training as soon as she enters the monastic order, spending many hours learning the relevant chants so that she could perform in ceremonies and memorizing the basic scriptures. The period as an apprentice is regarded as the most important in becoming accustomed to the monastic discipline and learning one's place in the communal hierarchy. In exceptional cases, even younger children are accepted on compassionate grounds. The Buddhist scriptures also record that many monks joined the sangha as young people with little knowledge of the Dharma.[29] In most cases, at the point of entry, a novice knows little beyond basic Buddhist ethics, which are mostly culturally specific notions of what constitutes good or bad behavior. In terms of general qualifications, senior members look for qualities such as obedience, intelligence, calm temperament, patience, generosity, a willingness to listen, and an ability to get along with others, which should enable a new member to immerse herself in the general ethos of the monastic community.

It is noteworthy that almost all senior monks and nuns in Myanmar who occupy important positions in the state monastic organization belong to a category called *nge-byu*, which means "young and pure," implying that they joined the monastic community before puberty.[30] This suggests that, if a candidate is to become fully and successfully socialized into a monastic vocation, he or she should be trained from a young age in matters of discipline and moral conduct, scriptural learning, teaching and preaching, and all aspects of social and communal protocol. Moreover, monastic training is long and arduous, and the qualities that enable a person to successfully endure it ultimately include innate good temperament, and commitment to the Triple Gem and serving the Buddhist community.

Variations in Ordination Practices and Ordained Status

Throughout Buddhism's long history, it has been normative for Buddhist women to be ordained only by monks, but in the last few decades, an increasing proportion of female candidates have undergone dual ordination, offered in Taiwan, Korea, and Sri Lanka. Taiwan has one of the largest contingents of highly educated *bhikṣunī*, who today outnumber monks by three to one. In their early struggle to re-establish a form of Chinese institutional Buddhism that was uninfluenced by either the Communist Party or the colonial legacy of Japanese Buddhism, leading monks such as Baisheng and Yinshun encouraged Taiwanese women to study the dharma and ordained them as female monastics.[31] However, it was only in 1976 that the first dual ordination was conducted in Taiwan, at the instigation of the nun Tianyi.[32] Beginning in the 1980s, the procedure has been greatly facilitated by the ever-increasing number of fully ordained nuns and trained ritual masters.

In Korea, whose Buddhist nuns are second only to Taiwan's in status relative to monks, the strong patriarchal values perpetuated by Confucianism have long presented a challenge for Buddhist women. In 1910, Myori Pophui was the first nun to receive ordination there, in what is widely regarded as a unique case of single ordination conferred by a group of senior nuns.[33] Korean nuns were initially dependent on monks for doctrinal studies and training, but after the country's liberation from Japan in 1945, many began transmitting their doctrinal knowledge to the next generation of nuns.[34] Korea's Buddhist nuns now constitute a self-sufficient group, and the tradition of nun masters teaching nun disciples in an independent environment seems to have contributed to a normalization of the practice of women's ordination being conferred by only women.

In Japan, Buddhist women have a long history of monasticism, launching their first monastic tradition during the sixth century, and a continuous stream of nuns have been ordained since then.[35] In the ninth century, the practice of women's ordination shifted to taking the Bodhisattva vows, which did not require a female candidate to have a quorum of monks present at her ordination. Within the many Buddhist sects in Japan, however, the treatment of female monastics has been varied, sometimes codifying unfair treatment in sect regulations. Notably, Arai describes how Sōtō nuns in the twentieth century fought for and won complete parity in its sect regulations.

There are many Buddhist women who undergo alternative forms of ordination, which can be defined as "self-ordination" or "community ordination." The majority of nuns in the Theravada tradition today observe eight precepts. Few observe ten. Although most are not fully ordained, a growing number of young women are joining their monastic communities. In Myanmar, for example, there are currently about 65,000 precept nuns called *thiláshin*, who since the 1980s have been co-opted into the state monastic organization and operate as ritual functionaries.[36] Registered with the Department of Religious Affairs of the Myanmar government, *thiláshin* are granted a monastic status in the category of "vocational members who serve the *sāsana*." Their position as "non-ordained" does not seem to speak decisively against the legitimacy of their monastic membership, however, since their official status is acknowledged by the state in their passports and other official documents that use their Buddhist titles conferred at the time of ordination.[37] In Thailand, there are some 20,000 precept nuns called *mae chi* who coexist with a small number of ordained *bhikkhunī*. While *mae chi* are self-ordained and are integrated into society, female candidates who seek *upasampadā* do so abroad, mostly in Sri Lanka. Nonetheless, their *bhikkhunī* status after return is not officially recognized by the Thai government. Another type of female monastic in Thailand, called *sikkhamat*, is affiliated with the reformed Buddhist group Santi Asoke. The Asoke group was established in the 1970s by the monk Phra Bodhiraksa, who was excommunicated by the Thai sangha in 1989.[38] He continues to ordain his members himself, but they cannot claim a legitimate religious status within mainstream Thailand and exist in several self-sustaining communes. Though *sikkhamat* are highly respected within the Asoke group, with a status said to be almost equal to that of male monastics, their total numbers are very low.

In countries where Buddhism is a minority religion and/or not deeply rooted in society, women's ordination has often been instigated by a lone Buddhist monk. For example, in Indonesia—the world's largest Muslim-majority nation—the first ordained Buddhist monk, Ashin Jinarakkhita, gave novice ordination to female candidates in the 1960s, and then sent them to Hong Kong to receive higher ordination.[39] Eventually, some of these nuns returned to Indonesia, where the lineage they established now trains and educates Buddhist nuns, supported by the international community of Buddhist women. In the case of nuns from the Zangskar region of the Indian Himalaya, several of them traveled to Lhasa in the 1950s and were ordained by the abbot of Ganden, who was then the prominent head of the Gelugpa sect.[40] Their newly ordained status allowed the nuns to found their first Buddhist nunnery in a remote part of northeast India, and this has developed into one of the largest and ritually active nunneries in the area.

Also in the West, where Buddhism is a relative newcomer as a religious tradition, there are homegrown Western Buddhist organizations such as the Triratna Buddhist Community, which has grown into one of the largest bodies in the United Kingdom and Europe.[41] The members of this group generally emphasize the collective sharing of spiritual experiences in ordination, rather than the preservation of monastic tradition through the strict observation of ordination procedures. As such, they have reinterpreted traditional notions of the sangha in a more open and inclusive manner, and in part as a result of this, their community is less gender-stratified than most of its Eastern counterparts. Triratna's ordination procedure is reported to be the same for both men and women, comprising two stages, one private and the other public, the latter being conducted by "public preceptors" who oversee the process and authorize the ordination. The candidate takes ten precepts, but ordination in this tradition does not necessarily make one into a "mendicant" in a traditional sense. Rather, the status change allows the newly ordained member to join advanced training retreats, to affiliate herself with the lineage of teachers, and generally to have more access to higher practices offered within the community.[42] Some of the Buddhist traditions in the East are also becoming more egalitarian and open to sharing across genders. For example, in the Chinese Chan school in Taiwan, the overall ordination procedure may take up to thirty days, to allow the candidates to break with old habits and prepare them for the status-change into a full monastic member. The main part of women's ordination is conferred by a quorum of ten *bhikṣu* and ten *bhikṣunī*, but the entire procedure leading up to it is a collective undertaking, instructed and led by a group of mentors who are both male and female ordained monastics with many years of training. They guide the female candidates through the intricate ritual process, instructing them how to walk, bow, and perform the recitation correctly, and ultimately supporting their full integration into the monastic community.[43]

The Procedures and Themes of Women's Ordination Rituals

The Buddhist ordination ceremony establishes a ritual threshold that allows the female candidate to break with her previous life and draw a line between being "this-worldly" and "otherworldly;" between the status of a laywoman and that of a monastic. Detailed communal rules maintain the physical separation between these two worlds, thus keeping the corrupting influences of the mundane at bay. The training in moral discipline that each novice receives from the community is considered essential to both protecting and reinforcing her renunciant status.

In Myanmar, the ceremony conducted to mark one's transition in status from a laywoman to a Buddhist nun is called *thiláshin wut-pwè*, "a ceremony of putting on the nun's robe." Traditionally, a woman's renunciation was a simple affair conducted in secret, attended only by members of the host nunnery, to avoid disputes with her family. Such conflicts were commonplace, due to the previously mentioned parental objections to girls' decisions to become nuns. In recent decades, there is more recognition of the nuns' scholarly achievements, and their rising popularity has led to increasing numbers of young women taking up temporary ordination in reputable nunneries. This trend has created new demands by lay supporters to make their status transition more viable. As a result, such ceremonies for Buddhist women have become more formal and structured and officially authenticated by the presence of monks. Thus, rather than conducted in a secretive private ritual, nuns' initiation in Myanmar has become a celebratory occasion attended by family, friends, and guests.

The status transition for a *thiláshin* candidate consists of two sections: the first part focusing on her renunciation of the world, and the second on her integration into the nuns' community. The religious significance of the ritual lies chiefly in the first half, in which a theatrical element is introduced to emphasize the act of renunciation: the candidate puts on a traditional costume in the manner of a celestial nymph and arrives adorned with much jewelry. Her mental preparation occurs *within* the ceremony when she goes through the outward transition from a wealthy princess to a plainly clothed shaven mendicant who leaves behind all her worldly possessions. The most important part of the status-change takes place while the hair is being cut off and the head shaved, which coincides with the "Mindfulness on the Thirty-two Parts of the Body" being recited in the Pali language by the participating nuns. Repeated in a loop, it begins with "hair" and finishes with "urine," listing the thirty-two anatomical parts of the body and bodily fluids, which conforms with the traditional procedure stipulated in the Theravada Vinaya.[44] The recitation is instrumental in reminding the candidate about the transient nature of one's physical existence and the deep implication of renunciation and the sacrifice she makes in casting away her female gender. There is an added sense of sadness that comes with her taking the eight precepts, which implies that the newly ordained can no longer use items commonly used by women, such as makeup or perfume, nor is she allowed to sing or dance. The candidate takes the Three Refuges, committing to the Buddha, the Dharma, and the sangha that she will adhere to a monastic way of life. She then asks the preceptor nun to grant her monastic robes, and changes into them, becoming outwardly transformed into a Buddhist nun.

Now as in the past, the first part of the ceremony is generally conducted by senior nuns who confer the eight precepts on a new nun, without any monks being present. But the second half of the ceremony has, in recent decades, come to be officiated by a monk who arrives at that point to sanction her status-change. Specifically, he does this by reciting the special attributes of the Buddha, and again summons the congregation to the Triple Gem, after which the new nun is given a formal Buddhist title in Pali language. At the end of the ceremony, the main donors—normally, the new nun's parents—pour water from a jug onto a plate on the floor, both to mark the public endorsement of her status change by the sangha and to confirm the meritorious act of the woman who has just been formally accepted into the nuns' community.[45]

The purpose of ordaining a *mae chi* in Thailand is similar to that for initiating a *thiláshin* in Myanmar, but while women's ordination is increasingly treated as an occasion for celebration in Myanmar, no similar movement is visible in Thailand. As Falk has explained of the Thai case, the difference between a woman's ordination conducted at a temple and at a *samnak chii* is that, while the former is a simple procedure officiated by a monk, the latter is conducted in a self-governed venue by the nuns, and it is a much more public occasion.[46] Moreover, while in Myanmar the ritual focuses on the transient nature of the physical body, Thai ordination is experienced far more explicitly as the "death" of the female candidate. This theme is acted out in the ritual procedure when the candidate passes around a tray laden with flowers and asks for forgiveness for any wrongdoing she has committed during her lifetime, more or less as a dying person would normally do. As well as putting an end to her secular persona, however, the ritual expresses a strong aspiration to be "born again."[47] The candidate's family and relatives participate in the shaving sequence, each cutting a snippet of her hair, before a senior nun takes over to complete the shaving of the head and eyebrows, after which the candidate receives a new set of robes. The ritual sequence that follows includes the candidate taking refuge in the Triple Gem, receiving the eight precepts from the officiating monk, and receiving his blessings (which appear broadly similar to those in a Myanmar ceremony). In the end, the monk grants her an official religious identity and communal affiliation.

In Mahayana Buddhist countries, an ordination ceremony constitutes a similar presentation of a major transition in a woman's life. Prior to the ceremony in Japan's Sōtō Zen tradition, the female candidate goes through an intense period of purification of both mind and body as she casts off all the attributes of her previous secular life, as well as relationships with family and friends. This process of separation starts when the candidate is still a laywoman, to ease what might otherwise be the drastic transition into a monastic life. On the day of ordination, a female candidate—who was until recent years around the typical age for marriage—sometimes (though rarer today) entered the worship hall wearing a formal bridal kimono, probably satisfying her wish to wear such a garment at some point in her life, and symbolizing her determination to enter a life of abstinence.[48] She thanks her parents and ritually bids them farewell before being led into another room where her head is shaved, except for a patch at the top.[49] When she reappears to the public, the female candidate has been transformed into a white-clad figure with a shorn head, and then she is given a last chance to decide whether to return to her previous life as a laywoman. If she professes her commitment to the monastic life at this stage, however, the last remnant of her hair is removed from the crown of her head, and she puts on the black outer robe. After she vows to adhere to her sect's set of customary precepts, it completes the final stage of her status-change. The day of her ordination is regarded as her "new birthday," which indicates the end of the old and start of the new.[50] As already mentioned, Buddhist women's ordination is often represented as an experience akin to the "death" of her former identity, as socially defined by marriage and reproduction; and the departure from her secular existence is represented as both sad and profoundly liberating.

Final Remarks on Women's Ordination

In recent decades, the international movement to revive the *bhikkhunī* order has provided Buddhist women with a new leeway to become fully ordained in many Asian countries where the *bhikkhunī* lineage had gone extinct or where there was never a full ordination. The movement has emphasized the historical links made between the Theravada and Mahayana traditions, and has brought Buddhist nuns affiliated with many different traditions to work together toward achieving the goal of reintroducing the *bhikkhunī* lineage. Proponents of the revival movement also hoped that, especially in relatively poor and remote areas, nuns could translate the renewed recognition of their ordained status into more public support and increase their donation incomes. The movement has been particularly successful in Sri Lanka, where almost 4,000 female candidates have been ordained as *bhikkhunī* in the past two decades. However, the newly restored order has also exposed tensions between those who promote progressive ideals of gender equality and individual rights, and those who seek to defend the collective interests of their community via maintaining harmonious coexistence with both monks and the laity. These differing viewpoints are prominent among the nuns themselves; many have refused to become ordained in other Buddhist traditions and have opted to remain as precept nuns in their own monastic communities, while others have joined the international movement in the spirit of Buddhist sisterhood. On the other hand, there are growing numbers of Western women ordained in and affiliated with particular Buddhist traditions in the East; but in many cases, they find it difficult to sustain themselves as ordained nuns in non-Buddhist societies that lack both monastic communities and the material support that, in Asia, would be offered them by their lay supporters.[51] This highlights the importance of the community's guidance and support for new entrants after ordination, especially in non-Buddhist cultural contexts, as well as fostering an interdependent relationship between monastic members and the wider society.

Meanwhile, many alternative modes of female Buddhist ordination are now available, having developed out of particular local situations; and the large numbers of female monastics in countries where monks and/or the state refuse to accept formal female ordination is a measure of Buddhist women's success in transmitting their own lineages and winning public recognition. In practice, however, senior nuns in Asia are more concerned about the ritual efficacy of ordination: whether the rhythm and pronunciation of the ceremonial recitation is correct enough for the ordination to take effect vis-à-vis the candidate's status-change, and may spend many hours rehearsing prior to it to perfect their ritual performance. As women's ordination becomes a more public and international event, the mixing of the procedural details of multiple Buddhist traditions, and especially the effects of such mixing on the manner in which the oral recitations are conducted, are matters of obvious concern to the monastic participants.[52] By the same token, if a particular ceremony is perceived as truly efficacious, the status of the newly ordained nun will be endorsed by her lay supporters and fellow nuns, and she will be accepted as a legitimate monastic within the local Buddhist community. In other words, the legitimacy of her status cannot be fully undermined by legal criteria alone, even if such criteria are drawn from canonical procedures in the Vinaya.

As a final point, it is worth noting that few scholars have looked into the actual ordination experiences of Buddhist women, partly because ordinations have traditionally been esoteric rituals, closed to outside researchers, and the subject of few firsthand accounts.[53] Yet it has to be acknowledged that every ordination experience leaves a profound effect on the female candidate, since it is a de facto departure from the familiar into an unknown world of monastic vows and moral discipline. Accounts by nuns often reveal the agonizing soul-searching that led them to leave their previous life and become a vocational monastic, in many cases defying the pressure from family members to accept conventional notions of womanhood. Once ordained, a woman is in effect adopted by the host community of nuns, which takes on the sole responsibility for guiding and training her into full membership in their society; and in this respect, the ordination ceremony itself is only the start of a long journey.

Notes

1. Mohan Wijayaratna, *Buddhist Monastic Life*, trans. Claude Grangier and Steven Collins (Cambridge: Cambridge University Press, 1990), 117; Vinaya I, 23.
2. Vinaya I, 83; Dhp-a I, 98.
3. *Garudhamma* in Pali.
4. Analayo, *Vinaya Studies* (Taipei: Dharma Drum, 2017), 303.
5. They are generally known as eight-precept or ten-precept observing nuns.
6. http://www.congress-on-buddhist-women.org/; see *Dignity and Discipline: Reviving Full Ordination for Buddhist Nuns*, ed. Thea Mohr and Jampa Tsedroen (Boston: Wisdom Publications, 2009).
7. https://tnp.org/tibetan-nuns-geshema-graduation-ceremony-december-2016/; accessed September 21, 2020.
8. Janet Gyatso, "Female Ordination in Buddhism: Looking into a Crystal Ball, Making a Future," in *Dignity & Discipline: Reviving Full Ordination for Buddhist Nuns*, ed. Thea Mohr and Jampa Tsedroen (Boston: Wisdom Publications, 2009), 1–21.
9. Vinaya II 256, 34 to 257, 25.
10. Analayo, *Vinaya Studies*, 279.
11. In Myanmar, where conservatism is the pervasive dominant viewpoint, any public discussion of the *bhikkhunī* revival remains banned, following a major controversy in 2004: see Hiroko Kawanami, "The *Bhikkhuni* Ordination Debate: Global Aspirations, Local Concerns, with Special Emphasis on the Views of the Monastic Community in Burma." *Buddhist Studies Review* 24, no. 2 (2007): 226–44.
12. Conservative Theravada monks criticized a restored woman's ordination that had been conferred by a mixed quorum of international sangha in the 1990s as insufficient. The abbot of Dambula monastery thereafter started to re-confer ordination on Sinhalese *bhikkhunī* previously ordained in India to legitimate their status in Sri Lanka. Moreover, those Sinhalese *bhikkhunī* who had received *upasampadā* in India came under heavy criticism from members of their own tradition for dressing in Mahayana robes and taking the Bodhisattva vow. Kawanami, "Ordination Debate," 227.
13. Kawanami, "Ordination Debate," 238.
14. A candidate cannot be forced to renounce, so she has to make a formal request to initiate an ordination ritual called *pravrajya*.

15. Bhikshuni Wu Yin, *Choosing Simplicity: A Commentary on Bhikshuni Pratimoksha*, trans. Jendy Shih; ed. Bhikshuni Thubten Chodron (Ithaca, NY: Snow Lion Publications, 2001),105–7.
16. These include being lustful, consenting to be touched, stroked, grabbed, fondled, or squeezed in the area between her collarbones and knees: Vinaya IV, 34, 213.
17. Vinaya IV, 6, 337; Shih 2000, 399.
18. There seem to be regional differences within Thailand regarding women's entry into an ordination hall, and in central parts of the country, women can enter the building called *bot*. See Monica Lindberg Falk, *Making Fields of Merit: Buddhist Female Ascetics and Gendered Orders in Thailand* (Copenhagen: NIAS, 2007), 98–99.
19. Ann Heirman, *"The Discipline in Four Parts": Rules for Nuns According to the Dharmaguptakavinaya* (Delhi: Motilal Banarsidass, 2002), 63–69.
20. Wu Yin, *Choosing Simplicity*, 92–95.
21. Leprosy, boils, intestinal worms, tuberculosis or asthma, epilepsy, as well as mental imbalance.
22. Vinaya II, 271, 17; 272, 12.
23. Vinaya II, 271.
24. Vinaya IV, 317–34.
25. Hiroko Kawanami, *Renunciation and Empowerment of Buddhist Nuns in Myanmar-Burma: Building a Community of Female Faithful* (Leiden: Brill, 2013), 77.
26. Bhikkhu Bodhi, "The Revival of Bhikkhunī Ordination in the Theravāda Tradition," in *Dignity and Discipline, Reviving Full Ordination for Buddhist Nuns*, ed. Thea Mohr and Jampa Tsedroen (Boston: Wisdom Publications, 2009), 102–3; Vinaya IV, 320, 21.
27. Bodhi, "The Revival," 103.
28. In Thailand the minimum age seems to be about 14, and in Myanmar it is normally after the completion of a state primary education, when the child is about 12.
29. Wijayaratna, *Buddhist Monastic Life*, 13–14.
30. Kawanami, *Renunciation and Empowerment*, 44–45.
31. Elise Anne DeVido, *Taiwan's Buddhist Nuns* (Albany: State University of New York Press, 2010), 16.
32. DeVido, *Taiwan's Buddhist Nuns*, 17.
33. Eun-Su Cho, "Female Buddhist Practice in Korea: A Historical Account," in *Korean Buddhist Nuns and Laywomen: Hidden Histories, Enduring Vitality*, ed. Eun-Su Cho (Albany: State University of New York Press, 2011), 31.
34. Pori Park, "The Establishment of Buddhist Nunneries in Contemporary Korea," in *Korean Buddhist Nuns and Laywomen: Hidden Histories, Enduring Vitality*, ed. Eun-Su Cho (Albany: State University of New York Press, 2011), 166–67.
35. Paula Kane Robinson Arai, *Women Living Zen: Japanese Sōtō Buddhist Nuns* (Oxford: Oxford University Press, 1999), 31–48.
36. There were 64,519 precept nuns (*thiláshin*) in Myanmar in 2017, according to the statistics published by the Department of Religious Affairs of the Myanmar government. Since 1980 they are officially registered with the Ministry of Religious Affairs.
37. *Bhikkhunīs* from Thailand and Sri Lanka, in contrast, are still referred to by their lay names in official documents.
38. Falk estimates the number of *mae chi* in Thailand to be about 20,000, as compared to just 100 fully ordained *bhikkhunī* and female novices there. Heikkila-Horn states that there are currently 25 female *sikkhamat* in the Asoke community. This information was obtained via discussions at a conference panel (August 16, 2017, EUROSEAS, Oxford University) attended by myself and both speakers.

39. At his first ordination of a female novice in 1963, he gave her a Pali title: Jinakumari. In 1966, he sent Jinakumari and eight other novice nuns to Po Lin Monastery in Hong Kong so that they could receive higher ordination. See Jack Meng-Tat Chia, "Toward a Modern Indonesian Buddhism: The Buddhist Nationalism of Ashin Jinarakkhita," *History of Religions* 57, no. 4 (2018): 38.
40. Gutschow reports that despite their initial reluctance to ordain, the nuns were persuaded to go through it by a fellow monk who insisted that the resultant "merit would outweigh any ritual mistake." Kim Gutschow, *Being a Buddhist Nun: The Struggle for Enlightenment in the Himalayas* (Cambridge, MA: Harvard University Press, 2004), 22.
41. Initially called Friends of the Western Buddhist Order, and later simply the Western Buddhist Order, it was founded in 1967 by Sangharakshita, an English Buddhist monk.
42. *Handbook for Women Who Have Asked for Ordination into the Triratna Buddhist Order*, 3–19. https://manchesterbuddhistcentre.org.uk; accessed September 3, 2018.
43. For the description of Chinese Chan ordination, see Jian Cheng-shi, "Mindfulness as Ancient Wisdom in Contemporary Chan Monasteries in China and Taiwan," paper presented at the annual conference of the UK Association for Buddhist Studies (July 1, 2017, SOAS, University of London).
44. *Satipatthana Sutta*, MN10 and MN I, 57, 16.
45. Apparently, this pouring of water and confirming the meritorious act is not performed in Thailand for female candidates as it is for male novices, which seems to confirm the ambiguous/non-societally sanctioned nature of women's ordination there.
46. For a detailed description of the ordination procedure of Thai *mae chi*, see Falk, *Making Fields of Merit*, 92–101.
47. Falk, *Making Fields of Merit*, 92.
48. Arai, *Women Living Zen*, 102–3.
49. In the Sōtō Zen tradition, she is presented with the essentials, such as a set of black bowls, a black monastic robe, a surplice for formal occasions, a mini-surplice for informal occasions, and a cloth for kneeling and prostrations.
50. Arai, *Women Living Zen*, 102.
51. Jetsunma Tenzin Palmo has highlighted the problems in "Some Challenges Facing Non-Himalayan Nuns in the Tibetan Buddhist Tradition," in the 14th Sakyadhita International Conference proceedings: *Compassion and Social Justice*, edited by Karma Lekshe Tsomo (Yogyakarta: Sakyadhita, 2015), 111–14. Also see Michelle Hannah, "Colliding Gender Imaginaries: Transnational Debates about Full Ordination for Tibetan Buddhist Nuns," *Asian Journal of Women's Studies* 18, no. 4 (2012): 18–22.
52. This issue of ritual language was addressed by the 14th Dalai Lama at the Hamburg Conference in 2007 when he told a group of international *bhikkhunī* that they had to learn Tibetan language and memorize the ritual formula if they were to conduct legitimate ordinations of Tibetan nuns in the Mulasarvastivada tradition.
53. Gutschow, *Being a Buddhist Nun*, 180.

Further Reading

Analayo. *Vinaya Studies*. Taipei: Dharma Drum, 2017.

Arai, Paula Kane Robinson. *Women Living Zen: Japanese Sōtō Buddhist Nuns*. Oxford: Oxford University Press, 1999.

Cho, Eun-Su, ed. *Korean Buddhist Nuns and Laywomen: Hidden Histories, Enduring Vitality.* Albany: State University of New York Press, 2011.
DeVido, Elise Anne. *Taiwan's Buddhist Nuns.* Albany: State University of New York Press, 2010.
Falk, Monica Lindberg. *Making Fields of Merit: Buddhist Female Ascetics and Gendered Orders in Thailand.* Copenhagen: NIAS, 2007.
Gutschow, Kim. *Being a Buddhist Nun: The Struggle for Enlightenment in the Himalayas.* Cambridge, MA: Harvard University Press, 2004.
Heikkilä-Horn, Marja-Leena. *Buddhism with Open Eyes: Belief and Practice of Santi Asoke.* Bangkok: Santi Asoke, 1997.
Heirman, Ann. *"The Discipline in Four Parts": Rules for Nuns According to the Dharmaguptakavinaya.* Delhi: Motilal Banarsidass, 2002.
Kawanami, Hiroko. "The *Bhikkhunī* Ordination Debate: Global Aspirations, Local Concerns, with Special Emphasis on the Views of the Monastic Community in Burma." *Buddhist Studies Review* 24, no. 2 (2007): 226–44.
Kawanami, Hiroko. *Renunciation and Empowerment of Buddhist Nuns in Myanmar-Burma: Building a Community of Female Faithful.* Leiden: Brill, 2013.
Mohr, Thea, and Jampa Tsedroen, eds. *Dignity and Discipline: Reviving Full Ordination for Buddhist Nuns.* Boston: Wisdom Publications, 2009.
Thubten Chodron, Bhikkhuni, ed. *Choosing Simplicity: A Commentary on Bhikshuni Pratimoksha*, trans. Jendy Shih. Ithaca, NY: Snow Lion Publications, 2001.
Wijayaratna, Mohan. *Buddhist Monastic Life: According to the Texts of the Theravāda Tradition*, trans. Claude Grangier and Steven Collins. Cambridge: Cambridge University Press, 1990.

CHAPTER 24

MONASTIC AUTHORITY IN MEDIEVAL JAPAN

The Case of the Convent Hokkeji

LORI MEEKS

THE methods by which monastic authority is established and transmitted in Buddhist communities are likely as diverse as the tradition itself. In this chapter I will consider some of the processes by which nuns at the medieval Japanese convent Hokkeji established and maintained authority at their newly revived institution. The methods I outline here are by no means representative of Buddhism as a whole, but they do tell us a lot about the broader religious culture of pre-modern Japan. To a certain extent, they also reflect the challenges faced by female monastics in particular.

The convent Hokkeji (the "Lotus Temple") was first established around 741 under the auspices of Queen-Consort Kōmyō (701–760), the consort and co-ruler of Emperor Shōmu (701–756). The convent appears to have flourished for at least a century after its initial founding but later came to experience, from at least the tenth century, numerous periods of decline and restoration.[1] With the help of Eison (1201–1290), a Shingon monk interested in restoring the Vinaya monastic precepts in Japan, a small but diverse group of women staged a large-scale revival of Hokkeji in the 1240s. They did this during a time when official monastic roles for women had all but disappeared in Japan. Attention to the methods by which Hokkeji nuns established and maintained monastic authority are especially telling, then, for these nuns had to assert themselves in an environment that privileged male leadership.

In thinking through the various means by which Hokkeji nuns created a sense of authority, there are three major areas that come to mind. First, the nuns derived a great deal of authority by fashioning themselves as the curators of the celebrated legacy of their founder, Kōmyō. Close connections to the court and influential aristocratic families enabled them to claim Kōmyō's legacy as their own. Second, they received the precepts, as well as doctrinal and ritual training, from established priests and created teaching lineages of their own. And finally, they mastered a long list of complex rituals and performed them on a regular basis. This was the common "work," or *otsutome*, of Japanese temples, and it was one of the primary methods by which temples attracted donors: they performed rituals that were deemed efficacious.

In the sections that follow, I will examine each of these areas, considering how particular connections, areas of expertise, and skills enabled Hokkeji nuns to establish themselves as authoritative religious professionals.

Drawing on the Authority of the Founder and Her Courtly Culture

In literature written by the nuns who revived Hokkeji, the most commonly celebrated source of monastic authority is the convent's founder, Queen-Consort Kōmyō. The clearest example of this is evident in the 1304 *Hokke metsuzaiji engi* (Origins of the Lotus Temple for the Eradication of Transgressions). In this origin narrative, which would have been recited to pilgrims who visited Hokkeji, the nuns celebrate Kōmyō on many levels. First, she is described as a wise and generous co-ruler, as a devout Buddhist who converted her personal residence into the temple Hokkeji, and as a filial daughter of Fujiwara no Fuhito (659–720). According to the *Hokke metsuzaiji engi*, Kōmyō was fiercely committed to creating a monastic order that would be staffed by women. The text reports that, upon learning that Tōdaiji, the male counterpart of Hokkeji, would be off-limits to women, the Queen-Consort vowed to fill all of Hokkeji's lofty positions (such as the "five masters," or *goshi*, and "three cabinet members," or *sangō*) with nuns.[2]

After establishing Kōmyō's virtuousness as the founder of Hokkeji, the text identifies the ways in which Kōmyō continues to assert authority over the life of the convent. It would require no exaggeration to say that the nuns appear to have regarded Kōmyō as a deified individual; indeed, they repeatedly identify her as a manifestation of the bodhisattva Kannon (Avalokiteśvara). The *Hokke metsuzaiji engi* asserts this identity in numerous ways, the most obvious being its description of miracles associated with the Queen-Consort, both in the distant past and during the time of the convent's thirteenth-century revival. Among the miracles related, perhaps the most relevant is that in which a king from Gandhāra makes a vow to worship a living manifestation of Avalokiteśvara and then learns in a dream that Avalokiteśvara is living in Japan, as the Queen-Consort Kōmyō. He dispatches artisans to travel to Japan and "copy her form." This endeavor results in the artisans creating six images that match the iconographical characteristics of the bodhisattva Kannon. The *engi* asserts that one of these six images is the primary statue of Hokkeji, an eleven-faced Kannon said to have been made in the Queen-Consort's own likeness.[3]

And thus the *honzon*, or primary image, at Hokkeji is said to be both the bodhisattva Kannon and the Queen-Consort herself. The *engi* states this explicitly: "She [Kōmyō] is a trace manifestation (*suijaku*) of the eleven-faced Kannon." The *engi* furthermore describes Kōmyō's presence as an enduring one; as a living deity made present through the temple's main image, she continues to express her will to the nuns. In another section from the *Hokke metsuzaiji engi*, for example, Kōmyō uses the temple's main image—the statue said to be a representation of her—to communicate her will. In this episode, the nuns tell of a time when a certain Buddhist teacher, the Master Tankū (Tankū Shōnin, 1176–1253) came to visit Hokkeji to pay respects to its celebrated Kannon image. The nuns staying at Hokkeji at the time asked the Master for help, citing the dilapidated state of the convent's buildings and their lack of proper robes. According to the *Hokke metsuzaiji engi*, Tankū initially refuses but then experiences a vision in which the temple's main image begins to cry. When he sees the beautiful image of Kannon shedding tears, the story relates, Tankū begins to cry himself and agrees that he will help rebuild Hokkeji's gate and walls. In the same section, the *engi* also offers another example of how Kōmyō uses the image of Kannon to convey her will. In this other example, Kōmyō causes the nuns to see rays of light shining forth from her image; then, she delivers an oracle through one of the nuns who investigated the rays of light and explains that the image should no longer be left on display now that Hokkeji has been restored.[4]

From these examples, it is clear that the nuns of medieval Hokkeji drew upon the legacy of the Queen-Consort as one of the primary sources of their authority. In constructing the *Hokke metsuzaiji engi*, they establish Kōmyō's many virtues and express that she remains a powerful, living force at the convent, especially through the temple's primary image, said to have been created in her own image. But this connection to Kōmyō was more complex, of course, than can be garnered through a reading of the *engi* alone. It is also important to emphasize that, as a figure of both history and legend, Kōmyō had already achieved a celebrated status, especially among the educated classes. In appealing to their connection to the Queen-Consort, then, the nuns did not have to rely merely on the praises they themselves heaped upon her in the *engi*, for the Queen-Consort's importance was already well established in popular literature.[5] It is also important to contextualize Kōmyō's role as a representative of both the imperial family and the Fujiwara, pre-modern Japan's most celebrated aristocratic lineage. Nuns affiliated with the restoration of Hokkeji also relied on connections they themselves had to courtly life, to the imperial family, and to Fujiwara lineages.

Indeed, at the heart of Hokkeji's medieval revival were women with intimate ties to the Japanese court. Jizen, the first abbess of the revived Hokkeji, and Kūnyo, her teacher, are clear examples of this. Kūnyo appears to have been the product of an illicit relationship between the Imperial Lady Takamatsu (Takamatsu-in), daughter of Emperor Toba (1103–1156) and his queen-consort Bifukumon-in (1117–1160), and the priest Chōken. Her birth was concealed as a result, but thanks to the mediation of her powerful aunt Hachijō-in, scholars believe, she was raised in the household of the great poet Fujiwara no Shunzei and eventually brought back into the court of Hachijō-in as a lady-in-waiting.[6]

Even with her imperial birth obscured, then, Kūnyo grew up in a prominent Fujiwara household with extremely close connections to the court. Jizen, too, had served as a lady-in-waiting; she had been in the service of the Imperial Lady Shunkamon (Shunkamon-in, 1195–1211) and decided to take Buddhist vows after Her Highness Shunkamon-in passed away while still a very young adult. Jizen also appears to have had very close ties with Fujiwara no Shunzei's line, as Shunzei's own son, the highly celebrated poet Fujiwara no Teika (1162–1241), mentions Jizen's decision to take monastic vows in his journal, *Meigetsuki*. Teika praises Jizen, just twenty-five years old at the time, for having had the resolve to take vows, despite her young age. The passage suggests that he understood her decision to be based upon a deep sense of loyalty to her recently deceased master, the Imperial Lady Shunkamon.[7]

These ties with the world of the court were important on at least two levels. First, most powerful temples had close connections with the court during this period. Princes and members of aristocratic lineages, such as the Fujiwara and its many branches, commonly occupied the highest ranks at major Tendai and Shingon institutions, for example. Second, as noted earlier, Hokkeji's historical identity was closely linked to that of the Japanese court: after all, Empress Kōmyō had long been celebrated as the founder of Hokkeji, and it is believed that she and her daughter, who later ruled as Emperor Kōken and then again as Emperor Shōtoku, were personally committed to the advancement of Buddhist nuns and even encouraged some of their own ladies-in-waiting to become nuns. Some believe that from the time of the convent's inception, then, the boundary between Hokkeji and the royal women's household office was rather porous. Moreover, Hokkeji was originally built at the center of the *kokubunji-kokubunniji* ("state temple-state nunnery") initiative, in which a monastery-convent pair was to be built in every province of Japan. At these temples, monks and nuns, working as official bureaucrats of the state, were charged with chanting sutras for the protection of the realm.[8] The Nara priest Chinkai (1091–1152) recalls Hokkeji's close connection to the state and its court in an 1128 work:

> Incidentally, in the Heijō capital [Nara], there is a temple for nuns [*ama no tera*] called Hokkeji. Nuns are to live there and carry out the reading of the Lotus Sutra, and so it is named the Lotus Temple [Hokkeji]. In each of the over sixty provinces, state monasteries [*kokubunji*] and convents [*kokubunniji*] were built by the state. The convents were called Hokkeji, and the state also provided the nuns' food and clothing.[9]

There is also a great deal of evidence indicating that women of the court, and especially ladies-in-waiting, were familiar with Hokkeji during the Heian and Kamakura periods, even during the years when the convent was not especially thriving, and that they viewed the convent as an appropriate place for women of a certain class to undertake Buddhist practice.[10] And thus, we can say both that connections to the court gave certain women the confidence to assert personal connections to the Queen-Consort, whom they regarded as the convent's original source of authority, and at the same time, that courtly connections were generally understood as a vital source of authority in the Buddhist world of premodern Japan.

From a longer historical view, it seems clear that while more personal connections to the court and the Fujiwara family were important for the first generation of revivalists at Hokkeji, the cult to the Queen-Consort cultivated by these women and articulated in the *Hokke metsuzaiji engi* that they related to pilgrims visiting the temple eventually enabled even those women with less tangible ties to the Queen-Consort to nevertheless appeal to the power of her legend as a means of asserting monastic authority. While courtly ties did remain front and center through most of Hokkeji's history, the *engi* is suggestive of the ways in which Kōmyō could speak through her image at Hokkeji, suggesting that the nuns drawing on her authority did not necessarily have to be connected to her through their bloodlines, but could instead draw on her authority simply by being recognized as the rightful custodians of her image.[11]

Precepts and Training

Buddhist precepts and doctrinal training comprised a second essential source of monastic authority at medieval Hokkeji. The *Hokke metsuzaiji engi* makes note of this, as do other, external sources about Hokkeji's revival, such as the diaries and teaching records of the priest Eison.

Eison was a unique figure during this period of Japanese history, as he was committed to establishing in Japan what he believed to be a more authentic allegiance to the rules of the Vinaya. Although he had originally trained as a Shingon monk, he spent his career working to establish in Japan an order of monastics that lived in compliance with the Vinaya. This not only meant establishing precept platforms and ceremonies in line with those outlined in the Vinaya, but also performing other rituals, such as fortnightly confession assemblies, as specified in Vinaya texts. Related to these initiatives, Eison was also convinced that Japan needed to establish a properly ordained order of nuns. Although an order of fully ordained women (J. *bikuni*; Skt. *bhikṣunī*) had existed in Japan's Nara period—when Hokkeji was first established—the last ordination of *bikuni* to have taken place before Eison's revival dates to the early ninth century.[12]

It was during the mid-1240s that Jizen and her disciples began to align themselves with Eison's movement to revive the precepts in Japan. Eison's records indicate that he returned to Hokkeji regularly to bestow precepts on the nuns there. First, he conferred novice and probationary precepts at Hokkeji in the mid-1240s. Then he returned in the second month of 1249 to confer full *bikuni* precepts on twelve probationary nuns. Hokkeji's nuns appear to have viewed their identity as fully ordained *bikuni* with a deep sense of responsibility. In particular, it seems that they were committed to learning as much about the Vinaya as possible. Throughout the 1250s they regularly invited Eison to teach intensive seminars on texts central to his understanding of the Vinaya tradition as it was developed in East Asia. Many of these intensive lecture sessions were three to four weeks long. According to Eison's diary, for example, he spent three weeks lecturing at Hokkeji in 1250, this time focusing on two major Vinaya commentaries, Daoxuan's (J. Dōsen, 596-667) *Jiaojie xinxue biqiu xinghu lüyi* and the "Biaowubiao" Chapter from Kuiji's (J. Kiki, 632–682) *Dacheng fayuan yilinzhang*, plus Taehyŏn's (J. Taigen, fl. mid-eighth century) *Beommanggyeong bosal gyebon jong-yo*. Daoxuan's *Jiaojie xinxue biqiu xinghu lüyi* is an instructional manual on monastic decorum.[13] Eison visited Hokkeji for additional lectures in 1251, this time teaching Yuanzhao's (J. Ganjō, 1048–1116) *Sifenlü xingshichao zichiji*, yet another commentary on the Vinaya. He offered similar lecture sessions at Hokkeji in 1254, 1256, and 1257. Eison noted in his diary that some sixty-four nuns and four monks attended his lectures at Hokkeji in 1257, suggesting that by this time Hokkeji had become a major center of Buddhist learning for women.[14]

That the nuns who revived Hokkeji had received full *bikuni* precepts through the ordination procedures outlined in the Vinaya was a special point of pride, especially from the view of Eison's precept revival movement.[15] The *Hokke metsuzaiji engi* suggests that Hokkeji nuns, too, viewed their receipt of the precepts, as well as their doctrinal training, as an important marker of monastic authority. At the same time, however, it is important to note that the nuns' authority as monastic leaders did not stem solely from their association with Eison, or from the fact that they received precepts and doctrinal training from him *specifically*. Historical sources, as well as the *Hokke metsuzaiji engi*, suggest that Hokkeji nuns had, especially in the years before their association with Eison and his movement, sought and received both precepts and doctrinal training from other priests as well. In this sense, we may think of their monastic authority as deriving not simply from the ordinations and training they received from Eison specifically, but also from the fact that they had received ordinations and doctrinal training from recognized figures in the Buddhist world. In other words, they did not need to appeal to their connection with Eison solely, but rather to the fact that they had indeed received monastic precepts from different teachers and that they had studied Buddhist doctrine and ritual in a serious and focused way.

The aforementioned episode from the *Hokke metsuzaiji engi*, for example, suggests that some of the nuns of medieval Hokkeji had received precepts from the Tendai priest Tankū. And according to Fujiwara no Teika's *Meigetsuki*, Jizen first took the precepts from a Nara priest named Jirenbō;[16] it is this same "Ji" that she took in her Buddhist name "Jizen."

In terms of doctrinal learning, too, it is clear that many of the revivalist nuns of Hokkeji had embarked upon courses of Buddhist learning before and in addition to their encounters with Eison. Jizen and Kūnyo had studied at the Shingon temple Daigoji, for example, before they relocated to Hokkeji. At Daigoji, Kūnyo had studied at the sub-temple Shōkutei-in, under her cousin Jōken (1162–1231), a Daigoji abbott (*zasu*), and alongside another, female, cousin, Shin-Amidabutsu-ni. It appears that Jizen, too, studied and practiced with this group when she first took Buddhist vows, decades before moving to Hokkeji.[17]

Another prominent Hokkeji nun who studied with priests other than Eison was the nun Nyoen. Nyoen, who became the second rector or abbess at Hokkeji, following Jizen, came from what we might call a monastic family. She had been married to the Tōdaiji scholar-priest Genkan, and most of their offspring went on to monastic careers themselves: sons Enshō and Shōshu became prominent scholar-priests at Tōdaiji, for example, and daughter Enshō (pronounced the same as son "Enshō" but using a different character for "shō") became a nun at Hokkeji, along with her daughter Sonnyo.[18] According to his biography, Nyoen's son Enshō, who was regarded as a great scholar, regularly offered lectures on behalf of his female relatives and their colleagues. When his mother took up residence at Hokkeji in 1247 or 1248, Enshō's biographer notes, he moved to Kairyūōji, a Ritsu temple close to Hokkeji, so that he could visit his mother daily and assist her in her studies of Vinaya texts. The biography furthermore says that in the 1270s, Enshō gave lectures on the *Putixin lun* (Discourses on the mind of enlightenment, T. no. 1665) and the *Pini taoyao* (Requirements of the Vinaya, X. 44, no. 743), for his niece Sonnyo and her disciples at Kyoto's Tōrinji, where Sonnyo had become rector.[19]

In short, doctrinal and ritual training were very important at Hokkeji, and we can surmise that this training was an important source of monastic authority. Aspects of doctrinal training were mentioned previously; in the section that follows, I will consider the ritual activities of Hokkeji nuns. For now, it is useful to note that historical sources suggest how, in the years following its thirteenth-century revival, Hokkeji came to serve as a training ground for nuns who would eventually be sent out to lead smaller Ritsu- (Vinaya-) school convents in less populous areas. It was the training women received at Hokkeji that prepared them, we can assume, to become abbesses at other convents. Some of these branch convents included Kōdaiji, Tōrinji, Chūgūji, and Shōbōji in the western capital and its environs; Dōmyōji in the Karachi region; Keishō-in and Shana-in in Settsu; and Gokurakiji and Chisokuji in Kamakura.[20]

It should also be noted that, as was the case with monastic cultures throughout much of the world, we can think of Hokkeji not only as a religiously oriented institution of learning, but also as an intellectual hub with a rather broad scope. For example, we know that the poet and nun Abutsu-ni (1221–1283) spent some time at Hokkeji. Abutsu-ni's time at Hokkeji was somewhat short-lived, however, as she eventually left to marry Fujiwara no Teika's son, Tameie (1198–1275). It appears that Abutsu-ni first met Tameie when some ladies-in-waiting from Tameie's household hired her to copy *Genji monogatari*. Abutsu-ni, who became an accomplished poet herself, was known for her deep knowledge of *Genji monogatari*, which she taught to others in formal settings.[21] Some scholars speculate that it may have been Jizen herself who first introduced Abutsu-ni to Tameie's household, for Jizen had enjoyed a close friendship with Tameie's father, Fujiwara no Teika.[22] This example is suggestive of the ways in which Hokkeji nuns were part of broader intellectual networks that often superseded Buddhist doctrinal and ritual knowledge. Certainly the nuns' engagement in such elite intellectual networks also represented an important part of their monastic authority.

Ritual Performance

A third, crucial source of monastic authority was to be found in the regular performance of rituals. This realm of activity is inextricably linked to the first two discussed previously. First, Hokkeji materials make it clear that many of the rituals that nuns performed at Hokkeji were carried out with the express intent of serving Queen-Consort Kōmyō and her wishes. And second, rituals required a great deal of learning. Most of the rituals performed at Hokkeji involved written liturgies. Some required literacy only in the Japanese vernacular, but many others required one to read in Chinese or *kanbun*. And still others required basic familiarity with Sanskrit letters. Related to this point is the fact that ritual life at Hokkeji mirrored that found at men's temples and monasteries. Like their male counterparts, nuns at Hokkeji invested a great deal of time mastering and performing rituals, which they learned from their teachers and taught to their own successors.

Rituals have always constituted one of the primary functions of Buddhist institutions in Japan. Indeed, early narratives of Hokkeji's establishment suggest that the convent was built for the specific purpose of protecting the state through ritual activity, namely, the chanting of sutras. Ritual life conveyed authority on multiple levels: that the nuns had the knowledge and ability to perform the right rituals in the right way and at the right time certainly signaled their authority as nuns, but the fact that they were entrusted by numerous parties—such as elite donors, ordinary laypeople, and even the state—to carry out particular rituals is also an important marker of broader social trust and authority.

Fortunately, a ritual calendar, *Hokke metsuzaiji nenjū gyōji* (hereafter, *Nenjū gyōji*), survives from medieval Hokkeji. This fourteenth-century document, which contains lists of all of the liturgies carried out by the nuns of Hokkeji, is composed of six sections: Daily Rites (Morning, Midday, and Evening); All-Day Rites of Offering; All-Day and All-Night Continuous Ceremonies; Twice-a-Day Vinaya Discussions; Ceremonies for the First Month of the New Year; and Annual Ceremonies, Death Memorial Services, etc.[23] The *Nenjū gyōji* provides a rare glimpse into the ritual life of medieval Hokkeji. It is also suggestive of the ways in which ritual performance contributed to the monastic authority of the nuns.

First, there were daily rites that include four liturgies: one in the morning, two at midday, and one in the evening (followed by a session of seated meditation, or *zazen*). Each service contains five to seven chanted pieces. Many are sections of sutras, while others are *dhāranī*. Most of the texts to be chanted are in Chinese, although there are a few pieces included in the liturgies that would have been performed in *kundoku* style, as well as a few *dhāranī* written in Sanskrit. These daily services comprised the most basic ritual "work" of Buddhist temples. As such, their regular performance was an essential part of the larger cultural and symbolic apparatus that made a temple authoritative. That Hokkeji nuns knew how to perform these daily rites—which would have required a certain degree of facility in multiple languages, as well as training in Buddhist chant—and that they were committed to doing so throughout the day, each and every day, marked them as authentic Buddhist professionals.[24]

Next, let us consider the many large-scale ceremonies (*hōe*) and chanted lectures (*kōshiki*) that appear in many of the sections of the *Nenjū gyōji*. There are more than twenty-five large ceremonies and chanted lectures included in the ritual calendar. Many were held around the New Year, which appears to have been the busiest ritual season at Hokkeji. Some of these ceremonies, such as the Shushō-e (Service of the First Month), Shuni-e (Service of the Second Month), the Great Benevolent Kings Ceremony, and the Eight Chanted Lectures on the Lotus Sutra, were standards at many temples. Some, such as the Four-Part Vinaya Confession Ceremony and the Brahma Net Confession Ceremony, were linked to Hokkeji's identity as a Ritsu, or Vinaya, temple. Others were carried out in honor of particular figures, such as the Chanted Lecture on Kannon, Ceremonial Offerings to Kōbō Daishi, the Chanted Lecture on Prince Shōtoku, the Chanted Lecture on Mañjuśrī, the Chanted Lecture on Rāhula, and the Chanted Lecture on Ānanda. Still others were related to Hokkeji's history specifically, such as the Great Brahma Net Ceremony in Honor of the Death Anniversary of Our Founder [Queen-Consort Kōmyō], and the Chanted Lecture on the Favorable Rebirth of Our Founder [Queen-Consort Kōmyō]. Many of these large ceremonies were also multiple-day events.[25]

At least in part due to their complex nature and the degree of training they required, these larger-scale ceremonies and chanted lectures, like the daily rites, marked Hokkeji nuns as authoritative religious professionals. But the ceremonies bestowed and marked authority in other ways as well. Many of these ceremonies required significant investments of both time and money—the temple would need to prepare offerings, implements, embellishments, stages, and fabrics of various kinds, and to hire musicians and other performers. Only temples with significant resources, then, would have been able to organize the volume of large-scale ceremonies included in Hokkeji's ritual calendar. We can thus imagine that the robustness of Hokkeji's ceremonial calendar was yet another marker of the convent's prestige.

Moreover, it is likely the case that many of the rites at Hokkeji, including at least some of the daily services, were open to outsiders, including pilgrims, donors, and monastics from neighboring temples. Many of the large-scale ceremonies and chanted lectures, in particular, were outward-facing and served, at least partially, to educate the laity. This function is especially evident in the case of chanted lectures, or *kōshiki*, in which performers would chant in vernacular Japanese teachings about particular figures or ideas (Hokkeji performed *kōshiki* on Prince Shōtoku, on Buddha relics, and on Ānanda, among many other topics). These lectures were meant to be accessible to ordinary laypeople interested both in earning merit through the act of auditing a lecture and in learning more about Buddhist figures and practices. Both large-scale ceremonies and chanted lectures can also be understood as part of a larger culture of popular entertainment and teaching offered by Buddhist temples. That Hokkeji nuns were empowered by the Ritsu school to offer public teachings to lay devotees further bolstered their authority as Buddhist professionals.[26] Evidence that the ceremonies performed by Hokkeji nuns were held in high regard is found in *Daijōin jisha zōjiki,* the journal of the Kōfukuji Daijōin Monzeki priests. In his entries in the journal, the priest Jinson (1430–1508) regularly mentions attending the Great Brahma Net Ceremony held at Hokkeji on the seventh day of the sixth month in honor of Queen-Consort Kōmyō.[27] In an entry dated to 1464, Jinson, then abbot of the Daijō-in, describes his visit as follows:

> Today Queen-Consort Kōmyō's memorial service was carried out in the lecture hall [of Hokkeji]. I made a pilgrimage to Hokkeji's [performance] of the Queen-Consort's memorial service. I made the rounds, paying homage at every hall, and then settled down in the private room [provided for me]. After that, I entered the great bathhouse [*daiyuya*]. The significance of this bathwater is explained in a written divine oath [*onkimon*], which says that to avoid the three evil realms [of rebirth], one really should enter [this bath]. Next, I listened to the *hōe* in front of the Golden Hall, then I visited the rector's quarters, met with her, and presented an offering. Then I returned to the Zenjōin [at Kōfukuji]. My guards prepared my small perfumed robe and my palanquin, and my procession came to an end.[28]

The abbot Jinson was an elite figure: he was a member of the Ichijō line of the Fujiwara family, a prominent leader at the Kōfukuji-Kasuga complex, and a prolific writer of letters and documents.[29] That he regularly attended Hokkeji's Great Brahma Net Ceremony indicates that he held the ceremony in high esteem. His attendance both reflected and enhanced the monastic authority held by Hokkeji nuns. His support of the ceremony was likely linked to yet another marker of the convent's prestige: its connection to Queen-Consort Kōmyō. Fujiwara elites like Jinson probably viewed Kōmyō as one of their own illustrious ancestors. In the passage quoted here, we see that Jinson also placed a great deal of value on visiting the bath at Hokkeji, which was said to have been established by Kōmyō herself. He also mentions listening to the service, meeting with the convent's rector or abbess, and making an offering to her. In short, the passage suggests that Hokkeji and its rector were well regarded among religious elites in the ancient capital of Nara.

Finally, let us consider the death memorial services included in the last section of the *Nenjū gyōji.* Here we find that a number of such services had been commissioned by members of the ruling class. The Imperial Lady Muromachi (1228–1300), for example, had commissioned Hokkeji nuns to perform annual memorial services for four of her family members: for her grandfather, the retired sovereign Takakura; for her father, the emperor Go-Horikawa; for her grandmother, the Imperial Lady Kita Shirakawa-in; and for her aunt, Imperial Lady Shikikenmon-in. Services for individuals who had held important posts in the Bakufu warrior government also appear in the *Nenjū gyōji,* as do services for more ordinary members of the laity who had also served as donors to Hokkeji.[30]

The death memorial services included in the *Nenjū gyōji* indicate, then, that many laypeople, including some members of the ruling classes, had made a significant investment in ritual performances carried out by Hokkeji nuns. That members of the ruling classes entrusted the postmortem care of their loved ones to Hokkeji nuns further reflected and enhanced the institutional and ritual authority of the nuns. A perhaps even more impressive display of such entrustment by elites can be found in a colophon to the *Nenjū gyōji*, which reads:

> Outside of this, prayers for the shogunal household. Also prayers and *gongyō* (services) as needed in times of emergency. Depending on the time, these things are decided following the event or in accordance with the [particular] difficulty.[31]

This colophon suggests, of course, that Hokkeji was among the many temples the Bakufu (warrior) government would call upon for support during times of crisis. That the warrior government regarded Hokkeji nuns as capable of providing state protection further indicates that their rituals were regarded as both authoritative and efficacious.

Conclusion

Hokkeji's medieval revival highlights a number of strategies for establishing and maintaining monastic authority. First, Hokkeji nuns drew on the compelling and influential legacy of Queen-Consort Kōmyō. They did this not only though association with the royal and aristocratic lineages she represented, but also by emphasizing narratives about her virtuous character and miraculous deeds, and by using the temple's image of the Eleven-Faced Kannon, long associated with the Queen-Consort, to divine her will. The importance placed on Kōmyō's legacy at Hokkeji is instructive for thinking about other institutions as well: at many monasteries in Japan, miraculous stories about founders are utilized as a means of establishing and maintaining authority. Connections to royal and aristocratic lineages and to miraculous events are also commonly cited. Primary images, too, are often central in a temple's explanation of its efficacy. Images are often associated with particular miracles and sources of power, and as a result, those in the position of caring for those images are granted a great deal of religious authority.

Precepts and doctrinal training were another important source of monastic authority at Hokkeji. Receiving the precepts from a reputable teacher (or from reputable teachers) and undertaking formal training in ritual performance and doctrinal analysis were also essential markers of authenticity and authority. When it came to receiving the precepts and undergoing doctrinal training, there was a broad spectrum of possible formality and rigor. As conveyed previously, the nuns of medieval Hokkeji appear to have taken the precept ceremonies and doctrinal training very seriously. Many Hokkeji nuns also came from particularly educated backgrounds and were already well trained in broader scholarly endeavors, such as poetry and the study of *Genji monogatari*. Their literacy and scholarly engagement were undoubtedly important markers of monastic authority, as would have also been the case at male monasteries during this time.

Last but not least, ritual knowledge and performance were also central to the establishment and maintenance of religious authority at Hokkeji. Ritual performance—and faith in the idea that Hokkeji nuns knew how to conduct rituals properly—is what attracted lay supporters to a temple or monastery. As seen in the *Nenjū gyōji*, Hokkeji nuns managed to attract a great deal of support through its rituals. The nuns performed large-scale ceremonies that attracted pilgrims and auditors as elite as Kōfukuji's Jinson; they taught laypeople about Buddhist figures and topics through chanted lectures; they carried out memorial services for members of the royal family; and they prayed for the protection of the state when called upon to do so. These ritual activities reflected their authority and also enhanced it. The close link between monastic authority and ritual performance was by no means unique to Hokkeji; this dynamic can be found throughout religious life in pre-modern Japan. Those monasteries believed capable of carrying out effective rituals were deemed authoritative and worthy of patronage. Although one can imagine other possible means of establishing and maintaining monastic authority, these three strategies all worked rather well at medieval Hokkeji. They were strategies that combined broader cultural practices and values—such as using royal and aristocratic connections as markers of legitimacy—with those that were more squarely "Buddhist," such as precept lineages, doctrinal training, and ritual performance. This multipronged approach enabled Hokkeji nuns to assert themselves as religious professionals, and to attract patronage, establishing their integral position as members of the Buddhist clergy.

Notes

1. Lori Meeks, *Hokkeji and the Reemergence of Female Monastic Orders in Premodern Japan*. Kuroda Series in East Asian Buddhism (Honolulu: University of Hawai'i Press, 2010), 27–34.
2. *Hokke metsuzaiji engi* (hereafter, *HMZJE*) (1304) by Enkyō. In *Yamato koji taikan* 大和古寺大觀, 7 vols., ed. Ōta Hirotarō et al. (Tokyo: Iwanami Shoten, 1976–1978, 5:140a–43b), 140; Meeks, *Hokkeji*, 291.
3. *HMZJE* 140; Meeks, *Hokkeji*, 46.
4. *HMZJE* 141–42; also discussed in Meeks, *Hokkeji*.
5. See Abe Yasurō, *Yuya no kōgō: Chūsei no sei to seinaru mono* (Nagoya: Nagoya Daigaku Shuppankai, 1998).
6. See Tanaka Takako, *Gehō to aihō no chūsei* (Tokyo: Sunagoya Shobō, 2006)(orig. pub. 1993); KJGSK 1999, 210; Meeks, *Hokkeji*, 62.
7. *Kundoku Meigetsuki*, by Fujiwara no Teika (1162–1241), trans. Imagawa Fumio, 6 vols. (Tokyo: Kawade Shobō Shinsha, 1977-1979) 3:98b; *Kanjin gakushōki: Saidaiji Eison no jiden*, trans. and annotated by Hosokawa Ryōichi (Tokyo: Heibonsha, 1999), 213–15; Meeks, *Hokkeji*, 59–61.
8. For more, see Meeks, *Hokkeji*, 1–3, 29–30; Katsuura Noriko, *Nihon kodai no sōni to shakai* (Tokyo: Yoshikawa Kōbunkan, 2000).
9. *Bodai Shinshū* 菩提心集, by Chinkai, in *Jōdoshū zensho*, ed. Jōdoshū Shūten Kankōkai, 23 vols. (Kyōto: Jōdoshū Kaishū Happyaku Nen Kinen Kyōsan Junbi Kyoku, 1970–1974), 15:502–32, 26a, from translation in Meeks, *Hokkeji*, 33.
10. See Meeks, *Hokkeji*.

11. Indeed, courtly connections gained even more strength from the late medieval period, when the convent became a *bikuni gosho* that housed princesses and daughters of the shogunal families.
12. Until Eison's time, the last known record of a woman receiving full *bikuni* precepts in Japan dates to 828. See Ushiyama Yoshiyuki, *Kodai chūsei jiin soshiki no kenkyū* (Tokyo: Yoshikawa Kōbunkan, 1990), 16; Meeks, *Hokkeji*, 98.
13. T. no. 1897; *Kanjin gakushōki: Saidaiji Eison no jiden*, 199–200; cf. Hosokawa, *Kanjin gakushōki: Saidaiji Eison no jiden*, 200–3.
14. Meeks, *Hokkeji*, 126–27.
15. In ordaining monastics, Eison used a combination of the Vinaya precepts from *Shibun ritsu* (*Four-Part Vinaya*) and the bodhisattva precepts from *Fanwang jing (Brahma Net Sutra)*. Convinced that mainstream monastics of his day did not follow the Vinaya correctly, Eison did not believe that a full quorum necessary for ordination existed in Japan, and so he and a small group of other monks, including Kakujō, Ensen, and Ugon, took their initial vows in front of an image of Kannon in 1236. This was in following with the idea that precepts could be taken directly from a buddha or bodhisattva in cases where a quorum of ten monks could not be assembled. Even though this was an extreme measure, Eison believed that it accorded with the rules of the Vinaya. His records show that he was also very thoughtful in how he conferred precepts on nuns at Hokkeji: he carried the conferrals in a multi-step process that stretched over several years. First, he ordained a group of novice nuns at Hokkeji in 1245. Then, in 1247, he bestowed probationary (*shikishamana; śikṣamāṇā*) precepts, and finally, in 1249, *bikuni* precepts. These first ordinations took place, by necessity, without a group of fully ordained nuns to serve as witnesses. But it seems that once a group of *bikuni* had been ordained, they did serve as witnesses for later ordinations of women (see Meeks, *Hokkeji*, 119–26, and *passim*).
16. *Kundoku Meigetsuki*, 3:98b; *Kanjin gakushōki: Saidaiji Eison no jiden*, 213–15.
17. Meeks, *Hokkeji*, 63–64.
18. Meeks, *Hokkeji*, 167.
19. Meeks, *Hokkeji*, 108–9; *Tōdaiji Enshō Shōnin gyōjō*, ed. Tōdaiji Kyōgakubu (Nara: Tōdaiji Toshokan, 1977), 1, 8a; Hosokawa Ryōichi, *Onna no chūsei: Ononokomachi, tomoe, sono ta* (Tokyo: Nihon Editasukūru, 1989), 129–31; *Chūsei no jiin no fūkei: Chūsei minshū no seikatsu to shinsei* (Tokyo: Shin'yōsha, 1997), 97.
20. Meeks, *Hokkeji*, 2010, 183–96.
21. See Christina Laffin, *Rewriting Medieval Japanese Women: Politics, Personality, and Literary Production in the Life of Nun Abutsu* (Honolulu: University of Hawai'i Press, 2013), 101–4 and *passim*.
22. John R. Wallace, "Fitful Slumbers: Nun Abutsu's Utatane," *Monumenta Nipponica* 43, no. 4 (1988): 391–98; 391–92; Laffin, *Rewriting Medieval Japanese Women*, 104; Hosokawa, *Onna no chūsei*, 165–69; Meeks, *Hokkeji*, 85.
23. The *Nenjū gyōji* is dated to 1322 but contains a reference in the same handwriting to 1347, so the copy held in Hokkeji's archives must have been copied after 1347. See Meeks, *Hokkeji*, 215–16.
24. See *Hokke metsuzaiji nenjū [or nenchū] gyōji* [hereafter, *Nenjū gyōji*] (1322), by Yūshi, in *Yamato koji taikan*, 5:86a–87b.
25. See *Nenjū gyōji*.
26. Meeks, *Hokkeji*, 200, 228–29.
27. Meeks, *Hokkeji*, 241–42.

28. *Daijōin jisha zōjiki*, in *Zōho shiryō taisei*, vols. 26–37, ed. Zōho Shiryō Taisei Kankōkai (Kyoto: Rinsen Shoten, 1994), Kanshō 5 [1464] 6/7; translation in Meeks, *Hokkeji*, 241–42.
29. See Allan Grapard, *The Protocol of the Gods: A Study of the Kasuga Cult in Japanese History* (Berkeley: University of California Press, 1993), 171.
30. Meeks, *Hokkeji*, 201–2.
31. *Nenjū gyōji* 87b. Translation in Meeks, *Hokkeji*, 245.

Further Reading

Bodiford, William M., ed. *Going Forth: Visions of Buddhist Vinaya*. Honolulu: University of Hawai'i Press, 2005.

Brazell, Karen, trans. *The Confessions of Lady Nijō*. Garden City, NY: Anchor, 1973.

Groner, Paul. "Vicissitudes in the Ordination of Japanese 'Nuns' during the Eighth through the Tenth Centuries." In *Engendering Faith: Women and Buddhism in Premodern Japan*, ed. Barbara Ruch. Ann Arbor: Center for Japanese Studies, University of Michigan, 2002, 65–108.

Hosokawa Ryōichi. "Medieval Nuns and Nunneries: The Case of Hokkeji." Trans. Paul Groner. In *Women and Class in Japanese History*, ed. Hitomi Tonomura, Anne Walthall, and Wakita Haruko. Ann Arbor: Center for Japanese Studies, University of Michigan, 1999, 67–80.

Institute for Medieval Japanese Studies et al., eds. *Amamonzeki: A Hidden Heritage, Treasures of the Japanese Imperial Convents*. Tokyo: Sankei Shinbunsha, 2009.

Laffin, Christina. *Rewriting Medieval Japanese Women: Politics, Personality, and Literary Production in the Life of Nun Abutsu*. Honolulu: University of Hawai'i Press, 2013.

Meeks, Lori. "In Her Likeness: Female Divinity and Leadership at Medieval Chūgūji." *Japanese Journal of Religious Studies* 34, no. 2 (2007): 351–92.

Meeks, Lori. "Vows for the Masses: Eison and the Popular Expansion of Precept-Conferral Ceremonies in Premodern Japan." *Numen* 56, no. 1 (January 2009): 1–43.

Ruch, Barbara, ed. *Engendering Faith: Women and Buddhism in Premodern Japan*. Ann Arbor: Center for Japanese Studies, University of Michigan, 2002.

Tonomura Hitomi, Anne Walthall, and Wakita Haruko, eds. *Women and Class in Japanese History*. Ann Arbor: University of Michigan Press, 1999.

Wakita Haruko. *Women in Medieval Japan: Motherhood, Household Management and Sexuality*. Trans. Alison Tokita. Tokyo: University of Tokyo Press, 2006.

CHAPTER 25

MONASTIC DISCIPLINE AND LOCAL PRACTICE

VESNA A. WALLACE

TRADITIONAL Mongolian cultural norms that contradict the Vinaya are integrated into Mongolian Buddhist practice. Exploring substances that might be interpreted as counter to Vinaya regulations—especially fermented mare's milk (*airag*) and vodka—reveals ritual practices that approve of monks' consumption of such substances.[1] High-quality vodka (*arkhi*) is deemed necessary for a range of practices, including offerings to fierce mountain deities. These practices make the rituals for securing a successful production of good quality vodka prominent in Mongolian pastoral society. Seeing Mongolian Buddhist practice through an ethnographic lens offers a view of the significant cultural current that undergirds Mongolian monastic practice of the Vinaya, highlighting the primacy of traditional customs that preceded the Mongols' conversion to Buddhism. After many years of unsuccessful attempts made by the Fourteenth Dalai Lama to steer Mongolian monks away from drinking fermented mare's milk (*airag, tsegee*), he finally conceded during his visit to Mongolia in November 2017, permitting them to consume *airag*, recognizing the potency of this traditional custom in the Mongolian cultural sphere. At the same time, he appealed to them to abstain from vodka consumption. A cogent power of the customary drinking of *airag* with regard to the Vinaya becomes more understandable when the traditional views of the properties of *airag* are examined, as well as its various applications in different social and religious contexts.

Fermented mare's milk has been traditionally an important part in the life of the lay and monastic Mongols and their diet during summer season and early fall.[2] It has been essential in celebrations of special occasions, such as the royal festivals, state-sponsored Buddhist worship, weddings, a child's ceremonial haircutting, and in granting the titles of state officials, the titles of incarnate lamas (*khuvilgaans* and *khutugtus*), and the titles of monastic degrees. The custom of drinking and utilizing *airag* in various religious ceremonies precedes Mongols' conversion to Buddhism, as evidenced from the *Secret History of the Mongols* and from the pre-Buddhist Mongolian shamanic practices. *Airag* eventually became part of Buddhist tantric rituals with the appropriation of Tibetan

Buddhism in Mongolia. It has also been sprinkled on the rump of a winning horse in the race during the State *naadam* and Buddhist *danshug*[3] (Tib. *bstan bzugs*) festivals; it is ceremonially offered to equestrian and wrestling champions, and to Buddhist deities, to local spirits of the lands (*savdag*, Tib. *sa dag*), mountains, and waters, and to respected guests. *Airag* is also valued for its medicinal qualities and for giving strength and cheer after a long winter. In traditional Mongolian medicine, it has been used for destroying pathogenic microbes in the body, for improving metabolism, treating tuberculosis, hepatitis, diminishing inflammatory arthritis, and so on. The ubiquity of fermented mare's milk in Mongolian culture is such that Mongols of all ages and genders, including monastics, delight in consuming large quantities of *airag*. For all these reasons, *airag* is often referred to as "the paste of a white jade" (*tsagaan khasyn eeden*). The more *airag* matures, its level of alcohol content increases from 2% in the early summer to 14% in the fall. As we will see later, due to the common perception of the medicinal benefits of *airag*, the Vinaya precept of the abstinence from alcohol has been reinterpreted by Mongolian monastics. Thus, the traditional, pastoral custom of *airag* consumption at seasonal events became an integral part of monastic life and ceremonial activities, especially in summer and early fall when mares are being milked.[4]

At the beginning of the summer milking season, a festival of mare milk, which became a Mongolian Buddhist ritual adopted from a labor festival and the shamanic tradition,[5] has been held annually. At that time Buddhist versified *airag* benedictions and prayers for Buddhist celebrations of *airag* ritual festivals are read and specific preparations are made, as indicated in the ritual text titled *The Manner of Sprinkling a Mare's Milk* (*Rgod ma'i 'o ma gtor tshul*),[6] composed by Chakhar Geshe Luvsanchültemin (Tib. Cha har dge bshes Blo bzang Tsul khrims, 1740–1810).[7] According to the *The Manner of Sprinkling a Mare's Milk* (*Rgod ma'i 'o ma gtor tshul*),[8] in preparation for a ritual, a low table is set on a spread of white felt. Food is laid out on the table, and *airag* poured into a clean container is sprinkled three or nine times. Prior to the offering of incense, an officiating lama must recite the prayer of taking refuge in the Three Jewels, generate the altruistic motivation (*bodhicitta*), meditate on the Four Immeasurables, and recite the following three texts: the *Eight Appearances* (*Snang brgyad*, or *Gnam sa snang brgyad*), the *'Phags pa bkra shis rtsegs pa*, and the *Chos skyong* for auspiciousness and the removal of obstacles. After that, he must prepare the external and internal offerings and the offering cakes (Tib. *gtor ma*) that are to be presented to protective deities. Offering cakes are then blessed with six mantras and six *mudrās*. The officiating lama adds to mare's milk the so-called three whites (milk, curd, and ghee) and the ingredients containing three different types of taste in order to make mare's milk complete with six tastes. This is followed by recitations of the words of the corrective rite and purification by incense.[9]

The oblation of mare's milk is offered to numerous buddhas and bodhisattvas, to great Indian and Tibetan *yogīs* and *siddhas*, such as Tilopa, Nāropa, Saraha, and others, to the Sixteen Arhats, to renowned Indian, Tibetan, and Mongolian masters, such as Nāgārjuna, Asaṅga, Atiśa, Tsongkhapa and his main disciples, to Bogd Jebtsundamba, Khalkha Zaya Pandita, Blo bzang 'phrin las, etc., to the eight *nāga* kings, to the four *mahārājas*, to Brahmā, Indra, and other gods. It is then offered to sentient beings within the six realms of cyclic existence, to various spirits, and to the spirit-land owner of Jambudvīpa. Mare's milk is also offered to various mountains, lakes, and rivers, believed to be inhabited by various deities worshipped as protectors of Dharma and State, and by land-owning spirits and *nāgas*, who need to be appeased. It is also offered to important temples in the regions where the Khalkhas, the Ordos, and the so-called Upper Mongols (Degedü Mongɣol) reside in the Kökenuur region of Qinghai:

Let me sprinkle the ocean of the ambrosia of the best milk
To [a place] where Jebtsundamba, an emanation of Mañjuśrī was born,
To Altai and Khangai [mountains], to Orkhon, and Tuul [rivers],
To Ikh Khan, Bürenkhaan, and Even [mountains],
To Ider, Chuluut, and Urt Selenge [rivers],
To Erdemt Bulgan and to the elixir raters of Tamir [river],
To Erdene Zuu's temple and Sangiin Dalai lake,
And to Gorolgon Khairkhan and Ongi Khairkhan [mountains], etc.

I sprinkle milk eighteen times
To the Ordos Land called Brown Hills,
To the Relic Stūpa of Holly Chinggis Khaan,
To Khatni River, Arvui Alagsha,
To Khailmal Altan Ovoot, Four Highs, and Great Steppe,
Tsengel White Lake, Tsagaan Tokhoi.

I sprinkle milk eighteen times
To Loha [river], the Yellow River, and Unegen [river],
To Shandu, Kheiven, Dolnuur, Kharokhan,
To mountain lakes, water springs, temples, and the like
Of one's own country, to forty-nine *zasags*
To the Supreme Sky, *nāgas*, and spirit-land owners.[10]

A somewhat lesser adaptation of a ritual of the libation of mare's milk from the shamanic tradition is noticeable in the anonymous Mongolian text composed in the Mongolian language and titled *A Sūtra of Sprinkling Mare's Milk* (*Gegün-ü sün-ü sačuli-yin sudur orosibai*). The text shows its shamanic origin. Although it begins with the homage to the Three Jewels, the immediately following lines mention the offering of *airag* to the Tengri, Mother Etügen, stars, etc., which are characteristic of shamanic type of worship:

Homage to the Three Jewels!
Best among protections
Are Eternal Sky
And Mother Etügen!
Superior to all
Are Khan Eternal Sky,
Khan Earth and Water,

Ten thousand stars,
Round sun,
A crescent moon,
And planet Venus![11]

In this ritual text, mare's milk offerings are first made to different mountains and rivers of Mongolia, then to those of Tibet and China, some of which are also mentioned in Chakhar Geshe's text, and to Bodhgaya in India, the site of the Buddha's enlightenment. After that, mare's milk offerings are made to various shamanic deities (*tngri*), such as Atan, Baatar, Alman, Archlar, Altaan, Enkhsen, and other *tngris*, to Daisun, the emissary of the Mother Etügen, to the polar star in the north, and so on. Afterward, the offerings are made to the Buddhas Vajradhara, Amoghasiddhi, Amitābha, Akṣobhya, and to the Buddhas of the eight cardinal and intermediate directions. After that, the offerings are made to Mount Sumeru, to the kings of trees, waters, and so on. It is possible that this text was recited by both Shamans of the so-called Yellow Shamanic tradition, which adopted certain Buddhist elements, and by rural lamas of the pre-modern period. Boundaries between these two traditions, when practiced on the ground, as opposed to monastic, institutionalized practices, were more fluid than those between Buddhism and Black Shamanism, which, unlike Yellow Shamanism, has not been influenced by the Buddhist pantheon and cosmology.

In the Mongolian Buddhist context, the start of mare milk season has been deemed as the auspicious occasion for celebrating the Mongolian national, pastoral, and Buddhist identities, as well as for evoking prayers for the enlightenment of all sentient beings. For example, with his versified prayer "The Blessing of Mare's Milk," Gelek Palsang (Dge legs Dpal bzang, 1846–1923),[12] a well-known Khalkha Buddhist author of benedictions, celebrates the mare's milk festival as an auspicious event with these words:

All right! We, seniors,
Who enjoy our extensive virtues,
Surrounded by relatives and families,
Having received kindness from gracious noblemen,
And who are these days praised by everyone,
Have chosen the present day as auspicious.

Here on the great, wide earth,
Colorful flowers have blossomed, and the grass is swaying.

At this wide, spacious, and beautiful camp
A long stretched tethering rope has been laid out,
And neat, flexible halters and toggles have been prepared.

Many capable, young men have come together
In order to gather numerous horses,
Which have become strong and fat

Due to the nutriment of the grass abundantly grown
Owing to good rains.

The foals, as if wild asses,
Are also captured and tied here.

Here, the custom of Chinggis Khaan is upheld,
The firm genuine faith is determined, and
Those who are wise and have great qualities are being invited
To perform an incense offering of the wish-fulfilling jewel
And take on the ritual of summoning good fortunes.

By joyous friends, without distinction between yours and mine,
And by spirited foals, pushing forward as much as they are able,
The mares with swollen udders are being milked.

By offering, in a great voice, the choicest [sample of] drawn milk
To the protective and kind deities
And to the visible and invisible spirit-land owners,
Let's please them!

Distributing the prepared food [to everyone],
And serving out vodka that brings out wisdom,
Filled in small cups,
Let me say some wise hymns as following!

May the state of the king and noblemen be firm!
May the religious service of all holy beings spread wide!
May all discordant enemies
Of us, who have gathered here, be destroyed without a trace!
May we all always see the best of times!
May we all be filled with tea, milk, and dairy products
At all times!
May we all fully experience the result of boundless virtue!
May we all follow the law without deviation!
After passing beyond this lifetime,
May we all, mother-sentient beings, reach the supreme Buddhahood!

In the pre-modern and early modern periods, monasteries and lamas produced *airag* for recreational drinking from their own herds. In contemporary Mongolia, abundant supplies of *airag* are brought to monastic offices and temples by horse herders, relatives, and monasteries' benefactors. There is no social or moral stigma attached to monks' drinking *airag*. As contemporary Mongolian monks point out, although the Buddha prohibited the drinking of fermented fruit and sap of plants, nowhere in the Vinaya did he state that a *bhikṣu* should not drink fermented mare's milk. According to the oral accounts of Mongolian lamas, even the Thirteenth Dalai Lama (1876–1933) relished *airag* to such a degree during his visit to Mongolia from 1904 to 1906 that upon his return to Lhasa, he took seven Mongolian mares and four Mongolian monks skilled in making *airag*. In gratitude for the service of *airag*-making monks, he granted them higher monastic degrees.[13] Perhaps it is due to his liking of *airag* that when three Mongolian nobles requested him in the autumn of 1906 to compose regulations for monks of the philosophical colleges of Gandentsenpilin (Tib. Dga' ldan tshe phel ling) monastery[14] in Mongolia, the Thirteenth Dalai Lama prohibited only the drinking of vodka. There he states: "If [a monk] due to the lack of vigilance does a shameful deed, such as drinking vodka and the like, expel him out of monastery."[15]

However, Mongolian monastics considered vodka arkhi produced from *airag*—*but* not vodka that produced from fermented grains or fruits in Russia and China—to be a pure substance. It is deemed as the best part of the offering to fierce deities, especially to the fierce male mountain deities for whom a strong and purified drink is appropriate. In contrast, to peaceful mountain deities, milk is offered. Since fierce deities are the masters of a local terrain, only domestic Mongolian vodka made of *airag* is suitable.

Vodka made of *airag* has been also a part of the secret, inner offerings in Vajrayāna practice, in which vodka is transformed into nectar through tantric meditation. During the production of this type of vodka, lamas recite an incense offering text to secure the successful production of plentiful and good tasting vodka, saying:

> *Oṃ āḥ hūṃ*
> Aya, may the guardian black deity and his assistants be purified!
> May the harm of food, the harm of property, and the harm of milk be purified!
> May all milk, dairy products, and the like be purified!
> May all protective deities of the world be purified!
> May all the five destiny gods (*govyn lkha*, Tib. *'go ba'i lha*) be purified!
> May all male deities and tutelary deities (*süld tenger*) be purified!
> May all intoxicating vodkas, vodkas prosper!
> May the nutriment of all food increase under vodka!
> May the bee of the essence of vodka come to me!
> Destroy the harms of vodka *phaṭ*![16]
> *He, he*![17] May vodka, vodka, become abundant!
> Vodka, vodka become more plentiful, more plentiful *svāhā*!
> All food and vodka, vodka, come, come!
> Become more plentiful, become more plentiful *svāhā*![18]
>
> Write this mantra *oṃ hili hili svāhā* three times and hang it on a *bürkheer*:[19]
> Write this mantra *oṃ hrīḥ hrīḥ hūṃ hūṃ phaṭ* and hang it on a pennant.
> Recite this mantra *oṃ hūṃ don de ā* 21 times and install it as sacred.

Thus, at the conclusion of this prayer, three different types of mantras[20] are chanted, then written on a piece of paper and hung on a bottomless cask (*bürkheer*) placed on the top of the cauldron when distilling *airag* in the course of the production of vodka. The bottomless cask on top of the cauldron contains a pail to catch the vodka in a *bürkheer* and on a protective pennant, attached to the caldron for ensuring that no faults occur to the vodka during the process of distillation.

As we will see, since a recreational drinking of hard liquor, such as vodka, has been prohibited by Mongolian religious and ruling authorities, monks who drink vodka recreationally outside of a ritual context are not necessarily expelled from a monastery. Instead, they are provided opportunities for expiation through various other penal measures. Even in the case of monks' consumption of vodka, a restrictive field of monastic conduct marked by the Vinaya was to some degree made less restrictive by the regulations imposed on the temples and monasteries that were under the jurisdiction of different local princes and other governing nobles. For instance, according to regulations written in the early twentieth century by Dorjbold, a governing duke (*ǰasaɣ güng*) of Khalkha for the previously mentioned Gandentsenpilin monastery, a monk who is seen recreationally drinking vodka at three different occasions must be advised to abandon the habit. If he ignores the given council, then his conduct is to be announced at the assembly of monks, and he should be expelled from the monastery. But when a monk is seen drinking vodka only once or twice, he must offer 100 butter lamps and perform 500 prostrations for the sake of purification. After that, he must vow not to recreationally drink vodka in the future. According to the same regulations, monks also must not offer vodka to laypeople at social events, nor should they bring vodka to the temple as a tantric "inner offering" (Mong. *dotuɣadu takil*, Tib. *nang mcod*). This, however, does not mean that monks are not allowed to taste vodka during their personal practice in their private living quarters. In Dorjbold's view, the grave offence of recreationally drinking vodka stems not merely from the violation of a monastic vow, but also from the very nature of liquor, whose constituents originate from "the uterine blood of a single demoness holding wrong vows."[21] Dorjbold's association of vodka with the uterine blood of a demoness was most likely inspired by the association of tobacco with menstrual blood of Chinese demoness mentioned in Tibetan and Mongolian cautionary writings on the evils of tobacco smoking, when the habit of smoking of tobacco was introduced to Tibet and Mongolia from China and began to spread among monks. According to Dorjbold, if a monk becomes contaminated by drinking liquor, the power of his mantra decreases, and his tutelary deity (*yidam*), Dharma protectors, gods, *nāgas*, and the five Goviin Lkha (Tib. *'Go ba'i lha lnga*) who guard his virtuous deeds cease to protect him. In addition, at the time of his death, he will be unable to find a good monk who can perform for him the rite for the transference of consciousness (*'pho ba*).[22]

Dorjbold's association of vodka with a demoness refers to vodka produced and sold by Russian and Chinese merchants in Mongolia, who often took economic advantage over Mongols unskilled in trade. While Russian and Chinese vodka was most commonly made from potatoes, fermented fruit, and grains, which is prohibited in the Vinaya, Mongolian vodka was traditionally produced either from distilled *airag* or from the whey drawn from the milk of cows, sheep, or camels, and it has been considered by the Mongols as a pure substance. For this reason, it has been heralded as the best part of the offering to fierce deities and as a part of the inner offerings in tantric practice, in which a very small amount of vodka is consumed. Unlike *airag*, however, vodka has been prohibited as a recreational drink for monks in all Mongolian legal texts.

Similar to Dorjbold's regulations, in the Khalkha and Oirat Mongols' customary laws composed between the seventeenth and nineteenth centuries, penalties for monks who recreationally drank vodka involved fines in the form of livestock, and very rarely the expulsion from a monastic order. For example, in the "Supplementary Law" introduced by Kalmyk khan Dondogdash[23] into the *Great Law* (*Jeke Čaγaǰu*) of the Oirats in the mid-eighteenth century, which was originally instituted in 1640 as a law for western Mongolia, the penalty imposed on monks for drinking vodka was decided according to different ranks of monks' ordination. Thus, for a fully ordained monk (*gelüng*, Tib. *dge slong*), the penalty for drinking vodka was a four-year-old camel, which was to be given to the assembly's treasury. For a monastic novice (*getsül*, *gečül*, Tib. *dge tshul*), the fine was a four-year-old horse, and for a junior novice (*bandi*, Tib. *ban de*), it was a three-year-old sheep.[24]

Likewise, in the *Khalkha Regulations* (*Qalq-a-yin Jirum*), which were revised some twenty times from 1709 to 1795 by Khalkha dignitaries and high lamas, seven articles in the tenth chapter, which contains supplements introduced to the "Great Law" of the three administrative units (*khoshuu*) of Tüsheet Khan Province (*aimag*), pertain to monks' recreational drinking of vodka. According to article 199, if a fully ordained monk recreationally drinks vodka, he should be fined with nine five-year-old horses; if a novice drinks it, with five five-year-old horses; and if a junior novice drinks, with three five-year-old horses. Confiscated horses were to be given to the person who testified about the monks' recreational drinking. Statutes 202–203 offer different legal provisions for monks' recreational drinking of vodka, stating:

> If a fully ordained monk, a novice, or a junior novice drinks vodka, he must offer tea and meal (*manza*, Tib. *mang ja*), together with monetary donations (*ǰed*. Tib. *byed*), during a large religious service. The fully ordained monk must recite 21 scriptures; a novice must recite 14 scriptures, and a young novice must recite seven scriptures during a religious service in order to purify their bodies. If a monk is unable to offer these donations, he must pour six jars of water every day for three months instead.[25]

During a later revision of the *Khalkha Regulations*, four new statutes (that constitute the entire Chapter 14) were introduced. The first of these statutes concerns the varying penalties for monks recreationally drinking vodka, determined in accordance with the given monastic duties of the perpetrator. Thus, while a fully ordained monk, a novice, and a junior novice were to be fined with three, two, or one horse, respectively, penalties for attendants (*ki-ya lam-a*) to high-ranking *khutugtu*s and *khuvilgaan*s, and for a monastery's gatekeepers, who were accountable for the monastery's safety from arson, looting bandits, and unwanted visitors, were more severe than for ordinary monks. In addition to requiring the fine of two horses, the statute demanded that they be monastically disrobed and discharged to their individual *otog*s ("administrative units").[26] Likewise, according to the "Khalkha Regulations of the Chancellery," which applied to

Bogd Jebtsundambas' personal estate (Shavi) from 1789 to 1925, if a fully ordained monk was caught recreationally drinking vodka, he was to be penalized with a fine of nine horses, whereas the prescribed penalty for a novice was three horses. However, a monk seen drinking repeatedly was to be imprisoned for one year.

It is difficult, however, to know with certainty to what degree the aforementioned regulations were followed in practice. The very small number of court cases pertaining to monks recreationally drinking vodka suggests that very few monks were adjudicated. The record of 488 court cases dating to 1821–1913 and compiled in the book called the *Red Cover* (*Ulaɣan Qačartu*) contains only three cases that deal with such monks. One case, which involves a monastery's gatekeeper who was sentenced to the fine of nine heads of livestock instead of being expelled from his monastery, demonstrates a judicial laxity and judge's discreteness in overriding the law. Another case dealt with two drunken lamas who quarreled with a high government official, and the third case involved a monk who spread false rumors about a monastic disciplinarian (*gebküi*, Tib. *dge skos*) recreationally drinking vodka.[27]

During the period of the autonomous Mongolian state, followed by the fall of the Qing dynasty in 1912, the Mongolian government, headed by the Eighth Bogd Jebtsunamba, sought to solve the problem of excessive drinking among monks and laypeople through the newly instituted law titled the *Laws and Regulations to Actually Follow*. According to statute 24 of this law, anyone residing in the capital, whether a layperson or a monk, was not allowed to sell vodka to monks for recreational drinking. The prescribed penalty for breaking this regulation was bondage in a cangue (a flat, rectangular device made of wood for confining the neck of a criminal) for forty days and a hundred floggings. When vodka was needed for a religious ceremony in the monastic city of Ikh Khüree (present Ulaanbaatar), only a trusted official who had obtained a special permit could purchase it from herders. The law required that seven teams consisting of monks and government officials be formed to inspect whether monks were recreationally drinking vodka and to make a report if such an incident had occurred. Nowhere in this new *Laws and Regulations to Actually Follow* is it said that a monk who recreationally drinks vodka should be monastically disrobed. Statute 30 explicitly states that a monk who is seen recreationally drinking vodka but is unable to pay the fine should not be disrobed, but forced to attend 100 *pūjas* and to make 100 prostrations for each day of the designated period of punishment.[28] Likewise, for those who were offering or selling vodka to monks or who were not reporting a vodka-drinking monk to the authorities, various types of punishments, such as fines in livestock, flogging, imprisonment, and bondage in a cangue, were introduced.

As a recreational drinking of vodka among monks and laypeople, which began in the latter part of the nineteenth century, accelerated during the early twentieth century, influential Mongolian lamas and governmental authorities addressed the problem of alcoholism through edifying writings and legal statutes. Zhamtsarano and Baradin, who traveled through Khalkha and Buryatia in the early twentieth century (1917–1932), witnessed a wide dissemination of numerous didactic sources in those regions.[29] In one of several edifying epistles and edicts to the Khalkhas, the Eighth Bogd Jebtsundamba lamented, saying: "The amount of vodka that you drink resembles uncrossable rivers and oceans."[30] In another appeal, he wrote:

> Do not purchase and smoke any Russian and Chinese tobacco,
> Saying, "it is cheap," even if it is worth three coins.
>
> Do not purchase any kind of [their] vodka,
> Saying, "it is cheap," even if it is worth 100 coins.
> Do not drink it.
>
> If one consumes these,
> He will be affected by Chinese and Russian poison.[31]

The prevailing negative attitude of the Eighth Bogd Jebtsundamba's government and Mongolian nationalists toward Chinese and Russian merchants and settlers in Mongolia echoes the laws and decrees issued during the period of the Autonomous Mongol State. However, since the Eighth Jebtsundamba's reputation was declining due to his long periods of drunkenness, his appeals were ineffective. In his unpublished autobiography, Dilova Khutugtu (1883–1965) described the Eighth Jebtsundamba as he saw him in 1920, with these words:

> . . . for a week, drinking steadily night and day . . . he would go on drinking, never lying down to sleep and never moving except to go out to the toilet. At times he would seem to be completely unconscious, with his head lying on his chest; he would not seem to understand anything that was said to him. Then he would raise his hand and demand another drink; and the new drink would seem to sober him up so that he could conduct business. Even after a bout like this he would not sleep except in naps of two or three hours at a time. Yet, he was a very able politician and kept control of things within the limits of his rapidly vanishing power.[32]

The Fifth Noyon Khutugtu, Danzanravjaa (Bstan 'dzin rab rgyas, 1803–1856), a famous Mongolian *yogī*, writer, and composer who lived in the late nineteenth century, sometimes referred to as "a drunkard from the Gobi," reprimands his monastic disciples for recreationally drinking vodka in his didactic poem titled, "Verses That Prohibit Vodka Drinking," with these words of warning:

> If a novice [recreationally] drinks liquor,
> He will fall into Hot Hells.
> If a fully ordained monk [recreationally] drinks vodka,
> He will fall into the Intensely Hot Hells.
> If a group of monks
> Jointly drink vodka [recreationally],
> This is an omen of the decline of the teachings.
> Hence, completely abandon vodka!
> To those who say:

O' Danzanravjaa!
You said that there is no fault in drinking vodka
Because you offer it to deities,
By blessing it as an inner offering,
Chanting the recitations
Of purification, realization, and enlightening,
And considering it at as an elixir,

To them I respond with these words:

If you can eat dog meat
Mixing it with human excrement,
After chanting the purification and realization [recitations],
Then, having folded my hands,
I confess my faults in your presence.
I have been repeating myself
To all of my disciples that
If you drink vodka,
You are not [Danzan] Ravjaa's disciples.[33]

Danzanravjaa also composed verses for removing the harms of vodka and tobacco:

I offer this entire excellent offering of Great Bliss,
To the refuge Guru, to the Buddha of Great Bliss,
While enjoying myself with pledge substances of Great Bliss.
Please grant me swiftly the *siddhi* of Great Bliss.

Non-virtuous in a single moment, do not enjoy wrong and toxic goods
Such as the stupefying vodka, tobacco, and the like,
Negligent of the tradition to know what has been said.

"*Oṃ ā vajrasattva hūṃ, oṃ amini sani bara zali basanu svāhā.*"
Recite this mantra seven times.

In contemporary Mongolia, where social problems caused by alcoholism continue, the Pürevbat Lama published a book containing a collection of various Tibetan and Mongolian magic rites, mantras, and *sādhana*s for counteracting alcoholism, for removing the harms of heavy drinking of vodka, preventing intoxication from vodka when drinking it, and for transforming vodka into an elixir (*rashaan, rasiyan*, Skrt. *rasāyana*) suitable for a tantric, inner offering.[34] In one of the recommended rites for eliminating the addiction to vodka, a monk must prepare a mixture made of the root of aconite,[35] sweet flag,[36] and nutmeg (*zadi*, Skrt. *jāti*), write these letters—*oṃ cha ha pha la na sa kha ha* on a piece of paper, and then seven times eat the letters, together with the mentioned mixture.[37]

In another rite, after a monk takes a vow not to drink vodka again, he consumes a mixture made of the *Halerpestes* plant (*gets*), cinnamon, bark from the *Sympegma* plant,[38] black seed (*khar ür*), salt, *khadira*, camphor, vitrior, and other magic substances (*zai*,

Tib. *rdzas*). After that, he recites the mantra: "*oṃ kaṃkani kaṃkani rocani rocani troṭani troṭani trāsani trāsani pratihana pratihana sarva karma paraṃ parān ime sarvasattvān ca svāhā*" and "ye *dharmā hetu prabhavā hetuṃ teṣāṃ tathāgato hy avadat, teṣāṃ ca yo niroda evaṃ vādi mahāśramaṇaḥ, svāhā*" many times and drinks vodka. The introduction of a rite prescribed for keeping a monk sober while drinking vodka, which according to Pürevbat Lama was taught by Tsongkhapa (1357–1419), was symptomatic of the inability of the religious and legal authorities to deter some monks from recreational drinking of vodka.[39]

In his didactic book on the evils of drinking hard liquor, Pürevbat Lama also includes an anonymous, tantric yogic ritual text on transforming vodka into elixir:

> *raṃ yaṃ haṃ*
> *oṃ āḥ hūṃ ho hrī peṃ hrī*
> *e ma ho*
> The elixir vodka made of eight thousand roots,
> The ambrosia (*amṛta*) to remove the five poisons,
> In its outer appearance, it is seen as vodka that makes one drunk,
> In terms of the ultimate meaning, it is a medicine for healing mental afflictions.
> It is poured into an excellent skull-cup
> In order to eradicate the three poisons in their roots
> And for attaining the seed of the three bodies [of the Buddha].
> *Hūṃ* is blessed by the three fruits.
> At the center of the heart of
> My body, non-differentiable from the Buddha,
> There is the sun disc, and upon it,
> I arise in my mind in the form of peaceful and wrathful deities.
> I transform my channels and elements
> Into a residence of *ḍaka*s and *ḍākinī*s.
> I transform all my six sense faculties into the assembly of the Wisdom Buddhas.
> To sacred objects I make an offering with vodka produced from the essence of the seed,
> Seen as five types of ambrosias in the ultimate truth,
> In order to worship an assembly of the buddhas.
> Please grant me a *siddhi*
> By alcoholically enjoying in your mind, in pure bliss!
> At the center of the Dharma Body, which is inherently empty in nature.
> I taste it, *phaṭ* in the center of the clear light vision.[40]

As previously mentioned, along with the risks of ending in hot hells, connected to recreational drinking of vodka came a concern about the dangers of tobacco snuff and cigarette smoking. Although the Vinaya does not contain explicit prohibitions against smoking or snuffing tobacco, Tibetan and Mongolian tantric forms of Buddhism regard tobacco as a contaminant that pollutes and blocks the channels (Skrt. *nāḍī*) of vital energies (Skrt. *prāṇa*) in the body. Since these are closely related to mental states, blocking the channels hinders the practitioner's progress in yogic tantric practices. In Tibetan Buddhist literature and in the Mongolian Buddhist literature, one finds didactic works, some of which contain warnings against tobacco smoking and recreational drinking of hard liquor, often in the context of foretelling the future social disasters. A production of such works composed by Tibetan and Mongolian influential lamas flourished in the late nineteenth century. Their production intensified in the early twentieth century among the Khalkhas and Buryats. Diverse manuscript copies of Mongolian translations of the Thirteenth Dalai Lama's admonishments regarding tobacco smoking widely circulated among the Mongols. In one of the versions of the Dalai Lama's text, studied and translated into English by Sazykin under the title "Prophetic Messages of Holy Lamas about the Sinfulness and Perniciousness of Smoking Tobacco," the initial teaching about the evils of tobacco smoking is traced back to the future Buddha Maitreya, who transmitted it to Mañjuśrī. From Mañjuśrī it was passed in sequence to Padmasambhava, Avalokiteśvara, and Dalai Lama. In this prophetic didactic work, tobacco leaves originally grew in the navel of a mad and tobacco-smoking Chinese demoness, who was harming and devouring people at night, after her menstrual blood flew out of her sexual organ at the time when she was killed by Mañjuśrī. Various natural disasters, ranging from hail and lightning, poor harvest, human and animal diseases unrecognizable to physicians, or guardian spirits leaving the body, one's bad dreams, rebirth in eighteen types of hell, and disregard for Dharma are listed as manifold, negative results of one's close association with that demoness, which one forms through tobacco smoking.[41] The association of tobacco with the foul blood of the Chinese demoness is most likely due to the growing influx of tobacco from China to Tibet and Mongolia in the early twentieth century. A widespread habit of smoking tobacco was endemic in early-twentieth-century Mongolia, as stated in the previously mentioned epistle of the Eighth Bogd Jebtsundampa to the Khalkhas. In that letter he grieves in this way: "The time has arrived when the smoke of tobacco that you enjoy covers entirely the brightness of the sun and the moon."[42]

It is interesting that the habit of snuffing tobacco is not mentioned in either of the two previously discussed texts. Perhaps no social stigma is associated with monks snuffing tobacco in Mongolia in didactic texts like these, which are written by higher religious authorities, and do not mention tobacco snuffing. Indeed, lamas are regularly seen exchanging their snuff bottles at various social occasions.

However, the aforementioned Dorjbold, a governing duke of Khalkha, rebukes the monks of his Gandentsenpillin monastery for snuffing tobacco and smoking cigarettes during and right after their performance of *pūja*s. He warns that such conduct causes obstacles to the benefactors, devotees, and the recently deceased on whose behalf the *pūja*s are performed. He is concerned with the fact that acts like drinking vodka, smoking tobacco, and carrying a bag of tobacco are perceived in society as external signs of a layman, and therefore are contradictory to monastic vows. Monks who show these signs make a monastery's benefactors lose faith, and in this way engage in disgraceful acts of the Māra, who yearns to downgrade the Dharma. in Dorjbold's view, when one pollutes a consecrated Buddhist image with the smoke of tobacco, the sanctity of the image is lost. When a monk enters and sits in a temple with the breath smelling of tobacco, he creates obstacles to the temple's sacred objects and generates negative karma.[43]

Conclusion

In the early modern period, the prohibitions of monks' recreational drinking vodka and warnings against smoking tobacco, as discussed earlier, failed in part due to the inability of religious and state authorities to uphold the standards they set and the laws they instituted. The examples explored in this chapter in small part show how social customs and conditions of an adoptive culture that have been integrated into Buddhist monastic practices can take precedence over the Vinaya. In Mongolia, the Vinaya rule of abstinence from intoxicants lost its normativity to some degree when it became applicable only in relation to recreational drinking of vodka but not in relation to the traditionally popular consumption of *airag*. This tells us how the traditional, cultural norms that contradict the Vinaya bring to light the indeterminacy of how the Vinaya is applied. Obedience to the Vinaya seems nearly impossible in a pastoral society that is more committed to its cultural norms and conventions. As we have seen, the specificity of the Vinaya rule regarding what particular kinds of fermented drinks are prohibited for monks has facilitated the exclusion of the types of fermented drinks unknown to the compilers of the Vinaya. Thus, the absence of the mention of fermented mare's milk in the Vinaya formed the basis for Mongolian monks' justification for their consumption of fermented mare's milk. Moreover, if regional practices, reasoning, and language enable a society to modify Vinaya rules, then the Vinaya is not a self-contained, deductive system of monastic rules, nor can it be regarded as an absolute or universal Buddhist monastic law. Different, non-Vinayic, Buddhist laws in Mongolia, such as customary laws and minor local laws that admonish tobacco smoking, represent an intersection of monastic regulations and Mongolian pastoral culture.

Notes

1. Traditionally, there were no real nunneries or nuns in Mongolia, apart from *chavgants*, older laywomen who shaved their heads and lived in a male monastery as attendants to sick or old monks.
2. The *Secret History of the Mongols* mentions a milking of many mares in the home of Naqu-bayan's father Bogurchu, and of the leather sacks of *airag* offered as a provision for Temüjin's journey. See *The Secret History of the Mongols*, translated from Mongolian into English by N. Dorjgotov and Z. Erendo (Ulaanbaatar: National University of Mongolia, 2006), 41.
3. *Danshig*, or *danshug*, festival was first introduced in Mongolia in 1696 for securing a long of life of Öndör Gegeen Zanabazar, the First Bogd Jebtsundampa (1635–1723). It was performed once every three years. However, during the period of the Eighth Bogd Jebtsundamba (1869–1924) it was performed every year during the last month of summer. During the Communist period it was forbidden and was reintroduced in August 2015. Since then, it has been regularly performed on a yearly basis.
4. A mare is milked four to six times a day.

5. In the shamanic version of a mare milk ritual, in preparation for this ritual, foals were tied to new and green poles brought from a mountain, while two persons, holding together a bucket of milk, would sprinkle it with two wooden spoons used for ritual sprinkling (*tsatsal*), while reciting: "offering to the *ongods*, offering to the *ongods*." This is followed by prayer recitation, while requesting from the sky, *ongods*, mountains, and waters a new prosperous season and auspiciousness.
6. Cha har dge bshes Blo bzang Tsul khrims, *gsung 'bum*, Vol. *sa*, in L. Khürelbaatar, *Sudar Shastiryn Bilig* (Ulaanbaatar: National University of Mongolia and the Institute of Language and Literature of Academy of Science, 2002), 370–73.
7. A mare is milked four to six times a day. For instance, *The Manner of Sprinkling a Mare's Milk* (*Rgod ma'i 'o ma gtor tshul*), written in Tibetan by Chakhar Geshe Luvsančültemin (1740–1810). Aee Cha har dge bshes Blo bzang Tsul khrims, *gsung 'bum*, Vol. *sa* 4; Gelek Palsang's (1846–1923) *Airag Hymns*, etc.
8. Cha har dge bshes Blo bzang Tsul khrims, *gsung 'bum*, Vol. *sa*, 4. See Khürelbaatar, *Sudar Shastirın Bilig* (2002), 370–73.
9. Khürelbaatar, *Sudar Shastiryn Bilig* (2002), 370–71.
10. For the time being, my translation is based on Modern Mongolian rendition from Tibetan, available in Khüelbaatar, *Sudar Shastirın Bilig* (2002), 373, since I have not been able to acquire the original text at this time. Therefore, it may not perfectly reflect the original Tibetan.
11. The manuscript of the text *Gegün-ü* [*sün-ü*] *sačuli-yin sudur orosibai*, folio 1a (kept in my private collection) reads:

    ɣurban erdeni-dür mörgömüi.
    emüg-ün degedü erke-tü köke möngke tngri;
    el etügen eke;
    qamuɣ-un degedü qan möngke tngri;
    qan ɣaǰar usun tümen odun dügüregei saran;
    alaman saran altan saran graɣ odun.

    Cf. the *Gegün-ü sün-ü sačuli-yin sudur orosibai* in Damdinsürüng (Damdinüren), "Mongɣol uran ǰokiyal-un degeǰi ǰaɣun bilig orosibai," *Corpus Scriptorum Mongɣolum*, Vol. 14 (1959): 96–100; Khürelbaatar, *Sudar Shastirın Bilig* (2002), 371–73, where it reads: *altan odun* (Venus).
12. Gelek Palsang, born in the principality (*khoshuu*) of Govi Mergen of Tüsheet Khan Province (*aimag*), was monastically ordained in his childhood. During his early monastic training in the monastery of the Ongi River, he studied the Tibetan language and literature. He eventually abandoned a monastic life and became a herder but continued to study the Classical Mongolian script. In his early twenties, he was hired as a transporter of goods to China, which provided him with the opportunity to learn Chinese. On his journeys, he collected a considerable number of Mongolian texts, which he studied. It was in his thirties that he began to write benedictions of temples, *airag* and *naadam* festivals, weddings, greetings, and so on, for which he became widely known and in demand.
13. This account was given to me by monks in Gandantegchelin monastery in Ulaanbaatar in the summer of 2017.
14. The monastery was known also under the names of Sain Khaanı Khüree and Uyangın Khüree, whose construction began in 1660. It was located in what is today Övörkhangai province (*aimag*). By 1937, the monastery had over a thousand monks. According to Lkham

Pürevjav, the document containing monastic regulations was kept in Tsagaan Övöö *süm* of Khalkha's Central Province (Töv *aimag*) and was found in Züüt jas. See *Khüree Khiidiin Jayag*, comp. P. Lkham, ed. Kh. Eröölt (Ulaanbaatar: Private publication, 2011), 4.

15. "Mongol orond zakharch baisan XIII Dalai Lama Tüvdenjamts Gegeentnee Sain Noën Khan, Ded Daa, Janin Gün naraas güin ailtgaj gal morin jil buyu 1906 ony namryn ekhen sard Sain Noënı Khiid Gandantsenpillingd (Sain Noënı Khüree buyu Uyangın Khüree) zokhioson Gandanpunttsanglin Khidiin tsogchin Choirın Jayag," in *Khüree Khiidiin Jayag*, 30.
16. *Phat* is a mantric syllable that marks the end of fierce expression.
17. "*He he*" is an exclamatory expression.
18. G. Pürevbat, *Ükhliin Tsalmaas Chölöölgdökh Ertnii Uvdisuud: Arkhi, Tamkhi, Mörootei Togloom, Buruu Khurıtsal* (Ulaanbaatar: MIBA Publications, 2010), 67.
19. *Bürkheer* is a bottomless cask placed on the top of the cauldron when distilling *airag* to allow vodka flow out of it. It contains a pail to catch vodka.
20. "Write this mantra *oṃ hili hili svāhā* three times and hang on a *bürkheer*:
Write this mantra *oṃ hrīḥ hrīḥ ḥūṃ hūṃ phaṭ* and hang it on a pennant.
Recite this mantra *oṃ hūṃ don de ā* 21 times and install it as sacred.
If this protection is hung on the *bürkheer* that produces *tarag*, the harm to fermented *tarag* will not come. This is also a method of making vodka delicious."
21. The text does not specify what are these wrong vows.
22. "Khalkhyn Zasag Gün Dorjboldyn Zokhioson Jayag," in *Khüree Khiidiin Jayag*, 27–28. Even in the more rigid Qing laws for Mongolia, consumption of vodka did not necessitate the expulsion from the monastery. In the same text, Dorjbold references the order of the Ikh Khüree's Qing governor Sun Yun, issued in the twenty-first year of Jiaqing emperor (r. 1796–1820), which demanded that a monk who drinks alcohol has his vows taken away in order to be flogged 80 times, since a physical punishment of an ordained person was impermissible. If the monk confesses his fault and promises not to drink again, he can take his vows again, but if he has not learned his lesson, he is to be delivered to the office of external affairs.
23. Known also as Donrovravsh, an older son of Shagdarjav and a grandson of Ayukh Khan (r. 1669–1724), the powerful leader of Torghuds. Replacing Ayukh Khan after his death in 1742, he was granted the title of the Khaan of Kalmyks in 1757, and he died in 1761.
24. See B. Batbayar, *Ikh Tsaazın Ekh Bichgiin Sudalgaa* (Ulaanbaatar: Mongolian National University, School of Law, Research Center for Mongolian State and Law History, 2008), 67.
25. Kh. Jalan-Aajav, *Khalkh Juram* (Ulaanbaatar: Mongolian Ministry of Justice, 1995), 42.
26. Jalan-Aajav, *Khalkh Juram* (1995), 55.
27. In both cases, the penalty was nine heads of livestock. B. Bayarsaikhan, B. Batbayar, and B. Lhagvajav, *Mongolyn Shüün Taslakh Ajillagaanı Tüükhen Survalj Bichigt Khiisen Shinjligee* (*Ulaan Qačart*) (Ulaanbaatar: Law School of Mongolian National University, 2010): Section B, statues 126, 150, and 190 (2010), 76, 78, and 81.
28. *Jinkhene Yavakh Dagaj Khuuly Dürem: 1913–1918*, edited and transliterated into Cyrillic by B. Bayarsaikhan (Ulaanbaatar: University of Mongolia, School of Law, Research Center for Mongolian State and Law History, 2004).
29. "Spisok Materialam Ts. Zhamtsaranova and B. Baradina 1903–1904," in *Izvestiia Rossiskoi Akademii Nauk* (1918), 1553–54; Aleksei G. Sazykin, "Prophetic Messages of Holy Lamas about the Sinfulness and Perniciousness of Smoking Tobacco," *Mongolian Studies: Journal of the Mongolia Society* 21 (1998): 49–69.

30. Alice Sárkozi, *Political Prophecies in Mongolia in the 17th–20th Centuries* (Wiesbaden: Otto Harrassowitz, 1992), 123.
31. "Arkhi Tamkhiig Khorigloson VIII Bogd Jevszundamba Khutgtın Gerees Zarlig," in G. Pürevbat, *Ükhliin Tsalmaas Chölöölgdökh Ertnii Uvdisuud: Arkhi, Tamkhi, Möriitei Togloom, Buruu Khurıtsal* (Ulaanbaatar: MIBA Publications, 2010), 73–74.
32. Cited in Owen Lattimore, *Nationalism and Revolution in Mongolia: With a Translation from the Mongolian of Sh. Nachukdorji's Life of Sukebatur* (Leiden: E. J. Brill, 1955), 49–50.
33. Noën Khutagt Danzanravjaa, *Zürkhen Surgaaliud* (Ulaanbaatar: Jikom Press Kompani, 2001), 20–23.
34. As alcoholism and its effects on society continue to exert an influence to the present day, some of these practices have been recently reintroduced and compiled by Lama Pürevbat in his book *The Ancient Instructions on Becoming Liberated from the Mask of Death: Vodka, Tobacco, Gambling, and Wrong Sexual Desire*, or *Ükhliin Tsamaas Chölöölgdökh Ertnii Uvdisuud: Arkhi, Tamkhi, Möriitei Togloom, Buruu Khurıtsal* (2010).
35. *Aconitum variegatum* is one of 250 species of flowering plants belonging to the family *Ranunculaceae*. It is an herbaceous plant, native primarily to the mountainous parts of the Northern Hemisphere, growing in the moisture-retentive but well-draining soils of mountain meadows. Most species are extremely poisonous and must be dealt with carefully. The root of *A. ferox* contains large quantities of the alkaloid pseudaconitine, which is a deadly poison. The root of *A. luridum* of the Himalayas is said to be as poisonous as that of *A. ferox* or *A. napellus*.
36. *Acorus grammineus*; *Acorus calamus*, found in wetlands, particularly in marshes, shorelines, and flatlands, grows in Siberia, Mongolia, Korea, Himalayas. Products derived from it are toxic, containing carcinogenic ß-*asarone*.
37. G. Pürevbat, *Ükhliin Tsamaas Chölöölgdökh Ertnii Uvdisuud: Arkhi. Tamkhi, Möriitei Togloom, Buruu Khurytsal* (Ulaanbaatar: MIBA Publications, 2010), 66.
38. A sub-shrub with fissured bark, found in China, Mongolia, Kazaksthan.
39. According to Mongolian Lama Pürevbat, in this rite, having mixed together kidney beans and *arūra*, one puts them into water, recites the mantra *oṃ padma krodha kararaye svāhā* (*um badma gordiga rara ye suha*) 21 times, blesses water containing the mentioned substances by blowing into it, and drinks it. See G. Pürevabat, *Ükhliin Tsamaas Chölöölgdökh Ertnii Uvdisuud: Atkhi. Tamkhi, Möriitei Togloom, Buruu Khurytsal* (2010), 66.
40. Pürevabat, *Ükhliin Tsamaas Chölöölgdökh Ertnii Uvdisuud: Atkhi. Tamkhi, Möriitei Togloom, Buruu Khurıtsal* (2010), 70–71.
41. Sazykin, "Prophetic Messages of Holy Lamas about the Sinfulness and Perniciousness of Smoking Tobacco," 49–70.
42. Alice Sárkozi, *Political Prophecies in Mongolia* (Wiesbaden: Otto Harrassowitz, 1992), 223.
43. "Khalhyn Zasag Gün Dorjboldın Zokhioson Jayag," in *Khüree Khiidiin Jayag*, 8–10, 14.

Further Reading

Batbayar, B. *Ikh Tsaazın Ekh Bichgiin Sudalgaa*. Ulaanbaatar: Mongolian National University, School of Law, Research Center for Mongolian State and Law History, 2008.

Bayarsaikhan, B., B. Batbayar, and B. Lhagvajav. *Mongolyn Shüün Taslakh Ajillagaany Tüükhen Survalj Bichigt Khiisen Shinjligee* (*Ulaan Qačart*). Ulaanbaatar: Mongolian National University, School of Law, Research Center for Mongolian State and Law History 2010.

Damdinsürüng. "Mongɣol uran ǰokiyal-un degeǰi ǰaɣun bilig orosibai." *Corpus Scriptorum Mongɣolum* 14 (1959): 96–100.

Gegün-ü [sün-ü] sačuli-yin sudur orosibai. Ms, date unknown.

Jalan-Aajav, S. *Khalkh Juram*. Ulaanbaatar: Mongolian Ministry of Justice, 1995.

Jinkhene Yavakh Dagaj Khuuly Dürem: 1913–1918. Edited and transliterated into Cyrill by B. Bayarsaikhan. Ulaanbaatar: University of Mongolia, School of Law, Research Center for Mongolian State and Law History, 2004.

"Khalkhın Zasag Gün Dorjboldın Zokhioson Jayag," in *Khüree Khiidiin Jayag*. Compiled by P. Lkham and edited by Kh. Eröölt. Ulaanbaatar: Private publication, 2011.

Khüree Khiidiin Jayag. Compiled by P. Lkham and edited by Kh. Eröölt. Ulaanbaatar: Private publication, 2011.

Khürelbaatar, L. *Sudar Shastiryn Bilig*. Ulaanbaatar: National University of Mongolia and The Institute of Language and Literature of Academy of Science, 2002.

Noën Khutagt Danzanravjaa. *Zürkhen Surgaaliud*. Ulaanbaatar: Jikom Press Kompani, 2011.

Pürevbat, G. *Ükhliin Tsamaas Chölöölgdökh Ertnii Uvdisuud: Arkhi. Tamkhi, Möriitei Togloom, Buruu Khurıtsal*. Ulaanbaatar: MIBA Publications, 2010.

Sárközi, Alice. *Political Prophecies in Mongolia in the 17th–20th Centuries*. Wiesbaden: Otto Harrassowitz, 1992.

Sazykin, Aleksei, G. "Prophetic Messages of Holy Lamas about the Sinfulness and Perniciousness of Smoking Tobacco." *Mongolian Studies: Journal of the Society of Mongolia* 21 (1998): 49–70.

The Secret History of the Mongols. Translated from Mongolian into English by N. Dorjgotov and Z. Erendo. Ulaanbaatar: National University of Mongolia, 2006.

CHAPTER 26

DISCIPLINING THE BODY-MIND

CHARLES KORIN POKORNY

BUDDHIST traditions entering a new cultural sphere undergo a broad array of developments, some quite profound. This chapter examines how engaging Sōtō Zen monastic discipline in America functions for Western practitioners. Tassajara Zen Mountain Center serves as a case study of this phenomenon. Tassajara is among an array of transmissions and transformations of Zen monastic practice at training centers in the United States. While a spectrum of modalities, practice sensibilities, and training atmospheres are evolving among these centers, exploring diverse approaches to adapting Japanese Sōtō Zen, the cultural dynamics of developing monastic training that is accessible, relevant, meaningful, and transformative to Western practitioners is deeply shared. The raw "data" or "field research" for this discussion draws principally from my life of training at Tassajara for a total of eight years during three stays between 1994 and 2006, supplemented by conversations with current and former resident-practitioners. Taking Tassajara as an example of Western practice, I will explore the dynamics of disciplining the body-mind at Tassajara with reference to major points of continuity and discontinuity with Japanese Sōtō monastic practice.

MONASTIC LIFE AT TASSAJARA

In keeping with the tradition of locating training centers in remote natural environs, the monastery is nestled in a valley along Tassajara Creek, surrounded for miles on all sides by the wilderness of the Los Padres National Forest, inland from the Big Sur coastline in California. Natural hot springs drew Native Americans to the valley, and they named the place "Tassajara." A hot springs resort was opened in the nineteenth century. Tassajara was acquired by the San Francisco Zen Center in 1967 and was established as a monastery while continuing to function as a resort in the summer. The main buildings at the heart of Tassajara are the *zendō* (meditation hall), kitchen, and dining room/dorm. Smaller buildings, used for housing, offices, and maintenance, extend from the central area up and down creek. Further up the creek is the bathhouse, fed by the springs, a legacy of the site and a landscape feature that is woven into monastic practice. A daily bath is valued for hygiene, therapeutic relaxation, and bringing deep warmth to cold bodies in winter. Surrounded by the steep terrain of the Santa Lucia Mountains, off the grid and in a desert climate, the dry heat of summer and cold nights of winter are salient aspects of life.

The founding master of San Francisco Zen Center and Tassajara was Suzuki Shunryu, a Sōtō priest who came to the United States in 1959, interested in teaching Zen to Americans. While Suzuki focused on transmitting the spirit of Zen practice, other Japanese Zen priests, including Otogawa Kōbun, Katagiri Dainin, and Tatsugami Sotan, assisted Suzuki in developing formal monastic practice, imbuing Tassajara training with features of Japanese Zen culture. Efforts were made to carefully preserve traditional forms of practice while adapting to the cultural dispositions of Western practitioners and accommodating to Tassajara as a place, including its physical environment, buildings, and legacy as a resort. As an instance of Japanese Zen practice taking root in American soil, it could look like a transplantation of Japanese cultural forms, but from the outset, it was a new phenomenon, both Japanese and American. With an eye to honoring the founding teacher and caring for the vital spirit of Zen practice, Suzuki's American dharma successors have continued to carefully, and often cautiously, develop the forms of training in response to the needs, concerns, and proclivities of Tassajara practitioners, a community itself changing with the culture at large.

Following the model of Japanese Sōtō Zen, two approximately ninety-day monastic practice periods are held each year. At Tassajara, the annual schedule is built around the "guest season," which runs from late April to early September, when the center hosts sixty to eighty guests at a time. The monastic training periods then take place in autumn and winter between September and April.

In keeping with Sōtō tradition, *zazen* (sitting meditation) is the central practice of Tassajara. *Zazen* is simply to sit wholeheartedly engaged in upright stillness. As the central practice of Sōtō Zen, however, *zazen* has long been the subject of extensive, multifarious approaches and discourse. Following Sōtō tradition, *zazen* is practiced, and at times explicitly articulated, as a communal ritual of meditation. Depending on context, *zazen* is expounded in terms that may emphasize or de-emphasize its embodied, psychological, spiritual, or ritual dimensions. At Tassajara, the influence of Western frameworks, including a tendency to dichotomize ritual and meditation as well as other broad cultural perspectives and mindsets, is evident in an emphasis on psychological-experiential approaches to *zazen*.

The daily schedule during monastic training periods is similar to what takes place in many Sōtō monasteries in Japan. A typical day starts with the wake-up bell at 3:50 a.m. Practitioners gather in the meditation hall for *zazen* from 4:20 to 6:10 a.m. The *zendō* (meditation hall) at Tassajara is the main ritual hall. It hosts some of the functions of a *sōdō* (sangha hall) in a traditional Sōtō monastery, but practitioners do not sleep in the hall. Morning *zazen* is followed by a forty-minute chanting service and breakfast. Most chanting is in English, but the *Heart Sutra* is alternately recited in English and Japanese, and *dhāraṇī* texts not amenable to translation are recited in Japanese transliterations. Meals are held in the *zendō* following traditional monastic forms of the *ōryōki* (bowl that holds just enough) meal ritual.[1] Residents enjoy a high-quality, vegetarian, mostly organic diet. After breakfast, there is a one-hour study period, temple cleaning, and then either *zazen*, lecture, or class. At 11:20, a short chanting service is followed by *ōryōki* lunch. The first substantial break of the day takes place after lunch, lasting about an hour. The community gathers for work meeting at 1:15 p.m. Work during practice periods consists of food preparation, cleaning, grounds maintenance, and administration. Work ends at 4:15 with the daily "bath and exercise" time. Evening chanting at 5:50 p.m is followed by dinner in the *zendō*, another short break, and then *zazen* until 9:00 p.m., when the day closes with reciting the Three Refuges. Students wear traditional Japanese-style black robes to all *zendō* events. Practitioners are asked to observe silence from evening *zazen* through to the break after lunch the next day. Talking is permitted in the afternoon, although the recommendation during work is to limit talk to "functional speech."

Tassajara has taken a fairly conservative approach in adapting the ritual forms of Japanese Sōtō Zen. The ritual practice initially strikes Americans as foreign or "very Japanese." Ritual practice permeates a typical day during training periods. In addition to the central ritual practice of *zazen*, there are three chanting services, three formal meals, beginning and end-of-day rituals, and occasional ritual practices such as Buddha's awakening ceremony, practice period opening and closing ceremonies, etc. Ritual forms permeate daily life, including silence, holding hands in *shashu* (folded hands)[2] while in robes, and performing a bow in *gasshō* (palms joined) when passing another practitioner on the path. Ritual verses repeatedly invoke the bodhisattva vow to free all beings from suffering as the fundamental aspiration framing all monastic activities. While practitioners commonly arrive with some notion that ritual forms are either genuine expressions of inner sentiments or merely empty performances, many come to appreciate how deeply ritual forms function to shape attitudes, emotions, and dispositions, shifting from a sense of "mind leading body" to "body leading mind." Chanting enacts and promotes communal harmonization and intones central teachings of the tradition. Ritual procedures for entering the meditation hall, conducting services, and performing the meal ritual cultivate mindful embodiment in the Sōtō spirit of careful attention to fine detail. Mindfulness is actualized in attending carefully to one's bodily deportment and posture. Making mistakes, trying to be perfect, actively resisting, and becoming too loose or too tight around ritual forms afford numerous opportunities to study grasping and attachment. Daily ritualized performative speech acts include confession, refuge, offering, homage, invocation, vowing, and dedicating. In the spirit of Dōgen's teaching of practice-realization, ritual forms may also be wholeheartedly engaged as nothing more or less than "performances" or enactments of awakening.

Following Zen norms in Japan, Tassajara functions on a five-day week. Calendar days ending in four or nine are "personal days." Wake-up is one hour later. Breakfast or dinner is informal and individuals pack a picnic-style lunch. Students attend to personal matters such as laundry (done by hand) and cleaning eating bowl cloths. Four-and-nine days in Japanese Zen training involve some relaxing of the daily schedule and time for the weekly bath, but often do not include the chunk of personal "free" time afforded to Tassajara students to relax, socialize, hike, etc.

Sesshin (to collect the mind) are meditation intensives, three to ten days in length, which take place once per month. During *sesshin*, there is more *zazen*, no study period, a shorter work period, less break time, and silence is observed at all times. The signals calling practitioners to *zazen* are simplified and shortened, creating a different sense of time and urgency. *Sesshin* unfold with their own particular drama and quiet depths, inviting intensive focus and total exertion, sometimes with feelings of anticipation or trepidation beforehand, and afterward, permutations of relief, release, let-down, exhaustion, gratitude, etc.

There is no formal curriculum of study, but engagement with the teachings of Zen and the Buddhist tradition in general is encouraged through daily study periods, texts chanted in services, classes, lectures, and individual meetings with practice leaders. Practice period leaders often choose a teaching and study focus for each practice period, which could be a text such as Dongshan's *Jewel Mirror Samadhi*, a teaching such as dependent-arising or karma, or a practice such as compassion, precepts, or concentration.

Practitioners come to live, work, and train at Tassajara for a week up to multiple years. Students intending to stay for extended periods generally go through a process of leaving home, friends, and sometimes family, school, job or career, title, as well as various comforts, conveniences, and diversions of contemporary life. The hour-long drive on the fourteen-mile dirt road serves as a passage or transitional space, adding to the sense of retreat, "leaving the world," and separating from typical supports of identity and worldly life. There is no cell phone coverage, no internet access for students not on senior staff, and two phone lines for the entire community (both personal and business use). Mail and newspapers arrive once or twice per week. Students only leave for medical or family emergencies. Tassajara's isolation supports practitioners in renouncing, at least temporarily, worldly distractions and affairs.

Once at Tassajara, practitioners engage the forms of practice, become part of a community, and often form deep friendships. The community of practitioners itself constitutes one of the most vital, if ever-changing, dimensions of the training environment. The number of participants in practice periods ranges from forty-five to over seventy. Each practice period has its own particular culture and sense of community, accentuated by the personality, teaching, and leadership styles of the practice period leaders who rotate from among current and former abbots of San Francisco Zen Center.

Unlike contemporary Sōtō Zen in Japan, very few practitioners come to Tassajara as a kind of vocational training qualifying them to serve as full-time temple priests. People come with a range of motivations, interests, and intentions. Some come with an open curiosity to explore Zen training. Some come in response to deep suffering, including depression, death, and addiction. Activists come to retreat, recover, and recharge. Some seek a dramatic awakening, while others seek community, an alternative lifestyle, or escape from the pressures of urban life. Some come as part of priest training and particularly to receive training in ritual practice. The majority of practitioners are not ordained as priests. Priest ordination does not involve taking lifetime vows of celibacy. This follows the current norm in Japanese Zen among ordained men, most of whom function as married temple priests, and contrasts with women ordained in Japanese Sōtō Zen, most of whom do take lifetime vows of celibacy that carry through monastic training and functioning as temple priests. There is not a strong division of status or role between lay and priest at Tassajara, except that priests can lead ceremonies. Most practitioners do not classify easily into the "fourfold assembly," with residents assuming both lay and monastic qualities while training at Tassajara. The community is open to people of all genders. Ages of residents can range from eighteen to over eighty years old. Couples, and sometimes families, are welcome to practice at Tassajara, and couples sometimes form (practitioners are asked not to begin new sexual relationships in their first six months at Tassajara).

From this description of the life and rhythms of training at Tassajara, the discussion now turns to three dynamics of how this training functions for practitioners. The first is perhaps most traditional in emphasizing wholehearted engagement with ritual forms of practice to realize freedom through releasing self-grasping. The second dynamic turns on growth, emotional development, and maturity through practice in relationship and community. The third concerns broadening practice beyond monastic training, which takes place during the summer guest season when the world comes to the monastery.

The Core of Zen Training: When It's Cold, the Cold Kills You

Zen training has long prided itself on its uncompromising approach to intense communal practice, with long hours of meditation following a strict schedule, leaving little or no room for personal time or space. Following Dōgen's introduction of the sangha hall (*sōdō*) in Japan, monastics sit meditation, eat, and sleep in the same hall of communal practice. The training regimen is intentionally relentless and severe, ideally offering no escape hatches. Sitting meditation in extremes of heat and cold is idealized. The diet is very simple. Sleep and practically any form of comfort are minimized. It is a challenging, difficult modality of training, compared to squeezing a snake into a bamboo pole. It is also compared to pressure cooking, with cautions against any temptation to lift the lid off the pot lest it interfere with the cooking process.

This approach may be viewed as a ritual enactment of the profound determination of Shakyamuni Buddha as he endeavored to realize awakening. It may also be viewed as a means to address, challenge, and uproot grasping to the delusion of a separate self and the self-oriented tendencies based on, and deepening, that delusion. A Zen saying exhorts practitioners to "die on your cushion." The Chinese Chan master Dongshan taught, "When it's cold, the cold kills you. When it's hot, the heat kills you."[3] At Tassajara, this is heard as an encouragement to let the cold kill, or release, all resistance to the cold, and this releasing of resistance is ultimately letting go of the delusion of a self separate from the cold.

This release or relaxing of resistance is the soft inner dimension of meditation, with its outer, seemingly rigid stipulation of not moving. Practitioners are encouraged to sit still and upright, not as a form of stoic mastery over pain and discomfort, but as a practice and posture of vulnerability, of letting the cold and heat and all things touch one's life completely. In addition to cold and heat, practitioners sitting in meditation are commonly assailed by knee, back, and other bodily pains (cross-legged sitting often involves an intense and evolving encounter with physical pain and discomfort), itches, runny noses, flies, mosquitos, desires, fears, irritability, etc. Rather than moving and adjusting in response to such circumstances, likened to taking the lid off the pot, and rather than ignoring or blocking out such aspects of experience as "distractions," *zazen* is to be wholeheartedly present with, or as, whatever is happening. The practice of not moving in meditation is not realized by holding still, but through an engaged relaxation with what is. Pursued with diligence and care, this practice can release grasping to the delusion of separate self and open into liberation.

This same dynamic also underlies a central principle of communal monastic practice in Zen: to follow the schedule completely. When the hammer strikes the wooden *han* (board) announcing the beginning of *zazen*, practitioners go to the *zendō*. Ideally, everyone follows the schedule completely, except for those who are ill. It is not simply that by following the schedule one engages in practices that actualize the fundamental training, but that following the schedule is itself a key enactment and actualization of the fundamental training. Following the schedule itself is investigating the self and illuminating the mind. Just as practitioners do not move in *zazen*, they do not move from the schedule, nor do students leave Tassajara during monastic training periods. While following the schedule may seem to involve an unstinting adherence to a rigid external standard, this approach to practice likewise cultivates a soft, gracious presence with suffering, an inner tenderness, and compassion.

At Tassajara, not moving in meditation, following the schedule, and staying in the valley are all intended to support practitioners in releasing grasping and resistance. Such release opens into insight and a kind of freedom. It is a freedom *with* rather than a freedom *from*. When grasping is released, it does not give warmth when it is cold, nor do knee and back pain miraculously dissipate, nor does it solve the more intractable personal and interpersonal problems everyone faces. It is a freedom *within* problems, challenges, and restrictions, and as such, it is a freedom that has a dynamic function in supporting practitioners to embrace challenges and work with them productively. It is a liberation from unproductive struggle, freeing energies that may then be directed to vitalizing a practitioner's productive encounter with difficulties.

Grasping, even the subtle grasping of locating a "self" as the thinker of one's thoughts, is a psycho-physical event with mental and physical aspects. The embodied dimension of ritual forms is thus well-suited to an examination and release of grasping as the key psycho-physical underpinning of suffering. The ritual forms, from *zazen* to bowing on the path, to the detailed provisions of the eating ritual, put into question any substantial dichotomy of body and mind.

In this context, grasping concerns how one relates to what is being experienced. It is often subtle. While it shapes the field of awareness, it is not typically *in* the field of awareness. *Zazen*'s simplification of sensory input, with its release from expectations of practical productivity and interpersonal interaction, conduces to attending to this subtle phenomenon of grasping. A forceful approach is self-defeating in taking a grasping approach to the release of grasping. It is essential, rather, to carefully and thoroughly "feel" grasping. "Owning" the grasping in this way allows it to open and release.

On some level, practitioners may come seeking to escape from themselves, drawn by Buddhist teachings of selflessness, and idealized views of monastic training as a utopian life of communal selflessness. A great and often surprising irony of Zen practice is that practitioners come to be free from suffering only to find that monastic training is intended to promote a close intimacy with one's personal and interpersonal processes of suffering. Such intimacy is the vital function of renouncing the potential distractions and diversions of worldly life. Monastic discipline seeks to make a clear and transformative encounter with patterns of self-grasping unavoidable.

Compared to the rigors of Sōtō monastic training in Japan, Tassajara training can appear less strict, looser, easier, or watered down, and by extension, less effective, if not ineffectual, with respect to "pressure-cooking" patterns of grasping and suffering into freedom. While the diversity of training environments in Japan complicates comparison, differences may include more free time and personal space at Tassajara, along with abundant and delicious food, heated rooms (for some), less work, gentle encouragement with a lack of harsh feedback, daily bathing (rather than only on four-and-nine days), and the security of monthly stipends. While Tassajara has more scheduled *zazen* than some monasteries in Japan, the overall discipline may be less intense because practitioners are effectively released from the ritual-training space multiple times per day. With a critical eye toward American Zen in its early stages, one might regard these differences as accommodations to entitled Westerners, creating a comfortable "upper-middle way." On the other hand, the idealized tradition of uncompromising severity in Japanese Zen may be less concerned with liberation of suffering, and more concerned with upholding a reputation for strict training, endowing Zen priests with ritual charisma suitable to functioning as funerary masters. Whatever truth such perspectives, and others, may reflect, the focus here is on how training at Tassajara does indeed function.

We can explore how the relatively porous practice container at Tassajara works for Westerners by invoking the importance of an environment that is at once supportive as well as challenging, and appreciating how cultural differences lead to significant variations in how such a balanced environment is developed. In *Trust, Realization, and Self in Sōtō Zen Practice*, Daijaku Kinst engages insights of Western psychology in articulating how contemplative practice works.[4] Kinst notes a supportive function in providing the affirmation needed to fully engage the practice, and a transformative function that challenges practitioners appropriately. Rather than opposing each other or regarding the supportive function as inherently working to corrupt the transformative function, in this frame, these two functions necessarily work together. The "accommodations" of Tassajara may then be appreciated in terms of the positive functions of encouragement, affirmation, comfort, and allowances for personal space in monastic training environments. A good enough balance of support and challenge creates an effective training environment. Cultural differences need to be taken into account in how both the supportive and challenging functions are developed, established, and enacted. The relative severity of Sōtō training in Japan may be too austere for Westerners who often come to monastic practice with more questions than convictions.

A practice environment that is too challenging and "culturally other" will not be effective for most people. Without sufficient support, a challenging training environment may become overwhelming and may then be met with retreat, aversion, denial, or defensive self-protection. Forms of practice may be dismissed as overly strict, arbitrarily repressive, or authoritarian, or may even be rejected completely as abusive. Practitioners may withdraw from deep engagement with practice, and an intimate, transformative encounter with suffering is inhibited. Lacking sufficient support, the transformative efficacy of challenging environments may be severely limited and undermined. Toxic emotional and interpersonal environments can easily develop in intensive training. Kinst notes, "If the need for affirmation is ignored practice may become an arid spiritual athleticism lacking humility and a deepening connection to all beings that suffer and feel fear."[5] The heart of practice can be easily lost while its external forms are rigorously maintained. A merely abstract, ineffectual engagement with important, subtle teachings like emptiness and practice-realization may develop.

The supportive function is accordingly not of secondary importance, but is essential to actualizing the transformative potentials of monastic discipline. Westerners coming to train at Tassajara have not had long-term cultural exposure to the Zen tradition. The training environment itself needs to be adapted in order to be accessible and effectively introduce and inculcate intensive discipline. It is necessary to develop culturally appropriate approaches to the fragility and brokenness that brings some practitioners to step into the somewhat radical and unusual path of Zen monastic training. With enough support and affirmation, practitioners can relax and soften with what is happening while following the schedule and engaging the ritual forms. There needs to be enough confidence to be fully present with suffering before the underlying grasping can be explored, questioned, and released. The supportive function may be enacted or actualized in various ways, including community, beauty, nourishing food, adequate personal space, as well as ritual forms of respect, gratitude, and devotion. Relationships of mutual recognition and respect among practitioners and teachers provide ground for challenging, transformative interactions.

A supportive practice environment without sufficient challenge will also be ineffectual and will limit the transformative potential of practice. The transformative function may be enacted through the physical, emotional, intellectual, spiritual, and interpersonal challenges of monastic discipline. Such challenges include: sitting still for long periods in *zazen*, following a sufficiently rigorous schedule and set of guidelines, working with culturally foreign ritual forms, not being able to avoid or deny one's afflictions and patterns of suffering, and repeatedly engaging teachings such as impermanence, emptiness, and Zen koans that question one's sense of self and identity. Many aspects of monastic training environments have concurrent and overlapping functions of support and challenge. The food may be nourishing and delicious, but practitioners still have no choice about what is served for breakfast, lunch, and dinner.

The training model in Japanese Zen provides little or no time for practitioners to be alone—a significant, challenging dimension of the "pressure cooking" approach. At Tassajara, personal space and free time may provide a release of pressure that supports deep practice, but this spaciousness presents its own distinct challenges. With more time to be alone, breaks may become filled with stewing in one's problems or taking recourse to distractions or unhelpful patterns.

Some may benefit from more pressure or containment. Practitioners sometimes endeavor to create some additional pressure for themselves by taking up supplemental practices such as late-night *zazen*, performing prostrations during breaks, or maintaining silence at all times. This approach has weaknesses. A key value of following the schedule is challenging one's moment-to-moment inclinations, bringing up repeated encounters with grasping around preferences. Supplemental practices are generally permitted, but as they may easily become avenues of self-grasping, they are also accordingly challenged as such. On the other hand, there are important strengths in asking practitioners to challenge themselves beyond following the schedule. Following the schedule in itself is not sufficient. An inner diligence is necessary.

A relatively porous container places more responsibility on the individual for developing the intensity of practice. This may accord with cultural resistance to hierarchical authority and an ethic of "self-reliance." For many Tassajara practitioners, the fundamental motivation to engage discipline needs to be experienced as coming from within, rather than imposed from an external source, reflecting a more individualistic, and less relational, experience of self. A totally ritualized life may not provide sufficient avenues for uniquely individualistic self-expression which is valued as integral to practice. Spaciousness gives time for writing a poem, a long walk, or in-depth conversation. Practitioners also need to find an inner sense of discipline and commitment to draw on in their post-monastic lives. Most practitioners will leave Tassajara for lay lives in worldly contexts with no wake-up bells, practice schedules, or communities of like-minded students of Zen. Returning to the analogy of pressure-cooking, it may well be that this makes for a slower cooking process, but it is for many practitioners more accessible and effective.

The Sangha Jewel: The Rocks in the Creek Rub Together and Become Smooth

In both Japan and America, Sōtō Zen training thrives in highly relational, communal environments supporting a transformative encounter with interpersonal entanglements. A significant point of divergence lies in how these entanglements are processed, with the practice-culture at Tassajara leaning toward a more verbal and psychological approach. While the first dynamic concerns a softening and relaxing in relation to processes of suffering within the rigid strictures of monastic discipline, this dynamic concerns the development of this inner opening through interpersonal frictions to a multidimensional maturity in relationships. This extends the elemental practice principle of "letting the cold kill you" to the intricacies of interpersonal conflict. A traditional image of this aspect of communal practice points to how a "furry" variety of Japanese tuber is washed by rubbing them together in a tub of water. At Tassajara, the metaphor has been transposed to the ever-present flowing of Tassajara creek: the rocks in the creek rub together and become smooth. While in early Buddhism, the sangha treasure as a refuge is sometimes strictly defined as the awakened disciples of the Buddha, at Tassajara and following precedents in the Zen tradition, it is actually the unenlightened qualities, or rough edges, of community members that are honored as a refuge and treasure of mutually transformative potential within monastic training environments. Democratizing the teaching function, daily interactions are viewed as opportunities to "hear" the Dharma or "study the self." This dynamic turns on the maturing potential of practicing through the relational dimensions of both formal and informal spheres of monastic life. Many Tassajara practitioners regard this as a significant and valuable dimension of transformative practice.

While the central practice of *zazen* can appear non-relational, liberating insight into the nature of self is realizing how the self happens through relationship. This is part of the import of *zazen* as a communal ritual of enacting awakening. *Zazen* is not something an individual does. It is enacting and actualizing how individuals only ever happen *in relationship* (with each other, cold, pain, etc.). *Zazen* is becoming totally relational in silence. An individualistic frame of undertaking *zazen* as a means to personal attainment is challenged. Other ritual forms, such as bowing and chanting, are more explicitly relational. There are also rituals *of* relating, such as formal question and answer ceremonies.

During *zazen*, practice leaders frequently offer one-on-one interviews. Students sign up for fifteen- to forty-minute interviews one or more times per month. While practice interviews are not a form of psychotherapy, areas of overlap occur as practitioners seek deeper engagement and explore being honest and revealing. Teachers may enact receptive, non-judgmental listening and also challenge students directly, pointing to areas of grasping and limited views, or asking practitioners to bring forth a complete expression manifesting the heart of practice. Effective teachers sense when to be firm or soft, encouraging or questioning.

Lectures in the meditation hall are usually followed by questions and answers. Practitioners in their first training period often give a "way-seeking mind" talk, discussing how they have come to Zen practice and Tassajara. Work circle meetings are conducted in a fairly relaxed, pragmatic atmosphere, occasionally including humor, apologies, and frustrated pleas to accord with a request. While limited to "functional speech," work typically involves numerous interactions. Many crews have a weekly "check-in" where crew members speak in turn about their challenges, how they are doing, what they are feeling, and how this relates to practice. Along with emotional-relational processing, this practice of "checking-in" helps to frame work as a field of practice and to cultivate a collective sense of practicing together through work. Break times can involve socializing that itself may include "checking-in" and "studying the self."

Amid the silence, conversation functions as an essential medium in which practitioners find their way to wholehearted engagement with monastic discipline. Talking-practice encompasses working through doubts and questions about the teachings and practice regimen. Many practitioners do not arrive with a well-formed faith in purely embodied training, but need to cultivate a sense of understanding before fully entering the discipline. This may include bridging culturally foreign ritual forms, developing clarity regarding the teachings and history of Buddhist traditions, and reframing more "religious" aspects of practice that surface potentially confusing associations with Christianity (such as devotion or confession). As the discipline unfolds into encounters with patterns of suffering, verbally processing events becomes significant and helpful. The practice of "checking-in" can involve working through the challenges of honest and authentic expression/confession, emotional awareness, and being in touch with oneself. Talking-practice encompasses supportive and transformative functions.

Through communal training, work crews, and living arrangements, practitioners are continuously relating, making the valley "feel awfully small." Practice periods typically begin with a "honeymoon" period of relative harmony as the community and work crews settle in. Toward the middle of the three-month training period, difficult interactions typically arise as relationships are strained by frustration, mistrust, unskillfulness, and irritability in the midst of living closely together. Hard feelings may arise over a disagreement, a charged outburst, a perceived slight, or feeling triggered, pressured, judged, or corrected. As friction or strain develops between practitioners, they often find each other unavoidable. Rough edges keep bumping into rough edges. At some point, practitioners need to move from blaming interpersonal problems on the others involved, to taking responsibility for their own part in the difficulty. This turning may be precipitated by recognizing a repeating pattern of difficulty, or one relationship becoming extremely dysfunctional. Underlying narratives loosen, exposing how problems manifest scenarios and frames that are projected onto events and interactions. As practitioners "own" their problems, they work with them rather than being worked by them, uncovering processes of grasping that can then be released.

Interpersonal challenges are affirmed as a significant field of cultivation. Practitioners may work with the difficult emotions of contentious relationships in the quiet of *zazen*, in one-on-one practice interviews, "check-ins," and informally with friends. The various relational modalities, formal and informal, all work together in supporting practitioners to address problematic and undeveloped relational dispositions. While some problems are resolved inwardly in *zazen*, or through working with a teacher, some ultimately require a direct, honest, and vulnerable interaction explicitly addressing, confronting, and processing a conflict or difficulty. Highly combustible entanglements can be mediated by a practice leader. Skillfully giving and receiving feedback guides a relational approach to working with relational problems.

In comparison with Japanese training, the more verbal approach at Tassajara may point to how explicit processing of interpersonal difficulties can be vital to developing healthy, multicultural communities. The diversity of practitioners in the complex, multicultural society of the United States may call for explicitly addressing and talking through problems, as a lack of common ground undermines more indirect, intuitive, or nonverbal approaches. Two significant dimensions of diversity at Tassajara include age and gender, both of which come with certain challenges, as well as great gifts, to the training environment. Everyone who comes to Tassajara starts as a beginner. For some, this can be experienced as an acute loss of status, as one's supervisor may be younger, less experienced, and less qualified to function in leadership.

While gender bias is an issue, women have filled leadership roles at all levels of the San Francisco Zen Center organization. This has perhaps been facilitated by the non-hierarchical priest ordination in Sōtō Zen, employing the same precepts for lay and priest ordinations regardless of gender. While the practice period leader is honored as the principal teacher during a training period, there is also an egalitarian ethic and wariness of projecting perfect awakening on individuals. Most practitioners identify one practice leader as their primary teacher, and also develop significant "practice relationships" with other practice leaders. Democratization of the teaching function upholds all community members as potential teachers, and all interactions as potentially transformative. Teaching interactions are framed less in terms of hierarchy and more in terms of authentic, intimate meeting. Each practitioner may learn from everyone, allowing the diversity of practitioners to enrich the training environment with arrays of worldviews, sensibilities, life experiences, and approaches to practice. While LGBTQ practitioners are fairly well represented within San Francisco Zen Center, racial inclusiveness has been an area ripe for growth and development in the mostly white community.

Practice and growth in interpersonal relationships unfolds into a multidimensional maturity, affirmed as concretely manifesting awakening. Relational maturity at Tassajara includes emotional intelligence (as a form of self-knowledge and as empathy), psychological insight, practical wisdom including leadership and communication skills, virtues such as patience, equanimity, resilience, flexibility, and mutuality, as well as the ability to invite, give, receive, and work with feedback. In part, such maturity flows from how Dōgen's dictum to "study the self" is received in Western contexts—shaped, informed, and enriched by psychological perspectives and values. The core delusion of grasping a separate self is preserved, while a more developed psychology of how that delusion is elaborated through interpersonal and emotional processes is being assimilated and intertwined. "Studying the self" takes place through engaging ritual forms and psychological/verbal processing in various relational contexts. Single-mindedly striving for a spiritual breakthrough is not emphasized. Tassajara practice may easily frustrate those with a strong drive to attain a dramatic awakening. Rather than a seamless container devoted to developing one-pointed concentration and undertaking a heroic effort to penetrate ultimate truth, the relatively dispersed energy of diverse forms of relationality are embraced as a vital field of practice. The approach at Tassajara is geared toward a holistic maturity cultivated through multivalent practice, integrated across speech and silence, working to address patterns of suffering. This may in turn benefit post-monastic life. The path goes through where the rough edges rub together, rather than around or above them. In the dynamic life of the sangha, challenging relationships become supportive, and supportive relationships become challenging.

Traversing Formal and Informal Practice: The World Comes to the Monastery

The mode of discipline shifts considerably in moving from the fall and winter practice periods to the spring and summer guest season. From April through September, formal practice is reduced considerably. There is one hour of *zazen* and a twenty-minute chanting service in the morning, and in the evening, a forty-minute period of *zazen*. All meals are informal. Students work around seven hours per day on crews dedicated to caring for the guests and maintaining Tassajara. Work areas include the kitchen, dining room, office, cabins, grounds, maintenance, and administration or "senior staff." Most summer work positions are physically, interpersonally, and/or emotionally demanding. The guest season is at once a legacy of Tassajara as a beloved hot springs resort, a vital stream of economic support, an entry gate for new members of the community, and a field of practice in dynamic interplay with the monastic training periods.

The question of economic support, fundraising, and interfacing with communities of lay supporters is shared by all Sōtō training centers in the West. Rather than fully ordained monastics engaging in training with the support of lay community, Tassajara may be thought of as a community of hybrid lay-monastic practitioners who engage in training supported by income from the summer guest season. In one sense, Tassajara does not function on donations, but on guest fees. In another sense, summer guests become Tassajara's householder community of generosity and support, and practitioners who assume this perspective tend to embrace summer practice.

The summer guest season may be viewed as a potentially corrupting accommodation, or as a skillful means of adapting the ancient practice of settling in one place for the rains retreat and wandering from place to place during the rest of the year. At Tassajara, rather than leave the monastery to wander the world, the world is invited into the monastery. Year-round practitioners follow the rhythm of the seasons by staying put, while the world comes to the monastery as guests, volunteer workers, and new students. This is Tassajara's way of being neither separate from, nor entirely in, the world. Economic necessity opens into an annual rhythm of cold and heat, stillness and activity, turning inward and outward. It is uniquely challenging, and also uniquely beneficial, enriching, and deepening.

While Tassajara has long been appreciated for its hot springs, guests have come to appreciate the care that goes into the meals, grounds, decor, and peaceful atmosphere. The wilderness, lack of cell phone coverage, and sounds of the monastery combine with daily work efforts of practitioners to provide a deep sense of retreat. Along with monastic training, this is a significant offering of Tassajara as a place where guests can unwind, relax, appreciate natural beauty, and be refreshed by soaking in the springs. Guests are welcome to join residents for morning and evening meditation, and practice is a vital element of many workshops offered to summer guests.

While some practitioners long for year-round monastic training, many long-term residents appreciate the dynamics of turning from the intensity of stillness and silence in fall and winter, to the intensity of work, interpersonal engagement, and heat in summer. This annual rhythm actually makes long-term training at Tassajara sustainable and vital for multiyear practitioners. Summer practice has a key spiritual function in testing, expanding, and balancing the monastic intensity of winter practice amidst the pressures of running a kind of business. Attachment to stillness and quiet is exposed and challenged.

A widening of heart and deepening of maturity courses through both modalities of training. Tassajara works well for practitioners who appreciate the practice periods and summer guest season as mutually supporting and deepening, as synergistic rather than antagonistic. The dynamics of practice discussed earlier, releasing grasping and relational work, carry over into summer. "Leaving" the monastic retreat is preparation for eventually leaving Tassajara. Developing and deepening practice in the midst of work carries over into practitioners' lives and work after they leave the monastery.

Conclusion: Hearts Opening to the Bodhisattva Vow

Through the dynamics of disciplining body and mind, practitioners' hearts may turn from practicing for one's individual self to practicing for others. Inner softening and release of grasping opens into maturing interpersonal work, and both of these may open further into the deep, broad compassion of the bodhisattva vow dedicated to the welfare and awakening of all beings. The vow is opened and becomes particular, tangible, and concrete through the practitioner's personal encounter with suffering, as well as through rough edges rubbing together in communal practice. The spirit of sangha is not just getting along, but a deep appreciation and mutual recognition, which, in the summer, may be extended to everyone who comes to the valley.

While the way in which training at Tassajara works is unique to each practitioner, a deepening of the bodhisattva spirit may be the most vital transformation practitioners bring from monastic training into the world. The departing student ceremony includes a declaration that the departing student "now returns to the marketplace with gift-bestowing hands." Some will continue to sit *zazen*, some will not. Some will continue to practice in community, some will not. But many move forward in life after monastic training moved by a genuine, open-hearted urge to benefit others in meaningful ways. Clenched hands of grasping transform into open hands of giving and receiving, supporting and challenging.

Notes

1. See Dōgen's Fushukuhanpō, "The Dharma for Taking Food," in *Pure Standards for the Zen Community: A Translation of the Eihei Shingi*, ed. Taigen Dan Leighton and Shohaku Okumura (Albany: State University of New York Press, 1996), 83–108.
2. The right hand is folded around the left hand held in a fist at the solar plexus.
3. Thomas Cleary and J. C. Cleary, *The Blue Cliff Record* (Boston and London: Shambala, 1992), 258.
4. Daijaku Kinst, *Trust, Realization, and Self in Sōtō Zen Practice* (Moraga, CA: BDK America, 2015), 156–61.
5. Kinst, *Trust, Realization and Self*, 157.

Further Reading

Anderson, Reb. *Warm Smiles from Cold Mountains: Dharma Talks on Zen Meditation*. Berkeley, CA: Rodmell Press, 1999.

Arai, Paula Kane Robinson. *Bringing Zen Home: The Healing Heart of Japanese Women's Rituals*. Honolulu: University of Hawai'i Press, 2011.

Arai, Paula Kane Robinson. *Women Living Zen: Japanese Sōtō Buddhist Nuns*. Oxford: Oxford University Press, 1999.

Bunce, Renshin. *Entering the Monastery: A Memoir of 12 Years in and around San Francisco Zen Center*. San Francisco: Published on Amazon by author, 2014.

Buswell, Robert. *The Zen Monastic Experience: Buddhist Practice in Contemporary Korea*. Princeton, NJ: Princeton University Press, 1992.

Campbell, Patricia Q. *Knowing Body, Moving Mind: Ritualizing at Two Western Buddhist Centers*. Oxford: Oxford University Press, 2011.

Chadwick, David. *Crooked Cucumber: The Life and Zen Teaching of Shunryu Suzuki*. New York: Broadway Books, 1999.

Fischer, Norman. *Taking Our Places: The Buddhist Path to Truly Growing Up*. New York: HarperCollins, 2004.

Ford, James Ishmael. *Zen Master Who?: A Guide to the People and Stories of Zen*. Somerville, MA: Wisdom Publications, 2006.

Kinst, Daijaku. *Trust, Realization, and Self in Sōtō Zen Practice*. Moraga, CA: BDK America, 2015.

Rutschman-Byler, Jiryu Mark. *Two Shores of Zen: An American Monk's Japan*. Muir Beach, CA: Published by author, 2009.

San Francisco Zen Center. "Zenshinji Pure Standards (Guidelines of Conduct) for Practice Periods." SFZC.org. https://sfzc6.blob.core.windows.net/assets/ZMC-2018WinterPP_Shingi.pdf (accessed March 27, 2018).

Suzuki, Shunryu. *Zen Mind, Beginner's Mind.* Boston: Shambhala, 2011.

Wenger, Michael. *Wind Bell: Teachings from the San Francisco Zen Center 1968–2001.* Berkeley, CA: North Atlantic Books, 2001.

Yifa. *The Origins of Buddhist Monastic Codes in China: An Annotated Translation and Study of the Chanyuan Qinggui.* Honolulu: University of Hawai'i Press, 2002.

CHAPTER 27

HOME ALTARS

LINDA HO PECHÉ

THIS chapter grapples with the question: How do Buddhist Vietnamese American home altar practices organize domestic life? In the following analysis, I trace how domestic altars materialize as shifting *positions* in the realms of the diasporic, the political, and the civic. This approach goes beyond asking how religious objects are simple expressions of religious beliefs in material form, or representations (material signs) of the sacred, but rather asks how religious practices happen *materially* and *spatially*—what they might mean or do or say, and how they are inextricably bound in a matrix consisting of humans, spirits, things, places, and beliefs. I make three assertions. First, Vietnamese American home altar practices are organic, material spaces that practitioners manipulate to invoke the intersections between the homeland and a new home. Second, domestic altars can enact an individualized moral or spiritual orientation and also express a complex and politically engaged imaginary[1] through the particular positioning of objects and imagery. And third, they can reveal a creative, adaptable, and civically engaged Vietnamese American spirituality and subjectivity. My broader claim is that home altar practices organize and manifest religious embodiment, political and civic proclivities, and an appeal to diasporic and national belonging.

SITUATING VIETNAMESE RELIGIOUS PRACTICES

Although Vietnam is generally considered a Buddhist country, scholars agree that many Vietnamese practitioners have historically adhered to a locally specific kinship-based form of ancestor veneration. Historically, Confucianism, Taoism, and Buddhism from China and India, merged with an indigenous form of ancestor veneration[2] to produce a syncretic sense of "moral orientation." The formal religious practice of Buddhism was introduced to Vietnam during 1,000 years of Chinese colonization beginning around 200 BCE. Roman Catholicism gained influence with the upper middle class during the French occupation in the seventeenth century and today makes up about 10 percent of Vietnam's population. Two native religions, Cao Đài and Hòa Hảo, have added to Vietnam's religious diversity. Cao Đài is a blend of Buddhism, Confucianism, Taoism, and Catholicism. It is a relatively new monotheistic religion, officially established in 1926, that allows for the acceptance of the historical Buddha, Mohammed, and Jesus Christ as prophets. Hòa Hảo, which was founded in 1939 as a form of lay-Buddhist "protestantism," encourages practitioners to be ready for combat (for protection) and has a proscribed nationalist mission. It has more than 1.5 million followers and is located predominantly in the Mekong Delta; it emphasizes a highly disciplined personal prayer life and has no temples or formal liturgies. There are also smaller populations of Muslims among the Cham ethnic minority, Protestant Christians, and Taoists.[3]

In many households, practitioners more often than not maintain ancestral altar rituals in tandem and sometimes simultaneously with the religiously proscribed prayers, chants, and/or ritual behaviors of their religious faith. These Vietnamese ancestral altar practices, formally known as *thờ cúng tổ tiên* (worshipping the ancestors), are among the most commonly practiced ritual traditions in Southeast Asia, and offering incense *dang hương* is commonly seen as the most fundamental ritual act; for many Vietnamese, filial piety is seen as the heart of "moral personhood."[4] Indeed, these ancestral altar practices are central to negotiating and solidifying a sophisticated existential and ontological worldview. Rather than understanding domestic ancestral veneration practices as somehow peripheral to those of the East's "official religions," I would argue that such practices were, and in some cases still are, the official and recognized historical antecedents and primary belief systems within which such official religions were and are integrated into daily life. Hence, this analysis of Buddhist practice will center specifically on the practices associated with ancestral veneration.

Across the Pacific Ocean in the United States, Vietnamese American religious practitioners inherited the rich and diverse religious history associated with a wide range of folk religious practices and formal religious belief systems from the homeland. In the diaspora, most Vietnamese identify as Buddhists or practice a folk-traditional form of ancestral veneration; Vietnamese Catholics number about 20 percent of the total Vietnamese American population.[5] In the greater Houston area in Texas, where this research was conducted, there is a more even distribution; about 40 percent of the Vietnamese American population identify as Roman Catholic; 44 percent identify as Buddhists.[6] This analysis will focus on three different altar traditions as a lens with which to analyze the realms of the diasporic, the political, and the civic. The interviews associated with this research were conducted during my dissertation research and span between 2007 and 2011.

On Diaspora: Home Altar/Altar as Home

In one of the earliest interviews I conducted in 2007, a participant recounted that one of the first things she attended to when she came to the United States was to construct a makeshift altar in the tiny room where she was temporarily housed in her sponsor's Texas home. She was alone and frightened as she constructed a small space (made up of photos of living and deceased relatives and a small buddha statue) to commune with her ancestors and pray through her isolation, insecurities, and nervous apprehension of living in a new country. She sheepishly confessed that it was her elder brother's duty to maintain her family ancestral altar, but nevertheless, this sacred space that she carved for herself played a significant role in her peace of mind during that time of great transition. These quiet devotions of one woman provide an example of the elaboration of a "private religion focused on self-cultivation, the creation of a sense of home, and the intimate, individual transactions with the spiritual world."[7] The expressive objects on her altar clarified and materialized a religious and cultural epistemology, had the power to shape her memories of a lost country and home, possibly guided her through ritual transition, and allowed for a space to explore her feelings of liminality through this period of crisis. In the same vein, the following series of photos explore how, for many Vietnamese immigrants, home altars were, and still remain, a visual and spiritual expression of longing for a homeland and an articulation of a new diasporic religious and cultural aesthetic.

As observed in my various visits between 2007 and 2011 to Houston's south side, a woman I will call Cô Loan walked to pray at the Buddhist pagoda in her condominium complex. She lit incense, prayed, and chanted on her knees, perhaps for about thirty minutes (Figure 27.1). This was her ritual every morning and every evening. It usually took her no more than a few paces to reach her front door, where she had decked out the entire entrance of her first-floor exterior with decorative tiles of colorfully painted flowers among an array of plastic fruits and flowers, tinsel streamers, lanterns, and paper votives. She often cared for another altar in front of a side window, dedicated to the wandering spirits; incense, bowls of water, silk flowers, and fruit are offered here as well.

On one occasion, Cô Loan led me through her front door into a front room that housed a visually provocative floor-to-ceiling assemblage of framed prints and photos, religious iconography, adornments, and the mixed scents of incense, fruit, and Vietnamese cooking. In the past, she cooked meals out of her home for many of the residents of the apartment complex, so my father, a resident himself, had been acquainted with her before. I had heard from other residents that she maintained an impressive altar in her living room that was half Catholic (her husband's faith) and half Buddhist (her own). From my own childhood experiences, I know that small apartments, especially where multiple religious practices are found, demand spatial

FIGURE 27.1. Buddhist pagoda, Thái Xuân Village complex; Houston, Texas, 2011.
Photo: Linda Ho Peché (all photos were taken with permission).

compromises. Apparently, the altar has since grown into two full-scale altars occupying almost the entire one-room apartment. A statue of the Virgin Mary has been placed front and center above the (at least 60-inch) flat-screen TV, and the wall is entirely decorated with plastic fruit, rosaries, candles, plastic candelabras, Christmas lights, and ornaments. A large plastic mold-made statue of the bodhisattva Bố Đại occupies the left of center floor beside the television. Endearingly called the "fat" or "happy" buddha, this figure is based on the story of an ancient Chinese historical monk known through folk tradition to bestow fortune and happiness. A couple of black leather couches line the walls on either side, and framed photographs of many children and grandchildren adorn the walls along with lacquered decorative panels.

A few steps beyond the living room, a Buddhist altar occupies the entire wall of the room adjoining the kitchen. A similarly dizzying array of religious iconography, fruit, incense holders, and carefully chosen and placed decorative containers and artifacts lines each of the three shelves that comprise this altar. A table holds fruit as well as uncooked noodles and sweets, offerings given to the spirits or treats for the living (Figure 27.2).

The ancestral altar is situated above a cabinet with a mirrored door. Loan has constructed a seamless sacred environment that extends to the external thresholds of her home, bridging the contours of public and private space and blurring religious, aesthetic, and cultural mores. As a religious space, her home is carefully positioned

FIGURE 27.2. Buddhist altar in dining room area; Houston, Texas, 2007.
Photo: Linda Ho Peché.

to engage in Catholic, Buddhist, and ancestral ritual activity. Her aesthetic choices—the prevalent colors of red and gold, her preference for bamboo and plastic foliage, and the multivalent visual references to Vietnam through such representations as the wall displays of a wooden contour map of Vietnam—reveal deeply meaningful material and spiritual ties to the homeland. This elaborate altar communicates several messages to her relatives, neighbors, and broader religious community. First, it may indicate her exemplary fulfillment of her filial duties and suggests that she must have a good relationship with benevolent ancestral spirits; it signals her "responsible nature and virtuous character"[8] and may also signal her relative economic success, especially amidst a condominium complex known to house the working poor. But this is only the most surface, sociological range of meanings associated with Cô Loan's richly semiotic construction. In order to understand some of the deeper levels of meaning, it is important first to explore the context in which she maintains her altars, that is, the immediate surroundings of her neighborhood. By doing so, we gain important insights into a community which was built very much around the idea of recreating home, although well-integrated into both the benefits and difficulties of American urban life, thousands of miles away from "home."

At that time, Cô Loan lived in the Thái Xuân Village condominium complex located in South Houston, a few blocks from Houston Hobby International Airport. The apartments are composed of a series of buildings with age-worn pitched roofs, wrought iron fringes, and painted grey brick siding, vaguely reminiscent of a French colonial style. Father John Chin Tran established the complex in the 1980s to house refugees and recent immigrants displaced by war and poverty in Vietnam. Many of his parishioners originally came from North Vietnam's Thái Bình province. In the 1950s, they fled to the South during the partition of the country in accordance with the 1954 Geneva Accords, which ceded North Vietnam to communist supporters, many of whom had designated Catholics as "colonial sympathizers." The priest renamed the complex after Thái Xuân, the hamlet in Xuân Lộc, South Vietnam, where his fellow villagers and parishioners had established a new residence. When they found asylum for a second time in the United States, they arrived here, a complex that originally housed white middle-class residents who had vacated the apartments after they lost their livelihoods during Houston's 1980s oil bust.[9]

Currently, the complex hosts two public altars, a Catholic statue of the Virgin Mary in the chapel, and a Buddhist statue in an outdoor structure referred to as the pagoda. Although daily mass is rarely conducted due to waning attendance, residents still hold ceremonies, celebrations, and New Year's dragon dances in the complex's courtyards. There are Vietnamese gardens tended by residents, a one-room library dedicated to Mayor Lee Brown, and the Tân Hiệp Food Market, which offers fish sauce and pickled leeks. Many of the contemporary residents are recent immigrants who tend to be Buddhist practitioners, live in extended family units, mostly working class, and are less educated than the previous waves of Vietnamese immigrants. In keeping with middle-class Vietnamese aspirations, many participants, including Loan, participate in a number of Vietnamese American cultural rituals that indicate middle-class status, such as community-organized beauty pageants that highlight Vietnamese traditional clothing, the *áo dài*, at local Vietnamese churches.[10] A *Houston Press* article describes ways in which these extended cultural traditions—including religious worship—function to maintain a sense of group identity and a "village-like" sense of community for these residents:

> Religion is literally at the center of daily life in the village—just as it was in Vietnam. Nestled behind a central courtyard, the small Thai Xuan chapel hosts a daily prayer hour and two weekly masses delivered in Vietnamese. On a recent Friday, men in the congregation occupied one side of the aisle, near a tinsel-decked Christmas tree, and women sat on the other. . . . Thai Xuan village was installed with a chapel . . . and even sported a courtyard garden with a larger-than-life Virgin Mary surrounded by stalagmites, which are common in the caves of Ha Long Bay.[11]

Even so, Houston's infamous suburban sprawl requires that residents have a broad understanding of the city landscape beyond this seemingly idealized ethnic enclave. Loan's daily cartography extends well beyond the Thái Xuân Village—every day she navigates the suburban landscape of Houston. Her daily movements involve getting in her car to travel miles around Houston to go to temple or to her children's homes in the suburbs in Pearland and Spring, Texas. Her friends live in places like Bellaire (known as the lengthiest Little Saigon District, street-wise, in the country), where she shops for wares and produce; but they also live in gated communities like those in Sugarland and Katy, in nondescript, racially and socioeconomically homogenous master-planned communities. She calls Vietnam a few times a month and mails her relatives packages of consumer goods such as electronics and gadgets. They mail her DVDs or photographs of relatives' funerals or weddings, as a way to stay socially connected through visual representations of life-cycle events in Vietnam. Residents like Loan constantly interact with and transform their immediate environments through expressive objects and interactions with people on local, regional, and transnational fields. This contemporary moment reframes religious (as well as social, economic, and political) practice as translocal, hetero-local, diasporic, and increasingly global. Indeed, Mihaly Csikszentmihalyi has noted that in the context of an increasingly mobile American society, "things play an important role in reminding us of who we are with respect to whom we belong."[12] It should not be a surprise that in a diasporic community, religio-cultural objects become tangible ways to communicate and identify with kin and the homeland.

Thomas Tweed offers a way of attending to the religious lives of transnational migrants through the spatial metaphors of "dwelling and crossing." Drawing on a number of classic theoretical insights of Deleuze and Guattari (borrowing the hydraulic model), Arjun Appadurai (on cultural flows), and Clifford Geertz (on dwelling-in-travel), he concludes, "religions are flows, translocative and transtemporal crossings."[13] Using this approach, we can understand Loan's home altar as a semiotically rich resource for negotiating, performing, and celebrating real and symbolic spatial connections to networks of related kin between the homeland and across the diaspora. Indeed, there is a way in which it makes sense, theoretically, to explore altars such as Loan's, not only in terms of the multiple meanings and localities that they encode locally, but also in terms of the multiple meanings and localities they encode transnationally. Thus, a translocative analysis accounts for the practices that move people symbolically (and physically) between the domestic home, the surrounding community, and the diasporic homeland. These intersections of the local and the global allow both the first-generation Vietnamese refugee and immigrant and the American-born second generation to participate and experience "home" through the practice of religious and filial piety.

My interest is thus to illuminate how a broad spectrum of expressive objects, such as those comprising Cô Loan's home, reflect multivalent personal and communal relationships and influences. This particular altar/home is clearly an example of the ways material things both define and negotiate the public, domestic, and private spheres, as well as the geopolitically wider diasporic spheres of culturally shared values, tastes, and connections. For Loan, her altar serves as a centerpiece of ritual action, religious activity and homeland connection. It is a personal and meaningful expression of a sense of home, deeply connected physically and aesthetically to her surrounding community.

On Politics: "Thank You for Your Service"

Dr. Thiet bowed reverently in her meditation room in her large home located in one of Austin's prestigious west-side neighborhoods. We are both sitting on the floor as she explains all the levels of her altar. Symbolically and physically, she occupies the lowest level, the ground, where she meditates kneeling on a small mat and pillow. She keeps a box of tissues handy as well. On a small table to her right she has a large bowl-like gong and striker, carefully placed on a pillow, which helps her call herself to the present moment during her meditations. She has a white tablecloth on a short elongated table barely higher than the ground, where she places her prayer books and incense box, and another wooden meditation device with a striker on a small pillow to her left. Facing the altar, on eye level while kneeling (because according to Thiet one should never meditate with an altar below eye level), a dark mahogany coffee table displays black and white photographs of her husband's parents on the left, and hers on the right. In the images, her father-in-law is dressed like a mandarin court official, as was common until the end of the French occupation. The rest of the images, placed within the two large framed photos, show her ancestors in various phases of their lives, and even include a few other relatives who passed away recently. In the center, she has placed a wooden statuette of the buddha with a walking stick as a reminder to follow a spiritual path, and a small white bowl of rice as an incense holder. Two star-shaped candle holders and a small vase of flowers flank his sides. An elegant teacup of water is placed on one side, a fresh apple on a plate on the other. Electric candleholders brighten up the altar on each end of the table, along with two fresh potted plants. On a box covered with a white tablecloth sits a white statuette of the first historical buddha, and directly behind she has placed a framed print of a buddha drawn in the Pure Land tradition, common for Mahayana Buddhists throughout Vietnam. Two tiny statues of buddhas are placed in front, brought back from a three-day meditation session that she attended in Houston. On either side stand statuettes of the female bodhisattva of compassion, Quán Thế Âm, also known by her Chinese name, Guanyin.

She reads me the Buddhist tenets etched on lacquered panels on the right wall. Directly below on the floor, she has placed her stereo system and two speakers to play music for her meditation session. In the corner along the left wall is a smaller altar dedicated specifically to the female bodhisattva. She explains that the bodhisattva wants to help eliminate all the bad in the world, and would go to hell to bring everyone up if she could. As if to reiterate her devotion to Quán Thế Âm, Dr. Thiet points to her jade pendant in the image of the bodhisattva. The small altar set on a small shelf seems to be a more private, intimate space. A large lacquered panel of Quán Thế Âm leans on the wall, which shares space with taped handwritten notes and petitions from friends or family in English and Vietnamese that ask her to pray for sick relatives or acquaintances. A small statue of a buddha is displayed, along with the ritually necessary teacup of water on one side, symbolizing purity and peace, and the apple on a plate on the other. She also has placed candles, a potted plant, and a small gong on this level. The bottom shelves hold an array of scented candles, incense, and matchsticks (Figure 27.3).

On the wall directly next to the altar are newspaper clippings displaying images of soldiers recently killed in Iraq over an article titled, "Thank You for Your Service." Above the soldiers' images, she placed postcards of statues of buddhas sent from friends in different areas of the world; their placement above the soldiers' profiles is designed, according to her, with the hope that this would bring peace to their souls. She explains, "Every time I see new faces of soldiers in the newspaper, I put them up. It is a memorial to remember and to pay respect to them in hopes that this atmosphere [in my altar room] brings them some peace." It was 2010 when the interview took place, two months

FIGURE 27.3. Newspaper clippings and postcards of Buddha by Quán Thế Âm altar; Austin, Texas, 2007.

Photo: Linda Ho Peché.

before the official pullback of US troops from an unpopular and controversial war in Iraq. She says, "We do not condemn or judge in our tradition. We do not say, 'yes' and we do not say 'no,' we just try to stop people from doing it [killing each other]." As a follower of the peace activist Thích Nhất Hạnh, she does not believe in war, but also does not judge, boycott, or believe in causing any social conflict. Nevertheless, she believed it was important to thank and support the country that had taken in so many Vietnamese refugees. Interestingly, she herself was not one of these refugees. She had arrived as a doctoral student in the early 1970s and married another Vietnamese graduate student here while the war raged on. They had no recourse but to remain in the United States and thankfully their families back home remained relatively safe. Nevertheless, she felt bound and obligated to give thanks to the country that had accepted the South Vietnamese community. So, every time the local newspaper displays the images of US soldiers, she places their images next to her altar.

Altars and shrines—ubiquitous in many homes, yet often overlooked—provide the lens and starting point through which to explore the intersections of the religious, the social, and the political dimensions of Vietnamese American life. There are a number of possible avenues to explore the blurring of civic/political life and religious belief and practice. One approach calls attention to the religious dimensions of political life, a civil religion. Popularized by Robert Bellah,[14] this theoretical framework calls attention to the subtle and overt ways in which ethical principles emerge in discourse and practice when invoking American identity and nationalism. Another approach calls attention to the ways in which politics emerges in the context and practice of religion. In other words, this approach illuminates the ways in which institutionalized religious beliefs and practices structure hegemonic social and civic life, and the ways in which practitioners resist structures of oppression that seem to be religiously justified in hegemonic or religious discourse and practice. It also calls attention to the opposite function: the ways in which oppressed and marginalized peoples garner strength and sustenance for counter-hegemonic acts through their religious constructions and connections. For example, Thomas Tweed[15] has addressed the ways in which Cuban Americans in Miami have found religious solace and (anti-communist) political expression in constructing and maintaining a shrine dedicated to Our Lady of the Exile. Thuy Vo Dang[16] has argued that the highly charged and ethically imbued discourses of anti-communism do "cultural work" among Vietnamese Americans, who claim sociopolitical agency and collective identity in the process.

Dr. Thiet's prayer room expresses a range of political discourses that are manifest on her altars. The objects and images on and contiguous to her altars orient her as a practitioner to a religious and social moral order and situates her as an individual with filial, religious, and civic obligations. Additionally, it is common to find the South Vietnamese (staunchly anti-communist) flags and military photographs on home altars, at Buddhist temples, Catholic churches, and pilgrimage sites, and even adorning the covers of religious hymnals. Through the purposeful elaboration of altars and religious spaces with American nationalist symbols, practitioners counter the hegemonic erasure of Vietnamese Americans' participation in broader national political discourses. As previous participants in a similarly unpopular war, these visible manifestations of support for American soldiers give visibility to what Yen Le Espiritu[17] has called the ghostly aspects of war, that is, "the experiential realities of social and political life that have been systematically hidden or erased." They reveal the intimately spiritual ways in which altar practitioners call attention to, and engage with, an adopted nation and the familiar loss of life—through the personal invocation of individual soldiers. These altar practices demonstrate ways in which religious piety and the political and civic realms intersect.

On Civic Belonging and Religion: "We Don't Want to Bother the Neighbors"

In this section, I examine the ways in which ancestral altars are oriented (both through physical positioning and social positioning) in and outside of homes across a range of neighborhoods, including in emerging ethnic suburban communities. In so doing, I call further attention to the specific and multilayered ways in which Vietnamese religious practitioners in America both spatially and spiritually perform, negotiate, and mitigate their multiple identities as Americans, as Vietnamese, and as Hòa Hảo practitioners.

I visited a Hòa Hảo practitioner's home in Sugarland, Texas, a few times between 2010 and 2013. Often, several members would congregate to pray. They bowed five times at the altar erected in honor of the sacred directions, sometimes referred to as an altar for the King of the Earth. I was told that Hòa Hảo is an overtly nationalist religion founded in 1939—sometimes referred to as Protestant Buddhism—that came under particular oppression during the French occupation in Vietnam and more recently under communist rule. Many practitioners have since fled in exile and have continued to practice in the United States. The religion's founder was nineteen-year-old Huỳnh Phú Sổ, a native of the Mekong River Delta region of southern Vietnam, who gave spiritual priority and loyalty to the "nation" in order to more directly speak to the societal issues practitioners faced during that time. Practitioners first bow in reverence for their ancestors, again for the nation of Vietnam, again for Buddha and the sangha, and lastly for all humanity. A reverend explains:

> First, we thank for our ancestors. Second, we thank for our country. Third we thank for Buddha and sangha and the Buddha bible and four[th] we thank for mankind, human beings. So when Hòa Hảo people go outside, they practice religion, that mean[s] we devote our time for all, for thanks.

He continues, "we repay and give thanks for all that is given us. We owe for everything that we have. We must repay our ancestors, who gave us names, and even gave us their own blood. Even our clothes, many people touched our clothes so that we may use them. For all this, we repay." The altar's owner, an older Hòa Hảo practitioner named Nancy, decided not to call her Houston suburb's homeowner's association (HOA) to ask about erecting her altar in the front of her home, as dictated by her religious tradition.

> I thought if I build it in front yard, I need a permit. I can build in the backyard if not higher than the fence, so people cannot look at it; [we are] not allow[ed] to build too high. [Besides,] Buddha is inside [our minds] in the spiritual, not outside in the physical.

Thus, she erected her altar in the backyard. Members of her religious community often visit and pray together there (Figure 27.4).

FIGURE 27.4. Hòa Hảo practitioner and altar to the cardinal directions; Sugarland, Texas, 2013.
Photo: Linda Ho Peché.

John Pham, another Hòa Hảo practitioner who resides in another suburb outside of Houston, was able to erect his altar without permission from his HOA or trouble from the neighbors. His significantly downplayed altar allowed him to "fly under the radar," so to speak:

> HOA did not send me a letter and did not do anything. I like decorat[ing] it in front, and I pray, burn incense in the morning and the evening. It does not disturb neighbors; maybe that's why HOA [does] not say anything.

However, not all attempts were so amicably resolved. Another Sugarland family brought legal action to both the HOA and the City of Sugarland to maintain the right to erect their altar, in the style and size that they deemed necessary. Indeed, residents in gated neighborhoods and master-planned communities are often obligated to join an HOA, which legally guarantees aesthetically consistent appearances through administered covenants, conditions, and restrictions that limit exterior changes to neighborhood homes. In the process, these legal entities impose and establish a certain sense of belonging (and not belonging) through the governing of the visual and material components of homes. HOAs also have the right to govern the racial, ethnic, or sexual orientation of their members, something that has been problematic for Vietnamese Americans, especially in Texas.

Debates about proper community appearance are not new. Politicians, city planners, and design professionals have often been implicated in moderating debates about community appearance, often wielding power that socially and visually shapes urban communities. Historically, established Anglo communities have sought to curtail the visually and linguistically coded enclaves of immigrant communities through specific policies that would "assist" newcomers to better assimilate into greater society. Eventually, some of those neighborhoods (like Chinatowns) became marketable and cities went through great lengths to sanitize and prepare them as tourist attractions. Debates about community appearance continue to be hotly contested, especially among newer immigrants who face the scrutiny of their remodeling practices that run counter to their established neighbors' sense of aesthetic expression.[18] Drawing on Foucault, Asher Ghertner identifies an "aesthetic governmentality" to account for the ways in which a community's dominant aesthetic is imposed through micro-practices, which in turn change the way people perceive environments and their place in them, promoting the state's vision and illusion of order.[19] As this case reveals, the religio-aesthetic choices that practitioners make (or are forced to make) are a lesson in citizenship and belonging.

While these practitioners were variously successful in their attempts to erect an altar on their front lawns, the fact that they actively engaged both informal and formal (legal) strategies to do so foregrounds and highlights the uneven and unpredictable nature of "belonging" and the relative sense of entitlement to civic rights as citizens. This case calls attention to the politics of religion and the contestation of space. Among classic works, Jonathan Z. Smith and, somewhat more recently, Chidester and Linenthal[20] outlined the importance of the production, practice, and representation of space, and its relationship with knowledge and power. These "micro-practices"—the small but significant cases of power struggles with different HOAs—exemplify how the process of "situating of altars" is a lens with through which to explore how immigrants are negotiating, contesting, and acquiescing to socially derived (and some would say, imposed) notions of civic belonging. In other words, altars are organic, active spaces that practitioners manipulate to orient themselves socially in the context of private, public, and spiritual landscapes.

Altars can be vehicles to express the aspiration of "belonging" through the use and expression of dominant Anglo middle-class suburban aesthetics, even in the intimate spaces of the home. For example, Chú Phong[21] explains how he revised his traditions and his altar to fit into an Anglo-suburban aesthetic:

> In Vietnam, my family keeps the culture more than us; they celebrate the death anniversary of our ancestors on the exact dates. They have more time and relatives live closer to each other. I am the son, the leader of the family, so the responsibilities should fall to me, but my sister organizes the *đám giỗ* every year because we are not living in Vietnam, we are living here. In Vietnam, in the past, we wore a white headband for three years to mourn when your mother or father passed away. Nowadays, we wear a small white ribbon on our lapel after wearing the white band at church for the funeral. Because we live in another culture, we only keep some of the traditions. We don't want to bother our neighbors, so they don't complain about us. Over here, we have to be aware of city ordinances, or take consideration of the limitations of carrying on our traditions.

His choice for a self-described "simple" altar reflects particular tastes informed by the conservative religious beliefs of the Vietnamese Catholic Church, as well as a preference for fitting in with the mostly Anglo, suburban neighborhood.

The poetics of religious space and how to situate altars engages competing concerns, including shifting cultural contexts, institutional demands, and notions of civic space. Lived religion depends on place to constitute a myriad of cultural expressions.[22] On its most transcendental level, an ancestral altar is a sacred space with access to the spiritual plane for the communication with ancestors, spirits, and the divine. As many of my previous examples have illustrated, ancestral altars are meticulously produced, with rigorous attention to detail and intensive ritualization, and are experienced first and foremost through the senses and emotions of embodied dwelling.

Conclusion

In this chapter, I have examined how embodied practices of physical and spiritual attention materialize and ground Buddhist religious experience, while simultaneously expressing a broad range of ideologies and desires. I examined three altars that I situated analytically in the realms of the diasporic, the political, and the civic in order to examine ways in which practitioners can shape and interact with the material and spatial articulations of home altars in a myriad of complex ways. Each practitioner expressed their own personal emotions and aspirations, nevertheless clearly enmeshed in the cultural politics of their local, national, and diasporic communities. Thus, I make the case for a focus on the negotiated and porous boundaries of what practitioners claim constitutes religious practice; on the fuzzy contours of the spiritual and the secular; on what demarcates private and public spaces; and how "Buddhist" or "Vietnamese" and/or "American" values or political discourses manifest aesthetically through domestic religious practices. These varied practices and perspectives urge us to be more fluid with what constitutes being Buddhist, being Vietnamese, and/or being American.

In conclusion, I assert that altars are particularly good to "think through." I address various facets of what they are constituted of and how they work—as ways to express a familial or diasporic imaginary; or as assemblages of things that are both intimately meaningful and private, yet situated at the intersections of geopolitical engagements and cultural politics. As a collection of things, altar assemblages are constituted through the purposeful and chance encounters of the practitioner(s), which is a way to talk about the global (as zones of engagement of people, ideas, and historical specificity) through the intimately local.[23] As organic and malleable spaces, they are useful in negotiating one's place in the world—within the family, local neighborhoods, the nation, and the diasporic community. They orient practitioners by encouraging certain modes of embodiment and social and moral proclivities. Beyond functioning as religious objects, a number of images, icons, and artifacts function as mnemonic devices and mediums for the expression and materialization of what it means to be Vietnamese in America, or for some, Vietnamese American (a subtle, but significant difference). But at its crux, this analysis is about spiritual traversing—how individuals and groups of Vietnamese Americans access, experience, and/or transform relationships with and between spirits and gods, benevolent ancestors, transnational kin, American neighbors, the nation-state, and the diaspora at large. This all happens in the materiality of everyday life and in the domestic ritual practices associated with the ancestral veneration tradition.

Notes

1. This refers to Benedict Anderson's (1983) concept of a national imaginary, a socially constructed community of persons that, through their beliefs and values, see themselves as participants in a broader collective of people they may not know personally.
2. Many scholars refer to this practice of veneration as "ancestor worship," although Jonathan Lee aptly points out that this connotes a Christian-centered understanding of altar practices. Ancestor "veneration" may be a better alternative to express the mutual respect and relationships maintained between the living and the dead through the ancestral altar. See Jonathan Lee, "Ancestral Veneration in Vietnamese Spiritualities," *The Review* 3 (2003): 16.
3. Paul Rutledge provides a good overview of religions in Vietnam in *The Role of Religion in Ethnic Self-Identity: A Vietnamese Community*, 1st ed. (Lanham, MD: University Press of America, 1984).

4. Kate Jellema, "Everywhere Incense Burning: Remembering Ancestors in Đổi Mới Vietnam," *Journal of Southeast Asian Studies* 38, no. 3 (2007): 467–92.
5. For more on this topic, see Pei-Te Lien and Tony Carnes, "The Religious Demography of Asian American Boundary Crossings," in *Asian American Religions: The Making and Remaking of Borders and Boundaries*, ed. Fenggang Yang (New York: New York University Press, 2004): 38–54.
6. Terry A. Rambo, in *Searching for Vietnam: Selected Writings on Vietnamese Culture and Society* (Kyoto: Kyoto University Press, 2005), discusses how historically, the Catholic institution was scrutinized and persecuted, possibly for "its strong and cohesive organization, its wealth, its self-conscious militancy and above all, its foreign origins and identification with Western colonialism" (90). As a result, a large number of practitioners have sought asylum in the United States and comprise a large proportion of the Vietnamese American community.
7. Jellema, "Everywhere Incense Burning," 467–92.
8. Jellema, "Everywhere Incense Burning," 476.
9. See news article by Josh Harkinson, "Tale of Two Cities," *Houston Press*, December 15, 2005. https://www.houstonpress.com/news/tale-of-two-cities-6547193.
10. Nhi T. Lieu, *The American Dream in Vietnamese* (Minneapolis: University of Minnesota Press, 2011).
11. Harkinson, "Tale of Two Cities," https://www.houstonpress.com/news/tale-of-two-cities-6547193.
12. In Mihaly Csikszentmihalyi, "Why We Need Things," in *History from Things: Essays on Material Culture*, ed. Steven Lubar and W. David Kingery (Washington, DC, and London: Smithsonian Institution Press, 1993), 27.
13. Thomas Tweed offers his theory of religion in *Crossing and Dwelling: A Theory of Religion* (Cambridge, MA: Harvard University Press, 2008), 158. See also Tweed, *Our Lady of the Exile: Diasporic Religion at a Cuban Catholic Shrine in Miami* (New York: Oxford University Press, 2002).
14. Robert Neelly Bellah, "Civil Religion in America," in his volume *Beyond Belief: Essays on Religion in a Post-Traditional World* (Berkeley: University of California Press, 1991), 168–92.
15. Tweed, *Our Lady of the Exile*.
16. See Thuy Thanh Vo Dang's dissertation, "Anticommunism as Cultural Praxis: South Vietnam, War, and Refugee Memories in the Vietnamese American Community," PhD diss., University of California, San Diego, Ethnic Studies, 2008, ProQuest, UMI Dissertation.
17. Yen Le Espiritu, "About Ghost Stories: The Vietnam War and 'Rememoration,'" *Modern Language Association of America* 123, no. 5 (2008): 1700–2.
18. For more discussion on immigrants and place, see Denise Lawrence-Zuniga, "Contested Landscapes: Movement, Exile and Place," *American Anthropologist* 105, no. 3 (2003): 639–40.
19. For more discussion on governmentality, see D. A. Ghertner, "Calculating Without Numbers: Aesthetic Governmentality in Delhi's Slums," *Economy and Society* 39, no. 2 (2010): 185–217.
20. For a more thorough discussion on space, knowledge, and power, see Jonathan Z. Smith's classic work, Map Is *Not Territory: Studies in the History of Religions* (Leiden: Brill Academic, 1978); and a somewhat more recent work by David Chidester and Edward Linenthal, *American Sacred Space* (Bloomington: Indiana University Press, 1995).

21. *Chú* here is a pronoun indicating a formal reference and a sign of respect on my part; in some dialects *chú* is used to address an older man of the same age as one's father. Vietnamese pronouns are a complex sociolinguistic practice that indicate the social status between speakers and other persons in the context of everyday discourse.
22. See Steven Feld and Keith H. Basso, ed., *Senses of Place*, 1st ed. School of American Research Advanced Seminar Series (Santa Fe, NM, and Seattle: School of American Research Press, distributed by the University of Washington Press, 1996); see also Rhys H. Williams, "Religion, Community, and Place: Locating the Transcendent," *Religion and American Culture: A Journal of Interpretation* 12, no. 2 (July 1, 2002): 249–63.
23. For an excellent ethnographic analysis of the intersections between the local and the global, see Anna Lowenhaupt, *Friction: An Ethnography of Global Connection* (Princeton, NJ: Princeton University Press, 2004).

Further Reading

Bellah, Robert N. "Civil Religion in America." In *Beyond Belief: Essays on Religion in a Post-Traditional World*. Berkeley: University of California Press, 1991, 168–92.

Chidester, David, and Edward Linenthal, ed. *American Sacred Space*. Bloomington: Indiana University Press, 1995.

Dang, Thanh Thuy Vo. "Anticommunism as Cultural Praxis: South Vietnam, War, and Refugee Memories in the Vietnamese American Community." PhD diss., University of California, San Diego, Ethnic Studies. ProQuest, UMI Dissertation, 2008.

Espiritu, Yen Le. "About Ghost Stories: The Vietnam War and 'Rememoration.'" *PMLA: Modern Language Association of America* 123, no. 5 (2008): 1700–2.

Jellema, Kate. "Everywhere Incense Burning: Remembering Ancestors in Đổi Mới Vietnam." *Journal of Southeast Asian Studies* 38, no. 3 (2007): 467–92.

Lee, Jonathan. "Ancestral Veneration in Vietnamese Spiritualities." *The Review* 3, no. 1 (2013):16.

Lien, Pei-Te, and Tony Carnes. "The Religious Demography of Asian American Boundary Crossings." In *Asian American Religions: The Making and Remaking of Borders and Boundaries*, ed. Fenggang Yang. New York: New York University Press, 2004, 38–54.

Lieu, Nhi T. *The American Dream in Vietnamese*. Minneapolis: University of Minnesota Press, 2011.

Rambo, A. Terry. *Searching for Vietnam: Selected Writings on Vietnamese Culture and Society*. Kyoto: Kyoto University Press, 2005.

Smith, Jonathan Z. *Map Is Not Territory: Studies in the History of Religions*. Leiden: Brill Academic, 1978.

Tweed, Thomas A. *Crossing and Dwelling: A Theory of Religion*. Cambridge, MA: Harvard University Press, 2008.

Tweed, Thomas A. *Our Lady of the Exile: Diasporic Religion at a Cuban Catholic Shrine in Miami*. New York: Oxford University Press, 2002.

Williams, Rhys H. "Religion, Community, and Place: Locating the Transcendent." *Religion and American Culture: A Journal of Interpretation* 12, no. 2 (July 1, 2002): 249–63.

CHAPTER 28

CALENDRICAL, LIFE-CYCLE, AND PERIODIC RITUALS

JONATHAN S. WALTERS

INTRODUCTION: MAKING THE WORLD BUDDHIST

THE Buddhist-ness of the contemporary moment in a country like Sri Lanka is in one sense a given. Space—the island of Sri Lanka itself—is widely landmarked by Buddhist temples, monuments, and historical sites. Mythical and historical narratives portray the island as possessing a special Buddhist destiny: predicted by the Buddha to be the special home of a future Buddhism and protected by the gods[1] as a result, infused with the Buddha's presence through his three visits to the island, and documented by historians to possess the world's oldest continuous Buddhist civilization. Time, correspondingly, is sometimes calculated according to the Buddha Era (BE), a temporal system known in Sri Lanka since at least the fourth century CE and shared throughout the Theravada Buddhist world. This system understands the present in relation to the traditional date of the Buddha's final nirvana. 2020 CE corresponds to 2563 BE,[2] just a little past the halfway mark of the 5,000-year life span that Gotama Buddha's *sāsana* is expected to enjoy.[3] Throughout South and Southeast Asian Buddhist societies, the Western reckoning of months and days is often retained even when the year is calculated according to the Buddha Era, but in Sri Lanka, as elsewhere, Buddhists also maintain an overlapping lunar calendar for determining the year's twelve-month cycle (and for periodic adjustments corresponding to "leap years"). Thus, the Buddha's passing is dated on the full moon day of the lunar month of Wesak (Pali Vesakkha), which variously overlaps April and/or May in the Western calendar. Even more specifically, a lunar calculation of the day, based on two half-days of thirty units each, and finer distinctions still corresponding to minutes and seconds, has persisted into the present for certain purposes, such as astrological calculation.[4]

Despite mythological, historical, nationalist, scholarly, and tourist representations of Sri Lanka as Buddhist, however, not all spaces there are Buddhist, and not all Buddhist spaces are equally so, nor of one sort. The Buddhist-ness of certain places, let alone of the entire island, is constructed—partly ideologically, partly materially—and requires regular maintenance. Ideas and material commitments to them are periodically expanded, challenged, reinterpreted, or newly affirmed, and survive only if they are transmitted as meaningful to the changing circumstances of the ever-next generation. Buildings and monuments decay, require additions or renovations to meet changing needs, or find themselves affected by the changing geographies and demographies of the locales that ground them. From small villages to the Buddhist nationalist constituencies operative in twentieth- to twenty-first-century Sri Lankan politics, some Buddhists with differing views and/or non-Buddhists may also question or challenge claims about the Buddhist-ness of particular spaces, producing conflicts and resolutions with their differing effects on Buddhist considerations.

Similarly, the use of Western months and days even when the Buddha Era is invoked betrays the deeper way in which the Buddha Era exists within, and largely is dominated today by, the so-called Common Era. While the latter serves obvious and useful purposes, the designation is less "common" or universal than its name implies, and what universality it does enjoy was largely imposed in the Western colonialisms and imperialisms of the nineteenth and twentieth centuries that are specifically eschewed in the globalism it now signifies. BCE and CE are new global names for an older reckoning of time specific to Euro-American religious self-understandings, which conceived of time according to Christian soteriology and eschatology; the Buddha Era imposes its own, different soteriological and eschatological frameworks on human experience.

The Buddhist-ness of space and of time is thus a condition in need of making and remaking, especially when viewed within broader spatial and temporal frames. Being reborn human in a Buddhist place during a Buddhist time is considered a rare opportunity for progress toward the eventual goal of nirvana (Sinh. *nivan*, Pali *nibbāna*). Most of the world's space is not and never has been Buddhist. The same is true of most of time, when it is conceived on a scale of eons (*kalpa*, Pali *kappa*, the time that elapses between the creation and destruction of a world). But in Sri Lanka many spaces remain Buddhist, and this present time proceeds in a rare Buddha Era—traditionally there have been only twenty-five of them in the last 100,000+ eons—when a Buddha is known and present in relics and other reminders, in his teachings, and in his monks and nuns. Buddhist time is not only a time (including this present time) when those who encounter the Buddha, as relic, teaching, and/or adept, have thereby been enabled to escape from the otherwise interminable cycle of suffering and rebirth (samsara), or at least to make progress toward that nirvana in some future existence. It is also a time more than halfway to the inevitable decline and disappearance of this presence and possibility less than 2,500 years from the present; life spans and social graces will likewise continue to decrease into nonexistence until a new Buddha (Skt. Maitreya, Pali Metteyya, Sinh. Maitri) arises to create a new Buddhism within which such opportunity will exist again, until it too declines and finally disappears.

This naming and calculating of time as Buddhist give shape to and motivate particular religious practices designed to navigate it accordingly. These practices facilitate reaping the soteriological benefits of existence during a Buddha Era, and weathering the impending destruction of that Buddhism and the world that supports it. For most Sri Lankan Buddhists, this navigation involves the accumulation of merit (Pali *puñña*, Sinh. *pin*) and other wholesome (*kusala*) types of karma, expected to bear fruit in nirvana, whether later in the present lifetime or (more likely) during some future one. In particular, such karma is hoped to effect rebirth when and where the coming Buddha Maitreya has arisen, and time and space themselves will once again be maximally auspicious for soteriological progress. Simultaneously, navigating Buddhist time involves moral restraint (Pali *sīla*, Sinh. *sil*) to avoid demerit (Pali *pāpa*, Sinh. *paw*) and other unwholesome (*akusala*) types of karma, grounded in fear of their negative effects on future existence (*saṃsāra-bhaya*). Since before Buddhism was brought to Sri Lanka, this eschatology has been narrated as a prediction made by the present (Gotama) Buddha himself, and has informed the self-understanding in time of successive generations of Buddhists. This navigation of time is also one of space, as Buddhists perform these acts by traveling to Buddhist parts of the home, village, neighborhood, country, and/or world.

This framing of the present informs all Buddhist practice, including even the most advanced forms of moral discipline, wisdom, and meditation. But it is especially significant for the ordinary Buddhists who expect to continue thus navigating existence in time and space at least until the arising of Maitreya Buddha, and conceivably much longer. Contemporary Sri Lankan Buddhists draw on a repertoire of navigational tools, that is, specific practices aimed at productively moving forward through time by (re) making its Buddhist-ness, taking advantage of and contributing to the Buddhist-ness of space within which those efficacious practices can proceed. Despite considerable regional and historical variation, the rituals themselves, like the soteriology they forward and the eschatology they address, have been remarkably stable, shared across the island (and beyond), and already largely in place before Buddhism was first taken there.

Many of these practices are rituals tied directly to Buddhist time, calculated according to the Buddhist calendar and in many cases entailing recollection and celebration of its historical landmarks. They are performed in spaces designated Buddhist, whether permanently (such as temples and pilgrimage sites) or temporarily for this very purpose (such as makeshift altars or curtained-off parts of a room). Such rituals, which for convenience can be designated "calendrical," regularize making the world Buddhist within the calendrical movements of the day, week, month, year, and in some cases longer units of time.

In addition to these "calendrical" rituals, the repertoire of available Buddhist practices includes others that occur only periodically. Rituals associated with individual or institutional life cycles may well be "once in a lifetime" performances, and may be timed primarily around circumstances or considerations separate from the calendar as such, and/or in circumstances made Buddhist somewhat haphazardly and temporarily. Other occasional rituals lack even the structure of time and space still implied in life-cycle rituals, whether they concern an individual life span or the historical "life" of an institution such as a temple or monument. Such "periodic" rituals might include those undertaken when accident or illness strikes, in conjunction with a journey, or because the opportunity just happens to arise. But all of these assert and enact the reality of Buddhist time and space in their ability to occur at all, as well as in their power to move an individual or community forward along the gradual path to nirvana, actualized in time and space through the performance itself.

The following two sections explore these main ritual types with further specificity, in the process enlarging upon the ways they seek to make space and time Buddhist. The first section details the lived ritual calendar that shapes many Buddhist days, weeks, months, and years in contemporary Sri Lanka. The second section takes up the non-calendrical, "life-cycle," and "periodic" rituals that likewise instantiate the soteriological promise and sometimes worldly benefit of Buddhist time within the actual space of lived experience. The conclusion returns to larger issues that confront this temporal and spatial impulse to make the world Buddhist.

Calendrical Rituals

The significance of making and maintaining the Buddhist-ness of time and space is manifest at multiple levels of each. These levels can be scaled in terms of complexity, such that the daily rituals in a modest home and national-level celebrations of major full-moon (Sinh. *poya*, Pali *uposatha*) holidays differ more in degree than kind. They all share basic structures, commencing with the same introductory chants (praising the Buddha, taking refuge in the Triple Gem, affirming the five precepts) and taking place where Buddhist-ness has been enhanced, whether in front of a simple household shrine (typically containing one or more Buddha images or pictures on a shelf suitable for offerings of incense, oil lamps, and flowers) or at a shrine, stupa, temple image house, and/or pilgrimage site.

At least once daily, and in more pious households twice or thrice daily, the simple act of recitation and offering (*pūjā*) establishes the day, and the home, as Buddhist. The chants cultivate a basic, existential orientation of reverential regard for the Buddha, refuge in him and his ongoing teachings (Dharma), and monks and nuns (sangha), and moral restraint. The Buddha is praised in Pali as the fully accomplished "Blessed One" (*bhagavan*) and "Worthy One" (*arahant*); refuge in him, the Dharma, and the sangha—the Triple Gem—is repeated three times, a small meditation on and reaffirmation of commitment to pursuing the goal of existence. Moral restraint entails embracing guiding principles or "trainings" (*sikkhāpada*). For most ordinary Buddhists, this is encapsulated in the five precepts (Pali *pañca sīla*, Sinh. *pansil*) to cultivate avoidance of killing, taking what is not given, unchastity, speaking falsely, and dulling moral faculties with alcohol. These too are chanted in formulaic Pali. More pious members of the household might enlarge the list of precepts (see later discussion) and/or the ritual liturgy by chanting additional well-known Pali verses—typical ones embellish the praises of the

Buddha and articulate similar ones of the Dharma and the sangha, deepening the recollection of and commitment to each; invoke the merit of all forms of offerings, and of all the places where they are made; harness the power and protection (*paritta*, Sinh. *pirit*) of the Triple Gem for the obstacles the day might entail—or they might add meditative practices such as reading the *Satipaṭṭhāna sūtraya* or cultivating loving-kindness (*maitri bhāvanā*), but in its most typical, basic form the whole performance takes only a few minutes.

In addition to its mental affect, infusing the day with meaning and comforting notions of refuge and protection focused on the domestic shrine—itself situated to mark the home as centrally and actively Buddhist—this short ritual also fills the home with incense whose lingering fragrance reminds those living in it or visiting it that the day occurs in Buddhist time and the home constitutes Buddhist space in which to live guided by the refuges, and the moral trainings, whose chanting lingers in the mind. Likewise, the handful of beautiful but already decaying flowers creates a day-long visual reminder of Buddhist teachings of impermanence (as reiterated in one of the best-known additional verses sometimes chanted in these rituals, "like my body this flower will decay and die"). Sound is central to the chanting itself, punctuating the air with more or less skillful ornamental Pali recitation. Professional chanting often continues to constitute sound as Buddhist in the house, whether emanating from daily radio or television broadcasts of elaborate versions of the liturgy (especially *pirit*), from CD-players or computers, or from the loudspeakers of local temples, where such professional chanting and the ringing of the temple bell mark the whole village or neighborhood as Buddhist with sound during the morning, midday, and evening *pūjā*. The daily ritual necessitates bodily practice, too; preparations involve tactile experiences like gathering and arranging flowers, lighting and placing sticks of incense and oil lamps, while the chanting is variously performed with the hands held up clasped together (*añjali*) and/or kneeling or sitting in a meditative cross-legged posture. In temple rituals, anyway, even taste comes into play, since the provision of *pūjā* in front of the Buddha image is followed by the actual consumption of alms by the resident monks or other adepts, after which the assembled laypeople eat. Indeed, for children, taste is often a major attraction of village-wide temple festivals or national-scale pilgrimages, where ordinarily unavailable delicacies are sure to be found.

These daily rituals to make the home Buddhist tend to be the concern of women and children, the former initiating the latter into the practice by having them gather flowers and teaching them the chants from an early age until at a certain point they may take on the full responsibility, a transmission underscored in the Buddhism curriculum in the public schools and in Buddhist Sunday schools. Women's lives are especially regulated along with their children's implicit weekly cycles, and women and children likewise dominate overlapping weekly and monthly calendrical rituals of two sorts. On the one hand, households typically provide alms-food to the resident monks or nuns of their primary (village or neighborhood) temple, on a monthly, twice-monthly, or similar schedule; while the whole family might present the food or receive the recipients' blessings (*anumodana*), the preparation of it is typically women's responsibility. As once-isolated villagers have become more accustomed to travel throughout the island, the result of better infrastructure as well as new educational, occupational, and marital opportunities, it is now common for large groups to provide alms for forest retreats or monastic schools on an annual or biannual calendar. This scheduling of one or more day each (solar) month for almsgiving is paralleled, on the other hand, by weekly and monthly (lunar) sabbaths, among which the full-moon day is especially significant.

Those especially committed laypeople who adopt an enlarged moral restraint in eight precepts (Pali *aṭṭha sīla*, Sinh. *atasil*), typically do so according to the lunar calendar. The longer and more arduous list of precepts transforms the third into a commitment to complete celibacy, and adds trainings to refrain from eating after noontime, watching entertainments and wearing perfumes and ornaments, and sitting or lying on a luxurious seat or couch. Eight-precept holders (*upāsaka, upāsikā*) ordinarily gather in local temples on the four lunar sabbaths (*poya*) each month (corresponding to the days of no moon, waxing moon, full moon, and waning moon) to collectively undertake the work to make that day each week especially Buddhist, and to make the full-moon day each month (when all Buddhists are expected to visit the local temple) even more so. These *upāsaka/ikā*s adopt for the day—or, for the most committed at that level, always adopt—a range of attendant, quasi-monastic practices that include adopting special dress (white sarong, shirt, and sash; "rosary" beads) reminiscent of monastic robes; the avoidance or transformation of ordinary daily practices; devoting the day to chanting, study, and meditation; active participation in temple *pūjā*s; formal "receipt" of the precepts from monks or nuns; and being addressed in the honorific language typically reserved for monks and nuns. These all signal that for that day, at least, these especially pious Buddhists practice a lifestyle believed to hasten the movement toward nirvana while producing peace of mind, physical health, domestic calm, and similar worldly benefits.

The "holiday" status of the full moon days was highly contentious during colonial times, because these days punctuate the Buddhist year in important ways. It was on full-moon days that the great events, not only of the Buddha's life but of subsequent Buddhist history, occurred. Annually these events are retold, enacted, illustrated, and/or interpreted in full-moon-day sermons on the *poya* days to which they correspond. These are reminders that, like the basic chants of the daily ritual, are reinforced in school curricular and extra-curricular projects, Sunday school lessons and other activities, radio and television broadcasts, and in associated festivities (including carnivals, "haunted houses," dramas and musical shows, street markets, parades and processions, sporting events, and so on, that are variously associated with the different *poya* days in the places where the celebration of each is centered).

These conjunctions of specific Buddhist times (*poya* days) and specific Buddhist places (the sites most popularly associated with particular such full-moon days) constitute Sri Lanka's largest and most important Buddhist festivals, attracting sometimes millions of pilgrims to be in Colombo for Wesak (the day of the Buddha's final nirvana/passing away, and also of his birth, and his Awakening), or Anuradhapura and Mihintale for Poson (the day on which Buddhism was first brought to Sri Lanka), or Kandy for Esala (corresponding to annual festival processions of the Buddha's tooth relic and the island's protector deities). For locals this may be the year's most practically demanding time, as they engage in welcoming those vast numbers of pilgrims in their distinctive ways. Thus, villages, schools, and other associations across Sri Lanka's North Central Province rally and fundraise to provide free potables, food, sweets, flowers for worship, and similar necessities to hundreds of thousands of Poson pilgrims each year, in "charity booths" (*dansäl,* Pali *dānasāla*) erected at major sites and along major roadways for several days on each side of the Poson full moon. The comparatively small collectivities that sponsor these "charity booths"—in some places so numerously so that they raucously compete for takers—dissolve into a totality of provision that blankets the whole region, surveyed by youths from each village and neighborhood who travel from spot to spot sampling the goodies on offer, a practice euphemistically called "worshipping the charity booths" (*dansäl vandinawā*). Through practices like these, Buddhists' collective, specifically Buddhist, identity is simultaneously affirmed, transmitted, and subtly transformed in step with changing social expectations, potentials, or mores, not to mention considerable attention from politicians, and in political rhetoric. Distinctly modern elements such as the ubiquitous sending of greeting cards to celebrate Wesak or elaborate traffic schemes directing vehicles around the maze of temporary tableaus (*pandol*) painted with scenes of the Buddha's life, previous lives (*jātaka*), or events from Buddhist history, illuminated with blinking lights and sometimes with Buddhist devotional music blaring over loudspeakers, constructed at major junctions, are new trappings conjoined to truly ancient practices, which likewise made festivals associated with these lunar sabbaths into celebrations of Buddhist time throughout the year.

Simultaneously, since the earliest days of Indian Buddhism these lunar sabbaths have been the occasion for major calendrical monastic rituals that similarly mark Buddhist time in the lived experiences of monks and nuns. Monks and nuns in a particular space congregate to collectively affirm the uprightness of the sangha (each other) on a calendrical cycle corresponding to the *poya* days. The *pāṭimokkha*, held every full-moon day and intervening no-moon day, entails chanting of the 227 (or for nuns, 235) rules of monastic discipline (*vinaya*) in unison to affirm collective adherence to them during the previous lunar month, and to create a space in which to confess any breaches. Monks and nuns also participate in the full-moon-day rituals at their temples, "giving" the eight precepts to those who want to observe them, leading *pūja*s, preaching, and leading meditation. Monastic life is on a continuum with more pious forms of lay life, an enhanced version of the same commitment to the Buddha, Dharma, and sangha and the practice of moral restraint. But the absence of laypeople in monastic rituals serves to mark them off as distinct. The practical connection of the two spheres, as well as the distinction between them, is most markedly enacted in the annual robes-giving ceremony (*kaṭhina-pinkama*) at the conclusion of the monks' and nuns' annual rains retreat (Pali *vassa*, Sinh. *vas*). Having just completed the three- or four-month retreat, a time of intensified study, meditation, and staying in the home temple or monastery, the annual "accusing" ceremony (*pavāraṇā*) on the full-moon day that marks its end replaces the ordinary calendrical *pāṭimokkha* rite, adding to it the once-a-year invitation to the collective sangha to call out breaches committed by others as witnessed during the preceding year. The especially reaffirmed sangha is then presented an enlarged version of the usual offerings made on full-moon days, including new monastic robes and new stocks of the basic requisites for the coming year. But the reciprocal relationship of monastic and lay spheres most highlighted during the robes-giving ceremony is regularized in all the calendrical rites, which punctuate the entire year with Buddhist-ness: specific times on regular schedules are designated especially Buddhist, and spaces are created, cleaned, ornamented, and supplied with necessities to facilitate collective recognition and enactment of that Buddhist-ness.

Life-Cycle and other Periodic Rituals

Calendrical rituals thus make and remake time and space Buddhist, regularizing collective recollections and affirmations of that Buddhist-ness while motivating and occasioning the merit-making practices that help Buddhists navigate their way to rebirth during the time of the future Buddha, avoiding the cataclysm that will precede it. To an extent, the messy and irregular real world can be made to conform to that calendar. Plans might be made around temple visits and responsibilities on full-moon days; the daily *pūjā* can be performed quickly when necessary; a temple restoration project might involve hundreds of individual workers and donors and extend over many months or years, but can be inaugurated or declared complete on a single chosen full-moon day. Even with this flexibility, however, the calendrical rites cannot cover all the times and all the spaces in which, depending upon circumstance, practices of these sorts might be needed, desired, or otherwise appropriate. Some of these non-calendrical rituals reflect the overlapping regularity of the stages in the individual biographical process, or parallel landmark anniversaries in the "life" of a particular institution. Other non-calendrical practices lack even that level of regularity, responding instead to whatever hurdles and serendipitous opportunities may arise, irrespective of any calendrical system or correspondence to individual life-stages or institutional histories. However varied, these different non-calendrical rituals, like the calendrical ones, draw on that same repertoire of practices that make and remake time and space Buddhist, though sometimes with different emphases and urgency.

In comparison with some other religions, such as Christianity or Hinduism, Buddhism actually prescribes comparatively few life-cycle rituals. A strictly Buddhist perspective does not celebrate many of the most central such moments singled out in other religions, such as birth, puberty, and marriage, given the negative valuation of becoming and attachment, and of celebration itself. Birth announcements, birthday parties, and birthday gifts have emerged quite recently, through international media beamed into television sets; puberty rites for girls are elaborate and ancient, but grounded so thoroughly in astrological and quasi-Hindu structures as to be palpably non-Buddhist; marriages are conducted with obvious borrowings from

Christian ceremony, often even in dress and basic liturgy, and traditionally it has been considered inauspicious for a bride and groom to even see a Buddhist monk or nun on their wedding day.

The major exception here is death; Buddhist practices are integral to the performance of a funeral. Monks and nuns do attend funerals, preach, and receive robes and other alms to produce merit for the deceased person; space is arranged for their visits, just as it would be for any almsgiving or sermon, employing platforms, room dividers, banners, special seats with white covers, and/or simply designating a certain part of the "death house" as the place for the monks, as means allow. The immediate family typically or at least ideally takes the eight precepts and dresses in white for the duration of the funeral, serving the people who visit the body over several days while it remains in state; attendees' analyses (for example, taking the loss as exemplary of impermanence, or speculating about the person's karma) and blessings (most commonly, "let the comfort of nirvana be attained," Sinh. *nivan suva läbēvā*) are often couched in specifically Buddhist terms. But even at funerals, non-Buddhist elements drawn mostly from Hindu traditions provide the ritual material surrounding the keeping and then the burial or cremation of the corpse, and even un-Buddhist activities including drinking alcohol, gambling, feasting, flirting, ill-speaking, theft, and so on may emerge in the crowds to limit the event's overall Buddhist-ness, especially during those stretches when no monks and nuns are present; the "death house" allows far more such lapse than does the temple or for that matter the ordinary home. Still, the Buddhist aspect persists in a series of postmortem almsgiving rituals typically on the seventh day, first month, third month, sixth month, and/or first year anniversaries of the death, depending on the will and means of the bereaved. These are strictly Buddhist practices, focused on monks and nuns and conducted in a space made Buddhist for the occasion, or in a permanently Buddhist space such as a temple. Alms are provided to the monks or nuns, who accept them after establishing the bereaved in the precepts, then guide the family through transferring the merit to the deceased, and preach sermons.

Other occasional rites might also fruitfully be seen within the range of life-cycle rituals, in distinctively Buddhist modes. Thus certain pilgrimages may be considered "must do's" in a lifetime, whether it be to one of the major Buddhist pilgrimage sites within the island (e.g., the mountain pilgrimages to the Buddha's footprint [Adam's Peak] and the site of Buddhism's coming to Sri Lanka [Mihintale]) or in India (monks and nuns sometimes lead tours for groups of lay pilgrims, who spend weeks or months touring the sites of significance in Buddhist history). Likewise, taking the eight precepts is usefully seen as marking life-cycle benchmarks, especially for women. Many men never take the eight precepts, whereas a mature woman who does not do so at least on full-moon days would be considered unusual in traditional settings. When men do take the eight precepts it sometimes involves considerable drama, corresponding to major transformations in their lives (such as retirement, surviving a major illness, or, notably, giving up alcohol). Women tend to take the additional precepts at a much younger age than men, and in much greater numbers, enabled in part by the simultaneous expectation that children will join them at the temple when they do so. That expectation is reinforced by Sunday school (*daham pasal*) teachers, who require practicing *sil* (taking the eight precepts) during these school holidays, and create age-appropriate activities to coincide with them. Thus the practice of taking the eight precepts may mark the time of childhood (and, when children eventually have other things to do on full-moon days, childhood's end), for both girls and boys, after which the former will likely resume the practice sometime in the future as a first renegotiation of her domestic status, one day each lunar month; as a second renegotiation if, with increasing commitment, *atasil* is taken four times monthly; a third renegotiation if, with further commitment still, *atasil* is adopted as a full-time lifestyle (this roughly corresponds with retirement, and entails full-time celibacy); and a fourth, as old age becomes incapacitating, if she withdraws into quasi-monastic existence by relocating in a temple (especially at the Bodhi tree of Anuradhapura), or remaining homebound in practice. A smaller number of eight-precept holders eventually adopt the ten precepts (Pali *dasa sīla*, Sinh. *dasasil*), which divide the seventh precept into two (not to view entertainments, not to adorn the body) and add one more (not to handle money). Males who do so become monastic novices, as do some females in newly created "official" (*bhikkhunī*) nuns' lineages. But most female ten-precept holders, called "ten-precept mother" (*dasasil mātā*) or "discipline reverend" (*sil mäniyā*) nuns, overlap more seamlessly with eight-precept holders, perhaps withdrawing to a separate space for undistracted practice as nuns (some may even start a temple around them), but often maintaining close domestic ties.

"Life cycle" also usefully describes the wide range of practices required to maintain public spaces as Buddhist, especially the construction and upkeep of temples and their edifices. Projects to expand or repair temples engage all the families of a village or neighborhood in ritual as well as manual practices that make and maintain the space's Buddhist-ness, paralleling the ways that individual families make (by installing a shrine) and remake (in the daily ritual) the Buddhist-ness of their individual homes. Enlarging, embellishing, restoring, or otherwise improving the stupa, bodhi tree shrine, image house, monastic residence, or preaching hall of one's local temple involves sometimes expensive and elaborate acts of donation (*dāna*), performance of *pūjā*s, listening to sermons and similar practices, heaping up merit for participants while creating the space in which future Buddhists will similarly perform meritorious deeds, and generating even more merit for the original donors in the process. These projects also involve sometimes onerous gifts of labor (*śramadāna*), especially by those unable to donate money or materials. Because temples and other Buddhist monuments are public spaces, these projects construct Buddhist community along with the edifices, engaging people of all ages, men and women, insiders as well as outside donors, in a shared merit-making activity, each according to his or her abilities and will, which ennobles collective practice as a collective karma bound eventually to bear fruit in collective future-life arahantship. The collective responsibility for life-cycle maintenance of the shared public space can also make it a site of contention, requiring another layer of maintenance that, if unsuccessful, can reach the point of splitting temple congregations. Resident monks and nuns play important roles in these contexts, as does the temple donors' association (*dāyaka sabhā*). Elected officers call and run meetings, often scheduled for *poya* days when everyone with a stake is likely to visit the temple anyway, but the work that culminates there is more ongoing, and it is not always possible to know in advance when some crisis might emerge (like storm damage), or some transformative change might occur (like the succession of resident monastics).

Similarly, even with these broadened understandings, the life-cycle designation cannot contain all the occasions that, in particular spaces and circumstances, ordinary Buddhists make Buddhist. The number of such occasions is limitless, because any situation might be approached in a particularly Buddhist way. For example, throngs of Buddhists make (and later "prove") vows (*bara*) at the Bodhi tree in Anuradhapura, administered by lay Buddhist priests and modeled on parallel Hindu practices. These vows might be written on cloth and tied to branches or railings of the tree, especially if they are exorcistic ("let the astrological curse on so-and-so be lifted"), or oral promises to "prove" the vow if successful (for example, provide a donation after the desired result has been obtained). The latter vows are typically for good things, especially safe delivery in childbirth, safe return from a journey, and success in the London exams that determine children's career plans. Similar vowing practices focus on the Temple of the Tooth in Kandy, Kelaniya temple near Colombo, and other temples well-known for efficacy in particular domains, as well as local temples.

The underlying power (*anubhāva*), emanating from the Bodhi tree or Tooth Relic or even the shrines at the local temple, is also accessible through protective texts (*pirit*). Drawing on collections of ancient sermons (*suttas*) believed powerful in confronting particular situations, supplemented through the centuries with later compositions designed to enlarge the range of situations that can be dealt with in this fashion and to reduce the amount of time required to do so, *pirit* allows such *anubhāva* to be called forth anytime and anywhere Buddhists encounter illness, danger, or other such troubles, or they simply want to maximize the Buddhist-ness of some particular event or space. *Pirit* may be recited individually (typically in some abbreviated fashion) or collectively, in which case it may entail elaborate preparations including decorated pavilions and provisions for multiple monks or nuns who tag-team to prolong the chanting for hours or even days. Specific *pirit* texts are also diagrammed as protective devices for the home (such as the *Ratana-sūtra-yantra*ya) or to bring wealth (such as *Sīvali-yantraya*). *Pirit* even allows a bit of Buddhist-ness to slip into those life-cycle moments with which it does not easily sit. Buddhist weddings, despite the absence of monks and nuns, typically include recitation of the *Jayamaṅgalagāthā* (*pirit*) to bless the marriage. Likewise, in rural Anuradhapura the lay *pirit* troupe (*gihi pirit kandāyama*) in a particular village will perform all-night *pirit* for successful childbirth in the expectant mother's home, late in her term, mixing practices employed by monks when they chant *pirit* with the offerings, creation of sacred space, and other elements typical of Hindu-origin thaumaturgical practices in that region.

Conclusion

Contemporary Sri Lankan Buddhists thus possess a variety of tools with which to make any particular time or space Buddhist, or more Buddhist. Performing *pūjā*, chanting Pali praises, refuges, or *pirit*, adopting precepts, visiting temples, constructing and maintaining shrines in the home and/or in temples, participating in pilgrimages and festivals or even sending Wesak cards, Buddhists make time and space as fully Buddhist as they will. Undertaking these practices may be generated by any number of overlapping motivations. Each practice produces merit, promising soteriological results in future lives, culminating in nirvana. This promise is accepted not only because Buddhist teachings and teachers repeatedly affirm its truth, but because the practices themselves cultivate the basic trainings in moral restraint (Pali *sīla*), wisdom (Pali *paññā*), and meditation (Pali *samādhi*) that, fully perfected, constitute the goal itself. These practices allow ordinary Buddhists to "practice" controlling bodily actions, honing intelligence, and cultivating mental calm and insight in emulation of the Buddha, accordance with the Dharma, and participation in the sangha. At the further end—adopting the ten precepts—these practices overlap seamlessly with the full-time commitment to being Buddhist entailed by monasticism. Even a full-time eight-precept holder will spend as much of her or his time chanting, studying, and meditating as possible, and embellish the home and attend the temple and pilgrimages to locate himself or herself in Buddhist space as fully as possible, too. Many develop a lifestyle and demeanor that closely overlaps with those of monks and nuns. Though the majority of Buddhists do not make that sort of full-time commitment, or at least postpone it until retirement, even if it is only an occasional performance of the daily ritual or visit to the temple, Buddhist hagiography makes clear that the very smallest such Buddhist action can have exponentially greater results later in life, or in future lives.

These practices, moreover, help Buddhists cope in the face of life's uncertainties. Even the five precepts cultivate a quelling of desire that might help one face want in a time of drought; the central Buddhist teachings emphasized in sermons and Sunday school lessons, like the impermanence of all things and the universality of suffering, might help a practitioner face loss or illness with detached resignation; the small meditations practiced on *poya* days might help her or him remain calm and clear-headed when suffering an emergency; a lifetime of practice ideally culminates in a peaceful death and favorable rebirth as the dying person recalls meritorious things done, rehearses Dharma teachings learned, and enters into the meditative states that have been cultivated. This repertoire of practices also allows tangible interventions in situations over which one otherwise can exert little control. Thus the response to drought might include a more proactive, large-scale *pirit* ceremony to bring rain and blessings on the environment; pitched chanting of "Buddha!" (Pali *Buddho*) or "My Revered Buddha King!" (Sinh. *magē budu rajānan vahansē*) might allow a Buddhist to remain focused and dispel fear in the midst of attending to another's medical emergency; worship verses might be loudly recited to keep wild elephants out of one's path at night; a properly executed funeral and postmortem alms-giving ceremonies maximize the merit of departed loved ones (as well as the survivors) unable, as is often emphasized, to carry anything else with them into the next life.

The will to practice is also inflected by worldly commitments. Most basically, it may well be the case that some Buddhists (especially men and children) are compelled to what level of practice they achieve by the will of others (especially more committed wives, mothers, and grandmothers). Outside such family pressures, "Buddhist" is a sociological as well as soteriological identity, and in Sri Lanka's multiethnic and multi-religious society, attempts to make certain spaces and times Buddhist can clash with the desires of others even as it affirms communal identity among Buddhist participants. At this level the marking of public space or time as Buddhist might become a source of contention, as when Buddhist temples broadcast *pirit* over loudspeakers that compete with Muslim calls to prayer or Hindu temple *pūjās*, or claims about their Buddhist-ness in earlier times become arguments over the ownership of particular spaces in the present. In such situations, being Buddhist can sometimes become so closely identified with baser economic or political interests that even some Buddhists might contest some manifestations of it. But such multi-religious contention is by no means inevitable, and one advantage of the need to make and remake time and space as Buddhist is that it allows for grace in not making other times and spaces so. This same flexibility allows individuals and communities to reach the levels of practice that they choose, and that they can. And it allows them to extend the creative process of making time and space Buddhist in new ways, as the world itself changes. Thus since only about 2010, it has become quite a ubiquitous practice for Sri Lankan Buddhists conversing with other Buddhists to conclude telephone calls or text messages with the salutation *Budu saranai*, "refuge in the Buddha," or sometimes simply "B.S." Buddhist memes, sacred images, *pirit* and other chanted texts, popular music, sermons, and news proliferate widely on social media, a new virtual space made Buddhist in contemporary times.

Notes

1. Deities and a wide range of lesser supernatural beings, originating in various forms of Hinduism as well as indigenous religion, have long played and continue to play important roles in Sinhala Buddhist lives and communities. Some Buddhists consider these beings agentive in daily life and manipulable for purposes both good and bad; various overlapping calendrical, life-cycle, and periodic ritual traditions have developed in association with them. They are not specifically Buddhist in that they are fellow participants in, rather than the focus of, Buddhist practices; the practices associated with them are not believed to produce Buddhist soteriological ends such as the acquisition of merit, cultivation of Buddhist virtues, and eventual achievement of nirvana. Though they are hence largely outside the

scope of this chapter, the gods as well as the practices associated with them are in various ways susceptible to being made Buddhist. They might be understood, as fellow participants in the Buddhist world, as being subject to the effects of their own good and bad karma, requiring merit for better rebirth leading toward nirvana; they might be celebrated in conjunction with Buddhist festivals, their own statues and festivals might be located within Buddhist temples, they might be offered Buddhist merit in exchange for worldly favors, they might be called on as protectors and enforcers of Buddhist institutions and values (in particular *pirit*, see later discussion), and so on.

2. Or BV, *Buddha-varṣa*, lit. "Buddha Year."
3. The halfway point (2500 BE = 1956 CE) was widely anticipated and celebrated throughout the Buddhist world, and led to a surge of Buddhist nationalism, publication, and expansion in Sri Lanka as elsewhere, an impulse that corresponded to the emergence of the postcolonial "new nations."
4. Like rituals associated with the gods (see n. 1), astrological sciences and practices imported from Hindu traditions on the mainland have maintained important roles among Sinhala Buddhists despite not being Buddhist per se; astrology is especially central in scheduling Buddhist festivals, observing auspicious rituals associated with the Sinhala New Year (April 13–14), and arranging and holding weddings.

Further Readings

Abeysekara, Ananda. *Colors of the Robe: Religion, Identity, and Difference*. Columbia: University of South Carolina Press, 2002.

Ānandajoti Bhikkhu, ed. and tr. *Safeguard Recitals*. Kandy: Buddhist Publication Society, 2004.

Bond, George D. *The Buddhist Revival in Sri Lanka: Religious Tradition, Reinterpretation and Response*. Columbia: University of South Carolina Press, 1988.

Carter, John Ross. *On Understanding Buddhists: Essays on the Theravāda Tradition in Sri Lanka*. Albany: State University of New York Press, 1993.

Gombrich, Richard F. *Precept and Practice: Traditional Buddhism in the Rural Highlands of Ceylon*. Oxford: Clarendon, 1971.

Gombrich, Richard, and Gananath Obeyesekere. *Buddhism Transformed: Religious Change in Sri Lanka*. Princeton, NJ: Princeton University Press, 1989.

Holt, John Clifford. *The Buddhist Viṣṇu: Religious Transformation, Politics, and Culture*. New York: Columbia University Press, 2004.

Holt, John Clifford, ed. *Buddhist Extremists and Muslim Minorities: Religious Conflict in Contemporary Sri Lanka*. Oxford: Oxford University Press, 2016.

Langer, Rita. *Buddhist Rituals of Death and Rebirth: Contemporary Sri Lankan Practice and Its Origins*. London and New York: Routledge, 2007.

Nārada Thera and Bhikkhu Kassapa. *The Mirror of the Dhamma: A Manual of Buddhist Chanting and Devotional Texts*. Kandy: Buddhist Publication Society, 1963. Rev. ed. Bhikkhu Khantipālo (Kandy, 2008): https://what-buddha-said.net/library/Wheels/wh054.pdf.

Salgado, Nirmala S. *Buddhist Nuns and Gendered Practice: In Search of the Female Renunciant*. Oxford: Oxford University Press, 2013.

Samuels, Jeffrey. *Attracting the Heart: Social Relations and the Aesthetics of Emotion in Sri Lankan Monastic Culture*. Honolulu: University of Hawaiʻi Press, 2010.

Samuels, Jeffrey, Justin Thomas McDaniel, and Mark Michael Rowe, eds. *Figures of Buddhist Modernity in Asia*. Honolulu: University of Hawaiʻi Press, 2016.
Seneviratne, H. L. *The Work of Kings: The New Buddhism in Sri Lanka*. Chicago: University of Chicago Press, 1999.
Southwold, Martin. *Buddhism in Life: The Anthropological Study of Religion and the Sinhalese Practice of Buddhism*. Manchester: Manchester University Press, 1983.

CHAPTER 29

FOOD PRACTICES

LISA GRUMBACH

Attitudes toward Food within Buddhist Traditions

In order to understand the use of food within Buddhist practices, it is helpful to consider how Buddhists have thought about food in various times and places. Compared to many other Asian religions, the Buddhist tradition has tended to take a relatively material view of food. In contrast to Hinduism, where food offerings to deities are considered to be imbued with spiritual essence that is incorporated into the body of the devotee who eats the deity's leftovers (*prasāda*), or Daoism, in which the practitioner ingests specific food items (avoiding "grains," eating special "foods" such as pine bark, talismans, and elixirs) to achieve the goal of immortality, Buddhists primarily see food in terms of nourishment. The Buddhist tradition advocates neither extreme food abstinence nor overindulgence, but rather a "middle way" of moderation. In this way, food is not overvalued, but it is essential for life and proper practice. Anthropologist H. L. Seneviratne notes that the role of food in Buddhist thought and practice

> . . . is signified in the Buddhist "first question" (*eko dhammo*) and its answer, "all beings subsist on food" ("*sabbe satta aharaṭṭhitika*"). This statement is so important that to fully understand it would release one from *saṁsāra*. In it is condensed a very high valuation of food as subsistence, as well as an equally strong devaluation of food as having any significance beyond the purely subsistive. Subsistence is understood as a necessary condition of proper contemplation and mental discipline which leads to enlightenment.[1]

In Buddhism, food does not need to have magical or spiritual power of its own for it to be an essential part of practice.[2]

While the Buddhist tradition does not tend to invest food with spiritual power, food is nevertheless not without social value. Within Indian society, food is perhaps the most highly charged marker of social bonds and distinctions.[3] Buddhists, as part of Indian society, could not ignore the social ramifications of eating. We find in the early Vinaya elaborate rules for how monastics are to receive and eat food (discussed later in the chapter). In other words, in Buddhist practice, *what* people eat is typically of less concern than *how* they receive it and eat it (with a few important exceptions developing in the East Asian sphere).

A second characteristic of Buddhist attitudes toward food is the definition of food, i.e., what kinds of things may be *thought of* as food. The Buddhist tradition takes a rather wide view of what to count as food, and this is related to Buddhist cosmology and doctrine. The basic position of Buddhist cosmology is that, since beings undergo countless rebirths, every being has at some time been a human, an animal, a god, etc. This is often expressed in Buddhism as the idea that all beings have at some point been our mothers and fathers. To put it another way, all beings, including ourselves, have been food for others. Combined with ideas of no-self, interdependence, and compassion, this worldview calls into question the boundaries between self and others. Thus the body itself can also be considered food that can be offered to others (see later discussion). The Buddhist teachings of emptiness (*śūnyatā*) and interdependence (*pratītyasamutpāda*) have also impacted ideas of food. The idea that all things (dharmas) are empty of an inherently existing self—that all things arise dependent upon other things—tends in the later Mahayana traditions toward a radical non-duality in which discriminating views (i.e., good vs. bad, like vs. dislike) are negated. In terms of food practices, this is seen particularly in the context of higher-level tantric ritual, where the practitioner is enjoined to consider things that would normally be reviled, such as feces, the flesh of dead bodies, blood, and pus, as no different from other food, at least within the instructions of ritual texts. It must be stressed, however, that this extreme view of food is not taken up as actual practice by the vast majority of Buddhists. Yet these ideas should not be ignored or dismissed. There are many stories and occasional anecdotes of bodhisattvas and advanced masters performing such practices.[4] These stories are often held to express the highest teachings of Buddhism, and the tradition generally maintains that only those who have cultivated this kind of attitude—one might say, an awakened view of food—are capable of achieving the highest goal of the religion: enlightenment.

A third point to keep in mind is that food forms the basis of practices that link various "classes" of beings into karmic and dharmic relationships. The most prominent of these is the relationship created between monastics and their surrounding communities (the laity), which is defined through food. The basic form of the lay–monastic relationship is that laypeople provide food to monastics, and in exchange monastics provide the Dharma to laypeople. Additionally, food is offered by both lay and monastics to a host of other beings, such as gods, spirits, ghosts, demons, and ancestors. In many Buddhist countries, these ritual observances are among the most important events of the year and form the basis for the ways in which people engage in Buddhist practice itself: requesting aid from deities for good harvests, health, and prosperity; memorializing ancestors (both lay and monastic); and managing potentially harmful spirits of various kinds. In these many practices and rituals, food is an indispensable element.

However, regardless of the prominent and extensive use of food, we must note that Buddhist discussions never suggest that the food itself has any efficacy within ritual. Again, this is in marked contrast to other Indian and Asian religions. In Buddhism, while food is essential in ritual, it is not the most important thing. This status is reserved for the Dharma. If laypeople give food to monastics, those people in return receive something much more valuable than food: the teaching. If in a ritual, food is offered to a troublesome ghost, the food provides some comfort to the spirit, but it is the monastic's preaching of the Dharma (and possibly use of Buddhist incantations) that opens the path for the ghost's moving on to the Pure Land or some other rebirth. The most profound aspects of this hierarchy of Dharma and food perhaps appear in the context of gendered relationships, as seen in the relationship between Gautama and his aunt *cum* foster mother Mahaprajapati. When the Buddha refuses to ordain women, he is reminded of the "milk-debt": that a child owes its mother an unrepayable debt for the mother's breastfeeding.[5] Within Indian society, the milk-debt defines a whole host of relationships and beliefs that idealize mothers.[6] Yet the early Buddhist tradition seems to have been uncomfortable with this idea, as such an unrepayable debt would place Mahaprajapati (the mother) in a position higher than the Buddha. The textual tradition develops the idea that it is rather Mahaprajapati who owes a debt to the Buddha since she received his teaching of the Dharma.[7] In the end, no food offering—even that most rarified of foods, mother's milk—occupies a position superior to the Dharma, and this valuation of Dharma over food and monastics over mothers continued to influence the creation of ritual practices in the centuries to come.[8]

Finally, the preceding point reminds us that food is intimately connected to gendered practice. Generally, people of any gender may perform or take part in all food-related religious practice in Buddhism, from making offerings, to participating in festivals, or adopting a vegetarian diet. However, in a particular place or time, a practice may become more associated with a specific gender or may become an important factor in the expression of gendered practice. A complete review or analysis of gendered food practices is not possible in this chapter, but I will attempt to point out areas where gender becomes an important consideration.

While there are innumerable regional and local variations of food practices, I have selected practices from various parts of the Buddhist world that illustrate the ideas and attitudes related to food reviewed previously. We begin with the practice of giving food, which is a part of Buddhist practice everywhere, first examining the importance of food offerings within the sangha (food offerings to monastics by the laity), and second, the feeding of other types of beings, such as buddhas, ancestors, ghosts, and spirits. Next, we examine food-related festivals, which are major religious events throughout Asia, focusing on the role Buddhism plays in the production of food. Another well-known aspect of Buddhist food practice is vegetarianism, which is mostly but not exclusively associated with the Mahayana tradition of East Asia. Lastly, we survey a range of ritualized eating, drinking, and cooking practices that have become associated with Buddhism, particularly through the Chan/Zen schools, such as formalized tea drinking, procedures for eating during monastic training, and cooking as a form of Zen practice.

Offering and Receiving Food

The most important and widely performed type of Buddhist practice is perhaps *dāna*, or giving, and the giving of food is undoubtedly the most common kind of giving. The giving of food is a practice that can be performed by anyone. Laypeople give food to monastics; both laypeople and monastics give food to buddhas and deities. Home and temple altars are provided with daily food offerings, and the many ritual observances throughout the year require more elaborate offerings. Within the contexts of both domestic and monastic life, food offerings are ubiquitous.

Indeed, the beginnings of Buddhism as a religious path might arguably be said to start with a food offering. In the well-known story of Gautama's search for enlightenment, the Buddha-to-be tries out several types of religious practice but finds none of them to be satisfactory or leading to liberation from suffering. Realizing the limitations of these teachings, Gautama, emaciated from having performed ascetic practices including fasting, rejects the idea of such severe regimens. At this point the woman Sujātā offers him a bowl of milk-rice, which Gautama accepts and eats. Refreshed and strengthened, Gautama then completes the path to enlightenment, becoming the Buddha. Note the importance of food in this episode: this acceptance of food by Gautama marks his departure from the other existing religious paths and his setting out on the "middle way" that defines Buddhism. Sujātā's offering sustains the bodhisattva during his seven-week ordeal of meditative practice to reach enlightenment, at the conclusion of which the new Buddha receives another food offering (rice cakes and sweets) from the merchants Trapaṣa and Bhallika. Notably, the tradition holds that Sujātā is the first laywoman follower of the Buddha, and Trapuṣa and Bhallika the first laymen followers.[9]

These stories of food offerings define the proper relationship between the laity and monastics. Laypeople should offer food; monastics should receive it. Like Sujātā, lay Buddhists make offerings of various sorts to the Buddha(s) and the sangha. These can be simple things, such as daily offerings of rice and water on Buddhist altars. In Southeast Asia, the daily alms rounds remain an important part of Buddhist practice for both monastics and laypeople. The laity accrue merit by giving food to monastics, and it is the duty of the monastics to act as the "field of merit" for the laypeople; that is, providing food to monastics is the primary way that laypeople accrue the merit necessary for advancement on the Buddhist path. Although the act of giving in itself is sufficient to produce merit, giving food also presents opportunities for monastics to provide the teaching of the Dharma to the laity, particularly when food is given at religious services held at monasteries, or when laypeople invite monastics to a meal.[10] Thus, it is important that monastics accept whatever food is offered to them. For a monastic to refuse a food offering would be tantamount to refusing to act as a field of merit or to provide the Dharma.

The *pāṭimokkha* rules pertaining to the foods that monastics may receive list several categories of food, beginning with staple foods, which are listed in five types: cooked grains, *kummāsa* (a grain-based confection), *sattu* (any grain dried and ground into meal), fish, and meat.[11] Monastics may also receive non-staple foods: any other kind of food not included among the staples, such as vegetable products (leaves, stems, flowers, etc.), nuts, tubers and roots, and flour-based goods like cake, bread, and pasta. Besides food received for meals that should be eaten before noon, fruit juices and various types of medicinals may be consumed at other times of the day. Note that the monastic rules allow for the eating of meat. However, there are three conditions for meat to be "pure" (*tikoṭiparisuddha*): monastics should not have seen, heard, or otherwise known that an animal was killed specifically for them.[12] If these three conditions are not met, the monastic should refuse the meat.

In addition to listing the types of food, the *pāṭimokkha* also specifies how to receive and eat food. The rules include injunctions such as "I will accept almsfood attentively," "I will eat almsfood which has curry in the proper proportion," "I will not look at another's bowl enviously," and "I will not throw away bowl-washing water which has rice-grains [in it] amidst the houses."[13] Additionally, when eating, the food in the bowl should be mixed together rather than eaten separately. These various rules are intended to create harmonious relationships between monastics and the lay community, and to maintain order among the monastics themselves, as well as inculcating bodily habits conducive to Buddhist practice. For example, the mixing of food together in the bowl is intended to make the taste of the various foods uniform, discouraging one from expressing like or dislike of any particular item, thus aiding in the reduction of attachments.

Feeding Others

In addition to food given to the human sangha, equally important are food offerings made to other kinds of beings—buddhas, ancestors, deities, spirits, and animals. Here we will focus on two examples representative of these kinds of offerings: ritual offerings for deities and spirits in Tibetan practice; and the feeding of ancestors through the example of Kūkai (774–835), the founder of the Japanese Shingon school who is still fed even today.

Before looking at these examples, however, a word about feeding in Buddhist practice will help us understand its importance. While there is some overlap with the practice of offering food to the sangha described earlier, the feeding of others includes a larger set of beings, most of which are not human (or not living human beings). Making offerings to the monastic sangha entails the expectation of specific Buddhist returns (receiving the teaching of the Dharma or accumulating merit), whereas feeding others has different objectives. Within ritual, the feeding of spirits serves to draw the spirits into some kind of relationship with the ritual agent or community. The feeding of ancestors provides sustenance, helps the ancestors avoid falling into a hell realm, and maintains good relationships with the deceased, who will continue to watch over and protect the family. Alternatively, sometimes an act of feeding is performed without expectation of any return. This kind of feeding of others represents the perfection (*paramitā*) of giving, in which giving is performed completely altruistically. This latter practice is especially associated with the bodhisattva, who through the six perfections completes the path to Buddhahood. The ultimate example is the former life story of Shakyamuni, who as a bodhisattva gives his body as food to feed a starving tigress and her cubs. In later Mahayana formulations of practice based on ideas of suchness and buddha-nature, in which all beings are already fully possessed of buddhahood, feeding others comes to represent one of the highest forms of practice, as evidenced by the following medieval Japanese text:

> When you eat, visualize [this act] as making offerings to the thirty-seven honored ones [i.e., the Buddhas and bodhisattvas depicted on the Diamond-realm mandala of esoteric Buddhism], and when you feed others, form the thought that you are, upwardly, making offerings to the Buddhas of the ten directions and three periods of time, and downwardly, giving alms to hell-dwellers, hungry ghosts and those in the animal realm. And you should likewise form this thought when you feed your servants and retainers, or give food to horses and cattle, birds and beasts. For lay people, men and women engaged in public and private affairs, what practice could possibly be superior?[14]

The act of feeding thus serves many purposes, from creating relationships with others to demonstrating the highest forms of Buddhist altruism and understandings of buddhahood.

We turn now to our first example, a Tibetan ritual of feeding used to create and maintain relationships between all types of beings. The Accomplishing Medicine (*sman sgrub*) ritual, as studied by Frances Garrett, Andrew Erlich, Nicholas Field, Barbara Hazelton, and Matthew King, consists of elaborate food offerings that feed and thereby connect a wide variety of beings. Garret et al. explain that the main purpose of the ritual is to transform various food substances into medicine, but "it also accomplishes much more than this, bestowing on the practitioner long life, miraculous powers, or an understanding of the mind's true nature, blessing a community of practitioners and lay people, alchemically transforming impurity into purity, attacking disease-causing demonic forces, and so forth."[15] The most important part of the ritual is the creation of *torma* (*gtor ma*), "offering cakes," made in conformity to the likes and dislikes of special "guests" (buddhas, gods, demons, etc.).[16] The ritualists use *torma* to offer hospitality to invited beings, such as buddhas, ancient sages, local deities, *yakṣa*s, and hungry ghosts, and to command malevolent spirits to leave the ritual space.[17] The medicines created in the course of the week-long ritual are also distributed to all people observing or attending the ritual, so that human beings are linked together with the nonhuman.[18] In sum, the benefits sought through the performance of ritual are realized through creating and maintaining relationships with various beings, specifically by feeding them.

Our second example is the feeding of ancestors, often associated with East Asian veneration of ancestors, but found widely throughout South Asia as well.[19] Providing food to ancestors has many purposes: saving the dead from falling into hell, ensuring that they are happy in the afterlife, and maintaining family ties so that the ancestors will help the living family. Giving food to the ancestors is the central purpose of the Chinese ghost festival and the Japanese *obon* celebration.[20] Additionally, the feeding of monastic ancestors features prominently in the ritual of all East Asian Buddhist schools. Here we look at the example of Kūkai, the founder of the Shingon school in Japan. As a revered ancestor and proponent of the Shingon doctrine of buddhahood in this very body (*sokushin jōbutsu*), we might expect Kūkai to receive food appropriate to the status of an ancestor or even a buddha. Focusing on the kinds of food that are provided can help determine how specific figures are categorized. As an ancestor or buddha, we might expect him to be given cooked rice, water, and fruits. Food is taken to Kūkai in a ceremony called the *shōshingu* ("feeding the living body"). At approximately 6 a.m. every day, a meal is placed in a large wooden box, which is carried by two monks and first set before the Ajimi Jizō, or "Tasting Jizō." After Jizō "tastes" the food, the box is carried to Kūkai's mausoleum (Gobyō). And what is given to Kūkai? According to the monks, the food items vary from day to day and contain a sampling of the same foods that all the monks eat—on occasion, even pasta carbonara.[21] This example demonstrates the place of Kūkai within the monastery. It is believed that Kūkai continues to "live" in a mummified state, and his daily feeding is different from those for regular ancestors and buddhas.[22] Giving him the same foods that the other monks eat places him firmly within the realm of the living practitioners. However, Kūkai's portion is given the special distinction of being "tasted" by Jizō, indicating the elevated status of the master.

These two examples show how feeding others operates within ritual and daily practice to foster relationships among various kinds of beings. The logic of ritual feeding additionally allows us to discern the status of beings by paying attention to what kinds of foods are offered to them.

Festivals and Food Production

We have seen in the previous discussion how food functions within and is essential to Buddhist ritual. It is equally true that Buddhist ritual is necessary for food. The history of Buddhism is filled with rituals and prayers for the success of food crops, and festivals focused on food production, especially rice, form the core of annual ritual observances in many Buddhist cultures. Festivals in the northeast region of Thailand are representative of how Buddhism is used together with other belief systems to ensure food production. These festivals take place at the beginning of the rainy season to welcome and worship male and female spirits who protect the village and ensure the fertility of the crops.[23] Two of the most important rites, marking the beginning and end of the festival, center on Buddhist figures. The first rite involves the Indian Buddhist monk Upagupta, called Phra Upakut in Thai, who is represented by a small stone kept in the village's Buddhist temple. The day before the festival, the stone is removed from the temple and hidden in the nearby river. The festival begins with an elaborate ritual of finding the Phra Upakut stone and reinstalling it in the temple. The festival ends with a parade in which another important Buddhist figure, Prince Vessantara, is carried through the village on an elaborately decorated carriage accompanied by his wife and two children.[24]

Why are these Buddhist figures included in a fertility festival? Both Upagupta and Vessantara are famed throughout Southeast Asia for associations with water and rain. John Strong's study of Upagupta details this monk's mythic associations with water.[25] It is well known that Māra disrupts Buddhist festivals and causes torrential rains, which not only ruin the festival but also damage the crops.[26] Tales of Upagupta defeating Māra earned him a reputation as a figure who protects festivals and helps to ensure proper rainfall.[27] Thus, Upagupta/Uphakut is invoked at the beginning of these festivals to protect the proceedings generally and the crops in particular.

The story of Prince Vessantara is one of the most famous tales in Buddhist literature.[28] In this *jātaka* story, Vessantara is the last incarnation of the bodhisattva before his final birth as Gautama. The prince embodies the Buddhist teaching of compassionate giving, perhaps being generous to a fault. He gives away the kingdom's auspicious white elephant, which ensures plentiful rain. Vessantara and his family are banished from the kingdom, and in the course of their travels he even gives away his wife and children. However, the story ends with Vessantara's triumphal return to the kingdom, reunion with his family, and ostensibly the return of rains and good harvests. Like Upagupta, the inclusion of the Vessantara narrative in Southeast Asian fertility rituals marks the bringing of auspiciousness, rain, and fertility to the village.

In this example, rituals of fertility and food production are interwoven with rites for Buddhist figures known for their associations with water and rain. Although here we have discussed but one festival, the use of Buddhist rituals for the success of food crops is found throughout Asia.

Buddhist Vegetarianism

Although vegetarianism is not completely unknown in South Asian, Southeast Asian, or Tibetan Buddhist traditions, monastics in these areas continue to follow the traditional Vinaya, which allows meat eating, and most laypeople eat meat.[29] A vegetarian diet is most associated with East Asian Buddhism, where vegetarianism is defined not only by the avoidance of meat but also the five pungent vegetables (garlic, onions, Chinese chives, scallions, leeks) that are thought to inflame the passions. As part of religious practice, vegetarianism is related to specific Buddhist goals: the Mahayana sutras promote meat avoidance as a way for the practitioner to cultivate compassion; avoiding the pungent vegetables decreases the passions that can be an obstacle to practice; and maintaining the Buddhist vegetarian diet is sometimes seen as necessary for spiritual advancement.[30]

In East Asia, vegetarianism has been considered a standard Buddhist practice for both lay and monastic practitioners since approximately the sixth century. The shift to vegetarianism in East Asia rests on a combination of religious, social, and political factors. In China, Mahayana sutras, which never gained popularity in India, became the standard Buddhist scriptures. In comparison to earlier (non-Mahayana) material, some of these texts severely criticize meat eating. The *Mahāaparinirvāṇa-sūtra*, for example, says that meat eating "destroys one's capacity for great compassion" and results in a "smell of murder" that causes fear in beings.[31] Additionally, new precepts for lay followers found in the *Fanwangjing* (Brahma's Net Sutra), likely composed in China, created a rule against meat eating for the laity.[32] Early moves toward vegetarianism seem to have come first from the laity, who combined Buddhist ideas of compassion and karmic retribution with native Chinese ideas of the cultivated and virtuous person to argue that one who eats meat is as culpable as the butcher in killing animals—an idea that is not found in Indian Buddhism.[33] These developments resulted in a dilemma for Chinese Buddhists, who saw the contradiction between the Vinaya teachings, which allow meat eating, and the teachings of the sutras, which forbid it. Resolution came in the form of the vegetarian layperson Emperor Wu (r. 502–549) of the Liang dynasty: after debating the issue with the monks and nuns of his kingdom—who were loath to decide whether Vinaya or sutra was superior—he unilaterally declared that monastics too had to keep a vegetarian diet.[34] That is, Chinese states began to regulate the lives of religious practitioners, and vegetarianism became a state-ordered requirement for monks and nuns. This insertion of a rule against meat eating into the monastic regulations is a significant difference between East Asian Mahayana Buddhism and the rest of the Buddhist world.

In contemporary East Asia, vegetarianism remains a central part of Buddhist identity. Vegetarian halls (*zhaitang* or *fotang*, "buddha hall"), for example, are popular in Taiwan and have been spread throughout Southeast Asia by Chinese immigrants.[35] Members are known by appellations referencing vegetarianism: vegetarian friends (*caiyou*), vegetarian women (*caigu*), and vegetarian men (*caigong*); in Taiwan, these groups are called the Vegetarian Teachings (Zhaijiao).[36] The vegetarian halls are maintained largely by women who are often non-ordained "vegetarian nuns" (*zhaigu*, literally, "vegetarian aunts"). Maintaining a vegetarian diet is a central part their religious identity and practice. The Taiwanese vegetarian nun Cai Zhichan (1900–1958) gives a prominent place in her writing for vegetarianism as the basis of religious practice:

> In order to repay the debts of my parents, I devoted my life to religious training (to become Buddha's disciple) in solitude since I was sixteen years old. A Bodhi tree bears a Bodhi seed, a bright mirror is free from dust and does not require wiping. When I am searching for the flavour (true nature) of Chan, I found it to be similar to the flavour of the Way (Dao); after vegetable roots are consumed (to lead a simple vegetarian life), you will be able to uncover the root of wisdom.[37]

In fact, vegetarianism is essential in this tradition to achieving the higher levels of teaching and practice.[38]

In contrast to vegetarianism as the norm for Chinese monastics, the Mahayana tradition has also viewed transgressing the rule against meat eating as evidence of the highest spiritual achievement. Stories of eminent monks often extoll the virtues of monks who maintain a vegetarian diet; however, there are also stories of monks who eat meat, drink wine, and otherwise transgress the Buddhist precepts.[39] In the main, these stories are hagiography, not history, serving the didactic purpose of pointing to important Mahayana principles and teachings, such as emptiness and non-discriminatory judgment and action. A story of the early Chinese monk Daoxuan (596–667) and the Indian tantric master Śubhakarasiṃha (637–735) as roommates illustrates the point:

> Tripitaka Śubhakarasiṃha drank wine and ate meat; in word and deed he was crude and uncouth, always getting drunk, raising a ruckus and vomiting on the mat. Master of the Regulations Daoxuan could not tolerate him in the least. Once, in the middle of the night, Daoxuan caught a flea and was about to toss it to the ground when Śubhakarasiṃha, half-drunk, repeatedly called out, "You've killed a child of the Buddha!" Only then did Daoxuan realize that Śubhakarasiṃha was an exceptional man.[40]

Historically, only a few figures are associated with such behaviors, like the Korean monk Wonhyo (617–686) and the Japanese monk Ikkyū (1394–1481), both of whom are said to have visited brothels, drunk alcohol, and eaten meat.

Finally, it is well known that Japanese Buddhists have almost entirely given up the practice of vegetarianism, along with other precepts (Japanese monastics may also marry and drink alcohol). The reasons for this are complex and cannot be adequately dealt with in this short review. A few things should be noted, however. The Jōdo Shinshū school, founded by Shinran (1173–1263), rejected all monastic regulations, including vegetarianism, from the thirteenth century. Jōdo Shinshū clerics were routinely criticized by those of other schools, all of which continued to maintain the precepts and monastic regulations as required by the state. When the Japanese government changed the regulations in 1872, stating that "[f]rom now on Buddhist clerics shall be free to eat meat, marry, grow their hair, and so on," a full-fledged debate began within and between the various Buddhist schools, with some advocating that monastics should continue to uphold the precepts, while others argued in favor of eating meat for a variety of reasons.[41] Although these arguments continued for several decades after the legal change, during that time eating meat became commonplace. Today in Japan, most people, lay or ordained, eat meat. However, vegetarianism is maintained during monastic training periods, and nuns often keep the precepts, including a vegetarian diet.[42] Even the Jōdo Shinshū often serves vegetarian meals (*otoki*) to participants at important annual events.[43]

Ritualized Drinking, Eating, and Cooking

Besides the use of food in religious ritual, East Asian Buddhist traditions are often noted for the ritualization of everyday food habits and actions, such as drinking tea and cooking. However, some care must be exercised not to think of these as exclusively Buddhist practices. Other religious traditions have also contributed to the creation of ritualized food rules, and these food practices have been widely adopted into society generally. This is perhaps best seen in the examples of tea drinking and the tea ceremony. Tea became consumed as a beverage from about the eighth century in China, and drinking tea became widespread in China during the Song period (960–1279). During this time, Chan monasteries were also developing "pure rules" (*qinggui*) for monastic behavior in which eating and drinking became highly ritualized. Buddhist scholar and nun Yifa has shown that new rules involving living spaces and food practices were incorporated from Confucian-based aristocratic society, including procedures for serving tea: "The extremely meticulous tea service etiquette outlined in monastic regulations—including instructions on where each person should walk, who should bow or speak to whom and when—cannot be found in the original Vinaya; it is an invention of Chinese Buddhism that reflects a culture rooted in classical Confucian works, particularly the *Yili*."[44] That is, ritualized tea drinking within Chinese Buddhism derived from customs that were already part of elite Chinese life.

Although tea etiquette and ceremonial tea drinking are not unique to Buddhism, the habit of tea drinking nevertheless became associated with monastic life in part because the Buddhist precepts forbid alcohol. James Benn's study of tea in Chinese history enumerates the many ways in which tea was used by Buddhists. Already in the Tang period (618–907), the *Chajiu lun* ("A discussion of tea and alcohol") indicates that tea was associated with monastic life. In the text, the anthropomorphized characters of Tea and Alcohol argue over who is better, with Tea stating at one point: "Famous monks, 'great worthies' (*dade*, *bhadanta*s, or elder monks) and recluses in groves of meditation (*chanlin*, monasteries) all take me while making discourses, for I can clear away their dullness and weariness."[45] Within monasteries, tea was and is used in offerings and rituals, is served to guests, and is consumed by monastics for its stimulant effects, social functions, and medicinal properties. Yet all of these things could also be said of Daoists, the imperial court, Confucian literati, and even general society. It is often noted that tea figures prominently in Chan literature, but Benn also cautions that these references tell us more about the ubiquity of tea in daily life than about any special relationship between Chan and tea.[46] Buddhists participated in and contributed to tea culture in China, but no more or less than other important groups in society. The same may be said of Japan, where aristocrats, warriors, merchants, and monastics all contributed to the social and material culture of the tea ceremony. The difference was that all of these other groups could also drink alcohol, whereas Buddhists did not; thus tea was seen as the Buddhists' preferred beverage.

In Japan, the Sōtō monk Dōgen (1200–1253) added further commentary and refinement to the Chan regulations in his *Eihei shingi*.[47] The text has separate chapters on instructions for the head cook (*Tenzō kyōkun*) and rules on receiving and eating food (*Fushuku hanpō*, "the Dharma for taking food"), including how to sit, how to arrange one's bowls, how to receive food, how to deport oneself while eating (for example, one should not make loud noises), and how to cultivate gratitude while eating. These procedures are still part of Sōtō Zen monastic life today. However, it should be noted that an attitude of care toward food is not limited to the Zen schools. All schools of Buddhism in Japan espouse the idea that people should express gratitude for food they receive. These attitudes are expressed in common Japanese words such as *mottainai* (not to waste food/things) and *itadakimasu* ("I humbly receive [this food]," interpreted within Buddhism as the expression of gratitude for the life one receives from the food and for the work of the people who created the food/meal).[48]

Finally, the idea that cooking can be considered practice has gained particular attention from Western Zen Buddhists, for whom this idea applies to cooking in everyday life and not just the monastery.[49] Dōgen's instructions for the cook circulate as a separate book, which has become very popular in Western-language translations.[50] The great number of cookbooks about "Zen cooking" and *shōjin ryōri* (monastic vegetarian food) written or translated in English and other Western languages attests to interest in cooking as practice.

Conclusion

In the preceding examples, we have seen how Buddhist teachings and goals are supported through a variety of food practices. First, in various contexts, how people eat is often more important than what they eat. Even in East Asia, where there are rules about what one may eat, once these rules are set, attention returns to the "how" of eating. A greater Buddhist ethic underlies these practices, namely that how one behaves and deports oneself is one of the first steps in the cultivation of practice. This insight is fundamental to all forms of Buddhism. Food practices also demonstrate the continuity of religious teaching across lay and monastic communities. Although laypeople do not usually follow the many rules of monastic life, the food practices they participate in serve to teach and continually reinforce Buddhist ideals. The daily giving of food by the laity to monastics in South Asia allows people to constantly practice generosity. In East Asia, attention to food fosters a sense of gratitude to all beings. Finally, as Buddhism has moved into various geographical regions, food has always provided ways for the religion to integrate itself into the multiple cultures it has encountered. In feeding rituals in Tibet and food festivals in Southeast Asia, Buddhist figures, themes, and rituals fuse seamlessly with local traditions. Although such practices may not be aimed at the enlightenment sought by the individual practitioner, these important religious events are opportunities for Buddhism to be fully involved with all kinds of community concerns. Food provides many different ways for Buddhists to practice and live the Dharma.

Notes

1. H. L. Seneviratne, "Food Essence and the Essence of Experience," in *The Eternal Food: Gastronomic Ideas and Experiences of Hindus and Buddhists*, ed. R. S. Khare (Albany: State University of New York Press, 1992), 179–200; 187–88.
2. Buddhists, too, sometimes consume talismans, healing water, or other food/medicinal items used for health. See, for example, Paula Arai, *Bringing Zen Home: The Healing Heart of Japanese Women's Rituals* (Honolulu: University of Hawai'i Press, 2011), 113–20.
3. On the meanings and uses of food in Hindu ritual, see R. S. Khare, "Food with Saints: An Aspect of Hindu Gastrosemantics," in *The Eternal Food*, 27–52; and Manuel Moreno, "*Pañcāmirtam*: God's Washings as Food," in *The Eternal Food*, 147–78.
4. For an example of this kind of extreme view of food, see the story of the Chinese monk Shi Wangming, who eats the flesh of a rotting corpse in order to teach other monks, in John Kieschnick, *The Eminent Monk: Buddhist Ideals in Medieval Chinese Hagiography* (Honolulu: University of Hawai'i Press, 1997), 57–58.
5. Reiko Ohnuma, "Debt to the Mother: A Neglected Aspect of the Founding of the Buddhist Order of Nuns," *Journal of the American Academy of Religion* 74, no. 4 (2006): 861–901. See also Ohnuma's book, *Ties That Bind: Maternal Imagery and Discourse in Indian Buddhism* (Oxford: Oxford University Press, 2012), especially 94–112.
6. The folkloricist Alan Dundes has shown that the indebtedness of the child to the mother for her giving of milk is linked to the valuation of both mothers and cows in Indian society. See his study of Indian social relationships, *Two Tales of Crow and Sparrow: A Freudian Folkloristic Essay on Caste and Untouchablility* (Lanham, MD: Rowman and Littlefield, 1997), especially 98–105.
7. Ohnuma, "Debt to the Mother," 873–74.
8. For example, the origins of the Chinese ghost festival (*yulanpen hui*) lie partly in concerns with repaying the "breast-feeding kindness" of mothers; Alan Cole, *Mothers and Sons in Chinese Buddhism* (Stanford, CA: Stanford University Press, 1998), 82. In Southeast Asia, the remembrance of the milk-debt remains an important part of monastic ordination; Ohnuma, *Ties That Bind*, 171.
9. For the stories of Sujātā and Tapassu and Ballika, see John Strong, *The Experience of Buddhism: Sources and Interpretations* (Belmont, CA: Wadsworth, 2002), 2nd edition, 44–48.
10. On lay-monastic relationships, see Anthony Fiorucci, "Food Fights and Table Manners: Food, Bodies, and Ideology in the *dāna* Encounter of Pāli Buddhism," master's thesis (revised), University of Stockholm, n.d.
11. There are ten types of food (meat) that monastics may not receive: human flesh, elephant, yellow tiger, tiger, leopard, bear, lion, snake, dog, and horse. For a discussion of these categories of food, see Thānissaro Bhikkhu, *The Buddhist Monastic Code I*, "Pācittiya Four: The Food Chapter," at Dhammatalks.org (Talks, Writings, and Translations of Thānisarro Bhikkhu), https://www.dhammatalks.org/vinaya/bmc/Section0019.html.
12. On the three types of pure meat, see John Kieschnick, "Buddhist Vegetarianism in China," in *Of Tripod and Palate: Food, Politics, and Religion in Traditional China*, ed. Roel Sterckx

(New York: Palgrave MacMillan, 2005), 187–89. On Buddhist meat eating in ancient India, see Fiorucci, "Food Fights and Table Manners," 49–60. See also Katherine Ulrich's study of sixth-century dietary polemics among Buddhists, Jains, and Saivites (Hindus), "Food Fights: Buddhist, Hindu, and Jain Dietary Polemics in South India," *History of Religions* 46, no. 3 (2007): 228–61.

13. Fiorucci, "Food Fights and Table Manners," 91–92.
14. *A Collection of Treasures* (*Hōbutsu shū*), attributed to Taira Yasuyori (*Dai Nihon Bukkyō zensho*, ed. Bussho kankō kai, 147: 426), translated by Jacqueline I. Stone, "The Contemplation of Suchness," in *Religions of Japan in Practice*, ed. George J. Tanabe, Jr. (Princeton, NJ: Princeton University Press, 1999), 201.
15. Frances Garrett, Andrew Erlich, Nicholas Field, Barbara Hazelton, and Matthew King, "Narratives of Hospitality and Feeding in Tibetan Ritual," *Journal of the American Academy of Religion* 8, no.1–2 (2013): 493, citing Frances Garrett, "The Alchemy of Accomplishing Medicine (*sman sgrub*): Situating the *Yuthok Heart Essence* Ritual Tradition," *Journal of Indian Philosophy* 37, no. 3 (2009): 210.
16. Garrett et al., "Narratives of Hospitality and Feeding," 498.
17. Garrett et al., "Narratives of Hospitality and Feeding," 502–4.
18. Garrett et al., "Narratives of Hospitality and Feeding," 511.
19. On South Asian ancestor rituals, see Matthew R. Sayers, *Feeding the Dead: Ancestor Worship in Ancient India* (Oxford and New York: Oxford University Press, 2013), and Patrice Ladwig, "Feeding the Dead: Ghosts, Materiality, and Merit in a Lao Buddhist Festival for the Deceased," in *Buddhist Funeral Cultures of Southeast Asia and China*, ed. Paul Williams and Patrice Ladwig (Cambridge: Cambridge University Press, 2012), 119–41.
20. On the creation of the Chinese ghost festival, see Steven Teiser, *The Ghost Festival in Medieval China* (Princeton, NJ: Princeton University Press, 1988), and Cole, *Mothers and Sons in Chinese Buddhism*.
21. Personal communication, August 28, 2019, with thanks to Nasu Eisho for help with collecting this information.
22. On mummification practices in Japan, see Tullio Federico Lobetti, *Ascetic Practices in Japanese Religion* (New York: Routledge, 2014), 130–36.
23. Ruth Gerson, "The Ghost Festival of Dan Sai, Loei Province, Thailand," in *The Art of Rice: Spirit and Sustenance in Asia*, ed. Roy W. Hamilton (Los Angeles: UCLA Fowler Museum of Cultural History, 2003), 184–99. On this festival in the village of Ban Huay Cho, see John S. Strong, *The Legend and Cult of Upagupta: Sanskrit Buddhism in North India and Southeast Asia* (Princeton, NJ: Princeton University Press, 1992), 253–72.
24. Gerson, "The Ghost Festival of Dan Sai," 199.
25. Strong, *The Legend and Cult of Upagupta*, 212–21. In Southeast Asian stories, Upagupta is the son of a fish-maiden and a monk (or sometimes the Buddha himself) and lives in the ocean.
26. Strong, *The Legend and Cult of Upagupta*, 269.
27. Strong, *The Legend and Cult of Upagupta*, 188–202.
28. An English translation of the Vessantara story can be found in Strong, *The Experience of Buddhism*, 23–26.
29. In South Asia, for example, lay practitioners may choose to be vegetarian, but monastics generally stress that it is unnecessary to avoid meat and take a conservative approach to maintaining the Vinaya. See James Stewart, *Vegetarianism and Animal Ethics in Contemporary Buddhism* (London: Routledge, 2016), 120. In Tibet, there is a long tradition

of vegetarianism linked to ideas of monastic rules and the bodhisattva ideals, and in recent years some monasteries have changed to a vegetarian diet. See Geoffrey Barstow, "Monastic Meat: The Question of Meat Eating and Vegetarianism in Tibetan Buddhist Monastic Guidelines (*bca' yig*)," *Religions* 10, no. 4 (2019): 240 (doi:10.3390/rel10040240). See also his book-length study, *Food of Sinful Demons: Meat, Vegetarianism, and the Limits of Buddhism in Tibet* (New York: Columbia University Press, 2017).

30. On vegetarianism in Mahayana texts, see Kieschnick, "Buddhist Vegetarianism in China," 187–93.
31. Kieschnick, "Buddhist Vegetarianism in China," 189–90.
32. Kieschnick, "Buddhist Vegetarianism in China," 191. For the complete list of the lay precepts of the *Fanwangjng*, see Alicia Matsunaga, *The Buddhist Philosophy of Assimilation: The Historical Development of the Honji-Suijaku Theory* (Tokyo: Charles E. Tuttle, 1969), 152–54.
33. Kieschnick, "Buddhist Vegetarianism in China," 195–98.
34. Kieschnick, "Buddhist Vegetarianism in China," 198–201.
35. Show Ying Ruo, "Chinese Buddhist Vegetarian Halls (*Zhaitang*) in Southeast Asia: Their Origins and Historical Implications." Nalanda-Sriwijaya Centre Working Paper No. 28 (July 2018): 1–51. Show's study focuses on lay Buddhist groups called the Great Way of Former Heaven (Xiantian Dadao).
36. Show, "Chinese Buddhist Vegetarian Halls," 19, 38.
37. Show, "Chinese Buddhist Vegetarian Halls," 25.
38. Show, "Chinese Buddhist Vegetarian Halls," 39.
39. On the "meat-eating, wine-drinking" monks, see John Kieschnick, *The Eminent Monk*, 51–63.
40. Kieschnick, *The Eminent Monk*, 59.
41. Richard Jaffe, "The Debate over Meat Eating in Japanese Buddhism," in *Going Forth: Visions of Buddhist Vinaya*, ed. William M. Bodiford (Honolulu: Kuroda Institute, University of Hawai'i Press, 2005), especially 262–73.
42. For Sōtō Zen nuns' attitudes on precepts, see Paula Kane Robinson Arai, *Women Living Zen: Japanese Sōtō Buddhist Nuns* (Oxford and New York: Oxford University Press, 1999), 99, 137–48.
43. On the *otoki* meal, see Jessica Starling, *Guardians of the Buddha's Home: Domestic Religion in Contemporary Jōdo Shinshū* (Honolulu: University of Hawai'i Press), 30–31, 56–58.
44. Yifa, "From the Chinese Vinaya Tradition to Chan Regulations: Continuity and Adaptation," in *Going Forth: Visions of Buddhist Vinaya*, ed. William M. Bodiford (Honolulu: Kuroda Institute, University of Hawai'i Press, 2005), 131.
45. James Benn, *Tea in China: A Religious and Cultural History* (Honolulu: University of Hawai'i Press, 2015), 49.
46. Benn, *Tea in China*, 128–30.
47. For a translation of Dōgen's *Eihei shingi*, see Taigen Dan Leighton and Shohaku Okamura, trans., *Dōgen's Pure Standards for the Zen Community* (Albany: State University of New York Press, 1995).
48. For a study critical of how gratitude is used to justify meat-eating, see Barbara R. Ambros, "*Partaking of Life*: Buddhism, Meat-Eating, and Sacrificial Discourses of Gratitude in Contemporary Japan," *Religions* 10, no. 4 (2019): 279 (doi:10.3390/rel10040279).
49. On the official website of the Sōtō Zen school, the foreign-language part of the site has, under the heading "Practice," an explanation of "Food as Practice," with teachings about "Cooking in Buddhism," an explanation of *ōryōoki* (procedures for monastic meals),

approximately two dozen recipes, and videos about *shōjin ryōri* (https://global.sotozen-net.or.jp/eng/practice/food/index.html). In contrast, the Japanese-language site does not have these links (https://www.sotozen-net.or.jp/).

50. See, for example, the English translation by Thomas Wright, published under two titles: *Refining Your Life: From the Zen Kitchen to Enlightenment* (New York: Weatherhill, 1983) and *How to Cook Your Life: From the Zen Kitchen to Enlightenment* (Boston: Shambala Publications, 2005). Additionally, a translation by Anzan Hoshin and Yasuda Joshu Dainen is available online: https://wwzc.org/dharma-text/tenzo-kyokun-instructions-tenzo.

Further Reading

Barstow, Geoffrey. *Food of Sinful Demons: Meat, Vegetarianism, and the Limits of Buddhism in Tibet*. New York: Columbia University Press, 2017.

Benn, James A. *Tea in China: A Religious and Cultural History*. Honolulu: University of Hawai'i Press, 2015.

Garrett, Frances, Andrew Erlich, Nicholas Field, Barbara Hazelton, and Matthew King. "Narratives of Hospitality and Feeding in Tibetan Ritual." *Journal of the American Academy of Religion* 81, no. 2 (2013): 491–515.

Hamilton, Roy, ed. *The Art of Rice: Spirit and Sustenance in Asia*. Los Angeles: UCLA Fowler Museum of Cultural History, 2003.

Jaffe, Richard. "The Debate over Meat Eating in Japanese Buddhism." In *Going Forth: Visions of Buddhist Vinaya*, ed. William M. Bodiford. Kuroda Institute Studies in East Asian Buddhism 18. Honolulu: University of Hawai'i Press, 2005, 255–75.

Khare, R.S., ed. *The Eternal Food: Gastronomic Ideas and Experiences of Hindus and Buddhists*. Albany: State University of New York Press, 1992.

Kieschnick, John. "Buddhist Vegetarianism in China." In *Of Tripod and Palate: Food, Politics, and Religion in Traditional China*, ed. Roel Sterckx. New York: Palgrave Macmillan, 2005, 186–212.

Ladwig, Patrice. "Feeding the Dead: Ghosts, Materiality, and Merit in a Lao Buddhist Festival for the Deceased." In *Buddhist Funeral Cultures of Southeast Asia and China*, ed. Paul Williams and Patrice Ladwig (Cambridge: Cambridge University Press, 2012, 119–41.

Sayers, Matthew R. *Feeding the Dead: Ancestor Worship in Ancient India*. Oxford and New York: Oxford University Press, 2013.

Show, Ying Ruo. "Chinese Buddhist Vegetarian Halls (*Zhaitang*) in Southeast Asia: Their Origins and Historical Implications." Nalanda-Sriwijaya Centre Working Paper No. 28 (July 2018): 1–51.

Sterckx, Roel, ed., *Of Tripod and Palate: Food, Politics, and Religion in Traditional China*. New York: Palgrave MacMillan, 2005.

Stewart, James. *Vegetarianism and Animal Ethics in Contemporary Buddhism*. London: Routledge, 2016.

Ulrich, Katherine E. "Food Fights: Buddhist, Hindu, and Jain Dietary Polemics in South India." *History of Religions* 46, no. 3 (2007): 228–61.

PART VII

MODERNITIES AND EMERGENT FORMS OF PRACTICE

For more than two millennia, the emergence and expansion of Asian Buddhist traditions have been characterized by movement across cultural and geographical boundaries, exemplified by the role of the Silk Road in facilitating the broad dissemination of Buddhist teachings, objects, and practices across a wide diversity of Asian linguistic and cultural communities. In this sense, Buddhist traditions have long been characterized by dynamics of adaptation and innovation as new communities have taken up Buddhist ideas and practices in response to local circumstances. Our focus on modernities in this section directs attention to some of the distinctive ways that Buddhist practice traditions have been shaped, beginning in the nineteenth century, by increased engagement with cultural and social dynamics centered in Europe and North America, including the emergence of a Euro-American discipline of Buddhist studies and the impacts of European colonialism, complemented more recently by the increasingly widespread establishment of diverse Buddhist practice traditions throughout Europe and North America.

The eight chapters in this section explore a number of important sites within which new forms of Buddhist practice are currently emerging, shaped by modes of Western modernity such as nationalism (often linked to ideals of secularity), capitalism, and scientific rationality. Thomas Borchert's Chapter 30 explores tensions between religious and political identities as Buddhist monks negotiate the demands of citizenship within modern Asian nation-states. Susan Darlington's Chapter 31, focused on tree ordination in Thailand, explores the role of Buddhist ritual in authorizing innovative practices committed to modern ideals of environmental sustainability. The authors of the next two chapters explore emerging dynamics within two new communities of Dharma practice in the United States. Drawing upon the perspectives of six queer-of-color practitioners, Jasmine Syedullah in Chapter 32 traces the emergence of a liberative Dharma of intersectionality within the practices of Radical Dharma centers. Tina Jitsujo Gauthier's Chapter 33 explores the development of new US Buddhist chaplaincy programs designed to train Dharma-based chaplains who are equipped to serve in a variety of settings, notably hospitals, which have been long dominated by Christian values and assumptions. In Chapter 34, Elizabeth Harris shifts away from the United States to examine new possibilities for dialogue and collaboration between Buddhists and non-Buddhists around the world, framed within the history of Christian missions and European imperialism. Louise Connelly's Chapter 35 explores possibilities for new forms of virtual Buddhist practice enabled by internet technology as she explores the challenges that virtuality poses for authentic Buddhist practice. In Chapter 36, John Dunne explores the history, critiques, and challenges of scientific research on Buddhist meditation practices. Finally, in Chapter 37, Erik Braun's study of the emergence of modern Western mindfulness practice explores its connections with a diversity of Asian and Euro-American sources of authority. Taken together, these chapters highlight the dynamic and emergent character of contemporary Buddhist practices, increasingly taking shape in local communities deeply influenced by complex translocal forms of communication.

CHAPTER 30

NATION-STATE AND MONASTIC IDENTITY

THOMAS BORCHERT

EVERY day throughout Thailand, at 8:00 a.m. and 6:00 p.m., the national anthem plays. In villages, it will play across a loudspeaker; on school grounds and campuses and in train stations, it blares across PA systems. The anthem, which dates to the late 1930s, a period when the monarchy was at an ebb in authority and the country's name changed from Siam to Thailand, talks about the unity and independence of the Thais, about their sovereignty and ownership of Thailand, and their willingness to shed their blood for the nation. The language is probably familiar to most Thais, though one can rarely understand the words of the anthem as they echo across campuses and stations. Indeed, most of the time, the versions played are instrumental only. Most Thais stand for the anthem, or they stop walking, standing still as the music plays. In my observation, there is very little emotion expressed. They do not hold their hands over their hearts; instead they pause, rushing off when it ends—except for Thai monks. Thai monks do not stand for the anthem. Up until a few years ago, the main railroad station in Bangkok, Hualomphong, had a section of seats in the main hall reserved for monks waiting for their trains.[1] This gave monks a modicum of privacy, and meant that they would not come in physical contact with women. When the anthem played at the station, everyone stood, except the group of monks in the center. I asked several monks about this, and they told me that they did not have to stand when the national anthem played. They *could*, but they did not have to. It is perhaps telling that in recent years, the section reserved for monks moved into a back hallway. This gave the monks more privacy, but it also removed from sight the overt conflict that the national anthem provided. The exemption from standing embodies a monastic exemption within Thailand that embodies and encapsulates a tension between being a monastic and a citizen.

This chapter begins with a straightforward observation: Buddhist monastics in the contemporary world embody two distinct identities, a religious and a national one. While there are men and women such as Tibetan monks and nuns in India who are long-term refugees and thus in some sense stateless, the vast majority of monks and nuns are citizens of a particular nation-state. Thus, when they travel from their home, they are subject to rules and regulations that govern the citizens of the state to which they belong. However, because the Buddhist world is decentralized along national lines and does not have a single governing institution (such as the Vatican within the Catholic Church), the rules that govern monastics are specific to each country. For example, Thai monks have identity cards that mark their ordination and are required to apply for passports that only monks carry. Japanese priests and monastics, on the other hand, do not. Meanwhile, Chinese monks and nuns have both ordination and national identification cards. Moreover, their ability to receive a passport may be affected by their status as a monastic, but it is just as likely to be affected by whether they are a member of a minority group.

In thinking about Buddhist practices, there is perhaps a tendency to ignore practices of the nation-state. In part, this is because we live in a world that tends to be unselfconsciously secularist, one in which, in particular, "proper" forms of Buddhism are differentiated from the public or political spheres.[2] This has been exacerbated by a tendency within the wider academic study of religion, which is sometimes still influenced by a crude Weberianism that sees Buddhism as focused on other-worldly matters, or the widespread (and problematic) view that Buddhism is at its core a peaceful religion. Buddhism, with its emphasis on meditation and mindfulness, would seem to be fundamentally differentiated, even alienated, from other parts of society and the politics of the nation-state. Yet as the movements—inspired by monks—against Muslims in Myanmar and Sri Lanka in the 2010s show, monastics (and by extension other Buddhists) are shaped by nationalism no less than other citizens of a given country.

This chapter suggests that national and Buddhist identities are both totalizing forms that have varied impacts on the lives and practices of Buddhist monastics. In one way, these identities may be in tension with one another. While monastics are inevitably within the world, the rhetorical stance (and sometimes literal act) of having left the world of "householders" can extend to the realm of politics and the nation-state. Some monks and nuns view their religious vocation as specifically apolitical, and thus nationalism imposes on them undue burdens. On the other hand, Buddhist institutions have always been enmeshed in political ones, and in the current era of nation-states, monastics are citizens, subject to citizenship education before and after ordination, as well as to specific legal regimes that are secular, ecclesiastical, and Vinaya-based. Thus there is a tension for monks and nuns between their religious and national identities. When the Dharma and the nation work in tandem, national ideals can give an affective force to Buddhist practices that they might not otherwise have. The goals of religion and nation are not always in conflict, but the potential is there.

Orienting Terms

Thinking about the relationship between monastic identity and citizenship requires explaining several parallel and entwined processes in the late nineteenth and early twentieth centuries. The first is the formation of the nation-states of Asia. While some of the countries of Asia have a substantial history as political entities, the region was transformed by the experience of European colonialism. Over the course of two centuries, what have become nation-states emerged from conditions of colonialism or semi-colonialism. This is plain enough, perhaps, but what is important to highlight is that the European forms of governance and categories of governance were both imposed upon and actively adapted by the polities of Asia in their effort to civilize and modernize and to resist colonialism (whether from an active colonized state such as India or from a semi-colonial status, such as Japan, Thailand, and China). The legacies of colonialism are profound, and scholars such as Partha Chatterjee have noted how postcolonial states resemble their colonial precursors.[3] Some of this is for matters of convenience (i.e., because institutions already existed), while some of it is also the result of colonial interests in determining what the postcolonial political order might look like. Reid has described this process in alchemical terms, as the transmutation of the "base-metal of empire" into the "gold of nationhood."[4]

One of the essential parts of this transmutation was the development of the categories of religion and Buddhism. Scholars have long understood that "religion" is not a native category to the region, even though a number of places had analogous categories to describe the phenomenon that we now call religion, and the past two decades have seen substantial work on the process by which this non-native term became naturalized in the newly developing nation-states.[5] What begins as a category in the context of treaties (Japan in the 1850s), and agreements to allow the free exercise of local religion under British colonialism (Burma and Sri Lanka in the early nineteenth century), ultimately is transformed into a category that colonial and national states use as a tool for the construction of a modern and civilized populace.[6] Mandair and Dressler have referred to this as "religion-making from above," a process where the state (colonial, national, democratic) establishes what it deems to be proper forms of religiosity. "Religion-making from below" is the process whereby non-state actors utilize the categories for religion and non-religion to accept, resist, or ignore the state's desires for creating the people.[7] What Mandair and Dressler, among others,[8] are pointing to is a dynamic process of the utilization of religion and related categories (like superstition, cults, secularity) by state and non-state, local and foreign actors, that is taking place in asymmetric, power-laden fields. One effect of this is that actors can change aspects of their practice to accord with the rules from above. For example, practices that are seen as legitimate (and therefore "religion") might be emphasized to make them more legible to the state. Alternatively, they might hide proscribed ("superstitious") practices. Despite this and the other effects of the asymmetric field of religious practice, religion-making from below can provide a resource for the destabilization of the nation-state.[9] Indeed, it is important to pay attention to where and how Asian actors engage with these categories, even when their agency is limited and constrained by the colonial state.[10]

Buddhism has a particular history within this process. In the early nineteenth century, "Buddhism," as we now understand it, did not exist. Buddhist sanghas had specific histories and relationships to the political systems of the polities where they existed (such as the use of Buddhist sects by the Tokugawa regime to maintain control of the population, or the way that the office of the Dalai Lama maintained political power in parts of Tibet), and there were transnational links between specific sanghas (such as the Theravada sanghas of Sri Lanka and mainland Southeast Asia). However, the idea of a single universal religion that is the descendant of the teachings of the Buddha, that the lamas and tulkus of Tibet, Mongolia, and Siberia share something important with the monks of Sri Lanka or the priests, nuns, and monks of Japan, only emerged in the course of the nineteenth century. While this idea relied on European notions of the centrality of texts as the essence of religion,[11] it was convincing to some state and non-state actors in Asia, and many Asian Buddhists were also nationalists. A unified notion of Buddhism became part of Asian efforts to build modern states, to resist colonialism, and to build international alliances in the Cold War. Moreover, throughout this process, the aspects of Buddhism that were most publicly a part of these linkages and movements were those that resembled a belief system, shorn of gods and superstition, a philosophy that resembled certain aspects of Protestant forms of Christianity. My point is not that this represented the sum total of what Buddhism was, or that Buddhism was specifically important to anti-colonialism, but that in the course of the nineteenth century, the ideas that (1) the nation-state was the ideal sovereign form, (2) "religion" is an important part of the culture group at the heart of a nation (and that has control of a nation-state), and (3) Buddhism is a transnational, universal religion, were all emerging simultaneously, entangled with one another. While the effects of this varied across the emerging nation-states of Asia, Buddhism, both as a philosophy and as an institutional structure, became a resource that Asians could use to foster the strength and independence of their nations.

For the purposes of this chapter, it is important to highlight that nation-states are political projects that are concerned with manufacturing a sense of unity and belonging in the populace. This work relies on practices of the nation that naturalize the feeling of belonging and fictive-kinship. By the late nineteenth century, "the nation form,"[12] had been transplanted into Asia, comprising technologies and practices of governance seen as necessary for a people or region to emerge into the "modern" world, both in competition with European powers (or at least to resist colonialism) and to attain their status as a legitimate nation among other nations. This meant that communities of people throughout Asian nation-states were subject to significant projects to remake them into a group that saw itself as a coherent nation. These projects varied across Buddhist (and non-Buddhist) Asia, but were enacted by national elites, as well as by states. They included the development of educational systems that naturalized (or sought to naturalize) an identification with the nation, and the effort to make or remake the category of religion so that it would be in line with European and American standards, as well as bringing Buddhism in line with the category of religion. We should understand that this project, one of making the people, as one that remains incomplete, but that has also entailed significant conceptual, and occasionally literal, violence.[13]

Part of this project entails understanding the formal status of Buddhism within the formation of the nation, as well as how monastics might be conceived as part of the

People (i.e., the national community). Again, conditions have varied across Asia (they have also varied over time within Asian nation-states), but it is possible to see several different ways that Buddhism has been recognized within the nation. On one side, there are nation-states where no particular religion is recognized within constitutions or other foundational documents, but where citizens are guaranteed the freedom to believe in whatever religion they choose, such as China or Japan.[14] In these countries, the status of being a monk or nun does not give one an exceptional status. It is effectively a job; a specific kind of a job, but there are few if any special dispensations as a result of it. On the other side are several of the Theravada countries of mainland Southeast Asia and Sri Lanka, as well as Bhutan, in which Buddhism is understood to have a special status within the nation. In Myanmar, the current constitution recognizes the "special position of Buddhism as the faith professed by the great majority of the citizens of the Union."[15] The situation is similar in Thailand, where constitutional documents have sought to privilege Buddhism without making it the official religion of the nation. In the 2017 constitution, the state is required to support and protect other religions in addition to Buddhism, but it should "promote and support education and dissemination of dharmic principles of Theravada Buddhism."[16] Moreover, it has "measures and mechanisms to prevent Buddhism from being undermined in any form."[17] It becomes clear that Buddhism plays different roles in the conceptions of the nation-state across Asia, ranging from playing a minimal role within the notion of the national community to being its core.

Just as the role of Buddhism in nationalist discourses varies, so do the conditions of individual monastics as citizens. As a concept, citizenship points to the relationship between an individual and the wider community, and scholars have discussed a variety of citizenships. These include political forms of citizenship, which highlight the relationship between the individual and the state, delineating her political rights in society, such as the right to the vote or that of free speech; social citizenship, denoting a right to access socioeconomic benefits in society; and cultural citizenship, the sense of belonging to a particular community, as felt by the individual and recognized by others.[18] While some scholars have resisted the expansion of the idea of citizenship beyond the formal discussion of rights,[19] notions of citizenship, both formal and informal, have become well established in Asian nation-states over the past century. This is similar to how other governing categories of modernity have become naturalized, but the strength and nature of these notions, as well as the rights that inhere to one's status as a citizen, are unevenly distributed. Throughout Asian nations, Buddhists are in majorities, pluralities, and minorities, and their rights as citizens, political or socioeconomic, vary as a result.[20] Moreover, ordination is treated unevenly within notions of citizenship: sometimes there are monastic exceptions, and sometimes monastics are no different from other citizens.[21]

While developing the national community of the nation is in part about transforming the identity of the people and so requires the development of knowledge about the nation, it also requires a series of practices to naturalize this identity. Thus, for example, the national anthem and the physical response to it is a particular example of the national community being formed (or reinforced) twice a day in Thailand. This chapter considers two types of acts where monastic identity and citizenship work on one another. First, it considers practices that are normally seen to be Buddhist or "religious" and thus not political. For monastics, these might include practices such as monastic education, giving Dharma talks, or performing rituals. Second, it considers rites of the nation that are ostensibly at least the provenance of all citizens. These would include questions of political participation, such as voting or holding political office, or participating in the military.[22] The following discussion highlights some of the ways that these practices manifest in different Asian nation-states from the end of the nineteenth century.

This chapter primarily focuses on Buddhists who have been ordained as a monk or a nun. While the distinction between lay and ordained is deeply embedded in the logic of the religion[23] and is emphasized through dress and bodily practices in many Buddhist contexts, relationships between lay and monastic vary across the Buddhist world. There are, moreover, a number of intermediary figures between fully ordained monastics who follow all of the precepts in the Vinaya and lay followers who might follow the *pañca sīla*. These include female renunciants such as the *dasasilmatava* of Sri Lanka who undertake ten precepts, as well as former monks in northern Thailand or southwest China who are lay, but have an important role in the local sangha. Ordained are not more important to Buddhist communities than laity. However, because monastics, broadly defined, might be subject to different rules (secular and religious) than the non-ordained, they are worth considering directly as an object of national imagination.[24]

Buddhist Practices in Service to (or against) the Nation

The "proper" role of monastics has long been a source of negotiation within monastic communities. In addition to the Weberian notion that Buddhist monastics are (or should be) oriented toward "other-worldly" goals such as nirvana, there are also internal dynamics that highlight the distance between monastics and politics. Some of this is rhetorical: men and women who ordain as monks or nuns go "from home into homelessness" (Pali: *pabbajjā*). Some of this is practical: monastics are not "householders," and they do not work for a living in a conventional sense, even if most monastics engage in work that preserves the teachings of the Buddha. At the same time, they have a connection to kings and states, and they rely on states as well as laypeople for support. Individual monks and nuns engage with society in their own ways, and some remain "outside" society. Yet even though the rhetoric of socially validated forms of Buddhism suggest that good monks and nuns should not be involved with politics, monastic life has often been entangled with politics in ways that are seen as legitimate.

Perhaps the most important way that we see Buddhist practices pulled into service of the nation is in the realm of education. From the end of the nineteenth century, Buddhist education became tied up with the development of the nation-state. Sometimes this was done by appropriating temple lands to develop public schools, visible in both Meiji-era Japan and Thailand.[25] Systems of monastic education were also realigned to the perceived needs of the nation by both states and monastic institutions. In Thailand, for example, from the start of the twentieth century, the Thai state based in Bangkok sought to nationalize the sangha as part of the process of turning a "galactic polity" into a nation-state. The Sangha Act of 1902 put the sangha of the entire country into the orbit of the sangha authorities in Bangkok. This process was accompanied by the process of tying appointment to offices in the sangha hierarchy to achievement in the system of monastic education that was being created in the first decades of the twentieth century.[26] Domesticating regional sanghas was a complicated process that required monks to be trained to think nationally rather than regionally or within their lineage. In Northern Thailand, for example, the famous monk Khrūbā Srivichai was placed under house arrest several times for resisting the authority of the Bangkok authorities and continuing to ordain novices, even though he did not have authorization from Bangkok.[27] In other words, developing monastic education that brought regional sanghas into the ambit of the nation-state was not an immediate process, but rather one that entailed negotiation, coercion, and accommodation.[28]

States have forged citizenship education with monastic education in different ways. Sometimes this has been through an indirect linkage, as was the case in Thailand. The Thai sangha is nationally organized (and administered through the Sangha Act), but the curriculum of monastic education is generally limited to Buddhism and Pali. In China, the curricula of monastic institutes have explicitly emphasized "patriotism" (*aiguo zhuyi*). The definition of patriotism has changed somewhat between that espoused by the Nationalists and that of the Communist Party in the past several decades, as has the degree to which monastic colleges are required to follow it. However, in each case, the idea of love for the nation has been a core part of the curriculum.[29]

While states have utilized monastic education to tie the vocations of monks and nuns to the nation-state, monastics have also actively engaged in this process. In the early decades of the twentieth century, the Chinese monk Taixu developed a monastic education system that would create modern monks. Citizenship education was central to this, and the schools became venues where student-nuns and student-monks could debate the meaning of citizenship.[30] This idea, that the training of monastics was itself essential to the development of a healthy nation, was not limited to China, but was articulated and developed in Sri Lanka, particularly at Vidyodaya Pirivena.[31]

Sermons, or dharma talks, are another monastic practice that can be shaped and transformed by nationalism and related forms of politics. Generally speaking, sermons occur in the context of a ritual of some sort (funeral, formal merit-making ceremony, or blessing) or a festival. Sermons vary significantly, and their content may do little more than explicate the meaning of a word or retell a *jataka* story. However, the context of the retelling may have deeply political circumstances. Brac de la Perrière discusses a monk in Myanmar who believed that Buddhism had suffered in its administration by the Burmese *junta*. He could not criticize the military directly, so he preached about the law of the Buddha, "in the religious idiom." In doing so, however, he indirectly challenged the military government.[32] Monastics also preach in support of the nation-state. Kent discusses sermons that took place in the context of rituals sponsored by the military in Sri Lanka in the early years of this century. The language of the sermons themselves was not necessarily exceptional: they included discussions of the qualities of the sangha, the qualities of the Buddha and the protective powers of his teachings, even in his absence. The rituals, however, were sponsored by the military and the sermons were given to soldiers to encourage them to protect the Dharma in the context of the civil war with the Liberation Tigers of Tamil Eelam (LTTE). In one of these, a lamp-lighting ceremony, 84,000 lamps were arranged with signs linking them to specific regiments, and in the shape of the island of Sri Lanka, with an eight-spoked Dharma wheel and a Sinhala lion.[33] Like the fusion of the goddess Bharat Mata and the map of India that has merged the cartographic and the sacred,[34] the lamps in this ritual fuse Buddhism and the imagination of the nation of Sri Lanka through the map. As Kent points out, the sermon, "transfer[ed] the words of the Buddha into the army's flag . . . to inspire soldiers to follow the example of defenders of Buddhism in the past."[35]

Buddhist practices have a certain ambiguity embedded into them. The actions of monastics may be explicitly and specifically "religious" or "Buddhist," but contexts may enable a nationalist meaning. Such flexibility of interpretation is visible in not only sermons and the education of monastics, but also other acts, such as the alms round (i.e., the Saffron Revolution in Myanmar, when monks "turned" over the alms bowls, to protest the military government raising oil prices);[36] annual ritual circumambulations in Lhasa, which precipitated clashes between Tibetan monks and the police;[37] or conferences and festivals.[38] As should be clear, there is not a single direction or meaning of these actions; some are in support of the nation as it is conceptualized by the government, some are against the state, and some are not against the state per se, but aim to move it in a different direction. The larger point is that Buddhist practices are not immune from becoming framed in nationalist ways.

Rites of National Belonging: Political Participation and Military Service

The flip side of Buddhist practices becoming fused with nationalist meaning is when monastics engage in activities that are more commonly associated with non-religious and non-ordained citizens. Debates over the appropriateness of certain types of practices for monks vary across Asia, both from inside and outside of sanghas. As is the case with other aspects of this chapter, standards, attention to the Vinaya, and the stakeholders that shape the conversation vary significantly around Asia. For example, in Thailand, there is a Supreme Sangha Council that has made numerous resolutions affirming that Thai monks should not participate in political activities by endorsing a candidate, for example.[39] Despite these kinds of injunctions, monastics do take part in military endeavors and political activities, particularly when they are framed in nationalist terms.

Military Service and Chaplaincy

There would seem to be a fundamental conflict between being an ordained Buddhist monastic and a soldier, not least because soldiers are trained to take the life of another. Yet at various moments, the lines between being a monk or nun and a soldier can become blurred, particularly when there is a threat to the national community. In the mid-twentieth century, Chinese monks and nuns faced significant challenges in trying to address the threat that the Japanese military posed to the survival of the Republic of China. While other citizens of the Republic of China had relatively straightforward (if futile) paths to resistance, monastics "somehow had to reconcile their constitutional duty of preparing for killing with their religious commitment of non-killing."[40] Many of the monastics studying in the new monastic schools, discussed earlier, that had been reformulated by Taixu to create modern monks that would serve society, saw that regardless of the complexity of their position, they had to fulfill their responsibilities to their motherland as well. As one declared, "We members of the sangha are also citizens of the nation. At this time when the mission of defending the nation against foreign invasion has been thrust upon us, we cannot refuse to fulfill our sacred duty to protect our country."[41] For other monastics, this was perhaps less about the way that the nation's peril superseded that of religious responsibilities, and more a concern that the persistence of Buddhism relied on the survival of China.[42] Yu highlights that while most monks and nuns agreed that they had a responsibility to the nation, they did not all agree on exactly how to fulfill it. Monks and novices in Buddhist institutes did undergo military training, sometimes willingly, and sometimes because the government required them to do so. Ultimately, though, the monastics who did not disrobe sought alternative ways to participate in the war effort: performing rites for the nation, gathering donations to give to soldiers, and participating in relief work and as ambulance drivers.[43]

It is this latter example that points to one of the ways that some monks in particular have served the nation-state most directly: as chaplains. Buddhist military chaplains have been present in Asia for much of the past century, with the first chaplains being a part of the Meiji government's campaigns in Asia in the late nineteenth century.[44] These early chaplains engaged in practices that would have been normal for Buddhist clerics, such as performing funeral rites. Some of them also sought a wider purview, proposing roles that resembled the military chaplaincies common in Europe. These included a "flag rite" in which the chaplains would bless a regiment, perform a rite to strengthen the spirits of the men, and a rite to pray for the victory of the army as a whole.[45]

If citizenship and monasticism are identities in tension, leaving monastics caught between two worlds, chaplains perhaps occupy an additional level of betweenness. They differ from monks like those who gave sermons to the soldiers in Sri Lanka, discussed previously, in that they are fully members of the military and also members of a given order. Vladimir Tikhonov speaks about Buddhist chaplains in the Korean military belonging to a "borderline zone of sorts": they are uniformed officers, but also belong to a special military division of the Chogye order. They are fully ordained monks, but only wear their robes when performing religious ceremonies.[46] Chaplains in the Thai military have a slightly different configuration. They are not monks, but they are required to be former monks, and they have to have passed the ninth level Pali exams that are the highest in Thailand's monastic education system. The rules that they are to follow also highlight their in-between state. Like laymen, they are to follow the five precepts, but they are also responsible for following the ethical frameworks described in other texts that are normally not relevant to lay men or lay women. They are to hold to sexual propriety by having one wife, and they cannot carry weapons. Significantly, they are also not to be a member of a political party, such that, like monks, they are "in the center" and "above politics."[47]

Not all Asian nation-states have Buddhist chaplains,[48] but Buddhist chaplaincy seems to be an institution that has developed to address some of the tension between the demands of the nation-state and being a monastic. Nation-states require the loyalty and service of their citizens (and the relationship is often spoken of in kinship terms). Buddhism has a long history of engaging in rites that are protective of the nation, but there are also Vinaya rules that limit monastic engagement with soldiers. These are merely *pacittaya*, offenses requiring confession, but they are nonetheless significant. Militaries have also found that soldiers require solace, but because of these limits, monks may find it difficult to comfort or aid soldiers.[49] In other words, the needs of the national community call into being a status or institution that is between soldier and monastic.

Political Participation

Among the most important rights and responsibility of citizens of nation-states is their capacity to participate as a political actor. This capacity varies, depending on whether or not the nation-state in question is a liberal democracy, but in the modern world, sovereignty generally rests in the people, regardless of whether the populace has much say in the matter. This is the case even in places like Thailand, where the link between the military and the palace and the use of *lèse-majesté* laws to protect the king have restricted criticism of both the monarchy and religious authorities,[50] or China, where the Communist Party asserts its leadership of the people. The capacity of people to act as independent actors is constrained, but in most Buddhist nation-states, even the authoritarian ones, the populace has the capacity to participate in matters of governance through holding political office, through participating in the government or lobbying it, and through the right to vote.

The capacity of monastics to take part in these rites of citizenship is uneven and is partly an effect of the legal status of monastics. In East Asia, where citizens in general are enfranchised (Japan, Taiwan, South Korea), monastics can also vote. In these places, the status of monastics as such is effectively invisible to the state. In a formal sense, Buddhist monastics are no different than other citizens. In Southeast Asia the situation is more complicated; the opportunities for monks and female renunciants such as the *mae chi* of Thailand or the *dasa sil mat* of Sri Lanka vary significantly. Monastics in Cambodia and Sri Lanka have the right to vote and there is even a political party primarily comprising monks in Sri Lanka, the *Jatika Hela Urumaya*. In Thailand, Myanmar, and Bhutan, monks are disenfranchised. In Thailand, one of the consistent aspects of the many constitutions since 1932 is that they have all prevented monks from voting in elections.[51] It is worth noting that not all monks agree with this disenfranchisement and argue that their rights as citizens are being abrogated.[52]

Other types of political participation can also be complicated in modern political systems for monastics. Even if Buddhism is never not political, the capacity of individual monks and nuns to speak openly about political matters is constrained. Monastics who feel that they should be outside of politics may constrain their speech or political participation; alternatively, their actions may be constrained by non-monastics through gossip and rumor. Richard Madsen notes that Hsing Yun, the founder of Fo Guang Shan Temple in Taiwan, has been referred to as a "political monk" because of his tendency to endorse certain candidates and engage informally with elections and other aspects of the political system in Taiwan.[53] For Hsing Yun, this was "not a laudatory term," but in other contexts preaching or talking about political matters could and can get a monk or nun arrested. In 1920s Burma, when the colonial state was concerned about the actions of the monks U Ottama and U Wissara, they "categorized them as 'political monks' and declared that political activism was in contravention of the Vinaya."[54] Part of what this has meant is that monks and nuns walk a fine line between their speech on politics and their status as monastics. When they do speak out on political matters, their language is most often couched in terms of the protection of the Buddha's dispensation. Monks and nuns can act politically and can participate as citizens in the life of the nation-state, but these acts are constrained to varying degrees by their coequal status as monastics.

Concluding Thoughts

In several recent essays, Ian Harris has analyzed how sanghas and states have interacted, showing that they have had a range of interactions across Buddhist history. These interactions have ranged from cases where the state had a singular authority over the sangha, to the reverse position when the sangha controlled (or indeed was) the state.[55] Sangha-state interactions thus should be seen on a continuum, not as constant. Schonthal and Walton remind us that Buddhist nationalism is not itself in fact a singular phenomenon, but rather the effect of a variety of contingent factors.[56] The contingencies can multiply as we consider practices of Buddhist monastics and their status as citizens. Throughout Asia we can see variations in the status of monks and nuns vis-à-vis the nation-state, the place of Buddhism in the imagination and legal formulation of the nation-state, and the ability of nuns and monks to act as citizens. Moreover, the contexts in which practices take place vary significantly. A simple sermon in one place can be read and heard like a nationalist screed in another.

In the era of nation-states, Buddhist monastics are troubled by split loyalties, pulled by their responsibility to their religion and to their national home. Conditions range from cases where this remains a simple tension to those that entail a terrible split in the lives of individual monastics, but it is in any case a division with which they are forced to contend. This tension is visible in the words of a Chinese monk in 1935, faced with the problem of how to respond to the challenge brought by the war with Japan: "The citizens of the country are duty-bound to love their nation, and they must perform this duty everyday. . . . One cannot be qualified as the citizen of a nation unless one loves the nation; otherwise one loses one's citizenship. Although I am a member of the sangha and a follower of the Buddha, I am always a citizen of China. The love of country and concern for people's welfare are constantly cherished in my heart."[57] Nationalism and becoming a monk or a nun both demand a full commitment from a person, which means that the potential for conflict will remain present in their lives. However, by examining Buddhist practices and those of the nation, we see that monastic citizens also often find ways to limit the tension between these two identities.

Notes

1. Thailand has female monastics who take eight or ten precepts. They do not normally sit in the areas reserved for monks, and their status is ambiguous. As is the case throughout the Theravada world, the reintroduction of a lineage of fully ordained nuns is contested, and beyond the scope of this chapter to discuss. In general in this chapter, monastics refers to both male and female ordained.
2. José Casanova, *Public Religions in the Modern World* (Chicago: University of Chicago Press, 1994).
3. Partha Chatterhee, *The Nation and Its Fragments: Colonial and Postcolonial Histories* (Princeton, NJ: Princeton University Press, 1993).
4. Anthony Reid, *Imperial Alchemy: Nationalism and Political Identity in Southeast Asia* (Cambridge: Cambridge University Press, 2010), 2.
5. See, e.g.: for Japan, Jason Ananda Josephson, *The Invention of Religion in Japan* (Chicago: University of Chicago Press, 2012); and Jolyon Baraka Thomas, *Faking Liberties: Religious Freedom in American-Occupied Japan* (Chicago: University of Chicago Press, 2019); for China, Rebecca Nedostup, *Superstitious Regimes: Religion and the Politics of Chinese Modernity* (Cambridge, MA: Harvard University Asia Center for China, 2009); for Thailand, Thongchai Winichakul "Buddhist Apologetics and a Genealogy of Comparative Religion in Siam," *Numen* 62 (2015), 76-99; for Burma, Alicia Turner, *Saving Buddhism: The Impermanence of Religion in Colonial Burma* (Honolulu: University of Hawai'i Press, 2014).
6. In addition to the citations in note 5, see Peter Gottschalk, *Religion, Science and Empire: Classifying Hinduism and Islam in Colonial India* (New York: Oxford University Press, 2013), on the impact of categories of "religion" in census and other technologies of government.

7. Arvind-Pal S. Mandair and Markus Dressler, "Introduction: Modernity, Religion-Making, and the Post-Secular," in *Secularism and Religion-Making*, ed. Markus Dressler and Arvind-Pal S. Mandair (Oxford: Oxford University Press, 2011), 20–22.
8. See Thomas, *Faking Liberties*; and Elizabeth Shakman Hurd, *Beyond Religious Freedom: The New Global Politics of Religion* (Princeton, NJ: Princeton University Press, 2015).
9. Bruce Lincoln, *Holy Terrors: Thinking about Religion after September 11* (Chicago: University of Chicago Press, 2003), 62–63.
10. Gottschalk, *Religion, Science*, 32.
11. Tomoko Masuzawa, *The Invention of World Religions: or, How European Universalism Was Preserved in the Language of Pluralism* (Chicago: University of Chicago Press, 2005), 126.
12. The ideal-typical nation-state included a national community whose sense of belonging was built on religion, language, or other forms of culture, that was governed by a state, whose sovereignty matched the territory occupied by the national community. The historical reality has rarely coincided with this ideal type, leading to destabilization discussed in Lincoln, *Holy Terrors*.
13. Paul Christopher Johnson, Pamela E. Klassen, and Winnifred Fallers Sullivan, *Ekklesia: Three Inquiries in Church and State* (Chicago: University of Chicago Press, 2018).
14. Most constitutions guarantee freedom of religion, but the degree to which this is framed in terms of belief or practice varies. The Chinese constitution, e.g., guarantees freedom of religious belief only, with practice subject to regulation.
15. Tomas Larsson, "Buddha or the Ballot: the Buddhist Exception to Universal Suffrage in Contemporary Asia," in *Buddhism and the Political Process*, ed. Hiroko Kawanami (Basingstoke, UK: Palgrave Macmillan, 2016), 79–80.
16. Thailand's Constitution of 2017, available at Constituteproject.org, accessed October 20, 2018, article 67.
17. Thailand's Constitution of 2017, available at Constituteproject.org, accessed October 20, 2018, article 67.
18. Vanessa L. Fong and Rachel Murphey, eds, *Chinese Citizenship: Views from the Margins* (New York: Routledge, 2006), 1–2.
19. Helen Irving, "Citizenship, Statehood, and Allegiance," in *Managing Diversity: Practices of Citizenship*, ed. Nicholas Brown and Linda Cardinal (Ottawa: University of Ottawa Press, 2007), 38.
20. See, e.g., Duncan McCargo, "Informal Citizens: Graduated Citizenship in Southern Thailand." *Ethnic and Racial Studies* 34, no. 5 (2011), 833-849, describes how being Buddhist (or not) affects notions of citizenship in Thailand.
21. Thomas Borchert, "On Being a Monk and a Citizen in Thailand and China," in *Buddhism and the Political Process*, ed. Hiroko Kawanami: 11–30 (Basingstoke, UK: Palgrave MacMillan, 2016).
22. There are other practices that could be considered: the recitation of pledges or anthems, support for sports teams, speaking a "national" language, etc.
23. Steven Collins and Justin McDaniel, "Buddhist 'Nuns' (*mae chi*) and the Teaching of Pali in Contemporary Thailand," *Modern Asian Studies* 44, no. 6 (April 2010): 1373–1408; 1376.
24. While it is beyond the scope of this chapter to fully consider how gender shapes monastic practices with regard to the nation, it is clear that it does. See Saroj Pathirana, "Sri Lanka's Bhikkhuni Nuns and Their Fight for Identity Papers," *BBC*, December 22, 2019, https://www.bbc.com/news/world-asia-49979978# (accessed May 25, 2020).

25. Tanigawa Yutaka, "The Age of Teaching: Buddhism, Proselytization of Citizens, the Cultivation of Monks, the Education of Laypeople during the Formative Period of Modern Japan," in *Modern Buddhism in Japan*, ed. Hayashi Makoto, Otani Eiichi, and Paul L. Swanson (Nagoya, Japan: Nanzan, 2014), 85-111; Charles E. Keyes, "The Proposed World of the School: Thai Villagers' Entry into a Bureaucratic State System," in *Reshaping Local Worlds: Formal Education and Rural Cultural Change in Southeast Asia*, ed. Charles E. Keyes, E. Jane Keyes, and Nancy Donnelly (New Haven, CT: Yale University Southeast Asian Studies, 1991), 1-18.
26. Craig Reynolds, "The Buddhist Monkhood in Nineteenth Century Thailand," PhD diss., Cornell University, 1972.
27. Katherine Bowie, "Of Buddhism and Militarism in Northern Thailand: Solving the Puzzle of the Saint Khruubaa Srivichai." *Journal of Asian Studies* 73, no. 3 (2014) 711-732.
28. Ratanaporn Sethakul, "Lanna Buddhism and Bangkok Centralization in Late Nineteenth to Early Twentieth century," in *Theravada Buddhism in Colonial Contexts*, ed. Thomas Borchert (New York: Routledge, 2018), 81-100.
29. Stefania Travagnin, "The Impact of Politics on the Minnan Buddhist Institute: *Sanmin zhuyi* and *aiguo zhuyi* in the Context of Sangha Education," *Review of Religion and Chinese Societies* 2 (2015): 35.
30. Travagnin. "Impact," 33; and Rongdao Lei Kuan Lai, "Praying for the Republic: Buddhist Education, Student-Monks, and Citizenship in Modern China, 1911–1949," PhD diss., McGill University, 2013.
31. H. L. Seneviratne, *The Work of Kings: The New Buddhism in Sri Lanka* (Chicago: University of Chicago Press, 1999).
32. Bénédicte Brac de la Perrière, "The 'Frying Pan' Abbot: The Rise and Fall of a Burmese Preaching Monk," *Contemporary Buddhism* 16, no. 1 (2015): 174.
33. Daniel W. Kent, "Preaching in a Time of Declining Dharma: History, Ethics and Protection in Sermons to the Sri Lankan Army," *Contemporary Buddhism: An Interdisciplinary Journal* 16, no. 1 (2015): 195.
34. Sumathi Ramaswamy, *The Goddess and the Nation: Mapping Mother India* (Durham, NC: Duke University Press, 2010); Benedict Anderson, *Imagined Communities: Reflections on the Origin and Spread of Nationalism* (London: Verso, 1991), 170–78.
35. Kent, "Preaching," 198.
36. Brac de la Perrière, "Abbot," 167–87.
37. Ronald D. Schwartz, *Circle of Protest: Political Ritual in the Tibetan Uprising* (New York: Columbia University Press, 1994).
38. On a Bodu Bala Sena conference, see Benjamin Schonthal and Matthew J. Walton, "The (New) Buddhist Nationalisms? Symmetries and Specificities in Sri Lanka and Myanmar," *Contemporary Buddhism* 17, no. 1 (2016), 81-115; on Chinese minorities, see Thomas Borchert, "Belt and Road Buddhists: Religion-Making and the Rebuilding of Minority Buddhism in the Reform Era," *Review of Religion and Chinese Society* 7 (2020), 92-119.
39. National Office of Buddhism, *Khūmeu Phra Sanghāthikān* (Sangha Administrative Officer Handbook) (Bangkok: National Office of Buddhism, 2011), 344.
40. Xue Yu, *Buddhism, War, and Nationalism: Chinese Monks in the Struggle against Japanese Aggressions, 1931–1945* (New York: Routledge, 2005), 45.
41. Yu, *Buddhism, War*, 45.
42. Yu, *Buddhism, War*, 53.
43. Yu, *Buddhism, War*, 113, 118.

44. Micah Auerback, "Paths Untrodden in Japanese Buddhist Chaplaincy to the Imperial Army," in *Military Chaplaincy in an Era of Religious Pluralism: Military-Religious Nexus in Asia, Europe, and USA*, ed. Torkel Brekke and Vladimir Tikhonov (Delhi: Oxford University Press, 2017), 62-80.
45. Auerback, "Paths Untrodden," 75.
46. Vladimir Tikhonov, "Militarized Masculinity with Buddhist Characteristics: Buddhist Chaplains and Their Role in the South Korean Army," in *Buddhist Modernities: Re-Inventing Tradition in the Globalizing Modern World*, ed. Hanna Havneviki, Ute Hüsken, Mark Teeuwen, Vladimir Tikhonov, and Koen Williams (New York: Routledge, 2017), 168.
47. Michael Jerryson, *If You Meet the Buddha on the Road: Buddhism, Politics, and Violence* (New York: Oxford University Press, 2018), 124–25.
48. Iselin Frydenlund, "'Operation Dhamma': The Sri Lankan Armed Forces as an Instrument of Buddhist Nationalism," in *Military Chaplaincy in an Era of Religious Pluralism: Military-Religious Nexus in Asia, Europe, and USA*, ed. Torkel Brekke and Vladimir Tikhonov (Delhi: Oxford University Press, 2017), 96. It is also worth highlighting that Asian Buddhist chaplains appear to be primarily if not solely men.
49. Jerryson, *If you Meet*, 121–22; Tikhonov, "Militarized," 169
50. David Streckfus, *Truth on Trial in Thailand: Defamation, Treason and Lèse-majesté* (New York: Routledge, 2011), 290.
51. Larsson, "Buddha."
52. Nanthachanok Wongsamut, "*Leuakdang* 2562: *Phakkānmeaung pheua Phutthasātsnā Khray cahā thāngawk haysitth thāngkānmeuang khong song*?" [Election 2019: Political Parties for Buddhism—Who will seek political rights of the sangha?], *BBC Thai*, January 2019, https://www.bbc.com/thai/thailand-46901485 (accessed January 20, 2019).
53. Richard Madsen, *Democracy's Dharma: Religious Renaissance and Political Development in Taiwan* (Berkeley: University of California Press, 2007), 68.
54. Brac de la Perrière, "Abbot," 175.
55. Ian Harris, "Introduction to Buddhism and the Political Process: Patterns of Interaction," in *Buddhism and the Political Process*, ed. Hiroko Kawanami (Basingstoke: Palgrave McMillan, 2016), 1-10; Ian Harris and Thomas Borchert, "In Defense of Dharma: Reflections on Buddhism and Politics," in *Teaching Buddhism*, ed. Gary DeAngelis and Todd Lewis (New York: Oxford University Press, 2017), 103-21.
56. Schonthal and Walton, "Buddhist Nationalisms," 83.
57. Yu, *Buddhism, War*, 61.

Further Reading

Brac de la Perrière, Bénédicte. "The 'Frying Pan' Abbot: The Rise and Fall of a Burmese Preaching Monk." *Contemporary Buddhism* 16, no. 1 (2015): 167–87.

Brekke, Torkel, and Vladimir Tikhonov, eds. *Military Chaplaincy in an Era of Religious Pluralism: Military-Religious Nexus in Asia, Europe, and USA*. Delhi: Oxford University Press, 2017.

Harris, Ian. "Introduction to Buddhism and the Political Process: Patterns of Interaction." In *Buddhism and the Political Process*, ed. Hiroko Kawanami. Basingstoke, UK: Palgrave Macmillan, 2016, 1–10.

Kent, Daniel W. "Preaching in a Time of Declining Dharma: History, Ethics and Protection in Sermons to the Sri Lankan Army." *Contemporary Buddhism: An Interdisciplinary Journal* 16, no. 1 (2015): 188–233.

Lai, Rongdao Lei Kuan. "Praying for the Republic: Buddhist Education, Student-Monks, and Citizenship in Modern China, 1911–1949," PhD diss., McGill University, 2013.

Larsson, Tomas. "Buddha or the Ballot: the Buddhist Exception to Universal Suffrage in Contemporary Asia." In *Buddhism and the Political Process*, ed. Hiroko Kawanami. Basingstoke, UK: Palgrave Macmillan, 2016, 78–96.

Mandair, Arvind-Pal S., and Markus Dressler. "Introduction: Modernity, Religion-Making, and the Post-Secular." In *Secularism and Religion-Making*, ed. Markus Dressler and Arvind-Pal S. Mandair. Oxford: Oxford University Press, 2011, 3–36.

McCargo, Duncan. "Informal Citizens: Graduated Citizenship in Southern Thailand." *Ethnic and Racial Studies* 34, no. 5 (2011): 833–49.

Nedostup, Rebecca. *Superstitious Regimes: Religion and the Politics of Chinese Modernity*. Cambridge, MA: Harvard University Asia Center, 2009.

Schonthal, Benjamin. *Buddhism, Politics, and the Limits of the Law: The Pyrrhic Constitutionalism of Sri Lanka*. Cambridge: Cambridge University Press, 2016.

Schonthal, Benjamin, and Matthew J. Walton. "The (New) Buddhist Nationalisms? Symmetries and Specificities in Sri Lanka and Myanmar." *Contemporary Buddhism* 17, no. 1 (2016): 81–115.

Thomas, Jolyon Baraka. *Faking Liberties: Religious Freedom in American-Occupied Japan*. Chicago: University of Chicago Press, 2019.

Travagnin, Stefania. "The Impact of Politics on the Minnan Buddhist Institute: *Sanmin zhuyi* and *aiguo zhuyi* in the Context of Sangha Education." *Review of Religion and Chinese Societies* 2 (2015): 21–50.

Yu, Xue. *Buddhism, War, and Nationalism: Chinese Monks in the Struggle against Japanese Aggressions, 1931–1945*. New York: Routledge, 2005.

CHAPTER 31

TREE ORDINATIONS AND GLOBAL SUSTAINABILITY

SUSAN M. DARLINGTON

WRAPPING an orange robe around a tree can be a subversive act for effecting social and environmental change. That was the case in 1988 when a tree ordination ritual was first performed in northern Thailand by the monk Phrakhru Manas Nathiphitak.[1] Adapting the ritual usually conducted for consecrating buddha images, the monk blessed a tree as a means of highlighting the problems of deforestation and drought faced by local farmers. He imbued the tree with sacred power through his words, entreating ritual participants to recognize their reliance upon trees and the forest. In a simple rethinking of Buddhist ritual, the monk challenged logging companies and the state policy that supported them. He simultaneously empowered villagers to take ownership of the forest and find means of breaking out of agricultural practices that both trap farmers into a cycle of debt and damage the natural environment upon which farmers depend.

Coined "tree ordination," this practice quickly expanded across Thailand and into neighboring countries, became appropriated by the state, and entered popular culture.[2] Tree ordinations provide a lens into Buddhist practice that aims not only to relieve suffering, Buddhism's ultimate goal, but to target underlying real-world problems that contribute to suffering. They help us understand one way in which ritual practice can promote global sustainability on a local level.

Buddhist rituals teach and enact the religion's teachings and values. They bring followers together and reinforce community as the practitioners work toward their salvation and that of those around them. They deal with power—beseeching, influencing, and obtaining power—on a spiritual plane. They provide guidance and solace for laypeople who are suffering in this world, enabling them to make spiritual merit for a better rebirth, and, some believe, improving one's situation in this life.[3]

Tree ordinations do all of these. The monks who perform them hold these spiritual aspects of the ritual as their primary goal. At the same time, these monks recognize the difficulties many Thai farmers face as both the government and seed corporations encourage mono-cropping and contract agriculture. The continual expansion of agricultural plots as farmers attempt to provide an adequate livelihood for their families results in deforestation and ecological damage to the natural environment. Monks and their supporters (often nongovernmental organizations) recognize the potential of ritual for teaching farmers the value of preserving the natural environment and using it in sustainable ways, and empowering them to break from non-sustainable agricultural methods.

In this chapter, I examine tree ordinations as used in northern Thailand to address issues of sustainability, especially agricultural sustainability. While global environmental problems have similar roots everywhere, the specific manifestations vary from place to place, as do the ways in which people deal with them. Yet common elements emerge: of community resilience, creative interpretation of religious teachings, and modes of agriculture and livelihood that reflect an increasing concern about human impact on the earth. Tree ordinations began in northern Thailand in a small community facing drought, soil degradation, and deforestation that turned to its spiritual values and practices as a response.

Drawing on ritual practices across the Theravada societies of South and Southeast Asia, John Holt argues that

> [r]eligious culture stands in reflexive relation to social, economic and political change. Religious cultures are dynamic rather than static, fluid rather than fixed. How various rites rise and fall in popularity may be accurate indices of social, economic, or political change.[4]

Examining tree ordinations, I would take this maxim a step further. Those who perform tree ordinations aim to effect not only social, economic, and political change, but also ecological change. The innovations incorporated into the ritual practice of tree ordinations are most effective when coupled with concrete projects designed to implement sustainable agricultural practices and aid smallholder farmers to establish sustainable livelihoods. While done on a local scale, tree ordinations offer a model of how religious ritual practice can contribute, albeit in a small way, to a broader movement toward global sustainability.

I draw from Roy A. Rappaport's seminal article, "The Obvious Aspects of Ritual," to unpack the practice of tree ordinations.[5] Key to this process is how the three main elements of Rappaport's analysis—formality, performance, and public acceptance—help us understand the local effectiveness of a new ritual practice in addressing the social and ecological impacts of environmental degradation and globalization.

Ordaining Trees?

The first tree ordination was performed in Mae Chai District, Phayao Province, in northern Thailand by the monk, Phrakhru Manas Nathiphitak. Drought hit the district in 1988. Villagers connected the drought with the effects of deforestation from logging concessions in the area. Feeling helpless, they turned to the monk, a well-respected local leader. Phrakhru Manas decided to perform what was to become known as a tree ordination. He adapted the text of a buddha image consecration ceremony (*buat phraphutta rup*), a traditional northern Thai ceremony,[6] to sanctify the largest remaining tree in the nearby forest. Villagers placed a new buddha image at the base of the tree, surrounded by donated saplings for reforestation. The image, the tree, and the saplings were all sanctified during the ritual. After the ceremony, villagers planted the saplings, which they called "ordained trees" (*ton mai thi buat lao*), coining the name for the adapted rite.[7] This ritual was not a *bhikkhu* (monk) ordination, and did not follow the format that ordaining a *bhikkhu* would involve. Instead, Manas's use of the adapted consecration ritual, along with wrapping a monk's robes around the tree, integrated sacred power, compassion, and concrete action to empower the farmers not only to challenge the logging companies and the government, but also to find sustainable approaches to using natural resources.

Despite open criticism and misunderstanding of the ritual, performance of it to preserve and protect forests spread. Soon tree ordinations were conducted across northern Thailand, and by the early 1990s, they could be found across the nation. Monks performed tree ordinations in areas that were threatened by deforestation or environmental degradation resulting from changes in agricultural practices. The most successful rituals used the rite to initiate and support sustainable agricultural projects.

In his first tree ordination ritual, Phrakhru Manas urged people to value the forest holistically and to break away from behavior that only treasured the forest for financial gain. Through a simple reframing of a popular ritual, that of consecrating a buddha image, to bring the values embodied through its practice to apply to nature (through the forest), Manas empowered farmers to regain control over their interactions with the environment and thereby their livelihoods. Wrapping the largest tree in the forest with a monk's robes and consecrating the surrounding forest not only helped to preserve the forest from deforestation. Manas symbolically equated the forest with the Buddha, not just through stories about the Buddha's connections with the forest, but also through establishing a ritual practice that embodied the relationship between the Buddha and nature, and his followers and the forest.

The case of Phrakhru Manas's first tree ordination and its spread across Thailand provide insight into the ways ritual can be used to raise awareness about environmental issues and to promote sustainable environmental practices. I focus on northern Thailand not only because the first tree ordination occurred there, but also because of the intensity of environmental problems faced by the farmers of the region. The first tree ordination was performed in northern Thailand for a reason: the rapid changes in agricultural methods and technologies impacted the land, the forest, and the water, as well as the livelihoods of the farmers over the latter half of the twentieth century and into the twenty-first. The rituals are used not only to highlight the environmental and economic problems farmers face, but to introduce programs aimed at addressing these issues, such as encouraging farmers to shift to integrated agriculture rather than contract or cash-farming.[8] The people of the region are predominantly Theravada Buddhist, and members of the sangha hold positions of respect and influence. When they become involved in dealing with laypeople's issues, their disciples pay attention. Using rituals increases people's engagement and commitment to projects such as those promoting integrated agriculture. While ritual practice does not hold the entire answer to global environmental problems, observing how ritual has been adapted and used to promote sustainable agriculture in this region demonstrates the potential of religious engagement in global sustainability.

The Practice Performed

In July 1991, I attended a tree ordination ceremony in Nan Province in northern Thailand conducted by Phrakhru Pitak Nanthakhun. Although the tree ordination was the culmination of months of preparation and was one aspect of a larger conservation program, the actual ceremony involved only a day and a half of activities. The purpose of the ritual was to consecrate and protect a community forest shared by ten villages in the local subdistrict and to initiate a program to promote sustainable agricultural practices.

The ordination ceremony began in the morning with a modification of a traditional ritual, in this case, *thaut phaa paa* (the giving of the forest robes). Normally, this ritual is performed by Thai laypeople to donate robes, money, and other necessities to monks for religious merit. The funds raised help the upkeep of the temple and support the monks. Since the 1980s this ritual has been increasingly used across the nation to raise funds for local development projects while still resulting in merit for those contributing. People's commitment to such projects is often stronger because of the religious connotations behind the source of the funds—they not only make merit from the original donations at the *phaa paa* ceremony, but from supporting the development project sanctioned through the ritual as well.

Phrakhru Pitak added a twist to this ceremony, as have other monks conducting tree ordinations. Patrons donated 12,000 saplings to the monks, along with robes and other necessities. Once the forest robes were ritually accepted by Phrakhru Pitak, he accepted the saplings, thus sanctifying them and conferring merit on the donors and the participants. The saplings were given to the villagers to reforest areas that had been denuded. These new trees were chosen carefully; they were species, such as fruit trees, that were valuable without having to be cut down. Because they had been sanctified and protected by the monks' blessing, the villagers saw cutting them as a form of religious demerit (*bap*).

After planting a few trees at the temple, participants made the five-kilometer trip into the mountains to the tree chosen to be ordained. Over 200 people accompanied twenty monks to the site. A four-foot-tall buddha image had been placed on a concrete stand at the base of the giant tree. Phrakhru Pitak commented that over twenty years ago, when he walked the eight kilometers from his village to school through the deep forest along this route, this tree was not unusual for its height or size. Now it clearly stood out as the tallest remaining tree. One could see for miles from it, across a landscape dotted with near vertical maize fields, visible because of the deforested hillsides.

The monks gathered under a tent, surrounded by the seated lay participants. After the monks lighted candles and incense, they led the laypeople in taking refuge in the Buddha, the Dharma, and the sangha. The monks then chanted, holding a long, white string that connected them together and led to the buddha image placed beneath the tree being ordained. The string (*sai sin*) conveyed the sacred power of the words from the chanting to the image and the tree, thereby imbuing the image and the tree with sanctity. (The string itself was also empowered through this ritual. Afterwards, participants would take pieces of the string home to use in protective rites typical across the Theravada world. Tied around people's wrists as an amulet, the string served to protect the wearer from malevolent spirits or the possibility of their *winyan* or "soul essence" escaping the physical body, leaving it vulnerable.) The laity sat with their palms together, signaling their involvement in the act.

After almost half an hour of chanting, two monks wrapped orange robes around the tree's trunk, marking its sanctification. The robes stood as a reminder that to harm or cut the tree—or any of the forest—was an act of demerit.

Phrakhru Pitak then gave a brief sermon on the history of the efforts to preserve the forest and the problems of drought resulting from deforestation in watershed areas. He emphasized the role of villagers in protecting the community forest. The main emphasis of Phrakhru Pitak's sermon was on the relationship between the Buddha and nature, and the interdependence between the conditions of the forest and the villagers' lives. The ceremony was used symbolically to remind people that nature is deserving of respect and vital for human as well as all life. The opportunity of the ordination was used to build spiritual commitment to preserving the forest and to teach in an active and creative way the value of conservation.

As in many Thai Buddhist rituals, the rite included the sanctification of water in a monk's alms bowl. A small buddha image was placed in the bowl and candle wax dripped into the water while the monks chanted. Traditionally, this holy water (*nam mon*) is sprinkled on the participants, conferring a blessing on them. The water is seen as ritually powerful, and people always make sure to receive some of the drops of it from the monk.[9] On this occasion, each of the headmen from the ten participating villages drank some of the water in front of the large buddha image to seal their pledge to protect the forest. This use of a sacred symbol to strengthen such an oath was another innovation that reinforced the notion of environmentalism as moral action. It made the protection or destruction of the forest karmic action: protecting it would confer good merit (*bun*), destroying it bringing bad (*bap*), the balance of which would ultimately affect one's rebirth or even quality of living in this life.

After the ceremony concluded, people planted some of the saplings around the now sacred tree. The participants divided the *sai sin* to take home for future rites, carrying sanctity from the tree ordination ritual with it. Local leaders established rules for protecting the community forest going forward, with anticipation for improved livelihoods and environmental conditions.

Why *Environmental* Rituals?

Northern Thai people perform many rituals throughout their lives, dealing with life-cycle events from birth to death, illness, house construction, and many other issues. They regularly make merit to improve future rebirths. They honor spirits of the land, family ancestors, and hungry ghosts as an integral aspect of their spiritual beliefs and practices. Why, then, develop a new practice focused on the forest? First, we must understand the changing environmental and social contexts within which these rituals are being practiced.

Since the mid-twentieth century, the central Thai government followed policies that promoted globalization, encouraged industrialization, and pushed intensive, export-oriented agriculture. While these policies helped Thailand develop its economy and overall standard of living, they had environmental and social consequences, especially on the local level. In northern Thailand, farmers were encouraged by the government, through loans from the national agricultural bank and large seed companies, to shift from predominantly subsistence farming to mono-cropping and contract farming.[10] This change rapidly led to multiple environmental issues, including deforestation, soil erosion, land degradation, alternating drought and flooding, and a loss of biodiversity. To meet the demands of their loans, farmers in Nan Province, as elsewhere, began to expand their fields and apply increasing amounts of chemical fertilizers, herbicides, and pesticides, which ran off into the waterways and ground water of the region. Seed companies lent farmers the seeds and chemicals, expecting repayment at the next harvest. Yet these companies held farmers to high standards for their produce, which farmers could not consistently meet. As loans were extended, farmer debt increased, creating a cycle of social and environmental degradation.

In Nan, the main commercial crop is corn, grown in vertical rows on the denuded mountainsides. The problem with corn is but one example of agricultural intensification in Nan. Other cash crops include long green beans, cassava, and, more recently, rubber. As each new cash crop is introduced into the province and farmers are encouraged by the agricultural corporations and the government to invest in them, the problems of deforestation, environmental degradation, and social and economic debt expand.

This cycle and related challenges are not unique to Nan. Across the globe, changes in agricultural practices impact the environment, the climate, and the social conditions of farmers. Nan is but a microcosm of global problems that are expanding at a rapid rate. The monks and their followers performing tree ordinations recognize the urgency of these problems and see a new form of Buddhist practice as offering a path toward sustainable agriculture and a more balanced way of life.

Rituals and Environmental Practice

Buddhism teaches a wide variety of values and ideal behaviors, including right livelihood (part of the noble eightfold path). One could ask why simply encouraging the lay farmers to enact these ideals is not sufficient to ensure their involvement in sustainable practices. Roy Rappaport lays out how rituals work and why.[11] Applying his analysis to this case offers understanding into how tree ordinations work to engage farmers in sustainable agriculture. The practice of ritual—the actual *doing* of the rite and its form—encodes basic meanings and conveys certain understandings to and among the participants. Rappaport argues that what makes ritual distinct from any other means of enacting the same function (in this case, getting farmers to change their agricultural practices) is "the social contract and the morality intrinsic in its structure."[12]

Rappaport defines ritual through several key features, each of which sheds insight into the effectiveness of tree ordinations and related rituals. These features include: formality, the invariance of the liturgical order, and the specific circumstances in which the ritual is performed;[13] performance, involving people as participants who are "doing something" and communicating that act to themselves and to others;[14] and performative pledges through which participants publicly accept the commitments encoded within the ritual.[15] Each of these "obvious aspects" of ritual can be examined as they are enacted within tree ordinations. Key here is Rappaport's argument that ritual performances make these public commitments stronger than any kind of conventional pledges or entreaties would do because of the morality embedded within the ritual act.

As tree ordinations at their core deal with the state of the natural environment and human responsibilities toward it, one could ask why educating farmers about the urgent need for sustainable practices and providing them with the technologies and methods are not enough. There are plenty of examples across Thailand that illustrate the success of such projects in promoting sustainability. Yet at the same time, there are examples of the failures of sustainable agricultural projects—projects in which farmers do not fully understand the urgency or do not have the wherewithal to withstand the pressures from corporations or the government to engage in contract or cash farming. I am not arguing here that these more secular projects should not be undertaken. Indeed, I have studied several in Nan Province, and fully support their efforts and hope for success. What I am arguing here is that by initiating such projects through ritual performances of tree ordinations, long-life ceremonies for waterways, and/or requesting support from the spiritual "lords of the land" (all forms of environmental rituals performed in northern Thailand), the chance of success and full engagement by farmer participants increases significantly for the reasons discussed by Rappaport on the effectiveness of rituals.

The features of ritual structure laid out by Rappaport provide a framework for seeing the ways in which both social contract and morality emerge from tree ordinations in northern Thailand. In particular, it is the public acceptance of the message contained within tree ordinations that makes these rituals both popular and effective. For this analysis, I focus on tree ordinations that I have personally attended, such as the one performed by Phrakhru Pitak Nanthakhun in Nan Province in 1991, described earlier.

Formality of Ritual

Tree ordinations usually take one of two forms. One is quite simple: a monk and a group of laypeople individually wrap monks' robes around trees within a forested area to be protected. The leadership of the monk (or a group of monks) makes the process carry greater weight and meaning than if the forest was merely demarcated as protected by laity. Yet this approach would not be considered a "ritual" by Rappaport due to the lack of formality involved.

The more common form of tree ordination is a ritual by Rappaport's definition. Since the first performance of a tree ordination by Phrakhru Manas Nathiphitak in 1988, the process has settled into a more-or-less set structure. There is more variation than Rappaport discusses in his article, although he allows for a range of differences depending on circumstances. The invariance for tree ordinations emerges in two ways: First, it is always performed by monks. They gather, along with the lay participants, around the tree to be "ordained," located within the forest to be consecrated. Second, the monks have choice in terms of the texts they recite, but they always pull from Buddhist scriptures. In his first ceremony, Phrakhru Manas adapted the text used for consecrating a buddha image. Other monks may choose different texts, such as the *Maṅgalasutta*, the *Seven Tamnan*, and the *Twelve Tamnan*. These texts are commonly used in consecration ceremonies and to teach life lessons. Phrakhru Pitak Nanthakhun told me he selects the texts carefully, depending on the community involved and the specific issues they face.[16] His main aim in selecting the text to use is getting the participants to think critically about the moral implications of economic development. He connects mainstream types of development, especially contract and cash farming, with the three root evils in Buddhism, desire/greed, anger/hatred, and ignorance.

Using texts that the Buddhist laity recognize brings the formality Rappaport discusses into tree ordinations. Even with the diversity of texts that individual monks choose to use in performing the ritual, the fact that they use texts from the Pali canon connects the ritual to the broader Buddhist tradition. Catherine Bell examines the processes through which rituals evolve, particularly in response to change: "Ritual can change when shifting social circumstances induce transmutations, when ritual is intentionally created or repurposed, or when ritual adopts new forms of expression or media."[17] This process can be seen clearly in the creation of tree ordinations by Phrakhru Manas, and the ways in which other monks have picked up, adapted, and solidified its ritual performance. Regardless of the exact text chanted during the rite, one can recognize it as a tree ordination and understand its purpose.

In their edited volume, *Ritual Innovation: Strategic Interventions in South Asian Religion*, Brian Pennington and Amy Allocco take Bell's analysis a step further. They push for unpacking the social, historical contexts as well as the maintenance of tradition: ". . . interrogating the social, political, or material conditions that trigger transformations in what, after all, are performances and acts that derive their legitimation from their connection to tradition."[18] It is this "connection to tradition" that is so important to Rappaport, as it provides the formality of ritual performance. Rituals are not simply invented on the spot, but carry meaning for the participants because of the formality—of when, where, and how the ritual is performed and its connections with the familiar and the sacred. At the same time, they carry the most meaning when they relate to contemporary circumstances in which the participants live.

The limits of Rappaport's analysis emerge here, as a tension exists between performing "traditional" rituals in the formal manner in which they have been done over time and the innovation that responds to changing needs and different places. Tree ordinations tap this tension, making references to the long-standing rituals while incorporating new elements and purposes. Key to the potential success of the adapted rituals lies with the reputation of the monks performing them. If the laity respect and trust the monks, then they accept the innovations as part of the ritual, which is still imbued with sanctity and meaning.

Ritual Performance

Another feature that makes rituals distinct from other events, according to Rappaport, is that they are performances that involve all the participants as the focus of the ritual rather than as some kind of audience.[19] All the participants, regardless of their specific role in the ritual, are "doing something."[20] The ritual itself and people's participation in it are communicating something, but they are communicating through *doing*. Participants are not just watching, but are engaging in the performance, thereby connecting themselves with the underlying morality on which the ritual is based.

For tree ordinations, it would appear that most of the "doing" is being done by the monks. They are chanting, holding the sacred string, the highest-ranking monk gives a dharma talk, and they wrap the tree with the monk's robes. Yet the lay participants are critical to the performance. They are not merely observing, but are listening with intent. Buddhism teaches that intention is the key to making merit—the other thing that participants are doing, to which I will return later—so the intention of participants to be engaged in the tree ordination is crucial. Intention is personal, but participation also signals public commitment to upholding the values and teachings contained within the ritual. Participants signal their engagement and intention through body language. At the right times, they bow, hold their palms together while listening to the chanting, and take refuge in the Buddha, the Dharma, and the sangha. The sangha lead the actions, and the laity follow, reflecting the social and religious hierarchy embedded in Buddhist practice and teachings. This dynamic interplay, however, is what enables the monks to help villagers more broadly in dealing with environmental and livelihood issues.

On a broader level, the "doing" involved in tree ordinations is the consecration of the forest. Forests can be marked as protected through signs and announcements. The ritual takes this a step further by making the entire forest sacred and specifying appropriate behaviors within the forest (for example, limiting tree cutting, stressing instead renewable resources like mushrooms and grasses for making brooms, or restricting hunting). This action parallels the consecration of a buddha image. Through the consecration ritual, the image is imbued with sacred power and becomes the Buddha, rather than just representing the Buddha.[21] In tree ordinations, the tree does not *become* the Buddha, but it does take on the sacred power of the words that the monks chant, transferred through the *sai sin*. Similarly, the forest becomes sacred, requiring a moral responsibility for caring for it. That said, in many cases villagers incorporate spirit beliefs along with their Buddhist practice, appealing to local guardian spirits to help protect the forest. The argument could be made that fear of the repercussion of going against the spirits motivates villagers' protection of the forest as much as, if not more than, the elements of Buddhist sanctity.[22]

Participants engage in this process of sanctification through their presence and participation in the ritual performance. Without the participants' hearing the chanted words, witnessing the act of wrapping the robes, and actively listening to the monk's sermon, the tree and the forest do not become sacred. No one would know of this changed status, nor how to behave appropriately.

Applying anthropologist Diana Taylor's analysis of protests, while not rituals by Rappaport's definition per se, as performances further shows how tree ordinations serve as performances. Taylor examined how children of the disappeared during Argentina's "Dirty War" publicly shamed the military and government agents responsible through public protests. They used theatrical and ritualistic techniques to gain attention and make people remember crimes that occurred one to two decades earlier.[23] Elsewhere, Taylor describes a performance's audience as "witnesses" to a traumatic event. Theater reveals an event, pulls the audience in, and shares the emotions and meanings with them. No longer can they claim ignorance. The goal is to provoke responsibility and empathy—even sympathy—on the part of the audience.[24] Similarly, tree ordinations in Thailand are performances, designed not to invoke traumatic memories but to gain people's commitment to the more mundane projects the rituals introduce. Here we can see a parallel to the "doing" stressed by Rappaport. Participants are actively witnessing, thereby creating and validating the performance of consecrating the forest. Through participation in a ritual, people publicly demonstrate their involvement in the project, taking oaths and making merit. Simply through their presence and engagement, the audience acknowledges the economic and political power imbalances that led to the need for the ritual in the first place.

Thai environmental monks are not retelling or rethinking history, but are transforming social hierarchies and power. Although eventually some tree ordinations served to reinforce social hierarchies,[25] initially they served to empower rural farmers to lay claim to their forests and land use. These rituals are embodied actions, ones that validate villagers' knowledge and abilities, especially against broader social structures that usually devalue or create idealized images of village life.

Perhaps the most common action in lay Buddhist ritual behavior is making merit. Merit (*bun*) is accumulated through good actions, undertaken with good intention. Demerit (*bap*) results from negative behavior, especially violating the five core precepts all Buddhists strive to uphold (refraining from: harming life, lying, stealing, engaging in sexual misconduct, and taking intoxicants that can cloud the mind). Through the accumulation of good merit, one can improve one's status in a future life (rebirth). Some in Thailand believe one can even improve one's current life through undertaking good deeds. Such deeds include engaging in rituals. While the purpose of tree ordinations is to consecrate a forest and ultimately protect it through encouraging people to change their behavior toward the natural environment, participants are acutely aware that they are gaining merit at the same time.

Tree ordinations initially shocked the broader public. Trees are not human, and although the monks do not claim to be turning them into *bhikkhu*s, as a performance the rites lead people to perceive them as such.[26] One of the criticisms of tree ordinations is that they challenge what people consider sacred—placing trees on the same level as monks goes against the established social hierarchy. Members of the media, the government, the sangha hierarchy, and even some mainstream monks accuse environmental monks of stepping beyond appropriate boundaries, manipulating the public through changing sacred relations, thereby challenging power relations. These very critiques indicate the effectiveness of the tree ordinations rites. As in the case of Argentina's children of the disappeared, a key aim of tree ordinations is to gain attention. If people are not watching—and witnessing—the performances are ineffectual. Tree ordinations captured the Thai imagination, pulled people in, and sparked lively debates about their appropriateness and the social, economic, and political circumstances that led to their performance.

Public Acceptance

Perhaps most relevant for my analysis of tree ordinations as rituals is Rappaport's argument that participation in ritual is a form of pledge to uphold the purpose of the rite. He refers to these as "performatives," through which conventions are established and made moral.[27] Rappaport states that "[b]y performing a liturgical order the performer accepts and indicates to himself and to others that he accepts whatever is encoded in the canons of the liturgical order in which he is participating."[28] The key here is the public performance in which each participant engages. For Rappaport, this moral commitment comes about because of the connection, even in innovative rituals, to the tradition in the form of the authority of the monks and the texts chanted.

Monks performing a tree ordination choose their texts depending on the situation and the participants. As mentioned previously, they may use texts from the consecration of a buddha image, or passages from the *Maṅgalasutta*. The specific text used is less important than the fact that they are drawing from the Pali canon, and the participants recognize the texts as sacred. These words carry sacred power and convey this sanctity to the project being initiated through the ritual. However, many alternative agriculture projects across Thailand begin without a ritual performance and are often successful. Using a ritual to initiate a project adds a layer of morality, increasing the likelihood of success as people feel a commitment toward the monk who performed the ritual and the sense that they are making merit by enacting the goals of the project. The rituals link merit-making with environmental protection. As with the five basic precepts in Buddhism, however, ultimately individual practitioners decide whether they will uphold the regulations of a given environmental project and accept the consequences, both environmental and spiritual.

In the tree ordination in which I participated, the headmen of the ten villages involved each made a pledge to protect the shared community forest that was sanctified through the ritual. They sipped some of the water that had also been sanctified through the monks' chanting. The *sai sin*, the string that conveyed the power of the chanted words to the buddha image and the tree, also connected an alms bowl filled with water to the monks. This water took up the sacred power from the words. Usually the monks bless the participants through sprinkling this water across the congregation toward the end of a ritual. In this case, however, the headmen each dipped a ladle into the water and took a sip to seal their pledge to protect the forest. Empowered by the monks performing the ritual, the headmen took on the responsibility to protect the forest and encouraged the villagers to do so as well. Village headmen carry their own social authority in Thai society; the involvement of these headmen in the tree ordination integrated their secular power with the spiritual authority of the monks.

Rappaport accurately describes the meaning of this act: "It is the visible, explicit, public act of acceptance, and not the invisible, ambiguous, private sentiment that is socially and morally binding."[29] More than any other aspect of performing a tree ordination, it is the visible display and affirmation of acceptance of the project that makes these rituals effective for their main purpose of getting people to enact sustainable practices. As villagers leave the ritual site and move into the hard work of changing their farming methods or protecting a community forest, the community knows which participants pledged commitment to the project. The pledges may be either explicit, as with the headmen discussed earlier, or implicit through participants' involvement in the ritual. Either way, a moral commitment strengthens the project and creates a communal bond for its success.

Conclusions

Phrakhru Pitak recognized that merely consecrating and protecting the forest were not going to solve any problems in themselves. He told me that these rituals needed to be integrated with projects aimed at helping farmers maintain their livelihoods without destroying the forest. They could not simply be denied access to forested land, but needed alternatives. Pitak, as with many of the monks who perform tree ordinations, used the ritual to promote integrated agriculture and to provide alternative means of livelihood that do not harm the forest or environment. These rituals are as much about helping farmers get out of debt and improving their social situations as they are about protecting the natural environment.

Integrated agricultural projects do not require connections with tree ordinations to achieve their goals. My argument here, though, is that through ritual participation, farmers publicly demonstrate their commitment to the agricultural projects and the protection of the forest. When successful, the tree ordinations and their related projects have the potential to decrease human impacts on the environment and to support farmers to break out of the cycle of debt and negative social consequences that contract farming incurs. In this way, tree ordinations contribute to achieving the ultimate goal of Buddhism in relieving suffering.

Notes

1. *Phrakhru* is an ecclesiastical title in Thai Buddhism. The monk's given name is Manas. Following Thai practice, I refer to Thai monks and scholars by their given names.
2. Susan M. Darlington, *The Ordination of a Tree: The Thai Buddhist Environmental Movement* (Albany: State University of New York Press, 2012).
3. Donald K. Swearer, *The Buddhist World of Southeast Asia* (Albany: State University of New York Press, 2010), part I.
4. John Clifford Holt, *Theravada Traditions: Buddhist Ritual Cultures in Contemporary Southeast Asia and Sri Lanka* (Honolulu: University of Hawai'i Press, 2017), 6.
5. Roy A. Rappaport, "The Obvious Aspects of Ritual," in his *Ecology, Meaning, and Religion* (Berkeley, CA: North Atlantic Books, 1979), 173–221.
6. On the buddha image consecration ceremony, see Donald K. Swearer, *Becoming the Buddha* (Princeton, NJ, and Oxford: Princeton University Press, 2004).
7. Pipob Udomittipong, personal communication, January 15, 2007.
8. Integrated agriculture (*kaseet phasom phasaam* in Thai) consciously entails mimicking nature, using environmentally friendly methods and domestic labor. According to Henry D. Delcore, "Development and the Life Story of a Thai Farmer Leader," *Ethnology* 43, no. 1 (2004): 37, "The goals of the method include decreasing land under cultivation (abandoned fields are ideally allowed to return to forest), use of domestic resources, avoidance of debt, and production of a variety of foods for household consumption with only a secondary emphasis on commercial production."
9. Grant Olson, "Cries over Split Holy Water," *Journal of Southeast Asian Studies* 22 (1991): 75–85.
10. On the pros and cons of contract farming, see Andrew Walker, *Thailand's Political Peasants: Power in the Modern Rural Economy* (Madison: University of Wisconsin Press, 2012), 119–31. Walker notes that whether contract farming is beneficial or harmful to farmers depends largely on the local economic and environmental context. In Nan

Province, from my conversations with farmers, NGO staff who work with farmers, and activist monks, it became clear that contract farming has resulted in high farmer debt and expansion of agricultural plots across the mountains.

11. Rappaport, "Obvious."
12. Rappaport, "Obvious," 175.
13. Rappaport, "Obvious," 175.
14. Rappaport, "Obvious," 177.
15. Rappaport, "Obvious," 189.
16. Phrakhru Pitak Nanthakhun, personal communication, October 27, 2010.
17. Catherine Bell, *Ritual: Perspectives and Dimensions* (New York: Oxford University Press, 1997), 212.
18. Brian Pennington and Amy Allocco, *Ritual Innovation: Strategic Interventions in South Asian Religion* (Albany: State University of New York Press, 2018), 4.
19. Rappaport, "Obvious," 176.
20. Rappaport, "Obvious," 177.
21. Swearer, *Becoming*, 109, 152.
22. Susan M. Darlington, "The Good Buddha and the Fierce Spirits: Protecting the Northern Thai Forest," *Contemporary Buddhism* 8, no. 2 (2007): 169–85.
23. Diana Taylor, "'You Are Here': The DNA of Performance," *TDR: The Drama Review* 46, no. 1 (2002): 149–69.
24. Diana Taylor, "Performing Ruins," in *Telling Ruins in Latin America*, ed. Michael J. Lazzara and Vicky Unruh (New York: Palgrave Macmillan, 2009), 25.
25. Henry D. Delcore, "Symbolic Politics or Generification? The Ambivalent Implications of Tree Ordinations in the Thai Environmental Movement," *Journal of Political Ecology* 11, no. 1 (2004): 8; Nicola Tannenbaum, "Protest, Tree Ordination, and the Changing Context of Political Ritual," *Ethnology* 39, no. 2 (2000): 109–27.
26. Mark L. Blum, "The Transcendental Ghost in EcoBuddhism," in *TransBuddhism: Transmission, Translation, and Transformation*, ed. Abraham Zablocki, Jay Garfield, and Nalini Bhushan (Amherst: University of Massachusetts Press, 2009), 209–38.
27. Rappaport, "Obvious," 189.
28. Rappaport, "Obvious," 193.
29. Rappaport, "Obvious," 195.

FURTHER READING

Brown, Kevin. "Spectacle as Resistance: Performing Tree Ordinations in Thailand." *Journal of Religion and Theatre* 5, no. 2 (2006): 91–103.

Clippard, Seth Devere. "The Lorax Wears Saffron: Towards a Buddhist Environmentalism." *Journal of Buddhist Ethics* 11 (2011): 212–48.

Darlington, Susan M. "Contemporary Buddhism and Ecology." In *The Oxford Handbook of Contemporary Buddhism*, ed. Michael Jerryson. Oxford: Oxford University Press, 2017, 487–503.

Darlington, Susan M. "The Good Buddha and the Fierce Spirits: Protecting the Northern Thai Forest." *Contemporary Buddhism* 8, no. 2 (2007): 169–85.

Darlington, Susan M. *The Ordination of a Tree: The Thai Buddhist Environmental Movement*. Albany: State University of New York Press, 2012.

Darlington, Susan M. "Translating Modernity: Buddhist Response to the Thai Environmental Crisis." In *TransBuddhism: Transmission, Translation and Transformation*, ed. Abraham Zablocki, Jay Garfield, and Nalini Bhushan. Amherst: University of Massachusetts Press, 2009, 183–208.

Delcore, Henry D. "Symbolic Politics or Generification? The Ambivalent Implications of Tree Ordinations in the Thai Environmental Movement." *Journal of Political Ecology* 11, no. 1 (2004): 1–30.

Eckel, M. David. "Is 'Buddhist Environmentalism' a Contradiction in Terms?" In *How Much Is Enough? Buddhism, Consumerism, and the Human Environment*, ed. Richard K. Payne. Somerville, MA: Wisdom Publications, 2010, 161–70.

Isager, L. and Ivarsson, S. "Contesting Landscapes in Thailand: Tree Ordination as Counterterriorialization." *Critical Asian Studies* 34, no. 3 (2002): 395–417.

Kaza, Stephanie and Kenneth Kraft, eds. *Dharma Rain: Sources of Buddhist Environmentalism*. Boston: Shambhala Publications, 2000.

Sponsel, Leslie E., and Poranee Natadecha-Sponsel. "The Role of Buddhism in Creating a More Sustainable Society in Thailand." In *Counting the Costs: Economic Grow and Environmental Change in Thailand*, ed. Jonathan Rigg. Singapore: Institute of Southeast Asian Studies, 1995, 27–46.

Sponsel, Leslie E., and Poranee Natadecha-Sponsel. "A Theorectical Analysis of the Potential Contribution of the Monastic Community in Promoting a Green Society in Thailand." In *Buddhism and Ecology: The Interconnection of Dharma and Deeds*, ed. Mary Evelyn Tucker and Duncan Ryuken Williams. Cambridge, MA: Harvard University Center for the Study of World Religions, 1997, 45–70.

Tannenbaum, Nicola. "Protest, Tree Ordination, and the Changing Context of Political Ritual." *Ethnology* 39, no. 2 (2000): 109–27.

Tucker, Mary Evelyn, and Duncan Ryuken Williams, eds. *Buddhism and Ecology: The Interconnection of Dharma and Deeds*. Cambridge, MA: Harvard University Center for the Study of World Religions Publications, 1997.

Yoon, Young-Hae, and Sherwin Jones. "Ecology, Dharma and Direct Action: A Brief Survey of Contemporary Eco-Buddhist Activism in Korea." *Buddhist Studies Review* 31, no. 2 (2014): 293–311.

CHAPTER 32

AN EMBODIED DHARMA OF RACE, GENDER, AND SEXUALITY

JASMINE SYEDULLAH

> Everyone and everything came out of darkness, therefore it is everywhere and in everything.
>
> Only our limited perception distorts this truth.[1]
>
> —Zenju Earthlyn Manuel, Sensei

Before the Buddha found enlightenment, he lived a life of privilege. He followed the path of his own dissatisfaction and stepped back from his birthright to see himself and the world more clearly. The Buddha bore witness to the suffering of sickness, old age, and death, and saw that they were inescapable. He found no safety in privilege. The violence of ignorance and resignation were everywhere inescapable. The only refuge from suffering lay in awakening.

Suffering became the first noble truth of the Buddha's teachings, the first truth of the human experience. But even timeless truths are subject to change. With the advent of modern colonialism, the rise of Western dominance across the globe further systematized, racialized, and gendered the truth of suffering. Sickness, old age, and death became more than inevitable truths; they were evermore "indissolubly wedded to the consolidation of capitalism," to borrow a phrase from scholar Angela Davis.[2] Industries of mass production came to profit off the labors of those who were forced to sacrifice their health and strength for mere survival. Predictive and strategic manipulations of forced migration, militarized borders, and weaponized piety conspired to silence any who posed threats to the modernized administration of national security, population control, wealth extraction, accumulation, and privatization.

Safety from suffering *is* freedom in this Western dialectic of piracy and privacy. No one escapes the seductions of this imagination of freedom that values property over people, contract over custom. Uncertainty, non-duality, and impermanence are not revelations from this perspective, but problems to be solved with instruments of risk assessment, insurance, and diversified asset allocations. The first truth of this logic of the Enlightenment is freedom without accountability, an imperative of liberation achieved by competition, entitlement, and displacement—deplete the land, colonize the people, and call their subjection "salvation." From these ideas, justifiable genocides ensue. While ancient India did not display the same technologies of piracy and privacy we might see at work in the lives of those struggling to survive colonialism and capitalism in any country today, the social constructions of power that shape and stratify humanity protect the well-being of the privileged, preserve their distance from sickness, old age, and death, and work to absolve those of us with close proximity to power from accountability for the unnecessary suffering of those lives we deem disposable.

Still deeply unsettling generations later, the many material consequences of Western histories of stolen land, lives, and futures continue to unfold today. Sitting with the truth of suffering that lives in our world is especially challenging for those most directly benefiting from their close proximity to power, be it by way of citizenship status, race, gender, or sexual orientation privilege, access to education, safe housing, and healthy food, or healthcare. That the strength and security of "our" well-being occasions far too many "others" to suffer premature death from the myriad sicknesses of the mind and body that plague the globe is untenable. When those of us who benefit from proximity to power infantilize, police, and punish what we do not understand in ourselves and in each other, we alienate ourselves from our own sense of humanity. What we are facing today is the need for a Dharma that faces the contradictions we inhabit; a retreat into the true birthright of Western "privilege."

The systemization of suffering, from colony to captive, from plantation to prison, from state-sanctioned violence to pandemic virus, is never totalizing. There have always been fugitives from proximities to power. It is only a matter of time. "Within Western norms," writes urban anthropologist Damien M. Sojoyner,

> time represents the ideological manifestation of freedom; the ability to wield time for one's material benefit is a central part of the Western educative process. . . . Black radical time is not something that is employed to be inflicted upon people; rather, it is central to organizing against structures of domination (such as prisons and education) . . . a means to analyze and break away from western-time-induced trappings . . . creating a politics based upon love of community and shared human experience.[3]

Put another way, proximity to power over time has never been exclusive to the will of any one person, or even wholly limited to the interests of the most privileged portions of the world's population. How we tell time, how we discern what time it is for ourselves and our communities, with or against the press of structural power, matters, not just for our own liberation, but for that of our ancestors and future generations.

Keeping time, time to sit, time to stay, time for the bell or to bow, time to "wait for the teacher" or to wake up, time keeping against the press of the outside world are all already part of the Dharma practice. There is a blueprint for another pedagogy of freedom to be learned from the stillness of sitting in close proximity to power over time. In retreats from the norms of urgency and productivity, a subversive space is seeded. From daily Dharma practices to the renegade choices of everyday people to "stay human," in the words of singer-songwriter Michael Franti, we can choose to prioritize relationship over recognition, freedom over security, collective safety over personal privilege. Along a continuum of radical disruptions of the tyranny of Western time and the press of progress, Dharma folks have been curating ways to pass on to future generations lessons for honoring life and living well, well before the West was "won." What we are seeing today, with the rise of queer-of-color practice circles and teachers, are people becoming fugitives from the tyranny of Western time-keeping through the transmission of the Dharma in meditation apps and zoom rooms, and the emergence of a future imagination of freedom, a practice of time-keeping born from the love that lives in the contradictions of so-called progress, in the truth of things as they are.

The Buddha's teachings ask us to take our seat in the world seriously, to see it, sit with it, wake up to it, and keep watch. Both those who benefit from global structures of domination and those who were never meant to survive have proximities to power to follow to collective liberation. Over time we follow the path of our own dissatisfaction and learn to make home wherever we are, transforming the very seat of our suffering from the inside out.[4] Bearing witness to ourselves and stepping back from the construct of the consciousness that sits is a powerful way to begin. But what there's just too little of in Western Buddhism today, frankly, are cultural traditions of practice that pass down everyday, practical ways to step back from the self that sits to more clearly see the constructs that situate that embodied consciousness in real-time and in asymmetrical relationship *to all our relations*. From ego to exceptionalism to supremacy, the eye's obscurations are inexhaustible—transforming them is a practice.

Relative and absolute distortions of perception are interconnecting and ever present in the Dharma, as Zen teacher Zenju Earthlyn Manuel explains:

> Even while wearing Zen robes, some students and teachers do not see me as a legitimate Zen teacher, even within the institution in which I was ordained. Of course, this is humbling and keeps my head from swelling up while wearing the brown okesa. As my late Zen teacher, Zenkei Blanche Hartman, shared, "When bothered with not being seen, ask yourself, *who do I think I am?*" There is no answer, only a sober moment and space for nothingness to do what it does. The silence enters and the mountain speaks.[5]

As practitioners we know the best defense against the tyranny of time is the space "for nothingness to do what it does." Curating it, clearing room for it, preparing our whole selves to be held by it—it is all the housekeeping needed to live by it, so we can take refuge there and return whenever necessary. When the Black experience meets the way of the Dharma, a space for healing emerges, a space for healing the wounds of white supremacy as it lands on Black peoples. Healing also emerges for what Rev. angel Kyodo williams Sensei refers to as healing backwards—healing the wounds of any whose liberation has been marred by the prevalence of white supremacy and anti-Blackness, and that means white-bodied people too. Nothingness holds all the creative love necessary for us to see each other anew and leverage this proximity to power together.

The space of stillness and the healing power of nothingness get beneath both the relative and absolute distortions of perception to break our addictions and transform our delusions as I recite with my sangha in the Meal Gatha whenever we gather for a community meal. African American Rev. Seiho Morris, an ordained Rinzai Zen Buddhist Monk, likens the work of waking up from delusions of racism and white supremacy, quite literally, to a process of substance recovery. In his Twelve Step recovery program for unconscious racial bias, Rev. Seiho brings the Four Noble Truths and Eightfold Path together with a revised expression of the Twelve Steps to name and formalize a process most often fail to see as interconnected. The first step is admitting that white supremacy is a problem in our Dharma communities.

If we who sit amid the inescapable distortions of modern consciousness passed down to us through traditions of nationalism, white supremacy, patriarchy, rape culture, and heterosexism, need support to bear witness, step back, and see clearly the ways we are passing as compassionate contemplative beings, while bypassing the effects of Western individualism, exceptionalism, and dominance within our own bodies and behavior, we have only to turn to those living in close proximity to power and its contradictions.

Those who take refuge in the Dharma as survivors of nationalism, white supremacy, patriarchy, rape culture, and heterosexism know what time it is. They are steeped in contemplative technologies of fugitive homemaking, breathing space for chosen family and ancestral wisdom traditions on altars, adding sage and palo santo to the lotus, the mandala, and the Buddha to ward off the seductions of suffering and oppression that seek to steal our time and attention. In the following observations, I turn to those who were never meant to survive for guidance on how practitioners of the Dharma, no matter what skin they are in, can take their seat, step back, and follow the path of their own dissatisfaction toward transformation.

"Turning the Wheel"

In October 2019, four women Dharma leaders, hailing from different meditation-based convert lineages of Buddhism, gathered at Spirit Rock Meditation Center in Northern California to convene The Fierce Urgency of Now: The Second Gathering of Buddhist Teachers of Black African Descent, hereafter called The Gathering II. Rev. angel Kyodo williams, Sensei and Myokei Shonan, Konda Mason, and Noliwe Alexander assembled more than seventy Black Dharma teachers and scholars from Dharma traditions across the United States, and two representatives from Canada and the United Kingdom.

The welcome message read, "It has been far too long (seventeen years!) since the last African American Retreat. . . . In these urgent, hyper-polarized times, now is the moment for dharma teachers and leaders of Black African Descent to come together, unify as sangha, and share our traditions and wisdom with one another as we go into deep inquiry about the healing roles we are being called to play in our communities."[6] We spent much needed time together in practice building kinship and beginning to name, own, and teach each other how we each draw from the Dharma in different ways to transform the traps of identity into openings for collective healing and awakening.

On our own, the presence of just one or two Black folks in a center or sangha is not enough to feel into the complete truth of our embodied experience. Tokenized representations at the margins of our centers are rarely enough to shift the culture or leadership. The Gathering II came at an auspicious time, mere weeks before the planet would be forever changed by pandemic, mere weeks before public outcry against anti-Black police brutality produced the largest mass protests ever recorded. We were "turning the wheel of the Dharma" as so many said that week, harmonizing the teachings of the Buddha with the liberation songs, lessons, and liturgies of the Black Prophetic Tradition. Being Buddhist (or Buddhish, as Rev. angel suggested), being Black, and being in this space of belonging brought a power all its own. There was strength in the embrace of this diasporic beloved community, with all the Dharma kinships and ancestral lineages of transmission we brought with us. Over the course of our ten-day retreat, many of us found new Dharma siblings in that spacious wine country landscape of rolling green hills and roving wild turkey. About six days in, we opened up the offering of space and, over the weekend, seventy swelled to include more than three hundred Black sangha siblings, all radiating freedom. The truth of suffering was both palpable and malleable, but we cannot heal what we cannot feel. In that space, taking that time, we could feel it all.

At each turn, wherever traditions of Dharma practice take root, they give rise to new expressions of themselves. At each instantiation of their transmission, new experiences of the truth of suffering change its texture, its inflection. From India to China, from China through Asia, from East to West, at each turn, new expressions of the Dharma have to contend with gatekeepers who guard its integrity against "change," or the insistence that it remain faithful to original interpretations of sacred texts. What we, who are Black, are sowing in this practice is space for direct experiences of close proximity with the relative and absolute truth of our own embodied relationship to suffering and strength, a shared experience with many mirrors for Western understandings of both, a truth so many are still learning to sit with, a truth about just how much Black lives matter.

The Radical Dharma

Over the last twenty years, my dear friend, mentor, and coauthor Rev. angel Kyodo williams has been sowing the seeds of a new Dharma informed by the truth of her embodied experience of intersectionality, awakening, and liberation. As Rev. angel writes in the introduction of *Radical Dharma*, there is only one way to observe the constructs that lead to harm and suffering out in the world; we must first see and account for those closest to home, those that make us feel most at home. Sitting is itself a simple practice for bearing witness to that which recedes from notice. Seeing and accounting for what is, stepping back from our patterns to observe them more clearly, without judgment we come to see truths hidden right under our nose. In the book and in the spaces the book has seeded throughout Western Buddhism and beyond, Radical Dharma is holding dynamic and embodied space for healing the harm of white supremacy backwards by noticing where we left parts of ourselves behind in order to belong, to progress, to feel at home. We notice when we choose security over freedom to reap the privileges of our belonging, rather than resist the seductions of individualism, exceptionalism, and dominance.

There is white supremacy present in our Dharma. In the welcome lies a navel-gazing presumption that white people have what Black and brown people want. The truth is that the freedom so many of us seek is something other than what most white folks currently enjoy or can even imagine. The Radical Dharma, or complete truth, is that we police and judge each other in ways that reinforce the police brutality that targets and kills Black people with impunity on a nearly daily basis.[7] We re-create delusions of superiority, even in our activist spaces and practice centers, even as we say we are about the work of liberation. No one escapes the violent effects of living in a violent culture. How each one of us accounts for our place on this land, our seat, our place, our role, our work in the world matters to our personal liberation as well as to our collective transformation.

Rather than avoid the dissatisfaction that racism and injustice give rise to in each of us, what if we turned toward the truth of that suffering and follow it through the wounding and loss to reclaim whatever has been left behind, as Rev. angel teaches: "[W]e're trying so hard to get away from it. We're trying to evade the grief and trauma of our own racism . . . and our continuous perpetuation of . . . oppression on ourselves and others every single day. Every single one of us."[8]

My coauthors Rev. angel and Lama Rod Owens are turning the wheel with many others to bring the Buddha's teachings on uncertainty, non-duality, and impermanence to bear on the trauma of white supremacy and its effects on our embodied experiences of race, gender, and sexuality. We each must reckon with our proximity to whiteness to transform the reality of its hold on our imaginations of freedom. No one escapes, but the whole truth is we, each of us, can support each other to be fugitives from the prison camps and plantations of our "privilege" to move closer to another vision of freedom.

A More Fugitive Freedom

What is your lineage? Who is your teacher? Where do you practice? These are the typical questions I hear from those familiar with Western Buddhism when they learn that I have a practice. Any one of these questions stops me in my tracks. The short answer is: I sit with Rev. angel and have for fifteen years. Radical Dharma is my lineage. As a lineage in formation, the ways I came to the cushion and the reasons I stayed there feel like departures from a traditional trajectory from curiosity to conversion, or from student to leader. I found Rev. angel's first book *Being Black* on the bookstore shelves at Brown University and bought it right then. "Black *and* Buddhist! Well at least I am not the first," I recall thinking to myself! The people I have come to recognize as my emergent sangha all found their way, in some part, through the words, witness, and wisdom of Rev. angel. We are mostly queer people-of-color from many root traditions; some hold other formal and informal relationships to teachers. Many consider themselves more "Buddhish" than Buddhist. Only the second Black person of her lineage, her own fugitive maverick relationship to Zen Buddhism is the full expression of the Dharma remixed through the embodied truth of her unique experience. As she writes in *Being Black: Zen and the Art of Living with Fearlessness and Grace* (2000), Rev. angel started as a formal student of Roshi Pat Enkyo O'Hara at the Village Zendo in New York City, but broke from her before receiving transmission. Shortly after the publication of her first book, she moved from Prospect Heights in Brooklyn to Northern California in 2001, and founded an urban monastery for practitioners-of-color in Oakland. She called it the newDharma Meditation Center and it became a residential practice center. I was fortunate to live just blocks away, close enough to bike to sits and dinners and talks and day-longs. I soon became her first dedicated practitioner, supporting her work within the Center, while apprenticing in the secular outposts of her efforts to bring the integrated elements of her newDharma practice and teaching to social change organizations and educators.

Along the way, our maroon-like sangha of largely radical, mostly queer-of-color activists and change agents has transformed from the real-time in-person tightly held container of wayward, awkward, and unrelenting practitioners, to an international network of people-of-color and white accomplices, many but not nearly all LBGTQ, each one utterly and unapologetically committed to divesting from the seductions of white supremacy in themselves while supporting others to do the same. Though I resonate with Zen and have since grade school, I never became a formal student of hers in the tradition of Zen. Many of our original sangha members did. Not following the formal protocols of belonging is not uncommon among those of us who come to a clearer vision of our own liberation in the company of Rev. angel's leadership, instruction, and guidance.[9]

To represent the breadth and depth of the community of practice Rev. angel has fostered, and to account for how sitting with the embodied Dharma of our intersectionality matters for the ways we hold the practice, I conducted interviews with six people, all part of the Dharma community inspired by Rev. angel and the work we do together. Each of these interviewees are people-of-color, all situated on some point of LGBTQ identity, most of whom identify as non-binary or nonconforming to traditional gender binaries and use they/them pronouns. They range in age from late twenties to early sixties. Their relationships to Buddhism range from formal Dharma and meditation teacher in the Shambhala tradition to "if I told my family they would worry about my soul," to "I don't call myself Buddhist but am deeply anchored by the practices and formal teachers, namely Rev. angel." There are, for many of us, what we might call fugitive elements present in our Dharma practice—practices and protocols of healing justice drawn from indigenous ceremony and spiritual survival passed down from ancestors, from the earth, from story, from river spirits, hot combs, *curanderismo*, and the intimacy of surviving shared trauma.

Though not all the interviewees are descendants of enslaved peoples, the elements of their journey to the cushion and commitment to practice are reminiscent of those who devised all kinds of invisible and undetected ways to escape slavery to move closer to freedom, by any means possible. While some historical fugitives fled north to the Free States or Canada, many took refuge in maroon communities, set up in the swamps or mountains far enough from those who sought their capture and subjection. The fugitive practices and maroon protocols of liberation from the antebellum era are a foundational piece of the Radical Dharma lineage precisely because it was in these spaces that the time of slavery was disrupted and the imagination of another future for freedom was born—one that did not require the ownership of another person to be authorized or recognized to exist. It is a lineage of rule-breaking that resonates in the throat with the recitation of the *Heart Sutra*, "O Shariputra, all Dharmas are inherently empty: not born, not destroyed, not defiled, not pure, neither lacking nor complete. . . ."

It was not until I was able to sit with Zen Master Bernie Glassman, Rev. angel's Dharma granddad in her lineage, that I came to understand myself as part of a lineage of irreverent rule-breakers. He spoke at Vassar, where I teach, in a lecture held just months before his transition. Listening to him talk about restorative justice circles in Rwanda and Auschwitz, listening to the playful combat between Bernie and his student Francisco "Paco" Lugoviña, who ordained Rev. angel and emerged out of nowhere from the audience, there was such love and electricity, an unapologetic relay of ways to reckon with the Dharma and the legacies of harm we carry in our bodies, one that lets the truth of that witness bear the path to liberation.

"When you're close to your suffering you're close to your humanity," as Lama Rod Owens teaches in a *Washington Post* interview that took place in the wake of the deaths of George Floyd, Breonna Taylor, and Ahmaud Arbery at the hands of police, weeks into a global pandemic. Lama Rod goes on:

> [A]nd when you're close to your humanity you become a mirror that reflects other people's humanity back to them. This is why I think Black and brown people are so situated to be the leaders of liberation and freedom, you know, because we're closer to what makes us human. We have not been able to wall ourselves off, or to numb ourselves, [in order] to participate in a system of oppressing others. That's going to keep us empathetic to others. And that empathy is really how that mirror works. It's like we're just reflecting back this reality that, yeah, everyone's hurting, you know, and we're close to our hurting. But the people who hurt us, they're the furthest away from their pain. And we're trying to draw people close, back to their pain, because that proximity is actually going to be the thing that disrupts them, to disrupt their participation in how systems are maintained by not being in a relationship to the suffering.[10]

Belonging beyond Adaptability

The people I interviewed for this project are all part of a growing maroon community of Radical Dharma sangha practitioners. We represent the non-white, non-heritage Buddhists, the queer, the non-binary. We bring many tendrils of liberation transmission with us to our cushions, those known and unnamed, from ancestors, elements, and stars. We are "creating a sense of world, an intergenerational world beyond what I can see," as one practice teacher interviewed shared. The generation of teacher/leader/spirit-guides who led our way demonstrate a deep dedication to embodying liberation as a practice in meeting and deconstructing or decentering the non-dual constructs of both self and structural injustice, because ego-death is the abolition of white supremacy in this realm.

As we, who represent the global majority, are often marginalized within discussions of Western Buddhism, we enter practice circles and centers knowing that we will likely encounter racism, sexism, or heterosexism along the way. The pressure to appear non-threatening, amicable, respectable, and articulate precede our arrival at our cushions. In fact, these modes of adaptivity are often the rule rather than the exception, a given to be anticipated anywhere whiteness and, as we say in Radical Dharma spaces, the principles and practices of white supremacy live. Many of us become so highly adaptable to whiteness that we only see how hard we are working to belong when we notice our resistance to predominantly white practice spaces. Our resistance and our desire are suddenly at cross-purposes. The habituated relationship to power, to invoke DuBois, is to appear as if you won't be a problem, even when you come wounded and in need of healing. As one non-binary Black practice leader of Caribbean descent shared in their interview,

> I am old enough, I've been through enough institutional spaces and non-institutional spaces to know that there are very few spaces where my whole being is accepted and seen.... At practice centers... the majority of the time... I am viewed as an "other"... there can be a lot of undue attention on me, because there's something different about me.... I'm walking in with my own comfort and I just adapt, make things my own, that's how I move. Most of the spaces I move into are like, "Hey! Come into our space and adapt to what we're doing"... I feel like I have to assess, and when I'm practicing my spiritual path I want to minimize that as much as possible—*I'm already doing that in so many other spaces.* In the relative sense, and I get to the absolute later, but in the relative sense there is something to protect. I guess I'm just trying to stay resourced so I can receive the teachings and receive whatever practices I am engaging inside an institution.

We practice inside institutions *and* out in the wild, with trees, in water, touching earth. We draw from several sites of practice to "stay resourced" and protect our energy, from indigenous traditions and ancestral lineages to the activist knowledges and intellectual traditions of Black and brown cultural workers like Gloria Anzaldúa and adrienne maree brown.

Most of those interviewed for this piece visited a formal center at some point, but left to find people-of-color retreats or found people-of-color circles, or joined queer affinity practice spaces, or connect to the Dharma through Rev. angel's leadership. One Black cisgender woman from Los Angeles shared that she visited a practice center in San Francisco on a whim. "It just so happened there was a Black woman there, and if she wasn't there I probably wouldn't be here today. She was nice and she was friendly and helpful and she wanted to engage with me so I came back a couple times." Like many of the interviewees, however, this woman ultimately sat with several sanghas and traditions, taking recommendations from friends for teachers about retreats for twenty years. In 2001 she met Rev. angel and many of the folks who would be our original sangha at Spirit Rock's People-of-Color retreat. It was that visit that inspired Rev. angel's move to hold her own sits in a house she rented at 65th and San Pablo in Oakland.

Another interviewee, a light-skinned Latinx practitioner, chose to stay in an existing formal practice place for the first links in her Dharma journey. "I always felt welcome in white spaces, until I started identifying as a person-of-color. Once I started identifying as a person-of-color I had different expectations." They told a story about asking their Vipassana teacher, a white woman, how come she did not talk about race, gender, sexuality? This interviewee said the teacher responded saying "There's no time!" "It wasn't that she thought it was irrelevant," the interviewee added, "but the other things they were teaching us were priority, the ancient wisdoms etc. There were token LGBT retreats, a young people's retreat, and a people-of-color retreat after some pushing by students. She did those . . . but there was very little content to discuss those issues—it was LITE—not *not* there but . . . quite limited."

A Black practitioner from New York found their way to their cushion predominantly through affinity spaces, starting with a people-of-color retreat at Blue Cliff Monastery in 2009, the East Coast monastery in the lineage of Thich Nhat Hanh. After hearing about it, this New York–based seeker decided to use their next vacation to retreat there. "Getting up to sit at six a.m. with a room full of very silent and still monastics I had the experience of 'Oh! This is what meditation is like. OK! I see!'" They picked up Thich Nhat Hanh's *Fragrant Palm Leaves* at Blue Cliff and fell in love. "Prior to that I had never felt anything other than a personal spirituality and never thought I would feel something that would connect me to other people." This interviewee went on to share of that first encounter,

> I remember two things about that time. I remember remembering my wish for having community and I was still at a point when I felt very much like a chameleon, feeling like I had to change to be in any space I was going into, this is also before I started psychotherapy and other things, but I remember feeling at home there. . . . Those memories stick with me still.

After that first encounter with the Dharma, taking refuge in stillness and silence, this New York–based practitioner sought sanctuary in a number of people-of-color sangha spaces held by emerging Black leaders over many years, one by Sebene Selassie in her home before she became the executive director at New York Insight Meditation Center. They migrated from practice leaders' homes to a colonic clinic in Fort Greene, then eventually they met at the Brooklyn Commons in downtown Brooklyn, and finally found home at Brooklyn Zen Center as the New York Insight POC and Allies sangha. This interviewee also noted the significant work that Gina Sharpe and Larry Yang did throughout this time to support people-of-color teaching cohorts in the Insight Theravada Lineage.

It was a few years later, at another retreat at Blue Cliff, when they were still offering people-of-color retreats, that this interviewee had a conversation about practice that led to an invitation to lead their own space. When asked if they felt called to share practice with others and hold space, my interviewee said, "I was terrified, but I trusted her and said 'I am open to it.' I felt strongly enough about practice and want to share it," they said. So began Love Circle Sangha in June 2014, as a practice group that centers on queer Black and indigenous people-of-color in the Thich Nhat Hanh tradition.

There is such richness inside these stories, in the mirroring and witness. Reading Ryūmon Zenji, Hilda Gutiérrez Baldoquín's introduction to *Dharma, Color and Culture*, it is clear that practitioners and teachers-of-color bring insight to the Buddha's teachings that have no bounds and are truly in service to all. Citing the teachings of Venerable Zen Master Thich Nhat Hanh, that "shine as a brilliant morning sun," Ryūmon Zenji's introduction situates a liberated experience in the intimacy of our embodiment in the world as it is. "He asks us, 'In your true home, is there any suffering?' He takes our hand and we learn to embrace the suffering; for without it, we cannot learn compassion."[11]

Staying resourced in Dharma spaces requires practitioners and people-of-color to lean into their own experience, learn to notice when and where the protocols of belonging we have inherited are not working for us, find our feet, as Rev. angel instructs in her Centering practice, and center into the truth transmitted to us when we turn inward and learn to listen to the language of the body. From the movement of the breath through it, we learn to tell time differently, to feel into the information vibrating through us, to better discern what is needed to be here now. Turning in without leaving embodiment behind is a contemplative approach; a practice in being radically receptive to and in alignment with the body, a practice in staying resourced enough to get what's needed to get free.

In addition to drawing on traditional practices of sitting, chanting, and taking refuge in ceremony, staying resourced looks like centering, time with nature, "popping a squat wherever," cleansing and detoxing with and near water, long walks. There are those who practice through storytelling, on a yoga mat, in dreams, through sound and voice, or writing, in any way we can "take the pain apart" to see it, hold it, more clearly. Another fugitive Latinx practitioner from Fort Collins, Colorado, shared, "there isn't a pathway of avoidance for queer people-of-color . . . taking the pain apart is a part of embodiment. I can't not confront that my body is a frontline of both colonizer and colonized, as someone who is mixed race, as someone who is mestiza, we are simultaneously situated at the confrontation of violence and resistance at a capillary level. It is in our nervous system." Even though avoidance isn't the pathway, they went on to say, there is liberation in transmuting the embodied effects of feeling like a contradiction. And indeed, I agreed, everyone's body can, if closely interrogated, evidence the contradictions of colonialism, but too many of us are not taught to sit with that non-duality and . . . let nothingness do what it does.

In the last days with these interviews, I was called into community with several new Dharma siblings. One, Theravadin practitioner, author, and filmmaker Aishah Shahidah Simmons, shared,

> I've been in the *fire* with my rage about systemic racism in my former lineage (asking myself, why . . . did I stay for seventeen years). The rage felt uncontrollable and I did all I could to contain it without publicly reacting. I'm grateful for the balm that Tuere Sala, one of my dhamma/dharma teachers, provided. Not to quiet the rage but to put it in a context. I stayed because I also received so much through my solitary sits for 10-, 20-, and 30-day periods. I stayed because I was taught that what I practiced was the *only* "real deal." Based on this, I was determined to not allow white supremacy, racism, and its inadvertent and intentional conduits prevent me from being enlightened. This understanding helped me cultivate *mettā* for myself because I was beating myself up royally for staying.[12]

She is not the only one on fire. We are heading into an era of reckoning with and awaking to the presence of white supremacy in the Western Dharma community. The world is on fire, and the love that is needed to make this fire cleanse as it consumes is a love fierce enough to sit with the violence of separation, to breathe space into the wounding, the rage, the emptiness, and the overwhelm, one that lets the practice alchemize the toughest, most indigestible, untenable truths into what Rev. angel calls a path of fearlessness and grace. Rather than leaving the work of reckoning to the racialized, gendered, and queerly oriented "others," instead of bypassing the parts that awaken us to the relative and absolute truth of suffering and leaving folks with the least access and least status to work twice as hard to get half the respect that white, cis-male, straight counterparts enjoy, what might it look like if those with the closest proximity to power turn to Black and brown leaders, note how they hold their seat, and join in working twice as hard so that we may end our addictions and transform our illusions, and find the awakened way together?

Inescapability and invisibility, violence and healing, binary and fluid, ascetic and audacious—we all live within the living contradictions of embodied experiences of identity. We walk the path by turning into that truth, bearing witness with love and meeting the suffering of division, exceptionalism, and domination where we stand, where we sit, in our circles and centers and lineages.

That question *who do I think I am?* is an invitation to become fugitive from the boundless ignorance of our bodyheartmindsouls. In the full realization of the relative and the absolute truth of being in the world, there is another way, across the river of suffering, free from all separation, in an embodied radical Dharma of sitting with fugitives.

Notes

1. Zenju Earthlyn Manuel, "Awakening Fueled by Rage," *Lion's Roar*, June 1, 2020, https://www.lionsroar.com/awakening-fueled-by-rage/.
2. Angela Y. Davis, "Women and Capitalism: Dialectics of Oppression and Liberation," in *The Black Feminist Reader*, ed. Joy James and T. Deneaan Sharpley-Whiting (Malden, MA: Blackwell, 2000), 148.
3. Damien M. Sojoyner, "Dissonance in Time: (Un)making and (Re)mapping of Blackness," in *Future of Black Radicalism*, ed. Gaye Theresa Johnson and Alex Lubin (London: Verso, 2017), 59–60.
4. For more on fugitive homemaking, see Jasmine Syedullah, "No Place like Home: Practicing Freedom in the Loopholes of Captivity," in *Pathways to Prison: Histories on the Architecture of Carcerality*, ed. Isabelle Kirkham-Lewitt (New York: Columbia University Press, 2020), 459-484.
5. Zenju Earthlyn Manuel, "Awakening Fueled by Rage," *Lion's Roar*, June 1, 2020, https://www.lionsroar.com/awakening-fueled-by-rage/.
6. Program for "The Fierce Urgency of Now: The Gathering of Buddhist Teachers of Black African Descent," *Spirit Rock Meditation Center*, Retreat Program, October 7–15, 2019, Woodacre, California, p. 2.
7. For more on the rates of Black people killed by the police, see https://mappingpoliceviolence.org/.
8. angel Kyodo williams, Rod Owens, and Jasmine Syedullah, *Radical Dharma: Talking Race Love and Liberation*. (Berkeley: North Atlantic Books, 2016), xx.
9. In conversation with the interviewees, I learned that nearly all of them have informal teacher/student relationships with Rev. angel. Some of us never asked to be a formal student, others of us asked three times. It is always "on the menu," as she makes clear, but that kind of nation-building for Zen is not exactly what she is up to. One said, "Ultimately Zen is a monastic transmission and what they are trying to do is train people in a monastery, super intensely, then throw them out into these lay centers, essentially trying to force lay people to be monastics. It is very hard. . . . I don't have any tension about it with regard to my own path . . . I've been very blessed to have a very close relationship with Rev. angel, and when I do reach out she's there. You know, and I have this whole other lineage that I have support from, and that works for me. . . . I think it works for me to have teachers in face, like Rev. angel, and in apparition like Thich Nhat Hanh, and I consider all my sangha siblings my teachers keeping me on the path by being themselves on the path."
10. Lama Rod Owens, "A Buddhist Teacher's Meditations on Confronting White Supremacy," interview by David Montgomery, *Washington Post*, July 21, 2020, https://www.washingtonpost.com/lifestyle/magazine/a-buddhist-teachers-meditations-on-confronting-white-supremacy/2020/07/20/3f9cf510-b71b-11ea-aca5-ebb63d27e1ff_story.html.
11. Hilda Gutiérrez Baldoquín, *Dharma, Color and Culture: New Voices of Western Buddhism* (Westminster: Parallax Press, 2004), 20.
12. Aishah Shahidah Simmons. Email message to author, July 26, 2020.

Further Reading

Baldoquín, Hilda Gutiérrez, ed. *Dharma, Color and Culture: New Voices of Western Buddhism.* Westminster: Parallax Press, 2004.
Glaude, Eddie S., Jr. *Exodus! Religion, Race, and Nation in Early Nineteenth-Century Black America.* Chicago: University of Chicago Press, 2000.
James, Joy, and T. Deneaan Sharpley-Whiting, eds. *The Black Feminist Reader.* Malden, MA: Blackwell, 2000.
Johnson, Gaye Theresa, and Alex Lubin, eds. *Futures of Black Radicalism.* London: Verso, 2017.
McGee, Rhonda V. *The Inner Work of Racial Justice: Healing Ourselves and Transforming Our Communities through Mindfulness.* New York: Penguin Random House, 2019.
Nishitani, Keiji. *Religion and Nothingness.* Berkeley: University of California Press, 1983.
Owens, Rod. *Love and Rage: The Path of Liberation through Anger.* Berkeley: North Atlantic Books, 2020.
williams, angel Kyodo. *Being Black: Zen and the Art of Living with Fearlessness and Grace.* Penguin Compass; New York, 2000.
williams, angel Kyodo, Rod Owens, and Jasmine Syedullah. *Radical Dharma: Talking Race Love and Liberation.* North Atlantic Press: Berkeley, 2016.
Willis, Jan. *Dharma Matters: Women, Race, and Tantra.* Boston: Wisdom Publications, 2020.
Yancy, George, and Emily McRae, eds. *Buddhism and Whiteness: Critical Reflections.* Lanham, MD: Lexington Press, 2019.

CHAPTER 33

BUDDHIST CHAPLAINCY

JITSUJO T. GAUTHIER

Story of the Cup

It was 5 p.m, when the call came for a chaplain to come to the Neonatal Critical Care Unit and do a baptism for a baby that was passing. I was the only one remaining in the Spiritual Care office. It was my first month in a Clinical Pastoral Education (CPE) residency. I had done only a half unit of CPE before this residency, had little experience doing bedside rituals, felt very uncomfortable in my authority to say spontaneous prayers, not to mention the fact that I was Buddhist. I remember my CPE supervisor telling us, "You are only called to things that you can handle." I took the generic document for a baby baptism from my hospital chaplain's handbook, and looked it over in the elevator as I headed up to the unit. When I got there, a nurse immediately approached me, "Are you here to do the baptism? The family is waiting for you in room 325." How did she know I was the chaplain? It was certainly not from my calm, centered demeanor or aura of spiritual presence, because the terror in my heart and mind was palpable.

When I reached the room, I took a deep breath, emptied my mind, and crossed over the threshold. I walked over to the family, and introduced myself as the hospital chaplain. Gazing down at the little baby lying there with so many tubes and wires taped to his body, I said, "Oh, he is so little, what is his name?" "This is Oscar," they said. I asked, "What is each of your relationship to Oscar?" Mom, dad, grandma, and a big sister told me about baby Oscar, how he suffered, and would soon die. They asked, "Could you baptize him? We want to make sure he will go to a better place, and be with God."

Though I felt ill prepared, I found my breath, looked into their eyes and received the sincerity of what they were asking me to do, and said okay. I realized I had forgotten the holy water, so I looked around for a clear pill cup or some small container for the water, but found nothing. Again, I connected with my breath, reached into my heart, placed my palms together, and began to read the baptism document folded between my now sweaty palms. I added some personal stories the family had told me into the reading. When it was time to perform the baptism, I walk over to the faucet, poured some water into my hand, breathed love into it, carried it over to the bedside, and said, "Why don't we all baptize him?" Holding out my palms, I motioned for mom to go first. Each dipped their finger in the holy water, and made a cross on the little baby boy's forehead. Following them, I did the same. It was so very tender. We finished by holding hands in a circle, I was holding baby Oscar's hand on one side, and mom on the other as I said a closing prayer. I prayed that baby Oscar have a peaceful passing, that he feel enveloped in God's love, and that the family feel comforted and supported in their grief.

The Heart of Buddhist Chaplaincy

The hospital gives chaplain interns/residents the authority to baptize dying infants. Usually there is not enough time to call in an outside priest or minister. After a baptized baby has passed, the Spiritual Care department mails the parents a certificate with a card. Some children's hospitals provide a baptism kit, which helps make the baby blessing/ baptism a more intimate and personal ritual. A kit may contain a bottle of holy water, a hand-knitted shawl to lay across the baby's chest, a candle, a hand-made card, and a certificate. The parents take the kit with them to memorialize the life created and lost, and/ or make a home altar to help them grieve.

When the family asked me to baptize baby Oscar, I wanted to say, "I am actually Buddhist, so what I can actually do is a baby blessing, so that Oscar feels peace, love, and safe in body and mind as he passes from this life to the next." But I knew in my heart that this would not serve them, this little baby boy, or the situation, so instead I looked into each of their eyes, mom, dad, older sister, grandma, and nodded my head yes. No one had taught me how to do a baptism. There were no Buddhist chaplaincy programs at the time. However, I had previously worked under a Buddhist CPE supervisor who always encouraged me to be authentic, offer what I had with an open heart, and to trust in this.

At the time I was also new to Buddhist practice, and had never heard of a purification ritual. So when I breathed love into the water it arose very naturally out of a genuine desire to serve this family and unite with them so that this baby felt completely loved and peaceful as he passed from this life to the next. As I gained experience, I made sure to come prepared, compiled a book of rituals, prayers, and poems from various religious/spiritual perspectives, developed many techniques as I did bedside rituals, and grew more comfortable standing in my role as a chaplain. There was something very special and touching about this first baptism when I knew nothing. An indescribable presence arose as we together created a ritual out of nothing, an interconnection that I will never forget.

Conceptual Overview of Buddhist Chaplains

Activities

Buddhist chaplains serve in US hospitals, hospices, behavioral health and psychiatric clinics, prisons, jails, military, law enforcement, fire departments, and colleges and universities. The question arises as to whether Buddhist chaplains should only see Buddhists, Jewish chaplains only Jewish care recipients, Christian chaplains only Christians, etc. The answer is that chaplains see people of all religious traditions and non-religious worldviews. In reality, Buddhist chaplains predominantly see non-Buddhist care recipients. Whatever their area of specialization, Buddhist chaplains are assigned to a particular unit and serve as a chaplain to all the people on that unit, no matter what their religion or worldview. Care recipients can request to see a chaplain of a particular religious tradition. The activities of a Buddhist chaplain range from conducting individual or group prayers, meditations, liturgy rituals, and weekly, monthly, or annual services in the interfaith chapel, to short-term individual spiritual care and counseling, and bearing witnessing practices. Bearing witness is the practice of deep listening from the heart, being inclusive, and seeing as many positions and perspectives as possible.

The majority of recipients seeking chaplaincy care in the United States are Christian and Catholic; there are also those who are Jewish, Buddhist, Hindu, and Muslim, as well as those who do not identify with any religion, are atheist, agnostic, humanist, multifaith, hold worldviews that are scientific, philosophical, or spiritual but not religious (SBNR). This usually raises the question of whether all chaplains have to know something about all world religions in order to provide adequate chaplaincy care. Likewise, do Buddhists need to know everything about Buddhism? Buddhist chaplaincy educator Daijaku Kinst notes the importance of training and knowledge in rituals from multiple Buddhist traditions, as well as a working knowledge of other non-Buddhist traditions for effective functioning in interfaith settings.[1] Rituals, liturgy, use of sacred texts, images, and objects are learned within one's own Buddhist tradition. Religious literacy, cultural sensitivity, interfaith and inter-Buddhist rituals, as well as awareness of power and privilege within the role, are part of chaplaincy education and clinical training.

Yet, it is impossible for Buddhist chaplains to know everything about every religion, and everything about Buddhism before working in the chaplaincy field. Rather, Buddhist chaplains bring their identity, practice, philosophy, cultural heritage, emotions, psychology, and training to work. During times of crisis, they practice "holding the space of the patient's inner life" and "bringing sanity to the scene" by "embodying a non-panicked mode of being," says Buddhist hospital chaplain Holly Hisamoto. Buddhist military chaplain Christopher Moore serves all soldiers by conducting invocations, prayers, meditations, rituals, and services for all religious traditions, bearing witness and counseling all soldiers through grief, loss, violence, and suicide, and creating meaningful Buddhist rituals concerning suffering, celebration, and other important transitions.[2] As Buddhist chaplains grow and mature, they continue to create innovative rituals that embody, transform, and acknowledge aspects of suffering for each new moment in time.

Roles and Competencies

When people are in the midst of a crisis, they often completely forget the resources that will help them navigate the difficultly. Just by self-introduction, a chaplain acts as a reminder of religious beliefs, practices, cultural heritage, and worldviews. This introduction is either a door opener or door closer. In either case, there is an opportunity to navigate this threshold and hear the story behind the opening or closing door. Buddhist chaplains undergo training in order to meet people in a way that is mutually human and from the heart. Buddhist chaplains receive educational training from Master of Divinity (MDiv) programs, clinical training from chaplaincy internship/residency programs in CPE, endorsement from the Buddhist community they identify with, and certification from the Association of Professional Chaplains (APC). APC is an umbrella organization that calls upon a Buddhist task force to advise them on their endorsement and certification processes. Requirements for chaplaincy board certification include both educational and clinical components, Dharma training and ministerial endorsement, and work experience.

The educational and clinical training that Buddhist chaplains receive teaches them skills to minister to people with worldviews, cultures, and faith systems different from their own. They learn to remain grounded in their own Buddhist practice without proselytizing their worldview onto the recipients of their care. Buddhist Chaplain Tim Ford explains:

> The chaplain's job as a religious person is to develop his or her own faith to the point where they can relax or surrender their beliefs enough to join another person in theirs. The patient's role is to apply their historical beliefs to a new and often difficult situation or to create new beliefs. Ultimately, it is the depth of relationship or synchronicity between these two roles that determines the depth of healing that will occur, not the homogeneity of their beliefs.[3]

Serving both religious and non-religious persons in crisis or distress, Buddhist chaplains support reintegration of physical, emotional, psychological, and spiritual lived experiences in relationships. At times, this kind of ministry follows quite nicely with foundational Buddhist teachings and tenets; at other times, this may challenge Buddhist chaplains to choose when to align with their own Buddhist identity, values, teachings, and tenets, and when to let them go. This chapter attempts to articulate the complexity of Buddhist chaplaincy as an emerging form of applied Buddhism.

Marginalization and Need

Anthropologist Frances Norwood conducted an ethnographic study with a group of hospital chaplains from varying religious traditions during their CPE internship, published in her 2006 article.[4] Norwood identifies the chaplain's role as ambivalent and marginal within a contemporary medical system, as she observes these CPE interns constantly shifting alliances between secular ideologies of medicine and religious ideologies of the care recipients. Interestingly, she also observes that from within their roles, these chaplains have agency. They strategically negotiate their power and place as they run up against the dominant structures, institutional ideologies, and different worldviews around them.

There are structural ideologies and expectations and projections of chaplaincy rooted in Christianity within healthcare, prison, military, and academic systems. Most chaplains, CPE supervisors, and directors of Spiritual/Pastoral Care departments in the United States are Christian. This makes it difficult for Buddhist chaplains to navigate, especially for those born in Asian countries. At the same time, there is opportunity to use their differences within the field as an asset. Many of their institutional coworkers and care recipients identify as agnostic, atheist, humanist, or SBNR, view Buddhism as "scientific" or "philosophical," and tend to be more open to Buddhist teachings and practices. As Buddhists are grounded in flexibility and fluidity, embody impermanence, suffering, and no-self, they bring different perspectives of spiritual care, which may in turn open new pathways for the field of chaplaincy overall.

Certification and Endorsement

The APC is considered the primary certifying body because it upholds the highest standards for becoming a board-certified professional chaplain. There are no certifying bodies for individual religions. Requirements for Buddhist chaplain certification follow national qualifications and competencies for the Board of Chaplaincy Certification Inc. (BCCI) common to all chaplains. Requirements include a bachelor's degree, 72 units from an accredited MDiv program, four units of CPE, endorsement by a recognized Buddhist community, one year of chaplaincy work, and a few essays that demonstrate professional competencies. Competencies for BCCI are within two levels. The first level is to develop and articulate integration of theory and practice. The second level is to develop a professional identity, conduct in relation to others, and skills in relation to systems, professional practice, and organizational leadership.[5]

The process of BCCI certification has been challenging for Buddhists over the years. Before there were Buddhist MDiv programs, APC worked with a Buddhist task force to create "A White Paper" (2006)[6] to assist Buddhist chaplains in developing equivalencies for certification utilizing Dharma training, mentorship, meditation retreats, and rituals. More recently, APC called upon a second Buddhist task force comprising individuals from the Buddhist MDiv and certificate programs in the United States. Their task in assisting APC is twofold: (1) to make an endorsement form that is user-friendly for both endorser, i.e., Buddhist teacher, and endorsee, i.e., Buddhist chaplain, and (2) to create a structure to ensure that those applying for certification are affiliated with a recognized Buddhist lineage/tradition/organization. Endorsement ensures that the endorsee is educationally, clinically, doctrinally, and developmentally qualified to represent their tradition and community within the chaplaincy setting in which they specialize.[7]

Training: Education and Dharma Practice

MDiv Degree Overview

Buddhist chaplains enroll in a university, or Buddhist certificate program, to get a Master of Divinity (MDiv). In order to become a board-certified chaplain, they will need an accredited educational degree. The MDiv is a 72-unit, three-year, full-time program. The APC and Association of Theological Schools (ATS) outline educational requirements and academic standards in the United States. Categories of study include courses in religious history, foundational religious teachings and tenets, sacred texts, ethical frameworks and development, world religions or comparative religions, ethnic and cultural diversity, chaplaincy, spiritual care and counseling, communications skills, spiritual/religious education, professional ethics, spiritual/religious leadership within communities/organizations, and supervised faith-based internships.

Buddhist MDiv programs devise curricula from these standards that combine religious studies classes and chaplaincy classes, along with psychology and organizational management classes. Religious studies classes teach the philosophy, hermeneutics, texts, and canonical languages of Buddhism. Students may choose an area of focus that interests them. Chaplaincy classes teach the history and theory of chaplaincy, spiritual formation, contemplative care and counseling practices, structures of power and privilege, Buddhist ministry, leadership, preaching, and pastoral theology. Buddhist educational programs weave in non-Buddhist sources and methods of spiritual formation, assessment, care, and counseling. Students learn how to build bridges to non-Buddhist faith-based systems and apply Buddhist scriptures to real-life situations. MDiv classes are interdisciplinary to practice basic communication and counseling skills for CPE.

Buddhist Institutions and Certificate Programs

Six universities offer Buddhist MDiv/MA degrees in Buddhist chaplaincy in the United States. Four universities are nationally accredited, two are regionally accredited, and there are four Buddhist chaplaincy certificate programs. Faculty from these institutions have been working together since 2016 within the Buddhist Ministry Working Group[8] to develop relationships, collaborate, and align professional competencies. Programs vary in philosophy, organization, and pedagogy, reflecting the founding Buddhist tradition, age of the program, geographic location, and faculty. Harvard Divinity School has a reputation of academic rigor and field placement rooted in Christianity. Naropa draws on the teachings of Trungpa Rinpoche, and it is well established in the integration of academia, embodiment, psychology, and service learning. The Institute of Buddhist Studies, based in Jodo Shinshu Buddhism, draws on the inter-religious consortia of the Graduate Theological Union. University of the West utilizes the pedagogy of Taiwanese Humanistic Buddhism, with a chaplaincy educational model that integrates the academic, practitioner, and caregiver.[9] Maitripa College, founded by Yangsi Rinpoche, identifies curriculum pillars of Buddhist philosophy, meditation, and community service. Won Buddhism stems from the Korean Zen tradition. These programs view Buddhist chaplaincy as applied Buddhism and emphasize the foundational teachings of the Three Jewels and the Threefold Training.

Buddhist chaplaincy certificate programs are strong in integrating Dharma training, but they lack academic components of Buddhist history, sacred texts, language, world religions, and comparative frameworks. However, some certificate programs are entering into agreements with seminaries or other Buddhist universities to complete the academic units for an MDiv degree. For example, the New York Zen Center for Contemplative Care has this agreement with Union Theological Seminary in New York City. Buddhist chaplains enhance their skills by engaging in other programs, such as those that offer a certificate in Buddhist contemplative care, counseling, or chaplaincy to professional caregivers from fields of medicine, psychology, and social work. Hospice and prison volunteers, Buddhist monastics, priests, and other serious practitioners may also seek to learn basic reflexive listening, contemplative care, Buddhist psychology, and chaplaincy skills to integrate with Dharma training. APC still accepts some MDiv equivalencies for certification, but this is becoming less frequent.

Spiritual Formation and Maturity

Many people ask why this MDiv requirement is 72 units as opposed to the usual 48 units. This is related not only to ATS educational requirements, but also to the maturing process, spiritual formation, and time necessary to grow into the chaplain role. Generally speaking, spiritual formation focuses on instruction, discipline, practice, or training intended to deepen faith and/or further spiritual development, growth, and transformation. MDiv students vary in the rate at which they attain formation and understanding of inner and outer pastoral/spiritual authority. This formation and maturing process goes beyond intellectual learning of theories and information. Vajrayana Buddhist CPE educator Tom Kilts introduces how the mandala principal and Buddha Families can be used as guides for pastoral formation, identity, and functioning in Buddhist ministry and as a CPE training methodology.[10] Articulating spiritual formation is a big part of the CPE application. It signifies self-understanding of conditioning and behavior patterns, self-responsibility, i.e., ability to identify inner and outer resources in difficult times, and micro and macro ministerial competencies about boundaries, power, and authority.

Many academic books have been published within the Judeo-Christian tradition on topics of spiritual formation and the development of pastoral/spiritual authority. There are no books specifically on Buddhist spiritual formation; therefore, MDiv and chaplaincy training programs turn to non-Buddhist texts, along with Buddhist articles and texts, in order to help students bridge Buddhist formation with Theistic approaches. When I teach Buddhist spiritual formation, I look at James Fowler's *Stages of Faith*[11] as archetypal energies,[12] which describe mind-body development, facets of mind, or aspects of understanding self/Self. I utilize Buddhist frameworks like the Ox-herding pictures,[13] Wheel of Life, Six Realms of Existence, the Threefold Training, and Eightfold Path to explore Buddhist spiritual formation with the students. Using Fowler's stages as a framework, Buddhist MDiv students reflect on their spiritual journey starting at birth, or even at conception within their mother's womb. Students explore their family of origin, cultural heritage, significant events, important persons, religious experiences, and other high-impact moments within mundane and ultimate reality.

Although Buddhism is not considered belief- or faith-based, there is a period when faith in the Buddha's Enlightenment experience is necessary. Once understanding is experienced inwardly, there is no need to rely on outside sources of authority. Zen Master Uchiyama identifies attitudes of the magnanimous mind, nurturing mind, and joyful mind as the ability to function as a true adult and mature person,[14] reflecting a developed pastoral/spiritual authority from a Zen Buddhist perspective. The Buddhist Ministry Working Group discussed what constitutes spiritual maturity and the ability to embody Buddhist ethics. Six elements of spiritual maturity were outlined as: (1) a clearly developed and practiced meditation technique, (2) ethical development, (3) a ritualized life, (4) perspective taking, i.e., the ability to see a variety of perspectives other than one's own, (5) identifying edge states within one's own development, e.g., discerning helpful/harmful, and the spiritual bypass, i.e., using prayer, meditation, or ritual to bypass suffering, and (6) the academic study of Buddha Dharma.

Contemplative Hours

Buddhist MDiv programs teach students theories of spiritual care and counseling, elements of spiritual maturity, stages of spiritual formation, notions of pastoral authority, and the academic study of Buddhism. However, integration requires contemplation. Contemplative practices include seated meditation, mindfulness practices like chanting, scripture recitation, yoga, walking, running, movement meditations, sangha work practices, spiritual/religious workshops and seminars, art, poetry, journaling, vigils and marches, group council/process, and day- or week-long spiritual, religious, or secular retreats. Educational programs make requirements for contemplative hours. MDiv programs find different ways for students to meet requirements, such as requiring a student to submit a log of contemplative hours, e.g., 180 hours per semester, providing students a faculty member as a meditation mentor, pairing them with a peer to create a buddy system, offering intensive retreats as part of the curriculum, and/or establishing connections with nearby sanghas. Like all spiritual journeys, it is really up to the MDiv students to seek out a Dharma teacher and sangha to connect with and support their chaplaincy formation and engaged work.

Dharma Training

Dharma training within a particular tradition is an important aspect of chaplaincy formation. Educational and clinical training are not enough. Taking refuge in the Three Jewels of Buddha, Dharma, and sangha and making vows to uphold the five precepts is the minimum requirement of a Buddhist chaplain. Monastics training from all traditions value a ritualized life, decorum, demeanor, and concentration practices. To embody Buddhist ethics takes a commitment to a Dharma tradition, teacher, and sangha.

Perspectives on authority may be best realized in relationship to a Dharma teacher. Attitudes of generosity, respect, and openness toward the Buddha, bodhisattvas, one's Dharma teacher, and even those who treat us poorly invoke compassion and develop authority and confidence from within. The vertical structure of the shepherd tending to the sheep from the mountaintop has been a strong image of a traditional Christian pastoral role,[15] i.e., a parental "power-over" modality. There is also the horizontal structure of the shepherd coming down off the mountaintop to walk among the sheep. Buddhist theologian Pamela Ayo Yetunde finds pastoral instances in the *Mahagopalaka-sutta*[16] of the cowherd raising and caring for cattle, and correlates this motif to the Buddha as a pastoral caregiver who tends to the sangha in a pastoral way.[17]

Many illustrations depict the Buddha seated on the ground in a circle among his disciples. This image of the pastoral role of being in conversation, i.e., "powerlessness-with" modality,[18] is sharing experience while remaining present in the midst of profound powerlessness to co-construct reality together. In this way, the pastoral role may be equated to a bodhisattva, spiritual friend (*kalyānamitra*), humanist, compassionate caregiver, engaged Buddhist, peacemaker, or student of life.[19] A Zen story likens sangha to a bag of sharp rocks continuously rubbing against each other to soften all their edges. We need others to rub up against our stuck or traumatized places if we are going to unearth deeper aspects of ourselves. We need the mirror of others to see Dharma and differences clearly, as we are only able to guide others to emotional, psychological, or spiritual places that we have gone ourselves.

Training: Clinical Pastoral Education (CPE)

CPE Internship/Residency

The Association for Clinical Pastoral Education (ACPE) has developed a chaplaincy internship/residency program called Clinical Pastoral Education (CPE). This is an interreligious, multifaith, clinical training program. CPE brings together a wide variety of Christian chaplains, e.g., Catholic, Protestant, Nazarene, Adventist, Eastern Orthodox, Quaker, along with Jewish, Hindu, Buddhist, and Muslim chaplains as the minorities. CPE is a form of experiential learning that can enhance careers in many fields. Diversity within the CPE groups adds to dialogue and learning by providing a forum for chaplains to engage directly with each other's different cultures and worldviews.

Most CPE programs are based in hospitals. However, there are developing CPE models that place chaplains in other settings to do clinical hours, e.g., universities, hospices, prisons, and nonprofit organizations, meeting weekly to do group educational hours. One unit of CPE is 400 hours of training, consisting of 100 hours of educational group work facilitated by a certified CPE educator, and 300 hours of clinical chaplaincy work. In this way CPE is multipurpose: (1) to train chaplains to work in the hospital setting, (2) to provide a forum for interreligious and multifaith group dialogue and learning among chaplains of different cultures and worldviews, and (3) to serve the spiritual needs of patients, families, and staff within the institution.

Similar to the medical doctor intern/resident program, CPE interns/residents are assigned to one to three hospital units where they serve as the chaplain for all the patients on that unit for the duration of their time there. CPE internships are offered on both a full- and part-time basis. A CPE internship equates to one unit of CPE over the course of several months, and a CPE residency equates to three to four units of CPE over the course of one year. The first few weeks of CPE are incredibly disorienting. Interns/residents are given chaplain badges, assigned to units, flooded with information about infection control, medical codes and terminology, patient visitation procedures, charting, advance directives, spiritual assessment, the course schedule, and on-call hours. Intern/residents are learning new structures and ideologies as they are getting to know each other. CPE supervisors focus on developing group intimacy and a community for learning. The CPE group may create a covenant to encourage direct communication and establish healthy boundaries, disclose their spiritual journey, their deeper call to chaplaincy, their aspirations of CPE, and share individual learning contracts.

The overarching learning model of spiritual care and counseling is called an Action-Reflection-Action model of practical theology.[20] This model encourages taking ministerial action in a spiritual care relationship, reflecting holistically and ethically on this interaction, and then taking another action. The founder of CPE, Anton Boisen, valued the study of human experience. He saw the spiritual care encounter as an opportunity for a spiritual quickening, and reading "living human documents" as an invaluable part of learning within ministry.[21] Studying one's own human experience as a living document requires the integration of theory and practice. Probably the most common question regarding spiritual care and counseling across traditions is: How does a chaplain address the needs of another without attempting to convert or proselytize? CPE trains chaplains of all religious traditions to be grounded in their own worldview, which facilitates spiritual care and counseling without proselytizing.

Buddhist Methods of Spiritual Assessment, Care, and Counseling

Zen Buddhist Chaplain Michael Monnet uses the Zen Peacemakers approach in his spiritual care and counseling work.[22] The Zen Peacemakers utilizes the Three Tenets of (1) not knowing, (2) bearing witness, and (3) taking action. These tenets restate the Three Mahayana Resolutions of (1) not doing evil, (2) doing good, and (3) doing good for others. To not do evil is to practice *not knowing* by giving up all fixed ideas, maintaining a willingness to be open within uncertainty, and cultivating a sense of wonder. The image Monnet uses to illustrate this approach is one of a cook who arrives on the scene empty-handed, using only the ingredients that are there in the present moment to create the meal. Similarly, Roshi Joan Halifax explains that the realization of impermanence in being with dying is to be thrust into uncharted territory, leaving behind everything familiar, and moving into a realm of not knowing, or a beginner's mind.[23]

To do good is *bearing witness* to the joys and sufferings of the world. To do good for others is *taking action* for the benefit of both self and other. Buddhist CPE Supervisor Trudi Jinpu Hirsch notes that "the story of Buddhism begins with Shakyamuni's foray outside the protective walls of his kingdom,"[24] thus coming face to face with old age, sickness, and death. This insight into suffering ultimately transformed his life. Hirsch creates a framework for chaplaincy based on the Four Noble Truths: (1) inquire about the disease of the care recipient's suffering; (2) identify the cause, i.e., attachments, aversions; (3) determine whether the care recipient is able to sit with and explore this suffering; and (4) see if a path to action arises through this process. Stepping outside the palace walls is moving out of the small isolated self, merging with the situation, into shared experience.

Buddhist chaplaincy educator Gil Fronsdal utilizes a Theravada approach to spiritual care by regarding notions of rebirth. Confronting life's deepest truths and transformations is preparing for death, easing the dying process, and learning how to care for the dying, the body after death, and rites of transition. He writes, "if we want to help a person die with as much peace, love and acceptance as possible, the caregiver needs to aim towards having these qualities established in him/herself."[25] Similarly, Tibetan Buddhist chaplaincy educator Kirstin Deleo utilizes the practice of "Essential Phowa" to create a calm and peaceful atmosphere to support the healing process of those who are ill or dying, and their caregivers. This practice involves invoking a presence that feels like the embodiment of infinite truth, wisdom, and compassion of all Buddha's, saints, masters, and enlightened beings. She then recommends imagining this presence as being deeply moved by your sincere wish, thus sending golden light that touches all aspects of being, including dark places of illness, fear, destructive emotions, negativity, and hidden sources of suffering.[26]

Buddhist chaplaincy educator Judith Simmer-Brown refers to genuine inter-religious dialogue as "listening dangerously." Simmer-Brown instills the peacemaking skills through contemplative pedagogies in the classroom. She teaches that by suspending judgment and opening our hearts and minds to the disparate voices, we have the opportunity to meet those unacknowledged parts of ourselves. She writes:

> When we truly listen to another, a resonance opens in our hearts, even if we have a conceptual reaction that closes doors between us; it is the human connection that speaks to us. If we are committed to suspending judgment, we find ourselves listening deeply. That listening leads us to hear our own hearts as well, and we begin to recognize the orphaned identities we carry.[27]

Likewise, Buddhist chaplain and educator Koshin Paley Ellison once told me to see an aspect of ourselves in each person we care for and reflect on. He asked: Who pushes your buttons? Who do you want to run away from? Who makes you scream? Cry? Who brings out the desire to sit and chat for hours? What kinds of illnesses are you comfortable with? What aren't you comfortable with? When chaplains utilize methods of concentration, ethics, and wisdom within their ministry they are able to listen deeply and close gaps between self and other. Leaning into suffering kindly and fearlessly, without overidentifying or denying that the care recipient reflects an aspect of ourselves, is being a competent chaplain.

Buddhist chaplaincy educators incorporate methods from their own Buddhist traditions, i.e., Theravada, Mahayana, Vajrayana, to train students. They encourage students to investigate and explore new methods based in their own Buddhist traditions. One basic guideline that I have taught to my MDiv students is to practice "not giving advice." Refraining from this allows the opportunity to join with the recipient of care. I also teach them to think of the hospital as a contemporary monastery and the hospital room doorway as a threshold, just as when they cross the threshold into a temple, monastery, devotional or meditation hall, they remove their shoes, step over the threshold, and make bows to honor the space with sincere practice. This is emptying, purifying, and entering a new mode free of agenda and expectation. I encourage them to be playful, and to explore chaplaincy from many different positions and roles.

Spiritual Assessment

Methods of Buddhist spiritual assessment are developing, though very little has been written. CPE offers assessment through documenting spiritual needs and resources on medical charts. In general, spiritual assessment tools examine spiritual history, needs, beliefs, concerns, rituals, and resources. Part of CPE is to present case studies, reflection papers, and "verbatims," spiritual care encounters written out verbatim to examine the technique. Verbatims also use spiritual assessment methods. A classic method of spiritual assessment is George Fitchett's 7 × 7 model,[28] which looks at seven dimensions of the care recipient: medical, psychological, psychosocial, family systems, ethnic/cultural, societal, and spiritual, along with further analysis of seven spiritual dimensions: belief-meaning, vocation-consequence, experience-emotion, courage-growth, ritual-practice, community, and authority-guidance. A more recent spiritual assessment method is Carrie Doering's model,[29] which distinguishes whether spiritual/religious resources are life-giving or life-limiting by identifying narrative themes, i.e., loss, violence, addiction, coping, and assesses social privileges, support, and disadvantages.

Vow, Vocation, and Right Livelihood

Chaplaincy work is tied to Buddhist vows, and a vocation of right-livelihood. Many have experienced an awakening, which called them to this path. Buddhist chaplains come from various cultural backgrounds, range in gender identity, socioeconomic background, as well as degrees of experience and training in Buddhism and pastoral skills. I have distinguished four types of people who pursue Buddhist chaplaincy training. The first are long-time Buddhist practitioners identified as the first generation of US-born Buddhist converts who received priest or lay ordination through lineages of Shambhala/Tibetan, Japanese Zen/Nichiren, Korean Won, or Insight Meditation. The second are Asian-born monastics, like Buddhist Army chaplain Lt. Tommy Nguyen, who enlisted in the Army after receiving many letters from Buddhist soldiers serving in Iraq and Afghanistan after September 11, 2001.[30] Other Asian-born monastics will utilize the chaplaincy training to learn how to teach Buddha-Dharma in English to new generations. For example, the displacement of families, loss of scriptures, religious culture, etc., have created a gap for Asian-born monastics after the Chinese Cultural Revolution and the Vietnamese-American war. Other monastics, like former Thai monastic Navy chaplain Lt. Aroon Seeda,[31] plan to take chaplaincy education and clinical models that they learn in the United States back to their home country to begin similar programs. The third are young Buddhists, Buddhist-hybrids, or Buddhist-interested seekers of various cultural heritages; many have taken vows, some are ordained in a tradition. The fourth are those looking for a midlife career change, or training to enhance their current career. These individuals often had direct experiences of suffering, loss, or trauma from which they have gained insight leading to a vocation change. The one thing all may have in common is an aspiration to take sincere vows, practice right livelihood, embody the Buddhist teachings, and to serve the underserved in ways that end suffering for all beings.

Challenges and Future Directions

Buddhist chaplains who do CPE will most likely have a Christian CPE educator. Their CPE educator and peer group will likely know very little about Buddhism, its main traditions, tenets, teachings, and values. Like members of any marginalized group, they will struggle to build most of the bridges and will find few bridges being built back toward them by the dominant culture. Most of the people they will minister to will be non-Buddhists, and at a certain point every Buddhist chaplain will experience an identity crisis. If they wear Western-style clothing, they will most likely withhold their Buddhist identity, unless directly asked, in order to be open to all recipients of care.

This acculturation process challenges Buddhist chaplains, facing fears of rejection, disowning their Buddhist identity, and adjusting their clothing attire. Clothing for chaplains varies; some hospitals expect chaplains to wear strictly "Western-style" business attire, while others allow ceremonial and/or religious attire. Traditional religious attire in US culture might be Amish, Hasidic, Mennonite, Mormon, Jesuit/Catholic, or Rabbinical. Because Buddhist monastic clothing has Asian cultural roots, the traditional clothing reflects these cultures, which may seem out of place in many secular chaplaincy settings. If an Asian monastic's donor, sponsor, Buddhist teacher, congregant, or monastic peer sees them wearing street clothes, they would interpret this as breaking their vows. Many Asian monastics who want to do CPE are trying to find the middle way between what to wear to satisfy the hospital, their supervisor, and sangha, while maintaining their vows and keeping the chaplaincy door open for future Buddhists.

The APC Buddhist task force is challenged to work out questions like: Where do we draw the line of legitimacy that allows for an "Americanized" sense of lineage and authorization and also vets out self-proclaimed Dharma teachers and traditions that may not support the healthy development of Buddhist chaplains? The Buddhist Churches of America (BCA) is the only endorsement agency that the Department of Defense recognizes, and it therefore finds itself in the position of acting as the umbrella endorser for Buddhist military chaplaincy. A future direction may be to establish a few umbrella endorsement agencies, or a group of consultants with multiple perspectives who have the capacity to objectively assess Buddhist communities and verify authorization that is both broad and inclusive.

Author Wendy Cage identifies a need for specific methodologies[32] for what Theistic traditions call a "ministry of presence" in chaplaincy work.[33] Buddhist chaplains in particular have the unique opportunity to articulate methodologies for a "ministry of presence," given Buddhism's long history of compiled systematic methods of critical and pragmatic reflexive praxis.[34] They have the opportunity to fill gaps within secular institutions and to create new pathways for chaplaincy in general. There is a need for academic textbooks that outline Buddhist approaches to spiritual formation, notions of spiritual assessment, and methods of spiritual care and counseling from several Buddhist perspectives and traditions.

We live in a multicultural, multi-religious, global society. Prisons are broken and serve as inhumane industrial complexes. The US military system is ill equipped to address the post-traumatic stress disorder (PTSD) that many soldiers return home with. Hospitals have become stressful environments where most people will end up dying. Buddhist chaplains are finding new ways to serve humanity and the earth by listening to stories of suffering, and hearing these stories as their own. From a range of religious locations, they offer adaptability, flexibility, deep listening, embodied ethics, and diversity. As non-competing agents, they allow space and time for stillness, silence, and open-ended notions of shared experience and authority. It takes courage to step over structural and ideological thresholds of difference, embrace diversity, and enter cultures, theologies, and worldviews other than our own. May we continue to strive to view difference and diversity as a teaching that we can all reflect.

Notes

1. Daijaku Judith Kinst, "Cultivating an Appropriate Response: Educational Foundations for Buddhist Chaplains and Pastoral Care Providers," in *The Arts of Contemplative Care: Pioneering Voices in Buddhist Chaplaincy and Pastoral Work*, ed. Cheryl A. Giles and Willa Miller (Boston: Wisdom Publications, 2012), 11–12.
2. Don Wagner, "Buddhist Chaplain Serves All Spiritual Needs," https://www.army.mil/article/191733/buddhist_chaplain_serves_all_spiritual_needs (accessed September 2018).
3. Tim Ford, "Interacting with Patients of a Different Faith: The Personal Reflection of a Buddhist Chaplain," *Southern Medical Journal* 99, no. 6 (2006): 658–59.
4. Frances Norwood, "The Ambivalent Chaplain: Negotiating Structural and Ideological Difference on the Margins of Modern-day Hospital Medicine," *Medical Anthropology* 25, no. 1 (2006): 1–29.
5. Association of Professional Chaplains, Board of Chaplaincy Inc. Common Qualifications, 2016, http://www.professionalchaplains.org/files/2017%20Common%20Qualifications%20and%20Competencies%20for%20Professional%20Chaplains.pdf (accessed October 25, 2018).
6. Association of Professional Chaplains, Board of Chaplaincy Inc. Common Qualifications, 2016, http://bcci.professionalchaplains.org/content.asp?pl=19&contentid=19 (accessed November 3, 2018).
7. Elaine Yun, "Professional Endorsement for Buddhist Chaplains," http://magazine.naropa.edu/wisdom-traditions-fall-2017/features/upaya-buddhist-ministry.php?fbclid=IwAR1UoO_yrtUnK_sdZOeKhFsg08urr9hfU7g8MuIRhrxUAkNLD9-oXhOE34c (accessed October 28, 2018).
8. Elaine Yun, "Faculty Explore Possibilities for Buddhist Chaplaincy in the West," https://hds.harvard.edu/news/2017/03/23/faculty-explore-possibilities-buddhist-chaplaincy-west# (accessed December 27, 2017).
9. Tina Jitsujo Gauthier, "Formation and Supervision in Buddhist Chaplaincy," *Reflective Practice: Formation and Supervision in Ministry*, 37 (2017): 3..
10. T. Kilts, "A Vajrayana Buddhist Perspective on Ministry Training," *Journal of Pastoral Care and Counseling* 62, no. 3 (2008): 273–82.
11. James W. Fowler, *Stages of Faith: The Psychology of Human Development and the Quest for Meaning* (San Francisco: Harper & Row, 1981).

12. Taigen Daniel Leighton, *Bodhisattva Archetypes: Classic Buddhist Guides to Awakening and Their Modern Expression* (New York: Penguin Arkana, 1998).
13. Gauthier, "Formation and Supervision in Buddhist Chaplaincy," 2017.
14. Kosho Uchiyama, *Opening the Hand of Thought: Foundations of Zen Buddhist Practice* (Boston: Wisdom Publications, 2004), 116–38.
15. G. R. Evans, *A History of Pastoral Care* (London: Cassell, 2000), 6.
16. Ñāṇamoli and Bhikkhu Bodhi, *The Middle Length Discourses of the Buddha: A Translation of the Majjhima Nikāya* (Somerville, MA: Wisdom Publications, 2015), 313.
17. Pamela Ayo Yetunde, "Dharma Care: Practice and Counseling from a Buddhist Perspective," http://www.dharmacare.com/Dharma-Care-Handbook.html (accessed November 27, 2017).
18. Bill Wallace, "Care of Dying: Power between, Power under, and Powerlessness with as a Means for Valuing and Balancing Boundaries and Mutuality," in *Boundary Wars: Intimacy and Distance in Healing Relationships*, ed. Katherine Hancock Ragsdale (Cleveland, OH: Pilgrim Press) 219–22.
19. Danny Fisher, "May I Always Be a Student," in *The Arts of Contemplative Care Pioneering Voices in Buddhist Chaplaincy and Pastoral Work*, ed. Cheryl A. Giles and Willa B. Miller (Somerville, MA: Wisdom Publications 2012), 173–84..
20. Carrie Doehring, *The Practice of Pastoral Care: A Postmodern Approach* (Louisville, KY: Westminster John Knox Press, 2015), 16–17.
21. Anton Boisen, "The Living Human Document," in *Images of Pastoral Care: Classic Readings*, ed. Robert C. Dykstra (St. Louis, MO: Chalice Press, 2005), 22–29.
22. Michael Monnet, "Developing a Buddhist Approach to Pastoral Care: A Peacemaker's View," *Journal of Pastoral Care and Counseling* 59, no. 1–2 (2005): 59.
23. Joan Halifax, *Being with Dying: Cultivating Compassion and Fearlessness in the Presence of Death* (Boston: Shambhala, 2009), 1.
24. Trudi Jinpu Hirsch, "The Four Noble Truths as a Framework for Contemplative Care," in *The Arts of Contemplative Care Pioneering Voices in Buddhist Chaplaincy and Pastoral Work*, ed. Cheryl A. Giles and Willa B. Miller (Somerville, MA: Wisdom Publications, 2012) 55–62.
25. Gil Fronsdal, "A Theravada Approach to Spiritual Care of the Dying and Deceased," in *Awake at the Bedside: Contemplative Palliative and End-of-Life Care*, ed. Koshin Paley Ellison (Somerville, MA: Wisdom Publications, 2016), 161–73.
26. Kirsten DeLeo, "More Than Just a Medical Event," in *Awake at the Bedside: Contemplative Palliative and End-of-Life Care*, ed. Koshin Paley Ellison (Somerville, MA: Wisdom Publications, 2016), 184–86
27. Judith Simmer-Brown, "Listening Dangerously: Dialogue Training as Contemplative Pedagogy," *Buddhist-Christian Studies* 33, no. 1 (2013): 38.
28. George Fitchett, *Assessing Spiritual Needs: A Guide for Caregivers* (Lima, OH: Academic Renewal Press, 2002).
29. Carrie Doehring, *The Practice of Pastoral Care*, 173–86.
30. Monica Sanford, Dharma Cowgirl, "The Monk and the Mercedes," May 3, 2011, https://dharmacowgirl.wordpress.com/2011/03/03/the-monk-and-the-mercedes/ (accessed September 7, 2018).
31. Sgt. Allison Beiswanger, "US Navy Buddhist Chaplain Gives Back to His Native Country," February 15, 2017, https://www.youtube.com/watch?v=OpWq25GaT50 (accessed September 7, 2018).

32. Wendy Cadge, *Paging God: Religion in the Halls of Medicine* (Chicago: University of Chicago Press, 2013), 77–127.
33. Donald Capps, "The Wise Fool Reframed," in *Images of Pastoral Care*, ed. Robert C. Dykstra (St. Louis: Chalice Press, 2005), 113.
34. B. L. Trinlae, "Prospects for a Buddhist Practical Theology," *International Journal of Practical Theology* 18, no. 1 (2014): 7–22.

Further Reading

Cadge, Wendy. *Paging God: Religion in the Halls of Medicine*. Chicago: University of Chicago Press, 2013.

Cooper-White, Pamela. *Shared Wisdom: Use of the Self in Pastoral Care and Counseling*. Minneapolis: Fortress Press, 2004.

De Silva, Padmasiri. *An Introduction to Buddhist Psychology and Counseling: Pathways of Mindfulness-based Therapies*. Basingstoke, Hampshire, UK: Palgrave Macmillan, 2014

Doehring, Carrie. *The Practice of Pastoral Care: A Postmodern Approach*. Louisville, KY: Westminster John Knox Press, 2015.

Ellison, Koshin Paley. *Awake at the Bedside: Contemplative Palliative and End-of-Life Care*. Somerville, MA: Wisdom Publications, 2016.

Evans, G. R. *A History of Pastoral Care*. London: Cassell, 2000.

Giles, Cheryl A., and Willa Miller. *The Arts of Contemplative Care: Pioneering Voices in Buddhist Chaplaincy and Pastoral Work*. Boston: Wisdom Publications, 2012.

Halifax, Joan. *Being with Dying: Cultivating Compassion and Fearlessness in the Presence of Death*. Boston: Shambhala, 2009.

Harvey, Peter. *An Introduction to Buddhist Ethics: Foundations, Values, and Issues*. Cambridge: Cambridge University Press, 2013.

Hu, Hsiao-Lan. *This-Worldly Nibbāna: A Buddhist-Feminist Social Ethic for Peacemaking in the Global Community*. Albany: State University of New York Press, 2012.

Palmer, Parker J. *The Courage to Teach: Exploring the Inner Landscape of a Teacher's Life*. San Francisco: Jossey-Bass, 2007.

Zhang, Shengyan, and Daniel B. Stevenson. *Hoofprint of the Ox: Principles of the Chan Buddhist Path as Taught by a Modern Chinese Master*. Oxford: Oxford University Press, 2002.

CHAPTER 34

BUDDHIST AND NON-BUDDHIST PRACTITIONER RELATIONS

ELIZABETH J. HARRIS

Themes from Pre-Modern Buddhism

From the birth of Buddhism in the fifth century BCE, followers of the historical Buddha engaged with non-Buddhist practitioners, for instance Jains and ascetics belonging to other *parivrājaka* ("wanderer") groups, Brahmins, and lay patrons of these groups. The Pali texts witness to this, but mask the level of competition present, by invariably casting the Buddha as victor in debate. There can be little doubt, however, that early Buddhists sharpened and modified their message through these exchanges.[1] Although it cannot be assumed that the Pali texts exactly represent what the historical Buddha taught, the strength of the oral tradition after the death of the Buddha suggests that they can be trusted as an indicator of the Buddha's message, filtered through the concerns of the Early Buddhist communities. Within the Pali texts, five broad approaches to non-Buddhist practitioners emerge: respectful yet rigorous debate; robust communication of ideas that challenged non-Buddhist groups; ridicule of non-Buddhist practitioners; the subordination of non-Buddhist beliefs and practices; the "appropriation and modification of practices/symbols" from non-Buddhist practitioners.[2] As the Buddhist traditions spread throughout Asia, these approaches developed further, informed by diverse political, economic, and religious contexts.

Risking generalization, however, a preferred Buddhist model emerged in Asia: respectful coexistence with non-Buddhist practitioners, if there was no perceived threat to the existence of Buddhism. Where Buddhism possessed political power, this usually occurred within a model that I have elsewhere termed "inclusivist subordination," namely a demotion of the Other within a Buddhist cosmological framework.[3] For instance, within the Kandyan Kingdom in Sri Lanka, before it was conquered by the British in 1815, non-Buddhist practitioners--Śaivite Hindus, Muslims, and Roman Catholics—were allowed religious freedom on the condition that they accepted their minority status, within a polity that prioritized Buddhism and the king as its guardian, and landscaped the capital to reflect this hierarchy.[4] This demotion or subordination was reflected in dance, temple murals, chants, and ritual. For instance, when the Buddha's tooth relic was incorporated within the annual Äsala Perahära in the eighteenth century, the processions from the *dēvāles* (shrines to the gods) were subordinated to it.[5] A study of nineteenth- and twentieth-century adaptations to an ancient dance, the Kohomba Kankariya, shows that, at one point, a Hindu priest from South India is trained to speak correct Sinhala, "demonstrating that he must learn to assimilate to the dominant culture."[6] There is no reason to believe that this kind of interlude was absent from earlier centuries. Within this model, Buddhists saw no problem in patronizing shrines and temples belonging to other religious groups for mundane blessings (the *laukika*), if the primacy of the Buddha over supra-mundane truth (*lokuttara*) was maintained.

When Buddhists did not hold power or were in danger of losing power, coexistence was still possible if courtesy and respect were shown to Buddhism. This seems to have happened in Central Asia when Buddhism first met Islam in the mid- to late seventh century.[7] The two religions held a common interest in trade and, at first, no threat was seen by Buddhists. In Sri Lanka, harmonious Buddhist-Muslim relationships existed into the period of British colonialism, although tension was emerging by the twentieth century.[8] However, when a non-Buddhist Other was perceived as a threat, coexistence and its corollary, courtesy, were jettisoned in favor of defense.

The Birth of Modernity

At the birth of modernity which, for the purposes of this chapter, I take to be the mid-nineteenth century, relations between Buddhist and non-Buddhist practitioners in Asia were conditioned by the power politics and socioeconomic realities of Western imperialism and/or influence, and the Christian mission that accompanied it. Within this context of asymmetrical power, boundaries between Buddhist practices and those of non-Buddhist practitioners became less permeable, less subject to "inclusivist subordination." Earlier coexistence models continued, but defense of Buddhism through vigorous confrontation and polemic eventually gained the upper hand.[9] In Japan, for instance, after the proscription of Christianity was lifted in the 1870s under pressure from the United States, a confrontational Buddhist reaction to Christian missionaries emerged, seen, for instance, in the work of Inoue Enryo (1858–1919).[10] Only at the beginning of the twentieth century, after Japanese Buddhists had experienced courtesy from Christians at the World's Parliament of Religions in Chicago (1893) and Japanese Christians were becoming more patriotic, did confrontation gradually change to coexistence and positive interchange.[11]

A similar pattern was present in Sri Lanka and Myanmar. In the second half of the nineteenth and early twentieth centuries, under British imperialism, Buddhists used printing presses, the visual arts, sound, Buddhist-Christian debates, Buddhist schools, and spatial strategies to undermine missionary activities. For instance, in Sri Lanka, the revivalist monk Mohoṭṭivatté Guṇānanda encouraged his followers to erect temporary preaching halls, *bana maḍuvas*, on land adjacent to Christian churches to challenge the missionary view that they could create Christianized space, free from Buddhist influence. Indigenous Methodist clergyman, David de Silva, for instance, reported in 1871 that Buddhists in Wellawatte, south of Colombo, had erected, "a poor temporary shed between our Chapel and my residence and invited the priest [Mohoṭṭivatté Guṇānanda] there too."[12] Drums and other instruments were also used to flood Christianized space with Buddhist rhythms.[13] In Myanmar, missionary preaching was disrupted, Christian schooling was boycotted, and Christians were challenged to debate.[14] In both Sri Lanka and Myanmar, indigenous Buddhists gained help from overseas sympathizers, for instance theosophists such as Henry Steel Olcott[15] and Frank Woodward in Sri Lanka, and Western Buddhist monks, such as Ananda Metteyya (Allan Bennett) and U. Dhammaloka in Myanmar, to whom this chapter will return.

In Cambodia, resistance emerged toward French Roman Catholic missionaries, who arrived, with a few individual exceptions, from the 1850s onward, before the country became a French Protectorate in 1864. For instance, a Roman Catholic priest, Father Barrea, was killed in 1867 and Christian expressions of social service were opposed.[16] The level of polemic, however, was not as great as under British rule.

In the early modern period, therefore, strands that had been present in earlier centuries were adapted to meet the challenges of Western imperialism. Within the twentieth century, this process continued, accompanied by growing Buddhist confidence that the message of the Buddha was needed in a failing, spiritually blind, and non-compassionate West.

Buddhist Mission to Non-Buddhist Practitioners in Western Countries

The Sri Lankan revivalist David Hewavitarne (1864–1933), who took the name Anagārika Dharmapāla, represented Theravada Buddhism in Chicago at the World's Parliament of Religions of 1893. Before giving his major speech, he wrote in his diary, "All expect to hear my paper and may it show to the world that there is light in Buddhism, more light than any other system."[17] Throughout his life, he spoke to numerous non-Buddhist audiences with the same aim: to demonstrate the superiority of Buddhism. Although he received hospitality from Christians in the United States and could engage positively with some Christian teachings,[18] this conviction of superiority was accompanied by an exclusivity that judged the non-Buddhist Other as dangerously destructive, with the exception of Jainism and some forms of Vedantism.[19]

This form of exclusivity, which developed from colonial exchanges, characterized what this chapter will call a Buddhist missionary movement in the late nineteenth and early twentieth centuries. It appealed to the spiritual blindness of the West, and its need of a higher wisdom to wake it from slumber. Both Asian Buddhists and Western converts to Buddhism were involved, not only at an elite level, as research into the Irish seaman who was ordained as U Dhammaloka in Myanmar demonstrates.[20] Charles Pfoundes, Allan Bennett, Dharmaduta activity from Sri Lanka, and D. T. Suzuki can be used as examples.

Charles James William Pfoundes (1840–1907) was an Irishman who spent most of his life in Japan, receiving a Japanese name, "Omoie Tetzunostzuke." He acted as a Western advocate of Japanese Buddhism and Japanese culture, and, during the latter part of a period of residence in London from 1879 to 1893, as the London representative of the Japanese Buddhist missionary society, the *Kaigai senkyōkai*, a Jōdo Shinshū-backed body.[21] He represents partnership, although at times an uneasy one, between Asian Buddhists and a Western convert for the purpose of making Buddhism better known in the West.[22]

Allan Bennett (1872–1923) was a British spiritual seeker who was a theosophist and a member of the Order of the Golden Dawn before he gained *upasaṃpadā* (higher ordination) in 1902 in Myanmar, eventually with the name Ananda Metteyya. He saw his life's mission as the bringing of Buddhism to the West. In July 1902, from Myanmar, he therefore founded the *Buddhasāsana Samāgama*, an international Buddhist organization with a journal, *Buddhism: An Illustrated Review*, which was eventually sent free to between 500 and 600 European libraries "on the condition that each copy be left on the Reading Room table until the next was received."[23] His conviction at this point in his life was that Buddhist principles needed "only to be better known to meet with wide-spread acceptance among the people of the West."[24] In 1908, he led a Buddhist mission to Britain in the hope that a Western monastic sangha could be founded there. Although this hope was disappointed, the mission was a key moment in the transmission of Buddhism to the United Kingdom. As with Dharmapāla, the main Buddhist Other for Ananda Metteyya was Christianity, and his attitude toward it can be seen in a triumphant article that he wrote for the first edition of *Buddhism*: "The Faith of the Future." Scientific discovery, he argued, was emptying the churches in Britain and proving that "there will be, there can be, no more adhesion to any form of religious Belief which maintains the existence of a Supreme Noumenon behind all Phenomena, of a Lawgiver behind those Laws, of a Hand whereby these worlds were made."[25] Christianity and all religions that looked toward a Creator God were, for Ananda Metteyya, doomed. They represented humanity in its infancy, when blind faith sufficed. Only Buddhism, with its ethical and compassionate vision, could work with science to create a better human future, although his experience of World War I dented his faith in science as a humanizing force.[26]

Asian Buddhists in countries such as Sri Lanka, Myanmar, and Cambodia gained greater freedom to engage in "missionary" activity after independence from European imperial powers. To take Sri Lanka as an example, a Lanka Dharmaduta Society (Society for the giving of the Dharma) was formed in the decade after independence, and training centers were established to equip *bhikkhus* to work overseas. Significantly, mission to Hindus and Muslims in the north and east of Sri Lanka was also mooted, in a move that went beyond the traditional model of "inclusivist subordination." "Buddhism Must Go to Jaffna [the major town in the Hindu North]," proclaimed an article of 1964, quoting the words of a V. L. Wijemanne at the centenary celebrations of a southern temple.[27] As late as 1984, within the context of nascent ethnic conflict, the same sentiment was expressed: that the monastic community should "spearhead a massive Dharmaduta mission in the North and East,"[28] with the aim of deflecting separatist sentiments. At the same time, criticism of Christian activities in the island appeared in the media. At the level of popular practice, however, there was much respectful coexistence between religions on the ground at this time. For every newspaper article framing Christianity as a threat, there were others that witnessed cooperation between Buddhists and Christians. For instance, a Buddhist monk addressing a Methodist meeting in Panadura, south of Colombo, in 1958, was reported as saying, "Let us all join hands irrespective of our religious differences, and unite in the national interest to serve the country."[29]

To move again to Japanese Buddhism, Daisetsu Teitarō Suzuki (1870–1966) should also be seen as a Buddhist missionary. Trained in the Zen tradition, he worked as an academic in both Japanese and US universities. Key to his life was the wish to communicate what he saw as the heart of Zen to the West, in a Western idiom. His many books, written in an accessible style, and his media presence gave him an influential voice. Unlike Dharmapāla and Bennett, however, he presented "Suzuki Zen" largely without condemning non-Buddhist practitioners. On the contrary, he read the works of the Christian mystic Meister Eckhart (ca. 1260–1327) and, finding resonances with Zen, wrote sympathetically on the touching points between Buddhist and Christian mysticism.[30]

By the mid-twentieth century, due to this mission and the Western orientalism that had preceded it, seen for instance, in Edwin Arnold's 1879 poem, *The Light of Asia*, Buddhism was, therefore, an established presence in the West. After the invasion of Tibet by China in the 1950s, a new "missionary" element entered as Tibetan refugee teachers settled in Europe and the United States. Chogyam Trungpa Rinpoche and Akong Tulku Rinpoche, for instance, took over a small Buddhist center on the borders of Scotland in 1967, naming it Kagyu Samye Ling. It became the largest Tibetan center in Europe. When Chogyam left for the United States in 1970, under a cloud of scandal, he continued to teach. In terms of practice, Tibetan missionary activities, however, did not seek to undermine the religious and non-religious practices of Westerners. Rather, they sought to communicate Buddhism in ways that would appeal to their Western audiences. Akong Rinpoche and Yeshe Losal at Samye Ling, for instance, eventually allowed Westerners to become novices for just one year so that they could sample what it was like to be a Buddhist monastic without having to make a lifetime commitment, and they developed residential courses that moved beyond traditional Buddhist practices.

Buddhist Responses to Calls for Inter-Religious Dialogue

In Asia, North America, and Europe, by the 1970s and 1980s, an important influence on Buddhist practice was the emerging, mainly Christian-dominated, field of inter-religious dialogue, which arose as Christians in both Asia and the West developed theologies and practices that were far less exclusivist than those of their nineteenth-century missionary forebears.[31] For instance, the British Anglican Bishop George Appleton (1902–1993), who worked for twenty years in Myanmar as a missionary with the Society for the Propagation of the Gospel, incorporated sensitivity toward Buddhism in his writings, for example in *Journey for a Soul*.[32] In the United States, the Benedictine David Steindl-Rast (b. 1926) became a student of Zen and sought to draw Buddhists into dialogue. In Sri Lanka, a group of indigenous Christians, including Aloysius Pieris S.J. (b. 1934), Michael Rodrigo O.M.I. (1927–1987), the Methodist Lynn de Silva (1919–1982), and the Anglican Yohan Devananda (1928–2016), sought to roll back the distrust toward Christianity that had been present in Sri Lanka since the colonial period, using debate, ritual, poetry, and art.[33] In Japan, two Jesuits, the German Hugo Enomiya Lassalle (1898–1990) and the Japanese Kakichi Kadowaki (1930–2017), studied Zen and sought to incorporate Zen methods into their Christian contemplative practice. Buddhists were invited to respond to these initiatives and, in the case of the Jesuits in Japan, to teach Christians.

Within Sri Lanka, the previously mentioned principle of courtesy being returned if courtesy was shown became operative among Buddhists. For instance, Pieris and de Silva drew Buddhists into dialogue on particular themes for their journal, *Dialogue*, published from Colombo. The responses they received ranged from blunt affirmation of the superiority of Buddhism to accommodative perspectives that explored the possibility of inter-religious rapprochement, but these were always voiced with courtesy. For example, in 1978, they invited Buddhist and Christian views on the religious dimension of humanity's relation to nature. Buddhist perspectives came from Sri Lankan academic Lily de Silva and Trevor Ling.[34] More ambitious was the edition that followed the death of de Silva in 1982, for which de Silva had invited Buddhists to reflect on a "Buddhist Approach to Christianity." Positive responses came from Maurice O'C. Walsh and Nyanaponika, a German Buddhist monk resident in Sri Lanka. A rigorous analysis of difference came from Sri Lankan academic Jotiya Dhirasekera, who stressed lack of continuity between the Christian concept of "eternal bliss" and the Buddhist concept of *nibbāna*.[35]

Notable examples can also be cited of Sri Lankan Buddhists responding warmly to Christian attempts to affirm Buddhism through the performative. For instance, when Rodrigo settled in a Buddhist village in the south of Sri Lanka in 1980, one Buddhist monk asked him to leave, believing he had come to convert. When he witnessed Rodrigo working with a Buddhist poet to write devotional songs based on the ten perfections (*pāramitā*) and then helping to perform them, his attitude changed. According to Rodrigo's account, after the performance, he declared:

> This group of ten Buddhist singers and one catholic priest and two sisters are Buddhist-Christians, Buddhists by their culture and the other group is Christian by belief and conduct. They have a large heart to honour the Buddha as a great Asian teacher. I regret having harassed him at the start saying he had come to baptize. Now, I know that was not his idea. So, now, I tell you, be free to come here or to go there to learn the dhamma. It is the same. He too can guide you.[36]

This Buddhist monk, through watching the actions of Rodrigo, was able to see that the Christian values inspiring him touched those of Buddhism. Pieris's use of art and the performative in dialogue was a response to a Buddhist initiative. In the 1960s, Charles de Silva, a Buddhist poet and linguist, showed Pieris a drama he had written on Jesus's crucifixion, which he had named, in Sinhala, "Supreme Sacrifice." He told Pieris he had watched a Roman Catholic passion play and had been disappointed. In a significant example of a Buddhist responding positively, if correctively, to the performative within the culture of non-Buddhist practitioners, he had, therefore, written his own version, which stressed the nature of Jesus's bodily sacrifice, using Buddhist perspectives. After all, Buddhists believe the historical Buddha prepared for buddhahood through mastering qualities such as the ability to give his body for the benefit of others.[37] The young Pieris was so impressed that he became convinced that Buddhists could help interpret Christianity to Christians. When he established a center for research and dialogue, Tulana, he therefore invited Buddhist artists to create works on Christian themes. One of the first was the monastic artist Hatigammana Uttarananda. Uttarananda responded positively to Pieris's request that he should read the Christian gospels and express in art a theme that he thought was unique to Christianity. He rightly did not see Pieris's request as an attempt at proselytization. He chose the theme of Jesus, the master, washing the feet of his disciples, exercising leadership through service, and an impressive, life-sized mural in Tulana's reception room resulted.[38] Other works of art followed by other Buddhist artists. Both de Silva's and Uttarananda's responses can be contrasted with the competitive nature of nineteenth-century encounters between Buddhist and Christian ritual and performance in the context of imperialism.

Some Buddhist responses to Christian calls for dialogue, however, resulted in non-connection and asymmetry, with Buddhists seeking to impress on Christians the superiority of Buddhism, and Christians seeking greater reciprocity. For example, Robert Sharf remembers an exchange between Steindl-Rast and Chinese Chan teacher Hsuan Hua in 1987 at the Berkeley conference that gave birth to the US-based Society for Buddhist-Christian Studies, to which this chapter will return, within which Hsuan Hua lectured "on the truths of Buddhism, showing little interest in an exchange of views."[39]

Four Spaces for Dialogue and Cooperation

Four main spaces emerged in the twentieth century for Buddhist exchange and cooperative action with non-Buddhist practitioners: inter-monastic exchange; societies/networks for formal dialogue; meditation retreats and comparative mysticism; and social engagement.

Inter-Monastic Exchange

Buddhist monastics probably met Christian contemplatives in Central Asia in the early centuries of Christian growth and, after the arising of Islam, Sufi devotion. Mutual influence cannot be ruled out. It was not, however, until the twentieth century that formal exchange began between Buddhist and Christian monastics. The Christian monk Thomas Merton (1915–1968) was a key influence in this, in spite of his tragic and premature death from accidental electrocution at a meeting in Bangkok in 1968, where he called for inter-monastic exchange. The history of this has been well documented on the Christian side[40] but not so well on the Buddhist side, suggesting an asymmetry of benefit between the two sides. The dominant Buddhist perspective has remained that Buddhism is supreme when it comes to the training and transformation of the mind and heart, and that Buddhists have little to learn from non-Buddhist monastic practitioners. However, the newsletters of Christian initiatives show that inter-monastic exchange has challenged this perspective for some Buddhist monastics, men and women.[41]

A key moment came when Christian monastic Patrick Henry, inspired by an inter-monastic meeting at Merton's Abby in Kentucky, Gethsemani, asked four US-based Buddhists, two men and two women, only one of whom was a celibate monastic, to reflect on the Christian monastic rule of St. Benedict. The four Buddhists—Norman Fischer (Sōto Zen), Joseph Goldstein (Theravada), Judith Simmer-Brown (Tibetan tradition), and Yifa, a nun within the Fo Guang Shan movement—responded with grace and courtesy. The four drew from their experience of relationships, working with the mind and heart, non-attachment, the nurturing of generosity and compassion, the stripping away of self-absorption, and conflict resolution in community to comment on the Rule. Differences between the Rule and Buddhist practices were not hidden, but the exercise moved beyond a stress on the obvious differences, such as a Creator God and rebirth, to issues connected with spiritual practice.[42]

Societies and Networks for Formal Dialogue

This chapter has shown that formal, intellectual exchange between Buddhists and Christians began in the mid-twentieth century, as Buddhists responded to Christian initiatives. In the late twentieth century, two further initiatives arose. The first, the Society of Buddhist-Christian Studies (SBCS), grew out of the East-West Project, started at the University of Hawai'i in 1980 by David Chappell, a Christian who later self-identified as a Buddhist. Chappell organized several conferences, the first of which, in the pioneering, inaugural year, took the theme "Buddhist-Christian Renewal and the Future of Humanity." It drew together almost 2,500 people and was, according to its participants, "a first of its kind."[43] In 1982, a Japanese chapter of the project began. In 1983, the International Buddhist-Christian Theological Encounter began, pioneered by Masao Abe, a Zen Buddhist influenced by the Kyoto School, and John Cobb, a Christian theologian.[44] Abe's approach to this dialogue drew greatly from the understanding of *śūnyatā* (emptiness) within the Kyoto School, and his realization that the Christian concept of God included self-emptying.[45] Dialogue with Christianity, in addition, enabled him to interrogate Buddhism, for instance on the topic of social ethics and justice, such that he argued that the realization of *śūnyatā* did not necessarily imply a going beyond good and evil but a "re-grasping" of the distinction between them through the operation of wisdom and compassion.[46]

It was at the 1987 conference of the East-West Project at Berkeley, California, that the SBCS was born. It has pioneered intellectual exchange on key issues in Buddhist-Christian relations through its journal, *Buddhist-Christian Studies*, and other publications, for instance, inviting Buddhists to reflect on Christianity and Christians to reflect on Buddhism.[47] Its published dialogue in honor of Frederick Streng was particularly innovative in terms of dialogical structure. The book had five sections on the following themes: Interreligious Dialogue; Ultimate Reality; Nature and Ecology; Social and Political Issues of Liberation; Ultimate Transformation or Liberation. Within each, two scholars, one writing from a Buddhist perspective and one from a Christian, dialogued with each other, by formally responding to the paper of the other, creating four chapters within each section.[48] Currently, the Society places emphasis on *Buddhist-Christian Studies*, a biannual newsletter, a blog to encourage debate in Buddhist-Christian Studies, the organizing of two panels at the annual American Academy of Religion, and an annual Frederick J. Streng Award for Excellence in Buddhist-Christian studies. In November 2017, the topics, first discussed by the Management Committee over lunch the year before, were: "What Buddhists and Christians Can Learn from Muslims" and "Uses and Misuses of Anger in Buddhism and Christianity."

A parallel organization, the European Network of Buddhist-Christian Studies, founded in 1997, grew from an initiative that brought together Christians who had written academically about or had enjoyed an in-depth encounter with Buddhism. Its main activity is a themed biennial conference, itself the result of Buddhist-Christian dialogue within the Board.[49] The topic of the 2017 conference, held at Montserrat in Spain, was "Meditation in Buddhist-Christian Encounter: A Critical Analysis," with case studies of Zen, mindfulness, and the hesychast tradition of Christian contemplation. When formed, the Network anticipated reciprocity between the two religions, and its Board includes both Buddhist and Christian members. However, the number of Christians involved in the Network has always been greater than the number of

Buddhists, again pointing to a significant asymmetry in Buddhist and Christian involvement in inter-religious academic exchange.

Inter-Religious Meditation Retreats and Comparative Mysticism

With reference to inter-religious meditation retreats, I take two examples of boundaries being blurred between Buddhist and non-Buddhist: Amaravati Buddhist monastery in Hertfordshire, United Kingdom, and Holy Isle, off the west coast of Scotland, owned by the afore-mentioned Kagyu Samye Ling Monastery. Amaravati was founded by the English Sangha Trust and opened in 1985. With a Thai Forest Tradition lineage, it is the home of both male and female renunciants, mainly Western, and offers a program of retreats and meditation sessions for non-monastics, who need not be Buddhist. Its current practice is to hold a Buddhist-Christian retreat once a year, in October, led by a Christian and a Buddhist monastic. During these retreats, images of the Buddha and Jesus Christ are placed side by side in the meditation room, and participants normally pay respect to each, breaking down exclusivist boundaries.

Holy Isle was acquired by the Kagyu Samye Ling Monastery in the 1990s. At one end of the island is an enclosed retreat center for Tibetan monastics. At the other is a Center for World Peace and Health, which, from its inception, aimed to bring together Buddhists and non-Buddhist practitioners, and the spiritual currents of East and West. From March to April each year, it offers a program of courses and retreat opportunities that move beyond an essentialized Buddhist model. For the goal of fostering peace and health, the line between what is Buddhist and non-Buddhist is blurred. Their program has included Iyengar Yoga, Secular Mindfulness retreats, The Healing Power of Vocal Sound, and Medical Qigong, as well as more traditional Buddhist topics. Inter-faith retreats and meetings are an important part of this, for instance courses that offer silence, spiritual reflection, and engagement with the Christian mystical tradition.

Within this context, the rising prominence of comparative mysticism is important. Abe's discovery of Meister Eckhart has already been mentioned. Cousins's seminal article of 1989 is also important. Comparing Teresa of Avila (1515–1582) and Buddhaghosa's *Visuddhimagga*, he did not downplay difference, but came to the conclusion that the "general structure" of the path was "remarkably similar" in the two.[50] The Western Buddhist nun Ayya Khema (1932–1997) went further when she spoke to the Eckhart Society shortly before her death. Drawing from her experience of inter-religious dialogue, she declared, "I have come to the conclusion that God (or Godhead) and *Nibbāna* are identical—that they cannot be anything else."[51] Within this area, Buddhists are beginning to see that the boundaries between techniques of meditation, or, within Christianity, contemplation, are not fixed.

Social Engagement

Masao Abe wrote, in the context of his conversation with Christians on social ethics and justice, "We must learn from Christianity how to solve the problem of society and history at large and interpret this in terms of the Buddhist standpoint of wisdom and compassion."[52] The story of the growth of engaged Buddhism is well documented. Less well documented are the controversies that arose over the issue of Christian influence. For the Vietnamese monk Thich Nhat Hanh, this was unproblematic. He was open in declaring that the inspiration he had gained from people such as Martin Luther King, Jr., and the Dutch Christian Hebe Kohlbrugge meant that he saw both the Buddha and Jesus as his "spiritual ancestors."[53] When Western feminist Rita Gross, however, suggested that Buddhists needed the prophetic tradition within Judaism and Christianity to struggle against patriarchy, the reaction she received was painful to her.[54]

Gross voiced her pain over this in her published dialogue with Christian feminist Rosemary Radford Ruether. Published in 2001 as *Religious Feminism and the Future of the Planet*, the exchange was intensely autobiographical—both women spoke about their route to dialogue, and what was most problematic and liberating in their own tradition—and intensely engaged. On the issue of the prophetic tradition, she shared,

> It still makes sense to me that Buddhist social engagement in general may well owe something to Buddhist interactions with non-Buddhist thought, including Christianity. Some Buddhists have said that the rise of Engaged Buddhist movements . . . proves that Buddhists don't need the prophetic voice because none of the leaders of these movements have appealed to it to develop their activist stances. But I would reply that such an observation is simplistic. . . . Nevertheless, my deeper question to such critics is "What's the problem? What's at stake in being so attached to the idea that Buddhism doesn't need and couldn't use any inspiration from anything non-Buddhist?"[55]

She then pointed out the failure of Jews and Christians to act on the prophetic voice and her belief that a Buddhist approach to social engagement could be developed without appeal to it, while nevertheless defending her appeal to non-Buddhist practice. The last book she wrote before her death, *Religious Diversity: What's the Problem?* continued this theme, utilizing insights that she gained from Buddhist meditative practices to argue that religious exclusivism was untenable and that religious diversity should be seen as gift and opportunity.[56]

Concluding Thoughts

In the twenty-first century, Buddhists in Asia and the West are divided in their attitude toward non-Buddhist practitioners. If the non-Buddhist practitioner can be subordinated to Buddhism, respectful coexistence remains a Buddhist ideal in line with long-established tradition. If non-Buddhist practitioners are seen as a threat, confrontation can still be chosen, as it was during the period of European expansionism and as it is now, in contemporary Myanmar and Sri Lanka, where Muslims are being attacked by Buddhist nationalists. With reference to the emerging practice of inter-religious dialogue and conversation, the suggestion that Buddhists can learn from non-Buddhist practitioners remains controversial, in spite of the writings of people such as Rita Gross. At the level of practical social engagement, however, there can be no doubt that Buddhists are currently sharing platforms with many non-Buddhist practitioners to work toward a more humane and compassionate world, and, at the level of meditation practice, fixed boundaries are breaking down, as comparative mysticism throws light on common structures and aims within the spiritual paths of different religious traditions.

Notes

1. This dialogic context is discussed in: Brian Black and Laurie Patton, eds., *Dialogues in Early South Asian Religions: Hindu, Buddhist, and Jain Traditions* (Abingdon, Routledge, UK: 2016) and Naomi Appleton, *Narrating Karma and Rebirth: Buddhists and Jain Multi-Life Stories* (Cambridge: Cambridge University Press, 2015).
2. Elizabeth J. Harris, "Buddhism and the Religious Other," in *Understanding Interreligious Relations*, ed. David Cheetham, Douglas Pratt, and David Thomas (Oxford: Oxford University Press, 2013), 88–117.
3. See, for instance, Elizabeth J. Harris, "Syncretism or Inclusivist Subordination? An Exploration into the Dynamics of Inter-Religious Cooperation," in *Theological and Philosophical Responses to Syncretism: Beyond the Mirage of Pure Religion*, ed. Patrik Fridlund and Mika Vähängas (Leiden and Boston: Brill, 2018), 209–25; Elizabeth J. Harris, *Religion, Space and Conflict in Sri Lanka: Colonial and Postcolonial Contexts* (Abingdon, UK: Routledge, 2020).
4. See James S. Duncan, *The City as Text: The Politics of Landscape in the Kandyan Kingdom* (Cambridge: Cambridge University Press, 1990); Harris, *Religion, Space and Conflict in Sri Lanka*.
5. Duncan, *The City as Text*, 128–39.
6. Susan A. Reed, *Dance and the Nation: Performance, Ritual, and Politics in Sri Lanka* (Madison: University of Wisconsin Press, 2010), 26.
7. Johan Elverskog, *Buddhism and Islam on the Silk Road* (Philadelphia: University of Philadelphia Press, 2000), 48–54.
8. Lorna Dewaraja, *The Muslims of Sri Lanka: One Thousand Years of Ethnic Harmony* (Colombo: The Lanka Islamic Foundation, 1994).
9. See Elizabeth J. Harris, *Theravāda Buddhism and the British Encounter: Religious, Missionary and Colonial Experience in Nineteenth Century Sri Lanka* (Abingdon, UK: Routledge, 2006), 189–204.
10. Notto R. Thelle, *Buddhism and Christianity in Japan: From Conflict to Dialogue 1854–1899* (Honolulu: University of Hawai'i Press, 1987), 27–33, 97, quoted in Harris, "Buddhism and the Religious Other," 104.

11. Thelle, *Buddhism and Christianity in Japan*, 163–213, quoted in Harris, "Buddhism and the Religious Other," 104–5.
12. David De Silva, *Quarterly Letter*, from Wellawatte, December 11, 1971, Vol. LXXVII (December–March 1871–1872): 132–34, here 132, quoted in Harris, *Religion, Space and Conflict*, 79-80.
13. See Harris, *Theravāda Buddhism and the British Encounter*, 189–204; Harris, *Religion, Space and Conflict*.
14. See Michael D. Leigh, *Conflict, Politics and Proselytisation: Methodist Missionaries in Colonial and Postcolonial Upper Burma 1887–1966* (Manchester: Manchester University Press, 2011), 78–87, quoted in Harris, "Buddhism and the Religious Other," 103.
15. Stephen Prothero, *The White Buddhist: The Asian Odyssey of Henry Steel Olcott* (Bloomington: Indiana University Press, 1996).
16. Ian Harris, *Cambodian Buddhism: History and Practice* (Honolulu: University of Hawai'i Press, 2005), 165, quoted in Elizabeth J. Harris, "The Impact of Colonialism on Theravāda Buddhist-Christian Relations: An Overview," in *Buddhist and Christian Attitudes to Religious Diversity*, ed. Hans-Peter Grosshans, Samuel Ngun Ling and Perry Schmidt-Leukel (Yangon: Ling's Family Publication, 2017), 183–207, here 202.
17. Diary entry for September 18, 1893: "Diary of the Later Anagarika Dharmapala, Typed from the Original Diary," held by the Mahabodhi Society, Colombo.
18. On April 23 and 24, 1892, for instance, his diary entries include numerous quotes from the New Testament concerning the ethical teaching of Jesus.
19. In the first chapter of a 1917 book, Dharmapala divided religions into the "Destructive and the non-Destructive." "Vedic Brahmanism, Zoroastrianism, Muhammedanism, Judaism, Christianity, Confucianism and Saiva Vedantism" were placed in the former. Buddhism, Jainism, and the bhakti Vedantism of the Caitanya movement were placed in the second; Ananda Guruge, ed., *Return to Righteousness: A Collection of Speeches, Essays and Letters of the Anagarika Dharmapala* (Colombo: Ministry of Cultural Affairs, 1991), 158–60.
20. See *Contemporary Buddhism* 11, no. 2 (November 2010): Special Issue edited by Alicia Turner, Laurence Cox, and Brian Bocking on "U Dhammaloka, 'The Irish Buddhist': Rewriting the History of Early Western Buddhist Monastics." See also Alicia Turner, Laurence Cox and Brian Bocking, *The Irish Buddhist: The Forgotten Monk Who Faced Down the British Empire* (Oxford: Oxford University Press, 2020).
21. Brian Bocking, "Flagging up Buddhism: Charles Pfoundes (Omoie Tetzunostzuke) among the International Congresses and Expositions, 1893–1905," *Contemporary Buddhism* 14, no. 1 (2013): 17–37; here 20–21.
22. Bocking, "Flagging up Buddhism," 28.
23. Elizabeth J. Harris, *Ananda Metteyya: The First British Emissary of Buddhism* (Kandy: Buddhist Publication Society, 1998), 10.
24. Ananda Metteyya, "Ourselves," *The Buddhist* 1.1, 163–67, quoted in Harris, *Ananda Metteyya: The First British Emissary*, 10; and Elizabeth J. Harris, "Ananda Metteyya: Controversial Networker, Passionate Critic," *Contemporary Buddhism* 14, no. 1 (May 2013): 78–93; here 83.
25. Ananda Metteyya, "The Faith of the Future," *Buddhism* 1.1 (1903): 6–38; here 10.
26. Harris, *The First Emissary of Buddhism*, 15–16.
27. Our Kalutara Correspondent, "Buddhism Must Go to Jaffna," *Daily News*, July 20, 1964: 3.
28. Victor Fernando, "Maha Sangha Spearheads Dharmaduta Mission in North and East," *Daily Mirror*, March 16, 1984: 1.

29. Panadura Correspondent, "Buddhists, Methodist Plea for Amity," *Daily News*, July 14, 1958: 3, quoted in Elizabeth J. Harris, *Theravāda Buddhism and the British Encounter: Religious, Missionary and Colonial Experience in Nineteenth Century Sri Lanka* (Abingdon and New York: Routledge, 2006), 211.
30. D. T. Suzuki, *Mysticism: Christian and Buddhist* (George Allen & Unwin, 1957). The first chapter relates his encounter with Eckhart, whom he then compares with Zen and the wider Buddhist tradition.
31. The process started with missionaries who, through study of the texts of religions other than Christianity and experience, moved beyond exclusivity to greater inclusivity, for example Timothy Richard (1845–1919) in China and J. N. Farquhar (1861–1929) in India, who voiced a fulfillment theology, namely that Christianity fulfilled all that was good in other traditions.
32. George Appleton, *Journey for a Soul: A Book of Prayers and Meditations* (London: Fontana, 1974).
33. See Elizabeth J. Harris, "Art, Literature and the Transformation of Memory: Christian Rapprochement with Buddhism in Post-independence Sri Lanka," *Religions of South Asia* 10, no. 1 (2016): 54–82. See also Elizabeth J. Harris and Perry Schmidt-Leukel eds, *A Visionary Approach: Lynn A. de Silva and the Prospects for Buddhist-Christian Encounter* (Sankt Ottilien: Editions of Sankt Ottilien, 2021).
34. Both in *Dialogue* V, no. 1 (January–April 1978): Lily de Silva, "Psychological and Ethical Dimensions of Humanity's Relation to Nature": 5–12; Trevor Ling, "Humanity's Relation to Nature in Buddhist Thought": 13–18.
35. All in *Dialogue*, new series IX, no. 1–3 (January–December 1982): M. O'C. Walshe, "Buddhism and Christianity: A Positive Approach": 3–39; Nynaponika Mahathera, "Christianity: Another Positive Response": 40–42; Jotiya Dhirasekere, "The Individual and Social Dimension of Salvation in Buddhism": 73–82.
36. Michael Rodrigo, *Buddhism and Christianity: Toward the Human Future: An Example of Village Dialogue of Life. Paper Read at the Berkeley Conference August 10–15 1987* (Buttala: Suba Seth Gedera Publications), 4, quoted in Harris, "Art, Liturgy and the Transformation of Memory," 71–72.
37. Aloysius Pieris, "Inculturation in Asia: A Theological Reflection on an Experience," in Pieris, *Fire and Water: Basic Issues in Asian Buddhism and Christianity* (Maryknoll, NY: Orbis): 127–37, quoted in Harris, "Art, Liturgy and the Transformation of Memory," 74–75.
38. Pieris, "Inculturation in Asia," 133–34, cited in Harris, "Art, Liturgy and the Transformation of Memory," 75.
39. Robert Sharf, "Why Buddhists Taught Zen to Christians," in *Meditation in Buddhist-Christian Encounter: A Critical Analysis*, ed. Elizabeth J. Harris and John O'Grady (St. Ottilien: EOS, 2019).
40. See, for example, Fabrice Blée (William Skudlarek with Mary Grady trans.), *The Third Desert: The Story of Monastic Interreligious Dialogue* (Collegeville, MN: Liturgican Press, 2011); Katrin Åmell, *Contemplation et Dialogue: Quelques exemples de dialogue entre spiritualités après le concile Vatican II* (Uppsala: Swedish Institute of Missionary Research, 1998). See also the online journal, *Dilatato Corde*, the organ of the different Roman Catholic Commissions for Inter-Monastic Dialogue.
41. Harris, "Buddhism and the Religious Other," 114. See also an early attempt in Sri Lanka to raise the question of Buddhist influence on Christian monasticism: Shantha Ratnayaka, "A Buddhist-Christian Monastic Dialogue," *Dialogue*, new series, VI, no. 3 (1979): 85–90.

42. Patrick Henry, ed., *Benedict's Dharma: Buddhists Reflect on the Rule of St Benedict* (London and New York: Continuum, 2002).
43. See Lynn de Silva, "Dialogue-Creative Transformation," *Dialogue*, new series VIII, no. 1–3 (January–December 1981): 1–5.
44. See Harris, "Buddhism and the Religious Other," 106.
45. Masao Abe (Steven Heine ed.), *Buddhism and Interfaith Dialogue* (Honolulu: University of Hawai'i Press, 1995), 1–16.
46. Abe, *Buddhism and Interfaith Dialogue*, 52–62.
47. For example, Rita M. Gross and Terry C. Muck, eds., *Christians Talk about Buddhist Meditation: Buddhists Talk about Christian Prayer* (New York: Continuum, 2003); and Rita M. Gross and Terry C. Muck, eds., *Buddhists Talk about Jesus: Christians Talk about the Buddha* (New York: Continuum, 2000).
48. Sallie B. King and Paul O. Ingram, *The Sound of Liberating Truth: Buddhist-Christian Dialogues in Honor of Frederick J. Streng* (Richmond, Surrey, UK: Curzon, 1999).
49. Previous publications have included: Perry Schmidt-Leukel, Köberlin, and Götz, eds., *Buddhist Perceptions of Jesus* (St. Ottilien: EOS, 2001); Perry Schmidt-Leukel, ed., *Buddhism, Christianity and the Question of Creation: Karmic or Divine* (Aldershot, UK: Ashgate, 2006); John D'Arcy May, ed., *Converging Ways: Conversion and Belonging in Buddhism and Christianity* (St. Ottilien: EOS, 2007); Perry Schmidt-Leukel, ed., *Buddhist Attitudes to Other Religions* (St. Ottilien: EOS, 2008); Elizabeth Harris, ed., *Hope: A Form of Delusion? Buddhist and Christian Perspectives* (St. Ottilien: EOS, 2013); Elizabeth J. Harris and John O'Grady, eds., *History as a Challenge of Buddhism and Christianity* (St. Ottilien: EOS, 2016); Perry Schmidt-Leukel, ed., *Buddhist-Christian Relations in Asia* (St. Ottilien: EOS, 2017).
50. Lance S. Cousins, "The Stages of Christian Mysticism and Buddhist Purification: Interior Castle of St Teresa of Ávila and the Path of Purification of Buddhaghosa," in *The Yogi and the Mystic: Studies in Indian and Comparative Mysticism*, ed. Karel Werner (Richmond, Surrey, UK: Curzon, 1996), 103–20, here 120.
51. Ayya Khema, "Mysticism Is no Mystery," *Eckhart Review* (Spring 1996): 45, cited in Harris, "Buddhism and the Religious Other," 110.
52. Abe, *Buddhism and Interfaith Dialogue*, 58.
53. Thich Nhat Hanh, *Living Buddha, Living Christ*, 6–7.
54. Rita M. Gross, *Buddhism after Patriarchy: A Feminist History, Analysis, and Reconstruction of Buddhism* (Albany: State University of New York Press, 1993).
55. Rita M. Gross and Rosemary Radford Ruether, *Religious Feminism and the Future of the Planet* (New York: Continuum, 2001), 171.
56. Rita M. Gross, *Religious Diversity: What's the Problem? Buddhist Advice for Flourishing with Religious Diversity* (Eugene, OR: Cascade, 2014).

Further Reading

Abe, Masao. *Buddhism and Interfaith Dialogue*, ed. Steven Heine. Honolulu: University of Hawai'i Press, 1995.

Black, Brian, and Laurie Patton, eds. *Dialogues in Early South Asian Religions: Hindu, Buddhist, and Jain Traditions*. Abingdon, Oxon, UK: Routledge, 2016.

Cox, Harvey G., and Daisaku Ikeda. *The Persistence of Religion: Comparative Perspectives on Modern Spirituality*. London: I. B. Tauris, 2009.

Gross, Rita M. *Religious Diversity: What's the Problem: Buddhist Advice for Flourishing with Religious Diversity*. Eugene, OR: Cascade Books, 2014.
Gross, Rita M., and Rosemary Radford Ruether. *Religious Feminism and the Future of the Planet*. New York: Continuum, 2001.
Harris, Elizabeth. *Religion, Space and Conflict in Sri Lanka: Colonial and Postcolonial Contexts*. Abingdon, Oxon: Routledge, 2018.
King, Sallie, B., and Paul O. Ingram, eds. *The Sound of Liberating Truth: Buddhist-Christian Dialogues in Honor of Frederick J. Streng*. Richmond, Surrey, UK: Curzon, 1999.
Lai, Whalen, and Michael von Brück. *Christianity and Buddhism: A Multi-Cultural History of Their Dialogue*, trans. Phyllis Jestice. Maryknoll, NY: Orbis, 2001.
Mitchell, Donald W., and James Wiseman. *The Gethesmani Encounter: A Dialogue on the Spiritual Life by Buddhist and Christian Monastics*. New York: Continuum, 1999.
Schmidt-Leukel, Perry, ed. *Buddhist Attitudes to Other Religions*. St. Ottilien: EOS, 2008.
Schmidt-Leukel, Perry, ed. *Buddhist-Christian Relations in Asia*. St. Ottilien: EOS, 2017.
Thelle, Notto R. *Buddhism and Christianity in Japan: From Conflict to Dialogue 1854–1899*. Honolulu: University of Hawai'i Press, 1987.
Vélez De Cea, J. Abraham. *The Buddha and Religious Diversity*. Abingdon, Oxon, UK: Routledge, 2013.

CHAPTER 35

INTERNET-BASED PRACTICES

LOUISE CONNELLY

Introduction

With the advent of cheaper, accessible internet access and the development of new technologies, including smartphones, social media, and virtual worlds, there has been a significant change in how we communicate with one another, share information, and even practice or "do" religion.[1] Digital culture, digital-social shaping of technology, and the digitization of religion have enabled new ways of engaging with religion, and this has resulted in redefining what we mean by "religious," "the sacred," or "tradition." Hoover argues that we need to appreciate how religion is "being expressed, understood, and performed through digital media" in order to truly understand how religion presents itself in the wider digital culture today.[2]

We may find our online and offline interactions blurring, as there is no longer the clear demarcation of online and offline engagement as was found in the early days of internet use.[3] Instead, the online/offline paradigm can now be integrated into daily life, and as a consequence, for some individuals, this has redefined how they engage with Buddhism and Buddhist practice. Examples of this include spinning a virtual prayer wheel in the online world of Second Life,[4] or lighting virtual incense on the iShrine mobile phone app, or leaving comments for a Buddhist monk on a website.

In order to better understand internet-based practice, we first need to understand what practice is within the digital context. Klassen defines practice as "a concept that attempts to bring together thought and action—both how people think about the world they live in and what they do in it."[5] Examining various forms of practice and ritual online enables us to understand how individuals are constructing and reimagining religious practice on the internet. For Helland, ritual is defined as "purposeful engagement with the sacred (whatever the sacred may be for those involved)," and it could be argued that cyberspace has become a sacred space, for some.[6] Moreover, Wagner posits that there is a "virtual sacred" that is current, visual, and in a constant state of flux, which is different from the sacred found offline.[7] This notion of practice and the sacred is aptly illustrated in many online spaces, for example the online world of Second Life, where creators (known as residents) can reimagine offline landscapes, buildings, and religious objects and create virtual versions. However, these virtual spaces can also be easily abandoned, may disappear altogether, or may be purchased and redesigned by other residents. Arguably, this epitomizes the ephemerality and transience of the "virtual sacred" and the Buddhist notion of impermanence (*anitya*).

While there are many examples of internet-based practice, scholars need to understand what might define internet-based practice as "Buddhist," whereas other actions or activities may be perceived as secular or quasi-Buddhist. For some participants, it may be the efficacy of the practice, or the sacredness that they prescribe to the activity. For others, it may be a partial substitute or extension of the practice they engage with offline. We also need to understand why someone would want to engage with Buddhist practice online, as opposed to offline in the "real world." Understanding the relationship between the individual, the aesthetics of an app or site, and the resulting experience can go some way toward explaining why some individuals will define what they do online as Buddhist practice.

Furthermore, sensory and emotional experience is intrinsic to offline practice, such as the significance of the relationship of haptic-vision and the associated religious experience,[8] which is embedded in many religions, including Buddhism. Seeing (and touching), as well as being seen by the deity (*darshan*)[9] can also provide a powerful sacred encounter. However, online, the platform (technology) can become a barrier to engaging in a full sensory (lack of taste, smell, touch) or embodied experience. This lack of sensory experience may devalue or diminish the practice, for example where digital artifacts can be viewed but cannot be physically touched, and this may be why some individuals do not consider internet-based practice to be "real." Therefore, when examining the concept of practice we need to consider how people think, act, and use practice as a tool for establishing religious identity, to engage with a community, and to experience the sacred.

Engagement with the "virtual sacred" does not necessarily have the same meaning or authenticity for everyone, and it is by examining online religious practice that scholars have uncovered the potential challenges to traditional notions of authority, the different forms and constructs of religion online, as well as questions about the efficacy of online practice. Using an ethnographic approach, Connelly's[10] research reveals that internet-based practice is considered "real" and has efficacy for those involved in some of the rituals in Second Life, as long as it is done with the same intention as it would offline. In contrast, Falcone's research presents a more complex picture of Buddhist practice, which varies depending on the type of person (searcher, student, or devotee) who is engaging with the practice.[11] These complexities highlight that Buddhist internet-based practice is often contextualized and dependent on or defined by the individual.

Moreover, this discussion should not be restricted to what is solely found on the internet; it can also include the use of mobile phone apps and technology that have been integrated into offline Buddhist practice. Examples include the recently launched Chinese robot Buddhist monk, who is designed to answer questions about Buddhism,[12] and a robot Buddhist priest in Japan who is live-streamed and leads a Buddhist funeral.[13] Buddhist internet-based practice therefore extends along a spectrum of digital Buddhism that now includes robotics and artificial intelligence.

Before turning to specific forms of internet-based practice, it is useful to provide a brief overview of Digital Religion research, including the four distinct waves of research that have aided our understanding of key themes (authority, community, identity, ritual) and have enabled a greater appreciation of how Buddhist internet-based practice materializes and what it means (if anything) to individuals and communities.

The following discourse includes examples of internet-based practice, giving specific attention to the different forms of Buddhist practice available in the virtual world of Second Life. The discussion will also highlight the potential challenges that may arise online, which include the redesigning of practice and resulting impact on authenticity, the dilution of authority, individualization of Buddhist practice, or the development of a "pick and mix" style of religiosity. In the conclusion, consideration will be given to the significance of internet-based practice in today's world, what the future of Buddhist practice may look like, and why researchers need to continually adapt methodological and theoretical approaches in line with technological and cultural changes in order to understand this constantly changing arena.[14]

The Study of Online Religion

Today, religious practice is no longer defined as either online or offline, since these spheres often merge and become blurred. Consequently, this requires digital methods and approaches to accommodate the examination of complex, contextualized, and culturally dependent religious practice. The field of Digital Religion research, which has emerged from internet studies and media, religion, and culture studies, finds scholars examining the internet and new media as "unique mediated contexts, spaces, and discourses where religion is performed and engaged."[15] Unlike the second wave of research (see later discussion), for example Helland's[16] early demarcation of online religion/religion online, Digital Religion research examines the blurring of online/offline spaces, technological affordances that shape religion, as well as the reimagining of spirituality and the sacred online.[17] This blurring can be found where online spaces and practices are normalized into everyday offline practice, for example the counting of virtual mala beads on a mobile phone app (My Mala).

If we review the developments of digital religion research over the past thirty years, it is often presented as four waves of research,[18] which can be summarized as (1) descriptive, (2) categorical, (3) theoretical, and (4) negotiation of the online/offline relationships.[19]

The first wave, which emerged in the early 1990s, is often described as the descriptive wave, which focused on how individuals and organizations were using the internet as an information source or a place to communicate with others. An example of this is what Prebish[20] refers to as the "cybersangha" and the emergence of the online Buddhist communities in chat rooms, online journals, and on websites. Internet-based practice at this time was primarily through text-based chat. However, early chat room platforms had a number of limitations, including the ease with which the internet could be accessed. Modem dial-up connections could be unreliable and webpages could take time to load, resulting in potential frustration for the user. Thirty years later, many people now have faster internet connections and real-time synchronous chat. Not only have the technological developments provided faster routes of communication; they have also dissipated geographical boundaries and have provided easier access to a larger community or a "networked global Sangha."[21]

The second research wave sought to understand why individuals were practicing religion online. Scholars focused on developing categories for the study of religion, such as Helland's conceptual framework of "online religion" (participatory/religious practice) and "religion online" (information about religion), which attempted to categorize the motivation of users and the types of online religious practice.[22]

By the middle of the first decade of the twenty-first century, the emergence of the third wave saw scholars developing methodological approaches and theoretical frameworks, and during this time, the themes of authority, community, identity, and ritual were studied in more detail.[23] The fourth and current wave focuses on how individuals negotiate online/offline spaces, the identification of benefits and potential challenges to religious authority and authenticity, as well as the creation of typologies and the development of new approaches for the study of religion online.[24] Examples include the use of virtual ethnography[25] to examine Buddhist practice in Second Life[26] and the creation of religious categorizations for mobile phone apps[27] and typologies for mapping Buddhist cyberspace.[28]

Understanding Buddhist internet-based practice is complex, as there are factors that are dissimilar to those found offline, for example, the ephemerality of the spaces and the technological affordances that influence and potentially transform or reshape religious practice online. Nonetheless, non-Buddhists, lay, and monastic Buddhists frequently use technology to negotiate relationships, build communities, curate identities, and practice Buddhism today.

Exploring Internet-Based Buddhist Practice

This section focuses on internet-based practice and the reasons why an individual engages with Buddhist practice online, how they practice online, the efficacy of the practice, and the significance of digital materiality and lack of embodiment in relation to internet-based practice.

For many, social media are firmly established in everyday life and used for a variety of purposes, including as a platform for religious questioning, self-discovery, or simply to satisfy a curiosity of the unknown. Social media are not confined to the layperson, as demonstrated by the Won Buddhist monks and nuns of Korea, who are using blogs (online-diaries or journals) as a means of self-discovery and communication. The blog provides an online space where discussion can take place via the comments feature, and this in turn creates a sense of community (sangha) online between the monks and nuns, as well as their blog followers. In addition, the act of blogging can provide a means by which to cultivate a sense of self, as the blogs can be used to reflect on the spiritual journey, thereby becoming a form of religious practice.[29]

Other social media platforms, such as the microblogging platform Twitter,[30] are used by a variety of Buddhists (lay and monastic), such as the Dalai Lama (@DalaiLama), who has over 19.2 million followers, and the Vietnamese Buddhist monk Thich Nhat Hanh (@thichnhathanh), who has 475,500 followers (as of November 2021). There are also a host of Facebook pages and YouTube channels used by non-Buddhists, as well as monastic and lay Buddhists. If we refer to the definition of practice, discussed previously, it could be argued that online spaces provide access to a community (sangha), information, and opportunities to engage with Buddhism, including access to scriptures and spiritual guidance. Some of these spaces could be said to offer a means for internet-based practice, including examples such as those found in Second Life.

In order to gain a better understanding of Buddhist internet-based practice, the following section focuses on two specific areas, namely mobile phone apps and virtual worlds (Second Life). These areas have been selected to provide two very different examples of Buddhist (and quasi-Buddhist practice), including the facilitation for capturing silence in the form of mindfulness and meditation. Due to the prolific rise of smartphones and the recent trend in using meditation/mindfulness mobile phone apps, this section highlights how mobile apps may influence and shape identity formation as well as challenge Buddhist authority. Furthermore, meditation, as well as other examples of internet-based practice found in Second Life, require us to consider the efficacy of the practice, the aesthetics of the environment, and how this can potentially shape the practice.

Mobile Phone Apps

According to Ofcom, 94 percent of UK adults own or use a mobile phone;[31] a US study claimed that 95 percent of Americans owned a mobile phone, with 77% owning a smartphone.[32] The increase of smartphones has resulted in an increase in the use of apps, including a plethora of apps relating to religion or spirituality.

There are a large variety of Buddhist and Buddhism-related apps, which offer the user a range of activities. Wagner classifies religious apps into six categories: (1) prayer, (2) ritual, (3) sacred text, (4) social media, (5) self-expression, and (6) focusing/

meditation apps.[33] Wagner and Accardo argue that this may be indicative of Western culture and the commercialization of Buddhism via platforms that facilitate "dharma for sale."[34] To appreciate the variety of Buddhist apps, it is useful to highlight a few, including Buddhify, which provides a series of guided meditations,[35] My Mala,[36] which allows the user to count virtual beads, and iShrine, which purports to be "a realistic and interactive Buddhist altar in the palm of your hand, [allowing you to] now practice meditation wherever you are even while away from home."[37] This app, while allowing the individualization of your altar, also provides a disconnectedness from a community. Other apps, such as the Buddhist Memory Game (no longer available),[38] have gamified Buddhism through the use of images, leading the user to search for and find pairs of cards. The gamification of Buddhism enables the user to attain a sense of achievement or progress that arguably trivializes or undermines the purpose of Buddhist practice, thus challenging Buddhist authority, authenticity, and traditional forms of practice.

Some newer and more sophisticated apps, such as Buddha Mind 2, are combining technology such as Bluetooth heart rate monitors with a meditation app, so that the user can measure their heart rate. The Buddha Mind website states: "This makes meditation addictive in a good way" and "track your meditations, eliminate anxiety, and live a better life."[39] App commercialization may be feeding on the anxieties arising from everyday life, such as uncertainty, stress, and mental health issues, and consequently are driving the market and increasing the popularity of mindfulness/meditation apps.

Wagner and Accardo argue that we need to consider apps using communication theory because this can help us to understand how practitioners practice Buddhism and how Buddhism is being reshaped and reimagined online.[40] Therefore, if we look more closely at apps and app usage, we begin to understand the types of Buddhist practice that are available and why someone would use an app. Apps can be accessed at a time that suits the user, thus providing flexibility and ease in fitting the practice into everyday life. A religious app may be used for different reasons, for example, as a means to access information, engage with others, perform rituals, as a form of "Dharma delivery," or to gain access to Buddhist teachings.[41] They can thus serve as tools for spiritual practice and access to the "virtual sacred,"[42] though one can ask if they provide the same experience and outcome as traditional offline forms of practice. They might provide this for some, but for others the mindfulness app is simply a means of dealing with the daily struggles of life, and it is incidental whether it resonates with or descends from Buddhist practice.

Moreover, the app can also shape our identity and, in some instances, provide an understanding of the self, albeit one that may be fluid and fragmented. The ephemerality of the technology and of the modes of engagement with the app can influence our understanding of the ways in which we engage with Buddhism and/or understand ourselves. We may even consider the iPhone or other smartphones as an extension of the self (the "iPod self"), since they are rarely shared with others, they can be highly personalized, and they express our identity through our choice of apps and settings.[43] Our phones can help us feel connected, but they can also cause us extreme anxiety if they are not working or are inaccessible, and we can find ourselves in a technology-dependent relationship.

While apps may help us curate and define our (religious) identity and our sense of self, Wagner and Accardo state that religious apps can result in an individualistic approach to religion because they allow the user to engage at a time convenient to them, without consequence or judgment from others, and in some instances, while multitasking and doing other things such as commuting to work.[44] This individualistic approach can result in self-centeredness, or can contribute to a sense of an autonomous self, which is at odds with the Buddhist ideal of selflessness. However, it is important to distinguish between the subtleties of engaging with Buddhism at an individual level and problematic forms of individualism. Engaging as an individual is not problematic per se, though it may be in tension with the development and centrality of the sangha (community). Whether engaged out of curiosity or because of the unavailability of offline Buddhist communities, Buddhist apps provide a means for individuals to engage with forms of Buddhist or quasi-Buddhist practice that may not be available to them offline.[45]

There are also concerns about app culture and how apps could potentially influence how we engage with and process Buddhist teachings (dharma), which may engender their dilution. While the app can be considered a tool for practice and the iPhone a "personalized Dharma tool" that could be used instead of traditional tools,[46] there are questions surrounding the authenticity of the practice and the authority of the information that the app provides, especially as many are commercial products.

This is further illustrated with apps that are not aligned with a specific school of Buddhism and thus could be considered eclectic forms of Buddhism. Consider, for example, the iShrine app, which allows the creation of a personalized altar with symbols extracted from Tibetan, Zen, and Theravada Buddhist traditions. It is this eclecticism and selective "pick-and-mix" style of religious seekership that some fear may dilute Buddhist authority and authenticity and contribute to the commercialization of religion, even if they also allow individuals to engage with forms of Buddhism that would have otherwise been out of reach.

Second Life

While apps and social media represent examples of internet-based practices, the online world Second Life showcases a much broader spectrum of internet-based Buddhist practice.[47] Created by Linden Lab, San Francisco, and launched in 2003, by 2013 the platform had established 36 million accounts. It provides an immersive experience where participants are known as "residents" and they use Linden dollars (L$, in-world currency) to purchase land, objects, clothes, and engage in a wide range of activities.

Unlike massive multiplayer role-playing games (MMPORGs), Second Life is not considered a game, as there is no reward structure or end goal per se.[48] Rather, it is a world where residents create an identity and can choose to join a community in which they can engage with different activities, such as attending pop concerts, shopping, socializing, as well as engaging with religious practice. While Second Life is to some extent similar to real life, as there are geographic locations, online behaviors, and accepted norms, there are also some fundamental differences. For example, residents can fly, instantly teleport from one location to another, dramatically change appearance, and potentially play with their identity online. Unlike real life, the environment is not permanent, depending on the funding for the land or the whim of the creators/builders. This aptly aligns with the Buddhist notion of impermanence (*anitya*).

Second Life also has similarities to real life, as it includes different religions and the associated but reimagined replicas of religious buildings and artifacts, for example virtual churches (Christianity), mosques (Islam), and stupas and temples (Buddhism). In order to better understand why someone would engage with Buddhism in Second Life, it is useful to consider who the residents are. Scholars such as Connelly,[49] Falcone,[50] and Grieve[51] identified and interviewed a number of residents, including non-Buddhists, lay-Buddhists, and ordained Buddhist priests (from different sects of Buddhism) in order to understand why so many individuals engage with Buddhism in Second Life. Taking a virtual ethnographic approach, both Connelly and Grieve noted that some individuals do not have access to a Buddhist community offline, their friends or families may not be supportive of their Buddhist practice, or they may have "real world" limitations such as a disability. For others, it means being part of a community and gaining a better understanding of Buddhism via an immersive online experience.

The Buddha Center in Second Life

There are a number of different Buddhist communities and locations in Second Life, including the Buddha Center (in-world address 137, 130, 21). Here, there are a variety of Buddhist practices on offer to residents, for example spinning virtual prayer wheels, sitting at the Deer Park where residents can listen to sermons from lay and monastic Buddhists, as well as participating in Zen Buddhist meditation in the Buddhist Temple. The recreation and reimagining of spaces, such as the Deer Park where the Buddha gave his first sermon, or the visualization of temples and artifacts found offline, arguably provide a sense of knowing and familiarity, as well as the associated expectations[52] of reverence and purpose. Therefore, the creators are reimagining offline artifacts and architecture and intentionally becoming custodians of iconographic authority.[53]

The Buddha Center was established in 2008; by 2010, the Center had over 2,500 residents,[54] and in 2017, they had 4,363 members.[55] The Center has both lay and monastic teachers from various Buddhist traditions, including Zen, Tibetan, and Theravada. The Center's sign, which hangs above the noticeboard, lists the names of the facilitators, times for practice and talks, and proclaims that the Buddha Center offers a "True Buddhism in Virtual Reality Second Life." This aligns with the founders' belief that the Center offers a "universal" type of Buddhism[56] to a wide range of individuals, who, for various reasons, may not have access to Buddhist teachers or community where they live. This ethos echoes Busch's understanding of Buddhist communities online, which enable a transcending of "boundaries between the variety of Buddhist traditions, sects and their distinctive cultural differences."[57]

While there are a variety of Buddhist practices at the Buddha Center, one type of practice held in the Buddha Temple is the silent meditation practice, known as *zazen*, which is often led by an ordained Buddhist priest. Grieve argues that to "make sense of online silent meditation," the practice needs to be examined in relation to "bodily practices, social roles, and the discourses that frame it."[58] Therefore, the virtual meditation practice may vary from one individual to other, and is dependent on various factors, such as why they choose to engage with the practice or the authenticity they assign to it.

Typically, the practice takes the format of the resident entering the main Buddha Temple, where some practitioners will instruct their avatar to prostrate. This is done by clicking on the "prostration" button (pose ball) and the avatar will automatically prostrate three times, which symbolizes the Three Refuges in Buddhism (Buddha, Dharma, and sangha). The aesthetics of the temple frequently change, including the use of visuals such as Buddha statues, paintings, photographs, water features, lotus flowers, and Zen meditation cushions (*zafu*). The visual and auditory experience in the temple provides a rich sensory experience for the participants, and instills a sense of realness and familiarity of the environment, which can contribute to the efficacy of the meditation practice for some residents.[59]

To begin the practice, the residents instruct their avatar to change their body position and to sit cross-legged on one of the twenty-three cushions, which are positioned in a semi-circle around a pond, which has lotus flowers floating on the water, all of which face a large gold Buddha statue. This is flanked by two smaller standing Buddha statues. There is virtual incense burning beside the meditation bowl, which emits a sound to signal the start and end of the session. The aesthetics of the space include the creation of an artifact that connotes the sense of smell (incense) and that is intended to provide the illusion of a full sensory experience such as one would find in an offline temple. There could also be the implication that the use of virtual incense is to remind the individual to light the incense in the offline context, as part of their practice.[60] Furthermore, the use of auspicious signs and artifacts provides a sense of iconographic authority, as the images such as the lotus flowers are associated with the birth of the Buddha,[61] and the religious tools, such as the meditation cushion and bowl, provide what Whitehead defines as a "mediating function in facilitating relationships between devotee and divine."[62] Furthermore, the meditation cushion can act as the symbol that joins the online avatar and the offline embodied person likely sitting in meditation, therefore blurring and merging the two realities.[63]

The meditation practice will often include audio (voice), text chat, and a virtual text-based note card containing scriptures, which is distributed to participants for them to keep in their inventory. The use of sound, including the sound of the water from the pool, the wind chimes hanging above the door, and the sound from the meditation bowl, provides an auditory sensory experience. This aligns with the importance that sound plays in some Buddhist practices, for example, the recitation of mantras, sermons, chanting, and sound-making artifacts, all of which provide sensory engagement and meaning-making, as defined by the individual engaged with the practice.[64] For some participants, they may assign merit to some online practices but not others, depending on the quality of the immersive experience or their own belief structure. This results in the participant (re)defining the efficacy and authenticity of the practice, as well as creating an individualistic interpretation of it.

In Second Life, there are also other Buddhist holy objects that relate to identity and can be interacted with, such as robes, mala beads, and prayer wheels. These might be worn as a means of curating an online Buddhist identity and as a symbol of authority or authenticity. For example, some facilitators choose to dress their avatar in monastic robes, wear mala prayer beads, or hold a small prayer wheel when they are visiting Buddhist sites in Second Life. In addition, many of the participants who engage with practice in the Buddha Temple may choose to dress more modestly than usual, further illustrating the recognition of the Buddha Temple as a sacred space, and transferring the religious, cultural, and societal norms found offline. Others may not recognize the space as sacred and inadvertently or intentionally act inappropriately. Generally, community members are very accepting; however, if there is any intentional inappropriate behavior, residents may speak to the participant or even ask them to leave.

The technological affordances can also have a negative impact on identity formation and social interaction, as Second Life requires the user to have a good internet connection and graphics card in order to participate. Consequently, avatars can often appear as a disembodied cloud, as their avatar has not "rezzed" properly. Other times, the avatar may be seen sinking through their meditation cushion and are half immersed into the floor, which provides a comical, dysfunctional, and disjointed experience (and practice). These technical issues make the experience incongruent with offline experiences and may contribute to some practitioners arguing that internet-based practices are not real, authentic, and cannot equate to the merit-making practices found offline due to their lack of genuine embodiment and sensory engagement. On the other hand, Grieve argues that virtual meditation can be authentic, simply because it bridges the gap between the real and the virtual, and the sacred and profane.[65]

While the principles of the online practice may be equated with those found offline, research has indicated that there can be blurring of online/offline practices. Interviews with the facilitators and participants found that 81.2 percent of the participants were simultaneously practicing meditation offline while their avatar was being led in meditation in Second Life.[66] The rationale for this simultaneous practice varies, and may include the practitioner's lack of access to a local offline community, their curiosity and desire to experiment with Buddhist practice,[67] and a desire to develop mindfulness and reduce anxiety.[68]

Online meditation is not the only practice that takes place at the Buddha Center; another is the spinning of a Buddhist prayer wheel, either held in the avatar's hand or found inside one of the virtual stupas. Thus, the soteriological meaning of the Tibetan Buddhist prayer wheel (wheel of Dharma) offline is reimagined and recreated in the online space. Offline, the person will touch and spin the prayer wheel, providing a tool for visualizing the mantra, releasing the prayer into the world, and accumulating merit. In

Second Life, the avatar needs to interact with the prayer wheels for them to spin; however, as there is not a physical person online, this "touch" is in fact accomplished with the click of the mouse and is therefore a kind of "imitation" touch.[69] For some residents, the lack of haptic interaction might negate the associated karmic result.

This situation has been discussed in interviews with online participants, and some individuals believe that there is merit (karma) attained from the online practice as long as it is done with the same intention as offline practice.[70] Falcone's research demonstrates that the efficacy of this practice differs depending on the type of individual, which she categorizes as either a student, searcher, or devotee.[71] Although all of them perceive the virtual artifact as having "some degree of virtue in their presence,"[72] the devotee typically does not view virtual artifacts as equivalent to those in real life because they are not consecrated. The student and searcher, however, view them as symbols (similar to those offline), and the student (those committed to following the Buddhist path) perceives the virtual and real-life objects with equivalency.

Therefore, whether a person engages with virtual objects or those found in real life, they are imbued with cultural and religious significance. What differs with internet-based practice are the inconsistencies of practice, intention, and outcome, all of which highlight the contextual complexities of virtual sacred spaces and practices. Therefore, the soteriological value of the virtual prayer wheel (and to some extent the virtual meditation) differs from that found offline, partly due to its lack of embodiment and full sensory experience, as well as the individuals' belief structure surrounding the soteriological value of the digital materiality in their practice. While digital meditation may blur the boundaries between online/offline realities, and some practices may be solely engaged with online, nonetheless these examples illustrate that, for some at least, internet-based practice supports their practice of Buddhism in ways that are equivalent or similar to offline practice.

Conclusion

This chapter has highlighted that internet-based practice is often contextualized and may vary from one individual to another, as well as between different types of media or platform. Furthermore, the technological and cultural context may dictate how we engage with Buddhist practice, and this may challenge traditional forms of Buddhism by reimagining sacred spaces and artifacts, as well as creating different levels of authenticity and efficacy of digital Buddhist practice. In this constantly changing environment, internet-based practice may need to be redefined by scholars as "Digital Dharma"[73] or "Digital Buddhism" in order to accommodate the wide spectrum of ways that technology is being used to engage with Buddhism and Buddhist practice.

We are entering an era where we need to re-evaluate definitions and notions of practice and consider whether we are experiencing the rise of a universal type of Buddhism or an eclectic type of Buddhism found through the use of apps and elsewhere online.

We may need to move away from the dichotomies and duality of thinking of online and offline and look instead at how technology is helping shape our understanding of Buddhism and engagement with Buddhist practice, which for some may have been previously out of reach. "This deconstruction of the assumption of static dualisms between here/there, sacred/profane, and online/offline"[74] is what researchers must grapple with, in order to truly understand how offline/online contexts and behaviors are manifesting and transforming in these spaces.[75]

Furthermore, we need to carefully consider how technology and internet-based practice are impacting traditional forms of Buddhism, as it could result in "Dharma dilution" or challenge traditional modes of authority[76] as the technology enables us to become consumers of religion where we can filter out and seek only what we want. Some of these spaces may be considered trustworthy, such as the Buddhanet information portal,[77] whereas others are not.[78] The eclectic pick-and-mix approach to Buddhism and practice can be found in Second Life, through the use of apps, as well as elsewhere online. While this can be exceptionally beneficial and can provide access to Buddhism for many individuals, it can also lead to fragmentation, division, and closed-mindedness, as the personalization of the practice provides safety rather than challenging personal belief structures.[79]

One of the noticeable elements of digital Buddhism is the ephemerality of digital spaces and, as a result, the constant state of flux of the sacred online. This can be disheartening and frustrating for participants, as it can have a direct impact on their sense of the authenticity of the practice, the strength of the community that develops, as well as one's sense of identity and curation of an online self. In addition, there may also be the individualization of internet-based practice, and this may have an impact on traditional notions of community formation (sangha), as illustrated with the use of some smartphone apps.

As technology changes and becomes more sophisticated, and our attitudes and behaviors change, our understanding of Buddhist internet-based practice also needs to be continuously re-evaluated. Scholars researching digital religion can use mediatization as a lens to examine digital Buddhism, including the affordances of technology, as well as how mediatization shapes communication and potentially challenges religious norms and authority. Furthermore, scholars need to ensure that there is "longitudinal and comparative work"[80] to identify where technology is actively and beneficially engaged with, such as the use of social media as a communication tool, as in the case of the Dalai Lama's Twitter account. On the other hand, scholars need to use appropriate and innovative approaches to examine both the subtle and more obvious changes to Buddhist identity, community, authority, and practice—both online and offline—if we are to truly understand who is practicing online, why they choose to do so, and what implications this may have for traditional forms of Buddhism.

Notes

1. Christopher Helland, "Ritual," in *Digital Religion: Understanding Religious Practice in New Media Worlds*, ed. Heidi A. Campbell (New York: London: Routledge, 2013), 25.
2. Stewart M. Hoover, "Foreword: Practice, Autonomy, and Authority in the Digitally Religious and Digitally Spiritual," in *Digital Religion, Social Media and Culture: Perspectives,*

Practices and Future ed. Pauline Hope Cheong, Peter Fischer-Nielsen, Stefan Gelfren, and Charles Ess (New York: Peter Lang, 2012), ix.

3. Christopher Helland, "Surfing for Salvation," *Religion* 32, no. 4 (2002): 293–302.
4. Second Life, http://secondlife.com/.
5. Pamela Klassen, "Practice," in *Key Words in Religion, Media and Culture*, ed. David Morgan (New York and London: Routledge, 2008), 137.
6. Helland, "Ritual," 27.
7. Rachel Wagner, *Godwired: Religion, Ritual, and Virtual Reality* (Abingdon, UK, and New York: Routledge, 2012), 79.
8. Stephen Pattison, *Seeing Things: Deepening Relations with Visual Artefacts* (London: SCM Press, 2007), 53.
9. For a detailed discussion, see Diana L. Eck, *Darsan: Seeing the Divine Image in India* (New York: Columbia University Press, 1998).
10. Louise Connelly, "Virtual Buddhism: An Analysis of Aesthetics in Relation to Religious Practice within Second Life," *Online Heidelberg Journal of Religion on the Internet* 4, no. 1 (2010): 12–34.
11. Jessica Falcone, "Our Virtual Materials: The Substance of Buddhist Holy Objects in a Virtual World," in *Buddhism, the Internet, and Digital Media: The Pixel in the Lotus*, ed. Gregory Price Grieve and Daniel Veidlinger (New York: Routledge, 2015), 179.
12. Harriet Sherwood, "Robot Monk to Spread Buddhist Wisdom to the Digital Generation," *The Guardian*, April, 26, 2016, https://www.theguardian.com/world/2016/apr/26/robot-monk-to-spread-buddhist-wisdom-to-the-digital-generation.
13. Samuel Gibbs, "The Future of Funerals? Robot Priest Launched to Undercut Human-Led Rights," *The Guardian*, August, 23, 2017, https://www.theguardian.com/technology/2017/aug/23/robot-funerals-priest-launched-softbank-humanoid-robot-pepper-live-streaming.
14. Cheong et al., *Digital Religion*.
15. Heidi Campbell, "Surveying Theoretical Approaches Within Digital Religion Studies," *New Media & Society* 19, no. 1 (2017): 16.
16. Helland, "Surfing," 293–302.
17. Campbell, "Surveying," 17.
18. Morten T. Højsgaard and Margit Warburg, *Religion and Cyberspace* (London: Routledge, 2005).
19. Campbell, "Surveying," 17.
20. Charles S. Prebish, "The Cybersangha: Buddhism on the Internet," in *Religion Online: Finding Faith on the Internet*, ed. Lorne L. Dawson and Douglas E. Cowan (New York: Routledge, 2004), 135–47.
21. Laura Busch, "To Come to a Correct Understanding of Buddhism: A Case Study on Spiritualizing Technology, Religious Authority, and the Boundaries of Orthodoxy and Identity in a Buddhist Web Forum," *New Media and Society* 13, no. 1 (2011): 62.
22. Helland, "Surfing," 293–302.
23. Heidi Campbell, *When Religion Meets New Media* (London: Routledge, 2010).
24. Heidi Campbell, *Digital Religion: Understanding Religious Practice in New Media Worlds* (Abingdon, UK, and New York: Routledge, 2013), 10.
25. See Christine Hine, *Ethnography for the Internet: Embedded, Embodied and Everyday* (London: Bloomsbury Academic, 2015).
26. Gregory Price Grieve, *Cyber Zen: Imagining Authentic Buddhist Identity, Community, and Practices in the Virtual World of Second Life* (Abingdon, UK: Routledge, 2017).

27. Wagner, *Godwired.*
28. Louise Connelly, "Towards a Typology and Mapping of the Buddhist Cyberspace," in *Buddhism, the Internet and Digital Media: The Pixel in the Lotus*, ed. Gregory Grieve and Daniel Veidlinger (New York: London: Routledge, 2015), 58–75.
29. Joonseong Lee, "Cultivating the Self in Cyberspace: The Use of Personal Blogs among Buddhist Priests," *Journal of Media and Religion* 8, no. 2 (2009): 97–114.
30. Twitter, https://twitter.com/.
31. Ofcom. 2017. "Fast Facts—internet," https://www.ofcom.org.uk/about-ofcom/latest/media/facts (accessed November 5, 2017).
32. PEW American Life Project, "Mobile Fact Sheet (12 Jan 2017)," http://www.pewinternet.org/fact-sheet/mobile/ (accessed November 5, 2017).
33. Wagner, *Godwired,* 102–5.
34. Rachel Wagner and Christopher Accardo, "Buddhist Apps: Skillful Means or Dharma Dilution?" in *Buddhism, the Internet, and Digital Media: The Pixel in the Lotus*, ed. Gregory Price Grieve and Daniel Veidlinger (New York: Routledge, 2015), 145.
35. "Mindfulness Everywhere," Buddhify, http://buddhify.com/ (accessed December 17, 2017).
36. "SynapseIndia," https://itunes.apple.com/gb/app/my-mala/id348337233?mt=8 (accessed November 27, 2017).
37. "iShrine," jChicken.com, -6?mt=8 https://appadvice.com/app/ishrine-virtual-buddhist-shrine/328373556 (accessed November, 18, 2021).
38. "Buddhist Memory Game," Foundation Mir, no longer available.
39. "BuddhaMind," http://www.buddhamindapp.com/ (accessed November 27, 2017).
40. Wagner and Accardo, "Buddhist Apps," 137.
41. Wagner and Accardo, "Buddhist Apps," 138.
42. Wagner, *Godwired,* 79.
43. Wagner, *Godwired,* 102–7.
44. Wagner and Accardo, "Buddhist Apps," 134.
45. Ally Ostrowski, "Buddha Browsing: American Buddhism and the Internet," *Contemporary Buddhism* 7, no. 1 (2006): 91–103.
46. Wagner and Accardo, "Buddhist Apps," 141.
47. Linden Lab, June 20, 2013, "Second Life Celebrates 10 year Anniversary," https://www.lindenlab.com/releases/second-life-celebrates-10-year-anniversary (accessed November 5, 2017).
48. Louise Connelly, "Virtual Buddhism: Buddhist Ritual *in Second Life*," in *Digital Religion: Understanding Religious Practice in New Media Worlds*, ed. Heidi A. Campbell (New York: London: Routledge, 2013), 128.
49. Connelly, "Virtual Buddhism: An Analysis," 12–34.
50. Falcone, "Virtual Materials."
51. Grieve, *Cyber Zen.*
52. Stephen Pattison, *Seeing Things: Deepening Relations with Visual Artefacts* (London: SCM Press, 2007).
53. Klemens Karlsson, "The Formation of Early Buddhist Visual Culture," *Material Religion* 2, no. 1 (2006): 68–96.
54. Connelly, "Virtual Buddhism: An Analysis," 14.
55. Buddha Center, http://www.thebuddhacenter.org/about/the-sangha-2/ (accessed November 5, 2017), site no longer available.
56. Connelly, "Virtual Buddhism: An Analysis," 15.

57. Busch, "To Come to a Correct Understanding," 62.
58. Grieve, *Cyber Zen*, 177.
59. Falcone, "Virtual Materials," 181.
60. Connelly, "Virtual Buddhism: An Analysis," 23.
61. Karlsson, "The Formation of Early Buddhist Visual Culture," 68–95.
62. Amy Whitehead, Conference Report: "Material Religion: Embodiment, Materiality, Technology," *Material Religion* 12, no. 4 (2016): 530.
63. Grieve, *Cyber Zen*, 177.
64. Dorothea E. Schulz, "Soundscape," in *Key Words in Religion, Media and Culture*, ed. David Morgan (New York: London: Routledge. 2008), 172–86.
65. Grieve, *Cyber Zen*, 212.
66. Grieve, *Cyber Zen*, 185.
67. Connelly, "Virtual Buddhism: An Analysis," 12–34.
68. Grieve, *Cyber Zen*, 188.
69. Connelly, "Virtual Buddhism: An Analysis," 17.
70. Connelly, "Virtual Buddhism: An Analysis," 17–18.
71. Falcone, "Virtual Materials," 179.
72. Falcone, "Virtual Materials," 185.
73. Grieve, *Cyber Zen*, 6.
74. Wagner and Accardo, "Buddhist Apps," 138.
75. Cheong et al., *Digital Religion*, 296.
76. Wagner and Accardo, "Buddhist Apps."
77. Buddhanet, http://www.buddhanet.net/ (accessed December 22, 2017).
78. Cheong et al., *Digital Religion*, 297.
79. Cheong et al., *Digital Religion*, 28.
80. Campbell, "Surveying," 22.

Further Reading

Campbell, Heidi. *When Religion Meets New Media*. London: Routledge, 2010.

Campbell, Heidi, ed. *Digital Religion: Understanding Religious Practice in New Media Worlds*. Abingdon, UK, and New York: Routledge, 2013.

Cheong, Pauline Hope, Peter Fischer-Nielsen, Stefan Gelfren, and Charles Ess, eds. *Digital Religion, Social Media and Culture: Perspectives, Practices and Future*. New York: Peter Lang, 2012.

Connelly, Louise. "Virtual Buddhism: An Analysis of Aesthetics in Relation to Religious Practice within Second Life." *Online Heidelberg Journal of Religion on the Internet* 4, no. 1 (2010): 12–34.

Connelly, Louise. "Virtual Buddhism: Buddhist Ritual in *Second Life*." In *Digital Religion: Understanding Religious Practice in New Media Worlds*, ed. Heidi A. Campbell. Abingdon, UK, and New York: Routledge, 2013, 128–35.

Falcone, Jessica. "Our Virtual Materials: The Substance of Buddhist Holy Objects in a Virtual World." In *Buddhism, the Internet, and Digital Media: The Pixel in the Lotus*, ed. Gregory Price Grieve and Daniel Veidlinger, 173–90. New York: Routledge, 2015.

Grieve, Gregory Price. *Cyber Zen: Imagining Authentic Buddhist Identity, Community, and Practices in the Virtual World of Second Life*. Abingdon, UK: Routledge, 2017.

Grieve, Gregory Price, and Daniel Veidlinger, eds. *Buddhism, the Internet and Digital Media: The Pixel in the Lotus*. New York: Routledge, 2015.

Wagner, Rachel. *Godwired: Religion, Ritual, and Virtual Reality*. Abingdon, UK, and New York: Routledge, 2012.

Wagner, Rachel, and Christopher Accardo. "Buddhist Apps: Skillful Means or Dharma Dilution?" In *Buddhism, the Internet, and Digital Media: The Pixel in the Lotus*, ed. Gregory Price Grieve and Daniel Veidlinger. New York: Routledge 2015, 134–54.

CHAPTER 36

CONTEMPLATIVE SCIENCE AND BUDDHIST SCIENCE

JOHN D. DUNNE

INTRODUCTION

WHILE the scientific study of contemplative practices located within or derived from Buddhist traditions can be traced back almost sixty years, most published studies have appeared in this century, with recent years witnessing the yearly publication of more than a thousand peer-reviewed articles on "mindfulness" alone.[1] This striking increase in scientific research on Buddhist or Buddhism-derived[2] practices emerges from a vibrant community of inquiry that often adopts the moniker of "contemplative science," a term that evokes the even more contentious notion of "Buddhist science." In this chapter, I will present a brief history of "contemplative science," with an emphasis on the pivotal role of the Mind and Life Institute, and then turn to "Buddhist science," along with the critiques it invokes. I will conclude by briefly exploring a particular feature of contemplative science and the challenges that it imposes.

A BRIEF HISTORY OF CONTEMPLATIVE SCIENCE

The earliest scientific publications on meditation emerged from studies conducted on Hindu practitioners as early as the 1950s.[3] Buddhist practices as the focus of scientific research first appear in 1966 in a study by Tomio Hirai and colleagues, who used electroencephalography (EEG) to examine Zen Buddhist *zazen*.[4] It is fitting that a Zen practice was the focus of the first such study to appear in print, since Zen was already playing a prominent role in the "East-West" dialogues around psychotherapy, while Buddhist practices from other traditions were at that time largely unknown in psychotherapeutic circles.[5] Despite Hirai's efforts, however, the scientific study of Buddhist and Buddhism-derived practices lay mostly dormant for some decades, at least as measured by the appearance of peer-reviewed publications. It is not until the twenty-first century that research on Buddhist and Buddhism-derived forms of meditation truly takes off. Zen practices occasionally appear in these later studies, but the vast majority are focused on "mindfulness," the main "Buddhism-derived" style of practice that has been the subject of scientific research. Despite the importance of mindfulness studies, their numerical dominance obscures other forces, beyond the cultural appeal of mindfulness, that have contributed to the remarkable growth of what many would call "contemplative science."

Some other forces that have spurred scientific studies of Buddhist or Buddhism-derived practices become evident through the history of "contemplative science" as a moniker for this research domain. The term emerges from a community of inquiry that formed around the Mind and Life Institute (MLI), and while it is certainly not the only institution to have a major impact in this arena, MLI's efforts correlate directly with the dramatic increase in peer-reviewed publications in the past fifteen years.[6] MLI began in 1987, motivated by earlier engagements between His Holiness the Dalai Lama XIV and scientists, including an event organized in 1984 by Robert Thurman at Amherst College.[7] These various events prompted the neuroscientist Francisco Varela to approach the Dalai Lama about an ongoing dialogue, and aided by the practical skills of the entrepreneur Adam Engle, the Mind and Life Institute inaugurated its first dialogue at the Dalai Lama's Indian home-in-exile in 1987. With the Dalai Lama as Honorary Chairperson, MLI continues to this day, having hosted thirty-three dialogues with the Dalai Lama that have spawned numerous publications and much media attention.[8]

The 1990s were crucial for MLI, when Varela and Engle used the dialogues to recruit individuals who have gone on to influential roles in the development of scientific research on Buddhist and Buddhism-derived practices.[9] B. Alan Wallace, a Buddhist scholar and meditation teacher, had already joined Varela for the first MLI dialogue as a Tibetan-language translator and an authority on Buddhist contemplative theory. In 1990, Jon Kabat-Zinn, the co-creator of Mindfulness-Based Stress Reduction (MBSR) and the founder of the Center for Mindfulness at the University of Massachusetts Medical School, joined an MLI dialogue on "Emotions and Health," and he was accompanied by Daniel Goleman, the author known for *Emotional Intelligence* and many other works. Goleman went on to write *Destructive Emotions*, the most widely read account of any MLI dialogue.[10] By 1992, Varela had recruited fellow neuroscientists Richard Davidson and Clifford Saron to join him on an expedition to the foothills above Dharamsala to conduct neuroscientific experiments on long-term practitioners or "adepts" living there, as suggested by the Dalai Lama. The expedition, which involved schlepping bulky and expensive equipment into this mountainous region, was an exercise in futility,[11] but it secured the ongoing engagement of Davidson and Saron, both of whom would go on to play prominent roles in "contemplative science."[12]

Along with the Dalai Lama dialogues, MLI created other initiatives that, while less visible, have had a tremendous impact on the emergence of contemplative science. Of particular importance is the "Mind and Life Summer Research Institute" (MLSRI, or simply the SRI). The yearly SRI meetings, which continue to this day, began in 2004 at the Garrison Institute, a retreat center created by philanthropists Jonathan and Dianna Rose in a former Catholic monastery on the banks of the Hudson River. The first few years featured Wallace, Davidson, Kabat-Zinn, and Goleman, all of whom were, by then, members of the MLI Board of Directors. They were joined by many other key collaborators, including the philosopher Evan Thompson and the philanthropist and filmmaker Barry Hershey. Orchestrated in the first several years by Adam Engle, the SRI was based upon the neuroscience "Boot Camp" programs that many universities still host. SRI provided intensive training for younger scholars, mostly scientists, in the theoretical and practical dimensions of studying various forms of meditation.

The 2004 to 2006 SRI programs included Wallace, who was then writing *Contemplative Science: Where Buddhism and Neuroscience Converge.*[13] The phrase used for the book's title offered a way to address a fundamental problem: namely, that a scientific paper could be on "meditation," without any specificity about the form of meditation being studied. Informal discussions suggested that part of the problem was simply the difficulty of pluralizing "meditation," which requires awkward phrasing, such as "forms of" or "kinds of" meditation. Likewise, "meditation" conjured the image of a seated practitioner engaged in quiet contemplation, and it thus did not encompass practices such as yoga and *taiji*. The term "contemplative science" offered a useful alternative, since its focus was understood to be "contemplative practices," in the plural, including many modalities where one is neither seated nor silent. The MLI leadership thus decided to deliberately promote "contemplative science" as a key focus of MLI's activities, including the SRI.[14]

As a term, "contemplative science" proved effective in demarcating the type of research that the SRI was intended to promote, but a moniker can only do so much. Many other factors contributed to the dramatic increase in scientific publications on mindfulness and other Buddhist or Buddhism-derived practices that began around 2004. Even before the first SRI in 2003, Davidson, Kabat-Zinn, and colleagues published the results of the first study to use functional magnetic resonance imaging (fMRI) to examine the effects of MBSR. While modest in its outcomes, the study featured a well-established neuroscientist who was willing to engage in meditation research, a career-ending choice for younger scientists prior to that point.[15] Davidson also conducted other fMRI studies that took some tentative steps toward "neurophenomenology," a method initially conceptualized by Francisco Varela that was especially suited to (and indeed, derived from) the study of contemplative practices.[16] At the same time, the cultural allure of mindfulness was becoming a hot topic in the United States and beyond, anticipating the famed (or infamous) *Time* magazine cover that depicted a "Mindful Revolution."[17] But along with all this was a philanthropic endeavor, funded by Barry Hershey, that may have had the greatest impact.

Named in memory of MLI cofounder Francisco Varela, who died at the age of fifty-four in 2001, the MLI Varela Research Award Program targeted a specific career-stage for young scientists, namely, the crucial period that stretches from the end of one's graduate education through one's early years as a tenure-track professor or postdoctoral fellow. The relatively modest grants sought to grow the ranks of academic scientists who conduct research in this domain, and the program has been a stunning success. Of the more than 150 awards granted since 2004, more than $55 million has been generated in follow-up grants. The list of awardees from the early years now reads like a "who's who" of the most prominent, mid-career researchers in this domain, many of whom hold positions at major universities.[18]

Much more could be said about the emergence of "contemplative science" and the exponential expansion of research in this area. Many other individuals, institutions, and cultural forces have played key roles, but a more complete account must be left as a desideratum. Instead, let us examine another term that emerges not long after MLI starts promoting contemplative science.

"Buddhist Science"

The interaction between Buddhism and science has attracted considerable attention in scholarly circles, with publications that range from cultural histories focused on the beginnings of this encounter in the nineteenth century to works on the most recent engagements.[19] This scholarship often questions the claim that Buddhism is especially compatible with science, and those critiques are easily provoked by speaking of "Buddhist science." While this term appeared in the archaic sense of a knowledge system in some nineteenth-century publications,[20] more recently, "Buddhist science" conveys the notion that, parallel to the scientific traditions that first appear in Europe, Buddhists have a similarly scientific account of our world, especially an "inner science" of the mind. This assertion appears most saliently in a series of volumes, commissioned by the Dalai Lama, on *Science and Philosophy in the Indian Buddhist Classics*.[21] In his introduction to these volumes, the Dalai Lama presents a novel, tripartite distinction of Buddhist science, Buddhist philosophy, and Buddhist religion. The Dalai Lama appears to have developed this distinction over the course of several MLI dialogues,[22] and it reflects his acuity in responding to late modernity, including the Western yearning for a "science" that somehow is fully compatible with contemporary spirituality, and yet also distinct from "religion."[23] This notion of "Buddhist science" is an especially direct way of claiming that Buddhism has always been "scientific," even before the emergence of science as we know it. This claim has evoked many critiques, but before examining it further, one issue must be addressed: namely, the way that "Buddhist science" seems to treat both "Buddhism" and "science" as monolithic entities.

The Dangers of the Monolith

Within Buddhist Studies, it is a truism that "Buddhism" is an invented term, foreign to the traditions we call "Buddhist," that suggests an unfounded uniformity across traditions.[24] This tendency toward monolithic treatment is especially problematic in the scientific study of Buddhist and Buddhism-derived practices, precisely because any scientific study must recognize that, since the practices, their contexts, and their conceptual frameworks differ significantly across traditions, the measurable effects of those practices will likely differ. As a historical matter, the vast majority of scientific studies concern the form of contemporary mindfulness found in "mindfulness-based interventions" (MBIs), the overall term for MBSR and its many derivatives.[25] Mindfulness practices in MBIs are properly called "Buddhism-derived," since Buddhist traditions provide the primary techniques and discursive elements, but mindfulness in MBIs is also a deliberate hybrid of modern Zen, *vipassanā*, and Tibetan Buddhist practices, not to mention other influences, such as Sufism. In this sense, MBIs are certainly "Buddhism-derived," but they do not map back to any particular Buddhist tradition as their source.[26] In short, there is no monolithic "Buddhism" that contemporary mindfulness emerges from. And given the variety of findings reported in studies of various practices, such as contemporary *vipassanā*[27] and advanced Tibetan practices,[28] the singularity of speaking about "Buddhist" practices is misleading.

While "Buddhist science" alludes to the insights that are allegedly cultivated through Buddhist practices, it primarily refers to Buddhist theoretical literature that gives an account of how those practices work (as well as accounts of other topics, such as the nature of the cosmos). Here, too, a monolithic treatment is problematic, since even when unpacking practices that could all be considered forms of "mindfulness," different Buddhist traditions offer divergent interpretations.[29] The heterogeneity of Buddhist accounts emerges in unpredictable ways in the scientific literature, where theories from multiple traditions are sometimes combined in novel ways by contemporary authors.[30] Likewise, theoretical constructs derived from a single tradition may be applied to practices from multiple traditions. A case in point is the distinction between "focused attention" (FA) and "open monitoring" (OM) styles of meditation, a distinction introduced in a 2007 publication with more than 2,500 citations, ranking it among the most cited meditation articles.[31] The FA/OM distinction was developed from Tibetan accounts, but it appears in numerous studies on non-Tibetan practices. Likewise, some of the most widely cited theoretical articles on mindfulness draw more-or-less explicitly on Theravada theory, but they are used to unpack the style of practice found in contemporary mindfulness, which does not map directly to Theravada practice.[32] So, too, James Austin's pioneering *Zen and the Brain* has often been cited to unpack meditation far beyond the boundaries of Zen.[33] Of course, a theoretical construct derived from one Buddhist tradition can turn out to be a useful tool when applied to contemplative practices from a wide variety of contexts. The point here is simply that "Buddhist science" in the singular obscures the considerable diversity in theories labeled "Buddhist," and researchers can thus lose track of how a tradition's commitments and agendas manifest in its particular contributions to the study of contemplative practices.

Beyond a singular notion of Buddhism, the monolithic use of the term "science" is perhaps even more problematic, not only because it invites the specter of scientism, but also because it suggests that all scientific disciplines are equal in their approach to contemplative practices. Here, a particular concern is the dominance of neuroscience, with the accompanying narrative that the brain is the center of all that matters, whether it be thought, emotion, culture, or consciousness itself.[34] Evan Thompson, the philosopher who was deeply involved in establishing the SRI, has become particularly vocal in his critique of the highly neurocentric features of the discourse that constitutes contemplative science. Thompson argues that the proper approach for this work should focus not on the brain, nor even on the brain and the "periphery" that is the body, but rather on the human organism embedded in an intrinsically social environment that emerges from complex, dynamic interactions on multiple levels. Thompson thus calls for a more holistic approach, drawing on the work of Edwin Hutchins and his notion of Cognitive Ecology, as a means to move beyond the neurocentrism that plagues contemplative science.[35] Thompson's critique of the neurocentrism in contemplative science is both biting and welcome. It includes a call for ongoing, reflexive attention to the way that our scientific practices construct and shape what we study. While sensitive to the tendency to idealize science, Thompson's critique might perhaps be even more effective if it addressed more directly the scientistic tendency to place not just the brain, but "science" itself on a monolithic pedestal around which we humanoids must dance.

Critiquing Buddhist Science: False Advertising and What's Lost

As noted earlier, an extensive literature on the interaction between Buddhism and science has emerged in recent years, and my aim here is to examine some salient points in the critiques of any special relationship between Buddhism and science. Overall, critics fall roughly into two camps: those who argue that crucial aspects of Buddhism are lost when one too closely construes Buddhism as scientific, and those who argue that any claim of some special relationship between Buddhism and science amounts to false advertising. Some critics fall into both camps, and a recent and persuasively argued example is Evan Thompson's *Why I Am Not a Buddhist*. The "something's lost" critiques have various motivations, but Thompson emphasizes the concern that "scientific" Buddhism is a "naturalized" Buddhism—one that is made fully compatible with modern science by excluding "supernatural" elements.[36] For these critiques, a naturalized Buddhism is an impoverished Buddhism because it necessarily lacks certain traditional elements, such as the very notion of transcendent nirvana, that are central to its normative account of human flourishing. In other words, without normative accounts of what it means to be human and what constitutes our highest aspirations, Buddhist traditions lose their transformative elements and become just another psychotherapeutic intervention.[37] This "what's lost" critique raises crucial issues that exceed the scope of this chapter, including the very question of whether the notion of a naturalized account of human flourishing is an oxymoron. Of greater relevance, for present purposes, is the "false advertising" critique, which essentially argues that to present

Buddhism as especially compatible with science is to misrepresent it. However, before examining Thompson's version of this critique, one oddity must be noted here: the absence of Asian voices.

When I say that Asian voices are largely absent in this discussion, I mean specifically that they are not heard in the critiques. Asian voices, most prominently the Dalai Lama's, are clearly heard in the arguments in favor of some special relationship between Buddhism and science, but this is not so for the critiques. A troubling asymmetry in this literature thus emerges. On the one hand, some Asian Buddhist intellectuals, concerned at least in part with colonialism, Western hegemony, and cultural survival, argue for the worth—or even the superiority—of Buddhist culture by appealing to something like "Buddhist science," and many modern Westerners, eager to find a spirituality compatible with science, become ready allies. Some Western intellectuals, however, respond by bemoaning the loss of what one author calls "naturalizing," in an appallingly orientalist moment, the "exotic" elements of Buddhism,[38] and some Western critics go on to reject the claim that Buddhism is exceptional in its compatibility with science. This is not to say that there are no traditional Asian Buddhists who are uncomfortable with a scientific Buddhism; indeed, some are, but they are very hard to find in print.[39] The absence of critical voices from traditional Buddhist communities is troubling. Is there a silent majority, opposed to a scientific rendering of Buddhism, who are reluctant to gainsay the Dalai Lama and other Asian Buddhist luminaries? Or is the program of casting Buddhism in a scientific light seen as a winning strategy by most Asian Buddhists? We do not know the answers to these questions, but given the devastation that Western modernity has wrought on the Buddhist cultures of Asia, perhaps it would be appropriate, in any case, to give Asian Buddhist intellectuals a bit more agency as they play the "science card" in the global game of cultural hegemony.

Be that as it may, turning now to Thompson's critique of the claim that Buddhism is especially "scientific," he targets a new formulation of Buddhism that has come to be known as "Buddhist modernism." For Thompson, Buddhist modernism preaches a form of Buddhist "exceptionalism," especially in terms of its compatibility with science. He says:[40]

> . . . [T]he dominant strand of modern Buddhism, known as "Buddhist modernism," is full of confused ideas. They coalesce around what I call "Buddhist exceptionalism." Buddhist exceptionalism is the belief that Buddhism is superior to other religions in being inherently rational and empirical, or that Buddhism isn't really a religion but rather is a kind of "mind science," therapy, philosophy, or way of life based on meditation.

Thompson's critique of this confused "Buddhist modernism" proceeds on various fronts, but at the outset, he emphasizes that he is "very sympathetic" to the Dalai Lama's goal of modernizing Buddhism, especially for Tibetans, but also as a "positive cultural force in the world" more generally.[41] Given this sympathetic stance, one of the opening moves in Thompson's critique seems ironic: he insists that Buddhism is a "religion" from which no alleged Buddhist science could be separated. Although Thompson acknowledges the European provenance of "religion" as a category,[42] he misses the irony of being a white, Western man who insists on imposing this category on Asian cultural practices, precisely in a context where at least some Asians are resisting that category and embracing "science" in a kind of counterattack to Euro-American hegemony.

In Thompson's defense, a Durkheimian account would certainly interpret Buddhism as a "religion" (although this might also be true for the "science" of scientism),[43] and admittedly, his main target is not traditional Asian Buddhists.[44] Instead, Thompson is especially concerned with Western Buddhists who have been deeply involved in the construction of Buddhist modernism, although again it is worth noting that this makes Asian Buddhists silent bystanders. Western Buddhists have other motivations for seeking a kind of scientific spirituality that is not "religious," and Thompson is right to unearth these motivations. Yet the larger problem here, beyond the troubling silence of Asian voices, is that in his rejection of Buddhist "exceptionalism," Thompson fails to notice the danger of the monolith. He remarks:[45]

> It's also not the case that Buddhist philosophy is inherently more scientific than the philosophies of other religions. For example, it's sometimes said that Buddhist philosophy relies on experience more than scripture, so that when there's a contradiction between the two, scripture is to be rejected in favor of perception and inference. But this assessment is partial and oversimplified. Some Indian Buddhist thinkers, as a matter of philosophical principle, reject testimony based on scripture as being a separate and distinct instrument of knowledge. This is mainly because they want to block appeals to the authority of the Vedas on the part of Brahminical philosophers. But other Buddhist philosophers accept testimony as a source of knowledge independent of perception and inference. . . . In either case, it's unthinkable in practice to reject the word of the Buddha or any of his conceptual and analytical frameworks (such as the so-called five aggregates or the mental and physical elements that are said to make up a person).

Thompson's assessment is highly problematic, and part of the problem is the monolithic treatment of a singular "Buddhism." Certainly, there are Buddhist philosophers for whom the Buddha's word is inviolable, and if the Buddha says that something is the case (for example, that our world is flat or that heat and moisture produce infection), then things could not possibly be otherwise. But the version of "Buddhist science" proposed by the Dalai Lama is explicitly drawing on a strand of Buddhist thought that emerges from the seventh-century CE philosopher Dharmakīrti. The Dalai Lama speaks of this philosophical style as the "Nalanda tradition," a coinage that refers to Nālandā monastery, among the most famed seats of higher learning in the history of Buddhism.[46] As a key figure in this intellectual tradition, Dharmakīrti explicitly affirms that the Buddha's words, as recorded in the discourses attributed to him, cannot be accepted if those words contradict empirical evidence.[47] This part of Dharmakīrti's philosophy has not escaped the Dalai Lama's attention, and it is the basis for his claim that Buddhists must abandon the traditional, "flat-earth" cosmology found in many Buddhist texts.[48]

But in the preceding passage, Thompson argues that, while "some" Buddhists adopt this Dharmakīrtian perspective on scripture, "others" do not, and since at least some Buddhists are not adopting this empirical attitude about scriptural inference, we must conclude that Buddhism is not "exceptional" in this regard. In this way, Thompson has effectively argued for a univocal "Buddhism" that not even Buddhist modernists would accept, since they recognize and then seek to compartmentalize or eliminate the "religious" or "supernatural" elements of Buddhist traditions. In short, an effective critique of Buddhist modernism cannot treat Buddhism as a whole; rather, it must specifically address the particular strands that Buddhist modernists wish to emphasize triumphantly.[49]

In this vein, beyond his perhaps inadvertent appeal to a monolithic Buddhism, Thompson is also simply incorrect about Dharmakīrti's account of scriptural inference, such that his critique of that strand of Buddhist intellectualism fails. Specifically, Dharmakīrti's argument is directed not just at Brahmanical philosophers, but also quite obviously at Buddhists. Dharmakīrti insists that the core elements of Buddhism—especially the Four Noble Truths—can be proven empirically, and he goes on to make the radical claim that, when allegedly referring to objects that are not amenable to empirical examination, the Buddha's words *do not prove anything*. In other words, any statement that the Buddha makes about entities that are beyond empirical examination is a mere assertion; it carries no epistemic weight, though it may have psychological value.[50] Thus, it is simply false for Thompson to claim that "it's unthinkable in practice to reject the word of the Buddha." This can only be said if one refuses to accept what Dharmakīrti has written, or else one claims special access to what Buddhist philosophers of the Dharmakīrtian ilk actually do "in practice," regardless of what they write. Indeed, it seems that "in practice" Dharmakīrti's radical rejection of scripture as probative becomes a kind of intellectual and elitist shibboleth for many Mahayana Buddhist philosophers at the end of the first millennium CE.[51] This is precisely the intellectual strand that the Dalai Lama wishes to evoke with his coinage of the "Nalanda tradition." And although this intellectual stance characterized a probably miniscule portion of the overall Buddhist population in Asia at the time, it was nevertheless a distinct, triumphalist posture through which some influential Buddhist philosophers proclaimed their alleged superiority. In this regard at least, there is a particular strand of intellectualism within Buddhism that is indeed "exceptional" precisely in the way that Thompson rejects. And since Buddhist modernists are content to choose certain strands or features of Buddhism over other features, there is no need, on their view, for their version of "Buddhism" to be one that all Buddhists have accepted historically. Of course, one might respond that the "real" Buddhism for a particular community is not what a small group of that community's highly educated elites hold it to be, but Thompson does not take this approach. And the highly intellectual and elitist strand of the Dharmakīrtian, "Nalanda tradition" would obviously object to the notion that the "real" Buddhism (or, more accurately, the "true dharma") is what the average Buddhist cowherd believes.[52] This is part of what makes that strand a particularly appealing thread for Buddhist modernists to use in weaving their version of "Buddhism."

Does the failure of Thompson's critique in this particular regard mean that the notion of "Buddhist science" should be straightforwardly accepted? No, it does not. I agree with Thompson that the rhetoric of "Buddhist science" is probably not the best strategy for ensuring Buddhism's flourishing in the twenty-first century, resisting Euro-American cultural hegemony, or enhancing Buddhism's cosmopolitan voice. Elsewhere, I have argued that, while the philosophical strand that the Dalai Lama calls the "Nalanda tradition" is indeed highly compatible with modern science, it diverges from the scientific method in important ways.[53] Even the contemporary Tibetan intellectual Thupten Jinpa, in an essay for the first volume of *Science and Philosophy in the Indian Buddhist Classics,* responds to the question of whether we can speak coherently of Buddhist science by answering both "yes" and "no." Jinpa notes that only a broad (and atypical) notion of "science" would allow for an affirmative answer.[54] Here, many of Thompson's critiques are well taken, but his vociferous rejection of Buddhist exceptionalism apparently blinds him to some readily available evidence: the enormous number of peer-reviewed publications mentioned earlier. To put it succinctly, this evidence strongly suggests that, in comparison to scholars and practitioners from other traditions, Buddhists have been unusually successful in their collaborations with mainstream scientists, and it is quite a stretch of the imagination to hold that this success is due entirely to the recent machinations of Western Buddhist modernists or the anti-colonial efforts of the nineteenth century. It seems far more likely that there is indeed something "exceptional" about the relevant Buddhist traditions in this regard, and while only one intellectual strand has drawn our attention here, there are other strands in other Buddhist traditions, such as the Abhidharma or Abhidhamma, that also seem unusually ready for appropriation into scientific contexts.[55] However, these apparently "exceptional" features of various strands of Buddhism do not in themselves justify the "modernizing" or "naturalizing" moves of Buddhist modernism. Much remains to be critiqued. Likewise, this "exceptional" success in scientific collaborations, as measured by the number of peer-reviewed publications, does not mean that the practical aspects of actually doing "contemplative science" on Buddhist or Buddhism-derived practices are all neatly resolved.

Doing Contemplative Science: The Challenge of Experience

Although diverse, much of the research characterized by "contemplative science" exhibits some common features and challenges, including those that emerge from the issues discussed previously. In this final section of the chapter, I will present just one, largely unrecognized feature of contemplative science that has several ramifications. I will then highlight three persistent challenges, emerging from that feature, that researchers face in this domain.

Contemplative Science: The Centrality of Experience

Some scientists only dabble in the study of contemplative practices, but most studies involve researchers for whom studies on mindfulness or other practices are a large part of their portfolios. Their work generally appears in two forms: clinical research and basic science. The former examines interventions with contemplative components for addressing ills such as stress or pain, although studies of interventions for enhancing performance—for example, in sports—use largely the same methods. Basic science, in contrast, examines fundamental processes of the mind-body system, such as visual perception or emotions, without any necessary connection to clinical outcomes. These areas of research overlap, such that a study in basic science might be designed to inform clinical research, and vice versa. In both areas, there are roughly two primary kinds of publications: theoretical papers and empirical studies. There are also two secondary publications: review papers, which summarize and analyze theoretical and/or empirical studies, and meta-analyses, which perform statistical analyses on the results of multiple empirical studies.[56]

Across these different domains of research and publication, I would argue that a key feature appears frequently, if sometimes implicitly: namely, the assumption that the experiential dimension of a practice—in short, the practice's phenomenology—must be intrinsic to the study. In other words, to the extent that some mechanism or process in the practice is having an observable outcome such as a measurable decrease in anxiety, this outcome is related to some phenomenally accessible aspect of the practice, such as the experience of no longer identifying with one's fear. This attitude contrasts sharply with the behaviorism that dominated psychology for much of the twentieth century,[57] and it also contrasts with pharmaceutical research, where the mechanisms of change are almost always assumed to be phenomenally inaccessible or unconscious. A pill can induce an outcome, such as a less anxious mood, that is accessible in the subject's experience, but the processes that induce that change are not. In contrast, a contemplative intervention such as MBSR seeks to alter experience in ways that the subject is invited to notice as implicitly linked to positive outcomes, even if those outcomes are not to be striven for.[58]

The centrality of experience in contemplative science echoes Francisco Varela's call for the integration of first- and third-person observation, where "first-person" refers to observations made from the standpoint of one's own experience, and "third-person" refers to observations from an impersonal standpoint, often using imaging technology such as EEG or fMRI.[59] For psychological science, especially with a behavioral bent, third-person observation is the norm, so Varela's call for integrating first-person accounts raised many issues, most especially the problem of how to gather that data. One outcome of Varela's call, which also resonated with the ethos of the MLI dialogues, was the need to collaborate with experienced contemplative practitioners, on the assumption that their contemplative training produced expertise in phenomenological observation.[60] A further implication was that scientists themselves should engage in the contemplative practices that they study. After all, a well-trained scientist would never use fMRI data if they had no idea how to gather or interpret it, so if phenomenological data is to be gathered, one must learn that, too. This attitude is concretely expressed in the schedule of the aforementioned SRI: each day involves multiple sessions of meditation, and significant time is devoted to a contemplative "retreat."[61] This emphasis on the experiential dimensions of contemplative practice is promising, but it also leads to a number of challenges.

Three Challenges for Contemplative Science

As a still nascent domain of research, contemplative science faces many challenges, including even the question of whether "contemplative science" itself will survive as a moniker. A full account of the various challenges is far beyond the scope of this chapter, and even just the challenges that emerge from the emphasis on experience would require yet another essay to unpack fully. To conclude this chapter, I will summarize challenges in just three areas: communication, phenomenology, and bias.

The challenge of "communication" concerns the interaction between a contemplative tradition and the contemplative scientist. To be sure, this problem includes the practical task of translation. In some of the early studies conducted on Tibetan adepts, our research team needed to be sure that the adepts, who mostly did not speak English, would understand the instructions guiding the experiment.[62] Beyond these practicalities, the main pitfall is the assumption that categories in the contemplative domain are directly translatable to the scientific domain. "Mindfulness" is a case in point, where the singularity of that term obscures the multiplicity of Buddhist approaches,[63] but another is the notion that nirvana could somehow be translated, more-or-less directly, into an empirically measurable paradigm.[64] Here, the cognitive scientist Larry Barsalou offers a useful approach. In a conference paper from 2010, Barsalou proposes that contemplative science is at a "pidgin" stage, where speakers of distinct, natural languages—in this case, the language of "science" and the language of "Buddhism"—are learning to communicate through functional, but loosely defined, hybrid terms and concepts. Eventually, with enough motivation and effort, this pidgin could become a "creole," a natural but hybrid language spoken by both communities.[65] Barsalou's model offers a clear pathway to avoid the dangers of assuming direct translatability between Buddhist and scientific theories.

A second challenge concerns phenomenology: How precisely does one gather "first-person" data? Theoretical accounts of contemplative practices clearly benefit from a phenomenological perspective,[66] but the process of gathering that data is far from obvious. Here, the issues that plague self-report measures emerge, including demand characteristics and social desirability, which prompt subjects to give the "right" answer on a questionnaire.[67] Microphenomenology, championed by Claire Petitmengin and colleagues, offers a promising approach, yet it involves a time-intensive process that can require as much as two hours of structured interviewing to unpack the phenomenological features in one minute of experience.[68] Using this method to gather sufficient data for a meaningful statistical analysis remains thus far impractical.

A third challenge is the problem of bias, both perceived and actual. Nicholas van Dam and colleagues have broached this issue in their critique of the "hype" around mindfulness in particular, and they argue, "[m]isinformation and poor methodology associated with past studies of mindfulness may lead public consumers to be harmed, misled, and disappointed."[69] Certainly, contemplative scientific research has its problems, even if many are common to other domains.[70] And while there is good evidence for the clinical efficacy of mindfulness in certain contexts,[71] the media "hype" tends to exaggerate such findings. Given the level of popular interest in meditation research, the scientific issues are exacerbated by the media attention, and the headline-grabbing publications on the alleged adverse effects of mindfulness practices are a case in point.[72] While intensive contemplative practice correlates with adverse outcomes in some individuals, the base rates of psychopathology in this population and the role of preexisting conditions make the question of causation speculative, to say the least. This nuance, however, does not make for good headlines, which are readily grabbed by reports of adverse outcomes,[73] and scientific publications that contradict these headlines[74] are unlikely to receive the same attention. The perception and reality of bias in contemplative science are likely related to the thematization of experience, including the experience of researchers themselves. A scientist who studies the contemplative practice that they do each day can easily be perceived as biased. At some point, contemplative science may move beyond this and the other challenges sketched here, but so far, even with the critique from Van Dam and colleagues, they remain largely unaddressed.

Notes

1. Nicholas T. Van Dam et al., "Mind the Hype: A Critical Evaluation and Prescriptive Agenda for Research on Mindfulness and Meditation," *Perspectives on Psychological Science* 13, no. 1 (January 2018): 36–61, https://doi.org/10.1177/1745691617709589.
2. "Buddhism-derived" contemplative practices originally appear in traditional Buddhist contexts but have been "secularized" as interventions for use by the general public. For a nuanced perspective on this "secularization" process, see Ira Helderman, *Prescribing the Dharma: Psychotherapists, Buddhist Traditions, and Defining Religion* (Chapel Hill: University of North Carolina Press, 2019). Broader treatments include David L. McMahan, *The Making of Buddhist Modernism* (New York: Oxford University Press, 2008); Jeff Wilson, *Mindful America: The Mutual Transformation of Buddhist Meditation and American Culture* (New York: Oxford University Press, 2014); Ann Gleig, *American Dharma: Buddhism beyond Modernity* (New Haven, CT: Yale University Press, 2019).
3. See, for example, B. K. Anand, G. S. Chhina, and Baldev Singh, "Some Aspects of Electroencephalographic Studies in Yogis," *Electroencephalography and Clinical Neurophysiology* 13, no. 3 (June 1, 1961): 452–56, https://doi.org/10.1016/0013-4694(61)90015-3.
4. A. Kasamatsu and T. Hirai, "An Electroencephalographic Study on the Zen Meditation (Zazen)," *Folia Psychiatrica Et Neurologica Japonica* 20, no. 4 (1966): 315–36.

5. Anne Harrington and John D. Dunne, "When Mindfulness Is Therapy: Ethical Qualms, Historical Perspectives," *American Psychologist* 70, no. 7 (2015): 621–31, https://doi.org/10.1037/a0039460.
6. Another especially influential institution was the Center for Mindfulness in Medicine, Health Care and Society at the University of Massachusetts Medical School, founded by Jon Kabat-Zinn and Saki Santorelli.
7. "Psychology of East Gaining Attention in Western World," *New York Times*, October 9, 1984, sec. Science, https://www.nytimes.com/1984/10/09/science/psychology-of-east-gaining-atention-in-western-world.html.
8. Daniel Goleman and Richard J. Davidson, *Altered Traits: Science Reveals How Meditation Changes Your Mind, Brain, and Body* (New York: Avery, 2017); Daniel Goleman, *Destructive Emotions: How Can We Overcome Them?: A Scientific Dialogue with the Dalai Lama* (New York: Bantam Books, 2004).
9. The complete list of dialogues and rosters of participants are available from the Mind and Life Institute, at "Event History," Mind & Life Institute, accessed April 4, 2021, https://www.mindandlife.org/events/event-history/.
10. Daniel Goleman, *Emotional Intelligence* (New York: Bantam Books, 1995); Goleman, *Destructive Emotions*.
11. Goleman and Davidson, *Altered Traits*, 209–11.
12. Davidson eventually founded the Center for Healthy Minds at the University of Wisconsin–Madison, and Saron was the co-creator and lead scientist for the Śamatha Project. See Goleman and Davidson, *Altered Traits*, 11, 93–95.
13. B. Alan Wallace, *Contemplative Science: Where Buddhism and Neuroscience Converge* (New York: Columbia University Press, 2007).
14. These observations come from my notes on the 2004 to 2009 SRIs, which I co-chaired or helped plan. Additional information comes from notes for meetings of the MLI Board of Directors, which I joined in 2007 for a three-year term.
15. Richard J. Davidson et al., "Alterations in Brain and Immune Function Produced by Mindfulness Meditation," *Psychosomatic Medicine* 65, no. 4 (August 2003): 564–70, https://doi.org/10.1097/01.psy.0000077505.67574.e3. For meditation research and career concerns, see Goleman and Davidson, *Altered Traits*, 13.
16. Antoine Lutz and Evan Thompson, "Neurophenomenology: Integrating Subjective Experience and Brain Dynamics in the Neuroscience of Consciousness," *Journal of Consciousness Studies* 10, no. 9–10 (2003): 31–52.
17. Kate Pickert, "The Mindful Revolution," *Time* 183, no. 4 (2014): 1. See also Gleig, *American Dharma*.
18. "Francisco J. Varela Research Awards," Mind & Life Institute, accessed April 4, 2021, https://www.mindandlife.org/insights/francisco-j-varela-research-awards/.
19. See, for example, Donald S. Lopez, *The Scientific Buddha: His Short and Happy Life*, 2012; Donald S. Lopez, *Buddhism and Science: A Guide for the Perplexed* (Chicago: University of Chicago Press, 2008); McMahan, *The Making of Buddhist Modernism*; Gleig, *American Dharma*.
20. See, for example, Evariste Régis Huc, *Souvenirs d'un voyage dans la Tartarie, le Thibet, et la Chine pendant les années 1844, 1845 et 1846*, 2. éd. (Paris: Librairie d'Adrien le Clerc, 1853).
21. First published in Tibetan, the series' first two volumes have been translated into English with additional contextual essays: John D. Dunne, Dalai Lama, and Compendium Selection Committee, *The Mind*, ed. Thupten Jinpa, trans. John D. Dunne and Dechen

Rochard, vol. 2, *Science and Philosophy in the Indian Buddhist Classics* (Somerville, MA: Wisdom Publications, 2020); Thupten Jinpa, Dalai Lama, and Compendium Selection Committee, *The Physical World*, ed. Thupten Jinpa, trans. Ian Coghlan, vol. 1, *Science and Philosophy in the Indian Buddhist Classics* (Somerville, MA: Wisdom Publications, 2017).

22. The Dalai Lama may have first alluded to this triad during the 2010 MLI dialogue. See John D. Dunne and Daniel Goleman, eds., *Ecology, Ethics, and Interdependence: The Dalai Lama in Conversation with Leading Thinkers on Climate Change* (Somerville: Wisdom Publications, 2018), 220–21.
23. For expressions of that yearning in contemporary mindfulness, see Erik Braun, "Mindful but Not Religious: Meditation and Enchantment in the Work of Jon Kabat-Zinn," in *Meditation, Buddhism, and Science*, ed. David McMahan and Erik Braun (New York: Oxford University Press, 2017), 173–97.
24. Charles Hallisey and Frank Reynolds, "Buddhism: An Overview," in *Encyclopedia of Religion*, ed. Lindsay Jones, Mircea Eliade, and Charles J. Adams (Detroit: Macmillan Reference USA, 2005), 1087–1101.
25. A publications search on Web of Science (1990–2020), restricted to scientific subject areas, yielded 15,059 results for "mindfulness" (TS = (mindfulness)). The same search for "meditation" excluding "mindfulness" (TS = (meditation) NOT TS = (mindfulness)) yielded 3,747 results, although many of these are also on mindfulness. The same search with topic set to "transcendental meditation" (TS = transcendental meditation) had 505 results.
26. Jon Kabat-Zinn, "Some Reflections on the Origins of MBSR, Skillful Means, and the Trouble with Maps," *Contemporary Buddhism* 12 (May 2011): 281–306, https://doi.org/10.1080/14639947.2011.564844.
27. One example is Heleen A. Slagter et al., "Mental Training Affects Distribution of Limited Brain Resources," *PLOS Biology* 5, no. 6 (May 8, 2007): e138, https://doi.org/10.1371/journal.pbio.0050138.
28. Examples include Antoine Lutz et al., "Long-Term Meditators Self-Induce High-Amplitude Gamma Synchrony during Mental Practice," *Proceedings of the National Academy of Sciences of the United States of America* 101, no. 46 (November 16, 2004): 16369–73, https://doi.org/10.1073/pnas.0407401101; Antoine Lutz et al., "Regulation of the Neural Circuitry of Emotion by Compassion Meditation: Effects of Meditative Expertise," *PloS One* 3, no. 3 (March 26, 2008): e1897, https://doi.org/10.1371/journal.pone.0001897.
29. John D. Dunne, "Buddhist Styles of Mindfulness: A Heuristic Approach," in *Handbook of Mindfulness and Self-Regulation*, ed. Brian D. Ostafin, Michael D. Robinson, and Brian P. Meier (New York: Springer, 2015), 251–70.
30. See, for example, David R. Vago and David A. Silbersweig, "Self-Awareness, Self-Regulation, and Self-Transcendence (S-ART): A Framework for Understanding the Neurobiological Mechanisms of Mindfulness," *Frontiers in Human Neuroscience* 6 (October 2012), https://doi.org/10.3389/fnhum.2012.00296.
31. Antoine Lutz et al., "Attention Regulation and Monitoring in Meditation," *Trends in Cognitive Sciences* 12, no. 4 (April 2008): 163–69, https://doi.org/10.1016/j.tics.2008.01.005. Citation rate is drawn from Google Scholar.
32. Examples include Britta K. Hölzel et al., "How Does Mindfulness Meditation Work? Proposing Mechanisms of Action from a Conceptual and Neural Perspective," *Perspectives on Psychological Science* 6, no. 6 (November 1, 2011): 537–59, https://doi.org/10.1177/1745691611419671; Kirk Warren Brown and Richard M. Ryan, "The Benefits of Being

Present: Mindfulness and Its Role in Psychological Well-Being," *Journal of Personality and Social Psychology* 84, no. 4 (2003): 822–48.

33. James H. Austin, *Zen and the Brain: Toward an Understanding of Meditation and Consciousness* (Cambridge, MA: MIT Press, 1998).
34. Marc De Kesel, "The Brain: A Nostalgic Dream: Some Notes on Neuroscience and the Problem of Modern Knowledge," in *Neuroscience and Critique: Exploring the Limits of the Neurological Turn*, ed. Jan De Vos and Ed Pluth (London: Routledge, 2015), 11–20, https://doi.org/10.4324/9781315714189.
35. Evan Thompson, "Looping Effects and the Cognitive Science of Mindfulness Meditation," in *Meditation, Buddhism, and Science*, ed. David McMahan and Erik Braun (New York: Oxford University Press, 2017), 47–61; Evan Thompson, *Why I Am Not a Buddhist* (New Haven, CT, and London: Yale University Press, 2020), 28–30, 125–32.
36. A scholarly version of naturalized Buddhism is found in Owen J. Flanagan, *The Bodhisattva's Brain: Buddhism Naturalized* (Cambridge, MA: MIT Press, 2011). For a popular version, see Robert Wright, *Why Buddhism Is True: The Science and Philosophy of Meditation and Enlightenment*, first Simon & Schuster hardcover edition (New York: Simon & Schuster, 2017).
37. Thompson, *Why I Am Not a Buddhist*, 77–85.
38. Wright, *Why Buddhism Is True*, 216.
39. Douglas Duckworth has reported on the writings of Tsültrim Lodrö, but the critique of science (primarily a "what's lost" version) is provided by Duckworth himself. See Douglas Duckworth, "Echoes of Tsültrim Lodrö: An Indigenous Voice from Contemporary Tibet on the 'Buddhism and Science Dialogue,'" *Contemporary Buddhism* 16, no. 2 (November 2015): 267–77, https://doi.org/10.1080/14639947.2015.1033811. Thupten Jinpa discusses Gendun Chöpel's engagement with science, but here too the overall tenor is not critical. See Thupten Jinpa, "Buddhism and Science: How Far Can the Dialogue Proceed?," *Zygon: Journal of Religion & Science* 45, no. 4 (December 2010): 871–82, https://doi.org/10.1111/j.1467-9744.2010.01138.x. At the 2009 conference on Buddhism and science held at the Central University for Tibetan Studies in Sarnath, India, one participant offered an impassioned defense of traditional Buddhist cosmology in opposition to scientific accounts, but his presentation was never published in English.
40. Thompson, *Why I Am Not a Buddhist*, 1–2.
41. Thompson, *Why I Am Not a Buddhist*, 58.
42. Thompson, *Why I Am Not a Buddhist*, 16.
43. David Chidester, *Empire of Religion: Imperialism and Comparative Religion* (Chicago: University of Chicago Press, 2014).
44. Thompson, *Why I Am Not a Buddhist*, 29 ff.
45. Thompson, *Why I Am Not a Buddhist*, 52.
46. Dalai Lama XIV Bstan 'dzin rgya mtsho, *The Universe in a Single Atom: The Convergence of Science and Spirituality* (New York: Morgan Road Books, 2005), 79.
47. John D. Dunne, *Foundations of Dharmakīrti's Philosophy*, Studies in Indian and Tibetan Buddhism (Boston: Wisdom Publications, 2004), 239–45.
48. Dalai Lama XIV Bstan 'dzin rgya mtsho, *The Universe in a Single Atom*, 79–80.
49. The Dalai Lama's own separation of "Buddhist religion" from "Buddhist science" and "Buddhist philosophy" can be interpreted as just this move, but a perhaps more obvious version of this compartmentalizing is found in the works of Buddhist naturalizers, such as Robert Wright and Owen Flanagan. See Wright, *Why Buddhism Is True*, and Flanagan, *The Bodhisattva's Brain*.

50. Dunne, *Foundations of Dharmakīrti's Philosophy*, 241. As noted there, perhaps the clearest statement of this position comes from the commentator Śākyabuddhi. Reflecting on Dharmakīrti's statement that scriptural inference is "not without problems," he says that scriptural inference is not a "real" (Sanskrit, *bhāvika*) source of epistemically reliable information.
51. Sara L. McClintock, *Omniscience and the Rhetoric of Reason: Śāntarakṣita and Kamalaśīla on Rationality, Argumentation, and Religious Authority* (Boston: Wisdom Publications, 2010).
52. The "cowherd" (Sanskrit, *gopāla*) is used as an example of the least educated person in Buddhist philosophical texts, both in Sanskrit and Tibetan, usually to indicate something incontestable because it is known "even down to the cowherds" (Sanskrit, *ā gopālam*). See, for example, Kamalaśīla, *Tattvasaṃgraha of Śāntarakṣita with the Commentary of Kamalaśīla*, vol. 1, Gaekwad's Oriental Series 30–31 (Baroda: Central Library, 1926), 277. A group of scholars have playfully and ironically adopted this term as a way of emphasizing their philosophical emphasis on the conventional; see Cowherds, *Moonshadows: Conventional Truth in Buddhist Philosophy* (Oxford and New York: Oxford University Press, 2011), v–vi. But while they interpret the metaphor to mean the average "man on the street," the metaphor points not to the average person, but to the least educated one.
53. John D. Dunne, "What Is Inner Science?," in *In Vimalakirti's House: A Festschrift in Honor of Robert A. F. Thurman on the Occasion of His 70th Birthday*, ed. Christian Wedemeyer, John D. Dunne, and Thomas Yarnall (New York: American Institute of Buddhist Studies, 2015), 317–41.
54. Jinpa, Dalai Lama, and Compendium Selection Committee, *Science and Philosophy in the Indian Buddhist Classics*, 1:43. I agree with Jinpa that, given a particular interpretation of "science," it makes sense to speak of "Buddhist science." The problem is that this definition does not align very well with the scientific method, although that too is often idealized. See Paul Feyerabend, *Against Method: Outline of an Anarchistic Theory of Knowledge* (London: Verso, 1986).
55. See, for example, the discussion of "psychologization" in McMahan, *Making of Buddhist Modernism*, 52–57.
56. Highly cited examples of these types of publications include, for an empirical study, Philippe R. Goldin and James J. Gross, "Effects of Mindfulness-Based Stress Reduction (MBSR) on Emotion Regulation in Social Anxiety Disorder," *Emotion* 10, no. 1 (February 2010): 83–91, https://doi.org/10.1037/a0018441; for a theoretical paper, Antoine Lutz et al., "Investigating the Phenomenological Matrix of Mindfulness-Related Practices from a Neurocognitive Perspective," *American Psychologist* 70, no. 7 (2015): 632–58, https://doi.org/10.1037/a0039585; for a review, Richard Chambers, Eleonora Gullone, and Nicholas B. Allen, "Mindful Emotion Regulation: An Integrative Review," *Clinical Psychology Review* 29, no. 6 (August 2009): 560–72, https://doi.org/10.1016/j.cpr.2009.06.005; and for a meta-analysis, Paul Grossman et al., "Mindfulness-Based Stress Reduction and Health Benefits. A Meta-Analysis," *Journal of Psychosomatic Research* 57, no. 1 (July 2004): 35–43, https://doi.org/10.1016/S0022-3999(03)00573-7.
57. George Graham, "Behaviorism," in *The Stanford Encyclopedia of Philosophy*, ed. Edward N. Zalta, Spring 2019 (Metaphysics Research Lab, Stanford University, 2019), https://plato.stanford.edu/archives/spr2019/entries/behaviorism/.
58. Jon Kabat-Zinn, *Full Catastrophe Living: Using the Wisdom of Your Body and Mind to Face Stress, Pain, and Illness*, revised and updated edition (New York: Bantam Books, 2013).

59. Lutz and Thompson, "Neurophenomenology"; F. J. Varela and Jonathan Shear, "First-Person Accounts: Why, What, and How," *Journal of Consciousness Studies* 6 (1999): 1–14.
60. Antoine Lutz, John D. Dunne, and Richard J. Davidson, "Meditation and the Neuroscience of Consciousness: An Introduction," in *The Cambridge Handbook of Consciousness*, ed. Philip David Zelazo, Morris Moscovitch, and Evan Thompson, 1st ed. (New York: Cambridge University Press, 2007), 499–551.
61. "Join Mind & Life for Our Summer Research Institute," Mind & Life Institute, https://www.mindandlife.org/event/2021-summer-research-institute/ (accessed April 14, 2021).
62. I served as an oral interpreter for these early "adept" studies. Resulting publications include: Lutz et al., "Long-Term Meditators Self-Induce High-Amplitude Gamma Synchrony during Mental Practice"; Lutz et al., "Regulation of the Neural Circuitry of Emotion by Compassion Meditation"; Antoine Lutz et al., "Guiding the Study of Brain Dynamics by Using First-Person Data: Synchrony Patterns Correlate with Ongoing Conscious States during a Simple Visual Task," *Proceedings of the National Academy of Sciences* 99, no. 3 (February 5, 2002): 1586–91, https://doi.org/10.1073/pnas.032658199.
63. Dunne, "Buddhist Styles of Mindfulness: A Heuristic Approach"; Rupert Gethin, "Buddhist Conceptualizations of Mindfulness," in *Handbook of Mindfulness: Theory, Research, and Practice*, ed. Kirk Warren Brown, J. David Creswell, and Richard M. Ryan (New York: Guilford Press, 2015), 9–41.
64. Jake H. Davis and David R. Vago, "Can Enlightenment Be Traced to Specific Neural Correlates, Cognition, or Behavior? No, and (a Qualified) Yes," *Frontiers in Psychology* 4 (November 22, 2013): 870, https://doi.org/10.3389/fpsyg.2013.00870.
65. Lawrence W. Barsalou, "Discussion Panel on Attention, Mindfulness, and Memory." (Workshop on Exploring the Language of Mental Life, Center for Compassion and Altruism Research and Education, Stanford University, Telluride, CO, July 2010).
66. Lutz et al., "Investigating the Phenomenological Matrix of Mindfulness-Related Practices from a Neurocognitive Perspective."
67. Richard J. Davidson and Alfred W. Kaszniak, "Conceptual and Methodological Issues in Research on Mindfulness and Meditation," *American Psychologist* 70, no. 7 (2015): 581–92, https://doi.org/10.1037/a0039512.
68. C. Petitmengin et al., "What Is It Like to Meditate?: Methods and Issues for a Micro-Phenomenological Description of Meditative Experience," *Journal of Consciousness Studies* 24, no. 5–6 (January 1, 2017): 170–98; Claire Petitmengin, "Describing One's Subjective Experience in the Second Person: An Interview Method for the Science of Consciousness," *Phenomenology and the Cognitive Sciences* 5, no. 3 (2006): 229–69, https://doi.org/10.1007/s11097-006-9022-2.
69. Van Dam et al., "Mind the Hype," 1.
70. Richard J. Davidson and Cortland J. Dahl, "Outstanding Challenges in Scientific Research on Mindfulness and Meditation," *Perspectives on Psychological Science* 13, no. 1 (January 1, 2018): 62–65, https://doi.org/10.1177/1745691617718358.
71. Simon B. Goldberg et al., "The Empirical Status of Mindfulness-Based Interventions: A Systematic Review of 44 Meta-Analyses of Randomized Controlled Trials," *Perspectives on Psychological Science: A Journal of the Association for Psychological Science*, February 16, 2021, https://doi.org/10.1177/1745691620968771.
72. Jared R. Lindahl et al., "The Varieties of Contemplative Experience: A Mixed-Methods Study of Meditation-Related Challenges in Western Buddhists," *PLOS ONE* 12, no. 5 (May 24, 2017): e0176239, https://doi.org/10.1371/journal.pone.0176239.

73. "The Times When Mindfulness Could Be Bad for You," *Psychology Today*, https://www.psychologytoday.com/blog/dont-forget-the-basil/202005/the-times-when-mindfulness-could-be-bad-you (accessed April 14, 2021).
74. Matthew J. Hirshberg et al., "Prevalence of Harm in Mindfulness-Based Stress Reduction," *Psychological Medicine* (August 18, 2020): 1–9, https://doi.org/10.1017/S0033291720002834.

Further Reading

Dahl, Cortland J., Antoine Lutz, and Richard J. Davidson. "Reconstructing and Deconstructing the Self: Cognitive Mechanisms in Meditation Practice." *Trends in Cognitive Sciences* 19, no. 9 (September 2015): 515–23. https://doi.org/10.1016/j.tics.2015.07.001.

Davidson, Richard J., and Alfred W. Kaszniak. "Conceptual and Methodological Issues in Research on Mindfulness and Meditation." *American Psychologist* 70, no. 7 (2015): 581–92. https://doi.org/10.1037/a0039512.

Dunne, John D. "Buddhist Styles of Mindfulness: A Heuristic Approach." In *Handbook of Mindfulness and Self-Regulation*, ed. Brian D. Ostafin, Michael D. Robinson, and Brian P. Meier. New York: Springer, 2015, 251–70.

Dunne, John D., Dalai Lama, and Compendium Selection Committee. *The Mind*, ed. Thupten Jinpa, trans. John D. Dunne and Dechen Rochard. Vol. 2. Science and Philosophy in the Indian Buddhist Classics. Somerville, MA: Wisdom Publications, 2020.

Goleman, Daniel, and Richard J. Davidson. *Altered Traits: Science Reveals How Meditation Changes Your Mind, Brain, and Body*. New York: Avery, 2017.

Harrington, Anne, and John D. Dunne. "When Mindfulness Is Therapy: Ethical Qualms, Historical Perspectives." *American Psychologist* 70, no. 7 (2015): 621–31. https://doi.org/10.1037/a0039460.

Helderman, Ira. *Prescribing the Dharma: Psychotherapists, Buddhist Traditions, and Defining Religion*. Chapel Hill: University of North Carolina Press, 2019.

Lutz, Antoine, John D. Dunne, and Richard J. Davidson. "Meditation and the Neuroscience of Consciousness: An Introduction." In *The Cambridge Handbook of Consciousness*, ed. Philip David Zelazo, Morris Moscovitch, and Evan Thompson, 1st ed. New York: Cambridge University Press, 2007, 499–551.

Lutz, Antoine, and Evan Thompson. "Neurophenomenology: Integrating Subjective Experience and Brain Dynamics in the Neuroscience of Consciousness." *Journal of Consciousness Studies* 10, no. 9–10 (2003): 31–52.

McMahan, David, and Erik Braun, eds. *Meditation, Buddhism, and Science*. New York: Oxford University Press, 2017.

Thompson, Evan. *Waking, Dreaming, Being: Self and Consciousness in Neuroscience, Meditation, and Philosophy*. New York: Columbia University Press, 2014.

Thompson, Evan. *Why I Am Not a Buddhist*. New Haven, CT: Yale University Press, 2020.

Van Dam, Nicholas T., Marieke K. van Vugt, David R. Vago, Laura Schmalzl, Clifford D. Saron, Andrew Olendzki, Ted Meissner, et al. "Mind the Hype: A Critical Evaluation and Prescriptive Agenda for Research on Mindfulness and Meditation." *Perspectives on Psychological Science* 13, no. 1 (January 2018): 36–61. https://doi.org/10.1177/1745691617709589.

CHAPTER 37

SEEING THROUGH MINDFULNESS PRACTICES

ERIK BRAUN

In the early 1980s, the anthropologist Nigel Barley observed a surprising fact when trying to assess the knowledge of wildlife among the Dowayo highlanders of Cameroon:

> In the end I managed to lay my hands on some postcards of African fauna. I had at least a lion and a leopard and showed them to people to see if they could spot the difference. Alas, they could not. The reason lay not in their classifications of animals but rather in the fact that they could not identify photographs. It is a fact that we tend to forget in the West that people have to learn to be able to see photographs. . . . Old men would stare at the cards, which were perfectly clear, turn them in all manner of directions, and then say something like "I do not know this man."[1]

This vignette, while seemingly far removed from the contexts of modern meditation, parallels an assumption about the practice of mindfulness. This form of meditation is often taken to be like seeing a photograph. We look—we employ the mindful gaze—and so see things as they actually are. A common definition of mindfulness as "a kind of nonelaborative, nonjudgmental, present-centered awareness in which each thought, feeling, or sensation that arises in the attentional field is acknowledged and accepted as it is" indicates this sense of epistemic transparency.[2] Yet, as the Dowayos' apparent difficulty making sense of pictures suggests, what is often taken to be meaningful "as it is" depends, in fact, on a deliberate formation. We forget that a historical process has created a way of seeing and the knowledge that comes from it.

Barley mentions the issue of how the Dowayos look at photographs only in passing. A reader may wish he had delved into the matter more deeply. Were the old men really not seeing the animals in the photographs at all? Perhaps their reactions to the postcards signaled an alternate but no less complex understanding of the representations? Or, could the Dowayos have simply been pulling Barley's leg? Regardless of the answers to these questions, the responses of the Dowayo informants when looking at the postcards make the point relevant here, namely that the act of seeing depends on interpretation.[3] No one can count on what will be seen by another, or whether the reaction will be what one expects. "I do not know this man" can be understood as a way of saying: "I do not see this the way you do." This point applies to us all.[4]

Members of the Dowayo tribe easily learned to recognize photographs in the way we would expect, Barley goes on to say, when the government introduced identity cards and textbooks containing images into local schools. Developing such a skill offered real empirical value; the images on the postcards were obviously not unconnected to reality. Along the same lines, coming to see through mindfulness may give valuable results in real-world circumstances (though there is debate about how much value).[5] In this chapter I am not arguing against mindfulness as an efficacious therapeutic practice, nor will I delve into philosophical issues of perception and consciousness. As with image recognition, seeing through mindfulness is also not a mere fabrication. The practice connects to reality for the practitioner in often useful, sometimes transformative, ways. But I am interested not so much in the results derived from mindfulness as in the origins and implications of a now-governing conception of it. In this chapter, we will trace how seeing through mindfulness, though a product of particular circumstances, develops the claim to be a universal human capacity.

This idea of mindfulness as an intrinsic feature of humanity has made it a popular practice with far-reaching effects on notions of meditation, Buddhism, and the self. Such a universalizing vision tends to see mindfulness as, at its root, secular, in the sense of being prior to any religious interpretation.[6] Yet the practice has Buddhist origins and continually negotiates its boundaries with Buddhist sources. This is not to claim that mindfulness is inherently Buddhist. On the contrary, mindfulness's variability contravenes any characterization of it as having a common core. To see through the assumptions about seeing through mindfulness, then, we should look not inward to some Cartesian theater of the mind where mindfulness supposedly resides untouched by history, but outward to the peoples and practices that have constructed its formations.

Defining *Sati* as Mindfulness

Modern formulations of mindfulness practice come from fairly recent interpretations, no earlier than the late nineteenth century. These are largely based on a relatively small functional canon of such Pali literature as the *Establishings of Mindfulness Sutta* (*Satipaṭṭhāna-sutta*), the *Mindfulness of Breathing Sutta* (*Ānāpānasati-sutta*), and the *Path of Purification* (*Visuddhimagga*). Regardless, modern presentations of mindfulness, both secular and Buddhist, will often take a hoary pedigree for granted, suggesting, if not outright asserting, that mindfulness has stayed essentially the same from the time of the historical Buddha (roughly, the fifth century BCE) up to the present day. One can make the case, certainly, that the texts just mentioned may extend back to the Buddha and even that certain techniques may have endured for long periods of time.[7] But when, for instance, an article in *Scientific American* (discussed at length later in the chapter) reviews scientific studies of the brain engaged in forms of meditation that it says "extend back thousands of years," the sense is given that an entire practice has remained unchanged, not only in the specifics of its methods but in its theoretical and cultural saliences.[8] To give another example, a frictionless transition from authoritative past to scientific present is suggested when the editors of a well-known volume about mindfulness talk of "the introduction of an *ancient* Buddhist meditation practice into mainstream medicine."[9] In an instance of how Buddhist and secular voices often sing in harmony on this score, Theravada Buddhists abet such claims by their own claims to unchanging teachings and practices that transcend the vagaries of history.[10]

The authors of the preceding examples, and many others besides, have clear objectives to benefit patients and push forward the boundaries of knowledge. These are highly worthy goals, but, to the extent that findings are based on acultural conceptions of mindfulness, they reinforce a collective amnesia. A sometimes passive (through ignorance), sometimes active (through an interpretive agenda) forgetting of the history of Buddhist-derived practices supports a sort of latent Orientalism that robs Buddhists of their agency in favor of an essentialized notion of meditation and its concomitant mental states.[11] Emphasizing the recent provenance of mindfulness, then, is not to ignore the histories of Asian forms of Buddhism, but to recognize them by highlighting modern mindfulness as only a recent permutation in a long series of causes and effects.

As a number of scholars have noted, the word "mindfulness" entered into English parlance in the late nineteenth century as a translation of the Pali term *sati*, thanks to its use—intermittently at first and then with standardizing regularity—by the influential translator and scholar T. W. Rhys Davids (1843–1922).[12] Rhys Davids observed in 1890 that, while a primary meaning of *sati* is simply memory, "it is one of the most difficult words (in its secondary, ethical, and more usual meaning) in the whole Buddhist system of ethical psychology to translate."[13] A number of sophisticated studies by scholars have recently sought to describe *sati* more fully as it is found in the Pali texts in both its primary and secondary senses noted by Rhys Davids.[14] In sum, their analyses describe a quality of mind that brings the object of attention to the forefront of awareness, sustains that object in awareness through its recollective function, and, by guarding the mind's focus and engendering a self-awareness about that focus, enables an ethical evaluation aiming at awakening.[15]

Yet *sati*, as subtle, complex, and important as it is in the preceding formulation, is not mindfulness as most people know it today. In current formulations, mindfulness *is* meditation. From the classical point of view, however, a meditator cannot rely on *sati* as the only quality of mind needed for purification and wisdom. Rather, it takes its place within various doctrinal retinues, such as the seven factors of awakening, the eight-fold path, and the faculties and powers.[16] Moreover, mindfulness is understood as a tool for development in all forms of meditation, including calming (*samatha*) meditation that typically precedes insight practice.[17] As ever-present, *sati* is subsumed within a larger category of *bhāvanā* or mental cultivation; it does not equate to the pursuit of insight from the classical perspective, as it is not exclusive to that practice.

Sati in the Spotlight

The possibility of the transformation of mindfulness from the technically constrained sense of *sati* in Pali literature to a stand-in for meditation as a whole began with the influential Burmese monk Ledi Sayadaw (1846–1923). Ledi had no intention of turning mindfulness into an all-encompassing practice, but he started the ball rolling in that direction in the late nineteenth and early twentieth centuries by popularizing a distinctive take on *vipassanā* or insight practice. Forgoing the need for first developing forms of calming meditation (*samatha*) and rarified states of absorption (*jhāna*)—as had been classically emphasized—Ledi taught that a person could start meditating just with what was called "momentary concentration" (*khaṇikasamādhi*). The pursuit of insight became plausible for not only monastics but laypeople, too, who now could more feasibly combine a relatively easier practice with worldly life.[18] But, while he made meditative practice far more accessible, mindfulness in his teaching remained closely tied to traditional conceptions of *sati*.[19]

Another Burmese monk called Mingun Sayadaw (1870–1955), over two decades younger than Ledi, also developed a form of insight practice that was accessible to laypeople. As in Ledi's teachings (and probably influenced by his efforts), it too largely cut out calming and concentration practice. Mingun's disciple, Mahāsi Sayadaw (1904–1982), would refine and spread this method far beyond the borders of Burma. In this form of practice, the meditator was to use mindful observation to label every sensory input—every sound, taste, touch, thought, what have you—that entered his or her consciousness. Like his forebears, Mahāsi's frequent references to mindfulness in his works place it within a larger scheme of practice. Because of his radical simplification of technique, however, that eschewed much initial doctrinal teaching to support the practice, Mahāsi's presentation left mindfulness relatively alone in the spotlight. It could become the crux of practice that overshadowed all else.[20]

To my knowledge, the first important work to use the English word "mindfulness" as a stand-in for meditation is by the Sri Lankan monk Soma Thera (1898–1960).[21] He was a student of Mahāsi and wrote, in the late 1930s, *The Way of Mindfulness*. This work is an anthology which contains a translation of the *Satipaṭṭhāna-sutta* into English, along with commentarial exegesis. In the introduction to Soma's work, he discusses the multifarious, though, from the commentarial perspective, ultimately unified and coherent understanding of mindfulness in the Pali sources. He notes the role of mindfulness as memory, but, following from that basic meaning, the sense of it as a quality of mind that is free from confusion, alert, and focused on an object (traditionally, that object would be one of the four "foundations" [*upaṭṭhāna*]). Mindfulness here remains closely tied to the valences of *sati* in the Pali texts, but Soma emphasizes its pride of place as the lynchpin of practice. This foregrounding would allow, with further developments, the autonomy of mindfulness to grow so that it would eventually (much later and in other cultural contexts) entirely detach itself from Buddhist traditions.

Sati as Bare Attention

Soma Thera's student, Nyanaponika Thera (1901–1994), took the next crucial step. Born Siegmund Feniger in Germany, he received full ordination in Sri Lanka in 1937. He would make a critical impact on the understanding of mindfulness through the publication of his book *The Heart of Buddhist Meditation*. It was "the book that started it all," as Jon Kabat-Zinn, the founder of Mindfulness-Based Stress Reduction (discussed later for his own impact), put it in the most recent edition of Nyanaponika's work.[22] The exercise of mindfulness in Nyanaponika's presentation follows Mahāsi as well as Soma. Nyanaponika mentions in *The Heart of Buddhist Meditation* the sense of *sati* as memory and its nuanced resonances in the classical literature. But he makes a powerful innovation, too. As a number of scholars have noted, he rearticulates the initial process of mindful observation as what he called "bare attention." Bhikkhu Bodhi, who was Nyanaponika's student, argues that the notion of bare attention may be practically helpful as what he calls "a procedural directive," in order to encourage novice meditators to avoid distorting conceptual elaborations of experience.[23] Nonetheless, Bodhi sees Nyanaponika's use of this term as a mistake. While Nyanaponika had a sophisticated understanding of mindfulness's functions and nature, employing the expression "bare attention" equated the technical notion of pre-conceptual attention, called *manasikāra*, with mindfulness proper. In Bodhi's view, this confusion of terms gives the impression that *sati* could be, like *manasikāra*, without the subtle qualities that imbue it with a sense of self-awareness and give it a wholesome valence (*kusala* or *sammā sati*).[24]

Bare attention certainly did not remain merely a pragmatic approach for the novice meditator. It has become a dominant sense of what mindfulness is. As with earlier figures, unintended consequences followed from its adoption. Writing in English, Nyanaponika's effects, at least initially, were largely limited to those who derived their understandings of practice from English-language sources. Later, conceptions of mindfulness shaped by Western ideas affected how it was understood and taught in Asia.[25] But the definitive break, in which the import of the term "mindfulness" left behind the constraints of canonical and commentarial senses of *sati*, first took place in America.

Bare Attention as Mindfulness

Mahāsi Sayadaw would travel to the United States in 1979. While there, he taught at the Insight Meditation Society (IMS). Founded in Barre, Massachusetts, in 1975, it became the hub of training and practice in Theravada-derived forms of meditation in the 1970s and 1980s, and has remained important for American lineages of mindfulness practice up to the present day.[26] The Burmese-born meditation teacher S. N. Goenka, a student of the Burmese meditation master U Ba Khin, who was in direct lineal descent from Ledi, seems to have provided the organizational structure for retreats at IMS. It was Mahāsi, however, who provided the charter technique. One of the IMS founders, Jack Kornfield, has described IMS as "primarily a Mahāsi-oriented center."[27]

Mahāsi, as far as I know, never taught using the term "bare attention," but his teaching formed an elective affinity with the concept as formulated by Nyanaponika. The insight meditation teacher Sylvia Boorstein, for instance, writes that Jack Kornfield recommended Nyanaponika's book as the first source for her formal training as a meditation teacher.[28] The scope of this chapter does not allow a full consideration of IMS teachers' complex and varied approaches to practice. The point here is that bare attention became fundamental to the overall IMS approach to mindfulness. Joseph Goldstein's influential 1976 work, *The Experience of Insight*, exemplifies this approach:

> There is one quality of mind which is the basis and foundation of all spiritual discovery, and that quality of mind is called "bare attention." Bare attention means observing things as they are, without choosing, without comparing, without evaluating, without laying our projections and expectations on to what is happening; cultivating instead a choiceless and non-interfering awareness.[29]

Bare attention here forms the basis of practice. The articulation of mindfulness as apparently bare of memory or ethical discrimination, however, does not signal an uprooting of the practice from its Buddhist setting. As with Nyanaponika, Goldstein remains tied to Buddhist systems of thought, as do many other teachers. Yet, as laypeople working in lay-run institutions teaching other laity, their formulation of a state of mind shorn of the complex nuances of *sati* found in traditional Theravada teachings weakened connections to authoritative systems of Buddhist thought. They thereby set the stage for the universalization of mindfulness.[30]

The idea of a "bare" state might seem to suggest a simplification of what's envisioned, a mental state stripped of content and a practice streamlined to brute sensory registration. But, in fact, mindfulness-as-bare-attention strikes me as potentially just as complex as *sati*. Admittedly, it is far less theorized, and, to that degree, simpler in its formulations. But, in terms of the implicit values that frame the context of presentation, especially deep-seated ideals of a therapeutic healing that typify American spirituality, its resonances are rich. For example, the prominent Buddhist psychiatrist Mark Epstein writes: "It is *the* fundamental tenet of Buddhist psychology that this kind of awareness [bare attention] is, in itself, healing: that by the constant application of this attentional strategy, all of the Buddha's insights can be realized for oneself."[31] Rather than aiming beyond existence in the round of rebirth, mindfulness can become a this-worldly practice for psychological health. One is reminded of the sensibility captured in the quotation from Ferdinand Galiani: "The important thing is not to be cured but to live with one's ailments."[32] This attitude suggests a profound divergence from the conceptions and aims of *sati* with which we started, but ones that are no less far-reaching and profound in their implications for shaping ways of life. As we continue to trace formations of mindfulness, these complex senses of subjectivity potentially present in bare attention should be kept in mind.

Mindfulness as a Universal State of Mind

The shift to mindfulness as bare attention within Buddhist settings was instrumental in the shift to mindfulness as a secular practice outside of them. A seminal development was the creation of the eight-week Mindfulness-Based Stress Reduction (MBSR) program by Jon Kabat-Zinn, first established at the University of Massachusetts hospital in Worcester, Mass.[33] This program and, subsequently, the books that Kabat-Zinn has written, beginning with *Full Catastrophe Living* in 1990, teach one how to reduce one's suffering by learning to observe—to be mindful—of one's experience instead of reacting to it.[34] Examination of Kabat-Zinn's thought and his MBSR program allows us to chart the reformulation of mindfulness as a secular and universal practice. But, first, it is important to note that understandings and uses of mindfulness have remained dynamic in the Buddhist scene. As will be discussed in detail later, developments in the conceptualizations of mindfulness cannot be hived off into entirely separate secular and religious spheres because people and groups are always talking and influencing each other across boundaries. At the same time, the formulations of mindfulness as a tool for medical intervention have proliferated beyond MBSR into treatments for depression, anxiety, and a host of other psychological ills, and it has also become a means for lifestyle optimization through weight loss, better sexual health, and increased work productivity, to name just a few of the many ways it has been applied. I focus here on MBSR for two reasons. First, while other, related uses are not unimportant, MBSR was the foundational application that has made an impact on notions of mindfulness that far exceeds that of other modalities. The other reason is more general. Mindfulness in the MBSR perspective exemplifies a distinct but broader tendency common to other therapeutic interventions to redefine mindfulness as something beyond Buddhism—or any religion, for that matter.

Kabat-Zinn has given the influential definition of mindfulness as "paying attention in a particular way: on purpose, in the present moment, and nonjudgmentally."[35] This definition is similar to the operational definition given at the start of this chapter; this is no surprise, as Kabat-Zinn's approach to mindfulness has profoundly shaped the research community's understanding of the practice as a therapeutic tool. This understanding of mindfulness is taught in his MBSR program, which consists of seated breath meditation, body scans to assess one's physical sensations, yogic movements, compassion exercises, and student/teacher dialogues. Recently, Kabat-Zinn has acknowledged, even at times celebrated, MBSR's Buddhist sources, but its appeal remains based in its secular framing, backed up by numerous scientific studies.[36] Despite criticisms of the rigor of some studies and of overstated claims of its benefits, mindfulness in the MBSR mode is justifiably understood as an empirically validated activity.[37] The studies and reports of its effects indicate it has helped many people. The analysis of it here is not meant to call into question its value as a health intervention, only to call attention to its role in shaping ideas about mindfulness. That role, thanks to its effects, is profound. The MBSR program, related off-shoot programs and centers, as well as the massive body of literature by Kabat-Zinn and others working within its ambit, now have a global reach.

The program makes no mention of Buddhism or Buddhist teachings as such. The logic of the program's instructions on how to reduce suffering through non-reactivity to pain, however, depends on a take on mindfulness as bare attention.[38] Such bare attention is understood as a common human capacity, bare not just in terms of the meditator's mental state, but bare of any cultural conditioning, too. Kabat-Zinn will claim that mindfulness conflicts with no religious belief or system.[39] Yet Kabat-Zinn readily acknowledges its Buddhist origins, observing "that MBSR is mostly vipassana practice (in the Theravada sense as taught by people like Joseph [Goldstein] and Jack [Kornfield] etc.) with a Zen attitude."[40] Indeed, Kabat-Zinn relates that the MBSR program was born out of a mystical vision he had in 1979 while attending a retreat at IMS.[41]

Mindfulness as typified in perspectives such as that of MBSR, however, also partakes of a variety of influences beyond Theravada-derived practices. Zen, as presented in D. T. Suzuki's influential works as a form of pure experience beyond religion, laid the basis in the 1950s for psychological uses of Buddhism in the United States as the means to an undistorted view of the self.[42] More generally, the "Zen boom" of mid-twentieth-century America set the stage for the adoption of an influential understanding of mindfulness as an inherently non-dual mode of perception.[43] This is a significant divergence from the classical Theravada view, which posits awakening as on one side of an utterly dualistic reality. In contrast, the non-dual view, drawing on images of interconnection in its own functional canon of Mahayana literature, depends on an idea of a mystical oneness. For MBSR, this sense comes most directly from Kabat-Zinn's own Son/Zen training. Mention should also be made, however, of Thich Nhat Hanh's *The Miracle of Mindfulness.*[44] This slim volume has served as an inspirational source—for Kabat-Zinn, but for many others, too—that has reinforced the sense of mindfulness as an openness to a meaningful non-dual experience.[45] In fact, Kabat-Zinn included a preface by Nhat Hanh in his *Full Catastrophe Living*. The attitude to experience in *The Miracle of Mindfulness* captures in part what Kabat-Zinn calls the "Zen attitude" of MBSR, which not only shapes a certain "dharma combat" dialogic style of teacher-student interaction in the program, but supports a sense of inherent potential that is understood as a basic human quality available to all. Infused with the non-dual viewpoint, bare observation can reveal the ever-present reality of oneness.

This non-dual perspective now pervades much of the thinking in the Theravada-oriented insight meditation (*vipassanā*) scene, too. A number of influential contemporary insight meditation teachers, particularly those associated with Spirit Rock, the institution Jack Kornfield took a lead role in founding when he moved to California in the 1980s, invoke a wide range of philosophical, aesthetic, and ethical perspectives that go beyond more traditional Theravada-based views. These perspectives include Advaita Vedanta, Tibetan Dzogchen, the Mahayana concept of Buddhanature, and Sufi poets (especially Rumi). A cultural predilection toward pure experience, informed by American understandings of Zen, dovetails with wider monistic impulses in the culture that have helped to reformulate the metaphysical underpinnings of mindfulness. Mindfulness taps into a sense of non-duality-as-oneness that goes beyond what one finds even in Mahayana Buddhist literature. Oneness becomes a positive good tied to a sense of self-flourishing.

As a program first born in a hospital setting, MBSR began with an emphasis (though by no means exclusively) on physical afflictions as the objects of the mindful gaze. This corporeal orientation highlights another critical component flowing from the intellectual developments described earlier and feeding back into them: the cultivation of the body not just as a means to confirm teachings, but as the very basis for seeing through mindfulness. The body scan, the incorporation of yoga, and above all the physicality of the breath and bodily pain are productive components of what now makes mindfulness what it is. This same sense is found in more explicitly Buddhist circles as well. In his book *A Path with Heart*, Jack Kornfield stresses the healing power of meditation and identifies the body as a means to understand the mind: "Most often the kinds of pains we encounter in meditative attention are not indications of physical problems. They are the painful, physical manifestations of our emotional, psychological, and spiritual holdings and contractions."[46]

As I have written about elsewhere, the power of a focus on pain is that its visceral nature makes it not just an arena where mental trauma can be played out, but a particularly effective form of experience which can turn an idea into a reality.[47] In the context of mindfulness as bare attention, bodily pain has become a powerful way to make mindfulness secular. For, when the secular is understood as prior to religious interpretation, what could be more immediate, more non-discursive, or less conceptualized (and so ostensibly prior to any interpretation) than pressing physical pain? As Talal Asad observes, pain is "the most immediate sign of this world, of the senses through which materiality, external and internal, is felt—and therefore it offers a kind of vindication of the secular."[48] Yet any attempt to make sense of this pain—as "holdings and contractions," or as something to which I can choose not to react through mere mindful watching of it—depends on interpretation. In other words, it is a learned way of seeing. The assumption of a "bare" looking, however, obscures this interpretive move. Bodily experience is taken to be just there in pre-conceptual observation, immediately obvious—in short, secular.

Mindfulness and (in?) the Brain

The body as a productive basis for secular conceptions of mindfulness brings us to the brain. The most recent development adding its powerful effect to formations of mindfulness is the neurological turn in the study of meditation. This turn goes beyond the numerous studies that have attempted to define and measure mindfulness as a medical or therapeutic intervention. Its principal impact has been through the use of third-person tools such as fMRI scans to find mindfulness or, at least, biological substrates of it in the brain.[49] We have circled back, then, to looking at pictures.

An article that appeared in the November 2014 issue of *Scientific American*, mentioned earlier, represents well how the neurological turn offers perhaps the fullest vindication of a secular take on mindfulness.[50] It is entitled "Mind of the Meditator" and has the following subtitle: "Contemplative practices that extend back thousands of years show a multitude of benefits to both body and mind." Unpacking this title reveals key features of contemporary mindfulness cast in universalist terms. While it is the mind of the meditator that is mentioned, it appears that what is most salient is the brain. And, despite the article having as one of its authors a Tibetan Buddhist monk, making numerous references to Buddhist traditions (especially Tibetan), and discussing techniques of meditation rooted in Buddhist practice, the title and subtitle suggest an elision from the specific to the universal, from the Buddhist to a common human potential located in what is seen in neuroimaging. Meditation becomes "contemplative practices" that are thousands of years old, now revealed by advances in technology.

A number of studies are surveyed in the article. All are governed by the effort to locate meditative activity in the brain. The implications of this are captured on a page of the article dominated by a graphic entitled "Brain Scanning: Varieties of Contemplative Experience." Beneath the title, three forms of meditation—focused attention, mindfulness, and compassion and loving kindness—are defined briefly in separate boxes. Underneath these definitions, the majority of the page is filled by four anatomical depictions of the brain of a meditator focusing on the breath. The images show what happens during the practice of focused attention rather than mindfulness, at least as the authors distinguish these two activities (a questionable distinction that I will discuss later). But the images still serve our purpose of highlighting the assumption that mindfulness exists beyond any particular context, as that assumption holds for all forms of practice.

The first brain image shows an inattentive mind as it appears in a scanner. The parts of the brain signifying wandering attention (components of the default-mode network) are highlighted in orange, green, blue, and red. The second image shows the mind as the anterior insula and the anterior cingulate cortex (parts of the salience network) light up in green and orange, respectively, when the meditator realizes that she or he has strayed from the object of focus. The third brain image depicts the parts of the brain (the inferior parietal lobe and the dorsolateral prefrontal cortex), colored green and blue, that are active as one reorients awareness to one's object of focus. And then the fourth reveals in a patch of blue the dorsolateral prefrontal cortex "that stays active when the meditator directs attention on the breath for long periods."[51] The implication is clear: attention, and, by extension, any form of meditation, are to be associated with particular parts of the brain.

I do not want to cast even the slightest doubt on the accuracy of these brain scans. What is more, it seems sensible to assume that particular meditational activities could cause activity in specific parts of the brain, though the philosopher Evan Thompson has recently criticized the notion that attention of any sort could be delimited to activity in particular parts of the brain.[52] The issue that concerns me is how the model creates the impression that a biological event represents the common core of a contemplative experience, such as mindfulness, that would be constant across cultures and millennia. The mistake is to read these images as revealing mindfulness (or any meditative state), defined in culturally specific terms, as mindfulness *tout court*. My point is akin to Ann Taves's about religious experience as a whole: to find a mindful experience in the brain defined in your particular terms is not to come close to defining all experiences that others deem mindful.[53] The implication of the images is that what makes meditation what it is can be seen in an image. But what of Dharma study that frames meditation for many? How can one include governing ideas of karma and rebirth? Or how does an image capture a moment as an accretive process of moral perfection? These questions span a range of issues as wide as the cultural and intellectual variations that shape experience.

As I mentioned earlier, the images in the article depict a brain engaged in focused attention meditation, not mindfulness. But not everyone would agree that one can separate focused attention from mindfulness in the way it is done in the article. Here, we come back to the matter of defining mindfulness as an encompassing practice as opposed to a subordinate, if still critical, component of a larger process of meditation. As the history explored here has shown, how we got to a secular vision of mindfulness is highly contingent. How can one find mindfulness in the brain if there is significant disagreement on what it is? Again, none of this is meant to dismiss the utility of brain scans, but to call into question any "common core" model that postulates mindfulness or any other form of meditation as an entity separate from its cultural conditioning.

Coexisting Formations of Mindfulness

Bhikkhu Bodhi remarks that "the last lap of [mindfulness's] journey is without parallel"[54] because of the ways it has been secularized and detached from its Buddhist framework as never before. What's interesting—even ironic—is that it is the Buddhist framework that makes this secularization possible. As the formulations and reformulations of mindfulness discussed in this chapter show, secular mindfulness is not a technique stripped of Buddhist concepts, notions, or explanations, as if mindfulness were some jewel taken from one setting and placed in another. Rather, the very possibility of a secular articulation of mindfulness has depended on Buddhism. In other words, Buddhism is integral to the secular practice of mindfulness. They are in complex—and fruitful—continuing relationships. To turn to Asad again: "The secular . . . is neither continuous with the religious that supposedly preceded it (that is, it is not the latest phase of a sacred origin) nor a simple break from it (that is, it is not the opposite, an essence that excludes the sacred)."[55] In other words, there is no simple progression or clean detachment. In contemporary understandings, mindfulness is often not presented as Buddhist—but not *not* Buddhist either.[56] And, even when mindfulness is framed in Buddhist terms, it is often taken as *not* Buddhist insofar as it is read as the articulation of universal qualities accessible by other means, above all through scientific study.

Similar to Taves's and Bender's observations about uses of the term "spiritual," the uses of mindfulness often point toward a "more than," a kind of "third term" that suggests some good or value beyond the Buddhist/secular divide.[57] This subversion of the binary is useful to both camps. On the one side, scientific formulations of mindfulness offer a scientific imprimatur to Buddhist perspectives and some claim to a universal character championed in the secular view. On the other side, the secular imports values from Buddhist concepts in apparently objective terms that give them a powerful purchase. The *Scientific American* article ends with the claim that what it calls "mental training" can help to develop "the foundation for an ethical framework unattached to any philosophy or religion. . . ."[58] This optimistic conclusion is appealing precisely because it seems to have broken free of the contamination of religious sectarianism.

Mindfulness has come to be seen by many as what Ricard, Davidson, and Lutz refer to as a "basic human quality." But, as this chapter has shown, such a view of mindfulness is learned and depends on a specific history. This fact does not negate the value of scientific studies or therapeutic interventions. Nor does it elevate any religious or other take on mindfulness as genuine or authentic. What it does do is call our attention to processes of the naturalization or materialization of mindfulness that abet a forgetting of its origins and varied definitions. By attending to its history, we learn to see it for what it is. Seeing through mindfulness means seeing it for the unfinished series of projects that make up its formations.

Notes

1. Nigel Barley, *The Innocent Anthropologist: Notes from a Mud Hut* (London: British Museum Publications, 1983), 96.
2. S. R. Bishop et al., "Mindfulness: A Proposed Operational Definition," *Clinical Psychology: Science and Practice* 11, no. 3 (2004): 4.
3. As Susan Sontag notes: "Although there is a sense in which the camera does indeed capture reality, not just interpret it, photographs are as much an interpretation of the world as paintings and drawings are"; Susan Sontag, *On Photography* (New York: Picador, 1977), Chapter One: "In Plato's Cave," Kindle edition, loc. 67.
4. My thanks to James McHugh and Sonam Kachru, whose comments helped me to develop this point.
5. See the survey article by Maria B. Ospina et al., "Meditation Practices for Health: State of the Research," Evidence Report/Technology Assessment No. 155 AHRQ Publication No. 07-E010 (June 2007), which is discussed in Donald Lopez, *The Scientific Buddha: His Short, Happy Life* (New Haven, CT: Yale University Press, 2012), 105–6.

6. The idea of the secular as the absence of religion comes from a common notion of secularity as what Charles Taylor calls "a subtraction story." See Charles Taylor, *A Secular Age* (Cambridge, MA: Harvard University Press, 2007), 22.
7. Rupert Gethin, "Buddhist Conceptualizations of Mindfulness," in *Handbook of Mindfulness: Theory, Research, and Practice*, ed. K. W. Brown, J. D. Creswell, and R. M. Ryan (New York: Guilford Publications, 2015), 36, fn.20, provides a valuable distinction. He notes that Bhikkhu Anālayo in "The Ancient Roots of the U Ba Khin Vipassanā Meditation," *Journal of the Center for Buddhist Studies, Sri Lanka* 4 (2006): 259–69, has argued for a significant continuity of practice within the U Ba Khin meditation tradition between modern and pre-modern times. But Gethin points out that a technique, even if quite old, does not carry with it the theoretical framework that gives it its meaning.
8. Matthieu Ricard, Antoine Lutz, and Richard J. Davidson, "Mind of the Meditator," *Scientific American* (November 2014): 39.
9. J. Mark G. Williams and Jon Kabat-Zinn, "Introduction," in *Mindfulness: Diverse Perspectives on Its Meaning, Origins and Applications*, ed. J. Mark G. Williams and Jon Kabat-Zinn (New York: Routledge, 2013), 11 [my italics].
10. Anne Blackburn, *Buddhist Learning and Textual Practice in Eighteenth-Century Lankan Monastic Culture* (Princeton, NJ: Princeton University Press, 2001), 8.
11. This notion of forgetting as both passive and active is drawn from Ricoeur's discussion of forgetting, though he describes forms of forgetting in sharper terms than I would apply here. See Paul Ricoeur, "From 'Memory—History—Forgetting,'" in *The Collective Memory Reader*, ed. Jeffrey K. Olick, Vered Vinitsky-Seroussi, and Daniel Levy (New York: Oxford University Press, 2011), 479.
12. For details on the use of mindfulness as the English word for *sati* and other early translations, see Rupert Gethin, "On Some Definitions of Mindfulness," in *Mindfulness: Diverse Perspectives on Its Meaning, Origins and Applications*, ed. J. Mark G. Williams and Jon Kabat-Zinn (New York: Routledge, 2013), 263–65; Lopez, *Scientific Buddha*, p. 93ff.; and Jeff Wilson, *Mindful America: The Mutual Transformation of Buddhist Meditation and American Culture* (New York: Oxford University Press, 2014), 15–19.
13. T. W. Rhys Davids, trans., *The Questions of King Milinda* (Oxford: Clarendon Press, 1890), 58.
14. Bhikkhu Bodhi, "What Does Mindfulness Really Mean? A Canonical Perspective," 19-40, and Georges Dreyfus, "Is Mindfulness Present-Centered and Non-Judgmental? A Discussion of the Cognitive Dimensions of Mindfulness," 41-54, in *Mindfulness: Diverse Perspectives on Its Meaning, Origins and Applications*, ed. J. Mark G. Williams and Jon Kabat-Zinn (New York: Routledge, 2013); Gethin, "Buddhist Conceptualizations" and "On Some Definitions"; Anālayo, *Satipaṭṭhāna: The Direct Path to Realization* (Birmingham, UK: Windhorse Publications, 2004) and *Early Buddhist Meditation Studies* (Barre, MA: Barre Center for Buddhist Studies, 2017).
15. Drawing on the *Visuddhimagga*, Bhikkhu Bodhi uses the phrase "lucid awareness" ("What Does Mindfulness Really Mean?," 19) to get at this notion of mindfulness as a quality of mind that knows the objects of experience and knows that it knows—and knowing that you know would be an aspect of memory ("What Does Mindfulness Really Mean?," 25). The Theravada tradition also sees mindfulness as inherently ethical, though it is not seen that way, for instance, in the Sarvāstivādin Abhidharma; Rupert Gethin, *The Buddhist Path to Awakening* (Oxford: Oneworld Publications, 2001), 40. Anālayo, *Early Buddhist Meditation Studies*, 23, argues that the early Buddhist perspective does not see mindfulness

as inherently wholesome either. These divergent views about *sati* underscore the point that understandings of it have never been monolithic.

16. Gethin, "On Some Definitions," 274–75; and Anālayo, *Satipaṭṭhāna*, 49.
17. Gethin, "Buddhist Conceptualizations," 13.
18. For details on Ledi Sayadaw and other meditation teachers, see Erik Braun, *The Birth of Insight: Meditation, Modern Buddhism, and the Monk Ledi Sayadaw* (Chicago: University of Chicago Press, 2013), esp. the conclusion.
19. Speaking more broadly, in the Burmese language the term *sati* is common but, so far as I know, has not been used widely as a general term for meditative practice. For example, it is used as the military command to call troops to attention.
20. The result of this tendency can be seen in a telling shift in translation in the English version of Mahāsi's magnum opus, the *Manual of Insight* (trans. The Vipassanā Mettā Foundation Translation Committee [Somerville, MA: Wisdom Publications, 2016]). The final section of Chapter Four is entitled "The Benefits of Mindfulness." But that section could be more literally rendered from the Burmese as "The Benefits of the Establishments of Mindfulness." The term used is the compound word *sati-paṭṭhāna*, not *sati*. The shift makes the difference between a conception of *sati* that resides within a meditative process versus one that stands in for it.
21. Soma, who resided at the prestigious Vajirārāma Temple in Columbo, was ordained in Burma. See George Bond, *The Buddhist Revival in Sri Lanka: Religious Tradition, Reinterpretation and Response* (Delhi: Motilal Banarsidass, 1992), 163. Along with the monk Kheminda Thera, he worked on the translation of the *Vimuttimagga*, along with Rev. N. R. M. Ehara of Nagasaki, Japan.
22. Nyanaponika Thera, *The Heart of Buddhist Meditation: The Buddha's Way of Mindfulness* (San Francisco: Weiser Books, 2014).
23. Bodhi, "What Does Mindfulness Really Mean?," 27.
24. Bodhi, "What Does Mindfulness Really Mean?," 32. For a discussion of philosophical objections to the characterization of *sati* as bare attention, see Robert Sharf, "Is Mindfulness Buddhist? (And Why It Matters)" in *Buddhism, Meditation, and Science*, ed. David McMahan and Erik Braun (New York: Oxford University Press, 2017), 204–8. But it is important to stress again that Nyanaponika did not intend to explain mindfulness proper as bare attention, only its initial exercise.
25. See, for example, Joanna Cook, *Meditation in Modern Buddhism: Renunciation and Change in Thai Monastic Life* (Cambridge: Cambridge University Press, 2010); and Julia Cassaniti, *Remembering the Present: Mindfulness in Buddhist Asia* (Ithaca, NY: Cornell University Press, 2017). See pp. 4–6 of *Remembering the Present* for a revealing incident in which a Thai MBSR teacher explains the cognitive dissonance between MBSR and Thai understandings of mindfulness.
26. Wendy Cadge, *Heartwood: The First Generation of Theravada Buddhism in America* (Chicago: University of Chicago Press, 2005), esp. chapter 3.
27. Jack Kornfield, "This Fantastic, Unfolding Experiment," *Buddhadharma: The Practitioner's Quarterly* (Summer 2007): 35.
28. Sylvia Boorstein, "Foreword," in Nyanaponika Thera, *The Heart of Buddhist Meditation: The Buddha's Way of Mindfulness* (San Francisco: Weiser Books, 2014), ix.
29. Goldstein, *The Experience of Insight: A Simple and Direct Guide to Buddhist Meditation* (Boston: Shambhala, 1976), 20. It is telling that Goldstein's most recent book, a series of commentarial reflections on the *Satipaṭṭhāna-sutta*, is entitled *Mindfulness*; Joseph

Goldstein, *Mindfulness: A Practical Guide to Awakening* (Boulder, CO: Sounds True, 2013). Bhante Gunaratana in his popular book *Mindfulness in Plain English*, first published in 1991, equates the two terms explicitly: "Mindfulness is non-conceptual awareness. Another English word for *sati* is 'bare attention.' It is not thinking. It does not get involved with thought or concepts.... It is, rather, the direct and immediate experiencing of whatever is happening, without the medium of thought. It comes before thought in the perceptual process"; Bhante Gunaratana, *Mindfulness in Plain English* (Somerville, MA: Wisdom Publications, 1991), quoted in Bodhi, "What Does Mindfulness Really Mean?," 28.

30. For a discussion of the impact of the handover of teaching authority from monastics to laypeople, see Bhikkhu Bodhi, "The Transformations of Mindfulness," in *Handbook of Mindfulness: Culture, Context, and Social Engagement*, ed. Ronald E. Purser, David Forbes, and Adam Burke (New York: Springer International, 2016), 3-14.
31. Mark Epstein, *Thoughts without a Thinker* (New York: Basic Books, 2013), 110.
32. Quoted in Philip Rieff, *Triumph of the Therapeutic: Uses of Faith after Freud* (Chicago: University of Chicago Press, 1987), 329.
33. For an extended analysis of MBSR and Kabat-Zinn's thought, see Erik Braun, "Mindful but Not Religious: Meditation and Enchantment in the Work of Jon Kabat-Zinn," in *Buddhism, Meditation, and Science*, ed. David McMahan and Erik Braun (New York: Oxford University Press, 2017), 173–97.
34. Jon Kabat-Zinn, *Full Catastrophe Living: Using the Wisdom of Your Body and Mind to Face Stress, Pain, and Illness* (New York: Bantam Books, 2013 [1990]).
35. Jon Kabat-Zinn, *Wherever You Go, There You Are: Mindfulness Meditation in Everyday Life* (New York: Hyperion, 2005), 4.
36. For recent reflections by Kabat-Zinn on how his efforts relate to Buddhism, see Jon Kabat-Zinn, "Too Early to Tell: The Potential Impact and Challenges—Ethical and Otherwise—Inherent in the Mainstreaming of Dharma in an Increasingly Dystopian World," *Mindfulness* 8, no. 5 (October 2017): 1125-1135.
37. See endnote 5 for a recent evaluation of research on mindfulness. For an account of its empirical validation, see Barry Boyce, "Introduction: *Anyone Can Do It, and It Changes Everything*," in *The Mindfulness Revolution: Leading Psychologists, Scientists, Artists, and Meditation Teachers on the Power of Mindfulness in Daily Life*, ed. Barry Boyce (Boston: Shambhala, 2011), xiv–xv.
38. Jon Kabat-Zinn, "Some Reflections on the Origins of MBSR, Skillful Means, and the Trouble with Maps," in *Mindfulness: Diverse Perspectives on Its Meaning, Origins and Applications*, ed. J. Mark G. Williams and Jon Kabat-Zinn (New York: Routledge, 2013), 282.
39. Braun, "Mindful but Not Religious," 179.
40. Richard Gilpin, "The Use of Theravāda Practices and Perspectives in Mindfulness-Based Cognitive Therapy," *Contemporary Buddhism* 9, no. 2 (November 2008): 238.
41. Kabat-Zinn, "Some Reflections," 287.
42. On Suzuki's influence, see also Anne Harrington and John D. Dunne, "When Mindfulness Is Therapy: Ethical Qualms, Historical Perspectives," *American Psychologist* 70, no. 7 (2015): 621-631, and Jane Iwamura, *Virtual Orientalism: Asian Religions and American Popular Culture* (Oxford: Oxford University Press, 2011), chapter 2.
43. John D. Dunne, "Toward an Understanding of Non-Dual Mindfulness," *Contemporary Buddhism* 12 (2011): 75–79.

44. Thich Nhat Hanh, *The Miracle of Mindfulness: An Introduction to the Practice of Meditation*, trans. Mobi Ho (Boston: Beacon Press, 1987 [1974]).
45. Wilson, *Mindful America*, 34, calls Nhat Hanh "the most important figure in Western Buddhism." Wilson's point that Nhat Hanh is a tremendously influential figure is well taken, though whether one could call him the most important would depend on the metric used. Nhat Hanh receives only passing mention in this chapter because, though he has shaped the American sensibility about mindfulness, he serves as a sort of force multiplier to the arc of development best revealed in the sources we have examined in detail.
46. Jack Kornfield, *A Path with Heart: A Guide through the Perils and Promises of Spiritual Life* (New York: Bantam, 1993), 43.
47. Braun, "Mindful but Not Religious," 175ff.
48. Talal Asad, *Formations of the Secular* (Stanford, CA: Stanford University Press, 2003), 68.
49. Another, more controversial aim is to use mindfulness as a first-person method, as what comes to be called an "inner science," to investigate directly the nature of consciousness. The most prominent example of this is the series of conversations among scientists, Buddhist (mostly Tibetan) monks, and the Dalai Lama, sponsored by the Mind and Life Institute.
50. Evan Thompson discusses this article along parallel lines to my points in his "Looping Effects and the Cognitive Science of Mindfulness Meditation," in *Buddhism, Meditation, and Science*, ed. David McMahan and Erik Braun (New York: Oxford University Press, 2017), 51ff.
51. Ricard, Lutz, and Davidson, "Mind of the Meditator," 41.
52. Thompson, "Looping Effects," 53–54.
53. Ann Taves, *Religious Experience Reconsidered: A Building-Block Approach to Religion and Other Special Things* (Princeton, NJ: Princeton University Press, 2009), 21–22.
54. Bodhi, "What Does Mindfulness Really Mean?," 35.
55. See Talal Asad, *Formations of the Secular*, 25, and Courtney Bender and Ann Taves, "Introduction: Things of Value" in *What Matters? Ethnographies of Value in a Not So Secular Age*, ed. Courtney Bender and Ann Taves (New York: Columbia University Press, 2012), 4.
56. See Candy Gunther Brown, "Can 'Secular' Mindfulness Be Separated from Religion?" in *Handbook of Mindfulness: Culture, Context, and Social Engagement*, ed. Ronald E. Purser, David Forbes, and Adam Burke (New York: Springer, 2016), 75-94.
57. See Bender and Taves, "Introduction: Things of Value," 7–8.
58. Ricard, Lutz, and Davidson, "Mind of the Meditator," 45.

Further Reading

Anālayo. *Satipaṭṭhāna: The Direct Path to Realization*. Birmingham, UK: Windhorse Publications, 2004.

Anālayo. *Early Buddhist Meditation Studies*. Barre, MA: Barre Center for Buddhist Studies, 2017.

Asad, Talal. *Formations of the Secular: Christianity, Islam, Modernity*. Stanford, CA: Stanford University Press, 2003.

Braun, Erik. *The Birth of Insight: Meditation, Modern Buddhism, and the Monk Ledi Sayadaw*. Chicago: University of Chicago Press, 2013.

Gethin, Rupert. "Buddhist Conceptualizations of Mindfulness." In *Handbook of Mindfulness: Theory, Research, and Practice*, ed. K. W. Brown, J. D. Creswell, and R. M. Ryan. New York: Guilford Publications, 2015, 9–41.
Gethin, Rupert. *The Buddhist Path to Awakening*. Oxford: Oneworld Publications, 2001.
Harrington, Anne, and John D. Dunne. "When Mindfulness Is Therapy: Ethical Qualms, Historical Perspectives." *American Psychologist* 70, no. 7 (2015): 621–31.
Kabat-Zinn, Jon. *Full Catastrophe Living: Using the Wisdom of Your Body and Mind to Face Stress, Pain, and Illness*. New York: Bantam Books, 2013 [1990].
Lopez, Donald S., Jr. *The Scientific Buddha: His Short and Happy Life*. New Haven, CT: Yale University Press, 2012.
Mahāsi Sayadaw. *Manual of Insight*. Translated by the Vipassanā Mettā Foundation Translation Committee. Somerville, MA: Wisdom Publications, 2016.
McMahan, David, and Erik Braun, eds. *Buddhism, Meditation, and Science*. New York: Oxford University Press, 2017.
Nyanaponika Thera. *The Heart of Buddhist Meditation: The Buddha's Way of Mindfulness*. San Francisco: Weiser Books, 2014.
Purser, Ronald E., David Forbes, and Adam Burke, eds. *Handbook of Mindfulness: Culture, Context, and Social Engagement*. New York: Springer, 2016.
Williams, J. Mark G., and Jon Kabat-Zinn, eds. *Mindfulness: Diverse Perspectives on Its Meaning, Origins and Applications*. New York: Routledge, 2013.
Wilson, Jeff. *Mindful America: The Mutual Transformation of Buddhist Meditation and American Culture*. New York: Oxford University Press, 2014.

Index

Due to the use of para id indexing, indexed terms that span two pages (e.g., 52–53) may, on occasion, appear on only one of those pages.

Figures are indicated by *f* following the page number

A

Abe, Masao, 588–89, 590–91
Abhayagiri, 39–40
Abhidhānottara-tantra, 269–70
Abhidharma, 386, 387–88, 392, 393–94
Abhidharmakośa, 390, 391, 392–93, 395
Abhirati, 28, 48, 389
abhiṣeka, 87–88, 154
Accardo, Christopher, 601–2
adaptation, 97, 98–100, 112, 371
adhiṣṭhāna, 390
agency, 7–16, 57, 150, 179, 277. *See also* images
Agni (J. Katen), 370–71
agnihotra, 370
Agonshū, 114–16, 369
ahiṃsā, 215
airag (*tsegee*), 435–36, 437, 439–42, 448, 450n.22, *See also* intoxicants
airag festival, 436
Ajahn Brahm, 107–8
Ajātaśatru, King, 135–36
Ajimi Jizō, 506–7
Akong Tulku Rinpoche, 585
Akṣobhya Buddha, 28, 357, 438
akuśala mūla, 375–76
ālayavijñāna, 376
alchemy, 375–76
Alexander, Noliwe, 553
Allocco, Amy, 543
altars, home, 469, 473*f*, 480*f*
ama no tera, 424
Amarapura Nikāya, 42–43
Amaravati Buddhist monastery, 590
Amchi (T. *a mchi*), 235, 240–41, 244–45
Amchi Gyatso Bista, 245–46, 247
America. *See* Buddhism: North American
Ames, Michael, 47–48
Amida triad, 148–49
Amitābha/Amitāyus (C. Āmítuófó, J. Amida), 28, 57, 58, 60–61, 63, 286, 320, 323, 327–31, 356–57, 375, 378, 388–89, 438
Amoghasiddhi Buddha, 357, 438
Anāgāmin, 391
anagarika, 90
Analayo, Venerable, 407
Ānanda, 134–35, 196, 304–5, 306, 405–6
Ananda Metteyya. *See* Bennet, Allen (Ananda Metteyya)
Ānāpānasati-sutta, 633–34
Anāthapiṇḍika, 387
anātman, 14, 98, 136, 387
Äṇavum Pirita, 313
ancestral veneration, 55, 469–70, 483n.2
aṇḍa (egg), 22–23
Aṅgulimāla, 226
Aṅgulimāla Paritta, 313
Aṅguttara Nikāya, 385, 394
aniconism, 136–37, 142
anitya, 136, 597–98, 603–4
Anthropocene, 214
antinomianism, 330
anubhāva, 496
Anumāna Sutta, 311–12
anumodana, 490–91
Anuttara Yoga Tantra, 269, 280
apacāyana, 362
Appell, Helen Fox, 275*f*

Appleton, George, 586
arahant, 489–90
Arai, Paula, 411
Archaeological Society of India, 191
Archaeological Survey of India, 220
archaeology, 191–93, 194, 213, 214–15
Arnold, Edwin, 585
Arthaśāstra, 221
Ārya-samantabhadra-caryā-praṇidhāna-rāja-sūtra, 321
Asad, Talal, 640, 642–43
Äsala Perahära, 581–82
āsana, 372, 392–93
Asaṅga, 386, 436–37
asceticism, 219, 257, 258
Asher, Frederik, 199–200
Ashoka, King, 72, 135–36, 183, 193, 194
Aṣṭāṅgahṛdayasaṃhitā, 238–40
Aṣṭa-sahasrikā-prajñāpāramitā, 32
Aśvaghoṣa, 25–26
Āṭānāṭiya-sutta, 24–25, 220–21, 388–89, 392–93
Aṭavisi Pirita, 313
Atīśa, 75, 436–37
Austin, James, 617
authenticity/authority, 2, 3, 5–6, 7–8, 12, 13, 347–48, 431, 600. *See also* monasticism
Āvadana Jātaka, 225–26
Avalokana-sūtra, 385–86
Avalokiteśvara (C. Guanyin, J. Kannon), 29, 30, 57, 60–61, 63, 81, 87*f*, 89–90, 199–200, 205, 255, 268, 269, 271, 275–77, 279, 357, 378, 389, 422–23, 431, 446–47
awakening, 11–12, 15, 28, 29, 32, 53, 118, 180, 346, 347, 371, 372–77. See also *bodhi*; *great doubt*; *koan*; *samyak-saṃbodhi*; *satori*
Awakening Mahayana Faith, 55–56
Āyuḥparyanta-sūtra, 385–86
Ayurveda, 224–25, 240, 243–44, 245
ayus, 388–89
Ayya Khema, 590

B

Baatar, 438
Babb, Lawrence A., 373–74
bad kan, 240, 245
bāhā, 86, 307–8
Baizhang Huaihai, 56–57, 348
Bajracharya, Badri, 89
Bajracharya, Naresh, 89
Bakraur stupa, 195–96
Baldoquín, Hilda Gutiérrez, 560
bap, 538, 539, 545
bara, 496
Baradin, 443–44
bardo, 244–45, 285–86, 287
bare attention, 636
Barley, Nigel, 632
Barsalou, Larry, 624
Batchelor, Stephen, 97
Baumann, Martin, 100
Bautze-Picron, Claudine, 203–4
Becker, Catherine, 191–93, 206–7
Beglar, J. D., 193–94
Being Black: Zen and the Art of Living with Fearlessness and Grace, 555
Bell, Catherine, 4, 542
Bellah, Robert, 478
Bender, Courtney, 643
benefit, 105, 154–55, 158, 247, 251–52, 257, 362
  this-worldly (*see* Buddhism: prosperity; *genze riyaku*)
Benn, James, 511–12
Bennet, Allen (Ananda Metteyya), 47, 584
Beommanggyeong bosal gyebonjong-yo, 425–26
Beopjeong, 61
bhakti, 142–43
Bhallika, 504
Bhaṭṭa Kumārila, 302–3
bhāvanā, 2, 199–200, 634
Bhāvaviveka, 389
Bhaya-bherava Sutta, 225
bhikkhu, 41–42
bhikkhunī (Skt. *bhikṣunī*), 9–10, 43, 49, 63, 73, 90, 406, 411, 415–16, 425–26, 494–95
Bhilsa Topes sites, 220
Bhṛkuṭī, 205
Bhutan, 70–71, 75, 77–78, 240–41, 360, 523
Bielefeldt, Carl, 104
bīja, 372
bikuni (Skt. *bhikṣunī*), 425–26
bioramas, 178
Bizot, François, 48–49
bla, 82, 248n.7, 285–86, 288–89, 291

Blackburn, Anne, 50
"Blessing of Mare's Milk, The," 438–39
Blo bzang 'phrin las, 436–37
Blue Cliff Record, 345–46
bodai, 253
Bodaishinron, 427
Bodawpaya, King, 42–43
Bodhgaya, 73, 130, 136, 152, 153*f*, 191–94, 195–207, 256, 261–62, 358, 438
Bodhi, Bhikkhu, 636, 642–43, 644–45n.15
Bodhi tree, 132, 152, 159, 194, 197, 496, 509
Bodhicaryāvatāra, 376–77
bodhicitta (T. *byang chub kyi sems*), 246, 376–77, 378–79, 436
bodhimaṇḍa, 179–80, 197
Bodhisattva Vow, 247, 411
Bodhi-seat, 197, 198, 204–5
Bodhisena, 199–200
body-mind, 16, 56–57, 66–67, 240, 299, 300, 453. *See also* Tassajara
Bogd Jebtsundamba, 436–37, 442–43
Boisen, Anton, 573–74
bombo, 83
Bond, George, 2
bóngthíng, 84
Boorstein, Sylvia, 637
borān kammatthān, 49
Borup, Jørn, 122
Brac de la Perrière, Bénédicte, 525–26
Brahmā, 46, 384–85
Brahmaloka, 385–86, 389, 390–91, 392
brahmavihāra, 8, 30–31, 390–91
"Brain Scanning: Varieties of Contemplative Experience," 641
Bramajāla Sūtra, 65–66
Brancaccio, Pia, 224
branding, 121–23
Braun, Erik, 98
bricolage, 113–14
Brinker, Helmut, 159–60
Bronkhorst, Johannes, 141–42
Broughton, Jeffrey, 344
buat phraphutta rup, 536–37
Buchanan, Francis Hamilton, 193
Buddha Gautama. *See* Shakyamuni/Sakkamuni
buddha-anusmṛti, 28–29, 388, 390, 391
Buddhacarita, 387–88
buddha-field. See *buddha-kṣetra*
Buddhaghosa, 134–35, 140, 224, 375–76, 388, 394
buddhakhetta, 390
buddha-kṣetra (buddha-field), 28–29, 375, 389
Buddhasāsana Samāgama, 584
Buddhasiṃha, 386
buddhavacana, 27, 177, 185–86, 300, 315–16
Buddhism. *See also* Chan Buddhism; Chosŏn Buddhism; Highland Buddhism; Jōdo Buddhism; Jōdo Shinshū Buddhism; Kamakura Buddhism; Mahayana Buddhism; Pure Land Buddhism; Sinhalla Buddhism; Sōtō Zen Buddhism; Tantric Buddhism; Theravada (Hinayana) Buddhism; Vajrayana Buddhism
  analysis of, 1–4
  Burmese, 43, 46, 49, 78, 148–49, 150–52, 159, 161–62, 256, 529, 635
  Canadian, 95–97
  Chinese, 54
  early, 22–30, 37–38, 39–40, 47
  engaged, 106, 591
  ethnic, 102
  European, 97–98
  exceptionalism and, 619, 620, 622
  field, 113–14
  globalized, 112–13
  Hawaiian, 94–95
  Himalayan, 73–77, 78–79, 83–84, 90–91 (*see also* Charya dance)
  humanistic, 330–31
  identity and, 100–3
  Japanese, 63–67
  Korean, 58–63
  Laotian, 38, 42–43, 47, 360
  modernism/modernity and, 2, 50, 118, 582–83, 619–22
  monolithic treatment of, 616–18
  New, 112–13
  North American, 3, 93, 95–97, 98–100, 107, 461–62 (*see also* Buddhist Churches of America; Tassajara Zen Mountain Center)
  practitioner relations with non-Buddhists, 581–82, 583–85

Chinkai, 424
Chinul, 58, 60
chö shé, 244–45
Chogyam Trungpa Rinpoche, 585
Chogye-jong Order of Korean Buddhism, 60
Chōken, 423
Choki Wangchuk, 85
chŏl, 60–61
Ch'ŏndoje, 60–61
Chōnen, 166
Chos skyong, 436
Chosŏn Buddhism, 58–59
Christian mission, 582
chú, 485n.21
Chú Phong, 481–82
Chuangzao renjian jingtu, 331
cintāmaṇi, 141
citizenship, 523–24
Claus-Bachmann, Martina, 26
cleansing, 373–74
Cobb, John, 588–89
Cognitive Ecology, 617–18
cognitive science. *See* mindfulness
Collins, Stephen, 384
colonialism, 50, 59, 182, 520–72
Commentary on the Contemplation Sutra, 323
communitas, 262
community, 13, 57, 70–71, 83–84, 87–88, 94–95, 98–99. See also *bhikkhu*; *bhikkhunī*; convent Hokkeji; Indra's Net; monasticism; nuns; ordination: women's; Paṭācārā; sangha
compassion (T. *snying rje*, Skt. *karuṇā*), 15, 29, 30–31, 57, 64, 106, 136, 237, 243–46, 255, 268, 270, 278, 331, 389, 391–92, 466
Confucianism, 54–55, 469–70
Connelly, Louise, 598, 603–4
consecration, 25, 88–89, 132–34, 138, 158, 159–61, 200. *See also* images *
Contemplation Sutra, 329
contemplative practice/science, 613–25. *See also* Buddhism: science; meditation; mindfulness
Contemplative Science: Where Buddhism and Neuroscience Converge, 615
convent Hokkeji, 421, 431
cooking, 65–67, 176, 177, 181, 457–61, 503, 511–12
Coomaraswamy, Ananda, 23
counseling. *See* chaplaincy
court. *See* convent Hokkeji
Crosby, Kate, 47, 49
Cūḷavaṃsa, 304–5
Cullavagga, 405–6, 409–10
cult of the book, 178–79, 206. *See also* text veneration
Cuṇḍa, 199–200, 205
Cunningham, Alexander, 193–96, 197, 198, 202–4

D

Da jingtu sishiba wen, 329
Daan, 329
Dacheng fayuan yilinzhang, 425–26
Daehaeng (Taehaeng), 62
daham pasal, 494–95
Dahui Zonggao, 341, 344–46, 347
Daibutsu, 160–61
daimoku, 64
Daisen, 438
Dalai Lama XIII, 439–40, 446–47
Dalai Lama XIV, 614, 616, 619–21, 622
đám giỗ, 482
dāna, 154, 219, 495–96, 504. *See also* food: offering; food: receiving; offerings
dance, 24, 25–26. *See also* Charya dance (Skt. *caryā-nṛtya*)
  Nepalese, 268–70
  "outer" and "secret," 269
  as Vajrayana practice, 87–88, 266–67, 270 (*see also* Charya dance; *Hevajra-tantra*)
dang hương, 470
danshug (*danshig*, Tib. *bstan bzugs*), 435–36, 448n.3
Danzanravjaa (Bstan 'dzin rab rgyas), 444, 445
dao, 54
Daochuo, 322
Daoxuan (J. Dōsen), 425–26, 510
darśan (darshan), 152, 377–78, 379, 598
Dasadhamma Sutta, 311–12
dasakusalakamma, 362
dasasil mātā/sil mäniyā (Sri Lan. *Thilashin*, Tai. *mae chi*, Khm. *don chi*), 43, 491–92, 494–95, 524, 528–29
Davidson, Richard, 375–76, 614–15, 643

Davidson, Ronald, 372–73
Davis, Angela, 550
Davis, Erik, 48
dāyaka sabhā, 495–96
de Silva, Charles, 587
de Silva, David, 583
de Silva, Lily, 303, 586
de Silva, Lynn, 586
death
  demon, 284–85
  disposal of remains after, 134–39, 288–90
  good, 326–27
  horoscope, 286, 289, 293
  karma and, 284
  memorial practices, 430–31
  monastic involvement with, 26–27, 292–93
  rituals, 295n.10, 326–27, 391–92, 393–94, 494
  sky burial, 289–90
  Tibetan concept of, 285–94
deathbed practice. *See also* rituals: deathbed practice
DeCaroli, Robert, 142–43
Deeg, Max, 194
Deep Ecology, 215
Dehejia, Vidya, 137
deity yoga (deva-yoga), 269, 377–78
Deleo, Kristin, 574–75
desanā, 307
Deshimaru Taisen, 119
Desi Sangye Gyatso (T. sDe srid Sangs rgyas rgya mtsho), 238–41
deva-anāgāmins, 387–88
deva-anusmṛti, 394, 395
deva-arhats, 387–88
dēvāles, 581–82
devaloka, 385, 386–87, 394
Devananda, Yohan, 586
devatā, 30, 225–26, 384–88, 394, 395, 396n.10
deva-yoga, 269. *See also* deity yoga
Devendra, Kusuma, 43
devotion, 8, 24, 25, 57, 60–61, 137, 154, 171–72, 206, 361, *See also* chanting; merit; offerings; pilgrimages
Dhammakaya temple, 116–17
Dhammapada, 9, 225, 301, 307, 312, 392
dhammapāṭha, 161–62
dhāraṇī, 29, 30, 183, 203–4, 391, 395, 454–55
Dharma, 358–59, 360, 503
  digital, 607
  dilution, 608
  "radical," 554–55, 558–61
  wheel of, 606–7
Dharma, Color and Culture, 560
dharma-bhāṇaka, 27–28, 180–81
dharma-dhātu, 29–30, 31–32
dharmadhātu-jñāna, 274
Dharmaguptaka lineage, 42, 43, 406, 408, 423–24
Dharmaguptaka-vinaya, 406, 409
dharmakāya, 64–65, 142, 178
Dharmakīrti, 620–21
Dharmapāla, Anagārika, 95, 583–84
Dharmasvamin, 75
dhutaṅga, 42
Dial, The, 95
dialogue
  inter-monastic, 588
  inter-religious, 586–87
  societies/networks for formal, 588–90
  spaces for, 588–91
Dialogue, 586
Dīgha Nikāya, 196, 220–21, 386, 391
digital practice. *See* Dharma; meditation; practice
Dilova Khutugtu, 444
Discernments of the Dharmadhatu of Avatamsaka (*Huayan Fajie Guanmen*), 55–56
discipline, 270, 272, 277, 278, 279, 341. *See also* monasticism
doctrine, 85, 100, 254, 361–62, 379, 387, 502. See also *dharmakāya*
Doering, Carrie, 575–76
Dōgen, 64, 457–61, 464–65, 512
dōgyō ninin, 254
dōjō, 115, 116, 120
dokusan (J. *sanzen*), 103, 348
Dongshan, 456, 457–58
Dorjbold, 441, 447
Dowayo tribe, 632–33
Dressler, Markus, 521
Droṇa, 134–35
Ducor, Jérôme, 385–86
dug gsum (Skt. *klesha*), 240
duḥkha, 7, 98, 215, 217–18
dveṣa, 272
Dyaḥ Pyākhaṃ, 279

E

East Bay Meditation Center (EBMC), 101–2
Eastern Monachism, 303
Eckhart, Master, 585, 590
ecology. *See* Cognitive Ecology; Deep Ecology; environment
"Ehibhikkhu," 405
Eight Appearances (*Snang brgyad, Gnam sa snang brgyad*), 436
Eight precept holders (*upāsaka, upāsikā*), 491
Eight Precepts (Pali *aṭṭha sīla*, Sinh. *atasil*), 491, 494–95
Eighth Bogd Jebtsundamba, 443–44, 446–47
Eihei shingi, 512
Eison, 421, 425–26, 433n.15
elections, 528–29
Ellison, Koshin Paley, 575
Elverskog, Johan, 219, 226–27
embodiment, 2, 7–16, 233
Emerald Buddha, 158
emotion, 5–10
Emotional Intelligence, 614
Engle, Adam, 614–15
enliven, 24, 137–38, 148–49, 156, 158, 159, 160, 162–64, 167, 171
Ennin, 253
Enomiya Lassalle, Hugo, 586
Enshō, 427
entangling vines, 341
environment
  built, 191, 204, 207 (*see also* stupa)
  natural. 215–27. (*see also* food; gardens, monastic)
environmental humanities, 213–14
Enyō Imamura, 94–95
Epstein, Mark, 637–38
Esala, 491–92
Essentials of Chan, 342
European Network of Buddhist-Christian Studies, 589–90
Evans-Wentz, W. Y., 287
Experience of Insight, The, 637
Ezen-ni, 63

F

"Faith of the Future, The," 584
Falcone, Jessica, 603–4, 607
Falk, N. E., 220, 414–15
Fanwangjing, 509
Faxian, 193
feeding other beings, 506. *See also* food: offering/receiving/social value of
Feniger, Siegmund. *See* Nyanaponika Thera (Siegmund Feniger)
festival of mare milk, 436
Field, Nicholas, 506
Fierce Urgency of Now, The, 553–54
fire-walking, 256
Fischer, Norman, 588
Fitchett, George, 575–76
"Five Hundred *Bhikkhus*," 225
"Five Periods and Eight Teachings," 56
Five Precepts (Pali *pañca sīla*, Sinh. *pansil*), 45, 487, 489–90, 497, 524
fMRI, 615, 623–24, 640–41
Fo Guang Shan, 106, 116–17
Foard, James, 260
Fogelin, Lars, 191–93
food, 501, 513n.11, 515–16n.49
  Buddhist attitudes toward, 501–3
  festivals, 512–13
  offering/receiving/social value of, 501–2, 504–7
  production, 507–8
footprint, Buddha's, 309–10
Ford, Tim, 567
forests, 220–26
Foulk, T. Griffith, 347, 348
Four Noble Truths, 574, 621
Fowler, James, 571
fragmentation, 140, 608
Franti, Michael, 552
Fronsdal, Gil, 574–75
Fudō Myōō (Acalanātha Vidyārāja), 371–72
fugitive, 551, 555–57, 561
Fujiwara no Fuhito, 422, 423
Fujiwara no Teika, 423–24, 426, 427
funerary rites/rituals/practices. *See* rituals: death
Fushuku hanpō, 512

G

Galiani, Ferdinand, 637–38
gandakuṭī, 170–71, 196
Gaṇḍavyūha, 30
Gandhara Lokanātha, 167*f*
gandharvas, 386
Gaṇeśa, 269

Gaofeng Yuanmiao, 342, 344
gaosheng nian, 324
garbha, 22–23
Garbhadhātu mandala, 381n.15
gardens, monastic, 215–17, 220–26
Garrett, Frances, 506
garudhammā, 43
gasshō, 455
gāthās, 301, 305, 308
gebküi (Tib. *dge skos*), 443
Geertz, Clifford, 4, 475
Gelek Palsang (Dge legs Dpal bzang), 438–39, 449n.12
Gelugpa tradition, 406–7
gelüng (Tib. *dge slong*), 442
gender, 21–24, 45, 101, 292, 456–57, 464, 490–91, 494–95, 503, 509. *See also* convent Hokkeji; generativity (female); ordination: women's
generativity (female), 21–22, 23, 29
Genji monogatari, 427, 431
genjō-kōan, 337
genze riyaku, 66
geography, 30–31, 38–40, 54–55, 238, 246–47
Gerke, Barbara, 237
Gethin, Rupert, 360, 388, 390
getsül, gečül (Tib. *dge tshul*), 442
Getz, Daniel, 325
Ghatikāra, 387
Ghertner, Asher, 481
Ghosa, 388
Ghost Festival, 55
ghyewa (*gral*), 82
Giác Lâm Pagoda, 358
Glassman, Bernie, 106, 557
Gleig, Ann, 101–2, 104
goddess, 21–22, 47, 200. See also *devatā*; Hāritī; Prajñāpāramitā; Vajrayoginī (Vajradevī, Vajravārāhī)
Goenka, S. N., 90, 636–37
Gōhō, 162–64
Goldstein, Joseph, 588, 637, 639
Goleman, Daniel, 614–15
goma. See *homa* (J. *goma*)
Gombrich, Richard, 47, 50, 178–79
gompa, 85
gong'an. *See* koans
gongfu (J. *kufū*), 344
Gopaka, 386
Goviin Lkha (Tib. *'Go ba'i lha lnga*), 441
Granoff, Phyllis, 223, 224
Great Brahma Net Ceremony, 429–30
great doubt, 153, 336–37, 340, 341, 342, 343
Grieve, Price, 603–4, 605, 606
Gross, Rita, 591
gter, 185
gtor ma, 292–93, 436
gTsan-smyon Heruka, 75–76
guanxiang, 324
Guanyin. *See* Avalokiteśvara
Guishan Lingyou, 339, 347
Gunaratana, Bhante, 363–64, 645–46n.29
Gurney, Sir Henry, 363–64
gurudharma, 405–6
Gurung, 79–80, 84, 85–86
gyudpi, 85

H

Hakuin Ekaku, 340, 342
Halifax, Roshi Joan, 574
Han, Chenxing, 102
Hanmaŭm Sŏn Center, 62
Hansen, Anne, 50
Hardy, Robert Spence, 303
Hārītī, 26, 218, 278–79
Harris, Ian, 529–30
Harris, Stephen E., 376–77
Hartman, Zenkei Blanche, 552
Hathaka, 386–87
Hayagrīva, 205
Hayashi, Yokio, 48
Hazelton, Barbara, 506
healing, 238–43. *See also* medicine
Heart Sutra, 63, 115, 268, 368, 454–55
heavens, attaining, 384
Heim, Maria, 373–74
Helland, Christopher, 597–98, 599, 600
henro. *See* Shikoku Pilgrimage *(henro)*
Henry, Patrick, 588
heritage, 260, 303, 566–67. *See also* pilgrimage
Hershey, Barry, 614–15
Hevajra, 269, 357
Hevajra-tantra, 269–70
hibutsu, 158

Hickey, Shannon, 102–3
Highland Buddhism, 72–73
Himachal Pradesh, 74–75
Himagata Varṇanāva, 309, 310
Himavat, 71, 72
Hirsch, Trudi Jinpu, 574
Hisamoto, Holly, 566–67
Hòa Hảo, 469–70, 479–81
hōe, 429, 430
Hoguk Pulgyo, 59
Hokke metsuzaiji engi, 422–23, 425, 426, 430–31, 432
Hokke metsuzaiji nenjū gyōji (Nenjū gyōji), 428–29
Hokkeji convent. *See* convent Hokkeji
Holt, John, 48, 358, 536
Holy Isle, 590
homa (J. *goma*), 64, 87–88, 115, 368–73, 378–79, 380n.2
Hōnen, 64, 327–28
hongaku, 63–64
Hongren, 374
honji-suijaku, 63
honzon, 371–72
Hori, Victor Sogen, 346–47
hosshin, 253
hosshin seppō, 64–65
Hsing Yun, 529
Hsuan Hua, 587
huatou, 341, 344–45
huatu, 322–23
Huayan (K. Hwaŏm) school, 55–57, 58
Huber, Toni, 258–59
Huineng, 337–38, 374
Huiyuan, 54–55, 321–22, 326
human realm, 330–31
Hunt, Ernest and Dorothy, 94–95
Huntington, Susan, 137, 199–200
Hutchins, Edwin, 617–18
Huvishka, King, 198
Huỳnh Phú Sổ, 479
Hwadu (C. *huatou*; J. *koan*), 58, 344
hwajaeng, 59
Hwaŏm, 58

I

ichi nengi, 328
iconophobia, 139, 142–43
identity, 6, 12, 57, 100–3, 259–61, 365, 491–92, 498, 561. *See also* chaplaincy; monasticism; ordination: women's
ihai, 66
Ikkyū, 510
images, 131, 132–34, 139–43
  agency of, 156, 159–66
  aniconic, 136–37
  anthropomorphic, 132, 136–39
  cache, 159–60
  iconophobia/iconophilia, 142–43
  originals and replicas of, 166
  shadow, 162–64
  veneration of, 150–56, 167–71
Imamura, Enyō, 94–95
impermanence (T. *mi rtag pa*, Skt. *anitya*), 237, 490
impurity, 12, 139–40, 142, 506
incense offering, 6, 24, 27–28, 66, 154–55, 206, 313, 356, 357–58, 359
inclusivist subordination, 581–82, 584
Indasālagūha, 224
Indra, 46
Indra's Net Community, 61–62
inner breathing, 286
inner science, 647n.49
insight meditation. See *vipassanā*
Insight Meditation Society (IMS), 636–37
inter-monastic exchange. *See* dialogue: inter-monastic
inter-religious debate. *See* dialogue: inter-religious
interdependence, 15
interfaith ministry. *See* chaplaincy
International Buddhist-Christian Theological Encounter, 588–89
internet. *See* Dharma: digital; practice: internet
intersectionality, 554–55
intoxicants, 435, 437, 441–45, 450n.22. See also *airag* (*tsegee*)
Ippen, 327–28
iṣṭadevatā, 158
itadakimasu, 512
iti pi so, 45

J

jātaka, 359, 388, 491–92
Jātaka Pota, 301

Jatika Hela Urumaya, 528–29
Jaya Sthiti Malla, King, 85–86
Jayamaṅgala Gāthā (pirit), 305, 496
Jewel Mirror Samadhi, 456
jhāna, 392–93, 635
Jianshe renjian jingtu lun, 330–31
Jiaojie xinxue biqiu xinghu lüyi, 425–26
Jigwang (Chigwang), 62
Jinapañjaraya, 313
jinen, 327–28
Jingtu huowen, 324
Jingwan, 182
Jinson, 429–30
jirinkan, 372
Jishū, 327
Jizen, 423–24, 426
Jizō, 63, 103–4
Jñānamalla Bhajans, 89
Jōdo Buddhism, 64
Jōdo Shinshū Buddhism, 64, 65–66, 327, 510
Jōken, 426
Jokhang Temple, 358
Jotiya Dhirasekera, 586
Journey for a Soul, 586
Jowo Shakyamuni, 148–49
Jungto (Pure Land) Society, 61–62
junrei, 253
juzu, 66

K

Kabat-Zinn, Jon, 104, 119, 614–15, 636, 638–40
Kagyu Samye Ling Monastery, 585, 590
Kaigai senkyōkai, 584
Kakichi Kadowaki, 586
Kakudha, 387
Kālacakra, 357
kali yuga, 237
Kalmyk khan Dondogdash, 442
kalpa (Pali *kappa*), 487
kalyānamitra, 572
Kamakura Buddhism, 64
kanhua (*hwadu*), 60–61
Kaniṣka, Emperor, 72
Kannon. *See* Avalokiteśvara (J. Kannon)
Kannon Pilgrimage, 66–67
kapha, 240
Kapilavastu, 71
Kapstein, Matthew, 73, 85
Kāraṇḍavyūha, 29
karma, 3, 4, 55, 84, 284, 607*
Kashmir, 70, 72–73
Kassapa V, King, 304–5
Kāśyapa, 135
Katagiri Dainin, 454
Kataragama (Tam. Skanda, Murugan), 260
kaṭhina, 45–46, 312–13
Kathmandu Valley, 73–74, 75–76, 78, 80, 85, 86, 89–90, 268, 269, 278–79
katikāvatas, 311–12
kaze no denwa, 67
Kelaniya Raja Maha Vihara stupa, 41*f*
kenshō, 346
Kent, Daniel W., 525–26
kha btags, 289
Khalkha Regulations (*Qalq-a-yin Jirum*), 442–43
Khalkha Zaya Pandita, 436–37
khilbri, 84
Khrūbā Srivichai, 524–25
Khuddasikkhā, 311–12
Kibok Pulgyo, 60–61
kido, 60–61
Kilys, Tim, 570–71
Kim, Jinah, 32
King, Martin Luther, Jr., 591
King, Matthew, 506
kinhin, 119
kinji hoto mandara, 183–84
Kinmei, Emperor, 148–49
Kinnard, Jacob, 204
Kinst, Daijaku Judith, 459–60, 566
Kiri kōḍu, 311
Kiriyama, Seiyū, 114–16
Kirsch, Thomas, 47–48
Kīrtī Śrī Rājasiṅha, King, 304–5
ki-ya lam-a, 442–43
Klassen, Pamela, 597–98
kleśa, 272, 376–77
kleṣāvaraṇa, 372–73
klu, 235–36
Knox, Robert, 314
koan (Ch. *kong'an*), 56–57, 336, 337–40, 345–48
  practice, 341–43
Kōbō Daishi, 254, 260–61
Kōfuku no Kagaku, 116

Kohlbrugge, Hebe, 591
Kohomba Kankariya, 581–82
kōjō, 344
Kōken, Emperor, 424
kokubunji-kokubunniji, 424
Kōmyō, Queen-Consort, 421–23, 428, 430, 431–32
Konāgamana, 135
Kornfield, Jack, 636–37, 639–40
koromo (kesa), 119
kōshiki, 429–30
Kriyāsaṃgraha, 281n.9
kṣānti, 272
Kṣitigarbha, 357
Kuiji (J. Kiki), 324, 425–26
Kūkai, 64–65, 66–67, 152, 361, 505, 506–7
kundoku, 428–29
kusala/akusala (Skt. *kuśala/akuśala*), 8, 15, 381–82n.32, 488
Kushinara, 358
Kusuma Devendra, 43
kuyō, 66–67
kyi-dug, 244

L

la (T. *bla*), 237
Lakṣmī, 30
Lalitavistāra, 194, 387–88
lama, 80–81, 84
lambu, 83
Lan Xang, 39
landscapes, 215–19
Laṅkāvatāra-sūtra, 376
Larger Sukhāvatīvyūha-sūtra, 323, 326
las (Skt. *karma*), 237
Laws and Regulations to Actually Follow, 443
Layman, Emma, 102
leaving home, 55
Ledi Sayadaw, 49, 635
legitimacy, 412, 416, 432, 577
lena, 214, 221–22, 223–24, 227
Leoshko, Janice, 198, 199–200
Lepcha. *See* Rong-pa
Lhasa Mentsikhang, 249n.24
li, 55–57
Liberation Tigers of Tamil Eelam (LTTE), 525–26
Licchavi, 73–74
Light of Asia, The, 585
Lim Teong Aik, 364
Linenthal, Edward, 481–82
Ling, Trevor, 586
Linji (J. Rinzai), 347
Linji Yixuan, 339
Lion's Roar, 107
Liuquan, 160
localization (Indianization), 38–39
Lofton, Kathryn, 122–23
Loi Krathong festival, 45–46
Lokeśvara, 268
lokuttara, 581–82
Longquan temple, 116–17
Lopez, Carlos, 370
lotus (Skt. *padma*), 23, 26–27, 31, 32–33, 205, 218, 386, 553, 605
Lotus Sutra (daimoku, *namyō-hō-renge-kyō*), 56, 63, 64, 95, 105, 135, 139, 179, 184–85, 238–40, 376
"Lotus Temple." *See* convent Hokkeji
lowland-upland interactions, 218–19
Luang Pho Thuat, 361
Luang Phor Toh. *See* Somdet Toh, Venerable
lucid awareness, 644–45n.15
Lugoviña, Francisco, 557
Lumbini, 73, 358
lunzang, 184
Lutz, Antoine, 643

M

Machida, Soho, 327
Madhyāmaka (Sanron) school, 58
Madsen, Richard, 529
Maḍugallē Siddhārtha, Venerable, 312–13
mae chi (don chi), 412, 414–15, 528–29
Mae Nak, 361
Mahā Jaya Maṅgala Gāthā, 313
Mahā Parākramabāhu Katikāvata, 311–12
Mahabodhi Society of India, 193–94, 258–59
Mahābodhi Temple Complex, 192*f*, 194–96, 195*f*, 198, 204–7, 255, 261–62
Mahābrahma, 386–87
Mahagopalaka-sutta, 572
Mahākāla, 269, 357
Mahākāla-tantra, 269–70

Min Bahadur Shakya, 89
Mind and Life Institute (MLI), 614
Mind and Life Summer Research Institute (MLSRI, or SRI), 614–15
"Mind of the Meditator," 641
mindfulness, 3, 97–98, 99, 119, 613–14, 624, 633, 635, 636–43. *See also* meditation; *sati*
"Mindfulness on the Thirty-two Parts of the Body," 414
"mindfulness-based interventions" (MBIs), 616–17
Mindfulness-Based Stress Reduction (MBSR), 614, 638–40
Mindon, King, 182
Mingun Sayadaw, 635
Minjung Pulgyo (People's Buddhism), 61–62
miracle, 132, 156, 158, 255, 358, 422, 431. *See also* Śrāvastī
Miracle of Mindfulness, The, 639
Mitra, R. L., 193–94
mizuko kuyō, 66, 103
mkhris pa, 240
mobile app. *See* practice: mobile phone apps
modernity. *See* Buddhism: modernism/modernity
Moggallāna, 386–87. *See also* Maudgalyāyana
Mohe Zhiguan, 56
Mohoṭṭivatté Guṇānanda, 583
mokṣa, 132
monastic governmentality. *See* monasticism
monasticism, 26–27, 65–67, 79–80, 213, 421. *See also* convent Hokkeji
Monghut, King (Rāma IV), 42–43
monlam, 244–45
Monnet, Michael, 574
mono no aware, 65
Moore, Christopher, 566–67
morality, Bramhanistic, 16n.6
mottainai, 512
mountains, 255–56
Mucalindanāga, 201*f*
mudrā, 30, 137, 266–67
  añjali, 153, 168–70, 205, 206, 490–91
  bhumisparśa, 199–200, 205, 224–25
  dhyāna, 200–2
Mujaku Dōchū, 343
Mūlasarvāstivāda Vinaya, 42, 135, 406–7
Mūlasikkhā, 311–12
Mumford, Stan Royal, 293
Muromachi, Imperial Lady, 430
Musoyu (*No Possession*), 61
Muzhou Daoming, 337, 340
Myori Pophui, 411

N

nāḍī, 446–47
Naess, Arne, 215
Nāgārjuna, 385–86, 394, 436–37
nāga/nāginī, 26, 218, 221, 225–26, 244, 441
Nairātmya Buddha, 31–32, 199–200, 269
Nakatsukasa Mōhei, 257
Nalanda tradition, 620–22
Namo Amitābha (C. namo Āmítuófó, J. namo Amida) Butsu, 357
Namo tassa bhavagato arahato sammāsambuddhassa, 45
Namsŏn, Ch'oe, 59
namu Amida butsu, 327–28
namu myōhō renge kyō, 116–17
Nanpo Jōmyō (Daiō Kokushi), 348
Naquin, Susan, 261
Nāropa, 75, 436–37
nationalism, 259–60, 498, 520, 525–26, 529–30, 553
nation-state, 519–26, 528–29, 531n.12. *See also* rituals of national belonging
Nattier, Jan, 102
natural disaster, 63–64, 66–67, 236–37, 446–47. *See also* Sowa Rigpa
nature, 214–15
nehan, 253
nembutsu, 64, 328, 329–30
Nepal, 21, 78–79
neurophenomenology, 615
Newar Buddhism, 73–74, 86–90, 277
Newar Vajrayana, 282n.17
Nguyen, Tommy, 576
nian, 325
nianfo (Ch.; K. yŏmbul; J. nembutsu), 56–57, 320, 324, 325, 326–27, 329, 331–32
nianfo mama, 57
nianfo samādhi, 321–22, 324–25
nibbāna. See nirvana (Sinh. *nivan*, Pali *nibbāna*)

Nichiren, 64
nikāyas, 39–40, 41–43, 385–86, 387–88, 392
Nippozan-Myōhōji, 105, 106
nirmāṇakāya, 164–65
nirvana (Sinh. *nivan*, Pali *nibbāna*), 43–44, 385, 487
Nittō guhō junrei koki, 253
Norwood, Frances, 568
Numrich, Paul, 99–100
Nŭng'in Sŏn Center, 62
nuns. See *bhikkhunī* (Skt. *bhikṣunī*)
Nyanaponika Thera (Siegmund Feniger), 586, 636, 637
Nyingma (T. *rnying ma*) lineage, 74–75, 79–80, 81, 236–37, 361
Nyoen, 427
nyūga ga nyū, 372
nyungne, 82

O

Obeyesekere, Gananath, 50
obon, 66
"Obvious Aspects of Ritual, The," 536
offering, 45, 56–57, 123–24, 206, 370–71, 436, 441–42, 489–93. See also *dāna*; food; incense offering; merit; pilgrimage; *tsha gsur*; veneration/offering; "Verses That Prohibit Vodka Drinking"; votive offerings
ofuda, 66–67
O'Hara, Roshi Pat Enkyo, 555
okaeri nasai, 115
Olcott, Henry Steel, 583
oṃ cha ha pha la nasa kha ha, 445
oṃ maṇi padme hūṃ, 29, 81, 268
omamori, 66–67
Omoie Tetzunostzuke. *See* Pfoundes, Charles (Omoie Tetzunostzuke)
onkimon, 430
ordination, 405, 409–11
  dual, 407, 409–11
  status, 411–13
  Theravada, 42–43
  tree, 535–40, 541–44, 546
  variations in, 411–13
  Vinaya, 62
  women's, 7, 407–9, 413–15, 503
ōryōki, 454–55
Otogawa, Kōbun, 454
Owens, Lama Rod, 555, 557

P

pabbajjā, 42, 524
pacittaya, 528
padabhañña, 307–8
padma. *See* lotus
Padmasambhava (Guru Rinpoche), 74–75, 81, 236–37, 361, 446–47
pagoda. *See* stupa
Pali
  Buddhism, 38–39
  canon, 2–3
  language, 40, 356
  Vinaya, 43
Pali Text Society, 97
Pañca Jina mandala, 269
paṇḍaka, 409–10
pandita, 86–87
Pang Yun, 338
paññā, 497
pāpa (Sinh. *paw*), 488
pārājika, 408, 409
Parākramabāhu I, King, 39–40
Parākramabāhu II, King, 304–5
paramitā, 505–6, 586–87
Paramopāsaka, 205–6
paribhogika, 196
parinirvāṇa, 25, 132, 134, 137–38, 177
paritta (Sinh. *pirit*), 26, 179–80, 301, 302–6, 315–16, 489–90, 496–97, 498
  maṇḍapa, 302*f*
  suttas, 308
Parittaśubha, 388–89
parivrājaka, 581
Pas, Julien, 389
Pashupati, 78
Paṭācārā, 9–10, 10*f*, 11*f*
Path with Heart, A, 640
pāṭimokkha, 41, 42, 43, 311–12, 492–93, 504–5
paṭipatti, 2
pavāraṇā, 492–93
Payne, K., 99
Peabody, Elizabeth Palmer, 95
Pennington, Brian, 543

Q

sahō, 118
sai sin, 539–40, 544, 546
Saichō, 65–66
Saikoku Kannon pilgrimage, 255
Sakkapañha sutta, 223–24
Śākyabhikṣu, 205–6
Śākyopāsaka, 205–6
samādhi, 28–29, 378, 497
Samanala Hälla, 310
sāmaṇera, 42
sāmaṇerī, 410
Samantabhadra, 321, 357
Samantakūṭa Vaṇṇanā, 310
Samantapāsadikā, 171
samatha, 634–35
sammā sati, 636
samnak chii, 414–15
samsara, 233, 268, 487, 501
samskaras, 87–88
Saṃvarodaya-tantra, 269–70
samyak-saṃbodhi, 269, 274
Samye Buddha, 151*f*
Samyutta Nikāya, 358–59
Sanchi Survey Project (SSP), 214, 215–16
saṅdēśas, 309
Sangha, 360–61, 461–65
Sangha Act of 1902, 524–25
saṅghadāna, 44, 45
saṅgharājas, 40
Sangs rgyas Sman bla (Skt. *Bhaiṣajyaguru*), 238–40
Sankhalipi, 222–23
sanmitsu, 372, 377–78
sanshi fo, 139
Santi Asoke Community, 412
Śāntideva, 376–77
sanzen. See *dokusan*
Saraha, 436–37
Sarasvatī, 30
Sariputta, 385–86, 405
sarīra, 134–35
Sarnath, 358
Saron, Clifford, 614
Sarva Giri, 193–94
sāsana, 176–77, 412, 486
sati, 633–36, 645n.20. *See also* mindfulness
Satipaṭṭhāna-sutta, 392, 489–90, 633–34, 635
satori, 103
sattu, 504–5
Sayka (T. *saskya*), 235
Schalk, Peter, 303
Schmithausen, Lambert, 215, 227
Schonthal, Benjamin, 529–30
Schopen, Gregory, 25, 178–79, 194, 196, 203–4, 205–6, 215, 219, 254–55, 321, 391
Schwegyin Sayadaw, 42–43
Science and Philosophy in the Indian Buddhist Classics, 616, 622
Scripture on the Production of Buddha Images, 159
Second Life, 600, 601, 603–7
secular, 3, 9, 79, 104–5, 106–7, 112–13, 119, 185–86, 262, 338, 362, 408, 415, 520, 541, 568, 577, 598, 633, 642, 643. *See also* mindfulness
Seeda, Aroon, 576
Seiho, Rev. Morris, 553
Seiryōji Buddha, 166
Sekhiyā, 311–12
Selasse, Sebene, 560
"self"/"other" power, 329–30
self-optimization, 117–21
semné, 244, 245
Seneviratne, H. L., 501
Sengji, 322, 326
sermon. *See* preaching
sesshin, 456
Seven Tamnan, 542
sexuality, 555, 556–57, 558, 559
sgrib, 242–43
Shakyamuni (Pali Sakkamuni) Buddha, 27, 60–61, 88*f*, 138, 161*f*, 163*f*, 165*f*, 246–47, 252–53, 355–56
  as a *bodhisattva*, 505–6
  buddhas before, 85–86
  and *buddha-vacana*, 27
  discourses, 56
  honoring, 25–26, 81, 86, 88*f*, 148–49
  images, 156–59
  jatakas of, 134
  meditation and, 117
  Prabhataratna and, 139, 356
  relics of, 137, 139
  Samantapāsadikā and, 171
  Theravada Buddhism and, 356

shakyō, 66–67
Shamanism, 53, 83–84, 435–36, 437–38
Shandao, 322–23, 324, 326–27
Shankara, 85–86
Sharf, Robert, 118, 587
Sharpe, Gina, 560
shashu, 103, 455
Sheng Yen (Shengyan), 331
Shenxiu, 374
Sherpas, 85–86
shes rab. *See* wisdom
shi, 55–56
shikantaza, 64
Shikoku Pilgrimage *(henro)*, 253, 254, 257, 258, 260–61, 263n.5, 361
Shin Shūkyō, 66–67
Shin-Amidabutsu-ni, 426
Shingon, 369, 372
shinian, 323
shinjin, 327–28, 329–30
Shinnyo-en, 95, 116, 369
Shinran, 64, 327–28, 510
Shinshin Shūkyō, 67
Shinto, 53
Shitou Xiqian, 338, 340
shixiang nian, 325
shōjin ryōri, 65–67, 512
Shōmu, Emperor, 421
Shonan, Sensei and Myokei, 553
shōnenju, 372
shōshingu, 506–7
Shōtoku, Emperor, 424
shugyō, 253
Shunkamon (Shunkamon-in), Imperial Lady, 423–24
shushō-ittō, 60, 64
Shwe Dagon Pagoda, 256, 259–60, 358
Shwegyin Nakaya, 42–43
Shwesandaw Shakyamuni, 162*f*
Si zhong nianfo, 325
Siam, 39
siddham, 64
Siddhartha Gautama, 312–13. *See also* Shakyamuni/Sakkamuni Buddha
Sifenlü xingshichao zichiji, 425–26
SikhavaḷaňdaVinisa, 311–12
sikkhamānā, 410
sikkhamat, 412
Sikkim, 70, 77–78, 84. *See also* Rong-pa
Śikṣāsamuccaya, 385–86
sīla (Skt. *śīla*, Sinh. *sil*), 487, 489–90, 497. *See also* Five Precepts
sīmā, 41, 408–9
Simmer-Brown, Judith, 575, 588
Simmons, Aishah Shahidah, 561
Sinhala Buddhism, 307, 309, 356, 499n.4
Sirimā, 387
Śiva, 38–39, 46
Sīvali-yantraya, 496
Siyam Nikāya, 42–43
Skanda (Murugan). *See* Kataragama (Tam. Skanda, Murugan)
skillful means (T. *thabs*, Skt. *upāya*), 31, 237, 244, 280
Skilling, Peter, 47
smansbyinpa, 243
Smith, Jonathan Z., 191–93, 481–82
smoking, 446–47
snuffing tobacco, 447
snying rje (Skt. *karuṇā*), 237
social engagement, 591
social interaction, 7, 606
social media, 62, 601–2, 603, 608
Society of Buddhist-Christian Studies (SBCS), 587, 588–89
sōdō, 454–55, 457
Soen, Shaku, 95
Soho Machida, 327
Sojoyner, Damien M., 551
Sōka Gakkai, 116–17
sokushin jōbutsu, 64, 506–7
solosmasthāna, 308, 358
Soḷosmasthāna Sāntiya, 308–9
Soma Thera, 635
Somdet Toh, Venerable (Luang Phor Toh), 361
sōmoku jōbutsu, 64–65
Sŏn (Ch. Chan; J. Zen), 58, 60
Song, King, 148–49
Sŏngch'ŏl, 60
Sonnyo, 427
Soryu Kugai, 94–95
sotāpanna, 386
Sōtō Zen Buddhism, 63, 64, 118, 299–300, 336, 374, 415

South Asia, 33n.1
Sowa Rigpa (T. *gso ba rig pa*), 235, 237, 238–46
speech, functional, 454–55, 462–63
Spencer, Anne, 102
Spirit Rock, 639–40
spiritual care. *See* chaplaincy
spiritual formation. *See* chaplaincy
Spiro, Melford, 47–48
śramadāna, 495–96
Śrāvastī, miracle at, 138, 164–65
Śrī Pāda, 309, 311
srog, 248n.7, 285–86
Stages of Faith, 571
statue, 160
Steindl-Rast, David, 587
Steng, Frederick, 589
Stevenson, Daniel, 326
Stone, Jacqueline, 327, 391–92
Strong, John, 178, 386, 508
stupas (*caityas*, *cetiyas*, pagodas), 22–27, 29–30, 31, 81, 105, 132, 134–36, 142, 191–93, 200–4, 203*f*, 356, 391
śubha, 388–89
Śubhakarasiṃha, 510
śuddha, 388–89
Sudhana, 30
Sujātā, 504
sukha, 388–89
sukha-duḥkha, 244
Sukhāvatī, 28, 321, 327, 328, 330–31, 357, 375, 385–86, 388–90, 391
Sukhāvatīvyūha, 321
Sukhothai, 39
Sunetta, 390–91
śūnyatā, 55–56, 501, 588–89
supernaturalism/animism, 47–48
"Supreme Sacrifice," 587
sustainability, environmental. *See* ordination: tree
Sutra of Utmost Golden Radiance, 183–84
Suzuki, DaisetsuTeitarō, 95, 103, 181, 584, 585, 639
Suzuki, Shunryu, 96, 454
Svarga, 388–89
svayambhū, 159
Swearer, Donald, 47, 180
syncretism, 48

T

ta nengi, 328
taechŏ,' 60
T'aego Order, 60
Taehyŏn (J. Taigen), 425–26
Taisen Miyata, Rev., 368
Taixu, 330–31, 525, 527
Takamatsu (Takamatsu-in), Imperial Lady, 423–24
takuhatsu, 257
Tamang lamas, 81–82
Tambiah, Stanley, 47–48
Tām̆bugala, 309
Tameie, 427
Tammayut Nikaya, 42–43
Tamu Pye, 85–86
Tankū, 426
Tanluan, 322
Tantra/tantras, 38–39, 164–65, 185, 269, 280, 370, 379
Tantric Buddhism, 30–31, 361. *See also* Vajrayana Buddhism
"Tantric Theravada," 48–49
Taoism/Daoism, 54–55, 469–70, 501
Tārā, 199–200, 205, 269, 357
Tassajara Zen Mountain Center, 457–61, 465–66
Tathāgata, 29–30, 180
Tathāgatagarbha-sūtra, 29–30, 55–56, 359
Tatsugami, Sotan, 454
Tāvatiṃsa, 386–87, 388, 394
Taves, Ann, 641–42, 643
Taylor, Diana, 544
tea drinking, 511–12
tejas, 176
Temiya, 388
Temple of the Tooth, 259–60
Ten Precepts (Pali *dasasīla*, Sinh. *dasasil*) 494–95
Tenjing Bista, 243–44
Tenzō kyōkun, 512
Terwiel, J., 47–48
text production, 178–79
text veneration, 27–28, 30–31, 32
textual body, Buddha's, 178–79
thabs (Skt. *Upāya*), 237
Thái Xuân Village, 473–75

Thailand, 38–39, 40, 42–44, 47, 49, 89–90, 116–17, 158, 261–62, 360, 388, 392, 412, 414–15, 507–8, 519, 524, 526–27, 537–38, 541, 545–46. *See also* Buddhism; Thai
Theravada Buddhism, 37–38, 40–41, 48–49, 50, 89–90, 356, 617, 633–34, 637
Theravada Buddhism, 47
Theravada Vinaya, 414
Thích Nhat Hanh, 477–78, 559, 560, 591, 639, 646n.40
thiláshin, 412
thiláshin wut-pwè, 413–14
thờ cúng tổ tiên, 470
Thompson, Evan, 614–15, 617–22
Three Gems/Jewels, 305, 306, 394
Three Mahayana Resolutions, 574
Three Mysteries, 372, 377–79
Three Refuges, 45, 605
Three Tenets (ZPO), 574
"Three Thousand Realms in a Single Thought," 56
Thudhamma Nikaya, 42–43
Thupten Jinpa, 622
Thupten Sangay, 292
Thurman, Robert, 280, 614
Thuy Vo Dang, 478
Tianru, 324
Tiantai school, 55–57
Tibet, 73–74, 75, 79–80, 85, 87–88, 131, 148–49, 160, 235, 238, 261–62, 293–94, 358, 359, 361, 438, 446–47, 512–13. *See also* Buddhism; Tibetan
Tikhonov, Vladimir, 527–28
Tilopa, 436–37
Tipiṭaka (Skt. *Tripiṭaka*), 37–38, 40, 384–85. See also *Tripiṭaka Koreana*
tiratana (Skt. *triratna*), 355
tōba, 115
Tobŏp, 61–62
Tōdaiji, 358, 422
Tomio, Hirai, 613–14
ton mai thi buat lao, 536–37
T'ong Pulgyo, 59
Tongdosa Temple, 358
torma (*gtor ma*), 506
tourism, 85–86, 105, 251–52, 262
Trailōkyavijaya, 199–200
Trainor, Kevin, 49, 136, 139, 194, 377
Tran, John Chin, 473–74
trance phenomena, 278–79
transference, 257
translocal landscapes, 217–19
transmutation, 375–77
Trapaṣa, 504
trauma, 237, 242–43, 246, 555, 640
Trautmann, T. R., 220
Trāyastriṃśa, 166, 386
Tricycle, 107
Trikamāla, King, 198
Tripiṭaka Koreana, 58
Triratna Buddhist Community, 412–13
tṛṣṇā, 376–77
Trust, Realization, and Self in Soto Zen Practice, 459–60
tsha tsha, 291
Tsongkhapa, 288, 375, 393, 436–37, 445–46
Tulana, 587
Tun Saraṇaya, 309
Tun Saraṇe, 310
Turner, Alicia, 50
Turner, Victor, 261–62
Turner, Victor and Edith, 253
Tweed, Thomas, 475
Twelve Tamnan, 542
Tworkov, Helen, 102

U

U Ba Khin, 636–37
U Dhammaloka (Laurence Carroll), 97, 583, 584
U Ottama, 529
U Wissara, 529
Udāyana, King, 137–38, 152, 159–60, 166
uddeśika, 152
Upagupta (T. Phra Upakut), 507–8
upasampadā, 42, 409, 412, 584
upaṭṭhāna, 635
upāya. See skillful means
upekśā, 8
Uposathā, 386
Uttarananda, Hatigammana, 587
Uttarapatha, 72

V

vahanse, 359
Vairocana, 357
vajra (T. *rdo rje*), 31, 235–36
vajrācārya, 86
Vajracharya, Prajwal Ratna, 267*f*, 268, 274*f*, 284–85
Vajracharya, Ratna Kaji, 268–69, 277
vajra-deha, 277
Vajradhara Buddha, 357, 438
Vajradhātu mandala, 381n.15
Vajrapāṇi, 30, 269, 272–74, 357, 387–88
Vajrasattva, 205
Vajravidāraṇa, 357
Vajrayana Buddhism, 21, 30–33, 207, 269. *See also* Tantric Buddhism
Vajrayoginī (Vajradevī, Vajravārāhī), 32–33, 151*f*, 269, 274, 278–79, 357
Vakkali Sutta, 177, 358–59
van Dam, Nicholas, 625
vandanā gāthā, 310
Varela, Francisco, 614, 615–16, 623–24
vassa (*vas*), 42, 492–93
Vasubandhu, 386, 387
vāta, 240
vegetarianism, 508–10, 514–15n.29
veneration/offering, 355–56, 357, 358, 361–65
"Verses That Prohibit Vodka Drinking," 444–45
Vesak, 312–13, 363–65
Vesākha Pūjā, 45–46
Vessantara, Prince, 507–8
Vessantara Jataka, 26, 226
vihāra, 26–27, 392–93
Vikramabāhu I, King, 304–5
Vimānavatthu, 390
Vinaya (Kyeyul) school, 9–10, 11–12, 58, 492–93
vipassanā, 48–49, 90, 616–17, 635, 639–40
Vipassī Buddha, 135, 386
vippakiṇṇa, 135
virtual sacred, 598
Viṣṇu, 38–39, 46
visualization, 28–29, 30–31, 48–49, 64, 206, 324, 325, 331–32
Visuddhimagga, 375–76, 386–87
Viśvamātā, 357
vodka, 439–46, 448
votive offerings, 140

W

Wagner, Rachel, 597–98, 601–2
Waldschmidt, E., 303
Wallace, B. Alan, 614–15
Walsh, Maurice O'C., 586
Walton, Matthew W., 529–30
wangsheng zhuan, 327
wat (*vat*, Bur. *kyaung*, Sri Lan. *vihāraya*), 40–41
Wat Pho, 358
Wat PhraKaeo, 358
water, 22–23
water cosmology, 23
Watts, Alan, 103
Way of Flowers (*kadō*), 65
Way of Fragrance (*kōdō*), 65
Way of Mindfulness, The, 635
Way of Poetry (*kadō*), 65
Way of Tea (*sadō*), 65
Welcoming Ceremony, 160
Wesak, 491–92
"White Lotus Society," 322, 325
white supremacy, 552–53, 554–55, 558
Whitehead, Amy, 605
Why I Am Not a Buddhist, 618–19
Wijemanne, V. L., 584–85
williams, angel Kyodo, 553, 554–57, 559, 560
Willis, Michael, 197, 198
Wilson, Jeff, 15
winyan, 539
wisdom (T. *shes rab*, Skt. *prajñā*), 29, 32, 237, 280
womb, 159, 571
Wŏnhyo, 58, 510
Woodward, Frank, 583
World Parliament of Religions, 95
Wu, Emperor, 509
Wu Zetian, Empress, 183
Wuliangshou rulai guanxing gongyang yigui, 378
Wumen guan, 338–40

Wumen Huikai, 338–39
wuwei, 54
Wuzu Fayan, 345–46

X

xiang jiao, 131, 148–49
Xiangyan Zhixian, 339–40
Xifang, 329
xinnian, 324
Xuanzang, 73, 193, 194, 204–5, 393
Xuedou Chongxian, 345
Xueyan Qin, 343

Y

yakṣa, 24–25, 26, 27, 142, 218, 220–21
yakṣī, 205–6, 215, 225–26
yakṣiṇī, 23–24, 26
Yang, Larry, 560
Yangsi Rinpoche, 569–70
Yanshou, 56–57
yantragala, 161–62
yantras, 48–49, 182–83
ye dharmā hetu..., 160
Yen Le Espiritu, 478–79
Yeshe Losal, 585
Yetende, Pamela Ayo, 572
yidam, 441
Yifa, 511, 588
Yijing, Śramaṇa, 154, 164–65
Yili, 511
Yinguang, 324
yoga, 29, 30–31, 32, 119, 269, 270, 271, 377–78
Yogācāra (Pŏpsang) school, 58
yogins, 389
yŏmbul, 58
yoni-rūpatvam, 31
Yü, Chün Fang, 261
Yuan Hongdao, 326–27, 329
Yuanwu Keqin, 345
Yuanzhao (J. Ganjō), 425–26
yuksik, 60
yul lha, 235–36
Yunmen Wenyan, 340–41, 342
Yunqi Zhuhong, 344
Yuthog Yontan Gompo (g.Yuthog Yon tan mgon po), 238–40

Z

zadi, 445
zafu, 605
zazen, 118, 119–21, 454–55, 458–60, 461, 462, 463, 465, 605, 613–14
Zen, 94–96, 97–98, 103–5, 112, 113–14, 118, 119–20, 336–37, 614, 639–40. *See also* Rinzai Zen Buddhism; Sōtō Zen Buddhism
Zen and the Brain, 617
Zen Peacemaker Order (ZPO), 106, 574
zendō, 453–55
Zenshin-ni, 63
Zenzō-ni, 63
Zhaijiao, 509
zhaitang (fotang), 509
Zhamtsarano, 443–44
Zhaozhou Congshen, 340
Zhiyi, 55–56
Zhiyu, 325, 326–27, 329
Zhongfeng Mingben, 347
Zhuhong, 325
zili, 322
Ziyong Chengru, 343
Zongmi, 324–25
zu, 320, 321